# KATHY COOKS

## Vegetarian, Low Cholesterol

*By*

# Kathy Hoshijo

A Fireside Book
Published by Simon & Schuster Inc.
New York   London   Toronto   Sydney   Tokyo

**FIRESIDE**
Simon & Schuster Building
Rockefeller Center
1230 Avenue of the Americas
New York, New York 10020
Copyright © 1986 by The Self-Sufficiency Association
All rights reserved
including the right of reproduction
in whole or in part in any form.

First Fireside Edition, 1989

Published by arrangement with the author.
Originally entitled *THE ART OF DIETING WITHOUT DIETING*
FIRESIDE and colophon are registered trademarks of Simon & Schuster Inc.
Designed by Raymund Capulong
Illustrator: Rico Garcia
Compositors: Pat Taylor, Cynthia Morris, The Memory Bank
Manufactured in the United States of America

3  5  7  9  10  8  6  4  2  Pbk.

Library of Congress Cataloging in Publication Data
Hoshijo, Kathy.
[Art of dieting without dieting]
Kathy cooks—vegetarian, low cholesterol/by Kathy Hoshijo.
p.   cm.
Originally published as: The art of dieting without dieting.
"A Fireside book."
Includes index.
1. Low-cholesterol diet—Recipes.   2. Vegetarian cookery.
RM237.75.H67    1989
641.5′636—dc19                                                                88-37319
CIP
ISBN 0-671-67805-1

The nutritionally-balanced diet and lifestyle practices recommended in this book will help you achieve optimum health. This kind of "preventive medicine" is the best medicine there is; however, the recipes and advice given in this book are by no means meant to be a prescription or treatment for any condition that requires medical attention. I am by no means a doctor attempting to treat you.

Especially if you're ill or on some sort of medication, be sure to consult with a physician knowledgeable about nutrition before starting any exercise or diet program. (A word of warning: Physicians aren't educated in the science of nutrition as part of their training, and few care enough to look into it themselves; so it may take a great deal of looking to find an appropriately knowledgeable physician, but it's worth the extra effort!)

# KATHY COOKS

*Vegetarian,*
*Low Cholesterol*

Thanks to all who made "Kathy's Kitchen" and this book possible.

Chris Butler, for being my guiding light, Stu Chaffet, Connie Stone and Stephanie Mullaley, for being there in the beginning.

My family for their support and patience. H. J. Brown, the Summit Production Crew, the behind-the-scenes cooking crew, Allen Compton and all the "Kathy's Kitchen" viewers.

Ray Capulong, Rico Garcia, Cynthia Morris and Pat Taylor for putting this book together.

*This book is dedicated to all of you who want to do something to attain and/or maintain a healthy balance (on the scales as well as in other aspects) in your own personal life, as well as a more even balance in the world between those suffering from excessive consumption . . .*

*. . . and those suffering from lack of enough.*

# Contents

# PREFACE

*To all of my viewers,*

*This book is especially written for you, because you are the reason why I was inspired to put this book together . . . and believe me when I tell you, it takes a lot of inspiration to cause me to sit down and write another book! I'm not one of those to whom writing comes easily. My family and friends will testify to that! When I'm separated from any of them by time and space for long periods of time, a letter from me is such a rarity — not because my thoughts aren't with them, but because it's so difficult for me to sit and put those thoughts onto a blank sheet of paper.*

*In response to the TV show, "Kathy's Kitchen," and my first book, Kathy Cooks . . . Naturally, I receive from hundreds to thousands of letters a week. At first I was appalled by the fact that a large percentage of these letters expressed, in one way or another, concern over being — or not wanting to become — overweight.*

*A great number of letters come from those of you who are obviously counting calories — inquiring about how many calories are in a specific food or recipe. Then there are the letters which frankly, and sometimes desperately, state that the person writing is (or feels) overweight and wants to know how to lose weight.*

*Answering each letter containing a specific question directly or indirectly connected to the subject of weight loss pushed me into research. Having never counted a calorie in my life, I had to look that information up. Because I've never had a weight problem, and therefore have never paid much attention to information pertaining to the subject, specific questions on weight loss-related subjects, other than calorie counts, sent me running to the library.*

*The answers found through researching the latest scientific and medical studies (discussed later in this book) both surprised and reassured me. I was surprised to find that many of the most common and widespread beliefs and practices published and adopted as means to shed unwanted pounds are not only erroneous, but are actually the very cause of a person's inability to permanently maintain their ideal body weight!*

It's also been reassuring to have the research prove that all the changes I made in my diet over 16 years ago to keep me healthy (which I've shared nationwide through the "Kathy's Kitchen" TV series and in my first book), are the same ones that keep me slim. How great it is to know that if you eat for optimum health, attaining and/or maintaining the ideal body weight comes as a natural fringe benefit! Having a trim body isn't something you have to strive for extraneously or, worse yet, ruin your health over, as many popular "diet" programs are set up to do.

Finding answers to specific questions on metabolism, quick ways to lose weight, permanent weight loss, etc., left me with feelings of frustration over the inadequacy of a letter to be able to relay information completely, as a thorough explanation would really take a book-length letter in response to each separate inquirer.

So, here it is — my "letter" in book length to each of you who wrote with questions about weight loss! Also included are new recipes as seen in the fourth, fifth, sixth and seventh "Kathy's Kitchen" series (recipes not included in my first book, Kathy Cooks . . . Naturally), which goes to show that cooking with healthy, whole foods is unlimitedly variegated when you spice up nutritional knowledge with a dash of imagination.

aloha,
Kathy
Hoshijo

*T*his is actually the introduction. I just put the "1" there so I'd get the chance to personally ask you to please read this, because I never read introductions either. This introduction will give you a sense of what the rest of the book is about and an idea of how to use it.

Eating is one of those things everyone has to do to maintain life and health. Considering this in a time and society which likes to consider itself scientifically and culturally advanced, it's amazing that there is so much widespread ignorance and apathy surrounding this basic necessity of life. Even though what we eat is so inseparably connected with health and life on an individual as well as a worldwide level, the importance of good nutrition, meal planning and preparation is so unappreciated that it's not taught in schools. More often than not, it is thought of as some kind of lowly drudgery that only an uncreative, dull-minded "wife-of-a-house" cannot escape. In fact, personal health and the world food situation can be improved greatly by making an art of using information provided by science on which foods are the healthiest and most ecologically sound in order to create palatable and beautiful meals.

For too long we have allowed what we eat to be dictated to us by habits and tastes developed in childhood, by advertisements created by companies who care more about seeing healthy profits than healthy customers, and by diet and food fads. The result? . . . A society plagued with dietary-related problems and diseases such as heart disease, atherosclerosis, cancer, diabetes, cirrhosis of the liver, osteoporosis, obesity, etc.

The subject matter of mail I get in

response to my TV show and cookbook, along with statistical figures and the number of best-selling "diet" books, all indicate to me that of all the problems caused by the typical American diet, people seem to be overwhelmingly concerned with obesity, or being even a little overweight!

Although this book does deal with the subject of being overweight (or even obese), and you will end up attaining and/or maintaining your ideal body "weight" by applying the contents to your life, this is not a "diet" book in the typical sense of the word. Between the covers of this book you'll find no miracle diet that promises to have you looking like the models you've seen in the latest fashion magazines in a week or two. Nor will you find any gadgets, gimmicks, or day-by-day programs laid out for you to follow for the next few weeks or months. Nor is this book written from the vantage point of someone who once struggled with a weight problem and can now lead you down the path to thinness.

You'll find that the emphasis of this book isn't on weight or thinness as much as it is on health. What is being offered is not a temporary diet consisting of avoiding certain foods, or eating some horrible tasting special foods till a desired result is achieved, but a healthful way of eating to stick to and benefit from for the rest of your life.

I have never had a weight problem, counted a calorie, or even owned a scale. I credit this all to the fact that 18 years ago I decided to — and did — eliminate all unhealthy foods from my diet.

Immediately after graduating from high school, I stopped eating all refined foods, as well as foods that were laden with saturated fat, cholesterol and/or chemical additives. I adopted a diet stressing fresh, whole foods, often referred to as complex carbohydrates (fruits, vegetables, whole grains and legumes). Since then, medical science has proven that a low cholesterol and saturated fat diet is necessary for optimum health — the best way to prevent atherosclerosis, heart disease, and even certain types of cancer.

And athletes now use a complex carbohydrate diet for the long-sustained energy it gives. The good news is that this healthy, energy-giving diet is not fattening!

Through the years of research that have gone into writing this book, I've come to understand that the ease with which my family and I have been able to maintain ideal weights is no coincidence. It turns out that the health-promoting foods my family and I have been eating are naturally slimming as well! That's why 18 years and six healthy children later, I still wear the same dress size I wore in high school.

In the following chapters, I'll explain the specific changes I made in my diet and lifestyle 18 years ago and how they work as natural slimmers. Because I know from experience that one of the hardest things about making healthy eating part of your lifestyle is not knowing *how* to do it, I've tried to include enough delicious recipes and ideas to make the change a pleasure to undergo and stick to for a lifetime.

Almost every recipe is accompanied by a nutritional analysis of the recipe which shows percentage of RDA for females 23 to 51 years old (Recommended Daily Allowance established by the National Academy of Sciences, latest revised edition, 1980) for the nutrients that an RDA has been established for; and amounts present are listed for nutrients for which an RDA hasn't been established. The analysis also includes a calorie count and tells what percent of the recipe is fat, protein, and carbohydrate.

I've included the recipe nutritional analysis in response to the many questions and requests I get for that sort of information, and also because I think once you see how many nutrients are naturally packed in fresh produce and whole foods, you'll be able to be more relaxed and not worry so much about this sort of information. As I admitted in my first book (*Kathy Cooks . . . Naturally*), I myself am not neurotic about counting calories, percentages and milligrams of this and that. I have been convinced by the continued good health of myself and my family, as well as from checking nutritional analysis tables as we were preparing them for this book, that there is such a perfect balance in nature that as long as a wide variety of fresh produce and whole foods are used, all necessary nutrients are naturally and easily provided.

I'd like to mention a few other things about these tables to really stress the point that I've included them for general information and not to make anyone neurotic about counting anything! The tables are based on laboratory tests done on foods, and the mineral content of foods will vary depending on the mineral content of the soil they were grown in. Some soils in parts of the country are deficient in certain minerals, and the foods grown there would be equally deficient in those minerals.

Another thing to bear in mind while studying these tables is that the "science" of nutrition is a relatively new one. How much information we now have in the field of nutrition in relation to how much there is to know can safely be compared to how much was known about the planet earth when Columbus proved it was actually round. There are still nutrients being "discovered," more and more is being learned every day about how nutrients interact with each other in the complex chemical system called the body, and the exact amount of nutrients needed for good, sound nutrition is not really certain. This is true of the RDA tables themselves.

There is a great debate in the scientific community itself on what the RDA's should be. Though there is general agreement that the present RDA tables need to be changed, attempts to do so have only led to more debate. The present RDA tables were established around the time of World War II in a relatively unscientific way. A panel of scientists given the task of determining the nutritional needs of U.S. combat troops developed the Minimum Daily Requirements (MDR) — what they felt were the minimum requirements of certain nutrients to prevent diseases such as scurvy, etc. The

MDR's were abandoned because it was decided that since the data was based on the nutritional needs of civilians, it could hardly be accurate for the greater needs of more active soldiers in combat. In the midst of lively debate over what an "average person" was, the original MDR's were taken, a 50 percent safety bonus was added, and thus the RDA's were created! That RDA table is the one presently used as a standard by everyone.

The National Academy of Science has made attempts to change them since so much more is known now than in the 1940's in the field of nutrition, but these attempts have only led to agreeing on the need for further study and deliberation.

Let's take vitamin C, for an example. The present RDA set at 60 milligrams will certainly prevent scurvy, but new studies done with monkeys raise real questions on the amount of vitamin C needed for promoting health (as opposed to preventing disease). Studies on monkeys, whose genetic makeup is 98 percent similar to humans, have shown that large amounts of vitamin C can counteract infections and stress, slow aging, and even prevent cancer. Monkeys and humans are among the very few living beings on earth (amongst bacteria, plants and animals) who don't manufacture their own vitamin C but must obtain it by eating. Studies of animals whose bodies produce their own vitamin C show that the amounts produced are always in direct proportion to their body size. Using the proportions to body size as a guideline would put the amount needed by a human adult at 3,000 to 4,000 milligrams (compare that to the RDA's 50 milligrams!). That gives an idea of the uncertainty over vitamin C, and it is only one of the 50 some odd known nutrients.

It should be sufficient to say that although I value the science of nutrition as being important, I also recognize the fact that there is not enough known to let a table run my life, or anyone else's for that matter! I've always found it interesting that before any such "science" existed with its weight and percentage tables, where people were farming and living in harmony with their surroundings, they naturally ended up eating the kinds of foods all these tables and figures end up advising us to eat. My approach towards nutrition has been to find out what foods are healthy, then get creative with them, to use a wide variety from day to day, and it all seems to balance out!

In Chapter 14 (p. 703) you'll find a list of some of the healthy foods that I keep in my kitchen on a regular basis. If the items are ones I think you might want some information on or would like to know where to get, that is provided as well. The foods listed in Chapter 14 aren't *all* the foods I consider to be healthy, but the staples. Along with every recipe there's a shopping list provided for the things I regularly keep in the kitchen. Alongside this list is a fresh produce list that tells all the produce and/or items that can normally be found in supermarkets needed for that specific recipe. If the recipe calls for an ingredient that requires shopping in a specialty store, those items will be listed in colored ink in the margin.

There really is no program laid out to make the changes in your diet and lifestyle described in the following chapters, although I can suggest a few. You know yourself better than I and can approach making the changes in the way that will best help you make this a lifelong commitment. You can read the whole book to get an overall view of all the information and just go "cold turkey"; if you are the type who generally makes a commitment, then jumps in without reservation and puts all your energy into whatever you've gotten yourself into, then this may work for you. This is what I did, although it took me years before I got it together! Hopefully, with the help of this book, that will be cut down to months for you. If you are the sort who likes to "test the waters" first and get in a little at a time, you may want to take one chapter at a time and just concentrate on making the changes in the one chapter for a week, or a month, or however long it takes till it is just part of your life; then go on to the next chapter. Of course, if you take the "cold turkey" route you'll see results sooner; but either way you go — be patient. This is not a quickie fad diet, but a way that a healthy, trim body can eventually be yours for a lifetime without having to be neurotic about charts, tables, scales, or counting calories.

Being liberated from having to spend so much time, energy, and attention on counting calories, etc., can make for a fuller and more meaningful life. Not having to center so much attention on ourselves frees up more time and energy to be able to center attention on others, the world around us, and higher pursuits in life. Rather than living to eat (or the other side of the coin — to avoid eating), everything gets put into perspective so we are eating to live and living to better ourselves and the world around us.

*O*n a personal or societal level, it's always important to know what the goal of any undertaking is, because only when the goal is clearly understood can we clearly assess whether we're progressing or regressing.

Of course, the goal must always be in touch with reality; if it isn't, it will inevitably result in disaster for the individual or society. Since this book is primarily written for those of you who want to attain and/or maintain body weight, let's look at . . .

# WHY OR WHY NOT . . . WHEN . . . WHAT . . . ?

# CHAPTER 1

# PUTTING THINGS IN PERSPECTIVE

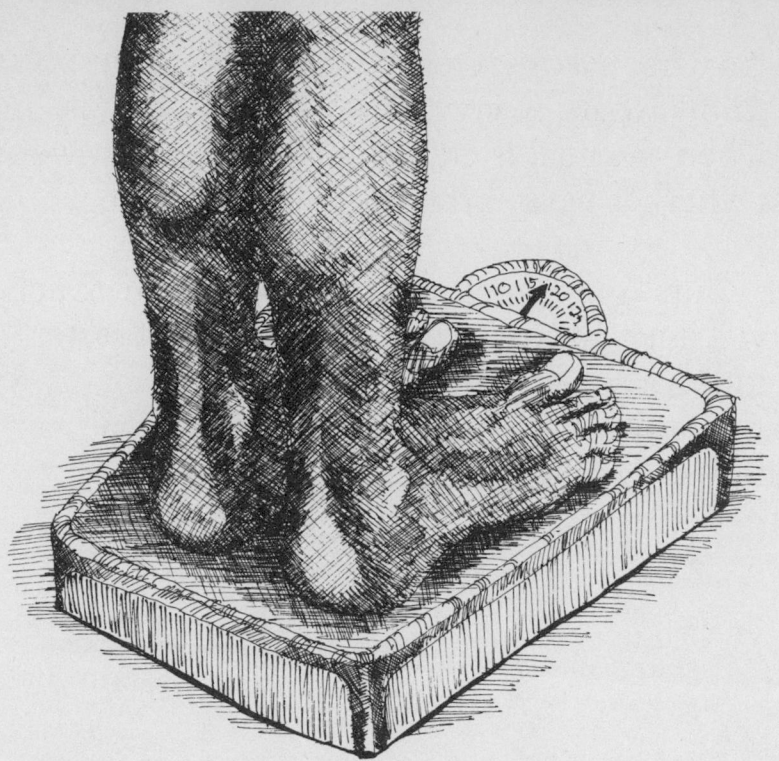

For everything in life, it's important to get things in perspective first; otherwise it's easy to get off on tangents (or out on limbs!). And the matter of attaining and/or maintaining an ideal body weight is no exception. The best way to get a clear perspective on anything is to stand back for a moment and take the time to examine what one is doing, why one is doing it and be sure one is working towards the right goal.

In the midst of the dieting mania with which people in America are obsessed, it's an important thing for each person to know what his ideal body weight is. Then, knowing whether one needs to lose, gain, or maintain body weight is simply a matter of finding out what needs to be done to attain that goal. The term "body weight" is really an inaccurate, yet very ingrained, way of describing the condition the body is in. It is so ingrained that I found myself having to allow the term to be used (up to this point, and even on the back cover of the book) because this is the way most people determine whether or not they're too fat. To correct this mistaken terminology would require more space than I've had up until now.

## THROW OUT THE SCALE

Rather than "body weight," the more accurate thing to say is "percentage of body fat." Most people decide to diet because they tip the scale at a figure they feel, or have read on height-weight charts, is undesirable. Many people, especially women, feel they're too fat when actually they aren't. Scales and height-weight charts measure and put concern on the wrong thing — weight; fat is what one should measure and be concerned about. While height-weight charts give a general indication (if you're 5'1" and weigh 200 pounds, you're most likely fat unless you happen to be Mr. Olympia!), they definitely aren't an accurate way to know if you are too fat. It's possible to be within the right weight range for your height and be too fat, or be extremely physically fit and be too heavy for your height on a height-weight chart. Many people who are only a little too fat and begin to watch their diet and start an exercise program, see no change (or even a gain) on the scale even though their body appears to be, and actually is losing fat. The reason for this is that muscle (and bones and organs) weighs more than fat does.

## HOW TO MEASURE BODY FAT

That doesn't mean you should decide you're "big-boned" and forget about the whole weight business. It just means that you need to go to a specialist with the proper equipment to measure the fat content of your body. Some physicians and many fitness centers are equipped with calipers (for the "pinch test") which measure the thickness of skin pinched up in different parts of the body, hydrostatic (underwater) weighing, or ultrasound machines with which they can give an accurate reading of the percentage of body fat. If you don't want to rely on going to someone else to find out your percentage of body fat, you should throw out your bathroom

. . . . . . . . . . . . . . . . . . . . . . . . . . . .

*The founder of modern dance, in her day a celebrated beauty and fashion trendsetter, Isadora Duncan, was described by the modern-day choreographer, George Balanchine, as a "fat lady rolling around the stage."*

. . . . . . . . . . . . . . . . . . . . . . . . . . . .

scale and invest in a caliper. (If you can't find a caliper locally, they are available from Creative Health Products, 5148 Saddle Ridge Road, Plymouth, Michigan 48170, for $21.95.)

## REMEMBER — BODY FAT'S NOT BAD . . .

For the 80 percent of the people in America who collectively spend over 10 billion dollars every year on some diet book, program, reduction or fitness center, special diet foods and drinks, and giz-mos to get rid of it — fat has become a dirty word. In the midst of so many people treating fat like the plague, it's hard to remember that it gives us energy, warmth, the capability to reproduce, helps to hydrate the body day and night, and stores and disperses essential fat-soluble vitamins. For good health, a certain amount of body fat is necessary and desirable. Medical science has established a healthy fat level for women to be between 18 and 25 percent, and 10 to 15 percent for men.

## . . . UNLESS THERE'S TOO MUCH

Although some experts feel that one can healthfully be a few percentage points above or below these guidelines, it's agreed across the board that if the percentage of body fat is ten percent or more above the higher healthy percentage point, then it's time to start getting rid of that extra fat! The risk of deterioration of the immune system, high blood pressure, heart disease, stroke, diabetes, arthritis, liver and kidney disorders, gallstones, blood clots and varicose veins increases the higher the percentage of body fat gets above what is considered to be healthy. Women have to face the additional increased risk of infertility or malnourishing a child in the womb and a difficult delivery, and cancer of the breast and/or uterus. All this, added to the effect on the ego and psyche, amount to good reasons to get rid of,

4

or never gain, too much body fat.

## ONLY ONE GOOD REASON FOR WATCHING PERCENTAGE OF BODY FAT

Our own health and well-being is really the only reason to concern ourselves with whether to gain, lose or maintain body fat. Surveys have shown that most men watch their diets and/or engage in a regular exercise program out of concern over the health problems being too fat can pose, but women are more concerned with what they look like.

Watching weight to try to conform to other's or society's idea of beauty (or what we perceive to be other's idea of beauty) can be unhealthy. Women's attempts to meet the modern-day standard of thin, willowy figures — so others will find them attractive or love them — has had a lot to do with the historically new development of eating disorders, such as anorexia and bulimia, sweeping this country in epidemic proportions. The causes of these eating disorders go much deeper, but the obsession with skinniness as a standard of beauty is what has gotten most women started. Skinniness hasn't always been associated with beauty. Women in history (and even in some parts of the globe today) would have to maintain fat levels hazardous to health to measure up to ideals of voluptuous, chubby and in some places downright obese beauty. Ideals of bodily beauty change as do fashion

trends that dictate what is acceptable to wear.

As long as we don't know our true identity and real value as the person or living being temporarily housed in a suit of skin, fat, muscle, blood, bones, etc., we'll find ourselves being pushed around

· · · · · · · · · · · · · · · · · · · · · · · · · · ·

*"Even if you hold to the theoretical tenets of materialism, you are most likely repelled by the sight of a corpse — even the corpse of a beautiful woman or a handsome man. Life is what attracts you . . . so it is this non-material person, this person whose essence is life itself, who is of real value. The material body is valuable only when the infinitely valuable person is present within the body. As soon as the person leaves the body, the body becomes worthless."*

*— Who Are You?*
*Discovering Your Real Identity*
*by Chris Butler*

· · · · · · · · · · · · · · · · · · · · · · · · · · ·

by the dictates of what the society we happen to live in deems to be fashionable for the moment. Attaining and being able to maintain a healthy percentage of body fat entails more than counting and limiting calories. It may

require behavior modification, change in lifestyles, and ultimately knowing one's own identity. For a thorough discussion and study of the question of identity in relation to practical life, the most thorough book I know of is *Who Are You — Discovering Your Real Identity* by Chris Butler. (If you can't find the book in a local bookstore, it can be ordered through Transcendental Sound, P.O. Box 27450, Honolulu, Hawaii 96827.)

I'm sure that as more and more people (especially women) get in touch with their true identity and know undoubtedly within themselves that their true value or worth isn't dependent on the shape of their silhouettes, and as more information about the intricate workings of the human body becomes available through science, many unhealthy dieting practices and myths will disappear.

While our bodies are, in a sense, like vehicles or clothing we're temporarily wearing and using (and, therefore, should care for), that's where all similarities end. Our bodies are made up of living cells and a wide array of chemical compounds that make them much more complex than a car or a jacket . . . So complex that modern-day science is still learning about the body's different systems and how they interact with each other and elements put into them. As new information surfaces, old misconceptions and practices need to be changed. Recent information provided through science disproves three main misconceptions upon which all fad and diet programs have been based.

## MISCONCEPTION #1: LOW-CALORIE DIETS ARE THE BEST WAY TO GET RID OF FAT

All weight-loss diets up until a year or two ago were based on the truth that if more calories are consumed than are burned, the body converts and stores those extra calories as fat. From that it would seem logical that the way to lose fat would be to cut back on calorie consumption. The myriad of old diets and weight-loss programs were set up to do just that in a number of different ways. Theoretically they should have worked, but didn't; thus, going on and off low-calorie diets practically became a lifestyle for many women. The reason low-calorie diets didn't work is because the body is run by many involuntary systems (systems which perform their functions without any conscious direction from us, like the heart beating, breathing, etc.) that have never taken lessons in logic.

One of the involuntary functions the body carries out is to store fat for emergencies. While the dangers of starving to death are very minute in this country, there's no way to tell our bodies not to worry and to discontinue that service. After observing the body's tendency to store certain amounts of fat under different circumstances, scientists have developed the "set-point theory."

According to the "set-point theory," there is a mechanism in each of our bodies which causes the body to create more fat than normal (and hold on to present fat stores) in times of emergency-like famine — to maintain whatever the amount of fat a person's body is "set" at. When anyone goes on a low-calorie diet, the body doesn't know that it's receiving less calories because the person is trying to get rid of fat. Instead, when the body suddenly starts receiving fewer calories than usual, its emergency alarm systems go off and the body gears up to cope with harder times ahead.

Metabolism (the process by which our bodies convert digested food into energy) slows down so the body can make more efficient use of the little food it is getting and turns more of it into fat than it normally would. To have as much fat in store as possible for the famine ahead, the body begins burning muscle protein so it can keep the present and newly-created fat on reserve.

The body keeps this up even after it starts receiving food again — just to be sure it's ready in case there's another famine. This is why many women experience getting fatter and gaining more weight when they return to eating normal amounts of food (or even a little less) after a low-calorie diet. When this happens, the usual reaction is to start looking for another crash or fad diet to try for awhile (at least one that works this time!). Thus the vicious cycle of on-and-off dieting is started.

The only way to get off this vicious cycle is to speed up the metabolism and lower the "set-point" by —

• *giving up on-and-off-again dieting forever;*

• *eating at regularly-scheduled times each day;*

• *eating at least 1,100 to 1,200 calories a day* (remembering that calories are not our enemy — just a way to measure energy);

• *making every calorie count by eating no empty-calorie foods;*

• and doing some sort of *aerobic exercise.*

## MISCONCEPTION #2: THE RIGHT PROGRAM WILL GET RID OF FAT FAST!

Another reason low-calorie diets and programs were accepted by so many for so long is that anyone on one would usually lose a good amount of weight quickly at first. That initial weight loss is not fat, but water which is quickly lost and regained. When the body has lost about five to seven pounds of water, the weight loss begins to level off. It is at this point, when constant checking with the scale shows no more quick progress and the body is demanding to be fed more by sending out strong hunger signals, that most women become discouraged and go off a low-calorie diet — having accomplished losing a little water and slowing their metabolisms down to produce and hold on to more fat. Having the fortitude to stick to a low-calorie diet much longer results in losing muscle mass, which is not healthy, nor is it desirable in terms of losing fat. Since muscle tissue can be used to burn stored fat and will burn more calories than any other active tissue in the body, it's a tissue you want to keep. Fatty tissue can only be lost gradually — at the rate of one to two pounds a week.

There is no quick way to get rid of fat. What is required is patience and determination, combined with —

- *eating foods that won't cause the body to make excess fat;*
- *eating at least 1,100 to 1,200 calories a day;*
- and some sort of *aerobic exercise.*

## MISCONCEPTION #3: ALL THE DIETING IN THE WORLD CAN'T HELP SOMEONE WITH A SLOW METABOLISM

As explained above (misconceptions #1 and #2), part of this is true; low-calorie fad diets not only don't help anyone with a slow metabolism lose extra fat, but actually set a person up to get even fatter by slowing the metabolism down further.

While some people are blessed with higher metabolisms than others, a person with a slow metabolism isn't stuck with a lifetime of fatness as inferred by this misconception. By learning more about

how the body works, modern science has established that a person with a slow metabolism can actually speed up their metabolism through a few commonsense and healthful changes in lifestyle and eating habits (as detailed in the next chapter).

In this day and age, when more and more people are equating new scientific information and advancement with new technology or "miracle pills" that are supposed to quickly solve our problems for us, it's ironic that new scientific information about body chemistry puts the responsibility for healthfully and permanently keeping an ideal level of body fat solely in the hands of each person.

# CHAPTER 2

# OFF TO A GOOD START

I t turns out that much of the new scientific information on how much and what to eat, how and when to eat it, and other healthy practices have been part of my life for the past 18 years because that's when I started studying and incorporating the science of yoga into my life. Although having a trim body (or perfect physical health) isn't the goal of yoga or the reason I began adopting activities recommended by the non-sectarian yogic science, it certainly has been a nice side-effect for me. In pursuit of living for a higher purpose rather than in pursuit of thinness, my family and I like to get every day off to a good start by waking up early enough to —

- *Stretch and exercise* a bit, then shower, to get the body systems revved up so we'll be mentally alert enough to . . .
- *Meditate* to become clear on and remember our true identities and purpose in life so, hopefully, we can function from that platform throughout the day.
- After this we have *breakfast*, which according to yogic guidelines is primarily made up of complex carbohydrates. Then everyone goes in whatever direction they need to for the day.

This simple schedule has naturally and effortlessly included many of the practices recommended by new scientific information about how to have a trim body. It's always interesting to me how "new scientific information" often backs up and explains why certain yogic practices actually work. It appears to me that modern-day scientists are very slowly — in a very roundabout way which is susceptible to so many mistakes — finding out a few of the things yogis have known for hundreds of thousands of

years by being able to accept information on faith from a higher source. Of course, modern-day scientists can only obtain information about matter through their process of using the senses and mind to observe and speculate on their observations. They'll not be able to approach any subject matter which is transcendental to matter, as the science of yoga does. Obviously, when talking about ideal levels of fat for the body, we're concerning ourselves with matter.

The things that count in connection with eating are . . .

• HOW MUCH

Concern over how much to eat has always been at the forefront when people want to lose fat or keep it off because unused calories are converted to fat. The surprise is that new scientific information shows an adult should eat a minimum of 1,100 to 1,200 calories a day, combined with some sort of aerobic exercise, to get or keep the body's metabolism revved up.

How many calories a person should eat to maintain an ideal percentage of body fat really depends on how physically fit and active they are. The body has to burn a certain amount of calories just to maintain bodily functions. This is called *basal metabolism*. An average basal metabolism for a healthy adult is about 60 calories an hour or 1,440 calories a day. This is why the minimum low-calorie diet shouldn't go below 1,100 or 1,200 calories a day. If the body receives fewer calories than the amount needed to carry out its basic functions (like keeping the heart beating, blood warmed, lungs breathing, etc.), it will automatically slow its metabolism down so it will take fewer calories to carry out these functions. Basal metabolism varies from person to person. It's generally higher in men than in women. The muscles burn more calories than any other part of the body, accounting for 90 percent of the

calories metabolized by the body. Thus, people who are more muscular and use their muscles a lot, have higher metabolisms.

This is another reason the repeated formula for losing fat is not to consume less than 1,100 to 1,200 calories a day and do some sort of aerobic exercise. This ensures keeping the metabolism up by giving the body what it needs to maintain bodily functions, and raising the metabolism, thus dipping into stored body

· · · · · · · · · · · · · · · · · · · · · · · · · · · ·

*"The growing interest taken by men in the practical results of science was both natural and legitimate; but it helped them to forget that science is knowledge, and the practical results but its by-products . . . "*

— *Etienne Gilson*
*French Historian of Philosophy*

· · · · · · · · · · · · · · · · · · · · · · · · · · · ·

fat by exercising. If trying to maintain weight, it's helpful to know about how many calories you burn through your day-to-day activities and eat around that many a day. If your day-to-day activities are pretty sedentary, it's a good idea to do some sort of physical exercise for health's sake.

This table, from *Ho-ping, Food For Everyone* by Medard Gabel, will give you an idea of approximately how many calories are burned through different activities.

## ENERGY REQUIREMENTS FOR VARIOUS ACTIVITIES
### (kilocalories/hour)

**Light Work**

| | | | | |
|---|---|---|---|---|
| Sitting | 19 | Writing | 20 |
| Standing relaxed | 20 | Typing | 16 - 40 |
| Sewing | 30 - 90 | Typing quickly | 55 |
| Dressing/undressing | 33 | Drawing | 40 - 50 |
| Lithography | 40 - 50 | Violin playing | 40 - 50 |
| Tailoring | 50 - 85 | Washing dishes | 60 |
| Ironing | 60 | Bookbinding | 45 - 90 |

**Moderate Work**

| | | | | |
|---|---|---|---|---|
| Shoemaking | 80 - 115 | Sweeping | 85 - 110 |
| Dusting | 110 | Washing | 125 - 215 |
| Metalworking | 120 - 140 | Walking | 130 - 240 |
| House painting | 145 - 160 | Carpentering | 150 - 180 |

**Hard Work**

| | | | | |
|---|---|---|---|---|
| Polishing | 175 | Joiner work | 195 |
| Blacksmithing | 275 - 350 | Riveting | 275 |
| Marching | 280 - 400 | Cycling | 180 - 600 |
| Rowing | 120 - 600 | Swimming | 200 - 700 |

**Very Hard Work**

| | | | | |
|---|---|---|---|---|
| | | Sawing wood | 420 |
| Stonemasonry | 350 | Running | 800 - 1000 |
| Coal mining (average for shift) | 320 | Climbing | 400 - 900 |
| Walking quickly | 570 | Rowing quickly | 1240 |
| Running quickly | 1240 | Skiing | 500 - 950 |
| Walking upstairs | 1000 | Wrestling | 1000 |

## • WHAT

New scientific studies have shown that as important as the *number* of calories consumed is *what* foods those calories are made of. The subject of what to eat (or not) and the reasons why are detailed in Sections 2 and 3 of this book. In a nutshell, the foods to avoid are flesh foods, refined foods, chemical additives, alcoholic beverages and any food or drink containing caffeine. The best foods to eat are complex carbohydrates, supplemented with a little bit of dairy products and six to eight glasses of clean water a day.

Calories are not all han-dled equally by the body. The sources of calories (energy) for the body are carbohydrates, protein and fat. Studies on rats that were all fed the same amounts of calories, but in different forms, showed that rats getting their calories primarily from fat were the fattest; rats getting their calories primarily from protein were next in line; rats getting their calories primarily from carbohydrates were the trimmest. The study, headed by Dr. Wayne C. Miller at the University of Illinois in Chicago, found that rats eating a lowfat diet (11 percent fat) had an average of 21 percent less body fat than rats fed high-fat diets (42 percent, 50 percent and 60 percent fat; most Americans get about 40 percent of their calories in the form of fat).

That fat is the most fattening source of calories shouldn't be a big surprise. It is the most concentrated form of energy, which is another way of saying that it is the most calorically dense, containing nine calories per gram. Compare that to the four calories per gram found in protein and carbohydrates.

Carbohydrates always get burned first, as they are the easiest for the human body to metabolize. Carbohydrates are easily converted into glucose, which is the primary fuel on which the body runs. Protein is broken down to amino acids which build and repair muscle tissue. Protein will be converted into glucose only in an emergency, when the body doesn't get enough carbohydrates. The body is forced to turn its own protein into glucose when the supply of protein through food is insufficient, resulting in loss of muscle tissue. A low-calorie diet of less than 1,100 calories a day would obviously provide insufficient amounts of carbohydrates and protein. Fat always remains fat and is either passed out of the body when absorbed in dietary fiber or stockpiled by the body. Fat is never converted to glucose. Stored fat is only burnable by the body when broken down by oxygen and special enzymes (amounts of which are both increased through aerobic exercise) into fatty acids, which are transferred to the muscles to be burned.

Dietary recommendations vary according to different sources, but all agree we should get the bulk of our calories from complex carbohydrates, followed by protein and a little fat. The 1977 "Dietary Goals for the U.S." report by the U.S. Senate Committee on Nutrition and Human Needs recommended we change our calorie consumption patterns from 46 percent carbohydrates (28 percent complex carbohydrates and 18 percent refined) to 58 percent carbohydrates

(48 percent complex carbohydrates, 10 percent refined); keep 12 percent protein where it is; and change from 42 percent fat (16 percent saturated, 19 percent monounsaturated, 7 percent polyunsaturated) to 30 percent fat (10 percent of each kind of fat). This change seems moderate when many health specialists today are recommending we get more like 75 percent of our calories from complex carbohydrates, 10 to 15 percent from protein and 10 to 15 percent from fat.

Just as a certain amount of fat is needed in the body for good health, so is a certain amount of fat needed in the diet. It's impossible to cut dietary fat out completely because it's contained in practically every food. There are a few well-known diets which exclude using any free-oils (vegetable oils, margarine, etc.) at all. However, some nutritionists feel that a diet so low in fat would lack essential linoleic acids to the point where the immune system would be depleted, making a person more susceptible to cancer, leukemia, etc. Another less scholarly problem with such diets is the food often tastes so bland that people tend to stay on them for only a short period of time. I feel it's better to use a moderate amount of free-oils in cooking so a healthy way of eating can be followed for a lifetime. Stir-frying and deep-frying are cooking techniques that have been used in the Far East for thousands of years, and

people in that part of the world have not had records of the diseases presently associated with too much fat consumption. (However, people in the Far East traditionally have eaten very little or no meat or dairy foods, which are both high in saturated fat.)

• HOW

As explained on p. 199, there are many good reasons for eating slowly and chewing food well. Fortunately, complex carbohydrates ensure that we have to do both to break down the dietary fiber so it can be swallowed.

• WHEN

Recent scientific studies have shown the question of *when* to do different activities is very important. It is so important that a new title has been given to those who specialize in studying how biological functions are governed by inner "clocks" — *chronobiologists*. In another way they are reconfirming something that most of our mothers stressed as a good nutritional practice and many dieters have chosen to ignore: breakfast is the most important meal of the day.

Anyone who has ever skipped breakfast in an attempt to cut down on calorie consumption by missing a meal, will benefit from information coming from a University of Minnesota study. After feeding the same women the same 2,000-calorie meal in the evening for a week, and then in the morning for a week, chronobiologists reported that the meal eaten in the morning brought about a weight loss; in the evening, a weight gain. The weight changes were due to loss of body fat and not just body fluid as one might expect.

The obvious reason for calories eaten at breakfast not to be converted to fat as readily as those at dinner is that you have all day to burn calories eaten in the morning. Food eaten later in the evening has every chance of being "slept on." While sleeping, the body's metabolism naturally slows down. As explained (on p. 10), the body burns a certain number of

calories just to maintain bodily functions — one of them being maintaining body temperature. In most people, body temperature peaks at about two to three o'clock in the afternoon and is lowest during sleep. This means the basal metabolism is lowest while asleep. Aside from this logical reason, chronobiologists have also found that levels of digestive-related hormones are highest in the morning. It's best to eat the largest meals at breakfast and lunch time, and a lighter, easier to digest meal at least six to eight hours before bed-

time. To keep the metabolism up, eat at regularly scheduled times.

A separate study at Kansas State University, headed by Dr. A. R. Wilcox, also found that joggers burned about the same number of calories when running in the morning or evening. *But* two-thirds of the calories burned by the morning joggers were fat, whereas only half of the calories the afternoon joggers burned were fat. Dr. Wilcox's conclusion was, "A pound of fat will be oxidized faster if you exercise on an empty stomach in the morning."

## EXERCISE ABSOLUTELY ESSENTIAL

Some sort of aerobic exercise (moderate exercises, sustained for one-half to one hour, that require more air to be breathed in — like jogging, swimming, dancing, bicycling, walking, etc.) keeps being emphasized as a way to burn body fat. It's not that your body won't benefit from other kinds of exercise, but aerobic exercise is the only kind that will raise the metabolism and cause a lot of stored body fat to be burned. Anaerobic exercises (exercises that call for short, intense bursts of energy — like sprinting, weight-lifting, calisthenics, etc.) burn the body's natural sugar, glycogen, more than fat. Anaerobics will strengthen muscles but have little effect on metabolism or burning stored body fat because a lot of oxygen must be present for the fat supply to be burned.

In the first few minutes of

an aerobic exercise the body also relies on burning glycogen, but as more oxygen is moved into the system through continued movement, along with more of the enzymes needed to break stored fat into fatty acids, the body begins to burn fat. To efficiently burn body fat, an aerobic exercise needs to be steadily and continually done for at least half an hour and must be done intensely enough to make you breathe harder, but not so hard that you have to stop to catch your

breath. The old school of thought on aerobics that you had to go for the burn — "no pain, no gain" — has recently been disproved. Fat is burned more efficiently by a low- to moderate-level workout. This means you don't have to hurt (mild discomfort is okay) or sweat a lot to get an effective workout. If trying to lose weight, it's important to do some sort of aerobic exercise at least four times a week and no more than six times a week. Another benefit of fat being released into the bloodstream during aerobic exercise is that it decreases appetite because blood-sugar levels stay pretty level while the body is burning fat (hunger is experienced when blood-sugar levels drop). Metabolism is raised during aerobic exercise and stays up about 25 percent for about 15 hours afterward and 10 percent for up to about 48 hours afterward. The basal metabolism actually increases with one's level of aerobic fitness.

Aside from burning fat, toning muscles and increasing cardiovascular and respiratory fitness, doing a low-intensity aerobic exercise regularly and sensibly offers many other healthy benefits:

• Moderate exercise throughout adult life helps you prevent decreasing your duration of life. A still ongoing Harvard-Stanford study of 17,000 men has shown, so far, that death rates in the non-exercising group were one-quarter to one-third higher than in the exercising group.

• The same study showed the risk of death from heart disease or cancer is significantly decreased by exercise.

• The same study showed that it's never too late to start an exercise program. The benefits of exercise were just as great for those who had been exercising since college and those who started in middle-age.

• Exercise helps to retard the aging process. The 1978 *Journal of Gerontology* reported that men in their 60's who did some sort of aerobic exercise for 20 years or more had reaction times equal to or better than inactive 20-year-olds.

• Besides benefiting brawn, exercising also benefits the brain. By increasing the flow of glucose to the brain, the ability to solve problems and think more systematically is increased.

• Not only muscles, but bones are made stronger through exercise. This is especially important for women to prevent osteoporosis in senior years.

• Overall cholesterol levels can be decreased and amounts of HDL (the good kind of cholesterol) can be increased through regular exercise.

• Blood pressure is naturally decreased as cardiovascular health is improved.

• A good workout helps to counteract stress by releasing endorphins (chemicals that calm the nervous system).

Since this is really a cookbook and there are so many excellent exercise books and videos on the market, as well as sports and classes available in local neighborhoods, I'd just like to recommend that you do some sort of regular exercise. For those of you who are curious about my personal exercise routine, I'll have to make it sufficient to say I've primarily done hatha yoga exercises for the past 18 years. These exercises have been ideal for me because I don't have to go anywhere to do them (with seven children, it's hard to find time to go to a separate location to exercise). I've been able to do hatha yoga exercises through all my pregnancies and am positive they had a lot to do with the ease of my labors. To me, hatha yoga exercises are ideal as they tone muscles while keeping them limber and are even aerobic (if you breathe properly), while benefiting all internal systems within the body ... But that's a whole other subject! Here are some recipes for getting the day off to a good start.

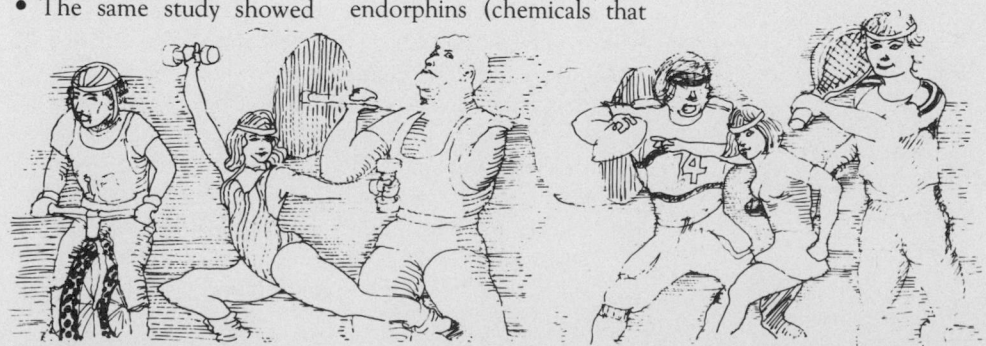

# OFF TO A GOOD START

In these days of increasing technological and scientific development, we would be wise to heed the words of one of the most respected scientists of our times as he spoke to a college class of future scientists. Albert Einstein said, "Concern for man and his fate must always form the chief interest of all technical endeavors in order that the creations of our mind shall be a blessing and not a curse to mankind. Never forget this in the midst of your diagrams and equations."

Almost all of us have heard that breakfast is the most important meal of the day, but most of us throughout America ignore this fact — or just can't seem to fit it into our busy schedules. Studies have shown that only 25 percent of families in America eat breakfast together any more — and in at least half of those households, at least one (and sometimes more) family member regularly skips the meal. Interestingly enough, the family members who skip breakfast are usually the ones with serious, unhealthy body fat levels, and are probably skipping this meal in an attempt to cut down on calories.

Little do they know that this one habit may be contributing to their problem. While people may start skipping breakfast because they have some body fat to lose, it's almost guaranteed that they will continue to have this problem as long as they skip the morning meal. The Health, Weight and Stress Program at John Hopkins Medical Center has reported that over half of the obese people in the United States skip breakfast most of the time.

Getting obesity under control is only one of the reasons staff members at the Institute of Human Nutrition at Columbia University developed a king/prince/pauper approach to meal planning (eat breakfast like a king, lunch like a prince, dinner like a pauper). Many medical reports have shown that low blood-sugar levels, diabetes, hyperactivity and even heart conditions can be effectively managed when breakfast is made a priority. After studying the lifestyles, illnesses and deaths of 7,000 men and women, researchers at the University of California listed eating breakfast regularly as one of the seven health habits that helps one attain longevity.

Of course, prioritizing breakfast doesn't only mean being sure to eat it, but to make sure it's made up of the healthiest ingredients. That means cereals that are so sugar-laden they could be classified as candy are out as a quick breakfast (40 percent of the leading commercial breakfast cereals found on supermarket shelves consist of one-third or more sugar) — and so is the traditional cholesterol, saturated fat and nitrate bacon and egg breakfast.

For about seven years, the following Breakfast Drink served with whole pieces of whatever fruit was in season was what I served for breakfast day in and day out. Something changed that: A move — part of the year spent in California. I find that my body craves heavier foods — like grains — in the morning when the weather is cooler. I found myself feeling a little chilled on winter mornings when I had fruit for breakfast. Maybe because their bodies were experiencing the same thing mine was, or because they were just tired of the same thing every morning for seven years, there was a minor revolution at breakfast time with everyone unanimously wanting something else to eat. Our breakfast menu now has a little more variety to it.

The Breakfast Drink was perfect (for so long) because it, combined with the fruit, was a nutritious meal that was quick and easy to prepare. Our lifestyle still demands quick and easy in the morning, so I've devised a number of short-order breakfasts and some that can be prepared the night before, like the ones that follow.

## TAKE A CLOSER LOOK AT YOUR FAVORITE CEREAL

| 1 OZ. | % SUGAR |
|---|---|
| Special K | 4.4 |
| Puffed Wheat | 3.5 |
| Cheerios | 2.2 |
| All Bran | 18.4 |
| Heartland | 23.1 |
| Country Morning | 31.0 |
| Quaker 100% Natural | 22.0 |
| 40% Bran Flakes | 15.8 |
| Post Grape Nuts | 6.6 |
| Wheaties | 4.7 |
| Shredded Wheat | 1.0 |
| Raisin Bran | 10.6 |
| Rice Crispies | 10.0 |
| Corn Flakes | 7.8 |
| Product 19 | 4.1 |
| Puffed Rice | 2.4 |
| Cocoa Puffs | 43.0 |
| Cap'n Crunch | 43.3 |
| Sugar Frosted Flakes | 44.0 |
| Sugar Pops | 37.0 |

I've given this recipe out before, but left the amount of raisins and which kind of nuts and seeds to use open-ended. I've gotten so many inquiries on this specific recipe that I decided to re-do it and make it more specific. One other question that needs frequent answering — yes, this is a thick "drink" that almost needs to be chewed.

A note about the graph: The vitamin content is higher than the graph indicates because the nuts and seeds are germinated (see p. 471). Unfortunately, there are no existing nutritional analyses for germinated nuts and seeds, and lab expenses were too much for me to afford . . .

# BREAKFAST DRINK

☆ Served with whole pieces of fresh fruit or whole grain toast, this makes a complete meal!

---

4 - 5 cups soaking water ("rejuvelac")
1 cup raw, hulled sunflower seeds
⅓ cup raw almonds
⅔ cup raisins

½ cup carob powder
¼ cup honey
4 heaping Tbsp. lecithin granules
2 tsp. grain coffee substitute

Soak first 4 ingredients together for 24 hours till tips of almonds and sunflower seeds begin to germinate. Pour all 4 ingredients into blender top and add next 4 ingredients. Blend till smooth. Serve as a breakfast drink along with pieces of fresh fruit. Makes six 1-cup servings.

| SHOPPING LIST | |
|---|---|
| Regularly Kept in the Kitchen (Listed in Chapter 14, p. 703) | Fresh Produce |
| Sunflower seeds<br>Almonds<br>Raisins<br>Carob powder<br>Honey<br>Grain coffee<br>Lecithin granules (or liquid lecithin) | (None) |

# NUTRITIONAL ANALYSIS FOR ONE SERVING BREAKFAST DRINK

```
NUTRIENT        Type: 14    FEMALE-23 TO 51 YEARS          % RDA   Amount
KCALORIES       A=======                                    15%   318.0 Kc
PROTEIN         A========                                   17%   7.800 Gm
CARBOHYDRATE    A                                         NO RDA  38.10 Gm
FAT             A                                         NO RDA  19.60 Gm
FIBER-CRUDE     A                                         NO RDA  2.010 Gm
CHOLESTEROL     A                                         NO RDA  0.000 Mg
SATURATED FA    A                                         NO RDA  2.950 Gm
OLEIC FA        A                                         NO RDA  4.930 Gm
LINOLEIC FA     A                                         NO RDA  7.900 Gm
SODIUM          A                                            0%   8.250 Mg
POTASSIUM       A=====                                      11%   417.0 Mg
MAGNESIUM       A===================                        38%   116.0 Mg
IRON            A=======                                    14%   2.530 Mg
ZINC            A=====                                      10%   1.570 Mg
VITAMIN A       A                                            0%   14.40 IU
VITAMIN D       A                                            0%   0.000 IU
VIT. E/TOTAL    A                                         NO RDA  14.40
VITAMIN C       A                                            0%   0.580 Mg
THIAMIN         A=============================              58%   0.590 Mg
RIBOFLAVIN      A=======                                    14%   0.170 Mg
NIACIN          A=====                                      12%   1.680 Mg
VITAMIN B6      A=========                                  19%   0.380 Mg
FOLACIN         A                                            1%   7.200 Ug
VITAMIN B12     A                                            0%   0.000 Ug
PANTO- ACID     A===                                        7%   0.410 Mg
CALCIUM         A=====                                      10%   87.00 Mg
PHOSPHORUS      A==============                             28%   229.0 Mg
TRYPTOPHAN      A==================================         66%   109.0 Mg
THREONINE       A==================================         66%   291.0 Mg
ISOLEUCINE      A===========================                54%   356.0 Mg
LEUCINE         A==============================             61%   535.0 Mg
LYSINE          A=====================                      42%   279.0 Mg
METHIONINE      A=========================                  51%   139.0 Mg
CYSTINE         A=========================                  50%   136.0 Mg
PHENYL-ANINE    A===========================================  86%  376.0 Mg
TYROSINE        A========================                   49%   217.0 Mg
VALINE          A==========================                 53%   409.0 Mg
HISTIDINE       A                                         NO RDA  206.0 Mg
ALCOHOL         A                                         NO RDA  0.000 Gm
ASH             A                                         NO RDA  1.340 Gm
COPPER          A===========                                22%   0.550 Mg
MANGANESE       A=========                                  18%   0.700 Mg
IODINE          A=========                                  18%   27.30 Ug
MONO FAT        A                                         NO RDA  4.680 Gm
POLY FAT        A                                         NO RDA  10.60 Gm
CAFFEINE        A                                         NO RDA  0.000 Mg
FLUORIDE        A                                            0%   20.30 Ug
MOLYBDENUM      A======================================     76%   250.0 Ug
VITAMIN K       A                                            0%   0.000 Ug
SELENIUM        A                                            0%   0.000 Mg
BIOTIN          A=                                           3%   4.630 Ug
CHLORIDE        A                                            0%   25.30 Mg
CHROMIUM        A===========                                24%   0.030 Mg
SUGAR           A                                         NO RDA  0.000 Gm
FIBER-DIET      A                                         NO RDA  3.350 Gm
VIT. E/AT       A=================================================  171%  13.70 Mg

% RDA:   |0      |20     |40     |60     |80     |100
```

Analysis does not include nutrients contained in "rejuvelac" (water that nuts and seeds were soaked in); uses raw almonds and sunflower seeds and does not include the increase in nutrients which occurs during germination.

An improvement on Dr. Bircher-Benner's muesli because the grains are sprouted, adding all the nutritional benefits that take place in that process! To germinate the wheatberries, soak in water overnight and drain. Put into a sprouting container or make your own by stretching some plastic or nylon window screen over the mouth of a jar and holding it intact with a strong rubber band; invert jar in a dish drainer or any place where it can be upside down so excess water can drain out and air can get in. Rinse germinating seeds 3 to 4 times a day, pour out water and turn upside down to drain each time. Germinate till little white tips grow to about ⅛" long and wheatberries are very sweet when eaten (takes 2 to 3 days).

# FRUITY MUESLI

☆ A fiber-filled, healthy breakfast cereal that's sweetened with the natural sugars that form from the starch in the grain during the germination process. Needs no additional sweetening.

---

3 cups fresh cut fruit (such as bananas, apples,
  peaches, apricots, strawberries, etc.)
¼ cup currants or raisins
¼ cup chopped nuts or seeds

3 cups ground wheatberry sprouts

1 Tbsp. grated fresh ginger root (optional)

Combine first 3 ingredients together in a bowl. Run wheatberries through a food grinder and add to ingredients in the bowl along with grated ginger (if you want to use it). Chill in refrigerator if you want to serve as a cold cereal; ideal to make the night before and refrigerate overnight, but is okay to make and let sit for about 15 minutes to allow juices to mix together. Makes six 1-cup servings.

| Special Shopping |
|---|
| Sprouted wheatberries — whole wheatberries can be found in natural food stores; wheatberries must be germinated at home. |

| SHOPPING LIST | |
|---|---|
| Regularly Kept in the Kitchen (Listed in Chapter 14, p. 703) | Fresh Produce |
| Raisins<br>Nuts or seeds | Fresh fruit of the season<br>Ginger root |

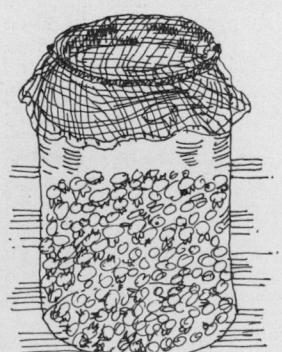

# SUN-BAKED TARTS

☆ These tarts are great served for breakfast, snacks, or can be decorated attractively with slices of fresh fruit to serve for dessert.

---

1 quart sprouted wheatberries
¼ cup chopped sunflower seeds
¼ cup chopped, pitted dates

Run all 3 ingredients through a food grinder. Mix ground ingredients together well. Break into balls and shape into tart shapes on an oiled cookie sheet. (Size of ball will depend on the size of tart you want. A good size for a small tart is ¼ cup.) To shape, just flatten ball out to about ¼" thick and pinch up sides like a pie shell. Leave tarts out in hot sun all day long to bake, or bake at 250 degrees for 4 to 6 hours. Shells should be dry on the outside and dry enough to hold their shape (but not totally dry) all the way through. Fill with desired no-cook filling like the following. The baked shells can be frozen so they are available for a quick treat. This recipe makes about 16 to 20 small tarts.

## Fig Filling:

½ cup chopped, dried figs
1 ripe banana
2 Tbsp. carob powder
2 Tbsp. water
2 tsp. cashew butter
1 tsp. honey

Blend all ingredients together till they form a fairly smooth paste. Scoop into already finished tarts.

## Apricot Filling:

½ cup orange juice
1 cup dried apricots

Soak overnight. Then blend together in blender till pureed, adding more juice as you blend if necessary.

| SHOPPING LIST | |
|---|---|
| **Regularly Kept in the Kitchen (Listed in Chapter 14, p. 703)** | **Fresh Produce** |
| Chopped sunflower seeds | Dried figs |
| Pitted dates | Banana |
| Carob powder | Orange juice |
| Cashew butter | Dried apricots |
| Honey | |

| Special Shopping |
|---|
| Sprouted wheatberries — whole wheatberries can be found in natural food stores; wheatberries must be germinated at home. |

# MISO SOUP

☆ Following Japanese tradition, my mother used to serve miso soup for breakfast sometimes. It's a fairly quick breakfast to make; with a little pre-planning you can make it the night before and simply heat up in the morning (it's good cold on hot summer days).

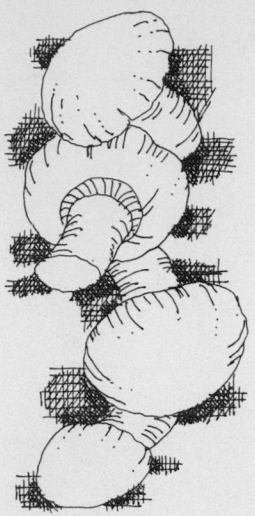

12 cups water
1-foot strip of kombu seaweed

½ cup slivered carrots
3 cups mild-flavored Chinese green (such as Chinese cabbage), cut in 1" pieces
2 cups watercress or Chinese mustard greens, cut in 1" chunks
1 cup sliced, fresh mushrooms

1½ cups dark miso

1 block tofu, cubed

Bring first 2 ingredients to a boil. (Use whole 1-foot strip of kombu seaweed if you want to remove it from the soup before serving; otherwise, cut it into fine julienne strips.) Then begin adding other ingredients to the water in the order listed. If not using ingredients specified in this recipe, just remember to add the hardest vegetables first since they will take longer to cook, and then end with the vegetables that cook very quickly. If you add each vegetable just after it's cut, the timing works out perfectly.

To add miso, place miso inside of a fairly fine-screened strainer. Immerse bottom part of strainer into boiling water and mash miso through the screen into the water with the back of a large spoon. This makes a smoother soup. Add cubes of tofu and cook long enough to warm. Serve with a scoop of brown rice or brown rice crackers. Makes six 2-cup servings.

For a long time in Japan, miso has been considered to be a very healthy food; and rightly so, as recent nutritional analysis has proved. Besides its nutritional benefits, there are some other benefits of miso that are especially pertinent to us in this day and age.

Back in the 1940's, a Dr. Akizuki, who personally drank miso soup daily to strengthen the frail body he was born with, got his whole family and hospital staff in Nagasaki to drink miso soup regularly. For two years after the atomic bomb hit Nagasaki, Dr. Akizuki and his staff worked very closely with fallout victims in areas of Nagasaki that had high radiation levels. When neither he nor his staff got radiation sickness as would be expected, Dr. Akizuki speculated that perhaps this was due to miso soup. A 1972 study by Japanese scientists, stimulated by Dr. Akizuki's writings, found that miso contains zybicolin (dipicolinic acid) which grabs onto heavy metals (radioactive strontium being one) and discharges them from the body.

Miso can also help to neutralize the effects of air pollution.

| SHOPPING LIST | |
|---|---|
| **Regularly Kept in the Kitchen** (Listed in Chapter 14, p. 703) | **Fresh Produce** |
| Miso<br>Tofu<br>Kombu or wakame seaweed | Carrots<br>Napa cabbage or other Chinese greens<br>Watercress or mustard greens<br>Mushrooms |

# NUTRITIONAL ANALYSIS FOR ONE SERVING MISO SOUP

```
NUTRIENT       Type: 14   FEMALE-23 TO 51 YEARS              % RDA   Amount
KCALORIES     Ã======                                         13%    276.0 Kc
PROTEIN       Ã===========================                    51%    22.50 Gm
CARBOHYDRATE  Ã                                              NO RDA  25.10 Gm
FAT           Ã                                              NO RDA  11.60 Gm
FIBER-CRUDE   Ã                                              NO RDA  2.280 Gm
CHOLESTEROL   Ã                                              NO RDA  0.000 Mg
SATURATED FA  Ã                                              NO RDA  1.680 Gm
OLEIC FA      Ã                                              NO RDA  0.840 Gm
LINOLEIC FA   Ã                                              NO RDA  1.660 Gm
SODIUM        Ã===========================================   116%    2554 Mg
POTASSIUM     Ã======                                         13%    510.0 Mg
MAGNESIUM     Ã===============                                30%    90.00 Mg
IRON          Ã===============================               62%    11.20 Mg
ZINC          Ã============                                   24%    3.710 Mg
VITAMIN A     Ã===========================================   109%    4361 IU
VITAMIN D     Ã                                               0%     0.000 IU
VIT. E/TOTAL  Ã                                              NO RDA  1.910 Mg
VITAMIN C     Ã==================                             36%    22.00 Mg
THIAMIN       Ã============                                   24%    0.240 Mg
RIBOFLAVIN    Ã==============                                 29%    0.350 Mg
NIACIN        Ã======                                         12%    1.660 Mg
VITAMIN B6    Ã======                                         13%    0.260 Mg
FOLACIN       Ã======                                         13%    52.00 Ug
VITAMIN B12   Ã====                                           8%     0.250 Ug
PANTO- ACID   Ã======                                         10%    0.600 Mg
CALCIUM       Ã=====================================          84%    678.0 Mg
PHOSPHORUS    Ã==================                             37%    300.0 Mg
TRYPTOPHAN    Ã==========================================    196%    320.0 Mg
THREONINE     Ã==========================================    235%    1026 Mg
ISOLEUCINE    Ã==========================================    194%    1268 Mg
LEUCINE       Ã==========================================    212%    1852 Mg
LYSINE        Ã==========================================    214%    1402 Mg
METHIONINE    Ã==========================================    104%    283.0 Mg
CYSTINE       Ã=======================================        94%    257.0 Mg
PHENYL-ANINE  Ã==========================================    252%    1097 Mg
TYROSINE      Ã==========================================    162%    709.0 Mg
VALINE        Ã==========================================    161%    1234 Mg
HISTIDINE     Ã                                              NO RDA  634.0 Mg
ALCOHOL       Ã                                              NO RDA  0.000 Gm
ASH           Ã                                              NO RDA  10.50 Gm
COPPER        Ã==============                                 29%    0.730 Mg
MANGANESE     Ã======================                         44%    1.660 Mg
IODINE        Ã==============================                 61%    91.60 Ug
MONO FAT      Ã                                              NO RDA  2.530 Gm
POLY FAT      Ã                                              NO RDA  6.550 Gm
CAFFEINE      Ã                                              NO RDA  0.000 Mg
FLUORIDE      Ã                                               0%     20.10 Ug
MOLYBDENUM    Ã==========================================    451%    1467 Ug
VITAMIN K     Ã========================                       47%    50.00 Ug
SELENIUM      Ã====                                           8%     0.010 Mg
BIOTIN        Ã==                                             5%     7.810 Ug
CHLORIDE      Ã========================                       47%    1619 Mg
CHROMIUM      Ã==========================================    208%    0.260 Mg
SUGAR         Ã                                              NO RDA  1.930 Gm
FIBER-DIET    Ã                                              NO RDA  2.680 Gm
VIT. E/AT     Ã============                                   25%    2.000 Mg

   % RDA:    |0      |20     |40     |60     |80     |100
```

Greens used in this analysis: watercress and pak-choy.

# EAT 'N RUN

Individuals looking at some of today's mammoth problems — like pollution, terrorism or the threat of a nuclear holocaust — are often left with a helpless feeling as they ask, "What can I do?"

In the last paragraph of his book Small is Beautiful, E. F. Schumacher replies, "The answer is as simple as it is disconcerting. We can, each of us, work to put our own inner house in order. The guidance we need for this work cannot be found in science or technology, the value of which utterly depends on the ends they serve; but it can still be found in the traditional wisdom of mankind."

Where breakfast is concerned, it's all right to eat and run; it's certainly better to do that than not eat breakfast at all. Unfortunately, more and more people in America are doing their AM eating and running in fast-food restaurants where they start the day with dishes full of cholesterol, fats, sugar and chemical additives. If only there were a profusion of healthy fast-food restaurants!

Without a healthy fast-food restaurant to run to, the better thing to do to safeguard one's health is do a little pre-planning to be able to make a healthy breakfast in short-order at home. One way to pre-plan breakfast is prepare it the night before (as the preceding recipe ideas are meant to be). If your morning schedule doesn't permit any sit-down-and-eat time, you can even pack a brown bag breakfast every night to take and eat on the bus, subway, etc.

If you do have a limited amount of time in the morning, the following recipes might give you some ideas on how to make some healthy, nutritious breakfasts quickly. This can be done by making your own (or buying from a natural food store) healthy mixes that just require mixing and sitting or baking. The muesli mix is a mix-and-sit recipe. There are a few whole grain muffin mixes available in natural food stores that take about 15 minutes to mix and bake. If you want to supplement these mixes with something fresh, or just have something fresh for breakfast, smoothie blender drinks offer unlimited possibilities; or try frying some tofu instead of the usual cholesterol-laden egg.

# SUGARLESS MUESLI MIX

☆ A mix that can be kept on hand to make a cold cereal. Since it should sit in liquid for at least 15 minutes, you may want to mix it immediately upon waking up (or the night before); that way, after exercising, showering, dressing, it'll be ready and waiting for you.

---

*4 cups raw rolled oats*
*1 cup finely grated, dried banana*
  *(grated on ⅛" holes)*
*1 cup finely diced, dried apple*
*1 cup date sugar*
*1 cup raisins*
*1 cup wheat germ*
*½ cup bran*
*½ cup chia seeds*

*2 cups sunflower seeds*
*1 cup almonds*

Combine first 8 ingredients in a bowl and mix with fingertips till dried fruit is evenly distributed throughout grains (don't leave any lumps of dried fruit). Run nuts and seeds in blender or food processor till they are a flour-like consistency; mix into other ingredients. Put in an airtight plastic container and refrigerate (to keep oils in wheat germ, nuts and seeds from getting rancid).

When you want to make muesli for breakfast, scoop 1 cup of muesli with 1 cup of yogurt, 1 cup of milk, a squeeze of lemon juice and 2 apples (grated) and/or as much fresh fruit of the season as desired. Mix well and allow to sit 15 minutes (or overnight), then serve. You can use fruit juice instead of the yogurt and/or milk . . . This is a dish you never get tired of because you can make it different every morning by changing the kind of fruit and/or juice used. The above proportions will make 2 to 3 servings.

Although I personally prefer the sprouted muesli (p. 19) for nutritional and taste reasons, this muesli mix is less work than the sprouted one and is good in a pinch — when there's no time to hand grind sprouted wheatberries. Many of the commercially-made muesli mixes contain sugar. This one is sweetened with dried fruit. You must still brush your teeth after eating this! Fruit sugar will cause tooth decay as much as white sugar does. Dried fruit has a tendency to stick to teeth, too.

| SHOPPING LIST | | |
| --- | --- | --- |
| **Regularly Kept in the Kitchen** (Listed in Chapter 14, p. 703) | | **Fresh Produce** |
| Oats Raisins Wheat germ Bran Sunflower seeds Almonds | | Dried apple |

| Special Shopping |
| --- |
| Dried banana, chia seeds — found in natural food stores. |

The assembly directions for all the "recipes" are the same. Just put all ingredients in the blender (except the toppings) and blend till completely smooth. Pour into serving container and, if you want to make it pretty, bother with the topping. This can be poured into a cup to drink as a smoothie or put in a bowl to be sipped as soup. If serving as a soup, you can cut small chunks of a compatible fruit (or vegetable) and mix in so you have something to sink your teeth into.

# BREAKFAST IN A CUP

☆ All of these can be made in a matter of minutes — especially if you don't measure. When making smoothie drinks, I only measure by eyeball.

To make 1 quart (4 servings):

| | Liquid | Protein | Fruit | Other | Topping |
|---|---|---|---|---|---|
| Peanut Butter Cups | 2 c. lowfat milk | ¼ c. peanut butter<br>¼ c. Bipro | 2 bananas | 2 c. crushed ice<br>1 Tbsp. honey | Chopped, roasted peanuts and drizzle of carob syrup (Carob Fondue, p.235) |
| A Berry Satisfying Frosty | ⅓ c. frozen orange juice concentrate<br>¼ c. water | 6 Tbsp. Bipro | 1½ c. berries in season or pitted cherries<br>2 bananas | 2½ to 3 c. crushed ice | Whole berry used in smoothie and fresh mint leaves |
| Peach Melba | 1 c. unsweetened apricot juice | 1 c. vanilla yogurt | 6 fresh or frozen medium peaches<br>1 ripe banana | 2 Tbsp. raw wheat germ<br>2 tsp. honey<br>Pinch of cinnamon | Whole grain honey- or juice-sweetened cookie crumbs |
| Light Summer Melon Drink | | | ½ honeydew melon<br>1 c. watermelon<br>1 c. cantaloupe | | Slice of kiwi fruit |
| Tropical Sunshine | 2 c. pineapple juice | | 2 papayas (about 2 c.)<br>2 frozen bananas | | Shredded coconut |
| Just Peachy Buttermilk | 2 c. buttermilk | | 4 frozen peaches | 6 pitted dates | Date sugar |
| Mango Milk | 3 c. lowfat milk | | 2 large mangoes | 1 tsp. honey | |
| Vegie Smoothie | 4 c. mixed vegetable juice | 3 Tbsp. Bipro | 1 small avocado (about 1 c.) | ¼ c. mixed sprouts<br>3 Tbsp. nutritional yeast<br>½ Tbsp. miso | Alfalfa sprouts |

# FRIED TOFU

☆ So simple to make, I hardly think of it as a recipe — but so many things can be done with the tofu once it's fried.

Quick breakfasts don't have to be cold. If you have time to fry an egg in the morning, you have time to do the same with cholesterol-free tofu.

---

*Butter or margarine or safflower oil*
*Japanese or Chinese firm tofu*
*Soy sauce*

Heat skillet and melt a tiny bit of whichever oil you want to use in the bottom. When oil is heated enough to make a drop of water sizzle, put ½"-thick slices of tofu in the bottom of skillet. Sprinkle lightly with soy sauce and flip. Cook to desired degree of brownness. Sprinkle soy sauce on uncooked side and flip to brown the same as the other side. Tofu can be browned only until parts of a side begin turning a yellow-gold and tofu is still soft, or fried till darkly browned and tofu crisps on the outside.

These are only a few of the things that can be done with the Fried Tofu for a quick breakfast:
• Lightly fry, place on top of a toasted whole grain English muffin, top with a little cheese and broil till cheese melts. Top with a tomato slice and alfalfa sprouts.
• Put on top of whole grain toast and top with spaghetti sauce.
• Put slimmer slices on a whole wheat or corn tortilla and top with salsa, sliced avocado, lettuce and sprouts.
• Put in a sandwich with your favorite sandwich fillings between two pieces of whole grain bread.
• Serve as a cutlet alongside some leftover brown rice and salad.
• Layer a toasted English muffin with a whole canned Ortega chili, Fried Tofu, tomato slice, sprinkles of Tabasco and grated cheese (in that order) and broil till cheese melts.
• The list could go on, but I think you have the idea by now!

26

# VALMIKI'S EGGLESS SCRAMBLE

☆ I'm proudly presenting this recipe that my second son, Valmiki, created and makes quite often for himself and for the whole family. Like most creative chefs, he doesn't follow recipes or measure with cups and spoons, so his creations are a little different each time.

---

2 Tbsp. margarine or butter
3 cups mashed Chinese firm tofu
¼ cup nutritional yeast
1 Tbsp. soy sauce
½ tsp. asafetida or garlic powder
½ tsp. turmeric
Dash black pepper

Combine all ingredients together in a heated skillet and cook, stirring constantly, mashing the mixture with the back of the spatula till tofu is hot and nutritional yeast has melted. You can make variations, as you would with scrambled eggs, by adding one of the following to the mixture as you cook it — or use your imagination to add other special flavorings.

Makes 2 to 3 servings.

¼ cup finely chopped chives and
   ¼ cup imitation bacon bits
   made from soy protein

¼ cup each of diced tomato and
   diced bell or green chili pepper,
   plus 1 teaspoon chili powder

## SUGGESTED BREAKFAST MENU

*Yuba bacon
(prepare as in
Hot Vegi-Bacon Dressing
recipe, but cut yuba
in long strips)*

*Valmiki's Eggless Scramble*

*Whole grain toast*

| SHOPPING LIST | |
|---|---|
| **Regularly Kept in the Kitchen** (Listed in Chapter 14, p. 703) | **Fresh Produce** |
| Margarine or butter<br>Tofu<br>Nutritional yeast<br>Soy sauce<br>Asafetida<br>Turmeric<br>Black pepper | (None) |

# NUTRITIONAL ANALYSIS FOR ONE SERVING
## VALMIKI'S EGGLESS SCRAMBLE

| NUTRIENT | Type: 14 FEMALE-23 TO 51 YEARS | % RDA | Amount |
|---|---|---|---|
| KCALORIES | X==================== | 35% | 709.0 Kc |
| PROTEIN | X=========================================== | 154% | 68.00 Gm |
| CARBOHYDRATE | X | NO RDA | 22.60 Gm |
| FAT | X | NO RDA | 44.40 Gm |
| FIBER-CRUDE | X | NO RDA | 0.590 Gm |
| CHOLESTEROL | X | NO RDA | 0.000 Mg |
| SATURATED FA | X | NO RDA | 6.600 |
| OLEIC FA | X | NO RDA | 3.780 Gm |
| LINOLEIC FA | X | NO RDA | 7.550 Gm |
| SODIUM | X================ | 32% | 714.0 Mg |
| POTASSIUM | X================ | 33% | 1240 Mg |
| MAGNESIUM | X============================================ | 83% | 249.0 Mg |
| IRON | X===================================================== | 226% | 40.70 Mg |
| ZINC | X============================== | 57% | 8.550 Mg |
| VITAMIN A | X============= | 27% | 1095 IU |
| VITAMIN D | X | 0% | 0.000 IU |
| VIT. E/TOTAL | X | NO RDA | 0.010 Mg |
| VITAMIN C | X | 1% | 1.060 Mg |
| THIAMIN | X===================================================== | 960% | 9.600 Mg |
| RIBOFLAVIN | X===================================================== | 783% | 9.400 Mg |
| NIACIN | X===================================================== | 411% | 53.50 Mg |
| VITAMIN B6 | X===================================================== | 467% | 9.350 Mg |
| FOLACIN | X========================== | 57% | 231.0 Ug |
| VITAMIN B12 | X===================================================== | 233% | 7.000 Ug |
| PANTO- ACID | X================ | 30% | 1.650 Mg |
| CALCIUM | X===================================================== | 325% | 2600 Mg |
| PHOSPHORUS | X===================================================== | 118% | 945.0 Mg |
| TRYPTOPHAN | X===================================================== | 622% | 1015 Mg |
| THREONINE | X===================================================== | 650% | 2828 Mg |
| ISOLEUCINE | X===================================================== | 513% | 3356 Mg |
| LEUCINE | X===================================================== | 592% | 5159 Mg |
| LYSINE | X===================================================== | 700% | 4575 Mg |
| METHIONINE | X===================================================== | 327% | 892.0 Mg |
| CYSTINE | X===================================================== | 348% | 947.0 Mg |
| PHENYL-ANINE | X===================================================== | 748% | 3257 Mg |
| TYROSINE | X===================================================== | 537% | 2338 Mg |
| VALINE | X===================================================== | 462% | 3528 Mg |
| HISTIDINE | X | NO RDA | 1981 Mg |
| ALCOHOL | X | NO RDA | 0.000 Gm |
| ASH | X | NO RDA | 15.00 Gm |
| COPPER | X============================== | 57% | 1.430 Mg |
| MANGANESE | X============================================ | 119% | 4.470 Mg |
| IODINE | X===================================================== | 274% | 412.0 Ug |
| MONO FAT | X | NO RDA | 12.60 Gm |
| POLY FAT | X | NO RDA | 22.30 Gm |
| CAFFEINE | X | NO RDA | 0.000 Mg |
| FLUORIDE | X | 0% | 0.000 Ug |
| MOLYBDENUM | X===================================================== | 1395% | 4536 Ug |
| VITAMIN K | X | 0% | 0.000 Ug |
| SELENIUM | X================ | 32% | 0.040 Mg |
| BIOTIN | X========= | 19% | 29.90 Ug |
| CHLORIDE | X========== | 21% | 718.0 Mg |
| CHROMIUM | X===================================================== | 943% | 1.180 Mg |
| SUGAR | X | NO RDA | 0.000 Gm |
| FIBER-DIET | X | NO RDA | 0.000 Gm |
| VIT. E/AT | X | 0% | 0.000 Mg |

```
% RDA:  |0      |20     |40     |60     |80     |100
```

Analysis does not include optional recipe variations; margarine used instead of butter.

**I**n the Bible it is written, "Those who live on the level of spirit have the spiritual outlook, and that is life and peace."

# SUNRISE GREETING FROM SOUTH·OF·THE·BORDER

**T**his breakfast, which takes its inspiration from Mexico, makes a breakfast of bacon and eggs pale in comparison. Not only is it better nutritionally, but it tastes better! What a great way to start the day when you have a little bit of extra time to spend on breakfast — maybe on a weekend or a lazy day.

But this kind of breakfast won't make you feel lazy for the rest of the day. As a whole meal practically made up of complex carbohydrates, it's the type of meal a jogger might eat while "carbohydrate-loading" for a marathon. Our days are like marathons, so we should fuel up properly for them with complex carbohydrate-based meals like these.

# PAPAYA ZINGER

☆ This is good served 15 to 30 minutes before or after
the rest of the meal, as all the enzymes in papaya will
really help to aid digestion. That's probably why a slice
of papaya is a common dessert with Mexican meals!

---

*4 cups diced papaya*

*¼ cup lemon juice*
*2 Tbsp. honey*
*2 tsp. grated fresh ginger root*
*1 tsp. finely grated lemon rind*

*Chilled fizzy water*

Cut papayas in half and de-seed. Cut dice shapes and
scoop out of peel into a mixing bowl. Mix next 4 ingredients
together in a little cup or bowl till honey is dissolved. Pour the
mixture onto the papaya and marinate for at least 30 minutes,
tossing occasionally.

Right before serving, spoon marinated fruit and sauce into
individual dessert cups and pour fizzy water over fruit to fill
the cups. Serve immediately. Makes 4 servings.

| SHOPPING LIST | |
|---|---|
| **Regularly Kept in the Kitchen** (Listed in Chapter 14, p. 703) | **Fresh Produce** |
| Honey | Papaya <br> Lemon <br> Ginger root <br> Sparkling water |

Give yourself a natural facial by
rubbing the inside of the papaya
peel over your face and allowing
it to dry. Then rinse off and
apply your moisturizer onto still
moist skin. Also, save the seeds
and try making some Papaya Seed
Pepper.

To make Papaya Seed Pepper . . .
Keep seeds that have been
scooped out of the papaya
(they're rich in enzymes and
other valuable nutrients; after all,
they contain the food the baby
plant would have grown on till it
established roots). The seeds have
a very pungent, peppery taste and
are delicious ground in salad
dressings or used instead of black
pepper. To make papaya pepper,
simply wash seeds in a colander
to remove bits of papaya and
stringy membranes that may be
attached. Drain, then spread the
seeds out on a cookie sheet and
place in a warm, dry place, like
inside a gas oven with only the
pilot light on. Leave the seeds till
they are crisp and dry. Now the
seeds can be placed in a pepper
mill and used in place of black
pepper.

# NUTRITIONAL ANALYSIS FOR ONE SERVING PAPAYA ZINGER

| NUTRIENT | Type: 14   FEMALE-23 TO 51 YEARS | % RDA | Amount |
|---|---|---|---|
| KCALORIES | A== | 4% | 90.70 Kc |
| PROTEIN | A= | 2% | 0.940 Gm |
| CARBOHYDRATE | A | NO RDA | 23.70 Gm |
| FAT | A | NO RDA | 0.200 Gm |
| FIBER-CRUDE | A | NO RDA | 1.100 Gm |
| CHOLESTEROL | A | NO RDA | 0.000 Mg |
| SATURATED FA | A | NO RDA | 0.060 Gm |
| OLEIC FA | A | NO RDA | 0.000 Gm |
| LINOLEIC FA | A | NO RDA | 0.000 Gm |
| SODIUM | A | 0% | 6.000 Mg |
| POTASSIUM | A===== | 10% | 388.0 Mg |
| MAGNESIUM | A== | 5% | 15.80 Mg |
| IRON | A | 1% | 0.200 Mg |
| ZINC | A | 0% | 0.110 Mg |
| VITAMIN A | A==================================== | 70% | 2822 IU |
| VITAMIN D | A | 0% | 0.000 IU |
| VIT. E/TOTAL | A | NO RDA | 0.000 Mg |
| VITAMIN C | A==================================================== | 156% | 94.00 Mg |
| THIAMIN | A== | 4% | 0.040 Mg |
| RIBOFLAVIN | A== | 4% | 0.050 Mg |
| NIACIN | A== | 4% | 0.540 Mg |
| VITAMIN B6 | A | 1% | 0.030 Mg |
| FOLACIN | A | 0% | 1.960 Ug |
| VITAMIN B12 | A | 0% | 0.000 Ug |
| PANTO- ACID | A=== | 6% | 0.340 Mg |
| CALCIUM | A== | 5% | 43.50 Mg |
| PHOSPHORUS | A | 1% | 8.750 Mg |
| TRYPTOPHAN | A=== | 6% | 11.10 Mg |
| THREONINE | A= | 3% | 15.30 Mg |
| ISOLEUCINE | A | 1% | 11.50 Mg |
| LEUCINE | A= | 2% | 22.70 Mg |
| LYSINE | A== | 5% | 35.50 Mg |
| METHIONINE | A | 1% | 3.120 Mg |
| CYSTINE | A | 0% | 0.080 Mg |
| PHENYL-ANINE | A= | 3% | 13.40 Mg |
| TYROSINE | A | 1% | 7.200 Mg |
| VALINE | A | 1% | 14.70 Mg |
| HISTIDINE | A | NO RDA | 7.270 Mg |
| ALCOHOL | A | NO RDA | 0.000 Gm |
| ASH | A | NO RDA | 0.930 Gm |
| COPPER | A | 1% | 0.030 Mg |
| MANGANESE | A | 0% | 0.010 Mg |
| IODINE | A | 0% | 0.000 Ug |
| MONO FAT | A | NO RDA | 0.050 Gm |
| POLY FAT | A | NO RDA | 0.040 Gm |
| CAFFEINE | A | NO RDA | 0.000 Mg |
| FLUORIDE | A | 0% | 10.50 Ug |
| MOLYBDENUM | A | 0% | 0.000 Ug |
| VITAMIN K | A | 0% | 0.000 Ug |
| SELENIUM | A | 0% | 0.000 Mg |
| BIOTIN | A | 0% | 0.000 Ug |
| CHLORIDE | A | 0% | 0.000 Mg |
| CHROMIUM | A | 0% | 0.000 Mg |
| SUGAR | A | NO RDA | 0.240 Gm |
| FIBER-DIET | A | NO RDA | 1.270 Gm |
| VIT. E/AT | A | 0% | 0.000 Mg |

```
% RDA:  |0      |20     |40     |60     |80    |100
```

# SOFT TORTILLAS

☆ Yes, you heard right (if you watched the show); I make about three dozen of these to serve five people. They're one of those things that everyone from the babies to the adults love to eat!

---

*Few dozen corn tortillas*
*Margarine or butter*

To make soft tortillas, heat skillet to hot. Take a very small dab of margarine or butter, put in the middle of the pan and sizzle to melt (use just enough to keep the tortillas from sticking to the pan). Put a tortilla in the skillet and swirl with fingertips so bottom of tortilla is evenly coated with margarine or butter. Let cook till little bubbles begin to appear on top surface of the tortilla (this should take 10 to 15 seconds).

Flip the tortilla over, cook another 10 seconds and remove from heat. Stack tortillas one on top of the other and cover with a bamboo lid to keep hot. The bamboo lid is ideal because it absorbs excess moisture from steam and keeps tortillas from getting soggy or sticking together; but if you don't have one, you may use an inverted bowl with a paper or tea towel inside the bowl to absorb the excess moisture.

| SHOPPING LIST | |
|---|---|
| Regularly Kept in the Kitchen (Listed in Chapter 14, p. 703) | Fresh Produce |
| Corn or whole wheat tortillas Butter or margarine | (None) |

I try to keep a stack of tortillas in the refrigerator because the children love to cook their own and snack on soft tortillas filled with whatever leftovers or other foods are available. To name a few ways they stuff soft tortillas:

- The babies love soft tortillas smeared with peanut butter and bananas
- Avocado sprinkled with sprouts and tabasco
- Refried beans with salsa and sprouts
- Leftover vegetables
- Sauteed tofu with leftover salad and salsa

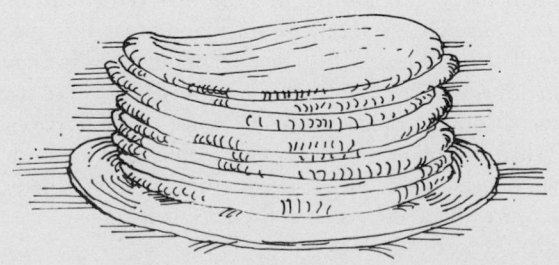

# TOFU RANCHEROS

1 tsp. vegetable oil
1½ tsp. asafetida and 1 cup finely slivered celery
 OR 1 cup finely slivered onion

2 Tbsp. finely chopped fresh cilantro or parsley
4 cups tomato wedges
⅓ cup chopped green chilies
¼ tsp. ground cumin
¼ tsp. black pepper
½ tsp. oregano
1½ tsp. soy sauce
⅛ tsp. cayenne (optional)

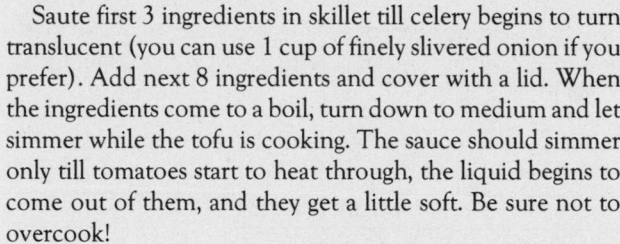

Oil for frying
1 lb. Chinese firm tofu, cut into eighths
Black pepper
Soy sauce
Cheddar cheese (optional)

Saute first 3 ingredients in skillet till celery begins to turn translucent (you can use 1 cup of finely slivered onion if you prefer). Add next 8 ingredients and cover with a lid. When the ingredients come to a boil, turn down to medium and let simmer while the tofu is cooking. The sauce should simmer only till tomatoes start to heat through, the liquid begins to come out of them, and they get a little soft. Be sure not to overcook!

Cut the tofu block into eighths width-wise. (This should give you about eight ½"-thick slices.) Oil another skillet and when oil is sizzling hot, place slices of tofu in skillet. While frying on the one side, sprinkle the other side with a little black pepper and soy sauce. Flip tofu and fry on the other side when the first side is heated. At this point, if you want to use the Cheddar cheese (which will add cholesterol to the meal), scoop a little well out of the middle of the tofu with a soup spoon, being careful not to scoop through to the bottom of the pan. Slice cheese about ⅛" thick and break into pieces that will fit into the well. Turn heat off under sauce and cover tofu with skillet lid. Cook till cheese melts, or if not using cheese, till bottom of tofu begins to brown a little. Serve each tofu slice on top of a soft-cooked tortilla or a mound of brown rice. Scoop about ½ cup of sauce on top of the tofu slice. Serve with a side dish of refried beans and a stack of soft tortillas. Makes 4 servings.

| SHOPPING LIST | |
|---|---|
| **Regularly Kept in the Kitchen**<br>(Listed in Chapter 14, p. 703) | **Fresh Produce** |
| Vegetable oil | Celery |
| Asafetida | Cilantro (also known as |
| Ground cumin | Chinese parsley or |
| Black pepper | coriander leaves) |
| Oregano | Tomatoes |
| Soy sauce | Green chilies |
| Cayenne | |
| Tofu | |
| Cheddar cheese (optional) | |

# SUGGESTED MENU FOR A SUNRISE GREETING BREAKFAST FROM SOUTH-OF-THE-BORDER

*Papaya Zinger*

*Soft Tortillas*

*Rice or refried beans*
*(with no lard)*

*Tossed salad*

*Tofu Rancheros*

*"Cafe" Con Leche*

# NUTRITIONAL ANALYSIS FOR ONE SERVING TOFU RANCHEROS
## WITH TWO CORN TORTILLAS

| NUTRIENT | Type: 14 FEMALE-23 TO 51 YEARS | % RDA | Amount |
|---|---|---|---|
| KCALORIES | A=========== | 20% | 403.0 Kc |
| PROTEIN | A================================ | 62% | 27.60 Gm |
| CARBOHYDRATE | A | NO RDA | 47.60 Gm |
| FAT | A | NO RDA | 15.10 Gm |
| FIBER-CRUDE | A | NO RDA | 2.550 Gm |
| CHOLESTEROL | A | NO RDA | 0.000 Mg |
| SATURATED FA | A | NO RDA | 1.800 Gm |
| OLEIC FA | A | NO RDA | 1.390 Gm |
| LINOLEIC FA | A | NO RDA | 3.350 Gm |
| SODIUM | A====== | 12% | 276.0 Mg |
| POTASSIUM | A=============== | 29% | 1095 Mg |
| MAGNESIUM | A========================= | 50% | 152.0 Mg |
| IRON | A================================================= | 90% | 16.30 Mg |
| ZINC | A=========== | 21% | 3.280 Mg |
| VITAMIN A | A=============================================== | 87% | 3506 IU |
| VITAMIN D | A | 0% | 0.000 IU |
| VIT. E/TOTAL | A | NO RDA | 1.940 Mg |
| VITAMIN C | A====================================================== | 138% | 83.30 Mg |
| THIAMIN | A========================= | 49% | 0.490 Mg |
| RIBOFLAVIN | A=============== | 28% | 0.340 Mg |
| NIACIN | A============ | 24% | 3.140 Mg |
| VITAMIN B6 | A============= | 26% | 0.530 Mg |
| FOLACIN | A=========== | 22% | 88.90 Ug |
| VITAMIN B12 | A | 0% | 0.000 Ug |
| PANTO- ACID | A========= | 18% | 1.030 Mg |
| CALCIUM | A==================================================== | 123% | 984.0 Mg |
| PHOSPHORUS | A============================ | 54% | 435.0 Mg |
| TRYPTOPHAN | A================================= | 217% | 355.0 Mg |
| THREONINE | A================================ | 232% | 1011 Mg |
| ISOLEUCINE | A================================ | 190% | 1242 Mg |
| LEUCINE | A================================ | 242% | 2114 Mg |
| LYSINE | A================================ | 232% | 1515 Mg |
| METHIONINE | A================================ | 125% | 340.0 Mg |
| CYSTINE | A================================ | 117% | 320.0 Mg |
| PHENYL-ANINE | A================================ | 271% | 1180 Mg |
| TYROSINE | A================================ | 163% | 712.0 Mg |
| VALINE | A================================ | 163% | 1244 Mg |
| HISTIDINE | A | NO RDA | 629.0 Mg |
| ALCOHOL | A | NO RDA | 0.000 Gm |
| ASH | A | NO RDA | 4.700 Gm |
| COPPER | A=================== | 36% | 0.900 Mg |
| MANGANESE | A========================= | 50% | 1.900 Mg |
| IODINE | A============================================ | 91% | 137.0 Ug |
| MONO FAT | A | NO RDA | 2.660 Gm |
| POLY FAT | A | NO RDA | 7.350 Gm |
| CAFFEINE | A | NO RDA | 0.000 Mg |
| FLUORIDE | A= | 3% | 92.10 Ug |
| MOLYBDENUM | A==================================================== | 465% | 1512 Ug |
| VITAMIN K | A====== | 12% | 12.70 Ug |
| SELENIUM | A==== | 8% | 0.010 Mg |
| BIOTIN | A==== | 9% | 14.90 Ug |
| CHLORIDE | A=== | 7% | 239.0 Mg |
| CHROMIUM | A================================================= | 360% | 0.450 Mg |
| SUGAR | A | NO RDA | 15.10 Gm |
| FIBER-DIET | A | NO RDA | 2.500 Gm |
| VIT. E/AT | A========= | 18% | 1.470 Mg |

% RDA:  |0    |20    |40    |60    |80    |100      10

Analysis does not include optional Cheddar cheese; parsley used instead of cilantro.

# "CAFE" CON LECHE

☆ Even children can drink this because it's caffeine-free.

---

*8 cups water*
*8" cinnamon stick*

*Grain coffee (4 times the amount per cup*
*    suggested on the label)*
*1 Tbsp. Barbados molasses or honey per cup*
*Nonfat milk to taste*

Follow instructions on the label for making grain coffee except boil 1" of cinnamon stick per cup of water. To make a very strong coffee flavor, add 4 times the amount of grain coffee to the water. Add sweetener and nonfat dairy milk to taste.

The unrefined sugar used in Mexico to make this and other sweet dishes is basically crystallized, unrefined sugar cane juice (much like the gur from India, p. 41) which is very nutritious. On a visit south-of-the-border, I remember looking at the blocks of this unrefined sugar but not tasting any, being unsure of what else might be in it (bugs, etc.). I use Barbados molasses as the closest thing to this Mexican sugar that's readily available.

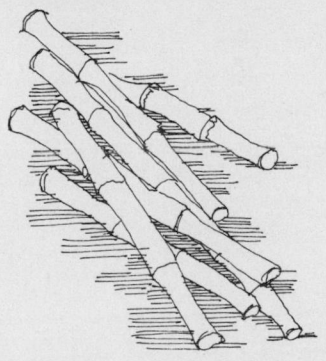

| SHOPPING LIST | |
|---|---|
| **Regularly Kept in the Kitchen** (Listed in Chapter 14, p. 703) | **Fresh Produce** |
| Cinnamon stick<br>Grain coffee<br>Barbados molasses<br>Milk | (None) |

In the Bhagavad-gita it is written, "The non-permanent appearance of happiness and distress and their disappearance in due course are like the appearance and disappearance of winter and summer seasons. They arise from sense perception, and one must tolerate them without being disturbed."

# EXOTIC INDIAN PANCAKES

Brunch buffets are nice meals to entertain with because they are a good way to gather family and friends together to pass the day . . . and into the evening. Brunches are usually easy-going, casual affairs — and when they have a theme, they're even more interesting and exciting. A buffet with an East Indian theme is a nice, spicy way to spice up any gathering.

One nice thing about this menu is that there are only four things to prepare on the day of the brunch (everything else can be done days ahead of time). On the morning of the brunch, the Carrot Halavah Cake and the Spicy Rice and Nuts should be made, each of which basically requires a few minutes of assembly time and then setting the timer to remind you when they're done cooking. The pancake batter should be blended and set aside to cook later — at the table with everyone sitting around. The Creamy Curry should be started about 20 minutes before everyone is scheduled to arrive.

Then it's time to sit at the table with all the dishes and condiments there and cook the pancakes right on the spot.

The cooked Savory Indian Pancakes can then be topped by each individual as they desire. The Creamy Curry, dollop of yogurt and Tamarind Chutney with some pieces of fresh vegetables (shredded lettuce, tomatoes) are a good combination — but with so many dishes and condiments available, mixing and matching is the way to go!

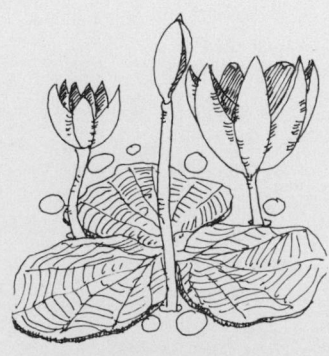

# FRESH GROUND CURRY POWDER

☆ Gram masala is another way to say "curry powder." Here is one that can be made from whole spice seeds and pods.

---

¼ cup turmeric
¼ cup cumin seeds
3 Tbsp. coriander seeds
1 Tbsp. ginger powder
1 Tbsp. black peppercorns
1 Tbsp. cardamom pods
2 tsp. whole cloves
1 tsp. fennel seeds
1 tsp. cayenne pepper
1 tsp. black mustard seeds
1 tsp. fenugreek seeds
1 tsp. nutmeg
1 tsp. cinnamon
1 tsp. asafetida or garlic or onion powder

You'll be pleased with how much fresher and tastier a fresh ground curry powder is. The idea is to grind all the spices, which are still in their whole form, to a powder. This can be accomplished by grinding the whole spices in a mortar and pestle or food grinder and then mixing them with the already powdered spices. Either that, or you can mix all the spices together in a blender and just blend till the whole ones are powdered. Use what you need immediately and store the rest in an airtight jar in the refrigerator. This makes a large spice jar's worth (about ¾ cup).

Curry mixes made with whole spices and ground on the spot are always fresher tasting because as soon as any seed is ground, the oils get a little rancid or stale. This applies to spice seeds as well. Grinding can be done with a good old mortar and pestle, your old coffee grinder (a good use for it now that you're not drinking coffee — right?!) or a blender. Although some swear it doesn't taste right unless done in a mortar and pestle, for lack of time I always do mine in a blender.

| SHOPPING LIST | |
|---|---|
| Regularly Kept in the Kitchen (Listed in Chapter 14, p. 703) | Fresh Produce |
| Turmeric | (None) |
| Cumin seeds | |
| Coriander seeds | |
| Ginger powder | |
| Black peppercorns | |
| Cardamom pods | |
| Whole cloves | |
| Fennel seeds | |
| Cayenne pepper | |
| Black mustard seeds | |
| Fenugreek seeds | |
| Nutmeg | |
| Cinnamon | |
| Asafetida | |

# CURRY POWDER MIX

☆ A garam masala you can make by mixing already
  ground spices common to spice racks in most kitchens.

1 tsp. ground cumin
1 tsp. cinnamon
1 tsp. turmeric
1 tsp. powdered ginger
½ tsp. cloves
½ tsp. mustard powder

Mix ingredients together and use whenever curry powder
is called for.

Turmeric is the "base" of all curries; the predominating flavor of the curry can be varied by changing the spicing added to the curry. Some curries have a strong ginger flavor; others clove or cumin. This recipe makes a fairly sweet, cinnamon-flavored one. Try getting adventurous and make a mix to suit your own tastes!

| SHOPPING LIST | |
|---|---|
| Regularly Kept in the Kitchen (Listed in Chapter 14, p. 703) | Fresh Produce |
| Turmeric | (None) |
| Cinnamon | |
| Ground cumin | |
| Powdered ginger | |
| Ground cloves | |
| Mustard powder | |

# FIERY HOT GREEN CHILIES

☆ An East Indian meal isn't complete without some hot chilies to mix in or sprinkle on here and there.

---

*½ lb. fresh, hot green chili peppers*

*2 Tbsp. mustard powder*
*1 Tbsp. salt*
*1 tsp. cayenne*
*1 Tbsp. very finely grated fresh ginger root*

*2 Tbsp. mustard oil*
*1 tsp. asafetida or 2 - 3 cloves garlic, crushed*

*¼ cup lemon juice*

Spread whole chilies out on a tray and leave in the sun or a food dehydrator to semi-dry. When withered a little bit, cut off stems and discard. Then cut into ⅛"-thick rounds. You may want to wear rubber gloves when handling the chilies, or be very careful not to rub fingertips into eyes or onto skin. Mix chilies with next 4 ingredients.

In a stainless steel measuring cup or butter melter, heat the next 2 ingredients till the oil just begins to smoke, then pour immediately onto the chili mixture. Pour this mixture into a crock or jar with a non-metallic lid that will hold 1 pint. Place the jar in a window or outside someplace where it will get sun all day long. After a full day of sun, shake the jar and add the lemon juice. Replace the lid and shake the jar to thoroughly mix in the juice. Now the jar must be kept warm, preferably by placing in the sun during the day and on top of a water heater or similar place at night. By the end of 4 to 7 days the chilies should be ready (the number of days will vary according to whether it is summer or winter). You can tell the chilies are ready when they have lost their bright green color and have turned a dull olive green. Refrigerate to store.

Here's a recipe to give you an idea of how to use mustard oil for cooking vegetables:

*¼ cup mustard oil*
*2 tsp. asafetida or 2 cloves garlic, crushed*

*2 lbs. whole collard greens*

*2 Tbsp. soy sauce*
*1 tsp. red chili flakes*
*2 - 4 whole, fresh, hot green chilies*
*½ cup water*

Heat oil in a large skillet or wok and saute asafetida (or garlic) for 5 to 10 seconds. Add washed, de-stemmed collard greens and cover. Allow to cook covered for about half a minute. Uncover and stir in last 4 ingredients. Cover and lower heat to simmer. Simmer for about 20 to 25 minutes till greens are tender. Remove lid and allow most of remaining liquid to cook off. Serve as a side dish. Makes 4 to 6 servings.

| SHOPPING LIST | |
|---|---|
| **Regularly Kept in the Kitchen** (Listed in Chapter 14, p. 703) | **Fresh Produce** |
| Mustard powder<br>Cayenne<br>Asafetida | Hot green chilies (like Serrano chilies)<br>Ginger root<br>Lemon |

| Special Shopping |
|---|
| Mustard oil — can be found in East Indian food stores. In India it's sometimes used medicinally to make packs to put on the chest or back for coughs, etc. Try cooking with it for a whole other flavor. |

## SUGGESTED MENU FOR AN EXOTIC EAST INDIAN PANCAKE BRUNCH

*Savory Indian Pancakes*

*Creamy Curry*

*Spicy Rice and Nuts*

*Tamarind Chutney*

*Plain yogurt*

*Shredded lettuce*

*Alfalfa sprouts*

*Tomatoes*

*Fiery Hot Green Chilies*

*Carrot Halavah Cake*

# TAMARIND CHUTNEY

☆ A tangy, sweet chutney that makes a flattering condiment for many meals. If no East Indian food stores are nearby and special ingredients can't be obtained, try the Fig-Date Chutney in *Kathy Cooks Naturally* (p.246) instead.

---

¼ cup chopped fresh cilantro (also called
    Chinese parsley or coriander leaves)
¼ cup chopped fresh mint leaves
2" chunk of peeled fresh ginger root
¼ cup gur (Indian sugar) or Barbados molasses
2½ tsp. soy sauce

1⅓ cups tamarind paste

2 Tbsp. vegetable oil
2 tsp. cumin powder
½ tsp. cayenne
¼ tsp. black pepper

Blend first 5 ingredients together in a blender to form a smooth paste. Pour into a mixing bowl and add tamarind paste. In a small stainless steel measuring cup or a butter melter, combine last ingredients and lightly roast over high flame till spices begin to sizzle and aroma can be smelled. Turn off heat and pour the spices into the mixing bowl as well. Mix thoroughly and try to refrigerate at least overnight before serving to allow flavors to mix together. This adds a wonderful sweet-sour flavor to a meal. It's especially tasty swirled on top of yogurt that's been dolloped on top of the Creamy Curry. Makes about 1½ cups.

| Special Shopping |
| --- |
| Gur (Indian sugar) — found in some East Indian food stores. It is simply crystallized sugar cane juice, so it contains all the good nutrients naturally contained in sugar cane before refining. The closest substitute is Barbados molasses.
Tamarind paste — in East Indian food stores. |

| SHOPPING LIST | |
| --- | --- |
| **Regularly Kept in the Kitchen** (Listed in Chapter 14, p. 703) | **Fresh Produce** |
| Soy sauce
Vegetable oil
Cumin powder
Cayenne
Black pepper | Cilantro
Mint
Ginger root |

# SPICY RICE AND NUTS

☆ A spicy, dynamic rice dish that proves grains aren't just a bland side dish to ladle gravy over.

---

3 Tbsp. vegetable oil or ghee
1 cup diced celery
1 tsp. asafetida OR 1 cup diced onion
   and 1 clove garlic, minced

1 Tbsp. finely grated fresh ginger root
¼ tsp. dry chili seeds
1 tsp. cumin seeds
1 tsp. garam masala

3 cups long grain brown rice

4½ cups water
1 Tbsp. soy sauce
¼ cup raisins

⅛ cup each of toasted cashews, peanuts,
   sliced almonds and sesame seeds

Saute first 3 ingredients together till celery and/or onion turns translucent. Add the next 4 ingredients and fry till spices begin to turn golden brown and you can smell them in the air. Add the rice and stir-fry till it begins to turn golden brown. Then add the next 3 ingredients, mix well with spoon and bring to a boil. Cover and turn heat down to medium-low so it maintains a gentle rolling boil for 10 to 15 minutes. Turn down and simmer for 15 to 20 minutes. Garnish with nuts and seeds before serving. Makes 6 to 8 servings.

Toasting grains before boiling is a good technique for cooking any grain. This recipe will work for other whole grains besides rice. Millet — which I think of as the king of all grains because it's the only alkaline grain — is especially good made like this. Pre-toasting the grain makes it cook up light and fluffy.

| SHOPPING LIST | |
|---|---|
| Regularly Kept in the Kitchen (Listed in Chapter 14, p. 703) | Fresh Produce |
| Asafetida<br>Red chili flakes<br>Cumin seeds<br>Raisins<br>Cashews<br>Peanuts<br>Slivered almonds<br>Sesame seeds<br>Brown rice<br>Soy sauce | Celery<br>Ginger root |

| Special Shopping |
|---|
| Ghee — in East Indian food stores; or make your own at home by clarifying butter over a low heat, removing all cloudy milk solids till only the clear fat is left.<br>Garam masala — in East Indian food stores; or make your own with one of the curry mix recipes. |

# NUTRITIONAL ANALYSIS FOR ONE SERVING
## SPICY RICE AND NUTS

| NUTRIENT | Type: 14 FEMALE-23 TO 51 YEARS | % RDA | Amount |
|---|---|---|---|
| KCALORIES | Å====== | 13% | 278.0 Kc |
| PROTEIN | Å====== | 13% | 5.800 Gm |
| CARBOHYDRATE | Å | NO RDA | 35.90 Gm |
| FAT | Å | NO RDA | 13.30 Gm |
| FIBER-CRUDE | Å | NO RDA | 0.990 Gm |
| CHOLESTEROL | Å | NO RDA | 0.000 Mg |
| SATURATED FA | Å | NO RDA | 1.470 Gm |
| OLEIC FA | Å | NO RDA | 6.930 Gm |
| LINOLEIC FA | Å | NO RDA | 6.480 Gm |
| SODIUM | Å==== | 8% | 194.0 Mg |
| POTASSIUM | Å==== | 8% | 308.0 Mg |
| MAGNESIUM | Å============= | 26% | 79.00 Mg |
| IRON | Å===== | 10% | 1.920 Mg |
| ZINC | Å==== | 8% | 1.340 Mg |
| VITAMIN A | Å | 0% | 30.50 IU |
| VITAMIN D | Å | 0% | 0.000 IU |
| VIT. E/TOTAL | Å | NO RDA | 6.820 Mg |
| VITAMIN C | Å=== | 6% | 4.090 Mg |
| THIAMIN | Å======== | 17% | 0.170 Mg |
| RIBOFLAVIN | Å== | 5% | 0.070 Mg |
| NIACIN | Å======== | 17% | 2.320 Mg |
| VITAMIN B6 | Å====== | 13% | 0.270 Mg |
| FOLACIN | Å== | 5% | 21.70 Ug |
| VITAMIN B12 | Å | 0% | 0.000 Ug |
| PANTO- ACID | Å====== | 13% | 0.760 Mg |
| CALCIUM | Å==== | 9% | 75.70 Mg |
| PHOSPHORUS | Å=========== | 22% | 181.0 Mg |
| TRYPTOPHAN | Å===================== | 45% | 74.70 Mg |
| THREONINE | Å==================== | 43% | 188.0 Mg |
| ISOLEUCINE | Å================== | 39% | 255.0 Mg |
| LEUCINE | Å======================== | 52% | 455.0 Mg |
| LYSINE | Å=============== | 32% | 215.0 Mg |
| METHIONINE | Å================ | 34% | 93.80 Mg |
| CYSTINE | Å=============== | 31% | 85.70 Mg |
| PHENYL-ANINE | Å================================ | 67% | 293.0 Mg |
| TYROSINE | Å=================== | 40% | 177.0 Mg |
| VALINE | Å=================== | 39% | 298.0 Mg |
| HISTIDINE | Å | NO RDA | 173.0 Mg |
| ALCOHOL | Å | NO RDA | 0.000 Gm |
| ASH | Å | NO RDA | 1.730 Gm |
| COPPER | Å======= | 14% | 0.370 Mg |
| MANGANESE | Å=============== | 33% | 1.250 Mg |
| IODINE | Å=================================================== | 116% | 175.0 Ug |
| MONO FAT | Å | NO RDA | 3.830 Gm |
| POLY FAT | Å | NO RDA | 6.750 Gm |
| CAFFEINE | Å | NO RDA | 0.000 Mg |
| FLUORIDE | Å | 0% | 22.20 Ug |
| MOLYBDENUM | Å==================================================== | 122% | 398.0 Ug |
| VITAMIN K | Å | 0% | 0.000 Ug |
| SELENIUM | Å==== | 8% | 0.010 Mg |
| BIOTIN | Å= | 2% | 3.450 Ug |
| CHLORIDE | Å | 1% | 59.80 Mg |
| CHROMIUM | Å========================================================== | 168% | 0.210 Mg |
| SUGAR | Å | NO RDA | 2.100 Gm |
| FIBER-DIET | Å | NO RDA | 0.530 Gm |
| VIT. E/AT | Å========================= | 51% | 4.120 Mg |

```
% RDA:    |0      |20      |40      |60      |80      |100
```

Analysis does not include dry chili seeds or garam masala; vegetable oil used instead of ghee.

# CREAMY CURRY

☆ Steaming vegetables retains more nutrients; the dish as a whole isn't *that* rich with only four ounces of Neufchatel, yogurt or cream cheese in the whole potful.

1 lb. cauliflower
1 lb. potatoes

2 Tbsp. butter or margarine
2 tsp. curry powder
1 tsp. ground sage
½ tsp. paprika
¼ tsp. asafetida or ¼ cup finely diced onion

1 tsp. Spike or other vegetable-seasoned salt
¼ tsp. black pepper
4 oz. Neufchatel or cream cheese
2 Tbsp. tomato paste
½ cup milk

Wash and cut vegetables into bite-sized pieces. Place in steamer and steam till tender. In the meantime, make the sauce by combining the next 5 ingredients in a pot and toasting spices over a medium-high heat. Add the last 5 ingredients and mix till smooth and creamy. Add steamed vegetables and stir into sauce thoroughly. Vegetables can be left as they are or gently mashed with a potato masher. Makes 6 to 8 servings.

| SHOPPING LIST | |
|---|---|
| **Regularly Kept in the Kitchen** (Listed in Chapter 14, p. 703) | **Fresh Produce** |
| Butter or margarine<br>Curry powder<br>Sage<br>Paprika<br>Asafetida<br>Spike<br>Black pepper<br>Milk | Cauliflower<br>Potato<br>Tomato paste |

| Special Shopping |
|---|
| Neufchatel cheese — in supermarket cheese departments or gourmet cheese specialty stores; or use cream cheese (which has more saturated fat and cholesterol) or Yogurt Cheese (p. 319), which adds much less cholesterol and saturated fat and a nice, tart flavor. |

# NUTRITIONAL ANALYSIS FOR ONE SERVING CREAMY CURRY

| NUTRIENT | Type: 14   FEMALE-23 TO 51 YEARS | % RDA | Amount |
|---|---|---|---|
| KCALORIES | ౠ==== | 9% | 187.0 Kc |
| PROTEIN | ౠ====== | 13% | 5.940 Gm |
| CARBOHYDRATE | ౠ | NO RDA | 22.50 Gm |
| FAT | ౠ | NO RDA | 9.090 Gm |
| FIBER-CRUDE | ౠ | NO RDA | 1.140 Gm |
| CHOLESTEROL | ౠ | NO RDA | 16.30 Mg |
| SATURATED FA | ౠ | NO RDA | 3.760 Gm |
| OLEIC FA | ౠ | NO RDA | 1.780 Gm |
| LINOLEIC FA | ౠ | NO RDA | 0.140 Gm |
| SODIUM | ౠ======= | 14% | 312.0 Mg |
| POTASSIUM | ౠ========= | 18% | 686.0 Mg |
| MAGNESIUM | ౠ====== | 12% | 37.50 Mg |
| IRON | ౠ=== | 6% | 1.220 Mg |
| ZINC | ౠ== | 4% | 0.630 Mg |
| VITAMIN A | ౠ======== | 17% | 681.0 IU |
| VITAMIN D | ౠ== | 4% | 8.500 IU |
| VIT. E/TOTAL | ౠ | NO RDA | 0.150 Mg |
| VITAMIN C | ౠ=================================================== | 111% | 67.10 Mg |
| THIAMIN | ౠ========= | 16% | 0.160 Mg |
| RIBOFLAVIN | ౠ===== | 11% | 0.140 Mg |
| NIACIN | ౠ======= | 14% | 1.840 Mg |
| VITAMIN B6 | ౠ=========== | 22% | 0.440 Mg |
| FOLACIN | ౠ======= | 15% | 61.90 Ug |
| VITAMIN B12 | ౠ== | 4% | 0.120 Ug |
| PANTO- ACID | ౠ====== | 13% | 0.750 Mg |
| CALCIUM | ౠ==== | 9% | 77.00 Mg |
| PHOSPHORUS | ౠ======= | 15% | 124.0 Mg |
| TRYPTOPHAN | ౠ==================== | 43% | 70.80 Mg |
| THREONINE | ౠ======================== | 51% | 225.0 Mg |
| ISOLEUCINE | ౠ=================== | 40% | 265.0 Mg |
| LEUCINE | ౠ======================= | 49% | 435.0 Mg |
| LYSINE | ౠ============================= | 61% | 403.0 Mg |
| METHIONINE | ౠ=================== | 40% | 109.0 Mg |
| CYSTINE | ౠ=========== | 22% | 61.80 Mg |
| PHENYL-ANINE | ౠ============================= | 60% | 263.0 Mg |
| TYROSINE | ౠ======================= | 49% | 214.0 Mg |
| VALINE | ౠ=================== | 41% | 320.0 Mg |
| HISTIDINE | ౠ | NO RDA | 153.0 Mg |
| ALCOHOL | ౠ | NO RDA | 0.000 Gm |
| ASH | ౠ | NO RDA | 1.930 Gm |
| COPPER | ౠ==== | 8% | 0.200 Mg |
| MANGANESE | ౠ=== | 6% | 0.260 Mg |
| IODINE | ౠ===== | 11% | 17.50 Ug |
| MONO FAT | ౠ | NO RDA | 3.200 Gm |
| POLY FAT | ౠ | NO RDA | 2.070 Gm |
| CAFFEINE | ౠ | NO RDA | 0.000 Mg |
| FLUORIDE | ౠ==== | 8% | 238.0 Ug |
| MOLYBDENUM | ౠ | 0% | 0.000 Ug |
| VITAMIN K | ౠ==================================================== | 2650% | 2783 Ug |
| SELENIUM | ౠ | 0% | 0.000 Mg |
| BIOTIN | ౠ==== | 9% | 13.70 Ug |
| CHLORIDE | ౠ | 0% | 0.000 Mg |
| CHROMIUM | ౠ==== | 8% | 0.010 Mg |
| SUGAR | ౠ | NO RDA | 5.150 Gm |
| FIBER-DIET | ౠ | NO RDA | 0.050 Gm |
| VIT. E/AT | ౠ= | 2% | 0.200 Mg |

```
  % RDA:  |0      |20     |40     |60     |80     |100
```

Neufchatel cheese used instead of cream cheese; margarine used instead of butter.

# CARROT HALAVA CAKE

☆ Tastes a lot like the carrot halavah so popular in India; for those of us who don't have the time to spend hours stirring carrots and sugar or carrots, milk and sugar down to a thick, candy consistency.

Ghee, which is used to make East Indian sweets, has its own distinctive flavor. If plain butter is used, this cake will taste delicious, but not like an East Indian sweetmeat.

---

¼ cup yogurt
¼ cup ghee
½ cup honey

1 cup whole wheat flour
½ tsp. cardamom powder
1 tsp. baking soda
1 tsp. baking powder

1½ cups finely grated or ground carrots
   (packed firmly)
¼ cup shredded coconut
⅛ cup chopped pistachios
¼ cup coarsely chopped raisins

Sliced almonds

2 Tbsp. ghee
2 Tbsp. honey

Preheat oven to 350 degrees.

Cream first 3 ingredients together. Sift in next 4 ingredients and mix well to get lumps out. Add next 4 ingredients and stir in thoroughly. Pour into an oiled, floured 9" square or 9" diameter cake pan. Spread evenly and sprinkle some sliced almonds on top. Bake at 350 degrees for about 35 to 40 minutes or till a toothpick inserted in the middle comes out clean. Baste top of cake with the final honey and ghee mixture as soon as cake comes out of the oven. Makes one 9" cake.

| SHOPPING LIST | |
|---|---|
| **Regularly Kept in the Kitchen** (Listed in Chapter 14, p. 703) | **Fresh Produce** |
| Yogurt | Carrots |
| Honey | |
| Whole wheat flour | |
| Cardamom | |
| Baking soda | |
| Baking powder | |
| Pistachio nuts | |
| Raisins | |
| Almonds | |

| Special Shopping |
|---|
| Ghee — in East Indian food stores; or make your own at home by clarifying butter over a low heat, removing all cloudy milk solids till only the clear fat is left. |

# NUTRITIONAL ANALYSIS FOR ONE SERVING
## CARROT HALAVA CAKE

```
NUTRIENT      Type: 14   FEMALE-23 TO 51 YEARS        % RDA   Amount
KCALORIES     X===                                     7%    146.0 Kc
PROTEIN       X==                                      4%    1.970 Gm
CARBOHYDRATE  X                                      NO RDA  19.90 Gm
FAT           X                                      NO RDA  7.300 Gm
FIBER-CRUDE   X                                      NO RDA  0.440 Gm
CHOLESTEROL   X                                      NO RDA  13.20 Mg
SATURATED FA  X                                      NO RDA  3.770 Gm
OLEIC FA      X                                      NO RDA  1.150 Gm
LINOLEIC FA   X                                      NO RDA  0.380 Gm
SODIUM        X=                                       3%    85.70 Mg
POTASSIUM     X=                                       3%    122.0 Mg
MAGNESIUM     X===                                     6%    19.40 Mg
IRON          X=                                       3%    0.540 Mg
ZINC          X=                                       2%    0.330 Mg
VITAMIN A     X=======================================77%    3094 IU
VITAMIN D     X                                        0%    0.000 IU
VIT. E/TOTAL  X                                      NO RDA  0.840 Mg
VITAMIN C     X                                        1%    1.110 Mg
THIAMIN       X===                                     6%    0.060 Mg
RIBOFLAVIN    X=                                       3%    0.040 Mg
NIACIN        X==                                      4%    0.590 Mg
VITAMIN B6    X=                                       2%    0.050 Mg
FOLACIN       X                                        1%    7.480 Ug
VITAMIN B12   X                                        0%    0.020 Ug
PANTO- ACID   X=                                       2%    0.160 Mg
CALCIUM       X==                                      4%    35.30 Mg
PHOSPHORUS    X====                                    9%    79.40 Mg
TRYPTOPHAN    X=======                                14%    24.20 Mg
THREONINE     X=======                                14%    62.10 Mg
ISOLEUCINE    X=======                                12%    84.00 Mg
LEUCINE       X=======                                15%    136.0 Mg
LYSINE        X=====                                  11%    72.80 Mg
METHIONINE    X=====                                  10%    29.60 Mg
CYSTINE       X======                                 12%    34.40 Mg
PHENYL-ANINE  X===========                            22%    96.00 Mg
TYROSINE      X=======                                15%    69.40 Mg
VALINE        X======                                 13%    99.70 Mg
HISTIDINE     X                                      NO RDA  42.70 Mg
ALCOHOL       X                                      NO RDA  0.000 Gm
ASH           X                                      NO RDA  0.380 Gm
COPPER        X=                                       3%    0.090 Mg
MANGANESE     X======                                 12%    0.460 Mg
IODINE        X===========                            22%    33.30 Ug
MONO FAT      X                                      NO RDA  2.540 Gm
POLY FAT      X                                      NO RDA  0.500 Gm
CAFFEINE      X                                      NO RDA  0.000 Mg
FLUORIDE      X                                        0%    19.00 Ug
MOLYBDENUM    X=====================================138%    450.0 Ug
VITAMIN K     X                                        0%    0.000 Ug
SELENIUM      X                                        0%    0.000 Mg
BIOTIN        X                                        0%    1.240 Ug
CHLORIDE      X                                        0%    14.20 Mg
CHROMIUM      X================                       32%    0.040 Mg
SUGAR         X                                      NO RDA  0.480 Gm
FIBER-DIET    X                                      NO RDA  1.380 Gm
VIT. E/AT     X====                                    8%    0.660 Mg

   % RDA:   |0      |20     |40    |60     |80    |100
```

47

# SAVORY INDIAN PANCAKES

☆ This is like the Japanese dish Sukiyaki in that it's best cooked right at the table, with conversation flowing all around.

---

*2 cups dry mung beans*

*¾" cube of peeled, fresh ginger root*

**For every 1 cup of soaked beans, add:**
*½ cup water*
*½ tsp. Spike or other vegetable-seasoned salt*
*½ tsp. asafetida or 1 clove garlic*
*¼ tsp. baking soda*
*⅛ tsp. cayenne*
*⅛ tsp. black pepper*

Soak mung beans overnight to soften. The next day, mung beans must be ground, so drain the beans to prepare for grinder. Grinding can be done in a food processor or a blender. If in a food processor, do the whole batch of beans and multiply the other ingredients by 4. If in a blender, do 1 cup of beans at a time with the amount of other ingredients as listed *per batch*. Whether in a blender or a food processor, first drop chunk of ginger root in and allow it to get chopped up. Add soaked, drained mung beans and run machine till beans are fairly ground up (in a blender you can only do 1 cup at a time to avoid burning out the motor). Add the next 6 ingredients and grind to a smooth, fluffy paste. The batter is now ready to be made into pancakes, which takes mastering a light touch on the spoon. Just remember — practice makes perfect!

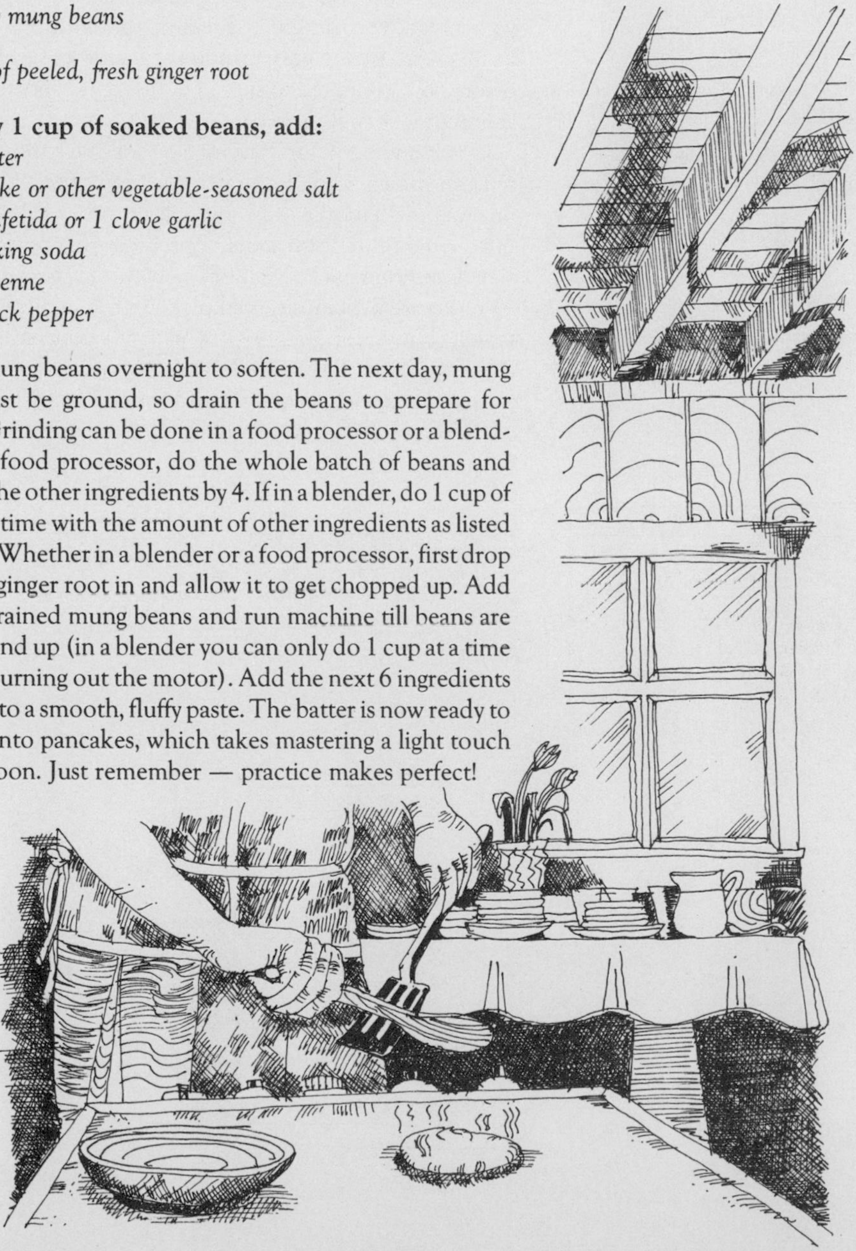

Heat a non-stick skillet or griddle over a medium flame and pour ½ to 1 teaspoon of oil into the skillet or griddle. With a spoon, mix batter thoroughly (batter must be mixed before each pancake is poured because it separates very quickly) and scoop out ⅓ to ½ cup of batter. Pour batter into the middle of the skillet and place the rounded bottom of a broad spoon (like a soup spoon) very lightly in the center of the batter. Then use a slow, gentle and continuous spiral motion to spread the batter outward with the back of the soup spoon till pancake is about 7" to 8" in diameter. If batter is sticking to the spoon and making holes in the pancake as you spread, you are either pressing too hard or you didn't begin pressing soon enough and the batter was semi-cooked before you attempted to spread it. Just try to spread with the spoon immediately and lighten the touch.

Cover and cook for 2 minutes, or till the pancake turns a reddish-brown color. Remove cover and drizzle a tiny bit of oil over the pancake. Flip to cook on other side and cook uncovered till reddish spots begin appearing on the second side. Continue cooking all of the batter in the same way.

These are delicious served plain with side dishes of vegetables, chutneys and yogurt; or you may want to stuff the pancake by placing filling inside and folding it over to form a turnover shape. This one recipe makes 18 to 20 pancakes.

| Special Shopping |
|---|
| Dry mung beans — in Oriental food aisles of supermarkets, Japanese or Chinese groceries, East Indian food stores (called "moong" there), and some natural food stores. |

| SHOPPING LIST | |
|---|---|
| **Regularly Kept in the Kitchen** (Listed in Chapter 14, p. 703) | **Fresh Produce** |
| Spike<br>Asafetida<br>Baking soda<br>Cayenne<br>Black pepper | Ginger root |

# NUTRITIONAL ANALYSIS FOR ONE SERVING
## SAVORY INDIAN PANCAKES

| NUTRIENT | Type: 14 FEMALE-23 TO 51 YEARS | % RDA | Amount |
|---|---|---|---|
| KCALORIES | Å | 1% | 22.90 Kc |
| PROTEIN | Å== | 4% | 1.860 Gm |
| CARBOHYDRATE | Å | NO RDA | 4.700 Gm |
| FAT | Å | NO RDA | 0.180 Gm |
| FIBER-CRUDE | Å | NO RDA | 0.580 Gm |
| CHOLESTEROL | Å | NO RDA | 0.000 Mg |
| SATURATED FA | Å | NO RDA | 0.080 Gm |
| OLEIC FA | Å | NO RDA | 0.000 Gm |
| LINOLEIC FA | Å | NO RDA | 0.000 Gm |
| SODIUM | Å================ | 31% | 699.0 Mg |
| POTASSIUM | Å= | 2% | 105.0 Mg |
| MAGNESIUM | Å== | 4% | 13.80 Mg |
| IRON | Å= | 3% | 0.630 Mg |
| ZINC | Å | 1% | 0.230 Mg |
| VITAMIN A | Å= | 2% | 105.0 IU |
| VITAMIN D | Å | 0% | 0.000 IU |
| VIT. E/TOTAL | Å | NO RDA | 1.030 Mg |
| VITAMIN C | Å====== | 13% | 7.970 Mg |
| THIAMIN | Å== | 5% | 0.050 Mg |
| RIBOFLAVIN | Å== | 5% | 0.070 Mg |
| NIACIN | Å= | 3% | 0.440 Mg |
| VITAMIN B6 | Å= | 2% | 0.040 Mg |
| FOLACIN | Å=== | 7% | 31.50 Ug |
| VITAMIN B12 | Å | 0% | 0.000 Ug |
| PANTO- ACID | Å= | 3% | 0.200 Mg |
| CALCIUM | Å= | 2% | 18.50 Mg |
| PHOSPHORUS | Å== | 4% | 35.00 Mg |
| TRYPTOPHAN | Å====== | 13% | 21.20 Mg |
| THREONINE | Å===== | 10% | 46.70 Mg |
| ISOLEUCINE | Å===== | 11% | 77.00 Mg |
| LEUCINE | Å===== | 11% | 101.0 Mg |
| LYSINE | Å======= | 14% | 95.20 Mg |
| METHIONINE | Å=== | 7% | 20.20 Mg |
| CYSTINE | Å== | 4% | 11.10 Mg |
| PHENYL-ANINE | Å======= | 15% | 67.00 Mg |
| TYROSINE | Å=== | 6% | 29.20 Mg |
| VALINE | Å===== | 10% | 78.50 Mg |
| HISTIDINE | Å | NO RDA | 39.50 Mg |
| ALCOHOL | Å | NO RDA | 0.000 Gm |
| ASH | Å | NO RDA | 0.320 Gm |
| COPPER | Å== | 4% | 0.100 Mg |
| MANGANESE | Å= | 2% | 0.090 Mg |
| IODINE | Å================== | 35% | 52.50 Ug |
| MONO FAT | Å | NO RDA | 0.020 Gm |
| POLY FAT | Å | NO RDA | 0.060 Gm |
| CAFFEINE | Å | NO RDA | 0.000 Mg |
| FLUORIDE | Å | 0% | 0.000 Ug |
| MOLYBDENUM | Å | 0% | 0.000 Ug |
| VITAMIN K | Å | 0% | 0.000 Ug |
| SELENIUM | Å | 0% | 0.000 Mg |
| BIOTIN | Å | 0% | 0.000 Ug |
| CHLORIDE | Å | 0% | 2.240 Mg |
| CHROMIUM | Å | 0% | 0.000 Mg |
| SUGAR | Å | NO RDA | 0.000 Gm |
| FIBER-DIET | Å | NO RDA | 0.570 Gm |
| VIT. E/AT | Å | 0% | 0.000 Mg |

% RDA:  |0      |20     |40     |60     |80     |100

Data for sprouted mung beans was used in this analysis for lack of data on soaked mung beans. The nutritional changes that occur during the germinating process are actually somewhere between dry mung beans and mung bean sprouts.

# NEGATE NEGATIVE INTAKE WITH POSITIVE ALTERNATIVES

Over 18 years ago I took a look at the diet on which I had been raised, which was pretty much the average American diet with a few Oriental touches thrown in. Through "eyes" sharpened by a desire to always be in the best of health and information accumulated from publications that were, at that time, available only in "health food" stores, I saw certain "foods" that had to go. In the next six chapters I'll list the "foods" that I've eliminated from my diet in what I feel is the order of importance.

I purposely put the word "food" in quotes when talking about the elements I eliminated because a more proper word would be "poisons." Webster's dictionary defines the word "poison" as "a substance . . . causing illness or death when eaten, drunk or absorbed in relatively small quantities." What a "relatively small quantity" is may be open to debate, but there's no question that the "foods" described in the next six chapters do cause illness or death when eaten or drunk over a period of time. Sitting around slowly poisoning ourselves hardly makes sense, and we only keep doing so because we've been conditioned to think of these poisons as "food."

# CHAPTER 3

# FLESH FOODS (MAKE YOU FLESHY)

The category of "foods" that I think is the most important to eliminate actually contains substances that are readily accepted as poisons. The most important "food" group to eliminate in terms of health as well as weight loss and control are all types of meat and eggs. If you do this, in one fell swoop you will cut out a major portion of cholesterol and saturated fats, as well as poisonous pesticides, antibiotics and hormones from your diet.

I should clarify here that by the word *meat* I mean all flesh foods, which includes poultry and any fish or shellfish. It seemed necessary to mention because for some strange reason people seem not to consider poultry or seafood to be meat, even though the substance is the flesh or muscle which helped the creature move around.

## . . . CONTAIN CHOLESTEROL AND SATURATED FAT

Eighteen years ago, when I cut all meat and eggs out of my diet for health reasons, I did so because it made logical sense to me to stop consuming these sources of saturated fats and cholesterol, though there was no real confirming scientific data available. Today that isn't the case! There has been so much media publicity on the 10-year, 150-million-dollar study released in 1984 by the federal government (National Heart, Lung and Blood Institute), that conclusively established the link between cholesterol levels and heart disease, that I feel there's not much need for me to go into detail on the detrimental effects on health that the consumption of cholesterol and saturated fat plays.

It seems that everyone is aware of the necessity to cut back on the consumption of cholesterol and saturated fat. Most people are wisely trying to do so as a preventive measure. In fact, public awareness and concern is so widespread that it's not surprising to see the different food industry businesses reacting to, or trying to cash in on it. The meat and egg industries are trying to confuse the issue by doing things like disseminating information on how the body needs cholesterol, or producing ads promoting meat as a natural food. The words "no cholesterol" can be seen on labels throughout the supermarket on products that aren't necessarily healthy. Maybe

avocado growers should consider labeling avocados; sales have gone down on avocados because many people trying to avoid cholesterol and saturated fats mistakenly think these buttery fruits are a source when they contain neither. Things can get real muddled and confusing in the marketplace without complete information.

·····································

*"For every 1% reduction in total cholesterol level, there's a 2% reduction of heart disease risk."*

*— Dr. Charles Glueck, Director University of Cincinnati Lipid Research Center*

·····································

You don't have to go and get a college degree as a nutritionist to be able to select a healthy diet. There are just a few basic things you need to know to be able to make intelligent selections. Some may feel that this is oversimplified, but these are the basics that helped me in connection with cholesterol and saturated fat:

• The human body *does* need cholesterol to function properly, but it manufactures its own. The body produces 500 to 1,000 milligrams of cholesterol a day and doesn't need to get any through foods eaten.

• There are two kinds of cholesterol in the human body: LDL (Low-Density Lip-

oprotein) and HDL (High-Density Lipoprotein). LDL is generally thought of as the bad kind; LDL delivers fat and cholesterol to cells, and the higher the level of LDL, the higher the risk of atherosclerosis and therefore heart attack. HDL is generally thought of as the good kind; it actually removes cholesterol from circulation and reduces the risk of heart disease. Though HDL is the more desirable of the two types of cholesterol to have in the bloodstream, it is possible to have too much of a "good" thing! The HDL level must be considered in relationship to the total amount of cholesterol in the bloodstream (serum cholesterol) because HDL is a product of cholesterol metabolism. A high HDL level in a high total serum cholesterol level is not healthy; a lower HDL level in a low level of total serum cholesterol makes for a low heart disease risk.

• Cholesterol is produced in the liver, so a food must have had a liver to produce cholesterol. In other words, only animal flesh (including fish) and animal products (dairy foods and eggs) contain cholesterol. Plants and products made from plants contain no cholesterol.

• The above rule applies for saturated fats as well. Saturated fats are found in animal flesh and products and not in plant foods, *with the exception of coconut and cocoa oils*, which are the only commonly used plant fats that are saturated. Plants contain polyunsaturated and monounsaturated fats. Saturated fats harden when refrigerated, whereas monounsaturated fats cloud and polyunsaturated fats remain clear and free-flowing when refrigerated.

• The cholesterol content of meat, poultry and fish is pretty much the same and all cause the serum cholesterol level to rise in whoever consumes them. Of all flesh foods, fish is the only one whose fat is polyunsaturated.

• Polyunsaturated fats and, more recently, monounsat-

......................................

*Synthetic pesticide production in the U.S. increased from 124 million pounds in 1947 to 1.8 billion pounds in 1981. Did this eradicate the pests? . . .*

......................................

urated fats have been credited with lowering the LDL levels in the blood; whereas saturated fats tend to cause LDL levels to rise.

### . . . AND PESTICIDES

A few years after I had eliminated meat from my diet, I became even more convinced that my decision to do so was safeguarding my health when I read the first issue of *Diet for a Small Planet* by Frances Moore Lappe. Sitting there on page 21 (in the 1971 edition), staring me in the face, was a graph that first introduced me to the fact that

meat (including fish and poultry) is the highest source of pesticide (and drug) residues in the human diet.

That was back in 1971, and until recently I assumed that, in the 15 years since, it had become common knowledge. Imagine my surprise when I got a call from one of the PBS stations that airs "Kathy's Kitchen" asking me on what grounds I had made statements about pesticide residues in meat and to send along documentation!

• Pesticides pose a number of threats to human health in that some are carcinogenic, while others may cause neurotoxicity, fetotoxicity, birth defects, mutations or bone marrow effects.

• Pesticides make their way into the human diet in two different ways: 1) those applied in agricultural practices; and 2) those which are in the ecosystem.

• There are basically two families of pesticides: those that are water-soluble and those that are fat-soluble. Not to diminish the hazard they pose, but relatively speaking, water-soluble pesticides pose less of a threat because they can be washed off more easily (from the surface of fruits and vegetables sprayed with them) and they travel through and out of the body in body fluids. Fat-soluble pesticides (organochlorines) aren't easily removed from plant life or anything else on which they're applied, and get stored in the fat cells of animals that consume the tainted food.

• The higher up the food chain a living being eats, the more stored pesticides it will consume and, in turn, store. Animals eat many times their weight in vegetation within a lifetime. Pesticides on the vegetation are stored and collected in the animal's fat cells throughout its lifetime, and animals eating these animals receive and store the concentrated pesticides. Through this process, called *biomagnification*, an animal eating at the top of the food chain can have stored within

......................................

*. . . "Environmental Action" reports a 31.4% pre-harvest crop loss in 1942; a 33% pre-harvest crop loss in 1975.*

......................................

its body more pesticides than are in the environment.

All the points mentioned above are common scientific knowledge. The awareness of this information is the basis of a great deal of concern to scientists and physicians, environmentalists and consumer action groups, as well as being the reason for the existence of government monitoring programs carried out by the USDA and FDA.

Every few years, the Environmental Protection Agency printed a "Pesticide Residues in Total Diet Samples" report in their Pesticide Monitoring Journal. The Meat, Fish and Poultry category was always the highest source of pesticide residues, followed by Dairy Products and the Oils, Fats and Shortenings categories (because they are all high-fat foods). Pesticide levels found on fruits, vegetables, grains and legumes were consistently around *12 times lower* than those in meat, fish and poultry.

For what it's worth, I should mention that all levels — including the levels for meat, fish and poultry — were below the legally "acceptable" levels. Whether the acceptable levels are actually safe and whether government agencies can effectively monitor levels of pesticides and drugs is of great concern in the scientific community and to the federal government departments involved, as discussed in the Comptroller General's 1979 report to Congress ("Problems in Preventing the Marketing of Raw Meat and Poultry Containing Potentially Harmful Residues").

This report emphasizes that acceptable levels are often set for a pesticide 1) for which a final determination hasn't been made as to the exact effects the element has on the human body, but it hasn't been proven yet to cause cancer; and/or 2) the element is known to be harmful to humans, but residues are unavoidable because of their persistence in the environment. DDT, DDE and TDE

are good examples of this. Residues of these pesticides were found in all food reported on in "Pesticide Residues in Total Diet Samples" up until the most recent, printed in 1977. It's disturbing to find them mentioned in the 1977 report at all considering that DDT, etc., were banned 12 years ago. This is due to the fact that scientists estimate DDT will take a good 40 years

······································

*"I have never been more appalled than I was at the recent advertising campaign which had as its basis, 'Since dioxin has been around for centuries, we shouldn't worry about it.' One of the most toxic substances known to man, and we're being conditioned to accept it."*

— Lester Crawford
DVM, Director FDA

······································

to make its way out of the soil, etc., in the United States; and it's questionable when it will be out of the ecosystem since U.S. chemical firms still market DDT to Third World countries for use in agriculture. It's guesstimated that even if all pesticide usage were to stop immediately, the pesticides currently in the ecosystem wouldn't reach equilibrium for another 100

to 200 years.

At this point I should mention that even though they're not fed by humans, environmental pollution is so high that fish and shellfish contain high levels of pesticides and other environmental contaminants (lead, mercury, etc.). How much is contained depends on how high up the food chain the particular species eats and where it lives. Considering that there have been DDT and lead residues found in as remote a place as the Antarctic, it's not surprising that in some parts of the world certain kinds of fish and shellfish can't be legally sold.

All the bickering over what "acceptable" or "safe" levels are seems silly anyway remembering the problem of biomagnification. A human being eating at the top of the food chain is not just eating concentrations of pesticides, but in doing so repeatedly stores whatever residues are present as many timesfold as he consumes the food. How much the human body serves as a storehouse of pesticides is well illustrated by a brochure printed by the Environmental Defense Fund (EDF) entitled "Bottle or Breast . . . Deciding Which is Best."

As pointed out in the brochure, a nursing infant "gets a large dose of harmful chemical residues . . . sometimes more than *several hundred times* the acceptable daily intake" via mother's milk. The amount of residues found in breast milk is a direct measurement of residues in the mother's body.

Studies done on human mother's milk are a good barometer of pesticide storage in human beings. The only way the human body can eliminate fat-soluble pesticides is through lactation or burning away fat (as in a true reduction program where fat is lost, not water).

In the report "Diet as a Factor Affecting Organochlorine Contamination of Breast Milk," also printed by the EDF, it's documented and advised that the best way to cut down on residue intake (and, therefore, storage) is to cut down on or eliminate meats from the diet, and to consume lowfat dairy products. The important point demonstrated by this report is that a human being eating at the top of the food chain can be a walking storehouse of hundreds of times what is considered to be a "safe" level of residues, even though his or her diet is made up of foods that contained residues that were at what U.S. government regulations deem as safe.

### ...AND UNPRESCRIBED DRUGS

A report released by the Subcommittee on Government Operations, headed by Rep. Ted Weiss (D-NY), in 1985 ("Human Food Safety and Regulation of Animal Drugs") indicates that pesticide residues aren't the only chemical threat to human health to be found in meat. Like other sectors of society today, the livestock "industry" has become increasingly dependent on drugs. The extent of drug abuse in the industry is shocking. The report charges that 90 percent of the 20,000 to 30,000 animal drugs being used on livestock aren't even approved by the FDA.

Two specific categories of drugs found in meat pose significant threats to human health, and could also have something to do with the fattening of America. These substances are administered or fed to commercially raised

• • • • • • • • • • • • • • • • • • • • • • • • • •

*"Officials of the FDA acknowledged that it had identified and inventoried only 7% of the thousands of animal drugs on the market . . ."*

— New York Times

• • • • • • • • • • • • • • • • • • • • • • • • • •

livestock to fatten them up, and it seems only logical that those substances, passed on to humans through residues in animal tissues, would have the same fattening effects on our bodies.

### ANTIBIOTICS

Surprisingly, one of the fattening agents is antibiotics which are fed to livestock in subtherapeutic amounts (doses below those required to treat an actual disease). This is a practice used by farmers since the early 1950's to prevent disease and to promote growth.

No one knows why subtherapeutic doses of antibiotics cause weight gains of 10 to 20 percent above normal, but there are some theories:

1) The bodies of livestock can grow faster and more efficiently because they're not having to fight off disease; otherwise, bodies are using a certain amount of energy to fight off and defeat diseases that never surface.

2) The drugs somehow alter metabolism.

3) The drugs increase the absorption of nutrients in the intestinal tract.

Whether or not the residues of antibiotics in meat can cause weight gain in humans has never been the subject of scientific studies. The scientific community has mostly concerned itself with the graver issues of whether antibiotic residues in meat can cause allergic reactions or allergies in humans to the antibiotics themselves, or worse, whether widespread use of antibiotics in animals can or is breeding resistant strains of bacteria. For example, there have been cases where salmonella bacteria passed on to humans through meat were fatal because the bacteria proved to be resistant to the usual antibiotic treatment. Because of the gravity of this issue, the FDA is now being pressured to ban the use of tetracycline and penicillin in animal feed.

### GROWTH HORMONES

The other substance administered to livestock, residues of which could possibly lead to weight gain in humans, are growth hormones. This never occurred to me until 1979 when DES, the most widely used growth hormone at the time, was banned by the FDA. It wasn't banned because it was found to be fattening to humans, but because it was proven to cause cancer in humans! This did call to my attention for the first time the fact that hormone residues

........................................

*"Widespread use of antibiotics to stimulate growth of food animals is a major source of serious — sometimes fatal — disease in humans, according to researchers from the Federal Centers for Disease Control and two state health departments."*

— Washington Post
Sept. 6, 1984

........................................

were left in meat in large enough quantities to affect humans. Since then, I've read a publication called "Thumper" in which Diane Broughton has well-documented information on growth hormones used in livestock. It has convinced me that growth hormones used in livestock have a good deal to do with the fattening of America.

The history of DES is worth reviewing briefly be-

cause it demonstrates some important points. DES is a synthetic hormone that was used legally (approved by the FDA) since the 1950's to promote growth in livestock, causing a 15 to 19 percent weight gain before slaughtering. What led to the banning of DES in 1979 was the discovery — accompanied by a great deal of media coverage in the 1970's — that DES caused cancer in humans (more specifically, vaginal cancer in daughters whose mothers were given DES during pregnancy to prevent a miscarriage). The studies and findings, led and published by Dr. Arthur L. Herbst, also gave grounds for medical science to suspect, for the first time, that other estrogenic hormone compounds might also be carcinogenic. A 1980 tally showed that 57 of 429 women who had developed this rare form of cancer had mothers who were treated with other types of hormonal therapies during their pregnancies.

These findings were accompanied in the 1970's by improved technology which allowed residues to be detected in parts per billion and trillion, where they had passed undetected previously.

In a 1970 report, the National Cancer Institute, the Surgeon General of the U.S. and the National Institute of Environmental Health Sciences all favored the banning of DES. The FDA moved to ban DES in livestock feed in 1972; implants in 1973. The

livestock industry managed to have the ban overturned on a technicality — the FDA had neglected to hold a legally required hearing before banning DES. It wasn't until 1976 that the FDA began legal proceedings again, and not until 1979 was it finally banned.

Despite the banning of DES in 1979, discoveries of feedlots flagrantly disregarding the law occurred in 1980 and as recently as 1983.

........................................

*"At least when people take medication or prescription drugs, they know what they're swallowing; but this way, when they eat meat, they have no way of knowing what they're taking. It's dangerous."*

— Ted Weiss
Chairman of House Government
Operations Committee (D-NY)

........................................

The history of DES is important, as it demonstrates: 1) The government often approves and sets "tolerance" or "safety" levels for residues of elements of which it has no idea, at the time, of whether the substance is actually safe or what the long-term effects will be. 2) Once something is approved and is later proven to be unsafe for human consumption, it takes a long time to get it removed from the market. 3) The USDA and FDA aren't able to properly monitor all the regulations they're supposed to be enforcing, as is proven in the 1985 27th report by the Committee on Government Operations ("Human Food Safety

> "I can't speak for the whole universe on regulation, but in the animal drug and animal feed area, we are an under-regulated society . . .

and the Regulation of Animal Drugs"). Knowing this, people aren't careful about following regulations too closely. In short, we shouldn't assume that since the FDA has approved something, or set a "safety" level for it, that it is actually safe!

Since the banning of DES, an array of hormones have made a niche for themselves in that upwards of 20-million-dollar-a-year market.

The leading brands are:

1) Synovex (H:S) — a combination of (H) estradoil and testosteron and (S) ostradiol and progesterone. According to their own brochure, Synovex is implanted in over 50 percent of feedlot cattle in the U.S.

2) Zenarol (also known as Ralgro) — an anabolic steroid, in the same family as Dianabol and Winstrol, which are anabolic steroids most commonly used by athletes. This growth hormone has received unfavorable findings and press in Europe. Ralgro was the predominately used hormone in Puerto Rico a few years ago in the much publicized cases of puberty in infants being caused by hormone residues in meat and chicken.

3) Steeroid — a relatively newly-approved progesterone/estrogen mixture. (Androgens, as testerone, are male hormones; progesterones are female hormones. Estrogens are hormones produced in the ovary and placenta, and in the testes in very small amounts.)

Growth hormones have an anabolic effect on cells that are sensitive to them that causes the cells to synthesize protein and convert nutritive matter more rapidly than normal, resulting in a 15 to 19 percent weight gain and a bulkier profile. This effect of hormones has made them invaluable to livestock growers and popular amongst certain athletes. Some athletes take anabolic steroids to increase weight and body mass.

Interestingly enough, the cattle industry and FDA claim that anabolic hormones go in and out of the body very quickly, which explains the 60-day withdrawal period before slaughter (for anabolic steroids — not for sex hormones). Contrarily, Olympic officials proudly announced that their testing could detect anabolics in the bodies of athletes up to six months after an athlete has taken hormones . . . And their testing only picks up parts-per-billion, whereas hormones can cause changes in metabolism in amounts as small as parts-per-trillion!

Hormones are very potent agents. It only takes a miniscule amount to throw off, or at least alter, the very delicate balance of the endocrine system which regulates a host of body functions such as growth, metabolism, reproduction, etc. An extremely small amount of a hormone — whether due to an internal malfunction of a gland, or being introduced from outside — can affect an important bodily function.

There have been cases recorded in medical journals that document how even a little hormone absorbed

> . . . I think we've been both efficient and thorough in handling the DES scandal, but we're strained to the point of breaking, and I wonder how many contamination incidents we're missing."
>
> — Lester Crawford
> DVM, Director FDA
> May 1980

through the skin caused changes in sex organs:
• 1) A five-year-old boy developed breasts after using a hair cream containing fe-

male hormones. The breasts disappeared after he discontinued use of the cream for two months ("American Journal of Diseases of Chidren," vol. 136, 1982, pp. 587-8).

• 2) In Spain, a male hairdresser developed breasts and his libido decreased after massaging bald customers' scalps with a hormone-laced product. Two months after discontinuing use of the product, his sex life returned to normal, but the breasts had to be surgically removed ("British Journal of Plastic Surgery," vol. 35, 1982, pp. 209-10).

• 3) Similar cases have occurred at plants that produce birth control pills, in factory workers who absorbed hormones through their hands. ("Pharmacological Basis of Therapeutics," 1975, p. 1429).

These and similar cases are just examples of what extremely small traces of hormones absorbed through the skin can do. Imagine how much worse the effects would be if ingested and accumulated in the body. The properties of the hormones implanted in livestock are such that they do accumulate in the body. They are *hydrophobic*, which means they stay away from water and head for fat cells where tiny residues accumulate and remain metabolically active. They're also heat and acid resistant, which means that they're not broken down by cooking or by acids in the stomach.

As with antibiotics, the scientific community has concerned itself primarily with effects on human health rather than whether or not hormones implanted in livestock are fattening to humans, who eat the meat from those animals. Since research and studies have centered mostly on how carcinogenic hormone residues in meat might be, the evidence as to whether these same residues cause humans to fatten remains circumstantial.

················

*"Anyone that spreads the half-truth about having to eat a carload of this or that in order to get cancer is guilty of contributing to the national confusion that is crippling us."*

— *Lester Crawford*
*DVM, Director FDA*

················

## CONSIDER THIS CIRCUMSTANTIAL EVIDENCE ...

Though circumstantial, it is certainly logical and makes perfect sense. National statistics certainly would suggest that Americans are being fattened by hormone residues in meat. The American diet craze started in the late 1950's, a few short years after the use of antibiotics and hormone agents to add bulk to livestock became a common practice in feedlots. A recent USDA Food Consumption Survey showed that Americans are consuming fewer calories but gaining more weight than ever. Could this phenomenon be America experiencing what is known in feedlots as "feed efficiency" (the ability of livestock implanted with hormones to gain more weight on less food)?

The question is very pertinent considering that a very small percentage of Americans are grossly obese; the majority of overweight Americans fighting the battle of the bulge are concerned with losing the extra 15 to 20 pounds of excess weight they are carrying around. This 15 to 20 pounds roughly equals 10 to 20 percent of the average adult's weight; livestock implanted with hormones generally gain 15 to 19 percent more than their usual weight.

In addition to the battle with excess weight, the American public is struggling with other problems that are side-effects of ingesting hormones — knowingly in the form of birth control pills, or purposely to bulk-out as some athletes do, or unknowingly in meats. These problems that have become so widespread include fluid retention, early puberty (on an average, the onset of puberty is about three years earlier than it used to be), hyper-insulinism and diabetes.

## AND THAT'S NOT ALL ...

After reading about all these undesirable residues, some might be considering a switch to organically grown meats to feed old tastes and habits — but any way it is grown, meat still contains cholesterol and saturated fats. Another thing to consider that requires us to widen our concern from just ourselves to others is that no matter how it's grown, meat makes the least efficient use of the world's food resources. This is discussed in great depth in Frances Moore Lappe's *Diet for a Small Planet*, which is especially worth reading to gain an understanding of greater issues concerning food than how much to eat or what it tastes like.

## NOW, THE GOOD NEWS . . .

The bright side of all this dismal news about these "foods" most of us have grown up with as the center of our meals is that we don't *have* to eat them, since we, and not food manufacturers, decide what we eat.

We don't *have* to eat meat or eggs for proper nutrition. These "foods" have traditionally been touted as superior protein foods because they contain all eight essential amino acids (the eight needed but not produced by the body to synthesize protein). However, the presence of cholesterol and saturated fat (not to mention pesticides and/or other environmental contaminants, antibiotics and hormones) makes meat and eggs inferior sources of protein in my book!

## WE CAN LIVE WITHOUT IT!

For good health, cholesterol-free sources of protein are whole grains, legumes, nuts and seeds. All of these foods are categorized as carbohydrates, but that doesn't mean that they are devoid of protein. In fact, by mixing grains, legumes, nuts and/or seeds in a meal, it is easy to get an adequate supply of protein containing all eight essential amino acids. I can't think of one menu in this book that this doesn't occur in!

Legumes and grains, with an occasional nut or seed mixed in, grow so well and make such good taste combinations that many countries around the world have gravitated to diets using these

........................................

*"It is nearly 50 years since I was assured by a conclave of doctors that if I did not eat meat I should die of starvation."*

— *George Bernard Shaw*

........................................

combinations as their staples. In the Orient, it has been soybeans and rice; in the Mideast, fava or garbanzos with wheat and sesame seeds; in the Mediterranean, lentils and wheat; in Mexico and South America, pinto beans and corn; and through Indian cooking (from the country of India), I have been introduced to a wide array of beans that I had never seen before mixed with wheat or rice. All this was arrived at without a single daily requirement chart!

While getting an adequate amount of protein is important, daily requirement charts can be misleading. As with other nutrients, the amount needed depends a great deal on body size, how active the person is, how much stress the body is under and other variables. In general, it's safe to say that anyone eating a diet consisting of a wide variety of whole grains, legumes, vegetables and fruits doesn't need to give extra thought to whether they're getting enough protein unless they are body builders or do some equally heavy physical labor, or are pregnant or breastfeeding mothers.

I don't know about the body builders, etc., but as a mother who's been pregnant with and nursed seven babies, I have to add that through my pregnant and breastfeeding years I never got neurotic about balancing out amino acids in foods, but just continued feeding myself and my family meals made from complex carbohydrates (whole grains, legumes, vegetables and fruits).

## TOO MUCH OF A GOOD THING

Such an overemphasis has been placed on the amount of protein needed in the diet that America is suffering from an overconsumption of protein. Excessive amounts of protein in the diet cause calcium to be leeched from the bones, which results in osteoporosis. Another good reason for eliminating meat from the diet is the fact that red meats have a high phosphate content, and consuming larger quantities of phosphorous than calcium causes the bones to lose calcium.

Large quantities of calcium in the system (either from consuming too much calcium or, what is more likely, losing it from the bones) can result in kidney stones.

In relation to the problem of being overweight, studies have shown that fat and protein are the most fattening sources of calories; carbohydrates the least. Test animals were put on diets that had the same amount of calories, but some were fed their calories in primarily fat, others were fed their calories in the form of protein and still others got their calories in the form of carbohydrates. The results showed that the animals fed mostly fat were the fattest, animals who ate mostly protein were next and the animals who ate carbohydrates were the slimmest. As we all know, meats and eggs contain large amounts of fat and protein.

### ONE LESS WORRY

Because of so much emphasis on protein, the first thing most people are concerned about when considering eliminating meat and eggs is, "Will I get enough protein?" Since adequate amounts of protein can be easily obtained through healthful and naturally slimming complex-carbohydrate foods, a more valid concern is, "Will I get enough vitamin B-12?" If anyone has eliminated or is planning to eliminate all animals and animal products — including dairy products — from their diet, this is the one nutrient that must be watched, as no

fresh plant food supplies it. If you're planning to consume dairy products in moderation (see Chapter 7) as I do, it's less of a concern. In actuality, vitamin B-12 is produced only by microorganisms — such as bacteria, friendly flori and algae. Animal foods contain B-12 because animals' bodies, like ours, store large amounts of B-12. Our bodies store so much B-12 that a deficiency in the diet can take 5 to 10 years to show up. Animals get a great deal of

..............................

*. . . Likewise, it has been eighteen years and six mentally and physically healthy children later since I was told by a doctor that if I did not eat meat, my baby would be mentally retarded and deformed.*

..............................

their B-12 from microorganisms in the soil, but since our bodies are built differently, this isn't advisable for humans!

Besides dairy products, a good way to include B-12 in a diet that excludes meat and eggs is through vegetable foods that have been fermented or cultured. In the recipes throughout this book, the fermented or cultured vegetable foods you'll find I use quite often that contain B-12 are

tempeh, miso, soy sauce, nutritional yeast (read the label as the amount varies from brand to brand) and algae-type foods such as seaweeds like hijiki, wakame and nori sheets. Some of these foods may be total strangers to you, but as you begin preparing the recipes in this book, I hope you'll become acquainted with them and learn to like these allies in eating for optimum health and ideal "weight."

### NOW WHAT'LL I EAT?

Now that I've given you reasons why (and not even *all* of them, as that would be a whole book in itself) it is desirable and advisable to exclude meat and eggs from the diet, I'd like to share some recipes that can help you do that. When I first made that decision 18 years ago, the only thing I could think of making was a green salad. That got old real fast! After a few days of that, I had to go into the kitchen and start experimenting. It took me years before I was able to cook up something palatable without making a disaster in the kitchen! But then I was an exceptionally bad case, as someone who previously knew and cared so little about how to function in the kitchen that I flunked Home Economics and got away with talking my husband into going out to eat every meal. In short, if I could do it, so can you — especially with the help of these recipes that work!

# SOYFRIENDS

In his studying to attain a universal understanding of the truth, which goes beyond sectarianism, Leo Tolstoy wrote, "Divide up what you possess with others, do not gather riches, do not exalt yourself, do not steal, do not cause suffering, do not kill anyone, do not do unto another what you would not have done to yourself. This was taught not only nineteen hundred years ago (in the Bible) but five thousand years ago (in the Bhagavadgita), and there can be no doubt of the truth of this law . . . he who does not do these things is doing wrong."

In eliminating meat from my diet, one food that has become a real friend in the kitchen is soybeans and by-products made from soybeans. From a nutritional standpoint, soybeans are a good cholesterol-free replacement for meat as they are the only legume which contain all eight essential amino acids. Though they contain all eight, they are a bit low in the amino acids methionine and cystine. That really presents no problem, as most grains are well-supplied with methionine (most grains are low in lysine, which soybeans are high in), and it's easy to use both together in the same recipe or meal. Even without combining soybeans with a grain so the body can utilize more protein, soybeans by themselves have a Net Protein Utilization about equal to that of beef and chicken.

Considering their great nutritional value, plus the fact that an acre of land can produce 20 times as much usable protein when used to grow soybeans instead of meat, it's not surprising that soybeans have been the staple of the densely-populated Far East for thousands of years. The earliest mention on record of soybeans dates back to 2000 B.C. in China.

When I say *soybeans*, I don't mean facing a bowl of boiled beans day in and day out. In the West, wheat is transformed into bread, pasta, pastries, etc.; in the Far East, soybeans have been transformed into other shapes and textures.

Here are some ideas for entrees using the three soybean by-products most easily obtained in the United States — tofu, yuba and tempeh. I should clarify that when I say "most easily obtained," it may not necessarily be real easy! Though these foods are becoming more popular, it may still mean a trip to a specialty shop to find them.

I can readily find tofu in any supermarket (but I don't know if that is the situation everywhere across the country), whereas yuba and tempeh mean a special trip. For the ingredients I have to go a little out of the way to obtain, I usually get enough at one time to last a few weeks and store them in the freezer.

# STUFFED TOFU LOAF

☆ A good example of how easy and tasty it is to combine legumes and grains!

☆ Leftovers are tasty sliced and put in sandwiches.

---

6 cups mashed Chinese firm tofu
¼ cup soy sauce
2 Tbsp. vegetable oil
2 Tbsp. whole wheat flour
½ tsp. thyme
½ tsp. savory
½ tsp. asafetida or ½ cup diced onion
2 tsp. basil
½ cup nutritional yeast

## SUGGESTED MENU

Stuffed Tofu Loaf

Mock Turkey Gravy

Mashed potatoes

Lightly steamed vegetables

Sugarless cranberry sauce

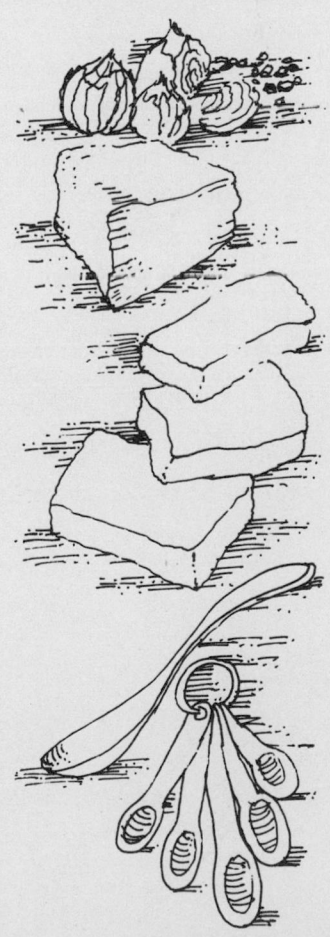

Preheat oven to 350 degrees. Oil bread pan. Prepare stuffing (see following recipe).

Combine all 9 ingredients together in a bowl and mix well. Press about ⅔ of mixture in an oiled bread pan so tofu is about 1" thick on bottom and up the sides of the pan. Stuff the center with stuffing and top with the remaining tofu mixture. Bake at 350 degrees for 30 minutes. Serve hot with gravy or cranberry sauce. I recommend using the Mock Turkey Gravy from *Kathy Cooks . . . Naturally.* Save leftovers to slice and use in sandwiches. Serves 6 to 8.

## Stuffing:

½ cup chopped walnuts or sunflower seeds
2 cups whole grain bread cubes and/or
    cooked brown rice

2 Tbsp. butter or margarine
¼ tsp. asafetida and 1 cup chopped
    celery OR 1 cup diced onion

½ cup tomato sauce
1 tsp. sage
2 Tbsp. chopped fresh parsley
½ tsp. thyme
½ tsp. Spike or other vegetable-seasoned salt

Combine first 2 ingredients in a bowl. Saute next 2 (or 3) ingredients together in a large skillet till celery or onion becomes translucent. Add next 5 ingredients and simmer together for about 5 minutes. Add first 2 ingredients and stuff Tofu Loaf immediately.

Makes a good, hot entree topped with the Mock Turkey Gravy or a sugarless cranberry sauce (use your favorite recipe, replacing sugar with half the amount of honey).

| SHOPPING LIST | |
|---|---|
| Regularly Kept in the Kitchen (Listed in Chapter 14, p. 703) | Fresh Produce |
| Tofu | Celery |
| Soy sauce | Parsley |
| Vegetable oil | |
| Whole wheat flour | |
| Nutritional yeast | |
| Whole wheat bread or brown rice | |
| Sunflower seeds or walnuts | |
| Butter or margarine | |
| Tomato sauce | |
| Asafetida | |
| Sage | |
| Savory | |
| Sweet basil | |
| Thyme | |
| Spike | |

# MOCK TURKEY GRAVY*

¼ cup butter or margarine
1 cup garbanzo flour (chickpea)
1 tsp. basil
½ tsp. thyme
½ tsp. black pepper

3 cups water

¼ cup soy sauce
2 tsp. lemon juice
2 - 3 Tbsp. nutritional yeast


Combine first 5 ingredients, stirring constantly over medium-high flame till lightly toasted. You may have to mash it with back side of the spoon. When toasted, gradually add water, stirring constantly to prevent lumping. (A whisk is ideal.) When blended, add last 3 ingredients and mix well. Makes about 1 quart.

* from *Kathy Cooks . . . Naturally*, p. 379

| SHOPPING LIST | |
| --- | --- |
| **Regularly Kept in the Kitchen** (Listed in Chapter 14, p. 703) | **Fresh Produce** |
| Margarine or butter | Lemon |
| Basil | |
| Thyme | |
| Black pepper | |
| Soy sauce | |
| Nutritional yeast | |

**Special Shopping**

Garbanzo flour (also known as chickpea flour) — in East Indian food stores and some natural food stores. If you can't find garbanzo flour, you can use whole wheat flour in its place in this recipe.

# NUTRITIONAL ANALYSIS FOR ONE SERVING
## STUFFED TOFU LOAF WITH MOCK TURKEY GRAVY

| NUTRIENT | Type: 14  FEMALE-23 TO 51 YEARS | % RDA | Amount |
|---|---|---|---|
| KCALORIES | Ã==================== | 39% | 789.0 Kc |
| PROTEIN | Ã======================================================= | 130% | 57.60 Gm |
| CARBOHYDRATE | Ã | NO RDA | 50.60 Gm |
| FAT | Ã | NO RDA | 45.30 Gm |
| FIBER-CRUDE | Ã | NO RDA | 2.150 Gm |
| CHOLESTEROL | Ã | NO RDA | 0.000 Mg |
| SATURATED FA | Ã | NO RDA | 6.280 Gm |
| OLEIC FA | Ã | NO RDA | 4.430 Gm |
| LINOLEIC FA | Ã | NO RDA | 12.40 Gm |
| SODIUM | Ã====================================== | 80% | 1778 Mg |
| POTASSIUM | Ã================ | 33% | 1259 Mg |
| MAGNESIUM | Ã============================================= | 92% | 277.0 Mg |
| IRON | Ã================================================= | 171% | 30.80 Mg |
| ZINC | Ã========================= | 53% | 8.010 Mg |
| VITAMIN A | Ã============= | 26% | 1054 IU |
| VITAMIN D | Ã | 0% | 0.000 IU |
| VIT. E/TOTAL | Ã | NO RDA | 9.280 Mg |
| VITAMIN C | Ã===== | 11% | 6.630 Mg |
| THIAMIN | Ã================================================ | 916% | 9.160 Mg |
| RIBOFLAVIN | Ã================================================= | 720% | 8.650 Mg |
| NIACIN | Ã================================================= | 398% | 51.80 Mg |
| VITAMIN B6 | Ã================================================= | 442% | 8.850 Mg |
| FOLACIN | Ã============================== | 55% | 221.0 Ug |
| VITAMIN B12 | Ã================================================= | 213% | 6.410 Ug |
| PANTO- ACID | Ã================== | 37% | 2.080 Mg |
| CALCIUM | Ã================================================= | 227% | 1818 Mg |
| PHOSPHORUS | Ã================================================= | 119% | 958.0 Mg |
| TRYPTOPHAN | Ã================================================= | 498% | 812.0 Mg |
| THREONINE | Ã================================================= | 520% | 2263 Mg |
| ISOLEUCINE | Ã================================================= | 416% | 2723 Mg |
| LEUCINE | Ã================================================= | 478% | 4171 Mg |
| LYSINE | Ã================================================= | 535% | 3500 Mg |
| METHIONINE | Ã================================================= | 283% | 770.0 Mg |
| CYSTINE | Ã================================================= | 290% | 791.0 Mg |
| PHENYL-ANINE | Ã================================================= | 614% | 2671 Mg |
| TYROSINE | Ã================================================= | 427% | 1859 Mg |
| VALINE | Ã================================================= | 379% | 2895 Mg |
| HISTIDINE | Ã | NO RDA | 1526 Mg |
| ALCOHOL | Ã | NO RDA | 0.000 Gm |
| ASH | Ã | NO RDA | 16.30 Gm |
| COPPER | Ã========================== | 55% | 1.390 Mg |
| MANGANESE | Ã================================================= | 117% | 4.400 Mg |
| IODINE | Ã================================================= | 252% | 379.0 Ug |
| MONO FAT | Ã | NO RDA | 11.80 Gm |
| POLY FAT | Ã | NO RDA | 23.30 Gm |
| CAFFEINE | Ã | NO RDA | 0.000 Mg |
| FLUORIDE | Ã | 0% | 26.60 Ug |
| MOLYBDENUM | Ã================================================= | 1361% | 4426 Ug |
| VITAMIN K | Ã | 0% | 0.000 Ug |
| SELENIUM | Ã==================== | 40% | 0.050 Mg |
| BIOTIN | Ã=========== | 18% | 27.50 Ug |
| CHLORIDE | Ã======= | 15% | 523.0 Mg |
| CHROMIUM | Ã================================================= | 760% | 0.950 Mg |
| SUGAR | Ã | NO RDA | 2.400 Gm |
| FIBER-DIET | Ã | NO RDA | 3.750 Gm |
| VIT. E/AT | Ã================================================= | 98% | 7.880 Mg |

```
% RDA:   |0      |20     |40     |60     |80     |100
```

Whole wheat flour was used in the gravy instead of garbanzo flour; sunflower seeds and whole grain bread cubes used in the stuffing; margarine used instead of butter.

# UN·RIBS

8 oz. dried bean curd (yuba) sticks

¼ cup nutritional yeast
¼ cup peanut butter (smooth)
2 Tbsp. miso
2 Tbsp. warm, melted margarine or butter
2 tsp. paprika

2 cups barbecue sauce

Soak dried bean curd sticks 4 to 6 hours or overnight in hot water. Drain out water and cut sticks into 4" to 6" lengths. Squeeze out excess water as you're cutting the yuba, and drain.

Preheat oven to 350 degrees. Oil cookie sheet.

In a large mixing bowl, mix next 5 ingredients together to form a smooth paste. Toss yuba sticks in and mix around till all sticks are evenly coated. Lay coated sticks side by side (touching each other), one layer thick, on an oiled cookie sheet. Bake at 350 degrees for 25 minutes, or till the bottoms become crisp and brown. Remove from oven. Pour into mixing bowl and toss with 2 cups of your favorite sugarless, natural food barbecue sauce. Lay out on baking sheet again and bake at 350 degrees for 10 to 15 minutes. Makes 5 to 6 servings.

## SUGGESTED MENU

Un-Ribs

Potato salad

Tossed green salad

Carob Brownies (p. 228)

| SHOPPING LIST | |
|---|---|
| **Regularly Kept in the Kitchen** (Listed in Chapter 14, p. 703) | **Fresh Produce** |
| Yuba<br>Miso<br>Nutritional yeast<br>Peanut butter<br>Butter or margarine<br>Paprika | (None) |

| Special Shopping |
|---|
| Your favorite sugarless, natural food barbecue sauce — most likely found in a natural food store. |

68

# NUTRITIONAL ANALYSIS COMPARING
# UN-RIBS WITH PORK SPARE RIBS

| NUTRIENT | Type: 14  FEMALE—23 TO 51 YEARS | Amount in Un-Ribs | Amount in pork spare ribs |
|---|---|---|---|
| KCALORIES | Ă============ | 458.0 Kc | 664.0 Kc |
| PROTEIN | Ă====================================== | 32.70 Gm | 48.30 Gm |
| CARBOHYDRATE | Ă | 28.50 Gm | 0.000 Gm |
| FAT | Ă | 27.00 Gm | 50.40 Gm |
| FIBER—CRUDE | Ă | 0.990 Gm | 0.000 Gm |
| CHOLESTEROL | Ă | 0.000 Mg | 201.0 Mg |
| SATURATED FA | Ă | 2.360 Gm | 19.50 Gm |
| OLEIC FA | Ă | 6.180 Gm | 0.000 Gm |
| LINOLEIC FA | Ă | 10.30 Gm | 0.000 Gm |
| SODIUM | Ă======================= | 1076 Mg | 154.0 Mg |
| POTASSIUM | Ă====== | 516.0 Mg | 533.0 Mg |
| MAGNESIUM | Ă==================== | 131.0 Mg | 41.10 Mg |
| IRON | Ă================= | 6.300 Mg | 3.090 Mg |
| ZINC | Ă===== | 1.700 Mg | 7.640 Mg |
| VITAMIN A | Ă============= | 1063 IU | 17.60 IU |
| VITAMIN D | Ă | 0.000 IU | 0.000 IU |
| VIT. E/TOTAL | Ă | 6.030 Mg | 0.990 Mg |
| VITAMIN C | Ă===== | 7.000 Mg | 0.000 Mg |
| THIAMIN | Ă================================================= | 3.830 Mg | 0.680 Mg |
| RIBOFLAVIN | Ă================================================= | 3.730 Mg | 0.630 Mg |
| NIACIN | Ă================================================= | 23.80 Mg | 9.110 Mg |
| VITAMIN B6 | Ă================================================= | 3.730 Mg | 0.580 Mg |
| FOLACIN | Ă======== | 64.20 Ug | 7.820 Ug |
| VITAMIN B12 | Ă================================================= | 2.830 Ug | 1.800 Ug |
| PANTO— ACID | Ă====== | 0.730 Mg | 1.250 Mg |
| CALCIUM | Ă========= | 157.0 Mg | 78.20 Mg |
| PHOSPHORUS | Ă========================= | 428.0 Mg | 435.0 Mg |
| TRYPTOPHAN | Ă================================================= | 320.0 Mg | 652.0 Mg |
| THREONINE | Ă================================================= | 1199 Mg | 2275 Mg |
| ISOLEUCINE | Ă================================================= | 1561 Mg | 2340 Mg |
| LEUCINE | Ă================================================= | 2445 Mg | 3933 Mg |
| LYSINE | Ă================================================= | 2072 Mg | 4768 Mg |
| METHIONINE | Ă================================================= | 411.0 Mg | 1193 Mg |
| CYSTINE | Ă================================================= | 407.0 Mg | 629.0 Mg |
| PHENYL—ANINE | Ă================================================= | 1590 Mg | 1.930 Mg |
| TYROSINE | Ă================================================= | 1312 Mg | 1722 Mg |
| VALINE | Ă================================================= | 1615 Mg | 2593 Mg |
| HISTIDINE | Ă | 928.0 Mg | 2457 Mg |
| ALCOHOL | Ă | 0.000 Gm | 0.000 Gm |
| ASH | Ă | 6.420 Gm | 1.860 Gm |
| COPPER | Ă========= | 0.450 Mg | 0.230 Mg |
| MANGANESE | Ă======================== | 1.810 Mg | 0.020 Mg |
| IODINE | Ă================================================= | 199.0 Ug | 0.000 Ug |
| MONO FAT | Ă | 5.960 Gm | 23.50 Gm |
| POLY FAT | Ă | 7.280 Gm | 5.860 Gm |
| CAFFEINE | Ă | 0.000 Mg | 0.000 Mg |
| FLUORIDE | Ă | 15.20 Ug | 0.000 Ug |
| MOLYBDENUM | Ă================================================= | 4551 Ug | 0.000 Ug |
| VITAMIN K | Ă | 0.000 Ug | 0.000 Ug |
| SELENIUM | Ă======== | 0.020 Mg | 0.020 Mg |
| BIOTIN | Ă======== | 24.30 Ug | 0.000 Ug |
| CHLORIDE | Ă=== | 217.0 Mg | 0.000 Mg |
| CHROMIUM | Ă================================================= | 0.410 Mg | 0.000 Mg |
| SUGAR | Ă | 0.560 Gm | 0.000 Gm |
| FIBER—DIET | Ă | 8.810 Gm | 0.000 Gm |
| VIT. E/AT | Ă================= | 2.850 Mg | 0.260 Mg |

```
% RDA:    |0      |20     |40     |60 ,   |80     |100
```

Dotted line indicates Un-Ribs. Straight line indicates pork spare ribs. Comparison is for an equal gram weight of Un-Ribs and pork spare ribs.

# STUFFED MUSHROOMS

☆ 2 - 3 very large mushrooms per person to serve as a main entree; or stuff medium-sized mushrooms to serve a gourmet hors d'oeuvres.

---

1 Tbsp. margarine or butter
16 large, fresh mushrooms

1 Tbsp. margarine or butter
Mushroom stems, finely chopped
8 oz. finely chopped tempeh
1 tsp. soy sauce

1 tsp. thyme
1 tsp. rosemary
⅛ tsp. black pepper

¼ cup chopped fresh chives
1 Tbsp. finely chopped fresh parsley
⅓ cup mashed tofu
⅓ cup Neufchatel cheese

¼ cup grated cheese

## SUGGESTED MENU

*Three-Onion
and Some Garden
Companions Soup
(without bread
and cheese), p. 673*

*Stuffed Mushrooms
topped with white sauce*

*Brown and/or wild rice*

*Caesar Salad (p. 539)*

Preheat oven to 375 degrees. Oil baking tray.

Rinse mushrooms and gently twist stems out. Melt margarine or butter in skillet and saute mushroom caps for about 2 minutes on each side over medium-high heat. Remove sauteed mushroom caps and, with stem sides up, line up in a lightly oiled baking tray.

Saute next 4 ingredients together till tempeh and mushrooms turn a golden brown. As soon as they are about done, add next 3 ingredients, stir in, and saute till you can smell the herbs cooking.

Turn off heat and add next 4 ingredients. Mix well and stuff mushroom caps, mounding the stuffing high. Sprinkle with grated cheese and bake at 375 degrees for about 15 minutes. Makes 16 caps for hors d'oeuvres, or about 4 servings if used as an entree.

| Special Shopping | SHOPPING LIST | |
|---|---|---|
| Neufchatel cheese — I can find this in supermarkets by the cream cheese; if not available there, try a specialty cheese store. | **Regularly Kept in the Kitchen (Listed in Chapter 14, p. 703)** | **Fresh Produce** |
| | Margarine or butter<br>Tempeh<br>Soy sauce<br>Thyme<br>Rosemary<br>Black pepper<br>Tofu<br>Cheese | Large, fresh mushrooms<br>Chives<br>Parsley |

# NUTRITIONAL ANALYSIS FOR ONE SERVING
## STUFFED MUSHROOMS

```
NUTRIENT      Type: 14    FEMALE-23 TO 51 YEARS              % RDA    Amount
KCALORIES     A=======                                       14%    292.0 Kc
PROTEIN       A=======================                       44%    19.40 Gm
CARBOHYDRATE  A                                            NO RDA    15.30 Gm
FAT           A                                            NO RDA    18.50 Gm
FIBER-CRUDE   A                                            NO RDA    2.420 Gm
CHOLESTEROL   A                                            NO RDA    21.40 Mg
SATURATED FA  A                                            NO RDA    6.020 Gm
OLEIC FA      A                                            NO RDA    3.220 Gm
LINOLEIC FA   A                                            NO RDA    2.800 Gm
SODIUM        A======                                        12%    277.0 Mg
POTASSIUM     A=======                                       15%    579.0 Mg
MAGNESIUM     A===========                                   22%    68.20 Mg
IRON          A===============                               28%    5.120 Mg
ZINC          A======                                        13%    2.060 Mg
VITAMIN A     A================                              30%    1204 IU
VITAMIN D     A                                               0%    0.000 IU
VIT. E/TOTAL  A                                            NO RDA    0.980 Mg
VITAMIN C     A=====                                         10%    6.000 Mg
THIAMIN       A=========                                     19%    0.190 Mg
RIBOFLAVIN    A====================                          40%    0.480 Mg
NIACIN        A=======================                       44%    5.750 Mg
VITAMIN B6    A======                                        14%    0.280 Mg
FOLACIN       A======                                        13%    55.70 Ug
VITAMIN B12   A=======                                       15%    0.450 Ug
PANTO- ACID   A==================                            36%    2.010 Mg
CALCIUM       A=================                             34%    279.0 Mg
PHOSPHORUS    A==================                            37%    299.0 Mg
TRYPTOPHAN    A=================================================   174%    285.0 Mg
THREONINE     A=================================================   180%    783.0 Mg
ISOLEUCINE    A=================================================   153%    1003 Mg
LEUCINE       A=================================================   186%    1625 Mg
LYSINE        A=================================================   203%    1326 Mg
METHIONINE    A=================================================   115%    314.0 Mg
CYSTINE       A=============================================        94%    256.0 Mg
PHENYL-ANINE  A=================================================   227%    991.0 Mg
TYROSINE      A=================================================   168%    734.0 Mg
VALINE        A=================================================   134%    1023 Mg
HISTIDINE     A                                            NO RDA    547.0 Mg
ALCOHOL       A                                            NO RDA    0.000 Gm
ASH           A                                            NO RDA    2.720 Gm
COPPER        A===========                                   22%    0.550 Mg
MANGANESE     A=============                                 27%    1.050 Mg
IODINE        A=================================================   176%    265.0 Ug
MONO FAT      A                                            NO RDA    5.900 Gm
POLY FAT      A                                            NO RDA    5.620 Gm
CAFFEINE      A                                            NO RDA    0.000 Mg
FLUORIDE      A                                               0%    22.80 Ug
MOLYBDENUM    A=================================================   320%    1043 Ug
VITAMIN K     A                                               0%    0.000 Ug
SELENIUM      A====                                           8%    0.010 Mg
BIOTIN        A===                                            6%    9.020 Ug
CHLORIDE      A=                                              3%    135.0 Mg
CHROMIUM      A=================================================   248%    0.310 Mg
SUGAR         A                                            NO RDA    0.000 Gm
FIBER-DIET    A                                            NO RDA    8.420 Gm
VIT. E/AT     A=                                              2%    0.230 Mg

  % RDA:  |0      |20     |40     |60     |80     |100
```

Margarine was used instead of butter in this analysis.

# AMERICAN HOLIDAY DINNER IDEAS

This is a thought Henry David Thoreau shared with us that is timely whether it is an election year or not: "The fate of the country does not depend on what kind of paper you drop into the ballot box once a year, but on what kind of man you drop from your chamber into the street every morning."

Special occasions and the holiday season sometimes present special problems to those who are trying to change their diet to a healthier one and/or are trying to watch their weight. Whether these times are a problem or not really depends on whether or not you let them be! There are a few things that you can do to help get yourself through any special occasion or holiday.

One of the most important things to remember when getting together with others is that the occasion and the company are the reason for getting together. Though some food almost always is served when people get together, the reason for gathering isn't just to eat.

If you are doing the entertaining, besides serving healthy, palatable food, you can plan activities centered around the particular occasion that everyone can take part in together that doesn't have anything to do with food. Taking walks, going skiing, doing skits, reading, singing, and/or playing music together are only a few of the kinds of things you can do with others. If you are a guest, remember that you've come to share company for whatever the occasion is and do that —eat or drink what is available that doesn't conflict with your dietary guidelines. Ideally, you are getting together on special occasions with family and friends who are near and dear enough that what you're eating or not eating won't be an issue.

When I'm doing the feeding, serving loved ones only the foods I know are good for them is part of caring. I've always found family members and friends to be willing and interested in trying a new dish they've never had before. When I'm on the receiving end, I've been fortunate to have family and friends who are loving enough to prepare a special meal of foods they know I'll eat, even though they themselves don't eat that way all the time.

However, over the years, more and more of my family and friends have begun making the lifesaving changes in their diets recommended in this book. The number of people in this country who are trying to make healthier changes in their diet is so great that it has become easier and easier through the years to be able to find something I can eat no matter where I go. (This was not the case 18 years ago.) You might arrive at the home of a friend only to find that they have made changes in their diet as you have. It's even possible that your family and/or friends are thinking about or actually trying to improve their diets and will find your dietary changes inspiring, rather than a problem.

Chances might be that if a special occasion takes place when you are just beginning to make the changes in your diet recommended in this book, the biggest problem you'll have may be the temptation and calling of old tastes and habits. About all you can do for that is call on your determination and intelligence to remember the reasons why some of your "old favorites" aren't healthy. The longer you stick with eating healthy, whole foods, the less of a problem this will be, because you actually will develop a higher taste. You will prefer the subtle flavors vegetables have to offer over salt; the natural sweetness of fruit over sugar. After the rich, nutty flavor of whole wheat bread, white bread holds about as much taste appeal as a soft sponge; after the good, clean taste of legumes and whole grains, you can actually taste (and smell as it cooks) the uric acid in meat. (For those of you who don't know what uric acid is, it's one of the waste products of the body. It would have been filtered from the bloodstream and passed out of the body through the bladder by the animal, bird, or fish, had it lived.)

If you are doing the cooking, the menu is in your hands, so plan a delicious meal that will simultaneously please your guests and not compromise your dietary commitments. If you don't make a point of talking about all the things you didn't use when serving a meal like this American Holiday Dinner, your guests will be so delighted that they probably won't even feel like they're missing anything.

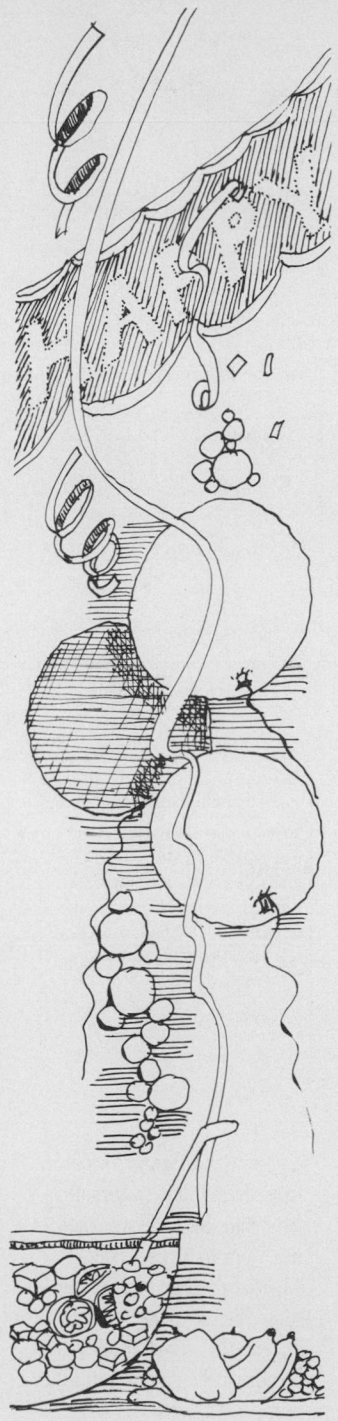

## AMERICAN HOLIDAY DINNER MENU

*Festive Mock
Stuffed Turkey*

*Mock Turkey Gravy (p. 66)*

*Sprouted Corn Patties*

*Fresh tossed salad*

*Potato Creamed Vegetables
(p. 560)*

*Mince*

*Fresh Fruit Tarts*

### Special Shopping

Whole corn kernels —
popcorn does not work. Get
a whole corn kernel from a
natural food store, preferably
Texas Deaf Smith County
corn or blue Hopi Indian
corn — if you can find it.

A dear friend, Sarai Stricklin,
once saved and then sprouted
some blue corn she was given
at a Hopi Indian reservation for
a special occasion feast at our
house. Before dinner, we ground
the corn in a food grinder and
deep-fried the patties. Thus this
recipe was created . . .

# SPROUTED CORN PATTIES

☆ A unique way to prepare this native American food.
Sprouting converts the starch in the corn to an easily
assimilated, natural sugar; enzymes released in sprouting make the protein more easy to digest; vitamin content is boosted.

*3 - 4 cups sprouted corn kernels*

This recipe must be started days ahead of time in the sense
that the corn needs to be germinated. I've found that I've had
the best luck sprouting Texas Deaf Smith County corn. Popcorn does not work. To germinate the corn, soak 2 cups of
whole corn kernels overnight in water. The next day, rubber
band a screen over the mouth of the jar with a very thick,
strong rubber band. Tip jar upside down in the sink to drain
out soaking water. Rinse the soaked corn kernels by running
water through the screen into the jar, swish the jar around
and drain again. Place jar upside down in a dish drainer, or any
place that excess water can drain out through the screen and
fresh air can circulate into the jar. Rinse sprouts 3 to 5 times a
day till the tip of the corn is germinated and about ⅛" to ¼"
long and the kernel is sweet when you bite it. Now the corn is
ready for preparation.

Simply grind germinated corn kernels in a food grinder.
Shape into patties about 2" in diameter and ⅜" thick. Heat oil
to about 375 degrees for deep-frying, and deep-fry patties till
they are a golden brown. These are best served hot. Recipe
makes enough for a few patties per person for 6 people.

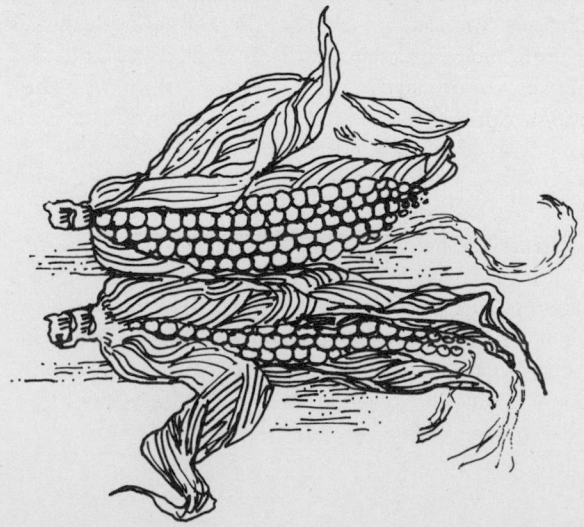

# STUFFING

☆ Excellent used to stuff the Festive Mock Turkey or served as a side dish at any compatible meal.

---

2 cups whole grain bread cubes
½ cup cooked lentils
½ cup chopped walnuts

2 - 3 Tbsp. butter or margarine
¼ tsp. asafetida and ½ cup diced
   celery OR ½ cup diced onion

½ cup blended tomatoes
1 tsp. ground sage
½ tsp. thyme
½ tsp. Spike or other vegetable-seasoned salt

½ cup chopped black olives
2 Tbsp. arrowroot mixed in ¼ cup water

Melted butter or margarine for basting

Preheat oven to 350 degrees and oil a loaf pan.

Combine first 3 ingredients and set aside. Saute next 3 ingredients in a skillet. When celery turns translucent, add next 4 ingredients and cook for about 5 minutes. Add next 2 ingredients and stir constantly till thickened. Pour into the mixture of dry ingredients.

Place in an oiled loaf pan and bake at 350 degrees for 1 hour. Baste the top every 15 minutes with melted butter or margarine. Serve as is for a dressing or stuff Festive Mock Stuffed Turkey (see following recipe) with this or your favorite stuffing recipe.

Besides stuffing tofu with this stuffing recipe, try stuffing vegetables such as bell peppers, tomatoes, zucchinis or winter squash (like acorn or butternut squash). Cover stuffed vegetable, or sprinkle some grated cheese on top, and bake at 350 degrees for about 30 to 45 minutes or till vegetable is lightly cooked and tender. Top with brown gravy or a white sauce.

| SHOPPING LIST | |
| --- | --- |
| **Regularly Kept in the Kitchen** (Listed in Chapter 14, p. 703) | **Fresh Produce** |
| Whole wheat bread<br>Lentils<br>Walnuts<br>Margarine or butter<br>Asafetida<br>Sage<br>Thyme<br>Spike<br>Arrowroot | Celery<br>Tomatoes<br>Chopped ripe olives |

I'm sure our fine-feathered friends would appreciate this thought expressed by Porphyry: "Who is to say birds are irrational because they cannot speak? Birds communicate with a language we cannot understand, nor can we understand the tongue of a foreigner — but do we pluck out his hair? A man who eats a harmless diet will be less inclined to slaughter another man's flesh, since the idea would be unthinkable."

# FESTIVE MOCK STUFFED TURKEY

☆ A special dish to prepare for special occasions. Takes longer to prepare than an everyday sort of meal; but nowhere near as long as it would to cook a turkey.

---

3 (1-lb.) blocks Chinese firm tofu

½ cup soy sauce
2 Tbsp. water

Stuffing

16 large sheets of dried bean curd (yuba), soaked

½ cup margarine or butter, melted

Have stuffing already prepared and soak yuba sheets.

Cut 1-pound blocks of tofu into fourths, cutting across the width of the block (some Chinese firm tofu comes already cut like this, with four slices per container). Mix soy sauce and water in an oblong cake pan and set tofu blocks in the soy sauce to soak for a few minutes on each side. (The tofu won't all fit in the cake pan at once, but you can just put a new slice in as you remove one to stuff.) Now set up an assembly line of sorts with the tofu, stuffing, yuba sheets, steamer racks, and the melted butter or margarine. Then, with each piece of tofu, assemble by going down the line.

First make a pocket in the tofu by gently (so it doesn't squash) holding a block in one hand and inserting a sharp knife into one of the thin ends. Then make a slit, leaving about ½" uncut on 2 sides and the bottom edges.

Stuff a few spoonfuls of stuffing into the pocket, being careful not to tear the sides of the tofu pocket. Wrap with a soaked yuba sheet like wrapping a gift box. Place in steamer rack. When the entire steamer rack is full of stuffed tofus, place over boiling water and steam for 10 minutes. Now remove from steamer, dip each piece in soy sauce and place on an oiled cookie sheet. Then paint a light coating of margarine or butter over each piece with a basting brush. Bake at 350 degrees till yuba begins to crisp and turn a golden brown — about 15 to 20 minutes. (You may want to baste with melted butter or margarine a few more times during this period.) Serve topped with Mock Turkey Gravy (p. 66). This will serve 5 to 6 people, allowing 2 pieces per person, which is plenty along with the rest of the meal!

If you're in a hurry, you can skip the steaming step and just bake the stuffed, wrapped tofu pieces at 425 to 450 degrees till yuba crisps and turns a golden brown, being sure to baste 3 or 4 times in the process.

| SHOPPING LIST | |
|---|---|
| **Regularly Kept in the Kitchen** (Listed in Chapter 14, p. 703) | **Fresh Produce** |
| Tofu<br>Soy sauce<br>Yuba sheets<br>Margarine or butter | (None) |

Also see shopping lists for Stuffing and Mock Turkey Gravy (p. 66).

A note for the frazzled hostess: The Festive Mock Stuffed Turkey can be prepared a few days ahead of time, up to the point of steaming. After steaming, cool, cover and refrigerate. Then just finish baking to crisp and brown it. Tofu keeps longer after it's been cooked.

# NUTRITIONAL ANALYSIS FOR ONE SERVING
## FESTIVE MOCK STUFFED TURKEY WITH MOCK TURKEY GRAVY

| NUTRIENT | Type: 14   FEMALE–23 TO 51 YEARS | % RDA | Amount |
|---|---|---|---|
| KCALORIES | A==================================================== | 93% | 1867 Kc |
| PROTEIN | A==================================================== | 352% | 155.0 Gm |
| CARBOHYDRATE | A | NO RDA | 83.10 Gm |
| FAT | A | NO RDA | 117.0 Gm |
| FIBER–CRUDE | A | NO RDA | 3.400 Gm |
| CHOLESTEROL | A | NO RDA | 0.000 Mg |
| SATURATED FA | A | NO RDA | 11.00 Gm |
| OLEIC FA | A | NO RDA | 16.60 Gm |
| LINOLEIC FA | A | NO RDA | 30.80 Gm |
| SODIUM | A==================================================== | 158% | 3481 Mg |
| POTASSIUM | A============================== | 56% | 2109 Mg |
| MAGNESIUM | A==================================================== | 212% | 637.0 Mg |
| IRON | A==================================================== | 296% | 53.40 Mg |
| ZINC | A======================= | 46% | 6.970 Mg |
| VITAMIN A | A==================================== | 71% | 2854 IU |
| VITAMIN D | A | 0% | 0.000 IU |
| VIT. E/TOTAL | A | NO RDA | 8.410 Mg |
| VITAMIN C | A====== | 12% | 7.580 Mg |
| THIAMIN | A==================================================== | 423% | 4.230 Mg |
| RIBOFLAVIN | A==================================================== | 288% | 3.460 Mg |
| NIACIN | A==================================================== | 186% | 24.20 Mg |
| VITAMIN B6 | A==================================================== | 171% | 3.420 Mg |
| FOLACIN | A======================= | 47% | 189.0 Ug |
| VITAMIN B12 | A==================================================== | 71% | 2.140 Ug |
| PANTO– ACID | A==================== | 41% | 2.280 Mg |
| CALCIUM | A==================================================== | 306% | 2448 Mg |
| PHOSPHORUS | A==================================================== | 251% | 2010 Mg |
| TRYPTOPHAN | A==================================================== | 1077% | 1756 Mg |
| THREONINE | A==================================================== | 1325% | 5767 Mg |
| ISOLEUCINE | A==================================================== | 1153% | 7532 Mg |
| LEUCINE | A==================================================== | 1330% | 11588 Mg |
| LYSINE | A==================================================== | 1520% | 9927 Mg |
| METHIONINE | A==================================================== | 740% | 2015 Mg |
| CYSTINE | A==================================================== | 737% | 2006 Mg |
| PHENYL–ANINE | A==================================================== | 1732% | 7536 Mg |
| TYROSINE | A==================================================== | 1298% | 5650 Mg |
| VALINE | A==================================================== | 1002% | 7641 Mg |
| HISTIDINE | A | NO RDA | 4342 Mg |
| ALCOHOL | A | NO RDA | 0.000 Gm |
| ASH | A | NO RDA | 20.90 Gm |
| COPPER | A==================================================== | 110% | 2.770 Mg |
| MANGANESE | A==================================================== | 298% | 11.20 Mg |
| IODINE | A==================================================== | 668% | 1002 Ug |
| MONO FAT | A | NO RDA | 26.00 Gm |
| POLY FAT | A | NO RDA | 31.50 Gm |
| CAFFEINE | A | NO RDA | 0.000 Mg |
| FLUORIDE | A | 0% | 15.60 Ug |
| MOLYBDENUM | A==================================================== | 6890% | 22395 Ug |
| VITAMIN K | A | 1% | 1.060 Ug |
| SELENIUM | A==================================================== | 120% | 0.150 Mg |
| BIOTIN | A======================= | 44% | 66.80 Ug |
| CHLORIDE | A============ | 25% | 865.0 Mg |
| CHROMIUM | A==================================================== | 1960% | 2.450 Mg |
| SUGAR | A | NO RDA | 2.050 Gm |
| FIBER–DIET | A | NO RDA | 39.30 Gm |
| VIT. E/AT | A== | 5% | 0.460 Mg |

```
% RDA:   |0      |20     |40     |60     |80     |100        in
```

Whole wheat flour was used for the gravy instead of garbanzo flour; margarine used instead of butter.

# MINCE

☆ Delicious as a side dish, a cold filling for a tart, or served piping hot over a honey-sweetened ice cream.

---

4 cups peeled, diced tart apples
2 cups tart cherries, pitted
2 cups green tomatoes or quinces, diced
1 cup raisins, packed
1 cup finely chopped walnuts
1 cup apple cider
½ cup honey
½ cup molasses
½ cup chopped Black Mission figs
¼ cup apple cider vinegar
¾ tsp. each of ground cloves,
   cinnamon, mace, nutmeg, and sea salt

Combine all ingredients in a pot and bring to a boil. Reduce heat and simmer, uncovered, for 1½ to 2 hours, stirring occasionally till thickened. Refrigerate. This will keep refrigerated for a few weeks or can be frozen. Makes about 2 quarts.

Since the tart tasting fruit, quince, has been declining in popularity since the medieval ages, you may have a hard time finding this fall/winter-bearing fruit. If I can't find something, or do and it's ridiculously expensive, I try to substitute something of similar texture and/or taste. In this case, it's green tomatoes, which may be equally hard to get unless you have a home garden . . . which is well worth considering, not just to be able to make this recipe, but to have a supply of fresh vegetables at your doorstep that you can control what gets sprayed on them or not!

| SHOPPING LIST | |
|---|---|
| **Regularly Kept in the Kitchen** (Listed in Chapter 14, p. 703) | **Fresh Produce** |
| Walnuts | Tart apples |
| Honey | Tart cherries |
| Molasses | Green tomatoes or quinces |
| Apple cider vinegar | Raisins |
| Ground cloves | Apple cider |
| Cinnamon | Dried Black Mission figs |
| Mace | |
| Nutmeg | |
| Salt | |

# NUTRITIONAL ANALYSIS FOR ONE SERVING MINCE

```
NUTRIENT      Type: 14   FEMALE-23 TO 51 YEARS          % RDA   Amount
KCALORIES     A==                                        4%   94.50 Kc
PROTEIN       A=                                         3%   1.500 Gm
CARBOHYDRATE  A                                        NO RDA 18.70 Gm
FAT           A                                        NO RDA  2.410 Gm
FIBER-CRUDE   A                                        NO RDA  0.570 Gm
CHOLESTEROL   A                                        NO RDA  0.000 Mg
SATURATED FA  A                                        NO RDA  0.190 Gm
OLEIC FA      A                                        NO RDA  0.410 Gm
LINOLEIC FA   A                                        NO RDA  1.420 Gm
SODIUM        A=                                         2%   50.30 Mg
POTASSIUM     A==                                        5%   200.0 Mg
MAGNESIUM     A==                                        4%   14.70 Mg
IRON          A==                                        4%   0.720 Mg
ZINC          A                                          1%   0.200 Mg
VITAMIN A     A===                                       6%   243.0 IU
VITAMIN D     A                                          0%   0.000 IU
VIT. E/TOTAL  A                                        NO RDA  0.850 Mg
VITAMIN C     A====                                      8%   5.310 Mg
THIAMIN       A=                                         3%   0.030 Mg
RIBOFLAVIN    A                                          1%   0.020 Mg
NIACIN        A                                          1%   0.240 Mg
VITAMIN B6    A=                                         2%   0.040 Mg
FOLACIN       A                                          0%   1.160 Ug
VITAMIN B12   A                                          0%   0.000 Ug
PANTO- ACID   A=                                         2%   0.140 Mg
CALCIUM       A=                                         2%   23.50 Mg
PHOSPHORUS    A==                                        4%   34.60 Mg
TRYPTOPHAN    A====                                      9%   14.80 Mg
THREONINE     A====                                      8%   36.70 Mg
ISOLEUCINE    A===                                       7%   46.30 Mg
LEUCINE       A====                                      9%   78.50 Mg
LYSINE        A===                                       6%   39.80 Mg
METHIONINE    A===                                       7%   21.00 Mg
CYSTINE       A====                                      8%   22.50 Mg
PHENYL-ANINE  A=====                                    11%   50.70 Mg
TYROSINE      A====                                      8%   36.90 Mg
VALINE        A===                                       7%   59.40 Mg
HISTIDINE     A                                        NO RDA 30.90 Mg
ALCOHOL       A                                        NO RDA  0.000 Gm
ASH           A                                        NO RDA  0.410 Gm
COPPER        A==                                        5%   0.140 Mg
MANGANESE     A===                                       6%   0.230 Mg
IODINE        A=                                         3%   4.900 Ug
MONO FAT      A                                        NO RDA  0.520 Gm
POLY FAT      A                                        NO RDA  1.520 Gm
CAFFEINE      A                                        NO RDA  0.000 Mg
FLUORIDE      A                                          0%   14.50 Ug
MOLYBDENUM    A                                          0%   0.000 Ug
VITAMIN K     A                                          0%   0.000 Ug
SELENIUM      A                                          0%   0.000 Mg
BIOTIN        A                                          1%   2.350 Ug
CHLORIDE      A                                          0%   0.000 Mg
CHROMIUM      A                                          0%   0.000 Mg
SUGAR         A                                        NO RDA  1.360 Gm
FIBER-DIET    A                                        NO RDA  0.400 Gm
VIT. E/AT     A=                                         2%   0.160 Mg

  % RDA:  |0      |20     |40     |60     |80     |100
```

Green tomatoes were used instead of quinces in this analysis.

# NUT BUTTER CUSTARD

☆ Not as rich as it sounds! It's sweetened with fruit juice and a tiny bit of honey and is completely cholesterol- and saturated fat-free.

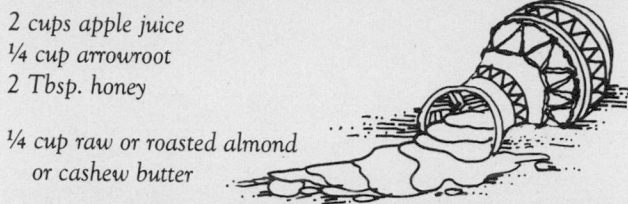

*2 cups apple juice*
*¼ cup arrowroot*
*2 Tbsp. honey*

*¼ cup raw or roasted almond*
*   or cashew butter*

In a pot off the heat, combine first 3 ingredients and mix till arrowroot is dissolved. Put on heat and add nut butter. Stir constantly till the pudding thickens and nut butter is thoroughly melted in. Cool and serve as a pudding in individual bowls, or use as a layer in a parfait, or as a pie or tart filling, etc. This makes 2 cups' worth of pudding — enough for four ½-cup servings or enough to fill tarts, layer parfaits, etc.

**Postscript:** This Nut Butter Custard recipe was originally included to be used as a thin, neutral base to put under the fresh fruit in the Fresh Fruit Tarts to keep the dough from getting soggy. For this reason I stressed using raw cashew or almond butter, as both these nut butters have a nice, sweet, and not overpowering, taste. However, when we were in the midst of producing the show, there were only the roasted almond and cashew butters available. Figuring we couldn't wait for the next shipment (Hawaii is unfortunately and precariously dependent on importing basic necessities), and that the camera wouldn't be able to taste the difference, I purchased some roasted almond butter. After making the tarts and presenting them on camera, the tarts were promptly eaten up by the crew, and — a new discovery for me — the roasted nut butter tarts were delicious in a different way from the raw nut butter tarts. They gave the tarts a fuller, richer flavor. So now I have rewritten the recipe to include raw or roasted almond or cashew butter.

This is as good an opportunity as any to remind you that I've given the recipes in this book as ideas that hopefully will introduce you to new ingredients, inspire you to use your imagination and experiment on your own, and substitute ingredients you don't have with ones that you do have.

To build a parfait:
1) use a tall-stemmed dessert or ice cream cup; 2) fill in first layer about 1" thick; 3) top with a ½"- to 1"-thick layer of another ingredient that contrasts in color and is compatible in flavor to the first layer; 4) sprinkle with chopped nuts or other bits and pieces of things; 5) repeat layering (steps 1 - 4) till cup is full. Refrigerate a few hours before serving.

Some parfait ideas using Nut Butter Custard as the base — just alternate layers of nut butter base with any of the following:
• Berry-Silly Pudding (p. 689) and sprinkle with Branola (p. 685)
• Carob Fondue (p. 235) sprinkled with sliced, toasted almonds
• Partially jelled filling for Jeweled Treasure Dessert (p. 381), with or without fruit, sprinkled with finely chopped fresh mint leaves

Got the idea? Now try some of your own innovations!

| SHOPPING LIST | |
| --- | --- |
| **Regularly Kept in the Kitchen** (Listed in Chapter 14, p. 703) | **Fresh Produce** |
| Arrowroot<br>Honey<br>Raw or roasted<br>Almond or cashew butter | Apple juice |

# NUTRITIONAL ANALYSIS FOR ONE SERVING
## NUT BUTTER CUSTARD

| NUTRIENT | Type: 14 | FEMALE-23 TO 51 YEARS | % RDA | Amount |
|---|---|---|---|---|
| KCALORIES | A===== | | 10% | 206.0 Kc |
| PROTEIN | A=== | | 6% | 2.950 Gm |
| CARBOHYDRATE | A | | NO RDA | 32.50 Gm |
| FAT | A | | NO RDA | 8.050 Gm |
| FIBER-CRUDE | A | | NO RDA | 0.390 Gm |
| CHOLESTEROL | A | | NO RDA | 0.000 Mg |
| SATURATED FA | A | | NO RDA | 1.580 Gm |
| OLEIC FA | A | | NO RDA | 0.000 Gm |
| LINOLEIC FA | A | | NO RDA | 0.000 Gm |
| SODIUM | A | | 0% | 6.000 Mg |
| POTASSIUM | A=== | | 6% | 240.0 Mg |
| MAGNESIUM | A======= | | 15% | 45.20 Mg |
| IRON | A==== | | 8% | 1.520 Mg |
| ZINC | A== | | 5% | 0.870 Mg |
| VITAMIN A | A | | 0% | 1.000 IU |
| VITAMIN D | A | | 0% | 0.000 IU |
| VIT. E/TOTAL | A | | NO RDA | 0.000 Mg |
| VITAMIN C | A | | 1% | 1.150 Mg |
| THIAMIN | A=== | | 7% | 0.070 Mg |
| RIBOFLAVIN | A== | | 4% | 0.050 Mg |
| NIACIN | A= | | 3% | 0.430 Mg |
| VITAMIN B6 | A= | | 3% | 0.070 Mg |
| FOLACIN | A= | | 2% | 11.00 Ug |
| VITAMIN B12 | A | | 0% | 0.000 Ug |
| PANTO- ACID | A= | | 3% | 0.210 Mg |
| CALCIUM | A= | | 2% | 16.60 Mg |
| PHOSPHORUS | A===== | | 10% | 85.70 Mg |
| TRYPTOPHAN | A============= | | 26% | 44.00 Mg |
| THREONINE | A============ | | 25% | 109.0 Mg |
| ISOLEUCINE | A========== | | 20% | 134.0 Mg |
| LEUCINE | A============ | | 27% | 236.0 Mg |
| LYSINE | A========= | | 22% | 150.0 Mg |
| METHIONINE | A========= | | 18% | 50.00 Mg |
| CYSTINE | A========= | | 19% | 52.00 Mg |
| PHENYL-ANINE | A================ | | 33% | 145.0 Mg |
| TYROSINE | A========== | | 20% | 90.00 Mg |
| VALINE | A============ | | 25% | 191.0 Mg |
| HISTIDINE | A | | NO RDA | 73.00 Mg |
| ALCOHOL | A | | NO RDA | 0.000 Gm |
| ASH | A | | NO RDA | 0.680 Gm |
| COPPER | A======= | | 15% | 0.380 Mg |
| MANGANESE | A= | | 3% | 0.140 Mg |
| IODINE | A | | 0% | 0.000 Ug |
| MONO FAT | A | | NO RDA | 4.650 Gm |
| POLY FAT | A | | NO RDA | 1.380 Gm |
| CAFFEINE | A | | NO RDA | 0.000 Mg |
| FLUORIDE | A | | 0% | 10.50 Ug |
| MOLYBDENUM | A | | 0% | 0.000 Ug |
| VITAMIN K | A | | 0% | 0.000 Ug |
| SELENIUM | A | | 0% | 0.000 Mg |
| BIOTIN | A | | 0% | 1.490 Ug |
| CHLORIDE | A | | 0% | 0.000 Mg |
| CHROMIUM | A | | 0% | 0.000 Mg |
| SUGAR | A | | NO RDA | 0.000 Gm |
| FIBER-DIET | A | | NO RDA | 0.000 Gm |
| VIT. E/AT | A | | 0% | 0.010 Mg |

```
% RDA:   |0        |20       |40       |60       |80       |100
```

Cashew butter was used instead of almond butter in analysis.

# FRESH FRUIT TARTS

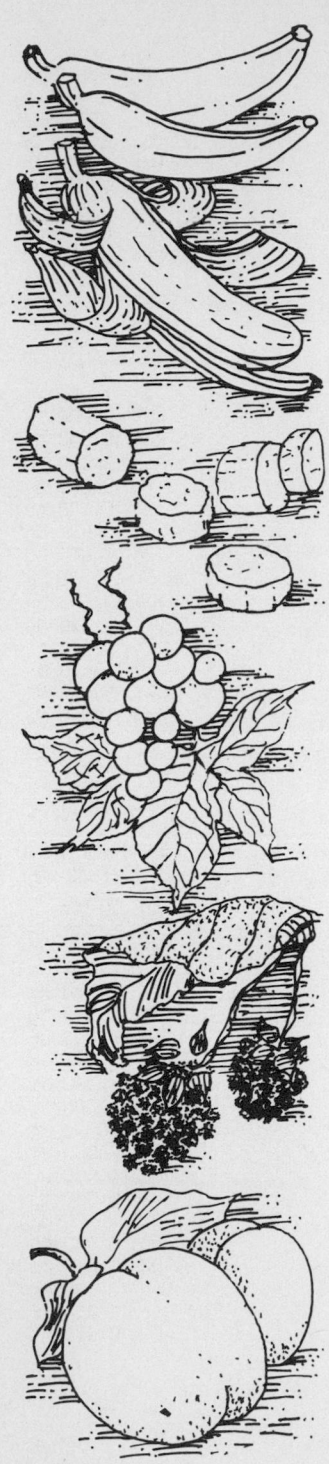

☆ A special way to serve fresh fruit for dessert; especially good to fill baked tart shells with Nut Butter Custard and then top with fruit and glaze.

---

*Baked whole wheat tart shells*

**Fruit Glaze:**

*½ cup sugarless jam*
*2 Tbsp. apple juice*

*Whole assorted fresh fruits*
  *such as strawberries, blueberries,*
  *raspberries, seedless grapes*
*Slices of banana, kiwi fruit, peaches,*
  *nectarines, apricots, plums, mango,*
  *fresh figs, melons, pineapple*

Use the Piroshki Quicker Dough recipe (see p. 334) or your favorite whole wheat pie crust. Roll dough out to about ⅛" thick and cut rounds using a cookie cutter or jar lid, and shape tarts on either oiled cookie sheets or on outside of oiled muffin tins. To shape rounds on cookie sheets, lay cut-out circles on sheets; then cut strips of dough about ½" thick and lay on top of the circles along the edges to form sides of tart shells. Crimp the double edge as you would with pie dough. For a deeper tart, you may prefer oiling the outside of the bottoms of muffin tins and wrapping the circles of dough over the bottoms and up the sides of the muffin wells. Or buy tart baking dishes in a gourmet cooking shop. (These are usually larger and deeper.) Bake tart shells at 425 degrees 12 to 15 minutes till golden brown.

**Fruit Glaze:**

Combine first 2 ingredients and stir over heat till the jam is watered down a tiny bit and apple juice is thoroughly mixed into jam. A little bit goes a long way. Now simply arrange prepared pieces of an assortment of such fresh fruits as whole strawberries, blueberries, raspberries, seedless grapes, etc. Slices of banana, kiwi, peaches, nectarines, apricots, plums, mango, fresh figs, melons, or pineapple can be artistically placed on top of baked tart crust or on top of a cream-type filling (see preceding Nut Butter Custard recipe) inside a baked tart shell. Use a basting brush to paint glaze over the fresh fruit arrangements. Makes about 1 dozen tarts.

| SHOPPING LIST | | | Special Shopping |
| --- | --- | --- | --- |
| **Regularly Kept in the Kitchen** (Listed in Chapter 14, p. 703) | **Fresh Produce** | | Sugarless jam — sweetened with honey or fruit juice; available in natural food stores. |
| (None) | Apple juice Your choice of assorted fresh fruits | | |

See also shopping list for Piroshki Quicker Dough recipe (p. 334) or other whole grain crust of your choice. (Suggestions: Quiche crust, p. 154, or Perfectly Nutty Crust, p. 271.)

At this time, when we are faced with an energy crisis and a world hunger problem — both of which are caused by overconsumption of the world's limited resources — we might be better citizens of the planet on which we live if we took heed of these simple words from Lao Tsu: "He who knows that enough is enough will always have enough."

# SZECHUAN KUNG FOOD

Here is a Chinese banquet fit for a king . . . or should I say an emperor? For a period of time in ancient China, Buddhist monks cooked for the emperors because they thought the emperors would be less warlike if they didn't eat meat. Because the monks were cooking for people who didn't necessarily want to stop eating meat, they made quite an art of making non-meat food taste and feel like meat. They refined the art to the point of doing things like laying fine bamboo splinters in tofu flavored like fish to resemble fish bones. Because the monks were such excellent cooks, the emperors accepted their cooking and made them their official cooks of sorts.

Although history shows us that many well-known philosophers and humanitarians did not eat meat, the examples of Hitler and Mussolini (who both eliminated meat from their diets) point to the fact that a person must change more than just his diet to become a more peaceful, gentle and compassionate person. It's possible for a self-centered, egocentric tyrant to remain that way after eliminating meat from the diet if the reasons for doing so originally were, and continue to be, self-centered. While there are many aspects of eliminating meat from the diet that can help to shift the center of concern from oneself to others, it isn't an automatic result of this dietary change.

That's why I'm always careful to keep the subject of eating in perspective in my own personal life as well as in anything I do with food in public. It's certainly important to make the change(s) to a healthier diet — but rather than seeing the new eating habits as *the* change to make, the ultimate goal, I just see it as common-sense knowledge. Unfortunately, it isn't as commonplace as it should be and needs to be learned and incorporated into our everyday lives so it takes little more thought or attention than breathing does. The point is to be able to carry out the bodily functions so vital to life and still have time and energy left to consider what to use that life for.

Even making a Chinese banquet to serve eight doesn't have to take a lot of time and energy. When planning a meal like this, presumably for dinner guests, you'll most likely want to plan and prepare it in such a way that at dinner time you can be with your guests at the table and not slaving away in the kitchen. This is easily accomplished as so much of this meal can be pre-prepared. Days beforehand you can make the Watercress Salad, Almond Nectar Float, Hot and Sour Soup, and the Mock Peking Duck (up to the point of steaming) and its sauce, and refrigerate all. On the day of serving, make the Steamed Buns dough about three hours before serving and assemble, and steam them about 45 minutes before serving time, right after you start the rice. As rice and buns are cooking, cut the vegetables for the Eggplant Szechuan and have them ready to slide off a cutting board. When guests are almost ready to be served, heat the Hot and Sour Soup and add last two ingredients. Serve this. After everyone has finished the soup, while digestive juices are beginning to flow, heat a wok and a skillet (or another wok) and quickly fry the Eggplant Szechuan dish in one and the steamed Mock Peking Duck in the other. Serve everything but dessert. After the main part of the meal is done, take the dessert out of the refrigerator, assemble and serve.

## SZECHUAN KUNG FOOD MENU

*Hot and Sour Soup*

*Watercress Salad*

*Mock Peking Duck and Sauce*

*Eggplant Szechuan*

*Steamed Buns (p. 604)*

*Perfect Brown Rice (p. 375)*

*Almond Nectar Float*

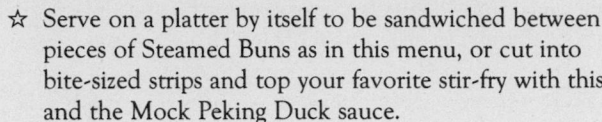

# MOCK PEKING DUCK

Chinese Buddhist monks used yuba a lot in their cooking. Sometimes used by itself in sheet or rope form; often wrapped around something to resemble the skin of an animal.

☆ Serve on a platter by itself to be sandwiched between pieces of Steamed Buns as in this menu, or cut into bite-sized strips and top your favorite stir-fry with this and the Mock Peking Duck sauce.

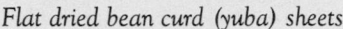

*Flat dried bean curd (yuba) sheets*

*2 Tbsp. plus 2 tsp. whole wheat flour*
*2 cups mashed Chinese firm tofu*
*2 cups water*
*3 Tbsp. honey*
*5 Tbsp. toasted sesame oil*
*1 tsp. asafetida or garlic powder*

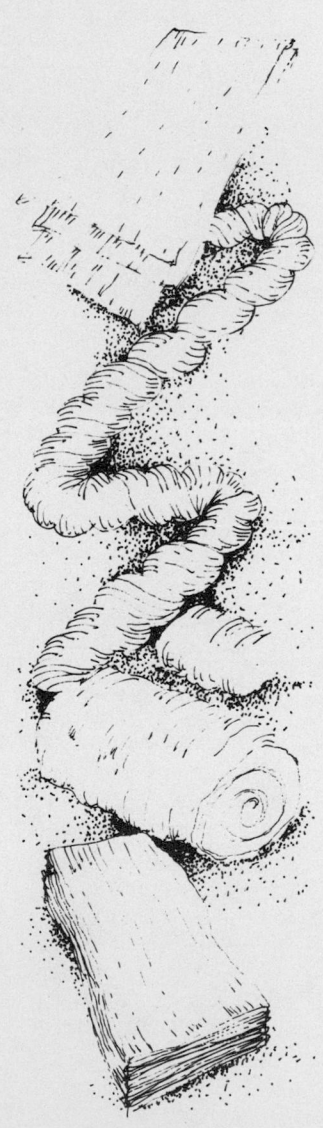

Soak yuba till it softens. Combine next 6 ingredients for the filling. Lay a sheet of yuba out flat on the counter. Spread a thin layer of filling onto half of the yuba sheet. Fold other half of yuba sheet over filling so the filling is sandwiched between 2 layers of yuba sheet. Spread again and fold again. Brush top with soy sauce. Place on steamer racks and steam for 30 minutes. Allow to cool at least a little.

Right before serving time, the pieces of Mock Peking Duck should be fried. Heat about ¼" of oil in the bottom of a skillet till oil is so hot that pieces sizzle when put in the oil. Dip pieces in soy sauce (or a mixture of 1 cup water and 2 teaspoons arrowroot which has been boiled and thickened to the consistency of a raw egg; and then dip into the Sesame Salt, see following recipe) and place in skillet. Fry on both sides till a crisp golden brown. Remove from skillet and cut into bite-sized strips. Serve on a platter with a separate bowl of the Mock Pecking Duck Sauce for people to put on as desired.

This is delicious served with Steamed Buns (see recipe, p. 604) so people can sandwich the Mock Peking Duck between the buns. It also adds a gourmet touch as a topping to a stir-fried vegetable. This recipe will make 8 Chinese banquet-sized servings. As dinner for a family of 2 to 4, it will make too much; but you may want to make a whole recipe anyway and freeze the extra already steamed slabs of Mock Peking Duck. They can be thawed and fried for another quick meal. To freeze, simply put layers of Mock Peking Duck in a plastic bag, seal and freeze. You might even consider multiplying the recipe a few times and steaming a great deal of slabs that can be frozen and easily thawed and fried later — especially if you like this as much as our family and friends do!

| SHOPPING LIST | |
|---|---|
| **Regularly Kept in the Kitchen**<br>**(Listed in Chapter 14, p. 703)** | **Fresh Produce** |
| Yuba sheets<br>Whole wheat flour<br>Tofu<br>Honey<br>Toasted sesame oil<br>Asafetida<br>Soy sauce | (None) |

# MOCK PEKING DUCK SAUCE

*½ cup water*
*¼ cup safflower oil*
*¼ cup miso*
*⅓ - ½ cup honey*
*1½ tsp. apple cider vinegar*

*1½ Tbsp. toasted sesame oil*
*½ tsp. or more red chili flakes*

Blend first 5 ingredients till smooth. Toast last 2 ingredients in skillet and pour into blended sauce. Serve on Mock Peking Duck; also good served on noodles or Chinese pancakes.

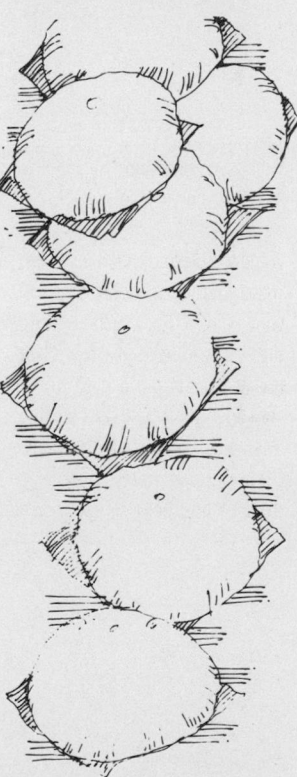

I prefer making my own sauce for the Mock Peking Duck since the hoisin sauce generally used and available in Chinese markets is usually full of sugar.

# WATERCRESS SALAD

☆ I've noticed that watercress bunches in produce sections vary in size from place to place. For example, a bunch of watercress in Hawaii is about 2 to 3 times larger than bunches are in California. For that reason, I need to specify that for this recipe you need enough watercress to end up with 3 to 4 cups of blanced watercress. Like any green, leafy vegetable, it'll shrink down quite a bit when cooked, so be sure to get enough. If you get too much watercress, you can always use it to add zest to a tossed salad or sandwiches.

2 bunches fresh watercress

2 Tbsp. soy sauce
1 tsp. honey
2 tsp. toasted sesame oil
1 tsp. apple cider vinegar

Whenever blanching vegetables like this, be sure to save the water. Don't throw it away, as you'll be tossing many of the water-soluble nutrients that come out of the vegetables into the water. Better to keep it and use it as a soup stock or to cook rice in. If you are making this whole Chinese banquet, use the watercress water to make the Hot and Sour Soup.

Wash the watercress and drain. Bring at least 4 cups of water (which can be saved and used later as stock for the following Hot and Sour Soup) to a boil. Place the watercress in the boiling water and leave in for 10 seconds. With tongs or a slotted spoon, remove watercress from boiling water and place in a colander. Immediately rinse under cold running water till watercress is cool (otherwise the heat retained by the watercress will cause it to cook more). Squeeze excess water out of watercress and chop into 1" lengths. You should have about 2 cups of blanched, chopped watercress. Mix next 4 ingredients together in a separate cup or small bowl, then pour over watercress and toss in to mix thoroughly. Refrigerate at least a few hours before serving. This is delicious served with Sesame Salt (see recipe, p. 93) sprinkled on top. Makes eight ¼-cup servings.

| SHOPPING LIST | |
|---|---|
| **Regularly Kept in the Kitchen** (Listed in Chapter 14, p. 703) | **Fresh Produce** |
| Soy sauce<br>Honey<br>Toasted sesame oil<br>Apple cider vinegar | Watercress |

## NUTRITIONAL ANALYSIS FOR ONE SERVING WATERCRESS SALAD

```
NUTRIENT        Type: 14    FEMALE-23 TO 51 YEARS              % RDA    Amount
KCALORIES       Ħ                                               0%     18.30 Kc
PROTEIN         Ħ=                                              2%      1.030 Gm
CARBOHYDRATE    Ħ                                            NO RDA     1.480 Gm
FAT             Ħ                                            NO RDA     1.150 Gm
FIBER-CRUDE     Ħ                                            NO RDA     0.190 Gm
CHOLESTEROL     Ħ                                            NO RDA     0.000 Mg
SATURATED FA    Ħ                                            NO RDA     0.160 Gm
OLEIC FA        Ħ                                            NO RDA     0.430 Gm
LINOLEIC FA     Ħ                                            NO RDA     0.470 Gm
SODIUM          Ħ======                                         12%    268.0 Mg
POTASSIUM       Ħ=                                              2%     110.0 Mg
MAGNESIUM       Ħ=                                              2%      7.950 Mg
IRON            Ħ                                               1%      0.180 Mg
ZINC            Ħ                                               0%      0.010 Mg
VITAMIN A       Ħ=================                              33%     1332 IU
VITAMIN D       Ħ                                               0%      0.000 IU
VIT. E/TOTAL    Ħ                                            NO RDA     0.330 Mg
VITAMIN C       Ħ==========                                     20%    12.10 Mg
THIAMIN         Ħ=                                              2%      0.020 Mg
RIBOFLAVIN      Ħ=                                              2%      0.030 Mg
NIACIN          Ħ                                               1%      0.210 Mg
VITAMIN B6      Ħ=                                              2%      0.040 Mg
FOLACIN         Ħ                                               0%      0.470 Ug
VITAMIN B12     Ħ                                               0%      0.000 Ug
PANTO- ACID     Ħ                                               1%      0.100 Mg
CALCIUM         Ħ==                                             4%     34.70 Mg
PHOSPHORUS      Ħ=                                              3%     26.40 Mg
TRYPTOPHAN      Ħ==                                             5%      8.330 Mg
THREONINE       Ħ====                                           8%     37.50 Mg
ISOLEUCINE      Ħ==                                             4%     26.50 Mg
LEUCINE         Ħ==                                             5%     46.50 Mg
LYSINE          Ħ==                                             5%     38.30 Mg
METHIONINE      Ħ=                                              2%      5.830 Mg
CYSTINE         Ħ                                               0%      1.660 Mg
PHENYL-ANINE    Ħ===                                            7%     32.50 Mg
TYROSINE        Ħ==                                             4%     17.50 Mg
VALINE          Ħ==                                             5%     39.00 Mg
HISTIDINE       Ħ                                            NO RDA    11.60 Mg
ALCOHOL         Ħ                                            NO RDA     0.000 Gm
ASH             Ħ                                            NO RDA     1.030 Gm
COPPER          Ħ                                               0%      0.020 Mg
MANGANESE       Ħ==                                             4%      0.150 Mg
IODINE          Ħ                                               0%      0.000 Ug
MONO FAT        Ħ                                            NO RDA     0.450 Gm
POLY FAT        Ħ                                            NO RDA     0.480 Gm
CAFFEINE        Ħ                                            NO RDA     0.000 Mg
FLUORIDE        Ħ                                               1%     29.10 Ug
MOLYBDENUM      Ħ                                               0%      0.000 Ug
VITAMIN K       Ħ=======                                        15%    15.80 Ug
SELENIUM        Ħ                                               0%      0.000 Mg
BIOTIN          Ħ                                               0%      0.110 Ug
CHLORIDE        Ħ                                               0%      0.000 Mg
CHROMIUM        Ħ                                               0%      0.000 Mg
SUGAR           Ħ                                            NO RDA     0.000 Gm
FIBER-DIET      Ħ                                            NO RDA     0.000 Gm
VIT. E/AT       Ħ=                                              3%      0.290 Mg

   % RDA:    |0        |20       |40       |60       |80       |100
```

# SESAME SALT

☆ Make enough to keep on hand (preferably in the refrigerator till serving time) to be put on the table instead of table salt. This is a good, flavorful way to cut down on salt consumption.

As you can see in the graph, which shows the nutritional amounts for a teaspoon of Sesame Salt, this is a much more nutritious condiment than plain table salt.

---

*1 cup toasted sesame seeds*
*3 Tbsp. salt*

Toast sesame seeds in a dry skillet over a medium heat by stirring constantly with a spatula till the seeds are lightly toasted. Be careful not to let seeds sit too long in one place in the hot skillet or cook too long because they will burn (burned sesame seeds have a very metallic taste). When the seeds are toasted, remove from heat and allow to cool. Blend in a blender with the salt till sesame seeds form a meal. It's important to cool the seeds completely because blending hot or warm seeds causes them to clump together to form more of a sesame butter than a meal.

This Sesame Salt is delicious sprinkled on vegetable dishes, salads, rice, etc., and is a tasty, nutritious substitute for salt. This recipe will make about 1 cup of Sesame Salt, which should last you a long time.

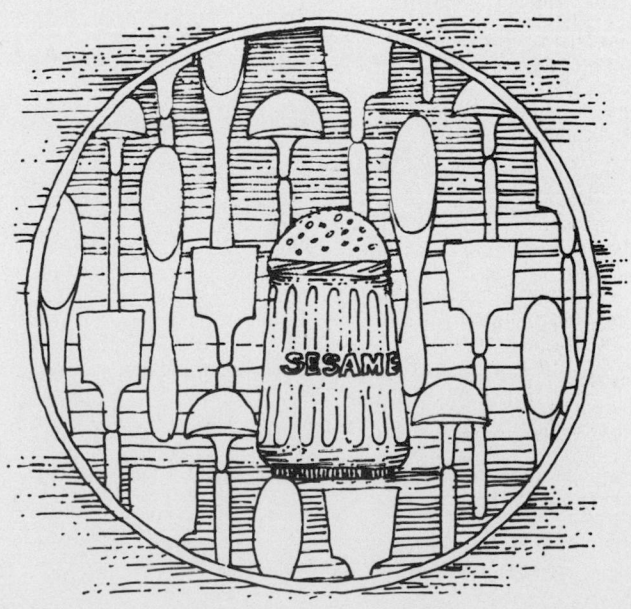

# NUTRITIONAL ANALYSIS FOR ONE CUP SESAME SALT

| NUTRIENT | Type: 14   FEMALE—23 TO 51 YEARS | % RDA | Amount |
|----------|--------|-------|--------|
| KCALORIES | A===================== | 40% | 816.0 Kc |
| PROTEIN | A============================ | 55% | 24.40 Gm |
| CARBOHYDRATE | A | NO RDA | 37.00 Gm |
| FAT | A | NO RDA | 68.90 Gm |
| FIBER—CRUDE | A | NO RDA | 12.20 Gm |
| CHOLESTEROL | A | NO RDA | 0.000 Mg |
| SATURATED FA | A | NO RDA | 9.680 Gm |
| OLEIC FA | A | NO RDA | 0.000 Gm |
| LINOLEIC FA | A | NO RDA | 0.000 Gm |
| SODIUM | A==================================================== | 800% | 17610 Mg |
| POTASSIUM | A========= | 18% | 687.0 Mg |
| MAGNESIUM | A==================================================== | 170% | 512.0 Mg |
| IRON | A==================================================== | 117% | 21.20 Mg |
| ZINC | A=================================== | 68% | 10.20 Mg |
| VITAMIN A | A | 0% | 0.000 IU |
| VITAMIN D | A | 0% | 0.000 IU |
| VIT. E/TOTAL | A | NO RDA | 32.70 Mg |
| VITAMIN C | A | 0% | 0.000 Mg |
| THIAMIN | A | 0% | 0.000 Mg |
| RIBOFLAVIN | A | 0% | 0.000 Mg |
| NIACIN | A | 0% | 0.000 Mg |
| VITAMIN B6 | A | 0% | 0.000 Mg |
| FOLACIN | A | 0% | 0.000 Ug |
| VITAMIN B12 | A | 0% | 0.000 Ug |
| PANTO— ACID | A | 0% | 0.000 Mg |
| CALCIUM | A=================================== | 193% | 1.550 Mg |
| PHOSPHORUS | A==================================================== | 116% | 935.0 Mg |
| TRYPTOPHAN | A==================================================== | 326% | 532.0 Mg |
| THREONINE | A==================================================== | 233% | 1014 Mg |
| ISOLEUCINE | A==================================================== | 160% | 1049 Mg |
| LEUCINE | A==================================================== | 214% | 1870 Mg |
| LYSINE | A==================================================== | 119% | 780.0 Mg |
| METHIONINE | A==================================================== | 296% | 806.0 Mg |
| CYSTINE | A==================================================== | 180% | 491.0 Mg |
| PHENYL—ANINE | A==================================================== | 297% | 1292 Mg |
| TYROSINE | A==================================================== | 235% | 1024 Mg |
| VALINE | A==================================================== | 178% | 1363 Mg |
| HISTIDINE | A | NO RDA | 720.0 Mg |
| ALCOHOL | A | NO RDA | 0.000 Gm |
| ASH | A | NO RDA | 8.610 Gm |
| COPPER | A==================================================== | 142% | 3.550 Mg |
| MANGANESE | A=============================================== | 95% | 3.590 Mg |
| IODINE | A==================================================== | 1260% | 1890 Ug |
| MONO FAT | A | NO RDA | 26.10 Gm |
| POLY FAT | A | NO RDA | 30.30 Gm |
| CAFFEINE | A | NO RDA | 0.000 Mg |
| FLUORIDE | A | 0% | 0.000 Ug |
| MOLYBDENUM | A | 0% | 0.000 Ug |
| VITAMIN K | A | 0% | 0.000 Ug |
| SELENIUM | A | 0% | 0.000 Mg |
| BIOTIN | A | 0% | 0.000 Ug |
| CHLORIDE | A | 0% | 0.000 Mg |
| CHROMIUM | A | 0% | 0.000 Mg |
| SUGAR | A | NO RDA | 0.000 Gm |
| FIBER—DIET | A | NO RDA | 0.000 Gm |
| VIT. E/AT | A | 0% | 0.000 Mg |

% RDA:   |0        |20      |40      |60      |80      |100

# HOT AND SOUR SOUP

☆ Some health buffs recommend drinking a warm cup of water with a tablespoon or two of apple cider vinegar in it before a meal to aid digestion (the enzymes in apple cider vinegar are supposed to help with digestion) . . . if this is true, it adds another good reason to the list of why to start the meal off with this version of an old Chinese favorite.

---

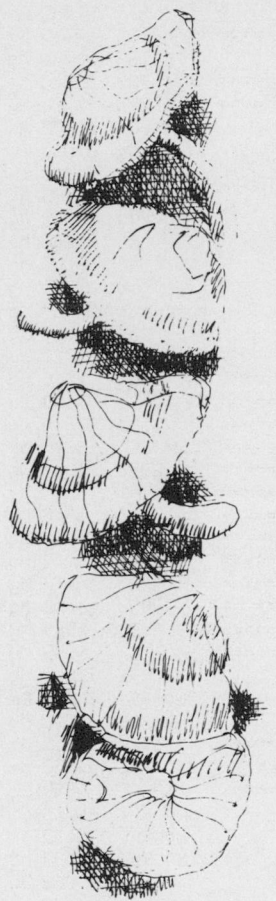

4 cups boiling vegetable broth or 4 cups
    water and 1 vegetable bouillon cube
1 oz. dried Oriental (shiitake)
    black mushrooms

4 cups water

½ lb. Chinese firm tofu
Soy sauce

¼ cup apple cider vinegar
1 Tbsp. soy sauce
½ tsp. black pepper

½ cup cold water
2 Tbsp. arrowroot

½ tsp. toasted sesame oil

Slivered green onions

Bring 4 cups of vegetable broth to a boil. Turn off heat and add dried mushrooms. Cover and allow to soak about 20 minutes. Drain mushroom soaking water into a large pot and add 4 cups of water. Turn on heat to bring liquid to a boil. As liquid is heating, cut stems off mushrooms and cut mushrooms into very thin slivers.

Cut tofu into very thin matchstick slivers and pour a little soy sauce on top of them. When liquid comes to a boil, reduce heat to medium, add slivered mushrooms and allow to simmer about 10 minutes. Then add slivered tofu and simmer another 5 minutes. Add next 3 ingredients and, in a little cup, quickly dissolve arrowroot in the cold water. Add to ingredients in the pot and stir constantly till the arrowroot thickens. (As the soup thickens, it will become clear again. It should take only 20 to 30 seconds after liquid comes to a boil for the arrowroot to thoroughly thicken.) Cover and turn off heat. Add sesame oil. The soup should be served immediately, topped with slivered green onions. Makes eight 1-cup servings.

| SHOPPING LIST | |
| --- | --- |
| **Regularly Kept in the Kitchen** (Listed in Chapter 14, p. 703) | **Fresh Produce** |
| Tofu<br>Soy sauce<br>Apple cider vinegar<br>Black pepper<br>Arrowroot<br>Toasted sesame oil | Scallions |

**Special Shopping**

Vegetable bouillon cubes — in natural food stores; no need for them if you have vegetable soup stock available.

Dried Oriental black mushrooms — found in Chinese groceries. Use dried shiitake mushrooms if you can't find black mushrooms.

# NUTRITIONAL ANALYSIS FOR ONE SERVING HOT AND SOUR SOUP

```
NUTRIENT       Type: 14   FEMALE-23 TO 51 YEARS            % RDA   Amount
KCALORIES     Å==                                             4%   80.50 Kc
PROTEIN       Å======                                        12%   5.670 Gm
CARBOHYDRATE  Å                                            NO RDA  9.200 Gm
FAT           Å                                            NO RDA  3.260 Gm
FIBER-CRUDE   Å                                            NO RDA  0.200 Gm
CHOLESTEROL   Å                                            NO RDA  0.000 Mg
SATURATED FA  Å                                            NO RDA  0.480 Gm
OLEIC FA      Å                                            NO RDA  0.390 Gm
LINOLEIC FA   Å                                            NO RDA  0.680 Gm
SODIUM        Å=========                                     17%   382.0 Mg
POTASSIUM     Å==                                             5%   201.0 Mg
MAGNESIUM     Å====                                           8%   25.20 Mg
IRON          Å=========                                     19%   3.560 Mg
ZINC          Å==                                             4%   0.600 Mg
VITAMIN A     Å===========                                   23%   954.0 IU
VITAMIN D     Å                                               0%   0.000 IU
VIT. E/TOTAL  Å                                            NO RDA  0.090 Mg
VITAMIN C     Å=                                              3%   1.800 Mg
THIAMIN       Å===                                            7%   0.070 Mg
RIBOFLAVIN    Å===                                            7%   0.090 Mg
NIACIN        Å===                                            7%   0.930 Mg
VITAMIN B6    Å=                                              2%   0.040 Mg
FOLACIN       Å=                                              2%   11.70 Ug
VITAMIN B12   Å                                               0%   0.000 Ug
PANTO- ACID   Å                                               1%   0.070 Mg
CALCIUM       Å=============                                 25%   204.0 Mg
PHOSPHORUS    Å=====                                         10%   82.10 Mg
TRYPTOPHAN    Å=====================                         43%   71.00 Mg
THREONINE     Å=======================                       46%   201.0 Mg
ISOLEUCINE    Å==================                            36%   238.0 Mg
LEUCINE       Å=====================                         42%   366.0 Mg
LYSINE        Å========================                      48%   314.0 Mg
METHIONINE    Å===========                                   23%   63.70 Mg
CYSTINE       Å============                                  25%   68.60 Mg
PHENYL-ANINE  Å===========================                   54%   236.0 Mg
TYROSINE      Å==================                            36%   160.0 Mg
VALINE        Å================                              32%   245.0 Mg
HISTIDINE     Å                                            NO RDA  137.0 Mg
ALCOHOL       Å                                            NO RDA  0.000 Gm
ASH           Å                                            NO RDA  1.020 Gm
COPPER        Å===                                            6%   0.150 Mg
MANGANESE     Å======                                        12%   0.450 Mg
IODINE        Å==========                                    20%   30.80 Ug
MONO FAT      Å                                            NO RDA  0.660 Gm
POLY FAT      Å                                            NO RDA  1.500 Gm
CAFFEINE      Å                                            NO RDA  0.000 Mg
FLUORIDE      Å                                               0%   1.870 Ug
MOLYBDENUM    Å==================================================  104%  340.0 Ug
VITAMIN K     Å                                               0%   0.000 Ug
SELENIUM      Å====                                           8%   0.010 Mg
BIOTIN        Å                                               0%   0.940 Ug
CHLORIDE      Å                                               1%   57.50 Mg
CHROMIUM      Å=================================             64%   0.080 Mg
SUGAR         Å                                            NO RDA  0.170 Gm
FIBER-DIET    Å                                            NO RDA  0.400 Gm
VIT. E/AT     Å                                               0%   0.000 Mg

   % RDA:    |0       |20     |40     |60     |80     |100
```

# ALMOND MILK

☆ Don't take this recipe for granted because it's little and buried amongst others. This is a very important basic recipe that can be used every day in the kitchen in drinks, baking — anywhere milk is called for.

---

*1 cup almonds (preferably whole ones which have soaked overnight and germinated)*
*4 cups water (if nuts were soaked, use water they were soaked in)*

Nut milks can be used in any recipe calling for cow's milk or soy milk. You can use any nut to make nut milk with, or any combination of nuts and/or seeds. Whole nuts or seeds blend up easier, are more digestible, and increase in nutritional value when they are soaked overnight and sprouted a bit.

To make the nut milk, just blend all the ingredients together in your blender till smooth. After ingredients are blended, you can leave pulp in for a smoothie-textured nut milk, or pour blended milk through a strainer to strain pulp out. Pulp should be saved and frozen for use in vegetable loaves, baking, candies, etc. Yields 4 servings (about 1 quart).

The nutritional analysis of Almond Milk is for water and whole, unsoaked almonds. I always make my Almond Milk with almonds I've soaked overnight because studies have shown this causes tremendous chemical changes in seeds that greatly boost their nutritional value. Unfortunately the studies have not been done on almonds but on beans such as lentils, mung, alfalfa, etc., but I'm sure the same changes take place in almonds (since they are a seed). Just soaking for 12 hours increases vitamin, mineral, amino acid and enzyme levels.

# NUTRITIONAL ANALYSIS FOR ONE SERVING ALMOND MILK

| NUTRIENT | Type: 14 FEMALE-23 TO 51 YEARS | % RDA | Amount |
|---|---|---|---|
| KCALORIES | A===== | 10% | 209.0 Kc |
| PROTEIN | A======== | 16% | 7.070 Gm |
| CARBOHYDRATE | A | NO RDA | 7.250 Gm |
| FAT | A | NO RDA | 18.50 Gm |
| FIBER-CRUDE | A | NO RDA | 0.960 Gm |
| CHOLESTEROL | A | NO RDA | 0.000 Mg |
| SATURATED FA | A | NO RDA | 1.750 Gm |
| OLEIC FA | A | NO RDA | 0.000 Gm |
| LINOLEIC FA | A | NO RDA | 0.000 Gm |
| SODIUM | A | 0% | 5.570 Mg |
| POTASSIUM | A=== | 6% | 259.0 Mg |
| MAGNESIUM | A=================== | 35% | 105.0 Mg |
| IRON | A=== | 7% | 1.300 Mg |
| ZINC | A=== | 6% | 1.050 Mg |
| VITAMIN A | A | 0% | 0.000 IU |
| VITAMIN D | A | 0% | 0.000 IU |
| VIT. E/TOTAL | A | NO RDA | 0.000 Mg |
| VITAMIN C | A | 0% | 0.220 Mg |
| THIAMIN | A=== | 7% | 0.070 Mg |
| RIBOFLAVIN | A=========== | 22% | 0.270 Mg |
| NIACIN | A==== | 9% | 1.190 Mg |
| VITAMIN B6 | A= | 2% | 0.040 Mg |
| FOLACIN | A== | 5% | 20.80 Ug |
| VITAMIN B12 | A | 0% | 0.000 Ug |
| PANTO- ACID | A= | 2% | 0.160 Mg |
| CALCIUM | A====== | 12% | 96.50 Mg |
| PHOSPHORUS | A=========== | 23% | 184.0 Mg |
| TRYPTOPHAN | A======================================== | 77% | 127.0 Mg |
| THREONINE | A=============================== | 60% | 262.0 Mg |
| ISOLEUCINE | A======================= | 47% | 307.0 Mg |
| LEUCINE | A================================ | 63% | 550.0 Mg |
| LYSINE | A================== | 36% | 236.0 Mg |
| METHIONINE | A============== | 29% | 80.50 Mg |
| CYSTINE | A======================= | 46% | 127.0 Mg |
| PHENYL-ANINE | A================================================ | 90% | 395.0 Mg |
| TYROSINE | A============================= | 57% | 250.0 Mg |
| VALINE | A======================= | 47% | 365.0 Mg |
| HISTIDINE | A | NO RDA | 198.0 Mg |
| ALCOHOL | A | NO RDA | 0.000 Gm |
| ASH | A | NO RDA | 1.070 Gm |
| COPPER | A======= | 14% | 0.350 Mg |
| MANGANESE | A========== | 21% | 0.800 Mg |
| IODINE | A | 0% | 0.000 Ug |
| MONO FAT | A | NO RDA | 12.00 Gm |
| POLY FAT | A | NO RDA | 3.900 Gm |
| CAFFEINE | A | NO RDA | 0.000 Mg |
| FLUORIDE | A | 0% | 0.000 Ug |
| MOLYBDENUM | A | 0% | 0.000 Ug |
| VITAMIN K | A | 0% | 0.000 Ug |
| SELENIUM | A | 0% | 0.000 Mg |
| BIOTIN | A | 0% | 0.000 Ug |
| CHLORIDE | A | 0% | 4.470 Mg |
| CHROMIUM | A | 0% | 0.000 Mg |
| SUGAR | A | NO RDA | 0.000 Gm |
| FIBER-DIET | A | NO RDA | 0.000 Gm |
| VIT. E/AT | A | 0% | 0.000 Mg |

% RDA:  |0     |20     |40     |60     |80     |100

Analysis uses raw almonds and does not include the increase in nutrients which occurs during germination; does not include nutrients contained in almond soaking water.

# ALMOND NECTAR FLOAT

☆ Another light dessert from the Orient to end a meal with.

---

4 sticks agar-agar (2 cups flakes)
5 cups Almond Milk (see preceding recipe)
½ cup honey
1 tsp. almond extract

4 cups chilled fruit juice
Honey to taste (optional)

Combine first 4 ingredients in a pot and let sit about 5 to 10 minutes to give agar-agar a chance to soften. Put over heat and bring to a boil, stirring occasionally to prevent sticking or burning. Boil gently till agar-agar is totally dissolved. Pour into square 9" x 9" cake pan or other flat container. Cool, then refrigerate. It should jell and be able to be cut into cubes. Cut into ½" cubes. Float cubes in last 2 ingredients which were previously blended together. Serve in individual dessert cups or small bowls. Makes 8½ cups.

The idea of floating a firm gel in a naturally sweet fruit juice leads to endless varieties of desserts (or snacks). Make the gels with different nut milks and/or fruit juices, or even beans (p. 473) and float them in compatibly-flavored juices. If this becomes a favorite, better make agar-agar a regular in the kitchen!

| SHOPPING LIST | |
|---|---|
| **Regularly Kept in the Kitchen** (Listed in Chapter 14, p. 703) | **Fresh Produce** |
| Almonds<br>Honey<br>Almond extract | Unsweetened fruit juice |

| Special Shopping |
|---|
| Agar-agar — in Japanese or Chinese groceries or Oriental food aisles in supermarkets; in some natural food stores. |

# NUTRITIONAL ANALYSIS FOR ONE SERVING
## ALMOND NECTAR FLOAT

| NUTRIENT | Type: 14   FEMALE-23 TO 51 YEARS | % RDA | Amount |
|---|---|---|---|
| KCALORIES | Ä===== | 11% | 225.0 Kc |
| PROTEIN | Ä==== | 8% | 3.700 Gm |
| CARBOHYDRATE | Ä | NO RDA | 34.30 Gm |
| FAT | Ä | NO RDA | 9.390 Gm |
| FIBER-CRUDE | Ä | NO RDA | 0.510 Gm |
| CHOLESTEROL | Ä | NO RDA | 0.000 Mg |
| SATURATED FA | Ä | NO RDA | 0.900 Gm |
| OLEIC FA | Ä | NO RDA | 0.000 Gm |
| LINOLEIC FA | Ä | NO RDA | 0.000 Gm |
| SODIUM | Ä | 0% | 12.20 Mg |
| POTASSIUM | Ä=== | 7% | 291.0 Mg |
| MAGNESIUM | Ä========= | 19% | 59.30 Mg |
| IRON | Ä=== | 6% | 1.150 Mg |
| ZINC | Ä= | 3% | 0.590 Mg |
| VITAMIN A | Ä | 0% | 0.000 IU |
| VITAMIN D | Ä | 0% | 0.000 IU |
| VIT. E/TOTAL | Ä | NO RDA | 0.000 Mg |
| VITAMIN C | Ä | 1% | 0.810 Mg |
| THIAMIN | Ä= | 3% | 0.030 Mg |
| RIBOFLAVIN | Ä====== | 13% | 0.160 Mg |
| NIACIN | Ä== | 5% | 0.740 Mg |
| VITAMIN B6 | Ä= | 3% | 0.060 Mg |
| FOLACIN | Ä= | 2% | 10.70 Ug |
| VITAMIN B12 | Ä | 0% | 0.000 Ug |
| PANTO- ACID | Ä= | 3% | 0.200 Mg |
| CALCIUM | Ä==== | 8% | 64.70 Mg |
| PHOSPHORUS | Ä=====■= | 12% | 101.0 Mg |
| TRYPTOPHAN | Ä==================== | 38% | 63.50 Mg |
| THREONINE | Ä=============== | 30% | 131.0 Mg |
| ISOLEUCINE | Ä=========== | 23% | 153.0 Mg |
| LEUCINE | Ä=============== | 31% | 275.0 Mg |
| LYSINE | Ä========= | 18% | 118.0 Mg |
| METHIONINE | Ä======= | 14% | 40.20 Mg |
| CYSTINE | Ä=========== | 23% | 63.50 Mg |
| PHENYL-ANINE | Ä====================== | 45% | 197.0 Mg |
| TYROSINE | Ä============== | 28% | 125.0 Mg |
| VALINE | Ä=========== | 23% | 182.0 Mg |
| HISTIDINE | Ä | NO RDA | 99.00 Mg |
| ALCOHOL | Ä | NO RDA | 0.000 Gm |
| ASH | Ä | NO RDA | 0.960 Gm |
| COPPER | Ä==== | 8% | 0.200 Mg |
| MANGANESE | Ä====== | 12% | 0.480 Mg |
| IODINE | Ä | 0% | 0.000 Ug |
| MONO FAT | Ä | NO RDA | 6.010 Gm |
| POLY FAT | Ä | NO RDA | 1.980 Gm |
| CAFFEINE | Ä | NO RDA | 0.000 Mg |
| FLUORIDE | Ä | 0% | 21.00 Ug |
| MOLYBDENUM | Ä | 0% | 0.000 Ug |
| VITAMIN K | Ä | 0% | 0.000 Ug |
| SELENIUM | Ä | 0% | 0.000 Ug |
| BIOTIN | Ä | 0% | 0.600 Ug |
| CHLORIDE | Ä | 0% | 2.230 Mg |
| CHROMIUM | Ä | 0% | 0.000 Mg |
| SUGAR | Ä | NO RDA | 0.000 Gm |
| FIBER-DIET | Ä | NO RDA | 0.000 Gm |
| VIT. E/AT | Ä | 0% | 0.010 Mg |

```
% RDA:   |0      |20     |40     |60     |80     |100
```

(See footnote for Almond Milk.) Juice used in analysis: apple. Optional honey not included.

# EGGPLANT SZECHUAN

☆ China is such a huge country, it's not surprising to find cuisine in one part of China worlds apart from the cuisine of another part. Szechuan cooking is typically very fiery; if you have a delicate palate, cut down on the amount of red chilies.

---

*At least 2 cups vegetable oil (for deep-frying)*
*8 cups eggplant spears*

*2 Tbsp. vegetable oil*

*1 tsp. toasted sesame oil*
*1½ tsp. crushed garlic*
*4 slices ginger, crushed*
*½ cup slivered scallions or green onions*
*½ - 1 tsp. crushed chili peppers*

*1 green bell pepper, slivered*
*1 red bell pepper, slivered*

*1 Tbsp. miso*
*1 tsp. honey*
*½ tsp. black pepper*

*¼ cup water*
*½ tsp. apple cider vinegar*
*2 tsp. arrowroot*

Chinese cooking is usually done with peanut oil because it will heat to a higher temperature without smoking than other oils. If you don't feel like buying peanut oil, especially for a few Chinese recipes, safflower or sunflower oil will work fine.

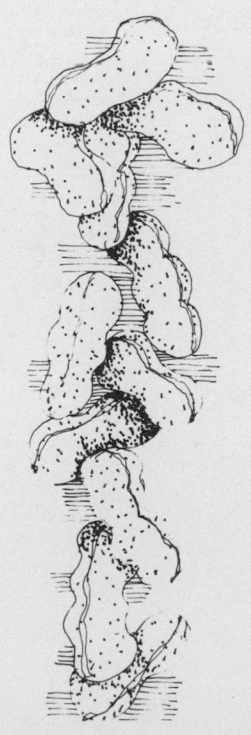

Heat oil for deep-frying in a wok. Wash eggplant and cut off stems. Cut into strips approximately 3" x 1" x 1". When oil is hot, deep-fry eggplant till it *begins* to soften and turn a golden brown. (Do not overcook till eggplant becomes tender.) Remove eggplant from oil and place in colander to let oil drain out thoroughly. Pour off all but 2 tablespoons of oil from the wok and stir-fry next 5 ingredients over high heat for about 30 seconds. Add bell peppers and stir-fry till bell peppers begin to look translucent. Push bell peppers up onto the sides of the wok. Then, in the center, add next 3 ingredients and mix till they dissolve into a thick sauce. Push bell peppers back into mixture and stir till bell peppers are evenly coated with the sauce. Then mix in previously deep-fried eggplant. In a separate cup, dissolve arrowroot in water and apple cider vinegar. Add this to bell pepper and eggplant mixture and toss till thoroughly mixed. Then cover and cook over medium

heat till the eggplant is tender. Pour onto serving platter and serve with hot Steamed Buns (see recipe, p. 604). The eggplant is delicious itself or sandwiched between the Steamed Buns. Serve immediately. Serves 8.

| SHOPPING LIST | |
|---|---|
| **Regularly Kept in the Kitchen (Listed in Chapter 14, p. 703)** | **Fresh Produce** |
| Vegetable oil | Eggplant |
| Toasted sesame oil | Garlic |
| Red chili flakes | Ginger root |
| Miso | Scallions |
| Honey | Green bell pepper |
| Black pepper | Red bell pepper |
| Apple cider vinegar | |
| Arrowroot | |

# NUTRITIONAL ANALYSIS FOR ONE SERVING
## EGGPLANT SZECHUAN

| NUTRIENT | Type: 14 FEMALE-23 TO 51 YEARS | % RDA | Amount |
|---|---|---|---|
| KCALORIES | A== | 4% | 80.70 Kc |
| PROTEIN | A= | 3% | 1.470 Gm |
| CARBOHYDRATE | A | NO RDA | 10.30 Gm |
| FAT | A | NO RDA | 4.430 Gm |
| FIBER-CRUDE | A | NO RDA | 1.380 Gm |
| CHOLESTEROL | A | NO RDA | 0.000 Mg |
| SATURATED FA | A | NO RDA | 0.470 Gm |
| OLEIC FA | A | NO RDA | 0.620 Gm |
| LINOLEIC FA | A | NO RDA | 2.730 Gm |
| SODIUM | A= | 3% | 85.20 Mg |
| POTASSIUM | A==== | 8% | 315.0 Mg |
| MAGNESIUM | A=== | 6% | 19.70 Mg |
| IRON | A== | 5% | 0.940 Mg |
| ZINC | A | 1% | 0.290 Mg |
| VITAMIN A | A========== | 20% | 823.0 IU |
| VITAMIN D | A | 0% | 0.000 IU |
| VIT. E/TOTAL | A | NO RDA | 1.550 Mg |
| VITAMIN C | A========================= | 49% | 29.70 Mg |
| THIAMIN | A===== | 10% | 0.100 Mg |
| RIBOFLAVIN | A== | 4% | 0.050 Mg |
| NIACIN | A== | 5% | 0.740 Mg |
| VITAMIN B6 | A== | 5% | 0.110 Mg |
| FOLACIN | A== | 4% | 19.00 Ug |
| VITAMIN B12 | A | 0% | 0.000 Ug |
| PANTO- ACID | A= | 3% | 0.170 Mg |
| CALCIUM | A= | 3% | 31.30 Mg |
| PHOSPHORUS | A== | 4% | 35.20 Mg |
| TRYPTOPHAN | A==== | 9% | 15.60 Mg |
| THREONINE | A====== | 13% | 57.00 Mg |
| ISOLEUCINE | A===== | 10% | 67.20 Mg |
| LEUCINE | A===== | 11% | 96.10 Mg |
| LYSINE | A====== | 13% | 87.10 Mg |
| METHIONINE | A=== | 6% | 16.50 Mg |
| CYSTINE | A= | 3% | 9.660 Mg |
| PHENYL-ANINE | A====== | 13% | 59.00 Mg |
| TYROSINE | A==== | 8% | 37.70 Mg |
| VALINE | A==== | 9% | 74.60 Mg |
| HISTIDINE | A | NO RDA | 32.30 Mg |
| ALCOHOL | A | NO RDA | 0.000 Gm |
| ASH | A | NO RDA | 0.920 Gm |
| COPPER | A== | 5% | 0.130 Mg |
| MANGANESE | A== | 4% | 0.170 Mg |
| IODINE | A | 0% | 0.000 Ug |
| MONO FAT | A | NO RDA | 0.690 Gm |
| POLY FAT | A | NO RDA | 2.970 Gm |
| CAFFEINE | A | NO RDA | 0.000 Mg |
| FLUORIDE | A | 1% | 45.20 Ug |
| MOLYBDENUM | A== | 4% | 14.20 Ug |
| VITAMIN K | A | 0% | 0.000 Ug |
| SELENIUM | A | 0% | 0.000 Mg |
| BIOTIN | A | 0% | 0.550 Ug |
| CHLORIDE | A | 1% | 45.30 Mg |
| CHROMIUM | A | 0% | 0.000 Mg |
| SUGAR | A | NO RDA | 4.230 Gm |
| FIBER-DIET | A | NO RDA | 0.280 Gm |
| VIT. E/AT | A======== | 17% | 1.380 Mg |

% RDA:  |0      |20      |40      |60      |80      |100

Green onions were used instead of scallions in this analysis.

# SOUTHERN HOSPITALITY . . . NATURALLY

O ftentimes in modern society, there is the tendency to look to an organization or politician to establish world peace. How few of us consider that peace starts with each separate individual as Spinoza did when he said, "Peace is not an absence of war; it is a virtue, a state of mind, a disposition for benevolence, confidence and justice."

I t is possible to still have some old favorite tastes and textures when switching to a diet that eliminates meat, poultry and fish. This menu is perfect for those who are going through "withdrawal" — finding their mouths watering at the thought of Southern-fried chicken — or to serve to friends who haven't made the change yet.

Many people stop eating red meat but continue eating white meat, like chicken, with the mistaken idea that it is somehow healthier. Meat, chicken and fish all contain about the same amount of cholesterol, while providing no vitamin C, little or no calcium, along with relatively high levels of phosphorous. Healthful changes in the ingredients for Southern-Fried Tofu, as well as the other dishes, provide a taste of Southern hospitality . . . naturally!

# SOUTHERN-FRIED TOFU

4 cups milk
¼ cup nutritional yeast
1 tsp. Spike or other vegetable-seasoned salt
¼ tsp. asafetida or ½ onion, diced
¼ tsp. black pepper

2 Tbsp. Tabasco (optional)

2 - 3 lbs. Chinese firm tofu

32 - 48 square, deep-fried tofu pouches (aburage)

4 cups whole wheat flour
½ cup nutritional yeast
4 tsp. black pepper
4 tsp. Spike or other vegetable-seasoned salt

1 quart cultured buttermilk

Oil for deep-frying

## SOUTHERN HOSPITALITY... NATURALLY MENU

*Southern-Fried Tofu
with Gravy*

*Murrieta Coleslaw*

*Mashed potatoes*

*Delightfully Refreshing
Inside-Out Torte*

Combine first 5 ingredients in a pot and simmer for about 20 minutes. Remove from heat and allow to cool to room temperature. If you wish to add Tabasco, mix in at this time.

As milk mixture is cooling, cut 1 pound of tofu into quarters by cutting across width of tofu block. Prick gently with a fork every inch or so. Cut each of these slabs into quarters by cutting through the 1" thickness so you end up with 4 cubes approximately 1½" x 1½" x 1". (Be sure not to cut across the 1" thickness so you end up with ½" cutlets.) One pound of tofu should make 16 cubes. Drop pierced tofu cubes into milk mixture. Cover and chill at least 3 hours or overnight.

Before cooking time, make aburage shells into pockets by slitting open on one end, pushing finger through the hole and separating the shell in the middle out to the outer edges. Stuff one soaked tofu cube into each aburage pocket and seal by "sewing" together with a toothpick. Drop all the stuffed pockets back into the milk mixture so they can absorb more milk.

Mix next 4 ingredients together in a large bowl. Pour buttermilk into a small bowl and fill a large skillet about 1" deep with vegetable oil. Line a large platter with 3 to 4 thicknesses of paper towels. This makes up the assembly line for cooking Southern-Fried Tofu.

One word of warning: These are cooked and served with toothpicks in them, so be sure to let everyone know before they bite in.

When it's time to cook, heat oil to 350 degrees on a cooking thermometer. Heat oven to 250 degrees (if you'll need to keep pieces warm; omit this step if the pieces will be gobbled up as soon as they're cooked!).

One at a time, remove stuffed pouch from milk, roll in flour mixture, then quickly dip into buttermilk and quickly roll in seasoned flour again. Put immediately into heated oil. Continue this process, moving quickly till skillet is filled. When batter is cooked golden brown on edges and underside, turn over and fry on the other side till crisp and golden brown. Remove from oil onto paper towels and allow excess oil to drain.

Serve hot, or place on cookie sheet lined with brown paper and set, uncovered, in heated oven. This is also delicious served cold, so don't be afraid of having leftovers. One recipe makes 32 to 48 pieces (depending on whether you use 2 or 3 pounds of tofu). At 3 pieces per serving, this makes 10 to 16 servings.

| Special Shopping |
| --- |
| Aburage (age) pouches — can be found in Japanese or Chinese groceries, but you'll find they're a bit expensive. I go straight to the tofu factory and buy a boxful of off-grade pouches for $1 to $2. |

| SHOPPING LIST | |
| --- | --- |
| **Regularly Kept in the Kitchen** (Listed in Chapter 14, p. 703) | **Fresh Produce** |
| Milk<br>Nutritional yeast<br>Spike<br>Asafetida<br>Black pepper<br>Tofu<br>Whole wheat flour<br>Cultured buttermilk<br>Safflower or sunflower oil | Tabasco (optional) |

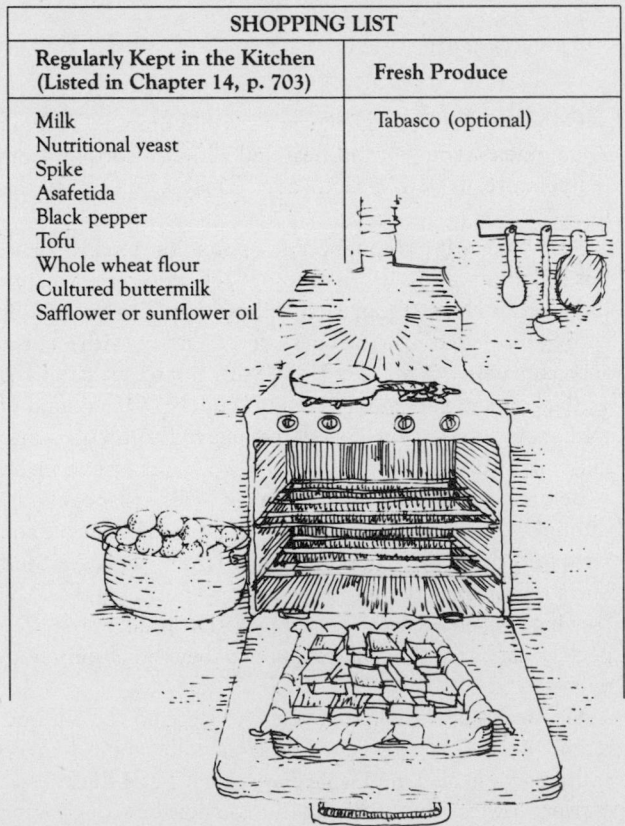

# NUTRITIONAL ANALYSIS COMPARING OUR SOUTHERN-FRIED TOFU DINNER WITH KENTUCKY FRIED CHICKEN DINNER

| NUTRIENT | Type: 14   FEMALE—23 TO 51 YEARS | Amount in our dinner | Amount in chicken dinner |
|----------|----------------------------------|----------------------|--------------------------|
| KCALORIES | ==================== | 906.0 Kc | 1471 Kc |
| PROTEIN | ======================================================= | 58.00 Gm | 80.10 Gm |
| CARBOHYDRATE | | 103.0 Gm | 105.0 Gm |
| FAT | | 30.40 Gm | 80.10 Gm |
| FIBER—CRUDE | | 3.100 Gm | 1.830 Gm |
| CHOLESTEROL | | 15.50 Mg | 412.0 Mg |
| SATURATED FA | | 5.050 Gm | 17.80 Gm |
| OLEIC FA | | 6.340 Gm | 0.000 Gm |
| LINOLEIC FA | | 8.760 Gm | 0.000 Gm |
| SODIUM | =============================== | 1658 Mg | 3298 Mg |
| POTASSIUM | ============================ | 2027 Mg | 1648 Mg |
| MAGNESIUM | ================================================= | 325.0 Mg | 151.0 Mg |
| IRON | ===================================================== | 22.40 Mg | 8.920 Mg |
| ZINC | ========================= | 8.770 Mg | 7.940 Mg |
| VITAMIN A | ===================================================== | 13094 IU | 583.0 IU |
| VITAMIN D | ========= | 40.90 IU | 89.20 IU |
| VIT. E/TOTAL | | 5.120 Mg | 0.000 Mg |
| VITAMIN C | =============================== | 44.40 Mg | 84.60 Mg |
| THIAMIN | ===================================================== | 6.250 Mg | 0.570 Mg |
| RIBOFLAVIN | ===================================================== | 6.090 Mg | 0.730 Mg |
| NIACIN | ===================================================== | 37.30 Mg | 19.40 Mg |
| VITAMIN B6 | ===================================================== | 6.440 Mg | 1.050 Mg |
| FOLACIN | ======================= | 201.0 Ug | 96.10 Ug |
| VITAMIN B12 | ===================================================== | 4.940 Mg | 3.500 Mg |
| PANTO— ACID | ========================= | 3.170 Mg | 2.470 Mg |
| CALCIUM | ==================================================== | 1602 Mg | 265.0 Mg |
| PHOSPHORUS | ===================================================== | 1045 Mg | 830.0 Mg |
| TRYPTOPHAN | ===================================================== | 960.0 Mg | 0.000 Mg |
| THREONINE | ===================================================== | 2891 Mg | 0.000 Mg |
| ISOLEUCINE | ===================================================== | 3807 Mg | 0.000 Mg |
| LEUCINE | ===================================================== | 5899 Mg | 0.000 Mg |
| LYSINE | ===================================================== | 4554 Mg | 0.000 Mg |
| METHIONINE | ===================================================== | 1038 Mg | 0.000 Mg |
| CYSTINE | ===================================================== | 902.0 Mg | 0.000 Mg |
| PHENYL—ANINE | ===================================================== | 3704 Mg | 0.000 Mg |
| TYROSINE | ===================================================== | 2802 Mg | 0.000 Mg |
| VALINE | ===================================================== | 3897 Mg | 0.000 Mg |
| HISTIDINE | | 2088 Mg | 0.000 Mg |
| ALCOHOL | | 0.000 Gm | 0.000 Gm |
| ASH | | 14.40 Gm | 0.000 Gm |
| COPPER | =============================== | 1.520 Mg | 0.450 Mg |
| MANGANESE | ===================================================== | 6.250 Mg | 1.100 Mg |
| IODINE | ============================ | 1857 Ug | 73.20 Ug |
| MONO FAT | | 4.390 Gm | 0.000 Gm |
| POLY FAT | | 9.440 Gm | 0.000 Gm |
| CAFFEINE | | 0.000 Mg | 0.000 Mg |
| FLUORIDE | ============ | 683.0 Ug | 0.000 Ug |
| MOLYBDENUM | ===================================================== | 6469 Ug | 0.000 Ug |
| VITAMIN K | ===================================================== | 235.0 Ug | 0.000 Ug |
| SELENIUM | ==================== | 0.050 Mg | 0.000 Mg |
| BIOTIN | ========= | 28.90 Ug | 26.70 Ug |
| CHLORIDE | ======= | 536.0 Mg | 0.000 Mg |
| CHROMIUM | ===================================================== | 1.600 Mg | 0.000 Mg |
| SUGAR | | 12.50 Gm | 0.000 Gm |
| FIBER—DIET | | 20.20 Gm | 0.000 Gm |
| VIT. E/AT | ============ | 2.000 Mg | 0.000 Mg |

```
% RDA:   |0      |20     |40     |60     |80     |100
```

Dotted line indicates our Southern-Fried Tofu dinner. Straight line indicates Kentucky Fried Chicken dinner.  Comparison is for an equal gram weight of each dinner.

# GRAVY

Don't waste the leftover milk and flour mixtures from the Southern-Fried Tofu! They make a delicious gravy, perfect for topping the Southern-Fried Tofu.

1 cup flour mixture used to dredge tofu in

2 tsp. sage
1 tsp. thyme

6 cups milk mixture used to soak tofu in

4 tsp. soy sauce
2 tsp. lemon juice

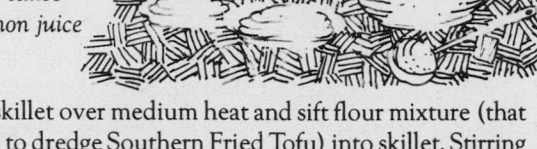

Heat skillet over medium heat and sift flour mixture (that was used to dredge Southern Fried Tofu) into skillet. Stirring constantly, lightly toast flour mixture till it begins to turn a slight bit darker. Add next 2 ingredients and mix in thoroughly.

Remove skillet from heat and pour in the leftover milk mixture that was used for soaking tofu in. With a wire whisk, thoroughly mix so all lumps are gone. Return to heat and continue whisking till gravy comes to a boil and thickens. Whisk in last 2 ingredients and turn off heat. If gravy thickens from sitting, just whisk in enough water to bring to desired consistency. Makes about 10 to 12 servings.

| SHOPPING LIST | |
|---|---|
| **Regularly Kept in the Kitchen** (Listed in Chapter 14, p. 703) | **Fresh Produce** |
| Sage Thyme Soy sauce | Lemon |

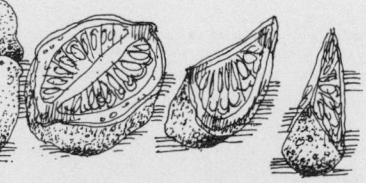

# MURRIETA COLESLAW

☆ Of the wide array of sumptuous dishes offered on the dinner menu at a wonderful spa, Murrieta Hot Springs — only a 2-hour drive from Los Angeles or San Diego — this simple salad was one of my favorites (salads are my favorite food!). I asked for the recipe, which they had none for; the best cooks create by feel. Their cook very kindly recreated the salad, and I cut the proportions down to be right for serving a large family or a dinner party instead of the close-to-a-thousand they serve every night at Murrieta.

4 cups finely julienned, grated carrots
5 cups thinly slivered cabbage
2 cups eggless or Tofu Mayonnaise
    (see recipe, p. 332) or Murrieta Hot
    Springs Mayonnaise (see following recipe)
½ cup Lowfat "Sour Cream"
    (see recipe, p. 186) or sour cream
2 Tbsp. plus 1 tsp. apple cider vinegar
2 tsp. honey or fructose
1½ tsp. dill weed
1 tsp. salt (I prefer less; try adding to taste)
1 tsp. black pepper

Combine all 9 ingredients in a bowl and mix thoroughly. Cover and refrigerate at least 3 to 4 hours before serving. Makes 10 to 12 servings.

| SHOPPING LIST | |
|---|---|
| **Regularly Kept in the Kitchen (Listed in Chapter 14, p. 703)** | **Fresh Produce** |
| Eggless mayonnaise<br>Apple cider vinegar<br>Honey<br>Dill weed<br>Salt<br>Black pepper | Carrots<br>Cabbage<br>Sour Cream (if not using<br>    Lowfat "Sour Cream") |

See shopping list for Lowfat "Sour Cream" (p. 186) if using it instead of real sour cream.

Their sumptuous vegetarian cuisine, mineral baths, mud baths, massages and workshops, all to be had in peaceful surroundings, make Murrieta Hot Springs a true oasis.
28779 Via Las Flores
Murrieta CA 92362
(714) 677-7451

# MURRIETA HOT SPRINGS MAYONNAISE*

☆ The only changes I made in the recipe — I use honey instead of fructose and sometimes my Tofu Mayonnaise (p. 332) instead of theirs which, delicious as it is, I've found to be a little rich.

---

2 cups milk powder
¾ cup vinegar
1½ cups water
1 tsp. salt
1 tsp. dry mustard

4 cups almond oil

Combine and blend together first 5 ingredients. While blending, slowly add almond oil till mayonnaise reaches desired consistency. As it sits, it will thicken. Keeps about 5 to 6 days in the refrigerator. Yields 8 cups.

* from the *Alive Polarity's Vegetarian Cookbook*, Alive Polarity Publications, p. 7.

# DELIGHTFULLY REFRESHING INSIDE-OUT TORTE

☆ A light version of the torte that puts one layer of cake between two jelled layers of fresh fruit.

If you can find the vegetable gelatin (carageenan), the recipe for the gel in the fruit torte can be used as a basic recipe for making healthy "jellos." Vary flavors by using different kinds of unsweetened fruit juices.

½ cup filtered apple juice, boiling
2 Tbsp. plus 2 tsp. vegetable gelatin

3½ cups cold filtered apple juice

¼ cup honey
2 Tbsp. margarine or butter
1 Tbsp. yogurt
1½ tsp. vanilla extract

¾ cup water

1 cup whole wheat flour
2 tsp. baking powder

2 - 3 fresh or stewed peaches, sliced

Bring ½ cup of filtered apple juice to a boil. Turn off heat and add vegetable gelatin to boiling hot water and stir till dissolved. Pour in cold juice and refrigerate till it just begins to jell.

In the meantime, or beforehand, start cake by preheating oven to 350 degrees and creaming next 4 ingredients together in a bowl. Add water and mix in thoroughly. Sift in dry ingredients and quickly stir till all lumps are gone. Pour into an oiled 9"-diameter cake pan and spread evenly on bottom of pan. Bake at 350 degrees for 15 to 20 minutes, or till a toothpick inserted in the center of the cake comes out clean. Remove from oven and allow to cool for a while. When warm, turn out of pan onto cooling rack and continue to cool.

When cake is cool and apple juice is partially jelled, it's time to assemble the torte. If gel is already firm, just dip pot in some warm water and it will soften up (hot water will liquify it again, so be careful!). Spread ½ cup of gel on bottom of the same cake pan that the cake was baked in (cleaned out, of

course!), or one of identical shape. Arrange peach slices in an attractive pattern in one layer across surface of gel. Pour half of the remaining gel over the peaches, top with cooled cake, then pour and spread the remaining gel over the cake. Cover the cake pan with plastic wrap and refrigerate till gel is completely set (about 2 hours). Gel is set when the ingredients don't slip to a side when pan is slightly tilted. Wet palm of hand and wipe over the surface of a flat serving platter, which torte will be inverted onto, and the top surface of the gel. Gently loosen edges of gel from sides of pan, then place tray or platter on top of cake pan with top side of platter facing gel. Invert tray and pan simultaneously so gel falls onto platter. Serve immediately or return to refrigerator immediately. Makes one 9"-diameter torte that will serve 8 to 10 people.

**Special Shopping**

Vegetable gelatin — try a Jewish food store for Kosher gelatin made from carageenan. As a second choice, use agar-agar, a seaweed which can be found in most natural food stores and Japanese or Chinese groceries. Carageenan jells like "Jell-o"; agar-agar sets thick and solid, doesn't wiggle.

| SHOPPING LIST | |
| --- | --- |
| **Regularly Kept in the Kitchen** (Listed in Chapter 14, p. 703) | **Fresh Produce** |
| Honey<br>Margarine or butter<br>Yogurt<br>Vanilla extract<br>Whole wheat flour<br>Baking powder | Filtered apple juice<br>Peaches (or nectarines or apricots) |

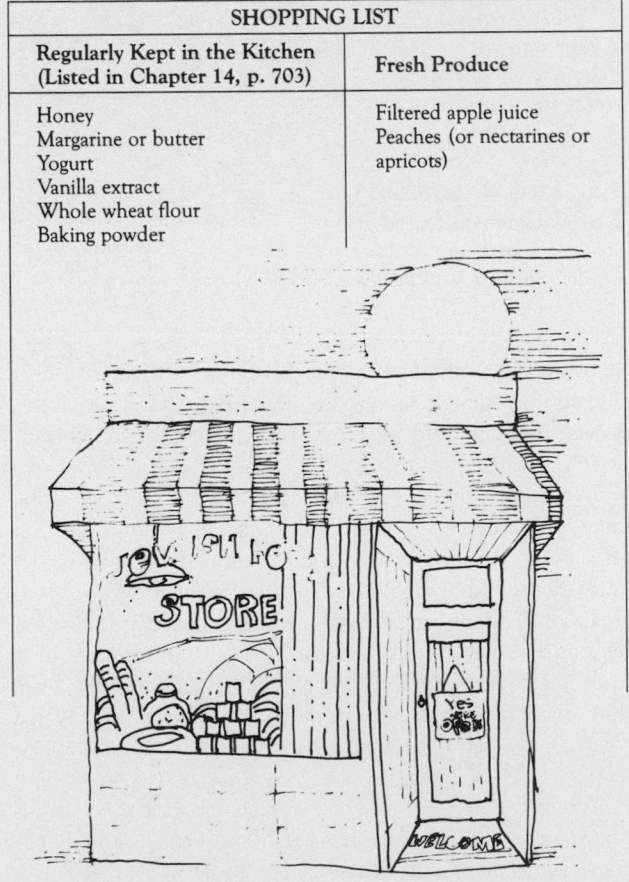

# NUTRITIONAL ANALYSIS FOR ONE SERVING
# DELIGHTFULLY REFRESHING INSIDE-OUT TORTE

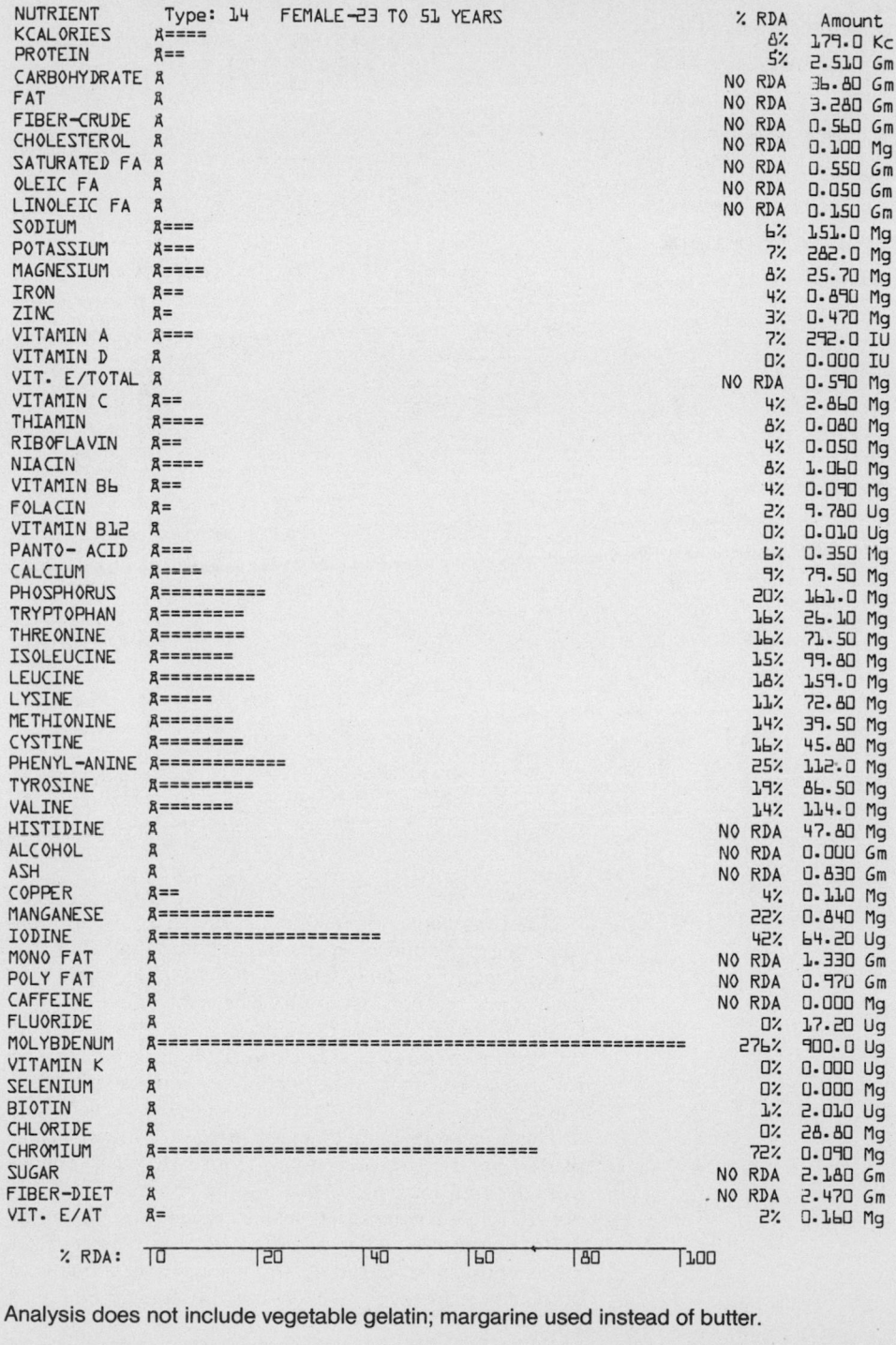

| NUTRIENT | Type: 14   FEMALE-23 TO 51 YEARS | % RDA | Amount |
|---|---|---|---|
| KCALORIES | A==== | 8% | 179.0 Kc |
| PROTEIN | A== | 5% | 2.510 Gm |
| CARBOHYDRATE | A | NO RDA | 36.80 Gm |
| FAT | A | NO RDA | 3.280 Gm |
| FIBER-CRUDE | A | NO RDA | 0.560 Gm |
| CHOLESTEROL | A | NO RDA | 0.100 Mg |
| SATURATED FA | A | NO RDA | 0.550 Gm |
| OLEIC FA | A | NO RDA | 0.050 Gm |
| LINOLEIC FA | A | NO RDA | 0.150 Gm |
| SODIUM | A=== | 6% | 151.0 Mg |
| POTASSIUM | A=== | 7% | 282.0 Mg |
| MAGNESIUM | A==== | 8% | 25.70 Mg |
| IRON | A== | 4% | 0.890 Mg |
| ZINC | A= | 3% | 0.470 Mg |
| VITAMIN A | A=== | 7% | 292.0 IU |
| VITAMIN D | A | 0% | 0.000 IU |
| VIT. E/TOTAL | A | NO RDA | 0.590 Mg |
| VITAMIN C | A== | 4% | 2.860 Mg |
| THIAMIN | A==== | 8% | 0.080 Mg |
| RIBOFLAVIN | A== | 4% | 0.050 Mg |
| NIACIN | A==== | 8% | 1.060 Mg |
| VITAMIN B6 | A== | 4% | 0.090 Mg |
| FOLACIN | A= | 2% | 9.780 Ug |
| VITAMIN B12 | A | 0% | 0.010 Ug |
| PANTO- ACID | A=== | 6% | 0.350 Mg |
| CALCIUM | A==== | 9% | 79.50 Mg |
| PHOSPHORUS | A========== | 20% | 161.0 Mg |
| TRYPTOPHAN | A======== | 16% | 26.10 Mg |
| THREONINE | A======== | 16% | 71.50 Mg |
| ISOLEUCINE | A======= | 15% | 99.80 Mg |
| LEUCINE | A========= | 18% | 159.0 Mg |
| LYSINE | A===== | 11% | 72.80 Mg |
| METHIONINE | A======= | 14% | 39.50 Mg |
| CYSTINE | A======== | 16% | 45.80 Mg |
| PHENYL-ANINE | A============ | 25% | 112.0 Mg |
| TYROSINE | A========= | 19% | 86.50 Mg |
| VALINE | A======= | 14% | 114.0 Mg |
| HISTIDINE | A | NO RDA | 47.80 Mg |
| ALCOHOL | A | NO RDA | 0.000 Gm |
| ASH | A | NO RDA | 0.830 Gm |
| COPPER | A== | 4% | 0.110 Mg |
| MANGANESE | A=========== | 22% | 0.840 Mg |
| IODINE | A===================== | 42% | 64.20 Ug |
| MONO FAT | A | NO RDA | 1.330 Gm |
| POLY FAT | A | NO RDA | 0.970 Gm |
| CAFFEINE | A | NO RDA | 0.000 Mg |
| FLUORIDE | A | 0% | 17.20 Ug |
| MOLYBDENUM | A==================================================== | 276% | 900.0 Ug |
| VITAMIN K | A | 0% | 0.000 Ug |
| SELENIUM | A | 0% | 0.000 Mg |
| BIOTIN | A | 1% | 2.010 Ug |
| CHLORIDE | A | 0% | 28.80 Mg |
| CHROMIUM | A==================================== | 72% | 0.090 Mg |
| SUGAR | A | NO RDA | 2.180 Gm |
| FIBER-DIET | A | NO RDA | 2.470 Gm |
| VIT. E/AT | A= | 2% | 0.160 Mg |

% RDA:  0    20    40    60    80    100

Analysis does not include vegetable gelatin; margarine used instead of butter.

The Buddha said, "The fool who knows he is a fool is that much wiser. The fool who thinks he is wise is a fool indeed." ... The first step towards attaining wisdom begins with recognizing one's lack of it.

# ANOTHER SHAPE FOR TOFU

As I started getting new recipes together to share with you, using my favorite inexpensive, cholesterol-free source of protein, tofu, I suddenly realized that there's a whole new form of tofu that you may not have been introduced to. The Chinese use a form of tofu that is made so firm that it is almost the texture of turkey, and being versatile as tofu is, can be flavored to resemble turkey or any of your favorite cold cuts.

This firmer form of tofu might give those of you who can't seem to get used to the texture of tofu a chance to benefit from the nutritional pluses that tofu has to offer. This firm-pressed tofu is condensed, much like cheese is, so the nutrients in the tofu are condensed in it as well. Tofu contains eight percent protein by weight; the firm-pressed tofu contains 22 percent protein (beef, chicken and fish contain about 20 percent).

Whenever we're talking about protein, it's important to talk about calcium because recent medical studies have shown that too much protein in a diet can leech calcium from bones. Tofu is unique, being a good source of high-quality protein and calcium as well. Tofu contains 146 milligrams of calcium, or 16 percent of the RDA (per 100 grams of tofu); the same amount of firm-pressed tofu contains 377 milligrams, or about 40 percent of the RDA for calcium. We're used to thinking of dairy products as good calcium and protein sources, but tofu supplies more of both than any dairy product (and remember — that's without cholesterol or saturated fat!). I was really surprised to learn that when milk is made into a firmer form, like curd or cottage cheese, calcium is actually lost. Milk contains 230 milligrams of calcium (per 100 grams); cottage cheese, 135 milligrams, and hard cheese, 204 milligrams of calcium.

Although not much is known yet about how other minerals affect the body's ability to assimilate and retain calcium, new information indicates it is an important consideration. One thing that is known is that the amount of calcium and phosphorous must be about equal, and if there is more phosphorous than calcium in a food, it will cause the bones to lose calcium. Tofu is an ideal calcium food in this respect because it contains about equal amounts of calcium and phosphorous. Dairy products generally contain almost twice as much phosphorous as calcium. Meat, chicken and fish are never even mentioned as sources of calcium because they contain anywhere from zero percent to five percent of the RDA, and anywhere from three to eight times the amount of phosphorous to calcium.

The only drawback about this firm-pressed tofu is that it's not as readily available as regular tofu is. That's why I've included a recipe for making this firm-pressed tofu from Chinese firm tofu, which is available in most supermarkets or natural food stores. Chinese firm tofu is, of course, also available in Chinatowns. But if you're going out of your way to find Chinese firm tofu in Chinatown, you can probably save yourself some trouble and find the firm-pressed version there.

The firm-pressed tofu takes a long time to make, but fortunately it's not stand-in-the-kitchen time. Because it's just as easy to make 10 pounds as 1 pound, and the hard-pressed tofu keeps well in the freezer or refrigerator, I recommend making more than you need at once and storing the extra for future use.

# PRESSED TOFU

☆ I'm fortunate enough to have some people who work
out by lifting weights in the family, which makes the 20
pounds needed to press the tofu easy for me to get.
But be innovative — you can use unopened sacks of
rice or flour, a large pot with rocks in it, or anything
lying around the house that will equal about 20 pounds.

---

2 lbs. Chinese firm tofu
Cheesecloth
Large cutting board
20 lbs. (of anything) to be used
   as a weight

Flavored stock of choice
   (see following recipes)

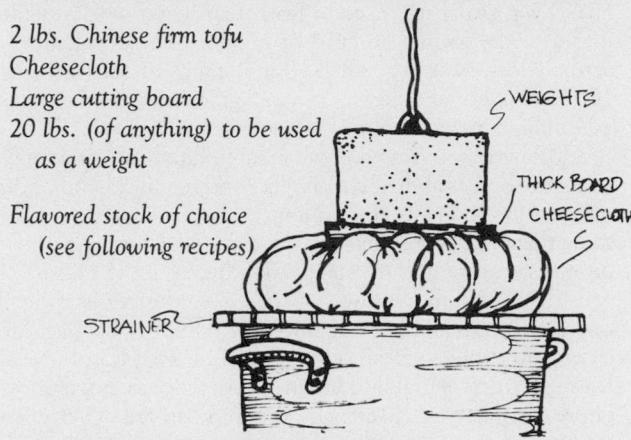

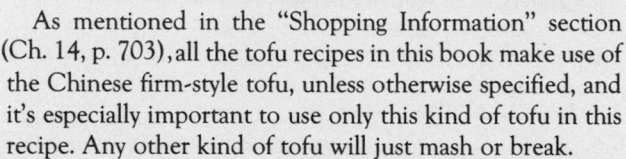

As mentioned in the "Shopping Information" section
(Ch. 14, p. 703), all the tofu recipes in this book make use of
the Chinese firm-style tofu, unless otherwise specified, and
it's especially important to use only this kind of tofu in this
recipe. Any other kind of tofu will just mash or break.

Most 1-pound containers of Chinese firm-style tofu come
with what appears to be a 1-pound block of tofu already cut in
quarters. If you happen to buy tofu made by a company that
sells its Chinese firm tofu in a solid block, cut the block into
quarters across the width of the block. You should end up
with 4 cutlets approximately 1" to 1¼" thick per pound of
tofu. This recipe makes use of 2 pounds of tofu, but you can
make more or less according to your need simply by increasing or decreasing the amount of liquid the pressed tofu is
boiled in, in proportion to the amount of tofu used.

Individually wrap each cutlet of tofu in a suitably-sized
piece of cheesecloth. Lay wrapped tofu pieces in a single layer
on a flat surface (preferably on the countertop that drains
into the kitchen sink). Lay a cutting board, or a clean piece of
some sort of untreated, non-poisonous wood, on top of the
wrapped tofu pieces so that all of them are covered. Place 20
pounds of weight on top of the board and allow to sit 8 hours
or overnight.

Unwrap the pressed pieces of tofu and boil them in any of the following flavored bases, or experiment with your own flavoring:

### Smoky-Flavored:

*3 cups water*
*½ cup soy sauce*
*2 Tbsp. liquid smoke*
*1 tsp. black pepper*

### Poultry-Flavored:

*3 cups water*
*½ cup soy sauce*
*⅓ cup nutritional yeast*
*4 tsp. poultry seasoning*
*1 tsp. thyme*
*1 tsp. summer savory*
*1 tsp. asafetida or onion powder*
*½ tsp. black pepper*

### Traditional Chinese-Style:

*3 cups water*
*½ cup soy sauce*
*2 - 4 pieces star anise*
*1 tsp. honey*
*1 tsp. Chinese five-spice powder*

Some ideas for serving:
• Good cold, sliced in ⅛" to ¼" thicknesses for sandwiches.
• Dice for salads.
• Slice thin and top with Mock Turkey Gravy (p. 66).
• Cut in matchsticks and use in stir-fry dishes.

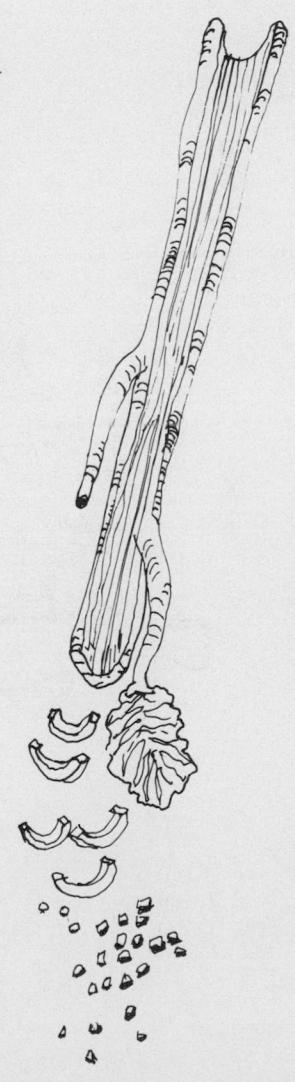

Each of the recipes given above provide enough to cover and flavor 2 pounds of pressed tofu. If you wish to do more tofu than 2 pounds, simply multiply the amount of base flavoring by the number of pounds of tofu. I like to press anywhere from 4 to 6 pounds of tofu and then make a few pots of different flavorings for the pressed pieces to go into.

No matter which flavor you use, do it in the following manner. In a saucepan, combine all ingredients, mix well and simmer for about 10 minutes over a very low flame. Add pressed tofu pieces to simmering liquid and bring gently to a boil, then turn heat down and cook at a gentle rolling boil for about 5 minutes. Remove from heat, cover and allow pressed tofu to soak for about 6 hours.

Remove cakes from liquid, drain, and bake at 250 degrees for about 2 hours. Allow to cool; refrigerate in plastic bags. The remaining liquid can be kept refrigerated for repeat use.

| Special Shopping |
|---|
| If making the Traditional Chinese-Style flavoring, you'll need — |
| Star anise |
| Chinese five-spice powder |
| Both can be found in Chinatown or Chinese grocery stores. |

| SHOPPING LIST | |
|---|---|
| Regularly Kept in the Kitchen (Listed in Chapter 14, p. 703) | Fresh Produce |
| Tofu<br>Soy sauce<br>Black pepper<br>Nutritional yeast<br>Poultry seasoning<br>Thyme<br>Summer savory<br>Liquid smoke | (None) |

Fig. 5. Composition of Nutrients in 100 grams of Tofu

Sources: *Standard Tables of Food Composition* (Japan), *FAO Food Composition Tables, and USDA Composition of Foods* (Wash., D.C.)

| Type of Tofu | Food Energy (Calories) | Moisture (Percent) | Protein (Percent) | Fat (Percent) | Sugars (Percent) | Fiber (Percent) | Ash (Percent) | Calcium (Mg) | Sodium (Mg) | Phosphorus (Mg) | Iron (Mg) | Vit. $B_1$ (Thiamine) (Mg) | Vit. $B_2$ (Riboflavin) (Mg) | Vit. $B_3$ (Niacin) (Mg) |
|---|---|---|---|---|---|---|---|---|---|---|---|---|---|---|
| Tofu | 72 | 84.9 | 7.8 | 4.3 | 2.3 | 0 | 0.7 | 146 | 6 | 105 | 1.7 | 0.02 | 0.02 | 0.5 |
| Doufu | 87 | 79.3 | 10.6 | 5.3 | 2.9 | 0 | 0.9 | 159 | 7 | 109 | 2.5 | 0.02 | 0.02 | 0.6 |
| Kinugoshi | 53 | 88.4 | 5.5 | 3.2 | 1.7 | 0 | 1.2 | 94 | 23 | 71 | 1.2 | 0.02 | 0.02 | 0.3 |
| Thick Agé | 05 | 79.0 | 10.1 | 7.0 | 2.8 | 0 | 1.1 | 240 | 15 | 150 | 2.6 | 0.02 | 0.02 | 0.5 |
| Agé | 346 | 44.0 | 18.6 | 31.4 | 4.5 | 0.1 | 1.4 | 300 | 20 | 230 | 4.2 | 0.02 | 0.02 | 0.5 |
| Soymilk | 42 | 90.8 | 3.6 | 2.0 | 2.9 | 0.02 | 0.5 | 15 | 2 | 49 | 1.2 | 0.03 | 0.02 | 0.5 |
| Doufu-ru | 175 | 52.0 | 13.5 | 8.4 | 13.6 | 1.2 | 11.6 | 165 | 458 | 182 | 5.7 | 0.04 | 0.18 | 0.6 |
| Ganmo | 192 | 64.0 | 15.4 | 14.0 | 5.1 | 0.1 | 1.4 | 270 | 17 | 200 | 3.6 | 0.01 | 0.03 | 1.0 |
| Grilled Tofu | 82 | 83.0 | 8.8 | 5.1 | 2.1 | 0 | 1.0 | 180 | 15 | 120 | 1.9 | 0.02 | 0.02 | 0.4 |
| Dried-Frozen Tofu | 436 | 10.4 | 53.4 | 26.4 | 7.0 | 0.2 | 2.6 | 590 | 18 | 710 | 9.4 | 0.05 | 0.04 | 0.6 |
| Okara | 65 | 84.5 | 3.5 | 1.9 | 6.9 | 2.3 | 0.9 | 76 | 4 | 43 | 1.4 | 0.05 | 0.02 | 0.3 |
| Dried Yuba | 432 | 8.7 | 52.3 | 24.1 | 11.9 | 0 | 3.0 | 270 | 80 | 590 | 11.0 | 0.20 | 0.08 | 2.0 |
| Pressed Tofu and Savory Tofu | 182 | 61.6 | 22.0 | 11.0 | 6.0 | 0.1 | 1.9 | 377 | 16 | 270 | 4.4 | 0.05 | 0.05 | 0.6 |
| Dry Soybeans | 392 | 12.0 | 34.3 | 17.5 | 26.7 | 4.5 | 5.0 | 190 | 3 | 470 | 7.0 | 0.50 | 0.20 | 2.0 |
| Defatted Soybean Meal | 322 | 8.0 | 49.0 | 0.4 | 33.6 | 3.0 | 6.0 | 220 | 4 | 550 | 8.4 | 0.45 | 0.15 | 2.0 |
| Kinako | 426 | 5.0 | 38.4 | 19.2 | 29.5 | 2.9 | 5.0 | 190 | 4 | 500 | 9.0 | 0.40 | 0.15 | 2.0 |

# SPECIAL LAYERED SALAD

☆ A special occasion salad that is a meal in itself.

☆ Ideal for entertaining, as it can be prepared a day ahead of time.

## SUGGESTED MENU

*Whole grain rolls or crusty bread*

*Special Layered Salad*

*Tropical Pleasure Candies (p. 401)*

4 cups torn Romaine lettuce
4 scallions, slivered
4 tomatoes, seeded and sliced
4 sun-dried tomatoes, cut into matchsticks
½ tsp. black pepper
1 cup slivered fresh basil leaves
¾ lb. smoked mozzarella cheese, sliced thin
2 cups alfalfa sprouts
½ cup slivered Greek olives

1 cup mashed Chinese firm tofu
2 scallions, slivered
3 Tbsp. nutritional yeast
2 Tbsp. soy sauce
½ tsp. black pepper

3 squares Smoke-Flavored Pressed Tofu (see preceding recipe), cut into matchsticks
1 bell pepper cut into rings
½ cup watercress leaves
6 oz. marinated artichoke hearts, sliced
4 cups small cauliflower flowerets, steamed and cooled

2 cups cooked garbanzo beans
⅓ cup parsley leaves

1½ cups eggless or Tofu Mayonnaise (see recipe, p. 332)
½ cup finely chopped celery
¼ cup lowfat yogurt
¼ cup sweet pickle relish
¼ cup nutritional yeast
2 Tbsp. soy sauce
1 Tbsp. Dijon mustard
1 tsp. kelp
1 tsp. Spike or other vegetable-seasoned salt
¼ tsp. black pepper
¼ tsp. asafetida or garlic powder

I always use a glass bowl to make this salad in because the different colored layers are so pretty!

In a large (1-gallon) glass pot or bowl, layer each ingredient separately in the order given for the first 9 ingredients, being sure to spread each ingredient evenly over the entire surface.

In a separate little bowl, mix next 5 ingredients together thoroughly. Spread as the next layer on top of the olives.

Layer the next 5 ingredients listed in the order given just as you did with the first 9 ingredients.

Put next 2 ingredients together in a food processor or blender and chop very fine. If you do not have either of these appliances, run the ingredients through a food grinder or chop very finely by hand. In a separate bowl, mix chopped garbanzos and parsley thoroughly with the last 11 ingredients and spread as the top layer of the salad. Cover with saran wrap or lid and refrigerate at least 6 hours (this salad will stay fresh, kept in layers in the refrigerator, for up to 24 hours).

To serve, be sure to dig down through all the layers so each serving contains all the layers. Makes 8 servings.

| SHOPPING LIST | | Special Shopping |
|---|---|---|
| **Regularly Kept in the Kitchen** (Listed in Chapter 14, p. 703) | **Fresh Produce** | Sun-dried tomatoes packed in olive oil; smoked mozzarella; Greek olives — can be found in Italian groceries or possibly gourmet food stores or delis. |
| Tofu and seasonings for preceding recipe | Romaine lettuce | Sugarless sweet pickle relish (sweetened with honey) — in natural food stores. |
| Black pepper | Scallions | |
| Tofu | Tomatoes | |
| Nutritional yeast | Basil | |
| Soy sauce | Alfalfa sprouts | |
| Garbanzo beans | Bell pepper | |
| Eggless mayonnaise | Watercress | |
| Yogurt | Marinated artichoke hearts | |
| Dijon mustard | Cauliflower | |
| Kelp powder | Parsley | |
| | Celery | |

# NUTRITIONAL ANALYSIS FOR ONE SERVING
## SPECIAL LAYERED SALAD

| NUTRIENT | Type: 14 FEMALE—23 TO 51 YEARS | % RDA | Amount |
|---|---|---|---|
| KCALORIES | A============= | 24% | 483.0 Kc |
| PROTEIN | A==================================== | 83% | 36.90 Gm |
| CARBOHYDRATE | A | NO RDA | 37.70 Gm |
| FAT | A | NO RDA | 23.70 Gm |
| FIBER—CRUDE | A | NO RDA | 3.420 Gm |
| CHOLESTEROL | A | NO RDA | 24.60 Mg |
| SATURATED FA | A | NO RDA | 6.400 Gm |
| OLEIC FA | A | NO RDA | 6.050 Gm |
| LINOLEIC FA | A | NO RDA | 2.950 Gm |
| SODIUM | A========================= | 50% | 1116 Mg |
| POTASSIUM | A=============== | 30% | 1146 Mg |
| MAGNESIUM | A==================== | 41% | 125.0 Mg |
| IRON | A================================== | 68% | 12.40 Mg |
| ZINC | A=============== | 30% | 4.500 Mg |
| VITAMIN A | A============================== | 60% | 2437 IU |
| VITAMIN D | A | 0% | 0.000 IU |
| VIT. E/TOTAL | A | NO RDA | 2.420 Mg |
| VITAMIN C | A=================================================== | 129% | 77.80 Mg |
| THIAMIN | A=================================================== | 421% | 4.220 Mg |
| RIBOFLAVIN | A=================================================== | 357% | 4.290 Mg |
| NIACIN | A=================================================== | 189% | 24.60 Mg |
| VITAMIN B6 | A=================================================== | 214% | 4.280 Mg |
| FOLACIN | A============================== | 61% | 245.0 Ug |
| VITAMIN B12 | A=================================================== | 115% | 3.450 Ug |
| PANTO- ACID | A========= | 19% | 1.090 Mg |
| CALCIUM | A=================================================== | 118% | 946.0 Mg |
| PHOSPHORUS | A==================================== | 83% | 666.0 Mg |
| TRYPTOPHAN | A=================================================== | 156% | 255.0 Mg |
| THREONINE | A=================================================== | 281% | 1224 Mg |
| ISOLEUCINE | A=================================================== | 221% | 1447 Mg |
| LEUCINE | A=================================================== | 285% | 2491 Mg |
| LYSINE | A=================================================== | 369% | 2411 Mg |
| METHIONINE | A=================================================== | 206% | 563.0 Mg |
| CYSTINE | A=================================================== | 119% | 325.0 Mg |
| PHENYL—ANINE | A=================================================== | 339% | 1476 Mg |
| TYROSINE | A=================================================== | 287% | 1252 Mg |
| VALINE | A=================================================== | 220% | 1678 Mg |
| HISTIDINE | A | NO RDA | 935.0 Mg |
| ALCOHOL | A | NO RDA | 0.000 Gm |
| ASH | A | NO RDA | 10.00 Gm |
| COPPER | A========== | 20% | 0.500 Mg |
| MANGANESE | A================== | 37% | 1.400 Mg |
| IODINE | A=================================================== | 114% | 172.0 Ug |
| MONO FAT | A | NO RDA | 6.070 Gm |
| POLY FAT | A | NO RDA | 6.100 Gm |
| CAFFEINE | A | NO RDA | 0.000 Mg |
| FLUORIDE | A= | 2% | 59.30 Ug |
| MOLYBDENUM | A=================================================== | 278% | 905.0 Ug |
| VITAMIN K | A=================================================== | 1752% | 1840 Ug |
| SELENIUM | A | 0% | 0.000 Mg |
| BIOTIN | A======= | 15% | 23.80 Ug |
| CHLORIDE | A= | 3% | 132.0 Mg |
| CHROMIUM | A=================================================== | 232% | 0.290 Mg |
| SUGAR | A | NO RDA | 4.950 Gm |
| FIBER—DIET | A | NO RDA | 5.030 Gm |
| VIT. E/AT | A=========== | 23% | 1.840 Mg |

```
% RDA:  |0     |20    |40    |60    |80    |100
```

Analysis uses Tofu Mayonnaise instead of commercial eggless; does not include sun-dried tomatoes.

# TOFU BALLS

☆ Another way to use this recipe: leave the horseradish and coriander powder out. These less spicy balls can then be served in spaghetti, in a brown gravy, or any recipe calling for meatballs.

1½ cups well-drained, mashed
  Chinese firm tofu

¼ cup sunflower seeds
¼ cup whole wheat flour
2 Tbsp. parsley flakes
⅛ tsp. black pepper
½ tsp. salt
½ tsp. asafetida or 2 cloves garlic,
  finely minced
2 Tbsp. nutritional yeast
¼ cup horseradish
2 tsp. coriander powder

Oil for deep-frying

2 cups raw, chopped vegetables
1 cup water chestnuts

Combine tofu with next 9 ingredients and mix together thoroughly. Heat up a wokful of oil to 350 to 400 degrees. As oil is heating, roll tofu mixture into balls the size of a large marble or walnut, depending on which size you prefer. When oil is the right temperature, drop balls in and deep-fry till golden brown. With a slotted spoon, remove balls from oil and set aside. If you want, you can make a large batch of these balls, and after frying they can be frozen for use on another day. Pour oil out of wok and stir-fry vegetables and water chestnuts in remaining oil till vegetables are tender. Pour vegetables on a platter to form a bed and place Tofu Balls on top. Pour a sweet-sour sauce over this.

## PINEAPPLE SWEET-SOUR SAUCE

(from *Kathy Cooks . . . Naturally*, p. 214)

2 Tbsp. oil
⅛ tsp. asafetida
1 tsp. grated fresh ginger
1 cup pineapple pieces

1 Tbsp. soy sauce
⅓ cup honey
¼ cup apple cider vinegar
¼ cup catsup
1 cup unsweetened pineapple
  juice
1 green bell pepper, sliced

2 Tbsp. arrowroot powder

Stir-fry first 4 ingredients together for a few minutes. Add next 6 ingredients. Dissolve arrowroot in a little bit of water and pour into cooking sauce, stir in and continue to stir until thick.

. . . or try using the Sate Sweet-Hot-Sour Sauce (p. 134) or Mushroom Sauce (p. 610) instead.

| SHOPPING LIST | |
|---|---|
| **Regularly Kept in the Kitchen** (Listed in Chapter 14, p. 703) | **Fresh Produce** |
| Tofu | Horseradish |
| Sunflower seeds | Assortment of fresh |
| Whole wheat flour | vegetables |
| Parsley flakes | |
| Salt | |
| Asafetida | |
| Nutritional yeast | |
| Coriander powder | |

# INDONESIAN SATE BARBECUE

Indonesian cooking is a good example of how borrowing ideas and ingredients from cuisines around the world can make for light, healthy meals that are excitingly palatable. Cooking from the Spice Islands, as Indonesia was once called by European traders, is a happy marriage of the cuisines from many different countries — curry tastes from India, stir-frying from China, along with many ideas from the Netherlands — and makes for contrasting, yet compatible meals.

One food that originated in Indonesia that we would do well to marry into our diets is tempeh. When I was working on my first book, I read about all the nutritional virtues of tempeh (some of which are described on p. 140) and decided it was really worth researching. I tried making some at home, and although it was successful, I decided not to include tempeh in my book at that time because it was such an endeavor to make that I figured most people probably wouldn't bother.

The philosopher king, Prahlad Maharaja, stated, "Just as the fruits and flowers of a tree in due course of time undergo six changes — birth, existence, growth, transformation, dwindling and death — the material body, which is obtained by the spirit soul under different circumstances, undergoes similar changes. However, there are no such changes for the spirit soul."

Eight years later, things have changed. There are a few commercial manufacturers of tempeh in this country, so now that tempeh is easier to get, I feel good about sharing some recipes that make use of it. If you don't usually shop in natural food stores, you may still have to go a little out of your way (while you're there, pick up a few other healthy new ingredients!), but at least you won't have to attempt making it at home! You'll find recipes in this book for using tempeh in more Western-style dishes, but the following recipes will give you a feel for how tempeh is used in Indonesian cooking.

The barbecue meal is meant to be served on individual platters with a mound of rice serving as a bed for the cooked kabobs and the Indonesian-Style Greens alongside the rice. You can provide whole lettuce leaves in a center bowl on the table for people to take and stuff Indonesian-style. In Indonesia they use lettuce leaves for a lighter version of the taco or sandwich. Just fill the lettuce leaf with the desired filling(s) and fold in half or wrap and eat. In this meal the lettuce leaves can be spread with the Sate Sweet-Hot-Sour Sauce and stuffed with rice, greens and/or pieces of the cooked kabobs. Another light but simpler to prepare meal is the Indonesian Salad. Both meals are certainly worth trying, and I hope the exciting flavors of the meals will inspire you to follow the example set by Indonesian cooking — to dare to combine the best ingredients and cooking techniques found throughout the world to make excitingly different meals.

# FLAVORED AND DEEP-FRIED TEMPEH

☆ This is a good basic recipe, as tempeh prepared this way can be used in many, many dishes.

½ cup water
2 Tbsp. soy sauce
2 tsp. asafetida or onion powder
2 cloves garlic, crushed
1½ tsp. ground coriander

Tempeh

Oil for deep-frying

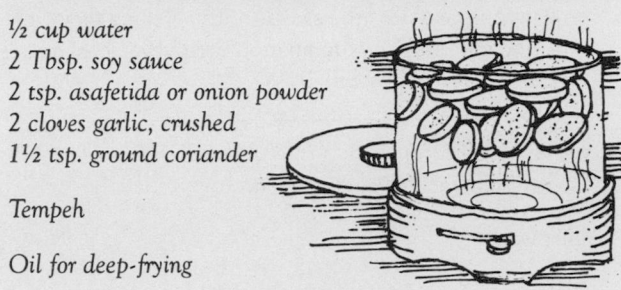

Combine first 5 ingredients in a shallow cake pan. Cut tempeh to whatever shape or size you will be using (patty shapes, thin 2½" x ¼" x ½" slivers, 1" cubes for sate, etc.) and soak in sauce for about 2 to 3 minutes on each side.

Heat oil and fry till tempeh turns a reddish-brown, then remove from oil and drain. Use as is or serve in desired dishes.

## INDONESIAN SATE BARBECUE MENU

Sate Kabobs

Golden Turmeric Rice

Indonesian-Style Greens

Loose lettuce leaves

Madhava's Favorite Candy
made with
toasted sesame seeds
and peanuts (p. 667)

| SHOPPING LIST | |
|---|---|
| Regularly Kept in the Kitchen (Listed in Chapter 14, p. 703) | Fresh Produce |
| Soy sauce<br>Asafetida<br>Ground coriander<br>Tempeh<br>Safflower oil | Garlic |

A study done at the University of California on legumes and their by-products found tempeh to be the easiest to digest; tofu, the second easiest.

# COCONUT MILK

☆ Though coconuts are one of the few plant sources of saturated fat, when no meat is eaten it doesn't hurt to use coconuts now and then. Coconut milk is used a lot in Indonesian cooking; cooking vegetables in coconut milk adds a whole other dimension to cooking with vegetables (the sweet, nutty, creamy flavor of the coconut milk in combination with vegetables makes them absolutely heavenly!).

---

*Meat of 1 fresh coconut, cut in ½" cubes,*
*    or 3 cups dry, shredded coconut (unsweetened)*

*Boiling water*

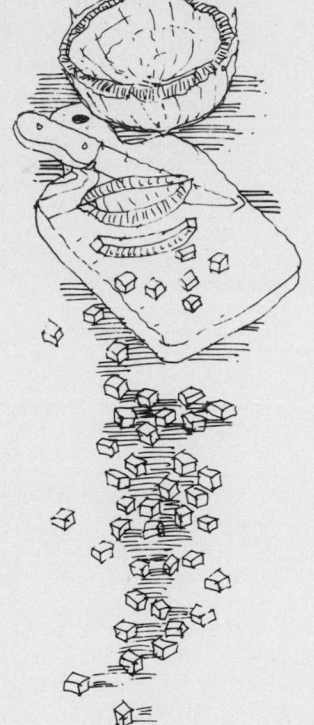

Blend only 2 cups of water and about ½ cup of coconut at a time so as not to burn out blender motor. Pour water into blender, put the lid on and turn the blender on. Open up the hole on the blender lid and drop coconut into the blending water. (Do not put all the coconut in the blender and then attempt to turn motor on because it's quite likely the blades will get stuck on some coconut and burn out the motor.)

Blend till coconut is very finely chopped and water is white like milk. Allow this to sit for about 10 minutes, then pour through a fine sieve or cheesecloth and press or squeeze as much water out as you can. One blenderful only makes about 1½ cups, so if you want to make more, do so in separate batches. I must admit that frozen or canned coconut milk is easier if you can find it.

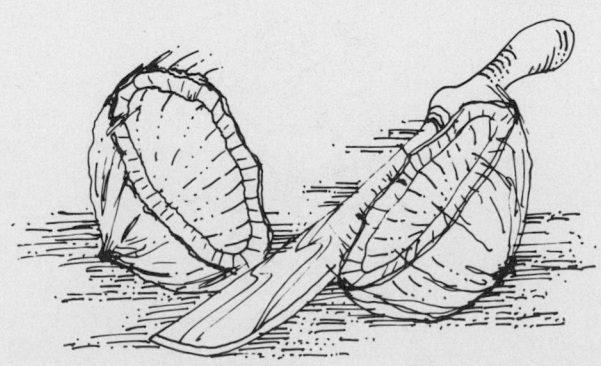

# GOLDEN TURMERIC RICE

*6 cups coconut milk*

*3 cups long grain brown rice*

*7" fresh lemon grass stalk,*
*or a tea ball filled with 3 tsp.*
*dried lemon grass herb tea*
*1 tsp. turmeric*

Bring coconut milk to a boil. Slowly drizzle in the rice so coconut milk never stops boiling. When all the rice is in the pot, add the last 2 ingredients and put the lid on the pot. Allow to boil a few minutes, then turn heat down and simmer for 45 minutes. Makes about four 2-cup servings as a bed for sate

| SHOPPING LIST | |
|---|---|
| Regularly Kept in the Kitchen (Listed in Chapter 14, p. 703) | Fresh Produce |
| Long grain brown rice Turmeric | (None) |

**Special Shopping**

Coconut milk — if not making your own (fresh coconuts are available in almost all fresh produce sections), you might be able to find canned coconut milk in grocery stores in the liquor department or some foreign food aisles;. sometimes frozen coconut milk is carried in the freezer section.
Lemon grass — fresh is preferred but hard to find; might be found in Indonesian groceries or restaurants. If they have roots on them, cut about 2" to 3" above the root and plant them, as it's a plant worth having around. Lemon grass is a good source of vitamin A and makes a delicious herb tea; iced and sweetened with a little honey, it tastes a little like lemonade.

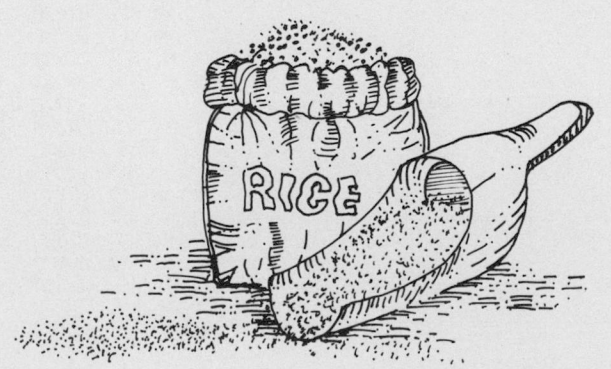

# NUTRITIONAL ANALYSIS FOR ONE SERVING
## GOLDEN TURMERIC RICE

```
NUTRIENT       Type: 14   FEMALE-23 TO 51 YEARS          % RDA  Amount
KCALORIES      X===========================             50%    1004 Kc
PROTEIN        X=============                           27%    11.90 Gm
CARBOHYDRATE   X                                        NO RDA 57.50 Gm
FAT            X                                        NO RDA 86.70 Gm
FIBER-CRUDE    X                                        NO RDA 0.480 Gm
CHOLESTEROL    X                                        NO RDA 0.000 Mg
SATURATED FA   X                                        NO RDA 76.00 Gm
OLEIC FA       X                                        NO RDA 4.350 Gm
LINOLEIC FA    X                                        NO RDA 0.000 Gm
SODIUM         X=                                       2%     56.00 Mg
POTASSIUM      X==============                          28%    1061 Mg
MAGNESIUM      X===============================         63%    189.0 Mg
IRON           X===================                     38%    6.870 Mg
ZINC           X==========                              21%    3.220 Mg
VITAMIN A      X                                        0%     0.000 IU
VITAMIN D      X                                        0%     0.000 IU
VIT. E/TOTAL   X                                        NO RDA 2.970 Mg
VITAMIN C      X========                                16%    10.10 Mg
THIAMIN        X===========                             22%    0.220 Mg
RIBOFLAVIN     X=                                       2%     0.030 Mg
NIACIN         X==================                      36%    4.770 Mg
VITAMIN B6     X=====                                   11%    0.230 Mg
FOLACIN        X                                        1%     6.250 Ug
VITAMIN B12    X                                        0%     0.000 Ug
PANTO- ACID    X=======                                 15%    0.840 Mg
CALCIUM        X====                                    9%     76.70 Mg
PHOSPHORUS     X===============================         62%    498.0 Mg
TRYPTOPHAN     X===========================================  87%  142.0 Mg
THREONINE      X=================================================  100%  438.0 Mg
ISOLEUCINE     X==========================================  81%  532.0 Mg
LEUCINE        X=========================================  114%  995.0 Mg
LYSINE         X=======================================  79%  517.0 Mg
METHIONINE     X=========================================  84%  229.0 Mg
CYSTINE        X========================================  81%  221.0 Mg
PHENYL-ANINE   X==================================================  148%  645.0 Mg
TYROSINE       X=========================================  83%  364.0 Mg
VALINE         X=============================================  96%  739.0 Mg
HISTIDINE      X                                        NO RDA 339.0 Mg
ALCOHOL        X                                        NO RDA 0.000 Gm
ASH            X                                        NO RDA 3.170 Gm
COPPER         X====================                    42%    1.060 Mg
MANGANESE      X=========================================  127%  4.770 Mg
IODINE         X=========================================  175%  263.0 Ug
MONO FAT       X                                        NO RDA 3.620 Gm
POLY FAT       X                                        NO RDA 0.930 Gm
CAFFEINE       X                                        NO RDA 0.000 Mg
FLUORIDE       X                                        0%     0.000 Ug
MOLYBDENUM     X=================================================  183%  597.0 Ug
VITAMIN K      X                                        0%     0.000 Ug
SELENIUM       X====                                    8%     0.010 Mg
BIOTIN         X                                        1%     1.890 Ug
CHLORIDE       X=                                       2%     84.70 Mg
CHROMIUM       X=================================================  240%  0.300 Mg
SUGAR          X                                        NO RDA 0.000 Gm
FIBER-DIET     X                                        NO RDA 0.000 Gm
VIT. E/AT      X======                                  12%    0.990 Mg

    % RDA:    |0      |20     |40     |60     |80     |100
```

Analysis does not include lemon grass.

# INDONESIAN-STYLE GREENS

☆ This is a typical way that greens are prepared in Indonesia, using a cooking method from their close neighbors in China.

¼ cup vegetable oil
½ cup shallots or green onions, slivered
1 fresh hot red chili, slivered

1 tsp. honey
1 Tbsp. soy sauce

2 lbs. spinach, choy sum or ong choy
   or other green leafy vegetable
   cut in 2"-wide strips

½ cup water

Fry first 3 ingredients together for 2 to 3 minutes over medium-high heat. Add next 2 ingredients and mix in.

Add greens and stir enough to coat leaves evenly with oil. Add water and cover. Cook for 3 to 5 minutes. Remove cover, mix thoroughly and serve immediately. The idea is to serve alongside a bed of rice so the rice can soak up the nice juices. Serves 4.

Frying (stir and deep) is used a lot in Asian cooking. It is a quick and therefore more energy-efficient method for cooking than baking. It takes less wood (or other fuel) to sustain heat long enough to cook something through by deep-frying than it does for baking. More densely populated areas of the world, like Asia, have developed practices in all aspects of their living, which have become almost part of their tradition, that make more efficient use of the world's resources. Interestingly enough, these Asian countries are the same ones that studies of world-wide statistics have shown very low rates of heart disease and various cancers. Traditionally in these countries, meat in the diet is either excluded or used very sparsely. With no or extremely little fat input coming from meat (and dairy products), it appears that a little oil in the diet from frying doesn't hurt.

| SHOPPING LIST | |
|---|---|
| Regularly Kept in the Kitchen (Listed in Chapter 14, p. 703) | Fresh Produce |
| Safflower oil<br>Honey<br>Soy sauce | Shallots or green onions<br>Hot red chili<br>Spinach, choy sum,<br>   ong choy or other dark<br>   green, leafy vegetable |

# NUTRITIONAL ANALYSIS FOR ONE SERVING
## INDONESIAN-STYLE GREENS

| NUTRIENT | Type: 14 FEMALE-23 TO 51 YEARS | % RDA | Amount |
|---|---|---|---|
| KCALORIES | A==== | 9% | 185.0 Kc |
| PROTEIN | A======== | 16% | 7.420 Gm |
| CARBOHYDRATE | A | NO RDA | 11.60 Gm |
| FAT | A | NO RDA | 14.40 Gm |
| FIBER-CRUDE | A | NO RDA | 2.370 Gm |
| CHOLESTEROL | A | NO RDA | 0.000 Mg |
| SATURATED FA | A | NO RDA | 1.410 Gm |
| OLEIC FA | A | NO RDA | 1.610 Gm |
| LINOLEIC FA | A | NO RDA | 10.00 Gm |
| SODIUM | A========== | 20% | 440.0 Mg |
| POTASSIUM | A================== | 36% | 1373 Mg |
| MAGNESIUM | A=============================== | 62% | 188.0 Mg |
| IRON | A================== | 37% | 6.750 Mg |
| ZINC | A==== | 8% | 1.330 Mg |
| VITAMIN A | A=================================================== | 405% | 16216 IU |
| VITAMIN D | A | 0% | 0.000 IU |
| VIT. E/TOTAL | A | NO RDA | 12.00 Gm |
| VITAMIN C | A=================================================== | 163% | 98.00 Mg |
| THIAMIN | A========== | 20% | 0.200 Mg |
| RIBOFLAVIN | A================== | 39% | 0.470 Mg |
| NIACIN | A======= | 14% | 1.940 Mg |
| VITAMIN B6 | A============ | 24% | 0.490 Mg |
| FOLACIN | A=================================================== | 112% | 450.0 Ug |
| VITAMIN B12 | A | 0% | 0.000 Ug |
| PANTO- ACID | A== | 5% | 0.280 Mg |
| CALCIUM | A=============== | 30% | 241.0 Mg |
| PHOSPHORUS | A======== | 16% | 134.0 Mg |
| TRYPTOPHAN | A============================ | 58% | 96.00 Mg |
| THREONINE | A================================= | 68% | 297.0 Mg |
| ISOLEUCINE | A========================== | 54% | 354.0 Mg |
| LEUCINE | A============================== | 61% | 536.0 Mg |
| LYSINE | A================================= | 68% | 446.0 Mg |
| METHIONINE | A======================= | 47% | 128.0 Mg |
| CYSTINE | A=============== | 31% | 86.70 Mg |
| PHENYL-ANINE | A=================================== | 71% | 310.0 Mg |
| TYROSINE | A============================= | 59% | 258.0 Mg |
| VALINE | A========================= | 51% | 390.0 Mg |
| HISTIDINE | A | NO RDA | 156.0 Mg |
| ALCOHOL | A | NO RDA | 0.000 Gm |
| ASH | A | NO RDA | 4.700 Gm |
| COPPER | A====== | 12% | 0.320 Mg |
| MANGANESE | A========================== | 55% | 2.090 Mg |
| IODINE | A | 0% | 0.000 Ug |
| MONO FAT | A | NO RDA | 1.660 Gm |
| POLY FAT | A | NO RDA | 10.40 Gm |
| CAFFEINE | A | NO RDA | 0.000 Mg |
| FLUORIDE | A==== | 8% | 236.0 Ug |
| MOLYBDENUM | A======== | 17% | 57.50 Ug |
| VITAMIN K | A=================================================== | 192% | 202.0 Ug |
| SELENIUM | A | 0% | 0.000 Ug |
| BIOTIN | A===== | 10% | 16.30 Ug |
| CHLORIDE | A | 0% | 0.560 Mg |
| CHROMIUM | A================ | 32% | 0.040 Mg |
| SUGAR | A | NO RDA | 1.830 Gm |
| FIBER-DIET | A | NO RDA | 7.250 Gm |
| VIT. E/AT | A=================================================== | 110% | 8.870 Mg |

% RDA:  |0        |20      |40      |60      |80      |100

Green onions used instead of shallots; spinach used as the green.

# SATE
# SWEET·HOT·SOUR SAUCE

☆ A real tongue zapper!

1½ cups coarsely chopped shallots
   or green onions
4 cloves garlic
6 - 8 fresh hot red chili peppers
2 Tbsp. grated fresh ginger root or 2 slivers
   dry galanga root, the size of quarters

3 Tbsp. tamarind paste
⅓ cup Barbados molasses
¼ cup soy sauce
⅓ cup water
¼ tsp. ground coriander
¼ tsp. black pepper

Grind first 4 ingredients together into a thick paste in a
large mortar and pestle or a blender. Add next 6 ingredients
and mix thoroughly. Dip Sate Kabobs into this sauce and
then place on grill (or under broiler) for about 3 minutes,
baste with sauce again, turn Sate Kabobs and grill (or broil)
another 3 minutes.

Remove from heat straight onto a bed of Golden Turmeric
Rice and baste again with the sauce. Serve a small bowl of this
sauce (about 2 tablespoons) along with the rice and Sate
Kabobs for individuals to pour more over their kabobs if
they desire.

This makes enough sauce for about 4 servings, providing
several kabobs per person.

| SHOPPING LIST | |
|---|---|
| **Regularly Kept in the Kitchen** (Listed in Chapter 14, p. 703) | **Fresh Produce** |
| Soy sauce | Shallots or green onions |
| Barbados molasses | Garlic |
| Ground coriander | Hot red chilies |
| Black pepper | Ginger or galanga root |

| Special Shopping |
|---|
| Tamarind paste — can be found in most East Indian food stores. |

# NUTRITIONAL ANALYSIS FOR ONE RECIPE
## SWEET-HOT-SOUR SAUCE

```
NUTRIENT        Type: 14   FEMALE-23 TO 51 YEARS          % RDA   Amount
KCALORIES       A===                                        6%   138.0 Kc
PROTEIN         A====                                       9%   4.210 Gm
CARBOHYDRATE    A                                        NO RDA  33.20 Gm
FAT             A                                        NO RDA  0.300 Gm
FIBER-CRUDE     A                                        NO RDA  2.140 Gm
CHOLESTEROL     A                                        NO RDA  0.000 Mg
SATURATED FA    A                                        NO RDA  0.040 Gm
OLEIC FA        A                                        NO RDA  0.000 Gm
LINOLEIC FA     A                                        NO RDA  0.000 Gm
SODIUM          A=========================                 47%   1044 Mg
POTASSIUM       A=========                                 19%   733.0 Mg
MAGNESIUM       A=======                                   14%   43.80 Mg
IRON            A==========                                20%   3.610 Mg
ZINC            A=                                          3%   0.450 Mg
VITAMIN A       A================================          62%   2484 IU
VITAMIN D       A                                           0%   0.000 IU
VIT. E/TOTAL    A                                        NO RDA  0.120 Mg
VITAMIN C       A===================================================  348%  209.0 Mg
THIAMIN         A=======                                   15%   0.150 Mg
RIBOFLAVIN      A=======                                   14%   0.170 Mg
NIACIN          A=====                                     11%   1.510 Mg
VITAMIN B6      A=======                                   15%   0.310 Mg
FOLACIN         A===                                        6%   25.50 Ug
VITAMIN B12     A                                           0%   0.000 Ug
PANTO- ACID     A====                                       9%   0.530 Mg
CALCIUM         A=====                                     11%   92.50 Mg
PHOSPHORUS      A======                                    13%   110.0 Mg
TRYPTOPHAN      A=========                                 18%   30.50 Mg
THREONINE       A===========                               20%   90.20 Mg
ISOLEUCINE      A======                                    13%   87.50 Mg
LEUCINE         A=======                                   15%   133.0 Mg
LYSINE          A==============                            28%   186.0 Mg
METHIONINE      A====                                       9%   26.20 Mg
CYSTINE         A=====                                     11%   32.50 Mg
PHENYL-ANINE    A========                                  17%   76.50 Mg
TYROSINE        A======                                    12%   54.70 Mg
VALINE          A======                                    13%   106.0 Mg
HISTIDINE       A                                        NO RDA  47.50 Mg
ALCOHOL         A                                        NO RDA  0.000 Gm
ASH             A                                        NO RDA  3.460 Gm
COPPER          A========                                  16%   0.420 Mg
MANGANESE       A==                                         4%   0.180 Mg
IODINE          A                                           0%   0.000 Ug
MONO FAT        A                                        NO RDA  0.030 Gm
POLY FAT        A                                        NO RDA  0.100 Gm
CAFFEINE        A                                        NO RDA  0.000 Mg
FLUORIDE        A                                           0%   22.50 Ug
MOLYBDENUM      A                                           0%   0.000 Ug
VITAMIN K       A                                           0%   0.000 Ug
SELENIUM        A============                              24%   0.030 Mg
BIOTIN          A=                                          2%   3.870 Ug
CHLORIDE        A                                           0%   0.360 Mg
CHROMIUM        A                                           0%   0.000 Mg
SUGAR           A                                        NO RDA  2.100 Gm
FIBER-DIET      A                                        NO RDA  0.000 Gm
VIT. E/AT       A                                           1%   0.150 Mg

    % RDA:   |0      |20      |40      |60      |80      |100
```

Green onions used instead of shallots; fresh ginger used instead of dry galanga root.

# SATE KABOBS

*1" cubes Flavored Deep-Fried Tempeh*

*Whole mushrooms*
*2" squares bell pepper*
*Whole cherry or plum tomatoes*

*2" cubes fresh pineapple (optional)*
*Whole water chestnuts (optional)*

Arrange some or all of the ingredients listed on bamboo skewers in whatever order or pattern you desire. (Bamboo is preferable to metal because metal heats and cooks the vegetables also from the inside, which causes them to fall off easier.)

Dip in Sate Sweet-Hot-Sour Sauce and grill for about 3 minutes. Baste with sauce again, turn kabob, and grill another 3 minutes or till all sides begin to get singed. Place kabobs on beds of Golden Turmeric rice and baste with sauce again.

| SHOPPING LIST | |
|---|---|
| **Regularly Kept in the Kitchen** (Listed in Chapter 14, p. 703) | **Fresh Produce** |
| Tempeh | Mushrooms Bell peppers Cherry or plum tomatoes Pineapple |

**Special Shopping**

Canned water chestnuts — in Japanese or Chinese groceries or the Oriental food aisles of supermarkets.

# INDONESIAN MEAL·IN·ONE SALAD

☆ Indonesians don't toss their salads as we do, but arrange each ingredient in separate piles on a plate (taking into consideration the aesthetics — which colored vegtables look good next to each other) with a small bowl of the dressing. Each person eats the salad by dipping selected pieces of salad into the dressing. I suppose the more Westernized way to eat this salad would be to pour the dressing over the vegetables and tempeh and mix them up a bit before eating! Either way it's done, this is a delicious meal or — made in smaller quantities — side dish.

---

*Golden fried pieces of Chinese firm tofu*
*and/or 1" cubes or strips of Flavored*
*Deep-Fried Tempeh*

*Raw mung bean sprouts*
*Raw cucumber, grated crosswise*
*into ⅛"-thick circles*
*Raw tomato wedges*
*Steamed ½" cubes potato*
*Steamed spinach, coarsely chopped*
*Steamed green beans, slivered*
*Steamed Chinese or regular cabbage, shredded*
*Steamed Chinese peas*
*Steamed carrot matchsticks*

Neatly arrange tofu and/or tempeh along with about 6 of the above ingredients — or any other favorite vegetable in season — in separate piles on each individual salad plate (the amounts of each are left to your discretion). Serve the following Peanut Dressing in a small bowl (about ¼ cup per person) for each individual serving and allow each person to pour the dressing on their salad as they like.

| SHOPPING LIST | |
|---|---|
| **Regularly Kept in the Kitchen** (Listed in Chapter 14, p. 703) | **Fresh Produce** |
| Tofu or tempeh | Mung bean sprouts |
| | Cucumbers |
| | Tomatoes |
| | Potatoes |
| | Spinach . |
| | Green beans |
| | Napa cabbage (bok choy) or regular cabbage |
| | Snow peas |
| | Carrots |

# PEANUT DRESSING

☆ Indonesian cooking also makes use of a lot of peanuts. George Washington Carver would be pleased!

10 fresh hot green chilies
12 cloves garlic
2 Tbsp. asafetida or garlic powder
¾ cup roasted peanuts
5 Tbsp. soy sauce
¼ cup lemon or lime juice
¼ cup tamarind paste
2 Tbsp. honey
⅝ cup water

Blend all ingredients together in a blender till smooth. The sauce should be the consistency of a prepared mustard, so add or subtract water as needed. This recipe makes eight ¼-cup servings.

| Special Shopping | SHOPPING LIST | |
| --- | --- | --- |
| | Regularly Kept in the Kitchen (Listed in Chapter 14, p. 703) | Fresh Produce |
| Tamarind paste — can be found in most (East) Indian food stores. | Asafetida<br>Peanuts<br>Soy sauce<br>Honey | Serrano (or other fresh, hot chilies)<br>Garlic<br>Lemons or limes |

# TEMPEH GOES WEST

RUSSIA

PACIFIC OCEAN

GCC

SAN FRANCISCO

LOS ANGELES

DALLAS

PEWAUKEE LAKE

HOUSTON

CHICAGO

Did you know that at least half of the world's population gets its protein from soybeans? And for good reason! Soybeans produce more protein per acre than just about any other kind of food, and the protein is of very high quality. The protein in soybeans about equals the protein in beef in quantity and digestibility. When the soybeans are made into tempeh, the nutritional attractions are even better.

Tempeh is a soybean product that originated in Indonesia and gives cooking with soybeans an added dimension. Tempeh is made by incubating soybeans in a friendly bacteria culture (rhizopus oligosporus) just as milk is made into yogurt with the introduction of another beneficial bacteria. The bacterial culture forms a fine white film around the soybeans, holding it together and replacing the beany flavor with a rich, mushroomy flavor. This soybean product can be sliced and cooked much like meat or chicken, to which some like to compare its new flavor. Fermenting soybeans cuts cooking time down to three minutes for stir- or deep-frying and 10 to 15 minutes for simmering or steaming, thus saving time and energy (both fuel and manual) used in the kitchen.

As more and more of us are concerned with taking care of the body through proper nutrition, exercise and living habits, we should take care not to forget *why*.

Ultimately, the reason to take care of the body must be more than to have a perfect body, as the body is bound to wither and die eventually.

Mahatma Gandhi had these thoughts to offer on why to care for the body: "I hope you clearly understand what I meant when I said you should cease to think of the body as yours. It is God's; but God has given it to you for the time being to keep it clean and healthy and to use it for His service. Take great care of the body as a trustee of God's property. Do not pamper or spoil it, fill it with dirt or overload it."

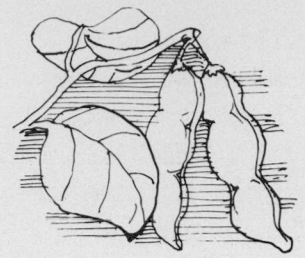

Not being limited to cooking soybeans as a lot of loose beans in a pot makes for exciting new meals with a lot of nutritional pluses added by the fermentation process. Because it is a fermented food, tempeh is a good — actually the best known in the West — vegetable source of vitamin B-12. Though nutritional amounts vary from one manufacturer to the next, a 3½-ounce serving of tempeh contains about 150 to 400 percent of the RDA for vitamin B-12. Enzymes produced by the bacterial culture actually predigest the protein in the soybeans, making them much more easy to digest. People who complain about having a hard time digesting soybeans often find they can eat tempeh with no problem. Tofu is another soybean by-product that's made easier to digest in the manufacturing process; unfortunately, when tofu is made the natural fiber of the soybean is removed. In tempeh it is left intact. These are all good reasons to find many new ways to use tempeh in everyday cooking.

Following are a few recipes for making the Tex-Mex favorite, Fajitas, with tempeh. Without that friendly bacteria, I would never have been able to slice soybeans so thin!

# TEMPEH "FAJITAS"

☆ The word "fajita" means flank steak that has been sliced very thin, but I'm slicing tempeh very thin for all the nutritional reasons described.

☆ There are directions provided for broiling this dish for those of you who are trying to avoid frying with extra oil.

---

1 lb. tempeh, sliced thin

⅝ cup soy sauce
⅝ cup red vine vinegar
⅝ cup water
2 tsp. white pepper
2 tsp. asafetida or garlic powder
2 tsp. oregano

2 Tbsp. safflower oil
4 fresh yellow chilies, halved
4 whole scallions

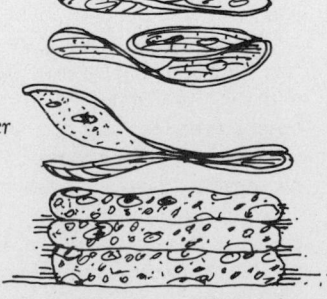

The correct pronunciation of *fajita* is fa-he-ta, not fa-je-ta, as I incorrectly said on the air.

141

2 cups tomato wedges

4 mild chilies, cut in chunks (canned
    Ortega, or prepared as in Pepper
    Antipasto Salad, p. 621)

2 Tbsp. marinade

1 Tbsp. lemon juice

1 dozen whole wheat or corn
    tortillas, steamed

1 recipe Guacamole (see recipe, p. 184)

Salsa

1 recipe Lowfat "Sour Cream"
    (see recipe, p. 186)

Shredded lettuce and alfalfa sprouts

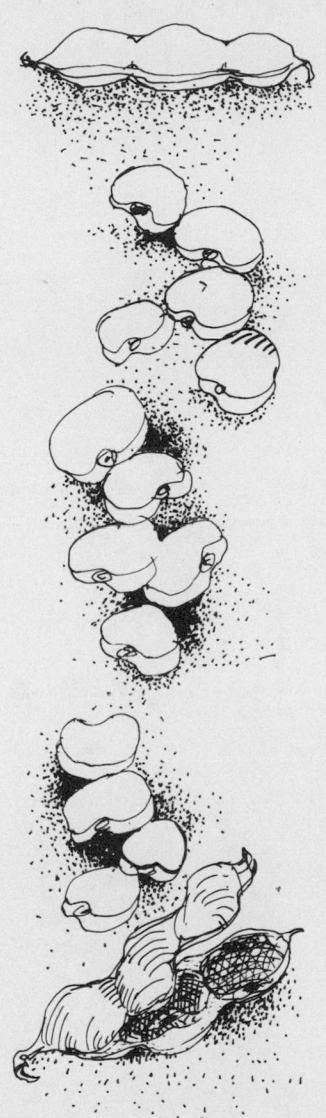

Prepare tempeh to be marinated in one of the following ways. If you plan to cook the tempeh by sauteing, slice 1 pound of tempeh into pieces about ⅛" thick and 2" to 3" long. If you wish to broil the tempeh, prick entire surface of tempeh slabs on both sides with a fork.

Make the marinade in a square cake pan by combining the next 6 ingredients. Put prepared tempeh into marinade, cover and marinate at least 6 hours or overnight in the refrigerator. Turn a few times while marinating to be sure that all surfaces are covered.

To cook, remove tempeh from marinade and reserve 2 tablespoons of the marinade in a little bowl. Cook by sauteing tempeh strips in a little oil over a medium-high heat, stirring occasionally, till nicely browned, or broil pricked slabs about 8 minutes on each side till browned and dark in spots.

A few minutes before tempeh is done cooking, heat a little oil in a separate skillet (if sauteing the tempeh) and put flame on high. Place yellow chilies and scallions in hot skillet and cook on both sides till vegetables become braised (browned) in spots and turn heat off.

Add yellow chilies to tempeh sauteing in other skillet along with tomatoes and other prepared whole chilies. Saute about 2 minutes. Lay scallions on top of mixture. Sprinkle with reserved marinade and lemon juice, remove from heat and serve immediately while still sizzling.

If broiling tempeh, add yellow chilies and scallions to the broiling pan a couple of minutes before tempeh is done cooking and cook till braised on both sides. Remove tempeh from broiler and slice into ⅛"-thick by 3"-long strips. Put a little oil in skillet and saute tempeh with yellow chilies, tomatoes and

Fajitas are a popular Tex-Mex dish that's brought to the table while still sizzling hot. This recipe makes a whole meal in itself. You'll end up with a buffet centered around the sizzling Fajitas.

other prepared whole chilies for about 2 minutes. Finish from this point as the sauteed tempeh was.

Serve sizzling tempeh buffet-style with the last 5 ingredients each in their own containers so each person can assemble their own the way they want. The idea is to lay a strip of the cooked tempeh down the center of a tortilla, top with whatever topping is desired, then roll up in the tortilla; ready to be picked up and eaten. Makes 4 to 6 servings.

| SHOPPING LIST | |
|---|---|
| Regularly Kept in the Kitchen (Listed in Chapter 14, p. 703) | Fresh Produce |
| Tempeh | Yellow chilies |
| Soy sauce | Scallions |
| Red wine vinegar | Tomatoes |
| White pepper | Anaheim or Ortega chilies |
| Oregano | Lemons |
| Safflower oil | Lettuce |
| Corn or whole wheat tortillas | Alfalfa sprouts |

Also see shopping lists for Guacamole (p. 184), Fresh Salsa, and Lowfat "Sour Cream" (p. 186).

Lemon

Lettuce

# NUTRITIONAL ANALYSIS COMPARING
# TEMPEH "FAJITAS" WITH BEEF FAJITAS*

| NUTRIENT | Type: 14 FEMALE-23 TO 51 YEARS | Amount in Tempeh "Fajitas" | Amount in beef fajitas |
|---|---|---|---|
| KCALORIES | A========================= | 900.0 Kc | 1115 Kc |
| PROTEIN | A================================================= | 47.30 Gm | 52.40 Gm |
| CARBOHYDRATE | A | 103.0 Gm | 84.00 Gm |
| FAT | A | 40.30 Gm | 68.20 Gm |
| FIBER-CRUDE | A | 10.50 Gm | 7.170 Gm |
| CHOLESTEROL | A | 5.310 Mg | 110.0 Mg |
| SATURATED FA | A | 5.770 Gm | 19.50 Gm |
| OLEIC FA | A | 14.50 Gm | 27.60 Gm |
| LINOLEIC FA | A | 11.40 Gm | 7.770 Gm |
| SODIUM | A=================================================== | 2859 Mg | 2920 Mg |
| POTASSIUM | A=============================== | 2367 Mg | 2245 Mg |
| MAGNESIUM | A====================================== | 251.0 Mg | 195.0 Mg |
| IRON | A====================== | 10.20 Mg | 10.90 Mg |
| ZINC | A================ | 4.840 Mg | 7.460 Mg |
| VITAMIN A | A=================================================== | 5572 IU | 4860 IU |
| VITAMIN D | A | 1.250 IU | 1.250 IU |
| VIT. E/TOTAL | A | 5.520 Mg | 4.620 Mg |
| VITAMIN C | A================================================ | 251.0 Mg | 251.0 Mg |
| THIAMIN | A=================================== | 0.710 Mg | 0.630 Mg |
| RIBOFLAVIN | A=========================== | 0.770 Mg | 0.850 Mg |
| NIACIN | A================================================ | 12.50 Mg | 12.60 Mg |
| VITAMIN B6 | A================================= | 1.300 Mg | 0.960 Mg |
| FOLACIN | A============================= | 259.0 Ug | 205.0 Ug |
| VITAMIN B12 | A=================== | 1.110 Ug | 1.780 Ug |
| PANTO- ACID | A=========== | 2.530 Mg | 2.130 Mg |
| CALCIUM | A====================== | 393.0 Mg | 300.0 Mg |
| PHOSPHORUS | A=============================================== | 751.0 Mg | 734.0 Mg |
| TRYPTOPHAN | A================================================ | 514.0 Mg | 423.0 Mg |
| THREONINE | A================================================ | 1695 Mg | 1688 Mg |
| ISOLEUCINE | A================================================ | 2177 Mg | 2067 Mg |
| LEUCINE | A================================================ | 3873 Mg | 3619 Mg |
| LYSINE | A================================================ | 2442 Mg | 2874 Mg |
| METHIONINE | A================================================ | 730.0 Mg | 917.0 Mg |
| CYSTINE | A================================================ | 535.0 Mg | 421.0 Mg |
| PHENYL-ANINE | A================================================ | 2024 Mg | 1682 Mg |
| TYROSINE | A================================================ | 1432 Mg | 1266 Mg |
| VALINE | A================================================ | 2196 Mg | 2174 Mg |
| HISTIDINE | A | 961.0 Mg | 1078 Mg |
| ALCOHOL | A | 0.000 Gm | 0.000 Gm |
| ASH | A | 11.90 Gm | 10.30 Gm |
| COPPER | A==================================== | 1.650 Mg | 0.940 Mg |
| MANGANESE | A============================== | 2.270 Mg | 0.650 Mg |
| IODINE | A | 564.0 Ug | 85.00 Ug |
| MONO FAT | A | 16.00 Gm | 14.10 Gm |
| POLY FAT | A | 12.80 Gm | 7.870 Gm |
| CAFFEINE | A | 0.000 Mg | 0.000 Mg |
| FLUORIDE | A= | 106.0 Ug | 106.0 Ug |
| MOLYBDENUM | A | 1588 Ug | 8.680 Ug |
| VITAMIN K | A============================ | 62.00 Ug | 62.00 Ug |
| SELENIUM | A==================== | 0.050 Mg | 0.070 Mg |
| BIOTIN | A======= | 25.40 Ug | 9.550 Ug |
| CHLORIDE | A== | 193.0 Mg | 0.460 Mg |
| CHROMIUM | A | 0.500 Mg | 0.050 Mg |
| SUGAR | A | 9.520 Gm | 9.520 Gm |
| FIBER-DIET | A | 21.80 Gm | 5.000 Gm |
| VIT. E/AT | A================================== | 5.490 Mg | 5.620 Mg |

% RDA:  0    20    40    60    80    100

Dotted line indicates Tempeh "Fajitas." Straight line indicates beef fajitas.

*Comparison is for our recipe Tempeh "Fajitas" with an equal weight of beef substituted for the tempeh.

144

# FRESH SALSA

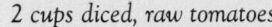

☆ This makes a fairly hot salsa; if you prefer a milder salsa, cut down on the number of Serrano chilies to suit your taste.

You can buy salsa in stores or make your own at home. If buying a commercial salsa be sure to read the label, as some of them contain sugar and/or preservatives (which we are trying to avoid!).

2 cups diced, raw tomatoes
2 cups diced, stewed tomatoes (see Moroccan Tomato-Pepper Salad, p. 420)
1 cup finely diced celery and 1 tsp. asafetida OR 1 cup diced onion
3 Tbsp. lemon juice
2 Tbsp. slivered scallions
1 Tbsp. chopped cilantro
1 Tbsp. soy sauce
2 tsp. honey
4 fresh Serrano (very hot) chilies, chopped very fine

Thoroughly mix all ingredients and refrigerate. Makes about 5 cups of salsa. (If you want to make a milder salsa, just add fewer chili peppers.)

| SHOPPING LIST | |
|---|---|
| **Regularly Kept in the Kitchen (Listed in Chapter 14, p. 703)** | **Fresh Produce** |
| Soy sauce<br>Honey | Tomatoes<br>Celery<br>Lemon<br>Scallions<br>Cilantro (same as Chinese parsley)<br>Serrano chilies |

# NUTRITIONAL ANALYSIS FOR ONE RECIPE FRESH SALSA

| NUTRIENT | Type: 14 FEMALE-23 TO 51 YEARS | % RDA | Amount |
|---|---|---|---|
| KCALORIES | A========= | 18% | 375.0 Kc |
| PROTEIN | A=============== | 30% | 13.50 Gm |
| CARBOHYDRATE | A | NO RDA | 87.20 Gm |
| FAT | A | NO RDA | 2.240 Gm |
| FIBER-CRUDE | A | NO RDA | 5.630 Gm |
| CHOLESTEROL | A | NO RDA | 0.000 Mg |
| SATURATED FA | A | NO RDA | 0.320 Gm |
| OLEIC FA | A | NO RDA | 0.000 Gm |
| LINOLEIC FA | A | NO RDA | 0.000 Gm |
| SODIUM | A===================================================== | 107% | 2369 Mg |
| POTASSIUM | A==================================== | 73% | 2749 Mg |
| MAGNESIUM | A====================== | 47% | 143.0 Mg |
| IRON | A==================== | 42% | 7.700 Mg |
| ZINC | A===== | 11% | 1.790 Mg |
| VITAMIN A | A===================================================== | 213% | 8549 IU |
| VITAMIN D | A | 0% | 0.000 IU |
| VIT. E/TOTAL | A | NO RDA | 6.550 Mg |
| VITAMIN C | A===================================================== | 373% | 224.0 Mg |
| THIAMIN | A================================ | 66% | 0.660 Mg |
| RIBOFLAVIN | A=================== | 40% | 0.480 Mg |
| NIACIN | A============================ | 58% | 7.650 Mg |
| VITAMIN B6 | A============== | 29% | 0.580 Mg |
| FOLACIN | A============= | 26% | 105.0 Ug |
| VITAMIN B12 | A | 0% | 0.000 Ug |
| PANTO- ACID | A============== | 28% | 1.560 Mg |
| CALCIUM | A================ | 32% | 262.0 Mg |
| PHOSPHORUS | A==================== | 40% | 323.0 Mg |
| TRYPTOPHAN | A================================ | 65% | 106.0 Mg |
| THREONINE | A================================== | 69% | 304.0 Mg |
| ISOLEUCINE | A======================= | 48% | 315.0 Mg |
| LEUCINE | A========================= | 51% | 451.0 Mg |
| LYSINE | A=================================== | 71% | 470.0 Mg |
| METHIONINE | A=================== | 38% | 104.0 Mg |
| CYSTINE | A============■■■■■=========== | 58% | 160.0 Mg |
| PHENYL-ANINE | A=================================== | 71% | 309.0 Mg |
| TYROSINE | A========================= | 51% | 222.0 Mg |
| VALINE | A==================== | 41% | 313.0 Mg |
| HISTIDINE | A | NO RDA | 182.0 Mg |
| ALCOHOL | A | NO RDA | 0.000 Gm |
| ASH | A | NO RDA | 12.60 Gm |
| COPPER | A==================== | 42% | 1.070 Mg |
| MANGANESE | A=========== | 22% | 0.860 Mg |
| IODINE | A | 0% | 0.000 Ug |
| MONO FAT | A | NO RDA | 0.320 Gm |
| POLY FAT | A | NO RDA | 0.910 Gm |
| CAFFEINE | A | NO RDA | 0.000 Mg |
| FLUORIDE | A==== | 8% | 234.0 Ug |
| MOLYBDENUM | A | 0% | 0.000 Ug |
| VITAMIN K | A=========== | 22% | 23.20 Ug |
| SELENIUM | A==== | 8% | 0.010 Mg |
| BIOTIN | A========= | 19% | 29.20 Ug |
| CHLORIDE | A | 0% | 0.000 Mg |
| CHROMIUM | A===================================================== | 120% | 0.150 Mg |
| SUGAR | A | NO RDA | 33.50 Gm |
| FIBER-DIET | A | NO RDA | 5.290 Gm |
| VIT. E/AT | A==================== | 42% | 3.360 Mg |

```
% RDA :  |0      |20     |40     |60     |80     |100
```

Onion was used instead of asafetida and celery in this analysis.

## SUGGESTED MENU

*Fresh tossed salad*

*Papaya Zinger (p. 30)*

*Tempehtillas*

# TEMPEHTILLAS

☆ This recipe turns the Tempeh "Fajitas" into a gourmet dish by adding a few extra ingredients to them and topping with the Heavenly Pepper Sauce.

---

*1 recipe Tempeh Fajitas,*
  *cooked and diced*

*½ cup slivered scallions*
*⅓ cup diced, chopped chilies (canned*
  *Ortega, or prepared as in Pepper*
  *Antipasto Salad, p. 621)*
*¼ cup roasted almonds*
*2 Tbsp. dried currants*

*1 cup mashed Chinese firm tofu*
  *(about ½ lb.)*
*1 tsp. black pepper*
*1 tsp. Spike or other vegetable-seasoned salt*
*¼ tsp. cinnamon*

*1 recipe Heavenly Pepper Sauce*
*½ lb. mild Cheddar cheese, grated*
*1 - 2 dozen corn tortillas*

Prepare 1 recipe's worth of the Tempeh Fajitas but dice tempeh into ¼" to ½" cubes instead of slices.

Combine next 4 ingredients in blender or food processor and chop till the almonds are finely and evenly chopped.

Pour into a mixing bowl, add next 4 ingredients and the cooked Tempeh Fajitas and mix thoroughly but gently, so as not to break tempeh cubes. Set mixture aside.

Prepare Heavenly Pepper Sauce (see following recipe). Grate cheese. Preheat oven to 450 degrees. Prepare soft tortillas by heating a small skillet (one that's only a little larger than the diameter of the tortilla). Drop about ½ teaspoon of margarine (or vegetable or olive oil) into skillet, drop a tortilla on top of the oil and spin tortilla with fingertips. Allow to cook about 5 seconds, flip and allow to cook about 10 seconds. Remove from heat and set on plate with a bowl inverted over it to keep it warm and moist. Do all the tortillas in this way (don't steam, as it makes the tortillas too tough for this recipe) and stack on top of each other under the bowl.

When all tortillas are done, assemble them one at a time by laying a strip (about 1" wide and ½" tall) of the tempeh mixture down the middle of the tortilla. Fold bare sides of the tortilla over the filling and place in baking utensil with fold side down. You can lay these side by side with sides touching in a rectangular cake tray, or place about 3 rolls on individual oven-proof plates (which the food will be served on). Stuff as many as needed, providing about 3 per serving, then pour Heavenly Pepper Sauce over the tortillas. Sprinkle with grated cheese and bake at 450 degrees till cheese melts. Serve immediately. Makes about 4 servings.

There's so much nutrition packed into these Tempehtillas that they make almost a whole meal-in-one dish made complete served alongside a fresh salad.

| SHOPPING LIST | |
|---|---|
| **Regularly Kept in the Kitchen** (Listed in Chapter 14, p. 703) | **Fresh Produce** |
| Almonds<br>Currants<br>Tofu<br>Black pepper<br>Spike<br>Cinnamon<br>Mild Cheddar cheese<br>Corn tortillas | Scallions<br>Anaheim or Ortega chilies |

Also see shopping lists for Tempeh "Fajitas" and Heavenly Pepper Sauce.

# NUTRITIONAL ANALYSIS FOR ONE SERVING TEMPEHTILLAS
## (including Tempeh "Fajitas," three corn tortillas and
## Heavenly Pepper Sauce)

| NUTRIENT | Type: 14   FEMALE—23 TO 51 YEARS | % RDA | Amount |
|---|---|---|---|
| KCALORIES | A============================= | 52% | 1042 Kc |
| PROTEIN | A====================================================== | 137% | 60.60 Gm |
| CARBOHYDRATE | A | NO RDA | 103.0 Gm |
| FAT | A | NO RDA | 49.10 Gm |
| FIBER—CRUDE | A | NO RDA | 11.00 Gm |
| CHOLESTEROL | A | NO RDA | 59.70 Mg |
| SATURATED FA | A | NO RDA | 15.20 Mg |
| OLEIC FA | A | NO RDA | 7.620 Gm |
| LINOLEIC FA | A | NO RDA | 11.80 Gm |
| SODIUM | A========================================================= | 141% | 3122 Mg |
| POTASSIUM | A======================== | 47% | 1791 Mg |
| MAGNESIUM | A================================================= | 94% | 284.0 Mg |
| IRON | A=================================================== | 98% | 17.80 Mg |
| ZINC | A========================= | 48% | 7.340 Mg |
| VITAMIN A | A=================================================== | 291% | 11662 IU |
| VITAMIN D | A | 0% | 0.000 IU |
| VIT. E/TOTAL | A | NO RDA | 5.140 Mg |
| VITAMIN C | A================================================= | 323% | 194.0 Mg |
| THIAMIN | A================================= | 63% | 0.630 Mg |
| RIBOFLAVIN | A==================================== | 72% | 0.870 Mg |
| NIACIN | A============================================ | 88% | 11.50 Mg |
| VITAMIN B6 | A========================= | 48% | 0.970 Mg |
| FOLACIN | A================== | 34% | 138.0 Ug |
| VITAMIN B12 | A==================== | 38% | 1.150 Ug |
| PANTO— ACID | A============= | 24% | 1.360 Mg |
| CALCIUM | A====================================================== | 150% | 1206 Mg |
| PHOSPHORUS | A==================================================== | 132% | 1060 Mg |
| TRYPTOPHAN | A==================================================== | 459% | 749.0 Mg |
| THREONINE | A==================================================== | 492% | 2144 Mg |
| ISOLEUCINE | A==================================================== | 453% | 2960 Mg |
| LEUCINE | A==================================================== | 573% | 4996 Mg |
| LYSINE | A==================================================== | 526% | 3439 Mg |
| METHIONINE | A==================================================== | 345% | 941.0 Mg |
| CYSTINE | A==================================================== | 236% | 643.0 Mg |
| PHENYL—ANINE | A==================================================== | 635% | 2763 Mg |
| TYROSINE | A==================================================== | 453% | 1972 Mg |
| VALINE | A==================================================== | 395% | 3012 Mg |
| HISTIDINE | A | NO RDA | 1458 Mg |
| ALCOHOL | A | NO RDA | 0.000 Gm |
| ASH | A | NO RDA | 12.60 Gm |
| COPPER | A=================================== | 66% | 1.660 Mg |
| MANGANESE | A======================================= | 75% | 2.820 Mg |
| IODINE | A=================================================== | 436% | 654.0 Ug |
| MONO FAT | A | NO RDA | 12.30 Gm |
| POLY FAT | A | NO RDA | 15.70 Gm |
| CAFFEINE | A | NO RDA | 0.000 Mg |
| FLUORIDE | A= | 2% | 79.30 Ug |
| MOLYBDENUM | A=================================================== | 720% | 2343 Ug |
| VITAMIN K | A== | 5% | 5.820 Ug |
| SELENIUM | A==================== | 40% | 0.050 Mg |
| BIOTIN | A========= | 16% | 24.00 Ug |
| CHLORIDE | A==== | 9% | 312.0 Mg |
| CHROMIUM | A=================================================== | 544% | 0.680 Mg |
| SUGAR | A | NO RDA | 6.900 Gm |
| FIBER—DIET | A | NO RDA | 18.20 Gm |
| VIT. E/AT | A======================== | 47% | 3.820 Mg |

```
% RDA:  |0      |20     |40     |60     |80     |100
```

Analysis for Heavenly Pepper Sauce does not include the optional Lowfat "Sour Cream." Safflower oil was used instead of margarine.

# HEAVENLY PEPPER SAUCE

☆ Don't limit use of this sauce to just Tempehtillas; it makes a heavenly addition to anything from other Mexican dishes to steamed vegetables.

---

Water
6 whole, dried New Mexican chilies

1 tsp. margarine or safflower oil
2 large red bell peppers, diced
6 Serrano chilies, chopped fine
2 jalapeno chilies, chopped fine
2 tsp. asafetida or 2 cloves garlic, crushed

1½ Tbsp. red wine vinegar
2 tsp. Spike or other vegetable-seasoned salt
2 tsp. chili powder
1½ tsp. grain coffee
½ tsp. oregano
½ tsp. ground cumin
¼ tsp. cayenne
12 cilantro leaves

½ cup Lowfat "Sour Cream" (p. 186), optional

Fill a 2-quart saucepan about ⅔ full with water. Place whole dried New Mexican chilies (the very large red ones) in water. Bring to a boil and boil chilies for about 5 minutes, being sure to push chilies down and submerge in boiling water. Cover and remove from heat, allowing to steep for at least 25 minutes.

In the meantime, combine next 5 ingredients in a skillet and saute over a low heat. If you want a mild sauce, core and deseed the Serrano and jalapeno chilies before chopping and/or use fewer chilies. For a truly hot sauce, use seeds and cores as they are the very hot part of the pepper. Cover skillet and simmer for 10 minutes, stirring occasionally to prevent sticking.

Put next 8 ingredients in blender. Pour in sauteed peppers. Remove boiled New Mexican chilies from water, slit open and, with a spoon, scrape the pulp from the peel into the blender. Blend all ingredients till they are pureed. Use the sauce as is, or for a creamier sauce, fold in ½ cup Lowfat "Sour Cream." This is an excellent garnish on any Mexican-type dish. Makes about 2 to 3 cups of sauce.

| Special Shopping |
| --- |
| Whole, dry New Mexican chilies — found in supermarkets that cater to Mexican clientele; sometimes strung on long strands in gourmet food stores. |

| SHOPPING LIST | |
| --- | --- |
| **Regularly Kept in the Kitchen (Listed in Chapter 14, p. 703)** | **Fresh Produce** |
| Margarine or safflower oil<br>Asafetida<br>Red wine vinegar<br>Spike<br>Chili powder<br>Grain coffee<br>Oregano<br>Ground cumin<br>Cayenne | Red bell peppers<br>Serrano chilies<br>Jalapeno chilies<br>Cilantro (same as Chinese parsley) |

Also see shopping list for Lowfat "Sour Cream" (p. 186).

# CHOLESTEROL-FREE NOUVELLE CUISINE

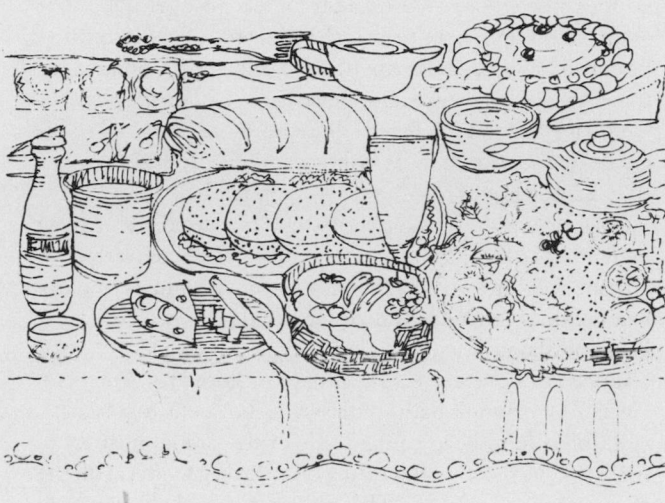

Today, when world peace is such a pressing issue, these words from "Maximus Supremes" give us a new slant on how to go about attaining it. "When a man finds no peace within himself, it is useless to seek it elsewhere."

Although there are exciting and exotic food and cooking methods to be found around the world, somehow or other gourmet cooking has become almost synonymous in our minds with French cuisine. All arts reflect the pulse of the times, and French cooking is no exception. French cooking, which traditionally dished out meat, eggs, cheese, butter and cream with a heavy hand, has had to lighten up a bit in recent years to keep in step with the issue of cholesterol and fat in the diet. This lighter version of French cuisine, which uses meat, eggs, cheese, butter and cream in lesser amounts, has been dubbed "Nouvelle Cuisine."

Guidelines for those watching their cholesterol intake, whether guided by their own wisdom for preventive measures or under a doctor's guidance, tell us that even "Nouvelle Cuisine" isn't light enough. The American Heart Association has introduced a three-part plan to help people lower or better manage their serum cholesterol levels.

## CHOLESTEROL-FREE NOUVELLE CUISINE MENU

*Cholesterol-Free
Spinach Quiche*

*Hot Vegi-Bacon Dressing*

*Pure Karrot-Gold Cake
topped with
Tofu Whipped Topping*

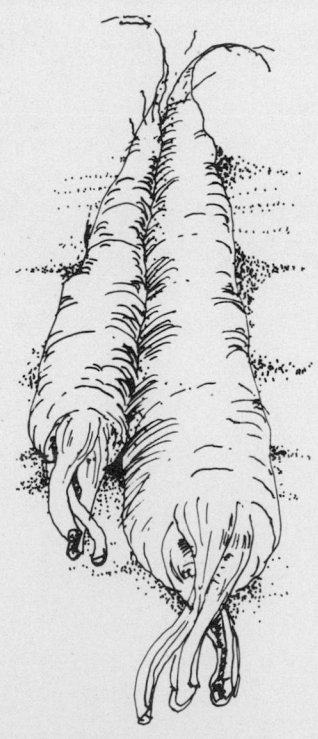

The first phase — the most excessive one in the plan — allows no more than 300 milligrams of cholesterol to be consumed in a day. This is what they recommend as a preventive diet meant for those interested in guarding their health; especially recommended for those whose cholesterol level is higher than average, or who have a family history of any coronary heart disease risk factors (like hypertension, hyperlipidemia, etc.), or have habits that increase the risk factor, like smoking cigarettes, etc. Phase II, especially recommended for those whose total cholesterol level is over 250 milligrams, allows no more than 200 milligrams of cholesterol to be consumed in a day. Phase III, especially recommended for those whose total cholesterol level is over 275 milligrams or who have a high LDL level, allows no more than 100 milligrams of cholesterol to be consumed in a day and no more than 22 percent of calories to be supplied by fat.

Eggs are one of the most cholesterol-rich food; a single egg contains 252 to 275 milligrams of cholesterol. Clearly eggs are one food it would be better to live without, as one egg nearly exhausts the day's cholesterol budget in even the most liberal allotment recommended by the American Heart Association. And there are some that consider the American Heart Association's daily cholesterol allotment too high!

To be able to keep eating some of the old familiar food, some people recommend eating only the egg white, as all the cholesterol is in the yolk. That's like throwing half your food budget away. Besides the foolishness of spending money to buy something you're going to throw half of away, eggs are a bad bargain for other reasons. They can contain salmonella bacteria, which makes the idea of eating raw eggs, as some health nuts promote, a bad one.

Although a lot of people have obviously developed a taste for eggs, they're not an appetizing food when you really think about it. In reality, a fertilized egg is an embryo — a baby bird — and an unfertilized egg is the menstrual period of a chicken.

Consider that and you may not be able to look at an egg in the same way again! But eliminating eggs from the shopping list doesn't mean having to leave any of your favorite food behind. I replace eggs in baking cakes, cookies, etc., with 2 to 3 tablespoons of yogurt per egg. This adds moisture to the product; and when the baked good begins warming in the oven, the bacteria in the yogurt start to multiply and grow, resulting in a light, leavened dish. I replace cooked egg dishes with tofu. Until recently, the only thing I couldn't do was whip up a meringue; now I can even do that with a whey-protein product that will be coming out on the market soon!

Though they've never had eggs, my family frequently requests meals centered around eggs, such as this cholesterol-free menu centered around an eggless quiche. Completely cholesterol-free Nouvelle Cuisine is a delicious possibility.

# CHOLESTEROL-FREE SPINACH QUICHE

☆ A completely eggless quiche; try making variations by changing vegetables and spicing. Remember . . . adding cheese will put cholesterol into this dish!

---

1 cup whole wheat flour
⅛ cup bran
⅜ cup margarine or butter

4 - 5 Tbsp. ice water

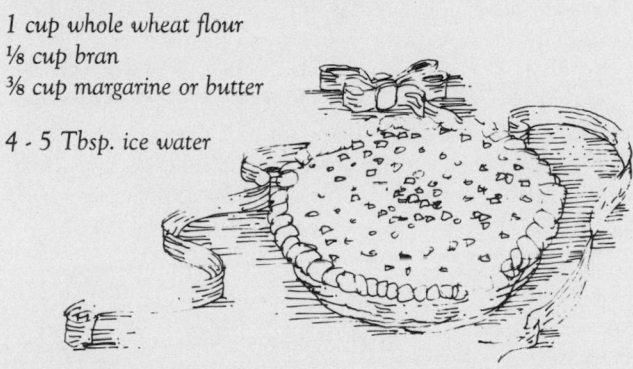

**Filling:**

1 Tbsp. margarine or butter
2 fresh scallions or green onions,
    chopped fine
10 cups finely chopped raw spinach leaves

½ cup water
¼ cup nutritional yeast
¼ cup Bipro
1 tsp. curry powder
1½ tsp. Spike or other vegetable-seasoned salt
2¼ cups mashed Chinese firm tofu

1 Tbsp. prepared Dijon mustard

⅛ cup nutritional yeast

Paprika

Besides not adding cholesterol to the system, recipes like this can actually help to remove cholesterol and fat from the system. Dietary fiber absorbs cholesterol and fat and takes them out of the body.

Preheat oven to 400 degrees. In the meantime, combine first 3 ingredients in bowl and, using fingertips or a pastry cutter, cut margarine or butter into flour till flour is a sand-like texture. Pour in ice water and mix till dough forms a crumbly ball. Roll ball out between 2 squares of wax paper to fit in a 9" pie pan. Place crust in pie pan, form edges, and prick with fork. Bake in preheated oven at 400 degrees for 10 minutes. While the crust is baking, wash and chop spinach and scallions and stir-fry next 3 ingredients over a very high heat till the spinach wilts down. (This amount will shrink down to about 2 cups. You can use 2 cups of frozen spinach instead, and just saute in pan long enough to wilt the scallions and warm the spinach.) This will take only a couple of minutes. Turn heat off spinach and blend next 6 ingredients together in a blender till smooth.

Remove crust from oven and turn heat down to 375 degrees. Spread the tablespoon of mustard evenly over the bottom of the crust. Take about a cup of the wilted spinach and spread it evenly over the bottom of the crust. Sprinkle ⅛ cup of nutritional yeast evenly over this spinach. Fold the rest of the wilted spinach into the blended tofu mixture and pour over the layer of spinach in the bottom of the pie pan. Spread the tofu mixture out evenly and sprinkle the top with paprika. Bake at 375 degrees for 30 to 40 minutes. Let the Quiche sit about 10 minutes before cutting. This is also delicious served cold. Makes one 9" pie — ample servings for 4.

| SHOPPING LIST | |
|---|---|
| **Regularly Kept in the Kitchen** (Listed in Chapter 14, p. 703) | **Fresh Produce** |
| Whole wheat flour<br>Bran<br>Margarine or butter<br>Nutritional yeast<br>Bipro<br>Curry powder<br>Spike<br>Tofu<br>Dijon mustard | Scallions<br>Spinach (fresh or frozen) |

# NUTRITIONAL ANALYSIS COMPARING OUR SPINACH QUICHE WITH SPINACH QUICHE (usually made with eggs, cheese and milk)

| NUTRIENT | Type: 14 FEMALE-23 TO 51 YEARS | Amount in our Spinach Quiche | Amount in spinach quiche made with eggs |
|---|---|---|---|
| KCALORIES | | 576.0 Kc | 697.0 Kc |
| PROTEIN | | 39.40 Gm | 25.50 Gm |
| CARBOHYDRATE | | 39.60 Gm | 40.50 Gm |
| FAT | | 33.70 Gm | 49.00 Gm |
| FIBER-CRUDE | | 2.520 Gm | 1.620 Gm |
| CHOLESTEROL | | 0.050 Mg | 264.0 Mg |
| SATURATED FA | | 5.240 Gm | 19.40 Gm |
| OLEIC FA | | 1.530 Gm | 17.40 Gm |
| LINOLEIC FA | | 3.200 Gm | 7.150 Gm |
| SODIUM | | 753.0 Mg | 1826 Mg |
| POTASSIUM | | 1529 Mg | 972.0 Mg |
| MAGNESIUM | | 262.0 Mg | 144.0 Mg |
| IRON | | 20.80 Mg | 6.950 Mg |
| ZINC | | 5.830 Mg | 3.570 Mg |
| VITAMIN A | | 10500 IU | 11573 IU |
| VITAMIN D | | 0.000 IU | 42.00 IU |
| VIT. E/TOTAL | | 5.550 Mg | 29.00 Mg |
| VITAMIN C | | 40.70 Mg | 30.00 Mg |
| THIAMIN | | 7.270 Mg | 0.450 Mg |
| RIBOFLAVIN | | 7.210 Mg | 0.780 Mg |
| NIACIN | | 42.40 Mg | 3.070 Mg |
| VITAMIN B6 | | 7.280 Mg | 0.410 Mg |
| FOLACIN | | 419.0 Ug | 207.0 Ug |
| VITAMIN B12 | | 5.270 Ug | 1.270 Ug |
| PANTO- ACID | | 1.610 Mg | 1.520 Mg |
| CALCIUM | | 1154 Mg | 620.0 Mg |
| PHOSPHORUS | | 650.0 Mg | 573.0 Mg |
| TRYPTOPHAN | | 611.0 Mg | 360.0 Mg |
| THREONINE | | 1658 Mg | 948.0 Mg |
| ISOLEUCINE | | 1937 Mg | 1288 Mg |
| LEUCINE | | 3089 Mg | 2166 Mg |
| LYSINE | | 2607 Mg | 1906 Mg |
| METHIONINE | | 591.0 Mg | 602.0 Mg |
| CYSTINE | | 607.0 Mg | 320.0 Mg |
| PHENYL-ANINE | | 1848 Mg | 1304 Mg |
| TYROSINE | | 1439 Mg | 1160 Mg |
| VALINE | | 2089 Mg | 1506 Mg |
| HISTIDINE | | 1074 Mg | 777.0 Mg |
| ALCOHOL | | 0.000 Gm | 0.000 Gm |
| ASH | | 11.60 Gm | 6.000 Gm |
| COPPER | | 0.890 Mg | 0.490 Mg |
| MANGANESE | | 4.600 Mg | 1.170 Mg |
| IODINE | | 326.0 Ug | 131.0 Ug |
| MONO FAT | | 12.00 Gm | 18.00 Gm |
| POLY FAT | | 13.60 Gm | 7.800 Gm |
| CAFFEINE | | 0.000 Mg | 0.000 Mg |
| FLUORIDE | | 137.0 Ug | 243.0 Ug |
| MOLYBDENUM | | 3625 Ug | 41.00 Ug |
| VITAMIN K | | 122.0 Ug | 106.0 Ug |
| SELENIUM | | 0.030 Mg | 0.020 Mg |
| BIOTIN | | 30.00 Ug | 20.30 Ug |
| CHLORIDE | | 331.0 Mg | 0.210 Mg |
| CHROMIUM | | 0.670 Mg | 0.050 Mg |
| SUGAR | | 0.690 Gm | 4.600 Gm |
| FIBER-DIET | | 10.00 Gm | 2.700 Gm |
| VIT. E/AT | | 2.900 Mg | 6.550 Mg |

% RDA:  |0  |20  |40  |60  |80  |100

Dotted line indicates our Cholesterol-Free Spinach Quiche. Straight line indicates spinach quiche usually made with eggs, cheese and milk. Comparison is for an equal gram weight of both.

# HOT VEGI·BACON DRESSING

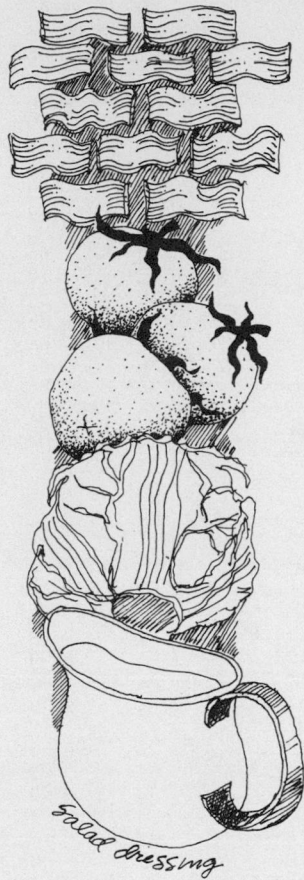

salad dressing

½ cup soy sauce
½ Tbsp. liquid smoke
1 cup soaked ¾" x 2" dried bean curd
   (yuba) strips

1 large head of lettuce, torn
2 cups chopped watercress
2 cups whole cherry tomatoes

¼ cup olive oil
1 Tbsp. apple cider vinegar
½ tsp. honey

A few minutes before serving time, combine first 3 ingredients and allow to soak together for a few minutes. In the meantime, combine salad fixings (using ones suggested in recipe or your favorites). The proportion of salad vegetables to yuba strips should be kept pretty much the same if you vary the vegetable ingredients. Heat olive oil in a skillet and lift yuba sheets out of soy sauce mixture (there should be some left for use at another time) to fry in olive oil. Fry over medium-high heat, stirring constantly till yuba turns a golden brown and one piece lifted out of pan turns crisp in a matter of seconds. (Yuba must be removed from heat before it will crisp.) Be careful, because once the yuba reaches this state, it burns very quickly. Remove all yuba strips and place on a separate platter to cool a bit. Turn off heat and while pan is still hot, add vinegar and honey and stir with a spatula till much of the oil is lifted off sides of pan. Then add yuba strips and toss into salad. Serve immediately so salad greens don't wilt. Serves 4 salad lovers.

Bacon lovers can cut the cholesterol-, saturated fat- and nitrate-free yuba into strips instead of bite-sized pieces and serve for breakfast (p. 27), in BLT's, or anywhere bacon would otherwise be used.

| SHOPPING LIST | |
|---|---|
| Regularly Kept in the Kitchen (Listed in Chapter 14, p. 703) | Fresh Produce |
| Soy sauce<br>Liquid smoke<br>Yuba<br>Olive oil<br>Apple cider vinegar<br>Honey | Lettuce<br>Watercress<br>Cherry tomatoes |

# NUTRITIONAL ANALYSIS FOR ONE SERVING
# SALAD WITH HOT VEGI-BACON DRESSING

| NUTRIENT | Type: 14   FEMALE-23 TO 51 YEARS | % RDA | Amount |
|---|---|---|---|
| KCALORIES | A===== | 10% | 203.0 Kc |
| PROTEIN | A========= | 19% | 8.490 Gm |
| CARBOHYDRATE | A | NO RDA | 12.20 Gm |
| FAT | A | NO RDA | 15.00 Gm |
| FIBER-CRUDE | A | NO RDA | 1.320 Gm |
| CHOLESTEROL | A | NO RDA | 0.000 Mg |
| SATURATED FA | A | NO RDA | 1.980 Gm |
| OLEIC FA | A | NO RDA | 9.900 Gm |
| LINOLEIC FA | A | NO RDA | 1.630 Gm |
| SODIUM | A================================================== | 94% | 2084 Mg |
| POTASSIUM | A========= | 19% | 717.0 Mg |
| MAGNESIUM | A======== | 16% | 48.90 Mg |
| IRON | A======== | 17% | 3.170 Mg |
| ZINC | A | 1% | 0.220 Mg |
| VITAMIN A | A======================================================= | 111% | 4477 IU |
| VITAMIN D | A | 0% | 0.000 IU |
| VIT. E/TOTAL | A | NO RDA | 3.080 Mg |
| VITAMIN C | A========================================== | 83% | 49.90 Mg |
| THIAMIN | A========== | 21% | 0.210 Mg |
| RIBOFLAVIN | A========= | 18% | 0.220 Mg |
| NIACIN | A========= | 19% | 2.510 Mg |
| VITAMIN B6 | A=== | 7% | 0.140 Mg |
| FOLACIN | A================ | 33% | 134.0 Ug |
| VITAMIN B12 | A | 0% | 0.000 Ug |
| PANTO- ACID | A==== | 8% | 0.480 Mg |
| CALCIUM | A==== | 9% | 79.40 Mg |
| PHOSPHORUS | A=========== | 22% | 183.0 Mg |
| TRYPTOPHAN | A============== | 28% | 46.70 Mg |
| THREONINE | A======================= | 47% | 208.0 Mg |
| ISOLEUCINE | A=================== | 39% | 257.0 Mg |
| LEUCINE | A=================== | 39% | 346.0 Mg |
| LYSINE | A======================== | 49% | 324.0 Mg |
| METHIONINE | A=========== | 23% | 65.00 Mg |
| CYSTINE | A===========■■ | 23% | 63.00 Mg |
| PHENYL-ANINE | A========================== | 53% | 232.0 Mg |
| TYROSINE | A================== | 37% | 163.0 Mg |
| VALINE | A================ | 32% | 251.0 Mg |
| HISTIDINE | A | NO RDA | 121.0 Mg |
| ALCOHOL | A | NO RDA | 0.000 Gm |
| ASH | A | NO RDA | 7.430 Gm |
| COPPER | A=== | 7% | 0.190 Mg |
| MANGANESE | A==== | 10% | 0.400 Mg |
| IODINE | A===== | 10% | 15.00 Ug |
| MONO FAT | A | NO RDA | 9.980 Gm |
| POLY FAT | A | NO RDA | 1.340 Gm |
| CAFFEINE | A | NO RDA | 0.000 Mg |
| FLUORIDE | A | 1% | 47.30 Ug |
| MOLYBDENUM | A===================================================== | 142% | 462.0 Ug |
| VITAMIN K | A===================================================== | 120% | 127.0 Ug |
| SELENIUM | A | 0% | 0.000 Mg |
| BIOTIN | A== | 5% | 8.750 Ug |
| CHLORIDE | A | 0% | 7.600 Mg |
| CHROMIUM | A=================================== | 64% | 0.080 Mg |
| SUGAR | A | NO RDA | 6.770 Gm |
| FIBER-DIET | A | NO RDA | 1.870 Gm |
| VIT. E/AT | A=============== | 31% | 2.540 Mg |

```
% RDA:  |0      |20    |40    |60    |80    |100
```

158

# PURE KARROT·GOLD CAKE

☆ Okara is soybean's answer to bran; incorporating it into the diet makes for healthy as well as delicious eating, as this cake (or cupcake) recipe proves.

## HOMEMADE SOY MILK

(from *Kathy Cooks . . . Naturally* p. 358)

*2 cups soaked soybeans*
*6 cups boiling water*

Soak soybeans overnight. Pour out water and rinse. Blend beans in 4 cups of boiling water. Strain through thin muslin. Pour remaining 2 cups of boiling water through cloth. Bring milk to a boil. While coming to a boil, stir occasionally to prevent sticking on bottom. After milk starts to boil, stirring isn't necessary. Boil over medium-high heat for ½ to 1 hour. The longer it's boiled, the thicker and richer the milk will be. Makes about 1 quart.

For more recipes using okara, see *Kathy Cooks . . . Naturallly.*

1 cup okara
2 cups whole wheat flour
¾ cup honey
1 Tbsp. poppy seeds
1 tsp. vanilla

½ cup vegetable oil
3 medium-sized carrots

1½ tsp. baking soda
1½ tsp. baking powder

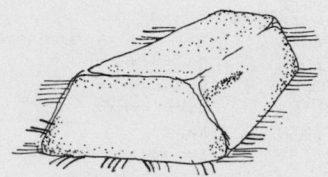

Preheat oven to 350 degrees and oil an 8" or 9" cake pan.

Combine first 5 ingredients in bowl. Blend next 2 ingredients in blender, dropping small chunks of carrot in oil one at a time till the blender shows about 1¼ to 1½ cups. Pour into the ingredients already mixed in the bowl. Add leavening. Mix enough to blend together and immediately pour into oiled cake pan (or individual muffin tins). Fill baking container only halfway up. Bake at 350 degrees for 45 minutes or till knife inserted comes out clean. Cool and frost.

| Special Shopping |
| --- |
| Okara — If you live close to a tofu factory, they usually give this away by the bucketful. Some Japanese food stores and supermarkets in Hawaii sell it by the bagful. Otherwise, make your own soy milk and save the pulp — that's what okara is. |

| SHOPPING LIST | |
| --- | --- |
| **Regularly Kept in the Kitchen** (Listed in Chapter 14, p. 703) | **Fresh Produce** |
| Honey<br>Poppy seeds<br>Vanilla extract<br>Safflower oil<br>Baking soda<br>Baking powder | Carrots |

# RAISIN ICING

☆ A different kind of an icing — full of vitamins, minerals and fiber; quite a contrast to the usual fat-laden, empty-calorie icings made with butter and sugar.

---

*2 cups boiling water*
*2 cups seedless raisins or currants*
*¼ tsp. grated lemon rind*

*1 cup water*
*4 tsp. arrowroot*

Bring water to a boil. Add raisins, turn off heat and allow to sit for 15 to 20 minutes to allow raisins to plump and soften. Pour this mixture in blender along with lemon rind and blend till smooth.

Pour back into pot and bring raisin liquid to a boil, stirring often to prevent burning. After boiling over medium heat for a few minutes, the raisin liquid will lose its cloudy appearance. At this point remove from heat and, in a separate container. mix the water and arrowroot till the arrowroot dissolves. Pour into heated raisin mixture and mix in thoroughly.

Return pot to heat and stir constantly till the pot's contents come to a boil and icing thickens. Cool and use to frost the Pure Karrot-Gold Cake (see preceding recipe). Top each serving with a dollop of Tofu Whipped Topping (see following recipe) at serving time.

| SHOPPING LIST | |
|---|---|
| **Regularly Kept in the Kitchen** (Listed in Chapter 14, p. 703) | **Fresh Produce** |
| Raisins Arrowroot | Lemon |

# NUTRITIONAL ANALYSIS FOR ONE SERVING
## PURE KARROT-GOLD CAKE WITH RAISIN ICING

```
NUTRIENT        Type: 14   FEMALE-23 TO 51 YEARS          % RDA   Amount
KCALORIES       A========                                  15%    313.0 Kc
PROTEIN         A=====                                     10%    4.530 Gm
CARBOHYDRATE    A                                        NO RDA   54.50 Gm
FAT             A                                        NO RDA   10.30 Gm
FIBER-CRUDE     A                                        NO RDA   1.520 Gm
CHOLESTEROL     A                                        NO RDA   0.000 Mg
SATURATED FA    A                                        NO RDA   0.990 Gm
OLEIC FA        A                                        NO RDA   1.130 Gm
LINOLEIC FA     A                                        NO RDA   6.860 Gm
SODIUM          A===                                        7%    168.0 Mg
POTASSIUM       A====                                       8%    330.0 Mg
MAGNESIUM       A======                                    12%    36.20 Mg
IRON            A====                                       9%    1.750 Mg
ZINC            A===                                        4%    0.680 Mg
VITAMIN A       A===================================================  126%  5064 IU
VITAMIN D       A                                           0%    0.000 IU
VIT. E/TOTAL    A                                        NO RDA   4.340 Mg
VITAMIN C       A==                                         4%    2.520 Mg
THIAMIN         A=========                                 18%    0.180 Mg
RIBOFLAVIN      A==                                         5%    0.070 Mg
NIACIN          A=====                                     10%    1.400 Mg
VITAMIN B6      A====                                       8%    0.160 Mg
FOLACIN         A=                                          3%    14.10 Ug
VITAMIN B12     A                                           0%    0.000 Ug
PANTO- ACID     A==                                         5%    0.300 Mg
CALCIUM         A=====                                     10%    83.50 Mg
PHOSPHORUS      A==========                                20%    167.0 Mg
TRYPTOPHAN      A===========                               22%    36.50 Mg
THREONINE       A==========                                20%    89.70 Mg
ISOLEUCINE      A=========                                 19%    129.0 Mg
LEUCINE         A===========                               22%    196.0 Mg
LYSINE          A=======                                   13%    87.90 Mg
METHIONINE      A========                                  16%    45.20 Mg
CYSTINE         A===========                               23%    62.80 Mg
PHENYL-ANINE    A=================                         32%    143.0 Mg
TYROSINE        A===========                               24%    107.0 Mg
VALINE          A=========                                 18%    140.0 Mg
HISTIDINE       A                                        NO RDA   60.80 Mg
ALCOHOL         A                                        NO RDA   0.000 Gm
ASH             A                                        NO RDA   1.130 Gm
COPPER          A===                                        7%    0.190 Mg
MANGANESE       A==============                            29%    1.100 Mg
IODINE          A============================              56%    84.60 Ug
MONO FAT        A                                        NO RDA   1.140 Gm
POLY FAT        A                                        NO RDA   7.010 Gm
CAFFEINE        A                                        NO RDA   0.000 Mg
FLUORIDE        A                                           1%    28.20 Ug
MOLYBDENUM      A===================================================  369%  1201 Ug
VITAMIN K       A                                           0%    0.000 Ug
SELENIUM        A                                           0%    0.000 Mg
BIOTIN          A                                           1%    2.740 Ug
CHLORIDE        A                                           1%    39.10 Mg
CHROMIUM        A===================================================  96%   0.120 Mg
SUGAR           A                                        NO RDA   0.840 Gm
FIBER-DIET      A                                        NO RDA   3.300 Gm
VIT. E/AT       A=====================                     43%    3.500 Mg

    % RDA:   |0      |20     |40     |60     |80     |100
```

# TOFU WHIPPED TOPPING

☆ Use for topping desserts and dishes you would usually add a dollop of whipped cream to.

---

1 cup mashed Chinese firm tofu
2 Tbsp. raw cashew butter
1 Tbsp. honey
¼ tsp. vanilla extract

½ tsp. lemon juice

Blend first 4 ingredients together in blender till smooth. Turn blender speed to whip and slowly drizzle lemon juice in from the top. The tofu mixture in the blender will actually solidify enough to form little peaks when a spoon is dipped in. Serve dollops on top of dishes in place of whipped cream for a nutritious, cholesterol- and chemical-free substitute. Makes a little over 1 cup.

It's nice to know that desserts can be nutritious food that nourish the body instead of empty calories that damage the body.

Whipped cream: 95% fat, 3% carbohydrate, 2% protein

Tofu Whipped Topping: 53% fat, 19% carbohydrate, 28% protein

(For other nutrients, see the graph.)

Although the Tofu Whipped Topping is lighter in fat, at 53% fat it should still obviously be reserved for special occasions.

| SHOPPING LIST | |
|---|---|
| Regularly Kept in the Kitchen (Listed in Chapter 14, p. 703) | Fresh Produce |
| Tofu<br>Raw cashew butter<br>Honey<br>Vanilla | Lemon |

# NUTRITIONAL ANALYSIS COMPARING
## TOFU WHIPPED TOPPING WITH WHIPPING CREAM

**Type: 14    FEMALE—23 TO 51 YEARS**

| NUTRIENT | Amount in Tofu Whipped Topping | Amount in whipping cream |
|---|---|---|
| KCALORIES | 619.0 Kc | 1060 Kc |
| PROTEIN | 45.40 Gm | 6.300 Gm |
| CARBOHYDRATE | 36.80 Gm | 8.580 Gm |
| FAT | 37.80 Gm | 113.0 Gm |
| FIBER—CRUDE | 0.620 Gm | 0.000 Gm |
| CHOLESTEROL | 0.000 Mg | 421.0 Mg |
| SATURATED FA | 6.300 Gm | 70.80 Gm |
| OLEIC FA | 2.520 Gm | 28.60 Gm |
| LINOLEIC FA | 5.040 Gm | 2.580 Gm |
| SODIUM | 39.00 Mg | 115.0 Mg |
| POTASSIUM | 784.0 Mg | 231.0 Mg |
| MAGNESIUM | 228.0 Mg | 21.90 Mg |
| IRON | 28.10 Mg | 0.090 Mg |
| ZINC | 5.640 Mg | 0.710 Mg |
| VITAMIN A | 418.0 IU | 4521 IU |
| VITAMIN D | 0.000 IU | 307.0 IU |
| VIT. E/TOTAL | 0.010 Mg | 1.930 Mg |
| VITAMIN C | 1.760 Mg | 1.780 Mg |
| THIAMIN | 0.500 Mg | 0.060 Mg |
| RIBOFLAVIN | 0.330 Mg | 0.330 Mg |
| NIACIN | 1.570 Mg | 0.120 Mg |
| VITAMIN B6 | 0.310 Mg | 0.080 Mg |
| FOLACIN | 95.90 Ug | 11.60 Ug |
| VITAMIN B12 | 0.000 Ug | 0.550 Ug |
| PANTO— ACID | 0.760 Mg | 0.780 Mg |
| CALCIUM | 1736 Mg | 198.0 Mg |
| PHOSPHORUS | 625.0 Mg | 192.0 Mg |
| TRYPTOPHAN | 708.0 Mg | 89.10 Mg |
| THREONINE | 1838 Mg | 284.0 Mg |
| ISOLEUCINE | 2238 Mg | 381.0 Mg |
| LEUCINE | 3492 Mg | 617.0 Mg |
| LYSINE | 2920 Mg | 500.0 Mg |
| METHIONINE | 610.0 Mg | 157.0 Mg |
| CYSTINE | 654.0 Mg | 58.10 Mg |
| PHENYL—ANINE | 2230 Mg | 304.0 Mg |
| TYROSINE | 1490 Mg | 304.0 Mg |
| VALINE | 2392 Mg | 422.0 Mg |
| HISTIDINE | 1306 Mg | 170.0 Mg |
| ALCOHOL | 0.000 Gm | 0.000 Gm |
| ASH | 4.320 Gm | 1.380 Gm |
| COPPER | 1.650 Mg | 0.000 Mg |
| MANGANESE | 2.980 Mg | 0.000 Mg |
| IODINE | 275.0 Ug | 0.000 Ug |
| MONO FAT | 14.10 Gm | 32.80 Gm |
| POLY FAT | 15.00 Gm | 4.220 Gm |
| CAFFEINE | 0.000 Mg | 0.000 Mg |
| FLUORIDE | 21.00 Ug | 92.20 Ug |
| MOLYBDENUM | 3024 Ug | 0.000 Ug |
| VITAMIN K | 0.000 Ug | 18.30 Ug |
| SELENIUM | 0.030 Mg | 0.000 Mg |
| BIOTIN | 7.310 Ug | 0.090 Ug |
| CHLORIDE | 479.0 Mg | 0.000 Mg |
| CHROMIUM | 0.760 Mg | 0.000 Mg |
| SUGAR | 0.040 Gm | 0.000 Gm |
| FIBER—DIET | 0.000 Gm | 0.000 Gm |
| VIT. E/AT | 0.000 Mg | 0.000 Mg |

% RDA:  |0    |20    |40    |60    |80    |100

Dotted line indicates Tofu Whipped Topping. Straight line indicates whipping cream. Comparison is for an equal gram weight of Tofu Whipped Topping and whipping cream.

163

# A BAGEL BUFFET

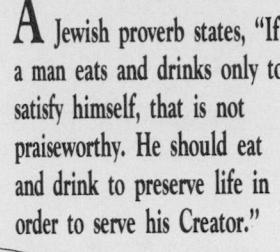

A Jewish proverb states, "If a man eats and drinks only to satisfy himself, that is not praiseworthy. He should eat and drink to preserve life in order to serve his Creator."

Bagels are a perfect bread with the emphasis on lowfat cooking nowadays . . . and when they're made with whole grains, they are doubly healthy! Since topping a lowfat whole grain bagel with lox and cream cheese would neutralize the benefits of eating such a bagel, there's a need for alternative toppings . . . like the cholesterol-free Tofu Cream Cheese, Deviled Eggless Salad and Mock Tuna Salad recipes here.

All these can be laid out on a table to make as elaborate or simple as you wish buffets. A wonderful thing about these bagel buffets is they are versatile. A bagel buffet spread can be served for breakfast, brunch, lunch, supper or late night get-togethers. That's not mentioning that whole grain bagels and cholesterol-free toppings make a satisfying anytime snack!

# BAGELS

☆ A basic recipe for whole wheat/soy bagels that, in a sense, is only as limited as your imagination. Make as many variations as you like with some of the suggested additions, or use your favorite condiments and food on or inside the bagel dough.

---

1 cup warm nut, soy, or cow's milk
¼ cup vegetable oil
1 Tbsp. honey
1 Tbsp. baking yeast
¼ tsp. salt

3¼ cups whole wheat flour
¼ cup soy flour

1 gallon water
2 Tbsp. honey

**For Variation:**
Poppy seeds
Sesame seeds
Black caraway seeds
Toasted wheat germ
Raisins
Sauteed finely chopped onion

Combine first 5 ingredients in a container and allow to sit for at least 5 minutes, or till yeast is dissolved. Combine next 2 ingredients in a mixing bowl and make a crater in the middle. Pour liquid ingredients into the crater and mix together thoroughly. When mixed, sprinkle a little flour onto dough and knead for at least 2 minutes. Pound and punch at least 3 times. Place dough back in mixing bowl and cover with a towel. Set in a warm place to rise till double in bulk. Punch down and knead again.

Break off pieces ¼-cup to ⅓-cup large and roll between palms to form a rope shape ¾" in diameter. Holding one end of the coil between thumb and forefinger, wrap coil around back of hand and pinch ends together till you can't see the seam. Place on an oiled and floured cookie sheet. When entire cookie sheet is full of bagels placed about 1" apart, put cookie sheet under a broiler for about 3 minutes.

In the meantime, bring water and honey to a boil in a wide-mouthed pot. Drop broiled bagels into gently boiling water and simmer for 15 to 20 minutes, turning over once.

Preheat oven to 375 degrees.

AN ELABORATE
BAGEL BUFFET
MENU

An assortment
of whole grain bagels

Tofu Cream Cheese and/or
a few of your favorite dips
made with
Tofu Cream Cheese

Deviled Eggless Salad

Mock Tuna Salad

Tossed salad

Platter of sprouts, sliced
avocado, onion rings,
olives, tomatoes, dill pickles

Peanut and/or other
nut butters

Assorted sugarless jams
and jellies

Remove bagels from water onto a towel to absorb extra moisture. At this point, if you want to make any of the variations, sprinkle surface of the bagel immediately with any of the suggested toppings, or any others you may want to try (except the raisins, as they must be mixed into the dough at mixing time — about ½ cup per recipe).

Place on an oiled cookie sheet and bake for 10 minutes at 375 degrees. Leaving bagels in, turn oven up to 400 degrees and bake another 10 to 15 minutes, or till they begin to turn golden brown. Makes about a dozen bagels.

| SHOPPING LIST | |
| --- | --- |
| **Regularly Kept in the Kitchen** (Listed in Chapter 14, p. 703) | **Fresh Produce** |
| Milk (or soy or nut milk) Safflower oil Honey Baking yeast Salt Whole wheat flour Sesame, poppy, caraway seeds | Raisins Onion |

| Special Shopping |
| --- |
| Soy flour — in natural food stores; soy powder is the same thing, just milled a little finer. |

# NUTRITIONAL ANALYSIS FOR TWO BAGELS

```
NUTRIENT        Type: 14   FEMALE-23 TO 51 YEARS           % RDA   Amount
KCALORIES       A=========                                  18%   366.0 Kc
PROTEIN         A==============                             27%   12.10 Gm
CARBOHYDRATE    A                                         NO RDA   58.30 Gm
FAT             A                                         NO RDA   11.20 Gm
FIBER-CRUDE     A                                         NO RDA   1.500 Gm
CHOLESTEROL     A                                         NO RDA   3.000 Mg
SATURATED FA    A                                         NO RDA   1.550 Gm
OLEIC FA        A                                         NO RDA   1.470 Gm
LINOLEIC FA     A                                         NO RDA   7.330 Gm
SODIUM          A==                                          4%   109.0 Mg
POTASSIUM       A=====                                      10%   400.0 Mg
MAGNESIUM       A==============                             26%   80.30 Mg
IRON            A=======                                    15%   2.760 Mg
ZINC            A=====                                      11%   1.780 Mg
VITAMIN A       A=                                           2%   86.10 IU
VITAMIN D       A====                                        8%   17.00 IU
VIT. E/TOTAL    A                                         NO RDA   6.060 Mg
VITAMIN C       A                                            0%   0.380 Mg
THIAMIN         A=====================                      43%   0.430 Mg
RIBOFLAVIN      A=========                                  18%   0.220 Mg
NIACIN          A=============                              26%   3.410 Mg
VITAMIN B6      A======                                     13%   0.260 Mg
FOLACIN         A==========                                 21%   84.60 Ug
VITAMIN B12     A==                                          4%   0.140 Ug
PANTO- ACID     A==========                                 18%   0.990 Mg
CALCIUM         A=====                                      11%   93.10 Mg
PHOSPHORUS      A===================                        39%   319.0 Mg
TRYPTOPHAN      A======================================    107%   176.0 Mg
THREONINE       A======================================    105%   459.0 Mg
ISOLEUCINE      A======================================    100%   658.0 Mg
LEUCINE         A======================================    115%   1004  Mg
LYSINE          A==================================         88%   581.0 Mg
METHIONINE      A================================           80%   218.0 Mg
CYSTINE         A=============================              74%   203.0 Mg
PHENYL-ANINE    A======================================    155%   676.0 Mg
TYROSINE        A===================================        90%   395.0 Mg
VALINE          A======================================    100%   764.0 Mg
HISTIDINE       A                                         NO RDA   216.0 Mg
ALCOHOL         A                                         NO RDA   0.000 Gm
ASH             A                                         NO RDA   1.270 Gm
COPPER          A=======                                    15%   0.380 Mg
MANGANESE       A=================================          86%   3.250 Mg
IODINE          A=================================         188%   283.0 Ug
MONO FAT        A                                         NO RDA   1.320 Gm
POLY FAT        A                                         NO RDA   6.760 Gm
CAFFEINE        A                                         NO RDA   0.000 Mg
FLUORIDE        A                                            0%   22.60 Ug
MOLYBDENUM      A=================================        1200%   3900  Ug
VITAMIN K       A=                                           2%   2.360 Ug
SELENIUM        A========                                   16%   0.020 Mg
BIOTIN          A==                                          5%   8.730 Ug
CHLORIDE        A=                                           3%   135.0 Mg
CHROMIUM        A=================================         312%   0.390 Mg
SUGAR           A                                         NO RDA   0.000 Gm
FIBER-DIET      A                                         NO RDA   9.850 Gm
VIT. E/AT       A======================                     45%   3.650 Mg

   % RDA:   |0      |20     |40      |60     |80     |100
```

Analysis does not include any of the optional variations; two percent lowfat cow's milk was used instead of nut or soy milk.

# PUMPERNICKEL BAGELS

☆ Try adding little chunks of dried apple and nuts to this hearty, earthy bagel.

---

¼ cup vegetable oil
2 Tbsp. baking yeast
2 Tbsp. blackstrap molasses
2 tsp. soy sauce
2 cups warm water (or potato or
    other vegetable water)

3 cups whole wheat flour
2½ cups whole rye flour

1 gallon water
2 Tbsp. honey

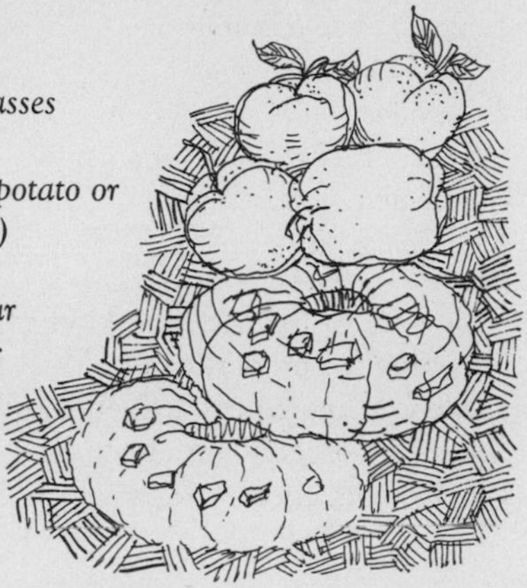

**For variation:**
½ cup raisins

Follow the same procedure as for Bagels in the preceding recipe.

Although the pumpernickel bagels in supermarkets have a healthy appearance because they're dark, a close look at the label will usually reveal they're made with refined flour (listed as wheat flour) and many times contain caramel coloring for the dark coloring, and preservatives.

| SHOPPING LIST | |
|---|---|
| **Regularly Kept in the Kitchen** (Listed in Chapter 14, p. 703) | **Fresh Produce** |
| Safflower oil | (None) |
| Baking yeast | |
| Blackstrap molasses | |
| Soy sauce | |
| Whole wheat flour | |
| Raisins | |

| Special Shopping |
|---|
| Whole rye flour — in natural food stores. |

# TOFU CREAM CHEESE

Peanut butter is popular, but did you know that just about any nut or seed can be made into a butter and each offers a different taste and nutritional value? In this recipe, the raw cashew butter provides the sweet, creamy taste found in cream cheese but not tofu.

☆ Use on top of whole grain bagels or to replace cream cheese in any recipe.

1 cup Chinese firm tofu
¼ cup raw cashew butter
2 tsp. honey
1½ tsp. - 1 Tbsp. Spike or other
   vegetable-seasoned salt
4 tsp. lemon juice

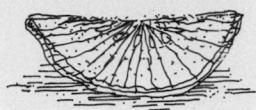

Be sure to use the right kind of tofu, as it is crucial for obtaining the proper texture.

Blend all ingredients in blender till smooth. Serve as cream cheese on bagels. This also makes a good base for dips in which cream cheese is normally used. Makes about 2 cups.

| SHOPPING LIST | |
|---|---|
| **Regularly Kept in the Kitchen** (Listed in Chapter 14, p. 703) | **Fresh Produce** |
| Tofu<br>Raw cashew butter<br>Honey<br>Spike | Lemon |

# NUTRITIONAL ANALYSIS FOR ONE RECIPE
## TOFU CREAM CHEESE

```
NUTRIENT        Type: 14   FEMALE-23 TO 51 YEARS              % RDA   Amount
KCALORIES       A====================                         39%    790.0 Kc
PROTEIN         A=================================================   116%   51.10 Gm
CARBOHYDRATE    A                                            NO RDA  41.50 Gm
FAT             A                                            NO RDA  53.60 Gm
FIBER-CRUDE     A                                            NO RDA  0.850 Gm
CHOLESTEROL     A                                            NO RDA  0.000 Mg
SATURATED FA    A                                            NO RDA  9.420 Gm
OLEIC FA        A                                            NO RDA  2.520 Gm
LINOLEIC FA     A                                            NO RDA  5.040 Gm
SODIUM          A===================================           68%   1509 Mg
POTASSIUM       A=============                                 26%   976.0 Mg
MAGNESIUM       A====================================================  103%  311.0 Mg
IRON            A====================================================  164%  29.60 Mg
ZINC            A========================                      48%   7.300 Mg
VITAMIN A       A=====                                         10%   422.0 IU
VITAMIN D       A                                              0%    0.000 IU
VIT. E/TOTAL    A                                            NO RDA  0.010 Mg
VITAMIN C       A========                                      16%   9.930 Mg
THIAMIN         A==============================                60%   0.600 Mg
RIBOFLAVIN      A===============                               31%   0.380 Mg
NIACIN          A=======                                       15%   2.070 Mg
VITAMIN B6      A==========                                    20%   0.400 Mg
FOLACIN         A===============                               30%   120.0 Ug
VITAMIN B12     A                                              0%    0.000 Ug
PANTO- ACID     A==========                                    20%   1.150 Mg
CALCIUM         A====================================================  220%  1761 Mg
PHOSPHORUS      A=================================================   96%   773.0 Mg
TRYPTOPHAN      A====================================================  488%  796.0 Mg
THREONINE       A====================================================  472%  2056 Mg
ISOLEUCINE      A====================================================  383%  2506 Mg
LEUCINE         A====================================================  455%  3964 Mg
LYSINE          A====================================================  493%  3220 Mg
METHIONINE      A====================================================  261%  710.0 Mg
CYSTINE         A====================================================  278%  758.0 Mg
PHENYL-ANINE    A====================================================  579%  2520 Mg
TYROSINE        A====================================================  383%  1670 Mg
VALINE          A====================================================  364%  2774 Mg
HISTIDINE       A                                            NO RDA  1452 Mg
ALCOHOL         A                                            NO RDA  0.000 Gm
ASH             A                                            NO RDA  5.170 Gm.
COPPER          A================================================    94%   2.360 Mg
MANGANESE       A=============================================   79%   2.980 Mg
IODINE          A====================================================  288%  432.0 Ug
MONO FAT        A                                            NO RDA  23.40 Gm
POLY FAT        A                                            NO RDA  17.70 Gm
CAFFEINE        A                                            NO RDA  0.000 Mg
FLUORIDE        A                                              0%    14.00 Ug
MOLYBDENUM      A====================================================  930%  3024 Ug
VITAMIN K       A                                              0%    0.000 Ug
SELENIUM        A=============                                 24%   0.030 Mg
BIOTIN          A==                                            4%    7.310 Ug
CHLORIDE        A=======                                       14%   479.0 Mg
CHROMIUM        A====================================================  608%  0.760 Mg
SUGAR           A                                            NO RDA  0.320 Gm
FIBER-DIET      A                                            NO RDA  0.000 Gm
VIT. E/AT       A                                              0%    0.000 Mg

    % RDA:   |0      |20     |40     |60     |80     |100
```

# DEVILED EGGLESS SALAD

☆ Good as a dip or spread, sandwich filling, or a scoop
on top of a salad.

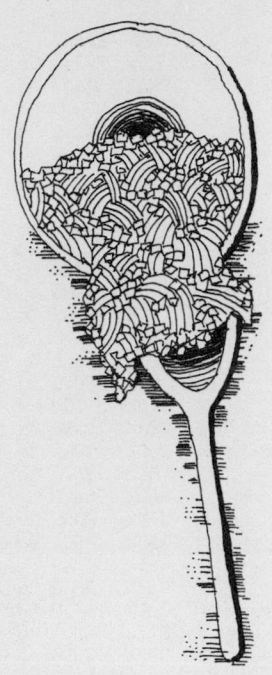

1 lb. Chinese firm tofu, mashed
⅓ cup eggless or Tofu Mayonnaise
    (see recipe, p. 332)
3 Tbsp. finely chopped celery
1 Tbsp. nutritional yeast
1 Tbsp. prepared mustard
1 tsp. Spike or other vegetable-seasoned salt

2 Tbsp. vegetable oil
¼ tsp. turmeric
½ tsp. black pepper
⅛ tsp. asafetida, or eliminate this and
    replace above 3 Tbsp. finely chopped
    celery with 3 Tbsp. finely chopped onion

Combine first 6 (or 5) ingredients together in a mixing
bowl. In a little butter melting pot, or something similar,
combine the next 4 ingredients and cook over heat till spices
begin to toast and you can smell them. Turn off heat and add
to other ingredients. Mix thoroughly. Makes about 2 cups of
Deviled Eggless Salad.

The Deviled Eggless Salad came
about when I realized how
much tofu resembles the texture of a hard-boiled egg, without cholesterol.

| SHOPPING LIST | |
|---|---|
| **Regularly Kept in the Kitchen** (Listed in Chapter 14, p. 703) | **Fresh Produce** |
| Tofu | Celery |
| Eggless mayonnaise | |
| Nutritional yeast | |
| Mustard | |
| Spike | |
| Safflower oil | |
| Turmeric | |
| Black pepper | |
| Asafetida | |

# NUTRITIONAL ANALYSIS FOR ONE RECIPE
## DEVILED EGGLESS SALAD

| NUTRIENT | Type: 14   FEMALE-23 TO 51 YEARS | % RDA | Amount |
|----------|----------------------------------|-------|--------|
| KCALORIES | A============================ | 53% | 1071 Kc |
| PROTEIN | A===================================================== | 192% | 84.50 Gm |
| CARBOHYDRATE | A | NO RDA | 31.00 Gm |
| FAT | A | NO RDA | 76.30 Gm |
| FIBER-CRUDE | A | NO RDA | 1.040 Gm |
| CHOLESTEROL | A | NO RDA | 0.000 Mg |
| SATURATED FA | A | NO RDA | 9.680 Gm |
| OLEIC FA | A | NO RDA | 8.630 Gm |
| LINOLEIC FA | A | NO RDA | 32.20 Gm |
| SODIUM | A========================== | 53% | 1170 Mg |
| POTASSIUM | A=================== | 38% | 1444 Mg |
| MAGNESIUM | A==================================================== | 103% | 311.0 Mg |
| IRON | A==================================================== | 300% | 54.00 Mg |
| ZINC | A=============================== | 62% | 9.300 Mg |
| VITAMIN A | A========== | 20% | 839.0 IU |
| VITAMIN D | A | 0% | 0.000 IU |
| VIT. E/TOTAL | A | NO RDA | 12.20 Mg |
| VITAMIN C | A===== | 11% | 7.130 Mg |
| THIAMIN | A==================================================== | 532% | 5.320 Mg |
| RIBOFLAVIN | A==================================================== | 418% | 5.020 Mg |
| NIACIN | A==================================================== | 215% | 28.00 Mg |
| VITAMIN B6 | A==================================================== | 250% | 5.010 Mg |
| FOLACIN | A=========================== | 53% | 214.0 Ug |
| VITAMIN B12 | A==================================================== | 116% | 3.500 Ug |
| PANTO- ACID | A=========== | 22% | 1.230 Mg |
| CALCIUM | A==================================================== | 435% | 3481 Mg |
| PHOSPHORUS | A==================================================== | 135% | 1083 Mg |
| TRYPTOPHAN | A==================================================== | 788% | 1286 Mg |
| THREONINE | A==================================================== | 791% | 3444 Mg |
| ISOLEUCINE | A==================================================== | 635% | 4148 Mg |
| LEUCINE | A==================================================== | 729% | 6358 Mg |
| LYSINE | A==================================================== | 853% | 5574 Mg |
| METHIONINE | A==================================================== | 398% | 1084 Mg |
| CYSTINE | A==================================================== | 428% | 1166 Mg |
| PHENYL-ANINE | A==================================================== | 932% | 4058 Mg |
| TYROSINE | A==================================================== | 646% | 2812 Mg |
| VALINE | A==================================================== | 561% | 4279 Mg |
| HISTIDINE | A | NO RDA | 2444 Mg |
| ALCOHOL | A | NO RDA | 0.000 Gm |
| ASH | A | NO RDA | 11.20 Gm |
| COPPER | A================================= | 76% | 1.910 Mg |
| MANGANESE | A==================================================== | 160% | 6.000 Mg |
| IODINE | A==================================================== | 444% | 667.0 Ug |
| MONO FAT | A | NO RDA | 13.30 Gm |
| POLY FAT | A | NO RDA | 48.00 Gm |
| CAFFEINE | A | NO RDA | 0.000 Mg |
| FLUORIDE | A | 0% | 21.40 Ug |
| MOLYBDENUM | A==================================================== | 1860% | 6047 Ug |
| VITAMIN K | A | 0% | 0.000 Ug |
| SELENIUM | A======================= | 48% | 0.060 Mg |
| BIOTIN | A======== | 16% | 24.40 Ug |
| CHLORIDE | A============== | 28% | 958.0 Mg |
| CHROMIUM | A==================================================== | 1240% | 1.550 Mg |
| SUGAR | A | NO RDA | 1.890 Gm |
| FIBER-DIET | A | NO RDA | 0.250 Gm |
| VIT. E/AT | A==================================================== | 132% | 10.60 Mg |

```
% RDA:  |0     |20    |40    |60    |80    |100
```

Tofu Mayonnaise was used instead of commercial eggless; onion used instead of asafetida and celery.

# MOCK TUNA SALAD

Kelp and other seaweeds add a seafood flavor to food without the cholesterol and environmental pollutants passed on by fish and shellfish.

☆ In this high-tech era, a hand food grinder may seem a bit archaic — but I prefer to think of it as appropriate technology. The children and I have fun grinding the beans this way instead of using our food processor for this recipe.

½ cup uncooked garbanzo beans
½ cup uncooked soybeans

½ cup sweet pickle relish
½ cup eggless or Tofu Mayonnaise
    (see recipe, p. 332)
½ tsp. salt
2 tsp. soy sauce
¼ cup nutritional yeast
1 Tbsp. kelp or dulse powder (or flakes)
⅛ tsp. asafetida and ½ cup diced celery
    OR ½ cup diced onion
⅛ tsp. black pepper

Soak beans overnight. Rinse, drain and boil in fresh water till tender. When they mash easily between fingers, rinse and drain. Mash well with a potato masher or run through a food grinder, Champion Juicer, or food processor. Combine with next 9 ingredients and mix thoroughly. Chill in refrigerator. Serve as a side dish, on crackers, in a sandwich, or on a salad.

| Special Shopping | SHOPPING LIST | |
| --- | --- | --- |
| | Regularly Kept in the Kitchen (Listed in Chapter 14, p. 703) | Fresh Produce |
| Sweet pickle relish — I always get the ones sweetened with honey at natural food stores. | Garbanzos (chickpeas) Soybeans Eggless mayonnaise Salt Soy sauce Nutritional yeast Kelp (or dulse) powder Asafetida Black pepper | Celery |

# NUTRITIONAL ANALYSIS FOR ONE RECIPE MOCK TUNA SALAD

```
NUTRIENT        Type: 14   FEMALE-23 TO 51 YEARS              % RDA   Amount
KCALORIES       X================================            62%    1240 Kc
PROTEIN         X=====================================================  183%  80.90 Gm
CARBOHYDRATE    X                                            NO RDA  163.0 Gm
FAT             X                                            NO RDA  35.30 Gm
FIBER-CRUDE     X                                            NO RDA  7.990 Gm
CHOLESTEROL     X                                            NO RDA  0.000 Mg
SATURATED FA    X                                            NO RDA  2.810 Gm
OLEIC FA        X                                            NO RDA  1.290 Gm
LINOLEIC FA     X                                            NO RDA  4.830 Gm
SODIUM          X=====================================       134%   2950 Mg
POTASSIUM       X==============================              83%    3143 Mg
MAGNESIUM       X===============================             86%    258.0 Mg
IRON            X======================================      143%   25.90 Mg
ZINC            X================================            70%    10.60 Mg
VITAMIN A       X===                                         7%     300.0 IU
VITAMIN D       X                                            0%     0.000 IU
VIT. E/TOTAL    X                                            NO RDA  5.440 Mg
VITAMIN C       X============                                25%    15.10 Mg
THIAMIN         X========================================    1900%  19.00 Mg
RIBOFLAVIN      X========================================    1541%  18.50 Mg
NIACIN          X========================================    823%   107.0 Mg
VITAMIN B6      X========================================    925%   18.50 Mg
FOLACIN         X========================================    188%   753.0 Ug
VITAMIN B12     X========================================    466%   14.00 Ug
PANTO- ACID     X===========================                 54%    2.970 Mg
CALCIUM         X========================================    119%   958.0 Mg
PHOSPHORUS      X========================================    190%   1523 Mg
TRYPTOPHAN      X========================================    359%   586.0 Mg
THREONINE       X========================================    486%   2115 Mg
ISOLEUCINE      X========================================    361%   2362 Mg
LEUCINE         X========================================    429%   3737 Mg
LYSINE          X========================================    548%   3579 Mg
METHIONINE      X========================================    256%   697.0 Mg
CYSTINE         X========================================    272%   742.0 Mg
PHENYL-ANINE    X========================================    566%   2463 Mg
TYROSINE        X========================================    390%   1697 Mg
VALINE          X========================================    335%   2560 Mg
HISTIDINE       X                                            NO RDA  1442 Mg
ALCOHOL         X                                            NO RDA  0.000 Gm
ASH             X                                            NO RDA  23.30 Gm
COPPER          X========================                    49%    1.230 Mg
MANGANESE       X===================================         95%    3.590 Mg
IODINE          X========================================    258%   388.0 Ug
MONO FAT        X                                            NO RDA  3.490 Gm
POLY FAT        X                                            NO RDA  11.00 Gm
CAFFEINE        X                                            NO RDA  0.000 Mg
FLUORIDE        X                                            1%     54.50 Mg
MOLYBDENUM      X========================================    623%   2026 Ug
VITAMIN K       X                                            0%     0.000 Ug
SELENIUM        X====                                        8%     0.010 Mg
BIOTIN          X=================                           32%    49.10 Ug
CHLORIDE        X===                                         7%     255.0 Mg
CHROMIUM        X========================================    608%   0.760 Mg
SUGAR           X                                            NO RDA  4.920 Gm
FIBER-DIET      X                                            NO RDA  25.80 Gm
VIT. E/AT       X============                                25%    2.040 Mg

    % RDA:   |0      |20      |40      |60      |80      |100
```

Tofu Mayonnaise was used instead of commercial eggless; kelp used instead of dulse powder; onion used instead of asafetida and celery.

Because we should eat to keep the body alive, to pursue higher things, there's the old saying, "Man doesn't live on bread alone . . . " In the Bible we find these words encouraging and advising us to pursue the highest purpose in life, "Lay not up for yourselves treasures upon earth, where moth and rust corrupt, and where thieves break through and steal; but lay up for yourselves treasures in heaven, where neither moth nor rust corrupt, and where thieves do not break through nor steal."

# SOUTH·OF·THE·BORDER AMERICAN STYLE

One soy product that's worth a mention while we're talking about texture and taste replacements for meat is TVP (texturized vegetable protein). Although it's certainly a better choice than ground beef, it isn't one of my personal favorites and really doesn't have a regular place in my kitchen.

I've personally found this particular soy product hard to digest and don't really care much for the chewy ground beef texture it has. However, I do know a lot of people like to use this product when they are just starting to eliminate meat from their diet, or are feeding family or friends who still eat meat. (In this case, I know of many people who have presented meals with TVP in them without telling anyone that there's no meat, and no one notices the difference.)

One handy thing about TVP is that it is relatively quick to make . . .just soak and add to the dish. Following are some recipes that have their roots and inspiration in Mexico. They are meant to all go together; to be piled on top of each other with some fresh lettuce or sprouts to make a meal-in-one dish. If you make everything as recommended and pile everything on top of each other, it should make enough to feed 4 to 6 people.

# NATIVE FRIED BREAD

☆ Mexican food lovers who want a break from the tortilla can try these breads that originated with the native Indians in Mexico. They can be topped with any number of toppings to make a complete meal. One possibility is listed at the right, to be stacked in the order given.

☆ Make breads 3 to 4 times smaller than described in the recipe, top and serve as an hors d'oeuvres.

---

*2 cups whole wheat flour*
*2½ tsp. baking powder*
*¼ tsp. salt*
*1 Tbsp. margarine or vegetable oil*

*¾ cup plus 2 Tbsp. warm water*

*Oil for deep-frying*

*Grated cheese*

Combine first 4 ingredients together in a mixing bowl, making sure to cut in margarine or vegetable oil until the flour is a sand-like consistency. Add water and mix until dough forms a large ball. Break dough into balls about 2" in diameter. Flour counter and roll dough balls into flat pancake-shaped breads about ⅛" to ¼" thick. As you roll each bread flat, poke a hole with your finger into the middle of the bread. Place the rolled bread onto an oiled cookie tray or oiled section of the counter so breads are lying side by side (do not stack the breads). Cover with a towel and allow breads to rise for 15 to 20 minutes. In the meantime, heat vegetable oil for deep-frying to about 350 to 375 degrees. Drop breads in and deep-fry till golden brown on one side. Flip over and fry till golden brown on the other side. Frying should only take 1 to 2 minutes. As breads are done, remove from oil. While breads are still hot, sprinkle grated cheese over them. Then top with Salpicon, lettuce strips and Green Chili Salsa (see following recipes).

## ONE SUGGESTED MEAL TO TOP NATIVE FRIED BREADS

*Native Fried Bread*

*Salpicon*

*Grated cheese*

*Shredded lettuce and/or alfalfa sprouts*

*Green Chili Salsa*

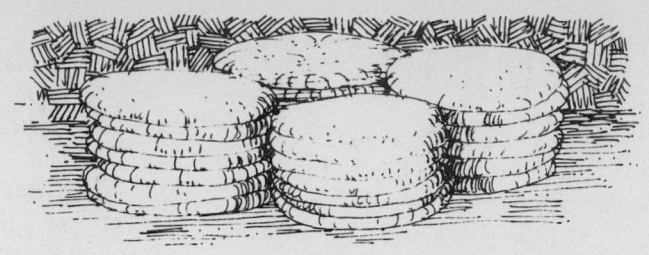

| SHOPPING LIST | |
|---|---|
| **Regularly Kept in the Kitchen**<br>**(Listed in Chapter 14, p. 703)** | **Fresh Produce** |
| Whole wheat flour<br>Baking powder<br>Salt<br>Margarine (or safflower oil)<br>Safflower oil | (None) |

"Salpicon" means little, teeny bits and pieces of things. In Mexico this dish is usually prepared with bits of beef or pork; bits of TVP will give the same general texture and taste without the undesirable cholesterol and saturated fat.

# SALPICON

☆ You won't be using all the vinegarette in the Salpicon — just enough to moisten the TVP. I usually make this much because the extra makes a delicious salad dressing!

2 cups TVP
2 cups water

### Vinegarette

2 tsp. asafetida or 2 cloves garlic
¼ cup packed cilantro leaves
1 tsp. chili powder
½ tsp. salt
½ tsp. dried oregano, crumbled
¼ tsp. mustard powder
⅓ cup vinegar
¾ cup vegetable oil
2 Pablano chilies, roasted, peeled, stemmed and seeded

Soak first 2 ingredients together. In a blender, blend next 8 ingredients. (These 8 ingredients also make a delicious vinegarette salad dressing.) Drain soaked TVP and place in skillet. Saute. Add enough of the blended vinegarette to nicely moisten the TVP. Chop the chilies and add them to the mixture in the skillet.

| SHOPPING LIST | |
| --- | --- |
| **Regularly Kept in the Kitchen (Listed in Chapter 14, p. 703)** | **Fresh Produce** |
| Asafetida<br>Chili powder<br>Salt<br>Oregano<br>Mustard powder<br>Vinegar<br>Safflower oil | Cilantro (the same as Chinese parsley)<br>Pablano chilies |

| Special Shopping |
| --- |
| TVP — Texturized vegetable protein is made from soybeans and are dry, almost dogfood-looking bits that resemble tough hamburger bits when soaked and cooked. Found in most natural food stores. |

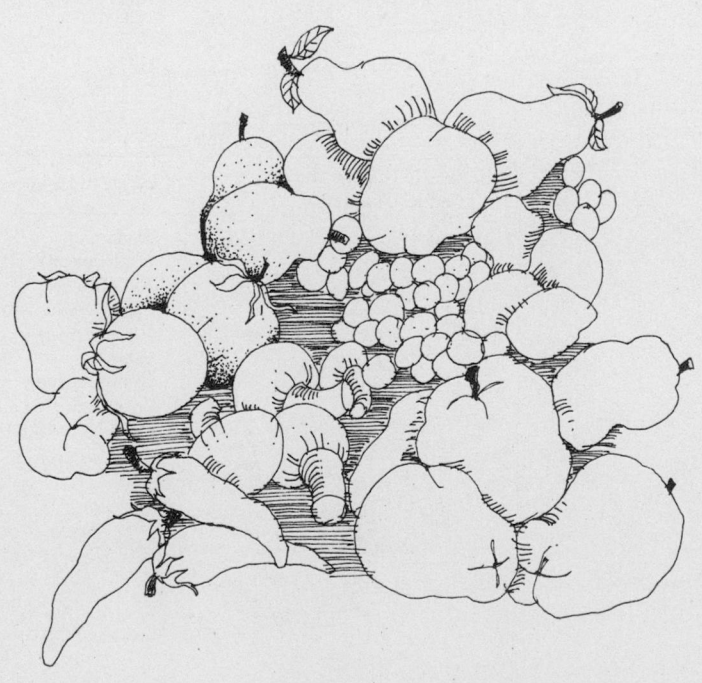

# GREEN CHILI SALSA

☆ This is a rich, creamy salsa that I like to reserve for serving only at parties or special-occasion dinners. For everyday Mexican meals I prefer a homemade Fresh Salsa (as on p. 145) or a commercial salsa from the supermarket that contains only vegetables and no preservatives!

---

*6 tomatillos*

*5 green Anaheim or Pablano chilies*
*1 tsp. asafetida or ¼ cup finely diced onion*
*½ avocado*
*¼ cup loosely packed cilantro leaves*
*½ tsp. salt (or to taste)*
*¾ cup sour cream or Lowfat*
*   "Sour Cream" (p. 186)*
*¼ cup whipping cream*
*1 tsp. lemon or lime juice*

Husk tomatillos, wash them and cut into quarters. Place in a covered skillet and simmer till tender. When they are tender, place in blender with the next 8 ingredients and blend till smooth.

| SHOPPING LIST | |
|---|---|
| **Regularly Kept in the Kitchen** (Listed in Chapter 14, p. 703) | **Fresh Produce** |
| (None) | Tomatillos<br>Anaheim or Pablano chilies<br>Avocado<br>Cilantro (the same as Chinese parsley)<br>Salt<br>Lemon or lime<br>Sour cream, or use Lowfat "Sour Cream" (p. 186)<br>Whipping cream |

# NUTRITIONAL ANALYSIS FOR ONE SERVING NATIVE FRIED BREAD WITH SALPICON AND GREEN CHILI SALSA

```
NUTRIENT         Type: 14   FEMALE-23 TO 51 YEARS          % RDA    Amount
KCALORIES      A=============                              26%      520.0 Kc
PROTEIN        A=================================          65%      29.00 Gm
CARBOHYDRATE   A                                           NO RDA   40.70 Gm
FAT            A                                           NO RDA   29.50 Gm
FIBER-CRUDE    A                                           NO RDA   1.690 Gm
CHOLESTEROL    A                                           NO RDA   8.170 Mg
SATURATED FA   A                                           NO RDA   3.950 Gm
OLEIC FA       A                                           NO RDA   2.840 Gm
LINOLEIC FA    A                                           NO RDA   10.40 Gm
SODIUM         A===============================            63%      1397 Mg
POTASSIUM      A========                                   17%      644.0 Mg
MAGNESIUM      A==================                         38%      115.0 Mg
IRON           A==============================             61%      11.10 Mg
ZINC           A==========                                 21%      3.160 Mg
VITAMIN A      A====================                       41%      1671 IU
VITAMIN D      A                                           1%       3.270 IU
VIT. E/TOTAL   A                                           NO RDA   6.360 Mg
VITAMIN C      A=====================================      76%      46.00 Mg
THIAMIN        A=====================                      43%      0.430 Mg
RIBOFLAVIN     A==============                             28%      0.340 Mg
NIACIN         A==========                                 21%      2.730 Mg
VITAMIN B6     A=======                                    15%      0.310 Mg
FOLACIN        A==========                                 21%      86.80 Ug
VITAMIN B12    A===                                        7%       0.230 Ug
PANTO- ACID    A=======                                    14%      0.820 Mg
CALCIUM        A=================================================  111%  892.0 Mg
PHOSPHORUS     A======================================     79%      633.0 Mg
TRYPTOPHAN     A=================================================  239%  391.0 Mg
THREONINE      A=================================================  250%  1090 Mg
ISOLEUCINE     A=================================================  226%  1477 Mg
LEUCINE        A=================================================  265%  2309 Mg
LYSINE         A=================================================  277%  1813 Mg
METHIONINE     A=================================================  188%  514.0 Mg
CYSTINE        A=================================================  138%  378.0 Mg
PHENYL-ANINE   A=================================================  327%  1423 Mg
TYROSINE       A=================================================  255%  1111 Mg
VALINE         A=================================================  202%  1543 Mg
HISTIDINE      A                                           NO RDA   821.0 Mg
ALCOHOL        A                                           NO RDA   0.000 Gm
ASH            A                                           NO RDA   4.060 Gm
COPPER         A============                               23%      0.590 Mg
MANGANESE      A=============================================  82%  3.090 Mg
IODINE         A=================================================  238%  357.0 Ug
MONO FAT       A                                           NO RDA   4.530 Gm
POLY FAT       A                                           NO RDA   13.30 Gm
CAFFEINE       A                                           NO RDA   0.000 Gm
FLUORIDE       A=                                          2%       62.20 Ug
MOLYBDENUM     A=================================================  1050%  3414 Ug
VITAMIN K      A==============                             27%      28.50 Ug
SELENIUM       A============                               24%      0.030 Mg
BIOTIN         A==                                         5%       7.630 Ug
CHLORIDE       A===                                        6%       237.0 Mg
CHROMIUM       A=================================================  400%  0.500 Mg
SUGAR          A                                           NO RDA   2.810 Gm
FIBER-DIET     A                                           NO RDA   6.480 Gm
VIT. E/AT      A============================               59%      4.750 Mg

   % RDA:   |0      |20     |40     |60     |80    |100
```

Lowfat "Sour Cream" was used instead of regular sour cream in the Green Chili Salsa; margarine used instead of vegetable oil in the Native Fried Bread.

# HEALTHY FAST-FOOD

We live in the midst of a society and culture that distracts one from being still enough to be with one's own thoughts and wonders. We are constantly bombarded with the distractions of radio and TV, sights and sounds, so many places to go and things to do. These strong words from Plato would do well to remind us that there is more to life than mindless consumption. Plato concluded, "The life which is unexamined is not worth living."

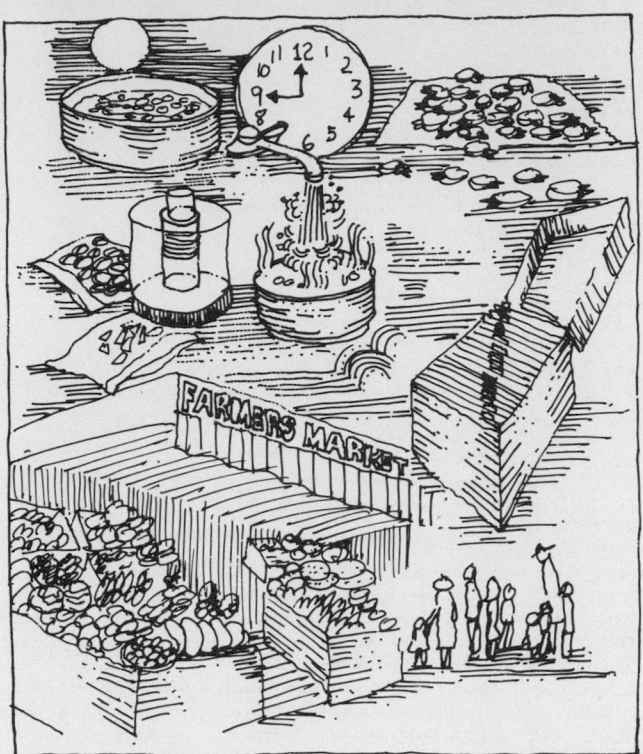

A lot of people have the mistaken idea that healthy food takes a long time to make, so as much as they'd like to eat a healthier diet, they think they just won't have the time to fit it into their already busy schedules. It's true that eating a healthier diet may take more time in the beginning, but becoming familiar with and learning something new always does. Once that hurdle is crossed and cooking with wholesome natural food becomes second nature, you'll find that preparing healthier meals takes no more time than denatured, chemical-laden "convenience" foods do.

It takes just as long to cook a steak or heat up a frozen TV dinner (or for that matter to drive to, park, order and receive an already prepared restaurant meal) as it does to prepare a *properly planned* natural food meal. Planning a natural food meal isn't that much different from planning any other kind of meal. As with planning any meal, it's good to know a day or two in advance what you'll be making so you're sure to have all the ingredients on hand and know if there are any pre-preparation steps necessary.

• The biggest time-saving preparation step for natural food that I know of is to get in the habit of soaking beans overnight the day before planning to use them. It's certainly an effortless task, and cuts cooking time in at least half. There are still times that I am not that well-planned, or I just plain old forget to soak them. I've learned a trick that has saved me many times . . . just turn your faucet water on to the hottest, scalding temperature and soak beans in this water for one to two hours before cooking time. This is about the equivalent of an overnight soaking.

• A more nutritious way to cut down on cooking time for beans is to lightly sprout your bean (till sprout is only ⅛-inch or so long). This will cut cooking time down to 10 to 15 minutes and gives you a completely different food nutrition-wise.

• Since boiling beans doesn't require personal presence in the kitchen, I don't even count it as cooking time. Just put a pot on with ample water and set a timer (or better yet, invest in a crock pot), then walk away and be free to use your valuable time for accomplishing something meaningful in your life.

• Whenever I cook beans or grains, I always cook more than I need for the one meal. The leftovers can be used in a dish the following day or frozen till needed. If frozen, again planning helps. If you know you're going to be making a dish with already frozen, cooked beans or grains in the morning, just remove them from the freezer at the beginning of the day so they'll be thawed and ready to cook with by afternoon or evening time.

• Speaking of freezing food, I have a friend to whom eating healthy meals is worth sacrificing a *little* time. This friend works during the week, so she shops once a week for her fresh produce (at farmer's markets where produce is freshest and cheapest), then comes home and spends a couple of hours with her food processor cutting and chopping all the produce. The chopped produce is then bagged and labeled for each day of the week and frozen. After work every day, my friend just pulls her pre-prepared vegetables out of the freezer and makes a dinner within half an hour. To be this well-planned and organized has certainly saved her lots of time and money.

• Although they are still quite expensive, there are a lot of healthy natural convenience foods making their appearance on store shelves. I've resorted to using these in a pinch, but am always sure to serve whatever it is with a fresh, lush salad. The salad can easily be made in the 10 to 45 minutes these convenience foods require to sit, cook, etc.

These are some ways to help cut down on time spent in the kitchen when preparing a natural food meal.

Another way is to have a few recipes you know will work that enable you to prepare a whole meal in a matter of 15 to 20 minutes from scratch. Following are a few standard "quickie" recipes that help me get the most out of my kitchen and get out of the kitchen simultaneously!

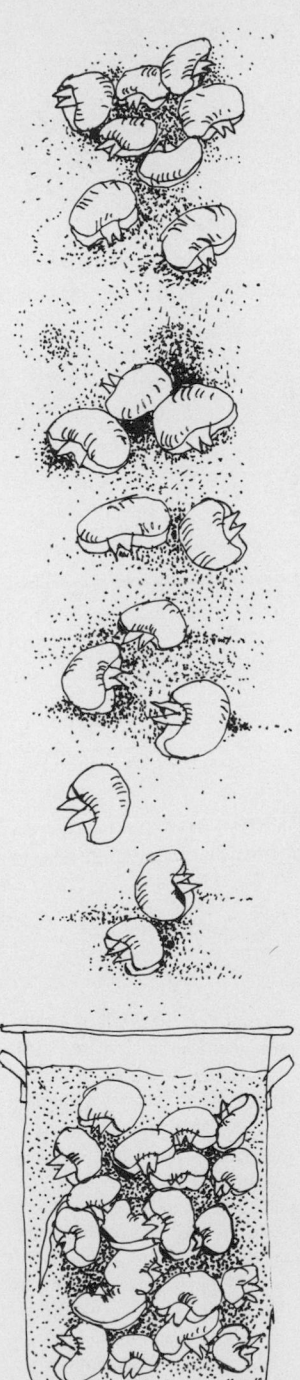

# NACHOS

☆ This dish, often served as an appetizer or snack at Mexican and natural food restaurants, can be turned into a one-dish meal by piling more nutrients on top of the chips and cheese.

---

½ lb. corn chips
½ lb. mild Cheddar cheese, grated

2 cups mashed or refried beans
4 oz. alfalfa sprouts
2 cups tomato wedges
2 cups slivered bell pepper
2½ cups Guacamole (1 Guacamole recipe)
1½ cups Lowfat "Sour Cream"

Salsa (commercial or see recipe, p. 145 or p. 644)

Preheat broiler.

Spread chips out evenly on a cookie sheet and sprinkle grated cheese evenly over the chips. Put under broiler to melt cheese. This just takes a minute or two, so watch carefully. I've actually burnt a few trayfuls and had one go up in flames!

Remove from heat and immediately layer each of the next 6 ingredients evenly in separate layers in the order listed, one on top of the next.

Top it all with salsa, or serve the salsa separately in a bowl for individuals to spoon over their individual servings if you think the salsa will be too hot for some tastes.

Serve immediately by picking up a whole section which includes every layer. This recipe makes 1 full cookie sheet which will yield 4 full-sized dinner portions or a dozen salad-sized portions. If you prefer, you can make individual-sized plates by placing layers on individual oven-proof plates.

Natural food stores sell corn chips that are usually a bit more expensive than the ones sold on grocery store shelves. The only difference is usually that natural food chips are fried in safflower oil (the most unsaturated fat, with essential linoleic acid), and grocery store chips are fried in a combination of oils that include coconut or palm oil, which are saturated fats. Considering the different effects of saturated and unsaturated fat on the cholesterol level in the blood, I feel it's worth paying a little extra for the unsaturated oil.

| SHOPPING LIST | |
|---|---|
| **Regularly Kept in the Kitchen** (Listed in Chapter 14, p. 703) | **Fresh Produce** |
| Mild Cheddar cheese<br>Refried beans | Corn chips<br>Alfalfa sprouts<br>Tomatoes<br>Bell peppers |

Also see shopping lists for Guacamole, Lowfat "Sour Cream" and Salsa (or use a commercial one).

# GUACAMOLE

☆ A helpful hint I learned from someone who spent a lot of time in Mexico: If you put the pit of the avocado in guacamole, or any other avocado preparation, it keeps the avocado from turning brown or spoiling so quickly.

2 cups mashed avocado
½ cup diced chilies (canned Ortega, or prepared as in Pepper Antipasto Salad, p. 621)
½ cup finely diced red bell pepper
2¼ tsp. Spike or other vegetable-seasoned salt
1½ tsp. lemon juice
¼ tsp. honey
¼ tsp. asafetida or ¼ cup finely diced onion

In an effort to avoid cholesterol and saturated fat, enough people have mistakenly stopped buying this buttery fruit to concern avocado farmers. The truth is that, rich as they are, avocados contain neither saturated fat nor cholesterol.

Combine all 7 ingredients and mix thoroughly. Makes about 2½ cups of Guacamole.

| SHOPPING LIST | |
|---|---|
| **Regularly Kept in the Kitchen** (Listed in Chapter 14, p. 703) | **Fresh Produce** |
| Spike<br>Honey<br>Asafetida | Avocados<br>Anaheim or Ortega chilies<br>Red bell pepper<br>Lemon |

# NUTRITIONAL ANALYSIS FOR ONE SERVING
## NACHOS WITH GUACAMOLE AND SALSA

| NUTRIENT | Type: 14  FEMALE-23 TO 51 YEARS | % RDA | Amount |
|---|---|---|---|
| KCALORIES | ============================ | 53% | 1068 Kc |
| PROTEIN | ================================================= | 97% | 42.70 Gm |
| CARBOHYDRATE | | NO RDA | 99.50 Gm |
| FAT | | NO RDA | 59.30 Gm |
| FIBER-CRUDE | | NO RDA | 5.010 Gm |
| CHOLESTEROL | | NO RDA | 65.00 Mg |
| SATURATED FA | | NO RDA | 15.80 Gm |
| OLEIC FA | | NO RDA | 16.20 Gm |
| LINOLEIC FA | | NO RDA | 2.340 Gm |
| SODIUM | ================================ | 60% | 1323 Mg |
| POTASSIUM | =================== | 39% | 1496 Mg |
| MAGNESIUM | ========================== | 51% | 154.0 Mg |
| IRON | =================== | 40% | 7.260 Mg |
| ZINC | ============= | 27% | 4.080 Mg |
| VITAMIN A | =============================================== | 95% | 3837 IU |
| VITAMIN D | | 0% | 1.250 IU |
| VIT. E/TOTAL | | NO RDA | 1.100 Mg |
| VITAMIN C | ================================================== | 283% | 170.0 Mg |
| THIAMIN | ===================================== | 77% | 0.770 Mg |
| RIBOFLAVIN | ================================== | 69% | 0.830 Mg |
| NIACIN | ======================= | 47% | 6.110 Mg |
| VITAMIN B6 | ================ | 33% | 0.670 Mg |
| FOLACIN | ================= | 34% | 138.0 Ug |
| VITAMIN B12 | =============== | 30% | 0.900 Ug |
| PANTO- ACID | =================== | 38% | 2.140 Mg |
| CALCIUM | ==================================== | 73% | 584.0 Mg |
| PHOSPHORUS | ================================= | 66% | 531.0 Mg |
| TRYPTOPHAN | ================================================== | 200% | 327.0 Mg |
| THREONINE | ================================================== | 245% | 1070 Mg |
| ISOLEUCINE | ================================================== | 240% | 1568 Mg |
| LEUCINE | ================================================== | 292% | 2547 Mg |
| LYSINE | ================================================== | 327% | 2137 Mg |
| METHIONINE | ================================================== | 252% | 687.0 Mg |
| CYSTINE | ====================================== | 79% | 216.0 Mg |
| PHENYL-ANINE | ================================================== | 310% | 1350 Mg |
| TYROSINE | ================================================== | 282% | 1229 Mg |
| VALINE | ================================================== | 224% | 1709 Mg |
| HISTIDINE | | NO RDA | 851.0 Mg |
| ALCOHOL | | NO RDA | 0.000 Gm |
| ASH | | NO RDA | 9.140 Gm |
| COPPER | =============== | 29% | 0.740 Mg |
| MANGANESE | ======== | 17% | 0.670 Mg |
| IODINE | ==================================== | 74% | 112.0 Ug |
| MONO FAT | | NO RDA | 18.60 Gm |
| POLY FAT | | NO RDA | 3.680 Gm |
| CAFFEINE | | NO RDA | 0.000 Mg |
| FLUORIDE | == | 5% | 156.0 Ug |
| MOLYBDENUM | =================== | 38% | 125.0 Ug |
| VITAMIN K | === | 7% | 8.160 Ug |
| SELENIUM | ================================================= | 304% | 0.380 Mg |
| BIOTIN | === | 7% | 10.90 Ug |
| CHLORIDE | | 0% | 0.000 Mg |
| CHROMIUM | ============================================ | 88% | 0.110 Mg |
| SUGAR | | NO RDA | 10.40 Gm |
| FIBER-DIET | | NO RDA | 5.810 Gm |
| VIT. E/AT | ======================= | 45% | 3.660 Mg |

```
% RDA:  |0      |20     |40     |60     |80     |100
```

The Fresh Salsa was used instead of a commercial one for this analysis.

# LOWFAT "SOUR CREAM"

☆ Feels and tastes enough like the "real thing," but with
much less fat and more of other desirable nutrients.
Use any time sour cream is called for.

---

*1 cup lowfat cottage cheese*
*¼ cup cultured buttermilk*
*2 Tbsp. lemon juice*
*½ tsp. honey*

Blend all ingredients together in blender till smooth. Cover
and refrigerate till needed. This recipe can be used in any
recipe instead of sour cream for a more nutritious, lowfat
dish.

| SHOPPING LIST | |
|---|---|
| **Regularly Kept in the Kitchen** (Listed in Chapter 14, p. 703) | **Fresh Produce** |
| Cultered buttermilk<br>Honey | Lowfat cottage cheese<br>Lemons |

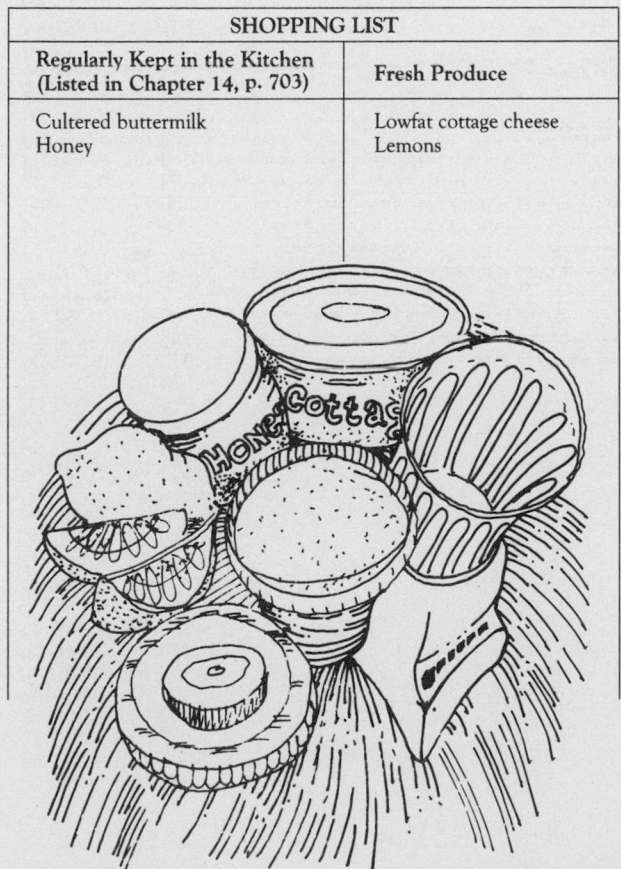

Regular Sour Cream:
86% fat
6% protein

This recipe for
Lowfat "Sour Cream":
17% fat
52% protein

# NUTRITIONAL ANALYSIS COMPARING
# LOWFAT "SOUR CREAM" WITH SOUR CREAM

| NUTRIENT | Type: 14   FEMALE-23 TO 51 YEARS | Amount in Lowfat Sour Cream | Amount in sour cream |
|---|---|---|---|
| KCALORIES | Ⱥ====== | 246.0 Kc | 688.0 Kc |
| PROTEIN | Ⱥ=================================== | 33.20 Gm | 10.10 Gm |
| CARBOHYDRATE | Ⱥ_____ | 16.50 Gm | 13.70 Gm |
| FAT | Ⱥ | 4.900 Gm | 67.30 Gm |
| FIBER-CRUDE | Ⱥ | 0.000 Gm | 0.000 Gm |
| CHOLESTEROL | Ⱥ | 21.20 Mg | 142.0 Mg |
| SATURATED FA | Ⱥ | 3.090 Gm | 41.90 Gm |
| OLEIC FA | Ⱥ | 1.120 Gm | 16.90 Gm |
| LINOLEIC FA | Ⱥ | 0.100 Gm | 1.530 Gm |
| SODIUM | Ⱥ===================== | 982.0 Mg | 171.0 Mg |
| POTASSIUM | Ⱥ==== | 349.0 Mg | 462.0 Mg |
| MAGNESIUM | Ⱥ=== | 22.80 Mg | 36.30 Mg |
| IRON | Ⱥ= | 0.410 Mg | 0.190 Mg |
| ZINC | Ⱥ==== | 1.220 Mg | 0.860 Mg |
| VITAMIN A | Ⱥ== | 184.0 IU | 2538 IU |
| VITAMIN D | Ⱥ= | 5.000 IU | 26.80 IU |
| VIT. E/TOTAL | Ⱥ | 0.240 Mg | 0.000 Mg |
| VITAMIN C | Ⱥ============ | 14.60 Mg | 2.760 Mg |
| THIAMIN | Ⱥ==== | 0.080 Mg | 0.110 Mg |
| RIBOFLAVIN | Ⱥ==================== | 0.510 Mg | 0.470 Mg |
| NIACIN | Ⱥ= | 0.400 Mg | 0.210 Mg |
| VITAMIN B6 | Ⱥ===== | 0.200 Mg | 0.050 Mg |
| FOLACIN | Ⱥ==== | 33.90 Ug | 34.90 Ug |
| VITAMIN B12 | Ⱥ============================= | 1.740 Ug | 0.960 Ug |
| PANTO- ACID | Ⱥ====== | 0.750 Mg | 1.150 Mg |
| CALCIUM | Ⱥ============== | 228.0 Mg | 374.0 Mg |
| PHOSPHORUS | Ⱥ======================= | 396.0 Mg | 272.0 Mg |
| TRYPTOPHAN | Ⱥ==================================================== | 368.0 Mg | 0.000 Mg |
| THREONINE | Ⱥ==================================================== | 1473 Mg | 0.000 Mg |
| ISOLEUCINE | Ⱥ==================================================== | 1950 Mg | 0.000 Mg |
| LEUCINE | Ⱥ==================================================== | 3394 Mg | 0.000 Mg |
| LYSINE | Ⱥ==================================================== | 2680 Mg | 0.000 Mg |
| METHIONINE | Ⱥ==================================================== | 983.0 Mg | 0.000 Mg |
| CYSTINE | Ⱥ==================================================== | 306.0 Mg | 0.000 Mg |
| PHENYL-ANINE | Ⱥ==================================================== | 1780 Mg | 0.000 Mg |
| TYROSINE | Ⱥ==================================================== | 1739 Mg | 0.000 Mg |
| VALINE | Ⱥ==================================================== | 2072 Mg | 0.000 Mg |
| HISTIDINE | Ⱥ | 1090 Mg | 0.000 Mg |
| ALCOHOL | Ⱥ | 0.000 Gm | 0.000 Gm |
| ASH | Ⱥ | 3.760 Gm | 2.120 Gm |
| COPPER | Ⱥ | 0.020 Mg | 0.000 Mg |
| MANGANESE | Ⱥ | 0.000 Mg | 0.000 Mg |
| IODINE | Ⱥ=================================== | 104.0 Ug | 0.000 Ug |
| MONO FAT | Ⱥ | 1.390 Gm | 19.40 Gm |
| POLY FAT | Ⱥ | 0.150 Gm | 2.500 Gm |
| CAFFEINE | Ⱥ | 0.000 Mg | 0.000 Mg |
| FLUORIDE | Ⱥ==== | 220.0 Ug | 0.000 Ug |
| MOLYBDENUM | Ⱥ | 0.000 Ug | 0.000 Ug |
| VITAMIN K | Ⱥ= | 3.550 Ug | 0.000 Ug |
| SELENIUM | Ⱥ==================== | 0.050 Mg | 0.000 Mg |
| BIOTIN | Ⱥ= | 5.770 Ug | 0.000 Ug |
| CHLORIDE | Ⱥ | 0.000 Mg | 0.000 Mg |
| CHROMIUM | Ⱥ | 0.000 Mg | 0.000 Mg |
| SUGAR | Ⱥ | 0.480 Gm | 0.000 Gm |
| FIBER-DIET | Ⱥ | 0.000 Gm | 0.000 Gm |
| VIT. E/AT | Ⱥ========= | 1.450 Mg | 0.000 Mg |

% RDA:   |0      |20      |40      |60      |80      |100

Dotted line indicates Lowfat "Sour Cream." Straight line indicates sour cream. Comparison is for an equal gram weight of Lowfat "Sour Cream" and sour cream.

# TEMPEH PIZZA

☆ Invented by one of the children, this has become a standard after-school snack around our house. When served with a fresh salad and some form of whole grain bread, it makes a complete meal.

8 oz. tempeh patty

¾ cup your favorite homemade or
    commercial pizza or spaghetti sauce
Assorted sliced vegetable toppings (olives,
    bell peppers, tomatoes, mushrooms, etc.)
½ cup grated mozzarella or Jack cheese

Steam tempeh patty for 15 minutes. In the meantime, slice enough vegetable toppings of your choice to sprinkle over the entire surface of the patty (about ½ cup's worth). Grate the cheese and preheat the oven to broil. Be sure to use toppings that really don't require a long cooking time, such as olives, mushrooms, bell peppers, tomatoes (stay away from eggplant, raw onions and hard vegetables like broccoli and cauliflower). If you still have time before the tempeh is done steaming, make a simple tossed salad and get out some form of whole grain bread or use the following recipe for Whole Wheat Breadsticks. (I recommend serving the Tempeh Pizza with these to make a whole meal.)

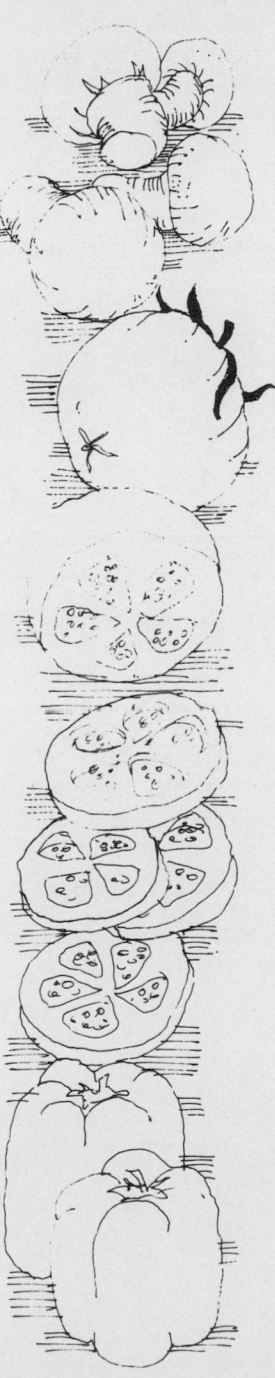

## SUGGESTED MENU

*Favorite green salad*

*Tempeh Pizza*

*Whole Wheat Breadsticks*

When tempeh is done steaming, place in an oiled cake pan and top with the next 3 ingredients put on in layers in the order listed. Place under broiler for about 5 to 7 minutes, till cheese is melted and beginning to brown. Remove from oven and serve immediately. Makes 1 serving, so just multiply this by the number of people being served.

| SHOPPING LIST | |
| --- | --- |
| **Regularly Kept in the Kitchen** (Listed in Chapter 14, p. 703) | **Fresh Produce** |
| Tempeh<br>Mozzarella or Jack cheese | Spaghetti sauce<br>Vegetables of your choice that require little or no cooking (olives, mushrooms, bell pepper, tomato) |

# NUTRITIONAL ANALYSIS FOR ONE SERVING TEMPEH PIZZA

| NUTRIENT | Type: 14   FEMALE-23 TO 51 YEARS | % RDA | Amount |
|---|---|---|---|
| KCALORIES | A=========================== | 49% | 994.0 Kc |
| PROTEIN | A===================================================== | 151% | 66.50 Gm |
| CARBOHYDRATE | A | NO RDA | 73.70 Gm |
| FAT | A | NO RDA | 52.00 Gm |
| FIBER-CRUDE | A | NO RDA | 9.470 Gm |
| CHOLESTEROL | A | NO RDA | 0.000 Mg |
| SATURATED FA | A | NO RDA | 4.160 Gm |
| OLEIC FA | A | NO RDA | 5.570 Gm |
| LINOLEIC FA | A | NO RDA | 9.040 Gm |
| SODIUM | A==================================== | 66% | 1460 Mg |
| POTASSIUM | A========================= | 49% | 1856 Mg |
| MAGNESIUM | A========================================== | 79% | 239.0 Mg |
| IRON | A======================= | 43% | 7.880 Mg |
| ZINC | A========================= | 47% | 7.070 Mg |
| VITAMIN A | A======================================= | 135% | 5432 IU |
| VITAMIN D | A | 0% | 0.000 IU |
| VIT. E/TOTAL | A | NO RDA | 3.370 Mg |
| VITAMIN C | A====================================================== | 107% | 64.30 Mg |
| THIAMIN | A======================= | 47% | 0.470 Mg |
| RIBOFLAVIN | A================================ | 65% | 0.780 Mg |
| NIACIN | A================================ | 111% | 14.50 Mg |
| VITAMIN B6 | A=================== | 38% | 0.760 Mg |
| FOLACIN | A================ | 32% | 131.0 Ug |
| VITAMIN B12 | A======================= | 45% | 1.360 Ug |
| PANTO- ACID | A============ | 24% | 1.350 Mg |
| CALCIUM | A■■■■■■■■■■■■■■■■■■■■■■■■ | 108% | 867.0 Mg |
| PHOSPHORUS | A==================================== | 115% | 920.0 Mg |
| TRYPTOPHAN | A================================================== | 565% | 922.0 Mg |
| THREONINE | A==================================================== | 584% | 2541 Mg |
| ISOLEUCINE | A=================================================== | 544% | 3556 Mg |
| LEUCINE | A==================================================== | 653% | 5688 Mg |
| LYSINE | A==================================================== | 659% | 4304 Mg |
| METHIONINE | A=================================================== | 416% | 1132 Mg |
| CYSTINE | A=================================================== | 313% | 852.0 Mg |
| PHENYL-ANINE | A==================================================== | 782% | 3404 Mg |
| TYROSINE | A==================================================== | 609% | 2650 Mg |
| VALINE | A=================================================== | 472% | 3602 Mg |
| HISTIDINE | A | NO RDA | 1877 Mg |
| ALCOHOL | A | NO RDA | 0.000 Gm |
| ASH | A | NO RDA | 10.50 Gm |
| COPPER | A===================================== | 73% | 1.840 Mg |
| MANGANESE | A============================================= | 89% | 3.340 Mg |
| IODINE | A================================================== | 639% | 959.0 Ug |
| MONO FAT | A | NO RDA | 8.410 Gm |
| POLY FAT | A | NO RDA | 12.40 Gm |
| CAFFEINE | A | NO RDA | 0.000 Mg |
| FLUORIDE | A= | 2% | 82.30 Ug |
| MOLYBDENUM | A===================================================== | 976% | 3175 Ug |
| VITAMIN K | A= | 2% | 2.910 Ug |
| SELENIUM | A============ | 24% | 0.030 Mg |
| BIOTIN | A============ | 22% | 34.10 Ug |
| CHLORIDE | A===== | 11% | 385.0 Mg |
| CHROMIUM | A==================================================== | 736% | 0.920 Mg |
| SUGAR | A | NO RDA | 3.600 Gm |
| FIBER-DIET | A | NO RDA | 34.50 Gm |
| VIT. E/AT | A===== | 11% | 0.880 Mg |

```
% RDA:  |0      |20     |40     |60     |80     |100
```

Jack cheese was used instead of mozzarella; a vegetable topping of olives, bell pepper, tomato and mushrooms used for this analysis.

# WHOLE WHEAT BREADSTICKS

*5 cups whole wheat flour*
*2 Tbsp. baking yeast*
*2 tsp. Spike or other vegetable-seasoned salt*
*2 tsp. coarse black pepper, Parmesan*
  *cheese, poppy seeds, or sesame seeds*

*2 cups warm water*
*2 Tbsp. olive oil*

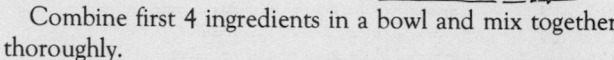

Combine first 4 ingredients in a bowl and mix together thoroughly.

Put next 2 ingredients together in a measuring cup and pour ¼ of it into dry ingredients. Mix in thoroughly and add ¼ more liquid; repeat till liquid is all used up. You should end up with a fairly soft, but unsticky, dough. Turn onto a lightly floured surface and knead 2 to 3 minutes. Oil mixing bowl and place kneaded dough in it. Cover with plastic wrap and allow to rise in a warm area for ½ hour.

Preheat oven to 450 degrees. Rub cookie sheet with olive oil. Now divide dough into walnut-sized balls and roll into thin sticks about 9" to 10" long. Place on cookie sheet about 1" apart and bake at 450 degrees for 12 to 15 minutes. Makes about 2 dozen breadsticks.

| SHOPPING LIST | |
| --- | --- |
| **Regularly Kept in the Kitchen** (Listed in Chapter 14, p. 703) | **Fresh Produce** |
| Whole wheat flour<br>Baking yeast<br>Spike<br>Black pepper (or Parmesan cheese, poppy seeds or sesame seeds)<br>Olive oil | (None) |

Make a few batches and keep on hand for snacking or to go with meals.

# RAW "STIR-FRY"

☆ A meal-in-one dish that resembles a stir-fry; but thickening the sauce is the only cooking needed in the whole recipe!

☆ You can make pressed tofu at home (p. 117) if you can't find it in Chinatown groceries.

## SUGGESTED MENU

*Raw "Stir-Fry"*

*Brown rice*

*Hot jasmine tea or caffeine-free green tea*

---

½ oz. dry shiitake mushrooms
3 cups water

3 cups Pressed Tofu, cut in matchsticks
   (see recipe, p. 117)

1½ cups raw mung sprouts
1 cup slivered green bell pepper
1 cup slivered yellow or red bell pepper
1 cup carrot matchsticks
1 cup fresh Chinese snow peas
2 cups finely slivered Napa cabbage
½ tsp. black pepper

1 tsp. oil
½ Tbsp. grated fresh ginger
½ tsp. asafetida or 1 clove garlic, crushed

Soaked mushrooms, de-stemmed and slivered
1 cup mushroom soaking water
2 tsp. soy sauce
1 Tbsp. arrowroot

¼ cup slivered scallions
½ cup sliced almonds, raw or toasted

Put first 2 ingredients together and bring to a boil, turn heat down and simmer 10 to 15 minutes. Remove from heat and allow to soak till needed.

192

In the meantime, cut Pressed Tofu in ⅛"-thick matchsticks and lay in a thin layer on serving platter.

Prepare vegetables by slivering and cutting into very thin matchsticks as specified. Combine next 7 ingredients in a bowl and toss together. Pour on top of tofu bed.

In a small skillet, combine next 3 ingredients and saute over medium heat till fresh ginger browns. Add next 4 ingredients and stir till they thicken and come to a boil. Immediately pour over vegetables and tofu. Sprinkle with last 2 ingredients and serve immediately. Makes 6 to 8 servings.

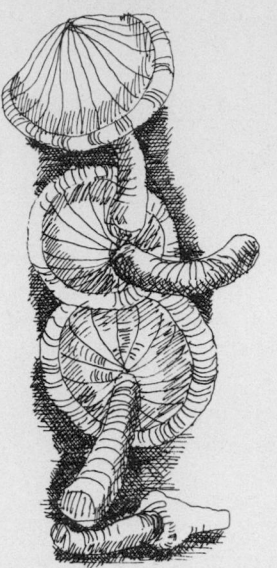

| SHOPPING LIST | |
|---|---|
| **Regularly Kept in the Kitchen** (Listed in Chapter 14, p. 703) | **Fresh Produce** |
| Dry shiitake mushrooms | Raw mung sprouts |
| Pressed Tofu (see recipe, p. 117) | Green bell pepper |
| Black pepper | Yellow or red bell pepper |
| Safflower oil | Carrots |
| Asafetida | Chinese snow peas |
| | Napa cabbage |
| | Fresh ginger root |

# NUTRITIONAL ANALYSIS FOR ONE SERVING RAW "STIR-FRY"

| NUTRIENT | Type: 14  FEMALE-23 TO 51 YEARS | % RDA | Amount |
|---|---|---|---|
| KCALORIES | A====== | 12% | 242.0 Kc |
| PROTEIN | A==================== | 42% | 18.60 Gm |
| CARBOHYDRATE | A | NO RDA | 18.00 Gm |
| FAT | A | NO RDA | 13.60 Gm |
| FIBER-CRUDE | A | NO RDA | 2.010 Gm |
| CHOLESTEROL | A | NO RDA | 0.000 Mg |
| SATURATED FA | A | NO RDA | 0.690 Gm |
| OLEIC FA | A | NO RDA | 4.050 Gm |
| LINOLEIC FA | A | NO RDA | 1.620 Gm |
| SODIUM | A=== | 6% | 153.0 Mg |
| POTASSIUM | A===== | 11% | 438.0 Mg |
| MAGNESIUM | A========== | 20% | 60.50 Mg |
| IRON | A============= | 26% | 4.850 Mg |
| ZINC | A= | 3% | 0.530 Mg |
| VITAMIN A | A================================================= | 191% | 7667 IU |
| VITAMIN D | A | 0% | 0.000 IU |
| VIT. E/TOTAL | A | NO RDA | 4.210 Mg |
| VITAMIN C | A================================================ | 123% | 73.80 Mg |
| THIAMIN | A========= | 18% | 0.180 Mg |
| RIBOFLAVIN | A========== | 20% | 0.240 Mg |
| NIACIN | A======== | 15% | 2.000 Mg |
| VITAMIN B6 | A==== | 8% | 0.160 Mg |
| FOLACIN | A=== | 7% | 31.10 Ug |
| VITAMIN B12 | A | 0% | 0.000 Ug |
| PANTO- ACID | A=== | 7% | 0.390 Mg |
| CALCIUM | A=================== | 39% | 316.0 Mg |
| PHOSPHORUS | A================= | 36% | 295.0 Mg |
| TRYPTOPHAN | A==================== | 41% | 67.60 Mg |
| THREONINE | A=================== | 40% | 174.0 Mg |
| ISOLEUCINE | A================= | 34% | 224.0 Mg |
| LEUCINE | A=================== | 39% | 342.0 Mg |
| LYSINE | A================= | 34% | 225.0 Mg |
| METHIONINE | A========= | 18% | 49.30 Mg |
| CYSTINE | A============ | 24% | 67.10 Mg |
| PHENYL-ANINE | A======================= | 49% | 217.0 Mg |
| TYROSINE | A================ | 33% | 144.0 Mg |
| VALINE | A================= | 35% | 269.0 Mg |
| HISTIDINE | A | NO RDA | 105.0 Mg |
| ALCOHOL | A | NO RDA | 0.000 Gm |
| ASH | A | NO RDA | 2.810 Gm |
| COPPER | A===== | 11% | 0.280 Mg |
| MANGANESE | A==== | 9% | 0.370 Mg |
| IODINE | A | 0% | 0.000 Ug |
| MONO FAT | A | NO RDA | 3.760 Gm |
| POLY FAT | A | NO RDA | 1.880 Gm |
| CAFFEINE | A | NO RDA | 0.000 Mg |
| FLUORIDE | A | 1% | 36.80 Ug |
| MOLYBDENUM | A | 0% | 2.060 Ug |
| VITAMIN K | A============================================ | 87% | 92.00 Ug |
| SELENIUM | A | NO DATA | NO DATA |
| BIOTIN | A= | 3% | 5.060 Ug |
| CHLORIDE | A | 0% | 0.740 Mg |
| CHROMIUM | A==== | 8% | 0.010 Mg |
| SUGAR | A | NO RDA | 4.160 Gm |
| FIBER-DIET | A | NO RDA | 2.230 Gm |
| VIT. E/AT | A==================== | 40% | 3.210 Mg |

```
% RDA:   |0      |20     |40     |60     |80     |100
```

Analysis does not include mushroom soaking water.

# CHAPTER 4

# MADE BY NATURE VS. MANMADE

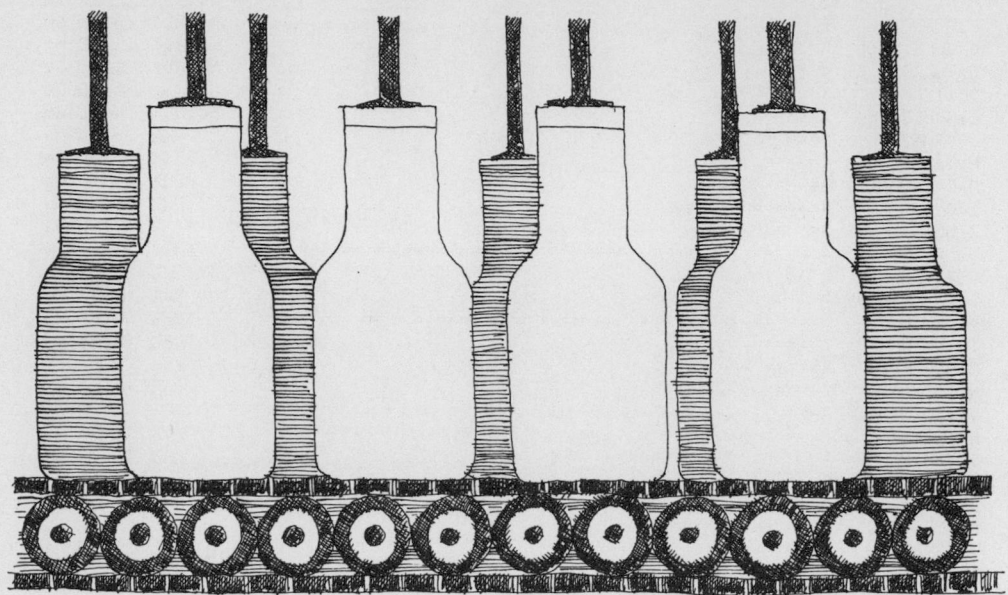

"Modern man does not experience himself as a part of nature but as an outside force destined to dominate and conquer it. He even talks of a battle with nature, forgetting that, if he won the battle, he would find himself on the losing side."

— *Small is Beautiful*
*Economics as if People Mattered*
by E. F. Schumacher

These words from the late British economist E. F. Schumacher on modern man's attitude toward nature, can be seen manifesting themselves in every aspect of life as we get further and further away from the natural order of things. The average person living in a "technologically-advanced" society eats a diet consisting of things he was never intended to eat (meat and chemicals), and food we are intended to eat (like grains) is adulterated beyond recognition. It's obvious that such a diet has put modern man on the losing side when statistics tell us that six of the 10 leading causes of death in the United States are diet-related diseases . . . a diet far removed from the one we are intended to eat, by nature.

## WE'RE NOT INTENDED TO EAT FLESH . . .

A study of the human body quickly reveals that it wasn't intended to eat flesh food of any kind.

### Herbivores (plant-eaters)—

• are equipped with flat teeth for cutting and grinding food.
• have saliva containing alpha-amylase, an enzyme whose only purpose is to digest complex carbohydrates.
• must chew food well, mixing it with saliva and swallowing small amounts down a small throat passage.
• have long, more complicated digestive tracts for digesting food high in dietary fiber, which means a longer period of time is needed for nutrients to be extracted.
• have intestines which are puckered and long.

### Carnivores (flesh-eaters)—

• are equipped with fangs for ripping flesh.
• are never found to have alpha-amylase in their saliva.
• don't chew their food, but tear off chunks and swallow them down a large throat passage.
• have short, simple digestive tracts for digesting food with little or no dietary fiber.
• have intestines which are smooth, like a pipe, and short.

## . . . NOR BE CHEMICAL DUMPING GROUNDS!

Although there are some who will debate whether the structure of the human body is evidence that we were never meant by the laws of nature to eat meat, I can't think of anyone in their right mind who would argue that we were intended to eat chemicals!

Because our bodies aren't made to ingest chemicals, I'm never surprised to hear that scientists, after long studies, have "discovered" that yet another chemical used in food causes (or plays a part in causing) cancer or other health problems. What surprises me is that chemical additives are allowed in food before the effect on human health is known (as was the case with saccharin). If experimenting on laboratory animals is considered inhumane, what should we consider using the U.S. "marketplace" (as industry calls all the people in the United States) as experimental ground?

Fortunately, we have more intelligence and freedom than laboratory animals. We can hear and weigh the debate between those in the food industry and health advocates. Food manufacturers, who continue to use chemical additives that have been proven in the lab to damage health, assert that laboratory animals are fed much larger quantities than people will ever eat at once. This implies that small amounts of a harmful chemical substance are safe to consume. Health advocates (and cancer experts) disagree, taking the stance that consuming even the most minute amount of a substance known to be car-cinogenic (or the cause of some other health problem) is too much; especially since chemical reactions between a few additives can compound the threat that only one substance poses to the health.

## BE AN INFORMED LABEL READER

Once an intelligent decision is made as to whether or not a particular element is good for us, we also have the ability to read labels and the freedom to buy or not buy a particular food product. With well over 2,000 food additives, it could be overwhelming to try to memorize a list of undesirables! On the other hand, I find the saying, "If you can't pronounce it, don't buy it!" too simplistic. There are some ingredients with long names that aren't harmful at all. I've found *A Consumer's Dictionary of Food Additives* by Ruth Winter to be an extremely valuable aid in weeding out chemical additives.

Reading labels is always a good practice, but one should be forewarned that a label may not necessarily tell what's in a food. Laws regarding labeling in this country are so inconsistent that the consumer who cares enough to read labels isn't served well by them. About 500 of more than 2,000 food additives don't have to be listed on labels. There are so many exceptions to the rule (of listing ingredients on the label in the order of predominance) that it makes me wonder why they bother to have a rule at all. It certainly gives the customer reading a label a false sense of security to feel he's being protected by labeling laws.

Some examples of how consumers can be misinformed by labels are as follows:

• Certain chemicals added in small quantities during processing of a food don't have to be listed.

• Rather than being required to list the specific chemical(s), the words "artificial coloring or flavoring" are enough.

• The government has made "recipes" or "formulas" for over 300 "standard foods" that list a variety of chemicals from which the food manufacturer can choose. As long as the manufacturer uses chemicals from the government "recipe" or "formula," he doesn't have to list them; the manufacturer only has to list ingredients on the label that are not included in the government's "recipe."

• If looking to avoid specific ingredients, one should know that an ingredient can sometimes be labeled differently. For example, refined white flour is listed as enriched flour, unbleached flour, or wheat flour (a product can be called "whole wheat bread" and still have refined flour in it; only "100% whole wheat" contains no refined flour). Corn syrup, raw and brown sugar, invert sugar, glucose, fructose and sucrose are only some of the words to look for if trying to eliminate simple sugars.

One thing that has made it easy for me to avoid chemical additives is the fact that they appear mostly in food I would not want to eat anyway. Many of these are foods we *are* intended by nature to eat, but which have been so altered and adulterated in the hands of man, we shouldn't. Through the process of refining, perfectly nutritious food is turned into a nutritional minus.

······························

"Although labeling regulations do not currently require the content of the different sugars to be described, if some sugar is listed as one of the first two or three ingredients, then one can reasonably assume that there is a lot of sugar added to the product. As noted earlier, use of fresh food enables greater protection against hidden refined and processed sugars."

— "Dietary Goals for the U.S."
U.S. Senate Select Committee
on Nutrition and Human Needs

······························

## THE BITTER TRUTH ABOUT SUGAR

As a source of empty calories, the number one food additive — sugar — is not only devoid of nutrients, but actually depletes B-vitamins from the body. In another sense, empty calories rob the body of all essential nutrients

because whatever percent of a person's diet is made up of empty calories could have consisted of wholesome, nutritious food. The chemical reactions sugar causes in the body lead to more sugar (and therefore empty-calorie) consumption. Looking at how the body reacts in response to sugar consumption makes me appreciate (and always leaves me in a little awe) what a complex, yet perfect creation the body is, complete with its own check-and-balance systems.

In its naturally perfect balance, the body has a normal blood-sugar level, and has naturally built-in mechanisms to regulate and keep the blood-sugar level as it should be. Sugar in the bloodstream in the form of glucose is necessary for the body to function properly; but we don't have to eat sugar to get sugar in the bloodstream. In fact, the most ideal way to get appropriate amounts of required sugar into the bloodstream is to eat whole (unrefined) plant food, also known as complex carbohydrates. Starches and sugars in whole plant food are converted to glucose very slowly, resulting in glucose trickling into the bloodstream over a long period of time. This gives the body energy to burn for a long period and a feeling of satiety. (The body doesn't feel hungry until enough glucose has been burned to make blood-sugar levels drop. At this point, the brain sends out hunger signals so we are forced to stop and refuel.) This is why many athletes favor a complex-carbohydrate diet.

As a matter of fact, the first time I was introduced to the fact that complex carbohydrates give long-sustained energy was when I was on a swim team in junior high. Amongst other dietary changes, our coach insisted that all team members stick to eating oranges at swim meets instead of chocolate bars.

He disproved the idea many of us had at the time that a chocolate bar eaten before our event would give us a winning burst of energy, by explaining the facts of body chemistry to us. When a candy bar — or any other food or drink with sugar in it — is consumed, the sugar enters the bloodstream almost immediately and all at once. This is because sugar is a simple carbohydrate; it doesn't have to be broken down or converted by the body and lacks fiber which, by itself, moderates and/or corrects blood-sugar and insulin levels.

When the bloodstream is overloaded with enough sugar all at once to push blood-sugar levels above normal, naturally built-in regulation systems are set off. The pancreas pumps out larger amounts of insulin than normal to compensate for the higher-than-normal amounts of glucose in the bloodstream (insulin burns or metabolizes glucose). The extra glucose is burned off very quickly by the extra insulin, which then stays in the bloodstream for hours, continuing to burn glucose and causing blood-sugar levels to fall below normal.

The initial lift a person feels (when glucose levels are high) quickly turns into a tired, hungry state (when glucose levels crash due to the rush of insulin sent into the bloodstream). Thus, instead of providing energy, eating sugar results in a person dragging around and not wanting or being able to do much due to a low-energy level, and

..............................

"If only a fraction of what is already known about the effects of sugar were to be revealed in relation to any other material used as a food additive, that material would promptly be banned . . . "

— Dr. John Yudkin
Physician, Biochemist and
Emeritus Professor of Nutrition
at London University

..............................

wanting to eat more — especially craving more sweets.

If that craving is followed, it can turn into a vicious cycle that throws the body's metabolism and blood-sugar levels off. Constantly setting blood-sugar and insulin levels off-kilter leads to hypoglycemia or diabetes, one of the 10 leading causes of death in the United States.

All of these chemical changes in the body caused by sugar have something to do with getting fatter. Following the hunger and sweet cravings caused by low blood-sugar levels (not an empty stomach) will lead to consuming more calories than needed. Most likely the food eaten will be another sweet, to satisfy the craving for sweets. Sweets made with sugar usually contain large amounts of fat (not to mention chemical additives!), which is the most fattening source of calories. Eating more calories than needed (those being mostly empty calories and fat), coupled with little physical activity due to the tired — even depressed — state of being in which low blood sugar leaves a person, is obviously a fattening combination. A little less obvious, but a fact of body chemistry, is that fat contributes to insulin resistance, a condition where the effects of insulin are blocked. When this takes place, the metabolizing of glucose in the bloodstream (by insulin) is blocked; as a result, blood-sugar levels remain high, which causes the pancreas to continue to pump out more and more insulin.

Insulin has other functions besides metabolizing glucose. Insulin also stimulates the production of some lipoproteins, the production of fat by the liver and the growth of the fatty tissue (andipose tissue) where the body's fat stores are kept.

## ESSENTIAL FIBER: ONE REASON NOT TO REFINE FOODS

What food doesn't stimulate insulin production? All unrefined complex carbohydrates (whole, unprocessed plant food). Fiber in complex carbohydrates has been found to moderate and even correct insulin levels in the bloodstream. Eating an orange with a certain amount of fruit sugar in it causes less of a rise in insulin levels than consuming the same amount of fruit sugar in orange juice.

From the time it enters the mouth to the time it leaves the body, dietary fiber plays a key role in helping to keep the body trim in a number of

..............................

*Many diet books and programs center around the myth that carbohydrates are fattening. This myth exists because the majority of carbohydrates Americans consume are simple (refined) carbohydrates.*

..............................

ways. First of all, food high in dietary fiber helps us to naturally limit the number of calories we consume. Since the foods high in dietary fiber are all unprocessed plant foods (whole grains, legumes, vegetables and fruit), we can also be assured that the calories are packed with nutrition (not empty calories).

I remember, when I first started eating whole grains, being amazed that I could only eat three to four slices of whole wheat bread where I could eat practically a whole

loaf of white bread. I have since learned that there are scientific explanations for this. The mechanisms in the body that regulate appetite are blood-sugar levels (as we've already discussed), a satiety system in the brain (the scientific word for this is "appestat"), and the state of fullness of the stomach.

Studies have shown that chewing and swallowing, and taking a long time to eat, are factors in setting off the satiety system in the brain to make a person feel full and make that feeling of satiety last for a longer period of time. The reasons why this is so aren't completely clear. Studies have shown that the activities of chewing and swallowing in themselves increase electrical activity in the part of the brain connected with satiety. It appears to take about five minutes after food first enters the mouth for any feeling of satiety to begin to register, and around 20 minutes before all mechanisms coordinate to communicate that the stomach is full, no matter how much food is eaten. Eating very quickly means very large quantities of calories can be gulped down before the body even gets a chance to turn its satiety signals on. Even though we may not all be fast eaters, I'm sure every one of us can recall having at least once hungrily and quickly gulped down a meal in 10 to 15 minutes, only to suddenly feel uncomfortably stuffed five to 10 minutes later (as the body's satiety mechanisms

caught up with us). Chewing well and eating slowly gives the body's satiety systems a chance to begin sending out signals before too many calories are consumed. Eating food high in dietary fiber forces us to chew well to break down cell walls, thus automatically slowing down eating time.

How dietary fiber makes the stomach feel full, thus cutting down on calorie intake, is more obvious. The stomach feels full because it is! Dietary fiber is bulk, so it takes up a lot of room and stays in the stomach longer than processed foods do. The cell walls of fiber contain no

..............................

*Simple carbohydrates are fattening; complex carbohydrates are not.*

..............................

calories.

Filling up on food high in dietary fiber naturally limits calorie intake and actually removes calories from the system at the other end. Fiber keeps a lot of fat and cholesterol from being digested and absorbs cholesterol and fat (as well as chemical toxins) from the bloodstream and removes them from the body. Cholesterol output in stool on a diet high in dietary fiber can be three times greater than on a diet low in dietary fiber.

This helps to keep the body slim while performing some life-saving work at the same time. Dietary fiber has been scientifically proven to prevent and even help reverse major killers like heart disease, cancer of the colon and diabetes. Lack of dietary fiber has even been linked to diverticular disease, varicose veins, constipation and hemorrhoids, ulcers, and appendicitis. Unfortunately, the process of refining strips essential fiber from whole grains along with the extremely nutritious germ.

## LIFE WITHOUT DENATURED FOODS

Other than the economics behind the fact that people have gotten used to the appearance of food made with refined grains (I remember not even touching brown rice the first time it was served to me after 14 years of white rice because it was *brown!*), people in the food industry also use refined grains — usually along with chemical preservatives — to preserve shelf life. Taking into account all the benefits to health (and contributions to a trim body) that unrefined, unprocessed food

offers, it appears that it really is time to consider "economics as if people mattered"! And possibly, through changing our diets to a more natural

......................................

*"We want enhanced food because all our lives we have been subjected to the beautiful pictures of foods in our magazines and on television. We have come to expect an advertiser's concept of perfection in color and texture, even though Mother Nature may not turn out all her products that way."*

— Ruth Winter
A Consumer's Dictionary
of Food Additives

......................................

one, we will experience and begin understanding the need and benefit of living in harmony with nature in all aspects of our lives.

Over 18 years ago, I stopped

eating anything with refined sugar, refined grains or chemical preservatives in it. A short tour of a supermarket will tell you this eliminated almost three-fourths of the foodstuffs appearing on supermarket shelves from my list. This has improved a little, as more and more shoppers are looking for food made from whole grains and sweeteners that contain at least some nutrients and are free from chemical preservatives. There are now some already-made products on store shelves that meet these specifications and, as the demand grows, food manufacturers will respond with more truly edible products. In the meantime, making these changes in your diet may mean preparing a lot of food at home.

The whole ninth chapter centers on whole grains. Since sweets play a small part in my family's diet (we eat sweets, other than fruit, only three to four times a month at most), they get an equally small part in this book.

# NATURALLY SWEET

Henry David Thoreau and Ralph Waldo Emerson were friends who shared thoughts and learned much from observing nature. In commenting on how observing the perfect order of things in nature taught him faith, Ralph Waldo Emerson wrote, "All that I have seen teaches me to trust the Creator for all I have not seen."

Sweets don't play a very big part in the diet around our home. As a matter of fact, even when sweets are offered to them, a few of the boys usually end up saying thanks, but they don't like sweets very much. Because sweets (other than fruit) are served only a few times a month, if that, the children have never really developed a sweet tooth. I guess that makes us "not very average Americans" as far as statistics go.

The importance of sweets to most Americans is demonstrated by the fact that Americans wrote more letters of concern to their congressmen about the saccharin controversy than they did about the Vietnam war! Saccharin is a potentially carcinogenic replacement for sugar, of which Americans eat enough to average out to 140 pounds per person in a year. That's about three-fourths cup of sugar per day! You may be thinking, "I never use that much sugar a day!" But this is true of almost everyone; much of the sugar we eat is hidden in the pre-prepared food we purchase. We may not realize how much sugar is in the sweets we buy; a one-cup serving of fruit-flavored yogurt contains as much sugar as a 12-ounce soda (about 2 tablespoons), 1 tablespoon of jam contains 1 tablespoon of sugar, etc. A quick scan of labels tells us that we get sugar in our diets even if we don't eat sweets. Sugar can be found in unsweet places like spaghetti sauce, salad dressings, pickles and relishes, crackers, breads, different flavored chips, some canned vegetables, treated meat and cold cuts, savory dry mixes (like gravies or breadings for meat), alchoholic beverages, etc. With sugar in almost everything, it's no wonder that we're practically a nation of sugar-addicts.

When trying to eliminate sugar from the diet, besides careful label reading, you will probably find yourself making a lot of things from scratch to be able to control what sweetener you put into your body. As far as chemical sweeteners go, I don't even consider them an alternative. Since they are made of chemicals that don't belong in our bodies, I'm assuming that in the long-run all chemical additives will end up going the way of saccharin and cyclamates. Besides the as yet unidentified hazards of chemical sweeteners, there are some undesirable known effects they have on the body. Where sugar produces a temporary feeling of satiety due to a rise in blood-sugar levels, chemical sweeteners don't give a feeling of satisfaction or fullness because they don't affect blood-sugar levels at all. They may even increase a craving for sweets by stimulating the sweet sensors on the tastebuds without supplying any sugar to the bloodstream to signal that craving being satisfied.

Sweetness is one of the four basic tastes the tongue recognizes, so in a sense a certain degree of desire for sweets is natural — best satisfied with natural sweets. I don't stretch the definition of "natural" as many food manufacturers do. Labeling laws specify the word "natural" can be applied to anything that comes from nature, no matter how far removed from its natural state a refining process has taken it. That's why food manufacturers get away with stamping "natural" all over labels and ads for food made with refined flour and sugar.

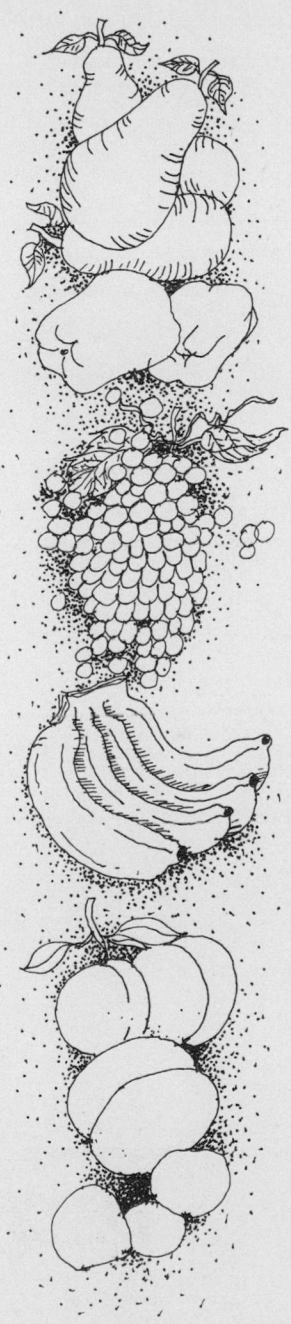

The most natural, and therefore most ideal, way to satisfy the taste for sweets is to eat whole pieces of fruit. Fresh fruit is one sweet eaten every day in our home. We keep a big basketful of fruit on a counter available to everyone all day long for snacking or a light meal. Sometimes the children choose to eat fruit for a meal instead of something else I've prepared, and I never object. Fruits are a complex carbohydrate, so I use them as much as I can in place of simple carbohydrates for sweetening.

Since the whole twelfth chapter contains recipes showing how to use whole fruit as a natural sweetener, I'll use this space to describe the simple carbohydrates that I use as sweeteners where fruit won't work. Before I describe them and their functions in recipes, I'd like to clarify some things about simple carbohydrates.

Technically speaking, the word "carbohydrate" is used to describe a chemical compound in which parts of hydrogen and oxygen are combined with carbon. All carbohydrates are formed by the process of photosynthesis, which is why all carbohydrate food is either a plant food or derived from a plant food. Man hasn't been able to completely figure out, much less reproduce the process of photosynthesis. Through the process of photosynthesis, sunlight, water and carbon dioxide in the atmosphere are transformed into energy in the form of plant sugars. There are two different kinds of carbohydrates — simple and complex.

Simple carbohydrates, as the name suggests, have a very simple structure, being made up of one or two simple sugars. A simple rule for finding simple carbohydrates is — any food that's sweet has simple carbohydrates in it. Fruits have simple sugars in them, but the fiber in fruit keeps the sugar from rushing into the bloodstream all at once.

Without the protection offered by fiber, any simple carbohydrate will cause blood-sugar levels to rise; for this reason, all simple sugars should be sensibly doled out. Because of this fact, some people erroneously present a half-truth by asserting there is no difference between eating white sugar and honey (or any other natural sweetener). All the natural sweeteners that I use in place of sugar do cause a rise in blood-sugar levels, but that's where the similarity ends.

As an empty calorie, refined white sugar provides nothing in the way of essential vitamins and minerals, whereas unrefined or less refined sweeteners do. Following are the sweeteners I keep in my kitchen to accomplish sweetening jobs where fruit won't do, in the order of desirability and frequency of use.

**Date sugar.** Technically, date sugar is still a complex carbohydrate as it is ground up, dried dates. Date sugar still contains dietary fiber as well as all the nutrients found in dates. It's a wonderful substitute for refined sugar in cases where it can be sprinkled on top of something (like breakfast cereal or yogurt), or used in a crumb topping, replacing a cup per cup (such as for cobblers or strudels). Unfortunately, cooking with date sugar is limited by some of its qualities; date sugar doesn't dissolve but just gets mushy when put in liquid or batters. It's also a little less sweet than white sugar.

**Frozen fruit juice concentrates.** For a processed food (stripped of essential fiber), juices and juice concentrates aren't bad because they retain a good amount of vitamins and minerals. The degree of sweetness varies from one kind of juice to another, as well as the flavor, which is the only drawback I can think of in using juice. Flavors of some concentrates are so strong that they may not be suitable for certain recipes. With the greater demand for "no sugar added" drinks, I've noticed more and more unsweetened juice concentrate flavors available in supermarket freezer sections. You'll have to experiment with substituting juice concentrates for sugar in your favorite recipes because of the wide variety of concentrate flavors, but always remember to subtract about ⅓ cup of liquid in the recipe for each cup of frozen concentrate used.

**Honey.** Pure, unheated, untreated honey is nature's only processed food; honey is nectar from flowers which is processed by the honeybee. The nice thing about this natural processing is that more is added in the process, as opposed to refining, where nutrients put there by nature are removed. The nutritional content and flavor of honey varies depending on what flower the nectar came from, what soil the plant grew in and other environmental conditions. No matter what kind of honey it is, it contains enzymes, propolis (added by the bees), pollen and minute amounts of vitamins and minerals, which is obviously preferable to no nutrients.

Honey is about twice as sweet as sugar, so in substituting honey for sugar you only need half as much. Be sure to subtract ¼ cup of the liquid in the recipe for each cup of honey used.

**Barbados molasses.** This is a molasses made from sugar cane juice for its own sake, whereas blackstrap molasses is a result of the first sugar extraction in the refining process of making white sugar from sugar cane. Barbados molasses is lighter in color and sweeter than blackstrap molasses and contains only slightly less iron, calcium, potassium and B-vitamins. I like to use Barbados molasses in baking recipes that call for the rich molasses-like flavor of brown sugar because the nutritional value of brown sugar is about the same as white sugar. To replace brown sugar, use the same amount of Barbados molasses and subtract ¼ cup of liquid in the recipe for each cup of molasses used.

**Maple syrup and maple syrup sugar.** I use these very rarely (like once a year, if that) because they're such expensive sweeteners. The distinctive maple syrup flavor adds a special taste to special dishes. When cooked down, maple syrup will actually crystallize and harden, whereas honey becomes sticky with a taffy-like hardness.

# ANY·KIND·OF·FRUIT CRISP

☆ Use 5 cups of your favorite fruit, or a combination of fruits on the bottom. Mainly I wanted to give you this recipe so you could get a feeling for using date sugar.

---

Baking with date sugar can be a little tricky because it burns quickly. The best way I've found to bake with it when sprinkled on top of something is to cover item being baked with foil and uncover only the last 10 minutes. (If mixed in or under other ingredients there won't be a burning problem as it's shielded by moisture.)

5 cups fruit (berries, cherries or apples, etc.)
¾ cup frozen 100% pineapple juice concentrate
3 Tbsp. minute tapioca
2 Tbsp. lemon juice
¼ tsp. cardamom
¼ tsp. very finely grated lemon rind

¾ cup almond or raw cashew butter
½ cup whole wheat flour
¼ cup rolled oats
2 Tbsp. bran
2 Tbsp. wheat germ

½ cup date sugar

Preheat oven to 375 degrees. Mix first 6 ingredients together thoroughly and pour evenly into an 8" or 9" cake pan. Cut next 5 ingredients together till nut butter is completely cut in and mixture is a sand-like texture. Add date sugar and mix in thoroughly. Sprinkle evenly over top of fruit.

Cover with foil and bake at 375 degrees for about 30 minutes. Remove foil and bake, uncovered, for another 10 to 15 minutes — till topping is browned and crisp. Makes 12 servings.

| Special Shopping | SHOPPING LIST | |
|---|---|---|
| | **Regularly Kept in the Kitchen** (Listed in Chapter 14, p. 703) | **Fresh Produce** |
| Date sugar — in some natural food stores. | Cardamom<br>Almond or raw cashew butter<br>Oats<br>Bran<br>Wheat germ | Fruit of your choice suitable for crisps (berries, cherries, apples)<br>Frozen 100% pineapple juice concentrate<br>Minute tapioca<br>Lemon |

# PINA·COLADA CAKE

☆ A cool, fruity cake; especially appreciated in warm to hot weather.

---

½ cup frozen 100% pineapple juice concentrate
⅓ cup frozen 100% apple juice concentrate
½ cup well-drained crushed pineapple
¼ cup butter or margarine
½ tsp. vanilla extract

2 cups whole wheat flour
2 tsp. baking powder
1 tsp. baking soda

½ cup well-drained crushed pineapple

1½ cups coconut milk
3 Tbsp. arrowroot

¼ cup frozen 100% pineapple or
apple juice concentrate

1½ cups crushed pineapple
1 Tbsp. arrowroot

Unsweetened shredded coconut

The icing is a watered-down version of a Hawaiian coconut pudding called "haupia." To make haupia, just add an extra 2 tablespoons of arrowroot to recipe, pour into a square cake pan, and refrigerate till chilled. Cut into squares or scoop into dessert cups. Especially good served topped with sprinkle of toasted coconut or slices of mango.

Get all ingredients out so they can come to room temperature. Preheat oven to 350 degrees and oil an 8" or 9" cake pan.

Blend first 5 ingredients together in a blender till smooth. Pour into mixing bowl and sift next 3 ingredients on top of blended mixture. Beat dry ingredients in well till all lumps are gone — but no longer. Be careful not to overmix. Fold pineapple into batter and pour into oiled cake pan. Bake at 350 degrees for 40 to 45 minutes, till a toothpick inserted in the middle comes out clean. Remove from oven and allow to sit in cake pan for about 15 minutes before turning onto a cooling rack. Sprinkle entire surface of warm cake with shredded coconut and allow cake to cool.

While cake is baking, mix coconut milk and arrowroot in a saucepan till arrowroot dissolves. Put pan on heat and stir constantly till mixture boils and thickens. Add juice concentrate and stir in, continuing till mixture re-boils and thickens. Remove from heat and cool. Do the same in a separate pot with crushed pineapple and arrowroot.

When cake, thickened pineapple and thickened coconut milk are cooled, split cake in half so you have two layers. Spread thickened pineapple over surface of bottom layer; top with second layer. Spread coconut milk over entire surface of cake like an icing. Sprinkle entire surface with shredded coconut and refrigerate till serving time. Makes one 9" cake (about 12 to 16 servings).

| SHOPPING LIST | |
|---|---|
| **Regularly Kept in the Kitchen** (Listed in Chapter 14, p. 703) | **Fresh Produce** |
| Butter or margarine<br>Vanilla<br>Whole wheat flour<br>Baking powder<br>Baking soda<br>Arrowroot | Frozen 100% pineapple<br>   juice concentrate<br>Frozen 100% apple<br>   juice concentrate<br>Fresh pineapple or can<br>   of unsweetened crushed<br>   pineapple<br>Coconut milk OR coconut<br>   (to make milk, p. 129)<br>Unsweetened shredded<br>   coconut |

# NUTRITIONAL ANALYSIS FOR ONE SERVING PINA-COLADA CAKE

```
NUTRIENT        Type: 14    FEMALE-23 TO 51 YEARS              % RDA    Amount
KCALORIES       A======                                        12%     244.0 Kc
PROTEIN         A====                                           8%     3.870 Gm
CARBOHYDRATE    A                                            NO RDA    33.00 Gm
FAT             A                                            NO RDA    12.00 Gm
FIBER-CRUDE     A                                            NO RDA    0.750 Gm
CHOLESTEROL     A                                            NO RDA    0.000 Mg
SATURATED FA    A                                            NO RDA    7.530 Gm
OLEIC FA        A                                            NO RDA    0.090 Gm
LINOLEIC FA     A                                            NO RDA    0.210 Gm
SODIUM          A====                                           8%     192.0 Mg
POTASSIUM       A====                                           8%     317.0 Mg
MAGNESIUM       A=======                                       15%     46.40 Mg
IRON            A====                                           8%     1.610 Mg
ZINC            A==                                             5%     0.800 Mg
VITAMIN A       A==                                             4%     172.0 IU
VITAMIN D       A                                               0%     0.000 IU
VIT. E/TOTAL    A                                            NO RDA    0.820 Mg
VITAMIN C       A===========                                   22%     13.50 Mg
THIAMIN         A=========                                     19%     0.190 Mg
RIBOFLAVIN      A==                                             4%     0.050 Mg
NIACIN          A=====                                         10%     1.400 Mg
VITAMIN B6      A===                                            7%     0.150 Mg
FOLACIN         A=                                              3%     14.70 Ug
VITAMIN B12     A                                               0%     0.000 Ug
PANTO- ACID     A===                                            7%     0.410 Mg
CALCIUM         A====                                           8%     65.70 Mg
PHOSPHORUS      A============                                  22%     177.0 Mg
TRYPTOPHAN      A=============                                 26%     43.80 Mg
THREONINE       A============                                  25%     109.0 Mg
ISOLEUCINE      A===========                                   23%     151.0 Mg
LEUCINE         A=============                                 27%     243.0 Mg
LYSINE          A========                                      17%     117.0 Mg
METHIONINE      A==========                                    21%     59.00 Mg
CYSTINE         A=============                                 27%     73.90 Mg
PHENYL-ANINE    A====================                          40%     174.0 Mg
TYROSINE        A==============                                29%     128.0 Mg
VALINE          A===========                                   23%     176.0 Mg
HISTIDINE       A                                            NO RDA    75.30 Mg
ALCOHOL         A                                            NO RDA    0.000 Gm
ASH             A                                            NO RDA    1.020 Gm
COPPER          A=====                                         11%     0.280 Mg
MANGANESE       A=================================             65%     2.460 Mg
IODINE          A============================                  56%     84.60 Ug
MONO FAT        A                                            NO RDA    2.110 Gm
POLY FAT        A                                            NO RDA    1.380 Gm
CAFFEINE        A                                            NO RDA    0.000 Mg
FLUORIDE        A                                               0%     4.510 Ug
MOLYBDENUM      A==================================================  369%  1200 Ug
VITAMIN K       A                                               0%     0.000 Ug
SELENIUM        A                                               0%     0.000 Mg
BIOTIN          A                                               0%     1.000 Ug
CHLORIDE        A                                               1%     38.00 Mg
CHROMIUM        A=================================================   96%  0.120 Mg
SUGAR           A                                            NO RDA    0.000 Gm
FIBER-DIET      A                                            NO RDA    3.520 Gm
VIT. E/AT       A=                                              2%     0.200 Mg

    % RDA:   |0        |20      |40     |60      |80     |100
```

Margarine used instead of butter in this analysis.

Whenever measuring honey in a measuring cup, pour oil in cup first (if recipe calls for it), then the honey; or (if recipe doesn't call for oil), lightly oil measuring cup before measuring honey. This makes honey slide right out of the cup.

# BASIC LIGHT WHOLE WHEAT CAKE

☆ A light cake that dispels the mistaken idea that "health food" desserts have to be heavy and taste like horse food.

☆ This recipe is here to give you an idea of how to convert a baking recipe. The original recipe ingredients are listed in the ingredient list in parentheses. The rules for substituting honey and eggs have previously been described; in addition, when baking cakes, for every egg left out I also add about ½ teaspoon of apple cider vinegar and ½ teaspoon baking soda for a lighter cake.

---

⅔ cup honey (1¼ cups sugar)
½ cup butter or margarine (¾ cup)

½ cup yogurt (3 eggs)
⅓ cup lowfat milk (½ cup)
1½ tsp. apple cider vinegar
2 tsp. vanilla extract (same)

2½ cups whole wheat flour
   (refined white flour)
1 Tbsp. baking powder (same)
1½ tsp. baking soda

Preheat oven to 350 degrees and oil two 8" or 9" cake pans. In mixing bowl, beat first 2 ingredients together till smooth. Pour next 4 ingredients on top of this; then sift next 3 ingredients on top and mix in thoroughly. Divide batter in half and spread each half in one of the oiled cake pans. Bake at 350 degrees for 20 minutes, till a toothpick inserted in the middle comes out clean. Allow to cool 15 minutes in cake pan, then remove cakes from pans and cool on cooling racks. Now you have two layers of a basic cake that can be dressed up with a sugarless icing and/or fillings between layers. You can also split each layer in half so you end up with four thin layers to layer something between.

The possibilities for dressing this cake are only as limited as your imagination. Using different fillings and icings will give you a completely different cake each time!

Some suggestions to get your imagination rolling:

1) Spread a honey- or fruit juice-sweetened jam between each layer and frost with the lemon variation of the Basic Icing recipe.
2) If you want a thicker, fruitier filling than the jam can provide, make your own fruit filling by cooking 3 cups fresh fruit with 2 tablespoons arrowroot till thickened (add a couple tablespoons of honey if using a tart fruit).
3) Fill between layers with Vanilla Filling (p. 448) and ice with fruity variation of the Basic Icing (strawberries are a nice choice, as they add their unique flavor and pretty color).
4) Fill between layers with carob icing or Carob Fondue (p. 235) and decorate top with roasted almonds.
5) Etc.

| SHOPPING LIST | |
| --- | --- |
| **Regularly Kept in the Kitchen** (Listed in Chapter 14, p. 703) | **Fresh Produce** |
| Honey Butter or margarine Yogurt Milk Apple cider vinegar Vanilla Whole wheat flour Baking powder Baking soda | |

And ingredients needed for making icing and desired filling between layers.

# NUTRITIONAL ANALYSIS FOR ONE SERVING
## BASIC LIGHT WHOLE WHEAT CAKE WITH BASIC ICING

| NUTRIENT | Type: 14    FEMALE-23 TO 51 YEARS | % RDA | Amount |
|----------|-----------------------------------|-------|--------|
| KCALORIES | ========= | 14% | 284.0 Kc |
| PROTEIN | ======= | 15% | 6.860 Gm |
| CARBOHYDRATE | | NO RDA | 43.50 Gm |
| FAT | | NO RDA | 10.20 Gm |
| FIBER-CRUDE | | NO RDA | 0.600 Gm |
| CHOLESTEROL | | NO RDA | 2.570 Mg |
| SATURATED FA | | NO RDA | 1.840 Gm |
| OLEIC FA | | NO RDA | 0.130 Gm |
| LINOLEIC FA | | NO RDA | 0.250 Gm |
| SODIUM | ========= | 16% | 373.0 Mg |
| POTASSIUM | ==== | 7% | 280.0 Mg |
| MAGNESIUM | ======= | 13% | 40.10 Mg |
| IRON | === | 5% | 0.990 Mg |
| ZINC | ==== | 6% | 1.040 Mg |
| VITAMIN A | ====== | 10% | 413.0 IU |
| VITAMIN D | | 1% | 2.800 IU |
| VIT. E/TOTAL | | NO RDA | 0.990 Mg |
| VITAMIN C | | 1% | 0.660 Mg |
| THIAMIN | ========= | 17% | 0.170 Mg |
| RIBOFLAVIN | ======== | 15% | 0.190 Mg |
| NIACIN | ===== | 9% | 1.290 Mg |
| VITAMIN B6 | ==== | 6% | 0.120 Mg |
| FOLACIN | === | 4% | 18.70 Ug |
| VITAMIN B12 | ======= | 13% | 0.390 Ug |
| PANTO- ACID | ======= | 13% | 0.760 Mg |
| CALCIUM | ============== | 24% | 194.0 Mg |
| PHOSPHORUS | ================== | 34% | 279.0 Mg |
| TRYPTOPHAN | ============================ | 53% | 86.60 Mg |
| THREONINE | =============================== | 58% | 253.0 Mg |
| ISOLEUCINE | ============================= | 54% | 354.0 Mg |
| LEUCINE | =================================== | 65% | 570.0 Mg |
| LYSINE | ============================== | 57% | 376.0 Mg |
| METHIONINE | =========================== | 51% | 141.0 Mg |
| CYSTINE | =================== | 36% | 100.0 Mg |
| PHENYL-ANINE | ========================================== | 77% | 337.0 Mg |
| TYROSINE | ==================================== | 67% | 295.0 Mg |
| VALINE | ============================ | 52% | 398.0 Mg |
| HISTIDINE | | NO RDA | 162.0 Mg |
| ALCOHOL | | NO RDA | 0.000 Gm |
| ASH | | NO RDA | 1.350 Gm |
| COPPER | === | 5% | 0.130 Mg |
| MANGANESE | ================= | 33% | 1.250 Mg |
| IODINE | ===================================== | 73% | 110.0 Ug |
| MONO FAT | | NO RDA | 4.520 Gm |
| POLY FAT | | NO RDA | 3.100 Gm |
| CAFFEINE | | NO RDA | 0.000 Mg |
| FLUORIDE | | 0% | 27.40 Ug |
| MOLYBDENUM | ================================================= | 461% | 1500 Ug |
| VITAMIN K | | 0% | 0.390 Ug |
| SELENIUM | | 0% | 0.000 Mg |
| BIOTIN | | 0% | 1.490 Ug |
| CHLORIDE | | 1% | 47.50 Mg |
| CHROMIUM | ==================================================== | 120% | 0.150 Mg |
| SUGAR | | NO RDA | 0.000 Gm |
| FIBER-DIET | | NO RDA | 3.790 Gm |
| VIT. E/AT | = | 2% | 0.200 Mg |

```
% RDA:   |0      |20     |40     |60     |80     |100
```

Margarine used instead of butter; analysis does not include optional variations.

# BASIC ICING

☆ Use this icing, or variations of it, to dress the Basic Light Whole Wheat Cake up in different ways.

¼ cup honey
2 Tbsp. butter or margarine
2 Tbsp. some liquid (depending on variation; water is okay for plain vanilla icing)
½ tsp. vanilla

¾ cup noninstant, nonfat milk powder

Cream first 4 ingredients together. Gradually add and mix in milk powder. Makes enough to cover one 9" cake.

Make variations on this icing by changing some of the ingredients and adding others. For example —

1) *Lemon variation:* Use 2 tablespoons lemon juice as the liquid and add ¼ teaspoon very finely grated lemon rind.
2) *Orange variation:* Use 2 tablespoons frozen orange juice concentrate and 1 teaspoon finely grated orange rind.
3) *Fruity variation:* Replace liquid with ½ cup of whatever mashed fruit you like (strawberries, pineapple, etc.).
4) *Carob variation:* Replace half of the noninstant, nonfat milk with carob powder and a tablespoon of grain coffee.
5) *Carob-mint variation:* Make changes as in #4 and replace vanilla with mint extract.

The variations go on and on . . . got the idea? Try some innovations of your own!

| SHOPPING LIST | |
|---|---|
| Regularly Kept in the Kitchen (Listed in Chapter 14, p. 703) | Fresh Produce |
| Honey<br>Butter or margarine<br>Vanilla | (None) |

Noninstant, nonfat milk powder and whatever ingredients needed for making variations.

Try dipping your finger in the milk powder and taste it to see how sweet it is. Lactose, the sugar found in milk, is another simple sugar; it provides some of the sweetness in this icing.

# MOM'S CONVERTED AUNT ESTHER'S CRISP COOKIES

☆ This is one of those recipes with a long history of hands it has passed through. It finally ended up in my aunt's, who then gave it to my mother. As I've mentioned throughout this book, my mother is good at converting recipes and especially does so to make her grandchildren something they will eat. She took my aunt's recipe and converted all the ingredients to healthier ones. My children loved the cookies, so I got the recipe from her; then one day I tried making them with Barbados molasses instead of honey because I thought it would go nicely with the spiciness of the cookie. Using Barbados molasses makes a less sweet cookie (than if honey is used), which is the way my children like it. If you want a sweeter cookie, use honey.

---

6 Tbsp. yogurt
¾ cup Barbardos molasses (or honey)
1 cup safflower oil

3 cups whole wheat flour
2 Tbsp. cinnamon
¼ tsp. cloves and/or nutmeg
1 tsp. baking powder, sifted
1 tsp. baking soda, sifted

1 cup chopped nuts and/or whole sunflower seeds
1 cup raisins

Honey is *hygroscopic*, meaning it attracts moisture. While this is great because it helps to keep any baked good it's in from getting stale, it's hard to make a crisp cookie with honey. As seen in this recipe, it is possible by using a low oven heat to dry out the moisture. Store in an airtight container to retain moisture.

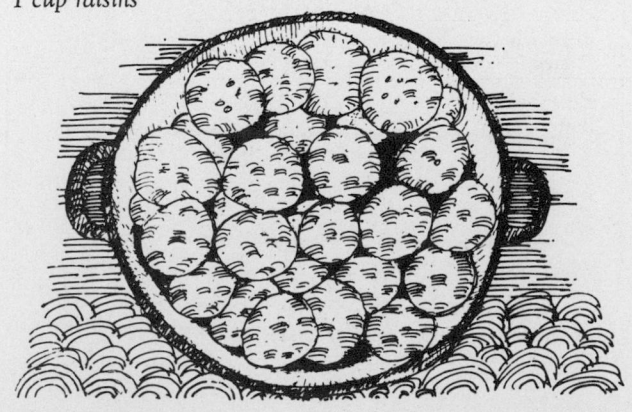

Preheat oven to 375 degrees and oil 2 cookie sheets. Cream first 3 ingredients together. Add next 5 ingredients and mix thoroughly. Sprinkle some flour over, and toss into, last 2 ingredients; then fold into dough. Refrigerate dough.

Divide dough into 4 and lay each fourth in a strip down the length of cookie sheets (2 strips on each sheet). Wet hands, flatten strips to about ⅜" thick and shape into even strips.

Bake 10 to 15 minutes till golden brown. Remove from oven and cut across width of strips to form bar-shaped cookies about 2" long by the width of the strip. Flip bars over in cookie sheet and return to oven. Bake another 5 to 10 minutes till brown. Remove from oven and turn cookies over again. Return to oven and turn heat off. Leave in oven till cookies get crisp. To test for crispness, remove one cookie from oven and allow to cool (cookie will be soft while warm). Length of time required in the unheated oven will vary, depending on how well your oven retains heat. For a moist bar cookie, just bake 15 minutes the first time and remove from heat. Makes about 2 dozen large cookies.

| SHOPPING LIST | |
| --- | --- |
| **Regularly Kept in the Kitchen** (Listed in Chapter 14, p. 703) | **Fresh Produce** |
| Yogurt | (None) |
| Barbados molasses | |
| Safflower oil | |
| Whole wheat flour | |
| Cinnamon | |
| Cloves and/or nutmeg | |
| Baking powder | |
| Baking soda | |
| Chopped nuts and/or sunflower seeds | |
| Raisins | |

# NUTRITIONAL ANALYSIS FOR TWO OF MOM'S CONVERTED AUNT ESTHER'S CRISP COOKIES

| NUTRIENT | Type: 14  FEMALE-23 TO 51 YEARS | % RDA | Amount |
|---|---|---|---|
| KCALORIES | Ȣ=========== | 20% | 418.0 Kc |
| PROTEIN | Ȣ======= | 15% | 6.960 Gm |
| CARBOHYDRATE | Ȣ | NO RDA | 47.50 Gm |
| FAT | Ȣ | NO RDA | 24.50 Gm |
| FIBER-CRUDE | Ȣ | NO RDA | 1.410 Gm |
| CHOLESTEROL | Ȣ | NO RDA | 0.430 Mg |
| SATURATED FA | Ȣ | NO RDA | 2.430 Gm |
| OLEIC FA | Ȣ | NO RDA | 6.240 Gm |
| LINOLEIC FA | Ȣ | NO RDA | 14.60 Gm |
| SODIUM | Ȣ== | 5% | 116.0 Mg |
| POTASSIUM | Ȣ====== | 12% | 487.0 Mg |
| MAGNESIUM | Ȣ============ | 23% | 71.90 Mg |
| IRON | Ȣ======== | 16% | 2.990 Mg |
| ZINC | Ȣ=== | 7% | 1.150 Mg |
| VITAMIN A | Ȣ | 0% | 8.830 IU |
| VITAMIN D | Ȣ | 0% | 0.000 IU |
| VIT. E/TOTAL | Ȣ | NO RDA | 10.70 Mg |
| VITAMIN C | Ȣ | 1% | 0.870 Mg |
| THIAMIN | Ȣ=========== | 22% | 0.220 Mg |
| RIBOFLAVIN | Ȣ====== | 12% | 0.150 Mg |
| NIACIN | Ȣ====== | 13% | 1.780 Mg |
| VITAMIN B6 | Ȣ==== | 9% | 0.180 Mg |
| FOLACIN | Ȣ== | 5% | 23.60 Ug |
| VITAMIN B12 | Ȣ | 1% | 0.040 Ug |
| PANTO- ACID | Ȣ==== | 8% | 0.490 Mg |
| CALCIUM | Ȣ======= | 15% | 127.0 Mg |
| PHOSPHORUS | Ȣ============== | 28% | 229.0 Mg |
| TRYPTOPHAN | Ȣ=========================== | 55% | 90.00 Mg |
| THREONINE | Ȣ======================== | 48% | 210.0 Mg |
| ISOLEUCINE | Ȣ==================== | 43% | 287.0 Mg |
| LEUCINE | Ȣ========================== | 54% | 473.0 Mg |
| LYSINE | Ȣ================ | 32% | 215.0 Mg |
| METHIONINE | Ȣ================= | 35% | 96.50 Mg |
| CYSTINE | Ȣ===================== | 46% | 126.0 Mg |
| PHENYL-ANINE | Ȣ===================================== | 77% | 337.0 Mg |
| TYROSINE | Ȣ====================== | 56% | 244.0 Mg |
| VALINE | Ȣ===================== | 42% | 326.0 Mg |
| HISTIDINE | Ȣ | NO RDA | 150.0 Mg |
| ALCOHOL | Ȣ | NO RDA | 0.000 Gm |
| ASH | Ȣ | NO RDA | 1.100 Gm |
| COPPER | Ȣ========= | 19% | 0.480 Mg |
| MANGANESE | Ȣ======================= | 47% | 1.770 Mg |
| IODINE | Ȣ============================================ | 86% | 130.0 Ug |
| MONO FAT | Ȣ | NO RDA | 5.900 Gm |
| POLY FAT | Ȣ | NO RDA | 14.60 Gm |
| CAFFEINE | Ȣ | NO RDA | 0.000 Mg |
| FLUORIDE | Ȣ | 0% | 9.750 Mg |
| MOLYBDENUM | Ȣ==================================================== | 553% | 1800 Ug |
| VITAMIN K | Ȣ | 0% | 0.000 Ug |
| SELENIUM | Ȣ============ | 24% | 0.030 Mg |
| BIOTIN | Ȣ== | 4% | 6.150 Ug |
| CHLORIDE | Ȣ | 1% | 57.00 Mg |
| CHROMIUM | Ȣ================================================ | 144% | 0.180 Mg |
| SUGAR | Ȣ | NO RDA | 0.000 Gm |
| FIBER-DIET | Ȣ | NO RDA | 5.050 Gm |
| VIT. E/AT | Ȣ================================================ | 114% | 9.160 Mg |

```
% RDA:   |0      |20     |40     |60     |80     |100
```

Chopped almonds used instead of sunflower seeds in this analysis.

# AMASAKE

One alternative sweetener I almost omitted mentioning is amasake, because I don't use it much in my kitchen. It happens to be a sweetener that people have very strong feelings about — either they really like it, or they don't. I personally like amasake, but most of the rest of my family describe amasake in words that aren't polite to put in a cookbook! So, being outnumbered, I don't use it much.

I might use it more, just for myself, if it wasn't such a chore to make. Unlike honey, or any of the other sweeteners I've mentioned which can be bought off the store shelf, amasake must be made at home. It's cultured in the same way that yogurt is.

Being a fermented food, amasake contains lots of vitamin B-12. Made from brown rice, all the nutrients of brown rice are included, except that amasake is easier to digest. In the fermenting process, the starch in the rice is converted to natural sugar — and that's what makes amasake sweet!

It's a new sweet — worth trying at least once to see if you like it. When changing eating habits, it helps to stay open to new ideas and foods!

The scholar Chanakya wrote, "Knowledge is called 'hidden wealth.' It can't be divided up by relatives; it can't be stolen by a thief. Bestowed on others, it does not diminish — the jewel of knowledge is the greatest wealth." Thus one should use his life to cultivate knowledge — enough material knowledge to be able to keep body and soul together, and most importantly, spiritual knowledge.

---

*½ cup Koji culture*
*4 cups raw brown rice*

Soak 4 cups brown rice overnight and then cook as you normally cook brown rice. When rice is cooked, remove from pot and place in large glass or glazed ceramic bowl or jar and allow to cool. When rice is cool enough to handle, mix in ½ cup Koji culture and cover bowl with a lid. Wrap the bowl in a towel and put in a warm place (like a gas oven with the pilot light on or an electric oven with the light bulb on). Allow to incubate for 4 hours, stirring occasionally with a wooden spoon. Don't allow to incubate longer than 4 hours or the rice will begin to ferment and sour. Place in cooking pot, mix in a few cups of water and bring to a boil on the stove. Turn heat down and simmer the incubated rice for 5 to 10 minutes. The amasake is now ready for use (good served like a porridge with no extra sweetener) or storage in the refrigerator.

You can also make an amasake concentrate by mashing the simmered amasake through a strainer. The amasake concentrate can be used instead of sugar (3 parts amasake concentrate for each 1 part of sugar) or honey in cooking and baking. Also, it can be used in beverages like the following one:

2 cups amasake concentrate
2 cups water
1 Tbsp. carob powder
2 tsp. grain coffee
½ tsp. vanilla

Blend together. This drink can also be frozen and then run through a Champion Juicer or food processor to make ice cream.

| Special Shopping | SHOPPING LIST | |
| --- | --- | --- |
| Koji culture — can be found in some natural food stores and some macrobiotic stores. | **Regularly Kept in the Kitchen** (Listed in Chapter 14, p. 703) | **Fresh Produce** |
| | Brown rice | (None) |

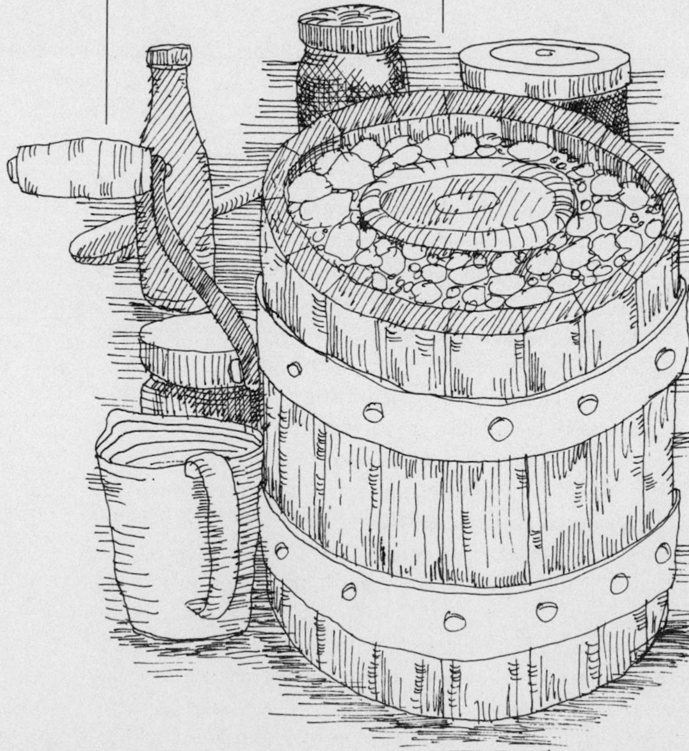

# CHAPTER 5

# CAFFEINE-FREE

If you've made the changes in your diet recommended up to this point, you've already made the majority of the changes needed for a healthier and naturally slimming way of eating! That's because the "average American diet" is made up primarily of flesh food, refined food and chemical additives; and you really start realizing just how much when you consciously try to drop anything that contains these items from your shopping list! Now it's time to take a look at another element worth eliminating from the "food" list — caffeine.

You probably have automatically left out caffeine in the process of eliminating sugar (as recommended in Chapter 4) because sugar is almost always put in products containing caffeine, either by manufacturers or individuals in their homes. Anything with chocolate in it, cola sodas, coffee and some teas are all sources of caffeine and are almost always sweetened with sugar because they would be so bitter otherwise.

Admittedly, this is something I'm not very well versed on. Food products containing caffeine have never been a big part of my diet, so I've never paid much attention to information on why they shouldn't be consumed. As a young girl growing up in Hawaii, I ate Chinese dried fruit preserves (more commonly and lovingly called "see-moi") instead of chocolate bars. Unfortunately for me, these are loaded with sugar and did ruin my teeth — but at least I never got addicted to chocolate. I did sneak a couple of cola sodas in my teen years. My parents never allowed any of us (my two brothers and me) to have any caffeine drinks — cola sodas, coffee or tea — on the grounds that caffeine wasn't good for us . . . and I believed them.

......................................

*"There have been findings of withdrawal symptoms of headache, nervousness and irritability among subjects deprived of normal coffee doses, as well as similar symptoms among those who may have ingested too much caffeine. The report said colas are of special concern since they are the major caffeine source for most children." (Cola drinks account for 65% of total U.S. drink consumption.)*

— *"Dietary Goals for the U.S."*
*(2nd Edition)*
*U.S. Senate Select Committee*
*on Nutrition and Human Needs*

......................................

I'm glad I did. It turns out that the consumption of caffeine has been linked to an increase in blood pressure and a change in the rate of heartbeat, increasing the risk of heart attack for those with high blood pressure or other factors (such as atherosclerosis, etc.). Caffeine constricts blood vessels while causing an increase in adrenalin and insulin levels. We already know from the information given in Chapter 4 that increasing insulin levels increases fat production and fat storage. An increase in adrenalin stimulates the nervous system and can manifest as irritability, nervousness or insomnia.

Caffeine also acts as a diuretic, causing the body to lose valuable stores of calcium, B-vitamins and vitamin C in the body fluids it flushes out.

All combined, these make good reasons for consciously putting an end to *any* caffeine consumption. Following are some recipes that may remind you of some old taste favorites. However, they won't help alleviate the chemical changes the body will go through during the withdrawal period from caffeine, which I've heard lasts only about one week.

# CAFFEINE-FREE COOKING

As one who lived to attain a higher understanding in life, the Chinese philosopher Lao Tsu spoke, "Knowing ignorance is strength; ignoring knowledge is sickness. If one is sick of sickness, then one is not sick. The sage is not sick because he is sick of sickness."

Two foods that I use a lot in place of caffeine-loaded chocolate and coffee are carob and grain coffee. To some degree they replace the flavor, and certainly the appearance of chocolate and/or coffee. Rather than getting bogged down in a comparison of the flavors, these two foods are better appreciated for what they are.

"In those days came John the Baptist, preaching in the wilderness . . . and the same John had his raiment of camel's hair, and a leather girdle about his loins; and his meat was locusts and wild honey." — *Matthew 3:1 -4*

Until I learned about carob, I always thought that John must have been a little mad to eat bugs (locusts)! It turns out that another name for carob is "St. John's Bread" because this is the locust (bean) that he lived on. It turns out he wasn't so mad after all . . . and knew what was good for him in more ways than one!

The legume, carob, is a food packed with nutrition — just the opposite of chocolate, which people like for its taste if they can overlook its nutritional drawbacks. Carob contains 4.5 percent protein compared to milk's 3.5 percent, and supplies three times the amount of calcium. Carob is also a good source of potassium and phosphorus.

Chocolate actually contains many elements that do any body a disservice. The presence of oxalic acid in chocolate inhibits calcium absorption, which is especially something women and children should think about every time they reach for something with chocolate in it. Whereas carob is a good source of protein, chocolate contains tannin, a substance which makes protein and iron indigestible. Studies have shown that foods containing tannin stunt growth in animals. A study of women who had cysts in their breasts found that the cysts disappeared in 67 percent of the women after they eliminated chocolate, tea and colas from their diets. The nitrogen compound menthylxanthine (found in chocolate, colas and some teas) is blamed for triggering the cell growth which promotes the growth of breast cells causing cysts. Last, but not least, there's caffeine . . .

Besides the fact that carob contains no caffeine, it's a naturally more slimming food than chocolate is for other reasons. Carob contains two times more dietary fiber than chocolate does, and its pectin has been shown to absorb fat and lower serum cholesterol levels. Carob contains only four percent fat, compared to chocolate's 75 percent — a saturated fat at that! With so much less fat, it figures that carob would have 43 percent fewer calories than chocolate does and an average of 70 percent fewer calories than an equal amount of sweet chocolate. The additional calories in sweet chocolate are added by the large amounts of sugar that have to be added to cut the bitter flavor of chocolate. A chocolate candy bar can easily contain ⅓ cup of sugar.

Since carob is made up of 46 percent natural sugars (compared to five percent in chocolate), it takes less outside sweetener (and therefore fewer calories) to sweeten it up. As a matter of fact, carob is sweet enough by itself for some things (as in the Carob Candy recipe, p. 223). I usually end up adding some, or quite a bit of grain coffee to carob in recipes where I'm trying to duplicate the bitter taste of chocolate.

That's only one way that I use grain coffee. I also use it in any recipe where a coffee beverage would otherwise be used. Here are some of my favorite caffeine-free recipes that make use of carob and grain coffee.

Carob

In this recipe, the sweetness is provided by carob with a little help from the lactose in the milk powder. Both supply nutrition as well, contributing to rather than robbing the body of valuable nutrients. If you want the candies a little sweeter and more moist, just add the optional honey or maple syrup.

# CAROB CANDIES

☆ A nutritious dessert or snack that's so simple to make, children can do it! . . . They can learn how to cook and about good nutrition at the same time.

---

*1 cup carob powder*
*1 cup noninstant nonfat milk powder*
*1 cup hot water*
*¼ cup margarine or butter*
*¼ cup safflower oil*
*1½ tsp. liquid lecithin*
*1 tsp. vanilla*

*2 cups roasted, unsalted nuts of your choice*
*2 cups raisins*

*¼ cup honey or maple syrup (optional —*
    *if you want it sweeter and not so dry)*

Combine first 7 ingredients together in mixing bowl and mix thoroughly. Stir in next 2 ingredients till evenly distributed. Add honey or maple syrup, if desired.

Drop by teaspoonfuls onto oiled cookie sheets and place on a shelf or counter space that doesn't get sun on it for 6 to 8 hours or overnight. This is the most energy-saving way to allow candies to dry out.

If you're in a hurry or just too impatient to wait, bake at 300 degrees for 15 to 20 minutes, or till tops of candies are shiny and candies can be removed from cookie sheets. Remove from sheets and place into airtight container or plastic bags. Store in refrigerator and/or keep some in the freezer. Makes about 40 candies.

| Special Shopping |
|---|
| Liquid lecithin — in natural food stores. |

| SHOPPING LIST | |
|---|---|
| **Regularly Kept in the Kitchen** (Listed in Chapter 14, p. 703) | **Fresh Produce** |
| Carob powder<br>Noninstant, nonfat milk powder<br>Margarine or butter<br>Safflower oil<br>Vanilla<br>Nuts<br>Raisins | (None) |

# NUTRITIONAL ANALYSIS FOR TWO CAROB CANDIES

```
NUTRIENT        Type: 14   FEMALE-23 TO 51 YEARS        % RDA   Amount
KCALORIES       A====                                    9%     198.0 Kc
PROTEIN         A======                                  12%    5.450 Gm
CARBOHYDRATE    A                                        NO RDA 21.80 Gm
FAT             A                                        NO RDA 12.30 Gm
FIBER-CRUDE     A                                        NO RDA 0.900 Gm
CHOLESTEROL     A                                        NO RDA 1.200 Mg
SATURATED FA    A                                        NO RDA 1.370 Gm
OLEIC FA        A                                        NO RDA 5.100 Gm
LINOLEIC FA     A                                        NO RDA 3.280 Gm
SODIUM          A=                                       2%     63.80 Mg
POTASSIUM       A====                                    9%     355.0 Mg
MAGNESIUM       A========                                17%    52.70 Mg
IRON            A==                                      5%     0.940 Mg
ZINC            A==                                      4%     0.710 Mg
VITAMIN A       A=                                       2%     97.70 IU
VITAMIN D       A                                        0%     0.000 IU
VIT. E/TOTAL    A                                        NO RDA 4.260 Mg
VITAMIN C       A                                        1%     0.970 Mg
THIAMIN         A===                                     7%     0.070 Mg
RIBOFLAVIN      A=========                               19%    0.230 Mg
NIACIN          A==                                      5%     0.710 Mg
VITAMIN B6      A==                                      4%     0.090 Mg
FOLACIN         A=                                       3%     12.60 Ug
VITAMIN B12     A====                                    8%     0.240 Ug
PANTO- ACID     A==                                      5%     0.300 Mg
CALCIUM         A========                                17%    136.0 Mg
PHOSPHORUS      A=========                               18%    144.0 Mg
TRYPTOPHAN      A=======================                 47%    77.90 Mg
THREONINE       A=======================                 47%    205.0 Mg
ISOLEUCINE      A==================                      39%    257.0 Mg
LEUCINE         A========================                49%    432.0 Mg
LYSINE          A===================                     40%    264.0 Mg
METHIONINE      A===============                         31%    87.00 Mg
CYSTINE         A============                            25%    68.30 Mg
PHENYL-ANINE    A=============================           59%    260.0 Mg
TYROSINE        A======================                  46%    201.0 Mg
VALINE          A==================                      38%    292.0 Mg
HISTIDINE       A                                        NO RDA 140.0 Mg
ALCOHOL         A                                        NO RDA 0.000 Gm
ASH             A                                        NO RDA 1.180 Gm
COPPER          A===                                     6%     0.160 Mg
MANGANESE       A====                                    8%     0.330 Mg
IODINE          A=====                                   10%    16.40 Ug
MONO FAT        A                                        NO RDA 5.800 Gm
POLY FAT        A                                        NO RDA 4.380 Gm
CAFFEINE        A                                        NO RDA 0.000 Mg
FLUORIDE        A                                        0%     11.70 Ug
MOLYBDENUM      A========================                46%    150.0 Ug
VITAMIN K       A                                        0%     0.000 Ug
SELENIUM        A                                        0%     0.000 Mg
BIOTIN          A=                                       3%     4.770 Ug
CHLORIDE        A                                        0%     13.60 Mg
CHROMIUM        A========                                16%    0.020 Mg
SUGAR           A                                        NO RDA 0.000 Gm
FIBER-DIET      A                                        NO RDA 2.420 Gm
VIT. E/AT       A==========================              51%    4.130 Mg

   % RDA:   |0      |20     |40     |60     |80     |100
```

Type of nuts used: chopped almonds. Analysis does not include optional honey or maple syrup.

As with all foods, appearance can make it more or less appealing. Taking the little bit of extra trouble to sprinkle the top of this pudding with the nuts and carob chips or shavings and serving it in a fancy dessert cup instead of plopping a brown glob in a bowl, increases the appeal of this dessert.

# BET 'YA THOUGHT IT WAS CHOCOLATE PUDDING

☆ It's so nice to serve desserts that you can feel good about dishing out! This one is a good example of a dessert that's a *food*. It makes a nice, light meal served with a few pieces of fresh fruit.

---

*1 cup Chinese firm tofu (drained)*
*1 banana*
*1 Tbsp. peanut butter*
*1 Tbsp. carob powder*
*1 Tbsp. grain coffee*
*3 Tbsp. honey*

*2 Tbsp. chopped sunflower seeds*

*Sliced almonds*
*Carob shavings or chopped carob chips*

Combine first 6 ingredients and mix in blender on low speed till smooth. Scoop into a bowl, add sunflower seeds, and mix. Top with sliced almonds. Shave a block of carob or a carob candy bar into fine slivers (or chop carob chips) and sprinkle on top. Set in freezer or refrigerator to chill. Makes 2 to 4 servings.

This pudding is very good when placed in little tarts made from Perfectly Nutty Crust recipe (see p. 271). Delicious!

| Special Shopping |
|---|
| Block of carob, or carob candy bar or chips — found in natural food stores. |

| SHOPPING LIST | |
|---|---|
| **Regularly Kept in the Kitchen** (Listed in Chapter 14, p. 703) | **Fresh Produce** |
| Tofu<br>Peanut butter<br>Carob powder<br>Honey<br>Sunflower seeds<br>Almonds | Banana |

# NUTRITIONAL ANALYSIS FOR ONE SERVING
# BET 'YA THOUGHT IT WAS CHOCOLATE PUDDING

```
NUTRIENT        Type: 14   FEMALE-23 TO 51 YEARS        % RDA   Amount
KCALORIES       Я======                                  12%   257.0 Kc
PROTEIN         Я================                        30%   13.60 Gm
CARBOHYDRATE    Я                                      NO RDA  32.20 Gm
FAT             Я                                      NO RDA  12.00 Gm
FIBER-CRUDE     Я                                      NO RDA   1.260 Gm
CHOLESTEROL     Я                                      NO RDA   0.000 Mg
SATURATED FA    Я                                      NO RDA   1.630 Gm
OLEIC FA        Я                                      NO RDA   3.500 Gm
LINOLEIC FA     Я                                      NO RDA   3.570 Gm
SODIUM          Я                                         1%   32.00 Mg
POTASSIUM       Я=====                                   11%   447.0 Mg
MAGNESIUM       Я==============                          28%   84.70 Mg
IRON            Я====================                    41%   7.550 Mg
ZINC            Я=====                                   10%   1.590 Mg
VITAMIN A       Я=                                        3%   132.0 IU
VITAMIN D       Я                                         0%   0.000 IU
VIT. E/TOTAL    Я                                      NO RDA   4.300 Mg
VITAMIN C       Я==                                       4%   2.870 Mg
THIAMIN         Я===========                             23%   0.230 Mg
RIBOFLAVIN      Я=======                                 15%   0.180 Mg
NIACIN          Я======                                  12%   1.630 Mg
VITAMIN B6      Я========                                16%   0.330 Mg
FOLACIN         Я====                                     8%   32.00 Ug
VITAMIN B12     Я                                         0%   0.000 Ug
PANTO- ACID     Я==                                       5%   0.310 Mg
CALCIUM         Я============================            59%   479.0 Mg
PHOSPHORUS      Я============                            25%   204.0 Mg
TRYPTOPHAN      Я======================================= 124%  203.0 Mg
THREONINE       Я======================================= 122%  535.0 Mg
ISOLEUCINE      Я======================================= 99%   652.0 Mg
LEUCINE         Я======================================= 117%  1024 Mg
LYSINE          Я======================================= 120%  788.0 Mg
METHIONINE      Я============================            65%   177.0 Mg
CYSTINE         Я==============================          71%   194.0 Mg
PHENYL-ANINE    Я======================================= 154%  674.0 Mg
TYROSINE        Я======================================= 104%  454.0 Mg
VALINE          Я===================================     90%   688.0 Mg
HISTIDINE       Я                                      NO RDA  412.0 Mg
ALCOHOL         Я                                      NO RDA   0.000 Gm
ASH             Я                                      NO RDA   1.570 Gm
COPPER          Я========                                16%   0.410 Mg
MANGANESE       Я=============                           27%   1.040 Mg
IODINE          Я================================        62%   94.20 Ug
MONO FAT        Я                                      NO RDA   4.000 Gm
POLY FAT        Я                                      NO RDA   5.650 Gm
CAFFEINE        Я                                      NO RDA   0.000 Mg
FLUORIDE        Я                                         0%   26.20 Ug
MOLYBDENUM      Я======================================= 304%  990.0 Ug
VITAMIN K       Я                                         0%   0.000 Ug
SELENIUM        Я                                         0%   0.000 Ug
BIOTIN          Я==                                       5%   7.670 Ug
CHLORIDE        Я==                                       4%   140.0 Mg
CHROMIUM        Я======================================= 184%  0.230 Mg
SUGAR           Я                                      NO RDA   4.170 Gm
FIBER-DIET      Я                                      NO RDA   3.420 Gm
VIT. E/AT       Я======================                  44%   3.550 Mg

    % RDA:  |0      |20     |40     |60     |80     |100
```

226

# HOMEMADE READY MIX

☆ In these days of convenience foods, how nice it is to have this healthful mix on hand to make cakes, brownies or cookies in a hurry.

---

*1½ cups whole wheat flour*
*¼ cup grain coffee*
*¼ cup carob powder*
*3 Tbsp. Bipro*
*1 tsp. baking soda*
*½ tsp. baking powder*

*½ cup vegetable oil*

Combine first 6 ingredients together in a bowl. Add vegetable oil and cut in with a pastry cutter or fingertips till the oil is thoroughly mixed in and the mix resembles the texture of sand. The mix should be sealed in a plastic bag and kept in the refrigerator (up to 1 month) or freezer (indefinitely) till needed.

You may want to make quite a few batches at a time to keep on hand. If you are going to make many batches, I strongly recommend mixing and bagging them separately so the amount of liquid added to make the final product is accurate. The mix can be used to make any of the following:

**CAROB CAKE:** 1 mix recipe makes one 9" x 13" cake or a 2-layer, 8" cake.

**Add to the mix:**
*1 tsp. vanilla (or mint, almond*
    *or orange) extract*
*¾ cup honey*
*1 cup boiling water*

Rules for substituting carob for chocolate: 1) replace 1 cup of cocoa with ½ cup carob and ½ cup grain coffee (or ¾ cup carob and ¼ cup grain coffee for a sweeter chocolate). 2) replace 1 ounce (a square) of baking chocolate with 1½ tablespoons carob, 1½ tablespoons grain coffee and 1 tablespoon water.

Preheat oven to 350 degrees.

Beat all ingredients together for 30 seconds. Pour mixture into oiled baking pans. Bake at 350 degrees for 20 to 25 minutes or till a toothpick inserted in the middle of the cake comes out clean. Cool in pans for 5 minutes, then turn onto cooling racks to thoroughly cool before icing.

**CUPCAKES:** Makes 12 to 16.

Preheat oven to 350 degrees.

Add same ingredients as for the cake mix. Pour batter into cupcake cups set inside muffin tins. Fill only ⅔ of the way up.

Bake at 350 degrees for 15 to 17 minutes. Allow to cool 5 minutes in muffin tins before removing cupcakes to cooling rack to thoroughly cool.

**BROWNIES:** Makes one 10" x 13" cookie sheet (approximately).

**Add to the mix:**
*½ cup margarine*
*1 tsp. vanilla*
*1¼ cups honey*
*2 Tbsp. water*

*½ cup chopped walnuts*

Preheat oven to 350 degrees.

Add first 4 ingredients to the mix. Then fold in chopped walnuts. Pour into oiled and floured cookie sheet and spread evenly. Bake at 350 degrees for 20 to 25 minutes or till toothpick inserted in center comes out clean.

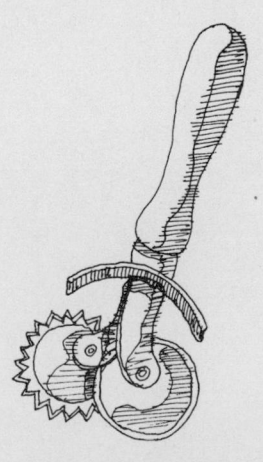

**COOKIES:** Makes about 2 dozen.

**Add to the mix:**
*1 tsp. vanilla*
*⅝ cup honey*
*¼ cup boiling water*

*½ cup raisins or carob chips*
*½ cup chopped nuts (optional)*

Preheat oven to 375 degrees.

Add first 3 ingredients and mix in till smooth. Add last ingredients, or any other tasty morsels that you may want to add to the cookie. Drop by heaping tablespoons onto oiled cookie sheets, leaving room in between for cookies to spread. Bake at 375 degrees for 10 to 12 minutes.

| SHOPPING LIST | |
|---|---|
| **Regularly Kept in the Kitchen (Listed in Chapter 14, p. 703)** | **Fresh Produce** |
| Whole wheat flour<br>Grain coffee<br>Carob powder<br>Bipro<br>Baking soda<br>Baking powder<br>Safflower oil | (None) |

# VERY CAROBY MOUSSE

☆ People usually think of gourmet food as unhealthy and very fattening (shrugging it off with "Who cares?"). Here's a healthy carob mousse that can be served as is, in parfaits or a bombe (see following recipe).

This mousse can be made without Bipro; it will just be a thicker and denser mousse.

---

2⅓ cups water
1¼ cups grain coffee
1 cup carob powder
1 cup honey
½ cup raw cashew butter (smooth)
¼ cup safflower or sunflower oil
2 Tbsp. liquid lecithin
2 Tbsp. carrageenan
2 Tbsp. arrowroot

1 cup plus 2 Tbsp. water
14 Tbsp. Bipro
¼ tsp. cream of tartar

Combine first 9 ingredients together in a pot. Using a wire whisk or electric mixer, mix and whip till smooth. Place over a medium-high flame and continue mixing at a high speed till it comes to a boil and the mixture thickens. Allow to cool to room temperature, then cover and refrigerate till cold (about 4 to 6 hours).

Whip last 3 ingredients together with an electric mixer for a few minutes till it is fluffy and forms soft peaks like a meringue. Gently fold into cooled carob pudding. Cover and place back in refrigerator to cool for at least 4 hours or overnight. This makes a wonderful mousse served as is or layered in parfaits; or can be used as the filling for the Unsinfully Rich Carob Bombe (see following recipe). Makes 10 to 12 servings.

| SHOPPING LIST | |
|---|---|
| **Regularly Kept in the Kitchen** (Listed in Chapter 14, p. 703) | **Fresh Produce** |
| Grain coffee | (None) |
| Carob | |
| Honey | |
| Raw cashew butter | |
| Safflower oil | |
| Arrowroot | |
| Bipro | |
| Cream of tartar | |

| Special Shopping |
|---|
| Liquid lecithin — in natural food stores. |
| Carrageenan — try looking in Jewish groceries for "kosher gelatin"; as a second choice replacement use agar-agar, which will make this mousse stiffer. |

# NUTRITIONAL ANALYSIS FOR ONE SERVING
## VERY CAROBY MOUSSE

```
NUTRIENT      Type: 14   FEMALE-23 TO 51 YEARS              % RDA    Amount
KCALORIES     A======                                        12%    252.0 Kc
PROTEIN       A=====                                         11%    5.250 Gm
CARBOHYDRATE  A                                            NO RDA   37.30 Gm
FAT           A                                            NO RDA   12.40 Gm
FIBER-CRUDE   A                                            NO RDA   0.720 Gm
CHOLESTEROL   A                                            NO RDA   0.050 Mg
SATURATED FA  A                                            NO RDA   1.810 Gm
OLEIC FA      A                                            NO RDA   0.570 Gm
LINOLEIC FA   A                                            NO RDA   3.340 Gm
SODIUM        A                                              0%     20.70 Mg
POTASSIUM     A===                                           7%     266.0 Mg
MAGNESIUM     A=====                                        11%     33.10 Mg
IRON          A===                                           6%     1.230 Mg
ZINC          A==                                            4%     0.660 Mg
VITAMIN A     A                                              0%     1.250 IU
VITAMIN D     A                                              0%     0.000 IU
VIT. E/TOTAL  A                                            NO RDA   1.800 Mg
VITAMIN C     A                                              0%     0.010 Mg
THIAMIN       A==                                            5%     0.050 Mg
RIBOFLAVIN    A===                                           6%     0.080 Mg
NIACIN        A=====                                        10%     1.350 Mg
VITAMIN B6    A=                                             3%     0.060 Mg
FOLACIN       A=                                             2%     9.750 Ug
VITAMIN B12   A                                              0%     0.000 Ug
PANTO- ACID   A=                                             3%     0.180 Mg
CALCIUM       A===                                           6%     49.80 Mg
PHOSPHORUS    A=====                                        10%     84.00 Mg
TRYPTOPHAN    A=========================================    80%     131.0 Mg
THREONINE     A=============================               57%     250.0 Mg
ISOLEUCINE    A==================                           38%     250.0 Mg
LEUCINE       A==============================               60%     525.0 Mg
LYSINE        A===============================             62%     410.0 Mg
METHIONINE    A====================                         41%     112.0 Mg
CYSTINE       A====================                         41%     113.0 Mg
PHENYL-ANINE  A=========================                    50%     221.0 Mg
TYROSINE      A=====================                        43%     188.0 Mg
VALINE        A==================                           39%     302.0 Mg
HISTIDINE     A                                            NO RDA   123.0 Mg
ALCOHOL       A                                            NO RDA   0.000 Gm
ASH           A                                            NO RDA   0.610 Gm
COPPER        A=====                                        10%     0.250 Mg
MANGANESE     A                                              0%     0.000 Mg
IODINE        A=========                                    18%     27.30 Ug
MONO FAT      A                                            NO RDA   3.650 Gm
POLY FAT      A                                            NO RDA   5.440 Gm
CAFFEINE      A                                            NO RDA   0.000 Mg
FLUORIDE      A                                              1%     28.00 Ug
MOLYBDENUM    A======================================      76%     250.0 Ug
VITAMIN K     A                                              0%     0.000 Ug
SELENIUM      A                                              0%     0.000 Mg
BIOTIN        A                                              1%     2.410 Ug
CHLORIDE      A                                              0%     23.70 Mg
CHROMIUM      A============                                 24%     0.030 Mg
SUGAR         A                                            NO RDA   0.010 Gm
FIBER-DIET    A                                            NO RDA   3.020 Gm
VIT. E/AT     A=========                                    19%     1.540 Mg

   % RDA:   |0       |20      |40      |60      |80      |100
```

Safflower oil used instead of sunflower oil; analysis does not include carrageenan and cream of tartar.

231

# UNSINFULLY RICH CAROB BOMBE

☆ Everyone has a hard time believing this rich dessert is cholesterol-free!

---

*2 recipes Carob Brownies, omitting nuts*
*(see recipe, p. 228)*

*1 recipe Very Caroby Mousse (see preceding recipe)*

*¼ recipe Carob Fondue (see following recipe)*

*Finely chopped walnuts*

Prepare 2 cookie trays Carob Brownies (from Homemade Ready Mix recipe), Very Caroby Mousse and Carob Fondue.

Now it's time to assemble everything. Trim outer ½" edges off the brownies, as they are too tough to use. Now cut pieces to fit a 2½-quart bowl. You'll need one smaller circle to fit the bottom of the bowl, wedges to fit the sides, and one large circle to fit the mouth of the bowl. If you are good at estimating, you might cut circles by placing the bottom of the bowl atop the brownies and cutting around it, leaving off enough on the edges of the circle so it will fit just inside the mouth of the bowl and not on top of it. Now cut wedges that are as tall as the bowl, minus the thickness of the top and bottom circles. Cut wedges so they meet together on the side edges. I cut one at a time, as the last wedge may have to be wider or thinner than the rest. If you feel uncertain about doing it this way, you may want to cut a pattern out of paper that you can lay in the bowl first to make sure the pieces fit, then cut the brownie around the paper patterns.

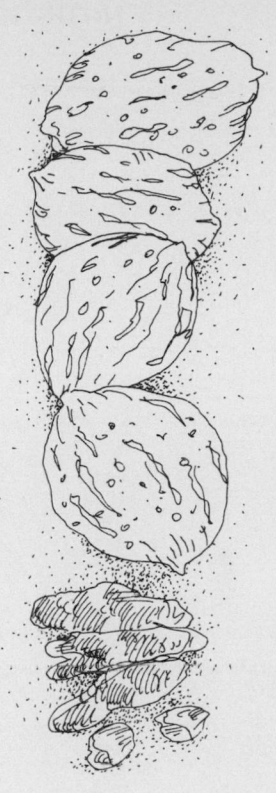

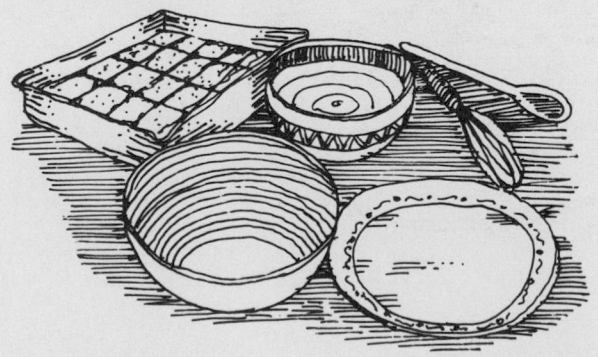

Another note about the wonder of carob: Carob seeds are so uniform in weight that they used to be used as a standard weight of measurement. The "carat" weight used for weighing precious gems came about because carob seeds were used as the standard for measuring such small, precious amounts.

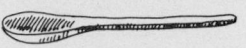

Line a 2½-quart mixing bowl with saran wrap and lay the brownie pieces in with the shiny side facing the bowl. Put in the bottom circle, then the side wedges so the bowl's surface is completely covered. Take whipped, chilled mousse from refrigerator and gently spoon into the bowl, filling halfway. Top this with a one-layer thickness of brownie scraps, then pour the rest of the mousse into the bowl. Cover with the large brownie circle and place a dinner platter over mouth of bowl with something from the refrigerator atop the dinner platter to weigh it down. Refrigerate 6 to 8 hours or overnight.

To unmold, remove dinner platter from bowl and replace it with the serving platter, putting serving side facing the bombe. (It is very important to be sure the serving platter is flat and not concave, because if the serving platter is concave, it will cause the center of the bombe to cave in.) Holding bowl onto plate, just invert and bombe will come out of bowl. Remove the saran wrap. This should be done just before serving time.

Pour ¼ recipe of warm Carob Fondue over top of the bombe and sprinkle with walnuts. Makes at least 12 servings.

See shopping lists for Carob Brownies from Homemade Ready Mix (p. 228), Very Caroby Mousse (p. 230) and Carob Fondue (following recipe).

# NUTRITIONAL ANALYSIS FOR ONE SERVING
## UNSINFULLY RICH CAROB BOMBE

| NUTRIENT | Type: 14 FEMALE-23 TO 51 YEARS | % RDA | Amount |
|---|---|---|---|
| KCALORIES | A=========================== | 48% | 960.0 Kc |
| PROTEIN | A============= | 26% | 11.80 Gm |
| CARBOHYDRATE | A | NO RDA | 132.0 Gm |
| FAT | A | NO RDA | 49.80 Gm |
| FIBER-CRUDE | A | NO RDA | 2.080 Gm |
| CHOLESTEROL | A | NO RDA | 0.080 Mg |
| SATURATED FA | A | NO RDA | 6.600 Gm |
| OLEIC FA | A | NO RDA | 3.010 Gm |
| LINOLEIC FA | A | NO RDA | 17.50 Gm |
| SODIUM | A======== | 17% | 386.0 Mg |
| POTASSIUM | A======= | 15% | 584.0 Mg |
| MAGNESIUM | A============= | 27% | 83.80 Mg |
| IRON | A======== | 17% | 3.160 Mg |
| ZINC | A===== | 11% | 1.700 Mg |
| VITAMIN A | A======= | 15% | 632.0 IU |
| VITAMIN D | A | 0% | 0.000 IU |
| VIT. E/TOTAL | A | NO RDA | 10.20 Mg |
| VITAMIN C | A | 0% | 0.050 Mg |
| THIAMIN | A============ | 25% | 0.250 Mg |
| RIBOFLAVIN | A======== | 16% | 0.200 Mg |
| NIACIN | A============== | 29% | 3.800 Mg |
| VITAMIN B6 | A===== | 10% | 0.210 Mg |
| FOLACIN | A=== | 7% | 29.70 Ug |
| VITAMIN B12 | A | 0% | 0.010 Ug |
| PANTO- ACID | A======= | 15% | 0.850 Mg |
| CALCIUM | A======= | 15% | 123.0 Mg |
| PHOSPHORUS | A=================== | 34% | 275.0 Mg |
| TRYPTOPHAN | A============================================ | 147% | 240.0 Mg |
| THREONINE | A============================================ | 111% | 484.0 Mg |
| ISOLEUCINE | A======================================= | 83% | 547.0 Mg |
| LEUCINE | A============================================ | 119% | 1043 Mg |
| LYSINE | A============================================ | 107% | 704.0 Mg |
| METHIONINE | A==================================== | 84% | 229.0 Mg |
| CYSTINE | A======================================= | 92% | 252.0 Mg |
| PHENYL-ANINE | A============================================ | 121% | 528.0 Mg |
| TYROSINE | A====================================== | 98% | 429.0 Mg |
| VALINE | A===================================== | 82% | 632.0 Mg |
| HISTIDINE | A | NO RDA | 269.0 Mg |
| ALCOHOL | A | NO RDA | 0.000 Gm |
| ASH | A | NO RDA | 1.760 Gm |
| COPPER | A========== | 20% | 0.500 Mg |
| MANGANESE | A====================== | 42% | 1.600 Mg |
| IODINE | A============================================ | 116% | 174.0 Ug |
| MONO FAT | A | NO RDA | 13.80 Gm |
| POLY FAT | A | NO RDA | 25.20 Gm |
| CAFFEINE | A | NO RDA | 0.000 Mg |
| FLUORIDE | A= | 3% | 108.0 Ug |
| MOLYBDENUM | A============================================ | 688% | 2238 Ug |
| VITAMIN K | A | 0% | 0.000 Ug |
| SELENIUM | A==== | 8% | 0.010 Ug |
| BIOTIN | A== | 4% | 6.340 Ug |
| CHLORIDE | A= | 2% | 97.60 Mg |
| CHROMIUM | A============================================ | 192% | 0.240 Mg |
| SUGAR | A | NO RDA | 0.010 Gm |
| FIBER-DIET | A | NO RDA | 9.830 Gm |
| VIT. E/AT | A=========================================== | 99% | 7.980 Mg |

```
% RDA:  |0     |20     |40     |60     |80     |100
```

Safflower oil used instead of sunflower oil; carrageenan and cream of tartar not included in Very Caroby Mousse; optional roasted almonds not included in Carob Fondue.

# CAROB FONDUE

☆ An elaborate dessert to present after a simple meal, or just have a Carob Fondue party.

---

1 cup carob powder
1¼ cups grain coffee
1½ cups honey
½ cup raw cashew butter (smooth)
1 cup water
1 tsp. vanilla extract

¼ cup liquid lecithin

½ tsp. almond extract
1½ cups finely chopped, roasted almonds (optional)

As you may have noticed, I use this fondue as an icing. It makes a moist, cholesterol-free addition to any cake, cupcake, brownie, etc.

Blend first 6 ingredients together in blender till smooth. Pour into pot and heat up. Add liquid lecithin and whisk in till smooth. Add last 2 ingredients (or omit nuts if you prefer to have a smooth fondue syrup). Keep mixture warm on serving table over a fondue flame and surround with already prepared platters of de-shelled nuts, whole grain cookies, bite-sized cubes of whole grain cakes, a cheese platter, and platters of fresh fruit of the season — both in whole form (such as strawberries, fresh figs, cherries, etc.) or sliced into bite-sized chunks (such as bananas, pineapple, apricots, peaches, pears, apples, etc.). An interesting treat is to freeze some of the fruit pieces beforehand (especially the banana, pineapple and grapes). When the frozen fruit is dipped into the carob sauce, it immediately hardens on the fruit and at the same time begins to melt on the outside edges of the fruit. Delicious!

235

This syrup also makes a good carob sauce to serve over ice cream sundaes, frozen bananas, etc.

You may want to serve a carob pate instead of the fondue as the center for all the accompaniments given above. To make the pate, just add half the amount of water and half the ground nuts. Allow carob mixture to cool and form a soft ball. Sprinkle remaining nuts on the counter and pour the soft carob pate ball onto the remaining ground nuts, rolling the ball around till the entire surface is coated with ground nuts. Place on serving platter, cover and refrigerate overnight. Makes about 3 cups.

| SHOPPING LIST | | Special Shopping |
| --- | --- | --- |
| **Regularly Kept in the Kitchen (Listed in Chapter 14, p. 703)** | **Fresh Produce** | Liquid lecithin — in natural food stores. |
| Carob powder | (None) | |
| Grain coffee | | |
| Honey | | |
| Raw cashew butter | | |
| Vanilla extract | | |
| Almond extract | | |
| Almonds | | |

# ENGLISH SUPPER

In his book *Small is Beautiful*, the late British economist E. F. Schumacher wrote, "I suggest that the foundations of peace cannot be laid by universal prosperity, in the modern sense, because such prosperity, if attainable at all, is attainable only by cultivating such drives of human nature as greed and envy, which destroy intelligence, happiness, serenity, and thereby the peacefulness of man."

If you're looking for supper ideas, why not try this meal fashioned after the British high tea. High tea is not synonymous with high brow; rather it's the working man's after-work meal. Rather than sandwiches and dainty little pastries laden with empty calories, this is a hearty, nutritious meal meant for replenishing energy expended through the working day.

I've taken fairly typical dishes that normally would be served at such a meal and made them healthier by changing cooking techniques or ingredients. Besides the changes made in the dishes to be served, I also make changes in the tea served.

By using different flavors of herbal teas, I'm able to serve family and friends such a wide array of differently flavored caffeine-free teas that they never tire of them. If you can find a natural food store with a complete herb section, or a specialty tea store in your neighborhood, you'll be amazed at the wide variety of caffein-free herbal teas available! Of course, some of them don't taste too good and are primarily used as medicine by people who choose to remedy ailments without the aid of potentially harmful drugs.

Some of our favorite herb tea flavors include —

1) Mint and/or spearmint — especially refreshing with the minty zing. With a little honey, it's our peppermint candy. Good served hot or iced.
2) Licorice — this is a bark tea that needs to be simmered. It tastes just like the candy. A little boiled in the tea water, before adding a leaf tea, eliminates the necessity of adding sweetener.
3) Sassafras — has an almost root beer flavor.
4) Red hibiscus and/or rosehips — makes a tart, tangy tea, full of viamin C.
5) Chamomile — a delicate, aromatic tea made from the

chamomile flower.

6) Raspberry leaf tea — one that I've drunk through all of my pregnancies, and I'm sure has helped make my labors easy. Although I personally don't know because I've never had menstrual cramps, it's also supposed to help alleviate them.

The list goes on and on, really. And that's not even mentioning some of the delicious caffeine-free commercial blends of herbal teas that are available. These blends have made their way onto supermarket shelves, in the tea section, as a few large companies have recognized the demand for caffeine-free products and moved to satisfy customers. Changes like this that are taking place on supermarket shelves show that we can make a difference by being particular about what we choose to buy. The fact is, whether in the marketplace or else where, individuals making what they may think are apparently insignificant choices and actions can and do make a difference.

# SUN TEA

The directions for cooking any type of caffeine-free herb tea are on the box. Usually, for leaf teas, it requires you to 1) boil water, 2) turn off heat and add leaves, 3) cover and steep for 3 to 5 minutes. It's important never to boil leaf teas or over-steep them, as this turns the oil in them rancid and causes a bitter taste. Bark or root teas need to be gently simmered to extract flavor from them.

An easier and more energy-efficient way to make tea that guarantees a sweet tea every time is to make sun tea. This just requires getting in the habit of every morning — or at least on the mornings of days you know you'll want tea later — putting as much water as you want and the correct amount of tea for it into a glass jar. Then just screw the lid on, place somewhere you know will get sun all day long and leave it there all day. This will gently steep the tea; won't turn oils rancid and bitter.

At the end of the day, remove tea bags or strain tea. For hot tea, heat strained tea. For iced tea, refrigerate strained tea. If you want to put a little honey in the tea to be iced, put about one cup of strained tea into a pot and almost bring to a boil. Add desired amount of honey to heated tea and stir till honey is dissolved. Pour this into the rest of the tea and refrigerate.

Other sources of caffeine, as well as menthylxanthine, are many nonprescription and prescription drugs. Because of this (and other undesirable elements found in these sorts of drugs) I prefer to use herb tea remedies. Most natural food stores have herbal remedy books that are very helpful.

# BRAISED VEGETABLES

☆ The best thing this recipe does is give you what may be a new cooking technique and an idea for how you can get a wide variety of vegetables in one dish. I would like to encourage you to deviate from the recipe by using whatever vegetables are in season — either growing in your backyard garden, or cheaper in price at the nearest farmer's market, roadside stand or super-market. When using other vegetables, just be sure to cook vegetables that cook at the same rate in batches together.

---

¼ cup olive or vegetable oil
1 cup diced carrots
1 cup diced potato

2 cups slivered celery

1 cup sliced green bell pepper
1 cup sliced red bell pepper

2 cups fresh or frozen peas
2 cups cut green beans

2 Tbsp. whole wheat flour

2 cups water
¼ cup nutritional yeast
1 tsp. asafetida or eliminate and saute 1 small,
   sliced onion in place of 1 cup celery
1 tsp. Spike or other vegetable-seasoned salt
2 tsp. soy sauce
½ tsp. black pepper

4 cups shredded cabbage

2 bunches fresh spinach, washed and de-stemmed

As you may have guessed if you've watched me cook, I think woks are one of the most ideal cooking utensils that can be owned. They're certainly ideal for this dish. The heat is distributed evenly up the sides of the wok, giving a large cooking (in this case, braising) surface. The vegetables can easily be slid up the side and flipped into a waiting baking tray, leaving oil at the bottom of the wok to braise more vegetables in.

Preheat oven to 425 degrees.

Heat the oil in a wok or cast iron skillet and add next 2 ingredients, stir-frying continuously till golden brown. Add the celery (or onion) and stir another few minutes. Then add the bell peppers and cook another few minutes (entire braising time thus far should be about 10 minutes). Remove vegetables and place in a 9" x 13" cake pan (or similar size baking dish).

Add the peas and beans to the oil that is left and fry them for a few minutes till they begin to brown on the edges. Mix them in with the other vegetables.

Add the whole wheat flour to the oil remaining in the pan and stir around to lightly toast the flour. Add the next 6 ingredients, stirring as you do so to prevent lumping, till the water thickens into a gravy. Add the cabbage and bring to a boil. Remove from heat and pour on top of the other vegetables.

Layer washed, de-stemmed spinach leaves on top of each other to cover the mixed vegetables already in the baking pan.

Brush top layer of spinach leaves with vegetable oil and bake at 425 degrees for 20 minutes. Makes enough for 4 or 5.

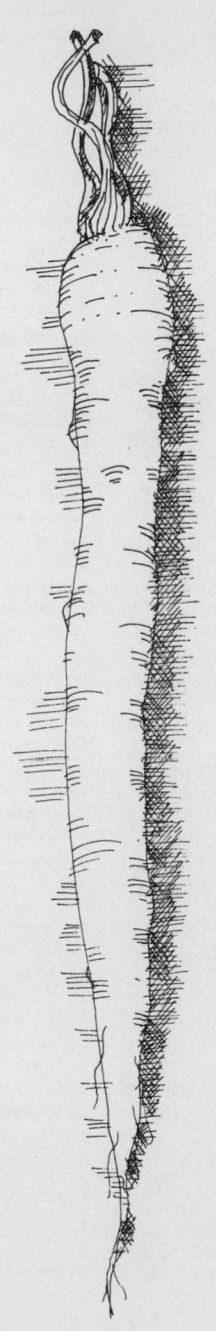

| SHOPPING LIST | |
|---|---|
| **Regularly Kept in the Kitchen** (Listed in Chapter 14, p. 703) | **Fresh Produce** |
| Olive or safflower oil | Carrots |
| Whole wheat flour | Potato |
| Nutritional yeast | Celery |
| Asafetida | Green bell pepper |
| Spike | Red bell pepper |
| Soy sauce | Fresh or frozen peas |
| Black pepper | String beans |
| | Cabbage |
| | Spinach |

# NUTRITIONAL ANALYSIS FOR ONE SERVING
## BRAISED VEGETABLES

| NUTRIENT | Type: 14  FEMALE-23 TO 51 YEARS | % RDA | Amount |
|---|---|---|---|
| KCALORIES | ========= | 17% | 348.0 Kc |
| PROTEIN | ===================== | 40% | 17.80 Gm |
| CARBOHYDRATE | | NO RDA | 43.30 Gm |
| FAT | | NO RDA | 15.30 Gm |
| FIBER-CRUDE | | NO RDA | 6.830 Gm |
| CHOLESTEROL | | NO RDA | 0.000 Mg |
| SATURATED FA | | NO RDA | 1.570 Gm |
| OLEIC FA | | NO RDA | 1.620 Gm |
| LINOLEIC FA | | NO RDA | 10.00 Gm |
| SODIUM | ================ | 30% | 661.0 Mg |
| POTASSIUM | =================================== | 67% | 2528 Mg |
| MAGNESIUM | ================================================ | 95% | 285.0 Mg |
| IRON | ================================ | 63% | 11.50 Mg |
| ZINC | ============ | 22% | 3.400 Mg |
| VITAMIN A | ==================================================== | 641% | 25677 IU |
| VITAMIN D | | 0% | 0.000 IU |
| VIT. E/TOTAL | | NO RDA | 16.50 Mg |
| VITAMIN C | ==================================================== | 405% | 243.0 Mg |
| THIAMIN | ==================================================== | 503% | 5.030 Mg |
| RIBOFLAVIN | ==================================================== | 432% | 5.190 Mg |
| NIACIN | ==================================================== | 233% | 30.40 Mg |
| VITAMIN B6 | ==================================================== | 276% | 5.530 Mg |
| FOLACIN | ==================================================== | 161% | 646.0 Ug |
| VITAMIN B12 | ==================================================== | 116% | 3.500 Ug |
| PANTO- ACID | ================ | 30% | 1.670 Mg |
| CALCIUM | ======================== | 47% | 380.0 Mg |
| PHOSPHORUS | ======================== | 47% | 378.0 Mg |
| TRYPTOPHAN | ==================================================== | 129% | 211.0 Mg |
| THREONINE | ==================================================== | 168% | 731.0 Mg |
| ISOLEUCINE | ==================================================== | 131% | 861.0 Mg |
| LEUCINE | ==================================================== | 146% | 1274 Mg |
| LYSINE | ==================================================== | 169% | 1109 Mg |
| METHIONINE | ============================================ | 94% | 257.0 Mg |
| CYSTINE | ====================================== | 83% | 227.0 Mg |
| PHENYL-ANINE | ==================================================== | 165% | 720.0 Mg |
| TYROSINE | ==================================================== | 146% | 637.0 Mg |
| VALINE | ==================================================== | 138% | 1056 Mg |
| HISTIDINE | | NO RDA | 379.0 Mg |
| ALCOHOL | | NO RDA | 0.000 Gm |
| ASH | | NO RDA | 11.40 Gm |
| COPPER | ================ | 31% | 0.790 Mg |
| MANGANESE | ======================================== | 80% | 3.020 Mg |
| IODINE | =============== | 28% | 42.10 Ug |
| MONO FAT | | NO RDA | 1.720 Gm |
| POLY FAT | | NO RDA | 10.80 Gm |
| CAFFEINE | | NO RDA | 0.000 Mg |
| FLUORIDE | ===== | 11% | 329.0 Ug |
| MOLYBDENUM | ============================================= | 89% | 292.0 Ug |
| VITAMIN K | ==================================================== | 499% | 524.0 Ug |
| SELENIUM | | 0% | 0.000 Ug |
| BIOTIN | ============ | 23% | 34.80 Ug |
| CHLORIDE | | 0% | 9.360 Mg |
| CHROMIUM | ==================================================== | 120% | 0.150 Mg |
| SUGAR | | NO RDA | 12.10 Gm |
| FIBER-DIET | | NO RDA | 12.00 Gm |
| VIT. E/AT | ==================================================== | 142% | 11.40 Mg |

```
% RDA:  |0      |20     |40     |60     |80     |100        10
```

Safflower oil used instead of olive oil; onion used instead of celery and asafetida.

# RAREBIT

☆ This sauce is excellent spooned over vegetables, toast, or toast topped with vegetables, tofu, etc. In this particular menu it can be spooned over the vegetables or the toasted English Muffin Loaf slices; or spread vegetables over top of English Muffin Loaf slices and spoon Rarebit over both.

2 Tbsp. butter or vegetable oil
3 Tbsp. whole wheat flour
1 tsp. mustard powder

1½ cups non-alcoholic malt beverage

1 lb. grated Cheddar cheese
2 tsp. prepared mustard
¼ tsp. Tabasco sauce
⅛ tsp. black pepper

Combine first 3 ingredients together in skillet and stir over medium heat till flour becomes lightly toasted. Little by little, pour in malt beverage, whisking constantly as you do so to prevent lumping. Cook and stir till thickened. Add next 4 ingredients and simmer for 10 minutes, stirring occasionally. Serve on toasted slices of English muffin loaf (or other kinds of toasted bread), or use as a sauce over raw or steamed vegetables, or put the vegetables on top of the toast and top them off with the Rarebit sauce. Makes enough for 6 to 8 servings.

| SHOPPING LIST | |
|---|---|
| **Regularly Kept in the Kitchen** (Listed in Chapter 14, p. 703) | **Fresh Produce** |
| Butter, margarine or safflower oil<br>Whole wheat flour<br>Mustard powder<br>Cheddar cheese<br>Black pepper | Prepared mustard<br>Tabasco |

| Special Shopping |
|---|
| Non-alchoholic malt beverage (there are many different brands now) — tastes like beer without the alchohol; can usually be found in natural food stores and some supermarkets. |

# NUTRITIONAL ANALYSIS FOR ONE SERVING RAREBIT

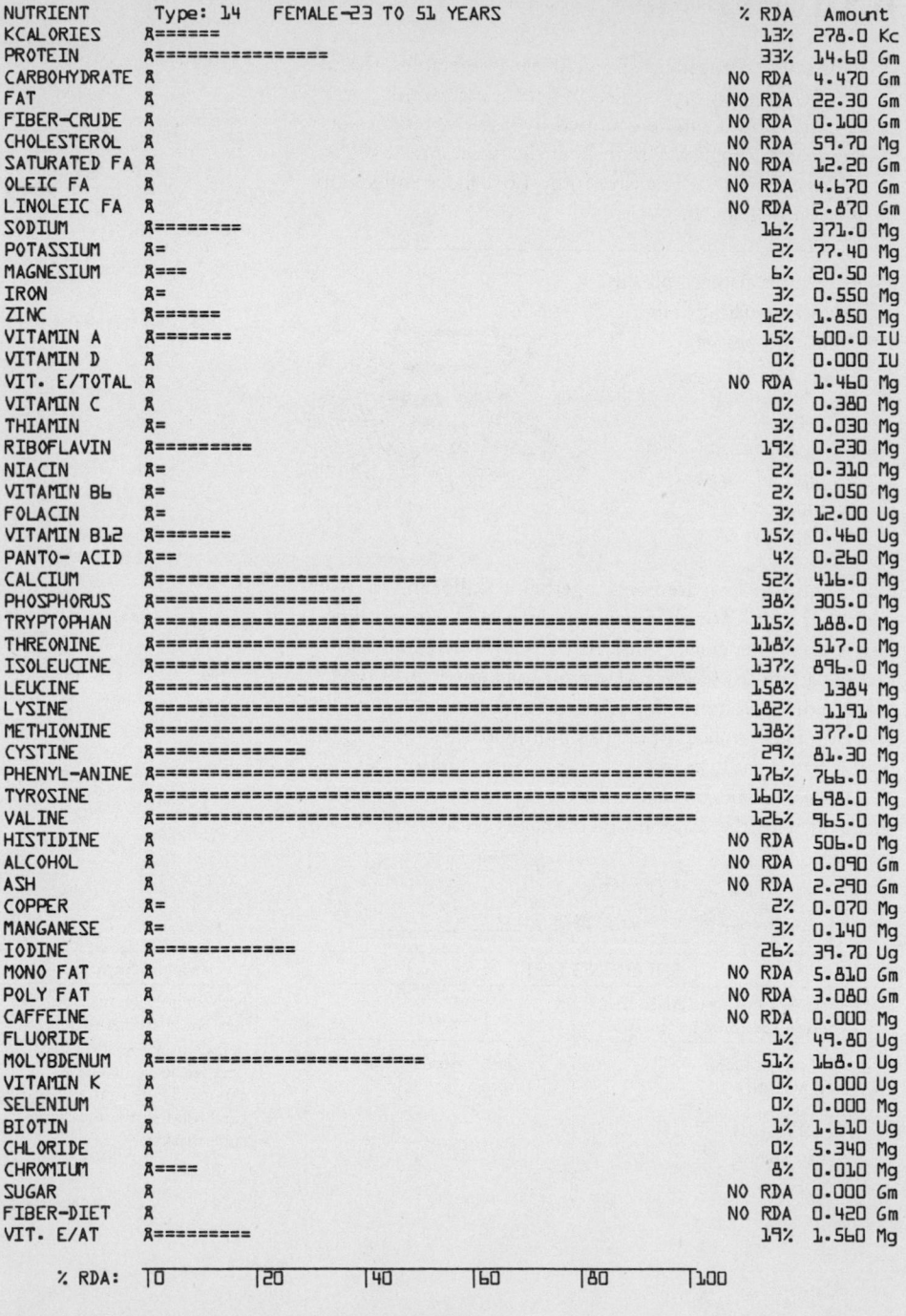

| NUTRIENT | Type: 14   FEMALE-23 TO 51 YEARS | % RDA | Amount |
|---|---|---|---|
| KCALORIES | A====== | 13% | 278.0 Kc |
| PROTEIN | A================ | 33% | 14.60 Gm |
| CARBOHYDRATE | A | NO RDA | 4.470 Gm |
| FAT | A | NO RDA | 22.30 Gm |
| FIBER-CRUDE | A | NO RDA | 0.100 Gm |
| CHOLESTEROL | A | NO RDA | 59.70 Mg |
| SATURATED FA | A | NO RDA | 12.20 Gm |
| OLEIC FA | A | NO RDA | 4.670 Gm |
| LINOLEIC FA | A | NO RDA | 2.870 Gm |
| SODIUM | A======== | 16% | 371.0 Mg |
| POTASSIUM | A= | 2% | 77.40 Mg |
| MAGNESIUM | A=== | 6% | 20.50 Mg |
| IRON | A= | 3% | 0.550 Mg |
| ZINC | A====== | 12% | 1.850 Mg |
| VITAMIN A | A======= | 15% | 600.0 IU |
| VITAMIN D | A | 0% | 0.000 IU |
| VIT. E/TOTAL | A | NO RDA | 1.460 Mg |
| VITAMIN C | A | 0% | 0.380 Mg |
| THIAMIN | A= | 3% | 0.030 Mg |
| RIBOFLAVIN | A========= | 19% | 0.230 Mg |
| NIACIN | A= | 2% | 0.310 Mg |
| VITAMIN B6 | A= | 2% | 0.050 Mg |
| FOLACIN | A= | 3% | 12.00 Ug |
| VITAMIN B12 | A======= | 15% | 0.460 Ug |
| PANTO- ACID | A== | 4% | 0.260 Mg |
| CALCIUM | A========================= | 52% | 416.0 Mg |
| PHOSPHORUS | A=================== | 38% | 305.0 Mg |
| TRYPTOPHAN | A=================================================== | 115% | 188.0 Mg |
| THREONINE | A=================================================== | 118% | 517.0 Mg |
| ISOLEUCINE | A=================================================== | 137% | 896.0 Mg |
| LEUCINE | A=================================================== | 158% | 1384 Mg |
| LYSINE | A=================================================== | 182% | 1191 Mg |
| METHIONINE | A=================================================== | 138% | 377.0 Mg |
| CYSTINE | A============= | 29% | 81.30 Mg |
| PHENYL-ANINE | A=================================================== | 176% | 766.0 Mg |
| TYROSINE | A=================================================== | 160% | 698.0 Mg |
| VALINE | A=================================================== | 126% | 965.0 Mg |
| HISTIDINE | A | NO RDA | 506.0 Mg |
| ALCOHOL | A | NO RDA | 0.090 Gm |
| ASH | A | NO RDA | 2.290 Gm |
| COPPER | A= | 2% | 0.070 Mg |
| MANGANESE | A= | 3% | 0.140 Mg |
| IODINE | A============= | 26% | 39.70 Ug |
| MONO FAT | A | NO RDA | 5.810 Gm |
| POLY FAT | A | NO RDA | 3.080 Gm |
| CAFFEINE | A | NO RDA | 0.000 Mg |
| FLUORIDE | A | 1% | 49.80 Ug |
| MOLYBDENUM | A========================= | 51% | 168.0 Ug |
| VITAMIN K | A | 0% | 0.000 Ug |
| SELENIUM | A | 0% | 0.000 Mg |
| BIOTIN | A | 1% | 1.610 Ug |
| CHLORIDE | A | 0% | 5.340 Mg |
| CHROMIUM | A==== | 8% | 0.010 Mg |
| SUGAR | A | NO RDA | 0.000 Gm |
| FIBER-DIET | A | NO RDA | 0.420 Gm |
| VIT. E/AT | A========= | 19% | 1.560 Mg |

```
% RDA:  |0      |20      |40      |60      |80      |100
```

Safflower oil used instead of butter in analysis.

# ENGLISH MUFFIN LOAF

☆ English muffins are one of our favorites — rarely had till my mother gave me this recipe. Of course we never buy the white flour/preservative versions and rarely buy the whole wheat ones because they're usually so expensive (do you know how many bags I have to buy to feed seven growing children and two adults?!). Now I can make English muffins inexpensively and relatively quickly.

---

2 Tbsp. baking yeast
1 tsp. salt
¼ tsp. baking soda
1½ cups bran
1½ cups whole wheat flour

2 cups milk
½ cup hot water from tap
1 Tbsp. honey

2½ -3 cups whole wheat flour

Mix first 5 ingredients together in a mixing bowl. Add next 3 ingredients and beat for about 5 minutes. Add the remaining flour a little at a time till the batter becomes very stiff, forming a soft, gooey ball of dough. (The amount of flour needed may vary by ½ cup depending on the humidity.) Oil two 8½" x 4½" x 3" bread loaf pans and flour with cornmeal. Divide dough in half and fill each loaf pan halfway up. Sprinkle the tops with cornmeal. Cover with a light towel or paper towel and allow to rise in a warm place till double in bulk.

Try making quickie pizzas like my sons do for quick after-school snacks. Spread a ½"-to ¾"-thick slice of the English Muffin Loaf with spaghetti sauce, sprinkle with grated cheese and a variety of fresh vegetables that don't need much cooking. Stick under broiler and cook till cheese thoroughly melts. Quite a far cry from quickie pizzas I failed to learn in Home Ec . . . white flour English muffins topped with tomato sauce and Vienna sausages — yuk!

Preheat oven to 400 degrees and bake for 25 minutes. Remove from loaf pans immediately and allow to cool on a rack. Slice bread in ½"- to ¾"-thick slices and toast well as with English muffins. Top with any of your favorite English muffin spreads (or some of the ones given here). This can be used anywhere and in any way you normally use English muffins. Makes 2 loaves.

| SHOPPING LIST | |
| --- | --- |
| **Regularly Kept in the Kitchen** (Listed in Chapter 14, p. 703) | **Fresh Produce** |
| Baking yeast<br>Salt<br>Baking soda<br>Bran<br>Whole wheat flour<br>Milk<br>Honey | (None) |

# NUTRITIONAL ANALYSIS FOR TWO SLICES ENGLISH MUFFIN LOAF

```
NUTRIENT        Type: 14    FEMALE-23 TO 51 YEARS         % RDA   Amount
KCALORIES       A====                                       8%    170.0 Kc
PROTEIN         A==========                                18%    8.020 Gm
CARBOHYDRATE    A                                         NO RDA  35.60 Gm
FAT             A                                         NO RDA  1.730 Gm
FIBER-CRUDE     A                                         NO RDA  1.620 Gm
CHOLESTEROL     A                                         NO RDA  2.570 Mg
SATURATED FA    A                                         NO RDA  0.540 Gm
OLEIC FA        A                                         NO RDA  0.390 Gm
LINOLEIC FA     A                                         NO RDA  0.620 Gm
SODIUM          A===                                        7%    173.0 Mg
POTASSIUM       A====                                       8%    308.0 Mg
MAGNESIUM       A=================                         34%    102.0 Mg
IRON            A=======                                   14%    2.670 Mg
ZINC            A=====                                     11%    1.710 Mg
VITAMIN A       A                                           1%    71.40 IU
VITAMIN D       A===                                        7%    14.50 IU
VIT. E/TOTAL    A                                         NO RDA  1.820 Mg
VITAMIN C       A                                           0%    0.330 Mg
THIAMIN         A================                         30%    0.300 Mg
RIBOFLAVIN      A=======                                   15%    0.180 Mg
NIACIN          A==============                            29%    3.780 Mg
VITAMIN B6      A======                                    13%    0.260 Mg
FOLACIN         A========                                  17%    70.10 Ug
VITAMIN B12     A==                                         4%    0.120 Ug
PANTO- ACID     A=======                                   14%    0.780 Mg
CALCIUM         A====                                       8%    69.40 Mg
PHOSPHORUS      A==================                        36%    293.0 Mg
TRYPTOPHAN      A===============================           58%    95.60 Mg
THREONINE       A==============================            57%    249.0 Mg
ISOLEUCINE      A===========================               53%    350.0 Mg
LEUCINE         A=================================         64%    560.0 Mg
LYSINE          A======================                    45%    296.0 Mg
METHIONINE      A=======================                   46%    126.0 Mg
CYSTINE         A=========================                 50%    136.0 Mg
PHENYL-ANINE    A===========================================  84%  366.0 Mg
TYROSINE        A=================================         64%    280.0 Mg
VALINE          A=========================                 50%    382.0 Mg
HISTIDINE       A                                         NO RDA  180.0 Mg
ALCOHOL         A                                         NO RDA  0.000 Gm
ASH             A                                         NO RDA  1.320 Gm
COPPER          A=====                                     11%    0.280 Mg
MANGANESE       A==================================        67%    2.520 Mg
IODINE          A==============================================  130%  195.0 Ug
MONO FAT        A                                         NO RDA  0.190 Gm
POLY FAT        A                                         NO RDA  0.020 Gm
CAFFEINE        A                                         NO RDA  0.000 Mg
FLUORIDE        A                                           0%    11.90 Ug
MOLYBDENUM      A=================================================  806%  2622 Ug
VITAMIN K       A                                           1%    2.020 Mg
SELENIUM        A====                                       8%    0.010 Mg
BIOTIN          A==                                         5%    8.650 Ug
CHLORIDE        A=                                          2%    88.80 Mg
CHROMIUM        A=================================================  200%  0.250 Mg
SUGAR           A                                         NO RDA  0.000 Gm
FIBER-DIET      A                                         NO RDA  9.760 Gm
VIT. E/AT       A==                                         4%    0.330 Mg

    % RDA:   |0      |20     |40     |60     |80     |100
```

246

# FRESH STRAWBERRY PRESERVES

☆ Use this recipe as a general idea guideline. Just about any fruit or combination of fruits can be used in place of the strawberries. Real sweet fruits, like mango, papaya, banana, etc., require no honey to be added.

---

*2 cups blended strawberry puree*
*2 Tbsp. lemon juice*
*¼ cup honey (more or less, according to taste)*

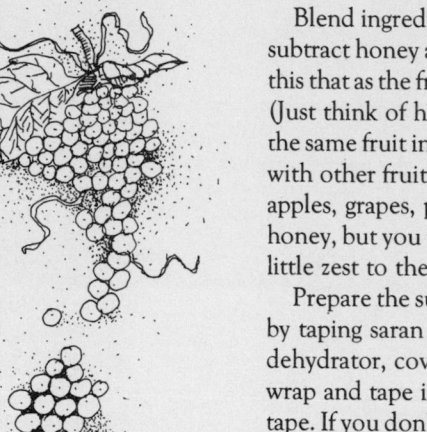

Blend ingredients together in blender till smooth. Add or subtract honey according to your taste. Remember as you do this that as the fruit dehydrates, it will naturally sweeten itself. (Just think of how much sweeter dried fruit is compared to the same fruit in its whole, fresh form.) This can also be done with other fruits. Some fruits (such as mangoes, pineapples, apples, grapes, papayas, etc.) will be sweet enough without honey, but you may want to add a squeeze of lemon to add a little zest to the taste.

Prepare the surface you are going to dehydrate the fruit on by taping saran wrap over the top of it. If you have a food dehydrator, cover entire top of dehydrating tray with saran wrap and tape it down at the corners with masking or clear tape. If you don't own a food dehydrator but it's a sunny, hot day, you can accomplish the same thing by spreading saran wrap over a cookie sheet and taping it down on the corners. Spread puree about ⅜" thick across the tray.

In the food dehydrator, dry the puree for about 3 to 3½ hours, gently stirring every hour or so. If drying outside in the sun and wind, you will just have to keep checking and stirring each time the top surface of the puree becomes thick. Drying time outside will vary a lot according to humidity, intensity of direct sun rays, time of day, etc., so you'll just have to keep an eye out. When the puree is a jam-like consistency, pour it into a glass jar and refrigerate it. This jam must be kept in the refrigerator and, because it hasn't been boiled, will keep only a few weeks.

If you allow the fruit puree to completely dry out, you will have fruit leather, which makes a delicious, nutritious and wonderful snack or dessert. The fruit leather can either be cut into strips and stored in an airtight container or the whole sheet can be rolled up. Makes a little less than a pint of preserves.

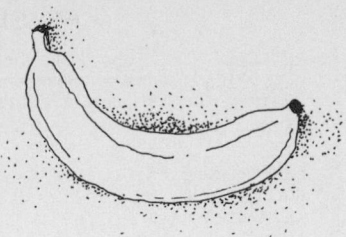

| SHOPPING LIST | |
|---|---|
| Regularly Kept in the Kitchen (Listed in Chapter 14, p. 703) | Fresh Produce |
| Honey | Strawberries<br>Lemon |

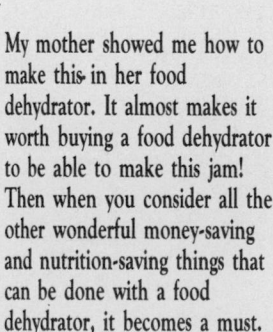

My mother showed me how to make this in her food dehydrator. It almost makes it worth buying a food dehydrator to be able to make this jam! Then when you consider all the other wonderful money-saving and nutrition-saving things that can be done with a food dehydrator, it becomes a must.

# NUTRITIONAL ANALYSIS FOR ONE RECIPE
## FRESH STRAWBERRY PRESERVES

```
NUTRIENT        Type: 14   FEMALE-23 TO 51 YEARS          % RDA   Amount
KCALORIES       A===============                           26%    528.0 Kc
PROTEIN         A======                                    12%    5.390 Gm
CARBOHYDRATE    A                                        NO RDA   131.0 Gm
FAT             A                                        NO RDA   3.180 Gm
FIBER-CRUDE     A                                        NO RDA   4.660 Gm
CHOLESTEROL     A                                        NO RDA   0.000 Mg
SATURATED FA    A                                        NO RDA   0.170 Gm
OLEIC FA        A                                        NO RDA   0.000 Gm
LINOLEIC FA     A                                        NO RDA   0.000 Gm
SODIUM          A                                           0%    15.80 Mg
POTASSIUM       A====================                      40%    1514 Mg
MAGNESIUM       A================                          32%    97.20 Mg
IRON            A==========                                20%    3.710 Mg
ZINC            A===                                        7%    1.190 Mg
VITAMIN A       A===                                        6%    243.0 IU
VITAMIN D       A                                           0%    0.000 IU
VIT. E/TOTAL    A                                        NO RDA   2.240 Mg
VITAMIN C       A=================================================  838%  503.0 Mg
THIAMIN         A=========                                 18%    0.180 Mg
RIBOFLAVIN      A=========================                 50%    0.610 Mg
NIACIN          A=========                                 18%    2.410 Mg
VITAMIN B6      A=============                              27%    0.540 Mg
FOLACIN         A==================                        39%    157.0 Ug
VITAMIN B12     A                                           0%    0.000 Ug
PANTO- ACID     A============================              56%    3.130 Mg
CALCIUM         A========                                  16%    128.0 Mg
PHOSPHORUS      A==========                                21%    168.0 Mg
TRYPTOPHAN      A================                          35%    57.90 Mg
THREONINE       A=================                         37%    162.0 Mg
ISOLEUCINE      A=========                                 18%    121.0 Mg
LEUCINE         A==============                            30%    266.0 Mg
LYSINE          A===============                           32%    214.0 Mg
METHIONINE      A=                                          2%    5.790 Mg
CYSTINE         A=======                                   14%    40.50 Mg
PHENYL-ANINE    A================                          35%    156.0 Mg
TYROSINE        A====================                      41%    179.0 Mg
VALINE          A==========                                20%    156.0 Mg
HISTIDINE       A                                        NO RDA   104.0 Mg
ALCOHOL         A                                        NO RDA   0.000 Gm
ASH             A                                        NO RDA   3.730 Gm
COPPER          A=========                                 18%    0.460 Mg
MANGANESE       A=================================         67%    2.530 Mg
IODINE          A                                           0%    0.000 Ug
MONO FAT        A                                        NO RDA   0.440 Gm
POLY FAT        A                                        NO RDA   1.600 Gm
CAFFEINE        A                                        NO RDA   0.000 Mg
FLUORIDE        A====                                       8%    239.0 Ug
MOLYBDENUM      A=================                         35%    115.0 Ug
VITAMIN K       A                                           0%    0.000 Ug
SELENIUM        A                                           0%    0.000 Mg
BIOTIN          A===                                        6%    9.500 Ug
CHLORIDE        A                                           0%    0.000 Mg
CHROMIUM        A                                           0%    0.000 Mg
SUGAR           A                                        NO RDA   45.40 Gm
FIBER-DIET      A                                        NO RDA   16.40 Gm
VIT. E/AT       A======                                    12%    1.030 Mg

    % RDA:   |0     |20    |40    |60    |80    |100
```

249

# APPLE CAKE

☆ A moist, just-the-right-sweetness apple upside-down cake.

Notice the date paste — a good sweetening idea to try in some of your favorite recipes.

---

2 Tbsp. butter or margarine
¼ cup honey

¼ cup date sugar
¼ tsp. cinnamon
Pinch cloves
Pinch nutmeg

1 apple, peeled, cored, and sliced about ⅛" thick

¼ cup butter or margarine

1 cup pitted dates filled with water
½ cup water

½ cup raisins
¼ cup chopped walnuts or pecans
1½ cups whole wheat flour
1 tsp. baking soda
1 tsp. baking powder

Preheat oven to 350 degrees.

Melt first 2 ingredients together in a 9"-square cake pan by putting the pan with the ingredients into the oven as it is preheating.

While the ingredients are melting, mix the next 4 ingredients together and then mix them into the melted butter and honey. Lay apple slices in the syrup to completely cover the bottom of the cake pan in an attractive way. (You may need more than one apple if you use a small one.)

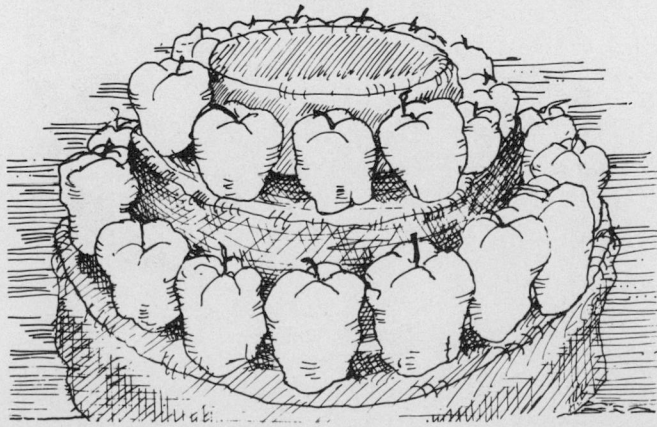

Fill a 1-cup measuring cup with pitted dates, but don't pack the dates into the cup. With the dates in the cup, fill the cup with water, then pour both dates and water into a blender. Add ½ cup more water into the blender. Now blend till it forms a smooth, thick paste. Add the ¼ cup butter or margarine and blend till totally whipped in. Put the blender mixture into a mixing bowl and add the last 5 dry ingredients. Mix just long enough to thoroughly blend in all the dry ingredients. Pour this batter on top of apple slices and spread evenly in the cake pan. Bake at 350 degrees for 35 to 40 minutes or till a toothpick inserted in the middle of the cake comes out clean. When done, remove from oven and immediately turn the cake pan upside down to empty out onto a serving platter. Makes one 9" x 9" cake.

| SHOPPING LIST | |
|---|---|
| **Regularly Kept in the Kitchen** (Listed in Chapter 14, p. 703) | **Fresh Produce** |
| Butter or margarine | Apple |
| Honey | Pitted dates |
| Date sugar | |
| Cinnamon | |
| Cloves | |
| Nutmeg | |
| Raisins | |
| Walnuts or pecans | |
| Whole wheat flour | |

# NUTRITIONAL ANALYSIS FOR ONE SERVING APPLE CAKE

```
NUTRIENT        Type: 14   FEMALE-23 TO 51 YEARS          % RDA   Amount
KCALORIES       Ã====                                      8%     174.0 Kc
PROTEIN         Ã==                                        5%     2.350 Gm
CARBOHYDRATE    Ã                                        NO RDA   29.20 Gm
FAT             Ã                                        NO RDA   6.540 Gm
FIBER-CRUDE     Ã                                        NO RDA   0.730 Gm
CHOLESTEROL     Ã                                        NO RDA   0.000 Mg
SATURATED FA    Ã                                        NO RDA   0.960 Gm
OLEIC FA        Ã                                        NO RDA   0.860 Gm
LINOLEIC FA     Ã                                        NO RDA   0.450 Gm
SODIUM          Ã===                                       6%     147.0 Mg
POTASSIUM       Ã==                                        5%     193.0 Mg
MAGNESIUM       Ã===                                       7%     23.80 Mg
IRON            Ã==                                        4%     0.770 Mg
ZINC            Ã=                                         3%     0.470 Mg
VITAMIN A       Ã==                                        5%     214.0 IU
VITAMIN D       Ã                                          0%     0.000 IU
VIT. E/TOTAL    Ã                                        NO RDA   0.950 Mg
VITAMIN C       Ã                                          1%     0.600 Mg
THIAMIN         Ã=====                                    10%     0.100 Mg
RIBOFLAVIN      Ã=                                         3%     0.040 Mg
NIACIN          Ã===                                       7%     0.930 Mg
VITAMIN B6      Ã==                                        4%     0.090 Mg
FOLACIN         Ã=                                         2%     9.570 Ug
VITAMIN B12     Ã                                          0%     0.000 Ug
PANTO- ACID     Ã===                                       6%     0.340 Mg
CALCIUM         Ã==                                        4%     32.80 Mg
PHOSPHORUS      Ã=====                                    11%     91.40 Mg
TRYPTOPHAN      Ã=========                                19%     31.80 Mg
THREONINE       Ã=======                                  14%     63.00 Mg
ISOLEUCINE      Ã======                                   13%     90.20 Mg
LEUCINE         Ã========                                 16%     141.0 Mg
LYSINE          Ã====                                      9%     65.10 Mg
METHIONINE      Ã======                                   12%     34.20 Mg
CYSTINE         Ã========                                 17%     48.30 Mg
PHENYL-ANINE    Ã===========                              23%     102.0 Mg
TYROSINE        Ã========                                 17%     76.60 Mg
VALINE          Ã======                                   13%     99.90 Mg
HISTIDINE       Ã                                        NO RDA   45.30 Mg
ALCOHOL         Ã                                        NO RDA   0.000 Gm
ASH             Ã                                        NO RDA   0.660 Gm
COPPER          Ã==                                        5%     0.140 Mg
MANGANESE       Ã==========                               20%     0.780 Mg
IODINE          Ã==================                       36%     54.40 Ug
MONO FAT        Ã                                        NO RDA   3.090 Gm
POLY FAT        Ã                                        NO RDA   1.920 Gm
CAFFEINE        Ã                                        NO RDA   0.000 Mg
FLUORIDE        Ã                                          0%     12.10 Ug
MOLYBDENUM      Ã=================================================237%   771.0 Ug
VITAMIN K       Ã                                          0%     0.000 Ug
SELENIUM        Ã                                          0%     0.000 Mg
BIOTIN          Ã                                          0%     0.990 Ug
CHLORIDE        Ã                                          0%     24.50 Mg
CHROMIUM        Ã=============================             56%     0.070 Mg
SUGAR           Ã                                        NO RDA   9.300 Gm
FIBER-DIET      Ã                                        NO RDA   2.800 Gm
VIT. E/AT       Ã=                                         3%     0.250 Mg

   % RDA:   |0      |20     |40     |60     |80     |100
```

Margarine used instead of butter; analysis does not include date sugar; chopped pecans used instead of walnuts.

# KEEPING OUT OF RUTS WITH "SUBSTITUTES"

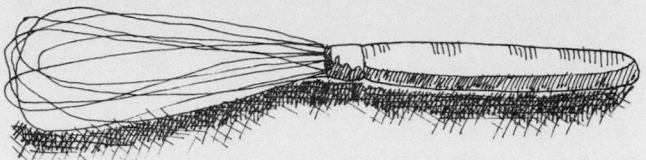

Throughout history, in every part of the world, there have been people who lived to aspire to higher understanding. Such individuals are sometimes called saintly persons, sages or philosophers for searching and teaching about the absolute truth. The Chinese Sage Lao Tsu tried to describe the absolute truth as such:

"There was Something undefined and yet complete in itself,
Existing before Heaven and Earth, Silent and Boundless,
Standing alone without change, yet pervading all without fail,
It may be regarded as the Mother of the World.
I do not know its name;
I call it 'Tao'
And, in the absence of a better word, call it 'the Great.'"

When talking about eliminating any familiar food from the diet and using something healthful in its place, it's easy to fall into the rut of trying to make the substitute taste and look as much like the old food as possible. This is certainly easy to do with carob and grain coffee because they look and taste enough like chocolate and coffee for comparisons to be inevitable.

A couple of important things to remember when trying to replace an old habit or food item with something else are —

1) The old habit or food doesn't have to be replaced with a taste-alike. Oftentimes it's good not to attempt a taste-alike as you'll just find yourself living in the world of trying to make things taste like the old habit or food you're trying to leave behind. No matter how good a substitute is, it'll never taste exactly like the food you're using it to replace. Better to venture out and try some completely different tastes. For example, try replacing your hot cup of coffee with a hot beverage that doesn't even attempt to replace the taste of coffee (as in some of the following idea-recipes).

2) Some of the foods being used as substitutes are foods on their own. When you stop thinking of them as substitutes and appreciate them for themselves, new dishes and tastes are possible. For example, I've used carob (usually used to replace chocolate) in the Mushroom Burger, which is an entree that isn't meant to replace chocolate in any way, shape or form.

Use these two guidelines to get adventurous and imaginative with new foods you're learning to eat!

# HAVE A LITTLE COFFEE IN YOUR CREAM (CHEESECAKE)

☆ A rich recipe, meant to be served only once in a great while — not every day of the week.

---

2⅔ cups moist, naturally sweetened
    whole grain cookie crumbs
⅓ cup seed or nut meal

2 cups Neufchatel cheese (two 8-oz. pkgs.)
2¾ cups sour cream
¾ cup honey
4 Tbsp. Bipro
1 tsp. vanilla

3 Tbsp. grain coffee
¼ cup honey

Preheat oven to 350 degrees.

Use a moist (preferably honey or fruit juice sweetened) whole grain cookie, and run this and nut or seed of your choice in a blender or food processor to make fine crumbs. Press into bottom of a springform cake pan. Blend next 5 ingredients together in blender or run through a food processor till absolutely smooth and a little whipped up. Pour 1 cup of blended mixture into a bowl and add next 2 ingredients to this (1 cup of blended mixture).

Pour half of the white mixture onto the crust in the bottom of the springform pan. Drizzle about ¾ cup of the 1 cup grain coffee mixture on top of this. You should now have a "marbleized" white and brown cheesecake mixture in the pan. Pour the remainder of the white mixture over this. Drizzle remainder of grain coffee mixture back and forth over surface of cake to make a pretty pattern.

Cheesecakes are the one place that substituting the Lowfat "Sour Cream" recipe (p. 186) for sour cream does not work. The cottage cheese in the Lowfat "Sour Cream" cooks into hard little lumps, making the cheesecake very grainy in texture.

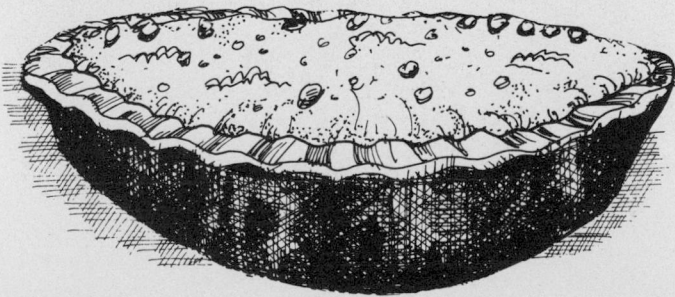

Bake at 350 degrees 60 to 70 minutes. Remove from oven and cool to room temperature. Cover with plastic wrap and refrigerate 6 to 8 hours before serving. Remove from springform pan and serve. Makes one cheesecake (about 10 servings).

| Special Shopping |
| --- |
| Moist whole grain cookie (honey or fruit juice sweetened) — in natural food stores. Neufchatel cheese — in some supermarket cheese departments or gourmet cheese shops. |

| SHOPPING LIST | |
| --- | --- |
| Regularly Kept in the Kitchen (Listed in Chapter 14, p. 703) | Fresh Produce |
| Nut or seed of choice Honey Bipro Vanilla Grain coffee Almond extract | Sour Cream |

# NUTRITIONAL ANALYSIS FOR ONE SERVING
## HAVE A LITTLE COFFEE IN YOUR CREAM (CHEESECAKE)

```
NUTRIENT        Type: 14   FEMALE-23 TO 51 YEARS        % RDA   Amount
KCALORIES     Ã=============                             24%   483.0 Kc
PROTEIN       Ã==========                               20%   9.220 Gm
CARBOHYDRATE  Ã                                        NO RDA  47.40 Gm
FAT           Ã                                        NO RDA  30.50 Gm
FIBER-CRUDE   Ã                                        NO RDA  0.990 Gm
CHOLESTEROL   Ã                                        NO RDA  38.80 Mg
SATURATED FA  Ã                                        NO RDA  10.80 Gm
OLEIC FA      Ã                                        NO RDA  7.940 Gm
LINOLEIC FA   Ã                                        NO RDA  8.540 Gm
SODIUM        Ã====                                      9%   199.0 Mg
POTASSIUM     Ã=====                                    10%   402.0 Mg
MAGNESIUM     Ã==========                               21%   63.10 Mg
IRON          Ã========                                 14%   2.580 Mg
ZINC          Ã====                                      9%   1.390 Mg
VITAMIN A     Ã=======                                  15%   627.0 IU
VITAMIN D     Ã                                          1%   3.300 IU
VIT. E/TOTAL  Ã                                        NO RDA  5.970 Mg
VITAMIN C     Ã                                          1%   0.820 Mg
THIAMIN       Ã=============                             26%   0.260 Mg
RIBOFLAVIN    Ã=========                                18%   0.220 Mg
NIACIN        Ã=======                                  14%   1.850 Mg
VITAMIN B6    Ã===                                       6%   0.130 Mg
FOLACIN       Ã==                                        5%   21.70 Ug
VITAMIN B12   Ã===                                       7%   0.210 Ug
PANTO- ACID   Ã======                                   13%   0.740 Mg
CALCIUM       Ã=========                                18%   146.0 Mg
PHOSPHORUS    Ã==============                            29%   238.0 Mg
TRYPTOPHAN    Ã=================================         69%   113.0 Mg
THREONINE     Ã================================         68%   299.0 Mg
ISOLEUCINE    Ã===========================               56%   366.0 Mg
LEUCINE       Ã====================================      75%   659.0 Mg
LYSINE        Ã=================================         69%   452.0 Mg
METHIONINE    Ã============================■■            59%   161.0 Mg
CYSTINE       Ã======================                    46%   126.0 Mg
PHENYL-ANINE  Ã============================================  92%   403.0 Mg
TYROSINE      Ã===================================       74%   324.0 Mg
VALINE        Ã==========================                54%   417.0 Mg
HISTIDINE     Ã                                        NO RDA  216.0 Mg
ALCOHOL       Ã                                        NO RDA  0.000 Gm
ASH           Ã                                        NO RDA  1.500 Gm
COPPER        Ã=====                                    10%   0.270 Mg
MANGANESE     Ã=============                             26%   0.990 Mg
IODINE        Ã=======================                   48%   72.20 Ug
MONO FAT      Ã                                        NO RDA  8.350 Gm
POLY FAT      Ã                                        NO RDA  9.630 Gm
CAFFEINE      Ã                                        NO RDA  0.000 Mg
FLUORIDE      Ã                                          1%   49.90 Ug
MOLYBDENUM    Ã=================================================  307%  999.0 Ug
VITAMIN K     Ã                                          0%   0.000 Ug
SELENIUM      Ã========                                 16%   0.020 Mg
BIOTIN        Ã=                                         2%   3.920 Ug
CHLORIDE      Ã                                          0%   31.60 Mg
CHROMIUM      Ã======================================    80%   0.100 Mg
SUGAR         Ã                                        NO RDA  0.000 Gm
FIBER-DIET    Ã                                        NO RDA  2.800 Gm
VIT. E/AT     Ã===============================           65%   5.270 Mg

   % RDA:   |0      |20     |40     |60     |80     |100
```

Cookie crumbs used for crust: Mom's Converted Aunt Esther's Crisp Cookies. Sesame meal used instead of nut meal.

# EXPRESS·O ICE

☆ A refreshing, simple-to-make hot weather dessert.

5 cups water
⅓ cup grain coffee

1 cup honey

Tofu Whipped Topping, p. 162 (optional)

Bring water to boil and pour onto grain coffee. Stir to dissolve grain coffee. Add honey and stir till honey dissolves. Cool to room temperature, then put in freezer and leave there till mixture turns slushy (let frozen crystals form, but don't freeze over solid). Remove from freezer and whisk to form a slush. Cover and put back in freezer. Just before serving, whisk again to form a chunky slush. Divide into dessert cups, top with Tofu Whipped Topping (add a dash of mint extract to tofu topping for a real refreshing change) and serve. Makes five 1-cup servings.

# MOLASSES WAKE·UP

☆ One tablespoon of blackstrap molasses contains about 17 percent of the RDA of calcium and iron, making this a true energy drink, unlike the temporary and illusory energy "boost" provided by coffee.

1 cup boiling water
1 Tbsp. blackstrap molasses

Squeeze of lemon juice

Bring water to a boil and pour into cup. Spoon molasses into hot water and stir till molasses dissolves. Squeeze lemon in and drink hot. Makes 1 individual serving.

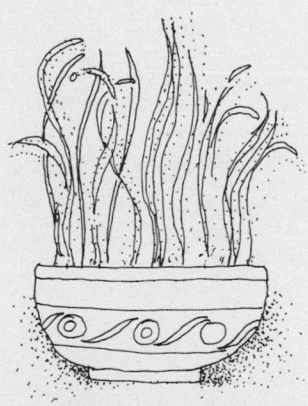

If you like starting the day off with a welcoming hot drink, try some of these drinks that don't even attempt to be coffee taste-alikes. You'll find, in the long-run, the nutritional pick-up far surpasses the caffeine "boost"!

# SUNRISE HERB TEA

☆ Start every day off differently, making a different flavored drink every morning by mixing different combinations of herb teas and frozen juice concentrates.

---

*4 cups water*
*Right quantity of herb tea of your choice*
 *(to go in 4 cups water)*

*3 -4 Tbsp. frozen 100% juice concentrate*
 *of your choice*

Bring water to a boil. Turn off heat and add proper amount of herb tea of your choice, cover and allow to steep 3 to 5 minutes. Strain tea or remove tea bags. Add frozen 100% fruit juice concentrate flavor of your choice. Makes 4 cups.

# GIN(·GER·SENG) TONIC

☆ A zingy way to start any day; but on days that you have a cold, drinking bottles full of this brew seems to make the cold pass more quickly.

☆ For centuries, ginseng has been a prized herb tea in the Orient. Credited with having rejuvenative powers, it's used by herbalists as a remedy for many diseases. Chinese doctors recommend a daily dose of this herb for maintaining good health, lots of energy, and increasing longevity. However, it's advised that women shouldn't drink ginseng on a daily basis; instead, they should drink another herb that's like the women's ginseng — Dong Quai (also known as Tang Kwai).

---

*4 cups water*
*3" fresh ginger root chunk, sliced thin*
*Right quantity of ginseng (to go in 4 cups water)*

*⅓ cup lemon juice*
*3 Tbsp. honey*
*Dash (up to ⅛ tsp.) cayenne (optional)*

Volumes of literature can, and in fact have been written about ginseng. There's so much about its history, effects on the body and romanticized background, but here I'll limit my comments to its preparation. If preparing ginseng from the root, it's interesting that real ginseng connoisseurs never touch the root with metal — from harvest to consumption. If you wish to prepare ginseng as they do, you'll need a bamboo steamer, a special wooden knife for cutting the root and a glass pot to simmer the cut root in. To prepare the ginseng root, place it in a steamer and steam till it is tender enough to slice with the wooden knife. Slice enough for desired amount of tea and let unsliced chunk of ginseng sit out so it will dry again. Simmer slices of ginseng in water in a covered glass pot.

Bring water to a boil. Turn down to simmer and add sliced ginger root. If you're using ginseng root, add at this time also; if using ginseng concentrate or instant tea, add later when ginger is being removed from water. (There are many different forms of ginseng available today. If using something besides slivers of ginseng root, just follow directions on package.) Cover and simmer for 15 minutes.

Strain and add next 2 or 3 ingredients. Stir till honey dissolves. Serve hot. This tea is also delicious and refreshing served cold over ice and fresh mint sprigs. Makes four 1-cup servings.

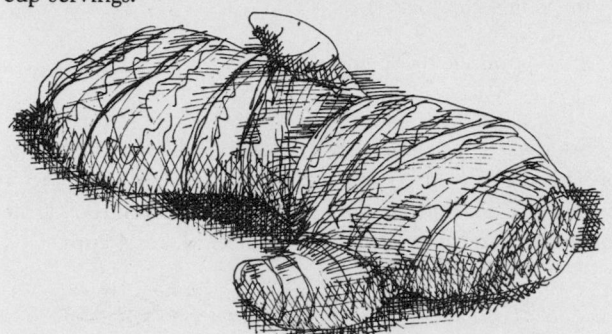

# FRUIT JUICE BREW

☆ Don't be afraid to use different flavors of fruit and vary the spices.

---

*2 cups unsweetened pineapple juice*
*2 cups unsweetened cranberry-apple*
*  or cherry-apple juice*
*1 cup water*
*1 cinnamon stick*
*6 -8 whole cloves*

Combine all ingredients in a pot and cover, allowing to sit overnight (in the refrigerator or on the kitchen counter, depending on whether the weather is hot enough to cause juice to spoil if left out).

Bring mixture to a boil, lower heat and simmer 5 to 10 minutes. Strain and serve. Makes four 1-cup servings.

If in a hurry, you can heat pineapple juice and sprinkle in a pinch of cinnamon and a sprinkle of powdered cloves; the flavor will be the same, but you will find the spices that sink to the bottom may tickle your throat.

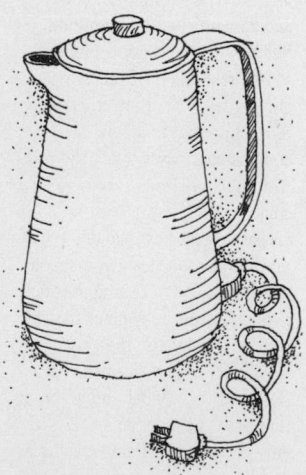

These juices can even be percolated in the old coffee percolator if you like . . . and will fill the room with different kinds of wonderful aromas.

259

# VEGETABLE JUICE BREW

☆ I usually use canned vegetable juice for this since it
gets cooked anyway. It would be a waste to make fresh
vegetable juice and then cook it! . . . Cold, fresh vegetable juice is another start-of-the-day beverage to try,
especially in the summer months!

---

4 cups tomato or mixed vegetable juice
1 cup chopped celery
2 bay leaves
¼ tsp. asafetida or ½ onion, diced
6 peppercorns

¼ cup lemon juice
⅛ tsp. or less cayenne (optional)

Put first 5 ingredients together in a pot, cover and leave
overnight (in the refrigerator or on the kitchen counter,
depending on whether the weather is hot enough to cause
juice to spoil if left out).

Bring mixture to a boil, lower heat and simmer for 10
minutes. Strain and serve like hot tea. Makes four 1-cup
servings.

# MUSHROOM BURGERS

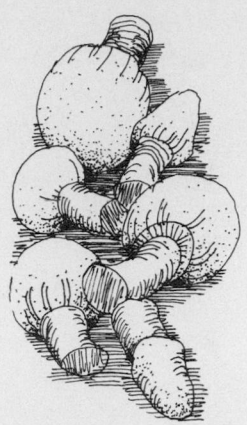

☆ Carob doesn't always have to be served as a sweet; it actually is a food and can be added to entrees like this one.

---

1 lb. finely chopped, fresh, raw mushrooms
1 cup finely ground, toasted almonds and/or sunflower seeds
2 cups whole wheat bread crumbs
⅓ cup tomato sauce or water
¼ cup carob powder
3 Tbsp. Bipro
¼ cup finely diced celery and 1 tsp. asafetida
    OR ¼ cup diced onion
2 Tbsp. nutritional yeast
1 Tbsp. prepared mustard
1½ tsp. soy sauce
¼ tsp. black pepper
Dash of Tabasco

Chop mushrooms very fine (most easily done in a food processor) so they *almost* form a puree; be very careful not to puree them. Combine with the rest of the ingredients and allow to sit for 15 minutes. In the meantime, preheat oven to 350 degrees. To form burger patties, pack enough mixture to fill a ½-cup measuring cup, turn onto an oiled cookie sheet and flatten to about ¾" thick. Bake at 350 degrees for 2 minutes, then remove from oven. Brush tops with melted margarine and bake for another 10 minutes. The burgers are now done. At this point you can top them with grated cheese and place under broiler till cheese melts, or serve plain. This is good on a whole wheat bun topped with lots of fresh sprouts, tomatoes, lettuce and bell pepper slivers. The burgers can also be served as an entree alongside rice or mashed potatoes topped with a brown gravy, and a nice fresh salad. Makes 6 burgers.

The carob tree is a beautiful, decorative tree and is useful as well. There's one in front of the library where I used to give my cooking classes. An evergreen tree with large, deep-green leaves, it makes a beautiful landscaping plant. It makes sense to landscape with useful plants, as suggested and demonstrated in *Edible Landscaping* by Rosalind Creasy, a worthwhile book to follow whether living in an apartment, on the farm or anything in between!

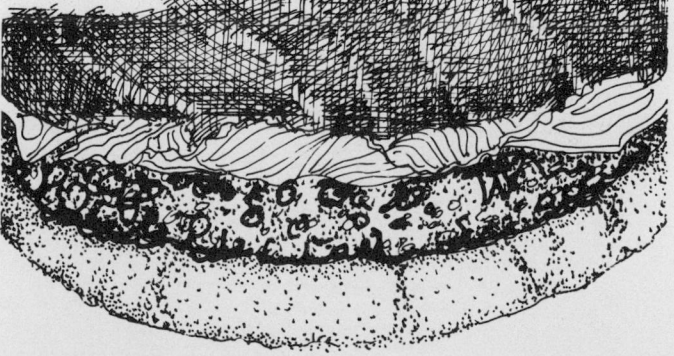

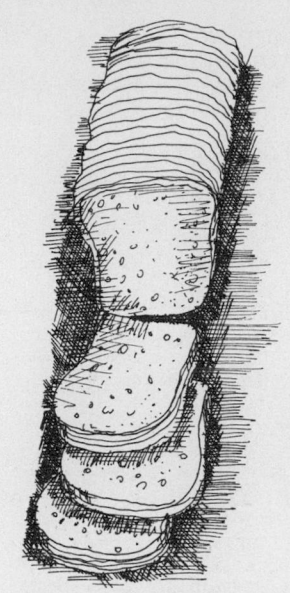

| SHOPPING LIST | |
|---|---|
| **Regularly Kept in the Kitchen (Listed in Chapter 14, p. 703)** | **Fresh Produce** |
| Almonds or sunflower seeds | Mushrooms |
| Whole wheat bread | Celery or onion |
| Carob powder | Tabasco |
| Bipro | |
| Asafetida | |
| Nutritional yeast | |
| Prepared mustard | |
| Soy sauce | |
| Black pepper | |
| Tomato sauce | |

# NUTRITIONAL ANALYSIS FOR ONE MUSHROOM BURGER

```
NUTRIENT       Type: 14   FEMALE-23 TO 51 YEARS            % RDA   Amount
KCALORIES      X=====                                       11%    239.0 Kc
PROTEIN        X==============                              27%    12.20 Gm
CARBOHYDRATE   X                                          NO RDA   23.60 Gm
FAT            X                                          NO RDA   13.30 Gm
FIBER-CRUDE    X                                          NO RDA   2.230 Gm
CHOLESTEROL    X                                          NO RDA   0.020 Mg
SATURATED FA   X                                          NO RDA   1.380 Gm
OLEIC FA       X                                          NO RDA   2.460 Gm
LINOLEIC FA    X                                          NO RDA   7.450 Gm
SODIUM         X=====                                       10%    236.0 Mg
POTASSIUM      X=======                                     15%    589.0 Mg
MAGNESIUM      X====================                        40%    121.0 Mg
IRON           X==========                                  20%    3.650 Mg
ZINC           X========                                    16%    2.410 Mg
VITAMIN A      X                                             0%    12.70 IU
VITAMIN D      X                                             0%    0.000 IU
VIT. E/TOTAL   X                                          NO RDA   13.10 Mg
VITAMIN C      X==                                           5%    3.180 Mg
THIAMIN        X==================================================  220%  2.200 Mg
RIBOFLAVIN     X==================================================  160%  1.930 Mg
NIACIN         X==================================================  106%  13.80 Mg
VITAMIN B6     X=================================================   96%   1.930 Mg
FOLACIN        X======                                      12%    50.50 Ug
VITAMIN B12    X==================                          38%    1.160 Ug
PANTO- ACID    X=====================                       42%    2.330 Mg
CALCIUM        X====                                         8%    70.00 Mg
PHOSPHORUS     X=====================                       43%    347.0 Mg
TRYPTOPHAN     X==================================================  125%  204.0 Mg
THREONINE      X==================================================  115%  504.0 Mg
ISOLEUCINE     X===========================================  87%   572.0 Mg
LEUCINE        X==================================================  104%  913.0 Mg
LYSINE         X==================================================  105%  692.0 Mg
METHIONINE     X===========================================  87%   238.0 Mg
CYSTINE        X==============================               61%   167.0 Mg
PHENYL-ANINE   X==================================================  129%  563.0 Mg
TYROSINE       X===================================          71%   312.0 Mg
VALINE         X==========================================   85%   655.0 Mg
HISTIDINE      X                                          NO RDA   268.0 Mg
ALCOHOL        X                                          NO RDA   0.000 Gm
ASH            X                                          NO RDA   3.630 Gm
COPPER         X============                                23%    0.580 Mg
MANGANESE      X======                                      13%    0.490 Mg
IODINE         X====                                         9%    13.60 Ug
MONO FAT       X                                          NO RDA   2.260 Gm
POLY FAT       X                                          NO RDA   7.980 Gm
CAFFEINE       X                                          NO RDA   0.000 Mg
FLUORIDE       X                                             0%    4.250 Ug
MOLYBDENUM     X========================                    48%    159.0 Ug
VITAMIN K      X                                             0%    0.000 Ug
SELENIUM       X========                                    16%    0.020 Mg
BIOTIN         X=                                            3%    5.710 Ug
CHLORIDE       X                                             0%    11.20 Mg
CHROMIUM       X====================                        40%    0.050 Mg
SUGAR          X                                          NO RDA   0.400 Gm
FIBER-DIET     X                                          NO RDA   1.560 Gm
VIT. E/AT      X==================================================  151%  12.10 Mg

    % RDA:   |0      |20     |40     |60     |80     |100
```

Sunflower seeds used instead of almonds; onion used instead of celery and asafetida.

# CHAPTER 6

# ALCOHOL AWARENESS

Throughout America more and more people are becoming aware of the damage done to individuals and society as a whole by alcohol. Many sobering facts have led the largest number of Americans since prohibition to voluntarily abstain from, or drastically cut back on consumption of alcoholic beverages. I see this new temperance movement, or mood, as being a great improvement over prohibition because individuals are making the decisions on their own, using their own intelligence and wisdom, rather than having it artificially forced upon them by legislation. And we certainly have been provided with enough facts and figures on which to base an intelligent decision.

## IS IT WORTH IT ON ANY LEVEL?

In 1975 the National Institute on Alcohol Abuse and Alcoholism compiled a conservative estimate of the monetary loss to society caused by alcohol of 42.75 billion dollars a year. That figure only takes into account those losses on which a price tag can be put: loss of production amongst male employees (19.63 billion dollars), health care (12.74 billion dollars), motor vehi-

> *"After all, a business or industry can only be considered healthy if the gross product substantially exceeds the investment required to produce it. The alcohol industry's contribution can therefore be known only after examining the price the American people have had to pay to receive it."*
>
> — Chris Butler
> *Drugs, Suicide, Divorce: Social Problems in the West*

cle accidents (5.14 billion dollars), violent crime (2.09 billion dollars), social services (2.7 billion dollars) and fire (.43 billion dollars).

The total doesn't include monetary losses such as those due to ineffectiveness of female employees (who make up about 41 percent of the labor force and 45 percent of the drinking population), nonviolent crimes (such as burglary, auto theft, fraud, vandalism, etc.) or the cost of investigations and calls law enforcement officials answer that don't result in arrests. And there are many other hidden costs that can't be accurately figured.

Of course, the amount of loss in lives ruined or lost can never be measured in dollars and cents. While under the influence of alcohol, a person often does things that result in physical/mental/emotional injuries or even death to himself and/or others. Not including deaths from diseases and damage to organs in the body caused by alcohol, there are over 200,000 alcohol-related deaths in America annually. Considering that 46,370 Americans died in the entire Vietnam War, it's not surprising that Americans are rallying in a different way to put an end to these unnecessary losses as urgently as we tried to end the Vietnam War.

## CHANGES AT WORK . . .

Though there haven't been any sit-in demonstrations, Americans are doing something to reduce the losses on every level, as articles in major newspapers and national magazines have reported. You know businesses are taking seriously losses due to inebriated workers when Anheuser-Busch (the country's largest brewer) does something as dramatic as ending the over century-old industry tradition of giving free beers to company employees and banning drinking on compa-

ny grounds (with the backing of the union). They are only one of the many companies who have taken action to end drunk driving and "inappropriate" drinking amongst their work force and executives by including in company policies actions that range from banning drinking on company grounds or during company hours, to paying for alcoholism treatment — or at least a taxi cab home — for employees in such need. Although most companies aren't under the pressure of public interest lawsuits, like the one filed in California to make it tougher for companies to write off

> *Society's annual losses due to alcohol: $42.75 billion.* — NIAAA, 1975
>
> *Federal taxes from alcohol sales and corporations: $5.4 billion.* — U.S. Treasury, Public Affairs, 1985

tabs for drinks bought while entertaining business associates, doing business over a drink is going the way of the dinosaur. Many executives are doing business over sparkling water or "power teas" by choice, or due to the social pressure of knowing that business associates frown on, or raise eyebrows at, anyone who smells like alcohol during work time.

## ON THE ROAD . . .

The business world isn't the only place where attitudes toward drinking are changing. A *Business Week*/Harris Poll showed that 65 percent favored jailing a drunk driver, even if he hadn't caused an accident, and 89 percent favored yanking his driver's license on the second offense. Under the pressure and publicity brought about by MADD (Mothers Against Drunk Driving) and other citizens' groups, most states have passed very stringent laws to penalize, and hopefully deter, drunk drivers.

....................................

*"More people are killed by eating and drinking than by the sword."*

— Sir William Osler

....................................

### WITHIN EACH PERSON

Society (and its attitudes) is made up of individuals. So many individuals are concerned with their own personal fitness and health that alcohol sales have dropped.

The fact that alcohol — another source of "empty calories" that give no nutrition — raises and lowers blood-sugar levels and can, therefore, be fattening, is one of its smaller drawbacks. Alcoholic beverages should actually be labeled "poison" because they contain ethyl alcohol (ethanol). It's this ethyl alcohol, found in all alcoholic beverages from beer to wine to the "hard stuff," that's so inebriating and causes so much damage to the body. Ethyl alcohol is extremely soluble in water, so as soon as it's put into the mouth it

begins to be absorbed into the body through the gums and tongue. This occurs before it's even swallowed. The rest is absorbed directly into the bloodstream through the stomach walls and small intestines, which quickly carry the alcohol to every part of the body, damaging every organ it passes through.

At one time in history, alcohol was thought to be a stimulant; we now know it does exactly the opposite. Alcohol causes blood cells to clump together, resulting in a thickening of the blood, which obviously slows circulation and transport of oxygen. The loss of oxygen affects the brain, causing what is called "tipsiness" or "drunkenness" while damaging brain cells. Every time an alcoholic beverage is consumed, thousands of brain cells are destroyed; since brain cells aren't repaired or replaced like other cells in the body, the damage is permanent. Besides the certain damage to the brain, damage to the digestive and nervous systems and other major organs of the body may be seen over a period of time.

The exact length of time it takes for damage to other systems and organs to show depends a great deal on the amount and frequency of alcohol consumption and the individual's body chemistry. Alcohol is known to ruin the nervous system and damage the heart, stomach, liver, kidneys and skin. It's a proven risk factor in heart disease, cancer and diabetes. Like any

other empty-calorie food, it not only deprives your body of proper nutrition by giving a full feeling, but it robs the body of its stores of vitamin A and C, the B-vitamins and many minerals. Women who drink during pregnancy harm the child in the womb; "fetal alcohol syndrome" is the name given to the deformities and mental retardation caused to the unborn infant by a drinking mother. To make matters worse, this potently harmful poison is addicting.

### ALL FOR THE BETTER!

Whatever the motivation is, the decision to leave alcoholic beverages out of one's life deserves a hearty toast ... of sparkling water, which is only one of the creative ways Americans are finding to replace alcoholic beverages.

....................................

*"It has become a sign of status, as a whole, sensuous human being, to have the ability to control your impulses."*

— Michael Sacks
Professor of Psychology
Cornell University
"Time" magazine
May 20, 1985, p. 70

....................................

Sometimes this is done by sticking to old rituals or patterns and just substituting a nonalcoholic drink, like "power teas" (mentioned previously) or putting one's feet up after work over a sparkling water, alcohol-free beer or wine, or exotic cooler. Varieties and sales of these non-alcoholic-type drinks have increased tremendously in the past few years.

Oftentimes old rituals and patterns are replaced with new activities. Many people who used to drink a little after work to relax and counteract stress are finding that exercising instead gives them the same desired results. Along with undesirable physiological changes that are set off in the body by alcohol, endorphins (chemicals that calm the nervous system) are released. A good workout releases endorphins while benefiting the body by keeping it fit. Whatever they are doing, less alcohol in the diet is definitely changing the how and the quality of Americans' work, play and social activity.

All of our bodies are temporary and bound to wither and die. Therefore, living to eat is a futile goal. Rather, we should eat to live, and live to pursue a higher goal as described simply by Henry David Thoreau, "Rather than love, than money, than fame, give me truth."

# DESSERT PARTY

The way Americans socialize and party is changing radically. Bartenders and professional caterers have all remarked on the drop in the sale of liquor (especially hard liquor) and the necessity of having to stock up on sparkling water and alcohol-free beer, wine and champagne. Some professional caterers I know have said that they think their customers often have full-bars set up at their parties just so they won't offend anyone. This may be an unfounded fear. I've been to parties given by a friend of mine, who owns a large chain of health spas, where he not only didn't provide a bar, but didn't allow any of his guests to bring any alcoholic beverages of their own (or smoke). Everyone seemed to be doing just fine without and I heard no complaints. Admittedly, most of the guests were health buffs and fitness pros, but more and more people are concerned with fitness nowadays.

Having a dessert party is one way to avoid centering a party around alcohol. It's a party that's meant to be held after mealtime or for a get-together after a big event. Depending on the time and setting of the party, it's one that can be given for children, family get-togethers or elegant, all-adult black-tie affairs.

Since sweets and alcoholic beverages don't mix well, people wouldn't necessarily be expecting alcoholic beverages to be provided. You can provide compatible beverages to quench the thirst usually brought on by sweets by providing the usual sparkling water or fruit coolers. If you want to give friends something they'll remember and talk about for a long time, why not be the first to hire a professional bartender and follow the example of the Long Beach Hyatt Regency Hotel by setting up a juice bar. Of course, the bartender would have to be one with sufficient experience or enough imagination to whip up smoothies or fruit-flavored coolers (like the Holiday Sparkler).

If you're not planning any dessert parties for the near future, you might want to serve one of these desserts as a sweet end to any meal.

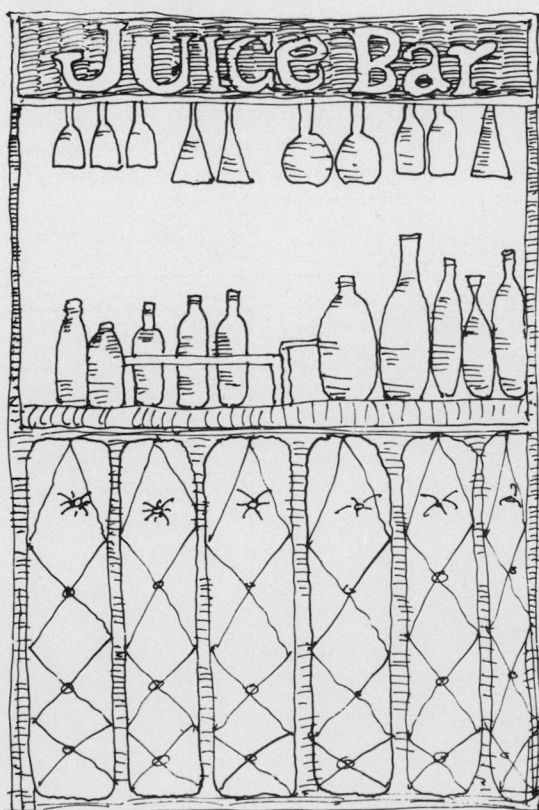

# PERFECTLY NUTTY CRUST

☆ This nutty and nutritious crust makes a perfect base for many cooked and raw fillings.

---

*3 cups whole wheat flour*
*2¼ cups nut meal (preferably*
 *almond, pecan or walnut)*
*1 cup margarine or butter*
*¼ cup honey*
*1 tsp. vanilla extract*

Preheat oven to 350 degrees.

Mix all ingredients together with pastry cutter or by hand. When thoroughly mixed, divide dough into 3 parts (if using 9" or 10" tart or pie pans), or into 12 parts (if using 3" tartlet pans). Press dough evenly into pans by hand. Cover and chill for at least 30 minutes. (The crusts can be frozen at this point for future baking.) Bake 20 to 25 minutes at 350 degrees till golden brown. Allow to cool and fill. Baked shells can be frozen for future use. This recipe makes three 9" tarts or a dozen 3" tartlets.

This is a delicious and nutritious pastry shell for many different fillings, such as those in the following recipes, or for any of your favorite pie fillings, ice cream pies, puddings, etc.

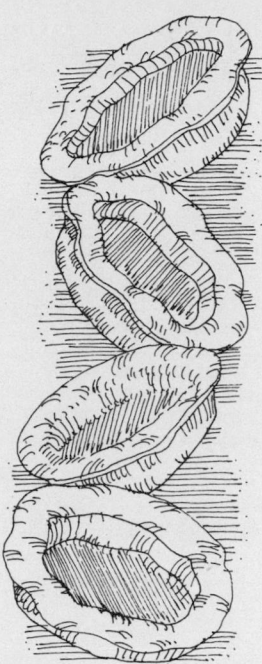

Although nut meals are available in some natural food stores, I prefer making my own. This way I can get whatever kind of nut in a meal that I want and can be sure of its freshness. As soon as a nut is ground or chopped, the oils in it begin to turn rancid, so it's actually impossible to buy a fresh nut meal. Making a nut meal is easy enough — just put desired nut (or seed) into a blender or food processor and run until nut or seed is the texture of sand. If there is extra nut meal, try to use it soon; and be sure to store in the refrigerator.

| SHOPPING LIST | |
|---|---|
| **Regularly Kept in the Kitchen** (Listed in Chapter 14, p. 703) | **Fresh Produce** |
| Whole wheat flour | (None) |
| Almonds, pecans or walnuts | |
| Margarine or butter | |
| Honey | |
| Vanilla extract | |

# NUTRITIONAL ANALYSIS FOR ONE PERFECTLY NUTTY PIE CRUST

| NUTRIENT | Type: 14  FEMALE-23 TO 51 YEARS | % RDA | Amount |
|---|---|---|---|
| KCALORIES | A===================================== | 86% | 1726 Kc |
| PROTEIN | A========================================== | 190% | 83.80 Gm |
| CARBOHYDRATE | A | NO RDA | 157.0 Gm |
| FAT | A | NO RDA | 94.20 Gm |
| FIBER-CRUDE | A | NO RDA | 6.680 Gm |
| CHOLESTEROL | A | NO RDA | 0.000 Mg |
| SATURATED FA | A | NO RDA | 13.20 Gm |
| OLEIC FA | A | NO RDA | 0.350 Gm |
| LINOLEIC FA | A | NO RDA | 1.210 Gm |
| SODIUM | A================ | 33% | 729.0 Mg |
| POTASSIUM | A==================================== | 76% | 2878 Mg |
| MAGNESIUM | A====================== | 46% | 138.0 Mg |
| IRON | A================================================ | 102% | 18.50 Mg |
| ZINC | A========= | 19% | 2.920 Mg |
| VITAMIN A | A============================== | 62% | 2500 IU |
| VITAMIN D | A | 0% | 0.000 IU |
| VIT. E/TOTAL | A | NO RDA | 4.740 Mg |
| VITAMIN C | A | 0% | 0.120 Mg |
| THIAMIN | A========================================== | 121% | 1.210 Mg |
| RIBOFLAVIN | A========================================== | 253% | 3.040 Mg |
| NIACIN | A========================================== | 123% | 16.00 Mg |
| VITAMIN B6 | A========== | 21% | 0.420 Mg |
| FOLACIN | A======== | 16% | 65.60 Ug |
| VITAMIN B12 | A= | 2% | 0.070 Ug |
| PANTO- ACID | A================== | 36% | 2.000 Mg |
| CALCIUM | A=============================================== | 99% | 792.0 Mg |
| PHOSPHORUS | A========================================== | 253% | 2024 Mg |
| TRYPTOPHAN | A========================================== | 866% | 1412 Mg |
| THREONINE | A========================================== | 686% | 2985 Mg |
| ISOLEUCINE | A========================================== | 559% | 3653 Mg |
| LEUCINE | A========================================== | 731% | 6371 Mg |
| LYSINE | A========================================== | 419% | 2739 Mg |
| METHIONINE | A========================================== | 377% | 1028 Mg |
| CYSTINE | A========================================== | 574% | 1562 Mg |
| PHENYL-ANINE | A========================================== | 1051% | 4574 Mg |
| TYROSINE | A========================================== | 690% | 3002 Mg |
| VALINE | A========================================== | 103% | 785.0 Mg |
| HISTIDINE | A | NO RDA | 344.0 Mg |
| ALCOHOL | A | NO RDA | 0.000 Gm |
| ASH | A | NO RDA | 13.70 Gm |
| COPPER | A============ | 24% | 0.610 Mg |
| MANGANESE | A========================================== | 160% | 6.000 Mg |
| IODINE | A========================================== | 338% | 508.0 Ug |
| MONO FAT | A | NO RDA | 48.60 Gm |
| POLY FAT | A | NO RDA | 26.30 Gm |
| CAFFEINE | A | NO RDA | 0.000 Mg |
| FLUORIDE | A | 1% | 28.00 Ug |
| MOLYBDENUM | A========================================== | 2215% | 7200 Ug |
| VITAMIN K | A | 0% | 0.000 Ug |
| SELENIUM | A================ | 32% | 0.040 Mg |
| BIOTIN | A== | 4% | 6.000 Ug |
| CHLORIDE | A=== | 6% | 228.0 Mg |
| CHROMIUM | A========================================== | 576% | 0.720 Mg |
| SUGAR | A | NO RDA | 0.000 Gm |
| FIBER-DIET | A | NO RDA | 18.20 Gm |
| VIT. E/AT | A====== | 12% | 0.980 Mg |

% RDA:  |0      |20      |40      |60      |80      |100

Margarine used instead of butter; almonds used for the nut meal in analysis.

# PEAR TART

☆ If serving this on a dessert party table, I suggest serving this piping hot to contrast some chilled fresh fruit tarts to be served side-by-side.

---

1 unbaked Perfectly Nutty Crust pie shell
  (see preceding recipe)

¾ cup sugarless apricot or pineapple preserves
3 Tbsp. pineapple, apricot or apple juice

½ cup almond meal
⅓ cup honey
1 Tbsp. whole wheat flour
⅓ tsp. finely grated lemon rind
⅛ tsp. ground cloves

6 ripe but firm pears

Prepare Perfectly Nutty Crust in a 9" or 10" tart or pie pan and preheat oven to 350 degrees.

Heat preserves and fruit juice till preserves are dissolved. Brush ¼ cup of the mixture evenly onto bottom layer of crust. Mix next 5 ingredients together and spread on bottom of crust.

Peel pears, cut in half, and cut out cores. Slice halves across width of pear about ⅛" thick, keeping halves together. Lay sliced halves on top of the almond mixture to cover entire surface. You can separate some of the sliced halves to fill in spaces.

Bake at 350 degrees for 30 minutes. Remove from oven, reheat preserve mixture, and brush evenly over entire surface of pears and crust. Put back into oven and bake another 10 minutes. Allow to sit at least 20 minutes before serving.

Delicious served hot, lukewarm or cold. If served alongside fresh, raw fruit tarts, it makes a nice contrast served hot.

| Special Shopping |
| --- |
| Sugarless apricot or pineapple preserves sweetened with honey or fruit juice — can be found in natural food stores. |

| SHOPPING LIST | |
| --- | --- |
| Regularly Kept in the Kitchen (Listed in Chapter 14, p. 703) | Fresh Produce |
| Almonds<br>Honey<br>Whole wheat flour<br>Cloves | Lemon<br>Pears |

# NUTRITIONAL ANALYSIS FOR ONE SERVING
# PEAR TART WITH PERFECTLY NUTTY CRUST

| NUTRIENT | Type: 14 FEMALE-23 TO 51 YEARS | % RDA | Amount |
|---|---|---|---|
| KCALORIES | A======== | 16% | 336.0 Kc |
| PROTEIN | A============ | 22% | 9.780 Gm |
| CARBOHYDRATE | A | NO RDA | 53.60 Gm |
| FAT | A | NO RDA | 11.60 Gm |
| FIBER-CRUDE | A | NO RDA | 2.670 Gm |
| CHOLESTEROL | A | NO RDA | 0.000 Mg |
| SATURATED FA | A | NO RDA | 1.610 Gm |
| OLEIC FA | A | NO RDA | 0.040 Gm |
| LINOLEIC FA | A | NO RDA | 0.160 Gm |
| SODIUM | A== | 4% | 92.00 Mg |
| POTASSIUM | A====== | 13% | 517.0 Mg |
| MAGNESIUM | A==== | 9% | 29.80 Mg |
| IRON | A======= | 14% | 2.520 Mg |
| ZINC | A= | 3% | 0.570 Mg |
| VITAMIN A | A==== | 8% | 341.0 IU |
| VITAMIN D | A | 0% | 0.000 IU |
| VIT. E/TOTAL | A | NO RDA | 0.650 Mg |
| VITAMIN C | A======== | 17% | 10.20 Mg |
| THIAMIN | A========= | 19% | 0.190 Mg |
| RIBOFLAVIN | A=============== | 31% | 0.380 Mg |
| NIACIN | A======== | 16% | 2.130 Mg |
| VITAMIN B6 | A== | 5% | 0.100 Mg |
| FOLACIN | A== | 5% | 20.80 Ug |
| VITAMIN B12 | A | 0% | 0.000 Ug |
| PANTO- ACID | A=== | 7% | 0.420 Mg |
| CALCIUM | A====== | 12% | 101.0 Mg |
| PHOSPHORUS | A============== | 29% | 239.0 Mg |
| TRYPTOPHAN | A==================================================== | 94% | 154.0 Mg |
| THREONINE | A========================================= | 77% | 339.0 Mg |
| ISOLEUCINE | A================================= | 63% | 414.0 Mg |
| LEUCINE | A=========================================== | 82% | 722.0 Mg |
| LYSINE | A========================= | 49% | 321.0 Mg |
| METHIONINE | A======================= | 45% | 123.0 Mg |
| CYSTINE | A=================================== | 65% | 178.0 Mg |
| PHENYL-ANINE | A============================================================= | 117% | 513.0 Mg |
| TYROSINE | A========================================= | 77% | 336.0 Mg |
| VALINE | A================================= | 63% | 484.0 Mg |
| HISTIDINE | A | NO RDA | 248.0 Mg |
| ALCOHOL | A | NO RDA | 0.000 Gm |
| ASH | A | NO RDA | 1.950 Gm |
| COPPER | A===== | 10% | 0.260 Mg |
| MANGANESE | A=================== | 36% | 1.370 Mg |
| IODINE | A======================= | 44% | 67.30 Ug |
| MONO FAT | A | NO RDA | 5.720 Gm |
| POLY FAT | A | NO RDA | 3.270 Gm |
| CAFFEINE | A | NO RDA | 0.000 Mg |
| FLUORIDE | A | 1% | 44.50 Ug |
| MOLYBDENUM | A==================================================== | 294% | 956.0 Ug |
| VITAMIN K | A | 0% | 0.000 Ug |
| SELENIUM | A | 0% | 0.000 Mg |
| BIOTIN | A | 0% | 1.070 Ug |
| CHLORIDE | A | 0% | 30.20 Mg |
| CHROMIUM | A================================================= | 88% | 0.110 Mg |
| SUGAR | A | NO RDA | 9.830 Gm |
| FIBER-DIET | A | NO RDA | 5.910 Gm |
| VIT. E/AT | A==== | 9% | 0.770 Mg |

```
% RDA:   |0      |20     |40     |60     |80     |100
```

Almond meal was used in the crust and margarine instead of butter; pineapple preserves and apple juice were used in the tart.

# BOUNTY·OF·THE·SEASON FRESH TARTS

☆ This recipe is to give a general idea for raw fruit tarts. Please feel free to use other flavored preserves for different color and taste combinations with whatever fruits are in season.

---

1 baked and cooled Perfectly Nutty Crust
    pie shell

Fruit of the season (strawberries and other
    berries, seedless grapes, peaches,
    apricots, sliced kiwi fruit, etc.)

6 oz. sugarless jam or conserves
½ cup apple juice
3 Tbsp. seaweed gelatin flakes
    (carrageenan or agar-agar flakes)
½ tsp. vanilla or almond extract (optional)

Fill a cooled Perfectly Nutty Crust pie shell with fresh fruit, nicely arranged. Fruits such as berries and seedless grapes should be left whole; fruits such as peaches and apricots should be cut in half, pitted and laid with the cut side down; fruits such as kiwi should be peeled and sliced.

If serving a few tarts on a dessert party table, I suggest making the most of the wonderful color palette provided by nature to make the table attractive by using different colored fruits in each tart.

Take a sugarless jam (there are plenty of honey-sweetened or just cooked down fruit conserves available in natural food stores) and simmer till the jam becomes liquidy. Try to choose a jam flavor that will enhance the appearance and flavor of the fruit you are using. Apricot and/or pineapple jams are safe additions to any fruit, as they are both a fairly neutral color and add a little bit of a pleasant tart flavor to any fruit. When jam is heated, add carrageenan or agar-agar seaweed gelatin and stir over low heat till it is dissolved. Spoon or brush over fruit in the crust. Refrigerate at least 2 hours before serving. Makes enough glaze for one 9" tart.

| SHOPPING LIST | | Special Shopping |
|---|---|---|
| **Regularly Kept in the Kitchen** (Listed in Chapter 14, p. 703) | **Fresh Produce** | Sugarless apricot or pineapple preserves sweetened with honey or fruit juice — can be found in natural food stores. |
| Vanilla or almond extract | Apple juice<br>Fruit of the season (berries, seedless grapes, peaches, apricots, kiwi, etc.) | Vegetable gelatin — try Jewish groceries for "kosher gelatin" made from carrageenan; as a second choice, use agar-agar flakes, a seaweed which can be found in most natural food stores, Japanese or Chinese groceries. |
| Also see shopping list for Perfectly Nutty Crust. | | |

# EGGLESS MERINGUE KISSES

☆ These should be whipped and cooked just before serving.

---

9 Tbsp. Bipro
⅓ cup water
2 Tbsp. honey
⅛ tsp. vanilla extract

¼ tsp. cream of tartar

Banana slices

Not just any whey protein powder will whip up into a meringue. Not to sound like an advertisement, but the Bipro whey protein powder is the only one I've found that will do this.

Combine first 4 ingredients together in a large, tall mixing bowl (large enough so meringue won't spill out when being whipped). Whip with wire whisk or electric beater till all ingredients are blended smoothly together. Add cream of tartar and, using an electric mixer, mix 3 to 4 minutes. With wire whisk, mix till stiff and will almost hold peaks (although will not hold peaks exactly like egg whites). Mix a few minutes longer, as this helps to dry it out a bit. The mixture will not deflate from too much mixing as egg whites do. Drop by tablespoons in kiss shapes onto oiled baking sheet and bake at 275 degrees for 4 to 5 minutes or till they begin to turn a golden brown — crisp on the outside but still moist inside. Lift gently from baking tray onto serving platter with a spatula.

Best served warm from oven as is or over slices of banana or fresh strawberries. Also nice for decorating cakes, mousses, etc. Makes 2 dozen kisses.

The whipped meringue, unbaked, makes an excellent icing. Simply ice the cooled cake and allow to sit at room temperature half an hour or so to allow it to dry on the surface a little.

**A variation on the kisses:** Fold chopped nuts (such as cashews or pecans) into whipped, unbaked meringues and then bake as above. Allow to cool and lift with spatula gently off baking tray. Place on top of fresh banana slices and serve. If you are serving Perfectly Nutty Crust tarts at the same time, I recommend leaving the nuts out of the meringue for a different texture.

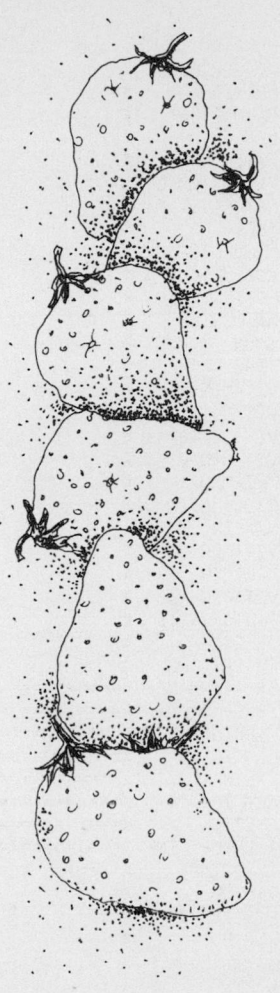

| SHOPPING LIST | |
| --- | --- |
| **Regularly Kept in the Kitchen (Listed in Chapter 14, p. 703)** | **Fresh Produce** |
| Bipro<br>Honey<br>Vanilla extract<br>Cream of tartar | (None) |

# NUTRITIONAL ANALYSIS FOR THREE EGGLESS MERINGUE KISSES

```
NUTRIENT      Type: 14    FEMALE-23 TO 51 YEARS            % RDA    Amount
  KCALORIES    A                                             1%    26.70 Kc
  PROTEIN      A==                                           5%     2.620 Gm
  CARBOHYDRATE A                                          NO RDA    4.260 Gm
  FAT          A                                          NO RDA    0.010 Gm
  FIBER-CRUDE  A                                          NO RDA    0.000 Gm
  CHOLESTEROL  A                                          NO RDA    0.050 Mg
  SATURATED FA A                                          NO RDA    0.010 Gm
  OLEIC FA     A                                          NO RDA    0.000 Gm
  LINOLEIC FA  A                                          NO RDA    0.000 Gm
  SODIUM       A                                             0%    10.70 Mg
  POTASSIUM    A                                             0%     7.470 Mg
  MAGNESIUM    A                                             0%     0.450 Mg
  IRON         A                                             0%     0.050 Mg
  ZINC         A                                             0%     0.000 Mg
  VITAMIN A    A                                             0%     0.000 IU
  VITAMIN D    A                                             0%     0.000 IU
  VIT. E/TOTAL A                                          NO RDA    0.000 Mg
  VITAMIN C    A                                             0%     0.000 Mg
  THIAMIN      A                                             0%     0.000 Mg
  RIBOFLAVIN   A                                             0%     0.000 Mg
  NIACIN       A                                             0%     0.020 Mg
  VITAMIN B6   A                                             0%     0.000 Mg
  FOLACIN      A                                             0%     0.000 Ug
  VITAMIN B12  A                                             0%     0.000 Ug
  PANTO- ACID  A                                             0%     0.010 Mg
  CALCIUM      A                                             0%     3.150 Mg
  PHOSPHORUS   A                                             0%     1.930 Mg
  TRYPTOPHAN   A===============================           60%    97.80 Mg
  THREONINE    A=================                         35%   155.0 Mg
  ISOLEUCINE   A==========                               20%   135.0 Mg
  LEUCINE      A==================                        37%   329.0 Mg
  LYSINE       A======================                    44%   292.0 Mg
  METHIONINE   A=============                             26%    72.30 Mg
  CYSTINE      A=============                             26%    73.10 Mg
  PHENYL-ANINE A===========                               23%   104.0 Mg
  TYROSINE     A=============                             26%   117.0 Mg
  VALINE       A=========                                 19%   148.0 Mg
  HISTIDINE    A                                          NO RDA   58.20 Mg
  ALCOHOL      A                                          NO RDA    0.000 Gm
  ASH          A                                          NO RDA    0.050 Gm
  COPPER       A                                             0%     0.000 Mg
  MANGANESE    A                                             0%     0.000 Mg
  IODINE       A                                             0%     0.000 Ug
  MONO FAT     A                                          NO RDA    0.000 Gm
  POLY FAT     A                                          NO RDA    0.010 Gm
  CAFFEINE     A                                          NO RDA    0.000 Mg
  FLUORIDE     A                                             0%     5.250 Ug
  MOLYBDENUM   A                                             0%     0.000 Ug
  VITAMIN K    A                                             0%     0.000 Ug
  SELENIUM     A                                             0%     0.000 Mg
  BIOTIN       A                                             0%     0.000 Ug
  CHLORIDE     A                                             0%     0.180 Mg
  CHROMIUM     A                                             0%     0.000 Mg
  SUGAR        A                                          NO RDA    0.010 Gm
  FIBER-DIET   A                                          NO RDA    0.000 Gm
  VIT. E/AT    A                                             0%     0.000 Mg

    % RDA:   |0       |20      |40      |60      |80      |100
```

# HOLIDAY SPARKLER

*1 part cranberry juice*
*1 part apple juice or cider*

*2 Tbsp. (approximately) natural*
*lemon-lime soda, chilled*
*Sparkling water, chilled*
*Lemon twist and fruit on a stick*

Mix enough (equal parts) of first 2 ingredients to fill a large punch bowl or container at an open "bar" and refrigerate.

Serve to order. Fill each glass ¾ of the way full with juice from the punch bowl or container. Add natural lemon-lime soda and fill the rest of the way with sparkling water. Garnish with lemon twist and cherry or strawberry on a beverage "sword."

| SHOPPING LIST | | Special Shopping |
|---|---|---|
| **Regularly Kept in the Kitchen** (Listed in Chapter 14, p. 703) | **Fresh Produce** | Cranberry juice — can be found sweetened with other fruit juices and sometimes unsweetened in natural food stores. |
| (None) | Unsweetened apple juice Sparkling water Lemon | Natural lemon-lime soda — get the ones sweetened with fruit juice in natural food stores. |

Sparkling water connoisseurs like their water and glass chilled — but no ice cubes, please! They say ice cubes "bruise" the bubbles.

# FESTIVE TROPICAL PUNCH

☆ You can make variations of this punch using different kinds of fruit juice and fruit purees — in that case, it won't be a tropical punch anymore; just call it a suitable name.

---

*1½ quarts apple juice*
*1½ quarts orange juice*
*3 cups grapefruit juice*
*3 cups pineapple juice*

*4 cups sweet tropical fruit, pureed*
*(mango, pineapple, papaya and/or banana)*

*3 quarts sparkling water*
*2 cups fresh strawberries, sliced*

Combine first 4 ingredients in a large pot or mixing bowl. Blend fresh fruit pieces together in blender till smooth and pour into juices. Mix well. Pour mixture into ice cube trays and/or children's popsicle trays (this makes delicious popsicles for children) and freeze solid. You will need quite a few ice cube trays for this.

Just before serving, pour fruit ice cubes into a large punch bowl and pour in sparkling water. Top with strawberries. Makes 2½ gallons.

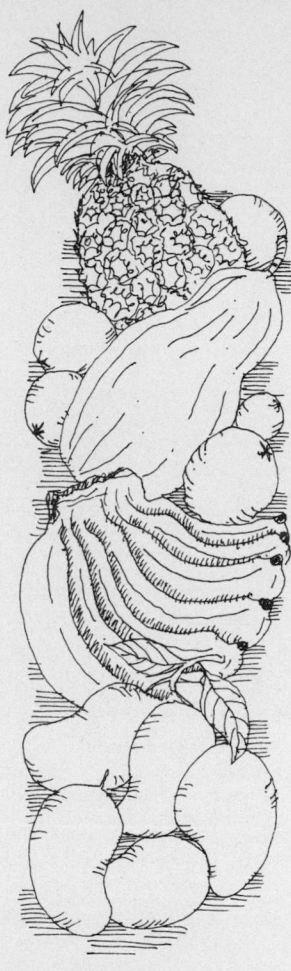

One of the tips the National Council on Alcoholism gives for party time is not to center the party around drinking. Providing attractive nonalcoholic beverages like this instead of alcoholic beverages makes the party better in more ways then one. Studies have shown that the quality and tone of parties improve when no alcohol is served; people actually get into conversations with each other, and nonalcohol parties tend to last longer.

| SHOPPING LIST | |
|---|---|
| **Regularly Kept in the Kitchen (Listed in Chapter 14, p. 703)** | **Fresh Produce** |
| (None) | Unsweetened apple juice<br>Unsweetened orange juice<br>Unsweetened grapefruit juice<br>Unsweetened pineapple juice<br>Tropical fruits (mango, pineapple, papaya and/or banana)<br>Sparkling water<br>Strawberries |

# NUTRITIONAL ANALYSIS FOR ONE SERVING
## FESTIVE TROPICAL PUNCH

| NUTRIENT | Type: 14 FEMALE-23 TO 51 YEARS | % RDA | Amount |
|---|---|---|---|
| KCALORIES | Ä= | 3% | 65.30 Kc |
| PROTEIN | Ä | 1% | 0.640 Gm |
| CARBOHYDRATE | Ä | NO RDA | 16.00 Gm |
| FAT | Ä | NO RDA | 0.180 Gm |
| FIBER-CRUDE | Ä | NO RDA | 0.240 Gm |
| CHOLESTEROL | Ä | NO RDA | 0.000 Mg |
| SATURATED FA | Ä | NO RDA | 0.020 Gm |
| OLEIC FA | Ä | NO RDA | 0.000 Gm |
| LINOLEIC FA | Ä | NO RDA | 0.000 Gm |
| SODIUM | Ä | 0% | 5.210 Mg |
| POTASSIUM | Ä== | 5% | 213.0 Mg |
| MAGNESIUM | Ä= | 3% | 11.80 Mg |
| IRON | Ä | 1% | 0.270 Mg |
| ZINC | Ä | 0% | 0.080 Mg |
| VITAMIN A | Ä======== | 16% | 678.0 IU |
| VITAMIN D | Ä | 0% | 0.000 IU |
| VIT. E/TOTAL | Ä | NO RDA | 0.140 Mg |
| VITAMIN C | Ä============================== | 58% | 34.90 Mg |
| THIAMIN | Ä=== | 6% | 0.060 Mg |
| RIBOFLAVIN | Ä= | 2% | 0.030 Mg |
| NIACIN | Ä= | 2% | 0.290 Mg |
| VITAMIN B6 | Ä= | 3% | 0.070 Mg |
| FOLACIN | Ä== | 4% | 19.30 Ug |
| VITAMIN B12 | Ä | 0% | 0.000 Ug |
| PANTO- ACID | Ä= | 3% | 0.200 Mg |
| CALCIUM | Ä= | 2% | 22.20 Mg |
| PHOSPHORUS | Ä= | 2% | 16.50 Mg |
| TRYPTOPHAN | Ä | 1% | 2.950 Mg |
| THREONINE | Ä | 1% | 8.470 Mg |
| ISOLEUCINE | Ä | 1% | 7.270 Mg |
| LEUCINE | Ä | 1% | 13.70 Mg |
| LYSINE | Ä= | 2% | 13.20 Mg |
| METHIONINE | Ä | 0% | 1.930 Mg |
| CYSTINE | Ä | 0% | 2.390 Mg |
| PHENYL-ANINE | Ä | 1% | 8.070 Mg |
| TYROSINE | Ä | 1% | 5.790 Mg |
| VALINE | Ä | 1% | 10.60 Mg |
| HISTIDINE | Ä | NO RDA | 4.560 Mg |
| ALCOHOL | Ä | NO RDA | 0.000 Gm |
| ASH | Ä | NO RDA | 0.530 Gm |
| COPPER | Ä= | 2% | 0.060 Mg |
| MANGANESE | Ä=== | 6% | 0.250 Mg |
| IODINE | Ä | 0% | 0.000 Ug |
| MONO FAT | Ä | NO RDA | 0.030 Gm |
| POLY FAT | Ä | NO RDA | 0.050 Gm |
| CAFFEINE | Ä | NO RDA | 0.000 Mg |
| FLUORIDE | Ä | 0% | 2.260 Ug |
| MOLYBDENUM | Ä | 0% | 1.690 Ug |
| VITAMIN K | Ä | 0% | 0.000 Ug |
| SELENIUM | Ä | 0% | 0.000 Mg |
| BIOTIN | Ä | 0% | 0.310 Ug |
| CHLORIDE | Ä | 0% | 0.000 Mg |
| CHROMIUM | Ä | 0% | 0.000 Mg |
| SUGAR | Ä | NO RDA | 0.650 Gm |
| FIBER-DIET | Ä | NO RDA | 0.410 Gm |
| VIT. E/AT | Ä= | 2% | 0.220 Mg |

```
% RDA :   |0      |20     |40     |60     |80     |100
```

Pureed fruit used in analysis was mango.

A materialist is a person who identifies himself as matter, as the material body, and lives striving to attain happiness through the body. The ironic thing is that attempting to satisfy the demands of the senses through communion with matter often leads to damaging and neglecting the body. We would take better care of the body and properly value it if we lived according to these words from the Greek philosopher Apothegm (550 B.C.), "The body is the soul's instrument, and the soul is God's instrument."

# THE HORN-OF-PLENTY PARTY TABLE

The holiday season usually finds us gathered together with the special people in our lives around tables that look like they've just been poured out of the horn-of-plenty. Although the spirit of the holiday season should be centered around the true meaning of the word "holy day," food has somehow come to play a dominant role for many. Unfortunately, for many hosts and hostesses this means being so preoccupied with food that there is little or no time left for contemplating or meditating on the true meaning of the holidays, not to mention spending time with family and friends.

It's actually possible to have time for these important things as well as provide nutritious and delicious refreshments by keeping things simple. One way I've found to accomplish this is to lay out a cornucopia hors d'oeuvres table which provides a wide array of healthy, natural foods and a festive air as well. And this hors d'oeuvres table, overflowing with an abundance of healthy refreshments, is a beautiful offering for guests at any party any time of the year.

The depiction of the cornucopia in sculptures, paintings, etc., shows a horn-of-plenty overflowing with fruit, flowers and grains, and that is exactly how to set the hors d'oeuvres table. I've simply purchased a woven wicker cornucopia that I elevate on the table so it looks like everything is pouring out of it. Then, instead of cut flowers, I take some flowering potted plants and put them here and there on the table because they last longer and the plant adds all the beauty of its form without having to cut off its life.

Now, for the food to go on the table! I usually go out and buy a wide variety of the ideal fast-food which comes individually wrapped — fruit, both fresh and dried.

Of course, the fruit available changes with the season, but while shopping, try to get fruits of different hue so there will be a colorful arrangement on the table. Where I buy the fruit depends on the number of people that will be coming to the party. If only a small amount of fruit is needed, I try to go to farmers' markets where the fruit is fresher and less expensive. However, if the guest list is in the hundreds, I go down to the wholesale produce market and purchase a case of each kind of fruit.

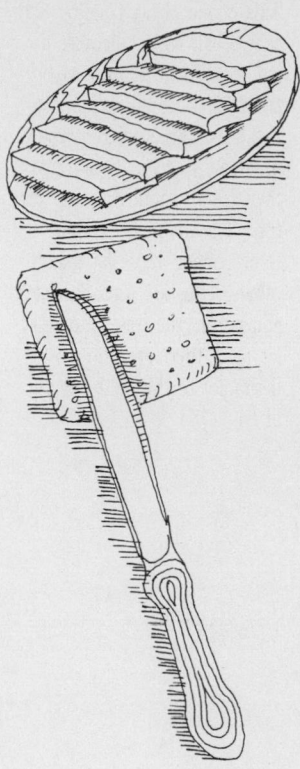

I also purchase a few different kinds of shelled nuts and some whole grain crackers and blocks of cheese. Although it's possible to bake one's own whole grain crackers at home, I've found that buying the ready-made ones in the stores to be the more practical thing to do, considering the amount of time homemade crackers take and how inexpensive the ready-made, store-bought ones are. It's quite amazing to see what a great selection of whole grain crackers there is in natural food stores. This is an example of a time when the all-important and good habit of reading labels is crucial. There are so many ready-made products on the market that are labeled "natural" which contain such unnaturally refined products as white flour (sometimes labeled "wheat flour" and mistaken by some people as meaning 100 percent whole wheat flour) and white sugar.

That ends the shopping list of foods that are just put out on the table as they are.

I then arrange all the fresh and dried fruit and nuts lavishly in piles on the table, being careful to take full advantage of the color spectrum provided by nature in the fresh fruit. I then slice a little bit of cheese from the cheese blocks and arrange the cheese slices, place the remainder of the cheese blocks with cheese knives stuck in them (for guests to cut once slices run out) and whole grain crackers on a few platters which are then placed in different places on the table.

Next to the platters of cheese and crackers, I try to place crudites (fresh vegetable sticks and pieces) and some of the following homemade items that can, fortunately, be made ahead of time. The fresh vegetables and crackers can then be spread with the pates or the cheese. Alongside these, I try to provide one or a few bowls of a fairly inexpensive salad like the Potato Salad a'la Paps, Pasta Primavera (p. 436), or Rigatoni in the Garden (p. 622). This table is then perfectly set for serving the nibbler as well as those that come hungry and need a whole meal.

This is one of my favorite cheese ball recipes because it has so many nice, fresh vegetables in it. You'll notice that I've listed three different kinds of cheese that can be used, as they are all about the same texture. The difference is that some contain more fat than others. They are listed in order, going from the least amount of fat (and, therefore, the most desirable) to the most amount of fat.

# VEGIE-NUT CHEESE BALL

☆ Instead of the blocks of cheese, this cheese ball can be used on top of the whole grain crackers or on the vegetable sticks.

_1 cup raw cauliflower, diced very fine_
_1 cup raw broccoli, diced very fine_
_1 cup raw bell pepper, diced very fine_
_1 cup yogurt cheese or Neufchatel cheese_
_or cream cheese_
_2 tsp. Spike or other vegetable-seasoned salt_
_1 tsp. dill_
_½ tsp. asafetida or ½ cup finely chopped chives_

Mix all ingredients together. This can be refrigerated as is and used as a stuffing for raw vegetables, sandwiches, etc. To make a cheese ball or two for a party table, blend 1 cup roasted peanuts and 1 cup sunflower seeds finely to make a nut meal. Mix ¼ of the nut meal in with the cheese mixture and then roll into a ball. Roll the ball in the remaining nut meal so the ball is evenly coated with nuts. Refrigerate at least 3 to 4 hours before serving.

| Special Shopping |
| --- |
| Yogurt cheese or Neufchatel cheese or cream cheese: Yogurt cheese is usually available in natural food stores, or you can make your own (p. 319); Neufchatel cheese is available in gourmet cheese specialty shops or some supermarket cheese departments; cream cheese can be found in any supermarket. |

| SHOPPING LIST | |
| --- | --- |
| **Regularly Kept in the Kitchen** (Listed in Chapter 14, p. 703) | **Fresh Produce** |
| Spike | Cauliflower |
| Asafetida | Broccoli |
| Nuts | Bell pepper |

# NUTRITIONAL ANALYSIS FOR ONE RECIPE
## VEGIE-NUT CHEESE BALL

| NUTRIENT | Type: 14  FEMALE-23 TO 51 YEARS | % RDA | Amount |
|---|---|---|---|
| KCALORIES | Ã================ | 32% | 650.0 Kc |
| PROTEIN | Ã================================ | 63% | 27.90 Gm |
| CARBOHYDRATE | Ã | NO RDA | 22.50 Gm |
| FAT | Ã | NO RDA | 51.90 Gm |
| FIBER-CRUDE | Ã | NO RDA | 3.390 Gm |
| CHOLESTEROL | Ã | NO RDA | 168.0 Mg |
| SATURATED FA | Ã | NO RDA | 32.30 Gm |
| OLEIC FA | Ã | NO RDA | 19.10 Gm |
| LINOLEIC FA | Ã | NO RDA | 1.530 Gm |
| SODIUM | Ã===================================================== | 130% | 2863 Mg |
| POTASSIUM | Ã=============== | 31% | 1177 Mg |
| MAGNESIUM | Ã============== | 28% | 85.80 Mg |
| IRON | Ã=========== | 22% | 4.130 Mg |
| ZINC | Ã====== | 12% | 1.880 Mg |
| VITAMIN A | Ã=========================================================== | 147% | 5896 IU |
| VITAMIN D | Ã | 0% | 0.000 IU |
| VIT. E/TOTAL | Ã | NO RDA | 0.650 Mg |
| VITAMIN C | Ã===================================================== | 500% | 300.0 Mg |
| THIAMIN | Ã============= | 27% | 0.270 Mg |
| RIBOFLAVIN | Ã========================== | 55% | 0.670 Mg |
| NIACIN | Ã======== | 17% | 2.210 Mg |
| VITAMIN B6 | Ã================ | 33% | 0.670 Mg |
| FOLACIN | Ã==================== | 41% | 167.0 Ug |
| VITAMIN B12 | Ã========= | 19% | 0.570 Ug |
| PANTO- ACID | Ã================ | 34% | 1.900 Mg |
| CALCIUM | Ã================= | 35% | 284.0 Mg |
| PHOSPHORUS | Ã========================== | 55% | 446.0 Mg |
| TRYPTOPHAN | Ã====================================================== | 160% | 262.0 Mg |
| THREONINE | Ã====================================================== | 258% | 1126 Mg |
| ISOLEUCINE | Ã====================================================== | 210% | 1372 Mg |
| LEUCINE | Ã====================================================== | 277% | 2415 Mg |
| LYSINE | Ã====================================================== | 342% | 2238 Mg |
| METHIONINE | Ã====================================================== | 219% | 596.0 Mg |
| CYSTINE | Ã=================================================== | 91% | 248.0 Mg |
| PHENYL-ANINE | Ã====================================================== | 320% | 1396 Mg |
| TYROSINE | Ã====================================================== | 268% | 1166 Mg |
| VALINE | Ã====================================================== | 203% | 1551 Mg |
| HISTIDINE | Ã | NO RDA | 882.0 Mg |
| ALCOHOL | Ã | NO RDA | 0.000 Gm |
| ASH | Ã | NO RDA | 5.510 Gm |
| COPPER | Ã=== | 7% | 0.190 Mg |
| MANGANESE | Ã======= | 14% | 0.540 Mg |
| IODINE | Ã==================================================== | 140% | 210.0 Ug |
| MONO FAT | Ã | NO RDA | 14.70 Gm |
| POLY FAT | Ã | NO RDA | 2.640 Gm |
| CAFFEINE | Ã | NO RDA | 0.000 Mg |
| FLUORIDE | Ã=== | 7% | 198.0 Ug |
| MOLYBDENUM | Ã | 0% | 0.000 Ug |
| VITAMIN K | Ã===================================================== | 3596% | 3776 Ug |
| SELENIUM | Ã | 0% | 0.000 Mg |
| BIOTIN | Ã======= | 14% | 21.40 Ug |
| CHLORIDE | Ã | 0% | 0.000 Mg |
| CHROMIUM | Ã============ | 24% | 0.030 Mg |
| SUGAR | Ã | NO RDA | 6.770 Gm |
| FIBER-DIET | Ã | NO RDA | 2.330 Gm |
| VIT. E/AT | Ã================ | 31% | 2.480 Mg |

```
% RDA:   |0     |20    |40    |60    |80    |100
```

Neufchatel cheese was used instead of yogurt cheese or cream cheese; chopped chives used instead of asafetida.

# ROASTED ALMOND BALL

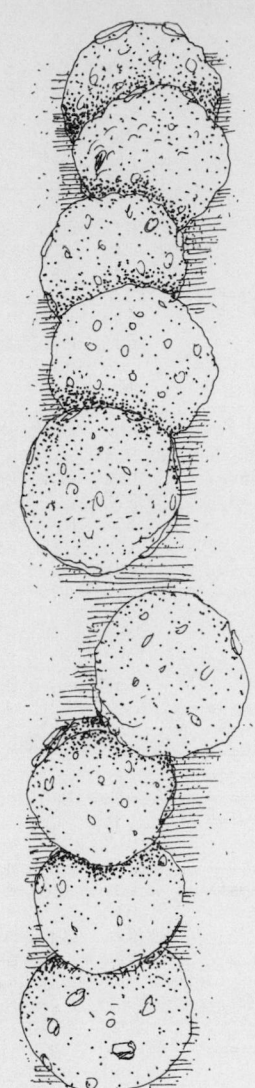

*1 lb. tempeh*

*2 cups eggless or Tofu Mayonnaise (see p. 332)*
*½ cup nutritional yeast*
*2 Tbsp. soy sauce*
*2 Tbsp. olive brine*
*2 Tbsp. lemon juice*
*1 tsp. black or white pepper*
*¼ tsp. Tabasco*

*½ cup chopped olives*
*2 cups finely chopped, roasted almonds*

*2 cups coarsely chopped, roasted almonds*

Steam tempeh for 20 minutes, cool and break into smaller chunks. Blend or mix next 7 ingredients together in a blender or food processor until smooth. Add chunks of tempeh slowly and run machine till tempeh is chopped and mixture is almost smooth. Pour mixture into a bowl and fold in the next 2 ingredients. Scrape ingredients together into the center of the bowl to form a gooey ball and pour onto a platter or cookie sheet that is covered with the remaining coarsely chopped nuts. Roll the ball in the nuts or spoon the nuts on top of the ball so the ball is evenly coated with chopped nuts. Refrigerate at least 3 to 4 hours, or even overnight, before serving. Makes about 6 cups. If you prefer a dip, simply add about 1 cup more olive brine or water to the mixture while blending it.

This recipe makes a delicious, dairyless "cheese ball" that I like to serve alongside a cheese ball made with dairy cheese to offer as an alternative to guests who are trying to avoid cholesterol.

| SHOPPING LIST | |
|---|---|
| **Regularly Kept in the Kitchen (Listed in Chapter 14, p. 703)** | **Fresh Produce** |
| Tempeh | Olives |
| Eggless mayonnaise | Lemon |
| Nutritional yeast | Tabasco |
| Soy sauce | |
| Black or white pepper | |
| Almonds | |

287

# NUTRITIONAL ANALYSIS FOR ONE RECIPE
## ROASTED ALMOND BALL

| NUTRIENT | Type: 14    FEMALE-23 TO 51 YEARS | % RDA | Amount |
|---|---|---|---|
| KCALORIES | A================================================= | 250% | 5017 Kc |
| PROTEIN | A================================================= | 556% | 245.0 Gm |
| CARBOHYDRATE | A | NO RDA | 259.0 Gm |
| FAT | A | NO RDA | 368.0 Gm |
| FIBER-CRUDE | A | NO RDA | 42.00 Gm |
| CHOLESTEROL | A | NO RDA | 0.000 Mg |
| SATURATED FA | A | NO RDA | 39.30 Gm |
| OLEIC FA | A | NO RDA | 19.00 Gm |
| LINOLEIC FA | A | NO RDA | 32.70 Gm |
| SODIUM | A================================== | 141% | 3113 Mg |
| POTASSIUM | A================================== | 208% | 7828 Mg |
| MAGNESIUM | A================================== | 749% | 2248 Mg |
| IRON | A================================== | 330% | 59.30 Mg |
| ZINC | A================================== | 328% | 49.20 Mg |
| VITAMIN A | A============================================ | 89% | 3565 IU |
| VITAMIN D | A | 0% | 0.000 IU |
| VIT. E/TOTAL | A | NO RDA | 11.20 Mg |
| VITAMIN C | A============================ | 54% | 32.50 Mg |
| THIAMIN | A================================== | 3770% | 37.70 Mg |
| RIBOFLAVIN | A================================== | 3341% | 40.10 Mg |
| NIACIN | A================================== | 1892% | 246.0 Mg |
| VITAMIN B6 | A================================== | 1900% | 38.00 Mg |
| FOLACIN | A================================== | 286% | 1145 Ug |
| VITAMIN B12 | A================================== | 1023% | 30.70 Ug |
| PANTO- ACID | A================================== | 136% | 7.520 Mg |
| CALCIUM | A================================== | 456% | 3651 Mg |
| PHOSPHORUS | A================================== | 661% | 5288 Mg |
| TRYPTOPHAN | A================================== | 2319% | 3781 Mg |
| THREONINE | A================================== | 2264% | 9851 Mg |
| ISOLEUCINE | A================================== | 1805% | 11791 Mg |
| LEUCINE | A================================== | 2249% | 19595 Mg |
| LYSINE | A================================== | 1990% | 13000 Mg |
| METHIONINE | A==========================------- | 1168% | 3178 Mg |
| CYSTINE | A================================== | 1484% | 4039 Mg |
| PHENYL-ANINE | A================================== | 2923% | 12718 Mg |
| TYROSINE | A================================== | 2104% | 9153 Mg |
| VALINE | A================================== | 1692% | 12899 Mg |
| HISTIDINE | A | NO RDA | 6772 Mg |
| ALCOHOL | A | NO RDA | 0.000 Gm |
| ASH | A | NO RDA | 74.30 Gm |
| COPPER | A================================== | 428% | 10.70 Mg |
| MANGANESE | A================================== | 533% | 20.00 Mg |
| IODINE | A================================== | 1478% | 2218 Ug |
| MONO FAT | A | NO RDA | 198.0 Gm |
| POLY FAT | A | NO RDA | 103.0 Gm |
| CAFFEINE | A | NO RDA | 0.000 Mg |
| FLUORIDE | A | 0% | 10.50 Ug |
| MOLYBDENUM | A================================== | 2791% | 9072 Ug |
| VITAMIN K | A | 0% | 0.000 Ug |
| SELENIUM | A====================================== | 72% | 0.090 Mg |
| BIOTIN | A================================================= | 96% | 145.0 Ug |
| CHLORIDE | A================== | 35% | 1201 Mg |
| CHROMIUM | A================================== | 2112% | 2.640 Mg |
| SUGAR | A | NO RDA | 0.970 Gm |
| FIBER-DIET | A | NO RDA | 67.40 Gm |
| VIT. E/AT | A============================ | 57% | 4.630 Mg |

| % RDA: | 0 | 20 | 40 | 60 | 80 | 100 | 10 |
|---|---|---|---|---|---|---|---|

Tofu Mayonnaise used instead of commercial eggless; olive brine and Tabasco sauce not included in analysis.

# EAST MEETS WEST WILD MUSHROOM PATE

☆ This pate is very seasonal, as chanterelle mushrooms and fresh shiitake mushrooms are seasonal. As no one (that I know of) is cultivating them, mushroom hunters can only find them growing in the wild in the spring and/or fall.

---

3 Tbsp. butter or margarine
1 lb. regular mushrooms
1 lb. fresh shiitake mushrooms
1 lb. chanterelle mushrooms

2 Tbsp. olive oil
1½ Tbsp. Bipro

2 Tbsp. finely chopped green onion
½ Tbsp. finely chopped chives
½ Tbsp. finely chopped Italian parsley
   or celery leaves

At upwards of $10 per pound for fresh shiitake and chanterelle mushrooms, this is a very expensive pate to save for serving on very special occasions. It sure tops goose liver pates any day! . . . Especially when you consider saving the goose unnecessary suffering and the fact that the liver is where many toxins are filtered from the bloodstream and collected.

Clean and drain each kind of mushroom separately. Preheat oven to 325 degrees and oil a small glass bread pan or casserole dish. In a small skillet, use 1 tablespoon of butter to saute regular mushrooms lightly. Pour into blender or food processor. Repeat with shiitake mushrooms. Saute chanterelle mushrooms in the same way, but only put half of them in the food processor or blender; set the other half aside for use later. Add next 2 ingredients to the mushrooms in the blender or food processor and blend till completely pureed.

Fold the last 3 ingredients into pureed mixture. Pour pureed mixture on bottom of bread pan or casserole dish so it's ½" thick. Slice or tear remaining whole chanterelles into thin strips and lay half of the strips over surface of puree in baking dish. Cover with rest of puree and top with remaining chanterelles. Cover baking dish with wax or parchment paper and bake for 1 hour at 325 degrees. Remove from oven and allow to set at least 4 hours. It can be covered and refrigerated a few days before the serving date.

Remove pate from baking dish by placing the serving platter on top of the baking dish and inverting platter and baking dish simultaneously. Pate should fall out onto platter easily. Serve in a mound with butter knives for guests to spread on crackers as an hors d'oeuvres. To serve as an entree, slice about ½" to ¾" thick and top with a sauce like the Au Gratin or Anything Sauce (p. 558). Makes about 6 cups of pate.

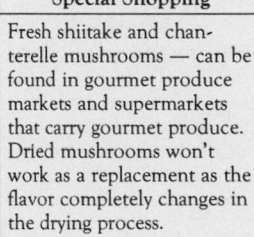

| SHOPPING LIST | |
|---|---|
| **Regularly Kept in the Kitchen** (Listed in Chapter 14, p. 703) | **Fresh Produce** |
| Butter or margarine<br>Olive oil<br>Bipro | Mushrooms<br>Green onions<br>Chives<br>Italian parsley or<br>    celery leaves |

**Special Shopping**

Fresh shiitake and chanterelle mushrooms — can be found in gourmet produce markets and supermarkets that carry gourmet produce. Dried mushrooms won't work as a replacement as the flavor completely changes in the drying process.

My secretary, right- and left-hand person and friend, Pat Taylor, lovingly called "Paps," whipped this salad up one Saturday afternoon for the crowd we knew would be coming over later. I was busy working on this book and just pulled all the this-and-that's lying around on shelves and in the refrigerator and decided we had the makings of potato salad. Paps put it together and flavored it so nicely that we spent the next two Saturdays trying to duplicate the original . . . Here it is!

# POTATO SALAD A'LA PAPS

☆ This recipe makes a quantity perfect for large parties or pot-lucks; cut this recipe down for a family-size salad.

---

10 lbs. potatoes

5 cups finely chopped celery
2 cups finely chopped bell peppers
12 oz. chopped, ripe olives
1 lb. fresh mushrooms, sliced
1 cup eggless or Tofu Mayonnaise (see recipe, p. 332)
3 cups Lowfat Sour Cream (see recipe, p. 186)
1 cup sweet pickle relish (honey-sweetened)
¼ cup prepared mustard
3 Tbsp. Spike or other vegetable-seasoned salt
5 tsp. asafetida or 2 onions, finely diced
½ lb. frozen peas
½ lb. frozen corn

Scrub potatoes well (but don't cut or peel). Put about 1" of water in bottom of pot large enough to hold all the potatoes. Cover, bring water and potatoes to a boil, turn heat down and simmer about 40 minutes till potatoes are done — tender enough to be poked with a fork. Drain water and set aside to cool to room temperature.

When potatoes are cooled, cut into ¾" chunks. Add remaining ingredients and mix thoroughly (frozen vegetables are to be added still frozen). This makes a very large amount. I've found the best way to mix this is in a very large bowl using hands and arms. Refrigerate if you want to. This large amount may not fit in a regular home refrigerator, but if you're serving this immediately, refrigeration isn't necessary as the frozen vegetables chill the salad just fine. Makes about 4 gallons — enough to feed quite a crowd!

| Special Shopping |
| --- |
| Honey-sweetened sweet pickle relish — in natural food stores. |

| SHOPPING LIST | |
| --- | --- |
| Regularly Kept in the Kitchen (Listed in Chapter 14, p. 703) | Fresh Produce |
| Eggless mayonnaise<br>Prepared mustard<br>Spike<br>Asafetida | Potatoes<br>Celery<br>Bell peppers<br>Ripe olives<br>Mushrooms |

Also see shopping list for Lowfat Sour Cream (p. 186).

# NUTRITIONAL ANALYSIS FOR ONE SERVING
## POTATO SALAD A'LA PAPS

```
NUTRIENT        Type: 14    FEMALE-23 TO 51 YEARS         % RDA   Amount
KCALORIES       A==                                         5%    118.0 Kc
PROTEIN         A====                                       9%    4.060 Gm
CARBOHYDRATE    A                                  NO RDA         22.20 Gm
FAT             A                                  NO RDA         1.980 Gm
FIBER-CRUDE     A                                  NO RDA         0.850 Gm
CHOLESTEROL     A                                  NO RDA         0.990 Mg
SATURATED FA    A                                  NO RDA         0.350 Gm
OLEIC FA        A                                  NO RDA         0.800 Gm
LINOLEIC FA     A                                  NO RDA         0.210 Gm
SODIUM          A======                                    12%    268.0 Mg
POTASSIUM       A=====                                     10%    396.0 Mg
MAGNESIUM       A====                                       8%    25.80 Mg
IRON            A====                                       8%    1.590 Mg
ZINC            A=                                          2%    0.410 Mg
VITAMIN A       A                                           1%    60.80 IU
VITAMIN D       A                                           0%    0.230 IU
VIT. E/TOTAL    A                                  NO RDA         0.360 Mg
VITAMIN C       A==============                            28%    17.20 Mg
THIAMIN         A=====                                     10%    0.100 Mg
RIBOFLAVIN      A===                                        7%    0.090 Mg
NIACIN          A======                                    12%    1.590 Mg
VITAMIN B6      A=======                                   14%    0.280 Mg
FOLACIN         A=                                          3%    14.30 Ug
VITAMIN B12     A=                                          2%    0.080 Ug
PANTO- ACID     A=====                                     11%    0.640 Mg
CALCIUM         A==                                         5%    47.90 Mg
PHOSPHORUS      A=====                                     10%    80.30 Mg
TRYPTOPHAN      A================                          33%    55.10 Mg
THREONINE       A==================                        37%    161.0 Mg
ISOLEUCINE      A==============                            29%    195.0 Mg
LEUCINE         A==================                        36%    319.0 Mg
LYSINE          A=====================                     43%    281.0 Mg
METHIONINE      A===============                           30%    82.90 Mg
CYSTINE         A========                                  16%    44.00 Mg
PHENYL-ANINE    A=====================                     43%    191.0 Mg
TYROSINE        A==================                        38%    167.0 Mg
VALINE          A==============                            30%    235.0 Mg
HISTIDINE       A                                  NO RDA         107.0 Mg
ALCOHOL         A                                  NO RDA         0.000 Gm
ASH             A                                  NO RDA         1.250 Gm
COPPER          A=====                                     10%    0.250 Mg
MANGANESE       A==                                         5%    0.210 Mg
IODINE          A=======                                   15%    22.70 Ug
MONO FAT        A                                  NO RDA         0.130 Gm
POLY FAT        A                                  NO RDA         0.320 Gm
CAFFEINE        A                                  NO RDA         0.000 Mg
FLUORIDE        A===                                        7%    215.0 Ug
MOLYBDENUM      A====                                       8%    28.20 Ug
VITAMIN K       A=================================         63%    66.20 Ug
SELENIUM        A                                           0%    0.000 Ug
BIOTIN          A                                           0%    0.980 Ug
CHLORIDE        A                                           0%    4.430 Mg
CHROMIUM        A========                                  16%    0.020 Mg
SUGAR           A                                  NO RDA         3.590 Gm
FIBER-DIET      A                                  NO RDA         0.280 Gm
VIT. E/AT       A=                                          2%    0.220 Mg

   % RDA:    |0      |20     |40     |60     |80     |100
```

Tofu Mayonnaise used instead of commercial eggless.

# HOT STICKS

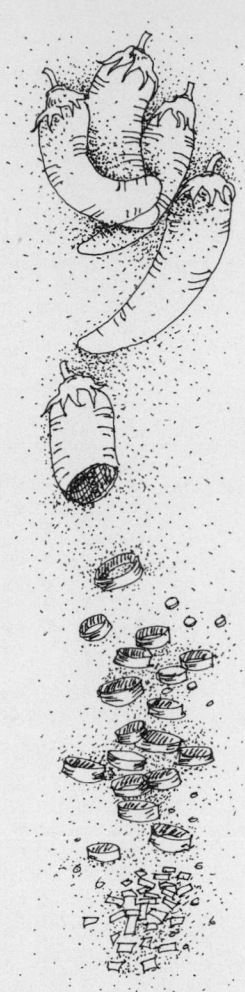

☆ A recipe for those who like spicy-hot food; if cooking
for a timid tongue, just cut the jalapeno peppers out or
down to two. My babies have eaten these breadsticks
made with two jalapeno peppers in them and said
nothing but "I like these!"

---

¼ cup warm water
1 Tbsp. baking yeast
1 tsp. honey

¼ cup olive oil
2 tsp. red chili flakes
1 tsp. whole cumin seeds

6 scallions, sliced thin
4 - 6 fresh jalapenos, cored and choppped fine
¼ cup chopped, ripe olives

1½ tsp. ground cumin
2 tsp. chili powder

1 cup corn meal
3½ cups whole wheat flour
½ tsp. Spike or other vegetable-seasoned salt
1½ cups grated Jack or Cheddar cheese (unpacked)

1¼ - 1½ cups cultured buttermilk

Olive oil
2 Tbsp. nutritional yeast
1 tsp. chili powder

Combine first 3 ingredients in a mixing bowl and set aside
so yeast can dissolve and begin to bubble. In the meantime,
put next 3 ingredients in a small skillet and saute till spices
brown, then add next 3 ingredients and saute till scallions
begin to wilt. Turn off heat and stir in next 2 ingredients.

This also makes nice rolls or a
loaf of bread if you don't want
to make breadsticks. To make
bread or rolls, don't knead
dough quite as long on the
floured counter, so dough
remains tender and moist.
Follow the rest of the recipe
instructions, but bake at 375
degrees for about 45 minutes.

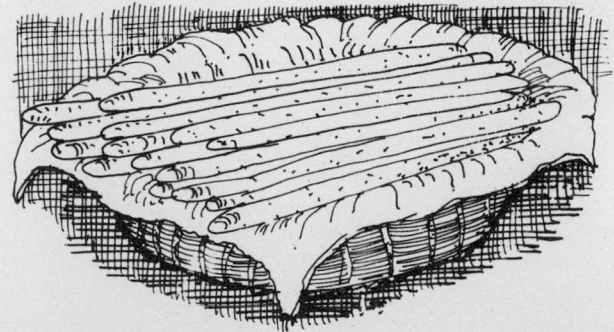

293

Put next 4 ingredients in the mixing bowl on top of the dissolved baking yeast and mix well with fingertips till cheese is evenly distributed throughout the grains. Pour buttermilk into the partially cooled skillet and stir to get all spices and flavoring vegetables off the sides and bottom of skillet. Pour this into mixing bowl and mix into dry ingredients thoroughly.

Flour counter and knead for about 15 minutes. Oil mixing bowl and put ball of dough into the bowl, covering with plastic wrap. Allow to sit in a warm place till dough doubles in bulk — about 1 hour. Punch the dough down and allow to sit about 5 minutes. Oil some cookie sheets. Break off balls of dough about 2 to 3 tablespoons large and roll between fingertips and counter to form long snake-shaped breadsticks about ¾" in diameter and 8" to 10" long. Put on oiled cookie sheet about 1½" apart. Cover cookie sheets with plastic wrap and allow breadsticks to rise for about 45 minutes.

Preheat oven to 400 degrees and bake breadsticks for about 10 minutes. Pull pans out, brush tops of breadsticks with a little olive oil and sprinkle with a mixture of the last 2 ingredients. Return to oven and bake another 5 minutes. Remove from oven and allow to cool. Makes about 2 dozen breadsticks.

| SHOPPING LIST | |
|---|---|
| Regularly Kept in the Kitchen (Listed in Chapter 14, p. 703) | Fresh Produce |
| Baking yeast | Scallions |
| Honey | Fresh jalapenos |
| Olive oil | Ripe olives |
| Red chili flakes | Corn meal |
| Whole cumin seeds | |
| Ground cumin | |
| Chili powder | |
| Whole wheat flour | |
| Spike | |
| Jack or cheddar cheese | |
| Cultured buttermilk | |
| Nutritional yeast | |

# NUTRITIONAL ANALYSIS FOR TWO HOT STICKS

```
NUTRIENT       Type: 14   FEMALE-23 TO 51 YEARS                    % RDA   Amount
KCALORIES      X=======                                            15%    314.0 Kc
PROTEIN        X===============                                    29%    13.00 Gm
CARBOHYDRATE   X                                                   NO RDA 39.50 Gm
FAT            X                                                   NO RDA 13.00 Gm
FIBER-CRUDE    X                                                   NO RDA 1.760 Gm
CHOLESTEROL    X                                                   NO RDA 1.120 Mg
SATURATED FA   X                                                   NO RDA 1.110 Gm
OLEIC FA       X                                                   NO RDA 4.260 Gm
LINOLEIC FA    X                                                   NO RDA 1.000 Gm
SODIUM         X====                                               9%     210.0 Mg
POTASSIUM      X=====                                              10%    389.0 Mg
MAGNESIUM      X=========                                          19%    59.70 Mg
IRON           X======                                             13%    2.510 Mg
ZINC           X=====                                              12%    1.880 Mg
VITAMIN A      X==========                                         21%    869.0 IU
VITAMIN D      X                                                   0%     0.000 IU
VIT. E/TOTAL   X                                                   NO RDA 2.320 Mg
VITAMIN C      X=============================================      93%    56.00 Mg
THIAMIN        X==============================================     103%   1.030 Mg
RIBOFLAVIN     X====================================              81%    0.980 Mg
NIACIN         X========================                           50%    6.620 Mg
VITAMIN B6     X=======================                            48%    0.970 Mg
FOLACIN        X=======                                            15%    60.40 Ug
VITAMIN B12    X==========                                         21%    0.650 Ug
PANTO- ACID    X======                                             12%    0.690 Mg
CALCIUM        X=============                                      26%    214.0 Mg
PHOSPHORUS     X==================                                 39%    314.0 Mg
TRYPTOPHAN     X=========================================          92%    150.0 Mg
THREONINE      X===============================================    103%   449.0 Mg
ISOLEUCINE     X===============================================    101%   660.0 Mg
LEUCINE        X================================================   123%   1078  Mg
LYSINE         X==============================================     110%   720.0 Mg
METHIONINE     X=================================------            93%    255.0 Mg
CYSTINE        X==========================                         61%    166.0 Mg
PHENYL-ANINE   X================================================   143%   625.0 Mg
TYROSINE       X===============================================    126%   550.0 Mg
VALINE         X=========================================          95%    726.0 Mg
HISTIDINE      X                                                   NO RDA 343.0 Mg
ALCOHOL        X                                                   NO RDA 0.000 Gm
ASH            X                                                   NO RDA 2.440 Gm
COPPER         X====                                               9%     0.240 Mg
MANGANESE      X========================                           48%    1.800 Mg
IODINE         X===============================================    108%   163.0 Ug
MONO FAT       X                                                   NO RDA 3.800 Gm
POLY FAT       X                                                   NO RDA 0.460 Gm
CAFFEINE       X                                                   NO RDA 0.000 Mg
FLUORIDE       X                                                   0%     26.30 Ug
MOLYBDENUM     X================================================   646%   2100  Ug
VITAMIN K      X                                                   1%     1.770 Ug
SELENIUM       X====                                               8%     0.010 Mg
BIOTIN         X==                                                 4%     6.650 Ug
CHLORIDE       X                                                   1%     66.50 Mg
CHROMIUM       X================================================   168%   0.210 Mg
SUGAR          X                                                   NO RDA 0.000 Gm
FIBER-DIET     X                                                   NO RDA 5.300 Gm
VIT. E/AT      X======                                             13%    1.040 Mg

  % RDA:    |0      |20     |40     |60     |80     |100
```

Monterey Jack cheese used instead of Cheddar in this analysis.

# FROM TIME TO TIME

Through the years of cooking and learning to cook, I've often come across and used recipes that call for using an alcoholic beverage for flavoring. Out of curiosity, more than anything else, I tried these recipes, attempting to substitute grape juice or grape juice and vinegar to see what they tasted like. Sometimes I'd serve them to friends who were familiar with the taste of alcoholic beverages to see what they thought.

I had to do this because I have no idea what different alcoholic beverages are supposed to taste like because I never began drinking them. I can thank my mother for that. I still remember very clearly the New Year's party when I was seven years old. All the adults were drinking and socializing and all the kids got together and were playing at being big. We were filling glasses with ice cubes and water, juices, etc., and pretending to drink and get drunk. My mother nipped in the bud even the desire to be doing what the big people were doing by serving us each a little cup of whiskey — straight. Needless to say, not only did I not finish mine, but I couldn't figure out *why* anyone would want to drink that stuff at all!

There are certain dishes, however, that are actually nicely flavored with different alcoholic beverages. What I've learned is that the alcohol evaporates or burns off. This means two things:

1)  The alcohol is gone; the alcohol is the part of any alcoholic beverage that is damaging to the body and extremely caloric.

2)  With the alcohol (which oftentimes masks the flavor of the drink) gone, the flavor of the drink will stand out. So, if using alcohol to cook with, one should get the finest available as opposed to cheap or "cooking" liquors.

Although I don't serve dishes with alcohol in them often at all (they take up proportionately as much of my menus as they do in this book), I've included these few recipes to give you some ideas and techniques for cooking off the alcohol. The flamed alcohol recipes are often made for special occasions for the dramatic effect they have.

I have often heard people remark with wonder as to why — with all the information confirmed by medical science about certain "foods" and habits that destroy the body — anyone would continue to consume these products. The Bhagavad-gita, an ancient book of wisdom, explains it very practically:

"As a boat in the water is swept away by a strong wind, even one of the senses on which the mind focuses can carry away a man's intelligence."

Controlling the senses, rather than being controlled by them, leads to physical, mental and spiritual well-being.

# YUBA BRISKET STEW

☆ I've made this into a pot pie by topping with whole grain biscuit crust and baking at 400 degrees for 25 to 30 minutes till crust is golden brown. As a pot pie, this is a meal-in-one dish served with a small salad.

## SUGGESTED MENU

*Tossed green salad*

*Whole grain rolls*

*Yuba Brisket Stew*

*Express-o Ice (p. 257)*

---

*8 oz. dried bean curd (yuba) sticks, soaked*

*2 Tbsp. soy sauce*
*2 Tbsp. melted butter or margarine*
*½ tsp. black pepper*

*1 Tbsp. safflower oil*
*½ cup diced carrot*
*½ cup diced celery*

*3 cups water*
*1 Tbsp. Vegex Bouillon Extract*
*2 oz. brandy*
*1 bay leaf*

*1 Tbsp. safflower oil*
*1 onion, sliced thin*
*1 turnip, cut in matchsticks*
*2 cups fresh peas*

*1 Tbsp. arrowroot*

Soak yuba sticks in water for a few hours (or all day) on the day of preparation. Just before time to make the stir-fry, drain water from yuba sticks and squeeze out as much water as you can. Cut into 3" to 4" lengths. Toss next 3 ingredients into the cut and drained yuba strips and allow to sit about 10 minutes.

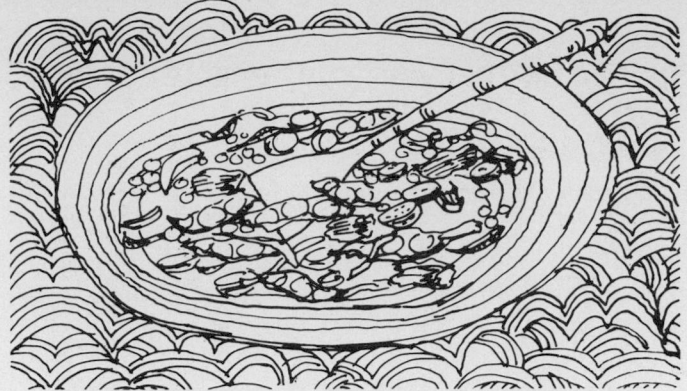

Heat wok or skillet and pour in seasoned yuba sticks, adding oil only if/when necessary to keep them from sticking to pan. Fry, stirring occasionally, till yuba is golden brown and slightly braised.

Remove from heat and pour into a rectangular roasting or cake pan. Put next 3 ingredients in empty heated skillet and saute till vegetables begin to brown. Toss in roasting pan with yuba sticks.

Preheat oven to 375 degrees. Add next 4 ingredients to cooked ingredients in roasting pan, making sure bouillon is thoroughly dissolved. Cover pan with lid or foil and bake at 375 degrees for about 1 hour.

Remove pan from oven and turn oven off. Pour juice from pan into a separate container.

Saute next 4 ingredients together in skillet till onions and turnips brown. Pour on top of baked vegetables and yuba.

Put arrowroot into about ¼ cup of stock which was previously poured off and set aside, and mix together to thoroughly dissolve arrowroot. Pour dissolved mixture and remaining stock into skillet and bring to a boil, stirring constantly till it slightly thickens. Pour on top of everything in pan and serve immediately. Makes about 4 to 6 servings.

| SHOPPING LIST | |
| --- | --- |
| Regularly Kept in the Kitchen (Listed in Chapter 14, p. 703) | Fresh Produce |
| Yuba sticks<br>Soy sauce<br>Butter or margarine<br>Black pepper<br>Safflower oil<br>Bay leaf<br>Arrowroot | Carrots<br>Celery<br>Onion<br>Turnip<br>Fresh peas |

| Special Shopping |
| --- |
| Vegex Bouillon Extract — found in some natural food stores; I prefer this to the cubes because it doesn't contain sugar, as the cubes do. Brandy — can be found just about everywhere, but it's on my special shopping list because it's an ingredient very rarely bought. |

# NUTRITIONAL ANALYSIS FOR ONE SERVING YUBA BRISKET STEW

```
NUTRIENT        Type: 14   FEMALE-23 TO 51 YEARS              % RDA    Amount
KCALORIES       Ʀ==========                                   21%    432.0 Kc
PROTEIN         Ʀ=====================================        76%     33.70 Gm
CARBOHYDRATE    Ʀ                                           NO RDA    24.10 Gm
FAT             Ʀ                                           NO RDA    25.70 Gm
FIBER-CRUDE     Ʀ                                           NO RDA     2.890 Gm
CHOLESTEROL     Ʀ                                           NO RDA     0.000 Mg
SATURATED FA    Ʀ                                           NO RDA     1.630 Gm
OLEIC FA        Ʀ                                           NO RDA     4.130 Gm
LINOLEIC FA     Ʀ                                           NO RDA    11.20 Gm
SODIUM          Ʀ================                             31%    693.0 Mg
POTASSIUM       Ʀ=========                                    18%    696.0 Mg
MAGNESIUM       Ʀ========================                     49%    149.0 Mg
IRON            Ʀ=======================                      47%     8.620 Mg
ZINC            Ʀ                                              0%     0.130 Mg
VITAMIN A       Ʀ====================================================  108%  4349 IU
VITAMIN D       Ʀ                                              0%     0.000 IU
VIT. E/TOTAL    Ʀ                                           NO RDA     6.240 Mg
VITAMIN C       Ʀ==================================================   102%    61.50 Mg
THIAMIN         Ʀ====================                         41%     0.410 Mg
RIBOFLAVIN      Ʀ=======                                      15%     0.190 Mg
NIACIN          Ʀ========                                     17%     2.330 Mg
VITAMIN B6      Ʀ=======                                      15%     0.310 Mg
FOLACIN         Ʀ==                                            4%    18.70 Ug
VITAMIN B12     Ʀ                                              0%     0.000 Ug
PANTO- ACID     Ʀ========                                     17%     0.960 Mg
CALCIUM         Ʀ==============                               28%    227.0 Mg
PHOSPHORUS      Ʀ===========================                  53%    429.0 Mg
TRYPTOPHAN      Ʀ===================================          197%   322.0 Mg
THREONINE       Ʀ===================================          279%  1217 Mg
ISOLEUCINE      Ʀ===================================          254%  1665 Mg
LEUCINE         Ʀ===================================          288%  2516 Mg
LYSINE          Ʀ===================================          341%  2228 Mg
METHIONINE      Ʀ===================================          151%   412.0 Mg
CYSTINE         Ʀ===================================          152%   414.0 Mg
PHENYL-ANINE    Ʀ===================================          366%  1596 Mg
TYROSINE        Ʀ===================================          297%  1296 Mg
VALINE          Ʀ===================================          226%  1729 Mg
HISTIDINE       Ʀ                                           NO RDA   909.0 Mg
ALCOHOL         Ʀ                                           NO RDA     0.000 Gm
ASH             Ʀ                                           NO RDA     4.410 Gm
COPPER          Ʀ=============                                24%     0.620 Mg
MANGANESE       Ʀ==========================                   53%     2.000 Mg
IODINE          Ʀ=================================            119%   179.0 Ug
MONO FAT        Ʀ                                           NO RDA     3.520 Gm
POLY FAT        Ʀ                                           NO RDA     7.060 Gm
CAFFEINE        Ʀ                                           NO RDA     0.000 Mg
FLUORIDE        Ʀ=                                             2%    66.10 Ug
MOLYBDENUM      Ʀ===================================          1692%  5501 Ug
VITAMIN K       Ʀ===================================          179%   188.0 Ug
SELENIUM        Ʀ============                                 24%     0.030 Mg
BIOTIN          Ʀ======                                       13%    20.90 Ug
CHLORIDE        Ʀ=                                             2%    94.00 Mg
CHROMIUM        Ʀ===================================          384%   0.480 Mg
SUGAR           Ʀ                                           NO RDA     5.770 Gm
FIBER-DIET      Ʀ                                           NO RDA    12.50 Gm
VIT. E/AT       Ʀ=================                            32%     2.600 Mg

     % RDA:    [0      [20     [40     [60     [80     [100
```

# STUFFED YUBA ROLL
# IN GINGER-BEER SAUCE

☆ A tangy, sweet, hot, spirited-tasting gourmet entree.

---

⅓ cup dried apricots covered with water

¼ cup water
2 cups diced celery and ½ tsp. asafetida
    OR 2 cups diced onion
1 tsp. Vegex Bouillon Extract

4 cups diced apple
1 cup crushed pineapple
1 Tbsp. grated fresh ginger root
¼ tsp. white pepper
⅛ tsp. cinnamon
Dash cayenne

½ cup ground nuts

1 cup water
¼ cup nutritional yeast
3 Tbsp. Dijon mustard
2 Tbsp. tomato paste
2 Tbsp. arrowroot
1 Tbsp. soy sauce

Yuba sheets approximately 8" x 10", soaked

2 Tbsp. safflower oil
1 onion, slivered
4 celery stalks, cut in sticks
2 large carrots, cut in sticks

2 (12-oz.) bottles or cans of beer

1½ cups water
3 Tbsp. tomato paste
1 Tbsp. Vegex Bouillon Extract

6 - 8 allspice berries or ½ tsp. ground allspice
2 bay leaves
4 garlic cloves, split
1" cinnamon stick
2 quarter-sized slices of fresh ginger root

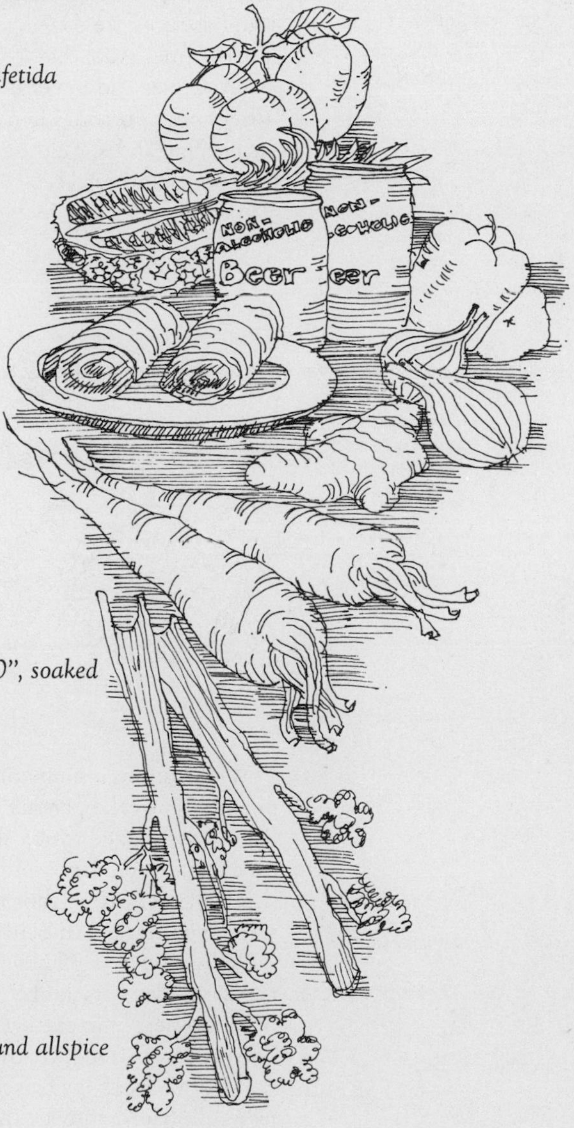

1 Tbsp. lemon juice
½ tsp. black pepper
½ tsp. Spike
2 Tbsp. fresh thyme or 1 Tbsp. dried thyme

## SUGGESTED MENU

*Tossed green salad*

*Mashed potatoes*

*Stuffed Yuba Roll in
Ginger-Beer Sauce*

*Yogurt Cheese Dessert
(p. 347)*

Put dried apricots in measuring cup, cover with hot water and soak till apricots soften. When dried apricots are softened, put next 4 (or 3) ingredients in a 13" skillet and saute over medium-low heat till celery gets tender. By this time the water in the skillet should almost be cooked out. Drain the liquid apricots are soaking in into skillet and quickly chop apricots fine. Add the apricots and next 6 ingredients to skillet. Cover and lower heat to simmer till apples get soft. When apples are soft, stir in nut meal and turn off heat. This is the stuffing and should be a thick, sticky, candied texture (not runny and juicy).

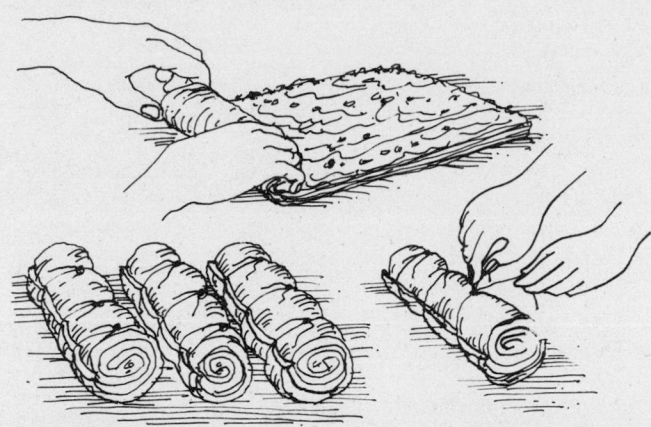

While stuffing is simmering, combine the next 6 ingredients in an oblong cake pan and whisk to make a smooth sauce. Place soft (soaked) yuba sheets in this sauce, 5 sheets at a time. You should have 4 groups of 5 sheets, with the outside sheets of each group thoroughly coated with the sauce and some sauce leaked in between the middle layers.

Preheat oven to 350 degrees. Divide stuffing into 4 equal parts. Now lay 1 stack of 5 yuba sheets (5 sheets piled on top of each other) onto cutting board. Put ¼ of the stuffing along one of the width edges of the yuba and spread evenly all along the width edge. Now roll stuffing up into rest of yuba sheet jelly-roll style. Gently tie the stuffed roll together in 3 places with dental floss or butcher's twine. Repeat with remaining yuba sheets and stuffing so you end up with 4 rolls of stuffed yuba.

301

Put oil in bottom of the same skillet stuffing was cooked in (no need to wash it out) and add vegetables. Saute till vegetables are browned. Push browned vegetables to edges of skillet and place all 4 yuba rolls side-by-side in center of skillet. Allow to brown on one side, flip and brown on second side. Pour beer into skillet over yuba rolls and vegetables. Mix next 3 ingredients in a bowl till smooth and pour into ingredients in skillet. In a large tea ball or a piece of cheesecloth, put the next 5 spices, close or tie shut and immerse in liquid in skillet.

Sprinkle next 4 ingredients over surface of contents in skillet. Cover, turn off stove heat and put in oven to bake at 350 degrees for 45 minutes. Remove from oven and remove strings. To serve, cut each roll in half across width of roll. Makes 8 servings.

| SHOPPING LIST | | Special Shopping |
|---|---|---|
| **Regularly Kept in the Kitchen** (Listed in Chapter 14, p. 703) | **Fresh Produce** | Vegex Bouillon Extract — found in some natural food stores; I prefer this to the cubes because it doesn't contain sugar, as the cubes do. Beer (either nonalcoholic or your favorite) — though beer can be found everywhere, I've put it on the special shopping list because this is one ingredient I rarely ever buy. |
| Asafetida | Dried apricots | |
| White pepper | Celery | |
| Cinnamon (ground and stick) | Apple | |
| Cayenne | Pineapple | |
| Nuts or seeds | Ginger root | |
| Nutritional yeast | Onion | |
| Dijon mustard | Carrots | |
| Tomato paste | Garlic | |
| Arrowroot | Lemon | |
| Soy sauce | Fresh thyme (or dried if fresh is unavailable) | |
| Yuba sheets | | |
| Safflower oil | | |
| Allspice (ground or berries) | | |
| Bay leaves | | |
| Black pepper | | |
| Spike | | |

# STUFFED YUBA ROLL IN GINGER-BEER SAUCE

```
NUTRIENT        Type: 14   FEMALE-23 TO 51 YEARS        % RDA    Amount
KCALORIES      A====================                     41%     829.0 Kc
PROTEIN        A=======================================  181%    79.90 Gm
CARBOHYDRATE   A                                         NO RDA  53.50 Gm
FAT            A                                         NO RDA  40.90 Gm
FIBER-CRUDE    A                                         NO RDA  2.150 Gm
CHOLESTEROL    A                                         NO RDA  0.000 Mg
SATURATED FA   A                                         NO RDA  0.850 Gm
OLEIC FA       A                                         NO RDA  8.670 Gm
LINOLEIC FA    A                                         NO RDA  18.10 Gm
SODIUM         A=========                                19%     423.0 Mg
POTASSIUM      A=================                        34%     1298 Mg
MAGNESIUM      A======================================== 114%    342.0 Mg
IRON           A======================================== 100%    18.10 Mg
ZINC           A====                                     9%      1.430 Mg
VITAMIN A      A======================================== 152%    6081 IU
VITAMIN D      A                                         0%      0.000 IU
VIT. E/TOTAL   A                                         NO RDA  5.870 Mg
VITAMIN C      A=================                        33%     20.20 Mg
THIAMIN        A======================================== 297%    2.970 Mg
RIBOFLAVIN     A======================================== 218%    2.620 Mg
NIACIN         A======================================== 133%    17.30 Mg
VITAMIN B6     A======================================== 131%    2.620 Mg
FOLACIN        A======                                   13%     54.80 Ug
VITAMIN B12    A============================             58%     1.750 Ug
PANTO- ACID    A========                                 16%     0.900 Mg
CALCIUM        A==============================           59%     477.0 Mg
PHOSPHORUS     A======================================== 124%    996.0 Mg
TRYPTOPHAN     A======================================== 484%    789.0 Mg
THREONINE      A======================================== 682%    2969 Mg
ISOLEUCINE     A======================================== 606%    3962 Mg
LEUCINE        A======================================== 697%    6073 Mg
LYSINE         A======================================== 818%    5347 Mg
METHIONINE     A======================================== 381%    1038 Mg
CYSTINE        A======================================== 376%    1023 Mg
PHENYL-ANINE   A======================================== 909%    3958 Mg
TYROSINE       A======================================== 729%    3175 Mg
VALINE         A======================================== 521%    3971 Mg
HISTIDINE      A                                         NO RDA  2315 Mg
ALCOHOL        A                                         NO RDA  0.180 Gm
ASH            A                                         NO RDA  8.160 Gm
COPPER         A=========================                51%     1.280 Mg
MANGANESE      A======================================== 145%    5.450 Mg
IODINE         A======================================== 302%    454.0 Ug
MONO FAT       A                                         NO RDA  3.370 Gm
POLY FAT       A                                         NO RDA  3.680 Gm
CAFFEINE       A                                         NO RDA  0.000 Mg
FLUORIDE       A=                                        2%      82.20 Ug
MOLYBDENUM     A======================================== 4216%   13704 Ug
VITAMIN K      A                                         0%      0.000 Ug
SELENIUM       A=============================            56%     0.070 Mg
BIOTIN         A==============                           26%     40.40 Ug
CHLORIDE       A===                                      6%      227.0 Mg
CHROMIUM       A======================================== 928%    1.160 Mg
SUGAR          A                                         NO RDA  9.930 Gm
FIBER-DIET     A                                         NO RDA  28.80 Gm
VIT. E/AT      A============                             24%     1.920 Mg

    % RDA:   |0      |20     |40     |60     |80     |100         10
```

Nuts used in analysis: almonds. Onion used instead of asafetida and celery; Vegex Bouillon
Extract not included.

303

# CAFFEINE-FREE CAFE BRULOT

☆ An elegant and dramatic way to end a formal dinner or begin a party (as in the Dessert Party, p. 269).

---

*1½ Tbsp. honey*
*Thinly peeled rind of 1 orange*
*1 vanilla pod or 1 tsp. vanilla extract*

*1½ cups brandy*

*6 cups hot grain coffee*

Place first 3 ingredients in a heat-proof serving bowl, and have piping hot grain coffee in attractive coffee pot. Pour brandy into a small saucepan and place over low heat till tiny bubbles begin to show along edge of pot. Quickly light with a long-handled match or flame at the end of an incense stick. Pour flaming liquor into serving bowl and stir constantly till flame dies out. Quickly pour in hot grain coffee, remove orange rind and vanilla pod and serve immediately. Makes about 20 dainty servings, traditionally served in demitasse cups.

This recipe originally calls for putting the flames out with coffee after a few seconds, but alcohol would still be present. So instead, I let the flame burn itself out (to get rid of the alcohol) and then pour in grain coffee. Though it's usually made with plain brandy, you might try some of the fruit-flavored brandies available.

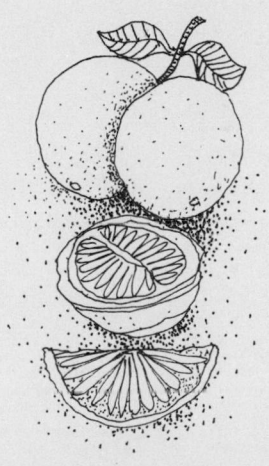

| SHOPPING LIST | |
|---|---|
| **Regularly Kept in the Kitchen** (Listed in Chapter 14, p. 703) | **Fresh Produce** |
| Honey Grain coffee | Orange |

| Special Shopping |
|---|
| Vanilla pod — in gourmet food stores. Brandy — can be found everywhere but is on this list because any alcoholic beverage is such a rarity on my shopping list. |

Points to remember for flambeing fruit:
- Both fruit and liquor must be slightly heated.
- Never bring liquor to a boil or alcohol will boil out and won't ignite. Just heat till tiny bubbles can be seen at the edge of the pot.
- Use a long-handled pot for heating and igniting liquor in.
- Use a long-handled (fireplace-type) match or incense stick for igniting liquor.

# CARIBBEAN FLAMBE

☆ All the ingredients are made in the Caribbean, hence the name. You can flambe any fruit, using the same general proportions and principles for igniting, for a simple, yet dramatic dessert. If using other fruit, try lightly sprinkling with cinnamon, nutmeg, cardamom or some other sweet spice instead of coconut.

---

*1 Tbsp. butter or margarine*

*2 fresh pineapple slices, ½" - ¾" thick*
*2 mangoes, split down flat sides of seeds*

*2 bananas, split lengthwise*
*1½ Tbsp. honey or Barbados molasses*

*¼ cup rum*
*Unsweetened shredded coconut*

Melt butter or margarine in a skillet and, over a medium-low heat, add next 2 ingredients. Fry till fruit lightly browns on one side, then flip and lightly brown other side. A few seconds before other fruit is done, add split bananas and cook about 10 seconds on each side. Drizzle honey or Barbados molasses lightly over fruit and pour in alcohol. Wait a few seconds to allow alcohol to warm, but be sure not to bring to a boil. Ignite with flame using a long-handled match or incense stick. Sprinkle on shredded coconut. When flame dies, serve immediately. Makes about 4 servings.

A fruit sauce can be made (for topping ice cream, cakes, pancakes, crepes, etc.) by cubing the fruit into ½" pieces and following the rest of the recipe.

| Special Shopping |
|---|
| Rum — again, though it can be found almost everywhere, I have put it on my special shopping list because it's so rarely a part of my shopping list. |

| SHOPPING LIST | |
|---|---|
| **Regularly Kept in the Kitchen** (Listed in Chapter 14, p. 703) | **Fresh Produce** |
| Butter or margarine<br>Honey | Pineapple<br>Mango<br>Bananas<br>Shredded coconut |

# CHAPTER 7

# DAIRY, BUT NOT TOO MUCH

D on't worry — I'm not going to tell you to eliminate all dairy products from your diet too! These last two chapters in this section are devoted to items that I use in a very limited way at home, and when I do use them I try to use the healthier choices.

I thought this chapter was important to include because many people, when cutting back on red meat consumption under doctor's advice or their own choice, make the mistake of using a lot of cheese and other dairy products. Some people even end up eating more cholesterol and saturated fat than they did when they were eating meat by consuming too many dairy products.

The overuse of dairy products usually stems from the overblown concern about getting enough protein that has been drummed into Americans. We have been conditioned to think (1) we need a lot of protein, and (2) that animals and animal products are "protein foods." As pointed out in depth in Chapter 3, we don't need as much protein as we have generally been led to believe, and animals and animal products definitely aren't the best sources of protein.

I use dairy products in my kitchen in a healthy way —by limiting the quantity and choosing the best quality products. With our budget, we are nicely limited to using dairy products one or two times a week, at the most; and, fortunately, in the case of dairy products and my way of viewing them, quality doesn't mean more expensive. In terms of health (and keeping the body trim), a quality dairy product is one with lesser amounts of cholesterol and saturated fat and is free from rennet (the enzyme juices of calves' stomachs used to curdle some cheeses) and gelatin (made from ground up bones and hooves).

Dairy products vary a great deal in cholesterol and saturated fat content from one product to the next, as can be seen in the table below. If everyone watched or counted their cholesterol intake as conscientiously as many people do their calories, we would find ourselves in better health and naturally trim (that is providing the cholesterol-free foods eaten are not empty-calorie foods). Because we've been conditioned to think of dairy products as being important sources of protein and calcium, I'm including that information as well, along with a small list (below the dotted line) of non-dairy foods you'll find I use a lot in my recipes, so you can easily compare healthful pluses and minuses.

## AMOUNTS CONTAINED IN A 100-GRAM (3½-OUNCE) PORTION:

| | Cholesterol (mg.) | Saturated Fat (gm.) | Protein (gm.) | Calcium (mg.) | Calories |
|---|---|---|---|---|---|
| Whole milk | 13.50 | 2.07 | 3.29 | 119.00 | 61.40 |
| *Lowfat milk | 7.37 | 1.19 | 3.32 | 121.00 | 49.50 |
| *Cultured buttermilk | 3.67 | .54 | 3.31 | 116.00 | 40.40 |
| *Lowfat yogurt | 6.16 | 1.00 | 5.24 | 182.00 | 63.40 |
| *2% lowfat cottage cheese | 8.40 | 1.22 | 13.70 | 68.50 | 89.80 |
| Cheddar cheese | 107.00 | 21.30 | 25.20 | 728.00 | 407.00 |
| *Provolone cheese | 71.40 | 17.20 | 25.80 | 764.00 | 357.00 |
| *Part-skim milk mozzarella | 57.10 | 10.20 | 24.50 | 653.00 | 257.00 |
| *Parmesan cheese | 79.00 | 19.10 | 41.60 | 1376.00 | 456.00 |
| *Cream cheese | 110.00 | 22.20 | 7.64 | 82.10 | 353.00 |
| *Neufchatel cheese | 78.50 | 15.00 | 10.00 | 75.00 | 264.00 |
| Soy milk | 0 | 0 (2.5 gm. unsaturated) | 4.40 | 18.50 | 52.00 |
| Tofu (curdled with calcium sulfate) | 0 | 0 (4.9 gm. unsaturated) | 15.70 | 682.00 | 145.00 |
| Hard-pressed tofu | 0 | 0 (11 gm. unsaturated) | 22.00 | 377.00 | 182.00 |

* more desirable to use

# LIMITING DAIRY PRODUCTS

In connection with dairy products, I have three policies: 1) replace them, whenever possible, with a cholesterol-free natural product that gives a similar texture, taste and/or nutritional value; 2) use a cultured dairy product whenever possible; and 3) use the product that is lower in cholesterol and saturated fat . . . And I follow them in that order.

Through the years I've found that soy milk and/or nut milks (p. 522) can be used in place of dairy milk just about anywhere. I say "just about" because my children love to drink their lowfat milk, whereas they balk at nonfat milk or soy milk (nut milk usually wins a hearty approval for its sweet, delicate flavor). Tofu can be used in place of cottage cheese in many recipes — especially recipes that have a flavorful sauce where the taste of cottage cheese won't be missed (as in the Simple Family Favorite, p. 311). There are a few soy-based cheeses making their way onto natural food store shelves; these contain about the same amount of fat as the real thing, but at least it is a polyunsaturated fat and it is cholesterol-free.

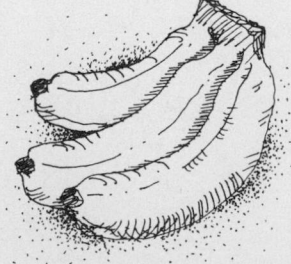

Though my husband and I don't drink milk, we do eat or drink cultured milk products (yogurt, kefir and cultured buttermilk) as they are, or when prepared as part of a dish. Cultured milk products are a superior form of dairy food because they provide all the good nutrients for which we eat dairy food (protein, calcium, etc.) along with the special benefits added by the bacteria culture. There are many scientifically-proven benefits which the bacteria culture performs and some benefits that science hasn't been able to explain the why's of yet.

The bacteria culture pre-digests the protein in milk, making it easier to digest. But besides that, the bacteria themselves are a healthy addition to our systems. The bacteria are friendly; they set up house in our intestinal tract, helping to produce some vitamins and other essential nutrients, and killing off harmful bacteria that doesn't belong. About 16 years ago, I got dysentery that weeks of taking antibiotics didn't get rid of. The tests kept turning up positive. Finally I placed a long-distance call to a friend who was into natural healing. His "prescription": eat lots of yogurt and take a yogurt enema every day. After two days of following his advice, my dysentery test finally came out negative! The lactobacillus acidophilus bacteria has been shown to inhibit the enzymes that activate carcinogens connected with cancer of the colon. The other benefits of yogurt have filled books, but for lack of space I'll end by saying that yogurt has been one of the central ingredients common to the Hunzas and Bulgarians (two societies where living to the age of 100 was common).

If you read the labels on yogurt, kefir or cultured buttermilk containers, you'll find that there are a number of different strains of bacteria cultures. They are all relatives of each other and perform similarly once in the body. They are not killed by stomach acid or the process of digestion and will thrive and multiply in the intestinal tract. One thing that does kill off this friendly flori is antibiotics. In our house, taking antibiotics is always the last resort, turned to only when absolutely necessary after all else has failed. Once every year or two, one person out of the 10 in our household may have to take them. Because antibiotics kill off the friendly bacteria, as well as the harmful ones that are causing a disease or infection, I always make sure the person who took antibiotics gets lots of yogurt, kefir or acidophilus supplements when their prescription runs out.

I prefer to make my own yogurt, kefir and buttermilk at home because I can do so for about a quarter of the store-shelf price. It's really very simple: just mix in thoroughly about ¼ cup of the cultured product per quart of milk and allow to incubate in a sterile glass or clay pot. Buttermilk and kefir are the easiest; they incubate by sitting, covered, at room temperature for 12 to 24 hours. Yogurt is a little harder, as it must be kept at about 110 to 115 degrees for eight hours. I've found the easiest way to do this is to wrap my sealed jar in a thick blanket and put the bundle in a gas oven with a pilot light or in an electric oven with the light on.

SUGGESTED MENU
FOR A SIMPLE MEAL

*Simple Family Favorite*

*Brown rice*

*Tossed green salad*

As far as hard cheeses go, remember that they are basically a concentrated form of milk — concentrating much of the cholesterol, saturated fat and protein (but losing some calcium in the whey). Cheddar cheese is an American favorite, but it's one of the highest in cholesterol and saturated fat. The Italian cheeses — provolone, mozzarella and Parmesan — are all relatively lower in cholesterol and saturated fat. Parmesan cheese is especially nice because it's so flavorful that only a little bit is needed. It would be hard to use a quarter-cup serving for one person of Parmesan cheese, whereas it's very easy to use a quarter cup per person of most other hard cheeses.

Following are some of my favorite yogurt recipes and some recipes that will give you an idea of how to use Parmesan cheese to cut down on cheese consumption.

# A SIMPLE FAMILY FAVORITE

☆ This is a simple, economic, tasty meal that can be prepared in minutes. My family never tires of different variations of this theme.

☆ Be sure to use a light hand in sprinkling the cheese on top of the dish. You'll find that though sprinkled lightly, the whole dish will be permeated with a cheesy flavor, as it is carried through the vegetable juices.

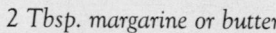

*2 Tbsp. margarine or butter*
*2 vegetable bouillon cubes*

*2 lbs. Chinese firm tofu, cubed*

*1 Tbsp. soy sauce*

*4 cups fresh mushroom slices*
*1 bell pepper, slivered*
*2 tomatoes, cut in wedges*
*1 tsp. rosemary*
*1 tsp. thyme*

*Parmesan cheese*
*Grated Monterey Jack cheese*

Put first 2 ingredients together in a large skillet over medium-high heat, mashing down bouillon cubes and mixing in with margarine or butter. Add tofu cubes (¾" to 1" large) and fry, stirring occasionally, till tofu begins browning. Sprinkle soy sauce over tofu and cook till thoroughly browned but the tofu is still moist.

While tofu is browning, cut vegetables in the following way: slice mushrooms about ¼" thick, sliver bell peppers about ¼" thick, slice thin ½" tomato wedges. All vegetables should be cut thin enough to finish cooking within 3 minutes. When tofu is browned, stir in the next 5 ingredients.

Sprinkle the whole surface with Parmesan cheese, then cover the whole surface with a layer of grated or thinly-sliced Monterey Jack cheese. Cover and continue to cook over medium-high heat for 3 minutes (don't over-cook). Serve on top or on the side of brown rice. Makes 6 to 8 servings.

| SHOPPING LIST | |
|---|---|
| Regularly Kept in the Kitchen (Listed in Chapter 14, p. 703) | Fresh Produce |
| Butter or margarine<br>Tofu<br>Soy sauce<br>Rosemary<br>Thyme<br>Grated Jack cheese<br>Parmesan cheese | Mushrooms<br>Bell pepper<br>Tomatoes |

**Special Shopping**

Vegetable bouillon cubes (made completely from vegetables with no animal fats or flavorings) — can be found in natural food stores.

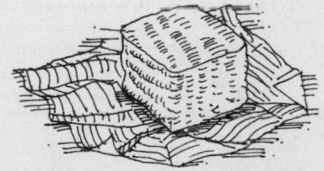

# NUTRITIONAL ANALYSIS FOR ONE SERVING
## OF A SIMPLE FAMILY FAVORITE

| NUTRIENT | Type: 14   FEMALE-23 TO 51 YEARS | % RDA | Amount |
|---|---|---|---|
| KCALORIES | A========= | 17% | 340.0 Kc |
| PROTEIN | A=================================== | 67% | 29.80 Gm |
| CARBOHYDRATE | A | NO RDA | 11.90 Gm |
| FAT | A | NO RDA | 22.10 Gm |
| FIBER-CRUDE | A | NO RDA | 1.000 Gm |
| CHOLESTEROL | A | NO RDA | 1.640 Mg |
| SATURATED FA | A | NO RDA | 2.980 Gm |
| OLEIC FA | A | NO RDA | 1.670 Gm |
| LINOLEIC FA | A | NO RDA | 3.030 Gm |
| SODIUM | A========= | 16% | 353.0 Mg |
| POTASSIUM | A========== | 18% | 677.0 Mg |
| MAGNESIUM | A================== | 35% | 106.0 Mg |
| IRON | A=================================================== | 96% | 17.30 Mg |
| ZINC | A=========== | 21% | 3.170 Mg |
| VITAMIN A | A============== | 28% | 1140 IU |
| VITAMIN D | A | 0% | 0.000 IU |
| VIT. E/TOTAL | A | NO RDA | 0.360 Mg |
| VITAMIN C | A==================== | 43% | 25.80 Mg |
| THIAMIN | A================ | 33% | 0.330 Mg |
| RIBOFLAVIN | A=================== | 38% | 0.460 Mg |
| NIACIN | A============ | 22% | 2.950 Mg |
| VITAMIN B6 | A====== | 11% | 0.230 Mg |
| FOLACIN | A======== | 15% | 61.00 Ug |
| VITAMIN B12 | A | 0% | 0.000 Ug |
| PANTO- ACID | A============= | 25% | 1.400 Mg |
| CALCIUM | A========================================== | 147% | 1177 Mg |
| PHOSPHORUS | A============================ | 54% | 432.0 Mg |
| TRYPTOPHAN | A========================================= | 277% | 452.0 Mg |
| THREONINE | A========================================= | 271% | 1181 Mg |
| ISOLEUCINE | A========================================= | 227% | 1488 Mg |
| LEUCINE | A========================================= | 263% | 2297 Mg |
| LYSINE | A========================================= | 313% | 2049 Mg |
| METHIONINE | A========================================= | 162% | 441.0 Mg |
| CYSTINE | A========================================= | 133% | 363.0 Mg |
| PHENYL-ANINE | A========================================= | 330% | 1438 Mg |
| TYROSINE | A========================================= | 236% | 1027 Mg |
| VALINE | A========================================= | 203% | 1549 Mg |
| HISTIDINE | A | NO RDA | 881.0 Mg |
| ALCOHOL | A | NO RDA | 0.000 Gm |
| ASH | A | NO RDA | 4.100 Gm |
| COPPER | A============= | 27% | 0.680 Mg |
| MANGANESE | A======================== | 49% | 1.860 Mg |
| IODINE | A================================================== | 110% | 165.0 Ug |
| MONO FAT | A | NO RDA | 4.880 Gm |
| POLY FAT | A | NO RDA | 8.840 Gm |
| CAFFEINE | A | NO RDA | 0.000 Mg |
| FLUORIDE | A | 0% | 24.30 Ug |
| MOLYBDENUM | A=================================================== | 558% | 1814 Ug |
| VITAMIN K | A= | 2% | 2.130 Ug |
| SELENIUM | A======== | 16% | 0.020 Mg |
| BIOTIN | A== | 4% | 6.240 Ug |
| CHLORIDE | A==== | 8% | 287.0 Mg |
| CHROMIUM | A=================================================== | 384% | 0.480 Ug |
| SUGAR | A | NO RDA | 2.470 Gm |
| FIBER-DIET | A | NO RDA | 0.490 Gm |
| VIT. E/AT | A== | 4% | 0.370 Mg |

```
% RDA:   |0      |20     |40     |60     |80     |100
```

Margarine used instead of butter; vegetable bouillon cubes not included in analysis.

# PESTO SAUCE

☆ A strong, pungent sauce that's delicious on pasta and salads; a little bit goes a long way!

Some people swear that pesto doesn't taste like pesto unless it's ground in a mortar and pestle. This may be true, but with my limited time I use the blender . . . and have had no one complain yet.

2 cups fresh basil leaves
2 Tbsp. de-shelled pine nuts, raw or lightly toasted
½ cup olive oil
1 tsp. asafetida or 3 cloves garlic

½ cup Parmesan cheese
2 Tbsp. Romano cheese
½ tsp. black pepper
½ tsp. soy sauce

Blend first 4 ingredients together till smooth. Stop blender, add last 4 ingredients, and blend till thoroughly mixed and sauce is the consistency of a tomato puree. It's now ready to serve over a whole grain pasta of your choice; or for a tasty new touch, incorporate into a salad like the one following. This recipe makes about 2 cups of Pesto Sauce.

| SHOPPING LIST | |
| --- | --- |
| Regularly Kept in the Kitchen (Listed in Chapter 14, p. 703) | Fresh Produce |
| Olive oil<br>Asafetida<br>Black pepper<br>Soy sauce<br>Parmesan cheese | Fresh basil<br>Pine nuts |

# TOMATO FANS

☆ A simple salad that makes the most of good flavor combinations.

Compared to most hard cheeses, provolone and mozzarella cheese are relatively low in cholesterol and saturated fat.

1 oz. cheddar cheese contains —
30.3 mg. cholesterol
6 gm. saturated fat

1 oz. provolone contains —
20 mg. cholesterol
4.9 gm. saturated fat

1 oz. part-skim milk mozzarella contains —
16.2 mg. cholesterol
2.9 gm. saturated fat

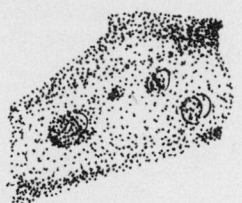

6 *large tomatoes*
*Pesto Sauce (see preceding recipe)*
*Provolone cheese slices*
*Watercress*

Cut tomatoes in half, cutting from top through to bottom, and remove brown spot where stem connects. Place tomato halves on cutting board with cut side facing down. With knife parallel to the cutting board, slice across tomatoes to make slices ¼" to ⅜" thick. Be sure to leave layered slices still joined on one end by not cutting all the way through. Fill alternating spaces between layers with thinly sliced provolone cheese (⅛" to ¼" thick) and Pesto Sauce. When each space between tomato layers is filled, insert 4 decorated toothpicks through all the layers. Then cut each tomato half into quarters so you end up with 4 stacks of layered tomato (from each half) held together with toothpicks.

Serve on a bed of watercress dressed with a light Italian or vinegarette dressing. As a small dinner salad, this makes 12 servings (½ tomato each).

| SHOPPING LIST | |
|---|---|
| **Regularly Kept in the Kitchen** (Listed in Chapter 14, p. 703) | **Fresh Produce** |
| Provolone or mozzarella cheese | Tomatoes Watercress |

# SAP SAGO CHEESE

☆ An herbed, therefore light-green, Swedish cheese that can be used as an even lower-fat replacement for Parmesan cheese.

Finely grate a cone of Sap Sago cheese in a food processor or with a very fine hand grater. (It should be grated as finely as Parmesan cheese.) Spread out on a baking sheet and bake at 275 degrees till golden brown, stirring from time to time. If grated, Sap Sago cheese clumps together a little while baking. Break it apart with fingertips or allow finished cheese to cool and run in blender or food processor again to break up small lumps.

Sap Sago cheese doesn't have to be baked; it can be used as is. I bake it to turn it a more appetizing golden brown (rather than pale green), and to mellow its strong smell and sharp taste.

# MOUNTAINOUS BREAKFAST

☆ One of those extremely nutritious breakfasts that help start the day off right.

1 banana, cubed
1 apple, cubed
½ papaya, cubed

¼ cup rolled oats
2 Tbsp. wheat germ
1 Tbsp. bran
2 Tbsp. raisins or diced dates

½ cup yogurt

Sliced almonds

Even though yogurt is a dairy product containing some cholesterol and saturated fat, studies have shown that it will actually lower serum cholesterol levels. Although there's some debate as to whether it's the bacteria culture, the calcium, or something else that brings this about, there's no debating that yogurt is a healthy way to consume dairy products.

Combine first 3 ingredients in a bowl. Sprinkle next 4 ingredients on top. Top with yogurt and sprinkle on sliced almonds. Makes 1 serving.

| SHOPPING LIST | |
|---|---|
| **Regularly Kept in the Kitchen**<br>**(Listed in Chapter 14, p. 703)** | **Fresh Produce** |
| Wheat germ<br>Bran<br>Raisins or dates<br>Yogurt<br>Almonds<br>Rolled oats | Banana<br>Apple<br>Papaya |

# NUTRITIONAL ANALYSIS FOR ONE SERVING
## MOUNTAINOUS BREAKFAST

| NUTRIENT | Type: 14   FEMALE-23 TO 51 YEARS | % RDA | Amount |
|---|---|---|---|
| KCALORIES | A================ | 30% | 614.0 Kc |
| PROTEIN | A==================== | 40% | 18.00 Gm |
| CARBOHYDRATE | A | NO RDA | 113.0 Gm |
| FAT | A | NO RDA | 15.30 Gm |
| FIBER-CRUDE | A | NO RDA | 4.330 Gm |
| CHOLESTEROL | A | NO RDA | 7.000 Mg |
| SATURATED FA | A | NO RDA | 6.050 Gm |
| OLEIC FA | A | NO RDA | 0.460 Gm |
| LINOLEIC FA | A | NO RDA | 0.170 Gm |
| SODIUM | A== | 4% | 100.0 Mg |
| POTASSIUM | A======================= | 47% | 1781 Mg |
| MAGNESIUM | A============================ | 57% | 171.0 Mg |
| IRON | A=========== | 23% | 4.270 Mg |
| ZINC | A======== | 17% | 2.660 Mg |
| VITAMIN A | A========================================= | 82% | 3307 IU |
| VITAMIN D | A | 0% | 0.000 IU |
| VIT. E/TOTAL | A | NO RDA | 1.450 Mg |
| VITAMIN C | A===================================================== | 188% | 113.0 Mg |
| THIAMIN | A============================ | 57% | 0.570 Mg |
| RIBOFLAVIN | A=============================== | 62% | 0.750 Mg |
| NIACIN | A=============== | 31% | 4.040 Mg |
| VITAMIN B6 | A========================= | 50% | 1.000 Mg |
| FOLACIN | A======= | 14% | 57.70 Ug |
| VITAMIN B12 | A========== | 21% | 0.640 Ug |
| PANTO- ACID | A=============== | 31% | 1.740 Mg |
| CALCIUM | A====================== | 44% | 354.0 Mg |
| PHOSPHORUS | A=================================== | 71% | 571.0 Mg |
| TRYPTOPHAN | A============================== | 62% | 102.0 Mg |
| THREONINE | A============================================= | 91% | 399.0 Mg |
| ISOLEUCINE | A===================================== | 75% | 492.0 Mg |
| LEUCINE | A==================================================== | 105% | 915.0 Mg |
| LYSINE | A====================================================== | 112% | 735.0 Mg |
| METHIONINE | A======================================== | 81% | 223.0 Mg |
| CYSTINE | A=========== | 22% | 62.50 Mg |
| PHENYL-ANINE | A========================================================= | 119% | 518.0 Mg |
| TYROSINE | A================================================ | 96% | 421.0 Mg |
| VALINE | A============================================= | 91% | 700.0 Mg |
| HISTIDINE | A | NO RDA | 328.0 Mg |
| ALCOHOL | A | NO RDA | 0.000 Gm |
| ASH | A | NO RDA | 4.870 Gm |
| COPPER | A========== | 20% | 0.510 Mg |
| MANGANESE | A================== | 35% | 1.330 Mg |
| IODINE | A==================== | 41% | 62.00 Ug |
| MONO FAT | A | NO RDA | 3.600 Gm |
| POLY FAT | A | NO RDA | 1.940 Gm |
| CAFFEINE | A | NO RDA | 0.000 Mg |
| FLUORIDE | A== | 4% | 120.0 Ug |
| MOLYBDENUM | A============================ | 55% | 179.0 Ug |
| VITAMIN K | A | 0% | 0.000 Ug |
| SELENIUM | A | 0% | 0.000 Mg |
| BIOTIN | A=== | 6% | 9.570 Ug |
| CHLORIDE | A | 0% | 9.000 Mg |
| CHROMIUM | A======== | 16% | 0.020 Mg |
| SUGAR | A | NO RDA | 30.40 Gm |
| FIBER-DIET | A | NO RDA | 8.130 Gm |
| VIT. E/AT | A======= | 15% | 1.260 Mg |

```
% RDA:   |0      |20      |40      |60      |80     |100
```

Raisins used instead of dates in analysis.

# YOGURT BANANA SPLIT

☆ A healthier version of a banana split; for equal weights, yogurt contains about 11 milligrams cholesterol to ice cream's 59 milligrams.

---

If buying commercially-made yogurt with fruit on the bottom instead of using homemade yogurt, you should know that most commercial yogurts contain as much sugar as a 12-ounce can of soda.

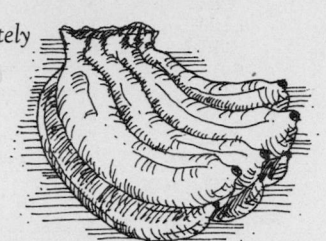

*1 banana, split lengthwise*
*3 different kinds of fruit, diced separately*

*1 cup yogurt with fruit or carob syrup*
  *(or use naturally sweetened*
  *fruit-flavored commercial yogurt)*
*Chopped nuts*
*Wheat germ*

Split banana in half lengthwise and place in long, shallow dish (like a banana split dish). Dice 3 different kinds of fruit and pile them in 3 separate mounds between banana slices. Pour yogurt on top of fruit and cover with fruit or carob syrup, or invert a naturally sweetened fruit-flavored yogurt on top. Sprinkle with nuts and wheat germ. Makes 1 serving.

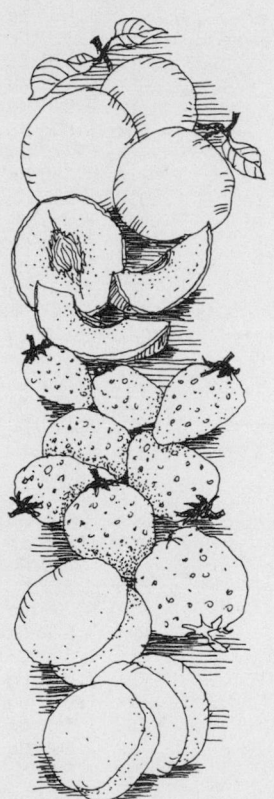

| SHOPPING LIST | |
|---|---|
| **Regularly Kept in the Kitchen** (Listed in Chapter 14, p. 703) | **Fresh Produce** |
| Yogurt or natural store-bought yogurt Nuts Wheat germ | Bananas 3 different kinds of fruit |

# YOGURT CHEESE

☆ Makes a cheese the texture of cream cheese with a pleasant yogurt tartness.

---

*1 quart nonfat plain yogurt*
*1 cup water*

Mix both ingredients together, then pour into a plain muslin teacloth or 3 thicknesses of cheesecloth. Tie ends of cloth together and hang somewhere to drain for 8 to 12 hours or overnight. The whey will drip out at the bottom of the cloth, so be sure to place something underneath to catch it. Makes about 2 cups.

Use in place of cream cheese. If you want to make a flavored cream cheese, mix in your favorite flavoring (such as fresh chives, dill, chili peppers, pimentos, or other combinations) either after your cheese has been made or beforehand as in the following recipe.

I prefer making my own yogurt cheese, although it is available in most natural food stores. It (and yogurt itself) can be made at home for about a quarter the cost of the shelf price in a store.

| SHOPPING LIST | |
|---|---|
| Regularly Kept in the Kitchen (Listed in Chapter 14, p. 703) | Fresh Produce |
| Yogurt | (None) |

# SOUTH·OF·THE·BORDER SPREAD

*4 cups yogurt*
*1 can pitted olives, sliced*
*2 tsp. chili powder*

*Salsa*

Mix brine of sliced olives and sliced olives into yogurt and spicing. Then hang as for Yogurt Cheese (see preceding recipe) for 6 to 8 hours or overnight.

Unmold onto serving platter and pour salsa over it. Serve with corn chips.

Use the same principle of this recipe to make different vegetable- or fruit-flavored yogurt cheeses, not unlike the cream cheeses speckled with different flavor combinations of vegetables or fruit found in many gourmet cheese shops.

| SHOPPING LIST | |
|---|---|
| Regularly Kept in the Kitchen (Listed in Chapter 14, p. 703) | Fresh Produce |
| Yogurt Chili powder | Ripe olives Salsa |

Whenever I have a choice of nuts, my personal preference is almonds. I choose them for their sweet flavor and the fact that they're a little lower in oil content than some other nuts.

# NOT·AS·RICH·
# AS·YOU·THINK PIE

☆ A wonderful dessert that takes a lot of pre-planning but very little time to make.

---

*1 cup commercial carob chips, or use carob mixture from Carob Candies recipe (see p. 223)*

*1¼ cups finely chopped nuts (cashews, almonds, or pecans preferred)*
*1 Tbsp. safflower oil*

*1 cup fruit-flavored yogurt*
*1 cup Yogurt Cheese*
*1 tsp. vanilla extract*

*1 cup evaporated skim milk, chilled in freezer 1½ - 2 hours*

*Finely chopped or shaved carob chips or candy bar*

Put mixing bowl and electric mixer blades in freezer the day before preparing; the can of evaporated skim milk, 2 hours before.

Melt commercial carob chips in top of a double boiler, or make 1 recipe of carob mixture for Carob Candies by omitting the nuts and raisins but being sure to include the honey or maple syrup sweetener.

Mix in next 2 ingredients thoroughly. Press mixture into a 9" pie pan and put in freezer.

In the meantime, whip next 3 ingredients together in a bowl till thoroughly mixed. Next, whip evaporated milk. (In order to whip evaporated milk, the can of skim milk must be chilled in the freezer for 1½ to 2 hours, and the whipper and bowl must be chilled in the freezer starting the night before. Whip with electric mixer till about tripled in volume. Fold gently into yogurt mixture and pour into frozen pie crust.

Return to freezer or refrigerator to chill. Just before serving, sprinkle with carob chips or shavings from carob bar. Makes one 9" pie.

# DIET CHEATER'S PEANUT BUTTER CHEESECAKE

*1 cup carob cookie crumbs*
*½ cup butter or margarine*

*3 (4-oz.) packages Neufchatel cheese*
*¾ cup chunky peanut butter*
*¾ cup honey*
*2 Tbsp. whole wheat flour*
*2 Tbsp. Bipro*
*1¼ cups milk*

*¼ cup honey*
*½ cup carob powder*
*½ cup noninstant, lowfat milk powder*
*1 tsp. vanilla*
*¾ cup nonfat or lowfat milk*

Blend old carob cookies in blender to make crumbs. Mix crumbs with ½ cup butter or margarine and press mixture into the bottom of a cheesecake pan. Be sure to dip hands in water while pressing to prevent crust from sticking to your hands. Mix next 6 ingredients together in a bowl till smooth and pour on top of crust. Mix next 5 ingredients and drizzle back and forth over top of cheesecake in the shell. With a butter knife, cut down into cheesecake mixture, being careful not to cut through to the crust. Cross syrup lines so syrup marbleizes cheesecake filling. Bake at 350 degrees for 1 hour

We can thank George Washington Carver for peanut butter. I'm sure that he would want us to thank God also! I'm not saying that lightly; the famed botanist wrote many times about how he felt that he wasn't doing the work but was simply an instrument of God. The story of how peanut butter came to be is exemplary of this. He got the farmers in the South to grow peanuts to replenish soil that had been depleted by year after year of cotton crops. When the farmers came to him for a solution as to what to do with all the peanuts, he went to the forest and prayed. Crediting God with giving him the intelligence, he then went into the laboratory and invented 300 different ways to use the peanut. Peanut butter was one of them!

and 10 minutes or till knife inserted in the middle comes out clean. Allow to cool and refrigerate overnight before serving.

| Special Shopping | SHOPPING LIST | |
|---|---|---|
| | **Regularly Kept in the Kitchen (Listed in Chapter 14, p. 703)** | **Fresh Produce** |
| Carob cookie crumbs — naturally sweetened cookies found in natural food stores, or use homemade (as on p. 229).<br>Neufchatel cheese — in some supermarket cheese sections or gourmet cheese shops. | Butter or margarine<br>Peanut butter<br>Honey<br>Whole wheat flour<br>Bipro<br>Milk<br>Carob<br>Vanilla | (None) |

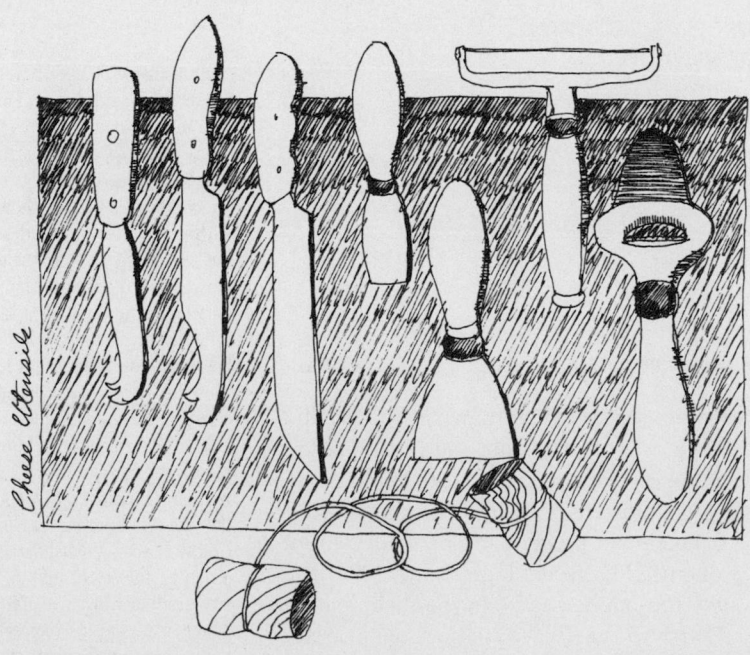

# NUTRITIONAL ANALYSIS FOR ONE SERVING
## DIET CHEATER'S PEANUT BUTTER CHEESECAKE

| NUTRIENT | Type: 14   FEMALE-23 TO 51 YEARS | % RDA | Amount |
|---|---|---|---|
| KCALORIES | A============ | 22% | 455.0 Kc |
| PROTEIN | A============ | 25% | 11.20 Gm |
| CARBOHYDRATE | A | NO RDA | 52.90 Gm |
| FAT | A | NO RDA | 25.00 Gm |
| FIBER-CRUDE | A | NO RDA | 1.230 Gm |
| CHOLESTEROL | A | NO RDA | 11.50 Mg |
| SATURATED FA | A | NO RDA | 5.150 Gm |
| OLEIC FA | A | NO RDA | 5.510 Gm |
| LINOLEIC FA | A | NO RDA | 6.940 Gm |
| SODIUM | A======= | 14% | 314.0 Mg |
| POTASSIUM | A===== | 10% | 404.0 Mg |
| MAGNESIUM | A========= | 18% | 56.90 Mg |
| IRON | A=== | 6% | 1.120 Mg |
| ZINC | A==== | 8% | 1.240 Mg |
| VITAMIN A | A====== | 12% | 507.0 IU |
| VITAMIN D | A==== | 8% | 17.00 IU |
| VIT. E/TOTAL | A | NO RDA | 6.020 Mg |
| VITAMIN C | A | 1% | 0.750 Mg |
| THIAMIN | A====== | 13% | 0.130 Mg |
| RIBOFLAVIN | A========== | 20% | 0.240 Mg |
| NIACIN | A============ | 24% | 3.140 Mg |
| VITAMIN B6 | A==== | 8% | 0.160 Mg |
| FOLACIN | A=== | 6% | 26.40 Ug |
| VITAMIN B12 | A====== | 12% | 0.380 Ug |
| PANTO- ACID | A======= | 14% | 0.790 Mg |
| CALCIUM | A========= | 20% | 162.0 Mg |
| PHOSPHORUS | A============== | 28% | 224.0 Mg |
| TRYPTOPHAN | A==================================================== | 96% | 157.0 Mg |
| THREONINE | A==================================================== | 96% | 419.0 Mg |
| ISOLEUCINE | A============================================= | 83% | 542.0 Mg |
| LEUCINE | A========================================================= | 111% | 968.0 Mg |
| LYSINE | A==================================================== | 99% | 651.0 Mg |
| METHIONINE | A====================================== | 72% | 178.0 Mg |
| CYSTINE | A============================ | 55% | 152.0 Mg |
| PHENYL-ANINE | A==================================================== | 134% | 585.0 Mg |
| TYROSINE | A==================================================== | 118% | 516.0 Mg |
| VALINE | A========================================= | 79% | 606.0 Mg |
| HISTIDINE | A | NO RDA | 312.0 Mg |
| ALCOHOL | A | NO RDA | 0.000 Gm |
| ASH | A | NO RDA | 1.760 Gm |
| COPPER | A=== | 6% | 0.160 Mg |
| MANGANESE | A=========== | 22% | 0.830 Mg |
| IODINE | A===================== | 43% | 65.70 Ug |
| MONO FAT | A | NO RDA | 9.080 Gm |
| POLY FAT | A | NO RDA | 9.500 Gm |
| CAFFEINE | A | NO RDA | 0.000 Mg |
| FLUORIDE | A= | 2% | 60.10 Ug |
| MOLYBDENUM | A================================= | 258% | 841.0 Ug |
| VITAMIN K | A= | 2% | 2.360 Ug |
| SELENIUM | A | 0% | 0.000 Mg |
| BIOTIN | A=== | 6% | 9.500 Ug |
| CHLORIDE | A | 1% | 36.20 Mg |
| CHROMIUM | A==================================================== | 104% | 0.130 Mg |
| SUGAR | A | NO RDA | 0.000 Gm |
| FIBER-DIET | A | NO RDA | 3.710 Gm |
| VIT. E/AT | A==================== | 41% | 3.340 Mg |

```
% RDA:   |0      |20     |40     |60     |80     |100
```

Margarine used instead of butter; lowfat milk used instead of nonfat; carob cookie crumbs from Homemade Ready Mix.

In his address to the Swedish Peace Congress, Leo Tolstoy said, "However much you may pervert the Christian teaching, however much you may hide its main principles, its fundamental teaching is the love of God and one's neighbor; of God, that is the highest perfection of virtue; and of one's neighbor, that is of all men without distinction. And, therefore, it would seem inevitable that we must repudiate one of the two — either the teaching of love of God and one's neighbors, or the state with its armies and wars."

# SOMETHING GOOD FROM RUSSIA

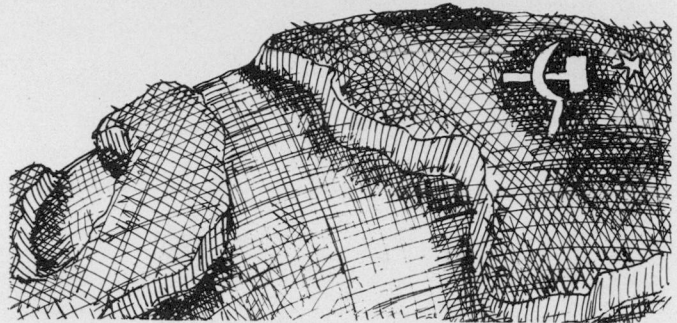

Having long thought of Russian food as boiled cabbage, lots of meat and Vodka, I was pleasantly surprised to be able to make a meal to be served as a light lunch or supper with a Russian theme, using some food and recipe ideas that originated there. The world would surely be in a different state of affairs if we could be as open-minded and -hearted about understanding other people and cultures as we are about their food. Although the typical Russian diet, like the average American diet, is not a healthful one, there are certain tribes that live in the Caucaus Mountains in Russia whose diet and lifestyle are worth studying.

In fact, the tribes of centenarians (people who live to the age of 100 or more) inhabiting Soviet Abkasia have been the subject of many studies, books and articles. Studies have shown that these mentally alert, sprightly and generally very slim centenarians eat an average of 1,700 to 1,900 calories a day (more than most elderly, or dieting, people in America consume), and that younger adults eat 2,500 to 3,000 calories a day. Those calories are made up of mostly complex carbohydrates, as they eat very moderate amounts of protein foods (between 15 and 20 percent) and sparse amounts of fat (less than 10 percent). About 70 to 75 percent of their diet is made up of plant foods, with milk and milk products being their primary protein food. One mainstay is a cultured milk product they call *matzoni*, which resembles cultured buttermilk. In a nutshell, other dietary habits that contribute to their good health are —

• They eat large quantities of fresh fruit, which is available about three-fourths of the year. Whole pieces of fresh fruit and matzoni are their healthful snack food.

• They use honey as a sweetener; no refined sugar (or any

325

other refined products, for that matter).

• Vegetables are most commonly served raw or cooked in very small amounts of water.

• They drink no coffee or tea, preferring spring water to well water.

Along with *what* they eat, how and when they eat also contributes to their physical well-being. The authors of all the articles and books I've read on the Azerbaijans have made mention of what small bites they take and how long they chew their food, so it must be done at such a rate as to stand out in contrast to our pace of eating. They eat an early, substantial breakfast (about 7 - 8 a.m.), a hearty dinner at around midday (2 - 3 p.m.), a very light snack or meal later in the afternoon, and avoid eating shortly before bedtime. In relation to how many calories they consume, it's necessary to point out that they are not a sedentary people. Rather, from youth to old age they are all very physically active and agile.

Of course, eating isn't the only thing to take into consideration. There are other practices and aspects of their society, especially detailed in *The Long Living People* by Sula Benet, which also contribute to their good health and longevity. However, since this is a cookbook, I'll leave you with the following recipes, recommending that you read Benet's book for information about other lifestyle practices that can make a difference in your life.

# COOLING BEET BORSCHT

☆ Such an amazingly pretty soup, you may want to just look at it . . . only until after the first bite!

---

2 large, fresh beets (about 3" in diameter)
3 cups water

½ cup very thinly grated cucumber rounds
¼ cup finely minced green onions or scallions
1 Tbsp. lemon juice
1 tsp. honey
2 tsp. fresh dill weed (or 1 tsp. dry)
½ tsp. black pepper
½ tsp. Spike or other vegetable-seasoned salt

2 cups buttermilk

Yogurt (optional)
Dill pickle (optional)

Borscht has many forms but is always made with beets. It is sometimes made as a hearty stew that is served hot. This borscht is a light, cold soup which makes a light, refreshing dish to serve on hot days.

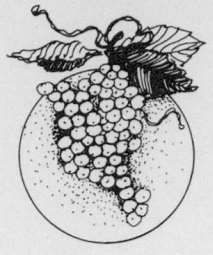

Wash beets and cut off long root and top. Quarter beets
and put them in a pot with the water. Bring to a boil, cover,
turn down heat and simmer for 15 minutes. Turn off heat and
remove lid. Allow to cool till beets can be handled. Slip beet
skin off and then coarsely grate all the beets right back into
the water they were cooked in. Add the next 7 ingredients
and refrigerate overnight, or place in the freezer for 2 hours if
you want to serve the borscht the same day. Right before serving, mix in the buttermilk. Serve in individual bowls with a
dollop of yogurt in the middle and topped with a thin slice of
dill pickle. Makes about 7 cups, which is 4 servings plus a little
for seconds.

| SHOPPING LIST | |
|---|---|
| Regularly Kept in the Kitchen (Listed in Chapter 14, p. 703) | Fresh Produce |
| Honey<br>Black pepper<br>Spike<br>Cultured buttermilk<br>Yogurt | Beets<br>Cucumber<br>Dill weed<br>Scallions<br>Lemon<br>Dill pickle |

# NUTRITIONAL ANALYSIS FOR ONE SERVING
## COOLING BEET BORSCHT

| NUTRIENT | Type: 14 FEMALE-23 TO 51 YEARS | % RDA | Amount |
|---|---|---|---|
| KCALORIES | A= | 3% | 72.10 Kc |
| PROTEIN | A===== | 10% | 4.720 Gm |
| CARBOHYDRATE | A | NO RDA | 11.10 Gm |
| FAT | A | NO RDA | 1.140 Gm |
| FIBER-CRUDE | A | NO RDA | 0.510 Gm |
| CHOLESTEROL | A | NO RDA | 4.500 Mg |
| SATURATED FA | A | NO RDA | 0.680 Gm |
| OLEIC FA | A | NO RDA | 0.250 Gm |
| LINOLEIC FA | A | NO RDA | 0.000 Gm |
| SODIUM | A====== | 12% | 271.0 Mg |
| POTASSIUM | A==== | 9% | 355.0 Mg |
| MAGNESIUM | A===== | 10% | 32.10 Mg |
| IRON | A= | 3% | 0.660 Mg |
| ZINC | A== | 4% | 0.690 Mg |
| VITAMIN A | A==== | 9% | 364.0 IU |
| VITAMIN D | A | 0% | 0.000 IU |
| VIT. E/TOTAL | A | NO RDA | 0.550 Mg |
| VITAMIN C | A======= | 14% | 8.430 Mg |
| THIAMIN | A=== | 6% | 0.060 Mg |
| RIBOFLAVIN | A======== | 16% | 0.200 Mg |
| NIACIN | A | 1% | 0.230 Mg |
| VITAMIN B6 | A= | 3% | 0.060 Mg |
| FOLACIN | A== | 5% | 23.10 Ug |
| VITAMIN B12 | A==== | 8% | 0.260 Ug |
| PANTO- ACID | A==== | 8% | 0.460 Mg |
| CALCIUM | A========== | 20% | 160.0 Mg |
| PHOSPHORUS | A======= | 15% | 124.0 Mg |
| TRYPTOPHAN | A=============== | 30% | 50.20 Mg |
| THREONINE | A======================= | 48% | 211.0 Mg |
| ISOLEUCINE | A==================== | 41% | 268.0 Mg |
| LEUCINE | A======================= | 49% | 430.0 Mg |
| LYSINE | A============================ | 56% | 372.0 Mg |
| METHIONINE | A=================== | 38% | 105.0 Mg |
| CYSTINE | A======== | 16% | 43.60 Mg |
| PHENYL-ANINE | A========================== | 52% | 230.0 Mg |
| TYROSINE | A===================== | 42% | 183.0 Mg |
| VALINE | A==================== | 41% | 319.0 Mg |
| HISTIDINE | A | NO RDA | 124.0 Mg |
| ALCOHOL | A | NO RDA | 0.000 Gm |
| ASH | A | NO RDA | 1.680 Gm |
| COPPER | A= | 2% | 0.060 Mg |
| MANGANESE | A= | 2% | 0.090 Mg |
| IODINE | A================== | 39% | 58.60 Ug |
| MONO FAT | A | NO RDA | 0.310 Gm |
| POLY FAT | A | NO RDA | 0.050 Gm |
| CAFFEINE | A | NO RDA | 0.000 Mg |
| FLUORIDE | A | 1% | 52.30 Ug |
| MOLYBDENUM | A | 0% | 0.120 Ug |
| VITAMIN K | A=== | 6% | 7.100 Ug |
| SELENIUM | A================================================= | 176% | 0.220 Mg |
| BIOTIN | A | 1% | 2.880 Ug |
| CHLORIDE | A | 0% | 3.360 Mg |
| CHROMIUM | A | 0% | 0.000 Mg |
| SUGAR | A | NO RDA | 3.920 Gm |
| FIBER-DIET | A | NO RDA | 0.060 Gm |
| VIT. E/AT | A | 0% | 0.030 Mg |

```
% RDA:   |0      |20     |40     |60     |80     |100
```

Green onions used instead of scallions; optional yogurt and dill pickle not included in analysis.

Sauerkraut is an example of how many people have benefited by being open-minded about what they can get and learn from other people and cultures. It originated in China as a way to preserve vegetables without refrigeration. The Tartars brought it to Russia, where it has become a staple. From Russia, sauerkraut was taken to Germany, where it's so widely used that most of us think of it as a German food. Though it's quite salty, a little bit of sauerkraut is healthy because enzymes created in the fermenting process help to aid digestion.

# RUEBEN SANDWICHES

☆ Replacing the usual ham or corned beef with seasoned yuba cuts down on the cholesterol and saturated fat.

---

*About 30 bacon-sized dried bean curd (yuba) strips*

*2 Tbsp. oil*
*1 tsp. black pepper*
*2 Tbsp. soy sauce*

*2 Tbsp. prepared mustard*

Soak the yuba strips in water till they soften. Cut into 30 bacon-sized strips and drain. Combine the next 3 ingredients and marinate the softened yuba strips for about 10 minutes. (You can be preparing the rest of the sandwich ingredients in the meantime. See list below.) Heat a skillet and saute the yuba strips and liquid till the liquid begins drying out. Add prepared mustard and turn off heat.

Now you can assemble the sandwiches provided you have already assembled and prepared the following:

1. Slices of whole grain pumpernickel/rye bread
2. Tofu Mayonnaise (see following recipe or use some other eggless mayonnaise)
3. Prepared mustard (optional)
4. Sauerkraut
5. Sliced tomatoes
6. Sliced Swiss cheese

Simply spread bread with eggless mayonnaise and some prepared mustard (depending on who wants the mustard and who doesn't). Next, put a layer of the Reuben Sandwich slices topped by a layer of sauerkraut, then a layer of tomato slices topped with slices of Swiss cheese. At this point you can make a hot, open-faced sandwich by placing sandwiches on an oiled cookie sheet and baking at 350 degrees for 10 minutes; or make a cold sandwich by enclosing it all with one final slice of pumpernickel/rye bread which has been spread with more Tofu Mayonnaise.

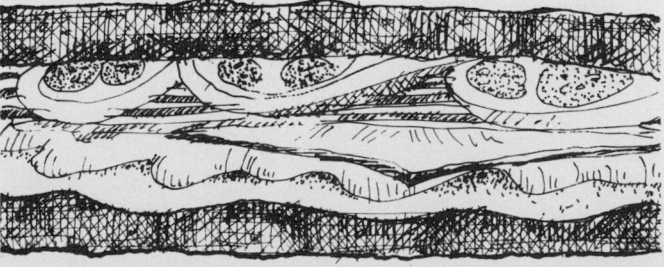

| SHOPPING LIST | |
| --- | --- |
| **Regularly Kept in the Kitchen (Listed in Chapter 14, p. 703)** | **Fresh Produce** |
| Yuba<br>Oil<br>Black pepper<br>Soy sauce<br>Prepared mustard<br>Eggless mayonnaise | Tomatoes<br>Swiss cheese |

**Special Shopping**

Whole grain rye or pumpernickel bread — read the label to make sure you are getting a whole grain bread rather than one that may be dark in color due to a caramel coloring which is often added to rye or pumpernickel breads; sometimes can be found in natural food stores, or make your own at home so you can be assured of the healthful ingredients.

# NUTRITIONAL ANALYSIS FOR ONE RUEBEN SANDWICH

| NUTRIENT | Type: 14  FEMALE-23 TO 51 YEARS | % RDA | Amount |
|----------|-------------------------------|-------|--------|
| KCALORIES | A==================== | 38% | 769.0 Kc |
| PROTEIN | A=================================================== | 162% | 71.50 Gm |
| CARBOHYDRATE | A | NO RDA | 45.60 Gm |
| FAT | A | NO RDA | 39.70 Gm |
| FIBER-CRUDE | A | NO RDA | 1.390 Gm |
| CHOLESTEROL | A | NO RDA | 13.90 Mg |
| SATURATED FA | A | NO RDA | 3.690 Gm |
| OLEIC FA | A | NO RDA | 8.740 Gm |
| LINOLEIC FA | A | NO RDA | 17.80 Gm |
| SODIUM | A===================== | 44% | 988.0 Mg |
| POTASSIUM | A=========== | 22% | 852.0 Mg |
| MAGNESIUM | A================================================= | 98% | 296.0 Mg |
| IRON | A=========================================== | 90% | 16.20 Mg |
| ZINC | A===== | 11% | 1.700 Mg |
| VITAMIN A | A============= | 26% | 1070 IU |
| VITAMIN D | A=== | 7% | 15.00 IU |
| VIT. E/TOTAL | A | NO RDA | 6.400 Mg |
| VITAMIN C | A=========== | 22% | 13.60 Mg |
| THIAMIN | A==================================== | 71% | 0.710 Mg |
| RIBOFLAVIN | A================ | 32% | 0.390 Mg |
| NIACIN | A================== | 37% | 4.840 Mg |
| VITAMIN B6 | A======= | 14% | 0.290 Mg |
| FOLACIN | A==== | 9% | 38.50 Ug |
| VITAMIN B12 | A==== | 8% | 0.250 Ug |
| PANTO- ACID | A======= | 15% | 0.870 Mg |
| CALCIUM | A==================================== | 72% | 577.0 Mg |
| PHOSPHORUS | A=========================================== | 118% | 948.0 Mg |
| TRYPTOPHAN | A=========================================== | 447% | 729.0 Mg |
| THREONINE | A=========================================== | 598% | 2605 Mg |
| ISOLEUCINE | A=========================================== | 543% | 3551 Mg |
| LEUCINE | A=========================================== | 636% | 5540 Mg |
| LYSINE | A=========================================== | 722% | 4717 Mg |
| METHIONINE | A=========================================== | 369% | 1004 Mg |
| CYSTINE | A=========================================== | 305% | 831.0 Mg |
| PHENYL-ANINE | A=========================================== | 825% | 3593 Mg |
| TYROSINE | A=========================================== | 623% | 2714 Mg |
| VALINE | A=========================================== | 477% | 3637 Mg |
| HISTIDINE | A | NO RDA | 1966 Mg |
| ALCOHOL | A | NO RDA | 0.000 Gm |
| ASH | A | NO RDA | 6.930 Gm |
| COPPER | A==================== | 43% | 1.090 Mg |
| MANGANESE | A=========================================== | 107% | 4.030 Mg |
| IODINE | A=========================================== | 247% | 371.0 Ug |
| MONO FAT | A | NO RDA | 2.030 Gm |
| POLY FAT | A | NO RDA | 5.330 Gm |
| CAFFEINE | A | NO RDA | 0.000 Mg |
| FLUORIDE | A | 1% | 28.30 Ug |
| MOLYBDENUM | A=========================================== | 3412% | 11091 Ug |
| VITAMIN K | A= | 2% | 2.900 Ug |
| SELENIUM | A================================ | 64% | 0.080 Mg |
| BIOTIN | A========== | 21% | 32.80 Ug |
| CHLORIDE | A== | 5% | 199.0 Mg |
| CHROMIUM | A=========================================== | 784% | 0.980 Mg |
| SUGAR | A | NO RDA | 2.920 Gm |
| FIBER-DIET | A | NO RDA | 21.60 Gm |
| VIT. E/AT | A================ | 32% | 2.600 Mg |

```
% RDA:   |0      |20     |40     |60     |80     |100
```

Tofu Mayonnaise used instead of commercial eggless in analysis.

# TOFU MAYONNAISE

☆ This makes a cholesterol-free mayonnaise which adds less fat and more nutrition than regular mayonnaise to whatever it's used in or on.

*½ lb. tofu*
*1 Tbsp. lecithin granules*
*1 Tbsp. oil*
*1½ tsp. honey*
*2 Tbsp. lemon juice*
*½ tsp. Spike or other vegetable-seasoned salt*
*⅛ tsp. asafetida or garlic powder*
*1 tsp. apple cider vinegar*

Put all ingredients in a blender and blend till smooth. Use on sandwiches or as a base for salad dressings. Unlike commercial mayonnaise, this will only keep a week or so, so it's better to make a small amount at a time. This makes 1½ to 2 cups.

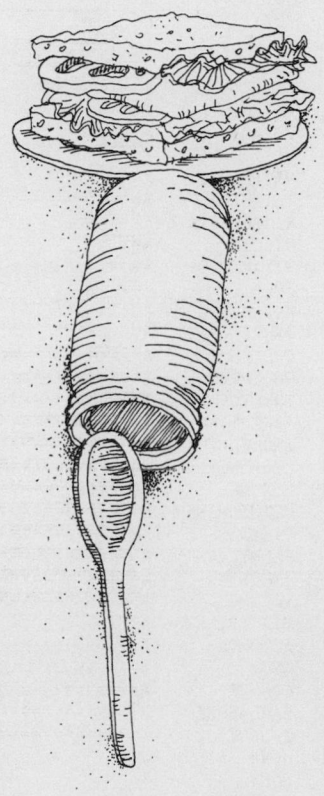

| SHOPPING LIST | |
| --- | --- |
| **Regularly Kept in the Kitchen** (Listed in Chapter 14, p. 703) | **Fresh Produce** |
| Tofu | Lemon |
| Safflower oil | |
| Honey | |
| Spike | |
| Asafetida | |
| Apple cider vinegar | |
| Lecithin granules | |

Only make as much as you need for a few days. Tofu is a very perishable food, and this Tofu Mayonnaise won't keep as long as regular mayonnaise.

# NUTRITIONAL ANALYSIS COMPARING
# TOFU MAYONNAISE WITH STANDARD MAYONNAISE

| NUTRIENT | Type: 14   FEMALE—23 TO 51 YEARS | Amount in Tofu Mayonnaise | Amount in standard mayonnaise |
|---|---|---|---|
| KCALORIES | ============ | 443.0 Kc | 1475 Kc |
| PROTEIN | ================================ | 29.70 Gm | 4.640 Gm |
| CARBOHYDRATE | ▆ | 16.60 Gm | 2.090 Gm |
| FAT | | 32.70 Gm | 164.0 Gm |
| FIBER—CRUDE | | 0.280 Gm | 0.070 Gm |
| CHOLESTEROL | | 0.000 Mg | 208.0 Mg |
| SATURATED FA | | 5.090 Gm | 28.20 Gm |
| OLEIC FA | | 3.220 Gm | 74.40 Gm |
| LINOLEIC FA | | 12.00 Gm | 50.00 Gm |
| SODIUM | ========== | 448.0 Mg | 772.0 Mg |
| POTASSIUM | ======= | 460.0 Mg | 77.30 Mg |
| MAGNESIUM | ================== | 109.0 Mg | 5.100 Mg |
| IRON | ================================================ | 19.70 Mg | 1.000 Mg |
| ZINC | ========= | 2.970 Mg | 0.590 Mg |
| VITAMIN A | === | 312.0 IU | 318.0 IU |
| VITAMIN D | ▆ | 0.000 IU | 21.20 IU |
| VIT. E/TOTAL | ▆ | 4.310 Mg | 40.40 Mg |
| VITAMIN C | = | 1.780 Mg | 0.220 Mg |
| THIAMIN | ================ | 0.300 Mg | 0.030 Mg |
| RIBOFLAVIN | ======= | 0.190 Mg | 0.110 Mg |
| NIACIN | == | 0.760 Mg | 0.040 Mg |
| VITAMIN B6 | ==== | 0.170 Mg | 0.040 Mg |
| FOLACIN | ====== | 55.50 Ug | 24.30 Ug |
| VITAMIN B12 | ▆ | 0.000 Ug | 0.580 Ug |
| PANTO— ACID | == | 0.270 Mg | 0.650 Mg |
| CALCIUM | ================================================= | 1289 Mg | 28.50 Mg |
| PHOSPHORUS | ===================== | 359.0 Mg | 71.40 Mg |
| TRYPTOPHAN | ================================================= | 463.0 Mg | 73.70 Mg |
| THREONINE | ======================================= | 1211 Mg | 226.0 Mg |
| ISOLEUCINE | ================================================= | 1473 Mg | 288.0 Mg |
| LEUCINE | ================================================= | 2258 Mg | 405.0 Mg |
| LYSINE | ================================================= | 1958 Mg | 311.0 Mg |
| METHIONINE | ================================= | 381.0 Mg | 148.0 Mg |
| CYSTINE | ================================================= | 411.0 Mg | 110.0 Mg |
| PHENYL—ANINE | ============================== | 1450 Mg | 260.0 Mg |
| TYROSINE | ================================================= | 979.0 Mg | 192.0 Mg |
| VALINE | ================================================= | 1503 Mg | 332.0 Mg |
| HISTIDINE | ============== | 867.0 Mg | 111.0 Mg |
| ALCOHOL | | 0.000 Gm | 0.000 Gm |
| ASH | | 2.640 Gm | 0.370 Gm |
| COPPER | ============== | 0.710 Mg | 0.080 Mg |
| MANGANESE | ============================== | 2.220 Mg | 0.020 Mg |
| IODINE | ================================================= | 250.0 Ug | 87.10 Ug |
| MONO FAT | | 4.980 Gm | 75.70 Gm |
| POLY FAT | | 20.10 Gm | 51.80 Gm |
| CAFFEINE | | 0.000 Mg | 0.000 Mg |
| FLUORIDE | | 8.720 Ug | 0.000 Ug |
| MOLYBDENUM | ================================================= | 2258 Ug | 0.000 Ug |
| VITAMIN K | | 0.000 Ug | 0.000 Ug |
| SELENIUM | ======== | 0.020 Mg | 0.020 Mg |
| BIOTIN | = | 5.460 Ug | 7.600 Ug |
| CHLORIDE | ===== | 357.0 Mg | 0.000 Mg |
| CHROMIUM | ================================================= | 0.560 Mg | 0.000 Mg |
| SUGAR | | 0.040 Gm | 0.000 Gm |
| FIBER—DIET | | 0.000 Gm | 0.000 Gm |
| VIT. E/AT | ======================== | 3.840 Mg | 18.80 Mg |

```
% RDA:    |0       |20      |40      |60      |80      |100        |0
```

Dotted line indicates Tofu Mayonnaise. Straight line indicates standard mayonnaise. Comparison is for an equal gram weight of Tofu Mayonnaise and standard mayonnaise.

# PIROSHKI QUICKER DOUGH

*2 cups whole wheat flour*
*2 tsp. baking powder*

*½ cup margarine or butter*

*⅓ cup water*

Preheat oven to 425 degrees and oil a cookie sheet.

Mix first 2 ingredients together in a mixing bowl. (Be sure to sift the baking powder so there won't be any lumps.) Add butter or margarine and cut into the dry ingredients till there are no large lumps of butter or margarine and the flour is a sand-like consistency. Make a little well in the middle of the flour and pour water into it. Mix thoroughly into a ball of dough and knead for 3 to 5 minutes. Cut ball of dough into eighths and roll each eighth into a ball. One at a time, roll each ball out about ⅛" thick on a very lightly floured counter and stuff with an eighth of the mushroom filling. Fold dough over filling to form a turnover. Pinch edges to seal together, then press edges with a fork. Place on an oiled cookie sheet and prick with a fork in 3 to 4 places on the top of turnover dough. Bake at 425 degrees for 15 minutes. Serve immediately. This recipe makes 8 large turnovers, ample and generous servings for 4 as the main part of the meal served along with the Borscht. These can also be made into many petite turnovers which can be served as hors d'oeuvres. Use this dough or the following Traditional Yeasted Dough.

| SHOPPING LIST | |
|---|---|
| **Regularly Kept in the Kitchen** (Listed in Chapter 14, p. 703) | **Fresh Produce** |
| Whole wheat flour<br>Baking powder<br>Butter or margarine | (None) |

Use one of these doughs for making Piroshki, depending on how much of a hurry you're in. The Traditional Yeasted Dough will take an extra 1½ to 2 hours to make.

# TRADITIONAL YEASTED DOUGH

*1½ tsp. baking yeast*
*1 cup warm water*
*2 tsp. honey*
*½ tsp. salt (optional)*

*3 cups whole wheat flour*

*Vegetable oil*

Combine first 4 ingredients together in a mixing bowl and allow to set about 5 minutes till baking yeast has dissolved. Mix in flour a little at a time till a firm ball of dough has formed. Then turn onto a floured counter and knead for 5 to 10 minutes. Rub vegetable oil on your hands and oil the ball of dough and the inside of the mixing bowl. Place dough back into bowl and allow to rise in a warm place till doubled in volume (about 1½ to 2 hours). You can prepare the filling, etc., as it is rising. This dough is cut, rolled and stuffed the same as the preceding Quicker Dough recipe but must be baked at 450 degrees for 20 minutes. Makes the same amount as the Piroshki Quicker Dough.

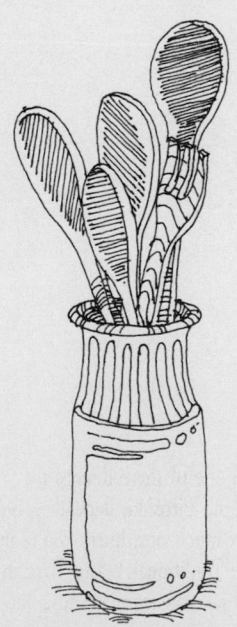

| SHOPPING LIST | |
|---|---|
| **Regularly Kept in the Kitchen** (Listed in Chapter 14, p. 703) | **Fresh Produce** |
| Baking yeast<br>Honey<br>Whole wheat flour<br>Vegetable oil | (None) |

# PIROSHKI FILLING

☆ Just cook the filling ever so lightly in the skillet;
  remember that it will cook more in the oven.

1 Tbsp. butter or vegetable oil
1 cup finely sliced celery
½ tsp. asafetida or 2 cloves garlic, minced

1 lb. mushrooms, chopped
1 Tbsp. lemon juice
½ tsp. black pepper

½ cup wheat germ or whole wheat bread crumbs
¼ cup chopped, toasted sunflower seeds
¼ cup finely chopped fresh parsley
2 cups cottage cheese
1 Tbsp. soy sauce

### SUGGESTED MENU FOR A LIGHT LUNCH OR SUPPER

*Borscht*

*Rueben Sandwiches
or Piroshki*

• *Tossed green salad*

Saute first 3 ingredients together till celery begins to turn
translucent. Add next 3 ingredients and saute 2 to 3 minutes.
(I usually add the mushrooms whole in the skillet and chop
them with the end of the spatula. By the time they're all
chopped, it's time to go on to the next step.) Turn off and
remove from heat. Add next 5 ingredients and mix in well. If
dough is divided into eighths, this filling should be also.
Makes 8 large turnovers (or many, many small ones) to serve
4 for dinner.

| SHOPPING LIST | |
| --- | --- |
| **Regularly Kept in the Kitchen (Listed in Chapter 14, p. 703)** | **Fresh Produce** |
| Butter or vegetable oil | Celery |
| Asafetida | Mushrooms |
| Black pepper | Lemon |
| Wheat germ or | Parsley |
|    whole wheat bread | |
| Sunflower seeds | |
| Cottage cheese | |
| Soy sauce | |

# NUTRITIONAL ANALYSIS FOR ONE SERVING
## TRADITIONAL YEASTED DOUGH WITH PIROSHKI FILLING

| NUTRIENT | Type: 14   FEMALE-23 TO 51 YEARS | % RDA | Amount |
|---|---|---|---|
| KCALORIES | Å================= | 30% | 611.0 Kc |
| PROTEIN | Å======================================== | 84% | 37.10 Gm |
| CARBOHYDRATE | Å | NO RDA | 87.60 Gm |
| FAT | Å | NO RDA | 15.90 Gm |
| FIBER-CRUDE | Å | NO RDA | 3.920 Gm |
| CHOLESTEROL | Å | NO RDA | 9.500 Mg |
| SATURATED FA | Å | NO RDA | 3.000 Gm |
| OLEIC FA | Å | NO RDA | 2.750 Gm |
| LINOLEIC FA | Å | NO RDA | 8.500 Gm |
| SODIUM | Å======================= | 45% | 996.0 Mg |
| POTASSIUM | Å================= | 32% | 1214 Mg |
| MAGNESIUM | Å=================================== | 69% | 207.0 Mg |
| IRON | Å==================== | 40% | 7.230 Mg |
| ZINC | Å==================== | 40% | 6.100 Mg |
| VITAMIN A | Å==== | 8% | 354.0 IU |
| VITAMIN D | Å= | 3% | 6.720 IU |
| VIT. E/TOTAL | Å | NO RDA | 14.30 Mg |
| VITAMIN C | Å========== | 20% | 12.40 Mg |
| THIAMIN | Å========================================================= | 111% | 1.110 Mg |
| RIBOFLAVIN | Å=========================================== | 85% | 1.030 Mg |
| NIACIN | Å========================================= | 80% | 10.50 Mg |
| VITAMIN B6 | Å================== | 39% | 0.790 Mg |
| FOLACIN | Å======================= | 46% | 184.0 Ug |
| VITAMIN B12 | Å============= | 26% | 0.800 Ug |
| PANTO- ACID | Å===================================== | 77% | 4.240 Mg |
| CALCIUM | Å========== | 20% | 161.0 Mg |
| PHOSPHORUS | Å======================================================= | 110% | 880.0 Mg |
| TRYPTOPHAN | Å================================================ | 274% | 447.0 Mg |
| THREONINE | Å================================================ | 329% | 1432 Mg |
| ISOLEUCINE | Å================================================ | 281% | 1835 Mg |
| LEUCINE | Å================================================ | 349% | 3044 Mg |
| LYSINE | Å================================================ | 349% | 2285 Mg |
| METHIONINE | Å================================================ | 305% | 832.0 Mg |
| CYSTINE | Å================================================ | 195% | 533.0 Mg |
| PHENYL-ANINE | Å================================================ | 421% | 1832 Mg |
| TYROSINE | Å================================================ | 347% | 1512 Mg |
| VALINE | Å================================================ | 263% | 2009 Mg |
| HISTIDINE | Å | NO RDA | 1057 Mg |
| ALCOHOL | Å | NO RDA | 0.000 Gm |
| ASH | Å | NO RDA | 6.020 Gm |
| COPPER | Å================= | 33% | 0.840 Mg |
| MANGANESE | Å============================================= | 182% | 6.850 Mg |
| IODINE | Å============================================= | 328% | 492.0 Ug |
| MONO FAT | Å | NO RDA | 2.390 Gm |
| POLY FAT | Å | NO RDA | 8.350 Gm |
| CAFFEINE | Å | NO RDA | 0.000 Mg |
| FLUORIDE | Å== | 5% | 145.0 Ug |
| MOLYBDENUM | Å============================================= | 1809% | 5880 Ug |
| VITAMIN K | Å | 0% | 0.000 Ug |
| SELENIUM | Å============================ | 64% | 0.080 Mg |
| BIOTIN | Å==== | 9% | 13.50 Ug |
| CHLORIDE | Å== | 5% | 203.0 Mg |
| CHROMIUM | Å============================================= | 488% | 0.610 Mg |
| SUGAR | Å | NO RDA | 0.840 Gm |
| FIBER-DIET | Å | NO RDA | 17.30 Gm |
| VIT. E/AT | Å============================================= | 126% | 10.10 Mg |

```
% RDA:   |0      |20     |40     |60     |80     |100
```

Optional salt was included in the dough; vegetable oil used instead of butter; wheat germ used instead of bread crumbs in the filling.

# SAY CHEESE!

Henry David Thoreau wrote —
"The finest qualities of our nature, like the bloom on fruits, can be preserved only by the most delicate handling. Yet we do not treat ourselves nor one another thus tenderly."

Years of material conditioning can cover our true nature so we appear hard to others and even ourselves. To be able to treat each other as Thoreau idealized, we need to become free from material conditioning — primarily from identifying ourselves and others as the material body — so we can relate to others as the sensitive living beings that they are.

Even in the category of "not used very often cheeses," there are some that are better choices than others.

Parmesan cheese is my first choice of hard cheeses, as it's relatively low in saturated fat and cholesterol and very little is needed; however, it doesn't always work because it doesn't melt like most hard cheeses do (due to its relatively low fat content). When a recipe calls for a melting cheese, I try to use part-skim mozzarella, unless the recipe would be ruined without the specific taste of a particular cheese (like Cheddar). Looking at the table (p. 308), part-skim mozzarella is the choice for obvious reasons; of all hard cheeses, it's about the lowest in cholesterol and saturated fat.

If I must use Cheddar — or some other cheese about as high in cholesterol and saturated fat content — for its flavor, I try to limit the amount I use. The amount of cheese most recipes call for usually can safely be cut in half. The technique of using a long, flat pan instead of a tall, deep one (as on p. 348) is one way of getting a good, cheesy flavor with less cheese.

For the creamy flavor and texture of cream cheese, I use Neufchatel cheese. This is one substitute where neither flavor nor texture is compromised. As can be seen in the table (p. 308), Neufchatel cheese is considerably lower in cholesterol, saturated fat and, therefore, caloric content, but it is still a very rich cheese. Reserve this cheese and the dishes made with it for special-occasion treats a few times a year.

# FRIED MOZZARELLA

☆ To be served as an entree, an accent to salads or an hors d'oeuvres plate, depending on what size the cheese is cut.

---

*Part-skim string or mozzarella cheese*

*¾ cup water*
*1 Tbsp. arrowroot*

*1 Tbsp. lemon juice*

*1 cup fine whole wheat bread crumbs*
*1 Tbsp. arrowroot*
*1 tsp. white pepper*
*1/16 tsp. cayenne*

Cut cheese. For serving as an entree, leave the string cheese the width it is and cut in 3" to 4" lengths; cut mozzarella in sticks ¾" x 3" to 4". For serving as an hors d'oeuvres or an addition to salad, leave string cheese the width it is and cut into 1" to 1½" lengths; cut mozzarella into ¾" cubes.

Mix next 2 ingredients together in a small pot till arrowroot dissolves. Put over flame and stir constantly till mixture comes to a boil and thickens. Remove from heat and stir in lemon juice. In a separate bowl, combine next 4 ingredients.

Prepare large skillet for frying; I use a well-seasoned cast iron skillet and lightly wipe it with a little vegetable oil. Whatever kind of skillet you have, use a small amount of oil because fat will come out of the cheese as it fries, which will help to keep it from sticking. Heat skillet over high heat; if skillet isn't hot enough, breading won't form a hard crust to hold heated cheese inside and it will melt all over the pan. Dip each piece of cheese into thickened arrowroot mixture and then into crumb mixture to bread the cheese and immediately put into skillet. Leave 1½" to 2" of space between each piece of cheese so cheese has room to melt and spread a bit. Fry till breading turns golden brown on one side, flip and cook on other side till breading turns a golden brown.

Remove from skillet. To serve as an entree, put 2 to 3 long pieces of fried cheese per plate on a bed of watercress and top with a sauce (either your favorite sugar-free spaghetti sauce, the Quicker Than "From Scratch" Pasta Sauce, p. 359, or the following Green Sauce). Small, flat patties are a nice addition to a crudite plate for hors d'oeuvres or placed on your favorite salad.

For sandwiches, try slicing part-skim mozzarella about ⅛" thick and fry in a well-seasoned cast iron skillet that's been wiped with oil. Cheese will spread out, so leave a few inches between each slice. Fry till cheese turns a reddish-brown on one side, flip and fry the same way on the other side. Put between your favorite whole grain bread and top with standard sandwich vegetables.

| SHOPPING LIST | |
|---|---|
| **Regularly Kept in the Kitchen (Listed in Chapter 14, p. 703)** | **Fresh Produce** |
| Part-skim mozzarella cheese<br>Arrowroot<br>Whole wheat bread<br>White pepper<br>Cayenne | Lemon |

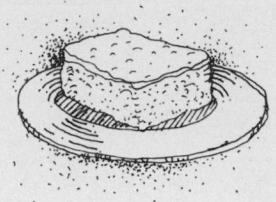

## NUTRITIONAL ANALYSIS FOR ONE RECIPE FRIED MOZZARELLA

| NUTRIENT | Type: 14   FEMALE-23 TO 51 YEARS | % RDA | Amount |
|---|---|---|---|
| KCALORIES | Ᾱ================================= | 71% | 1420 Kc |
| PROTEIN | Ᾱ===================================== | 268% | 118.0 Gm |
| CARBOHYDRATE | Ᾱ | NO RDA | 61.00 Gm |
| FAT | Ᾱ | NO RDA | 77.90 Gm |
| FIBER-CRUDE | Ᾱ | NO RDA | 1.100 Gm |
| CHOLESTEROL | Ᾱ | NO RDA | 259.0 Mg |
| SATURATED FA | Ᾱ | NO RDA | 46.40 Gm |
| OLEIC FA | Ᾱ | NO RDA | 19.40 Gm |
| LINOLEIC FA | Ᾱ | NO RDA | 1.620 Gm |
| SODIUM | Ᾱ===================================================== | 109% | 2407 Mg |
| POTASSIUM | Ᾱ======== | 17% | 666.0 Mg |
| MAGNESIUM | Ᾱ============================ | 62% | 186.0 Mg |
| IRON | Ᾱ========== | 20% | 3.760 Mg |
| ZINC | Ᾱ================================================= | 95% | 14.30 Mg |
| VITAMIN A | Ᾱ================================== | 69% | 2769 IU |
| VITAMIN D | Ᾱ | 0% | 0.000 IU |
| VIT. E/TOTAL | Ᾱ | NO RDA | 0.670 Mg |
| VITAMIN C | Ᾱ===== | 11% | 7.080 Mg |
| THIAMIN | Ᾱ============= | 29% | 0.290 Mg |
| RIBOFLAVIN | Ᾱ=============================================== | 125% | 1.510 Mg |
| NIACIN | Ᾱ=========== | 22% | 2.900 Mg |
| VITAMIN B6 | Ᾱ============ | 24% | 0.480 Mg |
| FOLACIN | Ᾱ======== | 17% | 71.20 Ug |
| VITAMIN B12 | Ᾱ=============================================== | 127% | 3.830 Ug |
| PANTO- ACID | Ᾱ======== | 17% | 0.980 Mg |
| CALCIUM | Ᾱ============================================= | 379% | 3035 Mg |
| PHOSPHORUS | Ᾱ============================================= | 290% | 2324 Mg |
| TRYPTOPHAN | Ᾱ=========================== | 58% | 96.00 Mg |
| THREONINE | Ᾱ============================================= | 1029% | 4478 Mg |
| ISOLEUCINE | Ᾱ============================================= | 871% | 5694 Mg |
| LEUCINE | Ᾱ============================================= | 1310% | 11413 Mg |
| LYSINE | Ᾱ============================================= | 1769% | 11554 Mg |
| METHIONINE | Ᾱ============================================= | 1187% | 3230 Mg |
| CYSTINE | Ᾱ============================================= | 244% | 664.0 Mg |
| PHENYL-ANINE | Ᾱ============================================= | 1425% | 6199 Mg |
| TYROSINE | Ᾱ============================================= | 1482% | 6447 Mg |
| VALINE | Ᾱ============================================= | 962% | 7335 Mg |
| HISTIDINE | Ᾱ | NO RDA | 4195 Mg |
| ALCOHOL | Ᾱ | NO RDA | 0.000 Gm |
| ASH | Ᾱ | NO RDA | 16.80 Gm |
| COPPER | Ᾱ====== | 13% | 0.340 Mg |
| MANGANESE | Ᾱ | 1% | 0.050 Mg |
| IODINE | Ᾱ============================================= | 369% | 554.0 Ug |
| MONO FAT | Ᾱ | NO RDA | 20.70 Gm |
| POLY FAT | Ᾱ | NO RDA | 2.110 Gm |
| CAFFEINE | Ᾱ | NO RDA | 0.000 Mg |
| FLUORIDE | Ᾱ======= | 14% | 398.0 Ug |
| MOLYBDENUM | Ᾱ | 0% | 0.000 Ug |
| VITAMIN K | Ᾱ | 0% | 0.000 Ug |
| SELENIUM | Ᾱ============ | 24% | 0.030 Mg |
| BIOTIN | Ᾱ== | 5% | 8.630 Ug |
| CHLORIDE | Ᾱ | 0% | 3.360 Mg |
| CHROMIUM | Ᾱ================ | 32% | 0.040 Mg |
| SUGAR | Ᾱ | NO RDA | 0.240 Gm |
| FIBER-DIET | Ᾱ | NO RDA | 0.000 Gm |
| VIT. E/AT | Ᾱ================== | 37% | 2.970 Mg |

```
% RDA:   |0      |20     |40     |60     |80     |100      10
```

Part-skim mozzarella used instead of string cheese.

# GREEN SAUCE

☆ This cool sauce makes a nice contrast when poured over hot, fried cheese.

---

½ cup frozen, chopped spinach
   or ½ lb. fresh spinach
1 cup watercress leaves

⅓ cup water
2 Tbsp. olive oil
1 Tbsp. red wine vinegar
½ tsp. miso
⅛ tsp. white pepper

½ cup chopped, stewed tomatoes

Wash fresh vegetables well. Bring a pot of water to a boil and fill a large mixing bowl with ice cold water. Put watercress in a strainer and submerge in boiling water till leaves turn a more brilliant green than when raw (takes about 15 to 20 seconds). Immediately lift strainer out of boiling water and plunge into cold water. This cools vegetables off so they don't continue cooking from the heat that they retain after being taken out of the boiling water. Wring water out of cooled vegetables and drop into blender top. Do the same with the fresh spinach; if using frozen spinach, you won't need to blanch — just place thawed spinach in the blender. Add next 5 ingredients and blend till leaves are pureed and form a thick sauce. Mix in chopped tomatoes and refrigerate at least a few hours before serving. Makes about 1 cup — enough to top off 10 to 12 servings of fried cheese.

Green Sauce is a good all-around sauce. Delicious served on top of pasta, steamed vegetables or even salad.

| SHOPPING LIST | |
| --- | --- |
| Regularly Kept in the Kitchen (Listed in Chapter 14, p. 703) | Fresh Produce |
| Olive oil<br>Red wine vinegar<br>Miso<br>White pepper | Spinach (fresh or frozen)<br>Watercress<br>Tomatoes |

# NUTRITIONAL ANALYSIS FOR ONE SERVING GREEN SAUCE

```
NUTRIENT        Type: 14   FEMALE-23 TO 51 YEARS            % RDA    Amount
KCALORIES       Å                                             1%   33.20 Kc
PROTEIN         Å=                                            2%    0.890 Gm
CARBOHYDRATE    Å                                          NO RDA   1.870 Gm
FAT             Å                                          NO RDA   2.820 Gm
FIBER-CRUDE     Å                                          NO RDA   0.290 Gm
CHOLESTEROL     Å                                          NO RDA   0.000 Mg
SATURATED FA    Å                                          NO RDA   0.400 Gm
OLEIC FA        Å                                          NO RDA   1.920 Gm
LINOLEIC FA     Å                                          NO RDA   0.220 Gm
SODIUM          Å=                                            2%   62.40 Mg
POTASSIUM       Å==                                          4%   172.0 Mg
MAGNESIUM       Å===                                         6%   20.40 Mg
IRON            Å==                                          4%    0.750 Mg
ZINC            Å                                            1%    0.150 Mg
VITAMIN A       Å========================                  44%    1781 IU
VITAMIN D       Å                                           0%    0.000 IU
VIT. E/TOTAL    Å                                        NO RDA   1.110 Mg
VITAMIN C       Å=========                                 16%    9.660 Mg
THIAMIN         Å=                                           2%    0.020 Mg
RIBOFLAVIN      Å==                                          4%    0.050 Mg
NIACIN          Å                                            2%    0.260 Mg
VITAMIN B6      Å=                                           2%    0.050 Mg
FOLACIN         Å=====                                      11%   44.90 Ug
VITAMIN B12     Å                                           0%    0.000 Ug
PANTO- ACID     Å                                           0%    0.020 Mg
CALCIUM         Å=                                           3%   31.80 Mg
PHOSPHORUS      Å=                                           2%   16.70 Mg
TRYPTOPHAN      Å===                                         6%   11.30 Mg
THREONINE       Å====                                        8%   37.30 Mg
ISOLEUCINE      Å===                                         6%   42.10 Mg
LEUCINE         Å===                                         7%   64.30 Mg
LYSINE          Å===                                         7%   51.20 Mg
METHIONINE      Å==                                          5%   14.40 Mg
CYSTINE         Å=                                           3%   10.20 Mg
PHENYL-ANINE    Å====                                        8%   38.30 Mg
TYROSINE        Å===                                         6%   29.90 Mg
VALINE          Å===                                         6%   46.90 Mg
HISTIDINE       Å                                        NO RDA  18.90 Mg
ALCOHOL         Å                                        NO RDA   0.000 Gm
ASH             Å                                        NO RDA   0.620 Gm
COPPER          Å=                                           2%    0.050 Mg
MANGANESE       Å==                                          5%    0.220 Mg
IODINE          Å                                           0%    0.000 Ug
MONO FAT        Å                                        NO RDA   1.990 Gm
POLY FAT        Å                                        NO RDA   0.270 Gm
CAFFEINE        Å                                        NO RDA   0.000 Mg
FLUORIDE        Å                                           0%   26.00 Ug
MOLYBDENUM      Å=                                           2%    7.680 Ug
VITAMIN K       Å==========                                21%   22.10 Ug
SELENIUM        Å                                           0%    0.000 Mg
BIOTIN          Å                                           1%    1.810 Ug
CHLORIDE        Å                                           0%    6.190 Mg
CHROMIUM        Å                                           0%    0.000 Mg
SUGAR           Å                                        NO RDA   0.110 Gm
FIBER-DIET      Å                                        NO RDA   0.730 Gm
VIT. E/AT       Å=====                                      10%    0.810 Mg

     % RDA:  |0      |20     |40     |60     |80     |100
```

# NO·BAKE CHEESECAKE

☆ This cheesecake would be higher in saturated fat and cholesterol if cream cheese and sour cream were used along with eggs to thicken them.

---

½ cup apple juice
½ cup honey
1 stick agar-agar (½ cup flakes)
2 tsp. vanilla extract

2 cups (two 8-oz. packages) Neufchatel cheese
1 cup Lowfat Sour Cream (p. 186)

1 cup chopped, pitted cherries

¾ cup naturally-sweetened whole grain
    cookie crumbs
2 Tbsp. honey
2 Tbsp. water

2 cups pitted cherries
½ cup apple juice
1 tsp. lemon juice
1 Tbsp. arrowroot

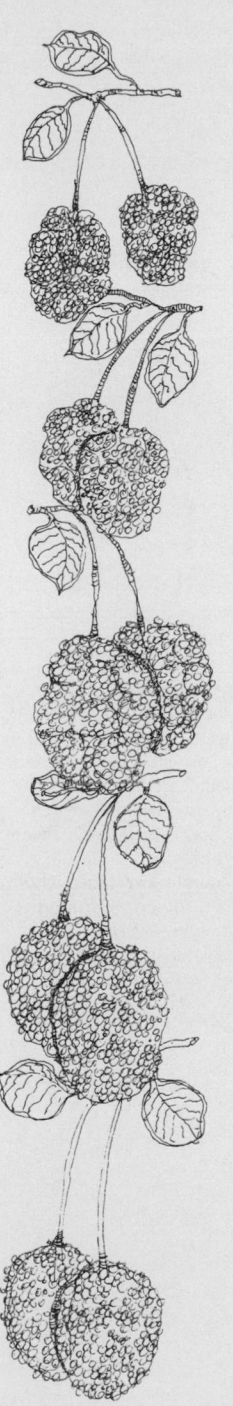

Allow dairy products and fruit to sit out to bring them to room temperature. Combine first 4 ingredients in a small pot, breaking agar-agar into small pieces. Allow mixture to soak till agar-agar softens. In the meantime, blend next 2 ingredients in a blender till completely smooth. Be very sure to blend Lowfat Sour Cream completely smooth, as lumps in the cheesecake are distracting. Place agar-agar mixture over a low heat and bring to a boil, stirring occasionally, till agar-agar melts. Pour dissolved agar-agar into blenderful of dairy products and run blender till everything is thoroughly blended in. Pour mixture back into small pot and allow to sit at room temperature for 20 minutes (not longer, as agar-agar will jell at room temperature), till agar-agar is beginning to thicken.

In the meantime, blend or run naturally-sweetened whole grain cookies (like Hawaiian Crunchies, p. 467, or your favorite commercial ones) in a food processor till they turn into fine crumbs. Mix crumbs with next 2 ingredients and press into bottom of a 9" or 10" springform pan. Chop fresh, pitted cherries into small (¼") chunks. Be sure fruit is not chilled, as it will cause the agar-agar to jell very quickly and form small lumps. Blend or whip dairy mixture to fluff it a bit. Pour chopped fruit (you can use other fruit besides cherries here) into mixture in pot after 20 minutes and quickly whip in. Pour this onto the crust in the springform pan, cover and chill for at least 6 to 8 hours (overnight and all day is fine).

At some point before serving time, combine last 4 ingredients in a small pot and mix till arrowroot dissolves. Put over heat and stir till mixture comes to a boil and thickens into a sauce. Refrigerate this. Just before serving, top cheesecake with the sauce (or try making ¼ of the Carob Fondue recipe and drizzle over top of cheesecake in place of the cherry sauce). Makes about 16 servings.

# NUTRITIONAL ANALYSIS FOR ONE SERVING
## NO-BAKE CHEESECAKE

| NUTRIENT | Type: 14    FEMALE-23 TO 51 YEARS | % RDA | Amount |
|---|---|---|---|
| KCALORIES | ‖===== | 10% | 216.0 Kc |
| PROTEIN | ‖======= | 14% | 6.290 Gm |
| CARBOHYDRATE | ‖ | NO RDA | 25.20 Gm |
| FAT | ‖ | NO RDA | 10.80 Gm |
| FIBER-CRUDE | ‖ | NO RDA | 0.310 Gm |
| CHOLESTEROL | ‖ | NO RDA | 23.60 Mg |
| SATURATED FA | ‖ | NO RDA | 4.840 Gm |
| OLEIC FA | ‖ | NO RDA | 3.530 Gm |
| LINOLEIC FA | ‖ | NO RDA | 2.410 Gm |
| SODIUM | ‖==== | 8% | 195.0 Mg |
| POTASSIUM | ‖== | 5% | 194.0 Mg |
| MAGNESIUM | ‖=== | 7% | 21.20 Mg |
| IRON | ‖== | 5% | 0.910 Mg |
| ZINC | ‖= | 3% | 0.450 Mg |
| VITAMIN A | ‖======= | 14% | 590.0 IU |
| VITAMIN D | ‖ | 0% | 0.310 IU |
| VIT. E/TOTAL | ‖ | NO RDA | 1.620 Mg |
| VITAMIN C | ‖= | 2% | 1.760 Mg |
| THIAMIN | ‖== | 5% | 0.050 Mg |
| RIBOFLAVIN | ‖===== | 10% | 0.130 Mg |
| NIACIN | ‖= | 3% | 0.430 Mg |
| VITAMIN B6 | ‖== | 4% | 0.080 Mg |
| FOLACIN | ‖= | 2% | 10.10 Ug |
| VITAMIN B12 | ‖=== | 6% | 0.190 Ug |
| PANTO- ACID | ‖=== | 6% | 0.370 Mg |
| CALCIUM | ‖=== | 7% | 62.70 Mg |
| PHOSPHORUS | ‖====== | 13% | 105.0 Mg |
| TRYPTOPHAN | ‖================== | 37% | 61.80 Mg |
| THREONINE | ‖============================ | 56% | 245.0 Mg |
| ISOLEUCINE | ‖======================== | 48% | 315.0 Mg |
| LEUCINE | ‖================================ | 64% | 560.0 Mg |
| LYSINE | ‖================================== | 69% | 455.0 Mg |
| METHIONINE | ‖========================== | 52% | 144.0 Mg |
| CYSTINE | ‖=========== | 23% | 63.30 Mg |
| PHENYL-ANINE | ‖==================================== | 73% | 320.0 Mg |
| TYROSINE | ‖================================ | 64% | 282.0 Mg |
| VALINE | ‖====================== | 45% | 346.0 Mg |
| HISTIDINE | ‖ | NO RDA | 193.0 Mg |
| ALCOHOL | ‖ | NO RDA | 0.000 Gm |
| ASH | ‖ | NO RDA | 1.000 Gm |
| COPPER | ‖== | 4% | 0.100 Mg |
| MANGANESE | ‖==== | 8% | 0.310 Mg |
| IODINE | ‖======== | 17% | 26.00 Ug |
| MONO FAT | ‖ | NO RDA | 2.950 Gm |
| POLY FAT | ‖ | NO RDA | 2.440 Gm |
| CAFFEINE | ‖ | NO RDA | 0.000 Mg |
| FLUORIDE | ‖ | 1% | 53.20 Ug |
| MOLYBDENUM | ‖========================================== | 83% | 270.0 Ug |
| VITAMIN K | ‖ | 0% | 0.220 Ug |
| SELENIUM | ‖ | 0% | 0.000 Mg |
| BIOTIN | ‖ | 1% | 2.010 Ug |
| CHLORIDE | ‖ | 0% | 8.580 Mg |
| CHROMIUM | ‖======== | 16% | 0.020 Mg |
| SUGAR | ‖ | NO RDA | 0.030 Gm |
| FIBER-DIET | ‖ | NO RDA | 0.750 Gm |
| VIT. E/AT | ‖========== | 20% | 1.650 Mg |

```
% RDA:  |0      |20     |40     |60     |80     |100
```

Cookie crumbs used in analysis: Mom's Converted Aunt Esther's Crisp Cookies.

The first time I had this dessert at an East Indian restaurant, friends and I sat around trying to figure out what it was! It came served in a tiny silver bowl in which a tiny ice cream scoop of the Yogurt Cheese Dessert had been placed. This simple dessert was so outrageously delicious, we finally broke down and asked the waiter what it was and how it was made!

# YOGURT CHEESE DESSERT

*1 cup Yogurt Cheese (see recipe, p. 319)*
*¼ cup honey*
*1 tsp. rose water*
*¼ tsp. ground cardamom*
*Dash nutmeg*

*Few saffron threads (optional)*
*Finely chopped almonds or pistachios*

Combine first 5 ingredients in a bowl and stir together well. Push this mixture through a very fine sieve (tea strainer-sized mesh) so mixture becomes silky smooth. Cover and refrigerate at least 3 to 4 hours before serving.

To serve, divide into fourths and place the tiny scoop in small dessert bowls. Sprinkle each scoop with a few strands of saffron (if you want to, and if you can find it) and very finely chopped nuts. Makes 4 servings (this is very rich and it's hard to eat much!).

**Special Shopping**

Rose water — found in East Indian food stores; the rose water sold in most pharmacies is also fine.
Yogurt cheese — found in natural food stores, or make your own at home.

| SHOPPING LIST | |
| --- | --- |
| **Regularly Kept in the Kitchen (Listed in Chapter 14, p. 703)** | **Fresh Produce** |
| Honey | (None) |
| Ground cardamom | |
| Nutmeg | |
| Saffron (optional) | |
| Almonds or pistachios | |

# MACARONI AND CHEESE

☆ This is a pretty standard macaroni and cheese recipe with half the cheese most such recipes call for. I'm able to cut down on the quantity of cheese by combining the following techniques:

☆ Nutritional yeast adds a nice, cheesy flavor.

☆ Broccoli absorbs and holds a lot of the flavored sauce in its flowerettes; the same recipe without broccoli won't taste as cheesy.

☆ Use sharp cheddar which has a stronger flavor.

☆ By using a flat, shallow pan instead of a deep one, the cheese sprinkled on top is included in every bite.

## SUGGESTED MENU

*Macaroni and Cheese*

*Tangy Herb Garden Salad*
*(p. 360)*

*Express-o Ice*
*(p. 257)*

1 lb. whole grain or lupini macaroni

1 Tbsp. butter or margarine
½ tsp. asafetida or ½ small onion, diced fine
½ tsp. white or black pepper

¼ cup arrowroot
3½ cups lowfat milk

¼ cup nutritional yeast
1 Tbsp. prepared mustard
1½ tsp. Spike or other vegetable-seasoned salt
¼ tsp. Tabasco

1½ cups chopped broccoli
1½ cups corn kernels or other vegetable

2 cups grated sharp cheddar cheese (½ lb.)

When serving a dish with a good amount of saturated fat and cholesterol, try to balance this by making the rest of the meal fat- and cholesterol-free.

Preheat oven to 350 degrees.

Bring water to a boil and boil noodles as directed on package. While water is coming to a boil, prepare sauce by sauteing next 3 ingredients together for a few seconds to toast spices. Mix next 2 ingredients together off of heat to dissolve arrowroot. Pour into toasted spices and stir constantly over medium-high heat till milk boils and thickens. Whisk in next 4 ingredients.

By this time, the noodles should be done cooking. When noodles are done cooking, drain in a colander. Pour drained noodles back into pot they were cooked in and mix in chopped vegetables, sauce and ¼ of the cheese (½ cup). Pour into an oblong cake pan that measures about 9" x 13" x 2". Sprinkle remainder of the grated cheese evenly over surface of noodles and bake at 350 degrees for about 15 minutes. Makes about 10 servings.

| SHOPPING LIST | |
|---|---|
| **Regularly Kept in the Kitchen** (Listed in Chapter 14, p. 703) | **Fresh Produce** |
| Butter or margarine | Tabasco |
| Asafetida | Broccoli (fresh or frozen) |
| White or black pepper | Corn or other vegetable |
| Arrowroot | (fresh or frozen) |
| Lowfat milk | |
| Nutritional yeast | |
| Prepared mustard | |
| Spike | |
| Sharp cheddar cheese | |

# NUTRITIONAL ANALYSIS FOR ONE SERVING
# MACARONI AND CHEESE

| NUTRIENT | Type: 14  FEMALE—23 TO 51 YEARS | % RDA | Amount |
|---|---|---|---|
| KCALORIES | A===== | 11% | 239.0 Kc |
| PROTEIN | A=============== | 30% | 13.50 Gm |
| CARBOHYDRATE | A | NO RDA | 22.10 Gm |
| FAT | A | NO RDA | 10.70 Gm |
| FIBER—CRUDE | A | NO RDA | 1.000 Gm |
| CHOLESTEROL | A | NO RDA | 30.10 Mg |
| SATURATED FA | A | NO RDA | 5.980 Gm |
| OLEIC FA | A | NO RDA | 2.190 Gm |
| LINOLEIC FA | A | NO RDA | 0.300 Gm |
| SODIUM | A======= | 15% | 351.0 Mg |
| POTASSIUM | A==== | 8% | 331.0 Mg |
| MAGNESIUM | A======= | 15% | 46.90 Mg |
| IRON | A==== | 9% | 1.630 Mg |
| ZINC | A====== | 13% | 2.060 Mg |
| VITAMIN A | A======== | 17% | 696.0 IU |
| VITAMIN D | A======== | 17% | 35.70 IU |
| VIT. E/TOTAL | A | NO RDA | 1.170 Mg |
| VITAMIN C | A===================== | 44% | 26.50 Mg |
| THIAMIN | A================================================= | 193% | 1.930 Mg |
| RIBOFLAVIN | A================================================= | 172% | 2.070 Mg |
| NIACIN | A========================================= | 84% | 11.00 Mg |
| VITAMIN B6 | A================================================= | 97% | 1.950 Mg |
| FOLACIN | A===== | 10% | 43.60 Ug |
| VITAMIN B12 | A============================== | 63% | 1.890 Ug |
| PANTO— ACID | A========= | 18% | 1.040 Mg |
| CALCIUM | A================= | 37% | 296.0 Mg |
| PHOSPHORUS | A================= | 37% | 303.0 Mg |
| TRYPTOPHAN | A================================================= | 109% | 179.0 Mg |
| THREONINE | A================================================= | 132% | 576.0 Mg |
| ISOLEUCINE | A================================================= | 127% | 833.0 Mg |
| LEUCINE | A================================================= | 119% | 1041 Mg |
| LYSINE | A================================================= | 155% | 1017 Mg |
| METHIONINE | A================================================= | 123% | 337.0 Mg |
| CYSTINE | A========================= | 52% | 144.0 Mg |
| PHENYL—ANINE | A================================================= | 170% | 740.0 Mg |
| TYROSINE | A================================================= | 139% | 605.0 Mg |
| VALINE | A================================================= | 121% | 929.0 Mg |
| HISTIDINE | A | NO RDA | 441.0 Mg |
| ALCOHOL | A | NO RDA | 0.000 Gm |
| ASH | A | NO RDA | 3.650 Gm |
| COPPER | A== | 5% | 0.130 Mg |
| MANGANESE | A======== | 17% | 0.650 Mg |
| IODINE | A=============================== | 61% | 92.40 Ug |
| MONO FAT | A | NO RDA | 3.130 Gm |
| POLY FAT | A | NO RDA | 0.690 Gm |
| CAFFEINE | A | NO RDA | 0.000 Mg |
| FLUORIDE | A= | 2% | 63.00 Ug |
| MOLYBDENUM | A================================================= | 132% | 431.0 Ug |
| VITAMIN K | A========================================= | 83% | 87.90 Ug |
| SELENIUM | A==== | 8% | 0.010 Mg |
| BIOTIN | A=== | 7% | 10.60 Ug |
| CHLORIDE | A | 0% | 16.90 Mg |
| CHROMIUM | A========================================== | 88% | 0.110 Mg |
| SUGAR | A | NO RDA | 1.510 Gm |
| FIBER—DIET | A | NO RDA | 1.770 Gm |
| VIT. E/AT | A== | 4% | 0.320 Mg |

```
% RDA:   |0      |20     |40     |60     |80     |100
```

Whole grain macaroni used instead of lupini in analysis; margarine used instead of butter; peas used instead of corn.

Mencius, an associate of Confucius, wrote the following words on one of the qualities that distinguishes a human from an animal: "Benevolence is the distinguishing characteristic of man to be embodied in man's conduct." . . . And this means in every aspect of man's conduct, down to his everyday activities such as eating. About eating, Mencius wrote further:

"If you see them in life, you can't bear to watch their death. If you hear their screams, you can't bear to eat their flesh. This is the nature of true benevolence."

# ITALIAN LUNCHEON

This Italian luncheon is centered around the calzone, which is actually a pizza folded in half and sealed on the edges. The new shape just offers a variation on the ever popular pizza, which makes it easy to pack in a lunch box or for on-the-road food. For an at-the-table meal, pouring a tasty sauce over the calzone and serving it with a fork and knife dresses it up for a more special meal.

Like the pizza, what is used for topping — in this case, filling — is only as limited as your imagination. I've included only two ideas for fillings due to the time limitations of a half-hour TV show. Both are good for the cholesterol and saturated fat conscious. The Dairyless Garden filling has no cholesterol; for the cheese filling, I recommend using a lowfat mozzarella (made partly with skim milk), as mozzarella is one of the cheeses with a lower cholesterol level. For taste's sake, I strongly recommend using smoked mozzarella if you can find it.

Whichever filling you use, I'm sure you'll find this a delightful luncheon or light late-afternoon dinner.

# RISING WHOLE WHEAT PIZZA DOUGH

☆ This rising pizza dough takes awhile to make; if in a hurry, you can use the Quick Whole Wheat Pizza Dough (p. 405) instead.

---

1 cup warm water
1 Tbsp. baking yeast

2 cups whole wheat flour
¼ cup olive oil
¼ tsp. salt
½ tsp. coarsely ground black pepper (optional)

1 cup whole wheat flour

Combine first 2 ingredients and allow to sit till yeast is dissolved.

Add next 3 (or 4) ingredients, using only 1 cup of the whole wheat flour. Stir all ingredients thoroughly with a wooden spoon. Add second cup of flour and mix in thoroughly. You should now have a soft, sticky dough.

Flour working surface and hands with ½ cup of the 1 cup whole wheat flour (last ingredient). Scrape dough onto floured surface and knead with the palm of the floured hand by pushing palm into dough and across the work surface. Fold dough in half, push palm into middle of dough and push across work surface. Repeat kneading in this way till the ½ cup of flour is absorbed. Sprinkle remaining flour on work surface sparsely, only as much at a time as is needed to keep dough from sticking to the work surface. Continue kneading till the dough no longer feels sticky. Test to see if it's kneaded enough by pushing palm into the middle of the dough and holding it there for 10 seconds. If the dough is done, your palm should come out clean; if there is some dough sticking to your palm, continue kneading on a lightly floured surface. This should take anywhere from 5 to 10 minutes.

When the dough is done being kneaded, lightly oil the mixing bowl and roll ball of dough around in it so dough is lightly covered with oil. Cover bowl with plastic wrap and allow to sit in a warm, draft-free area for 30 to 45 minutes till doubled in bulk. Punch dough down and knead for about 1 minute.

It's now ready to use for a pizza or calzone crust. Makes 1 pizza crust or 8 large, meal-sized calzones.

## MENU FOR AN ITALIAN LUNCHEON

*Dairyless Garden Calzone
and/or
Especially-Good-with-
Smoked-Cheese Calzone
topped with
Quicker than
"From Scratch"
Pasta Sauce*

*Tangy Herb Garden Salad*

*Neapolitan
Tofu Cheesecake*

# DAIRYLESS GARDEN CALZONE

☆ Calzones with this filling served at the same meal with the Neapolitan Cheesecake make a cholesterol-free meal with an ample amount of protein — supplied by the dessert!

2 Tbsp. olive oil
2 garlic cloves, crushed
2 cups thinly sliced celery and 2 tsp. asafetida OR 2 small onions, diced

2 cups seeded, chopped tomatoes
4 cups roughly chopped collard greens
2 tsp. Spike or other vegetable-seasoned salt
½ tsp. oregano
½ tsp. black pepper
¼ tsp. rosemary

⅔ cup mashed Chinese firm tofu
4 tsp. nutritional yeast
½ cup minced olives

Here in America when we think of Italian food, immediately the image of pasta or dough topped with tomato sauce and lots of cheese comes to mind. In reality, a great deal of Italian cooking is done with fresh vegetables — which grow abundantly in their California-like climate — using no cheese at all.

Saute first 4 ingredients till celery or onion becomes translucent.

Mix in next 6 ingredients (you can use any bitter greens in place of collards, such as escarole, kale, etc.). Then cover and allow to simmer over medium heat till collards turn a dark green.

Turn off heat and mix in last 3 ingredients.

Preheat oven to 450 degrees and assemble as in the Especially-Good-With-Smoked-Cheese Calzone (see following recipe). Bake at 450 degrees for 20 minutes or till golden brown.

Serve under your favorite commercial spaghetti or marinara sauce. Makes 8 large, meal-sized calzones.

| SHOPPING LIST | |
|---|---|
| **Regularly Kept in the Kitchen** (Listed in Chapter 14, p. 703) | **Fresh Produce** |
| Olive oil | Garlic |
| Spike | Celery |
| Oregano | Tomatoes |
| Black pepper | Collards |
| Rosemary | Olives |
| Tofu | |
| Nutritional yeast | |

Also see shopping list for Rising Whole Wheat Pizza Dough.

# NUTRITIONAL ANALYSIS FOR ONE DAIRYLESS GARDEN CALZONE
## (using Rising Whole Wheat Pizza Dough)

```
NUTRIENT        Type: 14    FEMALE-23 TO 51 YEARS           % RDA    Amount
KCALORIES       X=========                                    16%    324.0 Kc
PROTEIN         X===============                              28%    12.50 Gm
CARBOHYDRATE    X                                          NO RDA    41.10 Gm
FAT             X                                          NO RDA    14.70 Gm
FIBER-CRUDE     X                                          NO RDA    2.120 Gm
CHOLESTEROL     X                                          NO RDA    0.000 Mg
SATURATED FA    X                                          NO RDA    2.050 Gm
OLEIC FA        X                                          NO RDA    8.550 Gm
LINOLEIC FA     X                                          NO RDA    1.780 Gm
SODIUM          X========                                     17%    390.0 Mg
POTASSIUM       X=======                                      14%    550.0 Mg
MAGNESIUM       X===============                              30%    90.20 Mg
IRON            X==============                               28%    5.050 Mg
ZINC            X========                                     17%    2.650 Mg
VITAMIN A       X==========================================   96%    3844 IU
VITAMIN D       X                                             0%    0.000 IU
VIT. E/TOTAL    X                                          NO RDA    3.390 Mg
VITAMIN C       X============================                 56%    33.80 Mg
THIAMIN         X=======================================     112%    1.120 Mg
RIBOFLAVIN      X====================================         80%    0.960 Mg
NIACIN          X===========================                  57%    7.430 Mg
VITAMIN B6      X==========================                   52%    1.050 Mg
FOLACIN         X===========                                  23%    95.20 Ug
VITAMIN B12     X=========                                    19%    0.580 Ug
PANTO- ACID     X========                                     16%    0.930 Mg
CALCIUM         X==================                           36%    292.0 Mg
PHOSPHORUS      X================                             33%    270.0 Mg
TRYPTOPHAN      X==========================================   96%    158.0 Mg
THREONINE       X=========================================    94%    413.0 Mg
ISOLEUCINE      X====================================         82%    539.0 Mg
LEUCINE         X=========================================    95%    829.0 Mg
LYSINE          X====================================         82%    540.0 Mg
METHIONINE      X==============================               63%    172.0 Mg
CYSTINE         X===================================          78%    213.0 Mg
PHENYL-ANINE    X=======================================     128%    560.0 Mg
TYROSINE        X==========================================   96%    419.0 Mg
VALINE          X===================================          76%    583.0 Mg
HISTIDINE       X                                          NO RDA    279.0 Mg
ALCOHOL         X                                          NO RDA    0.000 Gm
ASH             X                                          NO RDA    2.600 Gm
COPPER          X============                                 24%    0.600 Mg
MANGANESE       X===================================          78%    2.930 Mg
IODINE          X========================================    164%    246.0 Ug
MONO FAT        X                                          NO RDA    7.880 Gm
POLY FAT        X                                          NO RDA    1.950 Gm
CAFFEINE        X                                          NO RDA    0.000 Mg
FLUORIDE        X                                             0%    22.20 Ug
MOLYBDENUM      X========================================    907%    2949 Ug
VITAMIN K       X=                                            2%    2.910 Ug
SELENIUM        X====                                         8%    0.010 Mg
BIOTIN          X===                                          7%    10.50 Ug
CHLORIDE        X=                                            3%    125.0 Mg
CHROMIUM        X========================================    280%    0.350 Mg
SUGAR           X                                          NO RDA    3.600 Gm
FIBER-DIET      X                                          NO RDA    7.410 Gm
VIT. E/AT       X===========                                  22%    1.820 Mg

    % RDA:   |0      |20     |40     |60     |80     |100
```

Onions used instead of celery and asafetida in the filling.

# ESPECIALLY·GOOD·WITH· SMOKED·CHEESE CALZONE

☆ A friend first introduced me to smoked mozzarella cheese five years ago while I was visiting New York. He brought home a round of cheese, still warm from being smoked. It was delicious! Since then I've only been able to find smoked mozzarella twice. Since it's so hard to find, try substituting another smoked cheese or plain mozzarella; but this recipe is truly especially good with smoked mozzarella!

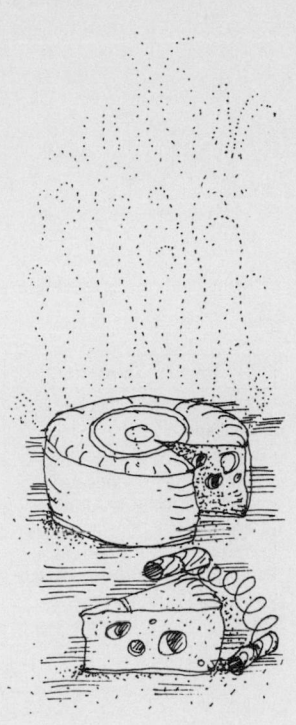

---

2 cups seeded tomato chunks
½ lb. coarsely grated, smoked (or plain)
  mozzarella cheese
¼ cup Parmesan cheese
10 fresh basil leaves, shredded
1 tsp. asafetida or 1 finely minced garlic clove
½ tsp. black pepper
1 Tbsp. arrowroot

1 recipe Rising Whole Wheat Pizza Dough

Prepare ripe tomatoes by cutting in half and pushing seeds out with fingertips. Cut into large ¾" chunks. Combine and mix thoroughly with all ingredients. If you can't find smoked mozzarella, plain mozzarella will be fine. This also makes a good pizza topping, or can be tossed into a pasta.

To make calzones, preheat oven to 450 degrees and cut 1 recipe of Rising Whole Wheat Pizza Dough into eighths. Lightly flour work surface and roll each eighth out to form a circle about 1/16" thick and 7" to 8" in diameter. Place about ½ cup of filling on half of the dough, leaving a ¾" border of uncovered dough around the edge. Fold uncovered half of the dough over the filling. Seal and crimp edges. Gently lift onto an oiled cookie sheet. Brush tops of crust with olive oil and bake at 450 degrees for 20 mninutes or till golden brown.

Remove from oven and serve as is. Calzones are especially good served with a spaghetti or marinara sauce ladled over them; either use your favorite commercial sauce or use the Quicker Than "From Scratch" Pasta Sauce recipe following. These particular calzones are delicious served at room temperature when made with the smoked mozzarella. Try serving them at room temperature with a chilled sauce ladled over them for a refreshing hot weather change! Makes 8 large, meal-sized calzones. You can make smaller, appetizer-sized calzones by cutting dough into smaller pieces.

| Special Shopping |
| --- |
| Smoked mozzarella cheese — a real specialty item which might be found in Italian food markets or gourmet cheese shops. If not able to find it, use regular mozzarella. One time when I couldn't find it, I used a smoked Gouda cheese instead. |

| SHOPPING LIST | |
| --- | --- |
| **Regularly Kept in the Kitchen (Listed in Chapter 14, p. 703)** | **Fresh Produce** |
| Asafetida<br>Black pepper<br>Arrowroot | Tomatoes<br>Basil |

Also see shopping list for Rising Whole Wheat Pizza Dough.

# NUTRITIONAL ANALYSIS FOR ONE
## ESPECIALLY-GOOD-WITH-SMOKED-CHEESE CALZONE
### (using Rising Whole Wheat Pizza Dough)

| NUTRIENT | Type: 14   FEMALE-23 TO 51 YEARS | % RDA | Amount |
|---|---|---|---|
| KCALORIES | A======= | 15% | 316.0 Kc |
| PROTEIN | A=================== | 34% | 15.30 Gm |
| CARBOHYDRATE | A | NO RDA | 36.90 Gm |
| FAT | A | NO RDA | 13.10 Gm |
| FIBER-CRUDE | A | NO RDA | 1.420 Gm |
| CHOLESTEROL | A | NO RDA | 18.60 Mg |
| SATURATED FA | A | NO RDA | 4.630 Gm |
| OLEIC FA | A | NO RDA | 6.400 Gm |
| LINOLEIC FA | A | NO RDA | 1.110 Gm |
| SODIUM | A===== | 11% | 259.0 Mg |
| POTASSIUM | A==== | 9% | 355.0 Mg |
| MAGNESIUM | A============ | 23% | 69.00 Mg |
| IRON | A====== | 12% | 2.300 Mg |
| ZINC | A====== | 13% | 2.070 Mg |
| VITAMIN A | A=========== | 23% | 920.0 IU |
| VITAMIN D | A | 0% | 0.000 IU |
| VIT. E/TOTAL | A | NO RDA | 2.930 Mg |
| VITAMIN C | A========= | 18% | 11.10 Mg |
| THIAMIN | A=============== | 31% | 0.310 Mg |
| RIBOFLAVIN | A========= | 19% | 0.230 Mg |
| NIACIN | A========== | 20% | 2.710 Mg |
| VITAMIN B6 | A===== | 11% | 0.220 Mg |
| FOLACIN | A======== | 17% | 68.10 Ug |
| VITAMIN B12 | A=== | 7% | 0.230 Ug |
| PANTO- ACID | A======= | 14% | 0.780 Mg |
| CALCIUM | A================ | 32% | 261.0 Mg |
| PHOSPHORUS | A====================== | 44% | 353.0 Mg |
| TRYPTOPHAN | A============================== | 59% | 97.60 Mg |
| THREONINE | A=================================================== | 116% | 507.0 Mg |
| ISOLEUCINE | A=================================================== | 104% | 683.0 Mg |
| LEUCINE | A=================================================== | 142% | 1241 Mg |
| LYSINE | A=================================================== | 156% | 1023 Mg |
| METHIONINE | A=================================================== | 120% | 328.0 Mg |
| CYSTINE | A=================================== | 69% | 190.0 Mg |
| PHENYL-ANINE | A=================================================== | 172% | 751.0 Mg |
| TYROSINE | A=================================================== | 164% | 714.0 Mg |
| VALINE | A=================================================== | 108% | 826.0 Mg |
| HISTIDINE | A | NO RDA | 447.0 Mg |
| ALCOHOL | A | NO RDA | 0.000 Gm |
| ASH | A | NO RDA | 2.280 Gm |
| COPPER | A====== | 12% | 0.300 Mg |
| MANGANESE | A================================ | 61% | 2.320 Mg |
| IODINE | A=================================================== | 154% | 231.0 Ug |
| MONO FAT | A | NO RDA | 6.560 Gm |
| POLY FAT | A | NO RDA | 0.770 Gm |
| CAFFEINE | A | NO RDA | 0.000 Mg |
| FLUORIDE | A | 1% | 42.40 Ug |
| MOLYBDENUM | A=================================================== | 830% | 2700 Ug |
| VITAMIN K | A= | 2% | 2.910 Ug |
| SELENIUM | A==== | 8% | 0.010 Mg |
| BIOTIN | A=== | 5% | 8.750 Ug |
| CHLORIDE | A= | 2% | 86.00 Mg |
| CHROMIUM | A=================================================== | 224% | 0.280 Mg |
| SUGAR | A | NO RDA | 2.900 Gm |
| FIBER-DIET | A | NO RDA | 7.310 Gm |
| VIT. E/AT | A========= | 19% | 1.580 Mg |

```
  % RDA:  |0       |20      |40      |60      |80      |100
```

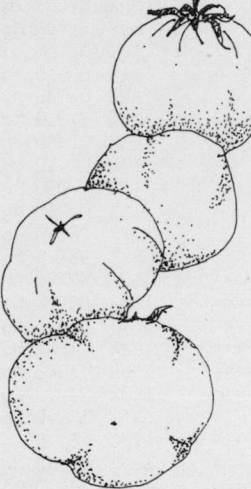

# QUICKER THAN "FROM SCRATCH" PASTA SAUCE

☆ How to dress up a can of tomato sauce or puree so it tastes like a pasta sauce that's been simmered for hours.

☆ As the recipe name suggests, this is delicious served over noodles as well as calzones.

---

1 Tbsp. olive oil
1 medium-sized onion, finely diced

6 cups canned tomato puree
1 bay leaf
1 Tbsp. basil
1 Tbsp. parsley flakes
1 Tbsp. oregano
2 tsp. thyme
½ tsp. asafetida or 1 clove garlic, crushed
½ tsp. grain coffee
¼ tsp. black pepper
⅛ tsp. cinnamon
⅛ tsp. cayenne pepper

1 Tbsp. soy sauce or miso (optional)

Saute first 2 ingredients in bottom of pot till onion becomes translucent.

Add next 11 ingredients and turn flame to simmer. Partially cover pot and leave to simmer for about a half-hour, stirring occasionally. Remove bay leaf and taste. If you want a saltier taste (although you may not miss that at all with the full flavoring provided by the herbs and spices), add 1 of the last 2 ingredients.

This is delicious served over pasta, pizza, calzones, or any similar dish. Makes about 5 cups of sauce.

Since most cans of commercial tomato puree have salt in them, I usually don't add any miso or soy sauce.

| SHOPPING LIST | |
| --- | --- |
| **Regularly Kept in the Kitchen** (Listed in Chapter 14, p. 703) | **Fresh Produce** |
| Olive oil | Onion |
| Tomato puree | |
| Bay leaf | |
| Basil | |
| Parsley flakes | |
| Oregano | |
| Thyme | |
| Asafetida | |
| Grain coffee | |
| Black pepper | |
| Cinnamon | |
| Cayenne | |
| Miso or soy sauce (optional) | |

# TANGY HERB GARDEN SALAD

☆ The fresh herbs and light vinegars are all the dressing this salad needs. Fresh herbs are so nice in salads (and other dishes), but so expensive, it's really worth growing your favorites at home.

☆ If you want to cut down on the amount of preparation that needs to be done at serving time, you can prepare the greens ahead of time and refrigerate in the salad bowl, covered with plastic wrap. Then at mealtime, all that needs to be done is to slice the sunchokes and toss in the vinegar.

---

*Approximately 8 cups fresh spinach leaves
    (unpacked in cup)*
*2 tsp. finely chopped fresh parsley*
*2 tsp. finely chopped fresh chives*
*2 tsp. finely chopped fresh basil*

*½ lb. thinly sliced sunchokes/Jerusalem artichokes*
*3 - 4 Tbsp. Balsamic vinegar*
*3 - 4 Tbsp. rice vinegar*

Rinse and drain spinach. Tear large leaves into quarters;

Sunchokes (Jerusalem artichokes) are a high-fiber, low-calorie tuber that's delicious served raw, like in this salad, or lightly sauteed. The plant is in the same family as the sunflower, growing to be 4 to 6 feet tall with sunflower-like blossoms. They are an attractive and useful plant if you have room in your yard (warning: they are a hardy plant that will take over whatever area you plant them in). A plant will grow from the little roots that sprout from the tuber; just cut off a small chunk of the tuber when the roots appear, put them in soil and care for them.

leave small leaves whole. Toss with chopped fresh herbs. This can be made beforehand, covered with saran wrap and refrigerated.

Just before serving, rinse sunchokes (but don't peel) and thinly slice so they are nearly paper thin. Do wait to do this just before serving, as they will brown otherwise. Toss slivered sunchokes with vinegar into salad and serve immediately. Makes about 8 servings.

| Special Shopping | SHOPPING LIST | |
|---|---|---|
| Balsamic vinegar — most likely found in a gourmet food store. | **Regularly Kept in the Kitchen** (Listed in Chapter 14, p. 703) | **Fresh Produce** |
| | Rice vinegar | Spinach<br>Parsley<br>Chives<br>Basil<br>Sunchokes (also called Jerusalem artichokes) |

# NEAPOLITAN TOFU CHEESECAKE

☆ For a change, make dessert a major source of nutrition in the meal by serving this cholesterol-free Tofu Cheesecake.

**Crust:**
*½ cup whole wheat flour*
*½ cup walnut meal*
*2 Tbsp. honey*
*1 Tbsp. margarine or butter*

**First layer:**
*12 oz. (¾ lb.) Chinese firm tofu, mashed*
*⅔ cup honey*
*⅔ cup carob powder*
*¼ cup grain coffee*
*1 Tbsp. arrowroot or Bipro*
*1 tsp. vanilla*
*1 tsp. almond extract*

½ cup carob chips

**Second layer:**
12 oz. (¾ lb.) Chinese firm tofu, mashed
1 ripe banana
½ cup honey
3 Tbsp. arrowroot or Bipro
4 tsp. vanilla

**Third layer:**
½ lb. Chinese firm tofu, mashed
1 cup mashed fresh strawberries
¼ cup honey
3 Tbsp. chemical- and sugar-free
    strawberry preserves
3 Tbsp. arrowroot
1 Tbsp. lemon juice

**Topping:**
2 cups sliced fresh strawberries
2 Tbsp. honey
1 tsp. arrowroot

I recommend serving this Tofu Cheesecake with the salad and Dairyless Garden Calzone, as I feel the cheese-filled calzone and the Tofu Cheesecake would be too heavy to serve in the same meal and might contain too much protein as well.

Preheat oven to 375 degrees.

Make walnut meal by running walnut halves in blender or food processor till chopped into a meal. Mix first 4 ingredients and press into a thin, even layer on the bottom of a 10" springform cake pan. To keep crust from sticking to your hands as you press it into place, wash hands and use moist hands to press with. When the crust begins sticking to your hands, dip hands in water again and continue pressing; repeat, dipping hands in water as often as necessary.

For the first layer of filling, blend the next 7 ingredients together till smooth. Pour on top of crust and spread out with a rubber spatula to form an even layer. Sprinkle carob chips evenly over entire surface.

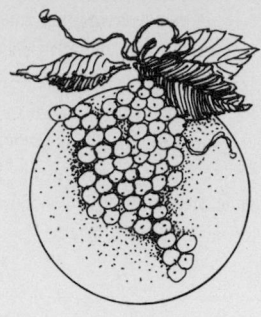

Rinse out blender and blend next 5 ingredients together till smooth to form the second layer. This must be very carefully poured onto the first layer so the stream of filling doesn't disrupt the first layer. I've found the best way to do this is to pour the mixture from the blender top against the rubber spatula and to move the spatula around the entire surface of the cheesecake while pouring; this seems to deflect the force of the mixture poured out of the blender so it doesn't dig into the previous layer. Smooth this layer out evenly.

Rinse blender top out and blend the next 6 ingredients together till smooth to form the next layer. Pour in the same way as the second layer and smooth out top layer. Bake at 375 degrees for 1¼ to 1½ hours, till a toothpick inserted in center comes out clean. The top of the Tofu Cheesecake should be a little puffy and have cracks in it. Remove from oven and allow to cool to room temperature on counter.

While Tofu Cheesecake is cooling, combine next 3 ingredients in a small pot and mix to dissolve arrowroot. Place over moderate heat and stir gently till mixture comes to a boil and thickens like a thin gravy. Allow this to cool, pour on top of Tofu Cheesecake and spread evenly. Cover with plastic wrap and refrigerate at least 3 to 4 hours or overnight.

To serve, undo springform pan and slice. Makes about 16 dessert-sized servings.

| Special Shopping |
| --- |
| Natural sugarless strawberry preserves (sweetened with honey or fruit juices) — available in natural food stores. |

| SHOPPING LIST | |
| --- | --- |
| Regularly Kept in the Kitchen (Listed in Chapter 14, p. 703) | Fresh Produce |
| Whole wheat flour<br>Walnut meal<br>Honey<br>Butter or margarine<br>Tofu<br>Carob<br>Grain coffee<br>Arrowroot<br>Bipro<br>Vanilla | Strawberries<br>Lemon |

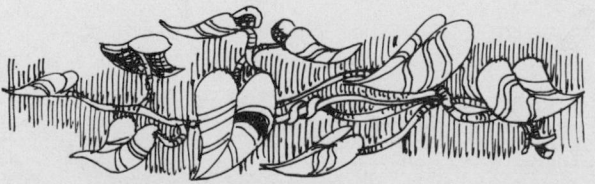

# NUTRITIONAL ANALYSIS FOR ONE SERVING
## NEAPOLITAN TOFU CHEESECAKE

| NUTRIENT | Type: 14   FEMALE-23 TO 51 YEARS | % RDA | Amount |
|---|---|---|---|
| KCALORIES | Ä======= | 15% | 308.0 Kc |
| PROTEIN | Ä============= | 27% | 12.10 Gm |
| CARBOHYDRATE | Ä | NO RDA | 48.70 Gm |
| FAT | Ä | NO RDA | 10.50 Gm |
| FIBER-CRUDE | Ä | NO RDA | 1.200 Gm |
| CHOLESTEROL | Ä | NO RDA | 0.380 Mg |
| SATURATED FA | Ä | NO RDA | 1.350 Gm |
| OLEIC FA | Ä | NO RDA | 1.150 Gm |
| LINOLEIC FA | Ä | NO RDA | 3.450 Gm |
| SODIUM | Ä | 1% | 42.50 Mg |
| POTASSIUM | Ä===== | 11% | 426.0 Mg |
| MAGNESIUM | Ä========== | 20% | 60.30 Mg |
| IRON | Ä=================== | 38% | 6.840 Mg |
| ZINC | Ä==== | 9% | 1.360 Mg |
| VITAMIN A | Ä== | 4% | 183.0 IU |
| VITAMIN D | Ä | 0% | 0.000 IU |
| VIT. E/TOTAL | Ä | NO RDA | 1.620 Mg |
| VITAMIN C | Ä============================= | 61% | 37.10 Mg |
| THIAMIN | Ä======= | 15% | 0.150 Mg |
| RIBOFLAVIN | Ä======= | 15% | 0.190 Mg |
| NIACIN | Ä==== | 8% | 1.040 Mg |
| VITAMIN B6 | Ä===== | 10% | 0.200 Mg |
| FOLACIN | Ä==== | 9% | 37.00 Ug |
| VITAMIN B12 | Ä= | 2% | 0.070 Ug |
| PANTO- ACID | Ä==== | 9% | 0.530 Mg |
| CALCIUM | Ä=========================== | 56% | 451.0 Mg |
| PHOSPHORUS | Ä=========== | 22% | 179.0 Mg |
| TRYPTOPHAN | Ä========================================== | 117% | 191.0 Mg |
| THREONINE | Ä======================================== | 112% | 491.0 Mg |
| ISOLEUCINE | Ä================================= | 90% | 588.0 Mg |
| LEUCINE | Ä======================================= | 108% | 943.0 Mg |
| LYSINE | Ä========================================== | 117% | 765.0 Mg |
| METHIONINE | Ä======================= | 63% | 173.0 Mg |
| CYSTINE | Ä======================= | 65% | 179.0 Mg |
| PHENYL-ANINE | Ä=============================================== | 131% | 572.0 Mg |
| TYROSINE | Ä================================== | 94% | 412.0 Mg |
| VALINE | Ä============================== | 80% | 617.0 Mg |
| HISTIDINE | Ä | NO RDA | 343.0 Mg |
| ALCOHOL | Ä | NO RDA | 0.000 Gm |
| ASH | Ä | NO RDA | 1.490 Gm |
| COPPER | Ä======= | 14% | 0.350 Mg |
| MANGANESE | Ä=============== | 31% | 1.190 Mg |
| IODINE | Ä================================ | 64% | 96.30 Ug |
| MONO FAT | Ä | NO RDA | 2.550 Gm |
| POLY FAT | Ä | NO RDA | 5.900 Gm |
| CAFFEINE | Ä | NO RDA | 0.000 Gm |
| FLUORIDE | Ä | 1% | 48.60 Ug |
| MOLYBDENUM | Ä=================================================== | 333% | 1084 Ug |
| VITAMIN K | Ä | 0% | 0.000 Ug |
| SELENIUM | Ä | 0% | 0.000 Mg |
| BIOTIN | Ä== | 4% | 6.200 Ug |
| CHLORIDE | Ä= | 3% | 130.0 Mg |
| CHROMIUM | Ä=================================================== | 168% | 0.210 Mg |
| SUGAR | Ä | NO RDA | 4.320 Gm |
| FIBER-DIET | Ä | NO RDA | 3.920 Gm |
| VIT. E/AT | Ä=== | 6% | 0.530 Mg |

```
% RDA:   |0      |20     |40     |60     |80     |100
```

Margarine used instead of butter; Bipro used instead of arrowroot in analysis.

# CHAPTER 8

# CUTTING DOWN ON SALT

Too much of a good thing is really the crux of the problem we have with salt nowadays. Excessive consumption of salt can cause the body problems just as excess consumption of many other essential nutrients can. With so much salt hidden in processed food and restaurant food, and tongues so accustomed to the taste of salt that they demand a few extra shakes of the salt shaker over almost every dish, it's easy to understand how we might get too much salt in our systems. All the publicity about salt's role in hypertension (high blood pressure) and heart disease makes it a little difficult to remember that salt is an essential nutrient.

In history, salt has often literally been worth its weight in gold. Pliny the Elder referred to salt as being one of the foremost of remedies for disease. Zen macrobiotics principles maintain that when salt is sprinkled on food, it is abrasive to the kidneys, but when added to a food and fermented, it has unique healing properties. Jesus called his disciples the "salt of the earth" to describe their great value. After Columbus bumped into America, different European countries sent trader ships to load up with salt. Does anyone remember Gandhi's words at the end of his famous march to the salt beds? "Man needs salt as he needs air and water . . . "

Good nutrition supplies what the body needs and doesn't throw off the body's natural, healthy balance. As with other nutrients, the amount required depends on a number of variables.

## AN ESSENTIAL NUTRIENT

How much salt a person needs will vary a great deal depending on —

• *Age.* Young children and senior citizens need less sodium.

• *Level of physical activity.* Those who perspire a lot need to replace more body salt.

• *Humidity and temperature of the environment.*

Depending on how much salt is lost or consumed, the body's salinity content can vary from meal to meal, but a healthy salinity level in the bloodstream is around one percent. If salinity levels are too low, the body can have trouble with diarrhea, weak intestinal muscle tone, or thin and weak blood, which can develop into a number of organ, glandular, or nervous disorders.

## NOT TO BE OVERCONSUMED

Most of us are more informed about the problems attributed to consuming too much salt, headed by hypertension and heart disease. Other problems excess salt consumption can result in are water retention, migraine headaches, kidney disorders, stomach cancer, and even overeating. While a low-sodium diet is a must for anyone whose body fluid salinity level is too high, I feel it's necessary to mention a study that shows excess salt consumption may not be the only factor to blame in hypertension.

University of Oregon researchers have reported that a diet deficient in calcium may have at least as much to do with high blood pressure as excess salt consumption does. About half of hypertension patients (subjects of the study) treated with calcium supplements had a drop in blood pressure levels. Studies headed by a Dr. McCarron are still in progress to see if long-term effects of calcium tablets and if increasing calcium consumption in the diet will lower blood pressure.

## HIGH-QUALITY WAYS TO SALT FOOD

I get a fair amount of mail from people asking why I so often use soy sauce or miso, even though they are so salty. Since no one in my family is suffering or has ever suffered from high salinity levels in body fluids, I use products that add a moderate amount of salt to our diet. Soy sauce and miso are both deceptively salty tasting. On the average, soy sauce contains about 14 percent salt (there are low-sodium soy sauces that contain seven to nine percent salt). This means a teaspoon of soy sauce provides about 286 milligrams of sodium, whereas a teaspoon of salt provides two grams (2,000 milligrams) of sodium. Miso usually contains about 12 percent sodium. And because of the full flavor present in soy sauce and miso, I end up using less than I would if I used salt.

Both soy sauce and miso add other nutrients along with the salt, which makes them a higher quality source of sodium than plain table salt. Soy sauce provides fewer nutrients because it's not a whole food, as miso is, and has a high water content. Since soy sauce and miso are both soybean products, they contain all the nutrients contained in soybeans (in small amounts) with some additional benefits as well. Being careful to buy naturally-fermented soy sauce or miso assures a pre-digested protein, some vitamin B-12, and friendly flora that help to aid digestion.

You may notice that I also use a vegetable-seasoned salt called Spike quite a bit in my recipes. Though there are many low-sodium, vegetable-seasoned salts on the market, Spike is not sold as a low-sodium product; but the presence of the vegetable seasonings definitely reduces the amount of salt I might have used if I were to use plain table salt.

There are really no special recipes showing how I use soy sauce, miso and Spike because the recipes spread throughout the book demonstrate that. Just remember, though, if your physician has placed you on a low- or no-sodium diet, to follow this until your blood salinity levels normalize (to about one percent). Then maybe you can try some soy sauce, miso or vegetable-seasoned salt to keep your system in healthy balance by using the right quantity and best quality sources of sodium.

# THE RIGHT STUFF

Negating all negative intake and eating all the right stuff for the rest of your life will ensure optimum health (of which a trim body is an integral part) for you and your loved ones. In case it hasn't been stated clearly enough in one place, the foods that have been right for my family and me for the last 18 years are mainly complex carbohydrates (whole grains and legumes, nuts, vegetables and fruits) and a tiny bit of dairy products. As can be seen by the variety of recipes in this book, these foods can be combined in so many delicious ways that eating healthfully never has to be boring or a tolerated austerity.

The word "carbohydrate" is a little misleading because complex carbohydrates contain more than just starch or sugars. A wide variety and good balance of complex carbohydrates contains enough protein, fat, vitamins, minerals and fiber that a body could thrive almost solely on them. They should make up at least 75 percent of food intake. Studies have shown that complex carbohydrate foods are the least fattening (see p. 11). The known scientific reasons for this are —

• Complex carbohydrates keep blood-sugar and insulin levels steady because they're broken down and absorbed into the bloodstream slowly. The fiber absorbs and helps the body pass out fat and toxins from the bloodstream.
• The combination of more even levels of blood-sugar and the bulk of dietary fiber keep one feeling fuller longer.
• Complex carbohydrates are usually transformed to glucose and burned by the body; they are rarely stored as fat.

# CHAPTER 9

# YOU CAN HAVE YOUR CAKE (PIZZA, PASTA, SUSHI AND FAVORITE DESSERTS) . . . PROVIDED THEY'RE MADE WITH WHOLE GRAINS

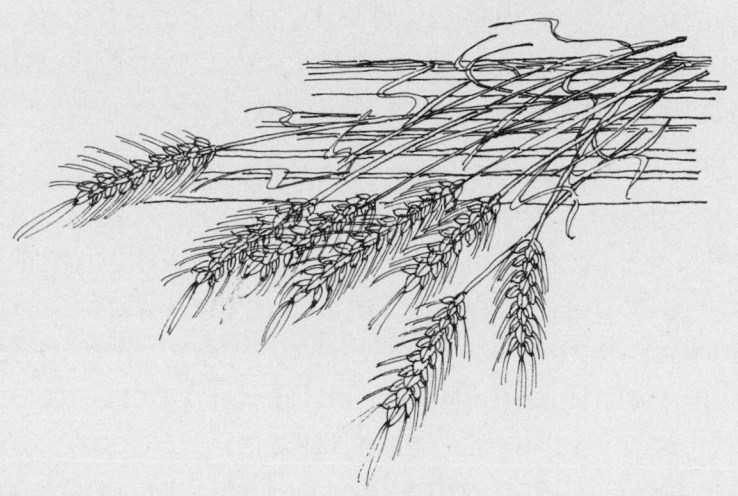

As a mother concerned for my family's and my own health, and as a cook, I prefer whole grains over refined grains. This hasn't always been the case. Being of Japanese descent, I grew up eating a lot of rice — a lot of *white* rice (and white bread) — so I know the trauma of changing from refined to whole foods.

When I was in junior high school, I was fortunate enough to have a swim coach, Halo Hirose, who managed to get my (as well as others') parents to make some small changes in our diets. He was the person who first introduced me to the fact that what I put into my body would make a difference in how it would feel and perform. Along with eating oranges and honey instead of chocolate bars for energy before swim events, came a couple of changes at home — eating whole wheat bread instead of white bread and brown rice instead of white rice.

Small changes like these seem gargantuous when trying to change habits and tastes acquired in a lifetime. When my mother made the first pots of brown rice, I remember my brother and I wouldn't touch the stuff because it was the wrong color. Now I'm happy that my mother was persistent; at the time, I was anything but appreciative. To make the change less drastic, my mother began cooking pots of half brown rice and half white rice so we could overcome our color prejudice and give the healthy stuff a try. Once we tasted the brown rice and decided it wasn't all that bad, it and whole wheat bread became part of my diet for life. After years of the nutty, rich flavor of whole grains, refined grains are unappealingly tasteless.

## YOU CAN CHANGE MORE THAN JUST YOUR DIET

More and more people across the country are rediscovering the wonderful taste and nutritional pluses of whole grains, as is evidenced by the increasing availability of 100 percent whole wheat breads and raw brown rice on grocery store shelves. The fact that these (and other natural products) are now gracing supermarket shelves, where 10 years ago one would have been hard-put to find these products anywhere but in health food stores, shows that votes (saying "yes" by purchasing, saying "no" by refraining from buying) registered in the marketplace of supply and demand are heard

and responded to. By refusing to buy non-nutritious, non-quality "plastic" foods, enough people in America have sent the clear message to food manufacturers that we want more wholesome, natural foods for ourselves.

Besides using the dollar to deliver messages about what we prefer to eat, this consumer power can be used to deliver messages of grave social concern, especially when it's fairly organized. The

.............................

*"Whether you choose to become an active member of a consumer organization, lobby your Congressional representatives for more food aid to needy nations, help set up a food cooperative in your community, or learn how to eat 'low off the food chain,' you are making a political decision."*

— Lerza and Jacobson
Food for People, Not for Profit

.............................

"Nestle's boycott" years ago let large, multi-national corporations know that American consumers do care about unethical, exploitative practices carried out by companies overseas.

A recent piece of mail I received brought to my attention an issue that is of importance to every one of us. The tropical rainforests (also befittingly called "the lungs of the

earth") are being destroyed at a rate of 100 acres a minute. Half of the world's rainforests are already gone, and if the bulldozing continues at the present rate, practically all the rainforests will be destroyed by the year 2050. Besides displacing and making local residents hungrier and poorer, and exterminating half of the plant and animal species on earth, losing the rainforests could accelerate the greenhouse effect (warming of the earth's atmosphere to the point of melting polar ice caps, which could "turn America's grain belt to desert and make Europe too cold and wet to grow food").

Since a great deal of the rainforests are being destroyed to raise beef cattle for export to affluent Western countries, the Rainforest Action Network is calling for a boycott of rainforest beef and companies (like Burger King) that import and sell rainforest beef.

*For more details, write to —*
*Rainforest Action Network*
*466 Green Street*
*San Francisco, CA*
*94133-9983*

. . . because I really should get back to the subject of whole grains. Let's see . . . I was talking about people across the country rediscovering whole grains, now that health and fitness have become "status symbols" in a sense. When you think of it, people everywhere latch on to the idea of status symbols. Status symbols usually become so because they are rare and hard to obtain. Since bad eating habits, coupled with a sedentary lifestyle, have made the majority of Americans unhealthy and unfit — even obese — it's easy to understand how health and fitness have become coveted goals to obtain.

Having to rediscover whole grains again is actually due to refined grains having been a status symbol at one time in history, and still presently is in some places on the planet. In ancient Japan, only Japanese princesses were allowed to eat white rice, which was very labor-intensive to produce. The peasants had to live on brown rice or even millet! As soon as modern milling methods made refined rice easy and inexpensive to obtain, everyone had to have it!

On a cultural exchange visit to the People's Republic of China a few years ago, I repeatedly asked our hosts for brown rice instead of white. The reply was always the same — in what would like to be a classless society — "Oh, no, that's peasant food." And because it's truly a rarity in that part of the world, being able to eat beef has become quite a status symbol as well. I sincerely hope that the citizens of the People's Republic of China and other "Third World" countries of the world who are striving to bring their standard of living up to that of the United States, can learn from our mistakes — without having to suffer the dietary-related diseases we have — and understand that many food status symbols are unhealthy.

Being of Japanese-American heritage, the whole grains that I'm most familiar with, and I therefore use the most,

> "The true food faddists are not those who eat raw broccoli, wheat germ and yogurt, but those who start the day on 'Breakfast Squares,' gulp down bottle after bottle of soda pop, and snack on candies and 'Twinkies' . . . people who eat a junk food diet constitute the norm, while individuals whose diets resemble those of our grandparents are labeled deviants."
>
> — Michael Jacobsen
> Center for Science
> in the Public Interest
> "Science" magazine
> May 16, 1975, vol. 188

are brown rice and whole wheat flour. They are both inexpensive and can be found in practically any supermarket. But aside from these, there is a wide array of other whole grains that are available (mostly in natural food stores) and worth trying.

• *Millet* — the topmost on my list of "other whole grains."
It is the only alkaline grain, making it easy to digest, and it contains more iron than any other grain. Millet provides more servings per pound than any other grain. Four to five parts of water to one part millet, simmered about 30 minutes, will yield about 4 to 5 cups of cooked millet.

• *Oats* — one grain that everyone is familiar with in its unrefined form. The oatmeal sold on supermarket shelves is the whole grain that has been rolled (or cut) into flakes. For regular rolled oats (not instant), use one part oats to two parts of water; simmer about 10 minutes.

• *Barley* — usually cooked in its whole form into stews and soups, but is also available in flake form (to be used like oatmeal) and as a flour. Simmer one part barley to four parts water for 40 to 50 minutes.

• *Bulgar* — a whole grain that is usually parboiled before it's pearled by manufacturers (pearling doesn't remove the germ of bulgar because of the seed structure). Because of being parboiled in the process, this is a quick-cooking grain at home; just use two parts water to one part grain, put grain in boiling water, cover and turn off heat, allow to sit 15 minutes.

• *Corn* — specifically meaning the seed of the maize plant native to America (Englishmen call wheat "corne"; Scotsmen call oats "corn"). Corn is very nutritious if you can find the grain and any flour or meal made from it in a whole form. All corn flour and corn meal on the market have been refined unless the label specifies "stoneground or unsifted, whole corn meal (or flour)." About the most common whole grain corn to be found is popcorn. While popcorn is a better alternative for snacking or dessert than anything made with refined grains, it is nutritionally the poorest of all the different varieties of corn that there are. Popcorn also cannot be used for sprouting where most other whole, dry corn varieties can be.

• *Rye* — can be cooked in whole kernel form like rice; its low-gluten flour makes dense, distinctive-flavored breads that some people prefer to whole wheat. The whole berry can also be germinated like wheatberries (p. 19).

• *Triticale* — a crossbreed of wheat and rye that offers an improved amino acid balance and a little more protein than whole wheat. It can be used about any way whole wheat is, but its softer gluten requires gentler handling. As a whole berry, simmer four parts water to one part grain for about one hour. The flour can be added to, or partly substituted for, whole wheat flour. The whole berry can also be germinated like wheatberries (p. 19).

• *Couscous* — especially important to use in making authentic Mid-Eastern dishes, as no other grain resembles its light, fluffy texture.

• *Buckwheat* — not really a grain at all in the scientific, botanical sense, although most people think of it and use it as a grain. It's actually related to rhubarb and is not of the seed-bearing grass family that all grains are. The whole buckwheat seed can be cooked like rice (except that it needs four parts water to one part grain), and buckwheat flour can be mixed with other lighter flours in baking. I personally use buckwheat the most by sprouting unhulled buckwheat seeds (see p. 530) for salads. Buckwheat is one of the best natural sources of rutic acid, which many herbalists recommend (usually in the form of rutin tablets) for clearing up varicose veins, atherosclerosis, high blood pressure and other circulatory problems.

• *Amaranth* — a newly reinstated, ancient food (of the Aztec Indians). It's quite nutritious cooked whole (three parts water to one part amaranth, simmered for about 25 minutes), sprouted or ground into a flour.

For lack of space, it's impossible for me to list all the different varieties that exist of each different grain and their separate nutritional values. In general, whole grains supply protein, essential fats, iron, B-vitamins (thiamine, riboflavin, niacin), vitamin E, folic acid, canthaxanthic acid, zinc, copper, chromium, magnesium, potassium, manganese and dietary fiber. To varying degrees, whole grains are usually lacking or low in the amino acids isoleucine and lysine, which are plentiful in legumes, nuts and seeds. It's not hard (and is really quite delicious) to make meals that combine whole grains and legumes and/or nuts.

Virtually all of the nutrients in whole grains are contained in the germ and bran, which are removed in refining. Since the oil-rich germ is intact in whole grains, they need to be stored properly to prevent spoilage. Whole grains last longest in their berry form; stored in a cool, dry place in an airtight container, they'll last one to two years. As soon as the grain is broken in some way, the oils in the germ begin to break down. This is why whole grain flours, meals or flakes should always be refrigerated in airtight containers where they will stay good for months. Some perfectionists prefer to grind their own flour at home in small flour mills; this certainly ensures the freshest flour possible!

In history, whole grains combined with legumes are unrivaled as the most important source of nutrients for man. Returning to a diet based on whole grains and legumes will help to improve personal health and could mean enough food for everyone in the world.

# SUSHI BUFFET

In commenting on the changing nature of this world, the ancient Chinese sage Lao Tsu wrote, "In fact, for all things there is a time for going ahead, and a time for following behind; a time for slow-breathing and a time for fast-breathing; a time to grow in strength and a time to decay; a time to be up and a time to be down . . . " Therefore the sage is not disturbed by such changes any more than by the changing of seasons.

If you are entertaining, or want to serve your family a special meal that's simple to prepare, this beautiful, exotic buffet with an Oriental theme may be what you're looking for! As all the dishes are cool and refreshing, this buffet spread is an excellent offering in hot weather. Since everything is prepared ahead of time, all that needs to be done at mealtime is to set the table and enjoy the company of loved ones while everyone makes their own sushi to suit their own taste.

The central dish or entree of this buffet is the Sushi Rice Salad; of course, I always make mine with brown rice. The Rice Salad is otherwise known in Japanese as "Badazushi." The Japanese words "bada-bada" mean "loose," so "Bada-zushi" translates to "loose sushi," which is exactly what the Sushi Rice Salad is. All the ingredients that would or could normally go into a sushi get tossed onto the rice salad-style, which saves the time, energy and skill that rolling or shaping sushis otherwise require.

To set the buffet table, center one, two or three large bowlfuls of the Sushi Rice Salad so they're easily reached. Around the Sushi Rice Salad, artfully arrange all the fixings for wrapping and filling sushi in individual bowls or platters.

For people to be able to make their own bite-sized sushis, provide an abundance of the following to be used for wrappers:
• *Nori seaweed sheets* — cut into sixths or eighths; available in the Oriental food aisle, if your local grocery store has one; some natural food stores carry these; for sure carried in Japanese grocery stores.
• *Whole Manoa or Bibb lettuce leaves* — an alternative to the

nori sheets for those who haven't yet acquired a taste for seaweed.

• *Chiso, also called beefsteak leaves* — a Japanese herb that adds its own unique piquant taste to the sushi; available in Japanese groceries or nurseries (if you want to try your hand at growing your own).

Just as for wrappers, there are no hard and fast rules for what condiments can be sprinkled on the rice for fillers. Here is a list of some things you can try, but also try to use your imagination and include some of your favorite vegetables:

• *3"- to 4"-long by ¼" or thinner carrot sticks.*
• *3"- to 4"-long by ¼" or thinner celery sticks and/or cucumber sticks sprinkled with soy sauce.*
• *3"- to 4"-long avocado slices or mashed avocado.*
• *Thinly-sliced tomato wedges.*
• *3"- to 4"-long radish sprouts* — available in some Japanese groceries or gourmet produce markets.
• *Soy sauce sprinkled on very finely grated daikon (white Japanese radish)* — available in Japanese groceries and some supermarket produce sections.
• *Authentic Japanese pickled vegetables* — a wide variety is available in Japanese groceries and some Oriental food aisles in supermarkets. Some to try:
*Tsukemono* (pickled greens), *Takuwan* (pickled daikon), *Nasubi-no-tsukemono* (pickled baby eggplant). Japanese pickled vegetables are extremely salty so only a tiny amount is used on top of rice.
• *Spinach Salad*
• *Soy sauce.*
• *Roasted, ground sesame seeds or Sesame Salt (p. 93).*

Some spreads to provide for putting on wrappers or rice:
• *Wasabe (hot Japanese mustard) mixed with a little soy sauce.*
• *Umeboshi plum paste* — this and wasabe mustard/horse-radish are available in Japanese groceries and sometimes in natural food stores or Oriental food aisles in grocery stores.
• *Miso-Sesame Barbecue Sauce (p. 602).*

Give everyone a plate for assembling rice and wrappers, fillings and spreads of their choice.

You may have to show everyone how to make their own sushis. The idea is that they can hold the wrapper of their choice in one hand, fill with rice down the center of the wrapper, and top rice with as many toppings and spreads as desired. Then, the wrapper should be folded over taco-style and eaten on the spot.

For guests that delight in a bit of a challenge and/or learning something new, you can make this a meal they'll never forget by providing a bamboo sushi roller at each place, instead of a plate, and whole nori sheets instead of the cut-up ones. Then, each guest will have to learn how to and actually assemble a real nori sushi roll on the spot. Either way you present this buffet, it's a memorable meal!

## MENU FOR A SUSHI BUFFET

*Sushi Rice Salad*

*Bibb lettuce and/or nori sheets*

*Various condiments (as listed in description of meal)*

*Spinach Salad*

*Jeweled Treasure*

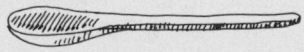

# PERFECT BROWN RICE

*4 cups water (or vegetable water)*

*2 cups brown rice*

Bring water, or vegetable water, to a boil. (This is a good way to use the mineral-rich water derived from steaming vegetables.) As soon as the water boils, slowly trickle the brown rice in so water keeps boiling. If you drop all the rice in at once, the water will stop boiling. It is crucial to keep the water boiling in order to end up with nice, fluffy rice. This is because the starch in the rice immediately cooks when it hits the boiling water and doesn't have time to soak out into the cooking water, causing it to thicken — which ends up making mushy cooked rice. After all the rice is in the pot and the water is still boiling, put a lid on the pot, turn heat down to simmer, and simmer for 45 minutes.

This much rice will serve 6. If you want to change portions, just remember: 1 part rice to 2 parts water.

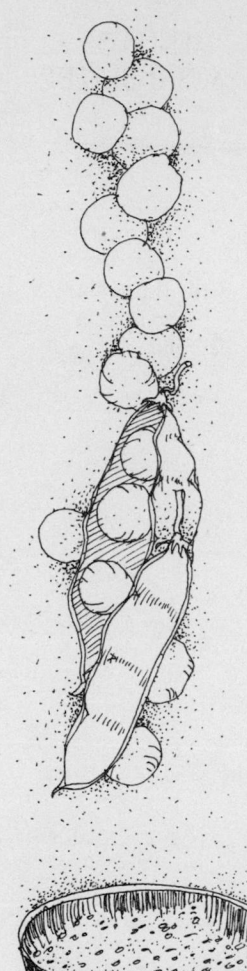

# SUSHI RICE SALAD

☆ In the Sushi Buffet, this is the entree; it also makes a delicious side dish.

*10 cups hot water*
*1 oz. dry shiitake mushrooms*

*4 cups raw brown rice*

*¼ cup rice vinegar (4.2% - 4.3% acidity)*
*5 Tbsp. water*
*2 Tbsp. honey*
*½ tsp. salt*

*2 Tbsp. water*
*2 Tbsp. soy sauce*
*1 Tbsp. honey*

*2 cups sliced age/aburage shells (optional)*

*2 cups matchstick or thinly sliced carrots*
*2 cups frozen or fresh peas*
*1 cup thinly slivered string beans*

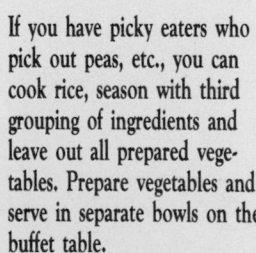

If you have picky eaters who pick out peas, etc., you can cook rice, season with third grouping of ingredients and leave out all prepared vegetables. Prepare vegetables and serve in separate bowls on the buffet table.

*1 cup slivered water chestnuts*

*½ cup toasted sesame seeds*
*5 sheets nori seaweed, crumbled*

Soak first 2 ingredients together for 25 minutes. Remove mushrooms from water and bring mushroom soaking water to a boil. Add rice, bring back to a boil and lower heat to medium-low to maintain a gentle rolling boil for 40 minutes. While rice is cooking, prepare vegetables. This dish is a delicious way to use leftover brown rice; in that case, the step of cooking rice in the mushroom soaking water is eliminated — just soak mushrooms in as little water as is necessary to cover them and keep water for cooking vegetables in later.

Uncover rice and scoop out into a large mixing bowl. Mix next 4 ingredients together and toss into rice. (Note: These 4 ingredients mixed together make a delicious oil-free dressing for salads.)

Boil age triangles in a small pot of water to remove oil. Discard water and rinse age in warm water and wring out. Cut into ¼"-thick slices. Slice soaked mushrooms into ¼"-thick slices.

Combine next 3 ingredients together in a small pot and bring to a boil. If you are using leftover rice, use the mushroom soaking water here.

Boil sliced mushrooms and age strips in water/soy sauce/honey mixture for 3 to 4 minutes, stirring occasionally to be sure every mushroom and age strip gets cooked in the liquid. Remove mushrooms and age strips from liquid with a slotted spoon, being sure to press liquid out of them by pressing mushrooms and age between the slotted spoon and a solid spoon.

Use remaining liquid to lightly cook prepared vegetables. (Carrots cut into matchsticks and/or pretty flower shapes; cut the flower shapes by using Japanese flower-shaped vegetable cutters on thinly-grated carrots or make four to five ⅛"-

deep grooves down the length of the carrot so the cross section of the carrot looks like a flower, then slice or grate into thin flowers. Thinly slice string beans diagonally.) Cook vegetables by adding to the boiling liquid all at once, or one vegetable type at a time, and stir gently, cooking till vegetables turn a more brilliant color than they are in their raw state. Remove from heat.

Toss prepared mushrooms, age, vegetables, and water chestnuts into rice. Cover with a damp cloth and allow rice to cool to room temperature, or cover and refrigerate overnight or a few hours before serving.

Just before serving, sprinkle top with whole or ground toasted sesame seeds and crumbled nori sheets. Makes 8 to 10 full-sized servings if served as a main dish on a bed of lettuce and mung bean sprouts, or will serve 30 as a dish on a buffet table.

| Special Shopping |
| --- |
| Dry shiitake mushrooms, age /aburage shells, canned water chestnuts — all three ingredients can be found in Japanese groceries and some supermarkets with Oriental food aisles. |

| SHOPPING LIST | |
| --- | --- |
| **Regularly Kept in the Kitchen** (Listed in Chapter 14, p. 703) | **Fresh Produce** |
| Brown rice<br>Rice vinegar<br>Honey<br>Soy sauce<br>Sesame seeds<br>Nori seaweed | Carrots<br>Peas (fresh or frozen)<br>String beans |

# NUTRITIONAL ANALYSIS FOR ONE SERVING SUSHI RICE SALAD

```
NUTRIENT      Type: 14   FEMALE-23 TO 51 YEARS              % RDA   Amount
KCALORIES     A=============                                 25%    512.0 Kc
PROTEIN       A===============                               29%    12.80 Gm
CARBOHYDRATE  A                                            NO RDA   98.30 Gm
FAT           A                                            NO RDA   7.480 Gm
FIBER-CRUDE   A                                            NO RDA   3.230 Gm
CHOLESTEROL   A                                            NO RDA   0.000 Mg
SATURATED FA  A                                            NO RDA   0.600 Gm
OLEIC. FA     A                                            NO RDA   9.210 Gm
LINOLEIC FA   A                                            NO RDA   0.630 Gm
SODIUM        A=========                                     18%    402.0 Mg
POTASSIUM     A========                                      17%    670.0 Mg
MAGNESIUM     A==============================                60%    181.0 Mg
IRON          A============                                  25%    4.570 Mg
ZINC          A========                                      17%    2.690 Mg
VITAMIN A     A=============================================260%   10409 IU
VITAMIN D     A                                               0%    0.000 IU
VIT. E/TOTAL  A                                            NO RDA   9.220 Mg
VITAMIN C     A=====================                         46%    28.10 Mg
THIAMIN       A====================                          40%    0.400 Mg
RIBOFLAVIN    A=========                                     18%    0.220 Mg
NIACIN        A=====================                         43%    5.600 Mg
VITAMIN B6    A==============                                30%    0.600 Mg
FOLACIN       A==                                             5%    23.20 Ug
VITAMIN B12   A                                               0%    0.000 Ug
PANTO- ACID   A==================                            37%    2.080 Mg
CALCIUM       A===========                                   22%    180.0 Mg
PHOSPHORUS    A==========================                    52%    416.0 Mg
TRYPTOPHAN    A=====================================        111%    181.0 Mg
THREONINE     A==========================================   129%    564.0 Mg
ISOLEUCINE    A=========================================    121%    794.0 Mg
LEUCINE       A=============================================155%    1355 Mg
LYSINE        A==========================================   106%    693.0 Mg
METHIONINE    A==================================            94%    256.0 Mg
CYSTINE       A=========================================     76%    207.0 Mg
PHENYL-ANINE  A=============================================188%    822.0 Mg
TYROSINE      A=============================================114%    499.0 Mg
VALINE        A=============================================118%    901.0 Mg
HISTIDINE     A                                            NO RDA   484.0 Mg
ALCOHOL       A                                            NO RDA   0.000 Gm
ASH           A                                            NO RDA   3.490 Gm
COPPER        A============                                  24%    0.620 Mg
MANGANESE     A============================================  94%    3.550 Mg
IODINE        A============================================ 502%    754.0 Ug
MONO FAT      A                                            NO RDA   1.520 Gm
POLY FAT      A                                            NO RDA   1.830 Gm
CAFFEINE      A                                            NO RDA   0.000 Mg
FLUORIDE      A                                               1%    46.00 Ug
MOLYBDENUM    A=============================================452%    1469 Ug
VITAMIN K     A=============================================132%    139.0 Ug
SELENIUM      A========                                      16%    0.020 Mg
BIOTIN        A==                                             5%    8.860 Ug
CHLORIDE      A==                                             5%    197.0 Mg
CHROMIUM      A=============================================592%    0.740 Mg
SUGAR         A                                            NO RDA   3.770 Gm
FIBER-DIET    A                                            NO RDA   3.750 Gm
VIT. E/AT     A=============                                 27%    2.220 Mg

    % RDA:   |0      |20     |40     |60     |80     |100
```

Optional aburage shells were included in analysis.

# SPINACH SALAD

☆ In quite a few countries, salads consist of lightly cooked vegetables as opposed to raw ones, like we're used to here.

---

*1 large bunch fresh spinach (about 1 lb.)*

*2 Tbsp. soy sauce*
*2 Tbsp. toasted, ground sesame seeds*
    *(preferably black sesame)*
*2 tsp. honey*

Bring large pot (large enough to fit whole spinach into) of water to a boil. Meanwhile, wash spinach off very well, as it usually has quite a bit of dirt and sand on it. Keep spinach in a bunch, leaving on roots and stems so you can use them as "handles" when blanching. When water comes to a boil, plunge whole bunch of spinach into boiling water till leaves turn a more brilliant green than when they are raw (only takes about half a minute). Remove wilted leaves from hot water and plunge into a bowlful of cold water to stop the cooking process and cool the leaves. Remove leaves from water with hands (they should be cool enough to do this) and wring out excess water as you would a towel. Place wrung-out roll of spinach on cutting board and cut into 1" to 1½" lengths. Mix next 3 ingredients together and toss into cut spinach. Allow to sit a few minutes if you wish to serve this warm, or cover and chill to serve cold. Just before serving, toss again and sprinkle with more toasted sesame seeds to garnish. Makes 8 very small Japanese-sized servings.

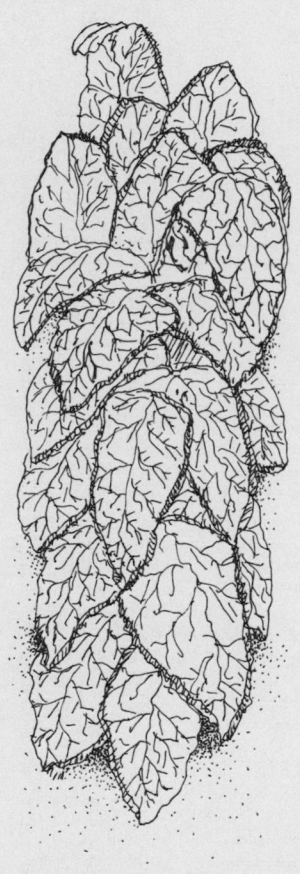

This salad is also delicious when made with watercress instead of spinach.

| SHOPPING LIST | |
|---|---|
| **Regularly Kept in the Kitchen** (Listed in Chapter 14, p. 703) | **Fresh Produce** |
| Soy sauce<br>Sesame seeds<br>Honey | Spinach |

# NUTRITIONAL ANALYSIS FOR ONE SERVING SPINACH SALAD

```
NUTRIENT        Type: 14   FEMALE-23 TO 51 YEARS                    % RDA    Amount
KCALORIES       A                                                     1%    32.20 Kc
PROTEIN         A==                                                   5%     2.390 Gm
CARBOHYDRATE    A                                                  NO RDA    4.330 Gm
FAT             A                                                  NO RDA    1.190 Gm
FIBER-CRUDE     A                                                  NO RDA    0.690 Gm
CHOLESTEROL     A                                                  NO RDA    0.000 Mg
SATURATED FA    A                                                  NO RDA    0.170 Gm
OLEIC FA        A                                                  NO RDA    0.000 Gm
LINOLEIC FA     A                                                  NO RDA    0.000 Gm
SODIUM          A======                                              13%    302.0 Mg
POTASSIUM       A====                                                9%     348.0 Mg
MAGNESIUM       A=========                                          18%     54.70 Mg
IRON            A=====                                              11%      2.000 Mg
ZINC            A=                                                   3%      0.460 Mg
VITAMIN A       A=================================================  96%    3876 IU
VITAMIN D       A                                                   0%      0.000 IU
VIT. E/TOTAL    A                                                NO RDA     2.170 Mg
VITAMIN C       A=============                                      27%     16.20 Mg
THIAMIN         A==                                                 4%      0.040 Mg
RIBOFLAVIN      A=====                                              9%      0.110 Mg
NIACIN          A==                                                 4%      0.570 Mg
VITAMIN B6      A===                                                6%      0.120 Mg
FOLACIN         A==============                                     27%    111.0 Ug
VITAMIN B12     A                                                   0%      0.000 Ug
PANTO- ACID     A                                                   0%      0.050 Mg
CALCIUM         A====                                               9%     78.90 Mg
PHOSPHORUS      A===                                                6%     51.60 Mg
TRYPTOPHAN      A=========                                         18%     30.30 Mg
THREONINE       A=========                                         19%     84.60 Mg
ISOLEUCINE      A=======                                           15%     99.50 Mg
LEUCINE         A========                                          17%    154.0 Mg
LYSINE          A=========                                         17%    112.0 Mg
METHIONINE      A=======                                           15%     42.40 Mg
CYSTINE         A=====                                             10%     27.60 Mg
PHENYL-ANINE    A==========                                        21%     92.70 Mg
TYROSINE        A========                                          17%     76.60 Mg
VALINE          A=======                                           14%    112.0 Mg
HISTIDINE       A                                                NO RDA    47.50 Mg
ALCOHOL         A                                                NO RDA     0.000 Gm
ASH             A                                                NO RDA     1.800 Gm
COPPER          A==                                                 4%      0.120 Mg
MANGANESE       A=======                                           14%      0.560 Mg
IODINE          A                                                   0%      0.000 Ug
MONO FAT        A                                                NO RDA     0.380 Gm
POLY FAT        A                                                NO RDA     0.520 Gm
CAFFEINE        A                                                NO RDA     0.000 Mg
FLUORIDE        A=                                                  2%     58.40 Ug
MOLYBDENUM      A==                                                 4%     14.40 Ug
VITAMIN K       A=========================                         48%     50.50 Ug
SELENIUM        A                                                   0%      0.000 Mg
BIOTIN          A=                                                  2%      3.960 Ug
CHLORIDE        A                                                   0%      0.000 Mg
CHROMIUM        A====                                               8%      0.010 Mg
SUGAR           A                                                NO RDA     0.280 Gm
FIBER-DIET      A                                                NO RDA     1.810 Gm
VIT. E/AT       A======                                            13%      1.060 Mg

    % RDA:  |0       |20      |40      |60      |80      |100      10
```

# JEWELED TREASURE

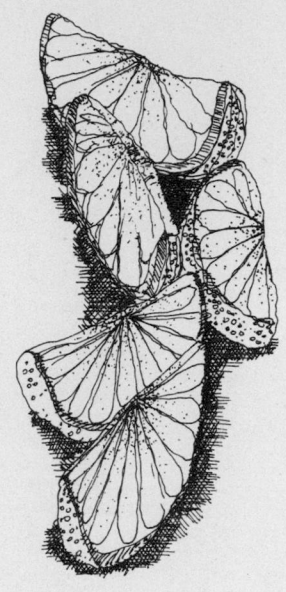

☆ The name of the recipe is appropriate. In Japan, honeydew melons are like treasures. On a trip to Japan, I discovered that a honeydew melon costs an equivalent of fifty U.S. dollars and are often taken as a special gift to someone.

☆ To get a melon is a special event, and the fruit is relished and much appreciated, not just thoughtlessly consumed.

☆ Like most Oriental desserts, this is light and refreshing, completely free of fat.

---

¼ cup water
2 Tbsp. vegetable gelatin

1¾ cups natural lemon-lime soda
  (or other flavor; can also use natural,
  unsweetened juices as well)

½ cup demembrained mandarin orange
  sections, cut in half

1 ripe honeydew melon, peeled and de-seeded

Bring ¼ cup water to a boil in small pot. Turn off heat and mix in vegetable gelatin till it dissolves. Pour in natural soda and mix thoroughly. Refrigerate till firmly set — so gel doesn't move when pot is tilted.

In the meantime, prepare fruit. Peel mandarin orange and break into sections. Peel membrane off each section and split in the middle, removing any seeds, till you have ½ cup's worth. To prepare melon, peel rind off the whole melon, then cut a cap off the top. Holding the melon upright in your hand, scoop out the seeds and membrane from the center of the melon, leaving the whole seed cavity intact. Put melon in refrigerator to chill.

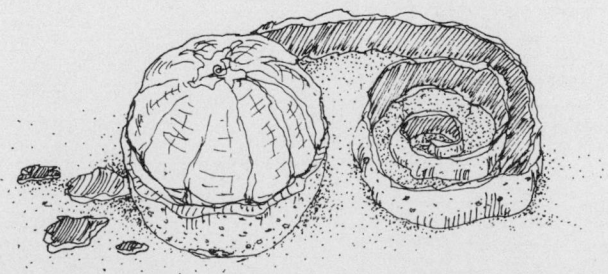

When the gel is firm, gently fold mandarin orange slices into the gel and stuff this mixture into the cavity of the melon. Return melon to the refrigerator with cavity tilted upright so softened gel doesn't spill out. Refrigerate till gel sets.

Just before serving time, cut a thin slice off the side of the melon so melon will sit flat on a serving platter with length of the stuffed cavity lying parallel to the platter. To serve, cut individual slices about ½" to ¾" thick, cutting across the width of the melon so you end up with a melon ring with a pretty fruit gel in the middle of the circle. Serve immediately. One melon serves 6 to 8.

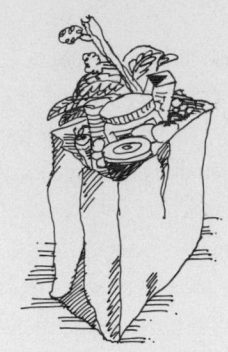

| SHOPPING LIST | | Special Shopping |
|---|---|---|
| **Regularly Kept in the Kitchen** (Listed in Chapter 14, p. 703) | **Fresh Produce** | Natural lemon-lime soda (honey- or fruit juice-sweetened) — all natural food stores and an increasing number of supermarkets are starting to carry these. Vegetable gelatin — try a Jewish food store for "kosher gelatin" made from carrageenan; as a second choice, use agar-agar, a seaweed which can be found in most natural food stores, Japanese or Chinese groceries. Carrageenan jells like "Jell-o"; agar-agar sets thick and solid, doesn't wiggle. |
| (None) | Mandarin oranges<br>Honeydew melon | |

# SANDWICHES FOR BROWN·BAGGING OR FANCY MEALS

Just to keep our bodies alive, we need clean air and water, energy and food. It's ironic that the economic and technological systems we've developed make so many of our unnecessary wants readily available; and, simultaneously, our basic needs (like clean air, water, energy and food) are becoming harder and harder to get. In commenting on this course of events, E. F. Schumacher wrote, "In the excitement of his scientific and technical prowess, modern man has built a system of production that ravishes nature and mutilates man."

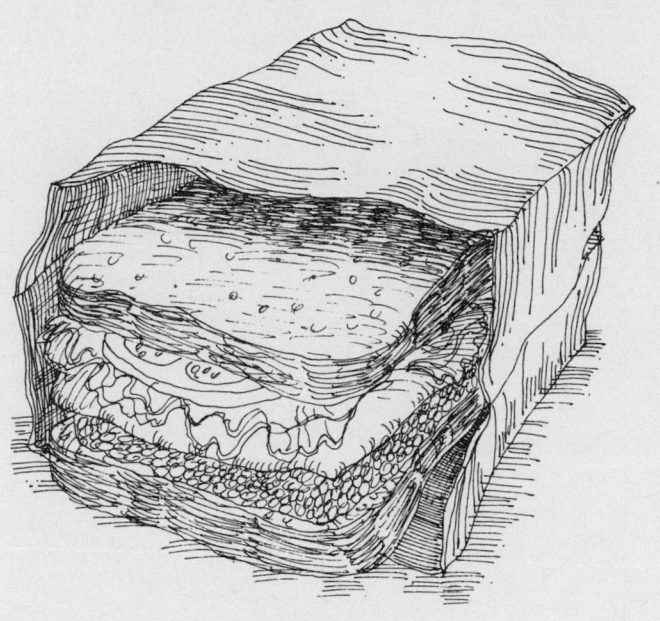

Slices of whole grain bread with fillings on or in them make satisfying, nutritious snacks or meals. Sandwiches can be served as the old-reliable in brown bag lunches or for fancy luncheons or light suppers. The main thing is to be sure the bread and the fillings are made of the healthiest ingredients.

This could be a little tricky in the marketplace today. After the word "free," the word "natural" has become one of the more widely-used consumer catchwords. Unfortunately, there are no laws defining what the term natural can or can't be used for. It's presently legal for the word "natural" to be used on products containing white sugar or white flour, which are both refined as far away from their original, natural forms as possible.

Many manufacturers are exploiting the public's growing concern and desire to eat a healthier diet by producing pseudo- or quasi-natural foods. The only way we can keep from being fooled is to educate ourselves on how to read labels. There are many dark-colored breads on store shelves labeled "whole wheat bread" that contain white flour (often listed as the first, therefore most abundant, ingredient. White flour is sometimes listed as wheat flour or unbleached wheat flour). If looking for a true loaf of whole wheat bread, look for the words "*100 percent* whole wheat."

Fortunately, there are enough 100 percent whole wheat breads on store shelves, making it easier and quicker for you and me to be able to make sandwiches, toast, etc., with whole grain bread. Though I love to fill the house with fresh, home-baked breads, and the children love to punch and knead the dough, I don't have the time to do it often. So, homemade bread is a special treat around our house.

There is a large variety of very interesting whole grain breads available in local natural food stores and supermarkets. Aside from whole wheat, there are breads made with other whole grains mixed in and some very interesting flourless breads that are made solely with sprouted grains and seeds. Unlike the Sweet Essene Bread, these commercial breads are leavened and taste like regular bread (not sweet like the Essene bread).

I like to start my sandwiches with whole grain breads and fill them with good, cholesterol-free fillings like those that follow. Some other good, cholesterol-free fillings are Deviled Eggless Salad (p. 171) and Mock Tuna Salad (p. 173).

# GROWING BOY'S SPECIAL

☆ When my 17-year-old son first invented this sandwich, he told me, "You have to taste this; you'll fall in love." It has become a standard after-school snack that takes only a few minutes to make.

4 slices whole grain bread
Eggless or Tofu Mayonnaise (see recipe, p. 332)
Dijon mustard

¼ block (¼ lb.) Chinese firm tofu
1 tsp. soy sauce
2 Tbsp. nutritional yeast
1 California avocado (1 cup's worth)
2 handfuls alfalfa sprouts

Lay bread slices on counter and spread 2 slices of bread with eggless mayonnaise and the other 2 slices with Dijon mustard.

Cut the tofu into 2 cutlets (cutting across the width of the block of tofu) about ⅝" thick. Lay each cutlet of tofu on top of each piece of bread which was spread with Dijon mustard. Mash each piece of tofu with fingertips or fork, just enough to break the tofu up. Sprinkle evenly with soy sauce and nutritional yeast. Top with slices of avocado and handful of sprouts. Top with remaining pieces of bread.

Makes 2 sandwiches — 1 serving for a 17-year-old, or possibly 2 servings for those with a slower metabolism!

As a growing boy, my son snacks on two of these sandwiches at a time. You may not want to eat that many unless you're very active or growing also. These sandwiches make a nutritious snack or a whole meal.

| SHOPPING LIST | |
|---|---|
| **Regularly Kept in the Kitchen** (Listed in Chapter 14, p. 703) | **Fresh Produce** |
| Whole grain bread | Avocado |
| Tofu | Alfalfa sprouts |
| Eggless mayonnaise | |
| Dijon mustard | |
| Soy sauce | |
| Nutritional yeast | |

# NUTRITIONAL ANALYSIS FOR
# TWO GROWING BOY'S SPECIAL SANDWICHES

```
NUTRIENT        Type: 14    FEMALE-23 TO 51 YEARS          % RDA   Amount
KCALORIES       Ã============                               23%   464.0 Kc
PROTEIN         Ã==========================                 50%   22.10 Gm
CARBOHYDRATE    Ã                                         NO RDA  37.50 Gm
FAT             Ã                                         NO RDA  28.80 Gm
FIBER-CRUDE     Ã                                         NO RDA   3.290 Gm
CHOLESTEROL     Ã                                         NO RDA   0.000 Mg
SATURATED FA    Ã                                         NO RDA   3.770 Gm
OLEIC FA        Ã                                         NO RDA  11.70 Gm
LINOLEIC FA     Ã                                         NO RDA   3.580 Gm
SODIUM          Ã=========                                  18%   400.0 Mg
POTASSIUM       Ã===============                            31%   1186 Mg
MAGNESIUM       Ã========================                   49%   147.0 Mg
IRON            Ã============================               56%   10.10 Mg
ZINC            Ã=============                              27%   4.050 Mg
VITAMIN A       Ã==========                                 20%   818.0 IU
VITAMIN D       Ã                                            0%   0.000 IU
VIT. E/TOTAL    Ã                                         NO RDA   0.870 Mg
VITAMIN C       Ã========                                   17%   10.60 Mg
THIAMIN         Ã==================================================  487%  4.870 Mg
RIBOFLAVIN      Ã==================================================  400%  4.800 Mg
NIACIN          Ã==================================================  231%  30.10 Mg
VITAMIN B6      Ã==================================================  248%  4.970 Mg
FOLACIN         Ã======================                     45%   181.0 Ug
VITAMIN B12     Ã==================================================  118%  3.550 Ug
PANTO- ACID     Ã==================                         39%   2.150 Mg
CALCIUM         Ã================================           64%   518.0 Mg
PHOSPHORUS      Ã==========================                 52%   420.0 Mg
TRYPTOPHAN      Ã==================================================  178%  291.0 Mg
THREONINE       Ã==================================================  200%  873.0 Mg
ISOLEUCINE      Ã==================================================  160%  1048 Mg
LEUCINE         Ã==================================================  188%  1645 Mg
LYSINE          Ã==================================================  199%  1301 Mg
METHIONINE      Ã=============================■■■            116%  316.0 Mg
CYSTINE         Ã=========================================   83%   228.0 Mg
PHENYL-ANINE    Ã==================================================  232%  1012 Mg
TYROSINE        Ã==================================================  133%  582.0 Mg
VALINE          Ã==================================================  151%  1158 Mg
HISTIDINE       Ã                                         NO RDA  455.0 Mg
ALCOHOL         Ã                                         NO RDA   0.000 Gm
ASH             Ã                                         NO RDA   7.710 Gm
COPPER          Ã=============                              27%   0.690 Mg
MANGANESE       Ã==============                             28%   1.070 Mg
IODINE          Ã========================                   49%   74.20 Ug
MONO FAT        Ã                                         NO RDA  13.40 Gm
POLY FAT        Ã                                         NO RDA   6.070 Gm
CAFFEINE        Ã                                         NO RDA   0.000 Mg
FLUORIDE        Ã                                            0%   0.440 Ug
MOLYBDENUM      Ã==================================================  244%  793.0 Ug
VITAMIN K       Ã                                            0%   0.000 Ug
SELENIUM        Ã============                               24%   0.030 Mg
BIOTIN          Ã====                                        8%   12.30 Ug
CHLORIDE        Ã=                                           3%   125.0 Mg
CHROMIUM        Ã==================================================  200%  0.250 Mg
SUGAR           Ã                                         NO RDA   0.020 Gm
FIBER-DIET      Ã                                         NO RDA   3.270 Gm
VIT. E/AT       Ã============                               25%   2.070 Mg

    % RDA:   |0      |20      |40      |60      |80      |100
```

Tofu Mayonnaise used instead of eggless commercial.

# SALAD·WICH

☆ A sub-type sandwich with lots of fresh vegetables in it.

---

¼ - ½ loaf large, whole grain, crusty bread
    (Italian or French) or small, individual-sized
    loaves, 6" long (see recipe, p. 541)

2 Tbsp. olive oil, 1 tsp. vinegar and
    ¼ tsp. asafetida or garlic powder
    OR favorite vinegarette dressing

3 - 4 leaves of loose-leaf lettuce
1 oz. alfalfa, red clover, or sunflower sprouts
2 oz. cheese, thinly sliced (preferably
    lowfat variety)
3 - 4 tomato slices
Leftover Antipasto Salad vegetables
    (see recipes, pp. 619 - 622)
Marinated artichoke hearts
Sliced olives
2 - 3 Tbsp. nutritional yeast or Parmesan cheese

Mustard
Red chilies (dried)
Oregano

Split bread in half lengthwise. Spread the bottom half with a mixture of the next 3 ingredients or your favorite vinegar-ette-type dressing. Layer next 8 ingredients on top of this in the order listed, starting with the lettuce and ending with nutritional yeast or Parmesan cheese. Spread top half of bread with mustard and sprinkle on the next 2 ingredients. Put on top of assembled sandwich and squeeze together. Hold intact by piercing it with a couple of toothpicks. This recipe is for one 6"- to 8"-long sandwich. If you want to make more, just multiply by the necessary number.

For health's sake, it's worth the extra work to make a whole grain, crusty bread if you can't find an already-made one in a store. Crusty Italian or French breads are very lowfat breads and have hardly any sweetener in them at all.

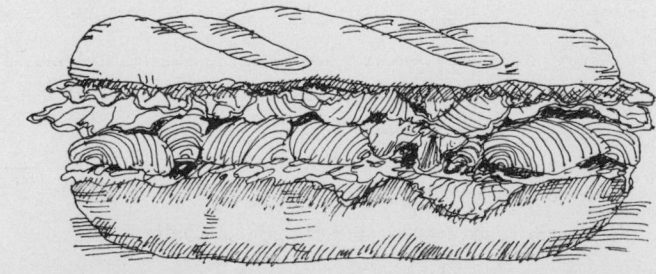

| SHOPPING LIST | |
|---|---|
| **Regularly Kept in the Kitchen (Listed in Chapter 14, p. 703)** | **Fresh Produce** |
| Olive oil<br>Vinegar<br>Asafetida<br>Cheese<br>Nutritional yeast or<br>    Parmesan cheese<br>Mustard<br>Red chili flakes<br>Oregano | Lettuce<br>Alfalfa, red clover or<br>    sunflower sprouts<br>Tomato slices<br>Marinated artichoke hearts<br>Sliced olives |

**Special Shopping**

Whole grain, crusty bread (Italian or French) — can sometimes be found in natural food stores, or make your own at home (p. 541).

Also some leftover Antipasto Salad; see shopping lists for Antipasto Salads (pp. 619 - 622).

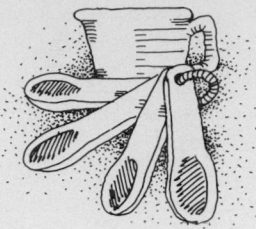

# WHOLE GRAIN FRENCH BREAD

1 pkg. baking yeast
1¼ cups warm water
1 Tbsp. honey
1 Tbsp. oil
1 tsp. salt (optional)

3½ cups whole wheat flour

Corn meal

2 Tbsp. oil
2 Tbsp. milk

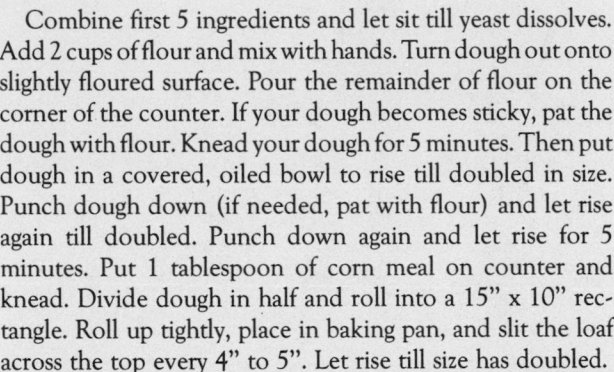

Combine first 5 ingredients and let sit till yeast dissolves. Add 2 cups of flour and mix with hands. Turn dough out onto slightly floured surface. Pour the remainder of flour on the corner of the counter. If your dough becomes sticky, pat the dough with flour. Knead your dough for 5 minutes. Then put dough in a covered, oiled bowl to rise till doubled in size. Punch dough down (if needed, pat with flour) and let rise again till doubled. Punch down again and let rise for 5 minutes. Put 1 tablespoon of corn meal on counter and knead. Divide dough in half and roll into a 15" x 10" rectangle. Roll up tightly, place in baking pan, and slit the loaf across the top every 4" to 5". Let rise till size has doubled.

Meanwhile, boil some water in a pot and preheat oven to 350 degrees. Put pan of boiling water on bottom shelf of oven. (This helps to keep dough from drying out.) Bake 20 minutes. Then remove loaf from oven and brush generously with a mixture of the oil and milk. Return to oven and bake 25 minutes longer.

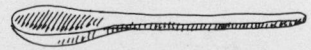

Though more and more whole grain breads can be found in stores, whole grain crusty breads are still hard to find. If you can't find any, for all the health benefits it's worth making your own. Even if you can find it in stores, you will be able to make the bread for about a quarter of the store shelf price.

| SHOPPING LIST | |
| --- | --- |
| Regularly Kept in the Kitchen (Listed in Chapter 14, p. 703) | Fresh Produce |
| Baking yeast<br>Honey<br>Oil<br>Whole wheat flour | (None) |

# SWEET ESSENE BREAD (Sun Bread)

☆ A naturally sweetened, unleavened bread. I like to spread slices with some nut butter, a natural fruit preserve, and then sprinkle with some bee pollen and raisins.

*Grind desired amount of sprouted wheatberries (2 - 3 days old) in food grinder. Shape into bread or biscuit shapes and bake as described in directions for variations that follow.*

### Variety #1:

2 cups ground, sprouted wheatberries
½ cup chopped nuts or seeds
½ cup chopped raisins
1 tsp. orange rind

### Variety #2:

2 cups ground, sprouted wheatberries
½ cup raisins
¼ tsp. cinnamon
⅛ tsp. cardamom
Few drops vanilla

### Variety #3:

2 cups ground, sprouted wheatberries
½ cup raisins
½ cup shredded coconut
⅓ cup carob powder

Combine ingredients and mix together well, kneading with hands if necessary. Form into one large, round loaf or several small ones. Place on a baking sheet covered with a thin screen (to keep bugs off) and set in the sun all day to bake; or set in the oven (without a screen) at 200 degrees to bake all day. Cool and serve by slicing into ½"- to ⅝"-thick slices. All varieties are good served just plain or with butter or cream cheese. One of my favorite ways to serve this, as a nutritious meal or a snack, is to spread a slice with a nut butter and a natural, sugarless preserve, then sprinkled with bee pollen. Keeps best in the refrigerator.

This recipe is originally given in the "Essene Gospel of Peace":
"Let the angels of God prepare your bread.
Moisten your wheat.
And leave it from morning to evening beneath the sun.
And the blessing of the angels of water,
air and sunshine will soon make the germ
of life to sprout in your wheat.
Then crush your grain, and make thin wafers.
Put them back beneath the sun . . .
and when it is risen to its highest in the heavens,
turn them over
on the other side
and leave them there until the sun be set."

| Special Shopping |
|---|
| Sprouted wheatberries — whole, dry wheatberries can be gotten in natural food stores; they must be sprouted at home (see p. 19). |

Since this recipe needs to be frozen, you may as well make the whole batch while you're taking the trouble to make some. That way you'll have more on hand when you need them. Freezing is crucial to the texture of the burger, as it toughens the tofu up.

# WORTH·THE·TROUBLE BURGERS

☆ Especially delicious cooked on an outdoor grill!

5 cups Granburger or other TVP
2 cups finely chopped celery and ¼ cup
    asafetida OR 2 cups diced onion
2 tsp. black pepper
2 lbs. tempeh, crumbled
¼ cup soy sauce
1 cup whole wheat flour
1 cup nutritional yeast
4 cups whole grain bread crumbs
1 cup walnut meal
¾ cup peanut butter
2 lbs. tofu, mashed

Oil for deep-frying

Melted butter or margarine

## Teriyaki Sauce:

1½ cups soy sauce
3 Tbsp. asafetida or 6 cloves garlic,
    finely minced
3 Tbsp. vinegar
2 Tbsp. honey
¼ lb. fresh ginger root
    -OR-

## Mild/Salty Sauce:

1 cup soy sauce
1 cup water

Soak Granburger or other TVP in hot water till moistened. Then combine with rest of first 11 ingredients and mix thoroughly. Heat oil to 425 degrees. As oil is heating, make sauce. For the Teriyaki Sauce, blend all 5 ingredients in blender till ginger is completely minced; or simply combine soy sauce and water for the Mild/Salty Sauce. Then pour sauce into Pyrex cake pan. Now measure ½ cup of mix at a time, shape into patties, and drop into hot oil as many as you can fit without covering each other. Deep-fry till brown and crisp on the surface. Remove from oil with slotted spoon, holding spoon over oil to allow excess oil to drain. Immediately place into sauce solution, flip over, then take out and place on another platter.

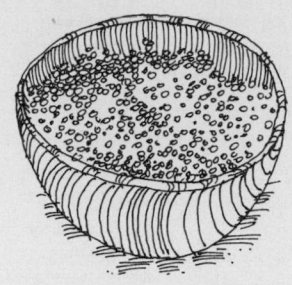

After mixture is done cooking and cooled, stack about 3 to 4 high on cookie or cake trays with squares of saran wrap between. Then wrap in plastic bags and freeze for at least a week. The day you plan to cook and serve the patties, remove from freezer (they can be cooked even when partially frozen), brush surfaces with melted butter or margarine, and place on grill to cook till surfaces get slightly singed and burgers are heated all the way through. Makes 28 burgers.

| SHOPPING LIST | |
|---|---|
| **Regularly Kept in the Kitchen** (Listed in Chapter 14, p. 703) | **Fresh Produce** |
| Asafetida<br>Black pepper<br>Tempeh<br>Soy sauce<br>Whole wheat flour<br>Nutritional yeast<br>Whole grain bread<br>Walnuts<br>Peanut butter<br>Tofu<br>Safflower oil<br>Vinegar<br>Honey | Celery |

| **Special Shopping** |
|---|
| TVP (Texturized Vegetable Protein) — in natural food stores. |

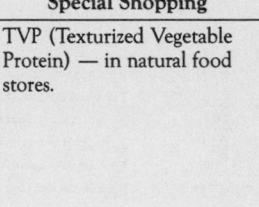

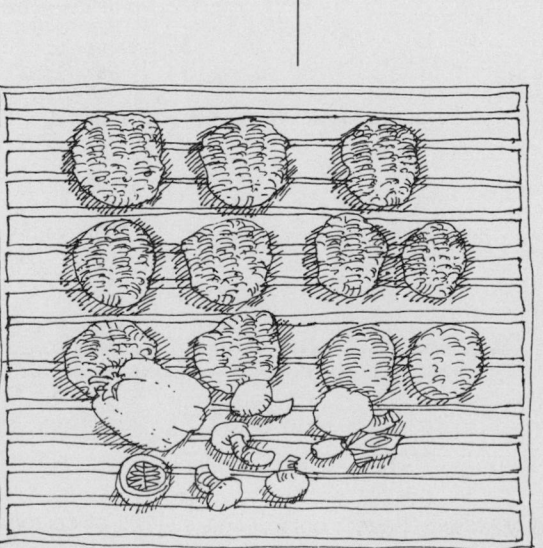

# NUTRITIONAL ANALYSIS FOR ONE
# WORTH-THE-TROUBLE BURGER

| NUTRIENT | Type: 14    FEMALE—23 TO 51 YEARS | % RDA | Amount |
|---|---|---|---|
| KCALORIES | ¤========= | 17% | 355.0 Kc |
| PROTEIN | ¤================================ | 60% | 26.80 Gm |
| CARBOHYDRATE | ¤ | NO RDA | 25.50 Gm |
| FAT | ¤ | NO RDA | 18.80 Gm |
| FIBER—CRUDE | ¤ | NO RDA | 1.940 Gm |
| CHOLESTEROL | ¤ | NO RDA | 0.000 Mg |
| SATURATED FA | ¤ | NO RDA | 2.500 Gm |
| OLEIC FA | ¤ | NO RDA | 3.780 Gm |
| LINOLEIC FA | ¤ | NO RDA | 7.630 Gm |
| SODIUM | ¤=================================== | 68% | 1501 Mg |
| POTASSIUM | ¤======== | 16% | 605.0 Mg |
| MAGNESIUM | ¤==================== | 40% | 122.0 Mg |
| IRON | ¤============================= | 57% | 10.40 Mg |
| ZINC | ¤========== | 21% | 3.230 Mg |
| VITAMIN A | ¤==== | 8% | 357.0 IU |
| VITAMIN D | ¤ | 0% | 0.000 IU |
| VIT. E/TOTAL | ¤ | NO RDA | 4.080 Mg |
| VITAMIN C | ¤= | 2% | 1.770 Mg |
| THIAMIN | ¤=================================================== | 284% | 2.840 Mg |
| RIBOFLAVIN | ¤=================================================== | 229% | 2.750 Mg |
| NIACIN | ¤=================================================== | 145% | 18.90 Mg |
| VITAMIN B6 | ¤=================================================== | 144% | 2.880 Mg |
| FOLACIN | ¤=========== | 23% | 95.60 Ug |
| VITAMIN B12 | ¤=============================== | 73% | 2.190 Ug |
| PANTO— ACID | ¤======= | 14% | 0.810 Mg |
| CALCIUM | ¤=================================================== | 73% | 589.0 Mg |
| PHOSPHORUS | ¤========================== | 50% | 405.0 Mg |
| TRYPTOPHAN | ¤=================================================== | 222% | 362.0 Mg |
| THREONINE | ¤=================================================== | 228% | 995.0 Mg |
| ISOLEUCINE | ¤=================================================== | 188% | 1230 Mg |
| LEUCINE | ¤=================================================== | 224% | 1957 Mg |
| LYSINE | ¤=================================================== | 230% | 1505 Mg |
| METHIONINE | ¤=================================================== | 125% | 340.0 Mg |
| CYSTINE | ¤=================================================== | 134% | 365.0 Mg |
| PHENYL—ANINE | ¤=================================================== | 288% | 1255 Mg |
| TYROSINE | ¤=================================================== | 203% | 887.0 Mg |
| VALINE | ¤=================================================== | 169% | 1291 Mg |
| HISTIDINE | ¤ | NO RDA | 677.0 Mg |
| ALCOHOL | ¤ | NO RDA | 0.000 Gm |
| ASH | ¤ | NO RDA | 7.560 Gm |
| COPPER | ¤=============== | 28% | 0.700 Mg |
| MANGANESE | ¤====================== | 49% | 1.870 Mg |
| IODINE | ¤=================================================== | 178% | 267.0 Ug |
| MONO FAT | ¤ | NO RDA | 4.790 Gm |
| POLY FAT | ¤ | NO RDA | 10.10 Gm |
| CAFFEINE | ¤ | NO RDA | 0.000 Mg |
| FLUORIDE | ¤ | 0% | 9.390 Ug |
| MOLYBDENUM | ¤=================================================== | 505% | 1643 Ug |
| VITAMIN K | ¤ | 0% | 0.000 Ug |
| SELENIUM | ¤======== | 16% | 0.020 Mg |
| BIOTIN | ¤===== | 11% | 17.90 Ug |
| CHLORIDE | ¤=== | 6% | 210.0 Mg |
| CHROMIUM | ¤=================================================== | 336% | 0.420 Mg |
| SUGAR | ¤ | NO RDA | 0.670 Gm |
| FIBER—DIET | ¤ | NO RDA | 5.530 Gm |
| VIT. E/AT | ¤========== | 19% | 1.530 Mg |

```
% RDA:  |0     |20    |40    |60    |80    |100    10
```

Teriyaki Sauce used instead of the Mild/Salty Sauce; onion used instead of celery and asafetida.

# MARINATED TEMPEH CUTLET

☆ A hearty, tasty sandwich filling.

---

*1 cup water*
*2 vegetable bouillon cubes*

*2 cups tomato sauce*
*¼ cup safflower oil*
*2 Tbsp. honey*
*2 Tbsp. prepared mustard*
*2 Tbsp. soy sauce*
*1 tsp. asafetida or 1 clove garlic, crushed*
*1 tsp. white pepper*
*⅛ - ½ tsp. Tabasco sauce*

*Tempeh cut into sandwich/burger-sized cutlets*
   *(sauce will marinate up to 4 lbs.*
   *which should make about 8 cutlets)*

Boil first 2 ingredients together till bouillon cubes dissolve. Add next 8 ingredients and mix well. Bring to a boil and add tempeh cutlets which have been pierced here and there with a fork. Turn down to simmer and simmer for 1 hour. Remove from heat and allow to sit 3 to 4 hours.

Preheat oven to 375 degrees and oil cookie sheet. Place prepared cutlets on oiled cookie sheet and bake at 375 degrees for 25 to 30 minutes.

To build a healthy, natural food sandwich, fill slices of whole grain bread with the "entree." Then pile generous servings of vegetables like —
- Lettuce and tomatoes
- Watercress
- Alfalfa, red clover and/or radish sprouts
- Thinly-sliced cucumber
- Whole green Ortega chilies
- Grated carrots
- Potato chips
- Your favorite, fresh herb . . .
My husband has introduced me to a tasty, refreshing addition to any savory sandwich: a few sprigs of fresh dill weed. Dill does grow like a weed, too, so if you end up liking the flavor of dill in sandwiches (also good in salad dressings, soups), plant a few in a flower bed or herb garden.

A special sandwich-eating tip from my husband is that you should always eat your sandwiches upside down. That is, put the bottom of the sandwich as you built it on top so your top teeth bite into that side. For the longest time I just laughed when he told me this, but I tried it and it really does make a difference in the way the sandwich tastes.

| SHOPPING LIST | |
|---|---|
| **Regularly Kept in the Kitchen** (Listed in Chapter 14, p. 703) | **Fresh Produce** |
| Safflower oil<br>Honey<br>Mustard<br>Soy sauce<br>Asafetida<br>White pepper<br>Tabasco<br>Tempeh | (None) |

| Special Shopping |
|---|
| Vegetable bouillon cubes — in natural food stores. These bouillon cubes have no beef or chicken flavoring. |

# POLYNESIAN PICNIC

In Hawaii the word "kamaaina" means a longtime resident of the Islands. One thing kamaainas learn to do is incorporate the best from East and West in their lives. For example, in the Bible we find this message:

"Now I say, brethren, that flesh and blood cannot inherit the Kingdom of God; that the perishable cannot inherit the imperishable."

And from the Far East, in the Bhagavad-gita, it is expressed:

"Know that that which pervades the entire body is indestructible. No one is able to destroy the imperishable soul."

We are not the perishable material bodies, but are the imperishable souls within different bodies. This truth transcends all geographical divisions and walls of sectarianism.

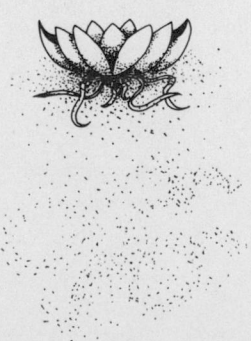

Like so much of present-day Hawaii, the foods for this outdoor picnic are a happy mixture of the meeting of East and West. On the next beautiful day, take this Polynesian picnic basket to your patio or backyard, a close-by park, or out to the country.

The nice thing about this picnic is that almost all of it can be made a day ahead of time. Everything can be made while frying the Noodle Cakes. Only the Basic Stir-Fry should be made just before packing up the picnic basket. I use a low, flat, open bamboo basket instead of the conventional picnic basket. To pack the basket, lay a couple of large, washed banana leaves on the bottom of the basket (or if those aren't available, some large, clean plastic sheets). Pile the Noodle Cakes in the center of the tray and pour the lightly stir-fried and/or fresh vegetables all around the noodles, leaving a spot to pile the Tossed Tofu Crisps in. Cover the top of the picnic basket with lightly singed banana leaves (or plastic sheeting) and hold this down by laying Tropical Pleasure Candies and whole pieces of fruit on top of the leaves (or plastic sheet) all around the edges. Carry separate containers of the Coconut Cream and Sesame Dressing.

To serve this picnic, unload pieces of fruit and candies onto table top or picnic cloth. Serve Noodle Cake onto a plate and cover with stir-fried vegetables, Fried Tofu Crisps and pour Sesame Dressing over all. For dessert, serve Noodle Cake with slices of fresh fruit and Coconut Cream — or just pieces of fruit and Tropical Pleasure Candies. Although this is an attractive and versatile picnic basket, it isn't transported too easily. I recommend using it for patio or backyard picnics.

# NOODLE CAKES

☆ I use any noodle but lupini noodles for this recipe, as noodles sticking together is actually desirable here.

___

*2 lbs. boiled whole grain spaghetti or*
*other long, thin noodle*

*2 cups ½" cubes cooked taro or sweet potato*

*Vegetable oil for frying*

*Black (or regular) sesame seeds*

Cook noodles till done but be sure not to overcook, as overcooked noodles don't work as well. Place noodles in a colander and rinse under cool water till cooled. Drain well, then roll loosely onto many layers of paper towels or a lint-free towel to blot off excess water. Mix the noodles together with the already cooked cubes of taro or sweet potato. Heat a 6" or 7" in diameter well-seasoned or non-stick skillet till it is hot enough that a drop of water sizzles away on contact. Pour ¼ cup of vegetable oil into skillet and heat oil till it sizzles when a single noodle is placed in it. Coil about 2 heaping cups' worth of noodle mixture into skillet and flatten evenly with a spatula to about ¾" to 1" thick. Cover and cook for about 5 to 7 minutes over medium-high heat till the bottom is golden brown. Uncover, flip, then cover and cook the second side. (If the pan is dry and it seems like the noodles will stick, be sure to dribble more oil into the skillet at this point by pouring oil along the sides of the skillet.) When the second side is browned, sprinkle top surface of Noodle Cake with sesame seeds and remove from heat. Drain on paper towel and cut into quarters.

These are to be served under or alongside your favorite stir-fry vegetable dish. They are also delicious in a sweet coconut milk syrup with pieces of fresh tropical fruit. To make a refreshing salad, top the Noodle Cakes with finely slivered and grated fresh vegetables and the Sesame Dressing (see following recipe). Makes 10 to 12 Noodle Cakes.

These Noodle Cakes can be used as a bed for the Basic Stir-Fry or fresh cut vegetables and topped with Tossed Tofu Crisps and some Seame Dressing. They can also be served as a sweet, topped with slices of fresh fruit and the Coconut Cream.

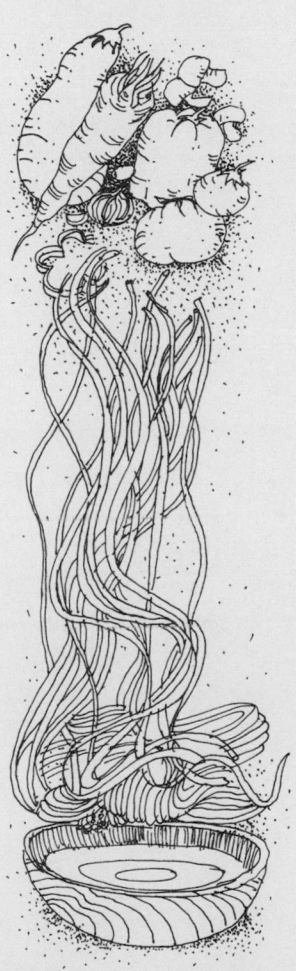

| SHOPPING LIST | |
|---|---|
| **Regularly Kept in the Kitchen** (Listed in Chapter 14, p. 703) | **Fresh Produce** |
| Vegetable oil Black or regular sesame seeds | Taro or sweet potato Assorted fresh vegetables |

| Special Shopping |
|---|
| Whole grain noodles — found in natural food stores. |

## SUGGESTED MENU FOR A POLYNESIAN PICNIC

*Noodle Cakes with Basic Stir-Fry and/or fresh vegetables*

*Tossed Tofu Crisps*

*Sesame Dressing*

*Coconut Cream*

*Tropical Pleasure Candies*

*Whole fresh fruit*

# SESAME DRESSING

*½ cup toasted sesame meal*

*½ cup toasted sesame oil*
*½ cup vegetable oil*
*¾ cup dried shiitake mushroom soaking water*
*⅔ cup soy sauce*
*¼ cup apple cider vinegar*
*¼ cup honey*
*½ tsp. black or white pepper*
*¼ tsp. cayenne*

To make sesame meal, toast whole sesame seeds, put in a blender and blend till seeds are chopped into a meal.

Soak a few dried shiitake mushrooms in a cup of warm water. If you're going to use shiitake mushrooms in a stir-fry, as in the following recipe, it's not necessary to separately prepare mushrooms just for the soaking water.

Blend toasted sesame meal with next 8 ingredients to form a smooth paste. Refrigerate overnight. Pour Sesame Dressing over Noodle Cakes topped with finely slivered fresh vegetables and/or Basic Stir-Fry vegetables (see following recipe) and serve on individual platters or in bowls. Makes about 3 cups of dressing.

| SHOPPING LIST | |
|---|---|
| **Regularly Kept in the Kitchen (Listed in Chapter 14, p. 703)** | **Fresh Produce** |
| Sesame seeds<br>Toasted sesame oil<br>Vegetable oil<br>Soy sauce<br>Apple cider vinegar<br>Honey<br>Black or white pepper<br>Cayenne<br>Dried shiitake mushrooms<br>   (if making the Basic Stir-Fry,<br>   use the soaking water from<br>   those) | (None) |

# BASIC STIR-FRY

1 oz. dried Oriental (shiitake) mushrooms,
   soaked, de-stemmed and slivered
¼ cup vegetable oil
¼ cup asafetida and 1 cup finely slivered celery
   OR 1 cup finely slivered onion

2 cups chopped mustard greens
12 cups chopped Chinese cabbage
12 cups chopped spinach leaves
2 cups slivered red bell peppers

Soak mushrooms, de-stem them and sliver about ¼" wide. (Be sure to save the mushroom soaking water for future use in gravies, soups, etc.) Prepare other vegetables by cutting celery into slivers about ⅛" thick, cutting leaves width-wise into 2" strips and cutting bell peppers into ¼"- to ½"-thick strips.

Stir-fry first 3 (or 4) ingredients together over high heat for about 2 minutes. Toss in remaining ingredients and stir-fry till all leaves are thoroughly coated with oil and the color of the leaves deepen (should only take about 30 seconds — be sure not to cook so long that vegetable juices begin coming out). Remove from heat and pour onto serving platter. Top with Sesame Dressing (see preceding recipe). Makes about 12 servings.

| SHOPPING LIST | |
|---|---|
| **Regularly Kept in the Kitchen**<br>**(Listed in Chapter 14, p. 703)** | **Fresh Produce** |
| Dried shiitake mushrooms<br>Vegetable oil<br>Asafetida | Celery<br>Mustard greens<br>Napa cabbage<br>Spinach<br>Red bell pepper |

Feel free to vary the vegetables in this simple stir-fry according to what's in season. The main thing is to cook the hard vegetables first since they will take longer to cook, then add the quick-cooking leaves last of all. Most importantly — don't overcook. Stir-frying retains more nutrients than boiling or even steaming, as the vegetables are cooked very quickly.

# NUTRITIONAL ANALYSIS FOR ONE SERVING BASIC STIR-FRY
# WITH NOODLE CAKE AND SESAME DRESSING

| NUTRIENT | Type: 14   FEMALE-23 TO 51 YEARS | % RDA | Amount |
|---|---|---|---|
| KCALORIES | Ā=========== | 20% | 417.0 Kc |
| PROTEIN | Ā============ | 22% | 9.840 Gm |
| CARBOHYDRATE | Ā | NO RDA | 41.50 Gm |
| FAT | Ā | NO RDA | 25.10 Gm |
| FIBER-CRUDE | Ā | NO RDA | 2.090 Gm |
| CHOLESTEROL | Ā | NO RDA | 0.000 Mg |
| SATURATED FA | Ā | NO RDA | 2.830 Gm |
| OLEIC FA | Ā | NO RDA | 5.370 Gm |
| LINOLEIC FA | Ā | NO RDA | 14.10 Gm |
| SODIUM | Ā===================== | 45% | 1009 Mg |
| POTASSIUM | Ā========== | 21% | 815.0 Mg |
| MAGNESIUM | Ā================== | 38% | 115.0 Mg |
| IRON | Ā============ | 25% | 4.580 Mg |
| ZINC | Ā===== | 10% | 1.520 Mg |
| VITAMIN A | Ā================================================= | 297% | 11916 IU |
| VITAMIN D | Ā | 0% | 0.000 IU |
| VIT. E/TOTAL | Ā | NO RDA | 11.40 Mg |
| VITAMIN C | Ā================================ | 137% | 82.50 Mg |
| THIAMIN | Ā============= | 29% | 0.290 Mg |
| RIBOFLAVIN | Ā============ | 24% | 0.290 Mg |
| NIACIN | Ā=========== | 22% | 2.880 Mg |
| VITAMIN B6 | Ā======= | 15% | 0.310 Mg |
| FOLACIN | Ā=============== | 30% | 123.0 Ug |
| VITAMIN B12 | Ā | 0% | 0.000 Ug |
| PANTO- ACID | Ā====== | 13% | 0.740 Mg |
| CALCIUM | Ā=========== | 22% | 177.0 Mg |
| PHOSPHORUS | Ā============= | 26% | 212.0 Mg |
| TRYPTOPHAN | Ā================================ | 76% | 124.0 Mg |
| THREONINE | Ā===================================== | 91% | 397.0 Mg |
| ISOLEUCINE | Ā================================ | 79% | 519.0 Mg |
| LEUCINE | Ā================== | 39% | 347.0 Mg |
| LYSINE | Ā============================ | 68% | 450.0 Mg |
| METHIONINE | Ā================================ | 79% | 217.0 Mg |
| CYSTINE | Ā======================== | 55% | 152.0 Mg |
| PHENYL-ANINE | Ā================================================ | 121% | 527.0 Mg |
| TYROSINE | Ā============================ | 68% | 299.0 Mg |
| VALINE | Ā============================ | 69% | 532.0 Mg |
| HISTIDINE | Ā | NO RDA | 271.0 Mg |
| ALCOHOL | Ā | NO RDA | 0.000 Gm |
| ASH | Ā | NO RDA | 5.150 Gm |
| COPPER | Ā======= | 15% | 0.380 Mg |
| MANGANESE | Ā==================== | 46% | 1.730 Mg |
| IODINE | Ā==================================- | 72% | 109.0 Ug |
| MONO FAT | Ā | NO RDA | 5.850 Gm |
| POLY FAT | Ā | NO RDA | 14.70 Gm |
| CAFFEINE | Ā | NO RDA | 0.000 Mg |
| FLUORIDE | Ā= | 2% | 81.00 Ug |
| MOLYBDENUM | Ā=============================================== | 225% | 733.0 Ug |
| VITAMIN K | Ā=============================================== | 129% | 136.0 Ug |
| SELENIUM | Ā======== | 16% | 0.020 Mg |
| BIOTIN | Ā=== | 6% | 9.180 Ug |
| CHLORIDE | Ā | 0% | 28.50 Mg |
| CHROMIUM | Ā=============================================== | 144% | 0.180 Mg |
| SUGAR | Ā | NO RDA | 5.540 Gm |
| FIBER-DIET | Ā | NO RDA | 4.650 Gm |
| VIT. E/AT | Ā==================================== | 89% | 7.190 Mg |

```
% RDA:  |0      |20     |40     |60     |80     |100
```

Sweet potato used instead of taro in Noodle Cake; onion used instead of celery and asafetida in Basic Stir-Fry.

# TOSSED TOFU CRISPS

☆ This dish gets made one day before serving so the flavors can mix together.

---

*½ lb. aburage shells (also called deep-fried tofu pouches)*

*1 clove garlic, minced*
*2 Tbsp. soy sauce*
*1 Tbsp. toasted sesame oil*
*1 Tbsp. vegetable oil*
*2 Tbsp. chopped green onion*
*⅛ tsp. chili powder*
*1½ tsp. honey*

Cut aburage shells into ¼"- to ½"- thick strips. Mix next 7 ingredients together to form a dressing. Put cut aburage shells into a mixing bowl and toss dressing in evenly. Refrigerate overnight. Makes about 12 servings.

| SHOPPING LIST | |
|---|---|
| **Regularly Kept in the Kitchen (Listed in Chapter 14, p. 703)** | **Fresh Produce** |
| Soy sauce<br>Vegetable oil<br>Chili powder<br>Honey<br>Toasted sesame oil | Garlic<br>Scallions |

| Special Shopping |
|---|
| Aburage (age) shells — found in Chinese and Japanese groceries; sometimes in Oriental food aisles in supermarkets. For a recipe like this, which calls for a lot of aburage shells (they're quite expensive in stores), I go to the local tofu factory and buy a boxful of off-grade ones (about four pounds) for about three dollars. |

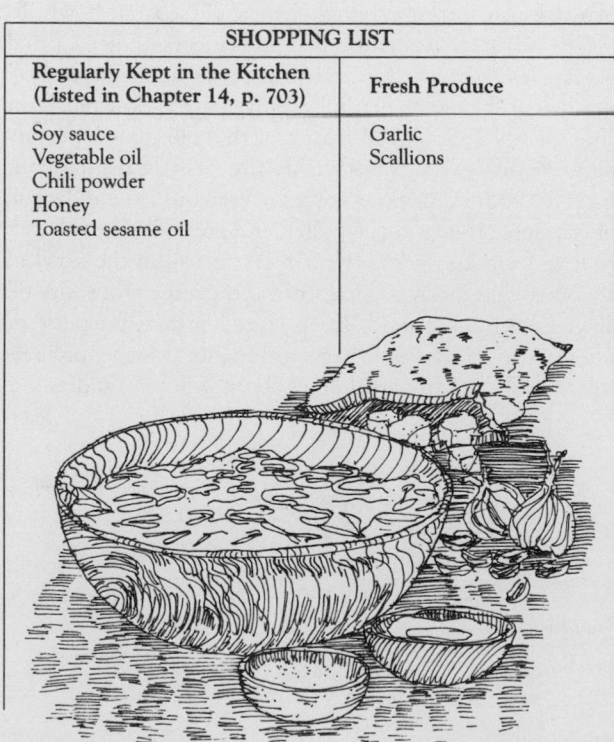

# TROPICAL PLEASURE CANDIES

☆ A milk-based candy with a surprise in the middle!

---

*¼ cup butter or margarine*
*½ cup honey*

*1 cup noninstant, nonfat powdered milk or*
*sweet-flavored soy protein powder*
*½ tsp. vanilla*
*½ cup macaroon coconut*

*2½ - 3 cups ¼" dices dried pineapple*

*Local bee pollen*

*Macaroon coconut*

Cream first 2 ingredients together. Add next 3 ingredients and mix thoroughly to form candy that is the texture of a ball of soft dough. Put last 3 ingredients each in separate bowls. To make one candy, wet hands and press pieces of diced, dried pineapple together to form a ball about ¾" in diameter. Roll this ball in the bee pollen till evenly coated. Now pinch off about a tablespoon-sized chunk of the milk powder candy mixture you've already made and flatten it in the palm of your hand to about ¼" thickness or less. Wrap this around the ball of pineapple rolled in bee pollen and press all edges closed. Roll to form a nice ball. Now roll this ball in the bowl of coconut. This candy is done. Follow the same procedure till all ingredients are used. Keep stored in a refrigerator or freezer in a sealed plastic bag — though it is highly unlikely that there'll be leftovers! Makes about 3 dozen candies.

### Special Shopping

Dried pineapple — found in natural food stores; some nut and dried fruit shops. Be sure to get pure dried pineapple; a lot of dried pineapple from Taiwan and the Philippines is cooked in sugar syrup and then dried. This kind of dried pineapple is usually a pale yellow and crystallized on the outside with sugar and moist and tender on the inside. Unadulterated dried pineapple is usually a little tough and is a brownish color.
Local bee pollen — in natural food stores.

| SHOPPING LIST | |
|---|---|
| **Regularly Kept in the Kitchen** (Listed in Chapter 14, p. 703) | **Fresh Produce** |
| Butter or margarine<br>Honey<br>Nonfat, noninstant milk powder or sweet-flavored soy protein powder<br>Vanilla | Unsweetened macaroon coconut |

# NUTRITIONAL ANALYSIS FOR ONE TROPICAL PLEASURE CANDY

| NUTRIENT | Type: 14 FEMALE-23 TO 51 YEARS | % RDA | Amount |
|---|---|---|---|
| KCALORIES | Ā= | 2% | 59.60 Kc |
| PROTEIN | Ā= | 3% | 1.400 Gm |
| CARBOHYDRATE | Ā | NO RDA | 8.890 Gm |
| FAT | Ā | NO RDA | 2.340 Gm |
| FIBER-CRUDE | Ā | NO RDA | 0.250 Gm |
| CHOLESTEROL | Ā | NO RDA | 0.660 Mg |
| SATURATED FA | Ā | NO RDA | 1.070 Gm |
| OLEIC FA | Ā | NO RDA | 0.050 Gm |
| LINOLEIC FA | Ā | NO RDA | 0.010 Gm |
| SODIUM | Ā | 1% | 33.60 Mg |
| POTASSIUM | Ā= | 2% | 99.70 Mg |
| MAGNESIUM | Ā= | 2% | 7.970 Mg |
| IRON | Ā | 1% | 0.180 Mg |
| ZINC | Ā | 1% | 0.190 Mg |
| VITAMIN A | Ā | 1% | 58.60 IU |
| VITAMIN D | Ā | 0% | 0.000 IU |
| VIT. E/TOTAL | Ā | NO RDA | 0.020 Mg |
| VITAMIN C | Ā=== | 6% | 3.970 Mg |
| THIAMIN | Ā= | 3% | 0.030 Mg |
| RIBOFLAVIN | Ā== | 5% | 0.060 Mg |
| NIACIN | Ā | 1% | 0.160 Mg |
| VITAMIN B6 | Ā | 1% | 0.030 Mg |
| FOLACIN | Ā | 1% | 4.930 Ug |
| VITAMIN B12 | Ā== | 4% | 0.130 Ug |
| PANTO- ACID | Ā= | 3% | 0.180 Mg |
| CALCIUM | Ā== | 5% | 44.60 Mg |
| PHOSPHORUS | Ā== | 4% | 37.70 Mg |
| TRYPTOPHAN | Ā===== | 11% | 19.50 Mg |
| THREONINE | Ā======= | 14% | 61.30 Mg |
| ISOLEUCINE | Ā====== | 12% | 80.50 Mg |
| LEUCINE | Ā======= | 14% | 130.0 Mg |
| LYSINE | Ā======== | 16% | 106.0 Mg |
| METHIONINE | Ā====== | 12% | 34.90 Mg |
| CYSTINE | Ā== | 4% | 13.50 Mg |
| PHENYL-ANINE | Ā======= | 15% | 66.50 Mg |
| TYROSINE | Ā======= | 14% | 64.60 Mg |
| VALINE | Ā===== | 11% | 91.10 Mg |
| HISTIDINE | Ā | NO RDA | 37.30 Mg |
| ALCOHOL | Ā | NO RDA | 0.000 Gm |
| ASH | Ā | NO RDA | 0.390 Gm |
| COPPER | Ā | 1% | 0.040 Mg |
| MANGANESE | Ā===== | 11% | 0.430 Mg |
| IODINE | Ā | 0% | 0.000 Ug |
| MONO FAT | Ā | NO RDA | 0.650 Gm |
| POLY FAT | Ā | NO RDA | 0.450 Gm |
| CAFFEINE | Ā | NO RDA | 0.000 Mg |
| FLUORIDE | Ā | 0% | 7.980 Ug |
| MOLYBDENUM | Ā | 0% | 0.000 Ug |
| VITAMIN K | Ā | 0% | 0.000 Ug |
| SELENIUM | Ā | 0% | 0.000 Mg |
| BIOTIN | Ā | 0% | 0.000 Ug |
| CHLORIDE | Ā | 0% | 0.000 Mg |
| CHROMIUM | Ā | 0% | 0.000 Mg |
| SUGAR | Ā | NO RDA | 0.000 Gm |
| FIBER-DIET | Ā | NO RDA | 0.360 Gm |
| VIT. E/AT | Ā | 0% | 0.040 Mg |

% RDA: |0    |20    |40    |60    |80    |100

Margarine used instead of butter; noninstant, nonfat powdered milk used instead of protein powder. Bee pollen not included in analysis.

# COCONUT CREAM

6½ cups coconut milk
¼ cup arrowroot
⅓ cup honey
Pinch ground cardamom

Mix ingredients together in a pot (off the heat) till arrowroot dissolves. Place over medium-high heat and, while stirring constantly, bring to a boil. Stir till it becomes as thick as a gravy. Remove from heat and allow to cool. Refrigerate overnight.

This is a delicious, light dessert served by itself in individual bowls and sprinkled with chopped nuts or dried fruit. It also makes a delicious base for cold fruit soups, or can be served with a Noodle Cake and slices of fresh tropical fruit.

| Special Shopping |
| --- |
| Coconut milk — found in some supermarket foreign food or liquor aisles, or in the freezer section. Otherwise, make your own at home (p. 129) with fresh coconut from the produce section (fresh coconut milk has a sweet, nutty flavor that gets lost in canning). |

| SHOPPING LIST | |
| --- | --- |
| **Regularly Kept in the Kitchen** (Listed in Chapter 14, p. 703) | **Fresh Produce** |
| Arrowroot<br>Honey<br>Cardamom | (None) |

# MORE THAN "JUST PIZZA"

These words of Ralph Waldo Emerson's can be adopted on an individual, community or even worldwide basis: "Every man takes care that his neighbor does not cheat him. But a day comes when he begins to care that he does not cheat his neighbor. Then all goes well."

Pizzas are one of those foods that everyone loves that can be a healthy, nutritious food. *Can be* — if you are selective about what is used as a topping and are sure to use a whole wheat crust instead of the usual white flour one. To be able to do this, you'll probably end up making your own pizzas from scratch at home, as there are very few pizza restaurants that serve a sugar- and chemical additive-free whole wheat crust.

By making your own pizza at home, you can control what the pizza is made of for about half the price. Considering the time it takes to drive to a pizza restaurant, park and order, it's just about as fast to make your own at home — especially when using the Quick Whole Wheat Pizza Dough which requires no rising!

# QUICK WHOLE WHEAT PIZZA DOUGH

☆ A pizza dough that requires no rising.

---

*1¼ cups warm water*
*1 Tbsp. baking yeast*
*2 Tbsp. honey*
*1 Tbsp. olive oil*
*¼ tsp. salt*

*3 cups whole wheat flour*
*½ tsp. baking powder*

Prepare all topping ingredients. Preheat oven to 475 degrees.

Combine first 5 ingredients and allow to sit 3 to 5 minutes till yeast dissolves. Add the next 2 ingredients and mix thoroughly to form a sticky dough. Oil a 10" x 14" cookie sheet with olive oil and oil hands as well. Turn dough onto oiled cookie sheet and pat surface of dough with oily hands so entire surface of dough is oiled and won't stick to rolling utensil. Roll dough out evenly onto cookie sheet, then use hands to push dough up edges of cookie sheet to form an edge on the crust. Fill with topping of your choice and bake at 475 degrees for 12 to 16 minutes till crust turns golden brown. Serve immediately. Makes 4 to 6 servings.

Besides making a pleasant-tasting pizza dough, this can also be shaped into rolls, buns, bread loaves, etc. that can be baked without rising. Bake bread loaves at 400 degrees for 20 to 25 minutes; rolls and buns at 350 degrees for 15 minutes.

| SHOPPING LIST | |
| --- | --- |
| **Regularly Kept in the Kitchen** (Listed in Chapter 14, p. 703) | **Fresh Produce** |
| Baking yeast<br>Honey<br>Olive oil<br>Salt<br>Whole wheat flour<br>Baking powder | (None) |

# EGGPLANT PIZZA

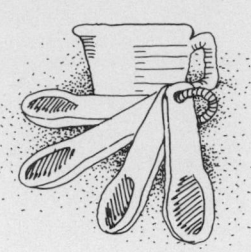

☆ A simple, yet elegant pizza that gets the most from a unique spicing technique borrowed from Indian cooking.

2 large eggplants, cut crosswise in
   ½" - ⅝" thicknesses
2 Tbsp. olive oil
2 Tbsp. safflower oil

1 Quick Whole Wheat Pizza Dough recipe
   (see preceding recipe)
1 Tbsp. olive oil
2 cups grated mozzarella or Monterey Jack cheese

2 Tbsp. olive oil
½ tsp. asafetida or ½ clove garlic, crushed
½ tsp. dried red chili flakes
½ tsp. black pepper
⅛ tsp. ground cloves

½ cup grated mozzarella or Monterey Jack cheese
2 Tbsp. Parmesan or Romano cheese

Wash eggplants and cut across the width into ½" to ⅝" fillets. Mix oils together in a cup. Heat a large skillet over a medium-low flame. Pour about half of the oil into the skillet; this should be just enough to keep eggplant from sticking to the skillet. (The eggplants should be large enough to have to be done in 2 batches in a 14"-diameter skillet; if using a smaller skillet, use less oil in each batch.) Lay as many slices as possible flat into pan. Cover and allow to simmer 3 minutes. Remove lid, flip, cover again and cook another 3 minutes. Remove eggplant from heat. Repeat till all eggplant is cooked. Preheat oven to 475 degrees.

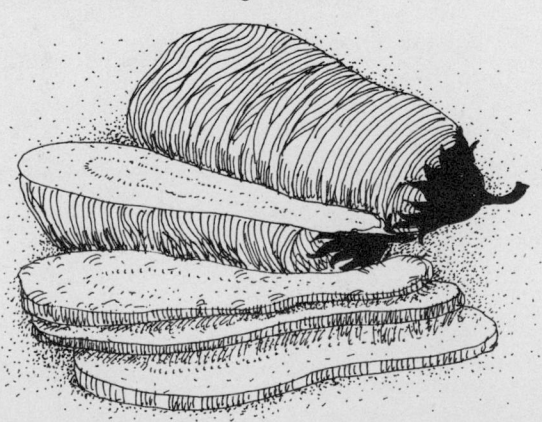

Try this or the Quick California Pizza with any salad to make a whole meal. Try this Pesto Salad in keeping with the Italian theme:

## PESTO SALAD

8 cups washed, fresh spinach
   leaves
2 cups small, fresh basil leaves

¼ cup olive oil
1½ tsp. asafetida or 2 crushed
   garlic cloves
¾ cup pine nuts

½ cup slivered, sun-dried
   tomatoes
¼ tsp. black pepper
¼ cup Parmesan cheese

Toss first 2 ingredients together and set aside (cover and refrigerate if you are making this in advance of serving time).

Just before serving time, toast next 3 ingredients together in a skillet till the pine nuts begin turning a golden brown. Remove garlic cloves and immediately pour this and the next 3 ingredients onto tossed greens. Toss well and serve immediately. Makes up to 8 servings.

While eggplant is cooking, prepare pizza dough and roll out onto cookie sheet. Pour 1 tablespoon of olive oil on top of rolled out dough and top with grated cheese. Lay cooked pieces of eggplant side by side, so sides overlap a little and surface of pizza is more or less covered with eggplant.

In a small pot or butter-melting cup, heat next 5 ingredients together and saute till spices become toasted. Remove from heat and drizzle evenly over the eggplant. Top by sprinkling evenly with last 2 ingredients.

Bake at 475 degrees for 12 to 16 minutes, till crust turns golden brown. Serve immediately. Makes 4 to 6 servings.

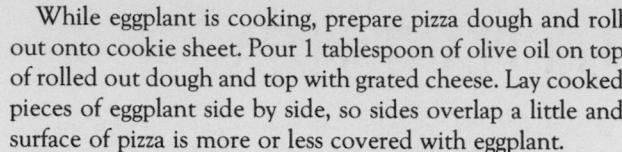

| SHOPPING LIST | |
| --- | --- |
| **Regularly Kept in the Kitchen** (Listed in Chapter 14, p. 703) | **Fresh Produce** |
| Olive oil | Eggplants |
| Safflower oil | |
| Mozzarella or Jack cheese | |
| Asafetida | |
| Red chili flakes | |
| Black pepper | |
| Ground cloves | |
| Parmesan cheese | |

Also see shopping list for Quick Whole Wheat Pizza Dough or Rising Whole Wheat Pizza Dough (p. 352).

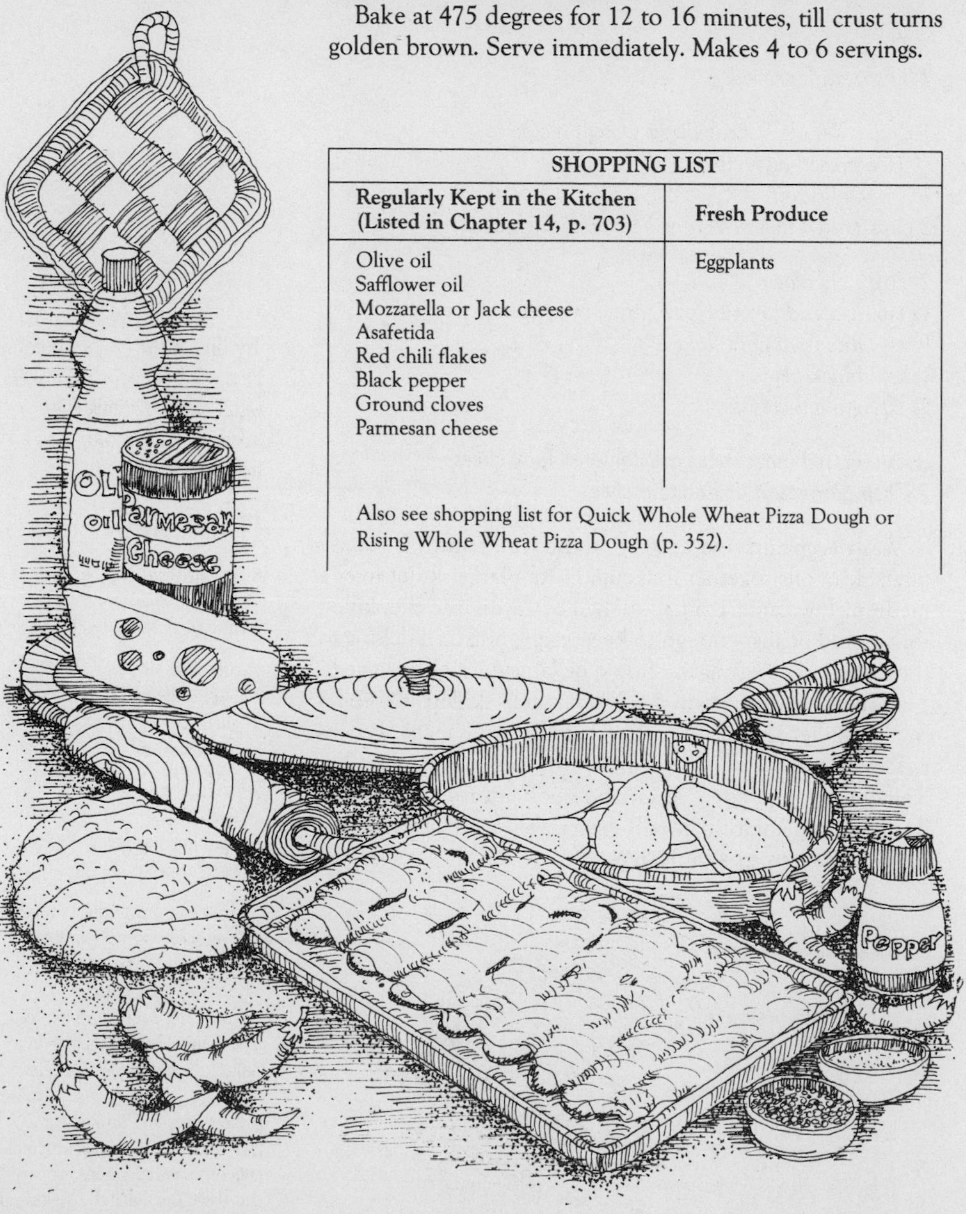

# NUTRITIONAL ANALYSIS FOR ONE SERVING EGGPLANT PIZZA
## (using Quick Whole Wheat Pizza Dough)

| NUTRIENT | Type: 14   FEMALE-23 TO 51 YEARS | % RDA | Amount |
|---|---|---|---|
| KCALORIES | Ȣ=========*====== | 30% | 618.0 Kc |
| PROTEIN | Ȣ=============================== | 62% | 27.40 Gm |
| CARBOHYDRATE | Ȣ | NO RDA | 65.00 Gm |
| FAT | Ȣ | NO RDA | 30.10 Gm |
| FIBER-CRUDE | Ȣ | NO RDA | 3.720 Gm |
| CHOLESTEROL | Ȣ | NO RDA | 37.90 Mg |
| SATURATED FA | Ȣ | NO RDA | 9.490 Gm |
| OLEIC FA | Ȣ | NO RDA | 13.20 Gm |
| LINOLEIC FA | Ȣ | NO RDA | 5.270 Gm |
| SODIUM | Ȣ=========== | 21% | 463.0 Mg |
| POTASSIUM | Ȣ========== | 21% | 807.0 Mg |
| MAGNESIUM | Ȣ================== | 37% | 113.0 Mg |
| IRON | Ȣ========== | 20% | 3.740 Mg |
| ZINC | Ȣ============ | 24% | 3.640 Mg |
| VITAMIN A | Ȣ======== | 16% | 659.0 IU |
| VITAMIN D | Ȣ | 0% | 0.000 IU |
| VIT. E/TOTAL | Ȣ | NO RDA | 5.800 Mg |
| VITAMIN C | Ȣ=== | 6% | 3.850 Mg |
| THIAMIN | Ȣ============================ | 57% | 0.570 Mg |
| RIBOFLAVIN | Ȣ============== | 31% | 0.380 Mg |
| NIACIN | Ȣ================ | 34% | 4.520 Mg |
| VITAMIN B6 | Ȣ============ | 24% | 0.480 Mg |
| FOLACIN | Ȣ=============== | 31% | 124.0 Ug |
| VITAMIN B12 | Ȣ======== | 17% | 0.530 Ug |
| PANTO- ACID | Ȣ========= | 18% | 1.040 Mg |
| CALCIUM | Ȣ=================================== | 71% | 571.0 Mg |
| PHOSPHORUS | Ȣ========================================= | 82% | 658.0 Mg |
| TRYPTOPHAN | Ȣ======================================= | 80% | 131.0 Mg |
| THREONINE | Ȣ=============================================== | 219% | 954.0 Mg |
| ISOLEUCINE | Ȣ=============================================== | 192% | 1255 Mg |
| LEUCINE | Ȣ=============================================== | 265% | 2310 Mg |
| LYSINE | Ȣ=============================================== | 308% | 2012 Mg |
| METHIONINE | Ȣ=============================================== | 223% | 609.0 Mg |
| CYSTINE | Ȣ=============================================== | 105% | 288.0 Mg |
| PHENYL-ANINE | Ȣ=============================================== | 313% | 1364 Mg |
| TYROSINE | Ȣ=============================================== | 303% | 1321 Mg |
| VALINE | Ȣ=============================================== | 202% | 1542 Mg |
| HISTIDINE | Ȣ | NO RDA | 844.0 Mg |
| ALCOHOL | Ȣ | NO RDA | 0.000 Gm |
| ASH | Ȣ | NO RDA | 4.540 Gm |
| COPPER | Ȣ============ | 23% | 0.590 Mg |
| MANGANESE | Ȣ========================================== | 88% | 3.320 Mg |
| IODINE | Ȣ=============================================== | 227% | 341.0 Ug |
| MONO FAT | Ȣ | NO RDA | 13.50 Gm |
| POLY FAT | Ȣ | NO RDA | 4.910 Gm |
| CAFFEINE | Ȣ | NO RDA | 0.000 Mg |
| FLUORIDE | Ȣ= | 2% | 64.80 Ug |
| MOLYBDENUM | Ȣ=============================================== | 1107% | 3600 Ug |
| VITAMIN K | Ȣ | 0% | 0.000 Ug |
| SELENIUM | Ȣ======== | 16% | 0.020 Mg |
| BIOTIN | Ȣ== | 5% | 8.740 Ug |
| CHLORIDE | Ȣ= | 3% | 114.0 Mg |
| CHROMIUM | Ȣ=============================================== | 288% | 0.360 Mg |
| SUGAR | Ȣ | NO RDA | 0.000 Gm |
| FIBER-DIET | Ȣ | NO RDA | 9.100 Gm |
| VIT. E/AT | Ȣ======================= | 50% | 4.060 Mg |

```
% RDA:  |0      |20     |40     |60     |80     |100
```

Mozzarella used instead of Monterey Jack cheese; Parmesan used instead of Romano.

Generally when people think of Italian cooking, visions of heavy pasta laden with cheese comes to mind. Italian cooking actually makes use of lots of fresh produce. Italy's climate is much like that of California's and makes for lots of fresh fruits and vegetables.

# QUICK CALIFORNIA PIZZA

☆ A pizza loaded with lots of fresh produce.

---

*1½ cups of your favorite meat/sugar-free commercial spaghetti sauce*

*¼ lb. Chinese firm tofu, drained and crumbled*
*1 large bell pepper, thinly sliced crosswise*
*1 cup thinly sliced tomato cross sections*
*1 cup thinly sliced mushrooms*
*1 cup thinly sliced olives*
*⅓ cup thinly sliced, pickled jalapeno peppers (optional)*
*½ Tbsp. pickled jalapeno pepper water (optional)*
*¾ lb. mozzarella or Monterey Jack cheese, grated*

*1 Quick Whole Wheat Pizza Dough recipe*

*1 avocado, sliced thin*

Prepare all the toppings first. Open your favorite meatless, sugar- and preservative-free commercial spaghetti sauce, or make your own sauce (this makes preparation time much longer, of course!).

Cut ¼ pound off tofu block, drain well, and crumble with fingertips (should make about ½ cup of soft curds). Slice bell peppers and tomatoes crosswise in thin slices (no thicker than ¼" thick). Slice mushrooms and olives. If you want a zesty, hot pizza, slice pickled jalapeno peppers crosswise and reserve some of the water they're soaking in.

Preheat oven to 475 degrees. Make the Quick Whole Wheat Pizza Dough and roll into cookie sheet. Layer the prepared ingredients evenly over the dough in the order listed. Bake at 475 degrees for 15 to 18 minutes. Remove from oven and top with sliced avocado. Serve immediately. Makes 4 to 6 servings.

| SHOPPING LIST | |
|---|---|
| **Regularly Kept in the Kitchen (Listed in Chapter 14, p. 703)** | **Fresh Produce** |
| Tofu<br>Mozzarella or Jack cheese | Favorite meat- and sugar-free commercial spaghetti sauce<br>Bell peppers<br>Tomatoes<br>Mushrooms<br>Pitted, ripe olives<br>Pickled jalapeno peppers<br>Avocado |

Also see shopping list for Quick Whole Wheat Pizza Dough or Rising Whole Wheat Pizza Dough (p. 352).

# NUTRITIONAL ANALYSIS FOR ONE SERVING
## QUICK CALIFORNIA PIZZA (using Quick Whole Wheat Pizza Dough)

| NUTRIENT | Type: 14 FEMALE-23 TO 51 YEARS | % RDA | Amount |
|---|---|---|---|
| KCALORIES | A===================== | 43% | 867.0 Kc |
| PROTEIN | A================================================ | 96% | 42.40 Gm |
| CARBOHYDRATE | A | NO RDA | 97.40 Gm |
| FAT | A | NO RDA | 40.20 Gm |
| FIBER-CRUDE | A | NO RDA | 5.610 Gm |
| CHOLESTEROL | A | NO RDA | 48.60 Mg |
| SATURATED FA | A | NO RDA | 12.30 Gm |
| OLEIC FA | A | NO RDA | 17.70 Gm |
| LINOLEIC FA | A | NO RDA | 3.470 Gm |
| SODIUM | A================== | 38% | 857.0 Mg |
| POTASSIUM | A==================== | 42% | 1601 Mg |
| MAGNESIUM | A================================ | 68% | 205.0 Mg |
| IRON | A========================== | 55% | 10.00 Mg |
| ZINC | A================== | 39% | 5.850 Mg |
| VITAMIN A | A======================================= | 83% | 3334 IU |
| VITAMIN D | A | 0% | 0.000 IU |
| VIT. E/TOTAL | A | NO RDA | 5.280 Mg |
| VITAMIN C | A=============================================== | 133% | 80.10 Mg |
| THIAMIN | A====================================== | 81% | 0.810 Mg |
| RIBOFLAVIN | A============================= | 61% | 0.740 Mg |
| NIACIN | A================================ | 69% | 9.030 Mg |
| VITAMIN B6 | A==================== | 42% | 0.840 Mg |
| FOLACIN | A====================== | 46% | 184.0 Ug |
| VITAMIN B12 | A=========== | 23% | 0.700 Ug |
| PANTO- ACID | A======================= | 52% | 2.890 Mg |
| CALCIUM | A==================================================== | 113% | 905.0 Mg |
| PHOSPHORUS | A==================================================== | 120% | 967.0 Mg |
| TRYPTOPHAN | A==================================================== | 160% | 261.0 Mg |
| THREONINE | A==================================================== | 334% | 1455 Mg |
| ISOLEUCINE | A==================================================== | 286% | 1869 Mg |
| LEUCINE | A==================================================== | 388% | 3382 Mg |
| LYSINE | A==================================================== | 450% | 2942 Mg |
| METHIONINE | A==================================================== | 321% | 875.0 Mg |
| CYSTINE | A==================================================== | 179% | 488.0 Mg |
| PHENYL-ANINE | A==================================================== | 465% | 2027 Mg |
| TYROSINE | A==================================================== | 434% | 1891 Mg |
| VALINE | A==================================================== | 293% | 2238 Mg |
| HISTIDINE | A | NO RDA | 1236 Mg |
| ALCOHOL | A | NO RDA | 0.000 Gm |
| ASH | A | NO RDA | 7.000 Gm |
| COPPER | A=================== | 40% | 1.010 Mg |
| MANGANESE | A======================================== | 135% | 5.090 Mg |
| IODINE | A==================================================== | 352% | 528.0 Ug |
| MONO FAT | A | NO RDA | 13.70 Gm |
| POLY FAT | A | NO RDA | 3.470 Gm |
| CAFFEINE | A | NO RDA | 0.000 Mg |
| FLUORIDE | A= | 3% | 104.0 Ug |
| MOLYBDENUM | A==================================================== | 1766% | 5740 Ug |
| VITAMIN K | A= | 2% | 2.910 Ug |
| SELENIUM | A============ | 24% | 0.030 Mg |
| BIOTIN | A===== | 10% | 16.20 Ug |
| CHLORIDE | A=== | 6% | 226.0 Mg |
| CHROMIUM | A==================================================== | 520% | 0.650 Mg |
| SUGAR | A | NO RDA | 3.840 Gm |
| FIBER-DIET | A | NO RDA | 15.80 Gm |
| VIT. E/AT | A================== | 41% | 3.290 Mg |

```
% RDA:    |0      |20     |40     |60     |80     |100
```

Quicker Than "From Scratch" Pasta Sauce used instead of commercial spaghetti sauce; mozzarella used instead of Monterey Jack cheese; optional pickled jalapeno peppers not included in analysis.

# DESSERT PIZZA

☆ Excellent, as described, for dessert or even as a main dish at a brunch.

___

## Crust:

1 Tbsp. baking yeast
¼ cup warm water
¼ cup honey

½ cup margarine or butter
2½ cups whole wheat flour

## Dairyless Filling:

1½ cups raw cashew butter
¼ lb. (about ½ cup) mashed Chinese firm tofu
¼ cup honey
¼ cup orange juice
2 Tbsp. lemon juice
2 Tbsp. arrowroot
1 Tbsp. finely grated orange rind
1 tsp. vanilla extract
⅛ tsp. cardamom
⅛ tsp. mace

## From Time-to-Time Filling:

2 cups Neufchatel cheese
5 Tbsp. honey
2 Tbsp. Lowfat "Sour Cream" (see recipe, p. 186)
2 Tbsp. Bipro
2 Tbsp. whole wheat flour
1 Tbsp. finely grated orange rind
1 tsp. vanilla extract
⅛ tsp. cardamom
⅛ tsp. mace

## Fruit Topping:

Green fruit — kiwi or seedless grapes
Yellow fruit — pineapple
Red fruit — strawberries or pitted cherries
Orange fruit — apricots, peaches, nectarines,
    mangoes, or papayas
Deep-colored fruit — red seedless grapes,
    blueberries or boysenberries, etc.
Bananas

*Kumquats (if available)*

*10 oz. sugarless apricot preserves*
*2 Tbsp. water or apple juice*

Combine first 3 ingredients and stir till yeast dissolves. Allow to sit about 10 minutes till mixture becomes bubbly. Add next 2 ingredients and mix in thoroughly till ingredients form a firm ball. Knead for about 10 minutes. Oil the ball of dough lightly and place in mixing bowl. Cover bowl with plastic wrap and allow to sit about 1 hour in a warm place.

Oil a cookie sheet or a 16" pizza pan or two 11" pie or tart tins. Pat and roll dough into pan so dough is evenly spread over the surface of the pan and up the sides. Allow crust to sit on counter in a warm place while making the filling (either Dairyless or Time-to-Time).

To make filling, blend all ingredients of chosen filling in blender till smooth. Spread finished filling evenly over rolled out Dessert Pizza crust. Bake at 350 degrees for 25 minutes, till crust turns golden brown.

Remove from oven and allow the whole pizza to completely cool. While it's cooling, prepare fruit topping by choosing one fruit from each color group (you don't have to use all the color groups, but try to think of the fruits you do choose in terms of how attractive they'll be side by side) and slice in ¼"-thick slices. Remember, fruit will be overlapped a little, so cut a little more than would be needed to just cover the surface of the pizza. Heat apricot (or other preserve of your choice) in water or juice till preserve melts and forms a thin glaze.

As soon as the baked pizza is cooled, layer sliced fruits in an artistic arrangement over the filling, being sure to overlap edges of fruit a bit. Brush with glaze made from apricot preserves. Serve as is or cover and refrigerate till serving time (you have up to 4 hours before crust starts to get soggy). Slice just before serving. Makes 4 to 6 meal-sized servings or a dozen dessert-sized slices.

| Special Shopping |
| --- |
| Sugarless apricot preserves (sweetened with honey or fruit juice) — available in natural food stores. |

| SHOPPING LIST | |
| --- | --- |
| **Regularly Kept in the Kitchen (Listed in Chapter 14, p. 703)** | **Fresh Produce** |
| Baking yeast<br>Honey<br>Margarine or butter<br>Whole wheat flour | Assorted fresh fruits to slice and cover top of pizza (try to vary colors)<br>Apple juice |

Also see shopping list for Lowfat "Sour Cream" (p. 186) and make a list of ingredients for Dairyless or Time-to-Time Filling.

# NUTRITIONAL ANALYSIS FOR ONE SERVING DESSERT PIZZA

| NUTRIENT | Type: 14   FEMALE-23 TO 51 YEARS | % RDA | Amount |
|---|---|---|---|
| KCALORIES | A======================= | 46% | 920.0 Kc |
| PROTEIN | A============================ | 52% | 23.30 Gm |
| CARBOHYDRATE | A | NO RDA | 105.0 Gm |
| FAT | A | NO RDA | 51.30 Gm |
| FIBER-CRUDE | A | NO RDA | 3.130 Gm |
| CHOLESTEROL | A | NO RDA | 0.000 Mg |
| SATURATED FA | A | NO RDA | 9.330 Gm |
| OLEIC FA | A | NO RDA | 0.330 Gm |
| LINOLEIC FA | A | NO RDA | 0.880 Gm |
| SODIUM | A==== | 9% | 198.0 Mg |
| POTASSIUM | A=============== | 28% | 1058 Mg |
| MAGNESIUM | A================================================ | 87% | 262.0 Mg |
| IRON | A====================== | 45% | 8.230 Mg |
| ZINC | A================== | 34% | 5.130 Mg |
| VITAMIN A | A===================== | 44% | 1780 IU |
| VITAMIN D | A | 0% | 0.000 IU |
| VIT. E/TOTAL | A | NO RDA | 2.100 Mg |
| VITAMIN C | A============================ | 57% | 34.20 Mg |
| THIAMIN | A============================== | 60% | 0.600 Mg |
| RIBOFLAVIN | A=============== | 31% | 0.380 Mg |
| NIACIN | A================= | 35% | 4.610 Mg |
| VITAMIN B6 | A============= | 27% | 0.550 Mg |
| FOLACIN | A================= | 35% | 141.0 Ug |
| VITAMIN B12 | A | 0% | 0.010 Ug |
| PANTO- ACID | A================== | 36% | 1.980 Mg |
| CALCIUM | A============= | 27% | 217.0 Mg |
| PHOSPHORUS | A==================================== | 72% | 580.0 Mg |
| TRYPTOPHAN | A=============================================== | 203% | 331.0 Mg |
| THREONINE | A=============================================== | 187% | 816.0 Mg |
| ISOLEUCINE | A=============================================== | 159% | 1041 Mg |
| LEUCINE | A=============================================== | 200% | 1743 Mg |
| LYSINE | A=============================================== | 164% | 1071 Mg |
| METHIONINE | A=============================================== | 133% | 362.0 Mg |
| CYSTINE | A■■■■■■■=========================== | 152% | 415.0 Mg |
| PHENYL-ANINE | A=============================================== | 260% | 1134 Mg |
| TYROSINE | A=============================================== | 175% | 762.0 Mg |
| VALINE | A=============================================== | 171% | 1308 Mg |
| HISTIDINE | A | NO RDA | 567.0 Mg |
| ALCOHOL | A | NO RDA | 0.000 Gm |
| ASH | A | NO RDA | 4.090 Gm |
| COPPER | A=================================== | 75% | 1.880 Mg |
| MANGANESE | A========================================= | 86% | 3.230 Mg |
| IODINE | A=============================================== | 154% | 232.0 Ug |
| MONO FAT | A | NO RDA | 27.10 Gm |
| POLY FAT | A | NO RDA | 11.60 Gm |
| CAFFEINE | A | NO RDA | 0.000 Mg |
| FLUORIDE | A | 1% | 37.50 Ug |
| MOLYBDENUM | A=============================================== | 993% | 3228 Ug |
| VITAMIN K | A | 0% | 0.000 Ug |
| SELENIUM | A======== | 16% | 0.020 Mg |
| BIOTIN | A== | 5% | 8.960 Ug |
| CHLORIDE | A= | 3% | 131.0 Mg |
| CHROMIUM | A=============================================== | 280% | 0.350 Mg |
| SUGAR | A | NO RDA | 5.100 Gm |
| FIBER-DIET | A | NO RDA | 8.870 Gm |
| VIT. E/AT | A=== | 6% | 0.550 Mg |

```
% RDA:  |0      |20     |40     |60     |80     |100
```

Margarine used instead of butter; Dairyless Filling used instead of From Time-to-Time Filling. Fruit used for topping: grapes, pineapple, strawberries, papaya, blueberries, banana, kumquats.

# A MOROCCAN FEAST

Henry David Thoreau jotted down this insight after a thoughtful walk in the forest: "As I stand over the insect crawling amid the pine needles on the forest floor, endeavoring to conceal itself from my sight, I ask myself why it will hide its head from me, who might be its benefactor, and impart to its race some cheering information ... I am reminded of the great Benefactor and Intelligence that stands over me, the human insect."

This Moroccan Feast is a festive meal with which to entertain. You might even set the right atmosphere for this meal by draping a tapestry-type bedspread from the ceiling (like a tent) — or better yet, set up a colorful tent or gazebo in the backyard on a warm day. Set the table with appropriate exotic brass vases and other decor.

To make and serve this feast authentically requires surprisingly little effort. The salads can all be made days ahead of time, refrigerated and taken out on the serving date so they can warm to room temperature. The Moroccan Relish should also be prepared well in advance and the Bisteeya can be prepared and frozen well in advance. All that needs to be done on the day of the feast is prepare the bread (doing this in the morning is fine), pop the Bisteeya in the oven, and attractively arrange a huge platter of whole fruits and nuts in shells (which is the traditional and healthful Moroccan dessert). The tea is made on the spot, after dinner, and takes but a few minutes.

Everything should be served in courses. All you need to set the table with are dinner plates. True Moroccan-style eating will be done with fingers, and the pieces of Moroccan Bread can also be used as eatable eating utensils to push food around the plate with. Provide knives and forks only for the squeamish; when you think of it, fingers are extremely efficient utensils for preparing and eating food — provided that they're clean.

So, start the meal by providing a finger wash bowl and towel. Then bring in baskets of the bread wedges and make them available through the whole meal. Serve salads in huge piles on central platters that everyone can take their share from. The Bisteeya should be served piping hot and unopen straight from the oven. A bisteeya is not a bisteeya if your fingers aren't burned a little when you poke through the crust to break off your piece. After the dishes are cleared, bring on the dessert platter and follow with the After-Dinner Mint tea. Since Islamic law forbids alchoholic beverages, you needn't feel pressured to provide an alchoholic drink! You'll know the feast is a success when you find yourself wondering where the belly dancers are!

# MOROCCAN BREAD

☆ A dense, earthy-flavored, crusty bread that's especially delicious when used to wipe up sauces from the different Moroccan salads or gravies.

2 Tbsp. baking yeast
1 tsp. honey
½ cup warm water

8½ cups whole wheat flour
2 Tbsp. anise seed
2 tsp. sesame seeds
1 tsp. salt

1 cup warm milk
Approximately 2 cups warm water

Corn meal

Combine first 3 ingredients in a small bowl and allow to sit 2 to 3 minutes till yeast dissolves. Stir and set aside on counter in a warm place and allow to rise till mixture is bubbly and doubles in volume.

In the meantime, mix the next 4 ingredients together in a mixing bowl and heat milk to lukewarm. Make a crater in the middle of the flour and pour in the risen, bubbly yeast mixture and the warm milk and mix in.

Add the warm water a little at a time to form a stiff dough (you may need a little more or less than 2 cups of water depending on variety of whole wheat flour used, humidity, etc.).

Serve the already cut wedges of this bread, cold or warm, in large, handwoven basket(s). Make them available through the whole meal.

Turn dough onto a lightly floured surface and knead for 10 to 15 minutes. The dough should be so stiff that it needs to be kneaded with fists. Divide dough into quarters and roll each piece into a ball. Allow to sit on floured surface about 5 minutes. In the meantime, sprinkle 2 cookie sheets with corn meal.

Form each ball of dough into a large cone shape. Place 2 cones on each cookie sheet and flatten each into round loaves that are slightly raised in the centers, about 6" in diameter.

Cover loaves with plastic wrap and allow to rise about 2 hours in a warm place. Preheat oven to 400 degrees.

Just before baking, gently prick bread around the sides in 4 places and bake at 400 degrees for 12 minutes. Turn heat down to 300 degrees and bake another 30 to 40 minutes till bread sounds hollow when tapped on the bottom. Remove from oven and allow to cool. Cut each loaf into 8 to 10 wedges just before serving. Makes 4 loaves of 8 to 10 wedges each.

| SHOPPING LIST | |
| --- | --- |
| **Regularly Kept in the Kitchen** (Listed in Chapter 14, p. 703) | **Fresh Produce** |
| Baking yeast<br>Honey<br>Whole wheat flour<br>Anise seeds<br>Sesame seeds<br>Milk<br>Corn meal | (None) |

# MOROCCAN EGGPLANT SALAD

Moroccan salads are made with cooked vegetables served at room temperature instead of raw vegetables like we're used to. The unique seasoning makes these memorable salads.

2 very large eggplants (approximately 3 lbs.)
3 cloves garlic, peeled and slivered

⅓ cup finely chopped, fresh parsley
6 sprigs fresh cilantro, chopped fine
¼ cup olive oil
2 Tbsp. soy sauce
¾ tsp. Spike or other vegetable-seasoned salt
1½ tsp. paprika

*1½ tsp. ground cumin*

*2 Tbsp. lemon juice*

Preheat oven to 400 degrees.

While oven is preheating, prepare eggplant for baking. Wash eggplant and leave whole. Use a paring knife to poke and drill a hole about 1" deep in the eggplant, and push one of the garlic slivers into the hole. Stud all the eggplants by following this procedure till all the garlic slivers are used up, trying to space holes as evenly as possible over the surface of the eggplant. Place eggplants on a cookie sheet and bake at 400 degrees for about 45 minutes. Eggplants should look collapsed and the skin will appear burnt. While eggplants are baking, cut and measure the next 7 ingredients into a skillet. Allow eggplant to cool enough to handle; then cut one in half and, placing hands over the center of the eggplant, squeeze as much of the liquid from the eggplant as possible without losing any of the eggplant pulp. Discard the liquid. With a spoon, scoop pulp out of peel into a strainer or food mill and mash and push through into the skillet, which already contains the next 7 ingredients. Saute ingredients together over a medium flame, stirring often, till eggplant turns a reddish-brown.

Turn off heat under the skillet. Cut remaining eggplant in half and squeeze out the liquid as with the first eggplant. Instead of mashing the eggplant, cut into large chunks and gently fold into the mixture in the skillet along with the lemon juice. Cover and refrigerate overnight or at least 2 to 3 hours before serving. Allow to sit at room temperature about 20 minutes before serving to take the chill off. Makes about 3 cups' worth of salad which, if served by itself as a salad or meal along with the Moroccan Bread, serves about 3 to 4 people. If served on a salad platter along with the Moroccan Carrot Salad and Moroccan Tomato-Pepper Salad and the bread, it altogether is enough to feed a dozen people.

| SHOPPING LIST | |
|---|---|
| **Regularly Kept in the Kitchen** (Listed in Chapter 14, p. 703) | **Fresh Produce** |
| Olive oil | Eggplants |
| Soy sauce | Garlic |
| Spike | Parsley |
| Paprika | Cilantro (same as Chinese parsley) |
| Ground cumin | Lemon |

# NUTRITIONAL ANALYSIS FOR ONE SERVING
## MOROCCAN EGGPLANT SALAD

| NUTRIENT | Type: 14    FEMALE-23 TO 51 YEARS | % RDA | Amount |
|---|---|---|---|
| KCALORIES | A======= | 15% | 301.0 Kc |
| PROTEIN | A======= | 15% | 6.770 Gm |
| CARBOHYDRATE | A | NO RDA | 32.80 Gm |
| FAT | A | NO RDA | 18.80 Gm |
| FIBER-CRUDE | A | NO RDA | 5.010 Gm |
| CHOLESTEROL | A | NO RDA | 0.000 Mg |
| SATURATED FA | A | NO RDA | 2.670 Gm |
| OLEIC FA | A | NO RDA | 12.80 Gm |
| LINOLEIC FA | A | NO RDA | 1.470 Gm |
| SODIUM | A===================== | 43% | 954.0 Mg |
| POTASSIUM | A=============== | 30% | 1147 Mg |
| MAGNESIUM | A=========== | 23% | 69.00 Mg |
| IRON | A============ | 24% | 4.320 Mg |
| ZINC | A== | 5% | 0.840 Mg |
| VITAMIN A | A================= | 34% | 1374 IU |
| VITAMIN D | A | 0% | 0.000 IU |
| VIT. E/TOTAL | A | NO RDA | 2.450 Mg |
| VITAMIN C | A================= | 34% | 20.40 Mg |
| THIAMIN | A====================== | 44% | 0.440 Mg |
| RIBOFLAVIN | A===== | 11% | 0.140 Mg |
| NIACIN | A============= | 26% | 3.420 Mg |
| VITAMIN B6 | A=========== | 23% | 0.460 Mg |
| FOLACIN | A=========== | 23% | 95.30 Ug |
| VITAMIN B12 | A | 0% | 0.000 Ug |
| PANTO- ACID | A=== | 7% | 0.430 Mg |
| CALCIUM | A=========== | 24% | 195.0 Mg |
| PHOSPHORUS | A============ | 24% | 192.0 Mg |
| TRYPTOPHAN | A=============== | 30% | 49.50 Mg |
| THREONINE | A===================== | 42% | 185.0 Mg |
| ISOLEUCINE | A================ | 33% | 222.0 Mg |
| LEUCINE | A================= | 36% | 321.0 Mg |
| LYSINE | A=================== | 39% | 257.0 Mg |
| METHIONINE | A========== | 20% | 56.60 Mg |
| CYSTINE | A===== | 10% | 28.40 Mg |
| PHENYL-ANINE | A======================== | 48% | 211.0 Mg |
| TYROSINE | A=============== | 30% | 134.0 Mg |
| VALINE | A================= | 35% | 268.0 Mg |
| HISTIDINE | A. | NO RDA | 117.0 Mg |
| ALCOHOL | A | NO RDA | 0.000 Gm |
| ASH | A | NO RDA | 5.040 Gm |
| COPPER | A========== | 21% | 0.540 Mg |
| MANGANESE | A======= | 17% | 0.640 Mg |
| IODINE | A======== | 17% | 26.20 Ug |
| MONO FAT | A | NO RDA | 13.30 Gm |
| POLY FAT | A | NO RDA | 1.790 Gm |
| CAFFEINE | A | NO RDA | 0.000 Mg |
| FLUORIDE | A | 0% | 6.390 Ug |
| MOLYBDENUM | A | 0% | 0.000 Ug |
| VITAMIN K | A | 0% | 0.000 Ug |
| SELENIUM | A | 0% | 0.000 Mg |
| BIOTIN | A | 0% | 0.020 Ug |
| CHLORIDE | A | 0% | 0.000 Mg |
| CHROMIUM | A | 0% | 0.000 Mg |
| SUGAR | A | NO RDA | 0.160 Gm |
| FIBER-DIET | A | NO RDA | 0.000 Gm |
| VIT. E/AT | A=============== | 28% | 2.260 Mg |

```
% RDA:  |0      |20     |40     |60     |80     |100
```

# MOROCCAN TOMATO-PEPPER SALAD

4 large, green bell peppers, peeled and seeded
4 large tomatoes, blanched, peeled and seeded

1 cucumber, diced
1 Tbsp. diced fresh chili pepper
2 - 3 Tbsp. lemon juice
2 Tbsp. finely chopped fresh parsley
2 Tbsp. olive oil
1 Tbsp. soy sauce
1 tsp. asafetida or 2 cloves garlic, crushed
1¼ tsp. black pepper
¼ tsp. ground cumin

Prepare bell peppers as in Pepper Antipasto Salad (see recipe, p. 621). If you are preparing the Moroccan Eggplant Salad, the peppers can be roasted in the broiler while the eggplant is baking.

Prepare tomatoes by bringing a pot full of water to a boil. Drop tomatoes in boiling water and boil for 15 seconds. Remove from water, slip peels off and cut out stems. Cut tomatoes in half crosswise and push the majority of seeds out with fingertips.

Cut prepared tomatoes and peppers into bite-sized chunks and toss with next 9 ingredients. Cover and refrigerate overnight, or at least for 2 to 3 hours before serving. Allow to sit at room temperature for about 20 minutes before serving to take the chill off. Makes about 1 to 1½ quarts of salad which, if served by itself as a salad or meal along with the Moroccan Bread, serves about 4 to 5 people. If served on a salad platter along with the Moroccan Eggplant Salad and Moroccan Carrot Salad and the bread, it altogether is enough to serve a dozen people.

## SUGGESTED MENU FOR A MOROCCAN FEAST

Moroccan Bread

1 to 3 of the
Moroccan salads

Brown Rice/Almond
Bisteeya

Moroccan Relish

Platter of whole fruits
and nuts in shells

Moroccan After-Dinner
Mint

| SHOPPING LIST | |
|---|---|
| **Regularly Kept in the Kitchen** (Listed in Chapter 14, p. 703) | **Fresh Produce** |
| Olive oil | Bell pepper |
| Soy sauce | Tomatoes |
| Asafetida | Cucumber |
| Black pepper | Chili pepper |
| Ground cumin | Lemon |
| | Parsley |

420

# NUTRITIONAL ANALYSIS FOR ONE SERVING
## MOROCCAN TOMATO-PEPPER SALAD

```
NUTRIENT        Type: 14    FEMALE-23 TO 51 YEARS          % RDA   Amount
KCALORIES       A===                                         6%   138.0 Kc
PROTEIN         A====                                        8%   3.520 Gm
CARBOHYDRATE    A                                         NO RDA  17.50 Gm
FAT             A                                         NO RDA  7.670 Gm
FIBER-CRUDE     A                                         NO RDA  2.470 Gm
CHOLESTEROL     A                                         NO RDA  0.000 Mg
SATURATED FA    A                                         NO RDA  1.100 Gm
OLEIC FA        A                                         NO RDA  4.810 Gm
LINOLEIC FA     A                                         NO RDA  0.550 Gm
SODIUM          A======                                     12%   278.0 Mg
POTASSIUM       A=========                                  19%   734.0 Mg
MAGNESIUM       A=======                                    15%   46.70 Mg
IRON            A=======                                    15%   2.710 Mg
ZINC            A=                                           3%   0.570 Mg
VITAMIN A       A===================================        70%    2819 IU
VITAMIN D       A                                            0%   0.000 IU
VIT. E/TOTAL    A                                         NO RDA  2.110 Mg
VITAMIN C       A=================================================  243%  146.0 Mg
THIAMIN         A==========                                 21%   0.210 Mg
RIBOFLAVIN      A======                                     13%   0.160 Mg
NIACIN          A=======                                    15%   2.050 Mg
VITAMIN B6      A======                                     13%   0.270 Mg
FOLACIN         A=====                                      11%   47.90 Ug
VITAMIN B12     A                                            0%   0.000 Ug
PANTO- ACID     A======                                     13%   0.740 Mg
CALCIUM         A==                                          4%   39.60 Mg
PHOSPHORUS      A=====                                      11%   91.30 Mg
TRYPTOPHAN      A========                                   16%   26.90 Mg
THREONINE       A=========                                  19%   82.90 Mg
ISOLEUCINE      A======                                     12%   79.20 Mg
LEUCINE         A=======                                    14%   123.0 Mg
LYSINE          A=========                                  18%   121.0 Mg
METHIONINE      A=====                                      10%   28.20 Mg
CYSTINE         A=======                                    14%   39.80 Mg
PHENYL-ANINE    A=========                                  18%   80.10 Mg
TYROSINE        A=====                                      11%   51.30 Mg
VALINE          A======                                     12%   92.10 Mg
HISTIDINE       A                                         NO RDA  48.10 Mg
ALCOHOL         A                                         NO RDA  0.000 Gm
ASH             A                                         NO RDA  2.810 Gm
COPPER          A=====                                      11%   0.280 Mg
MANGANESE       A=====                                      10%   0.400 Mg
IODINE          A                                            0%   0.000 Ug
MONO FAT        A                                         NO RDA  5.060 Gm
POLY FAT        A                                         NO RDA  0.970 Gm
CAFFEINE        A                                         NO RDA  0.000 Mg
FLUORIDE        A=                                           2%   64.80 Ug
MOLYBDENUM      A                                            0%   0.710 Ug
VITAMIN K       A====                                        9%   9.460 Ug
SELENIUM        A                                            0%   0.000 Mg
BIOTIN          A==                                          5%   8.760 Ug
CHLORIDE        A                                            0%   0.000 Mg
CHROMIUM        A=============================              56%   0.070 Mg
SUGAR           A                                         NO RDA  13.10 Gm
FIBER-DIET      A                                         NO RDA  2.790 Gm
VIT. E/AT       A=============                              26%   2.130 Mg

    % RDA:   |0      |20     |40     |60     |80     |100
```

421

# MOROCCAN CARROT SALAD

2 lbs. carrots, steamed and torn
    into bite-sized pieces

⅓ cup lemon juice
2 Tbsp. olive oil
2 tsp. finely chopped fresh parsley
1 tsp. paprika
½ tsp. ground cumin
½ tsp. asafetida or 2 cloves garlic, crushed
½ tsp. Spike or other vegetable-seasoned salt
¼ tsp. cinnamon
¼ tsp. honey

Scrub carrots well and cut tops and tips off. Steam carrots in a steamer till they are so tender they can be cut with a spoon easily. Remove from heat and take two forks to break carrots crosswise into bite-sized pieces. Add the next 9 ingredients and toss till thoroughly mixed. Cover and refrigerate overnight or at least for 2 to 3 hours before serving. Makes about 3 to 4 cups of salad which, if served by itself as a salad or meal along with the Moroccan Bread, serves 3 to 4 people. If served on a salad platter along with the Moroccan Eggplant Salad and Moroccan Tomato-Pepper Salad and the bread, it altogether is enough to feed a dozen people.

| SHOPPING LIST | |
| --- | --- |
| Regularly Kept in the Kitchen (Listed in Chapter 14, p. 703) | Fresh Produce |
| Olive oil | Lemon |
| Paprika | Parsley |
| Ground cumin | Carrots |
| Asafetida | |
| Spike | |
| Cinnamon | |
| Honey | |

# NUTRITIONAL ANALYSIS FOR ONE SERVING
## MOROCCAN CARROT SALAD

| NUTRIENT | Type: 14  FEMALE-23 TO 51 YEARS | % RDA | Amount |
|---|---|---|---|
| KCALORIES | A===== | 10% | 218.0 Kc |
| PROTEIN | A=== | 7% | 3.380 Gm |
| CARBOHYDRATE | A | NO RDA | 33.40 Gm |
| FAT | A | NO RDA | 9.750 Gm |
| FIBER-CRUDE | A | NO RDA | 3.270 Gm |
| CHOLESTEROL | A | NO RDA | 0.000 Mg |
| SATURATED FA | A | NO RDA | 1.380 Gm |
| OLEIC FA | A | NO RDA | 6.410 Gm |
| LINOLEIC FA | A | NO RDA | 0.730 Gm |
| SODIUM | A====== | 12% | 265.0 Mg |
| POTASSIUM | A============= | 26% | 1002 Mg |
| MAGNESIUM | A======== | 16% | 49.50 Mg |
| IRON | A===== | 11% | 2.040 Mg |
| ZINC | A== | 4% | 0.630 Mg |
| VITAMIN A | A=================================================== | 2037% | 81480 IU |
| VITAMIN D | A | 0% | 0.000 IU |
| VIT. E/TOTAL | A | NO RDA | 2.620 Mg |
| VITAMIN C | A================================= | 68% | 41.20 Mg |
| THIAMIN | A============== | 29% | 0.290 Mg |
| RIBOFLAVIN | A======= | 15% | 0.180 Mg |
| NIACIN | A========== | 21% | 2.840 Mg |
| VITAMIN B6 | A========== | 21% | 0.430 Mg |
| FOLACIN | A===== | 11% | 45.50 Ug |
| VITAMIN B12 | A | 0% | 0.000 Ug |
| PANTO- ACID | A===== | 10% | 0.590 Mg |
| CALCIUM | A===== | 11% | 90.60 Mg |
| PHOSPHORUS | A======== | 17% | 137.0 Mg |
| TRYPTOPHAN | A========== | 20% | 33.70 Mg |
| THREONINE | A============ | 25% | 111.0 Mg |
| ISOLEUCINE | A========= | 18% | 124.0 Mg |
| LEUCINE | A======= | 14% | 130.0 Mg |
| LYSINE | A========= | 18% | 123.0 Mg |
| METHIONINE | A=== | 7% | 21.50 Mg |
| CYSTINE | A==== | 9% | 25.30 Mg |
| PHENYL-ANINE | A========== | 21% | 95.30 Mg |
| TYROSINE | A====== | 13% | 57.30 Mg |
| VALINE | A======== | 17% | 134.0 Mg |
| HISTIDINE | A | NO RDA | 50.00 Mg |
| ALCOHOL | A | NO RDA | 0.000 Gm |
| ASH | A | NO RDA | 2.720 Gm |
| COPPER | A=== | 6% | 0.150 Mg |
| MANGANESE | A===== | 10% | 0.410 Mg |
| IODINE | A===== | 11% | 17.50 Ug |
| MONO FAT | A | NO RDA | 6.650 Gm |
| POLY FAT | A | NO RDA | 1.040 Gm |
| CAFFEINE | A | NO RDA | 0.000 Mg |
| FLUORIDE | A== | 4% | 116.0 Ug |
| MOLYBDENUM | A=== | 7% | 24.80 Ug |
| VITAMIN K | A | 0% | 0.000 Ug |
| SELENIUM | A | 0% | 0.000 Mg |
| BIOTIN | A== | 5% | 8.640 Ug |
| CHLORIDE | A | 0% | 0.000 Mg |
| CHROMIUM | A======== | 16% | 0.020 Mg |
| SUGAR | A | NO RDA | 13.90 Gm |
| FIBER-DIET | A | NO RDA | 4.320 Gm |
| VIT. E/AT | A============== | 29% | 2.350 Mg |

```
% RDA:    |0      |20     |40     |60     |80     |100
```

423

# BROWN RICE/ALMOND BISTEEYA

☆ Whole wheat Filo dough is very hard to find; I only know of one small "cottage industry" that makes whole wheat Filo dough. To try to make up for nutritional losses in refined white flour Filo dough, I try to sprinkle some wheat germ and bran between each sheet of Filo dough.

---

2 cups whole almonds, toasted

5 cups water
¾ cup finely chopped fresh parsley
¼ cup soy sauce
2 Tbsp. asafetida or 5 cloves garlic, crushed
3 cinnamon sticks
1 tsp. black pepper
¾ tsp. powdered ginger
¼ tsp. turmeric
¼ tsp. crushed saffron

½ lb. Chinese firm tofu (about 1 cup), crumbled

¼ cup lemon juice

¼ cup margarine or butter
1 tsp. poultry seasoning
2 cups long grain brown rice

⅓ cup date sugar
1½ tsp. cinnamon

10 Filo (Phyllo) dough sheets
½ cup margarine or butter
Wheat germ
Bran

½ cup fructose or maple syrup sugar
Cinnamon

If using raw, whole almonds, bake them in a 200-degree oven for 1 hour to lightly toast them. If almonds are already roasted, skip this step.

While almonds are baking, combine next 9 ingredients in a large pot (so liquid comes no more than halfway up the pot) and bring to a boil. Reduce heat to a slow boil.

Please don't take my using fructose in this one recipe as an endorsement of using fructose on a regular basis. I prefer to use fructose here instead of the usual confectioner's sugar, but am very wary of using fructose more than once or twice a year. Many products in natural food stores are made with fructose, but that doesn't make it a healthy food. Though studies are still being done on fructose, there are some who feel fructose is as damaging to the health as white sugar. I only use it here in this recipe for lack of anything else that will give a similar taste and texture.

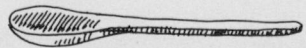

Crumble ½ pound (about 1 cup's worth) of tofu into a strainer. Set strainer into the boiling mixture so the tofu is covered by the liquid but remains contained in the strainer. Gently boil for about 20 minutes. Lift strainer out of liquid and set on lip of pot so excess liquid from the tofu drains back into the pot. After tofu is drained, pour the tofu into a small bowl and mix in ¼ cup lemon juice.

Add next 3 ingredients to the water boiling in the pot. Cover and cook over medium-low heat for 25 minutes. Turn off heat, remove cinnamon sticks, stir rice, and leave lid off.

Chop roasted almonds in a food processor or a blender to form an almond meal. In another bowl, mix chopped almonds with the next 2 ingredients (date sugar and cinnamon). Set aside.

It's now time to assemble the Bisteeya! All the steps previous to this point can be prepared days ahead of time, if desired. If you wish to assemble and bake the whole Bisteeya ahead of time, you can do that also, as in the Greek Spinach Pie (see recipe, p. 577) and freeze. Then take the already baked and frozen Bisteeya out, allow to thaw at room temperature, and bake at 350 degrees for about 20 minutes.

If you are assembling the Bisteeya fresh a short time before serving, be sure that it's timed so it can go straight from the assemblying into the oven, as sitting around at room temperature for a while will cause the bottom crust to get soggy.

Preheat the oven to 425 degrees. As the oven is preheating, melt the ½ cup of margarine or butter. Brush the bottom and sides of a 10" skillet or quiche dish with the melted butter. Lay in 1 sheet of Filo dough so edges hang out over the sides of the dish, brush entire surface of dough with margarine or butter, and sprinkle with a little wheat germ and bran. Add 5 more sheets of Filo dough, brushing each one with margarine or butter and sprinkling with wheat germ and bran, being sure to lay the dough so the corners aren't lying one on top of the other but are spread around the edge of the dish. Fold 2 Filo sheets in half and place in preheating oven for a few minutes till they get dry and crisp; this takes only a few minutes, so watch carefully — they burn quickly!

Pour rice mixture onto the 6 layers of Filo dough in baking dish and spread out evenly. Top this with the prepared tofu and spread evenly. Crumble the 2 crisp Filo sheets and spread evenly over the tofu layer. Sprinkle with ⅛ cup wheat germ and ⅛ cup bran. Sprinkle the almond meal/date sugar mixture evenly over this. Now fold the corners of the 6 layers of Filo dough that are hanging over the edges of the dish, over on top of the almond mixture. You should now have a crust of 6 layers of Filo dough wrapped over and encasing the rice, tofu, and almond layers. Lay 1 Filo dough sheet over the top of the dish and brush with margarine or butter. Repeat again with 1 more Filo dough sheet. Tuck the edges of the 2 top sheets of Filo dough down under the Bisteeya (like tucking in a sheet). Brush the top of the Bisteeya with the remaining margarine or butter.

Bake at 425 degrees for 20 minutes, till Bisteeya is a golden brown. Remove from oven and flip Bisteeya over onto a cookie sheet with bottom side up. Bake at 425 degrees for another 10 to 15 minutes till golden brown, but be careful not to burn. Remove from oven and flip onto serving platter with the bottom side against the plate. Sprinkle entire top surface with maple syrup sugar or fructose. (Usually the Bisteeya is topped with confectioner's sugar; maple syrup sugar is a healthier replacement, but if you object to the definite maple syrup flavor this adds, fructose is the next best choice.) Sprinkle cinnamon in abstract or geometric designs on top of the sugar topping with fingertips. Serve immediately. Bisteeya is always served so hot that burning the fingers is part of the dish! Makes about 8 servings. When served with preceding salads and bread, it will easily fill a dozen people.

| SHOPPING LIST | |
|---|---|
| **Regularly Kept in the Kitchen** (Listed in Chapter 14, p. 703) | **Fresh Produce** |
| Almonds | Parsley |
| Soy sauce | Lemon |
| Asafetida | |
| Cinnamon powder and sticks | |
| Black pepper | |
| Ginger powder | |
| Turmeric | |
| Saffron | |
| Tofu | |
| Margarine or butter | |
| Poultry seasoning | |
| Brown rice | |
| Date sugar | |
| Wheat germ | |
| Bran | |

**Special Shopping**

Filo (Phyllo) dough sheets — in the refrigerated or freezer section in gourmet food stores and some super-markets; also in Mid-Eastern and Greek groceries. Fructose or maple syrup sugar — found in most natural food stores. Maple syrup sugar imparts a definite maple syrup taste, so you may prefer fructose.

# NUTRITIONAL ANALYSIS FOR ONE SERVING
## BROWN RICE/ALMOND BISTEEYA

| NUTRIENT | Type: 14  FEMALE-23 TO 51 YEARS | % RDA | Amount |
|---|---|---|---|
| KCALORIES | Ħ=================== | 36% | 731.0 Kc |
| PROTEIN | Ħ===================== | 43% | 19.10 Gm |
| CARBOHYDRATE | Ħ | NO RDA | 82.20 Gm |
| FAT | Ħ | NO RDA | 39.10 Gm |
| FIBER-CRUDE | Ħ | NO RDA | 3.080 Gm |
| CHOLESTEROL | Ħ | NO RDA | 0.000 Mg |
| SATURATED FA | Ħ | NO RDA | 4.950 Gm |
| OLEIC FA | Ħ | NO RDA | 4.820 Gm |
| LINOLEIC FA | Ħ | NO RDA | 0.950 Gm |
| SODIUM | Ħ================ | 33% | 728.0 Mg |
| POTASSIUM | Ħ========= | 18% | 678.0 Mg |
| MAGNESIUM | Ħ====================================== | 75% | 227.0 Mg |
| IRON | Ħ==================== | 42% | 7.630 Mg |
| ZINC | Ħ============ | 27% | 4.170 Mg |
| VITAMIN A | Ħ============ | 27% | 1081 IU |
| VITAMIN D | Ħ | 0% | 1.310 IU |
| VIT. E/TOTAL | Ħ | NO RDA | 4.310 Mg |
| VITAMIN C | Ħ======== | 17% | 10.20 Mg |
| THIAMIN | Ħ======================= | 48% | 0.480 Mg |
| RIBOFLAVIN | Ħ================ | 35% | 0.430 Mg |
| NIACIN | Ħ===================== | 43% | 5.660 Mg |
| VITAMIN B6 | Ħ========== | 20% | 0.410 Mg |
| FOLACIN | Ħ========= | 18% | 73.10 Ug |
| VITAMIN B12 | Ħ | 0% | 0.020 Ug |
| PANTO- ACID | Ħ============ | 26% | 1.460 Mg |
| CALCIUM | Ħ===================== | 43% | 350.0 Mg |
| PHOSPHORUS | Ħ=============================== | 65% | 520.0 Mg |
| TRYPTOPHAN | Ħ================================================= | 165% | 270.0 Mg |
| THREONINE | Ħ================================================= | 157% | 687.0 Mg |
| ISOLEUCINE | Ħ================================================= | 134% | 876.0 Mg |
| LEUCINE | Ħ================================================= | 172% | 1501 Mg |
| LYSINE | Ħ================================================= | 130% | 855.0 Mg |
| METHIONINE | Ħ============================================== | 98% | 268.0 Mg |
| CYSTINE | Ħ================================================= | 111% | 302.0 Mg |
| PHENYL-ANINE | Ħ================================================= | 225% | 981.0 Mg |
| TYROSINE | Ħ================================================= | 136% | 592.0 Mg |
| VALINE | Ħ================================================= | 127% | 974.0 Mg |
| HISTIDINE | Ħ | NO RDA | 559.0 Mg |
| ALCOHOL | Ħ | NO RDA | 0.000 Gm |
| ASH | Ħ | NO RDA | 5.240 Gm |
| COPPER | Ħ=============== | 31% | 0.780 Mg |
| MANGANESE | Ħ============================================ | 90% | 3.410 Mg |
| IODINE | Ħ================================================= | 209% | 314.0 Ug |
| MONO FAT | Ħ | NO RDA | 20.10 Gm |
| POLY FAT | Ħ | NO RDA | 10.90 Gm |
| CAFFEINE | Ħ | NO RDA | 0.000 Mg |
| FLUORIDE | Ħ | 0% | 22.70 Ug |
| MOLYBDENUM | Ħ================================================= | 370% | 1205 Ug |
| VITAMIN K | Ħ | 0% | 0.000 Ug |
| SELENIUM | Ħ======== | 16% | 0.020 Mg |
| BIOTIN | Ħ= | 3% | 4.680 Ug |
| CHLORIDE | Ħ== | 4% | 156.0 Mg |
| CHROMIUM | Ħ================================================= | 328% | 0.410 Mg |
| SUGAR | Ħ | NO RDA | 4.760 Gm |
| FIBER-DIET | Ħ | NO RDA | 2.850 Gm |
| VIT. E/AT | Ħ========== | 21% | 1.720 Mg |

```
% RDA:  |0      |20     |40     |60     |80     |100
```

Due to lack of data for fructose and maple syrup sugar, powdered sugar was used instead.
Margarine was used instead of butter.

# MOROCCAN AFTER-DINNER MINT

☆ In Morocco, this tea is also served as a snack during the day and counts as a course at mealtime. Liquids are appreciated as the life-giving essentials that they are.

6 cups water

2 handfuls (approximately 2 cups)
  fresh spearmint leaves
⅓ cup honey
2 Tbsp. Ban-cha, San-cha or Kuki-cha tea

Bring water to a boil. Combine next 3 ingredients in a separate pot. If you can't find spearmint, fresh mint leaves will do, but the tea is really at its best with spearmint. Pour boiling water over ingredients in pot, cover and steep for 3 minutes. Stir gently, strain and serve immediately, or refrigerate and serve as an iced tea. Makes six 1-cup servings.

Drinking liquids is a healthy Moroccan practice we could all benefit from adopting. In Morocco, little roadside stands sell water much like soda is sold here. The wealthy drink perfumed water. As an exotic addition to any meal, try this perfumed water. Burn some gum arabic till it's charcoaled. Invert the water serving container over the burning gum arabic to catch the fumes. Immediately fill with cold water. Water will have a subtle perfumed flavor.

| SHOPPING LIST | |
|---|---|
| Regularly Kept in the Kitchen (Listed in Chapter 14, p. 703) | Fresh Produce |
| Honey | Fresh spearmint leaves |

| Special Shopping |
|---|
| Ban-cha, San-cha or Kuki-cha (caffeine-free green tea) — found in most natural food stores. |

# HOT MOROCCAN RELISH

☆ Serve in a small bowl for people who like hot dishes to dab onto their individual servings.

⅓ cup dried red chili flakes
⅓ cup water

1 tsp. caraway seeds
1 tsp. asafetida or 1 clove garlic, crushed
1 tsp. cumin seeds
½ tsp. coriander seeds
2 tsp. soy sauce

Olive oil to cover

Soak first 2 ingredients for about 1 hour. Place in blender, add the next 5 ingredients and blend till pureed. Pour into jar and pour olive oil over puree, cover and refrigerate.

This hot relish will keep 2 to 3 months when refrigerated. Serve this in a separate bowl for people to put on, or dunk in, their various Moroccan vegetable salads and/or Bisteeya. This relish can also be served by mixing with olives as a side dish. It's also delicious thinned with a little lemon juice and poured on top of cous-cous for flavoring.

| SHOPPING LIST | |
| --- | --- |
| Regularly Kept in the Kitchen (Listed in Chapter 14, p. 703) | Fresh Produce |
| Red chili flakes<br>Caraway seeds<br>Asafetida<br>Cumin seeds<br>Coriander seeds<br>Soy sauce<br>Olive oil | (None) |

# INTRODUCING LUPINI

To become fully conscious is the true goal in life, and everything we do helps or hinders us in progressing toward that goal. While there is certainly more to life than eating, being conscious of what we eat and why, can lead to being conscious of other things, as is expressed in this Jewish saying: "Some people have a foolish way of not minding, or pretending not to mind, what they eat. For my part, I mind my belly very studiously and carefully, for I look upon it that he who does not think about what he puts into his belly will hardly think about anything else."

A confession from a natural foods advocate: My family and I have never liked whole grain noodles. They are the one whole grain product we all barely tolerate because we know it's better for our health to eat whole grains instead of refined ones. (As can be seen from the recipes in this book, healthy foods don't have to taste bad!) We've found whole grain pastas to be generally unpalatable and have a tendency to stick together in a large, starchy clump. (Yes — even when we put a little oil in to prevent sticking!) So, imagine my excitement when I found a super whole grain/legume noodle that tastes really good, doesn't ever stick together, and that sauces adhere to better!

It is a noodle made with a combination of triticale flour and a bean called lupini. Those of us who frequent natural food stores are familiar with triticale — but lupini? The lupini bean may be new to us in America but has actually been known and used in Europe since the time of Babylon. Despite their being nutritional powerhouses, they've never gotten real popular as a food item because they have a very distinctive, bitter taste. However, for the past 30 years Dr. Fred Elliot and associates at Michigan State University have hybred a sweet lupini bean that some pioneering farmers in America have been growing.

The sweet lupini bean is at the point now where some farmers are beginning to accept it as livestock feed; although it is far from being widely accepted — much less known — as a food for humans, I feel it should be. Nutritionally, sweet lupini beans are at the top of any list of legumes and grains.

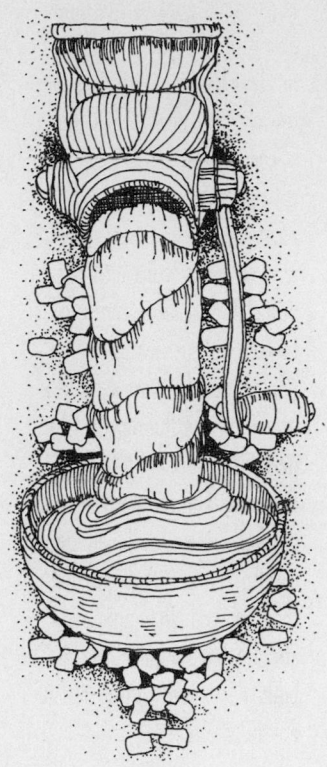

|  | Protein (%) | Lysine (%) | Dietary fiber (%) |
|---|---|---|---|
| Sweet lupini | 35.00 | 1.60 | 28.00 |
| Soybeans | 34.30 | 2.60 | 5.00 |
| Whole triticale | 16.00 | .88 | 14.00 |
| Whole wheat | 13.00 | .35 | 9.60 |
| High-lysine corn | 8.00 | .45 | 7.50 |
| Corn | 9.60 | .25 | 10.00 |
| Brown rice | .79 | .27 | 27.00 |

As you can see, nutritionally lupini beans are very close to soybeans. But one advantage the new sweet lupini beans have over soybeans is they don't have a beany flavor. I'm not proposing that lupini beans replace soybeans (the most commonly-used source of protein and other nutritional properties in my kitchen), but they certainly offer an alternative to soybeans in places where soybeans can't be grown, and in this way help to provide food for more people. Lupini beans will grow just about anywhere soybeans won't. The lupini plant is a hardy plant that will grow well in arid, slightly acidic soils and will tolerate cold very well.

I had the pleasure of meeting and learning about the lupini bean through one of the members of the family that's spearheading the farming of lupini beans in this country. He had developed a pasta made from lupini beans that by far surpassed any enriched pasta (admittedly, that's not so hard to do since virtually all nutrition is removed from the grain and only a few B-vitamins put back).

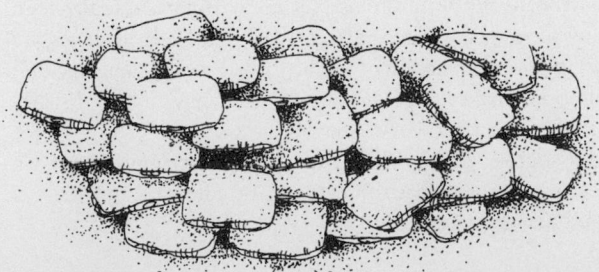

## PERCENTAGE OF U.S. RDA
### 4-oz. serving (dry)

|  | Lupini | Whole wheat pasta | Enriched |
|---|---|---|---|
| Protein | 46 | 33 | 28 |
| Dietary fiber | 42 | (No data) | 0 |
| Calcium | 25 | 6 | Trace |
| Vitamin A | 1 | 0 | 0 |
| Vitamin C | Trace | Trace | 0 |
| Thiamine | 64 | 60 | 82 |
| Niacin | 38 | 40 | 38 |
| Riboflavin | 40 | 10 | 40 |
| Iron | 38 | 12 | 18 |
| Calories (No RDA) | 365 | 412 | 420 |

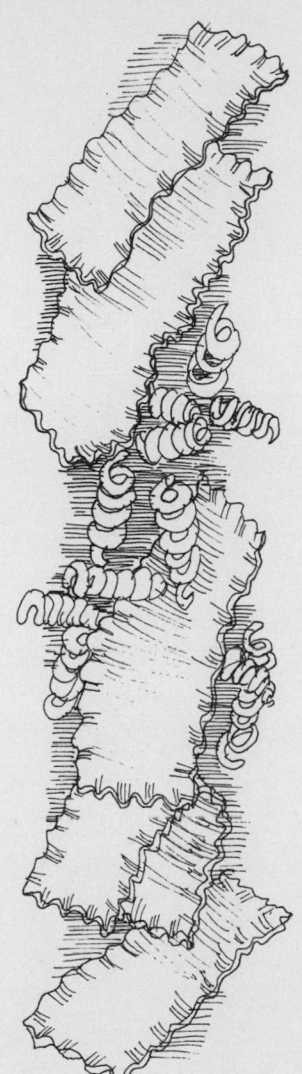

Excited about the many aspects of the lupini bean and the quality of the pasta made from them, I let my enthusiasm get the best of me and produced a show about lupini — prematurely. Unfortunately, lupini noodles aren't out on the market yet. I assume if and when they do appear on store shelves, it will first be in natural food stores. Please accept my apologies. I know how frustrating it can be to want to get or try something that isn't available yet.

Looking on the bright side of the picture — at least you have been introduced to lupini and know a little about it! Your information bank is that much more enriched, and when lupini products appear on the market for human consumption, your body can be that much more enriched as well!

# TOFU CROUTONS

☆ Besides served on top of whole grain noodles with the Zesty Creme Sauce, these croutons are a delicious addition to salads, soups, stews or any other entree.

*1 lb. Chinese firm tofu, cut in ⅝" cubes*
*Soy sauce*

*½ cup nutritional yeast*
*½ cup whole wheat flour*
*1 Tbsp. dry parsley flakes*

So as not to waste the energy it takes to heat up the oven, I usually multiply this recipe a few times. Then, after allowing the cooked Tofu Croutons to cool off, I put them in plastic bags to freeze for future use.

1 tsp. *Spike or other vegetable-seasoned salt*
¾ tsp. *tarragon*
¼ tsp. *nutmeg*
¼ tsp. *sage*
¼ tsp. *thyme*
¼ tsp. *crumbled rosemary leaves*
¼ tsp. *paprika*
¼ tsp. *black pepper*
¼ tsp. *asafetida or garlic powder*

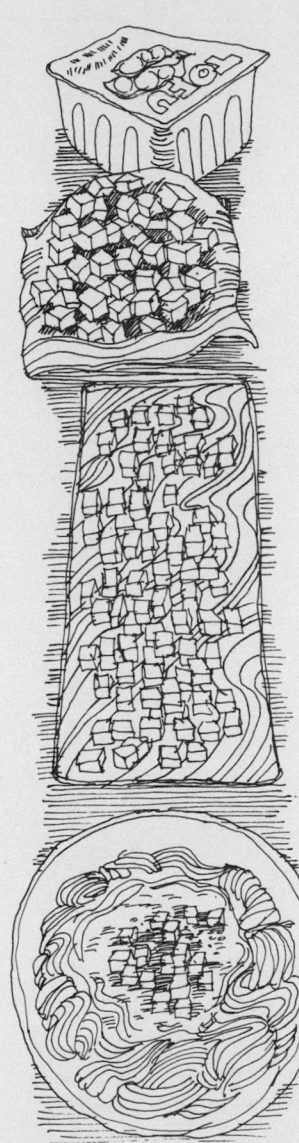

Preheat oven to 450 degrees.

Cut block of tofu into approximately ⅝" cubes. Put into a bowl large enough to scatter cubes in and sprinkle with soy sauce. Leave to sit a few minutes so tofu can absorb some soy sauce.

Mix the next 12 ingredients together in a strong plastic bag. Very gently with your fingertips, drop tofu cubes into the mixture in the bag. Twist top of bag shut and gently shake and rotate tofu in the mixture till it's evenly coated. Scatter tofu in a single layer on a large baking tray or cookie sheet that's been coated with about ⅛" of oil on the bottom (non-stick pans require only a thin film). Bake at 450 degrees for 15 to 20 minutes, till the cubes turn a golden brown and are crisp when cooled a little.

Serve on top of noodles with the following Zesty Creme Sauce. Also delicious tossed in salads, cooked vegetable dishes and entrees. Makes about 4 to 6 servings — certainly enough for 1 pound of noodles!

| SHOPPING LIST | |
|---|---|
| **Regularly Kept in the Kitchen** (Listed in Chapter 14, p. 703) | **Fresh Produce** |
| Tofu | (None) |
| Soy sauce | |
| Nutritional yeast | |
| Whole wheat flour | |
| Parsley flakes | |
| Spike | |
| Tarragon | |
| Nutmeg | |
| Sage | |
| Thyme | |
| Rosemary | |
| Paprika | |
| Black pepper | |
| Asafetida | |

# ZESTY CREME SAUCE

☆ An alternative to a tomato sauce to top noodles with.

---

2 cups diced potatoes
1½ cups diced carrots

1 cup fresh or frozen peas

4 cups nonfat or lowfat milk
⅔ cup nutritional yeast
2 Tbsp. plus 2 tsp. arrowroot
2 tsp. dry mustard powder
2 tsp. soy sauce
2 tsp. Spike or other vegetable-seasoned salt
½ tsp. black pepper

⅛ tsp. Tabasco (optional)

Put first 2 ingredients in a steamer to steam. When carrots turn a more brilliant orange than they were when raw, add peas. Steam 1 or 2 minutes longer and remove from heat to avoid over-cooking.

In the meantime, combine next 7 ingredients in a saucepan and whisk till arrowroot is dissolved. Put on medium-high heat and whisk or stir till sauce comes to a boil and thickens. After sauce is thickened, add hot sauce, if desired, and mix in well. Remove from heat and fold in the steamed vegetables. At this point, you can also mix in the Tofu Croutons, or else leave them aside to put on each individual serving.

Ladle sauce over cooked noodles and Tofu Croutons. Makes 1 quart. The number of servings this recipe makes depends on how thickly you pour on the sauce.

| SHOPPING LIST | |
|---|---|
| **Regularly Kept in the Kitchen** (Listed in Chapter 14, p. 703) | **Fresh Produce** |
| Milk | Potatoes |
| Nutritional yeast | Carrots |
| Arrowroot | Fresh or frozen peas |
| Dry mustard powder | Tabasco (optional) |
| Soy sauce | |
| Spike | |
| Black pepper | |

Of course, the Zesty Creme Sauce can be used over other than noodles. It adds life to steamed vegetables; it's delicious served on top of whole grain toast and Tofu Cutlets, on rice, baked potatoes, or can be used to replace a plain white sauce in any dish.

# NUTRITIONAL ANALYSIS FOR ONE SERVING LUPINI NOODLES
## WITH TOFU CROUTONS AND ZESTY CREME SAUCE

| NUTRIENT | Type: 14  FEMALE-23 TO 51 YEARS | % RDA | Amount |
|---|---|---|---|
| KCALORIES | A=========================== | 50% | 1,003 Kc |
| PROTEIN | A=================================================== | 164% | 72.40 Gm |
| CARBOHYDRATE | A | NO RDA | 138.0 Gm |
| FAT | A | NO RDA | 19.10 Gm |
| FIBER-CRUDE | A | NO RDA | 6.630 Gm |
| CHOLESTEROL | A | NO RDA | 18.00 Mg |
| SATURATED FA | A | NO RDA | 4.520 Gm |
| OLEIC FA | A | NO RDA | 2.370 Gm |
| LINOLEIC FA | A | NO RDA | 2.500 Gm |
| SODIUM | A============================= | 61% | 1359 Mg |
| POTASSIUM | A==================================== | 70% | 2654 Mg |
| MAGNESIUM | A==================================================== | 109% | 328.0 Mg |
| IRON | A====================================================== | 121% | 21.90 Mg |
| ZINC | A=============================================== | 98% | 14.70 Mg |
| VITAMIN A | A====================================================== | 319% | 12771 IU |
| VITAMIN D | A========================= | 51% | 102.0 IU |
| VIT. E/TOTAL | A | NO RDA | 2.000 Mg |
| VITAMIN C | A==================================== | 75% | 45.50 Mg |
| THIAMIN | A==================================================== | 2190% | 21.90 Mg |
| RIBOFLAVIN | A==================================================== | 1816% | 21.80 Mg |
| NIACIN | A==================================================== | 992% | 129.0 Mg |
| VITAMIN B6 | A==================================================== | 1085% | 21.70 Mg |
| FOLACIN | A============================================== | 94% | 378.0 Ug |
| VITAMIN B12 | A==================================================== | 573% | 17.20 Ug |
| PANTO- ACID | A========================================= | 86% | 4.730 Mg |
| CALCIUM | A==================================================== | 168% | 1345 Mg |
| PHOSPHORUS | A==================================================== | 189% | 1513 Mg |
| TRYPTOPHAN | A==================================================== | 403% | 657.0 Mg |
| THREONINE | A==================================================== | 542% | 2362 Mg |
| ISOLEUCINE | A==================================================== | 486% | 3176 Mg |
| LEUCINE | A==================================================== | 568% | 4950 Mg |
| LYSINE | A==================================================== | 664% | 4338 Mg |
| METHIONINE | A==================================================== | 376% | 1025 Mg |
| CYSTINE | A==================================================== | 355% | 967.0 Mg |
| PHENYL-ANINE | A==================================================== | 661% | 2879 Mg |
| TYROSINE | A==================================================== | 544% | 2369 Mg |
| VALINE | A==================================================== | 478% | 3643 Mg |
| HISTIDINE | A | NO RDA | 1730 Mg |
| ALCOHOL | A | NO RDA | 0.000 Gm |
| ASH | A | NO RDA | 27.80 Gm |
| COPPER | A========================= | 62% | 1.570 Mg |
| MANGANESE | A==================================================== | 1258% | 47.20 Mg |
| IODINE | A==================================================== | 177% | 266.0 Ug |
| MONO FAT | A | NO RDA | 3.870 Gm |
| POLY FAT | A | NO RDA | 5.950 Gm |
| CAFFEINE | A | NO RDA | 0.000 Mg |
| FLUORIDE | A== | 4% | 111.0 Mg |
| MOLYBDENUM | A==================================================== | 696% | 2264 Ug |
| VITAMIN K | A==================================================== | 102% | 108.0 Ug |
| SELENIUM | A============ | 24% | 0.030 Mg |
| BIOTIN | A==================== | 38% | 57.70 Ug |
| CHLORIDE | A=== | 7% | 244.0 Mg |
| CHROMIUM | A==================================================== | 432% | 0.540 Mg |
| SUGAR | A | NO RDA | 3.600 Gm |
| FIBER-DIET | A | NO RDA | 21.60 Gm |
| VIT. E/AT | A=== | 6% | 0.490 Mg |

```
% RDA:  |0     |20    |40    |60    |80    |100
```

Lowfat milk used instead of nonfat in the sauce.

# PRIMAVERA

☆ A garden fresh pasta dish to be served as a salad or an entree.

---

¼ cup butter or margarine
½ tsp. asafetida or 1 clove crushed garlic
   or ½ - 1 onion, slivered

1½ cups diced celery
1½ cups asparagus, in 1"- to 2"-long pieces
1½ cups sliced mushrooms
1½ cups cauliflowerettes
1½ cups thinly-sliced carrots
1½ cups sliced zucchini

1 cup whipping cream
1 vegetable bouillon cube
12 oz. whole grain noodles (preferably lupini)
½ tsp. black pepper
⅓ cup chopped fresh basil leaves
⅓ cup chopped fresh parsley
¼ cup nutritional yeast or Parmesan cheese
3 Tbsp. soy sauce

Saute first 2 ingredients a few seconds. Add vegetables and stir-fry till vegetables become translucent. Add next 8 ingredients and stir till mixed thoroughly. Remove from heat and serve. Makes 8 to 10 entree-sized servings; twice or three times as many side dish-sized servings.

If whipping cream is not on your list of "foods to eat" because of the high saturated fat and cholesterol content, try using Almond Milk (p. 98) with a tablespoon or two of raw cashew butter.

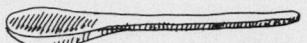

| SHOPPING LIST | |
|---|---|
| **Regularly Kept in the Kitchen** (Listed in Chapter 14, p. 703) | **Fresh Produce** |
| Butter or margarine | Celery |
| Asafetida | Asparagus |
| Black pepper | Mushrooms |
| Nutritional yeast or Parmesan cheese | Cauliflower |
| Soy sauce | Carrots |
| | Zucchini |
| | Fresh basil leaves |
| | Fresh parsley |

| Special Shopping |
|---|
| Whipping cream — found in any supermarket. I only put it on this list because it's a very rarely used food in my home that hardly ever makes it onto the shopping list. Vegetable bouillon cubes — found in natural food stores. Whole grain noodles — preferably lupini; but for lack of it, try different brands of whole grain pasta (found in natural food stores) till you find one that's not objectionable. |

# NUTRITIONAL ANALYSIS FOR ONE SERVING PRIMAVERA

```
NUTRIENT        Type: 14   FEMALE-23 TO 51 YEARS              % RDA   Amount
KCALORIES       A=====                                         10%   202.0 Kc
PROTEIN         A=======                                       14%   6.400 Gm
CARBOHYDRATE    A                                            NO RDA   17.70 Gm
FAT             A                                            NO RDA   12.40 Gm
FIBER-CRUDE     A                                            NO RDA   1.250 Gm
CHOLESTEROL     A                                            NO RDA   26.50 Mg
SATURATED FA    A                                            NO RDA   5.410 Gm
OLEIC FA        A                                            NO RDA   1.880 Gm
LINOLEIC FA     A                                            NO RDA   0.240 Gm
SODIUM          A=========                                     18%   400.0 Mg
POTASSIUM       A======                                        13%   504.0 Mg
MAGNESIUM       A=======                                       14%   43.10 Mg
IRON            A=====                                         10%   1.910 Mg
ZINC            A====                                           8%   1.310 Mg
VITAMIN A       A=================================================   140%   5602 IU
VITAMIN D       A===                                            6%   12.70 IU
VIT. E/TOTAL    A                                            NO RDA   1.320 Mg
VITAMIN C       A====================                          40%   24.40 Mg
THIAMIN         A=================================================  194%   1.940 Mg
RIBOFLAVIN      A=================================================  163%   1.960 Mg
NIACIN          A=====================================================   92%   12.00 Mg
VITAMIN B6      A=====================================================   99%   1.990 Mg
FOLACIN         A=========                                     19%   78.80 Ug
VITAMIN B12     A========================                      48%   1.450 Ug
PANTO- ACID     A========                                      16%   0.880 Mg
CALCIUM         A====                                           9%   76.20 Mg
PHOSPHORUS      A=========                                     19%   158.0 Mg
TRYPTOPHAN      A========================                      49%   79.90 Mg
THREONINE       A==============================                61%   267.0 Mg
ISOLEUCINE      A========================                      49%   322.0 Mg
LEUCINE         A=================                             34%   301.0 Mg
LYSINE          A============================                  58%   380.0 Mg
METHIONINE      A=======================                       46%   127.0 Mg
CYSTINE         A================                              33%   90.80 Mg
PHENYL-ANINE    A===================================           71%   311.0 Mg
TYROSINE        A=======================                       47%   208.0 Mg
VALINE          A=======================                       47%   359.0 Mg
HISTIDINE       A                                            NO RDA   180.0 Mg
ALCOHOL         A                                            NO RDA   0.000 Gm
ASH             A                                            NO RDA   3.810 Gm
COPPER          A==                                            4%   0.120 Mg
MANGANESE       A========                                      16%   0.630 Mg
IODINE          A================                              32%   49.10 Ug
MONO FAT        A                                            NO RDA   4.310 Gm
POLY FAT        A                                            NO RDA   1.920 Gm
CAFFEINE        A                                            NO RDA   0.000 Mg
FLUORIDE        A                                              0%   24.20 Ug
MOLYBDENUM      A=================================================  100%   325.0 Ug
VITAMIN K       A=================================================  529%   556.0 Ug
SELENIUM        A====                                           8%   0.010 Mg
BIOTIN          A==                                            5%   8.970 Ug
CHLORIDE        A                                              0%   12.70 Mg
CHROMIUM        A=================================            64%   0.080 Mg
SUGAR           A                                            NO RDA   3.340 Gm
FIBER-DIET      A                                            NO RDA   1.430 Gm
VIT. E/AT       A====                                          9%   0.770 Mg

    % RDA:   |0      |20     |40     |60     |80    |100
```

437

# TOFU PASTA SALAD

☆ Good served warm or cold; as a side dish or entree.

---

6 roasted and peeled peppers
  (see Pepper Antipasto Salad, p. 621)

12 oz. - 1 lb. lupini or other
  whole grain noodles, cooked

⅓ cup olive oil
3 Tbsp. tarragon vinegar
1 Tbsp. minced, fresh basil or 1 tsp. dried basil
2 tsp. asafetida or 4 cloves crushed garlic
½ tsp. black pepper
½ tsp. cayenne or Tabasco

1 (6-oz.) can pitted olives, sliced
½ the brine from pitted olives
  or 3 Tbsp. soy sauce
4 cups tomato wedges
⅓ cup Parmesan cheese or nutritional yeast
1 tsp. Spike or other vegetable-seasoned salt

2 lbs. Chinese firm tofu, drained
  and cut in 1" cubes

Prepare bell peppers by roasting as in Pepper Antipasto Salad (see recipe, p. 621).

Make marinade of next 6 ingredients. Toss in peppers so they can be marinating as the rest of the ingredients are being prepared.

Put water on for noodles and bring to boil. Cook noodles to "al dente" or till done. Rinse in colander and drain.

In a large bowl, mix next 5 ingredients and marinade mixture into warm noodles (or cold — see last paragraph), tossing thoroughly. After all ingredients are thoroughly mixed, gently mix in firm tofu that has been drained and cut into 1" cubes.

This salad is delicious served warm or chilled for a few hours on a bed of lettuce or sprouts. This is a good way to use leftover noodles — especially lupini noodles, which taste even better as a leftover refrigerated a few days.

One amazing thing about lupini noodles is that the cold leftovers don't even stick together as most any other type of noodle does. Some who have been fortunate enough to try them, feel that lupini noodles are even more delicious cold.

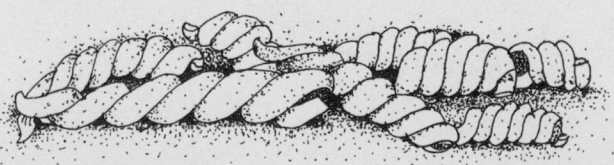

| Special Shopping | SHOPPING LIST | |
|---|---|---|
| | **Regularly Kept in the Kitchen (Listed in Chapter 14, p. 703)** | **Fresh Produce** |
| Lupini noodles — unfortunately, this show came out prematurely. The noodles were to be on the market, but at this writing aren't yet. If you can't find them, use whole grain noodles from a natural foods store, or write to me at P.O. Box 1122, Glendale, CA 91209, for information on lupini noodles.<br><br>Tarragon vinegar — in gourmet food stores or gourmet sections of supermarkets; or make your own at home (p. 545)! | Olive oil<br>Asafetida<br>Black pepper<br>Cayenne (or Tabasco)<br>Parmesan cheese<br>Spike<br>Tofu | Anaheim or bell peppers<br>Basil<br>Pitted, ripe olives<br>Tomatoes |

# NUTRITIONAL ANALYSIS FOR ONE SERVING TOFU PASTA SALAD

```
NUTRIENT        Type: 14   FEMALE-23 TO 51 YEARS         % RDA   Amount
KCALORIES       Ä=========                                16%    334.0 Kc
PROTEIN         Ä========================                 46%    20.60 Gm
CARBOHYDRATE    Ä                                        NO RDA  24.90 Gm
FAT             Ä                                        NO RDA  19.50 Gm
FIBER-CRUDE     Ä                                        NO RDA  1.730 Gm
CHOLESTEROL     Ä                                        NO RDA  0.000 Mg
SATURATED FA    Ä                                        NO RDA  2.600 Gm
OLEIC FA        Ä                                        NO RDA  8.380 Gm
LINOLEIC FA     Ä                                        NO RDA  2.710 Gm
SODIUM          Ä=============                            24%    542.0 Mg
POTASSIUM       Ä=========                                17%    640.0 Mg
MAGNESIUM       Ä===============                          31%    94.50 Mg
IRON            Ä===================================      65%    11.70 Mg
ZINC            Ä==========                               18%    2.830 Mg
VITAMIN A       Ä====================                     38%    1533 IU
VITAMIN D       Ä                                          0%    0.000 IU
VIT. E/TOTAL    Ä                                        NO RDA  1.740
VITAMIN C       Ä==================================================  124%   74.80 Mg
THIAMIN         Ä==================================================  269%   2.690 Mg
RIBOFLAVIN      Ä==================================================  215%   2.580 Mg
NIACIN          Ä==================================================  119%   15.50 Mg
VITAMIN B6      Ä==================================================  132%   2.640 Mg
FOLACIN         Ä==========                               19%    76.90 Ug
VITAMIN B12     Ä===============================          62%    1.860 Ug
PANTO- ACID     Ä=========                                16%    0.890 Mg
CALCIUM         Ä==========================================  82%   663.0 Mg
PHOSPHORUS      Ä===================                      39%    316.0 Mg
TRYPTOPHAN      Ä==================================================  182%   297.0 Mg
THREONINE       Ä==================================================  197%   860.0 Mg
ISOLEUCINE      Ä==================================================  157%   1031 Mg
LEUCINE         Ä==================================================  153%   1339 Mg
LYSINE          Ä==================================================  198%   1296 Mg
METHIONINE      Ä==================================================  115%   315.0 Mg
CYSTINE         Ä==================================================  112%   305.0 Mg
PHENYL-ANINE    Ä==================================================  237%   1032 Mg
TYROSINE        Ä==================================================  157%   683.0 Mg
VALINE          Ä==================================================  142%   1085 Mg
HISTIDINE       Ä                                        NO RDA  610.0 Mg
ALCOHOL         Ä                                        NO RDA  0.000 Gm
ASH             Ä                                        NO RDA  5.380 Gm
COPPER          Ä==========                               21%    0.530 Mg
MANGANESE       Ä=========================                49%    1.870 Mg
IODINE          Ä==================================================  116%   175.0 Ug
MONO FAT        Ä                                        NO RDA  7.080 Gm
POLY FAT        Ä                                        NO RDA  5.260 Gm
CAFFEINE        Ä                                        NO RDA  0.000 Mg
FLUORIDE        Ä                                          0%    23.60 Ug
MOLYBDENUM      Ä==================================================  467%   1520 Ug
VITAMIN K       Ä==                                        4%    4.650 Ug
SELENIUM        Ä========                                 16%    0.020 Mg
BIOTIN          Ä====                                      9%    14.00 Ug
CHLORIDE        Ä==                                        5%    189.0 Mg
CHROMIUM        Ä==================================================  328%   0.410 Mg
SUGAR           Ä                                        NO RDA  5.890 Gm
FIBER-DIET      Ä                                        NO RDA  2.400 Gm
VIT. E/AT       Ä=========                                18%    1.490 Mg

% RDA:    |0      |20     |40     |60     |80     |100
```

Whole grain noodles used instead of lupini; soy sauce used instead of olive brine; nutritional yeast used instead of Parmesan cheese in analysis.

In discussing the absence of, and the real need for, wisdom as the guiding light behind modern economics, science and technology, and its presence being the real foundation of peace, E. F. Schumacher has written — "The neglect, indeed the rejection, of wisdom has gone so far that most of our intellectuals have not even the faintest idea what the term could mean. What is wisdom? Where can it be found? It can be read about in numerous publications but it can be found only inside oneself. To be able to find it, one first has to liberate oneself from such masters as greed and envy. The stillness following liberation — even if only momentary — produces the insights of wisdom which are obtainable in no other way."

# PASTRIES CAN BE HEALTHY

You are in for a surprise if you thought that eating a healthier diet meant never eating a creme puff or eclair again! I thought so, too, for a long time. But I always keep my eye on the new products that are finding their way into natural food stores — and a new whey protein powder has changed all of that for me. Until I found this whey protein powder, I never thought I'd be able to make any of the gourmet-type dishes that call for whipped egg white.

The purity of this one particular whey protein powder (Bipro) makes it peak just like egg whites, and it can be used in place of eggs for just about any other cooking purpose as well. This whey protein powder has made it possible for me to make healthy, cholesterol-free (if a natural margarine is used), whole wheat choux pastries.

Of course, choux pastry shells can be filled with savory fillings and served as an entree or side dish, but most of us probably love them most when filled with sweets. Generally we think of creme puffs and eclairs as being fattening — because they are. They're generally made with refined foods, giving us fat and cholesterol-laden, empty calories. These choux pastries are full of nutrition; when made into desserts, they nourish the body while satisfying the tongue!

# CHOLESTEROL-FREE CHOUX PASTRY SHELLS

☆ Be careful to follow this recipe exactly. This is one of those temperamental recipes that must be done just right or it won't work right.

---

*1 cup water*
*6 Tbsp. margarine*

*½ cup water*
*6 Tbsp. Bipro*

*1 cup whole wheat flour*

*For savory fillings, add ⅛ tsp. each of*
*black pepper, nutmeg, and cayenne*
*to the above dough recipe*

*For sweet fillings, add ½ tsp. honey*
*to the dough recipe*

Preheat oven to 425 degrees.

Heat first 2 ingredients together in a pot over a medium heat till margarine melts. In the meantime, beat next 2 ingredients together in a separate mixing bowl with an electric mixer till Bipro is completely dissolved and mixture is foamy.

When margarine is melted, remove pot from heat and immediately mix in flour with a wooden spoon. Mix till all the flour is thoroughly mixed in. Put pot back on stove over a low heat and stir dough constantly with the wooden spoon for 2 to 3 minutes to evaporate some of the excess moisture. A little bit of the dough will begin forming a film on the bottom of the pot. Remove dough from heat and make a crater in the middle. Immediately pour in ¼ of the Bipro mixture and mix in (with the wooden spoon) till all of the liquid is absorbed. Add the remaining ¾ of Bipro water in the same way, using ¼ at a time. When all the Bipro water is thoroughly mixed in, the mixture must be shaped into desired sizes and shapes and put into a preheated oven immediately, or else they won't puff properly. Baking instructions differ according to the size of puffs desired.

*For small (about 1½" to 2" in diameter) balls:* Drop tablespoon-sized scoops onto an oiled cookie sheet about 1½" apart. Gently form into ball shapes. Bake at 425 degrees for about 20 minutes till puffs double in size and are crisp and

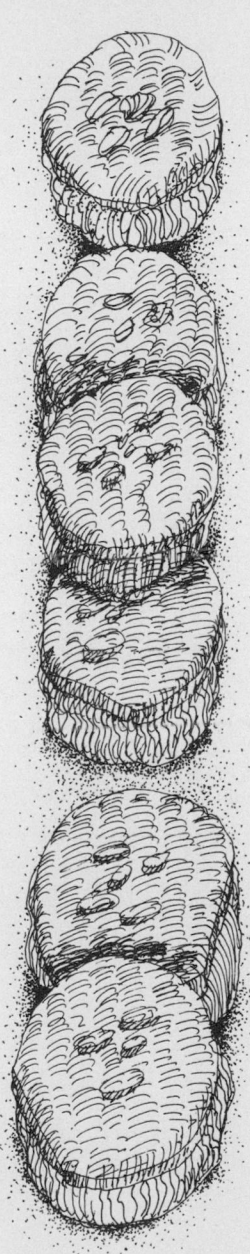

golden brown. Remove from oven and turn oven off. Pierce the side of each puff with a knife and return to the turned-off oven for 10 minutes. Cool. Makes about 15 small Cholesterol-Free Choux Pastry Shells.

After puffs are cooled, they can be frozen for future use or filled by using a ¼" tip on a pastry bag and squeezing the filling in through the hole already made on the side of the puff.

*For large (cupcake- or eclair-sized) puffs:* Drop ¼- to ⅓-cup-sized scoops (about 1" high by 2" in diameter) onto an oiled cookie sheet about 2" apart or into oiled muffin tins; or shape the same amount of dough into eclair-shaped logs that stand 1" high.

Bake at 425 degrees for 15 minutes. Without opening oven or removing puffs from the oven, turn heat down to 375 degrees and bake for another 15 minutes till doubled in size and a crisp, golden brown. Remove puffs from oven and turn oven off. Make a 1" slit in sides (or tips of eclairs) with a knife and return to turned-off oven for another 10 minutes. Remove from oven and allow to cool. After puffs are cooled, they can be frozen for future use or filled by cutting in half and filling (or piping a filling in with a pastry bag through the hole already made in the side). Makes about ½ dozen creme puff- or eclair-sized shells.

| Special Shopping |
| --- |
| Bipro — again, my apologies for prematurely using a product that isn't in the marketplace yet. When it comes out, it should be available in natural food stores. For information, write to me at P.O. Box 1122, Glendale, CA 91209. |

| SHOPPING LIST | |
| --- | --- |
| **Regularly Kept in the Kitchen** (Listed in Chapter 14, p. 703) | **Fresh Produce** |
| Margarine<br>Whole wheat flour | (None) |

# NUTRITIONAL ANALYSIS FOR ONE
# CHOLESTEROL-FREE CHOUX PASTRY SHELL

| NUTRIENT | Type: 14   FEMALE-23 TO 51 YEARS | % RDA | Amount |
|----------|-----------------------------------|-------|--------|
| KCALORIES | ᴿ===== | 10% | 213.0 Kc |
| PROTEIN | ᴿ======= | 14% | 6.160 Gm |
| CARBOHYDRATE | ᴿ | NO RDA | 17.20 Gm |
| ᶠAT | ᴿ | NO RDA | 14.10 Gm |
| FIBER-CRUDE | ᴿ | NO RDA | 0.570 Gm |
| CHOLESTEROL | ᴿ | NO RDA | 0.060 Mg |
| SATURATED FA | ᴿ | NO RDA | 2.340 Gm |
| OLEIC FA | ᴿ | NO RDA | 0.070 Gm |
| LINOLEIC FA | ᴿ | NO RDA | 0.240 Gm |
| SODIUM | ᴿ=== | 7% | 172.0 Mg |
| POTASSIUM | ᴿ= | 2% | 102.0 Mg |
| MAGNESIUM | ᴿ==== | 9% | 28.20 Mg |
| IRON | ᴿ== | 4% | 0.850 Mg |
| ZINC | ᴿ= | 3% | 0.580 Mg |
| VITAMIN A | ᴿ======= | 14% | 581.0 IU |
| VITAMIN D | ᴿ | 0% | 0.000 IU |
| VIT. E/TOTAL | ᴿ | NO RDA | 0.940 Mg |
| VITAMIN C | ᴿ | 0% | 0.060 Mg |
| THIAMIN | ᴿ====== | 13% | 0.130 Mg |
| RIBOFLAVIN | ᴿ= | 2% | 0.030 Mg |
| NIACIN | ᴿ==== | 8% | 1.040 Mg |
| VITAMIN B6 | ᴿ== | 4% | 0.080 Mg |
| FOLACIN | ᴿ= | 3% | 13.10 Ug |
| VITAMIN B12 | ᴿ | 0% | 0.010 Ug |
| PANTO- ACID | ᴿ=== | 7% | 0.400 Mg |
| CALCIUM | ᴿ= | 2% | 18.90 Mg |
| PHOSPHORUS | ᴿ===== | 11% | 95.20 Mg |
| TRYPTOPHAN | ᴿ=========================================== | 88% | 145.0 Mg |
| THREONINE | ᴿ=============================== | 60% | 264.0 Mg |
| ISOLEUCINE | ᴿ======================= | 44% | 291.0 Mg |
| LEUCINE | ᴿ================================= | 66% | 579.0 Mg |
| LYSINE | ᴿ=============================== | 62% | 411.0 Mg |
| METHIONINE | ᴿ======================= | 47% | 129.0 Mg |
| CYSTINE | ᴿ========================== | 54% | 149.0 Mg |
| PHENYL-ANINE | ᴿ================================ | 63% | 276.0 Mg |
| TYROSINE | ᴿ============================ | 57% | 250.0 Mg |
| VALINE | ᴿ==================== | 41% | 315.0 Mg |
| HISTIDINE | ᴿ | NO RDA | 131.0 Mg |
| ALCOHOL | ᴿ | NO RDA | 0.000 Gm |
| ASH | ᴿ | NO RDA | 0.770 Gm |
| COPPER | ᴿ== | 4% | 0.120 Mg |
| MANGANESE | ᴿ================ | 32% | 1.200 Mg |
| IODINE | ᴿ================================ | 67% | 101.0 Ug |
| MONO FAT | ᴿ | NO RDA | 6.390 Gm |
| POLY FAT | ᴿ | NO RDA | 4.470 Gm |
| CAFFEINE | ᴿ | NO RDA | 0.000 Mg |
| FLUORIDE | ᴿ | 0% | 0.000 Ug |
| MOLYBDENUM | ᴿ=========================================== | 443% | 1440 Ug |
| VITAMIN K | ᴿ | 0% | 0.000 Ug |
| SELENIUM | ᴿ==== | 8% | 0.010 Mg |
| BIOTIN | ᴿ | 0% | 1.200 Mg |
| CHLORIDE | ᴿ | 1% | 46.90 Mg |
| CHROMIUM | ᴿ============================================ | 112% | 0.140 Mg |
| SUGAR | ᴿ | NO RDA | 0.010 Gm |
| FIBER-DIET | ᴿ | NO RDA | 3.640 Gm |
| VIT. E/AT | ᴿ= | 2% | 0.190 Mg |

```
% RDA:  |0      |20     |40     |60     |80     |100
```

# TEMPEH SALAD

☆ A savory filling for Choux Pastry Shells or baked
potatoes, or to top a tossed salad with.

---

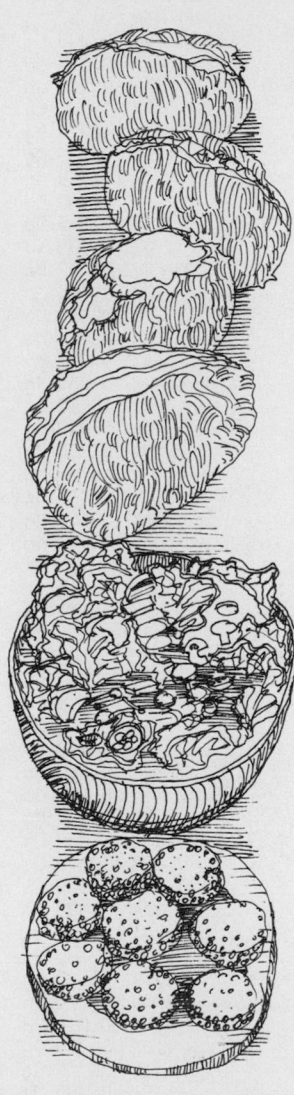

8 oz. steamed tempeh, cut in ¼" x ¾" strips

½ lb. Chinese firm tofu
½ cup honey-sweetened ketchup
¼ cup water
3 Tbsp. lemon juice
1 Tbsp. safflower oil
1 Tbsp. honey
1½ tsp. soy sauce
¼ tsp. asafetida or ½ tsp. garlic
  or onion powder
¼ tsp. Tabasco

1 Tbsp. safflower oil
1 Tbsp. soy sauce
1 tsp. lemon juice
1 tsp. kelp

1½ cups finely grated, julienned carrots
1 cup finely chopped celery

½ cup sliced green olives stuffed with pimientos

Alfalfa sprouts
Cucumbers, de-seeded and cut in matchsticks
Tomatoes, sliced

Steam tempeh for about 20 minutes. In the meantime,
blend next 9 ingredients in a blender till smooth and creamy.
Set aside.

Cut steamed tempeh into ¼"-wide by ¾"-long strips. Mix
next 4 ingredients together thoroughly and toss evenly onto
tempeh. Allow to sit for 5 to 10 minutes.

Heat a skillet and saute coated tempeh pieces over medium
heat, stirring occasionally to prevent sticking on the bottom.
When coating has been absorbed by tempeh and is forming a
dry coating on tempeh, turn off heat and set aside to cool.

Prepare vegetables. Mix carrots and celery into dressing
with cooled tempeh. Very gently — so as not to cause pimientos to fall out — fold in stuffed olives. This can be
served as is, but is much better if prepared ahead of time and
allowed to chill in the refrigerator a few hours.

This salad can be used to fill baked puffs (made from the

Cholesterol-Free Choux Pastry Shell recipe) by cutting puffs in half so there is a bottom and a lid. Then make a mixture of sprouts and cucumber matchsticks and put a little in the bottom of each puff. Place a scoop of Tempeh Salad on top of the sprout bed so it's overflowing. Top with tomato slice and top all with Choux Pastry lid. If you want to, you can leave lids off and use them as bottoms to fill as well. Chill till serving time. Makes about 10 filled pastries with lids or 20 without lids.

| SHOPPING LIST | | Special Shopping |
| --- | --- | --- |
| **Regularly Kept in the Kitchen** (Listed in Chapter 14, p. 703) | **Fresh Produce** | Honey-sweetened ketchup — in natural food stores. |
| Tofu | Lemons | |
| Safflower oil | Tabasco | |
| Honey | Carrots | |
| Soy sauce | Celery | |
| Asafetida | Green olives stuffed with pimientos | |
| Tempeh | Alfalfa sprouts | |
| Kelp powder | Cucumbers | |
| | Tomatoes | |

# NUTRITIONAL ANALYSIS FOR ONE CHOLESTEROL-FREE
# CHOUX PASTRY SHELL WITH TEMPEH SALAD FILLING

```
NUTRIENT       Type: 14   FEMALE-23 TO 51 YEARS              % RDA   Amount
KCALORIES      8========                                     17%    356.0 Kc
PROTEIN        8==================                           34%    15.20 Gm
CARBOHYDRATE   8                                             NO RDA 30.00 Gm
FAT            8                                             NO RDA 21.50 Gm
FIBER-CRUDE    8                                             NO RDA  1.910 Gm
CHOLESTEROL    8                                             NO RDA  0.060 Mg
SATURATED FA   8                                             NO RDA  3.250 Gm
OLEIC FA       8                                             NO RDA  1.530 Gm
LINOLEIC FA    8                                             NO RDA  3.620 Gm
SODIUM         8=============                                26%    576.0 Mg
POTASSIUM      8======                                       12%    467.0 Mg
MAGNESIUM      8===========                                  23%    69.80 Mg
IRON           8===========                                  24%     4.380 Mg
ZINC           8=====                                        10%     1.530 Mg
VITAMIN A      8=================================================== 147%   5915 IU
VITAMIN D      8                                              0%     0.000 IU
VIT. E/TOTAL   8                                             NO RDA  2.620 Mg
VITAMIN C      8=========                                    19%    11.70 Mg
THIAMIN        8============                                 25%     0.250 Mg
RIBOFLAVIN     8=====                                        10%     0.130 Mg
NIACIN         8==========                                   21%     2.850 Mg
VITAMIN B6     8=====                                        11%     0.220 Mg
FOLACIN        8=====                                        11%    44.00 Ug
VITAMIN B12    8==                                            5%     0.150 Ug
PANTO- ACID    8======                                       12%     0.700 Mg
CALCIUM        8=============                                27%    221.0 Mg
PHOSPHORUS     8=============                                27%    220.0 Mg
TRYPTOPHAN     8==================================================== 166%  271.0 Mg
THREONINE      8==================================================== 139%  607.0 Mg
ISOLEUCINE     8==================================================== 110%  720.0 Mg
LEUCINE        8==================================================== 144%   1258 Mg
LYSINE         8==================================================== 142%  933.0 Mg
METHIONINE     8===========================================          88%   240.0 Mg
CYSTINE        8==================================================== 101%  277.0 Mg
PHENYL-ANINE   8==================================================== 160%  697.0 Mg
TYROSINE       8==================================================== 125%  544.0 Mg
VALINE         8================================================     97%   745.0 Mg
HISTIDINE      8                                             NO RDA 357.0 Mg
ALCOHOL        8                                             NO RDA  0.000 Gm
ASH            8                                             NO RDA  2.390 Gm
COPPER         8========                                     16%     0.410 Mg
MANGANESE      8=========================                    50%     1.880 Mg
IODINE         8==================================================== 148%  222.0 Ug
MONO FAT       8                                             NO RDA  7.550 Gm
POLY FAT       8                                             NO RDA  8.650 Gm
CAFFEINE       8                                             NO RDA  0.000 Mg
FLUORIDE       8                                              0%    18.90 Ug
MOLYBDENUM     8==================================================== 624%   2031 Ug
VITAMIN K      8                                              1%     1.180 Ug
SELENIUM       8====                                          8%     0.010 Mg
BIOTIN         8==                                            4%     6.660 Ug
CHLORIDE       8=                                             3%    128.0 Mg
CHROMIUM       8==================================================== 248%   0.310 Mg
SUGAR          8                                             NO RDA  2.600 Gm
FIBER-DIET     8                                             NO RDA  7.720 Gm
VIT. E/AT      8========                                     16%     1.350 Mg

    % RDA:   |0      |20     |40     |60     |80     |100
```

# VANILLA FILLING

4 cups lowfat milk
½ cup honey
2 Tbsp. maple syrup
¼ cup arrowroot
2 Tbsp. tapioca flour

1 Tbsp. vanilla extract
Pinch turmeric (optional)

Combine first 5 ingredients in a pot large enough to allow for boiling up a bit. Whisk ingredients till all the tapioca and arrowroot flour is dissolved. Place pot over medium heat and stir often. As the mixture heats, the arrowroot and tapioca will begin lumping on the bottom. At this point, stir constantly till boiling. After mixture comes to a boil, continue stirring constantly for another minute. Turn off heat.

Add last 2 ingredients and mix in thoroughly (the turmeric is simply to add a little coloring and is, therefore, optional). Cover and allow to cool to room temperature, then put in refrigerator to chill.

This can be used as a pudding, or used to fill Cholesterol-Free Choux Pastries to make creme puffs or carob eclairs.

To make creme puffs, fill a pastry bag with Vanilla Filling and fit a large-mouthed tip on the bag. Using cooled puff-shaped pastries, insert the tip of the pastry bag into the hole that was poked into the side of the puff during the baking process, and squeeze enough pudding in to fill the puff. Remove tip and fill next puff. Sprinkle tops of creme puffs with maple sugar or date sugar, cover and refrigerate till serving time.

To make carob eclairs, follow same procedure as with creme puffs, although you will find with the long, log-like shape of the eclair, it's better to poke a hole on both of the tips to ensure that the hollow space gets completely filled. Fill eclair-shaped puffs and spread with icing made from the Carob Fondue recipe (see p. 235) or Carob Icing recipe from *Kathy Cooks . . . Naturally* (p. 510). After all eclairs are assembled, cover and refrigerate till serving time.

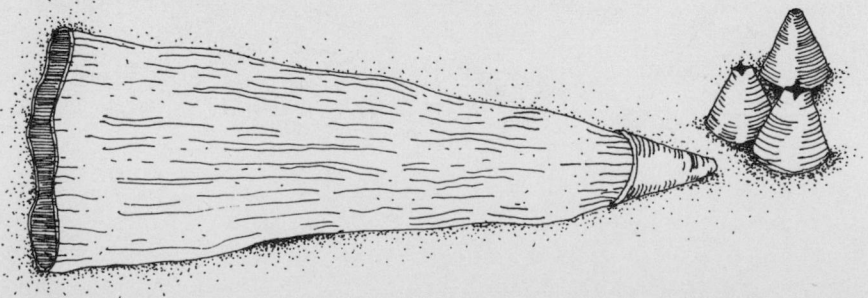

| Special Shopping |
|---|
| Maple syrup — found in most supermarkets and natural food stores. A word of warning: If buying maple syrup in supermarkets, read the labels carefully, checking for the words "100 percent" or "pure" maple syrup because there are syrups made with corn syrup and maple syrup flavoring. Though maple syrup is fairly easy to get, I rarely use it because it's so expensive. |

| SHOPPING LIST | |
|---|---|
| **Regularly Kept in the Kitchen** (Listed in Chapter 14, p. 703) | **Fresh Produce** |
| Milk<br>Honey<br>Arrowroot<br>Vanilla extract<br>Turmeric (optional) | (None) |

# NUTRITIONAL ANALYSIS FOR ONE CREME PUFF MADE WITH CHOLESTEROL-FREE CHOUX PASTRY AND VANILLA FILLING

| NUTRIENT | Type: 14  FEMALE-23 TO 51 YEARS | % RDA | Amount |
|---|---|---|---|
| KCALORIES | A=========== | 22% | 453.0 Kc |
| PROTEIN | A=============== | 28% | 12.70 Gm |
| CARBOHYDRATE | A | NO RDA | 63.60 Gm |
| FAT | A | NO RDA | 17.80 Gm |
| FIBER-CRUDE | A | NO RDA | 0.580 Gm |
| CHOLESTEROL | A | NO RDA | 14.40 Mg |
| SATURATED FA | A | NO RDA | 4.660 Gm |
| OLEIC FA | A | NO RDA | 1.030 Gm |
| LINOLEIC FA | A | NO RDA | 0.320 Gm |
| SODIUM | A====== | 12% | 273.0 Mg |
| POTASSIUM | A===== | 11% | 431.0 Mg |
| MAGNESIUM | A========= | 18% | 56.20 Mg |
| IRON | A=== | 7% | 1.350 Mg |
| ZINC | A=== | 9% | 1.370 Mg |
| VITAMIN A | A============ | 24% | 962.0 IU |
| VITAMIN D | A==================== | 40% | 81.60 IU |
| VIT. E/TOTAL | A | NO RDA | 1.120 Mg |
| VITAMIN C | A= | 3% | 1.880 Mg |
| THIAMIN | A========== | 20% | 0.200 Mg |
| RIBOFLAVIN | A=============== | 30% | 0.370 Mg |
| NIACIN | A===== | 10% | 1.370 Mg |
| VITAMIN B6 | A==== | 8% | 0.170 Mg |
| FOLACIN | A== | 5% | 22.70 Ug |
| VITAMIN B12 | A============ | 24% | 0.720 Ug |
| PANTO- ACID | A========= | 19% | 1.090 Ug |
| CALCIUM | A================ | 33% | 271.0 Mg |
| PHOSPHORUS | A================= | 35% | 286.0 Mg |
| TRYPTOPHAN | A================================================ | 145% | 237.0 Mg |
| THREONINE | A================================================ | 128% | 557.0 Mg |
| ISOLEUCINE | A================================================ | 104% | 684.0 Mg |
| LEUCINE | A================================================ | 139% | 1216 Mg |
| LYSINE | A================================================ | 141% | 926.0 Mg |
| METHIONINE | A================================================ | 107% | 292.0 Mg |
| CYSTINE | A====================================== | 76% | 209.0 Mg |
| PHENYL-ANINE | A================================================ | 135% | 590.0 Mg |
| TYROSINE | A================================================ | 129% | 564.0 Mg |
| VALINE | A=============================================== | 98% | 751.0 Mg |
| HISTIDINE | A | NO RDA | 307.0 Mg |
| ALCOHOL | A | NO RDA | 0.000 Gm |
| ASH | A | NO RDA | 2.220 Gm |
| COPPER | A== | 5% | 0.140 Mg |
| MANGANESE | A================ | 32% | 1.210 Mg |
| IODINE | A================================= | 67% | 101.0 Ug |
| MONO FAT | A | NO RDA | 7.470 Gm |
| POLY FAT | A | NO RDA | 4.600 Gm |
| CAFFEINE | A | NO RDA | 0.000 Gm |
| FLUORIDE | A= | 3% | 92.80 Ug |
| MOLYBDENUM | A================================================ | 443% | 1440 Ug |
| VITAMIN K | A===== | 10% | 11.30 Ug |
| SELENIUM | A==== | 8% | 0.010 Mg |
| BIOTIN | A= | 3% | 5.120 Ug |
| CHLORIDE | A | 1% | 46.90 Mg |
| CHROMIUM | A================================================ | 112% | 0.140 Mg |
| SUGAR | A | NO RDA | 0.010 Gm |
| FIBER-DIET | A | NO RDA | 3.640 Gm |
| VIT. E/AT | A= | 3% | 0.310 Mg |

```
% RDA:   |0        |20       |40       |60       |80       |100
```

Tapioca flour not included in analysis.

# DOWN·HOME BLUEBERRY PUDDING

☆ A hearty dessert — but try serving it as a breakfast dish, too!

1 cup whole wheat flour
1¼ tsp. baking powder
½ cup whole grain bread crumbs
½ cup butter or margarine

1 cup nonfat or lowfat milk
½ cup honey
1 tsp. Bipro or egg replacer

2½ cups blueberries

Mix together first 4 ingredients, cutting in the butter or margarine till flour is a sandy consistency. Beat next 3 ingredients together and thoroughly mix into the first 4. Fold in berries carefully so they don't break or smash. Pour pudding mixture into pyrex pudding dishes. Cover with foil, being careful to fill only halfway. Place rubber bands around the lids to keep the foil shut tightly. Place on steam rack and steam for 1 hour.

| SHOPPING LIST | |
| --- | --- |
| Regularly Kept in the Kitchen (Listed in Chapter 14, p. 703) | Fresh Produce |
| Whole wheat flour | Blueberries |
| Baking powder | |
| Whole grain bread crumbs | |
| Butter or margarine | |
| Nonfat or lowfat milk | |
| Honey | |
| Bipro | |

You can make variations of this recipe by using different kinds of berries . . . Try cranberries, raspberries, boysenberries, blackberries or very tiny strawberries (the large ones don't work well).

# NUTRITIONAL ANALYSIS FOR ONE SERVING
## DOWN-HOME BLUEBERRY PUDDING

| NUTRIENT | Type: 14   FEMALE—23 TO 51 YEARS | % RDA | Amount |
|---|---|---|---|
| KCALORIES | Ã========= | 18% | 361.0 Kc |
| PROTEIN | Ã====== | 12% | 5.280 Gm |
| CARBOHYDRATE | Ã | NO RDA | 50.60 Gm |
| FAT | Ã | NO RDA | 17.00 Gm |
| FIBER—CRUDE | Ã | NO RDA | 1.350 Gm |
| CHOLESTEROL | Ã | NO RDA | 3.000 Mg |
| SATURATED FA | Ã | NO RDA | 3.030 Gm |
| OLEIC FA | Ã | NO RDA | 0.250 Gm |
| LINOLEIC FA | Ã | NO RDA | 0.210 Gm |
| SODIUM | Ã======= | 14% | 316.0 Mg |
| POTASSIUM | Ã=== | 6% | 236.0 Mg |
| MAGNESIUM | Ã====== | 12% | 38.20 Mg |
| IRON | Ã=== | 6% | 1.080 Mg |
| ZINC | Ã== | 5% | 0.870 Mg |
| VITAMIN A | Ã========= | 19% | 771.0 IU |
| VITAMIN D | Ã==== | 8% | 17.00 IU |
| VIT. E/TOTAL | Ã | NO RDA | 0.880 Mg |
| VITAMIN C | Ã====== | 13% | 8.290 Mg |
| THIAMIN | Ã======== | 17% | 0.170 Mg |
| RIBOFLAVIN | Ã====== | 12% | 0.150 Mg |
| NIACIN | Ã===== | 11% | 1.450 Mg |
| VITAMIN B6 | Ã=== | 6% | 0.120 Mg |
| FOLACIN | Ã== | 4% | 19.90 Ug |
| VITAMIN B12 | Ã== | 5% | 0.170 Ug |
| PANTO- ACID | Ã====== | 12% | 0.670 Mg |
| CALCIUM | Ã======= | 15% | 123.0 Mg |
| PHOSPHORUS | Ã============= | 26% | 215.0 Mg |
| TRYPTOPHAN | Ã==================== | 42% | 68.80 Mg |
| THREONINE | Ã==================== | 42% | 183.0 Mg |
| ISOLEUCINE | Ã================== | 39% | 255.0 Mg |
| LEUCINE | Ã======================= | 47% | 412.0 Mg |
| LYSINE | Ã================= | 35% | 233.0 Mg |
| METHIONINE | Ã================= | 36% | 98.90 Mg |
| CYSTINE | Ã============== | 29% | 80.10 Mg |
| PHENYL—ANINE | Ã============================= | 58% | 256.0 Mg |
| TYROSINE | Ã==================== | 42% | 183.0 Mg |
| VALINE | Ã================= | 36% | 279.0 Mg |
| HISTIDINE | Ã | NO RDA | 104.0 Mg |
| ALCOHOL | Ã | NO RDA | 0.000 Gm |
| ASH | Ã | NO RDA | 1.240 Gm |
| COPPER | Ã=== | 6% | 0.160 Mg |
| MANGANESE | Ã=============== | 31% | 1.170 Mg |
| IODINE | Ã========================== | 56% | 84.60 Ug |
| MONO FAT | Ã | NO RDA | 7.320 Gm |
| POLY FAT | Ã | NO RDA | 4.970 Gm |
| CAFFEINE | Ã | NO RDA | 0.000 Mg |
| FLUORIDE | Ã | 1% | 40.20 Ug |
| MOLYBDENUM | Ã================================================== | 369% | 1200 Ug |
| VITAMIN K | Ã= | 2% | 2.360 Ug |
| SELENIUM | Ã==== | 8% | 0.010 Mg |
| BIOTIN | Ã | 1% | 1.930 Ug |
| CHLORIDE | Ã | 1% | 38.00 Mg |
| CHROMIUM | Ã=============================================== | 96% | 0.120 Mg |
| SUGAR | Ã | NO RDA | 3.500 Gm |
| FIBER—DIET | Ã | NO RDA | 4.840 Gm |
| VIT. E/AT | Ã= | 2% | 0.190 Mg |

```
% RDA:   0      20      40      60      80     100
```

Margarine used instead of butter; Bipro used instead of egg replacer; lowfat milk used instead of nonfat in analysis.

I probably mispronounced this one on the air! I've never attended a cooking school, so I wouldn't know. I don't pretend to be an expert cook or gourmet. My interest in cooking is feeding my family good, nutritious meals.

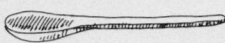

# CROQUEMBOUCHE

☆ Unless you have a huge refrigerator, the best thing to do is fill the balls and refrigerate on flat cookie sheets. Just before serving time, make the stack, drizzle with syrup and decorate.

---

*Small (1½" - 2" in diameter) Cholesterol-Free Choux Pastry Shells filled with Vanilla Filling (see preceding recipes)*

*3 cups maple syrup*

Prepare 5 or 6 times the Cholesterol-Free Choux Pastry Shell recipe, using directions for small balls, but mix and bake 1 batch at a time. Make 1 recipe of Vanilla Filling ahead of time so it's chilled. Fill each ball with Vanilla Filling in the same way as for creme or carob eclairs.

Put maple syrup in a pot that has walls 3 to 4 times taller than the surface of the syrup. Put a lid on the pot and bring to a boil over high heat. Remove lid, turn heat to medium-high and allow to boil without stirring for 4 to 5 minutes, till a ring of thick foam begins to form around the edge of the pot about 1" thick. Turn heat down to keep warm and mix syrup thoroughly.

Get out a decorative serving platter and lightly oil surface. Begin dipping each filled pastry shell in the warm maple syrup and arrange on oiled platter to form a solid bottom layer. Continue dipping balls and stacking on top of bottom layer to form a second layer, then a third, etc., each layer being a little smaller than the one below it. In this way, a pyramid of the balls is formed and the maple syrup helps to hold them together.

According to occasion, the mound can be decorated with fresh, non-poisonous flowers and leaves, or sprinkled with assorted chopped nuts and dried fruit. Another nice way to decorate the mountain of puffs is to dip whole berries (strawberries, raspberries, etc.) of your choice in the syrup and stick them here and there amongst the pastry balls. This can be topped at the last minute by pouring a cup or two of a sugarless preserve onto the mound.

Place decorated mound on table for people to pick pastries with their fingers and devour! Makes about 70 balls.

See shopping lists for Cholesterol-Free Choux Pastry Shells and Vanilla Filling.

453

# ADDING OTHER WHOLE GRAINS TO THE MENU

A visit to a well-stocked local natural food store can be an interesting and educating experience. When I first started shopping in health food stores, they were primarily "pill shops" with a few food items. The natural food industry has grown with the public demand for more healthy foods, and natural food stores have really changed in the past few years.

Most natural food stores are primarily stocked with food now, and a first-time visit to one will probably expose you to a lot of unfamiliar foods. If you're just starting to frequent natural food stores, may I suggest that each time you visit one you try to pick up a never-tried-before item, do a little skimming through cookbooks to find a suitable recipe and give the new item a try! Some of the items you might try exploring are whole grains, other than whole wheat flour and brown rice. Here are just a few recipes to give you an idea of how to use some of the "new" whole grains you might want to try.

Looking upon the land (that includes water, minerals, its rainforests, etc.) as an object or "factor of production" that exists only to be used or exploited for economic gain is resulting in pollution, scarcity of the earth's nonrenewable resources, and other as-of-yet unknown repercussions from throwing off the balance in nature that future generations may have to face. About this, E. F. Schumacher wrote — "They are, of course, factors of production, that is to say, means-to-ends, but that is their secondary, not their primary, nature. Before everything else they are ends in themselves; and it is therefore rationally justifiable to say that they are in a certain sense sacred. Man has not made them, and it is irrational for him to treat things he has not made and cannot make and cannot recreate once he has spoilt them, in the same manner and spirit as he is entitled to treat things of his own making."

The things "of his own making" are usually produced by, or of, nonrenewable resources, which means we should take care of those things as well. In Hawaii, this attitude is called "aloha aina" – that we should be caretaking the land with everything and everyone on it for the real Creator and ultimate Owner of everything.

BULGUR, dry
100 gm./3.5 oz.
(data from USDA)

Calories - 354
Protein - 11.2 gm.
Carbohydrate - 75.7 gm.
Fat - 1.5 gm.
Fiber - 1.7 gm.

Percentage of U.S. RDA:

Phosphorus - 42
Potassium - 6
Iron - 20
Thiamine - 28
Riboflavin - 11
Niacin - 34
Calcium - 3

# BULGUR SUMMER CHILI

☆ A chili that makes use of summer's bountiful harvest.

---

*2 cups water*
*1 cup bulgur*

*2 cups cooked pinto or kidney beans*

*2 Tbsp. olive oil*
*1 red onion*
*1 white onion*
*1 tsp. asafetida or 1 Tbsp. crushed garlic*
*½ cup diced celery*

*½ cup diced carrots*
*4 tsp. chili powder*
*2 tsp. ground cumin*
*½ tsp. black pepper*
*¼ - ½ tsp. cayenne*

*2 cups diced yellow crookneck squash*
*2 cups diced zucchini*
*2 cups diced green bell pepper*
*2 cups diced red bell pepper*
*½ lb. mushrooms, chopped*
*1 cup diced tomatoes*

*2 cups tomato sauce*
*1 cup alcohol-free beer or beer*
*1 Tbsp. miso*
*1 tsp. honey*

In a small pot, bring water to a boil. Add bulgur, cover, turn off heat and allow to sit 15 minutes. Also cook pinto beans in a separate pot, if you don't have any already-cooked ones on hand.

In the meantime, saute next 5 ingredients together in a large skillet till vegetables become tender and start to brown. Add next 5 ingredients and stir for a few minutes. Add next 6 ingredients, cover and simmer for 15 minutes. Add next 4 ingredients and the cooked beans and bulgur. Stir in completely, cover and simmer another 15 minutes. Makes 8 to 10 servings.

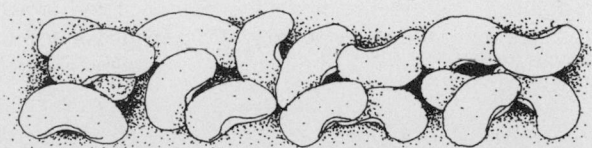

| SHOPPING LIST | |
|---|---|
| **Regularly Kept in the Kitchen** (Listed in Chapter 14, p. 703) | **Fresh Produce** |
| Pinto or kidney beans | Red and white onion |
| Olive oil | Celery |
| Asafetida | Carrots |
| Chili powder | Yellow crookneck squash |
| Ground cumin | Zucchini |
| Black pepper | Green and red bell pepper |
| Cayenne | Mushrooms |
| Miso | Tomatoes |
| Honey | |
| Tomato sauce | |

**Special Shopping**

Bulgur — found in natural food stores.
Alcohol-free beer — found in natural food stores; even some supermarkets and liquor stores. Regular beer is all right to use because the alcohol will cook out.

# NUTRITIONAL ANALYSIS FOR ONE SERVING
## BULGUR SUMMER CHILI

```
NUTRIENT      Type: 14   FEMALE-23 TO 51 YEARS                    % RDA   Amount
KCALORIES     A======                                             13%    263.0 Kc
PROTEIN       A============                                       22%    9.720 Gm
CARBOHYDRATE  A                                                   NO RDA 48.10 Gm
FAT           A                                                   NO RDA 5.090 Gm
FIBER-CRUDE   A                                                   NO RDA 2.720 Gm
CHOLESTEROL   A                                                   NO RDA 0.000 Mg
SATURATED FA  A                                                   NO RDA 0.610 Gm
OLEIC FA      A                                                   NO RDA 2.400 Gm
LINOLEIC FA   A                                                   NO RDA 0.270 Gm
SODIUM        A=======                                            15%    335.0 Mg
POTASSIUM     A============                                       22%    827.0 Mg
MAGNESIUM     A=======                                            15%    46.60 Mg
IRON          A============                                       24%    4.470 Mg
ZINC          A====                                               8%     1.210 Mg
VITAMIN A     A=========================================          82%    3306 IU
VITAMIN D     A                                                   0%     0.000 IU
VIT. E/TOTAL  A                                                   NO RDA 1.220 Mg
VITAMIN C     A====================================================  136% 81.70 Mg
THIAMIN       A=============                                      26%    0.260 Mg
RIBOFLAVIN    A============                                       24%    0.290 Mg
NIACIN        A==============                                     28%    3.710 Mg
VITAMIN B6    A=============                                      26%    0.520 Mg
FOLACIN       A======                                             12%    50.20 Ug
VITAMIN B12   A                                                   0%     0.000 Ug
PANTO- ACID   A===========                                        22%    1.210 Mg
CALCIUM       A====                                               9%     76.30 Mg
PHOSPHORUS    A===============                                    30%    246.0 Mg
TRYPTOPHAN    A=====================                              42%    69.80 Mg
THREONINE     A============================                       57%    250.0 Mg
ISOLEUCINE    A=======================                            47%    310.0 Mg
LEUCINE       A==========================                         53%    466.0 Mg
LYSINE        A=================================                  66%    434.0 Mg
METHIONINE    A=============  .                                   26%    72.10 Mg
CYSTINE       A============                                       24%    66.20 Mg
PHENYL  INE   A=================================                  67%    294.0 Mg
TYROSINE      A=======================                            46%    202.0 Mg
VALINE        A======================                             44%    337.0 Mg
HISTIDINE     A                                                   NO RDA 163.0 Mg
ALCOHOL       A                                                   NO RDA 0.060 Gm
ASH           A                                                   NO RDA 3.090 Gm
COPPER        A=======                                            14%    0.360 Mg
MANGANESE     A====                                               9%     0.350 Mg
IODINE        A                                                   0%     0.000 Ug
MONO FAT      A                                                   NO RDA 2.560 Gm
POLY FAT      A                                                   NO RDA 0.670 Gm
CAFFEINE      A                                                   NO RDA 0.000 Mg
FLUORIDE      A                                                   0%     27.00 Ug
MOLYBDENUM    A==========================                         53%    173.0 Ug
VITAMIN K     A                                                   1%     1.450 Ug
SELENIUM      A                                                   0%     0.000 Mg
BIOTIN        A                                                   1%     1.870 Ug
CHLORIDE      A                                                   1%     46.40 Mg
CHROMIUM      A============                                       24%    0.030 Mg
SUGAR         A                                                   NO RDA 6.750 Gm
FIBER-DIET    A                                                   NO RDA 1.740 Gm
VIT. E/AT     A=======                                            14%    1.180 Mg

% RDA:    |0      |20     |40     |60     |80     |100
```

Kidney beans used instead of pinto in analysis.

# WHOLE GRAIN CONFETTI SALAD

☆ Other whole grains work well in this salad. It's an especially good way to use up leftover grains. Simply replace first 3 ingredients with 4 cups of cooked grain.

---

4 cups water
1 cup millet
1 Tbsp. olive oil

1½ cups frozen or steamed, fresh peas
1 cup frozen or steamed, fresh corn
1 cup finely diced celery
1 cup diced red bell pepper
½ cup diced green bell pepper
½ cup finely chopped parsley
½ cup slivered water chestnuts

2 Tbsp. olive oil
2 Tbsp. safflower oil
3 Tbsp. balsamic or wine vinegar
¼ cup plain lowfat yogurt
2 Tbsp. nutritional yeast
1 Tbsp. soy sauce
1 Tbsp. Dijon mustard
1 tsp. asafetida or ½ cup slivered scallions
¾ tsp. black pepper

Bring first 3 ingredients to a boil, cover, turn down heat and simmer 30 minutes. Turn off heat, remove lid and allow to cool to room temperature. When cooled, add next 7 ingredients. If millet is warm, add frozen vegetables while still frozen and they will thaw and cool millet off at the same time; then add the remainder of vegetables after millet is cooled. If using peas and corn bought from the fresh produce shelf in the supermarket, lightly steam and allow to cool before adding to grain. If using freshly picked peas and corn from your own garden, try using them raw — why ruin the unmatchable, sweet flavor and nutritional value with heat!

In a small bowl, mix last 9 ingredients thoroughly; then toss into rice and vegetable mixture. Cover and refrigerate, as this tastes best when chilled for at least 2 hours before serving. Serve on top of a bed of lettuce and/or alfalfa sprouts. Makes 5 to 6 full servings or 15 to 18 small salad portions.

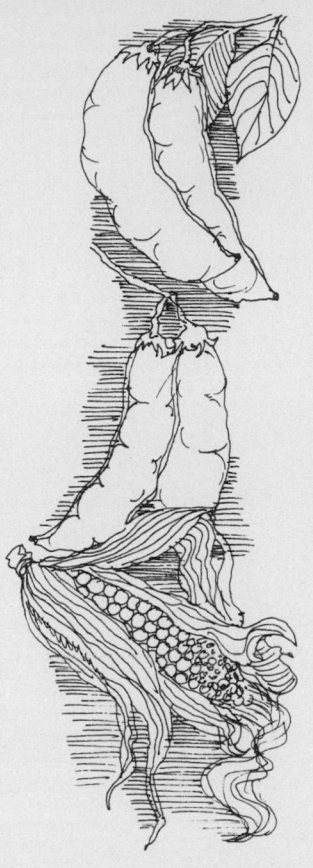

MILLET, dry
100 gm./3.5 oz.
(data from USDA)

Calories · 327
Protein · 9.9 gm.
Carbohydrate · 72.9 gm.
Fat · 2.9 gm.
Fiber · 3.2 gm.

Percentage of U.S. RDA:

Potassium · 11
Iron · 37
Thiamine · 73
Riboflavin · 31
Niacin · 17
Calcium · 2
Phosphorus · 38

| Special Shopping | SHOPPING LIST | |
|---|---|---|
| | **Regularly Kept in the Kitchen**<br>**(Listed in Chapter 14, p. 703)** | **Fresh Produce** |
| Millet — found in natural food stores. | Olive oil<br>Safflower oil<br>Wine or balsamic vinegar<br>Plain lowfat yogurt<br>Nutritional yeast<br>Soy sauce<br>Dijon mustard<br>Asafetida<br>Black pepper | Peas<br>Corn<br>Celery<br>Red bell pepper<br>Green bell pepper<br>Parsley<br>Canned water chestnuts |

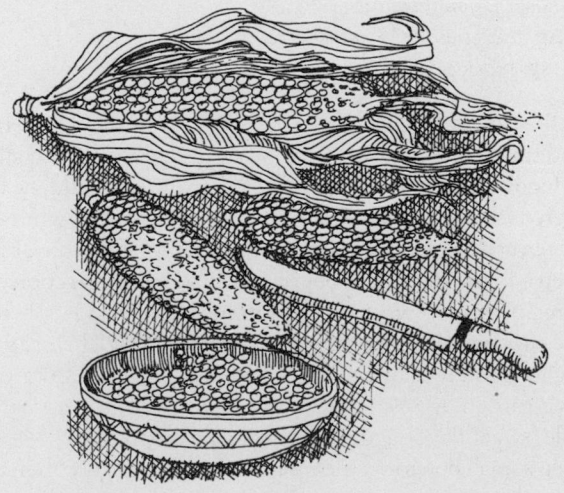

# NUTRITIONAL ANALYSIS FOR ONE SERVING
## WHOLE GRAIN CONFETTI SALAD

| NUTRIENT | Type: 14 FEMALE-23 TO 51 YEARS | % RDA | Amount |
|---|---|---|---|
| KCALORIES | A======= | 14% | 297.0 Kc |
| PROTEIN | A========= | 18% | 8.260 Gm |
| CARBOHYDRATE | A | NO RDA | 42.00 Gm |
| FAT | A | NO RDA | 12.80 Gm |
| FIBER-CRUDE | A | NO RDA | 2.800 Gm |
| CHOLESTEROL | A | NO RDA | 0.580 Mg |
| SATURATED FA | A | NO RDA | 1.520 Gm |
| OLEIC FA | A | NO RDA | 5.380 Gm |
| LINOLEIC FA | A | NO RDA | 3.880 Gm |
| SODIUM | A===== | 11% | 242.0 Mg |
| POTASSIUM | A======= | 15% | 580.0 Mg |
| MAGNESIUM | A===== | 10% | 31.50 Mg |
| IRON | A============ | 24% | 4.400 Mg |
| ZINC | A== | 4% | 0.740 Mg |
| VITAMIN A | A======= | 14% | 562.0 IU |
| VITAMIN D | A | 0% | 0.000 IU |
| VIT. E/TOTAL | A | NO RDA | 4.110 Mg |
| VITAMIN C | A================================================== | 103% | 62.00 Mg |
| THIAMIN | A================================================== | 186% | 1.860 Mg |
| RIBOFLAVIN | A================================================== | 144% | 1.730 Mg |
| NIACIN | A========================================= | 80% | 10.40 Mg |
| VITAMIN B6 | A========================================== | 82% | 1.650 Mg |
| FOLACIN | A===== | 10% | 42.60 Ug |
| VITAMIN B12 | A==================== | 40% | 1.220 Ug |
| PANTO- ACID | A===== | 11% | 0.620 Mg |
| CALCIUM | A==== | 8% | 70.30 Mg |
| PHOSPHORUS | A============== | 27% | 220.0 Mg |
| TRYPTOPHAN | A============= | 26% | 42.80 Mg |
| THREONINE | A==================== | 41% | 179.0 Mg |
| ISOLEUCINE | A================ | 31% | 208.0 Mg |
| LEUCINE | A==================== | 41% | 360.0 Mg |
| LYSINE | A======================= | 46% | 302.0 Mg |
| METHIONINE | A============ | 23% | 64.80 Mg |
| CYSTINE | A======= | 15% | 43.10 Mg |
| PHENYL-ANINE | A==================== | 40% | 175.0 Mg |
| TYROSINE | A=================== | 38% | 168.0 Mg |
| VALINE | A=================== | 39% | 299.0 Mg |
| HISTIDINE | A | NO RDA | 92.50 Mg |
| ALCOHOL | A | NO RDA | 0.000 Gm |
| ASH | A | NO RDA | 2.950 Gm |
| COPPER | A== | 5% | 0.140 Mg |
| MANGANESE | A= | 3% | 0.120 Mg |
| IODINE | A= | 2% | 4.330 Ug |
| MONO FAT | A | NO RDA | 5.580 Gm |
| POLY FAT | A | NO RDA | 4.060 Gm |
| CAFFEINE | A | NO RDA | 0.000 Mg |
| FLUORIDE | A | 1% | 39.60 Ug |
| MOLYBDENUM | A | 0% | 0.330 Ug |
| VITAMIN K | A============================================ | 89% | 94.10 Ug |
| SELENIUM | A | 0% | 0.000 Mg |
| BIOTIN | A== | 5% | 8.230 Ug |
| CHLORIDE | A | 0% | 2.980 Mg |
| CHROMIUM | A============ | 24% | 0.030 Mg |
| SUGAR | A | NO RDA | 3.910 Gm |
| FIBER-DIET | A | NO RDA | 1.710 Gm |
| VIT. E/AT | A================= | 35% | 2.800 Mg |

% RDA:  |0    |20    |40    |60    |80    |100

Scallions used instead of asafetida in analysis.

# HEARTY VEGETABLE SOUP

☆ This stick-to-the-ribs soup is made with spring/ summer vegetables, but can be just as delicious (and comforting) in the winter made with winter vegetables.

2 Tbsp. olive oil
1 large onion, diced
1 cup diced celery
½ cup diced carrots

11½ cups water
2 cups 1"- to 2"-long pieces of green
  and/or yellow string beans
2 cups diced zucchini and/or
  yellow crookneck squash
2 cups diced tomatoes
1½ cups small cauliflowerettes
1 cup fresh baby limas
½ cup tomato sauce
½ cup raw barley
3 Tbsp. miso
2 Tbsp. nutritional yeast
2 large, dry shiitake mushrooms
  blended to a powder
2 tsp. dry parsley leaves
1 tsp. turmeric
1 tsp. poultry seasoning
¼ tsp. black pepper
⅛ tsp. ground cumin

½ cup white wine

Saute first 4 ingredients together in soup pot till lightly browned. Add next 16 ingredients, cover and gently simmer for 30 minutes. Add wine, leave lid off and simmer for ·15 minutes. Like most soups, this tastes even better the next day, so I like to make it, cool it down and refrigerate overnight, then heat up for lunch or dinner. Makes 8 to 10 servings.

BARLEY, dry
100 gm./3.5 oz.
(data from USDA)

Calories - 349
Protein - 8.2 gm.
Carbohydrate - 78.8 gm.
Fat - 1.0 gm.
Fiber - .5 gm.

Percentage of U.S. RDA:

Potassium - 4
Iron - 11
Thiamine - 12
Riboflavin - 4
Niacin - 23
Calcium - 2
Phosphorus - 23

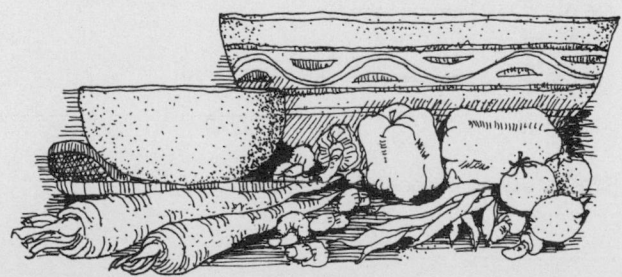

| SHOPPING LIST | | Special Shopping |
|---|---|---|
| **Regularly Kept in the Kitchen** (Listed in Chapter 14, p. 703) | **Fresh Produce** | Barley — found in natural food stores; some supermarkets. |
| Olive oil | Onion | |
| Tomato sauce | Celery | |
| Miso | Carrots | |
| Nutritional yeast | String beans | |
| Shiitake mushrooms | Zucchini and/or yellow | |
| Dry parsley leaves | crookneck squash | |
| Turmeric | Tomatoes | |
| Poultry seasoning | Cauliflower | |
| Black pepper | Fresh baby limas | |
| Ground cumin | White wine | |

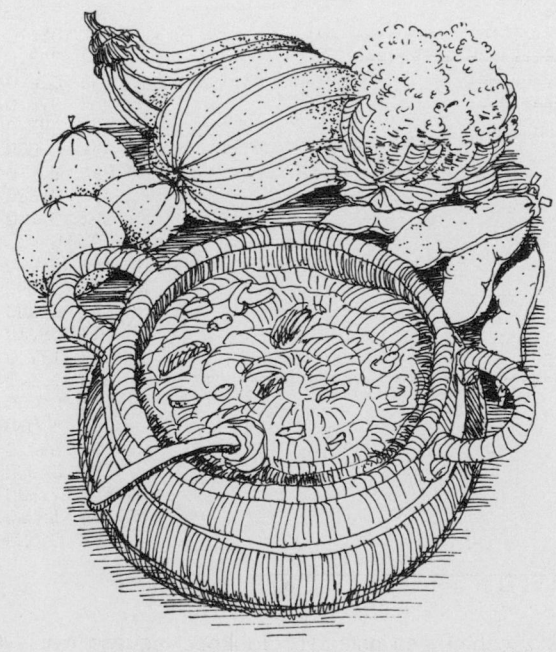

# NUTRITIONAL ANALYSIS FOR ONE SERVING
## HEARTY VEGETABLE SOUP

| NUTRIENT | Type: 14 FEMALE-23 TO 51 YEARS | % RDA | Amount |
|---|---|---|---|
| KCALORIES | A==== | 8% | 170.0 Kc |
| PROTEIN | A======= | 15% | 6.850 Gm |
| CARBOHYDRATE | A | NO RDA | 28.60 Gm |
| FAT | A | NO RDA | 4.380 Gm |
| FIBER-CRUDE | A | NO RDA | 1.980 Gm |
| CHOLESTEROL | A | NO RDA | 0.000 Mg |
| SATURATED FA | A | NO RDA | 0.640 Gm |
| OLEIC FA | A | NO RDA | 2.410 Gm |
| LINOLEIC FA | A | NO RDA | 0.320 Gm |
| SODIUM | A====== | 12% | 277.0 Mg |
| POTASSIUM | A======== | 17% | 652.0 Mg |
| MAGNESIUM | A========= | 18% | 55.50 Mg |
| IRON | A====== | 13% | 2.470 Mg |
| ZINC | A=== | 7% | 1.080 Mg |
| VITAMIN A | A==================================== | 75% | 3037 IU |
| VITAMIN D | A | 0% | 0.000 IU |
| VIT. E/TOTAL | A | NO RDA | 2.950 Mg |
| VITAMIN C | A============================ | 57% | 34.50 Mg |
| THIAMIN | A==================================================== | 128% | 1.280 Mg |
| RIBOFLAVIN | A==================================================== | 105% | 1.260 Mg |
| NIACIN | A================================ | 63% | 8.210 Mg |
| VITAMIN B6 | A================================= | 67% | 1.350 Mg |
| FOLACIN | A========= | 18% | 75.30 Ug |
| VITAMIN B12 | A============== | 29% | 0.890 Ug |
| PANTO- ACID | A==== | 9% | 0.530 Mg |
| CALCIUM | A=== | 7% | 62.50 Mg |
| PHOSPHORUS | A========= | 18% | 149.0 Mg |
| TRYPTOPHAN | A========================= | 50% | 82.20 Mg |
| THREONINE | A================================ | 65% | 283.0 Mg |
| ISOLEUCINE | A========================== | 52% | 343.0 Mg |
| LEUCINE | A============================ | 57% | 498.0 Mg |
| LYSINE | A============================= | 58% | 382.0 Mg |
| METHIONINE | A================= | 36% | 99.30 Mg |
| CYSTINE | A================= | 36% | 98.70 Mg |
| PHENYL-ANINE | A=================================== | 71% | 312.0 Mg |
| TYROSINE | A========================= | 51% | 226.0 Mg |
| VALINE | A======================== | 49% | 378.0 Mg |
| HISTIDINE | A | NO RDA | 173.0 Mg |
| ALCOHOL | A | NO RDA | 0.000 Gm |
| ASH | A | NO RDA | 3.410 Gm |
| COPPER | A==== | 8% | 0.220 Mg |
| MANGANESE | A======= | 14% | 0.560 Mg |
| IODINE | A | 0% | 0.000 Ug |
| MONO FAT | A | NO RDA | 2.610 Gm |
| POLY FAT | A | NO RDA | 0.840 Gm |
| CAFFEINE | A | NO RDA | 0.000 Mg |
| FLUORIDE | A | 1% | 35.10 Ug |
| MOLYBDENUM | A================== | 37% | 121.0 Ug |
| VITAMIN K | A==================================================== | 731% | 768.0 Ug |
| SELENIUM | A | 0% | 0.000 Mg |
| BIOTIN | A== | 5% | 8.960 Ug |
| CHLORIDE | A== | 4% | 142.0 Mg |
| CHROMIUM | A============ | 24% | 0.030 Mg |
| SUGAR | A | NO RDA | 7.500 Gm |
| FIBER-DIET | A | NO RDA | 1.910 Gm |
| VIT. E/AT | A====== | 12% | 0.960 Mg |

% RDA: |0  |20  |40  |60  |80  |100

Green beans used instead of yellow; zucchini used instead of crookneck squash in analysis.

# NUTTY·CRUST FLAT BREAD

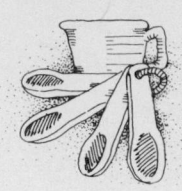

☆ An especially tasty bread that's perfect served with a large, special salad or a soup to make a complete meal.

☆ Other nuts can be used, but all are much harder than pine nuts. Pine nuts are a very soft, tender nut that don't get too hard when roasted.

---

½ cup warm water
2 Tbsp. baking yeast
2 Tbsp. olive oil
1 Tbsp. honey
¼ tsp. salt

½ cup white wine
2¼ cups whole wheat flour
½ cup rye flour
½ tsp. baking powder

1 tsp. Spike or other vegetable-seasoned salt
½ tsp. black pepper
¼ tsp. asafetida

Olive oil

1 - 1½ cups coarsely chopped pine nuts

Mix first 5 ingredients together and let sit about 10 minutes till yeast dissolves. Add next 4 ingredients and mix in thoroughly. Knead in mixing bowl about 5 minutes till dough is smooth and elastic. Shape into a round loaf about ½" thick.

In a small cup, mix next 3 ingredients and set aside. Oil a cookie sheet with olive oil and pour about 1 teaspoon of oil onto round loaf and rub all over both sides of loaf. Sprinkle half the spice mixture evenly over one side of loaf and rub in. Flip loaf over and do the same with the remaining spices.

Spread coarsely chopped pine nuts out on a cutting board and put round, flat loaf on top of them. Press down on top of the loaf (to embed pine nuts in the bottom) and push pine nuts up on sides to embed them in the side edges. Flip loaf over and push down on loaf (to embed pine nuts in other side). Once entire surface of bread is covered with pine nuts (embedded in), place on oiled cookie sheet and cover with plastic wrap. Place in a gas oven with a pilot light, or an electric oven with the light on, and allow to rise till doubled (about 1"

When baking breads, it's safe to use rye flour for up to a quarter of the flour called for in the recipe and still get a light loaf.

RYE FLOUR
100 gm./3.5 oz.
(data from USDA)

Calories - 327
Protein - 16.3 gm.
Carbohydrate - 68.1 gm.
Fat - 2.6 gm.
Fiber - 2.4 gm.

Percentage of U.S. RDA:

Potassium - 22
Iron - 25
Thiamine - 61
Riboflavin - 18
Niacin - 20
Calcium - 6
Phosphorus - 67

thick), about 1 hour.

Remove plastic wrap, close oven door, set heat to 350 degrees and bake for 35 minutes till golden brown and loaf sounds hollow when tapped. Makes about 8 servings.

| Special Shopping |
| --- |
| Rye flour — found in natural food stores. <br> Pine nuts — be sure to get ones with the shells already removed or you're in for a few hours of extra work! Can be found in natural food stores, nut houses, gourmet food stores. |

| SHOPPING LIST | |
| --- | --- |
| **Regularly Kept in the Kitchen** (Listed in Chapter 14, p. 703) | **Fresh Produce** |
| Baking yeast <br> Olive oil <br> Honey <br> Salt <br> Whole wheat flour <br> Baking powder <br> Spike <br> Black pepper <br> Asafetida | White wine |

# NUTRITIONAL ANALYSIS FOR ONE SERVING
## NUTTY-CRUST FLAT BREAD

| NUTRIENT | Type: 14   FEMALE-23 TO 51 YEARS | % RDA | Amount |
|---|---|---|---|
| KCALORIES | A======== | 14% | 287.0 Kc |
| PROTEIN | A============= | 25% | 11.20 Gm |
| CARBOHYDRATE | A | NO RDA | 35.30 Gm |
| FAT | A | NO RDA | 14.80 Gm |
| FIBER-CRUDE | A | NO RDA | 1.130 Gm |
| CHOLESTEROL | A | NO RDA | 0.000 Mg |
| SATURATED FA | A | NO RDA | 2.230 Gm |
| OLEIC FA | A | NO RDA | 2.900 Gm |
| LINOLEIC FA | A | NO RDA | 0.660 Gm |
| SODIUM | A==== | 9% | 212.0 Mg |
| POTASSIUM | A==== | 9% | 358.0 Mg |
| MAGNESIUM | A====== | 13% | 40.60 Mg |
| IRON | A=========== | 20% | 3.720 Mg |
| ZINC | A===== | 11% | 1.680 Mg |
| VITAMIN A | A | 0% | 0.250 IU |
| VITAMIN D | A | 0% | 0.000 IU |
| VIT. E/TOTAL | A | NO RDA | 1.830 Mg |
| VITAMIN C | A | 0% | 0.000 Mg |
| THIAMIN | A==================== | 43% | 0.430 Mg |
| RIBOFLAVIN | A======= | 15% | 0.190 Mg |
| NIACIN | A=========== | 23% | 3.050 Mg |
| VITAMIN B6 | A==== | 7% | 0.150 Mg |
| FOLACIN | A=========== | 22% | 89.70 Ug |
| VITAMIN B12 | A | 0% | 0.000 Ug |
| PANTO- ACID | A===== | 10% | 0.570 Mg |
| CALCIUM | A== | 5% | 42.60 Mg |
| PHOSPHORUS | A=================== | 39% | 314.0 Mg |
| TRYPTOPHAN | A==================================== | 71% | 117.0 Mg |
| THREONINE | A================================= | 67% | 292.0 Mg |
| ISOLEUCINE | A============================== | 60% | 392.0 Mg |
| LEUCINE | A====================================== | 76% | 667.0 Mg |
| LYSINE | A======================== | 48% | 319.0 Mg |
| METHIONINE | A============================= | 58% | 158.0 Mg |
| CYSTINE | A================================== | 69% | 188.0 Mg |
| PHENYL-ANINE | A============================================== | 95% | 416.0 Mg |
| TYROSINE | A======================================== | 81% | 353.0 Mg |
| VALINE | A============================== | 61% | 470.0 Mg |
| HISTIDINE | A | NO RDA | 213.0 Mg |
| ALCOHOL | A | NO RDA | 0.000 Gm |
| ASH | A | NO RDA | 1.470 Gm |
| COPPER | A======= | 15% | 0.380 Mg |
| MANGANESE | A====================== | 45% | 1.710 Mg |
| IODINE | A====================================================== | 108% | 162.0 Ug |
| MONO FAT | A | NO RDA | 6.720 Gm |
| POLY FAT | A | NO RDA | 4.590 Gm |
| CAFFEINE | A | NO RDA | 0.000 Mg |
| FLUORIDE | A | 0% | 5.110 Ug |
| MOLYBDENUM | A=============================================== | 623% | 2025 Ug |
| VITAMIN K | A | 0% | 0.000 Ug |
| SELENIUM | A==== | 8% | 0.010 Mg |
| BIOTIN | A== | 5% | 8.770 Ug |
| CHLORIDE | A | 1% | 64.40 Mg |
| CHROMIUM | A==================================================== | 160% | 0.200 Mg |
| SUGAR | A | NO RDA | 0.000 Gm |
| FIBER-DIET | A | NO RDA | 5.110 Gm |
| VIT. E/AT | A==== | 9% | 0.740 Mg |

% RDA:  |0       |20      |40      |60      |80     |100

Amaranth flour may be a little hard to find; amaranth seeds may be just a little easier to find as they're one of those ancient grains "new" to the American market. The whole seeds can be cooked like rice for a breakfast cereal, popped like popcorn, sprouted like alfalfa seeds, or ground at home into a fine flour or meal (through a flour mill or a blender). The amaranth greens are also high in nutrition. They can be eaten raw in salads or steamed.

AMARANTH (seeds)
2 oz./56.7 gm.
(data from Arrowhead Mills)

Calories - 200
Protein - 8 gm.
Carbohydrate - 35 gm.
Fat - 3 gm.
Fiber - 2 gm.

Percentage of U.S. RDA:

Iron - 100
Thiamine - 2
Riboflavin - 10
Niacin - 4
Calcium - 10
Phosphorus - 15

AMARANTH (plant/leaves)
100 gm./3.5 oz.
(data from USDA)

Calories - 36
Protein - 3.5 gm.
Carbohydrate - 6.5 gm.
Fat - .5 gm.
Fiber - 1.3 gm.

# HAWAIIAN CRUNCHIES

☆ These cookies can be made with other kinds of dried fruit and bran instead of coconut . . . but they won't be *Hawaiian* Crunchies anymore.

---

½ cup safflower or sunflower oil
½ cup frozen pineapple concentrate
½ cup honey

1 cup whole wheat flour
½ cup macaroon coconut
¼ cup amaranth flour
¼ cup finely chopped, rolled oats
¼ cup finely chopped, dried pineapple
2 Tbsp. finely chopped, dried papaya
2 Tbsp. finely chopped, sliced almonds
2 Tbsp. noninstant, nonfat milk powder
2 tsp. lecithin granules
⅔ tsp. baking soda
¼ tsp. very finely grated (almost pureed) orange rind

Preheat oven to 350 degrees and oil a cookie sheet.

Mix first 3 ingredients together. Add next 11 ingredients, being sure to chop rolled oats so they're as fine as the instant kind; run whole amaranth seeds in a blender or flour mill to form a flour (if you can't find amaranth flour). Mix thoroughly. Drop 2 tablespoons of batter onto oiled cookie sheet and flatten to about ¼" thick. Repeat, leaving 2" to 3" between each cookie. Bake at 350 degrees for 10 to 12 minutes. Leave oven door closed and turn off oven, leaving cookies in for another 10 to 15 minutes. Remove cookies from oven and loosen from cookie sheets with a spatula while cookies are still warm; if you let cookies cool on cookie sheets, they'll get very hard and stick to the sheets, making it hard to remove them without breaking. Makes about 20 cookies.

| SHOPPING LIST | | Special Shopping |
|---|---|---|
| **Regularly Kept in the Kitchen** (Listed in Chapter 14, p. 703) | **Fresh Produce** | Amaranth flour — found in natural food stores. |
| Safflower or sunflower oil<br>Honey<br>Whole wheat flour<br>Almonds<br>Noninstant, nonfat milk powder<br>Baking soda<br>Lecithin granules<br>Rolled oats | 100 percent frozen pine-apple concentrate<br>Macaroon coconut (be sure not to get shredded)<br>Orange | Dried pineapple and dried papaya — found in natural food stores; but be sure to check that they're not the ones that are cooked in sugar water before drying. Most of the dry pineapple and papaya from the Philippines and Taiwan are made this way. |

Percentage of U.S. RDA:

Potassium - 10
Iron - 21
Vitamin A - 152
Vitamin C - 133
Thiamine - 8
Riboflavin - 13
Niacin - 10
Calcium - 33
Phosphorus - 8

# NUTRITIONAL ANALYSIS FOR ONE HAWAIIAN CRUNCHIES COOKIE

```
NUTRIENT       Type: 14    FEMALE-23 TO 51 YEARS        % RDA    Amount
KCALORIES      A===                                       6%     137.0 Kc
PROTEIN        A==                                        4%     1.800 Gm
CARBOHYDRATE   A                                  NO RDA         17.50 Gm
FAT            A                                  NO RDA         7.150 Gm
FIBER-CRUDE    A                                  NO RDA         0.380 Gm
CHOLESTEROL    A                                  NO RDA         0.150 Mg
SATURATED FA   A                                  NO RDA         1.380 Gm
OLEIC FA       A                                  NO RDA         1.000 Gm
LINOLEIC FA    A                                  NO RDA         4.150 Gm
SODIUM         A                                          1%     33.00 Mg
POTASSIUM      A=                                         2%     100.0 Mg
MAGNESIUM      A==                                        5%     15.30 Mg
IRON           A==                                        5%     1.030 Mg
ZINC           A                                          1%     0.280 Mg
VITAMIN A      A                                          0%     39.90 IU
VITAMIN D      A                                          0%     0.000 IU
VIT. E/TOTAL   A                                  NO RDA         2.510 Mg
VITAMIN C      A====                                      8%     4.850 Mg
THIAMIN        A===                                       6%     0.060 Mg
RIBOFLAVIN     A=                                         3%     0.040 Mg
NIACIN         A=                                         3%     0.470 Mg
VITAMIN B6     A=                                         2%     0.050 Mg
FOLACIN        A                                          1%     5.300 Ug
VITAMIN B12    A                                          1%     0.030 Ug
PANTO- ACID    A=                                         2%     0.160 Mg
CALCIUM        A=                                         2%     22.60 Mg
PHOSPHORUS     A==                                        5%     46.40 Mg
TRYPTOPHAN     A=====                                    10%     17.60 Mg
THREONINE      A=====                                    10%     44.30 Mg
ISOLEUCINE     A====                                      9%     61.30 Mg
LEUCINE        A=====                                    11%     98.60 Mg
LYSINE         A====                                      8%     53.10 Mg
METHIONINE     A====                                      8%     22.50 Mg
CYSTINE        A====                                      8%     24.30 Mg
PHENYL-ANINE   A=======                                  15%     65.50 Mg
TYROSINE       A=====                                    11%     51.20 Mg
VALINE         A====                                      8%     68.30 Mg
HISTIDINE      A                                  NO RDA         30.10 Mg
ALCOHOL        A                                  NO RDA         0.000 Gm
ASH            A                                  NO RDA         0.300 Gm
COPPER         A=                                         3%     0.080 Mg
MANGANESE      A========                                 17%     0.670 Mg
IODINE         A========                                 16%     25.40 Ug
MONO FAT       A                                  NO RDA         0.960 Gm
POLY FAT       A                                  NO RDA         4.270 Gm
CAFFEINE       A                                  NO RDA         0.000 Mg
FLUORIDE       A                                          0%     9.650 Ug
MOLYBDENUM     A=====================================   110%     360.0 Ug
VITAMIN K      A                                          0%     0.000 Ug
SELENIUM       A                                          0%     0.000 Mg
BIOTIN         A                                          0%     0.460 Ug
CHLORIDE       A                                          0%     11.40 Mg
CHROMIUM       A=============                            24%     0.030 Mg
SUGAR          A                                  NO RDA         0.000 Gm
FIBER-DIET     A                                  NO RDA         1.020 Gm
VIT. E/AT      A=============                            26%     2.110 Mg

    % RDA:   |0      |20     |40     |60     |80     |100
```

Safflower oil used instead of sunflower; due to lack of data on dried pineapple and papaya, raw fruit was used in amounts which approximate the nutritional content of the dried.

# CHAPTER 10
# NUTS ABOUT LEGUMES AND NUTS

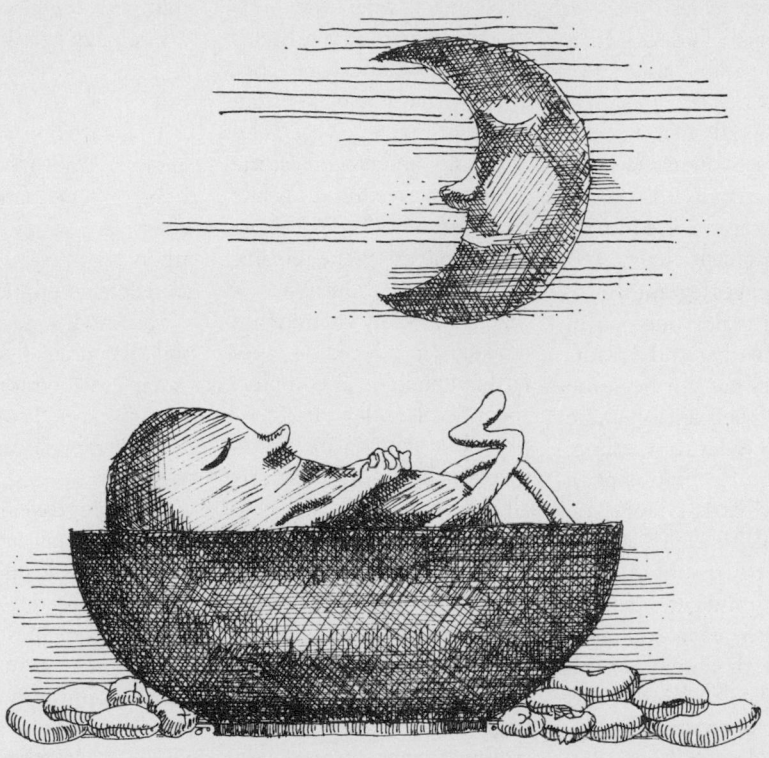

A longside whole grains, legumes and a touch of nuts form the center of two of our meals every day. (I usually serve one meal a day consisting of fruit; the other two meals are usually a large, fresh, tossed salad and an entree of legumes and grains.) The legume (and its by-products) that I use the most is soybeans. That's why they have their own chapter ("Soy-friends," Chapter 3) and are found in almost every chapter of this book.

I do occasionally use other legumes. This always takes a little pre-planning because legumes should always be soaked (at least) overnight before cooking. In a pinch, you can get away with soaking dry legumes for an hour in boiling hot water before cooking; this will reduce cooking time, as soaking overnight does, but you'll miss out on the nutritional benefit of an overnight soaking.

A long moistening of a legume (or any other seed-like grains or nuts) is exactly the condition required by nature to start the growth process. The chemical changes that take place as the seed readies itself to feed the new sprout, or actually does sprout, add an incredible amount of nutrients. Ideally, a legume should be allowed to germinate for two days (see pp. 528-529) before cooking; but even soaking the seed brings about significant changes.

The changes legumes, nuts, seeds and grains undergo in the germinating and sprouting process has not been the subject of enough scientific research to go into detail on. To complicate an attempt to describe what is known, the nutritional value of a germinated or sprouted seed changes from day to day and varies with each different kind of seed. Though I can't go into a day-by-day, detailed report on every kind of legume, nut, seed and grain due to lack of space and scientific data, there are certain chemical changes that take place in any seed that germinates or sprouts.

Besides the visible swelling of two to three times its dry size, soaking a seed (meaning any legume, nut, seed or grain) for eight to twelve hours activates and increases enzymes within the seed. These enzymes – alpha-amylase (p. 196) being one – are the same ones that are present in our mouths which begin the process of digestion. These enzymes predigest the food in the seed that is there for the baby plant to survive on till it can establish a healthy root system. Protein is hydrolyzed (broken down into the amino acids it is comprised of, as takes place when the body digests protein), amino acids increase, starches are converted to natural sugars found in freshly picked vegetables and fruits, and fat and calorie content are reduced. While some protein is lost in soaking and germinating, the remaining protein is about twice as digestible. Many vitamins are actually produced — especially vitamin C, B-complex, tocopherol and alpha-tocopherol (vitamin E) levels increase the longer the seed is allowed to sprout.

Soaking legumes overnight, and especially sprouting them for two to three days, cuts down on cooking time, increases valuable nutrients and decreases gassiness. If legumes are soaked overnight, then covered with three to four times water to beans, brought to a boil (don't add salt to boiling water as it keeps the beans hard longer) and simmered, they should take approximately this long to cook:

Black beans ........................1½ to 2 hours
Black-eyed peas............1½ to 2 hours
Garbanzos (chickpeas) ........2 to 3 hours
Kidney beans ......................1½ to 2 hours
Lentils............................1 hour
Limas (baby) ...............1 hour
Limas (large) ......................1½ to 2 hours
Pinto beans.........................1½ to 2 hours
Soybeans ................................2 to 3 hours
Split peas.......................1 hour
White navy beans .............1½ to 2 hours

These are only a few of the legumes more commonly found on supermarket shelves. There are a multitude of other legumes available in specialty and ethnic groceries.

Sprouted legumes can be boiled in a small amount of water, steamed or stir-fried for only about five minutes before they're thoroughly cooked.

In recipes that are suitable, I am always sure to germinate nuts and whole grains. Obviously germinated nuts can't be used in recipes calling for roasting nuts or nut meal, etc. I don't use nuts as often or in as great quantity as legumes or whole grains, partly because they're so much more expensive and also because they generally contain more fat. But used in dishes with legumes and/or whole grains, they help to boost the protein content and digestibility. Here are some ideas and menus that are examples of how to incorporate legumes and nuts deliciously into your meals.

# SUKIYAKI DINNER PARTY

A sukiyaki menu is perfect for a small, intimate dinner party because most of it can be prepared ahead of time and you can actually get your guests to cook their own meal (and they'll think it's fun) while sitting at the table sharing company!

The day before the party (or early the day of), I prepare the Japanese Bean Confection and Cooling Seaweed Salad. If you're not daring enough to try this wonderful, refreshing salad because it's made with seaweed, I suggest making the Miso Dressing ahead of time. Leave making the Touch-of-the-Orient Dinner Salad till just before guests arrive so it'll be nice and fresh. About 1½ hours before your guests are due, start the brown rice and prepare the sauce and a platter full of fresh vegetables and tofu to be cooked in the sukiyaki later, being sure to arrange attractively in piles on a platter. Also make the Touch-of-the-Orient Dinner Salad at this time if not making the Cooling Seaweed Salad.

When guests arrive and it's time to serve dinner, set the table with a large electric skillet, or a single gas burner with a skillet on top of it, in the center of the table and heat the skillet. Bring the cooked rice and salad to the table in large serving bowls with the proper serving utensils and give each person an empty platter and chopsticks (forks for the less adventurous). I've found that eating with chopsticks helps to slow down eating, so it may be a good utensil to get in the habit of using even when eating non-Oriental meals.

472

Start cooking the sukiyaki. Each person should be served some rice and salad and a little bit of each of the cooked sukiyaki vegetables and tofu. Keep adding ingredients to the sukiyaki pot as it is emptied. This makes for a leisurely meal that can last for hours.

Clear the table before serving the dessert. Japanese desserts are usually very simple and non-fattening. Often a piece of fruit served elegantly on a platter is the whole dessert . . . Whether it's the Bean Confection or a piece of fruit, always serve it simply and elegantly.

Aesthetics play an important part in Japanese meals. Most of us are probably familiar with the platters filled sparsely — but elegantly — that typify the Japanese way of presenting a meal. I'm afraid my appetite has become more Americanized! On a trip to Japan with a few other friends from Hawaii, our hosts took us out to dinner at a Japanese restaurant. The food was delicious, and we ordered many, many little platters of different foods. After our hosts dropped us off at the hotel, we all looked at each other and said, "Are you still hungry? Let's go and get something to eat!" This sukiyaki dinner shouldn't leave you with that feeling; but its exotic theme should be a real treat for family and/or friends. (I can't even begin to tell you how rewarding it was for me when I received a call from a viewer who said she had tried serving her family this sukiyaki dinner and they had so much *fun* spending a lot of time together and talking.)

# JAPANESE BEAN CONFECTION

☆ A *dessert* made with beans.

---

*1 lb. uncooked adzuki beans (red beans)*

*2 cups water*
*1 stick agar-agar*
*1 cup honey*

Soak beans in hot water overnight. Rinse and drain soaked beans. Put beans in large pot, cover with 3 times as much water, and bring to a boil for 5 to 10 minutes. Half-cover pot and turn to simmer. Simmer for at least 1 hour till beans are soft and mash easily between fingers.

While the beans are boiling, soak agar in 2 cups of water in a separate pot. When beans are close to being done, add honey to agar-agar and water and bring to a boil. Then simmer, stirring occasionally, till agar-agar completely dissolves. Turn off heat.

Pour cooked beans and the cooking liquid into a blender (liquid should be visible, but not above surface of the beans). Pour all the beans in if you want an absolutely smooth jell. Some people prefer having whole beans in their jell. If you're one of these people, reserve about 1 cup of drained beans. Blend beans in blender till smooth. Pour into strainer and press beans through strainer into the pot with the dissolved agar-agar. Discard remaining pulp and add reserved whole beans at this point. Stir in and turn heat on. Bring to a rolling boil and stir constantly till mixture thickens and resembles icing for a cake. Remove from heat and pour into a rectangular cake pan, filling to the lip. Refrigerate 6 to 8 hours or overnight.

To serve, cut lengthwise into fourths, forming 4 long strips. Put a strip on serving platter and slice across width of strip to make pieces ¼" thick.

Obviously, the number of servings this makes depends on how many pieces each person takes, but it should be sufficient to say that this recipe makes enough to serve a few dozen guests at a party and isn't a family-sized recipe. To make this recipe for family or just a few friends, cut the recipe in about a quarter and use a smaller mold.

| SHOPPING LIST | |
|---|---|
| Regularly Kept in the Kitchen (Listed in Chapter 14, p. 703) | Fresh Produce |
| Honey | (None) |

| Special Shopping |
|---|
| Agar-agar and adzuki beans — found in Japanese or Chinese groceries, in Oriental food aisles of supermarkets, and in some natural food stores. |

Does the thought of eating seaweed get the "yuk!" response from you? The fact is, you probably eat seaweed every day: it's used as a thickener in yogurts, ice creams, candies, salad dressings, gravies, etc. Just look for the words "carrageenan" or "agar"; those are seaweeds. Of course, not all seaweeds are tasteless as these are. Most seaweeds are very "seafoody" tasting. If you happen to like a seafood taste, seaweeds have a wealth of nutrients to offer.

WAKAME SEAWEED, raw
100 gm. edible portion
(data from USDA)

Calories - 45
Protein - 3.0 gm.
Fat - .6 gm.
Carbohydrate - 9.1 gm.
Fiber (crude) - .5 gm.
Calcium - 150 mg.
Iron - 2.2 mg.
Magnesium - 107 mg.
Phosphorus - 80 mg.
Potassium - 50 mg.
Zinc - .4 mg.
Copper - .3 mg.
Manganese - 1.4 mg.
Vitamin A - 360 IU
Vitamin C - 3.0 mg.
Thiamine - .06 mg.
Riboflavin - .23 mg.
Niacin - 1.60 mg.

# COOLING SEAWEED SALAD

☆ Vegetables from the sea provide plenty of minerals in this refreshing salad.

---

¼ cup rice vinegar
¼ cup honey
⅛"-thick slice of fresh ginger root, crushed

1 large cucumber, sliced paper thin
⅓ cup carrot, cut in fine julienne strips

3 - 6 long strands wakame seaweed, soaked and cut

Toasted sesame seeds

Soak wakame seaweed in water.

Combine first 3 ingredients together in a large bowl and allow to sit together as you slice the cucumber and carrot to allow flavor of ginger to permeate the vinegar. Then toss cucumber and carrot into vinegar mixture. Allow to sit as you prepare seaweed. This mildly "pickles" the vegetables, and the vegetable juices dilute the vinegar a bit. Squeeze as much water as you can out of the wakame seaweed and cut into bite-sized pieces. (If center stem is tough, cut this off; if it isn't tough, don't bother.) Toss into rest of salad. Cover and refrigerate 3 to 4 hours. Just before serving, sprinkle with sesame seeds. Makes 6 to 8 servings.

| SHOPPING LIST | |
|---|---|
| **Regularly Kept in the Kitchen** (Listed in Chapter 14, p. 703) | **Fresh Produce** |
| Rice vinegar | Ginger root |
| Honey | Cucumber |
| Wakame seaweed | Carrot |

# NUTRITIONAL ANALYSIS FOR ONE SERVING
## COOLING SEAWEED SALAD

```
NUTRIENT        Type: 14    FEMALE-23 TO 51 YEARS              % RDA   Amount
KCALORIES       Я=                                              3%   63.80 Kc
PROTEIN         Я                                               1%    0.710 Gm
CARBOHYDRATE    Я                                            NO RDA  15.20 Gm
FAT             Я                                            NO RDA   0.770 Gm
FIBER-CRUDE     Я                                            NO RDA   0.560 Gm
CHOLESTEROL     Я                                            NO RDA   0.000 Mg
SATURATED FA    Я                                            NO RDA   0.110 Gm
OLEIC FA        Я                                            NO RDA   0.000 Gm
LINOLEIC FA     Я                                            NO RDA   0.000 Gm
SODIUM          Я                                               1%   31.70 Mg
POTASSIUM       Я=                                              3%   136.0 Mg
MAGNESIUM       Я==                                             5%   15.80 Mg
IRON            Я=                                              3%    0.590 Mg
ZINC            Я                                               1%    0.270 Mg
VITAMIN A       Я======================================        73%   2939 IU
VITAMIN D       Я                                               0%    0.000 IU
VIT. E/TOTAL    Я                                           NO RDA   0.520 Mg
VITAMIN C       Я==                                             5%    3.440 Mg
THIAMIN         Я=                                              2%    0.020 Mg
RIBOFLAVIN      Я                                               1%    0.020 Mg
NIACIN          Я=                                              2%    0.360 Mg
VITAMIN B6      Я=                                              2%    0.040 Mg
FOLACIN         Я=                                              2%    8.400 Ug
VITAMIN B12     Я                                               0%    0.000 Ug
PANTO- ACID     Я=                                              3%    0.170 Mg
CALCIUM         Я=                                              3%   29.30 Mg
PHOSPHORUS      Я=                                              3%   25.70 Mg
TRYPTOPHAN      Я==                                             5%    9.370 Mg
THREONINE       Я===                                            6%   26.20 Mg
ISOLEUCINE      Я=                                              3%   25.80 Mg
LEUCINE         Я==                                             4%   42.20 Mg
LYSINE          Я==                                             4%   26.30 Mg
METHIONINE      Я==                                             4%   12.40 Mg
CYSTINE         Я=                                              2%    7.870 Mg
PHENYL-ANINE    Я===                                            6%   26.80 Mg
TYROSINE        Я==                                             4%   18.00 Mg
VALINE          Я==                                             4%   32.70 Mg
HISTIDINE       Я                                           NO RDA  13.20 Mg
ALCOHOL         Я                                           NO RDA   0.000 Gm
ASH             Я                                           NO RDA   0.580 Gm
COPPER          Я=                                              2%    0.070 Mg
MANGANESE       Я=                                              3%    0.120 Mg
IODINE          Я                                               0%    0.000 Ug
MONO FAT        Я                                           NO RDA   0.250 Gm
POLY FAT        Я                                           NO RDA   0.330 Gm
CAFFEINE        Я                                           NO RDA   0.000 Mg
FLUORIDE        Я                                               1%   28.10 Ug
MOLYBDENUM      Я                                               0%    1.370 Ug
VITAMIN K       Я                                               0%    0.000 Ug
SELENIUM        Я                                               0%    0.000 Mg
BIOTIN          Я                                               0%    0.810 Ug
CHLORIDE        Я                                               0%    0.000 Mg
CHROMIUM        Я                                               0%    0.000 Mg
SUGAR           Я                                           NO RDA   1.430 Gm
FIBER-DIET      Я                                           NO RDA   0.400 Gm
VIT. E/AT       Я                                               1%    0.120 Mg

    % RDA:   |0      |20     |40     |60     |80     |100
```

476

# MISO DRESSING

1½ cups water
⅓ cup nutritional yeast
¼ cup miso
3 Tbsp. sesame tahini (sesame butter)
¾" chunk fresh ginger root
2 tsp. rice vinegar
½ tsp. toasted sesame oil
¼ tsp. asafetida or ½ peeled clove garlic

Blend all ingredients in blender till ginger root is completely minced. Pour over salad. Makes almost a pint of dressing.

| SHOPPING LIST | |
|---|---|
| Regularly Kept in the Kitchen (Listed in Chapter 14, p. 703) | Fresh Produce |
| Nutritional yeast<br>Miso<br>Sesame tahini<br>Vinegar<br>Toasted sesame oil<br>Asafetida | Ginger root |

# MY BROWN BAG MISO DRESSING

☆ On the road I eat at salad bars a lot and find this acceptably healthy — with the exception of the dressings. So I always carry miso, tahini and nutritional yeast to make my dressing on the spot.

☆ This dressing on a salad bar salad, which includes cooked, dry beans of some sort and a whole grain cracker or bread (which can also be carried) make a whole meal.

---

1 part miso
1 part toasted or raw sesame tahini
2 parts nutritional yeast

Water

Diced tomato

This isn't written like a standard recipe due to the circumstances under which the dressing is made.

I use the spoons available at the table to measure first 3 ingredients into an empty water cup. Mix into a smooth paste and add water a little at a time till the dressing is thin enough to lightly coat the mixing spoon. Dice some tomato from the salad bar into ¼" cubes and add to dressing. Mix gently and pour over salad.

It sometimes requires taking a little bit of extra trouble to be able to eat healthy foods to maintain optimum health, but it's certainly worth it. You may find yourself having to adopt certain practices in order to do so, according to your personal lifestyle. One of the things I've learned to do while on the road or going to a luncheon or dinner where I'm not sure what will be served, is take along a little kit like this so I'll at least for sure be able to have the salad!

| SHOPPING LIST | |
| --- | --- |
| Regularly Kept in the Kitchen (Listed in Chapter 14, p. 703) | Fresh Produce |
| Miso Sesame tahini Nutritional yeast | Tomato |

**KOMBU SEAWEED**, raw
100 gm. edible portion
(data from USDA)

Calories - 43
Protein - 1.7 gm.
Fat - .6 gm.
Carbohydrate - 9.6 gm.
Fiber (crude) - 1.3 gm.
Calcium - 168 mg.
Iron - 2.9 mg.
Magnesium - 121 mg.
Phosphorus - 42 mg.
Potassium - 89 mg.
Zinc - 1.2 mg.
Copper - .1 mg.
Manganese - .2 mg.
Vitamin A - 116 IU
Thiamine - .05 mg.
Riboflavin - .15 mg.
Niacin - .47 mg.
Folacin - 180 mcg.

# TOUCH·OF·THE·ORIENT DINNER SALAD

☆ If you can't bring yourself to try the Cooling Seaweed Salad, you might try this salad — as the kombu seaweed is used sparcely.

---

*4 cups Napa cabbage, sliced in ½" strips*
*1 bunch watercress, cut in 2" lengths*
*1 red bell pepper, sliced thin*
*1 cucumber, sliced thin*
*½ cup finely slivered carrots*
*¼ cup julienne strips of kombu seaweed, soaked*

*Miso Dressing (see following recipe)*

Toss first 6 ingredients together (or mixtures of similar vegetables) in salad bowl. Serve salad in individual bowls and pour Miso Dressing on each serving. Serves 6 to 8.

| SHOPPING LIST | |
|---|---|
| **Regularly Kept in the Kitchen** (Listed in Chapter 14, p. 703) | **Fresh Produce** |
| Kombu seaweed | Napa cabbage |
| | Watercress |
| | Red bell pepper |
| | Cucumber |
| | Carrots |
| | Kombu seaweed |

# NUTRITIONAL ANALYSIS FOR ONE SERVING
## TOUCH-OF-THE-ORIENT DINNER SALAD WITH MISO DRESSING

| NUTRIENT | Type: 14 FEMALE-23 TO 51 YEARS | % RDA | Amount |
|---|---|---|---|
| KCALORIES | A== | 5% | 117.0 Kc |
| PROTEIN | A======== | 17% | 7.710 Gm |
| CARBOHYDRATE | A | NO RDA | 12.70 Gm |
| FAT | A | NO RDA | 4.950 Gm |
| FIBER-CRUDE | A | NO RDA | 1.700 Gm |
| CHOLESTEROL | A | NO RDA | 0.000 Mg |
| SATURATED FA | A | NO RDA | 0.700 Gm |
| OLEIC FA | A | NO RDA | 0.140 Gm |
| LINOLEIC FA | A | NO RDA | 0.150 Gm |
| SODIUM | A========== | 21% | 477.0 Mg |
| POTASSIUM | A====== | 13% | 515.0 Mg |
| MAGNESIUM | A======= | 15% | 47.00 Mg |
| IRON | A==== | 8% | 1.600 Mg |
| ZINC | A====== | 13% | 2.030 Mg |
| VITAMIN A | A=================================================== | 159% | 6371 IU |
| VITAMIN D | A | 0% | 0.000 IU |
| VIT. E/TOTAL | A | NO RDA | 0.690 Mg |
| VITAMIN C | A======================================= | 81% | 48.60 Mg |
| THIAMIN | A========================================== | 413% | 4.130 Mg |
| RIBOFLAVIN | A========================================== | 341% | 4.100 Mg |
| NIACIN | A========================================== | 184% | 24.00 Mg |
| VITAMIN B6 | A========================================== | 203% | 4.060 Mg |
| FOLACIN | A======== | 17% | 69.30 Ug |
| VITAMIN B12 | A========================================== | 103% | 3.110 Ug |
| PANTO- ACID | A====== | 12% | 0.690 Mg |
| CALCIUM | A======= | 16% | 130.0 Mg |
| PHOSPHORUS | A============= | 26% | 210.0 Mg |
| TRYPTOPHAN | A=============================== | 61% | 100.0 Mg |
| THREONINE | A=========================================== | 84% | 366.0 Mg |
| ISOLEUCINE | A=============================== | 61% | 400.0 Mg |
| LEUCINE | A================================== | 68% | 599.0 Mg |
| LYSINE | A===================================== | 74% | 488.0 Mg |
| METHIONINE | A======================= | 46% | 127.0 Mg |
| CYSTINE | A=================== | 38% | 105.0 Mg |
| PHENYL-ANINE | A======================================= | 79% | 347.0 Mg |
| TYROSINE | A================================= | 67% | 294.0 Mg |
| VALINE | A============================== | 60% | 459.0 Mg |
| HISTIDINE | A | NO RDA | 210.0 Mg |
| ALCOHOL | A | NO RDA | 0.000 Gm |
| ASH | A | NO RDA | 6.430 Gm |
| COPPER | A===== | 11% | 0.290 Mg |
| MANGANESE | A=== | 7% | 0.270 Mg |
| IODINE | A | 0% | 0.000 Ug |
| MONO FAT | A | NO RDA | 1.680 Gm |
| POLY FAT | A | NO RDA | 2.250 Gm |
| CAFFEINE | A | NO RDA | 0.000 Mg |
| FLUORIDE | A | 1% | 41.50 Ug |
| MOLYBDENUM | A============ | 24% | 78.00 Ug |
| VITAMIN K | A================================ | 65% | 68.80 Ug |
| SELENIUM | A | 0% | 0.000 Mg |
| BIOTIN | A=== | 6% | 10.20 Ug |
| CHLORIDE | A=== | 7% | 242.0 Mg |
| CHROMIUM | A============ | 24% | 0.030 Mg |
| SUGAR | A | NO RDA | 3.960 Gm |
| FIBER-DIET | A | NO RDA | 1.020 Gm |
| VIT. E/AT | A==== | 9% | 0.770 Mg |

% RDA:  |0     |20     |40     |60     |80     |100

The word sukiyaki translates to "on the blade of a plow" because this is how the dish originated. Farmers and travelers would heat up the blades of their plows or any other suitable metal over a fire to cook whatever foods were available. Certainly a far cry from the meal known in gourmet restaurants and books today! Another big difference — modern-day sukiyaki recipes often call for beef. Eating any four-legged animal was against the law and was enforced by the Emperor in Japan until the 19th century (although some Japanese who dealt with European traders and converted "Christians" knew the taste of beef from the 16th century on).

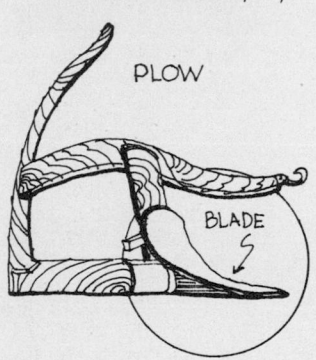

PLOW

BLADE

# SUKIYAKI

☆ The vegetables used in sukiyaki can always vary according to what is in season. This dish is a delicious and simple way to prepare any vegetable; some will require more cooking time than others.

---

*4 Tbsp. oil or margarine or butter*
*2 lbs. tofu, sliced or cubed*

*10 - 12 shiitake mushrooms*

*Assortment of fresh vegetables (sliced and arranged on separate platter), such as —*
   *Bamboo shoots and/or burdock root*
   *Fresh eunoki mushrooms*
   *Carrots*
   *String beans or snow peas*
   *Spinach, beet tops, or other dark greens*
   *Watercress or mustard greens*
   *Japanese radish (daikon) or turnip*
   *Leeks or onions*
   *Napa cabbage*
   *Mung bean sprouts*

## Sauce:

*½ cup shiitake mushroom soaking water*
*½ cup soy sauce*
*¼ cup honey*

Slice vegetables and tofu. Arrange in separate piles on a platter. Preheat a skillet on the stove (or use an electric one at the table) to 350 degrees.

Saute tofu in oil till browned. Push tofu into a pile in your skillet. Now put a pile of each kind of vegetable in the skillet and pour enough of the sauce in to cover the bottom of the skillet. Cook over medium heat for about 5 minutes, occasionally turning ingredients with chopsticks gently — taking care not to mix the separate piles together. Serve directly from the skillet onto plates by using chopsticks (or a fork if chopsticks are an impossibility!) to take a little from each pile and place on a platter. Sukiyaki is usually served with plain rice. Replenish the piles and sauce as they dwindle and while guests are eating. You can vary the number of servings this recipe makes by increasing or decreasing the amounts of vegetables and tofu.

| SHOPPING LIST | |
|---|---|
| **Regularly Kept in the Kitchen** (Listed in Chapter 14, p. 703) | **Fresh Produce** |
| Oil or margarine<br>Tofu<br>Dry shiitake mushrooms<br>Soy sauce<br>Honey | Bamboo shoots<br>Eunoki mushrooms<br>Carrots<br>String beans or snow peas<br>Spinach, beet tops, or other dark green<br>Watercress or mustard greens<br>Japanese radish (daikon) or turnip<br>Napa cabbage<br>Mung bean sprouts |

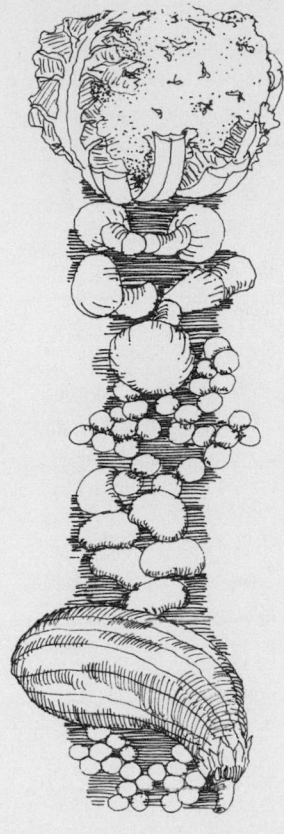

# POCKETFUL OF NUTRITION

The Chinese sage Lao Tsu wrote —
"Thirty spokes converge upon a single hub. It is on the hole in the center that the use of the cart hinges. We make a vessel from a lump of clay. It is the empty space within the vessel that makes it useful. We make doors and windows for a room. But it is the empty spaces within that make the room livable. Thus, while the tangible part of a thing, that which can be perceived by the senses exists, it is the intangible, that which cannot be perceived directly through the senses, that makes it valuable."

It is the intangible spirit soul or life force within the material body that makes the body valuable and attractive. Though the soul can't be seen with these eyes, smelled with this nose, touched with these hands, etc., even a small child can perceive when it's gone from a body. When the soul leaves the body, we no longer wish to live with the body and find it so repulsive that we bury it six feet under or burn it.

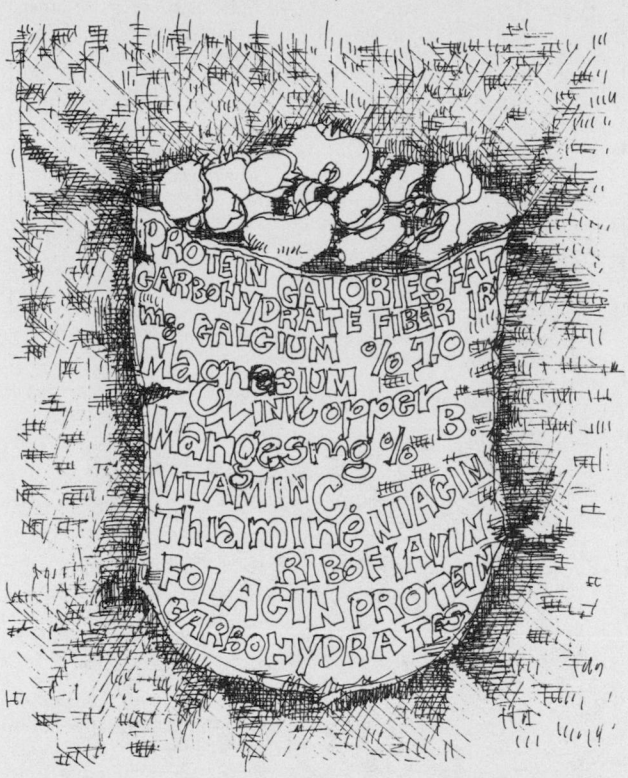

This is only an example of a meal that can be made with germinated and sprouted legumes and seeds. It makes a nice luncheon or early dinner. If you take the trouble to germinate the garbanzo (or other) beans, you'll find the Falafel won't feel uncomfortably heavy in your stomach as bean patties like this often do. I always cook — whether deep- or stir-fry, steam, saute or boil — large legumes like garbanzos, kidneys, pintos, etc., for at least five minutes to make them more digestible. Smaller legumes like sprouted lentils, mung beans, adzuki, etc., can be used raw (as in the salad) if you like. I hope this meal will give you some ideas and inspirations for using lightly germinated legumes, nuts and seeds in other meals on a regular basis.

# CACTUS COOLER

☆ A beneficial drink worth getting in the habit of having first thing in the morning or ½ to 1 hour before a meal.

---

*1 Tbsp. peeled and rinsed fresh aloe vera*
  *or aloe vera gel*
*2 Tbsp. lemon or lime juice*
*½ Tbsp. honey*

*1 cup chilled sparkling water or regular water*

Mix or blend first 3 ingredients together till honey dissolves. Pour into cup and stir in sparkling water. Makes 1 serving.

| SHOPPING LIST | |
|---|---|
| **Regularly Kept in the Kitchen** (Listed in Chapter 14, p. 703) | **Fresh Produce** |
| Honey | Lemon or lime Sparkling water |

**Special Shopping**

Aloe vera — bottled gel can be found in natural food stores; but be sure to check label to see if it's 100% aloe vera that can be taken internally. It's really worth growing your own aloe vera at home; to make drink with fresh aloe vera, cut off a chunk a little larger than one tablespoon and peel. Put peeled chunk of aloe vera in blender with next 2 ingredients and blend till smooth.

## SUGGESTED MENU FOR AN A-LIVE MEAL

*Cactus Cooler*

*Falafel sandwiches made with Falafels, Featuring Sprouts Tossed Salad, A-live Dressing and pita bread*

*Hummus*

*A tahini/dried fruit dessert*

# A·LIVE DRESSING!

☆ Use, as in this menu, to top Falafel sandwiches; or, as a salad dressing, pour over lightly steamed vegetables or a raw vegetable-nut loaf.

---

1 cup mixture of at least 3 kinds of germinated seeds and/or small beans (unhulled
  sesame, hulled sunflower, wheatberries,
  lentils, adzuki, mung and/or peas)
1 cup V-8 or other mixed vegetable juice
½ avocado (about ½ cup mashed)
½ cup salsa sauce (hot or mild —
  according to preference)
1 Tbsp. nutritional yeast
¼ tsp. miso (optional)

Blend ingredients in blender till thick and creamy. Pour liberally on top of salad. This dressing is best fresh and doesn't keep long, so make only as much as is needed just before serving time. Makes about 2½ cups of dressing.

| Special Shopping |
|---|
| Mixture of germinated seeds and beans — can be found in some natural food stores; or make at home (pp. 528 - 9) with your favorite combination of seeds and beans. |

| SHOPPING LIST | |
|---|---|
| **Regularly Kept in the Kitchen (Listed in Chapter 14, p. 703)** | **Fresh Produce** |
| Nutritional yeast<br>Miso (optional) | V-8 or other mixed vegetable juice<br>Avocado<br>Salsa sauce |

# NUTRITIONAL ANALYSIS FOR ONE RECIPE A-LIVE DRESSING

```
NUTRIENT        Type: 14    FEMALE-23 TO 51 YEARS              % RDA    Amount
KCALORIES       A========                                      17%     343.0 Kc
PROTEIN         A===============                               29%     13.10 Gm
CARBOHYDRATE    A                                              NO RDA  37.30 Gm
FAT             A                                              NO RDA  22.00 Gm
FIBER-CRUDE     A                                              NO RDA  4.110 Gm
CHOLESTEROL     A                                              NO RDA  0.000 Mg
SATURATED FA    A                                              NO RDA  2.910 Gm
OLEIC FA        A                                              NO RDA  11.00 Gm
LINOLEIC FA     A                                              NO RDA  1.850 Gm
SODIUM          A===============================               63%     1404 Mg
POTASSIUM       A=======================                       47%     1787 Mg
MAGNESIUM       A=================                             34%     103.0 Mg
IRON            A=============                                 27%     4.990 Mg
ZINC            A=========                                     19%     2.890 Mg
VITAMIN A       A==============================================   127%  5109 IU
VITAMIN D       A                                              0%      0.000 IU
VIT. E/TOTAL    A                                              NO RDA  1.050 Mg
VITAMIN C       A==============================================   201%  121.0 Mg
THIAMIN         A==============================================   489%  4.890 Mg
RIBOFLAVIN      A==============================================   402%  4.830 Mg
NIACIN          A==============================================   243%  31.60 Mg
VITAMIN B6      A==============================================   261%  5.220 Mg
FOLACIN         A=======================                       45%     181.0 Ug
VITAMIN B12     A==============================================   116%  3.500 Ug
PANTO- ACID     A=================                             34%     1.890 Mg
CALCIUM         A====                                          9%      76.20 Mg
PHOSPHORUS      A==================                            37%     297.0 Mg
TRYPTOPHAN      A========================                      48%     79.70 Mg
THREONINE       A==============================================   93%   405.0 Mg
ISOLEUCINE      A=================================             66%     432.0 Mg
LEUCINE         A========================================      81%     713.0 Mg
LYSINE          A==============================================   106%  696.0 Mg
METHIONINE      A==========================                    52%     144.0 Mg
CYSTINE         A================================              64%     176.0 Mg
PHENYL-ANINE    A=============================================    94%  409.0 Mg
TYROSINE        A=====================================         74%     326.0 Mg
VALINE          A===================================           70%     535.0 Mg
HISTIDINE       A                                              NO RDA  245.0 Mg
ALCOHOL         A                                              NO RDA  0.000 Gm
ASH             A                                              NO RDA  8.740 Gm
COPPER          A==================                            37%     0.940 Mg
MANGANESE       A=========                                     19%     0.730 Mg
IODINE          A                                              0%      0.000 Ug
MONO FAT        A                                              NO RDA  12.10 Gm
POLY FAT        A                                              NO RDA  2.460 Gm
CAFFEINE        A                                              NO RDA  0.000 Mg
FLUORIDE        A                                              0%      0.000 Ug
MOLYBDENUM      A====                                          8%      27.30 Ug
VITAMIN K       A                                              0%      0.000 Ug
SELENIUM        A                                              0%      0.000 Mg
BIOTIN          A===                                           6%      9.600 Ug
CHLORIDE        A                                              0%      30.20 Mg
CHROMIUM        A========                                      16%     0.020 Mg
SUGAR           A                                              NO RDA  0.000 Gm
FIBER-DIET      A                                              NO RDA  3.580 Gm
VIT. E/AT       A===========                                   22%     1.770 Mg

     % RDA:   |0      |20      |40      |60      |80      |100
```

Germinated seeds and beans used in analysis: lentils, mung and alfalfa. Optional miso included.

# FEATURING SPROUTS TOSSED SALAD

☆ I feel kind of silly giving a recipe for a tossed salad because I always toss mine together with what's available; however, I wanted to make a salad featuring sunflower greens and radish sprouts in case you've never used them. They're a great addition to any salad. I haven't found anyone who doesn't like them yet!

---

*3 oz. sunflower greens*
*2 oz. alfalfa sprouts*
*1 oz. radish sprouts*
*1 cucumber, sliced very thin*
*½ avocado, diced*

Separate sprouts and toss gently with each other. Just before serving, top with other ingredients. Makes 4 to 5 salads.

| Special Shopping |
| --- |
| Alfalfa sprouts, radish sprouts and sunflower greens — found in natural food stores; or grow your own at home (pp. 529 - 530). Alfalfa sprouts have become so commonplace, they can be found in most supermarket produce sections; if nothing else, at least get in the habit of always using alfalfa sprouts in salads, sandwiches, etc. |

| SHOPPING LIST | |
| --- | --- |
| Regularly Kept in the Kitchen (Listed in Chapter 14, p. 703) | Fresh Produce |
| (None) | Cucumber<br>Avocado |

# FALAFELS

☆ Little Mid-Eastern bean patties traditionally served in pita sandwiches; made in smaller sizes, they are delicious served in spaghetti sauce or anywhere else meatballs are called for.

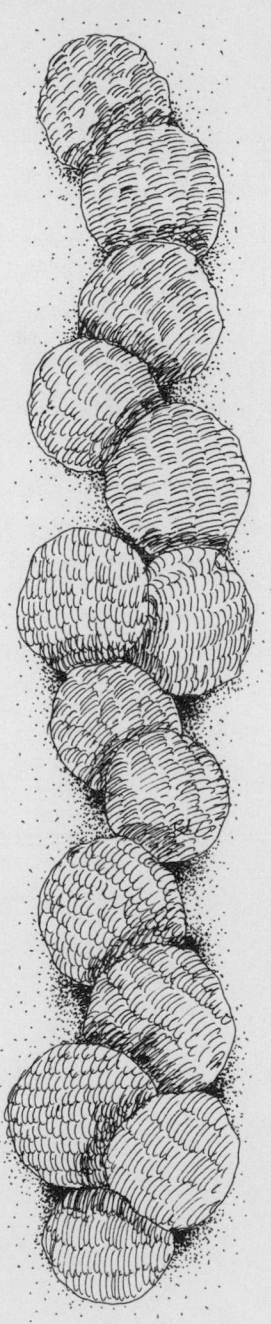

6 cups lightly germinated garbanzo
   beans (chickpeas)

¼ cup finely chopped parsley
2 tsp. ground cumin
2 tsp. ground coriander
1 tsp. baking soda
1 tsp. asafetida or 3 cloves crushed garlic
½ tsp. black pepper
½ tsp. turmeric
¼ - ½ tsp. cayenne
¼ tsp. salt

Oil for deep-frying

Heat oil for deep-frying. Put beans in food processor or run through food grinder to grind to a coarse pulp. Add next 9 ingredients and mix thoroughly. When oil is hot enough that a tiny bit of ground beans sizzles quickly to the top, begin dropping Falafel patties quickly into the oil. Take about 2 tablespoons of ground beans and lightly pat into a ½"-thick by 2¼" in diameter patty. Be sure not to mash and compress the patty together or the Falafel will end up with a very hard, dense texture. Just lightly pat into shape — and remember, it doesn't have to be neat. (If you live near a Mid-Eastern food store or like Falafels so much you want to have them often, you may want to buy a Falafel scoop that functions a little like an automatic ice cream scoop to make making the patties easier.) Drop patty into heated oil; repeat this as quickly as possible till desired number of patties are in the oil. Cook a couple of minutes, flip and cook another minute or so. Cooked Falafels should be hard and crisp on the outside and moist and tender on the inside; they should not be cooked till browned on the outside. Using beans that have been germinated for 2 to 3 days assures that they'll cook through enough to be easily digested in only a few minutes.

To make a Falafel sandwich, wrap whole wheat pita breads in foil and heat in a 350-degree oven for 10 to 15 minutes; warming helps to soften the bread. Remove one bread at a time from foil and cut a ½" strip off one end of the bread;

gently separate bread with fingertips to form a pocket. Depending on size of pita bread, lay 3 to 5 Falafels inside pita bread. Top with fresh salad and pour enough sauce into hole in pita bread to moisten contents. This recipe makes enough Falafels for about 8 sandwiches.

| Special Shopping | SHOPPING LIST | |
| --- | --- | --- |
| | Regularly Kept in the Kitchen (Listed in Chapter 14, p. 703) | Fresh Produce |
| Germinated garbanzos — germinate your own dry garbanzos at home. Garbanzos that have only been soaked overnight can be used instead, but they will take longer to cook through, and I've found germinated garbanzos don't leave me with an uncomfortably heavy feeling in my stomach. | Ground cumin<br>Ground coriander<br>Baking soda<br>Asafetida<br>Black pepper<br>Turmeric<br>Cayennne<br>Salt<br>Oil | Parsley |

# NUTRITIONAL ANALYSIS FOR ONE SERVING FALAFEL BALLS

```
NUTRIENT        Type: 14    FEMALE-23 TO 51 YEARS              % RDA   Amount
KCALORIES       A=====                                         10%     210.0 Kc
PROTEIN         A==============                                27%     11.90 Gm
CARBOHYDRATE    A                                              NO RDA  35.70 Gm
FAT             A                                              NO RDA  2.960 Gm
FIBER-CRUDE     A                                              NO RDA  3.110 Gm
CHOLESTEROL     A                                              NO RDA  0.000 Mg
SATURATED FA    A                                              NO RDA  0.360 Gm
OLEIC FA        A                                              NO RDA  0.730 Gm
LINOLEIC FA     A                                              NO RDA  1.470 Gm
SODIUM          A====                                          8%      181.0 Mg
POTASSIUM       A======                                        13%     490.0 Mg
MAGNESIUM       A============                                  23%     70.60 Mg
IRON            A=============                                 25%     4.570 Mg
ZINC            A======                                        13%     1.980 Mg
VITAMIN A       A==                                            4%      186.0 IU
VITAMIN D       A                                              0%      0.000 IU
VIT. E/TOTAL    A                                              NO RDA  0.050 Mg
VITAMIN C       A===                                           7%      4.560 Mg
THIAMIN         A=========                                     18%     0.180 Mg
RIBOFLAVIN      A===                                           7%      0.090 Mg
NIACIN          A====                                          9%      1.200 Mg
VITAMIN B6      A=======                                       15%     0.300 Mg
FOLACIN         A=======================================       79%     319.0 Ug
VITAMIN B12     A                                              0%      0.000 Ug
PANTO- ACID     A========                                      16%     0.910 Mg
CALCIUM         A======                                        12%     99.20 Mg
PHOSPHORUS      A=============                                 24%     195.0 Mg
TRYPTOPHAN      A================================              65%     106.0 Mg
THREONINE       A==============================================   93%   408.0 Mg
ISOLEUCINE      A===================================           72%     472.0 Mg
LEUCINE         A===========================================   89%     783.0 Mg
LYSINE          A=======================================================  113%  740.0 Mg
METHIONINE      A=========================                     52%     144.0 Mg
CYSTINE         A==========================                    54%     147.0 Mg
PHENYL-ANINE    A=================================================== 135%  588.0 Mg
TYROSINE        A==============================                62%     272.0 Mg
VALINE          A=============================                 60%     462.0 Mg
HISTIDINE       A                                              NO RDA  302.0 Mg
ALCOHOL         A                                              NO RDA  0.000 Gm
ASH             A                                              NO RDA  1.850 Gm
COPPER          A=========                                     19%     0.480 Mg
MANGANESE       A================                              33%     1.250 Mg
IODINE          A==                                            4%      6.560 Ug
MONO FAT        A                                              NO RDA  0.850 Gm
POLY FAT        A                                              NO RDA  1.550 Gm
CAFFEINE        A                                              NO RDA  0.000 Mg
FLUORIDE        A                                              0%      1.800 Ug
MOLYBDENUM      A                                              0%      0.000 Ug
VITAMIN K       A                                              0%      0.000 Ug
SELENIUM        A                                              0%      0.000 Mg
BIOTIN          A                                              0%      0.000 Ug
CHLORIDE        A                                              0%      0.000 Mg
CHROMIUM        A                                              0%      0.000 Mg
SUGAR           A                                              NO RDA  0.000 Gm
FIBER-DIET      A                                              NO RDA  0.000 Gm
VIT. E/AT       A                                              0%      0.030 Mg

  % RDA:  |0       |20      |40      |60      |80      |100
```

Due to lack of data for germinated garbanzo beans, dry garbanzos were used in an amount which approximates the nutritional content of the germinated.

# HUMMUS

1 cup cooked garbanzos *(preferably germinated)*
¼ cup sesame tahini
2 Tbsp. olive oil
¼ cup lemon juice
¼ tsp. asafetida
⅛ tsp. salt

Put into blender and blend.

## Special Shopping

Sesame tahini — sold raw or roasted; I use the raw tahini as I've found the roasted tahini to have a very strong, too dominating flavor. Can be found in natural food stores or Mid-Eastern food stores.
Preferably germinated garbanzos — germinate your own dry garbanzos at home. Garbanzos that have only been soaked overnight can be used instead, but they will take longer to cook through; and I've found germinated garbanzos don't leave me with an uncomfortably heavy feeling in my stomach.

| SHOPPING LIST | |
| --- | --- |
| **Regularly Kept in the Kitchen** (Listed in Chapter 14, p. 703) | **Fresh Produce** |
| Olive oil Asafetida Salt | Lemon |

A Lebanese woman told me her secret for making garlic less smelly. She puts the whole, unpeeled bulbs in the oven and bakes at 200 degrees (or lower if your oven will permit) till the bulbs begin to burst. Then remove from oven, allow to cool and just squeeze garlic cloves out of peels. I've tried it and it really does seem to help get rid of some of that garlic odor, makes it taste a little sweeter and definitely makes it easier to get the cloves out of the peel!

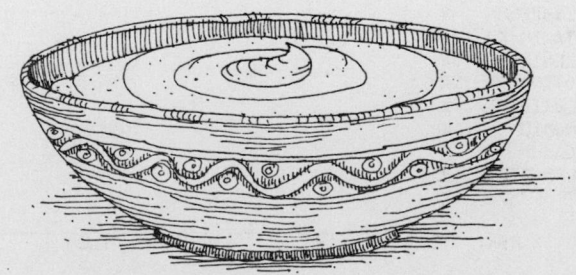

# NUTRITIONAL ANALYSIS FOR ONE RECIPE HUMMUS

| NUTRIENT | Type: 14 FEMALE-23 TO 51 YEARS | % RDA | Amount |
|---|---|---|---|
| KCALORIES | A===================== | 43% | 866.0 Kc |
| PROTEIN | A============================== | 57% | 25.40 Gm |
| CARBOHYDRATE | A | NO RDA | 65.90 Gm |
| FAT | A | NO RDA | 60.00 Gm |
| FIBER-CRUDE | A | NO RDA | 7.100 Gm |
| CHOLESTEROL | A | NO RDA | 0.000 Mg |
| SATURATED FA | A | NO RDA | 8.310 Gm |
| OLEIC FA | A | NO RDA | 19.20 Gm |
| LINOLEIC FA | A | NO RDA | 2.210 Gm |
| SODIUM | A====== | 13% | 299.0 Mg |
| POTASSIUM | A========== | 21% | 800.0 Mg |
| MAGNESIUM | A======================= | 46% | 138.0 Mg |
| IRON | A================= | 35% | 6.380 Mg |
| ZINC | A================ | 35% | 5.350 Mg |
| VITAMIN A | A | 1% | 56.20 IU |
| VITAMIN D | A | 0% | 0.000 IU |
| VIT. E/TOTAL | A | NO RDA | 5.710 Mg |
| VITAMIN C | A========================= | 50% | 30.10 Mg |
| THIAMIN | A================================================ | 97% | 0.970 Mg |
| RIBOFLAVIN | A================ | 34% | 0.410 Mg |
| NIACIN | A================ | 34% | 4.480 Mg |
| VITAMIN B6 | A====== | 12% | 0.250 Mg |
| FOLACIN | A===================================== | 72% | 289.0 Ug |
| VITAMIN B12 | A | 0% | 0.000 Ug |
| PANTO- ACID | A==== | 9% | 0.530 Mg |
| CALCIUM | A===================== | 42% | 338.0 Mg |
| PHOSPHORUS | A================================================ | 91% | 731.0 Mg |
| TRYPTOPHAN | A=================================================== | 230% | 375.0 Mg |
| THREONINE | A=================================================== | 226% | 984.0 Mg |
| ISOLEUCINE | A=================================================== | 165% | 1083 Mg |
| LEUCINE | A=================================================== | 212% | 1855 Mg |
| LYSINE | A=================================================== | 201% | 1317 Mg |
| METHIONINE | A=================================================== | 199% | 542.0 Mg |
| CYSTINE | A=================================================== | 151% | 411.0 Mg |
| PHENYL-ANINE | A=================================================== | 309% | 1347 Mg |
| TYROSINE | A=================================================== | 185% | 809.0 Mg |
| VALINE | A=================================================== | 158% | 1206 Mg |
| HISTIDINE | A | NO RDA | 716.0 Mg |
| ALCOHOL | A | NO RDA | 0.000 Gm |
| ASH | A | NO RDA | 4.670 Gm |
| COPPER | A================================ | 63% | 1.580 Mg |
| MANGANESE | A====================== | 45% | 1.690 Mg |
| IODINE | A================================================ | 98% | 148.0 Ug |
| MONO FAT | A | NO RDA | 31.70 Gm |
| POLY FAT | A | NO RDA | 16.80 Gm |
| CAFFEINE | A | NO RDA | 0.000 Mg |
| FLUORIDE | A | 0% | 0.000 Ug |
| MOLYBDENUM | A================================================ | 229% | 746.0 Ug |
| VITAMIN K | A | 0% | 0.000 Ug |
| SELENIUM | A | 0% | 0.000 Mg |
| BIOTIN | A= | 3% | 5.340 Ug |
| CHLORIDE | A= | 2% | 74.60 Mg |
| CHROMIUM | A================================================ | 232% | 0.290 Mg |
| SUGAR | A | NO RDA | 0.970 Gm |
| FIBER-DIET | A | NO RDA | 16.80 Gm |
| VIT. E/AT | A==================== | 40% | 3.210 Mg |

```
% RDA:  |0      |20     |40     |60     |80     |100
```

Analysis uses cooked garbanzo beans which were not germinated.

# A PIZZA — OF SORTS

☆ To be made with leftover Falafel sandwich fixings.

*Leftover pita breads*
*Your favorite sugar- and meat-free spaghetti sauce*
*Quick-cooking vegetables for topping pizza*
  *(like sliced olives, mushrooms,*
    *tomatoes, bell peppers)*
*Leftover Falafels*
*Grated carrot*

*Leftover Hummus*
*Nutritional yeast*
*Water*

Spread spaghetti sauce on top of pita breads. Top with sliced vegetables of your choice. Crumble leftover Falafel patties and sprinkle evenly over surface of covered pita breads. Sprinkle a thin layer of fresh grated carrot over all of it. Mix the leftover Hummus with nutritional yeast (about ¼ cup nutritional yeast per ½ cup of Hummus) and enough water to make a thick gravy consistency. Pour this sauce over entire surface of topped pita breads. Broil or bake in a hot oven only long enough to heat through.

| Special Shopping |
| --- |
| Whole grain pita breads — found in natural food stores; some supermarkets. |

| SHOPPING LIST | |
| --- | --- |
| **Regularly Kept in the Kitchen** (Listed in Chapter 14, p. 703) | **Fresh Produce** |
| Sugar- and meat-free spaghetti sauce<br>Nutritional yeast | Quick-cooking vegetables (olives, mushrooms, tomatoes, bell peppers, etc.)<br>Carrots |

Also see shopping lists for Falafels and Hummus, although you'll hopefully be using leftovers and won't have to be making them.

# FUDGY TAHINI

¼ cup raw sesame tahini
2 Tbsp. carob powder
2 Tbsp. mashed, moist, pitted dates
¼ cup water
4 tsp. noninstnat, nonfat milk powder
    or buttermilk powder

*Dried bananas*
*Finely chopped nuts  (toasted or raw)*

Blend first 5 ingredients together in a blender till they form a smooth, thick sauce and pour into a flat bowl. Roll pieces or whole, dried bananas into syrup to coat and then immediately roll into chopped nuts. Put finished pieces on platter and allow to sit for a day, or refrigerate a couple of hours to allow carob coating to thicken.

If you want to make a fudge-like candy, just add ¼ cup noninstant, nonfat milk powder or buttermilk powder to the carob coating mixture. Knead in some chopped nuts if desired and press into a tiny bread pan or bowl, cover and refrigerate at least a couple of hours. Cut desired shapes and serve. Should make enough dessert to serve 6 to 12.

| SHOPPING LIST | |
|---|---|
| **Regularly Kept in the Kitchen** (Listed in Chapter 14, p. 703) | **Fresh Produce** |
| Carob<br>Pitted dates<br>Noninstant, nonfat milk powder<br>Nuts | (None) |

### Special Shopping

Sesame tahini — sold raw or roasted; I use the raw tahini as I've found the roasted tahini to have a very strong, too dominating flavor. Can be found in natural food stores or Mid-Eastern food stores.
Dried bananas — found in natural food stores.

# NUTRITIONAL ANALYSIS FOR ONE SERVING FUDGY TAHINI

```
NUTRIENT      Type: 14    FEMALE-23 TO 51 YEARS            % RDA   Amount
KCALORIES     A===                                          6%    127.0 Kc
PROTEIN       A======                                       12%   5.440 Gm
CARBOHYDRATE  A                                          NO RDA   11.80 Gm
FAT           A                                          NO RDA   7.710 Gm
FIBER-CRUDE   A                                          NO RDA   0.880 Gm
CHOLESTEROL   A                                          NO RDA   1.330 Mg
SATURATED FA  A                                          NO RDA   0.970 Gm
OLEIC FA      A                                          NO RDA   1.990 Gm
LINOLEIC FA   A                                          NO RDA   0.530 Gm
SODIUM        A=                                            2%    44.50 Mg
POTASSIUM     A===                                          6%    242.0 Mg
MAGNESIUM     A=====                                        11%   35.10 Mg
IRON          A=                                            3%    0.570 Mg
ZINC          A===                                          6%    0.920 Mg
VITAMIN A     A                                             0%    4.550 IU
VITAMIN D     A                                             0%    0.000 IU
VIT. E/TOTAL  A                                          NO RDA   1.340 Mg
VITAMIN C     A                                             0%    0.480 Mg
THIAMIN       A========                                     17%   0.170 Mg
RIBOFLAVIN    A========                                     17%   0.210 Mg
NIACIN        A===                                          7%    0.960 Mg
VITAMIN B6    A=                                            2%    0.040 Mg
FOLACIN       A                                             1%    7.600 Ug
VITAMIN B12   A====                                         8%    0.260 Ug
PANTO- ACID   A==                                           5%    0.290 Mg
CALCIUM       A=========                                    18%   148.0 Mg
PHOSPHORUS    A==========                                   21%   171.0 Mg
TRYPTOPHAN    A=============================                58%   94.70 Mg
THREONINE     A==========================                   52%   228.0 Mg
ISOLEUCINE    A=====================                        42%   276.0 Mg
LEUCINE       A==========================                   53%   466.0 Mg
LYSINE        A======================                       44%   288.0 Mg
METHIONINE    A========================                     48%   133.0 Mg
CYSTINE       A==============                               29%   79.90 Mg
PHENYL-ANINE  A===============================              63%   277.0 Mg
TYROSINE      A==========================                   53%   232.0 Mg
VALINE        A=====================                        42%   323.0 Mg
HISTIDINE     A                                          NO RDA   153.0 Mg
ALCOHOL       A                                          NO RDA   0.000 Gm
ASH           A                                          NO RDA   1.250 Gm
COPPER        A====                                         8%    0.220 Mg
MANGANESE     A=                                            3%    0.130 Mg
IODINE        A==                                           4%    6.830 Ug
MONO FAT      A                                          NO RDA   3.660 Gm
POLY FAT      A                                          NO RDA   2.700 Gm
CAFFEINE      A                                          NO RDA   0.000 Gm
FLUORIDE      A                                             0%    4.870 Ug
MOLYBDENUM    A=========                                    19%   62.50 Ug
VITAMIN K     A                                             0%    0.000 Ug
SELENIUM      A                                             0%    0.000 Mg
BIOTIN        A                                             1%    1.680 Ug
CHLORIDE      A                                             0%    5.790 Mg
CHROMIUM      A                                             0%    0.000 Mg
SUGAR         A                                          NO RDA   2.430 Gm
FIBER-DIET    A                                          NO RDA   1.200 Gm
VIT. E/AT     A========                                     16%   1.290 Mg

   % RDA:   |0       |20      |40      |60      |80      |100
```

Analysis is for fudge candy and does not include dried bananas; includes additional ¼ cup noninstant nonfat milk powder plus ¼ cup chopped almonds.

# TAHINI'D DRIED FRUIT

2 Tbsp. raw sesame tahini
1½ tsp. honey
1 tsp. noninstant, nonfat milk powder
    or buttermilk powder
½ tsp. lemon juice
Tiny pinch (less than ⅛ tsp.)
    finely grated lemon rind

*Dried figs and/or pitted dates*

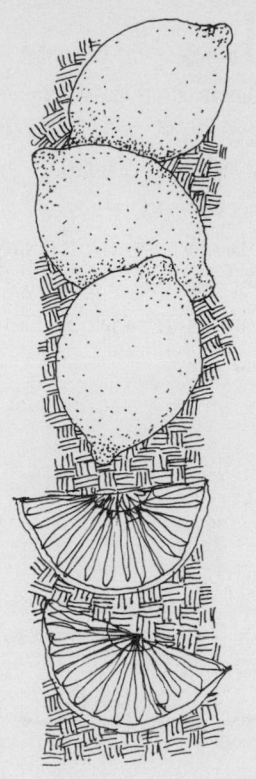

Mix first 5 ingredients together thoroughly and knead a few minutes with fingertips. Use this mixture to stuff dates or wrap around a whole dried fig. To stuff dates, slit date open on one side and remove pit and stem. Take enough sesame mixture to fill pit cavity and stuff the date. Sprinkle sesame filling with finely chopped nuts or press half an almond on top. To wrap figs, just pinch off a little less than a teaspoon of sesame mixture and squeeze as evenly as possible around dried fig, going only part way up to the stem; roll in finely chopped nuts or bee pollen if desired. Makes about 1 dozen pieces of dried fruit.

| SHOPPING LIST | |
| --- | --- |
| **Regularly Kept in the Kitchen** (Listed in Chapter 14, p. 703) | **Fresh Produce** |
| Honey<br>Noninstant, nonfat milk powder<br>Pitted dates and/or dried figs | Lemon |

| **Special Shopping** |
| --- |
| Sesame tahini — sold raw or roasted; I use the raw tahini as I've found the roasted tahini to have a very strong, too dominating flavor. Can be found in natural food stores or Mid-Eastern food stores. |

In making the point that human life is meant for pursuing the development of a higher consciousness, Socrates wrote —
"Bad men live that they may eat and drink, whereas good men eat and drink that they may live."

# A WINNING GREEK MEAL

## SUGGESTED MENU FOR A WINNING GREEK MEAL

*Mediterranean Salad*

*Lentil Soup*

*Greek Garlic Bread*

*Baklava*

Greek myth tells us that early man was originally a fruit-eating creature and that Greek athletes trained on dry figs and whole wheat meal. I find this entirely believable, as present scientific knowledge confirms that this kind of a diet (a high complex-carbohydrate diet) is the healthiest and gives long-sustained energy. Many present-day athletes — especially ones who participate in a sport that calls for high endurance, like marathon runners, triathalon competitors, swimmers, etc. — practice what they call "carbohydrate loading" days before their events.

Considering that good health and fitness are a form of wealth and are becoming today's coveted "status symbols," it's nice to know meals like this winning Greek one — which aid one in attaining both — are delicious and easy on the pocketbook as well!

# LENTIL SOUP

☆ Braising legumes or grains is a nice trick to make soups or stews even tastier.

---

*3 cups dry lentils or 7 cups germinated*
  *lentils (pp. 528 - 529)*
*1 gallon water*
*1 Tbsp. Spike or other vegetable-seasoned salt*

*½ cup olive oil*
*4 cups diced celery*
*1½ cups diced carrots*
*½ cup finely chopped fresh parsley*
*1½ Tbsp. asafetida or 1½ onions, diced*

*2 Tbsp. tomato paste*
*1 large bay leaf*

*½ tsp. oregano*
*1 tsp. Tabasco*
*1 Tbsp. soy sauce*

*3 Tbsp. tarragon vinegar (optional)*

Soak 3 cups of dry lentils overnight in about 3 quarts of water. About 1½ hours before serving time, drain lentils by pouring into a strainer and allowing to sit while carrying out the following steps.

Put the water and vegetable seasoning in a large soup pot and set on a back burner. In a large skillet, saute the next 5 ingredients together over a low heat for about 15 minutes, stirring occasionally. Add next 2 ingredients and the drained lentils to the ingredients in the skillet and turn heat up to medium. Saute, as above, about 10 minutes, stirring often. At the same time, turn heat under the pot of water up to high and bring to a boil. After sauteing the lentils and vegetables for 10 minutes, take a few cups of the boiling water, pour it into the skillet and use it to stir off any browning on the bottom of the skillet. Pour everything from the skillet into the pot of water, add the oregano, Tabasco and soy sauce, and bring to a boil. When the soup boils, cover with a lid and leave to simmer for about 45 minutes. (While the soup is simmering, you can make the following recipes for Greek Garlic Bread and the Mediterranean Salad.) When the soup is done simmering, turn off the heat and add the vinegar. You may decide you like the soup just fine without the vinegar, in which case you can leave it out.

In his "Pluto," Aristophanes writes of a man who became so rich "he didn't eat lentils anymore." What a pity! What we know about lentils today shows that that man was missing out on a wealth of healthy food by falling prey to giving up a healthy food for food "status symbols"! Not only are lentils an excellent source of protein, iron, phosphorus, folacin, thiamine and pantothenic acid, but a study in Australia showed that they also lower serum cholesterol levels.

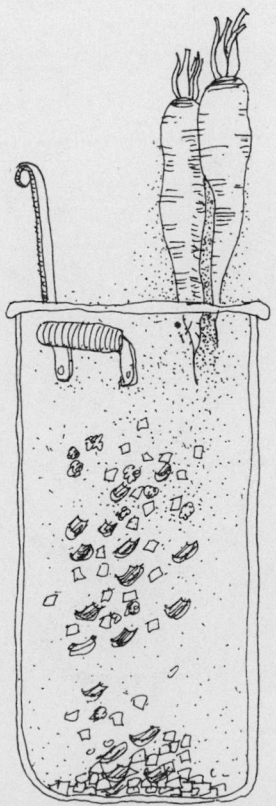

Serves 8 if used as the main dish in this menu. If used as a soup before another meal, it could serve up to 16.

| Special Shopping | SHOPPING LIST | |
| --- | --- | --- |
| Tarragon vinegar — found in gourmet food stores, or make your own (p. 545). | **Regularly Kept in the Kitchen** (Listed in Chapter 14, p. 703) | **Fresh Produce** |
| | Lentils | Celery |
| | Spike | Carrots |
| | Olive oil | Fresh parsley |
| | Asafetida | Tabasco |
| | Tomato paste | |
| | Bay leaf | |
| | Oregano | |
| | Soy sauce | |

# NUTRITIONAL ANALYSIS FOR ONE SERVING LENTIL SOUP

```
NUTRIENT        Type: 14    FEMALE-23 TO 51 YEARS                    % RDA    Amount
KCALORIES       Ā========                                            17%     352.0 Kc
PROTEIN         Ā===================                                 38%     16.90 Gm
CARBOHYDRATE    Ā                                                    NO RDA  42.20 Gm
FAT             Ā                                                    NO RDA  14.60 Gm
FIBER-CRUDE     Ā                                                    NO RDA  5.600 Gm
CHOLESTEROL     Ā                                                    NO RDA  0.000 Mg
SATURATED FA    Ā                                                    NO RDA  2.050 Gm
OLEIC FA        Ā                                                    NO RDA  9.870 Gm
LINOLEIC FA     Ā                                                    NO RDA  1.510 Gm
SODIUM          Ā============                                        25%     569.0 Mg
POTASSIUM       Ā=============                                       26%     981.0 Mg
MAGNESIUM       Ā=============                                       26%     79.30 Mg
IRON            Ā===================                                 38%     6.840 Mg
ZINC            Ā========                                            16%     2.490 Mg
VITAMIN A       Ā=================================================== 155%    6210 IU
VITAMIN D       Ā                                                    0%      0.000 IU
VIT. E/TOTAL    Ā                                                    NO RDA  3.040 Mg
VITAMIN C       Ā============                                        25%     15.10 Mg
THIAMIN         Ā=================                                   35%     0.350 Mg
RIBOFLAVIN      Ā=======                                             14%     0.170 Mg
NIACIN          Ā=========                                           19%     2.470 Mg
VITAMIN B6      Ā==========                                          20%     0.410 Mg
FOLACIN         Ā========================================            83%     332.0 Ug
VITAMIN B12     Ā                                                    0%      0.000 Ug
PANTO- ACID     Ā===========                                         23%     1.310 Mg
CALCIUM         Ā=====                                               10%     81.30 Mg
PHOSPHORUS      Ā======================                              44%     352.0 Mg
TRYPTOPHAN      Ā=================================================== 93%     153.0 Mg
THREONINE       Ā=================================================== 134%    587.0 Mg
ISOLEUCINE      Ā=================================================== 108%    706.0 Mg
LEUCINE         Ā=================================================== 134%    1173 Mg
LYSINE          Ā=================================================== 174%    1139 Mg
METHIONINE      Ā=========================                           51%     141.0 Mg
CYSTINE         Ā=====================================               78%     213.0 Mg
PHENYL-ANINE    Ā=================================================== 183%    797.0 Mg
TYROSINE        Ā=================================================== 99%     433.0 Mg
VALINE          Ā=================================================== 106%    809.0 Mg
HISTIDINE       Ā                                                    NO RDA  456.0 Mg
ALCOHOL         Ā                                                    NO RDA  0.000 Gm
ASH             Ā                                                    NO RDA  2.760 Gm
COPPER          Ā===========                                         22%     0.550 Mg
MANGANESE       Ā=============                                       26%     0.990 Mg
IODINE          Ā=================================================== 146%    220.0 Ug
MONO FAT        Ā                                                    NO RDA  10.00 Gm
POLY FAT        Ā                                                    NO RDA  1.530 Gm
CAFFEINE        Ā                                                    NO RDA  0.000 Mg
FLUORIDE        Ā                                                    1%      31.50 Mg
MOLYBDENUM      Ā=================================================== 405%    1317 Ug
VITAMIN K       Ā                                                    0%      0.000 Ug
SELENIUM        Ā                                                    0%      0.000 Mg
BIOTIN          Ā====                                                8%      12.30 Ug
CHLORIDE        Ā=                                                   2%      94.70 Mg
CHROMIUM        Ā=================================================== 96%     0.120 Mg
SUGAR           Ā                                                    NO RDA  3.570 Gm
FIBER-DIET      Ā                                                    NO RDA  14.00 Gm
VIT. E/AT       Ā============                                        25%     2.040 Mg

    % RDA:    |0      |20     |40     |60     |80     |100
```

Germinated lentils used instead of dry; onions used instead of asafetida.

To remove any bitterness in cucumbers, cut off both tips and score tips and open ends of cucumber with a knife. Rub cut side of tip around and around on open end of cucumber. If there is any bitterness in the cucumber, a thick, soapy, white foam will build up around the edges of the peel: Rinse this off, then prepare cucumber as recipe calls for.

# MEDITERRANEAN SALAD

☆ All the countries around the Mediterranean thrive on a pleasant, warm climate — much like that of California — which enables them to grow abundant crops; and the recipes from that area make abundant use of the crops!

*4 cups cucumber chunks*
*3 cups bell pepper chunks*
*6 cups tomato wedges*
*2 cups pitted ripe olives*
*2 cups washed and crumbled feta cheese*

*⅓ cup olive oil*
*3 Tbsp. apple cider vinegar*
*1 tsp. asafetida or 2 - cloves garlic, crushed*
*½ tsp. black pepper*
*½ tsp. Spike or other vegetable-seasoned salt*

Cut cucumbers, bell peppers and tomatoes into fairly large (about 1") bite-sized chunks. Put in salad bowl with olives and feta cheese. Combine next 5 ingredients in a separate container, pour onto ingredients in salad bowl and toss till dressing is thoroughly distributed. Cover and refrigerate about an hour before serving so flavors can distribute themselves nicely. This serves 8 to 10.

| Special Shopping |
|---|
| Feta cheese — found in most supermarket cheese sections; in cheese specialty shops. It's a very salty cheese, having been soaked in a brine. Rinsing the cheese helps to cut down on salt content a tiny bit. |

| SHOPPING LIST | |
|---|---|
| **Regularly Kept in the Kitchen** (Listed in Chapter 14, p. 703) | **Fresh Produce** |
| Olive oil | Cucumber |
| Apple cider vinegar | Bell pepper |
| Asafetida | Tomatoes |
| Black pepper | Pitted, ripe olives |
| Spike | |

# NUTRITIONAL ANALYSIS FOR ONE SERVING
## MEDITERRANEAN SALAD

| NUTRIENT | Type: 14 | FEMALE-23 TO 51 YEARS | % RDA | Amount |
|---|---|---|---|---|
| KCALORIES | A====== | | 13% | 261.0 Kc |
| PROTEIN | A======== | | 16% | 7.440 Gm |
| CARBOHYDRATE | A | | NO RDA | 13.60 Gm |
| FAT | A | | NO RDA | 21.60 Gm |
| FIBER-CRUDE | A | | NO RDA | 1.960 Gm |
| CHOLESTEROL | A | | NO RDA | 31.90 Mg |
| SATURATED FA | A | | NO RDA | 7.220 Gm |
| OLEIC FA | A | | NO RDA | 12.20 Gm |
| LINOLEIC FA | A | | NO RDA | 1.200 Gm |
| SODIUM | A============= | | 27% | 606.0 Mg |
| POTASSIUM | A======= | | 15% | 569.0 Mg |
| MAGNESIUM | A====== | | 12% | 38.30 Mg |
| IRON | A===== | | 11% | 2.060 Mg |
| ZINC | A===== | | 10% | 1.510 Mg |
| VITAMIN A | A============================= | | 58% | 2334 IU |
| VITAMIN D | A | | 0% | 0.000 IU |
| VIT. E/TOTAL | A | | NO RDA | 2.200 Mg |
| VITAMIN C | A==================================================== | | 138% | 83.10 Mg |
| THIAMIN | A======== | | 16% | 0.160 Mg |
| RIBOFLAVIN | A===== | | 10% | 0.120 Mg |
| NIACIN | A===== | | 11% | 1.470 Mg |
| VITAMIN B6 | A==== | | 8% | 0.170 Mg |
| FOLACIN | A=== | | 7% | 31.10 Ug |
| VITAMIN B12 | A | | 0% | 0.000 Ug |
| PANTO- ACID | A===== | | 10% | 0.600 Mg |
| CALCIUM | A============= | | 27% | 222.0 Mg |
| PHOSPHORUS | A=========== | | 23% | 186.0 Mg |
| TRYPTOPHAN | A===== | | 11% | 18.80 Mg |
| THREONINE | A======= | | 14% | 61.90 Mg |
| ISOLEUCINE | A==== | | 9% | 59.10 Mg |
| LEUCINE | A===== | | 10% | 92.40 Mg |
| LYSINE | A====== | | 13% | 88.60 Mg |
| METHIONINE | A=== | | 7% | 21.00 Mg |
| CYSTINE | A===== | | 11% | 30.40 Mg |
| PHENYL-ANINE | A======= | | 14% | 61.20 Mg |
| TYROSINE | A==== | | 9% | 39.40 Mg |
| VALINE | A==== | | 8% | 67.20 Mg |
| HISTIDINE | A | | NO RDA | 35.90 Mg |
| ALCOHOL | A | | NO RDA | 0.000 Gm |
| ASH | A | | NO RDA | 3.450 Gm |
| COPPER | A==== | | 8% | 0.210 Mg |
| MANGANESE | A==== | | 8% | 0.310 Mg |
| IODINE | A=== | | 6% | 9.060 Ug |
| MONO FAT | A | | NO RDA | 8.360 Gm |
| POLY FAT | A | | NO RDA | 1.250 Gm |
| CAFFEINE | A | | NO RDA | 0.000 Mg |
| FLUORIDE | A= | | 3% | 86.00 Ug |
| MOLYBDENUM | A | | 0% | 0.500 Ug |
| VITAMIN K | A==== | | 8% | 8.730 Ug |
| SELENIUM | A | | 0% | 0.000 Ug |
| BIOTIN | A== | | 5% | 7.900 Ug |
| CHLORIDE | A | | 0% | 0.000 Mg |
| CHROMIUM | A========================= | | 48% | 0.060 Mg |
| SUGAR | A | | NO RDA | 10.70 Gm |
| FIBER-DIET | A | | NO RDA | 2.140 Gm |
| VIT. E/AT | A============= | | 28% | 2.250 Mg |

```
% RDA:  |0      |20     |40     |60     |80     |100
```

# GREEK GARLIC BREAD

☆ A flavored, crusty bread to eat along with any soup or salad.

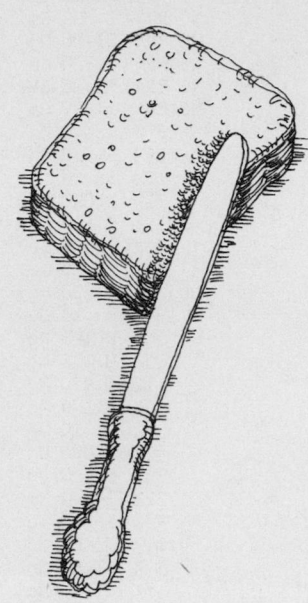

---

1 loaf whole grain French bread
  (or other long, crusty kind)
½ cup margarine or butter
1 Tbsp. asafetida or 3 - 4 cloves garlic, crushed

Nutritional yeast or grated kefalotyri
  or Parmesan cheese

If you can't find a loaf of whole grain French bread in the market, you can make your own at home (see p.---).

Cut bread into slices 1" thick. Mix asafetida or crushed garlic thoroughly into softened butter or margarine and spread on both sides of bread. Lay buttered pieces of bread out flat on a cookie sheet and sprinkle tops of bread with nutritional yeast (or cheeses mentioned). Place bread under broiler and broil till bread is toasted and sizzling. Turn pieces over, sprinkle with nutritional yeast and repeat. This takes only a few minutes to do. Best served hot, so wait till just a few minutes before serving time to make this. Make enough to allow 2 to 3 slices per person.

| Special Shopping |
| --- |
| Whole grain crusty bread (French or Italian) — found in natural food stores, or make your own (p. 389). |

| SHOPPING LIST | |
| --- | --- |
| **Regularly Kept in the Kitchen** (Listed in Chapter 14, p. 703) | **Fresh Produce** |
| Margarine or butter<br>Asafetida<br>Nutritional yeast or Parmesan cheese | (None) |

# BAKLAVA

☆ The filling for this Baklava takes a healthy departure from the traditional filling (which is not unhealthy!).

---

*1 lb. Filo (Phyllo) dough*

*4 cups very finely chopped nuts*
  *(pecans, almonds or walnuts)*
*½ cup date sugar*
*1 cup wheat germ*
*½ cup bran*
*Finely grated peel of 1 orange (or lemon)*
*1 tsp. vanilla extract*
*½ tsp. ground cloves*
*1 tsp. ground cinnamon*

*1 cup melted margarine or butter*

*2 cups water*
*1½ cups mild honey*

*3 Tbsp. lemon juice*

Most likely you'll use a frozen commercial Filo dough (also sometimes spelled "Phyllo"), which should be thawed according to the directions on the package. (If frozen Filo dough isn't available, and you're a fairly skilled baker, you might try the Whole Wheat Strudel Dough in *Kathy Cooks . . . Naturally*, p. 216.)

Get the thawed Filo dough ready to work with by laying it flat on a counter and covering it with a damp cloth to prevent the dough from drying out or becoming brittle. Combine next 8 ingredients in a bowl and mix thoroughly. Using a basting brush, or an unused paint brush, brush the bottom of a 13½" x 8¾" x 1¾" baking pan (you can vary the size of the pan a bit) with the melted butter or margarine. Now place 1 sheet of dough in the bottom of the pan with the edges of the dough coming up the sides of the pan. Brush the dough very lightly with the melted butter or margarine. Repeat this process till there's a stack of 8 sheets in the bottom of the pan. Sprinkle a quarter of the nut mixture evenly over the layers of Filo dough and then fold the edges of only 1 sheet of Filo dough directly under the nut mixture over onto the nut mixture. Now layer 4 more Filo dough sheets as was previously done, sprinkle with another quarter of the nut mixture, and fold the edges of the top layer of the dough onto the nut mixture as before. Repeat this process 2 more times (so you'll end

Especially the addition of wheat germ to the Baklava adds to its nutritional value. The additional wheat germ (and bran) replaces what was removed from the flour in the Filo dough and adds —

WHEAT GERM, 1 cup
(data from USDA)

Calories - 363
Protein - 26.6 gm.
Fat - 10.9 gm.
Carbohydrate - 46.7 gm.
Fiber (crude) - 2.5 gm.
Calcium - 72 mg.
Phosphorus - 1,118 mg.
Iron - 9.4 mg.
Sodium - 3 mg.
Potassium - 827 mg.
Thiamine - 2.01 mg.
Riboflavin - .68 mg.
Niacin - 4.2 mg.

BRAN, ½ cup
(data from USDA)

Calories - 81
Protein - 6.1 gm.
Fat - 1.7 gm.
Carbohydrate - 23.5 gm.
Fiber (crude) - 3.5 gm.
Calcium - 45.1 mg.
Phosphorus - 483.5 mg.
Iron - 5.7 mg.
Sodium - 3.4 mg.
Potassium - 424.5 mg.
Thiamine - .28 mg.
Riboflavin - .14 mg.
Niacin - 8.0 mg.

up with 4 layers of nut filling) till all of the nut mixture is used up. Add the top layer of Filo to the Baklava by adding on 7 Filo dough sheets as was previously done. Then fold all the loose edges over the 7th layer. Now add 1 more sheet, brush with butter and fold the edges of this 1 sheet down into the sides of the pan. With a very sharp knife, make cuts about ½" deep in the shape and size of the pieces you want to serve. They can be square, diamond-shaped or triangular.

Preheat oven to 350 degrees.

Now sprinkle the top of the Baklava with a few drops of water from your hand. This prevents dough from curling up when it bakes. Bake at 350 degrees for about 1½ hours or till top of dough is golden brown.

In the meantime, combine honey and water in a pot and bring to a boil. Turn heat down and lightly boil for about 10 minutes. (Be sure to use a pot 3 to 4 times larger than the amount needed to hold the liquid in order to prevent boil-overs.)

Turn off heat and add lemon juice. When Baklava is golden brown, remove from the oven and immediately use the sharp knife to cut all the way through to the bottom of the pan along the lines you made before baking. Pour the honey syrup over the hot Baklava and it will sizzle as it soaks into the pastry. Allow to sit for 3 hours, although overnight is preferable. The number of dessert servings this makes will depend on how the Baklava is cut. Because Baklava is very sweet and rich, small pieces are recommended. Cutting pieces approximately 2" square will give you 24 servings — which is too much for 1 person or family! You can either freeze some, or invite neighbors and/or friends over for some Baklava, herb tea and company.

| Special Shopping |
|---|
| Filo (Phyllo) dough sheets — found in the refrigerated or freezer section in gourmet food stores and some supermarkets; also in Mid-Eastern and Greek groceries. |

| SHOPPING LIST | |
|---|---|
| **Regularly Kept in the Kitchen** (Listed in Chapter 14, p. 703) | **Fresh Produce** |
| Pecans, almonds and/or walnuts<br>Date sugar<br>Wheat germ<br>Bran<br>Ground cloves<br>Vanilla<br>Cinnamon<br>Margarine or butter<br>Honey | Orange<br>Lemon |

# NUTRITIONAL ANALYSIS FOR ONE PIECE BAKLAVA

```
NUTRIENT        Type: 14    FEMALE-23 TO 51 YEARS          % RDA   Amount
KCALORIES       A=========                                 18%   362.0 Kc
PROTEIN         A=========                                 18%   8.100 Gm
CARBOHYDRATE    A                                        NO RDA   42.30 Gm
FAT             A                                        NO RDA   19.70 Gm
FIBER-CRUDE     A                                        NO RDA   1.020 Gm
CHOLESTEROL     A                                        NO RDA   0.000 Mg
SATURATED FA    A                                        NO RDA   2.430 Gm
OLEIC FA        A                                        NO RDA   8.140 Gm
LINOLEIC FA     A                                        NO RDA   2.490 Gm
SODIUM          A==                                          4%   93.60 Mg
POTASSIUM       A===                                         7%   280.0 Mg
MAGNESIUM       A================                           32%   96.90 Mg
IRON            A======                                     12%   2.190 Mg
ZINC            A=====                                      11%   1.710 Mg
VITAMIN A       A====                                        8%   323.0 IU
VITAMIN D       A                                            0%   1.410 IU
VIT. E/TOTAL    A                                        NO RDA   6.490 Mg
VITAMIN C       A=                                           2%   1.690 Mg
THIAMIN         A=============                              26%   0.260 Mg
RIBOFLAVIN      A============                               25%   0.300 Mg
NIACIN          A=========                                  19%   2.520 Mg
VITAMIN B6      A==                                          5%   0.110 Mg
FOLACIN         A====                                        8%   35.40 Ug
VITAMIN B12     A                                            0%   0.000 Ug
PANTO- ACID     A===                                         7%   0.430 Mg
CALCIUM         A====                                        8%   71.70 Mg
PHOSPHORUS      A=============                              26%   208.0 Mg
TRYPTOPHAN      A=====================================      73%   120.0 Mg
THREONINE       A==================================         68%   296.0 Mg
ISOLEUCINE      A============================               55%   360.0 Mg
LEUCINE         A====================================       72%   628.0 Mg
LYSINE          A========================                   49%   325.0 Mg
METHIONINE      A===================                        40%   110.0 Mg
CYSTINE         A==========================                 54%   148.0 Mg
PHENYL-ANINE    A=================================================  99%  432.0 Mg
TYROSINE        A===============================            62%   270.0 Mg
VALINE          A==========================                 53%   410.0 Mg
HISTIDINE       A                                        NO RDA   228.0 Mg
ALCOHOL         A                                        NO RDA   0.000 Gm
ASH             A                                        NO RDA   1.240 Gm
COPPER          A======                                     12%   0.300 Mg
MANGANESE       A=================                          35%   1.330 Mg
IODINE          A======                                     12%   18.20 Ug
MONO FAT        A                                        NO RDA   10.90 Gm
POLY FAT        A                                        NO RDA   5.140 Gm
CAFFEINE        A                                        NO RDA   0.000 Mg
FLUORIDE        A=                                           2%   57.90 Ug
MOLYBDENUM      A==================================         68%   224.0 Ug
VITAMIN K       A                                            0%   0.000 Ug
SELENIUM        A====                                        8%   0.010 Mg
BIOTIN          A=                                           3%   5.990 Ug
CHLORIDE        A                                            0%   13.80 Mg
CHROMIUM        A========                                   16%   0.020 Mg
SUGAR           A                                        NO RDA   2.350 Gm
FIBER-DIET      A                                        NO RDA   3.100 Gm
VIT. E/AT       A===================================        73%   5.850 Mg

   % RDA:    0      20      40      60      80      100
```

Nuts used in analysis: almonds. Margarine used instead of butter.

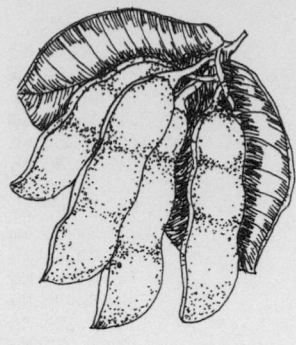

# SOY-GARBANZO ROAST

☆ Delicious served as a loaf; leftovers can be sliced and put in sandwiches.

---

*1 cup soaked soybeans*
*1 cup soaked garbanzo beans*

*1½ cups water*
*3 Tbsp. soy sauce*
*¼ tsp. asafetida or 1 clove garlic*
*½ tsp. black pepper*
*½ tsp. salt*
*1 tsp. basil*
*1 tsp. rosemary*
*2 bay leaves*

*¼ cup bran*
*1½ cups celery, diced fine*
*⅔ cup chopped sunflower seeds*
*½ cup whole wheat flour*

Soak first 2 ingredients overnight. Drain the soaked beans and blend in blender with next 8 ingredients. Combine blended mixture with next 4 ingredients. Pour into an oiled loaf pan, and if you want, place large (1" to 2") chunks of vegetables on top of loaf. Baste with some of the Basting Sauce. Cover and bake at 400 degrees for 45 minutes. Remove cover and baste again. Put back in oven and bake at least 15 minutes to brown the top.

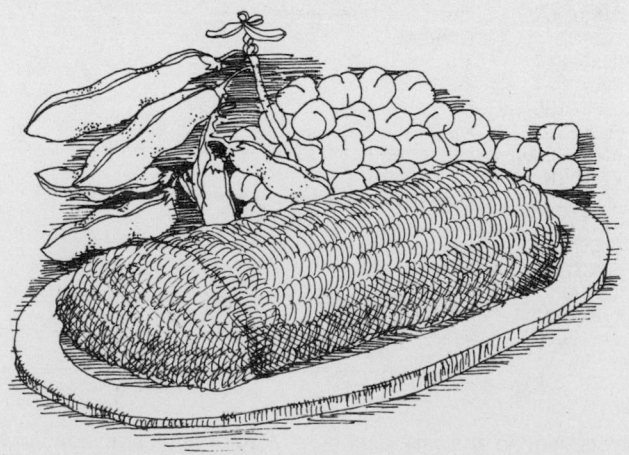

# NUTRITIONAL ANALYSIS FOR ONE SERVING
## SOY-GARBANZO ROAST WITH BASTING SAUCE

```
NUTRIENT        Type: 14   FEMALE-23 TO 51 YEARS          % RDA   Amount
KCALORIES       A=====                                     10%    205.0 Kc
PROTEIN         A=============                             25%    11.00 Gm
CARBOHYDRATE    A                                        NO RDA   20.20 Gm
FAT             A                                        NO RDA   10.60 Gm
FIBER-CRUDE     A                                        NO RDA   2.310 Gm
CHOLESTEROL     A                                        NO RDA   0.000 Mg
SATURATED FA    A                                        NO RDA   1.100 Gm
OLEIC FA        A                                        NO RDA   1.390 Gm
LINOLEIC FA     A                                        NO RDA   4.980 Gm
SODIUM          A==================                        36%    796.0 Mg
POTASSIUM       A====                                       8%    303.0 Mg
MAGNESIUM       A==============                            28%    84.40 Mg
IRON            A==========                                20%    3.690 Mg
ZINC            A====                                       9%    1.360 Mg
VITAMIN A       A=                                          3%    123.0 IU
VITAMIN D       A                                           0%    0.000 IU
VIT. E/TOTAL    A                                        NO RDA   7.770 Mg
VITAMIN C       A=========                                 18%    11.30 Mg
THIAMIN         A========================                  50%    0.500 Mg
RIBOFLAVIN      A=====                                     10%    0.130 Mg
NIACIN          A======                                    18%    2.380 Mg
VITAMIN B6      A======                                    12%    0.250 Mg
FOLACIN         A=====                                     11%    44.20 Ug
VITAMIN B12     A                                           0%    0.000 Ug
PANTO- ACID     A===                                        7%    0.410 Mg
CALCIUM         A=======                                   14%    112.0 Mg
PHOSPHORUS      A================                          33%    266.0 Mg
TRYPTOPHAN      A====================================      78%    128.0 Mg
THREONINE       A==========================================  89%  390.0 Mg
ISOLEUCINE      A===================================       70%    461.0 Mg
LEUCINE         A========================================  83%    728.0 Mg
LYSINE          A=======================================   81%    533.0 Mg
METHIONINE      A==========================                56%    154.0 Mg
CYSTINE         A========================                  52%    142.0 Mg
PHENYL-ANINE    A==========================================  113%  495.0 Mg
TYROSINE        A===================================       73%    321.0 Mg
VALINE          A===============================           64%    490.0 Mg
HISTIDINE       A                                        NO RDA   273.0 Mg
ALCOHOL         A                                        NO RDA   0.000 Gm
ASH             A                                        NO RDA   3.040 Gm
COPPER          A=======                                   14%    0.360 Mg
MANGANESE       A=============                             27%    1.030 Mg
IODINE          A==========================                53%    79.80 Ug
MONO FAT        A                                        NO RDA   1.700 Gm
POLY FAT        A                                        NO RDA   6.640 Gm
CAFFEINE        A                                        NO RDA   0.000 Mg
FLUORIDE        A                                           0%    3.150 Ug
MOLYBDENUM      A=================================        194%    633.0 Ug
VITAMIN K       A                                           0%    0.000 Ug
SELENIUM        A                                           0%    0.000 Mg
BIOTIN          A                                           1%    1.650 Ug
CHLORIDE        A                                           0%    28.90 Mg
CHROMIUM        A==================================        72%    0.090 Mg
SUGAR           A                                        NO RDA   0.580 Gm
FIBER-DIET      A                                        NO RDA   4.580 Gm
VIT. E/AT       A=====================================     83%    6.690 Mg

    % RDA:  |0       |20     |40     |60     |80      |100
```

The recipe for the sauce is enough to baste 6 to 8 times the recipe for the loaf; the recipe for the loaf is enough for one blenderful. I recommend making (all the way through, including baking) many loaves at a time and freezing the extra loaves for a day when you're too busy to cook. This certainly saves time and can help to conserve energy. If the oven is already on to bake one loaf, you may as well bake as many more as will fit, using the same heat.

# BASTING SAUCE

½ cup oil
½ cup soy sauce
3 Tbsp. Spike or other vegetable-seasoned salt

| SHOPPING LIST | |
|---|---|
| Regularly Kept in the Kitchen (Listed in Chapter 14, p. 703) | Fresh Produce |
| Soybeans | Celery |
| Garbanzos | |
| Soy sauce | |
| Asafetida | |
| Black pepper | |
| Salt | |
| Basil | |
| Rosemary | |
| Bay leaves | |
| Bran | |
| Sunflower seeds | |
| Whole wheat flour | |

# OH, NUTS!

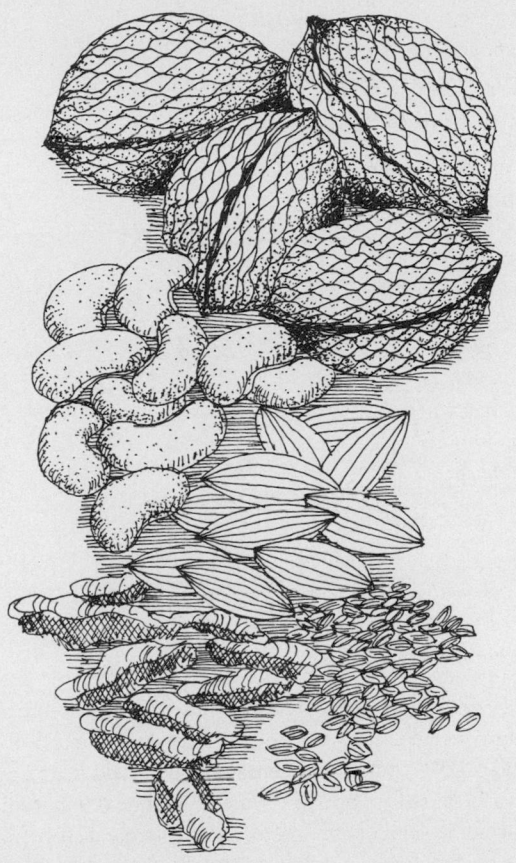

A realization of many philosophers and saintly persons is neatly summed up in these words from Plato: "The soul is immortal, and is clothed successively in many bodies."

Knowing this within our hearts could help put an end to wars between nations, religions, races, sexes or social classes. This knowledge makes us see that it's as silly to hate someone for having a body of a different nationality, religion, race, sex or social status as it would be to hate someone for wearing a shirt of a different color, shape, size or make.

In my home, nuts make their way into our tummies more often than during the holidays! Though they're concentrated packages of fat and protein (some more than others), they're valued for providing a lot of other nutrients and helping to make the protein in whole grains and legumes more digestible. My son, Valmiki, makes his own "trail mix" for energy food to get him through a day of surfing. This is about the only way the nuts are used on their own; usually I prepare nuts in dishes with whole grains and/or legumes. When you start using them, it's amazing how versatile they can be — adding wonderful tastes and textures, along with the nutrition packed in them, to any meal!

There's really no such thing as a "raw" cashew; that's why the whole ones won't germinate! The cashew nut hangs off the bottom of a large fruit called the cashew "apple." In many places where the cashew tree grows, people eat the apple and discard the nut because it's surrounded by an acrid fluid that blisters the skin on contact. Cashew nuts have to be roasted to remove this outer surrounding layer. However, "raw" cashews and nut butters bought in stores are much sweeter than the "roasted" versions. I prefer dry-roasting my nuts like this as opposed to deep-frying, which adds more fat to the already fatty nut. To dry-roast cashews or other nuts . . .

### DRY-ROASTING NUTS

Heat oven to 225 to 250 degrees. Spread nuts evenly on a cookie sheet, one layer deep, and place in oven. Turn every 20 minutes till nuts begin to turn golden and have a nice, toasted flavor. Remember, they will continue to cook from the retained heat for a little while after taken out of oven, so don't over-cook. It takes a little longer to roast nuts this way, but they'll cook evenly and will be less likely to burn — unless you forget about the whole tray altogether!

# NUTTY STROGANOFF

8 oz. whole grain fettuccine or other
  thin-shaped pasta

1 Tbsp. butter or margarine
1 cup diced celery and ¾ tsp. asafetida
  OR 1 cup diced onion

1 lb. small mushrooms, split
½ cup thinly sliced leeks

½ cup white wine
½ cup tomato sauce
1 Tbsp. Vegex Brewer's Yeast Extract
1 tsp. Spike or other vegetable-seasoned salt
½ tsp. nutmeg
½ tsp. black pepper
¼ tsp. Tabasco
½ tsp. basil
¼ tsp. thyme

½ cup water
1½ Tbsp. arrowroot
2 cups Lowfat Sour Cream (see p. 186)
1 cup roasted whole cashews

Roast cashews in oven if they're "raw." Bring water to a boil and drop noodles in to boil. Quickly saute next 3 (or 2) ingredients till vegetables turn translucent. Add next 2 ingredients and saute for about 5 minutes. Add next 9 ingredients and mix in thoroughly till Vegex is completely dissolved. In a small cup, mix next 2 ingredients together till arrowroot dissolves; then pour into sauce cooking on stove, stirring constantly till it thickens. Turn off heat and add last 2 ingredients, stirring till Lowfat Sour Cream is thoroughly incorporated.

Drain noodles when done cooking (follow directions on package). Pour drained noodles into other ingredients and mix in thoroughly. Serve immediately. Makes about 6 to 8 servings.

| SHOPPING LIST | | Special Shopping |
|---|---|---|
| **Regularly Kept in the Kitchen (Listed in Chapter 14, p. 703)** | **Fresh Produce** | Whole grain fettuccine — found in natural food stores. Vegex Brewer's Yeast Extract — found in natural food stores. I prefer this to the Vegex bouillon cubes which contain sugar. |
| Butter or margarine<br>Asafetida<br>Tomato sauce<br>Spike<br>Nutmeg<br>Black pepper<br>Tabasco<br>Basil<br>Thyme<br>Arrowroot | Celery<br>Mushrooms<br>Leeks<br>White wine<br>Cashews | |

Also see shopping list for Lowfat Sour Cream (p. 186).

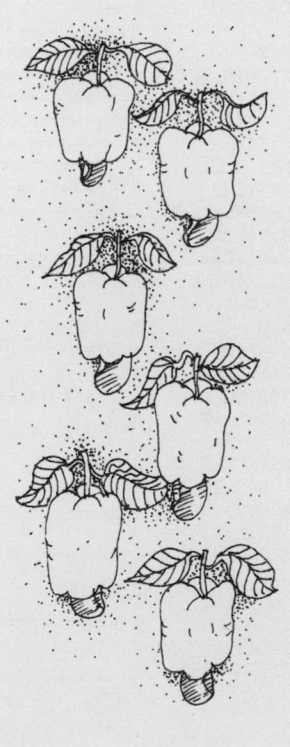

# NUTRITIONAL ANALYSIS FOR ONE SERVING NUTTY STROGANOFF

```
NUTRIENT        Type: 14    FEMALE-23 TO 51 YEARS              % RDA    Amount
KCALORIES       Ã=====                                          11%    232.0 Kc
PROTEIN         Ã================                               30%    13.60 Gm
CARBOHYDRATE    Ã                                             NO RDA    21.90 Gm
FAT             Ã                                             NO RDA    11.00 Gm
FIBER-CRUDE     Ã                                             NO RDA    0.880 Gm
CHOLESTEROL     Ã                                             NO RDA    5.310 Mg
SATURATED FA    Ã                                             NO RDA    2.650 Gm
OLEIC FA        Ã                                             NO RDA    5.790 Gm
LINOLEIC FA     Ã                                             NO RDA    0.610 Gm
SODIUM          Ã=========                                      18%    396.0 Mg
POTASSIUM       Ã======                                         12%    465.0 Mg
MAGNESIUM       Ã===========                                    22%    68.10 Mg
IRON            Ã======                                         13%    2.500 Mg
ZINC            Ã=====                                          11%    1.780 Mg
VITAMIN A       Ã=                                               3%    121.0 IU
VITAMIN D       Ã                                                0%    1.250 IU
VIT. E/TOTAL    Ã                                             NO RDA    2.290 Mg
VITAMIN C       Ã======                                         13%    8.210 Mg
THIAMIN         Ã=======                                        15%    0.150 Mg
RIBOFLAVIN      Ã=================                              35%    0.430 Mg
NIACIN          Ã===========                                    22%    2.860 Mg
VITAMIN B6      Ã====                                            9%    0.190 Mg
FOLACIN         Ã=====                                          10%    41.00 Ug
VITAMIN B12     Ã=======                                        14%    0.430 Ug
PANTO- ACID     Ã================                               32%    1.770 Mg
CALCIUM         Ã=====                                          10%    86.10 Mg
PHOSPHORUS      Ã================                               33%    268.0 Mg
TRYPTOPHAN      Ã====================================          108%    177.0 Mg
THREONINE       Ã====================================          133%    582.0 Mg
ISOLEUCINE      Ã====================================          113%    738.0 Mg
LEUCINE         Ã====================================          134%    1170  Mg
LYSINE          Ã====================================          152%    995.0 Mg
METHIONINE      Ã====================================          128%    350.0 Mg
CYSTINE         Ã============================                   56%    154.0 Mg
PHENYL-ANINE    Ã====================================          163%    711.0 Mg
TYROSINE        Ã====================================          134%    587.0 Mg
VALINE          Ã====================================          108%    828.0 Mg
HISTIDINE       Ã                                             NO RDA    418.0 Mg
ALCOHOL         Ã                                             NO RDA    0.000 Gm
ASH             Ã                                             NO RDA    2.500 Gm
COPPER          Ã=========                                      19%    0.480 Mg
MANGANESE       Ã===                                             7%    0.270 Mg
IODINE          Ã====================                           41%    62.60 Ug
MONO FAT        Ã                                             NO RDA    5.700 Gm
POLY FAT        Ã                                             NO RDA    1.970 Gm
CAFFEINE        Ã                                             NO RDA    0.000 Mg
FLUORIDE        Ã=                                               2%    70.40 Mg
MOLYBDENUM      Ã=============================                  59%    194.0 Ug
VITAMIN K       Ã                                                0%    0.880 Ug
SELENIUM        Ã============                                   24%    0.030 Mg
BIOTIN          Ã                                                1%    2.730 Ug
CHLORIDE        Ã                                                0%    6.350 Mg
CHROMIUM        Ã====================                           40%    0.050 Mg
SUGAR           Ã                                             NO RDA    1.530 Gm
FIBER-DIET      Ã                                             NO RDA    0.650 Gm
VIT. E/AT       Ã===                                             7%    0.630 Mg

      % RDA:   10      20      40      60      80      100
```

Margarine used instead of butter; onion used instead of celery and asafetida; Vegex Brewer's Yeast Extract not included in analysis.

# CASHEW BEARNAISE SAUCE

☆ This sauce is good served over the Nut Loaf or any other savory dish; it can also be used to uplift simple steamed vegetables, Fried Tofu (p. 26), etc.

---

¼ cup wine vinegar
¼ cup white wine
¼ cup finely diced celery and ¼ tsp. asafetida
   OR ¼ cup finely chopped scallions
1½ tsp. tarragon
½ tsp. Spike or other vegetable-seasoned salt
⅛ tsp. white pepper

2 Tbsp. butter or margarine

1 cup silken (Kinogoshi) tofu
¼ cup raw cashew butter

    Combine first 8 (or 7) ingredients in a small pot and simmer over a very low heat till liquid cooks down to 2 to 3 tablespoons. Add butter or margarine to the ingredients in pot to melt, and blend last 2 ingredients in a blender till smooth. Add ingredients in pot to blended tofu and blend a couple of seconds — only long enough to mix sauce ingredients evenly into tofu. Pour back into pot and heat through. Any leftovers are also good served cold as a salad dressing. Makes a little over 1 cup.

I don't know anyone who doesn't know what peanut butter is! But did you know that a butter can be made from any nut or seed? If you live close to a natural food store, you'll find a wide array of different nut and seed butters, both raw and roasted. If you can't find different kinds of nut butters on the natural food store shelves, ask for them or make them at home in your food processor.

| SHOPPING LIST | |
|---|---|
| **Regularly Kept in the Kitchen (Listed in Chapter 14, p. 703)** | **Fresh Produce** |
| Wine vinegar<br>Tarragon<br>Spike<br>White pepper<br>Butter or margarine<br>Raw cashew butter | White wine<br>Celery<br>Scallions |

| Special Shopping |
|---|
| Silken (Kinogoshi) tofu — found in Japanese groceries and some supermarkets alongside other tofus. |

# NUTRITIONAL ANALYSIS FOR ONE RECIPE
## CASHEW BEARNAISE SAUCE

| NUTRIENT | Type: 14 FEMALE-23 TO 51 YEARS | % RDA | Amount |
|---|---|---|---|
| KCALORIES | A========================= | 49% | 991.0 Kc |
| PROTEIN | A===================================================== | 120% | 52.90 Gm |
| CARBOHYDRATE | A | NO RDA | 41.70 Gm |
| FAT | A | NO RDA | 76.70 Gm |
| FIBER-CRUDE | A | NO RDA | 1.310 Gm |
| CHOLESTEROL | A | NO RDA | 0.000 Mg |
| SATURATED FA | A | NO RDA | 13.10 Gm |
| OLEIC FA | A | NO RDA | 2.520 Gm |
| LINOLEIC FA | A | NO RDA | 5.040 Gm |
| SODIUM | A=================== | 36% | 808.0 Mg |
| POTASSIUM | A================ | 32% | 1216 Mg |
| MAGNESIUM | A==================================================== | 108% | 324.0 Mg |
| IRON | A==================================================== | 173% | 31.20 Mg |
| ZINC | A======================== | 49% | 7.460 Mg |
| VITAMIN A | A=================== | 36% | 1456 IU |
| VITAMIN D | A | 0% | 0.000 IU |
| VIT. E/TOTAL | A | NO RDA | 0.010 Mg |
| VITAMIN C | A=== | 6% | 3.840 Mg |
| THIAMIN | A============================== | 63% | 0.630 Mg |
| RIBOFLAVIN | A================ | 35% | 0.430 Mg |
| NIACIN | A======== | 17% | 2.320 Mg |
| VITAMIN B6 | A========== | 20% | 0.400 Mg |
| FOLACIN | A============== | 29% | 117.0 Ug |
| VITAMIN B12 | A | 0% | 0.020 Ug |
| PANTO- ACID | A============ | 24% | 1.350 Mg |
| CALCIUM | A==================================================== | 226% | 1808 Mg |
| PHOSPHORUS | A==================================================== | 110% | 880.0 Mg |
| TRYPTOPHAN | A==================================================== | 497% | 811.0 Mg |
| THREONINE | A==================================================== | 484% | 2107 Mg |
| ISOLEUCINE | A==================================================== | 392% | 2564 Mg |
| LEUCINE | A==================================================== | 464% | 4047 Mg |
| LYSINE | A==================================================== | 503% | 3291 Mg |
| METHIONINE | A==================================================== | 267% | 728.0 Mg |
| CYSTINE | A==================================================== | 279% | 760.0 Mg |
| PHENYL-ANINE | A==================================================== | 589% | 2563 Mg |
| TYROSINE | A==================================================== | 392% | 1709 Mg |
| VALINE | A==================================================== | 371% | 2834 Mg |
| HISTIDINE | A | NO RDA | 1474 Mg |
| ALCOHOL | A | NO RDA | 0.000 Gm |
| ASH | A | NO RDA | 6.620 Gm |
| COPPER | A============================================= | 94% | 2.360 Mg |
| MANGANESE | A======================================= | 82% | 3.090 Mg |
| IODINE | A==================================================== | 218% | 327.0 Ug |
| MONO FAT | A | NO RDA | 34.10 Gm |
| POLY FAT | A | NO RDA | 25.20 Gm |
| CAFFEINE | A | NO RDA | 0.000 Mg |
| FLUORIDE | A | 0% | 9.950 Ug |
| MOLYBDENUM | A==================================================== | 930% | 3024 Ug |
| VITAMIN K | A | 0% | 0.000 Ug |
| SELENIUM | A================================ | 64% | 0.080 Mg |
| BIOTIN | A== | 5% | 7.640 Ug |
| CHLORIDE | A======= | 14% | 479.0 Mg |
| CHROMIUM | A==================================================== | 608% | 0.760 Mg |
| SUGAR | A | NO RDA | 0.000 Gm |
| FIBER-DIET | A | NO RDA | 0.000 Gm |
| VIT. E/AT | A | 1% | 0.080 Mg |

```
% RDA:   |0      |20     |40     |60     |80     |100
```

Scallions used instead of celery and asafetida; margarine used instead of butter; firm tofu used instead of silken (Kinogoshi) type in analysis.

# NUT LOAF

☆ Good served hot, topped with Cashew Bearnaise Sauce or Mock Turkey Gravy (p. 66); or cold on a tossed green salad bed topped with Au Gratin or Anything Sauce.

Although some natural food stores carry nut meal in their coolers, this is one item best made from scratch at home because the oils in the nut begin to turn rancid as soon as the nut is broken. It doesn't take that much effort . . .

---

2 cups raw almond meal
   (preferably from germinated nuts)
2 cups whole grain bread crumbs
3 Tbsp. Bipro
½ Tbsp. very finely grated lemon rind
2 tsp. Spike or other vegetable-seasoned salt
1 tsp. marjoram (1 Tbsp. if fresh)
1 tsp. basil (1 Tbsp. if fresh)
½ tsp. black pepper

1 Tbsp. butter or margarine
2 cups finely diced celery and ½ tsp. asafetida
   OR 2 cups finely diced onion

1 cup milk

1 Tbsp. olive oil
2 cups diced red bell pepper
½ cup diced zucchini
¼ cup chopped scallions
¼ cup parsley
¼ tsp. black pepper

1 cup grated sharp Cheddar cheese
1 Tbsp. lemon juice

   Preheat oven to 400 degrees and oil a 9" x 5" x 3" bread loaf pan. Combine first 8 ingredients in a bowl and mix thoroughly. Saute next 3 (or 2) ingredients in skillet till lightly browned and mix into mixture in bowl. Mix milk in till the mixture is evenly and thoroughly moistened. Divide in half and press half evenly in bottom of oiled loaf pan.

   Saute next 6 ingredients together till bell peppers become tender. Turn off heat and toss in next 2 ingredients. Pour on top of nut mixture in loaf pan and spread evenly. Top with remaining half of nut/bread mixture. Bake at 400 degrees for 40 to 50 minutes, till golden brown and crisp on the surface. Remove from oven and allow to sit at least 15 minutes before serving.

## NUT MEAL

Take raw or roasted, cooled nut of your choice and run in blender or food processor till they're chopped into a fine meal.

| SHOPPING LIST | |
|---|---|
| **Regularly Kept in the Kitchen** (Listed in Chapter 14, p. 703) | **Fresh Produce** |
| Almonds | Lemon |
| Whole grain bread | Celery or onion |
| Bipro | Red bell pepper |
| Spike | Zucchini |
| Marjoram | Scallions |
| Basil | Parsley |
| Black pepper | |
| Asafetida | |
| Lowfat milk | |
| Olive oil | |
| Sharp Cheddar cheese | |

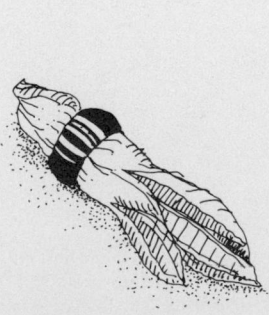

# NUTRITIONAL ANALYSIS FOR ONE SERVING NUT LOAF

```
NUTRIENT       Type: 14   FEMALE-23 TO 51 YEARS          % RDA   Amount
KCALORIES     A=====                                      11%    236.0 Kc
PROTEIN       A==================                         34%    15.30 Gm
CARBOHYDRATE  A                                        NO RDA    19.60 Gm
FAT           A                                        NO RDA    11.90 Gm
FIBER-CRUDE   A                                        NO RDA    1.230 Gm
CHOLESTEROL   A                                        NO RDA    13.70 Mg
SATURATED FA  A                                        NO RDA    3.470 Gm
OLEIC FA      A                                        NO RDA    1.930 Gm
LINOLEIC FA   A                                        NO RDA    0.190 Gm
SODIUM        A=======                                    15%    351.0 Mg
POTASSIUM     A=======                                    14%    557.0 Mg
MAGNESIUM     A====                                        9%    29.80 Mg
IRON          A========                                   17%    3.130 Mg
ZINC          A===                                         6%    0.910 Mg
VITAMIN A     A=====                                       11%    452.0 IU
VITAMIN D     A==                                          5%    10.20 IU
VIT. E/TOTAL  A                                        NO RDA    0.470 Mg
VITAMIN C     A==========================                 53%    32.20 Mg
THIAMIN       A========                                   17%    0.170 Mg
RIBOFLAVIN    A====================                       41%    0.500 Mg
NIACIN        A========                                   16%    2.130 Mg
VITAMIN B6    A===                                         7%    0.140 Mg
FOLACIN       A===                                         6%    25.30 Ug
VITAMIN B12   A===                                         6%    0.190 Ug
PANTO- ACID   A==                                          5%    0.320 Mg
CALCIUM       A===============                            30%    241.0 Mg
PHOSPHORUS    A=====================                      43%    347.0 Mg
TRYPTOPHAN    A=================================================  161%  264.0 Mg
THREONINE     A=================================================  132%  578.0 Mg
ISOLEUCINE    A=================================================  114%  745.0 Mg
LEUCINE       A=================================================  146%  1275  Mg
LYSINE        A=================================================  116%  762.0 Mg
METHIONINE    A===========================================        90%   247.0 Mg
CYSTINE       A=====================================              77%   212.0 Mg
PHENYL-ANINE  A=================================================  186%  813.0 Mg
TYROSINE      A=================================================  124%  540.0 Mg
VALINE        A=================================================  110%  841.0 Mg
HISTIDINE     A                                        NO RDA    400.0 Mg
ALCOHOL       A                                        NO RDA    0.000 Gm
ASH           A                                        NO RDA    2.770 Gm
COPPER        A=                                           3%    0.090 Mg
MANGANESE     A=                                           2%    0.080 Mg
IODINE        A========                                   17%    26.50 Ug
MONO FAT      A                                        NO RDA    5.410 Gm
POLY FAT      A                                        NO RDA    1.560 Gm
CAFFEINE      A                                        NO RDA    0.000 Mg
FLUORIDE      A                                           1%    39.10 Ug
MOLYBDENUM    A                                           0%    0.000 Ug
VITAMIN K     A                                           1%    1.420 Ug
SELENIUM      A====                                        8%    0.010 Mg
BIOTIN        A                                           0%    1.440 Ug
CHLORIDE      A                                           0%    0.000 Mg
CHROMIUM      A====                                        8%    0.010 Ug
SUGAR         A                                        NO RDA    2.620 Gm
FIBER-DIET    A                                        NO RDA    0.520 Gm
VIT. E/AT     A===                                         6%    0.540 Mg

   % RDA:  |0      |20     |40     |60     |80     |100
```

Margarine used instead of butter; onion used instead of celery and asafetida. Analysis does not include increase in nutrients which occurs if almond meal is made from germinated nuts.

# CAN BE SERVED RAW MIX

☆ Nuts are delicious raw, anyway; I certainly prefer mine that way! This mix makes a delicious raw loaf or burger patty that you don't have to worry about being raw in the center.

---

1 tsp. butter or margarine
½ cup diced celery and ½ tsp. asafetida
   OR ½ cup diced onion
1 cup chopped mushrooms
⅓ cup minced carrots

1¼ cups walnuts
⅓ cup hulled sunflower seeds
½ cup cooked garbanzos (preferably germinated)
2 Tbsp. wheat germ

⅔ cup cooked bulgur or brown rice
⅓ cup sesame seeds
2 Tbsp. nutritional yeast
8 sprigs fresh parsley
6 fresh basil leaves (large ones)
½ Tbsp. lemon juice
½ Tbsp. sesame tahini
½ tsp. miso
½ tsp. dried rosemary
½ tsp. ground cumin
¼ tsp. black pepper
¼ tsp. mint tea
¼ tsp. dried red pepper flakes

Combine first 5 (or 4) ingredients in a skillet and lightly saute till slightly tender; when done, turn off heat. In the meantime, run next 4 ingredients together in a blender, food processor or food mill (grinder) to form a meal (rough sand texture). Mix cooked, cooled vegetables and next 13 ingredients into nut meal and run in food processor a few more seconds, or run entire mix through a food mill. This can be patted into an oiled loaf pan and refrigerated to be served as a cool, raw loaf; excellent topped with a mild, creamy dressing. It can also be shaped into ½"-thick burger-sized patties and frozen with squares of wax paper between each patty. To make sandwiches or a warm entree, remove patties from freezer and fry over medium heat till browned on both sides. Smaller (2" diameter) patties can also be rolled in chopped nuts after shaping and served raw atop or alongside fresh salads. Makes 6 to 8 servings.

From the recipes so far, you may be thinking nuts must be cooked. On the contrary, they are quite delicious used raw — for savory or sweet dishes.

| SHOPPING LIST | | Special Shopping |
|---|---|---|
| **Regularly Kept in the Kitchen** (Listed in Chapter 14, p. 703) | **Fresh Produce** | Sesame tahini — found in natural food stores or Mid-Eastern food stores. Mint tea — found in natural food stores. |
| Butter or margarine<br>Asafetida<br>Walnuts<br>Sunflower seeds<br>Garbanzos<br>Wheat germ<br>Bulgar or brown rice<br>Sesame seeds<br>Nutritional yeast<br>Miso<br>Rosemary<br>Cumin<br>Black pepper<br>Red pepper flakes | Celery<br>Mushrooms<br>Carrots<br>Parsley<br>Basil leaves<br>Lemon | |

# NUTRITIONAL ANALYSIS FOR ONE SERVING
## CAN BE SERVED RAW MIX

| NUTRIENT | Type: 14   FEMALE-23 TO 51 YEARS | % RDA | Amount |
|---|---|---|---|
| KCALORIES | Ä====== | 12% | 258.0 Kc |
| PROTEIN | Ä============ | 24% | 10.60 Gm |
| CARBOHYDRATE | Ä | NO RDA | 16.40 Gm |
| FAT | Ä | NO RDA | 18.50 Gm |
| FIBER-CRUDE | Ä | NO RDA | 2.830 Gm |
| CHOLESTEROL | Ä | NO RDA | 0.000 Mg |
| SATURATED FA | Ä | NO RDA | 1.640 Gm |
| OLEIC FA | Ä | NO RDA | 3.180 Gm |
| LINOLEIC FA | Ä | NO RDA | 9.020 Gm |
| SODIUM | Ä | 1% | 25.80 Mg |
| POTASSIUM | Ä===== | 10% | 382.0 Mg |
| MAGNESIUM | Ä=================== | 37% | 111.0 Mg |
| IRON | Ä========= | 18% | 3.350 Mg |
| ZINC | Ä======== | 16% | 2.460 Mg |
| VITAMIN A | Ä=================== | 38% | 1553 IU |
| VITAMIN D | Ä | 0% | 0.520 IU |
| VIT. E/TOTAL | Ä | NO RDA | 9.340 Mg |
| VITAMIN C | Ä=== | 6% | 3.940 Mg |
| THIAMIN | Ä================================================= | 139% | 1.390 Mg |
| RIBOFLAVIN | Ä================================================= | 102% | 1.230 Mg |
| NIACIN | Ä============================== | 60% | 7.840 Mg |
| VITAMIN B6 | Ä================================ | 64% | 1.290 Mg |
| FOLACIN | Ä===== | 11% | 46.20 Ug |
| VITAMIN B12 | Ä============== | 29% | 0.870 Ug |
| PANTO- ACID | Ä===== | 10% | 0.580 Mg |
| CALCIUM | Ä======= | 15% | 122.0 Mg |
| PHOSPHORUS | Ä================= | 34% | 277.0 Mg |
| TRYPTOPHAN | Ä============================================= | 90% | 147.0 Mg |
| THREONINE | Ä=========================================== | 89% | 391.0 Mg |
| ISOLEUCINE | Ä==================================== | 71% | 468.0 Mg |
| LEUCINE | Ä=========================================== | 89% | 780.0 Mg |
| LYSINE | Ä==================================== | 72% | 473.0 Mg |
| METHIONINE | Ä======================================= | 79% | 215.0 Mg |
| CYSTINE | Ä=================================== | 69% | 190.0 Mg |
| PHENYL-ANINE | Ä========================================================= | 117% | 511.0 Mg |
| TYROSINE | Ä======================================= | 79% | 345.0 Mg |
| VALINE | Ä===================================== | 75% | 578.0 Mg |
| HISTIDINE | Ä | NO RDA | 309.0 Mg |
| ALCOHOL | Ä | NO RDA | 0.000 Gm |
| ASH | Ä | NO RDA | 2.790 Gm |
| COPPER | Ä========== | 21% | 0.540 Mg |
| MANGANESE | Ä===================== | 44% | 1.660 Mg |
| IODINE | Ä============== | 28% | 42.40 Ug |
| MONO FAT | Ä | NO RDA | 4.620 Gm |
| POLY FAT | Ä | NO RDA | 11.10 Gm |
| CAFFEINE | Ä | NO RDA | 0.000 Mg |
| FLUORIDE | Ä | 0% | 13.40 Ug |
| MOLYBDENUM | Ä========================== | 53% | 175.0 Ug |
| VITAMIN K | Ä | 0% | 0.000 Ug |
| SELENIUM | Ä | 0% | 0.000 Mg |
| BIOTIN | Ä=== | 7% | 10.80 Ug |
| CHLORIDE | Ä | 0% | 25.50 Mg |
| CHROMIUM | Ä======================= | 48% | 0.060 Mg |
| SUGAR | Ä | NO RDA | 0.820 Gm |
| FIBER-DIET | Ä | NO RDA | 1.640 Gm |
| VIT. E/AT | Ä===================== | 44% | 3.590 Mg |

```
% RDA:  |0      |20     |40     |60     |80     |100
```

Margarine used instead of butter; onion used instead of asafetida and celery; brown rice used instead of bulgur. Analysis uses cooked garbanzo beans which were not germinated.

# AN INDONESIAN DISH — FILIPINO STYLE

☆ Coconuts (and other palm relatives) are the only nuts that contain a saturated fat; so, like dairy products, limit your use of coconuts and coconut by-products to no more than once or twice a week.

---

*1 lb. Chinese firm tofu, cut in*
  *1" x 1" x ¼" cubes*
*Oil for deep-frying*

*¾ cup finely diced onion*
*1 tsp. asafetida or 2 cloves garlic, crushed*

*3 cups finely diced red bell pepper*

*5 oz. frozen spinach*
*2 cups cut string beans*
*3 cups coconut milk (fresh, frozen or canned)*
*1 (6 oz.) can tomato paste*
*1 Tbsp. soy sauce*
*2 tsp. fresh ginger root juice*
*2 tsp. honey*
*¼ tsp. black pepper*
*⅛ tsp. cayenne*

Heat oil for deep-frying till a cube of tofu sizzles and quickly rises to the surface. Drop all tofu into oil and deep-fry till golden brown, turning occasionally. Remove tofu from oil and put on paper towels to drain. Pour hot oil into a container (one that won't crack from the heat!).

With oil remaining on the surface of the wok (or pan), saute next 2 ingredients till onions become translucent. Add red bell pepper and saute till peppers get soft. Mix next 9 ingredients in thoroughly and simmer till beans are no longer crunchy. Serve as an entree over noodles or brown rice.

The following nut sauce makes use of an unstrained nut liquid. For a smoother nut milk, strain the pulp out as in the Almond Milk (p. 98) or homemade Coconut Milk (p. 129). Any nut or seed can be used to make a milk; nutritionally it's best to use soaked; lightly germinated nuts or seeds and the soaking water itself. The only nuts that won't benefit from this are whole, raw cashews (which are actually already cooked and therefore won't germinate), walnuts, pecans and coconuts (which would be impossible to soak and sprout in this fashion!). Nut milks can be used in any way cow milk is — as a beverage, in baking, puddings, etc.

| Special Shopping |
|---|
| Coconut milk — if not making your own, p. 129 (fresh coconuts are available in almost all fresh produce sections), you might be able to find canned coconut milk in grocery stores in the liquor department of some foreign food aisles; sometimes frozen coconut milk is carried in the freezer section. |

| SHOPPING LIST | |
|---|---|
| **Regularly Kept in the Kitchen (Listed in Chapter 14, p. 703)** | **Fresh Produce** |
| Tofu<br>Oil<br>Asafetida<br>Soy sauce<br>Honey<br>Black pepper<br>Cayenne | Onion<br>Spinach<br>String beans<br>Tomato paste<br>Ginger root |

# WARM ALMOND DRINK

1 cup nuts (preferably whole
    ones soaked overnight and
    sprouted a bit)
4 cups water (use water
    nuts were soaked in)
1 Tbsp. honey (optional)

Nutmeg

Make nut milk by blending first three ingredients together in a blender till smooth. After ingredients are blended, you can leave the pulp in for a smoothie-textured nut milk, or pour blended milk through a strainer to strain pulp out. (Pulp should be saved and frozen for use in vegetable loaves, baking, candies, etc.) Then place in a saucepan and warm over medium heat for 5 minutes. Serve with a dash of nutmeg. Makes 4 servings.

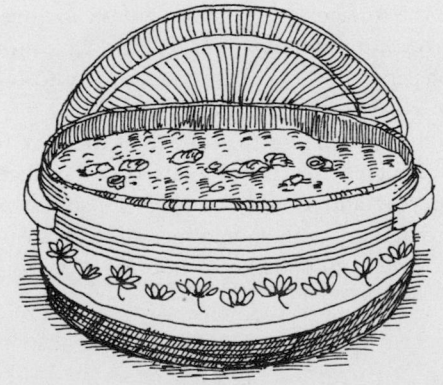

# NUTRITIONAL ANALYSIS FOR ONE SERVING OF
# AN INDONESIAN DISH — FILIPINO STYLE

```
NUTRIENT        Type: 14    FEMALE-23 TO 51 YEARS                  % RDA   Amount
KCALORIES       A========                                          17%    347.0 Kc
PROTEIN         A================                                  31%    13.70 Gm
CARBOHYDRATE    A                                                  NO RDA 20.20 Gm
FAT             A                                                  NO RDA 26.90 Gm
FIBER-CRUDE     A                                                  NO RDA 1.370 Gm
CHOLESTEROL     A                                                  NO RDA 0.000 Mg
SATURATED FA    A                                                  NO RDA 19.80 Gm
OLEIC FA        A                                                  NO RDA 0.560 Gm
LINOLEIC FA     A                                                  NO RDA 1.130 Gm
SODIUM          A====                                               8%    180.0 Mg
POTASSIUM       A============                                      22%    851.0 Mg
MAGNESIUM       A==================                                36%    110.0 Mg
IRON            A===========================                       53%    9.640 Mg
ZINC            A=======                                           13%    1.960 Mg
VITAMIN A       A===============================                   61%    2463 IU
VITAMIN D       A                                                   0%    0.000 IU
VIT. E/TOTAL    A                                                  NO RDA 0.580 Mg
VITAMIN C       A=========================================        113%    67.80 Mg
THIAMIN         A============                                      23%    0.230 Mg
RIBOFLAVIN      A=======                                           15%    0.190 Mg
NIACIN          A=========                                         17%    2.240 Mg
VITAMIN B6      A=======                                           14%    0.290 Mg
FOLACIN         A=======                                           15%    62.10 Ug
VITAMIN B12     A                                                   0%    0.000 Ug
PANTO- ACID     A===                                                6%    0.340 Mg
CALCIUM         A============================                      56%    452.0 Mg
PHOSPHORUS      A================                                  31%    255.0 Mg
TRYPTOPHAN      A==========================================       115%    189.0 Mg
THREONINE       A==========================================       119%    521.0 Mg
ISOLEUCINE      A====================================              92%    607.0 Mg
LEUCINE         A=========================================        109%    957.0 Mg
LYSINE          A==========================================       120%    789.0 Mg
METHIONINE      A=================================                 65%    179.0 Mg
CYSTINE         A==================================                69%    190.0 Mg
PHENYL-ANINE    A==========================================       142%    619.0 Mg
TYROSINE        A=========================================         95%    414.0 Mg
VALINE          A=====================================             88%    674.0 Mg
HISTIDINE       A                                                  NO RDA 354.0 Mg
ALCOHOL         A                                                  NO RDA 0.000 Gm
ASH             A                                                  NO RDA 3.180 Gm
COPPER          A=============                                     26%    0.670 Mg
MANGANESE       A=======================                           47%    1.790 Mg
IODINE          A====================                              41%    61.80 Ug
MONO FAT        A                                                  NO RDA 2.060 Gm
POLY FAT        A                                                  NO RDA 3.260 Gm
CAFFEINE        A                                                  NO RDA 0.000 Mg
FLUORIDE        A                                                   1%    29.00 Ug
MOLYBDENUM      A=================================================  210%    684.0 Ug
VITAMIN K       A=======                                           14%    15.70 Ug
SELENIUM        A                                                   0%    0.000 Mg
BIOTIN          A                                                   1%    2.940 Ug
CHLORIDE        A=                                                  3%    107.0 Mg
CHROMIUM        A=================================================  144%    0.180 Mg
SUGAR           A                                                  NO RDA 2.030 Gm
FIBER-DIET      A                                                  NO RDA 0.870 Gm
VIT. E/AT       A===                                                7%    0.630 Mg

   % RDA:   |0       |20      |40      |60      |80      |100
```

You don't always have to strain the pulp out (as in making nut milks) when blending soaked nuts or seeds with water. Leave the pulp in for a thicker drink, complete with all the healthy dietary fiber (as in the Breakfast Drink, p. 17). By adding even less water, you can get a fluffy mix that can be used in some ways to replace whipped cream.

# ALMOND FOOL

☆ The attractive, fruit-swirled desserts called "fools" are usually made with whipped cream, which we all know is loaded with saturated fat and cholesterol and contains hardly any nutritional value. This version, using blended almonds, offers much more nutrition without the "no-nos" of cholesterol and saturated fat.

☆ You can also make "fools" using Tofu Whipped Topping (p. 162) in place of the blended almond mixture.

---

⅔ cup raw almonds (or other nut)
1 cup water

1 Tbsp. honey
½ tsp. vanilla
⅛ tsp. cinnamon (optional)

Chilled, pureed fruit in season

Soak first 2 ingredients together for 24 hours or at least overnight. Put all of the nuts and ⅔ cup of soaking water in blender with next 2 (or 3) ingredients and blend till smooth and fluffy. Pour into bowl and refrigerate to chill.

This fluffy almond mixture can be used as is to top sliced fruit, pies, puddings, etc., or made into a "fool." To make a fool, puree enough fruit in the blender to equal about half the amount of fluffy almonds (sweeten with honey only if necessary) and chill in a separate bowl. At serving time, divide fluffy, blended almonds into serving bowls and spoon about half the amount of fruit puree on top. Fold the fruit puree into the blended almonds just enough to get a marbleized effect. Makes 4 servings.

| SHOPPING LIST | |
| --- | --- |
| Regularly Kept in the Kitchen (Listed in Chapter 14, p. 703) | Fresh Produce |
| Almonds<br>Honey<br>Vanilla<br>Cinnamon | Fruit of your choice |

# NUTRITIONAL ANALYSIS FOR ONE SERVING ALMOND FOOL

```
NUTRIENT        Type: 14    FEMALE-23 TO 51 YEARS                    % RDA   Amount
KCALORIES       A====                                                 9%    182.0 Kc
PROTEIN         A=====                                               11%     5.250 Gm
CARBOHYDRATE    A                                                  NO RDA   15.30 Gm
FAT             A                                                  NO RDA   12.60 Gm
FIBER-CRUDE     A                                                  NO RDA    1.120 Gm
CHOLESTEROL     A                                                  NO RDA    0.000 Mg
SATURATED FA    A                                                  NO RDA    1.180 Gm
OLEIC FA        A                                                  NO RDA    0.000 Gm
LINOLEIC FA     A                                                  NO RDA    0.000 Gm
SODIUM          A                                                    0%      4.410 Mg
POTASSIUM       A====                                                8%    324.0 Mg
MAGNESIUM       A==============                                     26%     79.90 Mg
IRON            A===                                                 6%      1.230 Mg
ZINC            A==                                                  5%      0.810 Mg
VITAMIN A       A                                                    0%     24.60 IU
VITAMIN D       A                                                    0%      0.000 IU
VIT. E/TOTAL    A                                                  NO RDA    0.230 Mg
VITAMIN C       A=========================================         84%     50.90 Mg
THIAMIN         A===                                                 6%      0.060 Mg
RIBOFLAVIN      A==========                                         20%      0.240 Mg
NIACIN          A===                                                 7%      1.020 Mg
VITAMIN B6      A==                                                  4%      0.080 Mg
FOLACIN         A===                                                 7%     29.70 Ug
VITAMIN B12     A                                                    0%      0.000 Ug
PANTO- ACID     A===                                                 7%      0.420 Mg
CALCIUM         A====                                                9%     76.20 Mg
PHOSPHORUS      A========                                           17%    139.0 Mg.
TRYPTOPHAN      A=============================                      55%     90.50 Mg
THREONINE       A=====================                              43%    191.0 Mg
ISOLEUCINE      A================                                   33%    217.0 Mg
LEUCINE         A======================                             45%    393.0 Mg
LYSINE          A=============                                      27%    179.0 Mg
METHIONINE      A=========                                          19%     54.20 Mg
CYSTINE         A================                                   32%     88.70 Mg
PHENYL-ANINE    A================================                   64%    279.0 Mg
TYROSINE        A====================                               42%    185.0 Mg
VALINE          A================                                   33%    259.0 Mg
HISTIDINE       A                                                  NO RDA  142.0 Mg
ALCOHOL         A                                                  NO RDA    0.000 Gm
ASH             A                                                  NO RDA    1.090 Gm
COPPER          A=====                                              10%      0.270 Mg
MANGANESE       A==========                                         21%      0.790 Mg
IODINE          A                                                    0%      0.000 Ug
MONO FAT        A                                                  NO RDA    8.050 Gm
POLY FAT        A                                                  NO RDA    2.760 Gm
CAFFEINE        A                                                  NO RDA    0.000 Gm
FLUORIDE        A                                                    0%     21.30 Ug
MOLYBDENUM      A=                                                   3%     12.00 Ug
VITAMIN K       A                                                    0%      0.000 Ug
SELENIUM        A                                                    0%      0.000 Mg
BIOTIN          A                                                    0%      0.980 Ug
CHLORIDE        A                                                    0%      1.120 Mg
CHROMIUM        A                                                    0%      0.000 Mg
SUGAR           A                                                  NO RDA    4.660 Gm
FIBER-DIET      A                                                  NO RDA    1.700 Gm
VIT. E/AT       A                                                    1%      0.100 Mg

    % RDA:   |0      |20     |40     |60     |80     |100
```

Pureed fruit used in analysis: strawberries.

# CHAPTER 11

# FOCUS ON VEGETABLES

All of us have heard — whether from our mothers, the U.S. Senate "Dietary Goals" report, or anyone else wishing us good health — that we should eat more vegetables. While vegetables are a source of a great variety of nutrients (each vegetable providing different ones and amounts), they are also naturally slimming foods.

Generally speaking, vegetables contain very few calories because they provide very little fat and little to fair amounts of protein (mostly incomplete protein), while contributing a wealth of vitamins, minerals, and sometimes enzymes that must be present for the body to properly metabolize proteins, carbohydrates and fats. Some vegetables contain more fiber than others, but — as we've already discussed — the presence of dietary fiber in vegetables can help to keep you slim by making you chew (p. 199) and filling your stomach with bulk that passes through the digestive tract. Dietary fiber is never converted to fat, and actually helps remove fat from the system.

I've provided some recipes here for vegetables, but have not come close to giving a recipe for all the different kinds of vegetables that exist or that we like to use. Rather, I've chosen these recipes to give you ideas of healthy preparation techniques.

# VEGETABLES, VEGETABLES, RAW! RAW! RAW!

It's easy to turn just about any nut, seed or legume into a vegetable through sprouting. Since growing and eating sprouts is something everyone can do and benefit from, I've exerpted the following instructions on how to grow sprouts from my first book, *Kathy Cooks . . . Naturally*.

Fortunately, one thing everyone can do is grow sprouts. Whether we live in condominiums, suburban houses, or have our own homesteads, growing sprouts is one easy way to become more self-sufficient for our food needs.

Sprouting is a foolproof way of gardening. You don't have to worry about warding off garden pests with sprays, etc. The result is cheap, organic, vital, fresh vegetables at your fingertips. No more paying high prices for lettuce or cabbage on supermarket shelves — food which has been sprayed with chemicals and has lost much of its nutritional value between the time of harvest and appearance on the supermarket shelf.

I would like to utilize the space available to give you the simple how-to's of sprouting and the benefits you can experience in your own life (the test of pudding is in the eating!).

Just about any whole seed, grain, nut or legume can be sprouted. One warning: when buying your seeds, be sure to get seeds that have not been treated with chemicals. Heat-treated and/or broken seeds will not sprout. Hulled seeds will not always sprout because they may be broken or bruised. Pick out all broken or shriveled seeds, for they will not sprout but may rot and ruin the whole batch.

Certain seeds and all nuts are better germinated (grown only till sprout emerges from seed — no longer than a half-inch) than actually sprouted.

**Nuts and seeds to be germinated only:**

| | |
|---|---|
| Wheatberries | Hulled sunflower seeds |
| Lentils | Corn |
| Garbanzos and all legumes | Pumpkin seeds |
| Almonds | Squash seeds |
| Hazelnuts | Sesame seeds |
| Peanuts | |

Some people like to keep things in their lives very shallow and superficial, surrounding themselves with a constant barrage of sights and sounds and things to do to fill in any quiet spaces that might give deep thoughts, doubts and questions a chance to pop up. It takes a certain amount of faith to inquire into the deeper meaning in life. The nature of this faith is described by Ralph Waldo Emerson:

"Undoubtedly we have no questions to ask which are unanswerable. We must trust the perfection of creation so far as to believe that whatever curiosity the Order of things has awakened in our minds, the Order of things can satisfy."

## SUGGESTED MENU FOR A SPROUTED FOOD MEAL

*Pineapple Wheatgrass Cooler*

*Special Packages with Mock Peking Duck Sauce (p. 90)*

*Sprouted Lentil Loaf Patties on salad bed with Au Gratin or Anything Sauce (p. 559)*

*Carrot Surprise or Carrot Ice Cream Float*

Germinating does so much for increasing nutritional value. For example, about 10 percent of the nutritional value is digestible when nuts are eaten raw. Soaking overnight increases the digestibility to 20 percent; when made into nut or seed milk, to 40 percent.

All you need to do is soak your seeds or nuts overnight. The following morning, drain off the water. (This is full of nutrients, so don't throw it away. It can be used for making nut or seed milk or used in salad dressing, etc.) Then just follow directions for the soiless sprouting method. The nutritional value of your nuts or seeds will double after sprouting for two days rather than using them immediately after overnight soaking.

There are basically two methods of sprouting — soiless and with soil. The first step for both is the same: soak seeds in enough water to cover overnight. You can save the water from soaking all seeds and nuts for use in nut milk smoothies, and all the water from wheat for rejuvelac — a very healthful drink. But the water from the legumes must be cooked before using.

### Soiless Method
(4 to 5 days sprouting time)

You will need —
- jar (wide mouth)
- plastic screen or thin cotton gauze
- strong rubber band
- seeds to be sprouted

### Seeds that do especially well with this method:
(amount per quart)

| | | | |
|---|---|---|---|
| Radish | 1½ Tbsp. | Cress | 1½ Tbsp. |
| Alfalfa | 1½ Tbsp. | Mustard | 1½ Tbsp. |
| Mung bean | ½ cup | Fenugreek | 1½ Tbsp. |
| Adzuki | ½ cup | Soybeans | ½ cup |

*Step 1:* Drain soaking water from seeds through the screen. Keep water either for drinking or to water plants. Rinse seeds well.

*Step 2:* Turn jar upside down in a dish drainer, wire stand or specially made sprout stand so excess water can drain out and fresh air can get to the seeds, and put in a dark, warm place.

*Step 3:* Rinse seeds through the screen two to four times a day. Keep the jar upside down; gently shake seeds evenly to distribute around walls of jar.

*Step 4:* After four to five days, or when sprouts are one to two inches long, put sprouts in the sun for a couple of hours to develop a bright green color, vitamin A and chlorophyll. All large beans, like soybeans and garbanzos, should be steamed or cooked for 10 to 15 minutes (unsprouted takes hours) before eating.

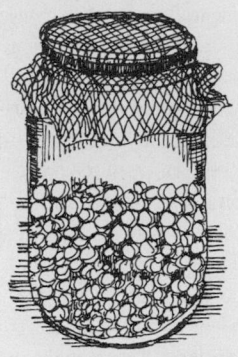

## With Soil Method
(1-week sprouting time)

You will need —
• 12" x 22" trays (the types of trays used in nurseries to grow and sell squares of lawn or ground cover)
• enough soil and peat moss (mixed together) to fill each tray halfway
• seeds for sprouting

### Seeds that do well in soil:
(amount per tray)

Unhulled buckwheat.............................................2 cups
Wheatberries.......................................................2 cups
Unhulled sunflower seeds...................................3 cups

*Step 1:* (the same as soiless sprouts)
*Step 2:* (the same as soiless sprouts)
*Step 3:* Let sprout one night in jar.
*Step 4:* Fill trays halfway with soil and peat moss mixture. Spread sprouted seeds evenly on smoothed out dirt which is damp but still crumbly (seeds should touch but not be on top of each other). Spread all the way to the edges.
*Step 5:* Water enough to keep soil moist. Don't over-water!

Wheatgrass is ready to eat when it is eight inches high. Cut with scissors just above the ground. Let it grow up again, cut, eat and start procedure again. Soil can be composted by putting in a special corner of your garden or in a trash can and left till all the roots die and compost — about three weeks. Soil is then ready to be used again. These trays can be grown on a balcony or lanai, a backyard, garage, or even inside your apartment. Sunflower and buckwheat only grow up once and are ready when the hulls fall off. Cut with scissors and use in a salad. You can cut these over a week's time. After a week, extra sprouts can be put in airtight containers in the refrigerator. They will keep a few days if properly covered.

The healthiest cooking technique to use on most vegetables (and fruit) is not cooking at all! Since cooking destroys so many of the valuable vitamins and enzymes that these foods have to offer, I like to serve mine raw as often as possible. The way I most commonly serve raw vegetables is as salads, which make up a third to a half of two of our daily meals.

I try to make our salads an interesting and varying mixture

"If the food value of germinated seeds is to be judged by their content of vitamins and readily available amino acids, then it appears the common use of sprouts in the diets of Oriental peoples rests on sound nutritional basis and should be introduced on a wide scale among Occidentals."
— Burkholder and McVeigh
"The Increase of B-vitamins in Germinating Seeds"
Proc. National Academy of Science #28

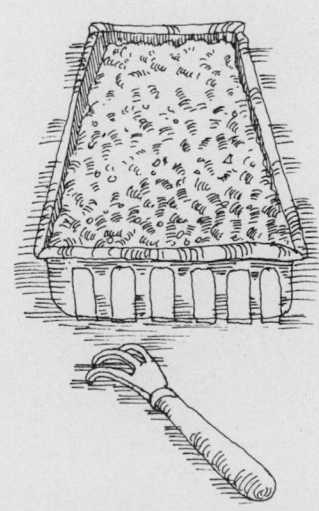

of different vegetables, but the one kind of vegetable I always include are sprouts. Sprouting seeds isn't a recent invention of the 60's hippies. Through ancient writings, we know that sprouts have been around for at least 4,800 years. It's a testimony to the health benefits of sprouts that the first written records about sprouts from both the East and West are in reference to using sprouts as a medicine.

Many Chinese classical herbal books recommend bean sprouts for treating maladies ranging from rheumatism, muscle cramps, digestive disorders, weakness of the lungs, to rough and spotted skin or damaged hair. Often quoting the *Classical Work on Herbal Medicines of Emperor Shen Nung*, these books date back to the 28th century B.C. Given this background and the extensive trade that took place between Western Europe and China, it's not surprising that the first book on the use of sprouts in Europe was also medicinal.

In the mid-1700's, the first European writing on using sprouts to prevent scurvy (caused by a vitamin C deficiency), by Dr. David McBride, impressed Britain's Captain Cook so much that he followed Dr. McBride's speculated program to a "T" on his journeys. Dr. McBride's prescription for preventing or curing scurvy was for each person to drink a daily dose of "wort." The wort drink consisted of one part malt powder (sprouted barley — dehydrated at temperatures not exceeding 140 degrees — which was ground to a powder) steeped like tea in three parts water.

In a time when scurvy was killing sailors in epidemic proportions (in the British Navy, one sailor in seven died of scurvy), Captain Cook's voyages set an ideal record! Not a single death from scurvy occurred in either of his two voyages, each of which lasted three years. For this, the Royal Society of London presented Captain Cook with their highest award, the Copley Medal, in 1776.

Instead of powdered sprouts, those of us land-bound today can easily grow our own sprouts in kitchen gardens, and through present-day nutritional information can understand why sprouts worked for Captain Cook and will work for us! Sprouts prevented and cured scurvy because they are a concentrated source of vitamin C. The seed manufacturing its own vitamin C is only one of the chemical changes that takes place during the sprouting process (see p. 471) that our bodies benefit from.

The nutritional content of sprouts varies a great deal, depending on the kind of sprout and what stage of maturity it is at. However, it is safe to say that all sprouts contain lots of enzymes (which pre-digest the protein in the sprouted seed and aid digestion in general), protein already broken down into amino acids, vitamin C and vitamin B-complex. No wonder people in China, Japan, Korea, India, Indonesia and the Philippines have used sprouts in their diets for hundreds of years!

The cuisine of these countries is a good place to look for recipes using sprouts. Following are some non-ethnic recipe ideas for using sprouts. The recipes are put together as if they are all to be served in one entirely sprouted food meal, but you can use each recipe separately as a single dish on another menu.

# PINEAPPLE WHEATGRASS COOLER

☆ An example of the kind of drink wheatgrass (raised in dirt, p. 530) can be incorporated in so a daily dose of wheatgrass can be taken palatably.

---

*1 pineapple, peeled, cored and chopped*
*1 cup ice cold water*
*½ cup wheatgrass, chopped*

Place in blender and blend till wheatgrass is blended. Pour liquid into muslin cloth over strainer and squeeze all the liquid out into a container, discard the pulp and serve your cocktails, full of chlorophyll and citric acid, in tall, chilled glasses. Makes 4 servings.

This cooler is best served ½ to 1 hour before a meal.

Probably because of the rarity of the fruit, pineapples were once reserved only for the royalty in Hawaii. About the only good thing I can think of that comes from modern agri-business in Hawaii and tropical Third World countries is the fact that pineapples are now more abundantly available. Besides being a good souce of manganese and citric acid, pine-apples also contain bromelin, a digestive enzyme which will, of course, aid digestion! Although there isn't much nutritional data from laboratories on wheatgrass, it's an element some (especially the Hippocrates Health Institute) credit with purifying and healing the body. Although I personally have never had an illness to test it out on, the theory is certainly logical, observing how many animals instinctively eat grass when sick.

| SHOPPING LIST | |
|---|---|
| **Regularly Kept in the Kitchen** (Listed in Chapter 14, p. 703) | **Fresh Produce** |
| (None) | Pineapple |

| Special Shopping |
|---|
| Wheatgrass — possibly found in a very well-stocked natural food store, but it's preferable to grow your own at home (p. 530) because it's usually sold already cut. Cutting your homegrown wheatgrass just before using ensures the freshest wheatgrass possible. |

# SPECIAL PACKAGES

☆ An all raw dish, using hulled sunflower seed sprouts and mung bean sprouts.

---

## SUGGESTED MENU FOR A DELIGHTFUL CHINESE MEAL

*Hot and Sour Soup (p. 95)*

*Special Packages*

*Brown rice*

*Japanese Bean Confection (p. 473)*

Lettuce leaves make a low-calorie, crispy and refreshing replacement for wheat or corn tortillas. Filling lettuce leaves for a light, refreshing dish can also be found in Indonesian and Greek cooking. The sauce and food used for filling can be varied so much that each dish can be made completely different. This Chinese-tasting version can be served with a menu like the above.

*⅔ cup finely minced Pressed Tofu (see p. 112)*
*½ cup finely minced, hulled sunflower seed sprouts (¼"-long sprouts)*
*½ cup finely minced jicima or water chestnuts*
*⅓ cup sesame seeds*
*¼ cup finely minced carrot*
*¼ cup coarsely chopped pine nuts*
*¼ cup finely minced celery*
*2 Tbsp. finely chopped, soaked seaweed*
*2 soaked shiitake mushrooms, finely minced*
*2 Tbsp. finely chopped scallions*
*2 tsp. finely chopped, fresh cilantro*
*2 tsp. soy sauce*
*2 tsp. toasted sesame oil*
*½ tsp. honey*
*⅛ tsp. white pepper*

*2 cups mung bean sprouts*

*Whole, crisp lettuce leaves*
*Mock Peking Duck Sauce (see p. 90)*

Toss first 15 ingredients together thoroughly. Set on top of bed of mung bean sprouts. Put washed, whole lettuce leaves in a large serving platter or bowl and Mock Peking Duck Sauce in a separate bowl. To serve, spread some Mock Peking Duck Sauce on a lettuce leaf and spoon some of the mixture onto the leaf. Fold the leaf up taco-style or roll it around filling. Hold it and eat; then build another one. Makes 6 to 8 servings.

| Special Shopping |
|---|
| Pressed tofu — found in Chinese groceries, some natural food stores, or make your own at home (p. 112). Hulled sunflower seed sprouts — possibly in very well-stocked natural food stores, but most likely you'll have to sprout your own (pp. 528 — 529). |

| SHOPPING LIST | |
|---|---|
| **Regularly Kept in the Kitchen (Listed in Chapter 14, p. 703)** | **Fresh Produce** |
| Sesame seeds<br>Pine nuts<br>Seaweed<br>Shiitake mushrooms<br>Soy sauce<br>Toasted sesame oil<br>Honey<br>White pepper | Jicima or water chestnuts<br>Carrot<br>Celery<br>Scallions<br>Cilantro (also called Chinese parsley or coriander leaves)<br>Mung bean sprouts<br>Lettuce |

Also see ingredients for Mock Peking Duck Sauce (p. 90).

# SPROUTED LENTIL LOAF

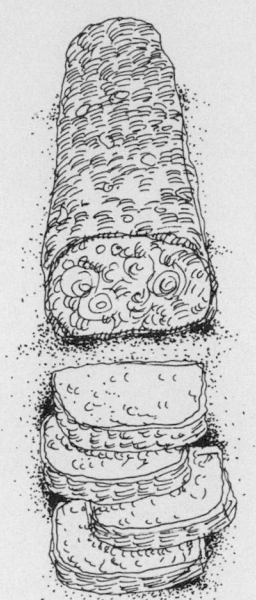

2 cups lentil sprouts (about ¼" long)
1 cup garden fresh or frozen, thawed corn kernels
½ cup diced celery
½ cup hulled sunflower seed sprouts
    (about ¼" long)
¼ cup chopped scallions

2 Tbsp. flaxseed meal
1 Tbsp. soy sauce
4 tsp. nutritional yeast

Run first 5 ingredients together in a food processor or food grinder till finely ground. Mix in last 3 ingredients thoroughly and allow mixture to sit about 5 minutes to give flaxseed meal a chance to solidify the mixture. Form into a loaf or large or small patties. Refrigerate about 1 hour before serving.

Serve slices of loaf with Au Gratin or Anything Sauce; or put patties on whole grain crackers or bread dressed with tomatoes, alfalfa sprouts and other desired vegetables; or serve on a bed of salad. Serves 4 to 6.

| SHOPPING LIST | |
| --- | --- |
| **Regularly Kept in the Kitchen** (Listed in Chapter 14, p. 703) | **Fresh Produce** |
| Soy sauce<br>Nutritional yeast | Garden fresh or frozen corn<br>Celery<br>Scallions |

| Special Shopping |
| --- |
| Lentil and hulled sunflower seed sprouts — possibly in very well-stocked natural food stores, but most likely you'll have to sprout your own.<br>Flaxseed meal — flaxseeds can be bought in natural food stores. Make a meal by running in a blender till ground to a powder. |

# CARROT ICE CREAM FLOAT

☆ Another way to use carrots for dessert.

1 glass freshly made carrot juice
2 scoops honey vanilla ice cream

Make fresh carrot juice in juicer. Pour into glass and drop scoops of ice cream into carrot juice.

When getting carrots for carrot juice or carrot dessert — or any time, really — be sure to get sweet carrots. I have found some carrots have a very bitter, disagreeable flavor.

# CARROT SURPRISE

☆ Vegetables can even be used to make dessert!

---

*2 cups ground carrots (about 1 lb.)*
*¾ cup date paste*
*½ cup ground, sprouted wheatberries or crumbled*
*    Sweet Essene Bread (see recipe, p. 390)*

*½ cup raw wheat germ*
*¼ cup raw cashew butter*
*¼ cup raisins*
*¼ cup sliced almonds*
*3 Tbsp. lemon juice*
*1 Tbsp. chia seeds*
*1 tsp. vanilla*
*¼ tsp. finely grated lemon rind*

Grind first 3 ingredients by running through a food grinder or Champion Juicer (with the solid attachment in; not the one with the holes in it); if using Essene bread instead of sprouted wheatberries, just crumble with fingertips — there's no need to run it through the grinder. Add next 8 ingredients and mix in thoroughly. Shape into desired shape — a large loaf or cake shape, or individual servings shaped in separate dessert bowls or platters. Cover and refrigerate for 2 to 3 hours before serving, till thoroughly chilled through. Serve by topping with a dollop of vanilla yogurt or an "icing" made of ¼ cup raw sesame tahini, 2 Tbsp. honey, 1 Tbsp. water, ⅛ tsp. vanilla. Makes 8 to 12 servings.

| Special Shopping |
| --- |
| Wheatberry sprouts or Essene bread — you'll probably have to grow your own wheatberry sprouts (p. 19) from wheatberries obtained in natural food stores. I find it easier to use Essene bread, which can be found in natural food stores or made at home (p. 390). |
| Chia seeds — found in natural food stores. |

| SHOPPING LIST | |
| --- | --- |
| **Regularly Kept in the Kitchen** (Listed in Chapter 14, p. 703) | **Fresh Produce** |
| Dates | Carrots |
| Wheat germ | Lemon |
| Cashew butter | |
| Raisins | |
| Sliced almonds | |
| Vanilla | |

# NUTRITIONAL ANALYSIS FOR ONE SERVING CARROT SURPRISE

| NUTRIENT | Type: 14   FEMALE—23 TO 51 YEARS | % RDA | Amount |
|---|---|---|---|
| KCALORIES | Ř====== | 12% | 252.0 Kc |
| PROTEIN | Ř====== | 13% | 5.870 Gm |
| CARBOHYDRATE | Ř | NO RDA | 47.10 Gm |
| FAT | Ř | NO RDA | 7.060 Gm |
| FIBER—CRUDE | Ř | NO RDA | 2.150 Gm |
| CHOLESTEROL | Ř | NO RDA | 0.000 Mg |
| SATURATED FA | Ř | NO RDA | 1.210 Gm |
| OLEIC FA | Ř | NO RDA | 1.460 Gm |
| LINOLEIC FA | Ř | NO RDA | 0.680 Gm |
| SODIUM | Ř | 0% | 21.80 Mg |
| POTASSIUM | Ř======== | 16% | 628.0 Mg |
| MAGNESIUM | Ř============ | 25% | 77.60 Mg |
| IRON | Ř===== | 11% | 2.120 Mg |
| ZINC | Ř====== | 13% | 1.980 Mg |
| VITAMIN A | Ř=================================================== | 399% | 15982 IU |
| VITAMIN D | Ř | 1% | 2.110 IU |
| VIT. E/TOTAL | Ř | NO RDA | 2.750 Mg |
| VITAMIN C | Ř======= | 14% | 8.570 Mg |
| THIAMIN | Ř============ | 26% | 0.260 Mg |
| RIBOFLAVIN | Ř======= | 14% | 0.170 Mg |
| NIACIN | Ř======== | 16% | 2.170 Mg |
| VITAMIN B6 | Ř====== | 13% | 0.270 Mg |
| FOLACIN | Ř===== | 11% | 46.20 Ug |
| VITAMIN B12 | Ř | 0% | 0.000 Ug |
| PANTO- ACID | Ř===== | 11% | 0.650 Mg |
| CALCIUM | Ř=== | 6% | 53.00 Mg |
| PHOSPHORUS | Ř=========== | 23% | 187.0 Mg |
| TRYPTOPHAN | Ř======================= | 49% | 81.10 Mg |
| THREONINE | Ř========================= | 51% | 226.0 Mg |
| ISOLEUCINE | Ř================= | 37% | 245.0 Mg |
| LEUCINE | Ř======================= | 46% | 408.0 Mg |
| LYSINE | Ř========================= | 50% | 329.0 Mg |
| METHIONINE | Ř================ | 34% | 94.90 Mg |
| CYSTINE | Ř================= | 37% | 102.0 Mg |
| PHENYL—ANINE | Ř============================= | 60% | 261.0 Mg |
| TYROSINE | Ř================= | 37% | 161.0 Mg |
| VALINE | Ř==================== | 41% | 318.0 Mg |
| HISTIDINE | Ř | NO RDA | 169.0 Mg |
| ALCOHOL | Ř | NO RDA | 0.000 Gm |
| ASH | Ř | NO RDA | 1.930 Gm |
| COPPER | Ř======== | 17% | 0.430 Mg |
| MANGANESE | Ř================= | 36% | 1.350 Mg |
| IODINE | Ř======= | 14% | 22.30 Ug |
| MONO FAT | Ř | NO RDA | 3.660 Gm |
| POLY FAT | Ř | NO RDA | 1.620 Gm |
| CAFFEINE | Ř | NO RDA | 0.000 Mg |
| FLUORIDE | Ř | 1% | 42.80 Ug |
| MOLYBDENUM | Ř===================================== | 75% | 245.0 Ug |
| VITAMIN K | Ř | 0% | 0.000 Ug |
| SELENIUM | Ř | 0% | 0.000 Mg |
| BIOTIN | Ř= | 2% | 4.220 Ug |
| CHLORIDE | Ř | 0% | 15.50 Mg |
| CHROMIUM | Ř======== | 16% | 0.020 Mg |
| SUGAR | Ř | NO RDA | 29.80 Gm |
| FIBER—DIET | Ř | NO RDA | 4.820 Gm |
| VIT. E/AT | Ř============ | 26% | 2.080 Mg |

```
% RDA:  ┌0      ┌20     ┌40     ┌60     ┌80     ┌100
```

Due to lack of data, analysis does not include ground, sprouted wheatberries.

# SALAD MEALS

The philosopher Epictetus wrote in *Enchorendean* — "Never say about anything: 'I have lost it,' but only, 'I have given it back.' Is your child dead? It has been given back. Is your wife dead? She has been given back. 'I have lost my farm and had it taken away.' Very well, this too has been given back. 'Yet it was a rascal who took it away.' But what concern is it of yours by whose instrumentality the Giver called for its return. So long as He gives it to you, take care of it as a thing that is not your own, just as travelers treat their inn."

Nice, fresh, crisp and juicy salads are my favorite kind of food! And nothing can match a salad made with vegetables just picked from the garden! Anyone who has ever had the pleasure of eating anything fresh from the garden knows what I'm talking about. Garden fresh vegetables taste completely different from the ones on supermarket shelves and are different in nutrition as well. As soon as a vegetable is picked, its vitamin content begins to deteriorate, even if refrigerated. Since the vegetables in supermarkets have been picked, trucked to a wholesaler who refrigerates the produce till a retail market buys them, where they sit in the cooler till there's room on the shelf — they usually have lost quite a bit by the time they're prepared at home. The ideal is to have your own backyard, organic garden so you can control what is applied to the plants you'll be eating, and also enrich the soil, which will in turn give you more mineral-rich produce. (There are many excellent books on organic gardening, especially the ones put out by the Rodale press.)

Whether from the garden or supermarket, I've been making vegetable salads at least once a day (sometimes twice) every day for 18 years. Two of the three meals a day are usually a legume and whole grain entree accompanied by a fresh tossed salad . . . but salads don't always have to be accompaniments. I often make salads as the whole meal. This doesn't mean I make my family live on lettuce leaves. By putting some more substantial and nutritious items together with vegetables usually used in salads, I'm able to serve nutritious and satisfying salad meals. Here are some of our favorites.

# HERBED CROUTONS

☆ Tasty herbed croutons that are a plus added to any soup or salad.

We try never to waste anything. Bread ends or stale bread can be used to make these croutons.

1½ tsp. dry parsley
¼ tsp. rubbed sage
¼ tsp. asafetida or garlic powder
¼ tsp. marjoram
½ tsp. basil
½ tsp. thyme
½ tsp. dill leaves
⅛ tsp. black pepper

2 Tbsp. olive oil

4 cups whole grain ½" bread cubes

Mix first 8 ingredients in a little bowl. Put oil in a skillet with herbs and mix herbs into oil completely. Pour cubes of stale whole grain bread into skillet and stir very quickly so bread becomes evenly coated with oil and herbs. Turn heat to simmer and leave it on while assembling the rest of the salad, being sure to stir every few minutes. Croutons are done when crisp and dry. Another way to dry and crisp the croutons is to bake on the lowest heat in the oven for 4 to 6 hours. If you are going to use the oven heat in this way, you may want to multiply the recipe 4 to 6 times and freeze or store the extra croutons for future use in soups or salads.

| SHOPPING LIST | |
|---|---|
| **Regularly Kept in the Kitchen** (Listed in Chapter 14, p. 703) | **Fresh Produce** |
| Parsley flakes<br>Sage<br>Asafetida<br>Marjoram<br>Basil<br>Thyme<br>Dill<br>Black pepper<br>Olive oil<br>Whole grain bread | (None) |

# CAESAR SALAD

☆ The "silken" (Kinogoshi) tofu used instead of the usual soft-boiled egg closely resembles the texture of one; if you can't find "silken" tofu, try to get the softest tofu possible.

---

*1 large head chilled Romaine lettuce*

*¼ cup olive oil*
*1 tsp. asafetida or 1 clove garlic*
*½ tsp. honey*
*½ tsp. black pepper*
*Shake of Tabasco or pinch cayenne pepper*

*¼ cup lemon juice*
*¼ block silken tofu (about ½ cup mashed)*

*1 recipe worth of Herbed Croutons*
   *(see previous recipe)*
*⅓ cup Parmesan cheese*
*¼ cup rinsed capers*

Rinse Romaine lettuce and tear into pieces as large as the inner leaves. (Do not tear into bite-sized pieces, as Caesar Salad is a salad traditionally served with a fork and knife. The larger leaf pieces also do not wilt down as quickly as small ones would once the dressing is applied.) Spin lettuce in a lettuce spinner or place on a tea towel to drain excess water. Combine next 5 ingredients together in a bowl. If you use garlic instead of the asafetida, you should crush the garlic clove and allow it to sit in the oil overnight. Before assembling the salad, strain out the garlic clove and add the rest of the flavorings. Pour the flavored oil over the lettuce leaves and toss gently till all leaves are evenly coated. Quickly blend the next 2 ingredients together in a blender and pour over lettuce. Toss in last 3 ingredients and serve immediately. Makes 4 to 6 servings if served as a whole meal salad with heated whole grain garlic bread.

If you've ever ordered this famous salad in your favorite restaurant, you've probably had them come and make a big production of tossing a softly boiled egg for a dressing right at the table. This recipe uses a "silken" tofu instead to avoid the cholesterol and slime of eggs. Getting in the habit of tossing dressings in at the last minute assures nice, crisp salads.

| Special Shopping |
|---|
| "Silken" (Kinogoshi) tofu — found in Japanese groceries or some supermarkets alongside other tofus. |

| SHOPPING LIST | |
|---|---|
| **Regularly Kept in the Kitchen** (Listed in Chapter 14, p. 703) | **Fresh Produce** |
| Olive oil | Romaine lettuce |
| Asafetida | Tabasco |
| Honey | Lemon |
| Black pepper | Capers |
| Cayenne | |
| Parmesan cheese | |

Also see shopping list for Herbed Croutons.

539

# NUTRITIONAL ANALYSIS FOR ONE SERVING
## CAESAR SALAD WITH HERBED CROUTONS

| NUTRIENT | Type: 14  FEMALE-23 TO 51 YEARS | % RDA | Amount |
|---|---|---|---|
| KCALORIES | A========= | 18% | 370.0 Kc |
| PROTEIN | A================ | 30% | 13.60 Gm |
| CARBOHYDRATE | A | NO RDA | 22.20 Gm |
| FAT | A | NO RDA | 27.20 Gm |
| FIBER-CRUDE | A | NO RDA | 1.530 Gm |
| CHOLESTEROL | A | NO RDA | 6.570 Mg |
| SATURATED FA | A | NO RDA | 5.040 Gm |
| OLEIC FA | A | NO RDA | 15.60 Gm |
| LINOLEIC FA | A | NO RDA | 2.710 Gm |
| SODIUM | A========= | 17% | 378.0 Mg |
| POTASSIUM | A====== | 13% | 501.0 Mg |
| MAGNESIUM | A=========== | 21% | 65.30 Mg |
| IRON | A================= | 35% | 6.320 Mg |
| ZINC | A==== | 9% | 1.380 Mg |
| VITAMIN A | A======================================= | 75% | 3022 IU |
| VITAMIN D | A | 0% | 0.000 IU |
| VIT. E/TOTAL | A | NO RDA | 3.690 Mg |
| VITAMIN C | A============================ | 56% | 34.10 Mg |
| THIAMIN | A============== | 28% | 0.280 Mg |
| RIBOFLAVIN | A=========== | 20% | 0.250 Mg |
| NIACIN | A======= | 15% | 2.020 Mg |
| VITAMIN B6 | A== | 5% | 0.100 Mg |
| FOLACIN | A====================== | 44% | 179.0 Ug |
| VITAMIN B12 | A | 0% | 0.000 Ug |
| PANTO- ACID | A=== | 6% | 0.340 Mg |
| CALCIUM | A========================= | 51% | 409.0 Mg |
| PHOSPHORUS | A================ | 33% | 269.0 Mg |
| TRYPTOPHAN | A==================================================== | 109% | 179.0 Mg |
| THREONINE | A==================================================== | 119% | 520.0 Mg |
| ISOLEUCINE | A==================================================== | 107% | 703.0 Mg |
| LEUCINE | A==================================================== | 122% | 1065 Mg |
| LYSINE | A==================================================== | 133% | 871.0 Mg |
| METHIONINE | A================================================ | 86% | 235.0 Mg |
| CYSTINE | A==================== | 41% | 112.0 Mg |
| PHENYL-ANINE | A==================================================== | 155% | 677.0 Mg |
| TYROSINE | A=============================================== | 92% | 402.0 Mg |
| VALINE | A==================================================== | 98% | 753.0 Mg |
| HISTIDINE | A | NO RDA | 312.0 Mg |
| ALCOHOL | A | NO RDA | 0.000 Gm |
| ASH | A | NO RDA | 2.930 Gm |
| COPPER | A===== | 11% | 0.280 Mg |
| MANGANESE | A==== | 9% | 0.370 Mg |
| IODINE | A=========== | 22% | 34.30 Ug |
| MONO FAT | A | NO RDA | 16.20 Gm |
| POLY FAT | A | NO RDA | 3.440 Gm |
| CAFFEINE | A | NO RDA | 0.000 Mg |
| FLUORIDE | A | 0% | 8.650 Ug |
| MOLYBDENUM | A==================================================== | 116% | 379.0 Ug |
| VITAMIN K | A==================================================== | 133% | 140.0 Ug |
| SELENIUM | A==== | 8% | 0.010 Mg |
| BIOTIN | A== | 4% | 6.430 Ug |
| CHLORIDE | A | 1% | 59.80 Mg |
| CHROMIUM | A==================================================== | 104% | 0.130 Mg |
| SUGAR | A | NO RDA | 1.450 Gm |
| FIBER-DIET | A | NO RDA | 0.000 Gm |
| VIT. E/AT | A=================== | 36% | 2.950 Mg |

```
% RDA:   |0      |20     |40     |60     |80     |100
```

Firm tofu used instead of silken; capers not included in analysis.

# DELICIOUS DISH(ES)

☆ Edible bowls! The dream of anyone who's ever washed dishes.

---

*French bread recipe (your favorite sour*
*dough kind) or use recipe on p. 389*
*and multiply 3 times*

¾ *cup olive oil*
¾ *cup nutritional yeast*
1½ *tsp. soy sauce*

If you are fortunate enough, perhaps you can buy already made whole grain French or Italian bread (nationality doesn't matter as long as it's crusty). Although it's getting easier to find sliced whole grain bread in just about any market, the crusty kind is often hard to find. For this reason I usually end up making my own, which is just as well when I have in mind using the bread as a bowl to serve a salad in. That way I can make the proper sizes and shapes.

The best shape is round or oval. The bread can be shaped into one large loaf (which must then be cut into thick wedges to serve), or small ones for each individual's serving. Whatever the size and shape, take a grapefruit knife and carve a circle on top of the baked bread about ½" to ¾" from the edge. Lift off the top and scoop out bread, leaving a shell with a ½" to ¾" crust wall.

Place hollowed out loaf (or loaves) on a cookie sheet and mix next 3 ingredients together. Butter the inside walls of the hollowed out loaf (or loaves) and bake at 400 degrees for 15 minutes or till bread is hot and the spread has melted in. Remove from oven and fill with salad (or other preferred filling) and serve immediately. This recipe makes enough for a whole meal for 6 to 8.

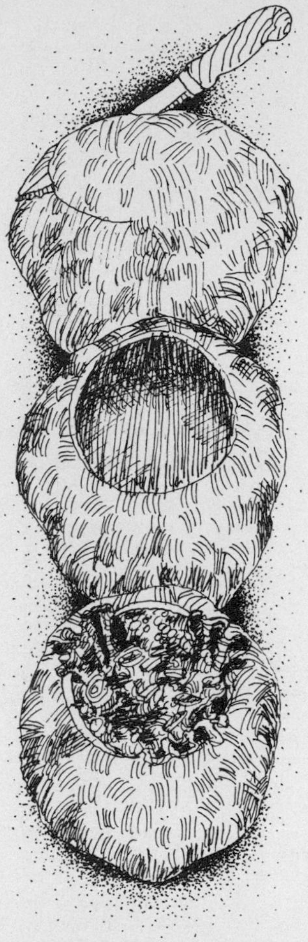

Delicious Dish(es) can be filled with just about anything. In the show, I filled them with Better Than Chicken Salad topped with alfalfa sprouts on a bed of tossed salad.

| Special Shopping |
| --- |
| Whole grain crusty bread or rolls (like French or Italian) — found in some natural food stores, or make your own (p. 389). |

| SHOPPING LIST | |
| --- | --- |
| **Regularly Kept in the Kitchen** (Listed in Chapter 14, p. 703) | **Fresh Produce** |
| Olive oil Nutritional yeast Soy sauce | (None) |

# BETTER THAN CHICKEN SALAD

1 lb. tempeh, steamed

4 oz. fresh spinach leaves (approximately 4 cups
    loosely packed) or ¼ cup frozen spinach

1½ cups eggless or Tofu Mayonnaise
    (see recipe, p. 332)
1 cup finely chopped celery
2 cups finely chopped watercress
1 Tbsp. Fines Herbes
½ tsp. asafetida or 2 Tbsp. chopped scallions
¼ cup nutritional yeast
1 Tbsp. Dijon mustard
2 tsp. soy sauce
⅛ tsp. black pepper
⅛ tsp. Tabasco sauce

2 cups cherry tomatoes
1½ bell peppers, cut into 1" chunks
1 cup sliced mushrooms

Alfalfa or red clover sprouts

Steam tempeh for 15 minutes. Cut into ½" to ¾" cubes
and allow to cool. While cooling, prepare dressing.

First get the spinach ready. If you are using fresh spinach
leaves, they must be parboiled for 2 minutes, then drained
and cooled. (To parboil, bring water to a boil and immerse
leaves till they wilt. Then pour into colander and run under
cold water.) Chop wilted or thawed frozen spinach leaves
fine. Blend next 10 ingredients together in blender till
smooth. Mix in chopped spinach. Pour green dressing into a
bowl with tempeh cubes and toss till everything is mixed
together thoroughly. Refrigerate 6 to 8 hours or overnight to
allow flavors to intermingle. Just before serving, toss in
next 3 ingredients.

This can be served on top of a bed of sprouts or your
everyday tossed salad. For a more gourmet touch, stuff red or
green chicory leaves, or bowls made out of a crusty bread or
rolls, and top with a handful of alfalfa sprouts.

Makes enough for 6 full meals and, of course, many more if
served on a small dinner salad or as an hors d'oeuvres.

This is one of those dishes that
is ideal for entertaining because
it's a little special and is ideally
prepared the day before serving
so flavors can intermingle.

| SHOPPING LIST | |
| --- | --- |
| **Regularly Kept in the Kitchen (Listed in Chapter 14, p. 703)** | **Fresh Produce** |
| Tempeh | Fresh or frozen spinach |
| Eggless mayonnaise | Celery |
| Fines Herbes | Watercress |
| Asafetida | Tabasco |
| Nutritional yeast | Cherry tomatoes |
| Dijon mustard | Bell peppers |
| Soy sauce | Mushrooms |
| Black pepper | Alfalfa or red clover sprouts |

# NUTRITIONAL ANALYSIS FOR ONE SERVING
# BETTER THAN CHICKEN SALAD WITH DELICIOUS DISH(ES)

| NUTRIENT | Type: 14    FEMALE-23 TO 51 YEARS | % RDA | Amount |
|---|---|---|---|
| KCALORIES | A=================================== | 76% | 1526 Kc |
| PROTEIN | A================================================ | 143% | 63.20 Gm |
| CARBOHYDRATE | A | NO RDA | 192.0 Gm |
| FAT | A | NO RDA | 63.80 Gm |
| FIBER-CRUDE | A | NO RDA | 8.340 Gm |
| CHOLESTEROL | A | NO RDA | 1.120 Mg |
| SATURATED FA | A | NO RDA | 8.560 Gm |
| OLEIC FA | A | NO RDA | 24.10 Gm |
| LINOLEIC FA | A | NO RDA | 24.60 Gm |
| SODIUM | A========================== | 61% | 1346 Mg |
| POTASSIUM | A======================= | 55% | 2078 Mg |
| MAGNESIUM | A=================================================== | 128% | 386.0 Mg |
| IRON | A=================================== | 88% | 16.00 Mg |
| ZINC | A============================== | 72% | 10.70 Mg |
| VITAMIN A | A====================================== | 90% | 3619 IU |
| VITAMIN D | A= | 3% | 6.360 IU |
| VIT. E/TOTAL | A | NO RDA | 22.50 Mg |
| VITAMIN C | A================================ | 78% | 47.30 Mg |
| THIAMIN | A============================================ | 1350% | 13.50 Mg |
| RIBOFLAVIN | A============================================ | 1058% | 12.70 Mg |
| NIACIN | A============================================ | 652% | 84.80 Mg |
| VITAMIN B6 | A============================================ | 660% | 13.20 Mg |
| FOLACIN | A=================================================== | 128% | 512.0 Ug |
| VITAMIN B12 | A============================================ | 327% | 9.830 Ug |
| PANTO- ACID | A======================================= | 90% | 5.000 Mg |
| CALCIUM | A============================== | 64% | 518.0 Mg |
| PHOSPHORUS | A=================================== | 177% | 1418 Mg |
| TRYPTOPHAN | A============================================ | 490% | 799.0 Mg |
| THREONINE | A============================================ | 527% | 2295 Mg |
| ISOLEUCINE | A============================================ | 449% | 2937 Mg |
| LEUCINE | A============================================ | 533% | 4646 Mg |
| LYSINE | A============================================ | 468% | 3061 Mg |
| METHIONINE | A============================================ | 338% | 921.0 Mg |
| CYSTINE | A============================================ | 415% | 1129 Mg |
| PHENYL-ANINE | A============================================ | 694% | 3021 Mg |
| TYROSINE | A============================================ | 551% | 2399 Mg |
| VALINE | A============================================ | 417% | 3181 Mg |
| HISTIDINE | A | NO RDA | 1507 Mg |
| ALCOHOL | A | NO RDA | 0.000 Gm |
| ASH | A | NO RDA | 17.30 Gm |
| COPPER | A================================== | 75% | 1.880 Mg |
| MANGANESE | A============================================ | 330% | 12.40 Mg |
| IODINE | A============================================ | 908% | 1363 Ug |
| MONO FAT | A | NO RDA | 24.60 Gm |
| POLY FAT | A | NO RDA | 24.90 Gm |
| CAFFEINE | A | NO RDA | 0.000 Mg |
| FLUORIDE | A= | 2% | 66.20 Ug |
| MOLYBDENUM | A============================================ | 4343% | 14117 Ug |
| VITAMIN K | A============ | 25% | 27.20 Mg |
| SELENIUM | A================================ | 72% | 0.090 Mg |
| BIOTIN | A==================== | 43% | 65.90 Ug |
| CHLORIDE | A======== | 17% | 602.0 Mg |
| CHROMIUM | A============================================ | 1400% | 1.750 Mg |
| SUGAR | A | NO RDA | 4.440 Gm |
| FIBER-DIET | A | NO RDA | 44.40 Gm |
| VIT. E/AT | A=========================================== | 170% | 13.60 Mg |

```
% RDA:  |0      |20     |40     |60     |80     |100
```

Scallions used instead of asafetida; alfalfa sprouts used instead of red clover in salad; optional salt included in bread dough.

# HERB VINEGARS

The method for making flavored herb vinegars is this simple! Wash and dry the fresh herb and put herb or combination of herbs you choose into a clean, boiled jar and fill with your favorite vinegar. I have found that apple cider vinegar has its own strong flavor, whereas wine vinegars or the excellent Japanese rice vinegars have a more neutral flavor and tend to impart the flavor of the herb better. Put the lid on and allow to sit in a cool, dark place (a closet or cabinet that stays fairly cool) for four weeks. (You may want to label the jars, specifying flavors and starting dates.)

Following is a list of fresh herbs to use in 1-pint portions:
- 3 sprigs tarragon or dill or thyme
- 2 - 3 sprigs basil (plus 10 peppercorns for zest)
- 1 sprig rosemary and 1 sprig lemon thyme plus 6 seedless grapes
- 2 sprigs mint and peel of 1 lemon cut off in a spiral, 10 dried currants
- 6 - 10 (depending on desired heat) hot jalapeno peppers, slit open, and 1 clove garlic
- Put a large piece of ginger root in a jar of vinegar in the refrigerator; the ginger will flavor the vinegar which in turn preserves the ginger. When using a recipe calling for fresh ginger root, use the chunk of ginger from the vinegar.

You've probably seen different flavored vinegars in gourmet stores or sections of supermarkets at outrageously expensive prices. You can easily make your own at home for a fraction of the price. Of course, it's ideal if you have an herb garden; but otherwise, fresh herbs from store produce departments can be used. Flavored vinegars make nice gifts for the gourmet cook; whether making as a gift with a personal touch or for use in the kitchen, the main thing is to plan enough ahead of time — allow one month to get the finished product.

# RASPBERRY (OR OTHER FRUIT) VINEGAR

*3 cups whole, fresh berries*
*½ cup white wine vinegar*

*⅝ cup honey*

This vinegar can be made using a number of different kinds of fruits, especially the kind that lean toward tartness, such as berries, currants, pineapple, peaches, apricots, plums or tart cherries. You may also want to try different combinations of fruit.

Place fruit of your choice and vinegar in a stainless steel or glass container. Crush the fruit and cover. Allow to stand 24 hours in a cool place. Strain fruit pulp out through a fine strainer or cheesecloth. Discard fruit pulp and pour liquid into cooking container. (This should make approximately 1¼ cups.) Add honey and bring liquid to a boil. Turn down to simmer and simmer for about 10 minutes. Cover and allow to sit out overnight. Gently and slowly (so sediment on bottom doesn't get stirred up) pour vinegar into bottle it will be stored in. Discard sediment in bottom of pot.

Use on fruit or vegetable salads as is or mixed in with other ingredients to make a dressing.

A couple of salad ideas using flavored vinegars . . .

# SUMMER REFRESHER SALAD

*2 cups honeydew melon balls*
*2 cups Crenshaw melon balls*

*⅓ - ½ cup strawberry vinegar*
*Cayenne pepper*

Cut melons in half, scoop out seeds, and cut out balls with a melon ball scooper. Mix balls together and carve melon halves decoratively so they can be used as "bowls." Refrigerate both the melon balls and skins. Just before serving, pour on enough strawberry vinegar to evenly toss into balls. Fill melon halves with dressed melon balls and sprinkle with cayenne pepper. Makes 2 to 4 servings.

## MENU SUGGESTION FOR FEATURING A SALAD AS THE MEAL

Salad
(like Night-Before Salad)

Nutty-Crust Flat Bread

Mint Sherbeto (p. 628)

# NIGHT-BEFORE SALAD

☆ Most of this salad should be made the night before you plan to serve it, making it a perfect meal to serve when you are feeding people you want to spend time with (instead of slaving away in the kitchen).

8 cups shredded Romaine lettuce
½ cup thinly sliced scallions
1 cup thinly sliced celery
2 (5-oz.) cans water chestnuts, sliced
1 (10-oz.) package frozen peas

1½ cups eggless or Tofu Mayonnaise
   (see recipe, p. 332)

2 tsp. honey
⅓ cup Parmesan cheese
1 tsp. Spike or other vegetable-seasoned salt
½ tsp. asafetida or garlic powder
¼ tsp. black pepper
1 tsp. paprika

½ block tofu, cut into ½" cubes
15 strips Mock Bacon (see recipe, p. 157)

2 large tomatoes, cut in wedges

Layer each of the first 5 ingredients on top of each other in the order given in a 4 to 5 quart see-through serving bowl. The only special instruction I can think of in regard to this step is to shred the Romaine lettuce (any other loose-leaf lettuce wilts too quickly) by cutting ½"-thick strips across the width of leaves. This is the bottom layer and foundation of the salad.

After all vegetables have been stacked one layer atop the next, spread the mayonnaise evenly on top of the whole surface. Sprinkle each of the next 6 ingredients as evenly atop the surface of the mayonnaise as possible. Cover and refrigerate at least 6 hours or overnight.

Just before serving, fry up Mock Bacon, cube tofu, and cut tomatoes. Now sprinkle cubed tofu over entire mayonnaise surface. Break Mock Bacon into almost bite-sized pieces and top with tomatoes. To serve, use a spoon and fork long enough to reach through all the layers so each serving gets some of each layer. Makes 6 to 8 servings. Makes a complete meal served with a whole grain bread.

| SHOPPING LIST | |
| --- | --- |
| **Regularly Kept in the Kitchen** (Listed in Chapter 14, p. 703) | **Fresh Produce** |
| Eggless mayonnaise | Romaine lettuce |
| Parmesan cheese | Scallions |
| Spike | Celery |
| Asafetida | Water chestnuts |
| Black pepper | Frozen peas |
| Paprika | Tomatoes |
| Tofu | |

Also see ingredients for Mock Bacon (p. 157).

# NUTRITIONAL ANALYSIS FOR ONE SERVING NIGHT-BEFORE SALAD

```
NUTRIENT        Type: 14    FEMALE-23 TO 51 YEARS              % RDA    Amount
KCALORIES       Ж============                                   25%    505.0 Kc
PROTEIN         Ж==================================================  102%    45.00 Gm
CARBOHYDRATE    Ж                                              NO RDA   34.70 Gm
FAT             Ж                                              NO RDA   25.10 Gm
FIBER-CRUDE     Ж                                              NO RDA   2.500 Gm
CHOLESTEROL     Ж                                              NO RDA   4.380 Mg
SATURATED FA    Ж                                              NO RDA   2.880 Gm
OLEIC FA        Ж                                              NO RDA   4.510 Gm
LINOLEIC FA     Ж                                              NO RDA   10.10 Gm
SODIUM          Ж==================                              36%    812.0 Mg
POTASSIUM       Ж=============                                   26%    1000 Mg
MAGNESIUM       Ж============================                    58%    175.0 Mg
IRON            Ж============================================    90%    16.30 Mg
ZINC            Ж=======                                         14%    2.160 Mg
VITAMIN A       Ж========================================        81%    3272 IU
VITAMIN D       Ж                                                 0%    0.000 IU
VIT. E/TOTAL    Ж                                              NO RDA   4.150 Mg
VITAMIN C       Ж=============================                   60%    36.10 Mg
THIAMIN         Ж============================                    58%    0.590 Mg
RIBOFLAVIN      Ж=============                                   29%    0.350 Mg
NIACIN          Ж============                                    24%    3.130 Mg
VITAMIN B6      Ж=====                                           11%    0.220 Mg
FOLACIN         Ж====================                            40%    160.0 Ug
VITAMIN B12     Ж                                                 0%    0.000 Ug
PANTO- ACID     Ж====                                            8%     0.480 Mg
CALCIUM         Ж================================================ 101%   809.0 Mg
PHOSPHORUS      Ж====================================            74%    599.0 Mg
TRYPTOPHAN      Ж===============================================  307%   501.0 Mg
THREONINE       Ж===============================================  389%   1695 Mg
ISOLEUCINE      Ж===============================================  335%   2188 Mg
LEUCINE         Ж===============================================  384%   3352 Mg
LYSINE          Ж===============================================  462%   3023 Mg
METHIONINE      Ж===============================================  224%   610.0 Mg
CYSTINE         Ж===============================================  198%   539.0 Mg
PHENYL-ANINE    Ж===============================================  494%   2152 Mg
TYROSINE        Ж===============================================  377%   1640 Mg
VALINE          Ж===============================================  293%   2234 Mg
HISTIDINE       Ж                                              NO RDA   1269 Mg
ALCOHOL         Ж                                              NO RDA   0.000 Gm
ASH             Ж                                              NO RDA   5.610 Gm
COPPER          Ж================                                32%    0.810 Mg
MANGANESE       Ж===================================             74%    2.810 Mg
IODINE          Ж==============================================   174%   262.0 Ug
MONO FAT        Ж                                              NO RDA   2.600 Gm
POLY FAT        Ж                                              NO RDA   8.050 Gm
CAFFEINE        Ж                                              NO RDA   0.000 Mg
FLUORIDE        Ж                                                 0%    22.50 Ug
MOLYBDENUM      Ж===============================================  1700%  5526 Ug
VITAMIN K       Ж===============================================  209%   220.0 Ug
SELENIUM        Ж============                                    24%    0.030 Mg
BIOTIN          Ж=====                                           11%    17.80 Ug
CHLORIDE        Ж===                                             6%     227.0 Mg
CHROMIUM        Ж===============================================  528%   0.660 Mg
SUGAR           Ж                                              NO RDA   5.710 Gm
FIBER-DIET      Ж                                              NO RDA   11.10 Gm
VIT. E/AT       Ж=============                                   27%    2.180 Mg

    % RDA:      |0      |20     |40     |60     |80     |100
```

549

# SAIMIN SALAD

☆ A gourmet salad with an Oriental flair.

---

8 oz. buckwheat soba or kudzu noodles

1 stick agar-agar
½ cup julienne strips of dry kombu

8 cups torn leafy lettuce
2 cups mung bean sprouts

2 cups fine julienne strips of carrot
2 Tbsp. scallions
1 bell pepper, slivered

4½ cups ice water
1¾ cups miso
1⅛ cups toasted sesame seeds
9 oz. fresh ginger root
3 Tbsp. honey

Age (aburage shells)
Soy sauce

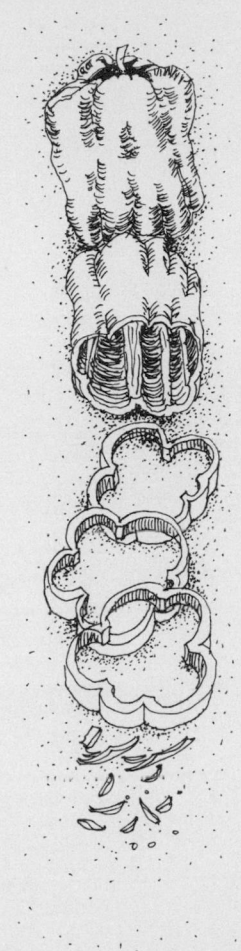

Boil noodles as directed on packet. Cut next 2 ingredients into julienne strips about ⅛" wide while they are still dry, then soak in a bowl full of hot water. By now (about 5 minutes) the noodles should be done cooking. When they are, pour them into a colander and rinse under cold running water to rinse off external starch and also to help cool the noodles off. Once they have cooled off, toss a tray full of ice cubes into the noodles and let them remain there as the rest of the ingredients are assembled. Sprinkle age crisps with soy sauce and place on baking tray to bake at 350 degrees for 20 minutes.

Toss lettuce and sprouts together in one bowl. In another bowl, toss the next 3 ingredients. Slice baked age crisps into thin julienne strips. Blend next 5 ingredients together in blender till ginger is thoroughly minced. (It's okay if some of the sesame seeds stay whole, but giant chunks of ginger are hot and strong to bite into!)

Now it's time to assemble each serving in individual bowls. This recipe makes 6 saimin bowl-sized servings, so divide ingredients evenly between 6 bowls in the following way. Line bowl with lettuce and mung bean sprouts, forming a bed on the bottom and up the sides of the bowl. Top this with a thin layer of the carrot, scallion and bell pepper mixture.

Remove ice cubes from noodles and drain water from the soaked seaweed. Toss seaweed into the noodles and fill center of each individual bowl with the noodle mixture. Top with slivers of baked age.

Pour about ½ cup of dressing into 6 individual-sized bowls (or one central server) for each person to put dressing on salad according to taste. This makes 6 servings.

| Special Shopping |
| --- |
| Buckwheat soba noodles/ agar-agar — found in Japanese groceries, Oriental aisles of supermarkets, or natural food stores.<br>Aburage shells (age) — found in Japanese or Chinese groceries; some Oriental food aisles in supermarkets. I go to the tofu factory and buy off-grade pouches for one to two dollars a box. |

| SHOPPING LIST | |
| --- | --- |
| **Regularly Kept in the Kitchen (Listed in Chapter 14, p. 703)** | **Fresh Produce** |
| Kombu<br>Miso<br>Sesame seeds<br>Honey<br>Soy sauce | Leafy lettuce<br>Mung sprouts<br>Carrots<br>Scallions<br>Bell pepper<br>Ginger root |

# NUTRITIONAL ANALYSIS FOR ONE SERVING SAIMIN SALAD

| NUTRIENT | Type: 14   FEMALE-23 TO 51 YEARS | % RDA | Amount |
|---|---|---|---|
| KCALORIES | Å=============== | 31% | 623.0 Kc |
| PROTEIN | Å============================== | 60% | 26.60 Gm |
| CARBOHYDRATE | Å | NO RDA | 82.70 Gm |
| FAT | Å | NO RDA | 21.70 Gm |
| FIBER-CRUDE | Å | NO RDA | 5.940 Gm |
| CHOLESTEROL | Å | NO RDA | 0.000 Mg |
| SATURATED FA | Å | NO RDA | 2.490 Gm |
| OLEIC FA | Å | NO RDA | 1.390 Gm |
| LINOLEIC FA | Å | NO RDA | 1.690 Gm |
| SODIUM | Å==================================================== | 142% | 3138 Mg |
| POTASSIUM | Å============= | 26% | 978.0 Mg |
| MAGNESIUM | Å======================================= | 81% | 245.0 Mg |
| IRON | Å============================ | 58% | 10.50 Mg |
| ZINC | Å==================== | 42% | 6.340 Mg |
| VITAMIN A | Å==================================================== | 297% | 11894 IU |
| VITAMIN D | Å | 0% | 0.000 IU |
| VIT. E/TOTAL | Å | NO RDA | 9.630 Mg |
| VITAMIN C | Å=============================== | 65% | 39.30 Mg |
| THIAMIN | Å================== | 38% | 0.380 Mg |
| RIBOFLAVIN | Å================ | 34% | 0.410 Mg |
| NIACIN | Å============= | 26% | 3.430 Mg |
| VITAMIN B6 | Å============ | 25% | 0.500 Mg |
| FOLACIN | Å===================== | 45% | 182.0 Ug |
| VITAMIN B12 | Å==== | 9% | 0.290 Ug |
| PANTO- ACID | Å============== | 30% | 1.650 Mg |
| CALCIUM | Å========================= | 56% | 448.0 Mg |
| PHOSPHORUS | Å============================== | 62% | 501.0 Mg |
| TRYPTOPHAN | Å=================================================== | 215% | 352.0 Mg |
| THREONINE | Å=================================================== | 269% | 1174 Mg |
| ISOLEUCINE | Å=================================================== | 237% | 1550 Mg |
| LEUCINE | Å=================================================== | 262% | 2287 Mg |
| LYSINE | Å=================================================== | 217% | 1423 Mg |
| METHIONINE | Å=================================================== | 148% | 405.0 Mg |
| CYSTINE | Å=================================================== | 102% | 279.0 Mg |
| PHENYL-ANINE | Å=================================================== | 318% | 1386 Mg |
| TYROSINE | Å=================================================== | 216% | 941.0 Mg |
| VALINE | Å=================================================== | 196% | 1496 Mg |
| HISTIDINE | Å | NO RDA | 765.0 Mg |
| ALCOHOL | Å | NO RDA | 0.000 Gm |
| ASH | Å | NO RDA | 15.40 Gm |
| COPPER | Å======================= | 51% | 1.290 Mg |
| MANGANESE | Å========================= | 57% | 2.160 Mg |
| IODINE | Å==================================================== | 381% | 572.0 Ug |
| MONO FAT | Å | NO RDA | 5.680 Gm |
| POLY FAT | Å | NO RDA | 8.260 Gm |
| CAFFEINE | Å | NO RDA | 0.000 Mg |
| FLUORIDE | Å | 0% | 25.10 Ug |
| MOLYBDENUM | Å==================================================== | 381% | 1239 Ug |
| VITAMIN K | Å============================================== | 89% | 94.10 Ug |
| SELENIUM | Å | 0% | 0.000 Mg |
| BIOTIN | Å=== | 7% | 11.10 Ug |
| CHLORIDE | Å======================= | 51% | 1755 Mg |
| CHROMIUM | Å=================================================== | 264% | 0.330 Mg |
| SUGAR | Å | NO RDA | 2.870 Gm |
| FIBER-DIET | Å | NO RDA | 8.940 Gm |
| VIT. E/AT | Å=============== | 33% | 2.650 Mg |

```
% RDA:   |0       |20      |40      |60      |80      |100
```

Buckwheat soba noodles used instead of kudzu in analysis.

# TOSSED ITALIAN STYLE

1 large head lettuce (about 8 to
   10 cups torn leaves)
2 oz. (about 2 cups) alfalfa, red
   clover or radish sprouts
3 bell peppers, sliced in ¼" rings
3 medium tomatoes, sliced into 16ths
6 oz. (2 cups) whole pitted ripe
   olives and/or avocado
1 tsp. oregano (dry)
2 tsp. basil (dry)
¼ tsp. black pepper
2 tsp. asafetida or ½ onion, very thinly sliced

¼ cup flaky nutritional yeast
½ cup Parmesan cheese
¼ cup olive oil
2 Tbsp. tarragon vinegar

Combine first 9 ingredients in a salad bowl. Use Romaine or any other dark green, loose-leaf lettuce (anything but iceberg). Just before serving, add last 4 ingredients and toss thoroughly. Serve immediately, as the dressing wilts the greens after awhile. Makes 6 to 8 servings if used as the main course for lunch or dinner, or 16 servings as a small salad to serve with a meal.

Both of these recipes are examples of what you can do with herb-flavored and fruit-flavored vinegars. Fruit-flavored vinegars aren't limited to just being used with fruit. The fruit-flavored vinegars add a nice flavor to savory sauces, vegetable dishes, salads, etc.

| SHOPPING LIST | |
|---|---|
| **Regularly Kept in the Kitchen (Listed in Chapter 14, p.703)** | **Fresh Produce** |
| Oregano<br>Basil<br>Black pepper<br>Asafetida<br>Nutritional yeast<br>Parmesan cheese<br>Olive oil<br>Tarragon vinegar | Lettuce<br>Sprouts<br>Bell peppers<br>Tomatoes<br>Olives and/or avocado |

# NUTRITIONAL ANALYSIS FOR ONE SERVING
## TOSSED ITALIAN STYLE

| NUTRIENT | Type: 14   FEMALE—23 TO 51 YEARS | % RDA | Amount |
|---|---|---|---|
| KCALORIES | ᴤ===== | 11% | 224.0 Kc |
| PROTEIN | ᴤ========== | 20% | 8.960 Gm |
| CARBOHYDRATE | ᴤ | NO RDA | 10.70 Gm |
| FAT | ᴤ | NO RDA | 18.40 Gm |
| FIBER—CRUDE | ᴤ | NO RDA | 2.190 Gm |
| CHOLESTEROL | ᴤ | NO RDA | 6.580 Mg |
| SATURATED FA | ᴤ | NO RDA | 3.590 Gm |
| OLEIC FA | ᴤ | NO RDA | 10.80 Gm |
| LINOLEIC FA | ᴤ | NO RDA | 1.070 Gm |
| SODIUM | ᴤ======== | 16% | 355.0 Mg |
| POTASSIUM | ᴤ======== | 17% | 638.0 Mg |
| MAGNESIUM | ᴤ====== | 12% | 37.80 Mg |
| IRON | ᴤ======== | 16% | 2.940 Mg |
| ZINC | ᴤ===== | 10% | 1.500 Mg |
| VITAMIN A | ᴤ=========================================== | 88% | 3553 IU |
| VITAMIN D | ᴤ | 0% | 0.000 IU |
| VIT. E/TOTAL | ᴤ | NO RDA | 2.190 Mg |
| VITAMIN C | ᴤ================================================= | 138% | 83.30 Mg |
| THIAMIN | ᴤ================================================= | 318% | 3.180 Mg |
| RIBOFLAVIN | ᴤ================================================= | 265% | 3.190 Mg |
| NIACIN | ᴤ================================================= | 142% | 18.50 Mg |
| VITAMIN B6 | ᴤ================================================= | 155% | 3.110 Mg |
| FOLACIN | ᴤ===================== | 46% | 185.0 Ug |
| VITAMIN B12 | ᴤ====================================== | 77% | 2.330 Ug |
| PANTO— ACID | ᴤ===== | 11% | 0.630 Mg |
| CALCIUM | ᴤ============ | 25% | 206.0 Mg |
| PHOSPHORUS | ᴤ============= | 27% | 217.0 Mg |
| TRYPTOPHAN | ᴤ=========================== | 58% | 94.90 Mg |
| THREONINE | ᴤ======================================= | 85% | 371.0 Mg |
| ISOLEUCINE | ᴤ=============================== | 69% | 453.0 Mg |
| LEUCINE | ᴤ===================================== | 80% | 700.0 Mg |
| LYSINE | ᴤ================================================ | 105% | 692.0 Mg |
| METHIONINE | ᴤ============================ | 60% | 164.0 Mg |
| CYSTINE | ᴤ================ | 35% | 95.90 Mg |
| PHENYL—ANINE | ᴤ========================================= | 90% | 393.0 Mg |
| TYROSINE | ᴤ======================================= | 85% | 372.0 Mg |
| VALINE | ᴤ=============================== | 69% | 532.0 Mg |
| HISTIDINE | ᴤ | NO RDA | 257.0 Mg |
| ALCOHOL | ᴤ | NO RDA | 0.000 Gm |
| ASH | ᴤ | NO RDA | 4.880 Gm |
| COPPER | ᴤ== | 5% | 0.140 Mg |
| MANGANESE | ᴤ== | 4% | 0.160 Mg |
| IODINE | ᴤ | 0% | 0.000 Ug |
| MONO FAT | ᴤ | NO RDA | 7.400 Gm |
| POLY FAT | ᴤ | NO RDA | 1.120 Gm |
| CAFFEINE | ᴤ | NO RDA | 0.000 Mg |
| FLUORIDE | ᴤ | 1% | 28.50 Ug |
| MOLYBDENUM | ᴤ | 0% | 1.660 Ug |
| VITAMIN K | ᴤ=================================================== | 117% | 123.0 Ug |
| SELENIUM | ᴤ | 0% | 0.000 Mg |
| BIOTIN | ᴤ==== | 8% | 12.10 Ug |
| CHLORIDE | ᴤ | 0% | 0.000 Mg |
| CHROMIUM | ᴤ================== | 40% | 0.050 Mg |
| SUGAR | ᴤ | NO RDA | 5.710 Gm |
| FIBER—DIET | ᴤ | NO RDA | 1.220 Gm |
| VIT. E/AT | ᴤ============ | 25% | 2.000 Mg |

```
% RDA:  |0      |20     |40     |60     |80     |100
```

Sprouts used: alfalfa. Olives used instead of avocado; onion used instead of asafetida.

When we stop to consider how the body must inevitably die no matter how futilely we try to prevent it, and the existence of the soul, or life force, which exists with or without a body, these words of Leo Tolstoy ring clear: "That Power cannot want of us what is irrational and impossible — the establishment of our temporary carnal life, the life of society, or the life of the State. It demands of us what alone is certain, rational and possible — the service of the Kingdom of God; that is, our cooperation in establishing the greatest possible unity among all living beings — a unity possible only in the truth. It therefore demands that we acknowledge and profess the truth revealed to us — the only thing that is within our power."

# VITAMIN·SAVING COOKING TECHNIQUES

As I've mentioned before, the healthiest way to prepare vegetables is raw (with the exception of some vegetables, like carrots, spinach, etc., in which cooking breaks elements down and makes the nutrients more accessible to our bodies). The easiest way I've found to get raw vegetables into our meals is to make salads. But I do cook vegetables as well. When it comes to cooking vegetables, some techniques are healthier than others. Boiling is out (unless making soup) because vitamins are destroyed by heat, and the water-soluble vitamins that aren't destroyed go into the water. The best ways to prepare vegetables are steaming, baking and sauteing or stir-frying. As can be seen in the following recipes, using these techniques (or combinations of them) will turn out highly palatable and nutritious dishes.

555

# CRUCIFEROUS AU GRATIN

☆ To make a healthy gratin, I lightly steam my vegetables instead of boiling to death (which destroys many vitamins and loses most of the rest in the water) as is usually done, and I try to make lighter sauces instead of the cholesterol- and saturated fat-laden cheese sauces usually used in French cooking. Be sure to save the steaming water to use in making the sauce, or refrigerate for later use — like in soups.

---

3 slices whole grain bread made into crumbs

2 Tbsp. nutritional yeast
1½ Tbsp. chives or other fresh herbs

3 - 4 lbs. (2 bunches) broccoli (about 8 cups)
1 large head cauliflower (about 4 cups)

1½ recipes Au Gratin or Anything Sauce

Preheat oven to 425 degrees.

Make bread into fine crumbs by running in a food processor or blender. Add next 2 ingredients and toss thoroughly together. Lightly steam vegetables till just tender (they can be easily pierced with a sharp knife). Gently toss steamed vegetables in Au Gratin or Anything Sauce to completely coat the vegetables with sauce. Place in baking trays 1½" to 2" deep. Sprinkle bread crumb mixture evenly over the surface of vegetables and bake at 425 degrees for 7 to 10 minutes, till crumbs begin to brown. Makes 6 to 8 entree-sized servings.

| SHOPPING LIST | |
|---|---|
| Regularly Kept in the Kitchen (Listed in Chapter 14, p. 703) | Fresh Produce |
| Whole grain bread Nutritional yeast | Chives or other fresh herb Broccoli Cauliflower |

Also see shopping list for Au Gratin or Anything Sauce (following recipe).

Research has shown that members of the cabbage family (cruciferous vegetables) — cabbage, cauliflower, broccoli, brussel sprouts, the Chinese "choy" vegetables — help to prevent cancer. That's just another good reason to use them often! This recipe features broccoli and cauliflower, but almost every vegetable is delicious served "au gratin." A vegetable gratin is a traditional French way to prepare vegetables that's simple and can be done healthfully. A gratin is basically any vegetable that's coated with a sauce, placed to cook in a shallow, casserole-type pan, sprinkled with bread crumbs and/or nuts (the French word "grantiner" means to prepare a dish with bread crumbs) and baked in the oven to brown and slightly toast the topping.

Endless numbers of variations of gratins can be made by varying combinations of vegetables, sauces and toppings.
• For vegetables: Use vegetables in season, each separately, or mix two or three kinds of vegetables together.
• For sauces: Use the Au Gratin or Anything Sauce, but try the "cream" sauce made of potatoes in Potato Creamed Vegetables, a tomato sauce, or occasionally the Zesty Creme Sauce (p. 434).
• For toppings: Try flavoring bread crumbs with fresh herbs (being sure flavors or herbs are compatible with specific vegetable being used), chopped nuts and/or a little bit of grated cheese instead of the nutritional yeast.

Just remember, every time you add cheese or a cheese sauce, you're adding cholesterol and saturated fat!

# NUTRITIONAL ANALYSIS FOR ONE SERVING
## CRUCIFEROUS AU GRATIN WITH AU GRATIN OR ANYTHING SAUCE

| NUTRIENT | Type: 14   FEMALE-23 TO 51 YEARS | % RDA | Amount |
|---|---|---|---|
| KCALORIES | A======== | 16% | 321.0 Kc |
| PROTEIN | A========================= | 48% | 21.20 Gm |
| CARBOHYDRATE | A | NO RDA | 32.30 Gm |
| FAT | A | NO RDA | 15.50 Gm |
| FIBER-CRUDE | A | NO RDA | 4.170 Gm |
| CHOLESTEROL | A | NO RDA | 0.000 Mg |
| SATURATED FA | A | NO RDA | 1.460 Gm |
| OLEIC FA | A | NO RDA | 1.610 Gm |
| LINOLEIC FA | A | NO RDA | 10.00 Gm |
| SODIUM | A======================= | 47% | 1054 Mg |
| POTASSIUM | A===================== | 44% | 1667 Mg |
| MAGNESIUM | A====================== | 45% | 136.0 Mg |
| IRON | A============ | 25% | 4.670 Mg |
| ZINC | A=============== | 31% | 4.660 Mg |
| VITAMIN A | A=================================================== | 119% | 4795 IU |
| VITAMIN D | A | 0% | 0.000 IU |
| VIT. E/TOTAL | A | NO RDA | 7.310 Mg |
| VITAMIN C | A=================================================== | 553% | 332.0 Mg |
| THIAMIN | A=================================================== | 1070% | 10.70 Mg |
| RIBOFLAVIN | A=================================================== | 908% | 10.90 Mg |
| NIACIN | A=================================================== | 488% | 63.50 Mg |
| VITAMIN B6 | A=================================================== | 555% | 11.10 Mg |
| FOLACIN | A=================================================== | 102% | 411.0 Ug |
| VITAMIN B12 | A=================================================== | 272% | 8.160 Ug |
| PANTO- ACID | A========================== | 54% | 3.010 Mg |
| CALCIUM | A============ | 25% | 201.0 Mg |
| PHOSPHORUS | A==================================== | 66% | 530.0 Mg |
| TRYPTOPHAN | A=================================================== | 135% | 221.0 Mg |
| THREONINE | A=================================================== | 188% | 822.0 Mg |
| ISOLEUCINE | A=================================================== | 137% | 900.0 Mg |
| LEUCINE | A=================================================== | 147% | 1287 Mg |
| LYSINE | A=================================================== | 196% | 1283 Mg |
| METHIONINE | A=================================================== | 105% | 286.0 Mg |
| CYSTINE | A========================================= | 80% | 220.0 Mg |
| PHENYL-ANINE | A=================================================== | 175% | 765.0 Mg |
| TYROSINE | A=================================================== | 149% | 650.0 Mg |
| VALINE | A=================================================== | 144% | 1104 Mg |
| HISTIDINE | A | NO RDA | 455.0 Mg |
| ALCOHOL | A | NO RDA | 0.000 Gm |
| ASH | A | NO RDA | 15.00 Gm |
| COPPER | A==== | 8% | 0.210 Mg |
| MANGANESE | A=========== | 22% | 0.830 Mg |
| IODINE | A==== | 8% | 13.10 Ug |
| MONO FAT | A | NO RDA | 1.700 Gm |
| POLY FAT | A | NO RDA | 11.10 Gm |
| CAFFEINE | A | NO RDA | 0.000 Mg |
| FLUORIDE | A | 1% | 34.00 Ug |
| MOLYBDENUM | A | 0% | 0.000 Ug |
| VITAMIN K | A=================================================== | 2860% | 3004 Ug |
| SELENIUM | A | 0% | 0.000 Mg |
| BIOTIN | A=========== | 23% | 35.10 Ug |
| CHLORIDE | A | 0% | 0.560 Mg |
| CHROMIUM | A====================================== | 88% | 0.110 Mg |
| SUGAR | A | NO RDA | 7.030 Gm |
| FIBER-DIET | A | NO RDA | 4.210 Gm |
| VIT. E/AT | A====================================== | 76% | 6.080 Mg |

```
% RDA:  |0      |20     |40     |60     |80     |100
```

# AU GRATIN OR ANYTHING SAUCE

☆ A cholesterol-free sauce that contains polyunsaturated oil instead of saturated fat; good for dressing vegetable gratins as well as other dishes!

½ cup water
½ cup nutritional yeast
¼ cup safflower (or other) oil
3 Tbsp. soy sauce
1½ tsp. lemon juice
1 tsp. kelp powder
½ tsp. Spike or other vegetable-seasoned salt
½ tsp. basil
½ tsp. asafetida or 2 cloves garlic

1 Tbsp. parsley flakes

Blend first 9 ingredients together in a blender till completely mixed. Add last ingredient. This sauce is delicious on vegetables prepared "au gratin," but can be used for many, many other purposes. Try it as a salad dressing (add a touch of vinegar if you like); as a light gravy over loaves, patties or other entree dishes; my children love this sauce on their brown rice, topped with some nutritional yeast. Makes a little over 1 cup.

| SHOPPING LIST | |
| --- | --- |
| **Regularly Kept in the Kitchen** (Listed in Chapter 14, p. 703) | **Fresh Produce** |
| Nutritional yeast<br>Safflower oil<br>Soy sauce<br>Lemon juice<br>Kelp powder<br>Spike<br>Basil<br>Asafetida<br>Parsley flakes | (None) |

If you're in a hurry, skip the baking with bread crumbs, as is done in making a gratin dish, and just toss this sauce onto lightly steamed vegetables to give them some zing. See — steamed vegetables don't have to be an uninteresting side dish!

You'll find throughout the book that I mention eating salad and an entree made of whole grains, legumes, nuts and seeds, and/or dairy products two times a day, and I list a tossed green salad in many menus. In my opinion, salads are one of the best ways to fix vegetables raw. This is a recipe that demonstrates why we never get tired of tossed salad! Growing your own herbs in a kitchen or backyard herb garden adds wonderful flavors to food at a fraction of store shelf prices! Though some of the gourmet-type vegetables make this salad so expensive that it should be reserved for special occasions, fresh herbs from a home garden make any everyday salad taste special!

# TOSSED SALADS CAN BE SPECIAL

☆ A tossed salad made special with fresh herbs and some harder-to-get vegetables.

---

*2 Tbsp. walnut oil*
*20 spears asparagus cut in 1" - 2" pieces*
*¼ lb. fresh shiitake mushrooms*

*1½ bunches lamb's lettuce (mache)*
*Leaves from 1 bunch arugula*
*    (about 2 cups unpacked)*
*Leaves from ½ bunch watercress*
*    (about 2 cups unpacked)*
*1 head loose-leaf lettuce (Romaine,*
*    red-leaf, green-leaf, etc.)*
*1 head limestone, butter or Manoa lettuce*
*1 head radicchio*

*¼ cup walnut oil*
*¼ cup pine nuts*
*3 scallions, finely chopped*
*½ tsp. asafetida or 2 cloves garlic, crushed*

*3 Tbsp. sherry or wine vinegar*
*3 Tbsp. each of finely chopped, fresh basil,*
*    tarragon, chives and thyme*
*1 tsp. soy sauce*
*¼ tsp. black or white pepper*

Saute first 3 ingredients together till asparagus and mushrooms are a little tender. Set aside to cool. Tear next 6 ingredients into bite-sized pieces and toss together in a bowl with cooled shiitake mushrooms and asparagus. Just before serving, saute next 4 ingredients together in same skillet (unrinsed) that shiitake and asparagus were sauted in, till pine nuts turn golden brown. Turn off heat and add next 7 ingredients; stir to thoroughly mix and toss into salad. Serve immediately after dressing the salad because dressing causes salad greens to wilt. Makes 10 to 12 servings.

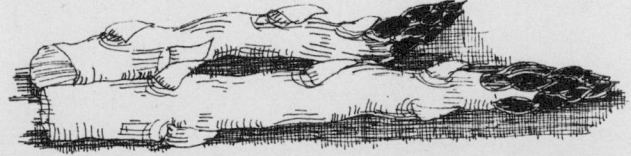

| Special Shopping |
|---|
| Walnut oil — found in gourmet food stores. You'll probably find a multitude of other kinds of oils worth trying (pecan, rape seed, etc.). Fresh shiitake mushrooms, mache, arugula, radicchio — found in gourmet produce stores or sections of supermarkets. |

# POTATO CREAMED VEGETABLES

☆ Just another recipe to demonstrate how you can turn steamed vegetables into more than "just steamed vegetables."

---

*Enough baked potatoes to make 4 cups of chunks*

*4 cups ½" slices of winter squash*
*2 cups ¾" chunks of carrot*
*2 cups cauliflowerets*

*4 cups fresh mushrooms, left whole or cut in half*
*2 cups frozen (or fresh) peas*
*1 cup frozen (or fresh) lima beans*

*4 cups lowfat milk*
*4 cups baked potato chunks*
*2 Tbsp. butter or margarine*
*2 tsp. Spike or other vegetable-seasoned salt*
*½ tsp. black pepper*

Preheat oven to 375 degrees.

Put at least enough scrubbed potatoes in the oven to make 4 cups' worth of potato chunks after they've done baking. I usually end up baking enough to use in a meal the following day as well. Bake at 375 degrees about 1 hour, or till a butter knife is easily poked into the middle of the biggest potato. While potatoes are baking, prepare hard vegetables by washing and cutting. Place all 3 hard vegetables in a steamer at

Oftentimes interesting and healthy dishes can be created from the simplest ingredients by combining cooking techniques as in this recipe. Here vegetables are being steamed, baked (one of the best ways to cook whole, uncut vegetables like potatoes, yams, winter squash, etc.) and blended.

The main thing to watch out for in cooking vegetables is never over-cook them!

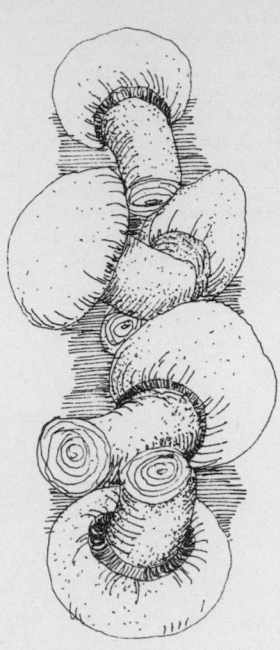

once and steam only till the color of the carrots and squash turn a more brilliant color than when they're raw; the vegetables should still be a little crunchy.

Pour the steamed vegetables into a rectangular baking pan (about 13" x 9" x 2") and gently mix in the next 3 vegetables.

Remove finished baked potatoes from oven, but leave heat on. Cut enough cooked potatoes into 1" to 2" large chunks to equal 4 cups. In two separate batches, blend the next 5 ingredients together with potato chunks in a blender till smooth (cut all ingredients in half for each blender batch). Pour blended mixture on top of assorted vegetables in the baking pan.

Cover with pan lid or tin foil and bake at 375 degrees for about 15 more minutes, till all vegetables are heated through and carrot chunks are tender. Makes 10 to 12 servings. This dish is also delicious served cold the following day.

| SHOPPING LIST | |
|---|---|
| Regularly Kept in the Kitchen (Listed in Chapter 14, p. 703) | Fresh Produce |
| Lowfat milk<br>Butter or margarine<br>Spike<br>Black pepper | Potatoes<br>Winter squash<br>Carrots<br>Cauliflower<br>Mushrooms<br>Fresh or frozen peas<br>Fresh or frozen lima beans |

# NUTRITIONAL ANALYSIS FOR ONE SERVING
## POTATO CREAMED VEGETABLES

| NUTRIENT | Type: 14  FEMALE—23 TO 51 YEARS | % RDA | Amount |
|---|---|---|---|
| KCALORIES | ᴁ===== | 10% | 204.0 Kc |
| PROTEIN | ᴁ========= | 18% | 8.170 Gm |
| CARBOHYDRATE | ᴁ | NO RDA | 34.10 Gm |
| FAT | ᴁ | NO RDA | 5.030 Gm |
| FIBER—CRUDE | ᴁ | NO RDA | 2.560 Gm |
| CHOLESTEROL | ᴁ | NO RDA | 7.200 Mg |
| SATURATED FA | ᴁ | NO RDA | 1.710 Gm |
| OLEIC FA | ᴁ | NO RDA | 0.480 Gm |
| LINOLEIC FA | ᴁ | NO RDA | 0.040 Gm |
| SODIUM | ᴁ====== | 13% | 297.0 Mg |
| POTASSIUM | ᴁ============== | 29% | 1088 Mg |
| MAGNESIUM | ᴁ========= | 18% | 55.10 Mg |
| IRON | ᴁ====== | 13% | 2.410 Mg |
| ZINC | ᴁ=== | 6% | 1.040 Mg |
| VITAMIN A | ᴁ=================================================== | 236% | 9476 IU |
| VITAMIN D | ᴁ========== | 20% | 40.80 IU |
| VIT. E/TOTAL | ᴁ | NO RDA | 2.410 Mg |
| VITAMIN C | ᴁ=========================================== | 86% | 51.90 Mg |
| THIAMIN | ᴁ============== | 28% | 0.280 Mg |
| RIBOFLAVIN | ᴁ=============== | 31% | 0.380 Mg |
| NIACIN | ᴁ============ | 25% | 3.300 Mg |
| VITAMIN B6 | ᴁ=========== | 22% | 0.440 Mg |
| FOLACIN | ᴁ======== | 16% | 66.40 Ug |
| VITAMIN B12 | ᴁ===== | 11% | 0.350 Ug |
| PANTO- ACID | ᴁ================ | 33% | 1.820 Mg |
| CALCIUM | ᴁ========== | 20% | 167.0 Mg |
| PHOSPHORUS | ᴁ============= | 27% | 216.0 Mg |
| TRYPTOPHAN | ᴁ=================================== | 71% | 116.0 Mg |
| THREONINE | ᴁ====================================== | 76% | 332.0 Mg |
| ISOLEUCINE | ᴁ================================ | 66% | 433.0 Mg |
| LEUCINE | ᴁ===================================== | 74% | 645.0 Mg |
| LYSINE | ᴁ========================================== | 87% | 571.0 Mg |
| METHIONINE | ᴁ========================= | 51% | 140.0 Mg |
| CYSTINE | ᴁ============== | 29% | 80.40 Mg |
| PHENYL-ANINE | ᴁ========================================= | 82% | 357.0 Mg |
| TYROSINE | ᴁ=================================== | 71% | 312.0 Mg |
| VALINE | ᴁ================================= | 67% | 516.0 Mg |
| HISTIDINE | ᴁ | NO RDA | 194.0 Mg |
| ALCOHOL | ᴁ | NO RDA | 0.000 Gm |
| ASH | ᴁ | NO RDA | 2.890 Gm |
| COPPER | ᴁ======= | 14% | 0.350 Mg |
| MANGANESE | ᴁ===== | 10% | 0.400 Mg |
| IODINE | ᴁ======= | 14% | 21.00 Ug |
| MONO FAT | ᴁ | NO RDA | 1.660 Gm |
| POLY FAT | ᴁ | NO RDA | 1.330 Gm |
| CAFFEINE | ᴁ | NO RDA | 0.000 Gm |
| FLUORIDE | ᴁ=== | 6% | 191.0 Ug |
| MOLYBDENUM | ᴁ= | 2% | 9.300 Ug |
| VITAMIN K | ᴁ==================================================== | 800% | 840.0 Ug |
| SELENIUM | ᴁ | 0% | 0.000 Mg |
| BIOTIN | ᴁ== | 5% | 8.680 Ug |
| CHLORIDE | ᴁ | 0% | 0.000 Mg |
| CHROMIUM | ᴁ======== | 16% | 0.020 Mg |
| SUGAR | ᴁ | NO RDA | 5.290 Gm |
| FIBER—DIET | ᴁ | NO RDA | 1.860 Gm |
| VIT. E/AT | ᴁ== | 4% | 0.330 Mg |

```
% RDA:   0      20     40     60     80     100
```

Margarine used instead of butter in analysis.

# QUICK, CREAMY VEGETABLE SOUP

10 cups water
1 lb. frozen mixed vegetables (or 1 lb. combination
   of fresh peas, corn, carrots, green beans)
2 heaping cups bite-sized broccoli pieces
1 heaping cup bite-sized zucchini
1 heaping cup bite-sized yellow crookneck squash
1 heaping cup bite-sized carrots
1 heaping cup bite-sized celery

1 lb. tofu, diced

1 Tbsp. butter or margarine
1 Tbsp. asafetida or 2 Tbsp. minced garlic
1 cup sliced mushrooms
1 Tbsp. soy sauce
1 Tbsp. Italian herb seasoning
2 tsp. oregano
1 tsp. basil

1½ Tbsp. honey
1 Tbsp. salt (or to your taste)

6 oz. tomato paste
8 oz. Neufchatel or cream cheese

½ lb. whole grain spiral (or other shape)
   noodles, cooked

Bring first 7 ingredients to a boil. When water boils, lower heat and add tofu. Simmer about 20 minutes — only till vegetables get soft. In the meantime, saute next 7 ingredients together till mushrooms absorb soy sauce. Add this to vegetables in pot along with next 2 ingredients. Put next 2 ingredients in a blender with a couple cups of only the soup broth and blend till smooth. Pour this and cooked noodles into soup and stir. Soup is done! Makes a little over 1 gallon.

| SHOPPING LIST | | Special Shopping |
| --- | --- | --- |
| **Regularly Kept in the Kitchen (Listed in Chapter 14, p. 703)** | **Fresh Produce** | Neufchatel or cream cheese — found in supermarket cheese section or cheese specialty shops. Even though it adds more fat, you might want to use cream cheese here because it definitely makes a creamier tasting soup. |
| Tofu<br>Butter or margarine<br>Asafetida<br>Soy sauce<br>Italian herb seasoning<br>Oregano<br>Basil<br>Honey<br>Salt<br>Whole grain noodle (preferably spiral or other shape that will hold soup well) | Fresh or frozen vegetable mix (peas, corn, carrots, green beans)<br>Broccoli<br>Zucchini<br>Yellow crookneck squash<br>Carrots<br>Celery<br>Mushrooms<br>Tomato paste | |

The only time I ever boil vegetables is when I make soup. Boiling vegetables destroys a lot of vitamins, and almost all of the ones that aren't destroyed end up in the water. At least with soup, the water is consumed and not thrown away!

A healthy practice to get into is to use water saved from steaming vegetables (p. 155) or soaking legumes, nuts and/or seeds (pp. 470 - 1) in the soup.

# NUTRITIONAL ANALYSIS FOR ONE SERVING
## QUICK, CREAMY VEGETABLE SOUP

```
NUTRIENT       Type: 14    FEMALE-23 TO 51 YEARS         % RDA    Amount
KCALORIES      Ä====                                        8%   173.0 Kc
PROTEIN        Ä==========                                 21%   9.560 Gm
CARBOHYDRATE   Ä                                         NO RDA  20.00 Gm
FAT            Ä                                         NO RDA   7.000 Gm
FIBER-CRUDE    Ä                                         NO RDA   1.150 Gm
CHOLESTEROL    Ä                                         NO RDA  11.10 Mg
SATURATED FA   Ä                                         NO RDA   2.650 Gm
OLEIC FA       Ä                                         NO RDA   1.600 Gm
LINOLEIC FA    Ä                                         NO RDA   0.750 Gm
SODIUM         Ä===========                                23%   524.0 Mg
POTASSIUM      Ä=====                                      11%   416.0 Mg
MAGNESIUM      Ä========                                   16%   50.00 Mg
IRON           Ä============                               25%   4.520 Mg
ZINC           Ä===                                         7%   1.150 Mg
VITAMIN A      Ä=================================================  118%  4758 IU
VITAMIN D      Ä                                            0%   0.000 IU
VIT. E/TOTAL   Ä                                         NO RDA   0.700 Mg
VITAMIN C      Ä==================                         39%   23.70 Mg
THIAMIN        Ä========                                   16%   0.160 Mg
RIBOFLAVIN     Ä======                                     12%   0.150 Mg
NIACIN         Ä=====                                      10%   1.420 Mg
VITAMIN B6     Ä====                                        9%   0.180 Mg
FOLACIN        Ä===                                         7%   29.40 Ug
VITAMIN B12    Ä                                            1%   0.030 Ug
PANTO- ACID    Ä=====                                      11%   0.650 Mg
CALCIUM        Ä===============                            30%   246.0 Mg
PHOSPHORUS     Ä=========                                  19%   152.0 Mg
TRYPTOPHAN     Ä=======================================    78%   128.0 Mg
THREONINE      Ä=============================================  91%  398.0 Mg
ISOLEUCINE     Ä=====================================      75%   493.0 Mg
LEUCINE        Ä==================================         69%   604.0 Mg
LYSINE         Ä=============================================  92%  605.0 Mg
METHIONINE     Ä===============================            63%   173.0 Mg
CYSTINE        Ä=======================                    47%   128.0 Mg
PHENYL-ANINE   Ä=========================================== 115%  503.0 Mg
TYROSINE       Ä====================================       74%   323.0 Mg
VALINE         Ä=================================          69%   528.0 Mg
HISTIDINE      Ä                                         NO RDA  291.0 Mg
ALCOHOL        Ä                                         NO RDA   0.000 Gm
ASH            Ä                                         NO RDA   1.810 Gm
COPPER         Ä=====                                      11%   0.280 Mg
MANGANESE      Ä===========                                23%   0.890 Mg
IODINE         Ä=======================================    78%   117.0 Ug
MONO FAT       Ä                                         NO RDA   1.870 Gm
POLY FAT       Ä                                         NO RDA   1.830 Gm
CAFFEINE       Ä                                         NO RDA   0.000 Mg
FLUORIDE       Ä                                            1%   30.10 Ug
MOLYBDENUM     Ä================================================  201%  655.0 Ug
VITAMIN K      Ä==============================             58%   61.00 Ug
SELENIUM       Ä====                                        8%   0.010 Mg
BIOTIN         Ä=                                           2%   4.400 Ug
CHLORIDE       Ä=                                           2%   68.80 Mg
CHROMIUM       Ä================================================  128%  0.160 Mg
SUGAR          Ä                                         NO RDA   2.010 Gm
FIBER-DIET     Ä                                         NO RDA   1.690 Gm
VIT. E/AT      Ä=                                           3%   0.250 Mg

   % RDA:   |0      |20     |40     |60     |80     |100
```

Margarine used instead of butter; Neufchatel used instead of cream cheese; peas, corn, carrots and green beans used as the mixed vegetable combination in analysis.

# MUSHROOM TERRINE

☆ A single vegetable terrine; make other terrines featuring other vegetables by replacing mushrooms with another vegetable and changing flavorings to suit the vegetable.

---

1 lb. Chinese firm tofu
2 Tbsp. Bipro
2 tsp. nutritional yeast
2 tsp. soy sauce
2 tsp. raw cashew butter
¼ tsp. asafetida

1 Tbsp. butter or margarine
½ cup chopped scallions
¾ lb. mushrooms, chopped

½ tsp. Spike or other vegetable-seasoned salt
¼ tsp. white pepper
⅛ tsp. mace
⅛ tsp. powdered ginger
2 tsp. very finely minced, fresh basil
1 tsp. very finely minced, fresh rosemary
1 tsp. very finely minced, fresh parsley

Preheat oven to 200 degrees.

Run first 6 ingredients together in blender or food processor till smooth. Saute next 3 ingredients together till scallions wilt (don't cook too long or liquid will come out of mushrooms. Mix last 7 ingredients into mushrooms and gently fold all into blended tofu mixture. Pour into lightly oiled baking pan. Heat a small pot of water to 175 degrees and pour into a shallow (pie or cake) pan. The mixture can also be poured into individual-sized molds (there are different shaped molds sold especially for this in gourmet stores, but a muffin tin will do).

Set the baking pan with the terrine in it inside of the water and bake in oven at 200 degrees for 45 to 50 minutes. Cool to room temperature and refrigerate. When ready to serve, unmold. Can be served as is or covered with a chaufroid or an aspic jelly, if desired, and served with a sauce if you like. Makes about 4 servings.

Make a filled terrine (like in timbales) by lining entire surface of terrine mold with the terrine mixture about ½" to 2" thick (depending on whether you're using individual- or loaf-sized molds). Pour a flavored cream sauce with vegetables into cavity and top with more terrine mixture to seal in. Cook as in cooking Mushroom Terrine.

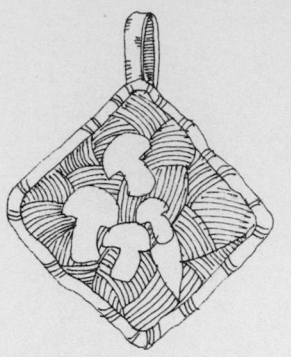

| SHOPPING LIST | |
| --- | --- |
| **Regularly Kept in the Kitchen (Listed in Chapter 14, p. 703)** | **Fresh Produce** |
| Chinese firm tofu | Scallions |
| Bipro | Mushrooms |
| Nutritional yeast | Basil |
| Soy sauce | Parsley |
| Raw cashew butter | Rosemary |
| Asafetida | |
| Butter or margarine | |
| Spike | |
| White pepper | |
| Mace | |
| Powdered ginger | |

# NUTRITIONAL ANALYSIS FOR ONE SERVING MUSHROOM TERRINE

```
NUTRIENT         Type: 14    FEMALE-23 TO 51 YEARS          % RDA    Amount
KCALORIES        A======                                     12%     254.0 Kc
PROTEIN          A==========================                 51%     22.70 Gm
CARBOHYDRATE     A                                          NO RDA   14.00 Gm
FAT              A                                          NO RDA   14.40 Gm
FIBER-CRUDE      A                                          NO RDA   1.020 Gm
CHOLESTEROL      A                                          NO RDA   0.020 Mg
SATURATED FA     A                                          NO RDA   2.220 Gm
OLEIC FA         A                                          NO RDA   1.130 Gm
LINOLEIC FA      A                                          NO RDA   2.260 Gm
SODIUM           A=========                                  16%     353.0 Mg
POTASSIUM        A=========                                  19%     715.0 Mg
MAGNESIUM        A===============                            29%     87.50 Mg
IRON             A=========================================  75%     13.60 Mg
ZINC             A=========                                  16%     2.540 Mg
VITAMIN A        A====                                        8%     336.0 IU
VITAMIN D        A                                            0%     0.000 IU
VIT. E/TOTAL     A                                          NO RDA   0.250 Mg
VITAMIN C        A====                                        8%     4.980 Mg
THIAMIN          A========================================= 103%    1.030 Mg
RIBOFLAVIN       A========================================= 105%    1.260 Mg
NIACIN           A==============================             64%     8.410 Mg
VITAMIN B6       A=======================                    47%     0.940 Mg
FOLACIN          A=======                                    15%     63.20 Ug
VITAMIN B12      A==========                                 19%     0.580 Ug
PANTO- ACID      A==================                         39%     2.170 Mg
CALCIUM          A========================================= 100%    800.0 Mg
PHOSPHORUS       A=====================                      44%     354.0 Mg
TRYPTOPHAN       A========================================= 234%    382.0 Mg
THREONINE        A========================================= 218%    952.0 Mg
ISOLEUCINE       A========================================= 168%    1098 Mg
LEUCINE          A========================================= 200%    1742 Mg
LYSINE           A========================================= 244%    1597 Mg
METHIONINE       A========================================= 118%    321.0 Mg
CYSTINE          A========================================= 111%    304.0 Mg
PHENYL-ANINE     A========================================= 243%    1059 Mg
TYROSINE         A========================================= 170%    742.0 Mg
VALINE           A========================================= 151%    1153 Mg
HISTIDINE        A                                          NO RDA   638.0 Mg
ALCOHOL          A                                          NO RDA   0.000 Gm
ASH              A                                          NO RDA   3.810 Gm
COPPER           A============                               23%     0.580 Mg
MANGANESE        A==================                         35%     1.340 Mg
IODINE           A=========================================  90%     136.0 Ug
MONO FAT         A                                          NO RDA   4.300 Gm
POLY FAT         A                                          NO RDA   6.870 Gm
CAFFEINE         A                                          NO RDA   0.000 Mg
FLUORIDE         A                                            0%     0.000 Ug
MOLYBDENUM       A========================================= 418%    136.0 Ug
VITAMIN K        A                                            0%     0.000 Ug
SELENIUM         A========                                   16%     0.020 Mg
BIOTIN           A=                                           3%     4.850 Ug
CHLORIDE         A===                                         6%     215.0 Mg
CHROMIUM         A========================================= 288%    0.360 Mg
SUGAR            A                                          NO RDA   0.000 Gm
FIBER-DIET       A                                          NO RDA   0.000 Gm
VIT. E/AT        A                                            1%     0.110 Mg

   % RDA:   |0      |20     |40     |60     |80     |100
```

Margarine used instead of butter in analysis.

# MULTI·VEGETABLE TERRINE

☆ A vegetable entree that can be served as everyday fare or dressed up for an appearance in a gourmet meal.

1 cup grated cheese (optional)

⅔ cup lowfat milk or water
2 lbs. Chinese firm tofu, crumbled
3 Tbsp. raw cashew butter
⅓ cup nutritional yeast
2 Tbsp. soy sauce
4 Tbsp. Bipro

2 Tbsp. wheat germ

½ Tbsp. butter or margarine
½ cup chopped shallots
1 Tbsp. chopped, fresh parsley

3 cups cooked brown rice
2 tsp. soy sauce
¼ tsp. black pepper
¼ lb. Chinese firm tofu, cut in
   less than ¼" cubes
1 Tbsp. nutritional yeast

1 Tbsp. butter or margarine
4 cups coarsely grated carrot
1 tsp. Spike or other vegetable-seasoned salt
⅛ tsp. white pepper

1 Tbsp. finely chopped, fresh dill weed

½ Tbsp. butter and/or water
2 cups finely chopped broccoli
¼ tsp. powdered ginger
¼ tsp. nutmeg
⅛ tsp. black pepper

2 cups grated yellow crookneck squash
1 cup finely chopped red bell pepper

1 Tbsp. lemon juice
½ tsp. honey
⅛ tsp. cayenne

Sauteing and stir-frying are another healthy way to cook vegetables because they cook quickly and aren't in any extra liquid that would draw water-soluble vitamins out of the vegetables. Lightly coating vegetables with oil or butter keeps oxygen from getting at them (oxygen causes vitamin loss) just as steam keeps oxygen from getting at steamed vegetables.

Preheat oven to 350 degrees. Oil a 9" x 5" x 3" bread loaf pan.

Grate cheese (if you're going to use it — the terrine is delicious without it!). Blend next 6 ingredients together in a blender till smooth and creamy. Sprinkle wheat germ all over surface of oiled bread loaf pan till all oiled surfaces are covered with wheat germ. Saute next 3 ingredients together till herbs wilt. Add next 5 ingredients and mix thoroughly. Divide rice mixture in half; set aside half and mix other half with 1/5 of the blended tofu mixture and pour this into bottom of bread pan to form an even layer. (If using cheese, sprinkle ¼ of it between each layer.) Saute next 4 ingredients for about 3 to 5 minutes. Pour sauted carrots out of skillet into a bowl and mix in dill and 1/5 of the blended tofu; spread this evenly on top of rice layer. Saute next 5 ingredients together, pour into a bowl and mix in with 1/5 of blended tofu; spread this evenly over carrot layer. Pour off extra juice from squash and red bell peppers; saute for 3 to 5 minutes, pour into bowl and mix in last 3 ingredients and 1/5 of blended tofu mixture; spread this evenly over broccoli layer. Mix remaining rice mixture with last 1/5 of tofu mixture and spread evenly on top of squash and bell pepper layer. Cover top with a sheet of parchment or wax paper and wrap entire bread pan in foil. Bake at 350 degrees for 1½ hours.

Allow to cool and set at least ½ hour before serving. To serve warm, unwrap pan from foil and invert pan onto a serving platter to turn terrine out. Cut slices about ¾" thick. To serve cold, allow baked terrine to sit out (still wrapped in foil) overnight, then refrigerate 6 to 8 hours. To dress this up into a real gourmet dish, "frost" the whole turned-out loaf with Cholesterol-Free Chaufroid Sauce, decorate with fresh herbs, vegetables, etc., and glaze with Quick Aspic. You can also slice the terrine into ¾" slices and dress and decorate each individual slice with Cholesterol-Free Chaufroid Sauce, vegetables and herbs, and Quick Aspic. Because of the different-colored layers, it's also attractive to glaze each individual slice only with the Quick Aspic. Makes about 10 servings.

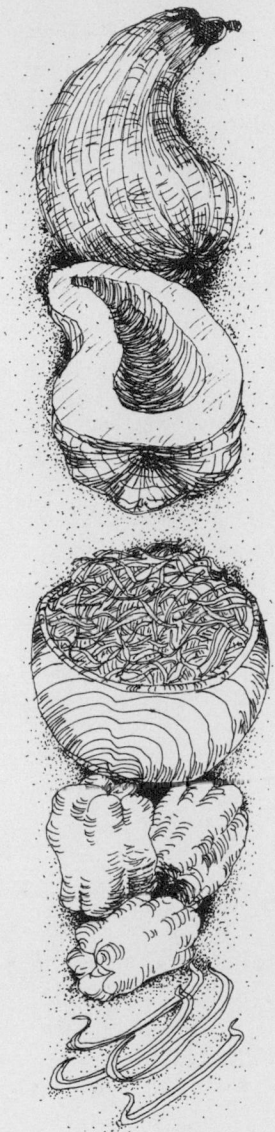

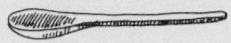

| SHOPPING LIST | |
| --- | --- |
| **Regularly Kept in the Kitchen**<br>**(Listed in Chapter 14, p. 703)** | **Fresh Produce** |
| Wheat germ<br>Butter or margarine<br>Brown rice<br>Soy sauce<br>Black pepper<br>Tofu<br>Nutritional yeast<br>Lowfat milk<br>Raw cashew butter<br>Bipro<br>Spike<br>White pepper<br>Ginger<br>Nutmeg<br>Honey<br>Cayenne | Shallots<br>Fresh parsley<br>Carrot<br>Fresh dill weed<br>Broccoli<br>Yellow crookneck squash<br>Red bell pepper<br>Lemon |

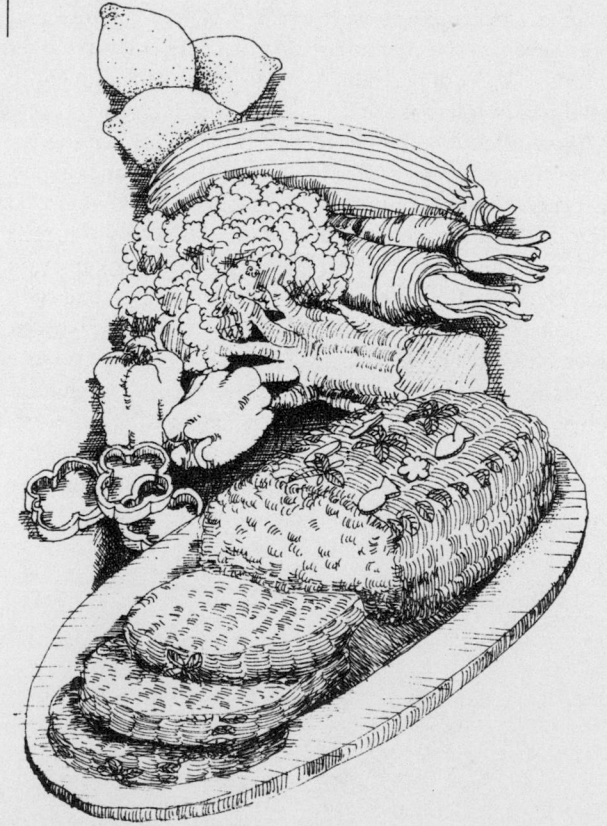

# NUTRITIONAL ANALYSIS FOR ONE SERVING MULTI-VEGETABLE TERRINE WITH CHAUFROID SAUCE AND QUICK ASPIC

| NUTRIENT | Type: 14 FEMALE–23 TO 51 YEARS | % RDA | Amount |
|---|---|---|---|
| KCALORIES | A=========== | 21% | 427.0 Kc |
| PROTEIN | A================================ | 63% | 28.10 Gm |
| CARBOHYDRATE | A | NO RDA | 43.40 Gm |
| FAT | A | NO RDA | 18.50 Gm |
| FIBER–CRUDE | A | NO RDA | 1.710 Gm |
| CHOLESTEROL | A | NO RDA | 1.210 Mg |
| SATURATED FA | A | NO RDA | 3.130 Gm |
| OLEIC FA | A | NO RDA | 2.930 Gm |
| LINOLEIC FA | A | NO RDA | 2.230 Gm |
| SODIUM | A================== | 36% | 803.0 Mg |
| POTASSIUM | A============ | 25% | 956.0 Mg |
| MAGNESIUM | A========================== | 53% | 161.0 Mg |
| IRON | A===================================== | 78% | 14.10 Mg |
| ZINC | A============== | 28% | 4.310 Mg |
| VITAMIN A | A=================================================== | 357% | 14308 IU |
| VITAMIN D | A= | 3% | 7.210 IU |
| VIT. E/TOTAL | A | NO RDA | 1.870 Mg |
| VITAMIN C | A================================ | 63% | 38.10 Mg |
| THIAMIN | A================================== | 368% | 3.680 Mg |
| RIBOFLAVIN | A================================== | 296% | 3.560 Mg |
| NIACIN | A================================== | 167% | 21.80 Mg |
| VITAMIN B6 | A================================== | 185% | 3.700 Mg |
| FOLACIN | A=============== | 30% | 123.0 Ug |
| VITAMIN B12 | A========================================== | 87% | 2.610 Ug |
| PANTO– ACID | A============ | 23% | 1.300 Mg |
| CALCIUM | A================================== | 103% | 831.0 Mg |
| PHOSPHORUS | A============================== | 62% | 496.0 Mg |
| TRYPTOPHAN | A================================== | 250% | 408.0 Mg |
| THREONINE | A================================== | 259% | 1127 Mg |
| ISOLEUCINE | A================================== | 203% | 1331 Mg |
| LEUCINE | A================================== | 244% | 2126 Mg |
| LYSINE | A================================== | 273% | 1784 Mg |
| METHIONINE | A=========================================■■■■ | 145% | 395.0 Mg |
| CYSTINE | A================================== | 143% | 391.0 Mg |
| PHENYL–ANINE | A================================== | 295% | 1286 Mg |
| TYROSINE | A================================== | 211% | 922.0 Mg |
| VALINE | A================================== | 191% | 1462 Mg |
| HISTIDINE | A | NO RDA | 776.0 Mg |
| ALCOHOL | A | NO RDA | 0.000 Gm |
| ASH | A | NO RDA | 6.970 Gm |
| COPPER | A================ | 32% | 0.820 Mg |
| MANGANESE | A============================= | 65% | 2.460 Mg |
| IODINE | A================================ | 160% | 241.0 Ug |
| MONO FAT | A | NO RDA | 6.250 Gm |
| POLY FAT | A | NO RDA | 7.040 Gm |
| CAFFEINE | A | NO RDA | 0.000 Mg |
| FLUORIDE | A | 1% | 30.20 Ug |
| MOLYBDENUM | A================================ | 489% | 1590 Ug |
| VITAMIN K | A================ | 34% | 36.10 Ug |
| SELENIUM | A==== | 8% | 0.010 Mg |
| BIOTIN | A==== | 8% | 12.90 Ug |
| CHLORIDE | A=== | 7% | 243.0 Mg |
| CHROMIUM | A================================== | 376% | 0.470 Mg |
| SUGAR | A | NO RDA | 2.690 Gm |
| FIBER–DIET | A | NO RDA | 1.430 Gm |
| VIT. E/AT | A====== | 12% | 0.970 Mg |

```
% RDA:   |0      |20     |40     |60     |80     |100
```

Water used instead of dry white wine in chaufroid sauce; optional grated cheese not included in terrine. Margarine used instead of butter.

# CHOLESTEROL-FREE CHAUFROID SAUCE

☆ Dressing up a loaf or individual-sized terrine with this "frosting" makes it a true gourmet dish.

---

*3 cups water*
*1 vegetable bouillon cube*
*2 Tbsp. chopped scallions*
*2 dried shiitake mushrooms*
*1 Tbsp. nutritional yeast*
*½ stick agar-agar (¼ cup flakes)*

*¼ cup raw cashew butter*
*¼ cup Chinese firm tofu*
*2 Tbsp. dry white wine or water*
*2 Tbsp. arrowroot*
*¼ tsp. Spike or other vegetable-seasoned salt*
*⅛ tsp. white pepper*

You may have seen photos of decorated terrines in French gourmet cookbooks. They're usually covered with a white or light-green chaufroid sauce and look somewhat like frosted cakes with beautiful vegetable decorations. The decorating of the chaufroid sauce is usually done with fresh herbs, vegetables cut in flower-like shapes and sometimes sliced nuts. The decorations are usually made to look like flowering plants. Use your imagination to create a pretty, colorful picture with vegetables and then glaze over with Quick Aspic to help decorations stick to chaufroid sauce and to add a shimmer to them as well.

Simmer first 6 ingredients together till they cook down to 1¼ to 1½ cups of broth. Remove and discard mushrooms and turn off heat. Blend last 6 ingredients together till smooth; leave blender on low and slowly strain broth through a strainer into running blender and blend till smooth, being sure all of tofu mixture is blended in (you may have to stop blender and scrape off sides). Pour through strainer back into pot that broth was cooked in and bring to a boil, stirring constantly to avoid lumping. Put ice cubes in a bowl that the broth pot can fit in easily. Set broth pot, with chaufroid sauce in it, in the bowl of ice cubes and gently stir chaufroid sauce till it cools and just begins to set. Immediately spread sauce on cold terrine (will not work on a warm or hot one), just like icing a cake. Decorate as desired, and glaze with Quick Aspic.

| SHOPPING LIST | |
|---|---|
| **Regularly Kept in the Kitchen** (Listed in Chapter 14, p. 703) | **Fresh Produce** |
| Shiitake mushrooms Nutritional yeast Raw cashew butter Tofu Arrowroot Spike White pepper | Scallions Dry white wine |

**Special Shopping**

Agar-agar — found in Japanese groceries, Oriental aisles in supermarkets, or natural food stores.
Vegetable bouillon cube — found in natural food stores (in case you're wondering, I use Morga bouillon cubes because they contain no sugar).

# QUICK ASPIC

*2 cups water and 1 vegetable bouillon cube*
   *(or 2 cups vegetable broth)*
*½ cup dry white wine*
*½ stick agar-agar (¼ cup flakes)*
*1 Tbsp. arrowroot*
*1 bay leaf*
*⅛ tsp. white pepper*

Combine all ingredients in a pot and mix till arrowroot is dissolved. Put on heat and bring to a boil, stirring constantly till agar-agar is completely dissolved. Remove bay leaf and while still warm, paint onto terrine that needs to be glazed.

Any leftover aspic can be poured into a small, shallow pan and allowed to cool. When jellied, cut into cubes and serve as an appetizer or on top of a salad at another meal.

| SHOPPING LIST | |
|---|---|
| **Regularly Kept in the Kitchen** (Listed in Chapter 14, p. 703) | **Fresh Produce** |
| Arrowroot Bay leaf White pepper | Dry white wine |

**Special Shopping**

Agar-agar — found in Japanese groceries, Oriental aisles in supermarkets, or natural food stores.
Vegetable bouillon cube — found in natural food stores.

# VEGETABLES STAR IN GOURMET MEALS

The Chinese philosopher, Lao Tsu, of ancient times wrote, "Under heaven, nothing is more soft and yielding than water. Yet for attacking the solid and strong, nothing is better. It has no equal. The weak can overcome the strong. The supple can overcome the stiff. Under heaven, everyone knows this. Yet no one puts it into practice."

I love to take vegetables out of the sidelines and feature them as the center of the meal in entrees that win rave reviews. The response I often get to this idea amazes me because most people are accustomed to eating vegetables as the "boiled to death" variety, or more healthfully steamed but still uninteresting side dish on a plate.

Very few have been served delicious, satisfying dishes consisting of mainly vegetables. If you are one of those people who have never featured fresh vegetables as an entree, please try the following recipes (at separate meals) for a pleasant surprise. If you already know what wonderful entrees fresh vegetables can make, you can add these recipes from around the world, and the different preparation techniques, to your collection.

# AVOCADO GAZPACHO

☆ Chilled soups make a light, refreshing meal on hot summer days!

---

3 medium avocados (about 3 cups' worth)
1 cup chopped cucumber
1 cup chopped bell pepper
2 tomatoes, chopped
¼ tsp. asafetida or ½ clove garlic juice
2 Tbsp. finely chopped fresh parsley
Pinch cayenne
1 Tbsp. soy sauce
⅛ tsp. black pepper
2 Tbsp. lemon juice
1 quart tomato juice
⅛ tsp. cumin
1 tsp. basil
½ tsp. oregano

Peel and cube avocados. In a large bowl, combine all ingredients. Stir to blend; chill. Makes about 2 quarts (8 servings).

## SUGGESTED LUNCH OR LIGHT SUPPER MENU FOR A HOT SUMMER DAY

Hot Sticks (p. 293)

Cheese platter

Avocado Gazpacho

Neapolitan Tofu
Cheesecake (p. 361)

| SHOPPING LIST | |
|---|---|
| **Regularly Kept in the Kitchen** (Listed in Chapter 14, p. 703) | **Fresh Produce** |
| Cayenne | Avocados |
| Soy sauce | Cucumber |
| Black pepper | Bell pepper |
| Cumin | Tomatoes |
| Basil | Parsley |
| Oregano | Lemon |
| | Tomato juice |

# GREEK SPINACH PIE

☆ This tasty gourmet entree may even please those who usually don't like spinach!

*½ lb. Filo dough*

*2 Tbsp. margarine or olive oil*
*2 cups diced celery and 2 tsp. asafetida*
*  OR 1 onion, diced*
*8 cups steamed or frozen spinach*

*½ lb. mashed tofu (about 1 cup)*
*1 cup water*
*2 Tbsp. Bipro*

*2 cups cottage cheese*
*1 cup crumbled feta cheese*
*¾ tsp. black pepper*
*¾ tsp. dill or tarragon*
*Juice of 1 lemon*

*1 cup melted butter or margarine OR 1 cup*
*  olive oil and ½ cup nutritional yeast*

*Wheat germ*
*Bran*

There are some vegetables that are more digestible when lightly steamed, like spinach and carrots. I often use frozen vegetables because studies have shown that frozen vegetables often contain more vitamins than the same ones "fresh" off the supermarket shelf. They can also be less expensive than the shelf ones (and available!) when the vegetable is out of season. When it comes to a dish in which spinach will be cooked, I always use frozen spinach because fresh spinach shrinks so incredibly when cooked that it's actually less expensive to get the frozen spinach!

Most likely you'll use a frozen commercial Filo dough (also sometimes spelled "Phyllo"), which should be thawed according to the directions on the package. (If frozen Filo dough isn't available and you are a fairly skilled baker, homemade strudel dough can be used in its place.)

Saute the next 3 ingredients till celery or onion becomes translucent. Add steamed spinach and cook on high heat, stirring often, till excess water cooks out. Remove from heat. Blend next 3 ingredients in blender till smooth. Pour this and the next 5 ingredients into the already cooked spinach and mix in thoroughly.

Preheat oven to 350 degrees.

Now get the thawed Filo dough ready to work with by unfolding the dough, laying it out flat on top of a counter and covering with a slightly moistened cloth to prevent dough from drying out or becoming brittle while you're fixing the pie. Using a basting brush or an unused paint brush, and the 1 cup of melted butter (or olive oil and yeast mixture), grease the bottom of a 13½" x 8¾" x 1¾" baking pan. (Size of pan can be varied a little.)

Now place 1 sheet of dough in bottom of pan with edges of dough coming up the sides of pan. If dough doesn't fit exactly, just tuck it in. It doesn't have to be neat. Brush very lightly with melted butter (or olive oil and yeast mixture). Sprinkle lightly with a little of the wheat germ and bran.

Repeat this process till there's a stack of 10 buttered sheets in bottom of pan. (As you layer the Filo dough, some of it may tear, but don't worry — the tear will be covered by the next few layers.)

Now spread the spinach filling evenly on top of the 10 layered Filo sheets and fold edges of dough over spinach filling. Top the filling off with another stack of 10 sheets, brushing each with butter and sprinkling with bran and wheat germ as before. Push edges of dough down into the sides of the pan and cut diamond or square serving-sized shapes in top crust layer with very sharp knife. Bake at 375 degrees for 15 minutes, then turn heat down to 350 degrees and bake for another 45 minutes, or till top of dough is golden brown and pie shrinks a bit from sides of pan. Allow to sit about 15 to 20 minutes before cutting; then cut along lines previously made in the top crust.

This Spinach Pie can be made ahead of time (before the day it's to be served) and then frozen. To do this, simply cover the pie tightly with foil after it's baked and cooled. Then, the night before or morning of the day it's to be served, remove the pie from the freezer and allow to sit at room temperature to thaw. Then bake at 350 degrees till heated all the way through. This usually takes about 20 to 30 minutes.

Serves 6 to 8 when cut in larger pieces and used as an entree. Can also be cut into 24 approximately 2" squares and used as an hors d'oeuvres.

| SHOPPING LIST | |
|---|---|
| Regularly Kept in the Kitchen (Listed in Chapter 14, p. 703) | Fresh Produce |
| Margarine or olive oil<br>Asafetida<br>Tofu<br>Bipro<br>Black pepper<br>Dill or tarragon<br>Wheat germ<br>Bran | Celery<br>Fresh or frozen spinach<br>Lowfat cottage cheese<br>Feta cheese<br>Lemon |

| Special Shopping |
|---|
| Filo (Phyllo) dough — found in the refrigerated or freezer section in gourmet food stores and some supermarkets; also in Mid-Eastern and Greek groceries. |

# NUTRITIONAL ANALYSIS FOR ONE SERVING GREEK SPINACH PIE

```
NUTRIENT       Type: 14   FEMALE-23 TO 51 YEARS            % RDA   Amount
KCALORIES      Å===============                             28%   575.0 Kc
PROTEIN        Å=================================           64%    28.40 Gm
CARBOHYDRATE   Å                                          NO RDA   34.60 Gm
FAT            Å                                          NO RDA   38.40 Gm
FIBER-CRUDE    Å                                          NO RDA    2.080 Gm
CHOLESTEROL    Å                                          NO RDA   20.70 Mg
SATURATED FA   Å                                          NO RDA    8.240 Gm
OLEIC FA       Å                                          NO RDA   21.50 Gm
LINOLEIC FA    Å                                          NO RDA    3.260 Gm
SODIUM         Å=============                               27%   605.0 Mg
POTASSIUM      Å=================                           32%   1231 Mg
MAGNESIUM      Å====================================        75%   227.0 Mg
IRON           Å===============================             63%    11.40 Mg
ZINC           Å=================                           32%    4.830 Mg
VITAMIN A      Å=====================================================  373%  14951 IU
VITAMIN D      Å                                             1%    2.300 IU
VIT. E/TOTAL   Å                                          NO RDA    9.800 Mg
VITAMIN C      Å===================                         37%    22.50 Mg
THIAMIN        Å=================================================== 494%   4.950 Mg
RIBOFLAVIN     Å=================================================== 431%   5.180 Mg
NIACIN         Å=================================================== 222%   28.90 Mg
VITAMIN B6     Å=================================================== 255%   5.100 Mg
FOLACIN        Å==============================================       90%   360.0 Ug
VITAMIN B12    Å=================================================== 130%   3.900 Ug
PANTO- ACID    Å==========                                  21%    1.180 Mg
CALCIUM        Å=====================================        73%   587.0 Mg
PHOSPHORUS     Å=============================                62%   496.0 Mg
TRYPTOPHAN     Å=================================================== 204%   334.0 Mg
THREONINE      Å=================================================== 256%   1115 Mg
ISOLEUCINE     Å=================================================== 206%   1350 Mg
LEUCINE        Å=================================================== 255%   2222 Mg
LYSINE         Å=================================================== 274%   1795 Mg
METHIONINE     Å=================================================== 193%   525.0 Mg
CYSTINE        Å=================================================== 126%   344.0 Mg
PHENYL-ANINE   Å=================================================== 290%   1263 Mg
TYROSINE       Å=================================================== 251%   1092 Mg
VALINE         Å=================================================== 193%   1473 Mg
HISTIDINE      Å                                          NO RDA   741.0 Mg
ALCOHOL        Å                                          NO RDA    0.000 Gm
ASH            Å                                          NO RDA    9.870 Gm
COPPER         Å==========                                  21%    0.530 Mg
MANGANESE      Å=====================================        72%    2.730 Mg
IODINE         Å=======================                      45%    68.70 Ug
MONO FAT       Å                                          NO RDA   22.90 Gm
POLY FAT       Å                                          NO RDA    5.180 Gm
CAFFEINE       Å                                          NO RDA    0.000 Mg
FLUORIDE       Å====                                         9%   268.0 Ug
MOLYBDENUM     Å=================================================== 184%   601.0 Ug
VITAMIN K      Å=================================================== 152%   160.0 Ug
SELENIUM       Å========                                    16%    0.020 Mg
BIOTIN         Å=========                                   16%    24.60 Ug
CHLORIDE       Å                                             1%    66.90 Mg
CHROMIUM       Å=================================================== 128%   0.160 Mg
SUGAR          Å                                          NO RDA    1.720 Gm
FIBER-DIET     Å                                          NO RDA    5.510 Gm
VIT. E/AT      Å==============================================       95%   7.610 Mg

   % RDA:  |0      |20      |40      |60      |80      |100
```

Onion used instead of celery and asafetida; olive oil and nutritional yeast used instead of melted butter or margarine in analysis.

# MID·EASTERN
# EGGPLANT ROLLS

☆ An elegant, yet simple, entree that's delicious served
warm or cold.

2 large eggplants
Olive oil for frying

3 Tbsp. olive oil
2 cups cooked, mashed garbanzo beans
2 tsp. asafetida or 3 - 4 cloves garlic, crushed
1 tsp. ground cumin
¼ tsp. ground coriander
½ tsp. black pepper
⅛ tsp. cayenne

2 cups finely chopped, fresh parsley
1 cup cooked bulgur
1 cup chopped frozen spinach
¼ cup lemon juice
3 Tbsp. raw sesame tahini
2 Tbsp. soy sauce

Make Yogurt Dressing (see following recipe) and cook garbanzo beans. Pour 1 cup boiling water over ½ cup uncooked
bulgar; then cover and allow grain to cook while preparing
the rest of the ingredients. To prepare eggplant, cut tops and
thin slices of round edges from opposite ends of eggplant.
Now cut ¼"-thick slices lengthwise.

Heat a little olive oil in a large skillet. Lay slices of eggplant
in to cook over medium heat with lid on, adding more oil if
needed. (Eggplant absorbs oil as it cooks, so watch to be sure
there is enough oil to keep eggplant from sticking to skillet.)
When you can see the top surface and edge of eggplant slices
take on a wet, almost translucent appearance, flip over and
cook for same length of time on other side. Remove from
heat when whole slice is cooked through and tender. Cook
all the slices in this way.

Make filling by pouring olive oil and garbanzo beans into
skillet and lightly mashing (so beans get crushed, but don't
mash into a paste). Add spices and saute together for a few
minutes to disperse flavor of spices. Turn off heat and add
next 6 ingredients. Mix well. Filling is now ready to go into
cooked eggplant slices.

Preheat oven to 350 degrees.

## SUGGESTED MENU

*Tossed salad with
Hot-Chaunce
Salad Dressing (p. 597)*

*Whole Grain
Confetti Salad
(p. 458)*

*Mid-Eastern
Eggplant Rolls
with Yogurt Dressing*

*Carrot Halavah Cake
(p. 46)*

A favorite sandwich around our
house is the Eggplant Sandwich.
Just put hot eggplant cutlets —
as made in the Mid-Eastern
Eggplant Rolls before they're
stuffed and rolled (perhaps cut
to ¾" thick instead of ¼") —
between dressed pieces of whole
grain bread with some grated
cheese and suitable sandwich
vegetables.

Spread ¼ to ⅓ cup of filling in a strip across width of cooked eggplant slice about ⅓ of the way up. Roll small edge over filling, continuing till eggplant is completely rolled. Place seam side down in a baking dish, securing with a toothpick if you like (it's not really necessary, though). Fill tray, arranging rolls in rows side by side. Bake at 350 degrees for 10 minutes. To serve, place 2 or 3 rolls on a plate, pour Yogurt Sauce over them, and sprinkle with paprika. Makes 6 to 8 servings.

| Special Shopping |
| --- |
| Raw sesame tahini — found in natural food stores or Mid-Eastern food stores. |

| SHOPPING LIST | |
| --- | --- |
| **Regularly Kept in the Kitchen (Listed in Chapter 14, p. 703)** | **Fresh Produce** |
| Olive oil | Eggplants |
| Garbanzo beans | Parsley |
| Asafetida | Spinach |
| Cumin | Lemon |
| Coriander | |
| Black pepper | |
| Cayenne | |
| Bulgar | |
| Soy sauce | |

# NUTRITIONAL ANALYSIS FOR ONE SERVING
## MID-EASTERN EGGPLANT ROLLS WITH YOGURT DRESSING

```
NUTRIENT        Type: 14   FEMALE-23 TO 51 YEARS          % RDA   Amount
KCALORIES       A==========                                20%    413.0 Kc
PROTEIN         A====================                      38%    17.00 Gm
CARBOHYDRATE    A                                          NO RDA 60.50 Gm
FAT             A                                          NO RDA 14.10 Gm
FIBER-CRUDE     A                                          NO RDA 5.090 Gm
CHOLESTEROL     A                                          NO RDA 4.660 Mg
SATURATED FA    A                                          NO RDA 2.490 Gm
OLEIC FA        A                                          NO RDA 5.070 Gm
LINOLEIC FA     A                                          NO RDA 0.580 Gm
SODIUM          A===========                               22%    502.0 Mg
POTASSIUM       A==================                        35%    1346 Mg
MAGNESIUM       A====================                      40%    122.0 Mg
IRON            A==================                        37%    6.690 Mg
ZINC            A========                                  17%    2.640 Mg
VITAMIN A       A=================================================== 101%  4056 IU
VITAMIN D       A                                          0%     0.000 IU
VIT. E/TOTAL    A                                          NO RDA 3.150 Mg
VITAMIN C       A==============================            59%    35.60 Mg
THIAMIN         A=========================                 49%    0.490 Mg
RIBOFLAVIN      A=================                         35%    0.420 Mg
NIACIN          A===============                           30%    3.910 Mg
VITAMIN B6      A===========                               22%    0.440 Mg
FOLACIN         A===========================               55%    221.0 Ug
VITAMIN B12     A=======                                   14%    0.420 Ug
PANTO- ACID     A========                                  17%    0.960 Mg
CALCIUM         A=====================                     42%    336.0 Mg
PHOSPHORUS      A===========================               54%    437.0 Mg
TRYPTOPHAN      A===========================================  87%  142.0 Mg
THREONINE       A============================================ 117% 513.0 Mg
ISOLEUCINE      A===========================================  94%  619.0 Mg
LEUCINE         A============================================ 120% 1048 Mg
LYSINE          A============================================ 141% 925.0 Mg
METHIONINE      A==========================================   99%  270.0 Mg
CYSTINE         A=====================                     42%    115.0 Mg
PHENYL-ANINE    A============================================ 155% 675.0 Mg
TYROSINE        A===========================================  106% 464.0 Mg
VALINE          A===========================================  100% 764.0 Mg
HISTIDINE       A                                          NO RDA 338.0 Mg
ALCOHOL         A                                          NO RDA 0.000 Gm
ASH             A                                          NO RDA 5.290 Gm
COPPER          A=============                             26%    0.650 Mg
MANGANESE       A================                          32%    1.210 Mg
IODINE          A=========================                 50%    75.30 Ug
MONO FAT        A                                          NO RDA 7.020 Gm
POLY FAT        A                                          NO RDA 3.090 Gm
CAFFEINE        A                                          NO RDA 0.000 Mg
FLUORIDE        A==                                        5%     144.0 Ug
MOLYBDENUM      A=====================================     78%    256.0 Ug
VITAMIN K       A=============                             26%    27.60 Ug
SELENIUM        A                                          0%     0.000 Mg
BIOTIN          A=                                         3%     5.480 Ug
CHLORIDE        A                                          0%     24.80 Mg
CHROMIUM        A======================================    80%    0.100 Mg
SUGAR           A                                          NO RDA 8.770 Gm
FIBER-DIET      A                                          NO RDA 6.330 Gm
VIT. E/AT       A===========                               23%    1.870 Mg

    % RDA:   |0      |20     |40     |60     |80     |100
```

Mint leaves not included in analysis for Yogurt Dressing.

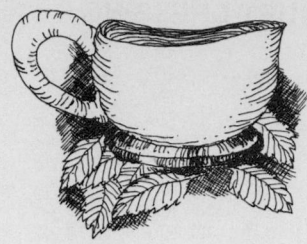

# YOGURT DRESSING

2 cups plain yogurt
32 finely chopped fresh mint leaves
½ cup finely diced tomato
2 tsp. dill leaves
1 tsp. soy sauce
⅛ tsp. black pepper

Paprika

Mix all ingredients together and refrigerate while making Eggplant Rolls to allow flavors to blend. Makes enough to pour over 6 to 8 servings.

| SHOPPING LIST | |
|---|---|
| Regularly Kept in the Kitchen (Listed in Chapter 14, p. 703) | Fresh Produce |
| Plain yogurt<br>Soy sauce<br>Black pepper<br>Paprika | Mint leaves<br>Tomato<br>Dill leaves |

# MID-EASTERN VEGETABLE DISH

☆ A one-dish meal; makes a whole meal served over a bed of brown rice or any other whole grain.

Perfect Brown Rice (see recipe, p. 375)

3 Tbsp. vegetable oil
1 Tbsp. asafetida or 2 onions, slivered (and minus 1 cup of assorted vegetables)
8 cups assorted, chopped vegetables

1 Tbsp. curry
2 tsp. cayenne
2 tsp. ground cumin
½ tsp. black pepper

As in stir-fries, or any other dish that cooking a mixture of vegetables is called for, always be sure to cook the hard vegetables (ones that'll take longer to cook — such as carrots, potatoes) a few minutes before adding soft vegetables (ones that cook quickly or are even okay eaten a little raw).

*2 Tbsp. tamarind paste*
*⅔ cup raisins*

*3 cups cooked garbanzo beans*

*2 cups water*

*2 large tomatoes*

*Paprika*

Cook 3 cups brown rice as directed for Perfect Brown Rice (p. 375). In a separate wok or large skillet, saute next 3 ingredients together till vegetables are lightly coated with oil. Add next 2 ingredients and mix till tamarind paste is completely dissolved and evenly mixed in. Add garbanzo beans and water. Cover pot and bring to a boil, then turn heat down and simmer till vegetables are tender (not mushy!). As vegetables are simmering, chop tomatoes into large chunks. When vegetables are tender, add the tomatoes and mix in. Make a bed of cooked rice on a large platter, then pour vegetables over it. This whole meal should take about an hour to cook. Serves 4 to 6.

| SHOPPING LIST | |
|---|---|
| **Regularly Kept in the Kitchen (Listed in Chapter 14, p. 703)** | **Fresh Produce** |
| Brown rice (or other whole grain)<br>Safflower oil<br>Asafetida<br>Curry<br>Cayenne<br>Ground cumin<br>Black pepper<br>Raisins<br>Garbanzo beans<br>Paprika | Assorted fresh vegetables of your choice (such as potatoes, carrots, bell peppers, zucchini)<br>Tomatoes |

| **Special Shopping** |
|---|
| Tamarind paste — in East Indian or Indonesian food stores. |

# NUTRITIONAL ANALYSIS FOR ONE SERVING
## MID-EASTERN VEGETABLE DISH

| NUTRIENT | Type: 14  FEMALE—23 TO 51 YEARS | % RDA | Amount |
|---|---|---|---|
| KCALORIES | A============================ | 52% | 1.050 Kc |
| PROTEIN | A================================== | 64% | 28.30 Gm |
| CARBOHYDRATE | A | NO RDA | 200.0 Gm |
| FAT | A | NO RDA | 17.60 Gm |
| FIBER—CRUDE | A | NO RDA | 8.690 Gm |
| CHOLESTEROL | A | NO RDA | 0.000 Mg |
| SATURATED FA | A | NO RDA | 1.530 Gm |
| OLEIC FA | A | NO RDA | 14.20 Gm |
| LINOLEIC FA | A | NO RDA | 7.500 Gm |
| SODIUM | A= | 3% | 69.60 Mg |
| POTASSIUM | A========================== | 53% | 2011 Mg |
| MAGNESIUM | A===================================================== | 107% | 323.0 Mg |
| IRON | A============================== | 58% | 10.50 Mg |
| ZINC | A================== | 36% | 5.420 Mg |
| VITAMIN A | A===================================================== | 320% | 12810 IU |
| VITAMIN D | A | 0% | 0.000 IU |
| VIT. E/TOTAL | A | NO RDA | 16.30 Mg |
| VITAMIN C | A===================================================== | 128% | 77.30 Mg |
| THIAMIN | A============================================= | 90% | 0.900 Mg |
| RIBOFLAVIN | A================= | 35% | 0.420 Mg |
| NIACIN | A===================================== | 75% | 9.830 Mg |
| VITAMIN B6 | A================================= | 68% | 1.370 Mg |
| FOLACIN | A============================================= | 86% | 345.0 Ug |
| VITAMIN B12 | A | 0% | 0.000 Ug |
| PANTO— ACID | A================================ | 65% | 3.590 Mg |
| CALCIUM | A============= | 27% | 218.0 Mg |
| PHOSPHORUS | A==================================================== | 100% | 804.0 Mg |
| TRYPTOPHAN | A=================================================== | 180% | 295.0 Mg |
| THREONINE | A===================================================== | 225% | 982.0 Mg |
| ISOLEUCINE | A===================================================== | 194% | 1271 Mg |
| LEUCINE | A===================================================== | 248% | 2167 Mg |
| LYSINE | A===================================================== | 221% | 1445 Mg |
| METHIONINE | A===================================================== | 155% | 422.0 Mg |
| CYSTINE | A===================================================== | 143% | 390.0 Mg |
| PHENYL—ANINE | A===================================================== | 328% | 1427 Mg |
| TYROSINE | A===================================================== | 164% | 714.0 Mg |
| VALINE | A===================================================== | 180% | 1373 Mg |
| HISTIDINE | A | NO RDA | 835.0 Mg |
| ALCOHOL | A | NO RDA | 0.000 Gm |
| ASH | A | NO RDA | 6.710 Gm |
| COPPER | A====================== | 47% | 1.190 Mg |
| MANGANESE | A===================================================== | 172% | 6.470 Mg |
| IODINE | A===================================================== | 587% | 881.0 Ug |
| MONO FAT | A | NO RDA | 2.070 Gm |
| POLY FAT | A | NO RDA | 9.500 Gm |
| CAFFEINE | A | NO RDA | 0.000 Mg |
| FLUORIDE | A=== | 6% | 166.0 Ug |
| MOLYBDENUM | A===================================================== | 730% | 2374 Ug |
| VITAMIN K | A===================================================== | 138% | 145.0 Ug |
| SELENIUM | A============ | 24% | 0.030 Mg |
| BIOTIN | A===== | 11% | 16.70 Ug |
| CHLORIDE | A==== | 9% | 312.0 Mg |
| CHROMIUM | A===================================================== | 928% | 1.160 Mg |
| SUGAR | A | NO RDA | 17.80 Gm |
| FIBER—DIET | A | NO RDA | 14.80 Gm |
| VIT. E/AT | A===================================================== | 104% | 8.380 Mg |

```
% RDA:   |0      |20     |40     |60     |80     |100
```

Onions (minus one cup of vegetables) used instead of asafetida. Vegetables used in analysis: potatoes, zucchini, beets, green beans, asparagus and bell pepper.

# EGGPLANT SUPREME CURRY

☆ An East Indian curry delicious served with brown or basmati rice.

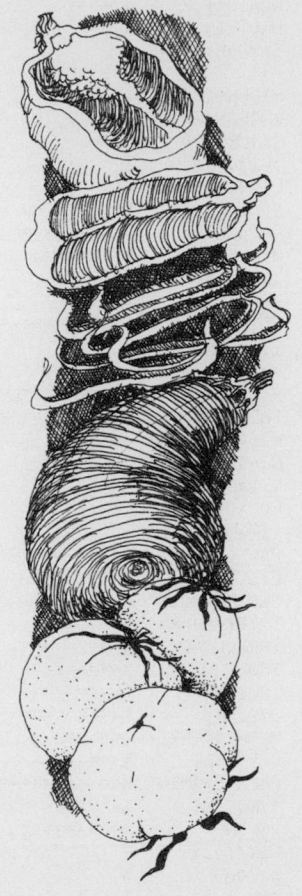

---

2 Tbsp. oil or ghee
1 tsp. asafetida or ½ cup finely sliced onion
1 eggplant in ½" cubes

1 green pepper, thinly sliced

3 tomatoes, cubed
¼ cup raisins

1 Tbsp. ghee or oil
1 tsp. cumin seeds
¼ tsp. chili seeds
2 tsp. curry powder
1 tsp. soy sauce

Saute first 3 ingredients together for about 5 minutes. Add bell peppers and saute for another 5 minutes. Add next 2 ingredients, cover the pan and cook over medium heat for another 5 minutes. In a separate, very small pot, mix together the next 4 ingredients and cook on high heat till spices are well-browned and the aroma of the spices fills the air. Uncover the skillet or wok with the vegetables cooking in it, and pour the oil with toasted spices into the vegetables. Add soy sauce, then stir spices and soy sauce into vegetables.

| SHOPPING LIST | |
|---|---|
| **Regularly Kept in the Kitchen (Listed in Chapter 14, p. 703)** | **Fresh Produce** |
| Asafetida | Eggplant |
| Raisins | Bell pepper |
| Cumin seeds | Tomatoes |
| Chili seeds | |
| 2 tsp. curry powder | |
| 1 tsp. soy sauce | |

| Special Shopping |
|---|
| Ghee — can be gotten already made at Indian import stores or made at home (see recipe in *Kathy Cooks . . . Naturally*, p. 42). To avoid saturated fat, you can use a polyunsaturated vegetable oil and it will taste all right, but ghee definitely adds its special, unique flavor to this dish! |

# NUTRITIONAL ANALYSIS FOR ONE SERVING
## EGGPLANT SUPREME CURRY

| NUTRIENT | Type: 14   FEMALE-23 TO 51 YEARS | % RDA | Amount |
|---|---|---|---|
| KCALORIES | A===== | 10% | 204.0 Kc |
| PROTEIN | A=== | 7% | 3.510 Gm |
| CARBOHYDRATE | A | NO RDA | 26.90 Gm |
| FAT | A | NO RDA | 11.20 Gm |
| FIBER-CRUDE | A | NO RDA | 2.860 Gm |
| CHOLESTEROL | A | NO RDA | 26.10 Mg |
| SATURATED FA | A | NO RDA | 6.470 Gm |
| OLEIC FA | A | NO RDA | 0.000 Gm |
| LINOLEIC FA | A | NO RDA | 0.000 Gm |
| SODIUM | A== | 4% | 105.0 Mg |
| POTASSIUM | A========== | 21% | 824.0 Mg |
| MAGNESIUM | A======== | 16% | 48.40 Mg |
| IRON | A====== | 13% | 2.350 Mg |
| ZINC | A= | 3% | 0.530 Mg |
| VITAMIN A | A======================= | 48% | 1938 IU |
| VITAMIN D | A | 0% | 0.000 IU |
| VIT. E/TOTAL | A | NO RDA | 0.610 Mg |
| VITAMIN C | A======================================== | 80% | 48.10 Mg |
| THIAMIN | A============ | 24% | 0.240 Mg |
| RIBOFLAVIN | A==== | 9% | 0.110 Mg |
| NIACIN | A======= | 15% | 2.010 Mg |
| VITAMIN B6 | A======= | 14% | 0.290 Mg |
| FOLACIN | A===== | 10% | 42.80 Ug |
| VITAMIN B12 | A | 0% | 0.000 Ug |
| PANTO- ACID | A==== | 8% | 0.440 Mg |
| CALCIUM | A==== | 8% | 64.70 Mg |
| PHOSPHORUS | A===== | 11% | 93.40 Mg |
| TRYPTOPHAN | A======== | 16% | 27.30 Mg |
| THREONINE | A========= | 20% | 88.10 Mg |
| ISOLEUCINE | A======= | 15% | 99.20 Mg |
| LEUCINE | A======== | 16% | 143.0 Mg |
| LYSINE | A========= | 18% | 121.0 Mg |
| METHIONINE | A===== | 10% | 28.90 Mg |
| CYSTINE | A===== | 10% | 27.90 Mg |
| PHENYL-ANINE | A=========== | 22% | 97.20 Mg |
| TYROSINE | A======= | 14% | 63.20 Mg |
| VALINE | A======= | 14% | 110.0 Mg |
| HISTIDINE | A | NO RDA | 54.10 Mg |
| ALCOHOL | A | NO RDA | 0.000 Gm |
| ASH | A | NO RDA | 2.290 Gm |
| COPPER | A====== | 12% | 0.320 Mg |
| MANGANESE | A====== | 12% | 0.450 Mg |
| IODINE | A | 0% | 0.000 Ug |
| MONO FAT | A | NO RDA | 3.010 Gm |
| POLY FAT | A | NO RDA | 0.710 Gm |
| CAFFEINE | A | NO RDA | 0.000 Mg |
| FLUORIDE | A= | 3% | 107.0 Ug |
| MOLYBDENUM | A | 0% | 0.000 Ug |
| VITAMIN K | A== | 5% | 5.320 Ug |
| SELENIUM | A | 0% | 0.000 Mg |
| BIOTIN | A= | 3% | 5.180 Ug |
| CHLORIDE | A | 0% | 0.000 Mg |
| CHROMIUM | A============ | 24% | 0.030 Mg |
| SUGAR | A | NO RDA | 12.60 Gm |
| FIBER-DIET | A | NO RDA | 1.270 Gm |
| VIT. E/AT | A==== | 8% | 0.680 Mg |

```
% RDA:   |0     |20    |40    |60    |80    |100
```

Ghee used instead of oil in analysis.

587

# EAST INDIAN INSPIRATIONS

We eat for the health of our bodies and minds, both of which are connected. The body and the mind are tools for us to use — properly or improperly. The ancient wisdom of the Bhagavad-gita has this to say about using the mind:

"For he who has conquered the mind, the mind is the best of friends; but for one who has failed to do so, his very mind will be the greatest enemy."

It may seem to you that I spend all my time in the kitchen because every time you see me on "Kathy's Kitchen," that's where I am — and this is a cookbook! In actuality, the opposite is true. I try to spend only as much time as is absolutely necessary in the kitchen because there is more to life than cooking and eating. Meals like this one, inspired by East Indian cooking, make it possible for me to feed my family nutritious meals that are tasty, but don't take a long time to prepare.

For a simple family dinner, I sometimes make — along with my born helpers — the Palak Tofu-Paneer and Chapatis. This satisfying meal, which the whole family loves (except Valmiki, who does not *love* spinach), can easily be expanded into a banquet for special occasions by adding the last four dishes listed on the menu to the meal. One delicious way to eat the banquet ingredients is to use the Chapati like a tortilla and fill it with some of the Palak Tofu-Paneer, and top this with some of the Hot-Chaunce Salad Dressing and Crispy Chutney. Like a lot of East Indian cooking, you end up with a gourmet feast that's inexpensive to make.

# PALAK TOFU·PANEER

☆ A simple-to-make, yet exotically delicious, nutritious entree which contains protein and the goodness of fresh vegetables.

1 lb. Chinese firm tofu, drained
  and cut in ¾" cubes
¼ cup soy sauce

Oil for deep-frying

2 Tbsp. margarine or butter
2½ lbs. (40 oz.) frozen, chopped spinach
6 cups ¾" cubes fresh tomatoes

2 Tbsp. ghee or safflower oil
2 tsp. curry powder
2 tsp. asafetida or 3 cloves crushed garlic
1½ tsp. ground cumin
1 tsp. ground coriander
¾ tsp. cayenne pepper
½ tsp. black pepper
½ tsp. cinnamon
¼ tsp. allspice
¼ tsp. cloves

2 Tbsp. soy sauce

Soak first 2 ingredients together while heating the oil to 350 degrees. Remove cubes from soy sauce and drain a few seconds in a strainer to remove excess soy sauce. Drop tofu cubes in heated oil all at once (or in a couple of separate batches if you desire) and cook till browned and a little crisp on the outside. Remove from oil and drain on plate covered with 2 to 3 thicknesses of paper towels. Leftover soy sauce can be kept and used later.

As the tofu cubes are cooking (or before you start frying them), combine the next 3 ingredients together in a skillet. Cover and put on medium flame to simmer for 10 minutes. Remove lid and mix well (the frozen spinach should be thawed and mixable by now).

Leave uncovered over medium flame to allow some of the juices to cook off as you make the chaunce. This is done by heating the ghee or oil in a butter-warming pot and adding all the spices listed. Toast in oil till the fragrance of the spices fills the kitchen and the spices appear to be browned. Pour into cooking vegetables immediately, add soy sauce and mix

## SUGGESTED MENU FOR AN EAST INDIAN BANQUET

Palak Tofu-Paneer

Chapatis

Brown or basmati rice

Crispy Chutney

Essence of Roses Drink

Hot-Chaunce Salad

thoroughly till tomatoes break up.

Turn off heat, add cooked tofu cubes, and cover for a few minutes before serving. Makes 8 entree-sized servings or twice as many side dish-sized servings.

| SHOPPING LIST | |
|---|---|
| **Regularly Kept in the Kitchen** (Listed in Chapter 14, p. 703) | **Fresh Produce** |
| Tofu | Frozen spinach |
| Soy sauce | Tomatoes |
| Safflower or sunflower oil | |
| Butter or margarine | |
| Curry powder | |
| Ground cumin | |
| Coriander | |
| Cayenne | |
| Black pepper | |
| Cinnamon | |
| Allspice | |
| Cloves | |

| Special Shopping |
|---|
| Ghee — can be gotten already made at Indian import stores or made at home (see recipe in *Kathy Cooks . . . Naturally*, p. 42). |

This dish has its roots in East Indian cooking. The few changes I've made —

• I use tofu instead of the milk curd usually used, as tofu is more readily available, and the curd is more time-consuming to make. Tofu is cholesterol-free, and curd will contain cholesterol and some saturated fat.

• I deep-fry the tofu in safflower oil instead of ghee to cut down on saturated fat, but use ghee to cook the chaunce (toast the spices in) because it imparts the heavenly taste of ghee throughout the dish by using a relatively small amount of this saturated fat.

# NUTRITIONAL ANALYSIS FOR ONE SERVING PALAK TOFU-PANEER

```
NUTRIENT        Type: 14   FEMALE-23 TO 51 YEARS              % RDA    Amount
KCALORIES     Ã=====                                          11%     221.0 Kc
PROTEIN       Ã==================                             36%     16.20 Gm
CARBOHYDRATE  Ã                                             NO RDA    18.20 Gm
FAT           Ã                                             NO RDA    12.20 Gm
FIBER-CRUDE   Ã                                             NO RDA    2.520 Gm
CHOLESTEROL   Ã                                             NO RDA    0.000 Mg
SATURATED FA  Ã                                             NO RDA    1.630 Gm
OLEIC FA      Ã                                             NO RDA    0.970 Gm
LINOLEIC FA   Ã                                             NO RDA    3.630 Gm
SODIUM        Ã=====================                          42%     928.0 Mg
POTASSIUM     Ã================                               33%     1254 Mg
MAGNESIUM     Ã==================================             62%     187.0 Mg
IRON          Ã=====================================          71%     12.80 Mg
ZINC          Ã=======                                        15%     2.260 Mg
VITAMIN A     Ã==========================================================  349%  13991 IU
VITAMIN D     Ã                                                0%     0.000 IU
VIT. E/TOTAL  Ã                                             NO RDA    6.450 Mg
VITAMIN C     Ã=======================================         78%     47.20 Mg
THIAMIN       Ã=================                               34%     0.340 Mg
RIBOFLAVIN    Ã=====================                           42%     0.510 Mg
NIACIN        Ã==========                                      19%     2.540 Mg
VITAMIN B6    Ã============                                    25%     0.500 Mg
FOLACIN       Ã==============================                  60%     241.0 Ug
VITAMIN B12   Ã                                                0%     0.000 Ug
PANTO- ACID   Ã=======                                         14%     0.810 Mg
CALCIUM       Ã======================================          76%     608.0 Mg
PHOSPHORUS    Ã================                                33%     265.0 Mg
TRYPTOPHAN    Ã=========================================       128%    209.0 Mg
THREONINE     Ã=========================================       135%    589.0 Mg
ISOLEUCINE    Ã=========================================       107%    701.0 Mg
LEUCINE       Ã=========================================       123%    1074 Mg
LYSINE        Ã=========================================       139%    914.0 Mg
METHIONINE    Ã======================================          76%     209.0 Mg
CYSTINE       Ã====================================            72%     196.0 Mg
PHENYL-ANINE  Ã=========================================       154%    671.0 Mg
TYROSINE      Ã=========================================       111%    484.0 Mg
VALINE        Ã===========================================     96%     737.0 Mg
HISTIDINE     Ã                                             NO RDA    381.0 Mg
ALCOHOL       Ã                                             NO RDA    0.000 Gm
ASH           Ã                                             NO RDA    6.750 Gm
COPPER        Ã============                                    24%     0.610 Mg
MANGANESE     Ã=============================                   58%     2.210 Mg
IODINE        Ã====================                            41%     61.80 Ug
MONO FAT      Ã                                             NO RDA    2.930 Gm
POLY FAT      Ã                                             NO RDA    6.580 Gm
CAFFEINE      Ã                                             NO RDA    0.000 Mg
FLUORIDE      Ã===                                             6%     186.0 Ug
MOLYBDENUM    Ã==================================              220%    716.0 Ug
VITAMIN K     Ã==================================              127%    134.0 Ug
SELENIUM      Ã                                                0%     0.000 Mg
BIOTIN        Ã======                                          12%     18.00 Ug
CHLORIDE      Ã=                                               3%     107.0 Mg
CHROMIUM      Ã==============================================  192%    0.240 Mg
SUGAR         Ã                                             NO RDA    9.420 Gm
FIBER-DIET    Ã                                             NO RDA    4.160 Gm
VIT. E/AT     Ã=========================                       55%     4.440 Mg

   % RDA:  |0      |20     |40     |60     |80     |100
```

Margarine used instead of butter; safflower oil used instead of ghee in analysis.

# CHAPATIS

☆ An unleavened bread that's very inexpensive to make. It's amazing how delicious a few simple ingredients can taste!

6 cups whole wheat flour
2 cups water

*Margarine or butter (optional)*

Mix first 2 ingredients together and knead a bit till dough is earlobe consistency. Cover the ball of dough with a bowl inverted on the counter and let dough sit 20 to 30 minutes (you can be making the rest of the dinner in the meantime). Flour counter liberally, heat a skillet to medium-high heat and break balls of dough about 1½" to 2" in diameter. One at a time, roll the balls out to about 4" to 5" in diameter and put the rolled chapati into the heated dry skillet. The chapati should get little bubbles on the top surface in 15 to 20 seconds. Using tongs, flip the chapati over on the other side and cook a few seconds. Remove chapati from skillet and immediately put it directly over a flame by holding an edge of the chapati with tongs. (Try not to touch the chapati to the grill or a hole may burn which releases the steam and prevents the chapati from ballooning up.) It should puff up like a balloon in a few seconds. Flip over to the other side as soon as it bubbles and let cook a few seconds on the other side. This ballooning up steams the chapati from the inside. Remove the chapati from the flame and put onto a platter. The chapati will deflate. At this point you can rub a little butter on one surface of the chapati or leave it dry and put the next chapati in the skillet.

Making Chapatis for a large family like mine would be very time-consuming if I didn't get them to help. With the number of children we have, we set up a little assembly line with one person making the dough balls, one person rolling and one person cooking. The babies are the cheering squad. They clap and cheer every time one of the Chapatis bubbles up. When a Chapati bubbles up like a balloon, that guarantees that it won't be raw inside, as the steam in the bubbling cooks the dough from the inside out.

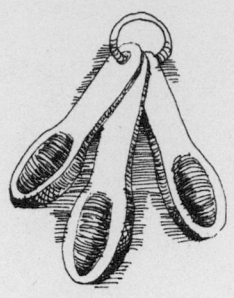

This recipe makes about 2 dozen chapatis (about 8 servings). You can cook a stack of chapatis and freeze them for future use if this whole process takes too long to consider doing often. A few crucial hints for making successful chapatis:

• The skillet must be the right temperature — too cool and the chapati will get hard and brittle before it gets little bubbles, and it won't balloon up. If you notice the chapati is turning a golden brown on the first surface, the heat is up too high and the chapati may burn, which prevents ballooning also.

• You may want to periodically wipe the burned excess flour out of the skillet to prevent burning.

• Gas stoves work best for this, but it is possible to balloon the chapati over an electric element turned to high.

| SHOPPING LIST | |
|---|---|
| **Regularly Kept in the Kitchen** (Listed in Chapter 14, p. 703) | **Fresh Produce** |
| Whole wheat flour<br>Butter or margarine (optional) | (None) |

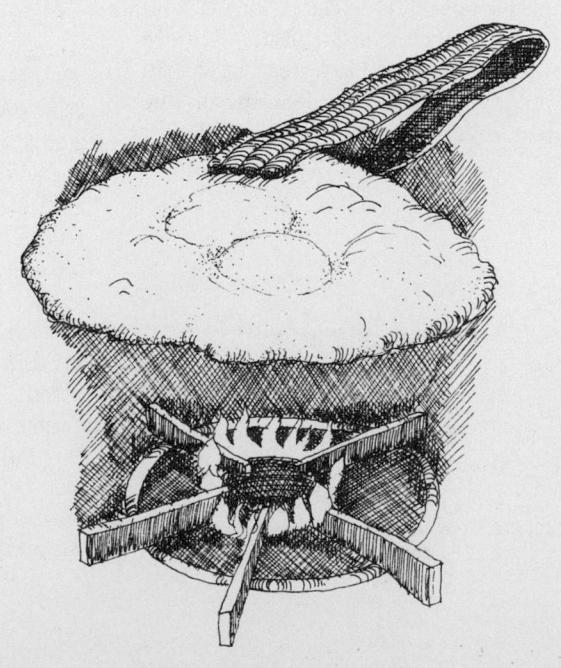

# NUTRITIONAL ANALYSIS FOR THREE CHAPATIS

```
NUTRIENT        Type: 14    FEMALE-23 TO 51 YEARS          % RDA    Amount
KCALORIES       Ã=======                                   15%     300.0 Kc
PROTEIN         Ã=============                             27%     12.00 Gm
CARBOHYDRATE    Ã                                         NO RDA   63.70 Gm
FAT             Ã                                         NO RDA   1.540 Gm
FIBER-CRUDE     Ã                                         NO RDA   2.070 Gm
CHOLESTEROL     Ã                                         NO RDA   0.000 Mg
SATURATED FA    Ã                                         NO RDA   0.300 Gm
OLEIC FA        Ã                                         NO RDA   0.260 Gm
LINOLEIC FA     Ã                                         NO RDA   0.900 Gm
SODIUM          Ã                                           0%     2.710 Mg
POTASSIUM       Ã====                                       8%     333.0 Mg
MAGNESIUM       Ã==================                        34%     102.0 Mg
IRON            Ã========                                  16%     3.000 Mg
ZINC            Ã=======                                   14%     2.180 Mg
VITAMIN A       Ã                                           0%     0.000 IU
VITAMIN D       Ã                                           0%     0.000 IU
VIT. E/TOTAL    Ã                                         NO RDA   3.550 Mg
VITAMIN C       Ã                                           0%     0.000 Mg
THIAMIN         Ã=========================                 49%     0.490 Mg
RIBOFLAVIN      Ã====                                       8%     0.100 Mg
NIACIN          Ã===============                           30%     3.900 Mg
VITAMIN B6      Ã=======                                   15%     0.300 Mg
FOLACIN         Ã======                                    12%     48.60 Ug
VITAMIN B12     Ã                                           0%     0.000 Ug
PANTO- ACID     Ã=========                                 18%     0.990 Mg
CALCIUM         Ã==                                         4%     37.30 Mg
PHOSPHORUS      Ã====================                      41%     334.0 Mg
TRYPTOPHAN      Ã=============================================  90%  147.0 Mg
THREONINE       Ã=======================================   79%     345.0 Mg
ISOLEUCINE      Ã=======================================   79%     519.0 Mg
LEUCINE         Ã==============================================  92%  802.0 Mg
LYSINE          Ã=========================                 50%     328.0 Mg
METHIONINE      Ã=================================         67%     183.0 Mg
CYSTINE         Ã===============================================  96%  262.0 Mg
PHENYL-ANINE    Ã===============================================  135%  591.0 Mg
TYROSINE        Ã===============================================  102%  447.0 Mg
VALINE          Ã===================================       72%     554.0 Mg
HISTIDINE       Ã                                         NO RDA   243.0 Mg
ALCOHOL         Ã                                         NO RDA   0.000 Gm
ASH             Ã                                         NO RDA   1.350 Gm
COPPER          Ã=========                                 18%     0.450 Mg
MANGANESE       Ã===============================================  120%  4.500 Mg
IODINE          Ã===============================================  254%  381.0 Ug
MONO FAT        Ã                                         NO RDA   0.000 Gm
POLY FAT        Ã                                         NO RDA   0.000 Gm
CAFFEINE        Ã                                         NO RDA   0.000 Mg
FLUORIDE        Ã                                           0%     0.000 Ug
MOLYBDENUM      Ã===============================================  1661%  5400 Ug
VITAMIN K       Ã                                           0%     0.000 Ug
SELENIUM        Ã===========                               24%     0.030 Mg
BIOTIN          Ã=                                          3%     4.500 Ug
CHLORIDE        Ã==                                         5%     172.0 Mg
CHROMIUM        Ã===============================================  432%  0.540 Mg
SUGAR           Ã                                         NO RDA   0.000 Gm
FIBER-DIET      Ã                                         NO RDA   13.60 Gm
VIT. E/AT       Ã====                                       9%     0.730 Mg

   % RDA:    |0      |20     |40     |60     |80     |100
```

Optional margarine or butter not included in analysis.

# CRISPY CHUTNEY

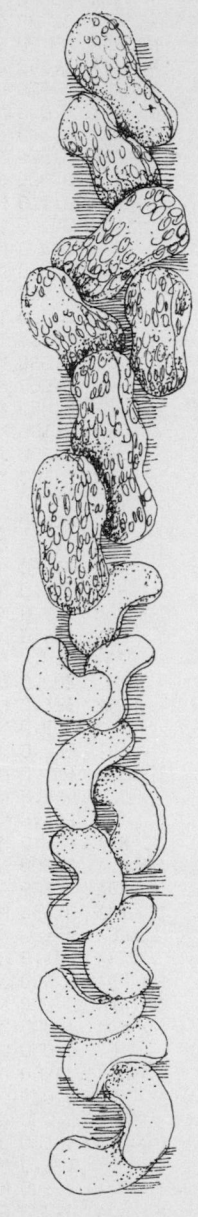

☆ A delicious condiment served on the side or sprinkled on top of other dishes.

---

1 cup roasted, blanched peanuts
1 cup roasted cashew pieces

Ghee or oil to cover bottom of a 2-quart pot

¼ cup popcorn kernels (to equal 3 cups
   popped popcorn) or 3 cups Brown
   Rice Crispies cereal

¼ cup raw sesame seeds
1½ tsp. black mustard seeds
½ tsp. asafetida or garlic powder
½ tsp. cinnamon
½ tsp. black pepper
¼ tsp. ground cloves

2½ tsp. maple or whole cane sugar
1½ tsp. green mango powder (called
   "amchoor" in Indian import stores)
1 tsp. cayenne (more or less, to taste)
½ tsp. (or less) salt
¼ tsp. turmeric

Either buy the first 2 ingredients already roasted, or toast raw nuts by baking in a single layer on a cookie sheet at 250 degrees till nuts turn golden and taste toasted (don't wait for them to brown, as heat already in nuts causes them to continue cooking after they're removed from heat).

Heat ghee or oil in bottom of 2-quart pot till a kernel of popcorn set in the oil pops. Quickly toss in popcorn kernels. As soon as the kernels begin sizzling, very quickly toss in next 6 ingredients, which have been pre-mixed, and stir to distribute evenly. Put lid on pot and pop corn over medium-low, the way popcorn is normally popped (shake pot over heat; don't let it sit in one place or kernels will burn).

After corn is popped, toss with roasted nuts. If using Brown Rice Crispies, toss them in with roasted nuts instead of popcorn. Then sprinkle on last 5 ingredients and toss thoroughly. Spread on cookie sheet in a single layer and bake at 250 degrees for 10 minutes. Allow to cool. Can be stored for weeks in an airtight container.

Make a few quarts at a time and keep in airtight containers for a delicious and nutritious snack.

| SHOPPING LIST | | Special Shopping |
|---|---|---|
| **Regularly Kept in the Kitchen** (Listed in Chapter 14, p. 703) | **Fresh Produce** | Ghee (if you want to use in place of oil) — for where to find, see Palak Tofu-Paneer recipe. |
| Blanched peanuts | (None) | Black mustard seeds — can be found in Indian food import stores; you can use regular mustard seeds found in the spice section of supermarkets instead. |
| Cashew pieces | | |
| Safflower oil | | |
| Popcorn | | |
| Sesame seeds | | |
| Asafetida | | Maple sugar or whole cane sugar — found in some natural food stores. |
| Cinnamon | | |
| Black pepper | | |
| Ground cloves | | Amchoor (green mango powder) — look in Indian food import stores. |
| Cayenne | | |
| Turmeric | | |
| Salt | | |

# ESSENCE OF ROSES DRINK

☆ This delicately-flavored drink doubles as a dessert that will aid digestion (thanks to the friendly bacterial culture in the yogurt!).

☆ Makes a refreshing, cooling snack on hot summer days.

*4 cups nonfat or lowfat yogurt*
*2 cups water*
*2 cups crushed ice*
*½ cup honey*
*1 Tbsp. rose water*

Blend all ingredients in blender till smooth. Serve immediately. Makes eight 1-cup servings.

| SHOPPING LIST | | Special Shopping |
|---|---|---|
| **Regularly Kept in the Kitchen** (Listed in Chapter 14, p. 703) | **Fresh Produce** | Rose water — found in Indian food import stores or pharmacies. |
| Yogurt | (None) | |
| Honey | | |
| Ice | | |

# HOT·CHAUNCE SALAD DRESSING

☆ A different kind of a hot dressing to spice up your salads; takes inspiration from the East Indian chaunce (toasting spices).

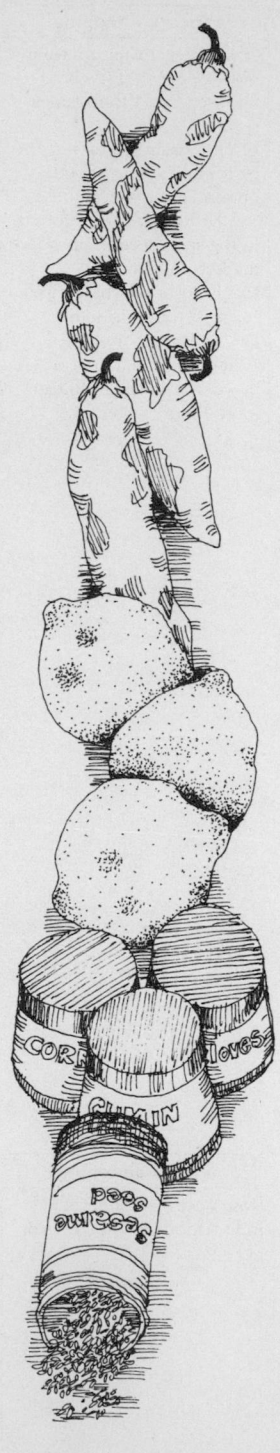

2 Tbsp. oil
¼ cup sunflower seeds

1 Tbsp. sesame seeds
1 tsp. coriander seeds
⅛ tsp. red chili seeds

½ tsp. cumin powder
⅛ tsp. cloves
⅛ tsp. asafetida or garlic powder
⅛ tsp. black pepper

1 Tbsp. lemon juice
1 tsp. soy sauce

This will dress about 2 quarts of your favorite tossed green salad.

Pre-measure seeds and spices, grouping separately in little containers in the groups they're listed in. Just before serving, toast oil and sunflower seeds till seeds just begin to get golden. Add next 3 ingredients and continue toasting till sesame seeds turn a light gold.

Add next 4 ingredients and continue toasting till all seeds are a golden brown and the spices can be smelled in the air. Remove from heat and pour onto prepared salad. Pour on last 2 ingredients and toss. Serve immediately. Makes eight 1-cup servings.

| SHOPPING LIST | |
|---|---|
| **Regularly Kept in the Kitchen** (Listed in Chapter 14, p. 703) | **Fresh Produce** |
| Safflower oil<br>Sunflower seeds<br>Sesame seeds<br>Coriander seeds<br>Red chili seeds<br>Ground cumin<br>Ground cloves<br>Asafetida<br>Black pepper<br>Soy sauce | Favorite salad ingredients for about 2 quarts of salad<br>Lemon |

# A LIGHT VEGETABLE BARBECUE

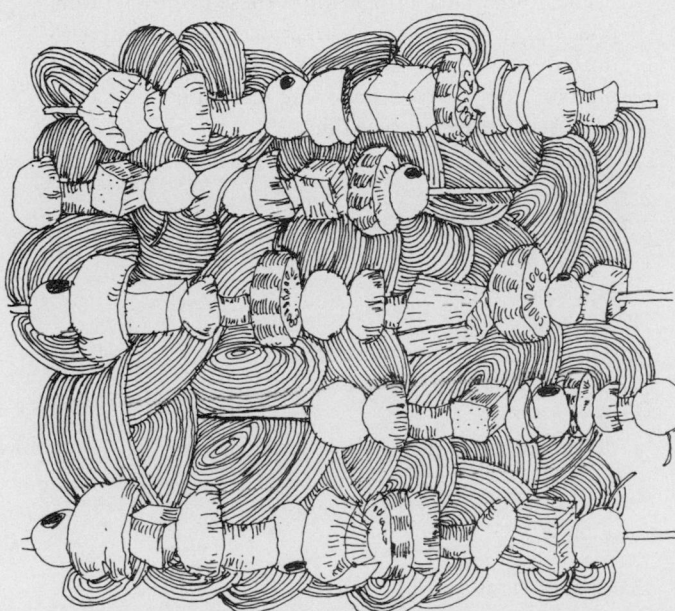

## SUGGESTED MENU

*Oriental-Style Protein Salad*

*Barbecued vegetables and/or kabobs in Miso-Sesame Barbecue Sauce and/or Korean Marinade*

*Steamed Bread or brown rice*

*As-the-Snow-Melts Dessert*

One way to get everyone to eat a good share of vegetables is to make them the center of attention at a barbecue. I grew up associating steak with the word "barbecue," but have since learned to appreciate and prefer a light vegetable barbecue to a carcinogenic barbecued steak. (Did you know that there's as much benzopyrene, a cancer-causing agent, in a two-pound, charcoal-broiled steak as there is in the smoke of 600 cigarettes?)

At most meals, and especially at barbecues, the "protein" dish is usually the center or entree, and vegetables are served as a side dish. In this meal, this order is reversed, with the vegetables served as the center, or entree, and the "protein" is served in the salad. The result is a light and refreshing meal that's perfect for a hot summer evening. Or, if you have an inside grill, it also makes a delicious winter dinner.

# ORIENTAL-STYE PROTEIN SALAD

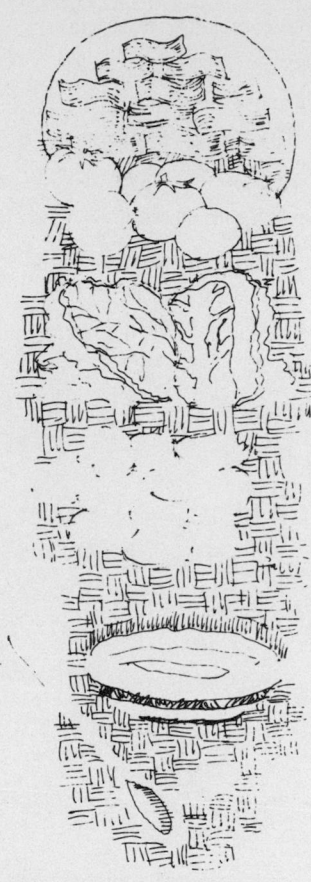

☆ This salad could be an expensive one to make, as small bags of aburage (age) pouches cost close to a dollar each. When I know that I'm going to be making this (or any other meal using a lot of these deep-fried tofu pouches), I head to the local tofu factory and buy a huge three- or four-pound box of their "off-grade" ones for one or two dollars. The unused pouches can be frozen for use another time.

---

2 Tbsp. soy sauce
2 Tbsp. rice vinegar
1 Tbsp. sesame oil
1 Tbsp. safflower oil
1½ tsp. peanut butter
¼ tsp asafetida or ½ clove garlic, crushed
¼ tsp. cayenne pepper
¼ tsp. honey
⅛ tsp. Japanese or Chinese hot mustard powder

8 oz. deep-fried tofu pouches (aburage)
  cut in ¼" - ½" strips

1 cucumber, cut in julienne strips
½ cup slivered scallions
2 Tbsp. finely chopped cilantro

1 large tomato, cut in thin wedges
1 Tbsp. toasted sesame seeds

Combine first 9 ingredients in blender top and blend till smooth.

Cut aburage/age pouches into ¼"- to ½"-wide strips and sprinkle blended dressing onto them. Toss till dressing is thoroughly mixed in.

In a separate bowl, toss next 3 ingredients together, using only half the cilantro. These can be stored separately in the refrigerator till just before serving time.

When ready to serve, toss aburage and mixed vegetables together. Evenly spread tomato wedges on top of mixture and sprinkle with sesame seeds and remaining cilantro.

Serve immediately. This makes an interesting side dish or a light and refreshing entree for hot summer meals. Makes 6 to 8 servings.

| SHOPPING LIST | | Special Shopping |
|---|---|---|
| **Regularly Kept in the Kitchen (Listed in Chapter 14, p. 703)** | **Fresh Produce** | Hot mustard powder — found in Japanese (called "wasabe") or Chinese groceries or the Oriental food aisle of a supermarket. If not available, use regular mustard powder. |
| Soy sauce<br>Rice vinegar<br>Safflower oil<br>Toasted sesame oil<br>Peanut butter<br>Asafetida<br>Cayenne<br>Honey<br>Sesame seeds | Cucumber<br>Scallions<br>Cilantro (same as Chinese parsley)<br>Tomatoes | Aburage (age) pouches — found in Japanese or Chinese groceries; some Oriental food aisles in supermarkets. I go to the tofu factory and buy off-grade pouches for one to two dollars a box. |

# NUTRITIONAL ANALYSIS FOR ONE SERVING
## ORIENTAL-STYLE PROTEIN SALAD

| NUTRIENT | Type: 14   FEMALE-23 TO 51 YEARS | % RDA | Amount |
|---|---|---|---|
| KCALORIES | ⊼===== | 10% | 214.0 Kc |
| PROTEIN | ⊼========== | 20% | 9.090 Gm |
| CARBOHYDRATE | ⊼ | NO RDA | 8.650 Gm |
| FAT | ⊼ | NO RDA | 13.40 Gm |
| FIBER-CRUDE | ⊼ | NO RDA | 0.770 Gm |
| CHOLESTEROL | ⊼ | NO RDA | 0.000 Mg |
| SATURATED FA | ⊼ | NO RDA | 0.760 Gm |
| OLEIC FA | ⊼ | NO RDA | 4.070 Gm |
| LINOLEIC FA | ⊼ | NO RDA | 6.010 Gm |
| SODIUM | ⊼======== | 16% | 362.0 Mg |
| POTASSIUM | ⊼=== | 7% | 283.0 Mg |
| MAGNESIUM | ⊼============= | 27% | 83.60 Mg |
| IRON | ⊼====== | 13% | 2.490 Mg |
| ZINC | ⊼====== | 12% | 1.820 Mg |
| VITAMIN A | ⊼====== | 13% | 522.0 IU |
| VITAMIN D | ⊼ | 0% | 0.000 IU |
| VIT. E/TOTAL | ⊼ | NO RDA | 3.300 Mg |
| VITAMIN C | ⊼======= | 15% | 9.470 Mg |
| THIAMIN | ⊼== | 5% | 0.050 Mg |
| RIBOFLAVIN | ⊼= | 3% | 0.040 Mg |
| NIACIN | ⊼=== | 7% | 0.950 Mg |
| VITAMIN B6 | ⊼== | 4% | 0.080 Mg |
| FOLACIN | ⊼= | 2% | 11.90 Ug |
| VITAMIN B12 | ⊼ | 0% | 0.000 Ug |
| PANTO- ACID | ⊼== | 4% | 0.270 Mg |
| CALCIUM | ⊼========= | 18% | 144.0 Mg |
| PHOSPHORUS | ⊼======== | 17% | 138.0 Mg |
| TRYPTOPHAN | ⊼=================================================== | 142% | 233.0 Mg |
| THREONINE | ⊼=================================================== | 175% | 763.0 Mg |
| ISOLEUCINE | ⊼=================================================== | 172% | 1125 Mg |
| LEUCINE | ⊼=================================================== | 201% | 1753 Mg |
| LYSINE | ⊼=================================================== | 180% | 1177 Mg |
| METHIONINE | ⊼============================================ | 85% | 232.0 Mg |
| CYSTINE | ⊼================================= | 68% | 185.0 Mg |
| PHENYL-ANINE | ⊼=================================================== | 259% | 1130 Mg |
| TYROSINE | ⊼=================================================== | 188% | 821.0 Mg |
| VALINE | ⊼=================================================== | 134% | 1025 Mg |
| HISTIDINE | ⊼ | NO RDA | 625.0 Mg |
| ALCOHOL | ⊼ | NO RDA | 0.000 Gm |
| ASH | ⊼ | NO RDA | 2.090 Gm |
| COPPER | ⊼======= | 14% | 0.350 Mg |
| MANGANESE | ⊼================== | 36% | 1.370 Mg |
| IODINE | ⊼=================================================== | 720% | 1081 Ug |
| MONO FAT | ⊼ | NO RDA | 1.760 Gm |
| POLY FAT | ⊼ | NO RDA | 3.200 Gm |
| CAFFEINE | ⊼ | NO RDA | 0.000 Mg |
| FLUORIDE | ⊼ | 0% | 18.30 Ug |
| MOLYBDENUM | ⊼=================================================== | 407% | 1323 Ug |
| VITAMIN K | ⊼ | 1% | 1.570 Ug |
| SELENIUM | ⊼==== | 8% | 0.010 Mg |
| BIOTIN | ⊼== | 4% | 6.140 Ug |
| CHLORIDE | ⊼= | 3% | 113.0 Mg |
| CHROMIUM | ⊼=================================================== | 496% | 0.620 Mg |
| SUGAR | ⊼ | NO RDA | 2.520 Gm |
| FIBER-DIET | ⊼ | NO RDA | 9.770 Gm |
| VIT. E/AT | ⊼====== | 13% | 1.110 Mg |

```
% RDA:  |0      |20     |40     |60     |80     |100
```

# MISO·SESAME BARBECUE SAUCE

☆ There are many different kinds of miso. For this recipe I prefer using white miso, as it's the mildest and sweetest of all misos and allows the delicate flavor of the vegetables to come through.

---

*Fresh shiitake mushrooms*
*½"-thick eggplant slices*
*½"-thick sliced, canned bamboo shoots*

### Sesame Basting Sauce:

*½ cup water*
*⅓ cup mild white miso*
*¼ cup ground, roasted sesame seeds*
*3 Tbsp. toasted sesame oil*
*3 Tbsp. safflower oil*
*1 Tbsp. honey*
*1 tsp. finely grated lemon rind*

*Ground, roasted sesame seeds for garnish*

Prepare vegetables and lay on platter. Mix next 7 ingredients thoroughly, cover and set aside. Put extra ground sesame seeds in a separate bowl to sprinkle on barbecued vegetables after they're cooked.

To barbecue vegetables, place a variety of vegetables on grill (or in broiler if you wish) and cook till side facing heat is tender and singed in places. Flip over using spatula or tongs and cook on the other side. While other side is cooking, baste the already grilled side that's now facing up with the Sesame Basting Sauce. When bottom side is tender and singed in places, flip vegetables over so basted side is facing heat. Grill till the basting begins to brown. Baste the side of the vegetables now facing up with the Sesame Basting Sauce and flip so this side can also brown.

Sprinkle top surface with ground, toasted sesame seeds and serve immediately. Cook as many vegetables as needed to fill everyone.

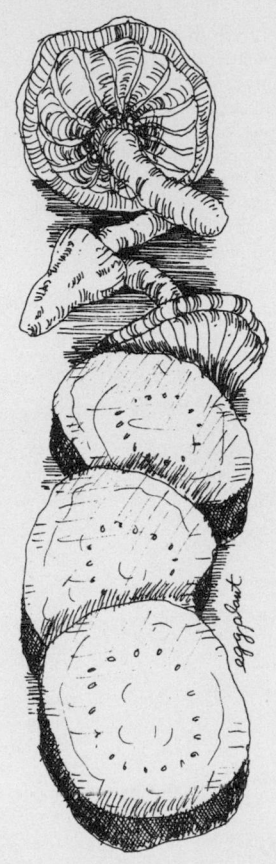

Fresh shiitake mushrooms are very expensive, but if you can find them and afford them, it's worth it to be able to serve each person one or even two.

| Special Shopping | SHOPPING LIST | |
|---|---|---|
| | **Regularly Kept in the Kitchen**<br>(Listed in Chapter 14, p. 703) | **Fresh Produce** |
| *Fresh shiitake mushrooms — found in Japanese groceries in the fresh produce section or in supermarkets in the gourmet produce section.<br>*Canned bamboo shoots — found in Japanese groceries or the Oriental food aisle of some supermarkets. | Mild white miso<br>Sesame seeds<br>Toasted sesame oil<br>Safflower oil<br>Honey | *Eggplant<br>Lemon |

*Suggested vegetables for this sauce.

# KOREAN MARINADE

☆ I try to provide a couple of different basting sauces or marinades at barbecues to offer people different flavors. This fiery sauce provides a nice contrast to the sweet Miso-Sesame Barbecue Sauce.

---

½ cup soy sauce
¼ cup honey
2 Tbsp. oil
1 Tbsp. toasted sesame seeds
½ Tbsp. finely minced or ground garlic
½ tsp. black pepper

2 Tbsp. chopped green onion
2 - 3 fresh red Serrano chilies, minced (optional)

Blend first 6 ingredients together in a blender and add last or last 2 ingredient(s). (The chilies make this very hot.)

Marinate vegetables in this sauce for about 15 to 20 minutes before cooking time. Vegetables that are good in this marinade are ½"-thick eggplant cutlets, tomatoes cut in half, bell peppers cut in quarters, and large, whole mushrooms. Tempeh and/or tofu are also good. The vegetables can also be cut into bite-sized cubes and used as shish kabobs instead.

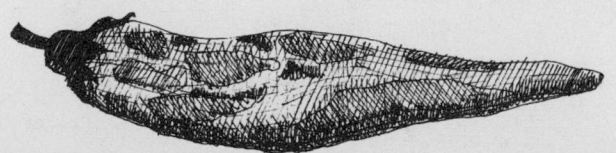

| SHOPPING LIST | |
|---|---|
| Regularly Kept in the Kitchen (Listed in Chapter 14, p. 703) | Fresh Produce |
| Soy sauce<br>Honey<br>Safflower oil<br>Sesame seeds<br>Black pepper | Garlic<br>Scallions<br>Serrano chilies<br>*Bell peppers<br>*Tomatoes<br>*Eggplant<br>*Mushrooms |

*Suggested vegetables for this marinade.

# STEAMED BREAD

☆ This recipe makes a steamed bread like the one often served in Chinese restaurants. It's a real basic recipe that you can use for innumerable purposes — like making stuffed buns; or shape into rose bud or sandwich shapes.

☆ For the vegetable barbecue, I recommend making the "sandwich" shape that will split open to insert pieces of the barbecued vegetable between.

☆ These little breads can be cooked, cooled and frozen. Then thaw and steam just before serving time to avoid having to make them at the last minute.

---

*2 Tbsp. baking yeast*
*2½ cups warm water*

*2 Tbsp. vegetable oil*
*½ cup honey*
*⅔ tsp. salt*

*6 cups whole wheat flour*
*1 tsp. baking powder*

Combine first 2 ingredients and allow to sit till yeast dissolves. Mix in next 3 ingredients. Sift in dry ingredients and mix thoroughly. Turn dough onto floured counter and knead till it forms a soft, firm dough.

This dough can be stuffed with a Chinese or other flavored filling and then steamed or baked. To make little steamed breads like those that are made in China to serve with vegetables, etc., use one or all of the following methods.

Steaming loaves of already baked bread is a good way to heat bread up. Warm, steamed bread resembles fresh-baked bread straight out of the oven in smell, texture and taste.

604

After preparing the dough, cut it in half. Shape each half on an oiled surface into a long, snake-like shape about 1½" in diameter. Slice across width of the roll at 1" intervals. Roll each section in hands coated with oil and place on little squares of wax paper cut to 2" x 2". Place breads in a steamer with enough space between each to allow for rising.

For buns that will split apart and can be used to sandwich things between them, use this method. After preparing the dough and cutting in half, roll on oiled surface into snake-like shape about ¾" in diameter and cut at ¾" intervals. Pair every 2 pieces together by stacking one atop the other with uncut surfaces touching. With flat side of a large enough knife, press each pair enough to flatten a bit and cause rounds to adhere to each other. Place each flattened pair on a 2" square of wax paper for cooking.

For a more decorative, festive shape, split dough in quarters and roll each quarter out on an oiled surface into a rectangle a little less than ¼" thick. Lightly oil surface of dough and roll up like a jelly roll so you end up with a long, snake-like shape about 1" in diameter. Cut at ¾" intervals and stack and press uncut edges together, as described in the second method (above). This time, lightly pinch edges together and gather all together in the middle on top of dough. Twist all edges together and place twisted side up on top of 2" squares of wax paper. These will cook up to look like a rose bud.

To cook, place steam rack and lid over cool water and turn heat on to high. When water begins to boil and you can see steam coming out from under lid, cook for 10 minutes.

If you make the whole recipe into Steamed Buns, there will be far more than enough for 8 servings. Fortunately, these freeze well. Just be sure to allow buns to thoroughly cool, then put in plastic bags, seal and freeze. (They can also be stored in a plastic bag for a week in the refrigerator.) To reheat, simply thaw and steam for 5 to 10 minutes.

Just a note: Steaming is a great way to heat a loaf of bread or a cake (with no icing) or sweet rolls. Just place the whole loaf in the steamer and steam till it's hot. It makes the bread as moist as, and taste like, a fresh-baked loaf!

If there is extra dough, you can also make the dough into a loaf, allow it to rise, and bake at 350 degrees for 30 to 45 minutes to make a delicious loaf of whole wheat bread.

# AS·THE·SNOW·MELTS DESSERT

☆ Another inspiration for a low-calorie, light dessert, typical of those served in the Orient.

---

*½ cup uncooked adzuki beans*
*7 cups water*

*¼ cup honey*

*¾ cup water*
*½ cup honey*

*Twice the amount of San-cha, Ban-cha or Kuki-cha*
*tea called for on tea box to make 1 cup tea*

*Large ice to shave*

Rinse beans, then soak them in water overnight or in very hot water for 1 hour before cooking. After beans have soaked, pour out soaking water and put in 7 cups water to cook beans in. Bring to boil, then cover and simmer 45 minutes, as in cooking rice. Add honey and cook at a gentle boil for 15 minutes, uncovered, so liquid can cook off. When most of the liquid is gone, remove from heat and cool to room temperature. Put in refrigerator to chill. After chilling, drain excess liquid and return beans to refrigerator. Reserve drained liquid to use in blender drinks or to jell for dessert another time.

Bring next 2 ingredients to a boil in pot and cook till honey is melted. Turn off heat and drop tea in a tea ball into hot honey water. Allow to steep the required amount of time. Remove tea ball, allow tea to cool, then refrigerate to chill. Everything up to this point can be done days ahead of time.

The shaved ice machine used to make this dessert has provided my family and friends with many a refreshing snack and dessert. Snow cones are the children's favorite. We shave the ice and pour unsweetened frozen fruit juice concentrates over the ice for a healthier version of these summertime beach favorites.

To serve, shave plain ice cubes in ice shaver and place about 1 cup of shaved ice in each serving bowl. Ladle on tea syrup till ice is saturated. Pour sweetened beans on top. Makes 6 to 8 servings.

Note: An ice shaving machine is an appliance that will bring your family and/or friends a lot of enjoyable, refreshing and low-calorie taste treats (for snacks or desserts). One of my children's favorites is pouring unsweetened fruit juice concentrates (found in the frozen department of grocery stores) over shaved ice to create dishes resembling snow cones that you buy at the beach in the summertime.

The only problem may be finding an ice shaving machine! The best place to try that I know of is a Japanese department store, if there is one in your city. Otherwise, I do know that they're available in the housewares section of Daiei Department Store, 500 Pearlridge Shopping Center, Aiea, Hawaii 96701. They sell a small household size for $25 plus tax and a larger commercial size for $250 plus tax.

| Special Shopping |
| --- |
| San-cha, Ban-cha or Kuki-cha (caffeine-free green tea) — found in most natural food stores. |

| SHOPPING LIST | |
| --- | --- |
| **Regularly Kept in the Kitchen** (Listed in Chapter 14, p. 703) | **Fresh Produce** |
| Adzuki beans<br>Honey<br>Ice | (None) |

# NUTRITIONAL ANALYSIS FOR ONE SERVING
## AS-THE-SNOW-MELTS DESSERT

| NUTRIENT | Type: 14 FEMALE-23 TO 51 YEARS | % RDA | Amount |
|---|---|---|---|
| KCALORIES | Ḁ==== | 8% | 176.0 Kc |
| PROTEIN | Ḁ=== | 6% | 3.040 Gm |
| CARBOHYDRATE | Ḁ | NO RDA | 42.20 Gm |
| FAT | Ḁ | NO RDA | 0.220 Gm |
| FIBER-CRUDE | Ḁ | NO RDA | 0.040 Gm |
| CHOLESTEROL | Ḁ | NO RDA | 0.000 Mg |
| SATURATED FA | Ḁ | NO RDA | 0.000 Gm |
| OLEIC FA | Ḁ | NO RDA | 0.000 Gm |
| LINOLEIC FA | Ḁ | NO RDA | 0.000 Gm |
| SODIUM | Ḁ | 0% | 4.370 Mg |
| POTASSIUM | Ḁ | 0% | 22.90 Mg |
| MAGNESIUM | Ḁ | 0% | 1.410 Mg |
| IRON | Ḁ | 1% | 0.210 Mg |
| ZINC | Ḁ | 0% | 0.060 Mg |
| VITAMIN A | Ḁ | 0% | 0.850 IU |
| VITAMIN D | Ḁ | 0% | 0.000 IU |
| VIT. E/TOTAL | Ḁ | NO RDA | 0.000 Mg |
| VITAMIN C | Ḁ | 0% | 0.000 Mg |
| THIAMIN | Ḁ=== | 7% | 0.070 Mg |
| RIBOFLAVIN | Ḁ= | 2% | 0.030 Mg |
| NIACIN | Ḁ== | 4% | 0.550 Mg |
| VITAMIN B6 | Ḁ | 0% | 0.000 Mg |
| FOLACIN | Ḁ | 0% | 0.000 Ug |
| VITAMIN B12 | Ḁ | 0% | 0.000 Ug |
| PANTO- ACID | Ḁ | 1% | 0.080 Mg |
| CALCIUM | Ḁ | 1% | 15.50 Mg |
| PHOSPHORUS | Ḁ=== | 6% | 51.60 Mg |
| TRYPTOPHAN | Ḁ======= | 14% | 24.00 Mg |
| THREONINE | Ḁ============ | 24% | 107.0 Mg |
| ISOLEUCINE | Ḁ========= | 18% | 121.0 Mg |
| LEUCINE | Ḁ============= | 27% | 243.0 Mg |
| LYSINE | Ḁ================== | 37% | 243.0 Mg |
| METHIONINE | Ḁ======= | 15% | 42.50 Mg |
| CYSTINE | Ḁ===== | 11% | 32.60 Mg |
| PHENYL-ANINE | Ḁ=================== | 39% | 170.0 Mg |
| TYROSINE | Ḁ============== | 28% | 126.0 Mg |
| VALINE | Ḁ========== | 20% | 155.0 Mg |
| HISTIDINE | Ḁ | NO RDA | 102.0 Mg |
| ALCOHOL | Ḁ | NO RDA | 0.000 Gm |
| ASH | Ḁ | NO RDA | 0.420 Gm |
| COPPER | Ḁ | 1% | 0.040 Mg |
| MANGANESE | Ḁ | 0% | 0.010 Mg |
| IODINE | Ḁ | 0% | 0.000 Ug |
| MONO FAT | Ḁ | NO RDA | 0.000 Gm |
| POLY FAT | Ḁ | NO RDA | 0.000 Gm |
| CAFFEINE | Ḁ | NO RDA | 0.000 Mg |
| FLUORIDE | Ḁ | 1% | 42.00 Ug |
| MOLYBDENUM | Ḁ | 0% | 0.000 Ug |
| VITAMIN K | Ḁ | 0% | 0.000 Ug |
| SELENIUM | Ḁ | 0% | 0.000 Mg |
| BIOTIN | Ḁ | 0% | 0.000 Ug |
| CHLORIDE | Ḁ | 0% | 5.780 Mg |
| CHROMIUM | Ḁ | 0% | 0.000 Mg |
| SUGAR | Ḁ | NO RDA | 0.000 Gm |
| FIBER-DIET | Ḁ | NO RDA | 0.000 Gm |
| VIT. E/AT | Ḁ | 0% | 0.000 Mg |

```
% RDA:  |0      |20     |40     |60     |80     |100
```

San-cha, Ban-cha or Kuki-cha tea not included in analysis.

The scholar Chanakya wrote —
"The petty mind thinks, 'This is mine. That's for others.' Whereas men of noble thought consider the whole earth as one family."

# BENEFICIAL CHINESE VEGETABLES

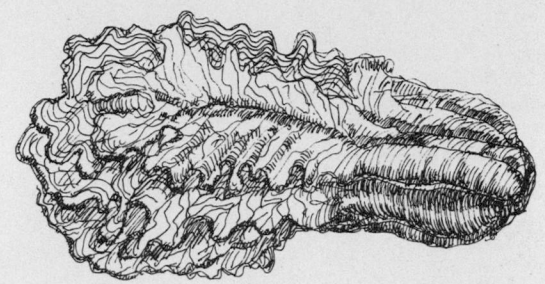

An interesting report caught my eye and increased my appreciation for many of the Chinese vegetables I grew up on. (People of the People's Republic of China and other Eastern Third World countries — are you listening?!) The report showed that dietary-caused diseases are on the rise as the diet in Japan and Taiwan have become Westernized throughout this last century to very closely resemble U.S. consumption patterns. (One hundred years ago, average fat consumption in one day was six grams; today, 55 grams — just like in the U.S.) While Taiwan's incidence of heart disease and heart attack has increased, it hasn't increased as drastically as Japan's.

Studies credit Chinese vegetables with being one of the factors that make the Taiwanese relatively immune to heart attacks even though they're consuming as much fat as the Japanese and Americans. The saving grace is Chinese vegetables; their higher levels (compared to our vegetables) of dietary fiber absorb cholesterol and bile salts and carry them out of the body. (High levels of cholesterol and bile salts in the system contribute to heart disease/heart attacks.)

Chinese vegetables have been as common in Hawaii produce departments as lettuce for as far back as I can remember due to the predominance and blending there of so many ethnic groups. Recently I've noticed more and more Chinese vegetables making their way onto mainland U.S. supermarket shelves and Chinese vegetable seeds becoming available in seed stands and catalogs. It's certainly worth using Chinese vegetables more often from the body's point of view as well as the tongue's.

# TOFU YUMS

☆ A cholesterol-free tofu version of egg-foo-yung.

½ tsp. black pepper
1 Tbsp. vegetable oil
2 cups Chinese peas, cut in 1" slivers
½ cup slivered green onion
½ cup slivered water chestnuts

2 cups fresh mung bean sprouts

½ cup mashed tofu
¾ cup whole wheat flour
¼ cup nutritional yeast
2 Tbsp. soy sauce
2 tsp. baking powder

3½ cups mashed tofu

Preheat oven to 350 degrees. Oil a cookie sheet.

Saute first 5 ingredients over very high heat till Chinese peas begin to turn translucent. Turn off heat and add raw mung bean sprouts. Mix the next 5 ingredients together in a mixing bowl. Blend the last 3½ cups of tofu till smooth and creamy. Pour ingredients into mixing bowl, add sauteed vegetables and mix thoroughly.

With a ¼-cup measuring cup, scoop dollops onto oiled cookie sheets, flattening the batter to form little patties. As with cookies, leave a little space between each patty. Bake at 350 degrees for about 20 to 25 minutes. Flip over and bake for another 15 minutes. While the Tofu Yums are baking, prepare the sauce. (Tofu Yums are delicious served with either the following recipe for Mushroom Sauce or Pineapple Sweet-Sour Sauce, p. 124.) To serve, place Tofu Yums into individual serving bowls and pour sauce over them. Allow to sit about 5 minutes before serving. Makes enough for 4 to 6 servings.

| SHOPPING LIST | |
|---|---|
| Regularly Kept in the Kitchen (Listed in Chapter 14, p. 703) | Fresh Produce |
| Black pepper<br>Vegetable oil<br>Tofu<br>Whole wheat flour<br>Nutritional yeast<br>Soy sauce<br>Baking powder | Chinese peas<br>Scallions<br>Water chestnuts<br>Mung bean sprouts |

## MUSHROOM SAUCE

6 cups cold water
1 oz. dried black (shiitake) Oriental mushrooms
½ cup soy sauce

1 cup water
⅓ cup arrowroot

Bring 6 cups water to a boil. Add dry mushrooms and turn off heat. Cover and let soak for at least 20 minutes, although overnight or all day is all right. (For instance, you can boil the water before going to work and come home to carry on.)

Remove mushrooms from soaking liquid and squeeze excess liquid out of mushrooms into pot. Keep the water. Cut stems off mushrooms and cut in long, thin strips. Return to the soaking water and add soy sauce. Simmer about 15 minutes.

In a separate bowl, mix water and arrowroot until arrowroot is dissolved. Now, bring the mushrooms and water to a boil. Remove from heat, pour in arrowroot mixture and mix in. Bring to a boil, stirring constantly until thickened. Pour into individual serving bowls over Tofu Yums.

# NUTRITIONAL ANALYSIS FOR ONE SERVING
## TOFU YUMS WITH PINEAPPLE SWEET-SOUR SAUCE

| NUTRIENT | Type: 14   FEMALE-23 TO 51 YEARS | % RDA | Amount |
|---|---|---|---|
| KCALORIES | A=================== | 39% | 795.0 Kc |
| PROTEIN | A==================================================== | 119% | 52.60 Gm |
| CARBOHYDRATE | A | NO RDA | 86.00 Gm |
| FAT | A | NO RDA | 33.10 Gm |
| FIBER-CRUDE | A | NO RDA | 3.900 Gm |
| CHOLESTEROL | A | NO RDA | 0.000 Mg |
| SATURATED FA | A | NO RDA | 4.350 Gm |
| OLEIC FA | A | NO RDA | 3.800 Gm |
| LINOLEIC FA | A | NO RDA | 12.70 Gm |
| SODIUM | A========================= | 51% | 1130 Mg |
| POTASSIUM | A=================== | 39% | 1472 Mg |
| MAGNESIUM | A======================================= | 79% | 239.0 Mg |
| IRON | A=================================================== | 173% | 31.20 Mg |
| ZINC | A==================== | 41% | 6.260 Mg |
| VITAMIN A | A================== | 37% | 1483 IU |
| VITAMIN D | A | 0% | 0.000 IU |
| VIT. E/TOTAL | A | NO RDA | 7.870 Mg |
| VITAMIN C | A================================================== | 160% | 96.30 Mg |
| THIAMIN | A==================================================== | 532% | 5.320 Mg |
| RIBOFLAVIN | A==================================================== | 419% | 5.030 Mg |
| NIACIN | A==================================================== | 231% | 30.10 Mg |
| VITAMIN B6 | A==================================================== | 255% | 5.100 Mg |
| FOLACIN | A======================= | 46% | 187.0 Ug |
| VITAMIN B12 | A==================================================== | 116% | 3.500 Ug |
| PANTO- ACID | A=================== | 39% | 2.180 Mg |
| CALCIUM | A==================================================== | 240% | 1926 Mg |
| PHOSPHORUS | A==================================================== | 121% | 975.0 Mg |
| TRYPTOPHAN | A==================================================== | 455% | 743.0 Mg |
| THREONINE | A==================================================== | 467% | 2033 Mg |
| ISOLEUCINE | A==================================================== | 382% | 2500 Mg |
| LEUCINE | A==================================================== | 437% | 3811 Mg |
| LYSINE | A==================================================== | 505% | 3300 Mg |
| METHIONINE | A==================================================== | 239% | 651.0 Mg |
| CYSTINE | A==================================================== | 261% | 711.0 Mg |
| PHENYL-ANINE | A==================================================== | 551% | 2400 Mg |
| TYROSINE | A==================================================== | 394% | 1718 Mg |
| VALINE | A==================================================== | 352% | 2688 Mg |
| HISTIDINE | A | NO RDA | 1398 Mg |
| ALCOHOL | A | NO RDA | 0.000 Gm |
| ASH | A | NO RDA | 11.10 Gm |
| COPPER | A============================= | 58% | 1.450 Mg |
| MANGANESE | A==================================================== | 146% | 5.490 Mg |
| IODINE | A==================================================== | 246% | 370.0 Ug |
| MONO FAT | A | NO RDA | 6.130 Gm |
| POLY FAT | A | NO RDA | 20.20 Gm |
| CAFFEINE | A | NO RDA | 0.000 Mg |
| FLUORIDE | A= | 3% | 84.30 Ug |
| MOLYBDENUM | A==================================================== | 1345% | 4374 Ug |
| VITAMIN K | A==================================================== | 179% | 188.0 Ug |
| SELENIUM | A==================== | 40% | 0.050 Mg |
| BIOTIN | A======== | 16% | 24.90 Ug |
| CHLORIDE | A======= | 15% | 521.0 Mg |
| CHROMIUM | A==================================================== | 752% | 0.940 Mg |
| SUGAR | A | NO RDA | 4.550 Gm |
| FIBER-DIET | A | NO RDA | 6.160 Gm |
| VIT. E/AT | A======================= | 49% | 3.930 Mg |

```
% RDA: |0      |20     |40     |60     |80     |100
```

611

# YUBA STIR·FRY

☆ Once you get the knack of stir-frying, you won't need recipes! The idea is to use whatever vegetables are in season in varying combinations with a soy-protein food if making an entree.

---

8 oz. dried bean curd sticks (yuba), soaked

2 Tbsp. soy sauce
2 Tbsp. toasted sesame oil
½ tsp. black pepper

1 oz. wakame seaweed

2 cups thinly sliced carrots
2 cups snow peas

2 Tbsp. safflower oil
1" chunk fresh ginger root, crushed
1 tsp. asafetida or 1 clove garlic, crushed

2 cakes furu (fermented soybean cake)
2 Tbsp. soybean cake brine
1 tsp. honey

8 cups tomato wedges
10 cups dark Chinese greens

1 Tbsp. arrowroot powder

Soak yuba sticks in water for a few hours (or all day) on the day of preparation. Just before time to make the stir-fry, drain water from the yuba sticks and cut into 2" to 3" lengths. Squeeze as much water out as you can while you are cutting the strips and drain again. Toss next 3 ingredients into the yuba strips and allow to sit about 10 minutes.

In the meantime, soak the seaweed in just enough water to cover it. Then prepare other ingredients by slicing carrots, rinsing and de-stemming snow peas, crushing ginger, washing and cutting tomatoes and whatever Chinese greens (or combination of greens) are available.

Heat wok and pour in the seasoned yuba sticks, adding oil only if it is necessary to keep them from sticking to the wok. Fry, stirring occasionally, till yuba is golden brown and slightly braised. The yuba strips should look (and taste) like fried chicken skin. Remove yuba from wok and set in a large bowl. Pour a couple of tablespoons of safflower oil into hot wok and put carrots into wok to stir-fry. Stir constantly till carrots

Some "dark Chinese greens" that can found in our supermarkets:
Bok-choy, You-tsai, Guy-lon, Guy-tsai, Hin-choy, Ong-choy.

On my visit to the People's Republic of China, I saw many dark-green, leafy vegetables growing in garden plots that I'd never seen before! I'm sure there's an even longer list of Chinese greens we know nothing about in the United States.

begin to turn a more brilliant orange than they were when raw. Remove from wok into the same bowl with the yuba. Now stir-fry snow peas in the same way as carrots, removing into the same bowl when peas begin to turn a brighter green than they were when raw. Stir-frying these vegetables (over the highest heat) should take only 30 seconds or so each.

Pour a couple more tablespoons of oil into empty heated wok; then add ginger and asafetida (or garlic). Allow to fry just about 30 seconds. Add the next 3 ingredients and stir quickly till they are dissolved. Add the next 2 ingredients along with the soaked seaweed (keeping the soaking water). Stir vegetables till Chinese greens wilt.

Add the ingredients that have already been fried and set aside in the bowl. You can pour in the yuba strips and mix with the vegetables, or just leave yuba in the bowl and pour on top of the vegetables on the serving platter. It is just a matter of your preference. Adding the yuba to the cooking vegetables makes it soft and juicy as it soaks up the gravy, while leaving it out to garnish the top of the vegetables after they're finished cooking allows yuba strips to remain crisp. Cover the vegetables and allow to simmer 3 to 5 minutes (till tomatoes begin to soften).

Stir arrowroot into water the seaweed was soaked in and pour into the vegetables. Stir very quickly so it thickens the whole vegetable gravy evenly. Makes 6 servings.

| SHOPPING LIST | |
| --- | --- |
| **Regularly Kept in the Kitchen (Listed in Chapter 14, p. 703)** | **Fresh Produce** |
| Yuba sticks | Carrots |
| Soy sauce | Snow peas |
| Toasted sesame oil | Ginger root |
| Black pepper | Tomatoes |
| Wakame seaweed | Dark Chinese greens of your |
| Safflower oil | choice |
| Asafetida | |
| Fermented bean cake (furu) | |
| Honey | |
| Arrowroot powder | |

Chinese peas, also known as snow peas or edible pod peas, absorb and remove 10 times more cholesterol from the body than American cucumbers.

# NUTRITIONAL ANALYSIS FOR ONE SERVING YUBA STIR-FRY

| NUTRIENT | Type: 14 FEMALE-23 TO 51 YEARS | % RDA | Amount |
|----------|-------------------------------|-------|--------|
| KCALORIES | Ã============= | 24% | 491.0 Kc |
| PROTEIN | Ã================================================= | 93% | 41.00 Gm |
| CARBOHYDRATE | Ã | NO RDA | 37.20 Gm |
| FAT | Ã | NO RDA | 25.70 Gm |
| FIBER-CRUDE | Ã | NO RDA | 3.970 Gm |
| CHOLESTEROL | Ã | NO RDA | 0.000 Mg |
| SATURATED FA | Ã | NO RDA | 1.230 Gm |
| OLEIC FA | Ã | NO RDA | 4.480 Gm |
| LINOLEIC FA | Ã | NO RDA | 9.420 Gm |
| SODIUM | Ã============ | 24% | 540.0 Mg |
| POTASSIUM | Ã================== | 37% | 1406 Mg |
| MAGNESIUM | Ã========================= | 53% | 160.0 Mg |
| IRON | Ã============================== | 63% | 11.50 Mg |
| ZINC | Ã= | 3% | 0.460 Mg |
| VITAMIN A | Ã============================================ | 442% | 17693 IU |
| VITAMIN D | Ã | 0% | 0.000 IU |
| VIT. E/TOTAL | Ã | NO RDA | 7.270 Mg |
| VITAMIN C | Ã================================================= | 238% | 143.0 Mg |
| THIAMIN | Ã========================= | 54% | 0.540 Mg |
| RIBOFLAVIN | Ã================ | 34% | 0.410 Mg |
| NIACIN | Ã================== | 38% | 5.040 Mg |
| VITAMIN B6 | Ã======== | 17% | 0.340 Mg |
| FOLACIN | Ã==== | 9% | 36.60 Ug |
| VITAMIN B12 | Ã | 0% | 0.000 Ug |
| PANTO- ACID | Ã============ | 24% | 1.350 Mg |
| CALCIUM | Ã=============================== | 62% | 500.0 Mg |
| PHOSPHORUS | Ã==================================== | 68% | 547.0 Mg |
| TRYPTOPHAN | Ã================================================= | 154% | 252.0 Mg |
| THREONINE | Ã================================================= | 216% | 942.0 Mg |
| ISOLEUCINE | Ã================================================= | 194% | 1269 Mg |
| LEUCINE | Ã================================================= | 216% | 1890 Mg |
| LYSINE | Ã================================================= | 258% | 1687 Mg |
| METHIONINE | Ã================================================= | 113% | 309.0 Mg |
| CYSTINE | Ã================================================= | 122% | 332.0 Mg |
| PHENYL-ANINE | Ã================================================= | 274% | 1192 Mg |
| TYROSINE | Ã================================================= | 216% | 942.0 Mg |
| VALINE | Ã================================================= | 171% | 1308 Mg |
| HISTIDINE | Ã | NO RDA | 675.0 Mg |
| ALCOHOL | Ã | NO RDA | 0.000 Gm |
| ASH | Ã | NO RDA | 7.120 Gm |
| COPPER | Ã================ | 32% | 0.810 Mg |
| MANGANESE | Ã======================== | 48% | 1.800 Mg |
| IODINE | Ã===================================== | 79% | 119.0 Ug |
| MONO FAT | Ã | NO RDA | 2.490 Gm |
| POLY FAT | Ã | NO RDA | 5.760 Gm |
| CAFFEINE | Ã | NO RDA | 0.000 Mg |
| FLUORIDE | Ã== | 5% | 141.0 Ug |
| MOLYBDENUM | Ã================================================= | 1129% | 3670 Ug |
| VITAMIN K | Ã================================================= | 273% | 287.0 Ug |
| SELENIUM | Ã======== | 16% | 0.020 Mg |
| BIOTIN | Ã========= | 18% | 27.80 Ug |
| CHLORIDE | Ã | 1% | 60.40 Mg |
| CHROMIUM | Ã================================================= | 328% | 0.410 Mg |
| SUGAR | Ã | NO RDA | 24.40 Gm |
| FIBER-DIET | Ã | NO RDA | 11.10 Gm |
| VIT. E/AT | Ã==================== | 38% | 3.090 Mg |

```
% RDA:   |0      |20     |40     |60     |80     |100
```

Chinese green used: pak-choy. Soybean cake brine not included in analysis.

Bok-choy has the additional benefit of being en excellent source of calcium. One cup of cooked Bok-choy contains 252 mg. calcuim with only 25 calories.

Compare to —

1 cup whole milk:
291 mg. calcium/150 calories

1 cup lowfat milk:
297 mg. calcium/120 calories

1 cup lowfat yogurt:
326 mg. calcium/145 calories

# LAYERED SALAD A'LA ORIENTAL

☆ An attractive layered salad that makes a whole meal served with rice or a whole grain noodle dish (also with an Oriental dash, of course!).

---

*2 blocks well-drained and cubed tofu*
*4 cups mung bean sprouts*
*6 cups chopped watercress*
*⅓ cup slivered scallions*
*4 cups cubed tomatoes*
*4 cups Napa cabbage (won-bok) or bok-choy*

*⅓ cup soy sauce*
*3 Tbsp. toasted sesame oil*
*3 Tbsp. safflower oil*
*2 Tbsp. rice vinegar*
*1 tsp. honey*
*1 cup toasted sesame seeds (or meal)*

In a 9" x 13" baking tray, layer each of the first 6 ingredients one on top of the other in the order given (starting with tofu on the bottom). Mix last 6 ingredients together in a jar and pour evenly over salad just a few minutes before serving. To serve, lift a segment of the salad, being sure to include every layer on each plate. The salad and dressing can be made the night before and stored in the refrigerator in separate containers. (This is important because the dressing makes the salad start to wilt and lose its water as soon as it's applied.)

Makes 6 servings if served as a meal-in-one salad. If served as a dinner salad, it will serve as many as 18.

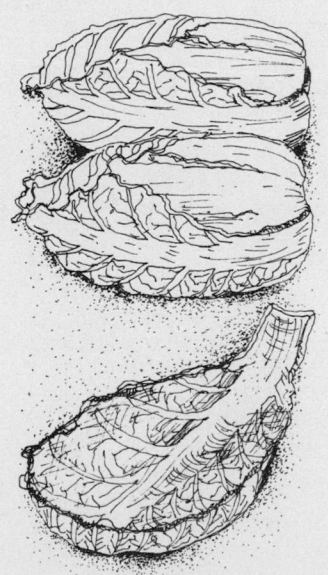

| SHOPPING LIST | |
|---|---|
| **Regularly Kept in the Kitchen** (Listed in Chapter 14, p. 703) | **Fresh Produce** |
| Tofu | Mung bean sprouts |
| Soy sauce | Watercress |
| Toasted sesame oil | Scallions |
| Safflower oil | Tomatoes |
| Rice vinegar | Napa cabbage |
| Honey | |
| Sesame seeds | |

# NUTRITIONAL ANALYSIS FOR ONE SERVING
## LAYERED SALAD A'LA ORIENTAL

| NUTRIENT | Type: 14   FEMALE-23 TO 51 YEARS | % RDA | Amount |
|----------|-----------------------------------|-------|--------|
| KCALORIES | Ã=============== | 28% | 573.0 Kc |
| PROTEIN | Ã============================================ | 83% | 36.90 Gm |
| CARBOHYDRATE | Ã | NO RDA | 29.60 Gm |
| FAT | Ã | NO RDA | 39.50 Gm |
| FIBER-CRUDE | Ã | NO RDA | 4.030 Gm |
| CHOLESTEROL | Ã | NO RDA | 0.000 Mg |
| SATURATED FA | Ã | NO RDA | 5.370 Gm |
| OLEIC FA | Ã | NO RDA | 5.080 Gm |
| LINOLEIC FA | Ã | NO RDA | 11.20 Gm |
| SODIUM | Ã======================= | 45% | 1000 Mg |
| POTASSIUM | Ã================= | 33% | 1261 Mg |
| MAGNESIUM | Ã======================================= | 77% | 231.0 Mg |
| IRON | Ã=================================================== | 128% | 23.20 Mg |
| ZINC | Ã================ | 31% | 4.710 Mg |
| VITAMIN A | Ã=================================================== | 128% | 5150 IU |
| VITAMIN D | Ã | 0% | 0.000 IU |
| VIT. E/TOTAL | Ã | NO RDA | 11.80 Mg |
| VITAMIN C | Ã================================================= | 124% | 74.60 Mg |
| THIAMIN | Ã======================== | 48% | 0.480 Mg |
| RIBOFLAVIN | Ã================= | 35% | 0.430 Mg |
| NIACIN | Ã=========== | 23% | 3.000 Mg |
| VITAMIN B6 | Ã========= | 18% | 0.360 Mg |
| FOLACIN | Ã============== | 27% | 108.0 Ug |
| VITAMIN B12 | Ã | 0% | 0.000 Ug |
| PANTO- ACID | Ã========= | 19% | 1.050 Mg |
| CALCIUM | Ã================================================== | 185% | 1483 Mg |
| PHOSPHORUS | Ã====================================== | 76% | 611.0 Mg |
| TRYPTOPHAN | Ã===================================================== | 338% | 551.0 Mg |
| THREONINE | Ã===================================================== | 322% | 1403 Mg |
| ISOLEUCINE | Ã===================================================== | 257% | 1682 Mg |
| LEUCINE | Ã===================================================== | 297% | 2587 Mg |
| LYSINE | Ã===================================================== | 326% | 2135 Mg |
| METHIONINE | Ã===================================================== | 189% | 515.0 Mg |
| CYSTINE | Ã==============████====================== | 177% | 483.0 Mg |
| PHENYL-ANINE | Ã===================================================== | 385% | 1678 Mg |
| TYROSINE | Ã===================================================== | 260% | 1131 Mg |
| VALINE | Ã===================================================== | 231% | 1765 Mg |
| HISTIDINE | Ã | NO RDA | 983.0 Mg |
| ALCOHOL | Ã | NO RDA | 0.000 Gm |
| ASH | Ã | NO RDA | 8.300 Gm |
| COPPER | Ã============================== | 60% | 1.520 Mg |
| MANGANESE | Ã========================================= | 81% | 3.060 Mg |
| IODINE | Ã================================================= | 122% | 183.0 Ug |
| MONO FAT | Ã | NO RDA | 10.80 Gm |
| POLY FAT | Ã | NO RDA | 21.00 Gm |
| CAFFEINE | Ã | NO RDA | 0.000 Mg |
| FLUORIDE | Ã= | 2% | 81.50 Ug |
| MOLYBDENUM | Ã===================================================== | 620% | 2016 Ug |
| VITAMIN K | Ã============================================= | 80% | 85.00 Ug |
| SELENIUM | Ã======== | 16% | 0.020 Mg |
| BIOTIN | Ã=== | 7% | 11.60 Ug |
| CHLORIDE | Ã==== | 9% | 319.0 Mg |
| CHROMIUM | Ã===================================================== | 440% | 0.550 Mg |
| SUGAR | Ã | NO RDA | 9.750 Gm |
| FIBER-DIET | Ã | NO RDA | 2.070 Gm |
| VIT. E/AT | Ã===================== | 42% | 3.390 Mg |

```
% RDA:  |0      |20      |40      |60      |80      |100
```

# ITALIAN GARDEN FEAST

Eating is something each of us must do to refuel our energies and maintain optimum health, and the foods we eat should be the ones best suited to do the job. Yet, as we eat, we should be ever mindful that we should be doing something constructive with our renewed energy and living for a higher purpose lest we fall into the plight described by these words of Leonardo da Vinci: "Lo, some can call themselves nothing more than a passage for food, producers of dung, fillers up of privies, for of them nothing else appears in this world, nor is there any virtue in their work, for nothing of them remains but full privies."

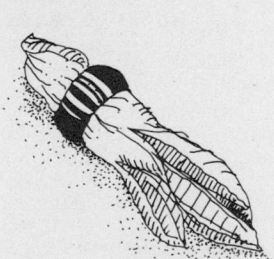

Most of us probably associate Italian cooking with a lot of heavy pastas topped with lots of cheese and tomato sauce. On the contrary, Italy has a climate similar to that of California, so they're able to grow an abundance of fresh produce. A lot of Italian cooking makes the best of Italy's abundance of fresh produce, making it a good place to look for recipe ideas using fresh vegetables.

It was interesting to me to find out that there was a great interest in the connection between diet and health during the Renaissance. Books written during the Renaissance indicate that there was an interest in the health-promoting aspects of food which spurred an increase in the use of vegetables in relation to the rest of the diet. There was even then a suspicion that the increased consumption of meat, ushered in with the increased prosperity in Europe, was undermining health. How interesting that modern-day, scientific research is now confirming the same information for us!

Scientific study in many fields (but here we'll stick to the subject of nutrition) is at the stage of blind men tapping the tip of an iceberg. Though we know something of our bodies and how they interact with different foods and elements put into them, there is so much more to learn! Even as I write this book, more information is being brought forth about fat in the diet that changes some of the things I've already written about fat and cholesterol (p. 55). I'm purposely leaving that and this in to graphically illustrate what an infantile stage the whole science of nutrition is in! Results of two different studies have led many in the scientific community to conclude that olive oil could possibly be the best fat to consume.

The "Seven Countries" study monitored 16 groups of healthy, middle-aged men in Japan, Yugoslavia, Finland, Italy, the Netherlands, Greece and the United States for 10 years. Finland had the highest rate of fatal heart attacks (628 per 10,000), followed by American men (424 per 10,000). All other groups followed with rates ranging from 317 to 50; except the group from Crete — they had no deaths from heart attacks during the whole 10 years (0 out of 655)!

After taking into consideration all the risk factors they could think of, researchers were at a loss to explain the Cretan's healthy hearts until a Dr. Scott Grundy of the University of Texas at Dallas revealed results of his studies. In 1985, Dr. Grundy put people on liquid formula diets that were high in different kinds of fat (40% saturated, polyunsaturated and monounsaturated), but low in cholesterol (less than 100 milligrams) for four weeks. His studies found that a high polyunsaturated diet reduced total cholesterol levels in the bloodstream — HDL (the good cholesterol that scientists think helps to reduce the risk of heart disease) as well as LDL levels. Monounsaturated fats (the kind of fat olive oil is) didn't lower HDL levels, while they did lower LDL levels.

Before Dr. Grundy's study, most scientists took the position that saturated fats increased serum cholesterol levels (especially LDL), polyunsaturated fats lowered serum cholesterol levels, and monounsaturated fats were neutral (neither raised nor lowered). This is why the American Heart Association has stressed using polyunsaturated fats for years. The Cancer Association has had trouble with this because animal studies have shown diets high in polyunsaturated fats cause cancer. A few recent studies have shown that animals fed diets high in olive oil developed no more tumors than those fed lowfat diets. This shouldn't be interpreted as meaning that drowning everything in olive oil is healthy. (Japanese, who eat overall very small amounts of fat, had the lowest total rates of breast and colon cancer and heart disease combined.) The above studies would lead us to keep fat levels safely low and to include olive oil as one of the fats used.

## SUGGESTED MENU

*Antipasto salad platter*

*Rigatoni in the Garden*

*Garden Harvest Pizza*

*Mint Sherbeto*

It may seem as though the marinades for each antipasto salad call for a lot of oil — because they do. But bear in mind that much of the dressing will be left over and can be used and reused many times.

# ANTIPASTO SALAD

☆ An antipasto salad is basically vegetables marinated in different dressings; they should be made ahead of time — preferably a day or two, or at least three hours before serving. Because they can be prepared ahead of time, along with the fact they're such an attractive dish (with all the pretty colors of different vegetables), antipasto salads are perfect for entertaining. You can make one, a few, or all of the following for an antipasto platter.

# GARDEN VEGETABLE ANTIPASTO SALAD

*1 small head cauliflower cut into 1" flowerets*
*1 large broccoli bunch cut into 1" flowerets*
*3 medium carrots cut into carrot sticks*

*¾ cup olive oil*
*¾ cup apple cider vinegar*
*1 tsp. asafetida or 2 - 3 cloves garlic, crushed*
*½ tsp. Spike or other vegetable-seasoned salt*
*¼ tsp. black pepper*

Make a large platter with a large variety of antipasto salads on it for hors d'oeuvres or appetizers. Individual platters of antipasto salad with thin slices of cheese and whole grain rolls or bread can be served as a whole meal.

Cut cauliflower and broccoli into bite-sized floweret chunks approximately 1" square. Cut carrots into regular-sized carrot sticks. Place all in a steamer and steam till broccoli turns a brilliant green and vegetables are tender but not mushy. Be very careful not to overcook. While vegetables are steaming, make the marinade in an airtight container or bottle with the next 5 ingredients. As soon as vegetables are done steaming, while still hot, put immediately into the marinade. Cover, turn container upside down and roll around till all the vegetables are coated. Leave to sit at room temperature till it cools; then either allow to sit in the marinade at least 3 more hours at room temperature or for several days in the refrigerator.

# MUSHROOM ANTIPASTO SALAD

*1 lb. fresh mushrooms*

*½ cup olive oil*
*1 Tbsp. apple cider vinegar*
*¼ cup lemon juice*
*¼ cup finely chopped, fresh parsley*
*1 tsp. dried thyme*
*2 tsp. asafetida or 4 - 6 cloves garlic, crushed*
*½ tsp. Spike or other vegetable-seasoned salt*
*⅛ tsp. black pepper*

Rinse the mushrooms and cut the stems off right under the caps. (You can save the stems to use in soups or sauces.) Steam the caps about 5 minutes. While steaming, make marinade with the next 8 ingredients and marinate as in preceding Garden Vegetable Antipasto Salad recipe.

# FRESH GREEN ANTIPASTO SALAD

*4 cups Swiss chard, cut crosswise in 1" strips*

*2 Tbsp. olive oil*
*1 tsp. dried oregano*

*2 Tbsp. lemon juice*
*½ tsp. Spike or other vegetable-seasoned salt*
*¼ tsp. black pepper*

Rinse chard and cut across leaves and stalk about 1" apart. Heat olive oil and oregano in a skillet over medium-high heat and stir-fry chard till it's wilted and turns a very deep green. Turn off heat, add next 3 ingredients and toss till thoroughly mixed. This can be served hot as is or covered and allowed to cool.

Leftover antipasto salad vegetables and a little of the dressing can be tossed into whole grain noodles with some Parmesan or Romano cheese to make a quick pasta salad.

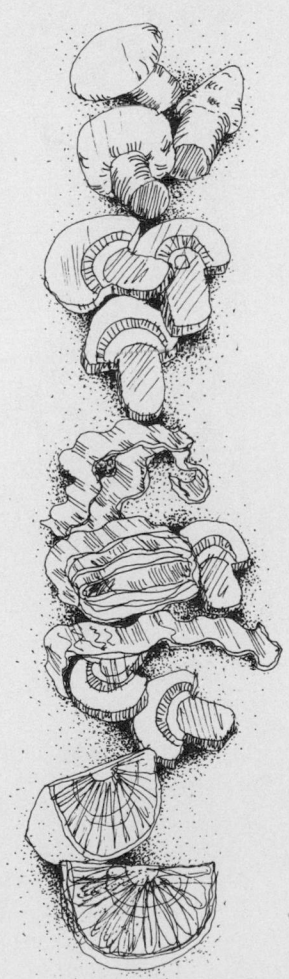

# PEPPER ANTIPASTO SALAD

*4 large bell peppers: red, green, yellow,*
   *and/or purple*

*2 Tbsp. lemon juice*
*1 Tbsp. apple cider vinegar*
*3 Tbsp. olive oil*
*1 Tbsp. soy sauce*

Prepare bell peppers for peeling by placing all of them at once under the broiler. (Chili peppers are also delicious prepared this way.) As soon as the peel close to the broiler blisters and is singed, turn the peppers so another side is facing the broiler. Do this till all the surfaces of the peppers are blistered. While peppers are under broiler, prepare marinade with the next 4 ingredients. Turn off the broiler and pull out broiling tray. Cover the peppers with a damp kitchen towel and allow them to sit till the peppers are cool enough to handle. Now the pepper skins will just slip off. Peel the peppers and de-stem them. Cut each pepper in half and remove seeds and inside membranes. Now cut each half into eighths (about ½" wide) and place in marinade. Marinate as done in the Garden Vegetable Antipasto Salad.

# TOMATO ANTIPASTO SALAD

*3 medium tomatoes, cut into wedges*
*2 cups thinly sliced celery*
*¼ cup thinly sliced red onion*
*½ cup pitted olives, chopped*
*1 dozen fresh basil leaves, chopped fine*
*¼ cup olive oil*
*2 Tbsp. apple cider vinegar*

Combine all the ingredients and mix thoroughly. Then cover and allow to marinate at room temperature a few hours before serving.

# AVOCADO·GARBANZO ANTIPASTO SALAD

2 cups garbanzo beans, cooked

1 Tbsp. olive oil
1 Tbsp. apple cider vinegar
¼ tsp. Tabasco sauce
¼ tsp. dried oregano
¼ tsp. paprika
½ tsp. asafetida or 1 - 2 cloves garlic, crushed

2 cups cubed avocado

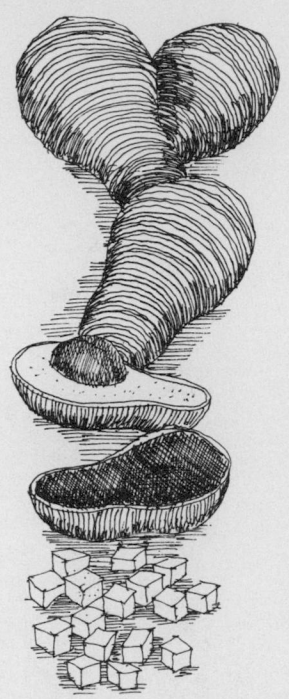

Cook the garbanzos — or better yet, use some that you had previously cooked and refrigerated or frozen. Prepare marinade by combining the next 6 ingredients. Pour cooked beans into marinade, stir thoroughly and allow to marinate as in the Garden Vegetable Antipasto Salad recipe. Right before serving time, cube avocados and mix in with marinated garbanzos.

# RIGATONI IN THE GARDEN

☆ If it sounds like the whole garden is in this dish . . . it practically is!

2 Tbsp. olive oil
1 tsp. asafetida or 1 onion, finely diced
½ cup finely chopped, fresh parsley
1 cup thinly sliced celery
½ cup thinly sliced radishes
1 cup thinly sliced carrots
1½ cups thinly sliced leeks
½ cup finely chopped fresh basil

1 cup finely chopped broccoli or cauliflower
2 cups diced zucchini
4 large tomatoes, cut in wedges
1 cup vegetable broth or 1 cup water

Italians cook their vegetables a great deal like the Chinese (which shouldn't be a surprise to us considering all the trade that went on between the two countries at one point in time!). Vegetables are considered perfectly cooked when done just enough to remove rawness, but still retaining flavor and firmness (firm, but soft enough to be cut with a fork).

*and 1 vegetable bouillon cube*
*1 tsp. Spike or other vegetable-seasoned salt*
*½ tsp. black pepper*

*1 lb. whole grain Rigatoni or other*
*    shaped noodles, cooked*
*2 Tbsp. olive oil (optional)*

Combine first 8 ingredients together in a large skillet or wok and stir-fry till celery is translucent. Then add next 6 ingredients, cover, and turn heat down to simmer for 10 to 15 minutes, stirring occasionally, till vegetables are tender. While vegetables are cooking, bring about 2 gallons of water and 1 tablespoon of olive or vegetable oil to a boil. Then add the pound of noodles.

All the previous procedures add up to noodles that will cook as individual noodles and not a starchy lump. By using 2 gallons of water per pound of dry noodles, you are giving the noodles enough "swimming room" that the surfaces of the noodles won't be touching and sticking together. The tablespoon of oil slightly coats the surface of the noodles and keeps them from sticking. And, of course, it is very important to bring the water to a boil before adding the noodles. (Placing noodles in cold water and letting them sit as the water heats guarantees that the noodles will stick together, as they have no boiling bubbles to keep them moving.)

Stir noodles with a wooden spoon till water returns to a boil. Boil noodles till they are what is called in Italy "al dente." "Al dente" describes the method for testing and the texture of the finished noodles all in one phrase. To test a noodle "al dente" means to use your teeth and simply bite into the noodle. The noodle is perfectly done when the starchy taste is gone but the noodle is still firm enough to have some resistance to the bite. Be careful not to overcook the noodles to the point where they're soft and almost mushy.

Drain noodles (don't rinse! — only rinse pasta if it's going to be served cold) and turn into a large bowl that won't be ruined by heat. Immediately pour the noodles on the garden vegetables along with the sauce they're in, and add the additional olive oil (optional). Toss noodles till vegetables are evenly distributed, and serve immediately in soup bowls.

Serves 10 to 12 people as one of the dishes in this menu. This dish can also be used as a one-dish meal served with a tossed salad. In that case, it will probably serve 4 to 5 people amply. When serving as a one-dish meal, you may want to supply protein by adding ⅓ cup each of grated Parmesan and grated Romano cheese at the same time you toss in the vegetables. By the way, we found leftovers to be delicious served cold the following day as a cold pasta salad on a bed of lettuce and/or sprouts.

| SHOPPING LIST | |
|---|---|
| **Regularly Kept in the Kitchen**<br>**(Listed in Chapter 14, p. 703)** | **Fresh Produce** |
| Olive oil<br>Asafetida<br>Spike<br>Black pepper | Parsley<br>Celery<br>Radishes<br>Carrots<br>Leeks<br>Basil<br>Broccoli and/or cauliflower<br>Zucchini<br>Tomatoes |

### Special Shopping

Whole grain rigatoni noodles — found in natural food stores. If you can't find rigatoni-shaped noodles, any whole grain noodle will do. All noodles are made of basically the same ingredients, just made into different shapes. Some shapes hold sauce better than others. Vegetable bouillon cubes — found in natural food stores; they are a quick and easy way to make a tasty vegetable broth. Even when shopping in a natural food store, be sure to read labels — some bouillon cubes contain sugar.

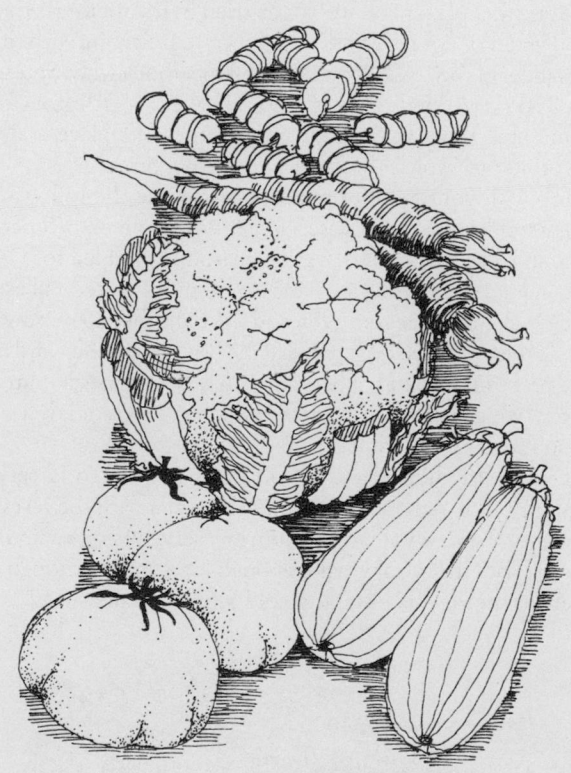

# GARDEN HARVEST PIZZA

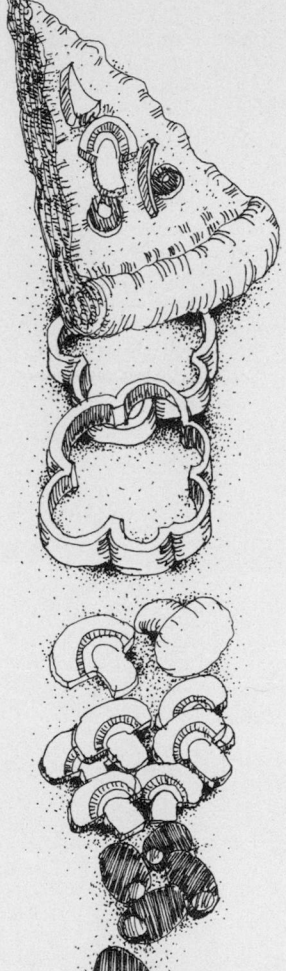

☆ A zucchini-crusted pizza held together with a little cheese and whole wheat flour; so skimp on, or skip, the cheese on top! (Nutritional yeast sprinkled on top of the pizza gives a cheesy flavor without adding any cholesterol or saturated fat.)

*4 cups grated zucchini (in large slivers)*
*½ cup whole wheat flour*
*1 cup grated mozzarella cheese*
*½ cup grated Parmesan cheese*
*1 tsp. dried basil or 2 Tbsp. fresh,*
*  minced basil leaves*
*½ tsp. black pepper*
*1 tsp. asafetida or 2 - 3 cloves garlic, crushed*

Preheat oven to 350 degrees and oil cookie sheet.

Grate the zucchini on the larger-sized holes of a four-sided hand grater or equivalent. Combine grated zucchini with the remainder of the crust ingredients and mix thoroughly. Spread evenly onto an oiled cookie sheet and bake at 350 degrees for 20 minutes. Remove from oven and, if needed, place under the broiler to brown the crust to a golden brown.

Top with your favorite pizza sauce (or use the following recipe) and toppings (slivered mushrooms, olives, bell peppers, and/or chili peppers, fresh tomatoes, crumbled tofu — to name a few possibilities) and some more grated cheese. Place back in 350-degree oven and bake another 20 minutes. While the pizza is baking, prepare the Rigatoni in the Garden (see preceding recipe). Then you can serve the pasta immediately, which will give the pizza enough time to cool down a bit so it can be cut and served.

This can be cut to make 10 to 12 pieces, or 10 to 12 servings at 1 piece each, which is ample if served with the rest of the menu here. If you are planning to serve just pizza and a tossed salad, this would make enough for 4, and (although it rarely happens) this pizza as a cold leftover is delicious!

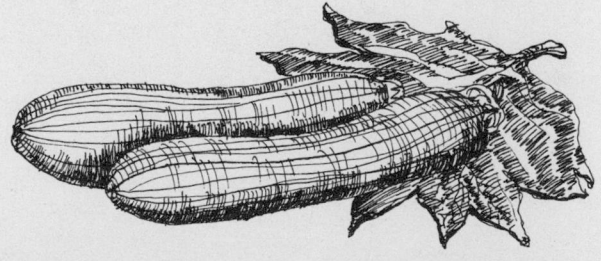

# NUTRITIONAL ANALYSIS FOR ONE SERVING
# GARDEN HARVEST PIZZA WITH PIZZA SAUCE

| NUTRIENT | Type: 14    FEMALE-23 TO 51 YEARS | % RDA | Amount |
|----------|-----------------------------------|-------|--------|
| KCALORIES | A======== | 17% | 350.0 Kc |
| PROTEIN | A==================== | 43% | 19.30 Gm |
| CARBOHYDRATE | A | NO RDA | 36.20 Gm |
| FAT | A | NO RDA | 16.60 Gm |
| FIBER-CRUDE | A | NO RDA | 2.630 Gm |
| CHOLESTEROL | A | NO RDA | 29.90 Mg |
| SATURATED FA | A | NO RDA | 6.920 Gm |
| OLEIC FA | A | NO RDA | 7.270 Gm |
| LINOLEIC FA | A | NO RDA | 0.870 Gm |
| SODIUM | A============= | 29% | 643.0 Mg |
| POTASSIUM | A============== | 30% | 1147 Mg |
| MAGNESIUM | A================ | 35% | 107.0 Mg |
| IRON | A========= | 19% | 3.490 Mg |
| ZINC | A======== | 16% | 2.440 Mg |
| VITAMIN A | A============================= | 63% | 2538 IU |
| VITAMIN D | A | 0% | 0.000 IU |
| VIT. E/TOTAL | A | NO RDA | 2.330 Mg |
| VITAMIN C | A========================================= | 90% | 54.30 Mg |
| THIAMIN | A============ | 27% | 0.270 Mg |
| RIBOFLAVIN | A============ | 26% | 0.320 Mg |
| NIACIN | A============= | 29% | 3.770 Mg |
| VITAMIN B6 | A========== | 20% | 0.410 Mg |
| FOLACIN | A===== | 10% | 42.00 Ug |
| VITAMIN B12 | A===== | 10% | 0.310 Ug |
| PANTO- ACID | A========= | 18% | 1.000 Mg |
| CALCIUM | A=========================== | 59% | 476.0 Mg |
| PHOSPHORUS | A========================== | 56% | 453.0 Mg |
| TRYPTOPHAN | A=============================== | 66% | 109.0 Mg |
| THREONINE | A==================================================== | 151% | 657.0 Mg |
| ISOLEUCINE | A=============================================== | 131% | 856.0 Mg |
| LEUCINE | A=============================================== | 183% | 1602 Mg |
| LYSINE | A=============================================== | 235% | 1540 Mg |
| METHIONINE | A=============================================== | 160% | 437.0 Mg |
| CYSTINE | A=========================== | 57% | 156.0 Mg |
| PHENYL-ANINE | A=============================================== | 209% | 912.0 Mg |
| TYROSINE | A=============================================== | 210% | 917.0 Mg |
| VALINE | A=============================================== | 141% | 1081 Mg |
| HISTIDINE | A | NO RDA | 622.0 Mg |
| ALCOHOL | A | NO RDA | 0.000 Gm |
| ASH | A | NO RDA | 4.780 Gm |
| COPPER | A========= | 19% | 0.490 Mg |
| MANGANESE | A============= | 28% | 1.070 Mg |
| IODINE | A========================================= | 90% | 136.0 Ug |
| MONO FAT | A | NO RDA | 7.630 Gm |
| POLY FAT | A | NO RDA | 0.940 Gm |
| CAFFEINE | A | NO RDA | 0.000 Mg |
| FLUORIDE | A | 1% | 44.30 Ug |
| MOLYBDENUM | A================================================= | 276% | 900.0 Ug |
| VITAMIN K | A | 0% | 0.000 Ug |
| SELENIUM | A==== | 8% | 0.010 Mg |
| BIOTIN | A | 1% | 1.660 Ug |
| CHLORIDE | A | 0% | 28.50 Mg |
| CHROMIUM | A======================================= | 72% | 0.090 Mg |
| SUGAR | A | NO RDA | 3.960 Gm |
| FIBER-DIET | A | NO RDA | 2.270 Gm |
| VIT. E/AT | A========== | 21% | 1.720 Mg |

```
% RDA:  |0      |20     |40     |60     |80     |100
```

For years I tried gagging down fruit drinks with brewer's or nutritional yeast in them because I'd heard how good nutritional yeast was for me. Then I discovered I really liked yeast in savory dishes (especially good in dishes with a little soy sauce in them!). In savory dishes, nutritional yeast gives an almost cheesy flavor. I've found that flavors and nutritional values can and do vary a great deal between different brands of nutritional yeast. Following is some of the nutritional information for the yeast I use the most (KAL brewer's yeast flakes).

Serving size:  Two heaping tablespoons (15 gm.)
Calories — 49
Protein — 7.5 gm.
Carbohydrate — 4.7 gm.
Fat — 0
Thiamine — 9 mg.
Riboflavin — 9 mg.
Niacin — 52 mg.
B6 — 9 mg.
B12 — 7 mcg.
Folic acid — 120 mcg.
Pantothenic acid — 1 mg.
Biotin — 19 mcg.
Inositol — 70 mg.
Choline — 60 mg.
PABA — 0.6 mg.
Potassium — 285.0 mg.
Phosphorus — 202.5 mg.
Sulphur — 58.5 mg.
Magnesium — 24.75 mg.
Sodium — 14.7 mg.
Calcium — 11.25 mg.
Zinc — 2.55 mg.
Iron — 0.6 mg.
Chromium — 33.0 mcg.
Selenium — 1.5 mcg.

Amino Acids:
Alanine — 611 mg.
Arginine — 401 mg.
Aspartic acid — 870 mg.
Glutamic acid — 1417 mg.
Glycine — 391 mg.
Histidine — 235 mg.
*Isoleucine — 389 mg.
Cystine — 120 mg.
Hydroxyproline — 337 mg.
*Leucine — 609 mg.
*Lysine — 632 mg.
*Methionine — 122 mg.
*Phenylalanine — 337 mg.
Proline — 357 mg.
*Threonine — 389 gm.
Serine — 377 mg.
*Tryptophane — 82 mg.
Tyrosine — 365 mg.
*Valine — 500 mg.

*Essential amino acids

# PIZZA SAUCE

2 Tbsp. olive oil
1 tsp. dried sweet basil
1 tsp. dried oregano leaves
1 tsp. dried marjoram
½ tsp. ground cumin
1 tsp. asafetida or 2 - 3 cloves garlic, crushed
⅛ tsp. cinnamon

2 cups tomato puree
1 tsp. honey
1 tsp. Spike or other vegetable-seasoned salt
2 Tbsp. apple cider vinegar

Combine first 7 ingredients in large skillet or saucepan and lightly toast. Add last 4 ingredients, bring to a boil, then lower heat and simmer for 10 to 15 minutes. Use this sauce for spaghetti or pizza if you don't already have a favorite sauce.

| SHOPPING LIST | |
|---|---|
| Regularly Kept in the Kitchen (Listed in Chapter 14, p. 703) | Fresh Produce |
| Whole wheat flour Mozzarella cheese Parmesan cheese Basil Black pepper Asafetida | Zucchini |

This list is just for the Garden Harvest Pizza crust; also add to your list whatever sauce and toppings you plan to use.

627

# MINT SHERBETO

☆ A refreshing, low-calorie sherbet.

4 cups water
1 cup lemon juice
1 cup honey
1 cup fresh mint leaves
½ tsp. pure mint extract

Blend all ingredients in blender till smooth. Freeze in ice trays. Right at the table, run through a Champion Juicer to make ice cream and catch in individual bowls. Serve immediately.

On the show, I use a Champion Juicer to make this and other fruit ice creams. It's a wonderful juicer that can be used to make juice, nut butters, or as a food grinder. If you have a food processor, it can be used to make this and other fruit ice creams (as on pp. 639 and 641).

| SHOPPING LIST | |
|---|---|
| **Regularly Kept in the Kitchen** (Listed in Chapter 14, p. 703) | **Fresh Produce** |
| Honey | Lemon<br>Mint leaves<br>Mint extract |

# CHAPTER 12

# FRESH IDEAS FOR FRUIT

Fresh fruit is my favorite fast-food! It contains lots of water, carbohydrates, vitamins and minerals (all essential nutrients!) — all pre-wrapped by nature. Even though the carbohydrate in fruit is primarily fruit sugar, it doesn't upset the body's blood-sugar levels or cause the body to store more fat (as refined sugars do) because of the way fruit sugar enters the bloodstream and the healthy presence of dietary fiber.

Dietary fiber has a lot to do with keeping the fruit sugar from entering into the bloodstream too quickly (which causes an undesired rise in insulin levels — see p. 198). When the fiber is removed from fruit, as is done when making juice, the fruit sugar will enter the bloodstream more quickly and cause a rise in insulin levels. Remember — a rise in insulin levels is undesirable because it causes the body to crave more sweets, increases its ability to store fat and, if it occurs too often, can lead to hypoglycemia and/or diabetes. I do use fruit juice (always unsweetened!) — but not excessively. The best thing to do is use fruit as nature made it, or only slightly alter it in preparation as demonstrated in the following recipes.

# HEALTHY SWEETS

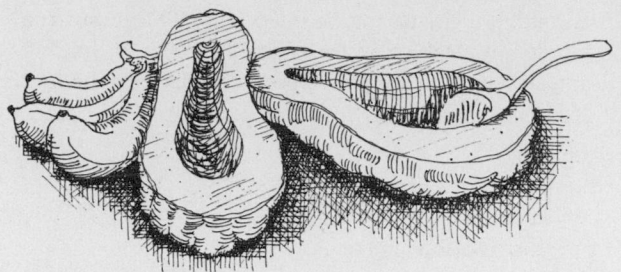

Summer weather puts us all in scantier, lighter clothes to beat the heat, and in swimsuits to take advantage of it. That's why, at this time of year, more people become aware of something they should be concerned about all year long — fitness.

However, fitness means a state of total health, not merely looking good in a swimsuit. Unfortunately, in order to quickly shed unwanted pounds to look fit and trim in a swimsuit, a lot of people resort to crash or fad dieting or other unhealthy practices. Many fad diets don't even work, and those that do help a person to temporarily shed some extra pounds end up wreaking havoc on the blood-sugar levels and internal organs. Better than putting the body on the unhealthy seesaw of dieting and then returning to the old consumption and lifestyle patterns that put the unwanted pounds there in the first place, is to make the effort it takes to change to a wholesome, natural foods diet that will keep the body at its ideal weight — naturally.

Nature provides the perfect foods for each season, too. In the heat of summer we are provided with a bounty of light and refreshing, juicy fresh fruits and vegetables. Here are some recipes that can help you make full use of summer fruits.

About 15 years ago, I lived on the North Shore of Oahu in a rural farming area close to the base of the mountains. In exchange for helping pick their crop, the local farmers used to give us crates and crates of their off-grade (too small, too large, too ripe to ship to market without bruising, or too odd-shaped — but just as delicious and nutritious as the fruit that made it to market) papayas, bananas and watermelons. With such an abundance of fruit, I had to get very innovative to use it all. One of my favorite innovations is raw pies.

Raw pies save time in the kitchen as well as saving valuable vitamins that would otherwise be destroyed when heated. Thus they make nutritious, as well as delicious, desserts, snacks or even whole meals. There has been many a day when my family started their day on raw pie for breakfast!

The basics behind making raw pies:

• For the crust, stick any number and combination of dry, healthy ingredients (bran, wheat germ, nut or seed meals, etc.) together with some healthy, sticky ingredients (nut butter, date paste or other dried fruit run through a food grinder, honey, etc.) so crust can be pressed into pie pan.

• For filling, use any fresh fruit in season, held together or thickened in such a way that the fruit doesn't have to be cooked.

• Since each crust and filling will taste different, fill crusts with a compatible tasting fruit, being sure the flavor of the crust enhances, and not over-powers, the flavor of the fruit.

The Raw Apple Pie is held together with psyllium seeds, a source of fiber which acts like bran in helping to clean out the intestinal tract. When wet, psyllium seeds form a gel.

# RAW "WHEAT" CRUST

☆ A mild, doughy-tasting crust; good for almost any fruit filling, but ideal for milder tasting fruit fillings (like apple) because it won't overpower the taste of the fruit.

---

½ cup bran
½ cup wheat germ (raw or toasted)
¼ cup date sugar
⅓ cup roasted cashew or almond butter

1 Tbsp. more nut butter

Honey or maple syrup (optional)

---

Combine first 4 ingredients in a bowl and mix together thoroughly. Remove ¼ cup of mixture and set aside to use as a crumb topping. Add 1 more tablespoon of the roasted cashew or almond butter to the mixture in the bowl. Clean your hands off and with wet hands (to keep the crust from sticking to your hands) press crust evenly into a pie pan. This can be filled with a raw filling. After filling the crust, take the mixture that was set aside earlier and crumble it on top of the filling so it looks like a crumb topping. Drizzle a little honey or maple syrup over the top of the crumbs, if desired. Refrigerate for a few hours before serving. Makes one 8" or 9" pie.

# RAW APPLE PIE

---

3½ cups grated apple
½ tsp. cinnamon

⅓ cup apple juice
1 Tbsp. lemon juice
4 tsp. psyllium seed powder
⅓ of a banana
2 Tbsp. raisins

Maple syrup (optional)

---

Combine first 2 ingredients together in a bowl. Blend the next 5 ingredients in a blender till raisins are chopped. Mix the blended ingredients in with the apples and pour into a raw pie crust. The Raw "Wheat" Crust is perfect for this. If you use the Raw "Wheat" Crust, sprinkle the ¼ cup of reserved crust on top for a crumb crust. Lightly drizzle maple syrup over crumb crust if desired. Refrigerate a few hours before serving. This makes a great breakfast for 4 or dessert for 8.

| SHOPPING LIST | | Special Shopping |
|---|---|---|
| **Regularly Kept in the Kitchen (Listed in Chapter 14, p. 703)** | **Fresh Produce** | Psyllium seed powder — found in natural food stores. Be sure to get the powder of the whole seed and not just the husks. |
| Bran<br>Wheat germ<br>Date sugar<br>Cashew or almond butter<br>Cinnamon<br>Raisins | Apple<br>Apple juice<br>Lemon<br>Banana | |

# NUTRITIONAL ANALYSIS FOR ONE SERVING RAW APPLE PIE
## WITH RAW "WHEAT" CRUST

| NUTRIENT | Type: 14   FEMALE-23 TO 51 YEARS | % RDA | Amount |
|---|---|---|---|
| KCALORIES | A======== | 17% | 342.0 Kc |
| PROTEIN | A============ | 24% | 10.70 Gm |
| CARBOHYDRATE | A | NO RDA | 51.40 Gm |
| FAT | A | NO RDA | 14.90 Gm |
| FIBER-CRUDE | A | NO RDA | 2.530 Gm |
| CHOLESTEROL | A | NO RDA | 0.000 Mg |
| SATURATED FA | A | NO RDA | 2.810 Gm |
| OLEIC FA | A | NO RDA | 0.580 Gm |
| LINOLEIC FA | A | NO RDA | 0.950 Gm |
| SODIUM | A | 0% | 7.720 Mg |
| POTASSIUM | A======== | 17% | 663.0 Mg |
| MAGNESIUM | A=============================== | 62% | 186.0 Mg |
| IRON | A============ | 25% | 4.550 Mg |
| ZINC | A=============== | 30% | 4.520 Mg |
| VITAMIN A | A= | 2% | 90.20 IU |
| VITAMIN D | A= | 2% | 4.230 IU |
| VIT. E/TOTAL | A | NO RDA | 4.260 Mg |
| VITAMIN C | A======= | 15% | 9.270 Mg |
| THIAMIN | A===================== | 42% | 0.420 Mg |
| RIBOFLAVIN | A========= | 19% | 0.230 Mg |
| NIACIN | A============= | 27% | 3.600 Mg |
| VITAMIN B6 | A=========== | 22% | 0.450 Mg |
| FOLACIN | A========== | 20% | 81.40 Ug |
| VITAMIN B12 | A | 0% | 0.000 Ug |
| PANTO- ACID | A======= | 15% | 0.850 Mg |
| CALCIUM | A== | 5% | 46.90 Mg |
| PHOSPHORUS | A========================== | 52% | 417.0 Mg |
| TRYPTOPHAN | A========================================= | 80% | 132.0 Mg |
| THREONINE | A==================================================== | 99% | 432.0 Mg |
| ISOLEUCINE | A===================================== | 73% | 479.0 Mg |
| LEUCINE | A================================================= | 95% | 833.0 Mg |
| LYSINE | A==================================================== | 102% | 672.0 Mg |
| METHIONINE | A==================================== | 70% | 191.0 Mg |
| CYSTINE | A================================== | 67% | 183.0 Mg |
| PHENYL-ANINE | A==================================================== | 114% | 498.0 Mg |
| TYROSINE | A================================== | 69% | 301.0 Mg |
| VALINE | A========================================== | 83% | 637.0 Mg |
| HISTIDINE | A | NO RDA | 345.0 Mg |
| ALCOHOL | A | NO RDA | 0.000 Gm |
| ASH | A | NO RDA | 2.560 Gm |
| COPPER | A================ | 33% | 0.840 Mg |
| MANGANESE | A=============================== | 78% | 2.930 Mg |
| IODINE | A==================== | 43% | 64.70 Ug |
| MONO FAT | A | NO RDA | 7.610 Gm |
| POLY FAT | A | NO RDA | 3.150 Gm |
| CAFFEINE | A | NO RDA | 0.000 Mg |
| FLUORIDE | A= | 3% | 101.0 Ug |
| MOLYBDENUM | A==================================================== | 258% | 839.0 Ug |
| VITAMIN K | A | 0% | 0.000 Ug |
| SELENIUM | A==== | 8% | 0.010 Mg |
| BIOTIN | A== | 4% | 7.280 Ug |
| CHLORIDE | A | 1% | 49.10 Mg |
| CHROMIUM | A=============================== | 64% | 0.080 Mg |
| SUGAR | A | NO RDA | 18.20 Gm |
| FIBER-DIET | A | NO RDA | 10.60 Gm |
| VIT. E/AT | A================ | 32% | 2.610 Mg |

```
% RDA:  |0      |20     |40     |60     |80     |100
```

Cashew butter used instead of almond; due to lack of data for date sugar, dates were used instead; optional honey or maple syrup not included in analysis for pie crust. Psyllium seed powder and optional maple syrup not included in analysis for pie.

# DATE-NUTTY CRUST

☆ A very sweet crust. I like the taste of coconut with dates, so I usually include coconut as one of the filling ingredients.

---

*1 cup soft, pitted dates*
*1¼ cups water or apple juice*

*2 cups nut or seed meal*
*2 Tbsp. poppy or chia seeds*

Cook first 2 ingredients together over medium-high heat, stirring constantly till dates dissolve and mixture thickens to form a date paste. Mix in nuts and seeds. (Sweet, mild-tasting nuts or seeds like almonds, sunflower seeds, sesame seeds, or mixtures of a few, are preferable.) Press with wet hands into a pie dish. Fill with a raw filling.

# TROPICAL DELIGHT

---

*2 cups commercial pineapple-coconut juice*
*4 Tbsp. arrowroot*

*Banana slices*
*Papaya slices*
*Shredded coconut (unsweetened)*

Mix first 2 ingredients together in a pot till the arrowroot is dissolved. Put over heat and stir constantly till it comes to a boil and thickens. Set aside to cool. Slice a layer of bananas on the bottom of a raw pie crust (the preceding recipe for the Date-Nutty Crust is delicious with this); then sprinkle a layer of shredded coconut on top of the bananas. Pour half of the cooled pineapple-coconut juice mixture on top of this. Now top this with a layer of thinly sliced papaya, another layer of shredded coconut, and the remainder of the pineapple-coconut mixture. Refrigerate at least 1 hour before serving. Makes perfect breakfast for 4 or dessert for 8.

The thickening that holds this Tropical Delight filling together is a combination of a commercial juice (one bought in a natural food store with no sugar in it) and arrowroot.

You can make endless kinds of fillings by picking a commercial juice to suit the flavor of whatever fruit (or fruits) you're using. Use 4 tablespoons arrowroot to 2 cups of juice.

| Special Shopping |
| --- |
| Pineapple-coconut juice with no sugar — found in natural food stores. |

| SHOPPING LIST | |
| --- | --- |
| **Regularly Kept in the Kitchen (Listed in Chapter 14, p. 703)** | **Fresh Produce** |
| Dates<br>Nuts or seeds<br>Poppy or chia seeds<br>Arrowroot | Apple juice<br>Banana<br>Papaya<br>Unsweetened, shredded coconut |

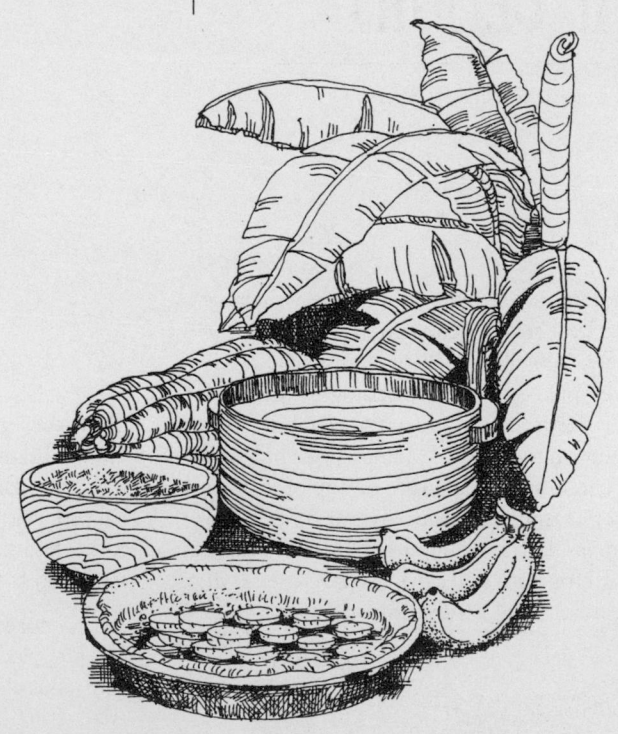

## NUTRITIONAL ANALYSIS FOR ONE SERVING
## TROPICAL DELIGHT WITH DATE-NUTTY CRUST

| NUTRIENT | Type: 14   FEMALE-23 TO 51 YEARS | % RDA | Amount |
|---|---|---|---|
| KCALORIES | A=============== | 30% | 603.0 Kc |
| PROTEIN | A============================ | 58% | 25.90 Gm |
| CARBOHYDRATE | A | NO RDA | 93.80 Gm |
| FAT | A | NO RDA | 18.80 Gm |
| FIBER-CRUDE | A | NO RDA | 5.060 Gm |
| CHOLESTEROL | A | NO RDA | 0.000 Mg |
| SATURATED FA | A | NO RDA | 7.500 Gm |
| OLEIC FA | A | NO RDA | 0.400 Gm |
| LINOLEIC FA | A | NO RDA | 0.120 Gm |
| SODIUM | A | 0% | 21.70 Mg |
| POTASSIUM | A====================== | 45% | 1695 Mg |
| MAGNESIUM | A======== | 16% | 49.90 Mg |
| IRON | A=================== | 39% | 7.090 Mg |
| ZINC | A== | 5% | 0.810 Mg |
| VITAMIN A | A=================== | 39% | 1586 IU |
| VITAMIN D | A | 0% | 0.000 IU |
| VIT. E/TOTAL | A | NO RDA | 0.090 Mg |
| VITAMIN C | A================================================ | 101% | 61.10 Mg |
| THIAMIN | A================= | 36% | 0.360 Mg |
| RIBOFLAVIN | A============================================ | 90% | 1.080 Mg |
| NIACIN | A==================== | 42% | 5.530 Mg |
| VITAMIN B6 | A========= | 18% | 0.360 Mg |
| FOLACIN | A== | 4% | 16.70 Ug |
| VITAMIN B12 | A | 0% | 0.000 Ug |
| PANTO- ACID | A======= | 14% | 0.800 Mg |
| CALCIUM | A=================== | 39% | 318.0 Mg |
| PHOSPHORUS | A===================================== | 76% | 610.0 Mg |
| TRYPTOPHAN | A================================================ | 276% | 450.0 Mg |
| THREONINE | A================================================ | 212% | 926.0 Mg |
| ISOLEUCINE | A================================================ | 163% | 1069 Mg |
| LEUCINE | A================================================ | 220% | 1919 Mg |
| LYSINE | A================================================ | 133% | 873.0 Mg |
| METHIONINE | A================================================== | 109% | 299.0 Mg |
| CYSTINE | A================================================ | 163% | 445.0 Mg |
| PHENYL-ANINE | A================================================ | 313% | 1364 Mg |
| TYROSINE | A================================================ | 198% | 865.0 Mg |
| VALINE | A================================================ | 168% | 1285 Mg |
| HISTIDINE | A | NO RDA | 703.0 Mg |
| ALCOHOL | A | NO RDA | 0.000 Gm |
| ASH | A | NO RDA | 5.710 Gm |
| COPPER | A======== | 16% | 0.410 Mg |
| MANGANESE | A=================== | 36% | 1.360 Mg |
| IODINE | A | 0% | 0.000 Ug |
| MONO FAT | A | NO RDA | 7.350 Gm |
| POLY FAT | A | NO RDA | 2.630 Gm |
| CAFFEINE | A | NO RDA | 0.000 Mg |
| FLUORIDE | A | 0% | 6.850 Ug |
| MOLYBDENUM | A | 0% | 0.000 Ug |
| VITAMIN K | A | 0% | 0.000 Ug |
| SELENIUM | A | 0% | 0.000 Mg |
| BIOTIN | A | 1% | 1.560 Ug |
| CHLORIDE | A | 0% | 0.000 Mg |
| CHROMIUM | A | 0% | 0.000 Mg |
| SUGAR | A | NO RDA | 33.40 Gm |
| FIBER-DIET | A | NO RDA | 3.370 Gm |
| VIT. E/AT | A= | 2% | 0.220 Mg |

```
% RDA:   |0       |20    |40    |60    |80    |100
```

Chia seeds used instead of poppy seeds; apple juice used instead of water; almond meal used in crust analysis.

The fruit (banana) used for this filling is a non-juicy one. Combined with dates, carob powder (which contains lots of pectin and therefore helps to thicken whatever it's in) and seeds make a thick enough filling that no thickening agent needs to be added.

# NO-BAKE BANANA PIE CRUST

☆ A crust held together with banana. Since bananas, carob and peanut butter are one of our favorite combinations, the Banana-Carob Pie filling is a natural choice.

---

½ cup toasted coconut
¼ cup bran
¼ cup wheat germ
¼ cup chopped dates or date sugar
1 banana, mashed
Few drops of lemon juice

Combine ingredients and press into a pie tin.

# BANANA-CAROB PIE

---

2 cups blended bananas
½ cup sunflower seeds
¼ cup carob powder
¼ cup pitted dates
1 tsp. vanilla or mint extract

Put all the above ingredients in a blender and blend till smooth. Pour into No-Bake Banana Pie Crust and decorate with slices of fruit.

| SHOPPING LIST | |
|---|---|
| Regularly Kept in the Kitchen (Listed in Chapter 14, p. 703) | Fresh Produce |
| Bran<br>Wheat germ<br>Dates or date sugar<br>Sunflower seeds<br>Carob powder<br>Vanilla or mint extract | Coconut<br>Bananas<br>Lemon |

# NUTRITIONAL ANALYSIS FOR ONE SERVING
## BANANA-CAROB PIE WITH NO-BAKE BANANA PIE CRUST

```
NUTRIENT        Type: 14   FEMALE-23 TO 51 YEARS              % RDA   Amount
KCALORIES       A=====                                         10%    208.0 Kc
PROTEIN         A=====                                         10%    4.820 Gm
CARBOHYDRATE    A                                            NO RDA   37.50 Gm
FAT             A                                            NO RDA   7.470 Gm
FIBER-CRUDE     A                                            NO RDA   1.670 Gm
CHOLESTEROL     A                                            NO RDA   0.000 Mg
SATURATED FA    A                                            NO RDA   2.510 Gm
OLEIC FA        A                                            NO RDA   1.150 Gm
LINOLEIC FA     A                                            NO RDA   2.940 Gm
SODIUM          A                                              0%     18.00 Mg
POTASSIUM       A=======                                       14%    558.0 Mg
MAGNESIUM       A================                             30%    90.60 Mg
IRON            A=====                                         10%    1.860 Mg
ZINC            A=====                                         10%    1.520 Mg
VITAMIN A       A=                                             2%     81.50 IU
VITAMIN D       A                                              0%     1.050 IU
VIT. E/TOTAL    A                                            NO RDA   5.910 Mg
VITAMIN C       A======                                        12%    7.590 Mg
THIAMIN         A=================                            33%    0.330 Mg
RIBOFLAVIN      A======                                        13%    0.160 Mg
NIACIN          A=======                                       14%    1.860 Mg
VITAMIN B6      A=================                            33%    0.670 Mg
FOLACIN         A====                                          8%     32.00 Ug
VITAMIN B12     A                                              0%     0.000 Ug
PANTO- ACID     A====                                          9%     0.510 Mg
CALCIUM         A==                                            4%     35.40 Mg
PHOSPHORUS      A==========                                   20%    163.0 Mg
TRYPTOPHAN      A===================                          38%    62.00 Mg
THREONINE       A=====================                        43%    189.0 Mg
ISOLEUCINE      A================                             32%    211.0 Mg
LEUCINE         A===================                          39%    346.0 Mg
LYSINE          A==================                           37%    242.0 Mg
METHIONINE      A==============                               31%    87.00 Mg
CYSTINE         A==============                               31%    86.30 Mg
PHENYL-ANINE    A=========================                    50%    220.0 Mg
TYROSINE        A==============                               29%    127.0 Mg
VALINE          A================                             34%    260.0 Mg
HISTIDINE       A                                            NO RDA   188.0 Mg
ALCOHOL         A                                            NO RDA   0.000 Gm
ASH             A                                            NO RDA   1.530 Gm
COPPER          A======                                        13%    0.330 Mg
MANGANESE       A==============                               31%    1.180 Mg
IODINE          A========                                      17%    26.40 Ug
MONO FAT        A                                            NO RDA   1.020 Gm
POLY FAT        A                                            NO RDA   3.260 Gm
CAFFEINE        A                                            NO RDA   0.000 Mg
FLUORIDE        A                                              0%     27.10 Ug
MOLYBDENUM      A===============================================  93%  303.0 Ug
VITAMIN K       A                                              0%     0.000 Ug
SELENIUM        A                                              0%     0.000 Mg
BIOTIN          A=                                             3%     5.520 Ug
CHLORIDE        A                                              0%     20.60 Mg
CHROMIUM        A============                                  24%    0.030 Mg
SUGAR           A                                            NO RDA   20.70 Gm
FIBER-DIET      A                                            NO RDA   4.820 Gm
VIT. E/AT       A================================             65%    5.230 Mg

      % RDA:   |0       |20      |40      |60      |80      |100
```

638

# NATURE'S OWN SODA

☆ While any fruit can be used, I like to use naturally sweet fruits that need no additional sweetening (like mango, pineapple, papaya).

---

*2 cups fruit puree (any kind)*
*Honey to taste (only if needed)*

*2 cups sparkling mineral water*

Blend fruit till smooth to make puree. (Add honey when blending only if necessary.) Pour into cups and add an equal amount of a naturally sparkling mineral water. Makes 4 cups.

For the soda, you can use juice instead of the fruit puree — but the big plus of using the fruit puree is that the fruit's natural fiber is still included. Drinking 100% fruit juice is preferable to drinking anything sweetened with sugar because juice contains lots of vitamins and minerals; but fiber is removed in the making of juice. Remember, fiber is important in the presence of sugar (even natural fruit sugar) to keep blood-sugar and insulin levels balanced. High insulin levels can lead to diabetes and always cause the body to store more fat. Fiber also helps to keep hunger pangs at bay and clean out the intestinal tract.

# FRESH FRUIT ICE CREAM

For this recipe, over-ripe fruits are the best to use. They are full of fruit sugar and are easily assimilated. Place chunks of pitted, cored and, if necessary, peeled fruit in plastic bags and place them in the freezer till frozen solid. Either a Champion Juicer or a Norwalk Juicer is needed. Just run the frozen fruit through the juicer and you have a nice, refreshing summer treat that is low in calories and very delicious. This kind of ice cream can also be made in a food processor by putting frozen fruit in the processor using the chopping blade. Turn on and leave on till fruit is whipped into a smooth, creamy-textured ice cream.

You can use one kind of fruit or combinations of fruits. I like to use frozen bananas as a way to sweeten tarter fruits like strawberries, raspberries, etc.

## NUTRITIONAL ANALYSIS FOR ONE SERVING NATURE'S OWN SODA

| NUTRIENT | Type: 14 FEMALE-23 TO 51 YEARS | % RDA | Amount |
|---|---|---|---|
| KCALORIES | Я= | 3% | 65.20 Kc |
| PROTEIN | Я= | 2% | 1.310 Gm |
| CARBOHYDRATE | Я | NO RDA | 15.20 Gm |
| FAT | Я | NO RDA | 0.790 Gm |
| FIBER-CRUDE | Я | NO RDA | 1.140 Gm |
| CHOLESTEROL | Я | NO RDA | 0.000 Mg |
| SATURATED FA | Я | NO RDA | 0.040 Gm |
| OLEIC FA | Я | NO RDA | 0.000 Gm |
| LINOLEIC FA | Я | NO RDA | 0.000 Gm |
| SODIUM | Я | 0% | 5.390 Mg |
| POTASSIUM | Я==== | 9% | 358.0 Mg |
| MAGNESIUM | Я=== | 7% | 23.10 Mg |
| IRON | Я== | 4% | 0.820 Mg |
| ZINC | Я | 1% | 0.270 Mg |
| VITAMIN A | Я | 1% | 59.40 IU |
| VITAMIN D | Я | 0% | 0.000 IU |
| VIT. E/TOTAL | Я | NO RDA | 0.560 Mg |
| VITAMIN C | Я================================================== | 203% | 122.0 Mg |
| THIAMIN | Я== | 4% | 0.040 Mg |
| RIBOFLAVIN | Я===== | 11% | 0.140 Mg |
| NIACIN | Я= | 3% | 0.490 Mg |
| VITAMIN B6 | Я=== | 6% | 0.120 Mg |
| FOLACIN | Я==== | 9% | 38.20 Ug |
| VITAMIN B12 | Я | 0% | 0.000 Ug |
| PANTO- ACID | Я====== | 13% | 0.730 Mg |
| CALCIUM | Я== | 5% | 46.90 Mg |
| PHOSPHORUS | Я== | 5% | 40.50 Mg |
| TRYPTOPHAN | Я==== | 8% | 14.40 Mg |
| THREONINE | Я==== | 9% | 40.50 Mg |
| ISOLEUCINE | Я== | 4% | 30.40 Mg |
| LEUCINE | Я==== | 7% | 66.60 Mg |
| LYSINE | Я==== | 8% | 53.60 Mg |
| METHIONINE | Я | 0% | 1.440 Mg |
| CYSTINE | Я= | 3% | 10.10 Mg |
| PHENYL-ANINE | Я==== | 8% | 39.10 Mg |
| TYROSINE | Я===== | 10% | 44.90 Mg |
| VALINE | Я== | 5% | 39.10 Mg |
| HISTIDINE | Я | NO RDA | 26.00 Mg |
| ALCOHOL | Я | NO RDA | 0.000 Gm |
| ASH | Я | NO RDA | 0.970 Gm |
| COPPER | Я== | 4% | 0.100 Mg |
| MANGANESE | Я======== | 16% | 0.620 Mg |
| IODINE | Я | 0% | 0.000 Ug |
| MONO FAT | Я | NO RDA | 0.110 Gm |
| POLY FAT | Я | NO RDA | 0.400 Gm |
| CAFFEINE | Я | NO RDA | 0.000 Mg |
| FLUORIDE | Я | 1% | 38.80 Ug |
| MOLYBDENUM | Я==== | 8% | 28.90 Ug |
| VITAMIN K | Я | 0% | 0.000 Ug |
| SELENIUM | Я | 0% | 0.000 Mg |
| BIOTIN | Я | 1% | 2.370 Ug |
| CHLORIDE | Я | 0% | 0.000 Mg |
| CHROMIUM | Я | 0% | 0.000 Mg |
| SUGAR | Я | NO RDA | 11.20 Gm |
| FIBER-DIET | Я | NO RDA | 4.100 Gm |
| VIT. E/AT | Я= | 3% | 0.250 Mg |

% RDA: |0      |20      |40      |60      |80      |100

Pureed fruit used: strawberries. Optional honey not included in analysis.

# PAPAYA ICE CREAM

☆ You can combine fruits by running varying chunks through the machine, or by pre-blending the fruits in a blender and freezing in ice cube trays as in the following recipe.

---

3 papayas
3 bananas
Juice of 3 lemons

Blend all 3 ingredients together in a blender and pour into ice cube trays. Freeze till solid. Remove frozen cubes and run through a Champion Juicer according to Champion Juicer directions for making ice cream, or in a food processor with chopping blade till fruit becomes whipped and creamy.

# DAIRYLESS CAROB ICE CREAM

---

¼ cup nut butter (preferably roasted
    almond or cashew)
2 cups water
⅓ cup carob powder
2 Tbsp. lecithin granules
6 - 8 dates
1 tsp. grain coffee
¼ tsp. vanilla

Blend ingredients together in blender till smooth. Pour into ice cube trays and freeze solid. Run through a Champion Juicer or food processor to make ice cream.

You can combine fruits to make ice cream by running varying chunks of frozen fruit through the machine or by pre-blending the fruits in a blender and freezing in ice cube trays as is done in the recipes on this page.

# NUTRITIONAL ANALYSIS FOR ONE SERVING
## DAIRYLESS CAROB ICE CREAM

| NUTRIENT | Type: 14   FEMALE—23 TO 51 YEARS | % RDA | Amount |
|---|---|---|---|
| KCALORIES | A==== | 9% | 180.0 Kc |
| PROTEIN | A==== | 8% | 3.540 Gm |
| CARBOHYDRATE | A | NO RDA | 24.90 Gm |
| FAT | A | NO RDA | 11.00 Gm |
| FIBER-CRUDE | A | NO RDA | 1.100 Gm |
| CHOLESTEROL | A | NO RDA | 0.000 Mg |
| SATURATED FA | A | NO RDA | 2.560 Gm |
| OLEIC FA | A | NO RDA | 0.030 Gm |
| LINOLEIC FA | A | NO RDA | 0.010 Gm |
| SODIUM | A | 0% | 6.570 Mg |
| POTASSIUM | A=== | 7% | 272.0 Mg |
| MAGNESIUM | A========= | 17% | 51.50 Mg |
| IRON | A=== | 7% | 1.260 Mg |
| ZINC | A=== | 6% | 0.960 Mg |
| VITAMIN A | A | 0% | 9.540 IU |
| VITAMIN D | A | 0% | 0.000 IU |
| VIT. E/TOTAL | A | NO RDA | 0.060 Mg |
| VITAMIN C | A | 0% | 0.010 Mg |
| THIAMIN | A=== | 7% | 0.070 Mg |
| RIBOFLAVIN | A=== | 6% | 0.080 Mg |
| NIACIN | A=== | 6% | 0.820 Mg |
| VITAMIN B6 | A== | 5% | 0.100 Mg |
| FOLACIN | A= | 3% | 15.40 Ug |
| VITAMIN B12 | A | 0% | 0.000 Ug |
| PANTO- ACID | A== | 5% | 0.320 Mg |
| CALCIUM | A== | 5% | 43.90 Mg |
| PHOSPHORUS | A===== | 10% | 87.50 Mg |
| TRYPTOPHAN | A================ | 32% | 53.10 Mg |
| THREONINE | A=============== | 30% | 134.0 Mg |
| ISOLEUCINE | A============ | 24% | 162.0 Mg |
| LEUCINE | A=============== | 31% | 277.0 Mg |
| LYSINE | A============ | 25% | 166.0 Mg |
| METHIONINE | A========== | 21% | 57.90 Mg |
| CYSTINE | A========== | 22% | 62.00 Mg |
| PHENYL-ANINE | A=================== | 39% | 170.0 Mg |
| TYROSINE | A========== | 23% | 101.0 Mg |
| VALINE | A============== | 29% | 222.0 Mg |
| HISTIDINE | A | NO RDA | 92.50 Mg |
| ALCOHOL | A | NO RDA | 0.000 Gm |
| ASH | A | NO RDA | 0.670 Gm |
| COPPER | A======== | 16% | 0.400 Mg |
| MANGANESE | A | 1% | 0.040 Mg |
| IODINE | A========= | 18% | 27.30 Ug |
| MONO FAT | A | NO RDA | 4.660 Gm |
| POLY FAT | A | NO RDA | 2.840 Gm |
| CAFFEINE | A | NO RDA | 0.000 Mg |
| FLUORIDE | A | 0% | 0.000 Ug |
| MOLYBDENUM | A=========================================== | 76% | 250.0 Ug |
| VITAMIN K | A | 0% | 0.000 Ug |
| SELENIUM | A | 0% | 0.000 Mg |
| BIOTIN | A | 1% | 2.410 Ug |
| CHLORIDE | A | 0% | 24.60 Mg |
| CHROMIUM | A============ | 24% | 0.030 Mg |
| SUGAR | A | NO RDA | 10.90 Gm |
| FIBER-DIET | A | NO RDA | 3.860 Gm |
| VIT. E/AT | A | 0% | 0.000 Mg |

```
% RDA:  |0      |20     |40     |60     |80     |100
```

Cashew butter used instead of almond in analysis.

Everyone wants to be happy. Everyone everywhere who is trying to attain happiness by different means might benefit by considering these words from the ancient book of wisdom, the Bhagavad-gita:

"One who is not in transcendental consciousness can have neither a controlled mind nor steady intelligence, without which there is no possibility of peace. And how can there be any happiness without peace?"

# FRUITY DISHES

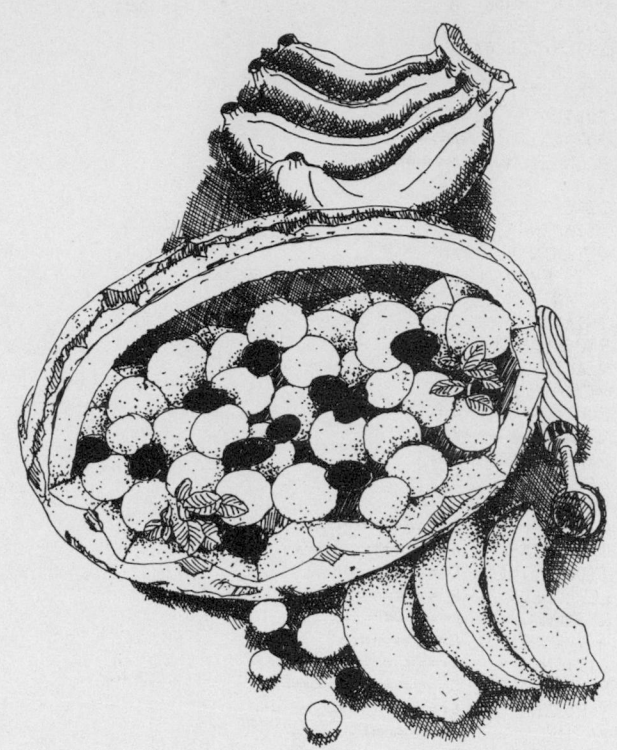

Whole pieces of fruit are glorious in themselves! They make the perfect fast-food for a meal or snack on the run. On the other hand, many a Japanese or Chinese meal is finished with whole pieces of fresh fruit presented elegantly on their own platters as dessert. One of my childhood memories is the whole family sitting at the table after dinner, patiently awaiting our dessert of grapes as my mother peeled, split and de-seeded each grape and set them in individual bowls. Grapes were quite a delicacy; they had to be imported and were quite costly. While whole fruits are relishable just as nature made them, they can also be turned into equally interesting and delicious entrees, side dishes or even gourmet desserts with a little preparation.

# FOUR "FRUIT" SALSA

☆ A delicious, fresh salsa that can be used anywhere salsa is called for.

1 cup chopped tomatoes
1 cup chopped red or green bell pepper
⅔ cup chopped cucumber
1 (or more) jalapeno pepper, finely minced
¼ cup chopped scallions
1 Tbsp. finely minced cilantro
1½ tsp. lime juice
1 tsp. miso
⅛ tsp. ground cumin
Dash asafetida or 1 clove garlic, minced

Combine all ingredients and mix thoroughly enough to dissolve miso. Allow to sit for at least 20 minutes so flavors can mingle.

| SHOPPING LIST | |
|---|---|
| **Regularly Kept in the Kitchen** (Listed in Chapter 14, p. 703) | **Fresh Produce** |
| Miso | Tomatoes |
| Cumin | Bell pepper |
| Asafetida | Cucumber |
| | Jalapeno pepper |
| | Scallions |
| | Cilantro |
| | Lime |

Avocados, cucumbers, eggplants, peppers, squash, tomatoes . . . Many of the foods we think of as vegetables are actually fruits. Technically speaking, any edible pod which contains plant-bearing seeds is a fruit.

# COOL·AS·A·CUCUMBER NOODLES

☆ These cucumber "noodles" can be topped with a sauce and served as a salad or added to a cold soup; try topping them with the Four "Fruit" Salsa to serve as a salad, or put them in the Avocado Creme Soup and top with the salsa.

---

*2 regular cucumbers or 1 hothouse cucumber*

*2 tsp. rice or wine vinegar*
*½ Tbsp. finely chopped, fresh cilantro, basil, chives or dill*
*¼ tsp. honey*
*⅛ tsp. white pepper*

Wash cucumbers (and de-seed if using regular cucumbers; hothouse variety doesn't need de-seeding), and with a sharp knife or appropriate grater, cut paper-thin strips the length of the cucumber to form "noodles." Toss last 4 ingredients into cucumber "noodles." Cover and refrigerate while making sauces, dressings, etc., to serve on noodles. Makes 3 to 4 servings.

I like using the hothouse (also known as "gas-less") variety of cucumbers most because they aren't waxed and are virtually seedless. The small, pickle-sized (Kirby) cucumbers are generally not waxed either, but their size is small for recipes such as this (recipes calling for chopped cucumbers wouldn't make any difference). The large, dark-green variety sold in super-markets are usually coated with a virtually unwashable wax (which seals in pesticides on skin, as well as moisture). Of course, if you grow your own, you can control what gets applied to them and have cheaper, fresher produce as well . . .

| SHOPPING LIST | |
|---|---|
| **Regularly Kept in the Kitchen** (Listed in Chapter 14, p. 703) | **Fresh Produce** |
| Rice or wine vinegar<br>Honey<br>White pepper | Cucumbers<br>Fresh herb of choice |

# AVOCADO CREME SOUP

*1 vegetable bouillon cube*
*1½ cups water*

*1 avocado (about 1 cup)*
*2 tsp. lemon juice*
*2 tsp. Neufchatel cheese*
*½ tsp. Spike or other vegetable-seasoned salt*
*⅛ tsp. white pepper*
*2 Tbsp. chopped chives*

Cook first 2 ingredients together to dissolve bouillon cube and allow to cool, or use 1½ cups cool vegetable broth. Put broth in blender or food processor with last 6 ingredients and run till smooth. Chill in refrigerator or by stirring a bowlful of soup set in a larger bowl full of ice cubes. Serve as is or topped with Cool-As-A-Cucumber Noodles and Four "Fruit" Salsa, or just the salsa.

Some of our favorite, yet extremely simple, ways to use avocados:
• an avocado guacamole on top of brown rice with a little soy sauce
• slices (or whole halves of avocados) sprinkled with Spike
• on whole grain toast with hot sauce or salsa

| SHOPPING LIST | |
| --- | --- |
| **Regularly Kept in the Kitchen** (Listed in Chapter 14, p. 703) | **Fresh Produce** |
| Spike<br>White pepper | Avocado<br>Lemon<br>Chives |

| Special Shopping |
| --- |
| Vegetable bouillon cubes — found in natural food stores. Neufchatel cheese — found in supermarket cheese sections or specialty cheese shops. |

# NUTRITIONAL ANALYSIS FOR ONE SERVING AVOCADO CREME SOUP WITH COOL-AS-A-CUCUMBER NOODLES AND FOUR "FRUIT" SALSA

```
NUTRIENT       Type: 14   FEMALE-23 TO 51 YEARS           % RDA   Amount
KCALORIES     %====                                          9%   190.0 Kc
PROTEIN       %====                                          8%   3.530 Gm
CARBOHYDRATE  %                                           NO RDA  15.40 Gm
FAT           %                                           NO RDA  14.00 Gm
FIBER-CRUDE   %                                           NO RDA  2.360 Gm
CHOLESTEROL   %                                           NO RDA  2.470 Mg
SATURATED FA  %                                           NO RDA  2.500 Gm
OLEIC FA      %                                           NO RDA  7.600 Gm
LINOLEIC FA   %                                           NO RDA  1.250 Gm
SODIUM        %===============                             28%   621.0 Mg
POTASSIUM     %==========                                  19%   728.0 Mg
MAGNESIUM     %=======                                     14%   43.50 Mg
IRON          %======                                      10%   1.850 Mg
ZINC          %==                                           4%   0.730 Mg
VITAMIN A     %==============================              58%    2343 IU
VITAMIN D     %                                             0%   0.000 IU
VIT. E/TOTAL  %                                          NO RDA  0.280 Mg
VITAMIN C     %===================                         36%   21.80 Mg
THIAMIN       %=====                                       11%   0.110 Mg
RIBOFLAVIN    %=====                                       10%   0.120 Mg
NIACIN        %========                                    16%   2.180 Mg
VITAMIN B6    %=======                                     13%   0.270 Mg
FOLACIN       %========                                    16%   64.10 Ug
VITAMIN B12   %                                             0%   0.000 Ug
PANTO- ACID   %========                                    16%   0.930 Mg
CALCIUM       %==                                           4%   36.10 Mg
PHOSPHORUS    %=====                                        8%   71.10 Mg
TRYPTOPHAN    %========                                     15%   24.50 Mg
THREONINE     %=========                                    19%   84.30 Mg
ISOLEUCINE    %=======                                      14%   94.00 Mg
LEUCINE       %=========                                    18%   158.0 Mg
LYSINE        %=========                                    19%   130.0 Mg
METHIONINE    %=======                                      14%   40.60 Mg
CYSTINE       %====                                          8%   23.60 Mg
PHENYL-ANINE  %==========                                   20%   89.60 Mg
TYROSINE      %=======                                      14%   65.00 Mg
VALINE        %=======                                      15%   116.0 Mg
HISTIDINE     %                                          NO RDA  43.30 Mg
ALCOHOL       %                                          NO RDA  0.000 Gm
ASH           %                                          NO RDA  1.320 Gm
COPPER        %=====                                       11%   0.280 Mg
MANGANESE     %======                                      12%   0.450 Mg
IODINE        %=====                                       11%   17.50 Ug
MONO FAT      %                                          NO RDA  8.060 Gm
POLY FAT      %                                          NO RDA  1.540 Gm
CAFFEINE      %                                          NO RDA  0.000 Mg
FLUORIDE      %                                             0%   20.30 Ug
MOLYBDENUM    %                                             0%   2.730 Ug
VITAMIN K     %                                             0%   0.610 Ug
SELENIUM      %                                        NO DATA  NO DATA
BIOTIN        %                                             0%   1.280 Ug
CHLORIDE      %                                             0%   6.360 Mg
CHROMIUM      %                                             0%   0.000 Mg
SUGAR         %                                          NO RDA  2.160 Gm
FIBER-DIET    %                                          NO RDA  2.420 Gm
VIT. E/AT     %========                                     17%   1.370 Mg

  % RDA:    |0      |20      |40      |60      |80      |100
```

647

# HOT PEPPER PRESERVE

☆ A change from the everyday fruit preserves; really wakes you up when eaten on whole grain toast for breakfast!

*1 cup ground red or green bell peppers*
*1 cup ground jalapeno peppers*

*4 cups honey*
*1½ cups apple cider vinegar*
*1 Tbsp. pure pectin powder*

Wash peppers and remove centers and seeds. Run in food processor or blender till very finely chopped (it should be quite juicy, with small pieces of pepper — don't puree). Add next 3 ingredients and stir till pectin dissolves. Place on heat over medium flame and bring to a boil, stirring constantly to avoid lumping. Allow to boil about 1 minute, stirring constantly. Remove from heat and, while still hot, pour through strainer or cheesecloth into sterilized jars and seal. Makes about 5 cups.

Don't throw the strained pepper out! This can be easily turned into a chutney by cooking with desired main ingredient (like pineapple, plums, mango, tomatoes, etc.) and spiced with a chaunce (see p. 597).

To make your own sugarless fruit preserves:

*¼ or ½ cup frozen 100% pineapple concentrate*
*¾ or ½ cup frozen 100% apple concentrate*
*2 Tbsp. pure pectin powder*

*1 lb. fruit, pureed or mashed*

Combine first 3 ingredients (whatever combination you want of concentrated frozen juices to total 1 cup) and mix till pectin dissolves. Place over heat and bring to a boil, stirring constantly till mixture thickens. Turn off heat and add fruit (puree for a smooth preserve; mashed if you like to run into chunks of fruit). Pour into jars and refrigerate. This jam must be stored in the refrigerator because the fruit hasn't been cooked.

To make a healthier "gum drop" type candy:

*4 cups pureed fruit or 4 cups 100% frozen fruit concentrate (or a mixture of the two to total 4 cups of liquid)*
*2 Tbsp. plus 1 tsp. pure pectin powder*

Combine all ingredients and stir till pectin dissolves. Place over heat and bring to a boil, stirring constantly till thickened. Spoon into a mold shape of your choice (gourmet kitchen stores often carry small and interestingly-shaped ice cube trays that work well for this). Allow to cool. When firm, pop out of ice cube trays.

| SHOPPING LIST | |
|---|---|
| **Regularly Kept in the Kitchen** (Listed in Chapter 14, p. 703) | **Fresh Produce** |
| Honey<br>Apple cider vinegar | Bell peppers<br>Jalapeno peppers |

| Special Shopping |
|---|
| Pure pectin powder — pectin is a natural dietary fiber found in many fruits. The pectins sold in supermarkets all have sugar in them. I've found a pure apple pectin powder that's sold in the vitamin section of natural food stores. If your local natural food store doesn't carry it, don't hesitate to ask them to special order it. (The one I've found is made by the Solgar Vitamin Company.) |

Sulfur dioxide is what forms when sulfur is burned; it is commonly used to treat dried fruit to keep them from browning. Like many elements on the FDA's GRAS list (Generally Regarded As Safe), the actual safety of the element for human consumption is debatable and the FDA has asked for further studies. At the same time, the FDA has nó regulating figure on the maximum amount of sulfur dioxide that can be used. Sulfur dioxide itself is very poisonous; inhalation of the gas can be highly irritating to the lungs and even cause death (in concentrated amounts). Although sulfur dioxide fumes aren't inhaled by the consumer of dried fruit treated with the gas, the residues left on the fruit alter its nutritional value and can affect the body. Besides destroying part of the B-vitamin complex contained in food treated with sulfur dioxide, a 1933 report (called "100,000,000 Guinea Pigs; Dangers in Everyday Foods, Drugs and Cosmetics") found that daily portions of 3/10 to 1 gram (about as much as is found in 6 ounces of dried fruit) over a period of months caused different problems in individuals, including "destruction of corpuscles in the blood, anemia, belching of sulfur dioxide gas, inflammation of the mucous membrane of the mouth, symptoms of malaise, headache, backache, nausea, albumin in the urine, sensation of cold, etc."

Needless to say, I think it's worth the little bit of extra effort and expense to get unsulfured dried fruit!

| Special Shopping |
| --- |
| Unsulfured prunes or other dried fruit, licorice root tea — found in natural food stores. Chinese five-spice — found in Chinese groceries or Oriental food aisles of supermarkets. |

# RAW APRICOT BUTTER

*1½ cups apple juice*
*1 cup unsulfured, dried apricots*
*¼ cup whole almonds*

Combine all 3 ingredients, cover and soak overnight. Blend all together in blender till smooth. Use as a jam or fruit butter on sandwiches, crackers, etc. This must be kept in the refrigerator. Makes about 1 pint.

# HAWAIIAN-STYLE PRUNES

☆ A way to make prunes (or other dried fruit) with a Chinese sweet and sour taste.

*¾ cup lemon or lime juice*
*¼ cup honey*
*3 - 4 lemon slices, ⅛" thick (fruit and rind)*
*½ tsp. salt*
*½ tsp. licorice root tea*
*¼ tsp. Chinese five-spice*
*1 whole clove*

*1 lb. unsulfured prunes*

Bring first 7 ingredients to a boil and stir till honey dissolves. Turn off heat and allow to sit 5 to 10 minutes. Strain hot liquid onto prunes in a jar and put lemon slices in jar too. Cover and allow to sit 3 days, turning jar whenever you think of it. Makes about 1 quart.

Keep prunes in refrigerator and serve two with the fruit meal of the day. To serve as a compote, spoon a few prunes with a little syrup into a small dessert cup (on top of some fresh fruit or the prunes by themselves). Pour about ¼ cup of chilled, naturally-sweetened ginger-ale over each serving; can be served topped with a dollop of plain yogurt.

| SHOPPING LIST | |
| --- | --- |
| Regularly Kept in the Kitchen (Listed in Chapter 14, p. 703) | Fresh Produce |
| Honey Salt Cloves | Lemon |

# NUTRITIONAL ANALYSIS FOR ONE RECIPE RAW APRICOT BUTTER

```
NUTRIENT        Type: 14   FEMALE-23 TO 51 YEARS              % RDA   Amount
KCALORIES       A==================                           34%   685.0 Kc
PROTEIN         A==============                               27%   12.30 Gm
CARBOHYDRATE    A                                          NO RDA   128.0 Gm
FAT             A                                          NO RDA   19.50 Gm
FIBER-CRUDE     A                                          NO RDA   4.790 Gm
CHOLESTEROL     A                                          NO RDA   0.000 Mg
SATURATED FA    A                                          NO RDA   1.860 Gm
OLEIC FA        A                                          NO RDA   0.000 Gm
LINOLEIC FA     A                                          NO RDA   0.000 Gm
SODIUM          A                                              1%   42.20 Mg
POTASSIUM       A================================             66%    2502 Mg
MAGNESIUM       A==============================               61%   184.0 Mg
IRON            A======================                       46%   8.320 Mg
ZINC            A=======                                      14%   2.140 Mg
VITAMIN A       A=================================================== 235%   9412 IU
VITAMIN D       A                                              0%   0.000 IU
VIT. E/TOTAL    A                                          NO RDA   0.000 Mg
VITAMIN C       A====                                          9%   5.420 Mg
THIAMIN         A====                                          8%   0.080 Mg
RIBOFLAVIN      A=====================                        43%   0.520 Mg
NIACIN          A====================                         40%   5.220 Mg
VITAMIN B6      A=========                                    18%   0.360 Mg
FOLACIN         A====                                          8%   35.20 Ug
VITAMIN B12     A                                              0%   0.000 Ug
PANTO- ACID     A============                                 24%   1.370 Mg
CALCIUM         A===========                                  21%   174.0 Mg
PHOSPHORUS      A======================                       45%   360.0 Mg
TRYPTOPHAN      A==================================================== 130%   212.0 Mg
THREONINE       A=================================================    99%   432.0 Mg
ISOLEUCINE      A==================================           69%   453.0 Mg
LEUCINE         A===============================================      95%   828.0 Mg
LYSINE          A===========================================          86%   565.0 Mg
METHIONINE      A==================                           37%   103.0 Mg
CYSTINE         A=========================                    52%   143.0 Mg
PHENYL-ANINE    A==================================================== 135%   591.0 Mg
TYROSINE        A========================================     82%   361.0 Mg
VALINE          A===================================          70%   538.0 Mg
HISTIDINE       A                                          NO RDA   276.0 Mg
ALCOHOL         A                                          NO RDA   0.000 Gm
ASH             A                                          NO RDA   6.170 Gm
COPPER          A=================                            37%   0.940 Mg
MANGANESE       A=================                            37%   1.390 Mg
IODINE          A                                              0%   0.000 Ug
MONO FAT        A                                          NO RDA   12.20 Gm
POLY FAT        A                                          NO RDA   4.120 Gm
CAFFEINE        A                                          NO RDA   0.000 Gm
FLUORIDE        A                                              0%   0.000 Ug
MOLYBDENUM      A                                              0%   0.000 Ug
VITAMIN K       A                                              0%   0.000 Ug
SELENIUM        A                                              0%   0.000 Mg
BIOTIN          A                                              1%   1.800 Ug
CHLORIDE        A                                              0%   0.000 Mg
CHROMIUM        A                                              0%   0.000 Mg
SUGAR           A                                          NO RDA   0.000 Gm
FIBER-DIET      A                                          NO RDA   0.000 Gm
VIT. E/AT       A                                              0%   0.030 Mg

   % RDA:  |0       |20      |40      |60      |80      |100
```

# COMPOTES

I hate to give a recipe for a compote because recipes tend to cut down on people's imaginative and artistic tendencies sometimes. The most important thing in making a compote is to use perfect produce. I use a lot of off-grade fruit, especially to freeze for use in fruit ice creams, smoothies, etc., or for cooking — but for compotes the fruit must be in perfect condition because the fruit is being featured as the center of attention. That means it should be perfectly ripe and unbruised.

When picking fruit for compotes, reject any with bruises or cracks or rotten spots. Pineapples, watermelons, apples, oranges, grapefruits, grapes and berries must be bought ripe — they don't ripen any more than they were when picked. Cantaloupes and honeydews, bananas, avocados, pears, peaches, nectarines and apricots can be bought a little underripe, if you like, because they will continue to ripen.

To make a compote, leave bite-sized fruit whole; cut other fruit into bite-sized pieces. Gently coat with desired sauce, refrigerate to chill. Serve in chilled goblets or champagne flute-type glasses.

"Compote" is a fancy French word for a simple but well composed fruit salad served in a fancy goblet or champagne flute. Any fruit, or combination of fruits, can be used in making a compote; the main thing to consider is coordinating colors and flavors. Compotes are traditionally dressed with alcoholic beverages or syrups containing alcoholic beverages. I healthfully prefer to use nonalcoholic drinks, flavored sparkling waters, naturally-sweetened sodas or fruit smoothie-type sauces with none of the preceding instead.

# LOWFAT AND CHOLESTEROL-FREE BAKED ALASKA

☆ A way to serve Fresh Fruit Ice Cream as a gourmet dessert!

_____

*1 naturally-sweetened 9" cake layer, cooked and cooled*

*Enough frozen fruit to make 2 quarts of Fresh Fruit Ice Cream (p. 639)*

*1½ recipes of Eggless Meringue Kisses (p. 277)*

Bake a whole grain, naturally-sweetened cake (layer should be about 1" thick), cool and split in half to form two thin layers. Cut one layer to fit in bowl or mold about halfway up and cut other layer to fit over mouth of bowl. Run frozen fruit of your choice through a food processor or Champion Juicer to make two different flavors of Fresh Fruit Ice Cream (p. 639): I always use banana in combination with another fruit (about half-half) because the bananas will act as a natural sweetener for fruits that need a little sweetening (like strawberries, peaches, etc.). Line a 2-quart bowl (or larger if you desire) with plastic wrap. Put enough of the first flavor of Fresh Fruit Ice Cream in bowl to fill halfway. Place cut layer of cake on top of this. Put bowl in freezer while making second layer of Fresh Fruit Ice Cream; when it's made, fill bowl to brim and top with larger layer of cake. Wrap totally with plastic wrap and freeze till hard. It's ideal to do all of this a day or two before you plan to serve the Baked Alaska so it can freeze real solid.

Before serving, preheat oven to 425 degrees and make 1½ recipes of the Eggless Meringue Kisses. Line a baking tray with foil and remove plastic wrap from cake and ice cream mold. Invert frozen cake and fruit ice cream onto it (you may have to slide a knife between the bowl and plastic wrap to loosen the ice cream from the mold) and remove plastic wrap. Quickly "frost" fruit ice cream and cake with meringue and put in oven. Bake at 425 degrees for 1 to 2 minutes, till tips of ridges on meringue brown a bit. Immediately remove from oven, cut into wedges with a serrated knife that's been dipped in hot water, and serve. Makes 10 to 12 servings (unless you use a larger bowl).

Hopefully by now you've gotten into the habit of keeping frozen fruit in your freezer (a good way to use an abundance of ripened fruit — in smoothie drinks, fruit ice creams, jams, or to have on hand for future baking).

As can be seen by this recipe, the fruit ice creams can be used in any recipe that saturated fat- and cholesterol-laden ice cream is.

Make a shopping list for your favorite whole grain cake, Fresh Fruit Ice Cream (p. 639) using fruits of your choice, and Eggless Meringue Kisses (p. 277).

# CHAPTER 13

# THE GIFT OF HEALTH

The gift of health is one of the more valuable gifts a person can give to oneself and loved ones. Even though the value of good health goes unquestioned, it's sometimes met with a great deal of resistance when it means changing habits acquired over a lifetime. Young children who are fortunate enough to be brought up on a healthy diet from the start, reap the gift of health in a number of different ways.

Feeding children a well-balanced diet (free from cholesterol and chemically-laden flesh foods and eggs, refined flours and sugar, caffeine, artificial flavorings, colorings and preservatives) will build strong, healthy bodies that will be less susceptible to such diet-related problems and diseases as obesity, atherosclerosis, heart disease, stroke, several types of cancer and diabetes. This kind of a diet also makes for a mind that can concentrate and maintain longer attention spans (*Why Your Child Is Hyperactive* by Dr. Feingold, M.D.).

Since the body is similar to a car in the sense that it is a vehicle we are using for awhile, eating a wholesome, natural diet in the early years can be likened to the crucial "break-in" period on a new car: if it's done properly, you get a lot more mileage out of the vehicle in the long-run. Animal experiments and studies of centenarians (people who live past 100) around the world have shown that a low-calorie diet in early life extends the total life span.

Why this is so is extremely logical. Factors that contribute to heart disease — one of the biggest killer diseases in America — build up over a long period of time. Autopsies on young soldiers (the average age being 22) killed in the Korean War showed that 77 percent of the young American soldiers already had badly narrowed blood vessels (atherosclerosis). Koreans, who are raised on a diet consisting mainly of rice and vegetables, showed no such damage.

A (June 24) 1983 *American Medical News* article ("Health Risk Factors Found Among L.A. Children") showed that out of the 1,500 fourth and fifth graders studied, 24 percent had high blood pressure; 23 percent had excessively high cholesterol levels — the children's average cholesterol level was 40 milligrams higher than what is considered to be healthy; and 32 percent were obese.

Studies have reported that being fat in infancy has no bearing on whether a person will grow up to be a fat adult. (Don't ever put an infant on a diet! They need that "baby fat.") My trim 17-year-old got so plump on mother's milk that at one point (before he started crawling and moving around) he had four chins! But 75 percent of children who are fat between the ages of nine and 12 grow up to be fat adults, and 90 percent of fat teenagers remain that way for life! It appears that the chances of an obese person becoming slim decrease the longer a person has to multiply the number of fat cells in their body and become set in bad eating habits and sedentary ways.

The number of fat cells in a body naturally and healthfully increases during times of rapid growth — before birth, during infancy, the two years before puberty, and for women, during pregnancy. Bad eating habits and a sedentary lifestyle can cause the body to unhealthfully increase the number of fat cells when they're not needed. Although researchers don't know how new fat cells are created by the body, they do know certain conditions that lead to this happening. As was already described (p. 198), insulin causes the body to store more fat. It does this by driving fat and sugar out of the bloodstream and into the appropriate cells. Fat driven out of the bloodstream gets stored in fat cells. When all of the existing fat cells are completely full and can't take bearing on whether a person body's self-preservation mechanisms somehow make the body increasingly insensitive to insulin. Thus blood-sugar levels rise, so the pancreas pumps out more and more insulin, increasing insulin levels as well. At this point, the body copes with this unhealthy condition by producing new fat cells. Once fat cells are created, they're with you for life!

While the number of fat cells you have can always increase, modern science tells us they will never decrease. Obviously, the best way to never have to worry about fat is to never get fat in the first place (keep the number of fat cells down to what's healthy and normal). But fat people needn't despair! . . . it's possible to get slim by slimming the fat cells themselves.

According to the "fat cell theory," which was presented in 1967 by Dr. Jules Hirsch (Rockefeller University, N.Y.), and research findings since have made it more a fact than theory, there are two causes of obesity: having obese fat cells and having too many fat cells. Fat cells can be reduced, or emptied and shrunk almost to the point of invisibility, so a person with either problem can slim down accordingly. Obviously, the person with more fat cells will just have to work a little harder.

It appears that some people start off with more fat cells and/or a tendency to produce new fat cells more readily and rapidly than others. Exactly why this is so has not been determined. It's the old debate between whether genes or the environment are the cause for something. In the case of fat, it's a question of whether a person inherits a predisposition to being thin or fat through their parents' genes or due to eating habits and activity levels. As in other areas where the heredity vs. environment question exists, "scientific" research pretty much shows that it's not an either/or situation. Both are factors in whether a person will be fat or not. Of the two, environment is the more important.

A person who has inherited a tendency to be fat can transcend his or her genetic tendencies through proper diet and physical activity. Although this can be done at any point in life, fortunate is the child whose parents know and care enough to give him a healthy start in life, because patterns established in childhood usually carry over into adult life unless someone makes a conscious effort to change them.

It's amazing how tastes and habits can be conditioned into us. Even as I write this, my three-year-old daughter has served herself a bowl of unsweetened oatmeal (she also likes her whole grain, cold breakfast cereal unsweetened). When I asked her if she wanted honey on it, she looked at me like I was crazy and said, "Nope." I could never eat my breakfast cereal or oats unsweetened — and that may be something I've

been conditioned to; whereas my daughter's tastes haven't become so conditioned yet.

Many years ago, I read about a study made on infants who were not fed "balanced" meals, but were allowed to pick and choose whatever they wanted to eat. Interestingly enough, each infant ended up choosing a well-balanced diet, answering their body's demands.

Of course, this study was done on infants whose taste buds had not yet become conditioned through years of being fed adulterated, refined foods or persuaded by countless commercials and advertisements into thinking that a particular taste was good. To my knowledge, no such study has been done on the average American teenager or adult. It would be my guess that the results would be very different. In an infant there is still a "virgin" tongue, unadulterated by years of poor eating habits and conditioning. After a few years the tongue becomes conditioned, or trained, to like or accept tastes of things not meant for, and definitely not good for, human consumption.

All of us can probably remember some tastes that we "learned" to like, and then there are some that we can't remember learning at all. The one event that caused my husband to start looking at and thinking about how we become conditioned to liking certain things or accepting them as "normal," took place soon after his first child was

born. This infant absolutely refused to eat meat, and when my husband mentioned this to his mother, she remarked, "Oh, they're all like that. You just have to keep feeding it to them and after awhile they'll learn to eat it."

About 18 years ago, when I took a good, hard look at my conditioning and eating habits, it resulted in making a lot of changes. One of them was a decision to change my eating habits to more healthful ones (described in this book).

Having made this resolution, I started coming face-to-face with exactly how deeply conditioned my eating habits and tastes were — starting with my inability to try brown rice because it was the wrong color, to craving all the sweets and junk food my reading and studying told me was so bad for me!

Of course, this craving came from many years of taste conditioning and not from my body needing the nutrients contained in the junk food, as it was all deficient in nutrients anyway. Knowing this, I ate only the healthy, complex-carbohydrate foods (whole grains, legumes, nuts, fruits and vegetables) that I knew were good for me.

After going through an initial "withdrawal" period, I noticed that my tastes changed a great deal, much like an ex-smoker's do. I no longer crave junk food and have learned to listen to my body's messages.

Paying attention to messages from my body is one of

the reasons that meal and menu planning vary a little between my first book and this one. My first book was written in Hawaii; this one primarily in California. I have found that in cooler weather I feel hungrier and tend to crave more grains and hearty legume foods. When the weather is hot (as it always is in Hawaii), I don't get hungry as often and tend to crave and eat light meals that feature fresh fruits and vegetables. I also notice the kinds of snacks my children ask for seem to change with the seasons.

Yes — of course I allow snacking . . . as long as it's healthy food that's being eaten! Looking at my children (and myself), I see that snack-ing isn't necessarily a fattening habit. I even think it's a good one because it has helped my children learn about what foods are healthy, since they choose and prepare their own snacks (and are expected to clean up after themselves).

I don't want you to get the idea that the gift of health comes through snacking. But since children snack so much, that is the subject of the bulk of this chapter. The gift of health is something anyone can have at any point in their life by making the necessary lifestyle changes; but it's so wonderful to give this to children from the very begin-ning of their lives! This starts in the beginning with just feeding them the right foods and, as they get older, teach-ing them what the right foods are and why.

And a word about exer-cise: physically active child-ren will be healthy and trim. This is accomplished by get-ting them active and being active yourself, since children learn so much from example. Especially for the moms who "never have time to exercise because they're so busy with the children" — take half an hour a day to do your exercis-ing. You'll feel so much better and have so much energy as a result that you'll be able to get much more done in a day. Your children will learn from watching you that exercise is important and may even join in!

# HEALTHY SNACKS

In these times when the need for peace — both individual and worldwide — is obvious, the Bhagavad-gita offers us this to consider: "A person who is not disturbed by the incessant flow of desires that enter like rivers into the ocean, which is ever being filled but is always still — that person can alone achieve peace, and not the man who strives to satisfy such desires."

Snacking is something everyone thinks is okay — even good for you, if you're a kid. It's accepted that active, growing bodies need to be refueled between meals. The idea of an adult snacking is associated in most people's minds with future pounds to lose. This isn't necessarily true. Snacking can contribute to good health and a trim body even for an adult.

The important thing for adults (and children) is to choose the right foods as snacks. The simple rules to go by: think whole grains, fresh foods and fiber; minimize fatty foods, sources of cholesterol, and empty calories (white sugar and flour) ... the same general guidelines to eating healthy food found throughout this book. Eating snacks consisting of these recommended foods helps to keep the body trim by keeping the metabolism revved up and making it so a person will be less likely to overeat at mealtime.

# FROZEN GRAPES

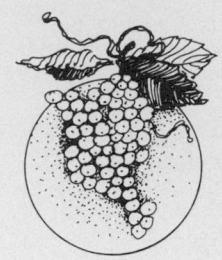

*Seedless grapes*

Wash grapes well and allow to drain. Place in freezer in plastic bags overnight. Eat like little popsicles. How many you freeze determines the number of servings.

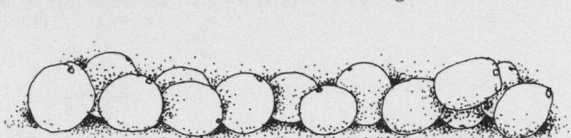

# VITAMIN AND MINERAL DRINK

*2 cups orange juice*
*1 apple, cored and quartered*
*3 frozen bananas*
*8 frozen peach or apricot halves*
*1 cup fresh pineapple cubes*
*2 Tbsp. wheat germ*
*2 Tbsp. lemon juice*
*2 Tbsp. lecithin granules*
*1 Tbsp. nutritional yeast*

Blend all ingredients in blender till smooth and frothy. Serve immediately. Makes 2 to 3 large servings.

| SHOPPING LIST | |
|---|---|
| **Regularly Kept in the Kitchen (Listed in Chapter 14, p. 703)** | **Fresh Produce** |
| Wheat germ | Orange juice |
| Lecithin granules | Apple |
| Nutritional yeast | Banana |
| | Peach or apricot |
| | Pineapple |
| | Lemon |

We make a lot of frozen fruit in our house. That way we have it on hand for snacking — whole (like frozen grapes) or in fruit smoothie drinks. My children's taste for simple fruit snacks really showed up while taping this show. Chintamani (then two) came in to help, but as soon as she saw the frozen fruit, decided it was time to eat instead! That's one thing about having the children help on the air — we never know what they'll do!

I do make sure they learn safety rules as soon as they start helping in the kitchen. Rules for running the blender:
1) Always put the lid on before starting! It sure makes a mess all over the walls (and even the ceiling) if this rule is forgotten.
2) Never, never, never stick anything in the blender or any other electrical appliance when it's running!

# NUTRITIONAL ANALYSIS FOR ONE SERVING
## VITAMIN AND MINERAL DRINK

| NUTRIENT | Type: 14   FEMALE-23 TO 51 YEARS | % RDA | Amount |
|---|---|---|---|
| KCALORIES | Ȣ=============== | 26% | 521.0 Kc |
| PROTEIN | Ȣ=========== | 20% | 9.160 Gm |
| CARBOHYDRATE | Ȣ | NO RDA | 115.0 Gm |
| FAT | Ȣ | NO RDA | 8.480 Gm |
| FIBER-CRUDE | Ȣ | NO RDA | 3.250 Gm |
| CHOLESTEROL | Ȣ | NO RDA | 0.000 Mg |
| SATURATED FA | Ȣ | NO RDA | 2.560 Gm |
| OLEIC FA | Ȣ | NO RDA | 0.230 Gm |
| LINOLEIC FA | Ȣ | NO RDA | 0.350 Gm |
| SODIUM | Ȣ | 0% | 8.830 Mg |
| POTASSIUM | Ȣ========================= | 49% | 1846 Mg |
| MAGNESIUM | Ȣ===================== | 43% | 131.0 Mg |
| IRON | Ȣ====== | 12% | 2.200 Mg |
| ZINC | Ȣ======== | 17% | 2.560 Mg |
| VITAMIN A | Ȣ================ | 33% | 1337 IU |
| VITAMIN D | Ȣ | 1% | 2.110 IU |
| VIT. E/TOTAL | Ȣ | NO RDA | 3.240 Mg |
| VITAMIN C | Ȣ=================================================== | 245% | 147.0 Mg |
| THIAMIN | Ȣ=================================================== | 276% | 2.760 Mg |
| RIBOFLAVIN | Ȣ=================================================== | 220% | 2.640 Mg |
| NIACIN | Ȣ=================================================== | 130% | 16.90 Mg |
| VITAMIN B6 | Ȣ=================================================== | 180% | 3.600 Mg |
| FOLACIN | Ȣ========================== | 54% | 216.0 Ug |
| VITAMIN B12 | Ȣ============================ | 58% | 1.750 Ug |
| PANTO- ACID | Ȣ================ | 30% | 1.680 Mg |
| CALCIUM | Ȣ=== | 7% | 60.20 Mg |
| PHOSPHORUS | Ȣ================ | 30% | 240.0 Mg |
| TRYPTOPHAN | Ȣ===================== | 45% | 74.30 Mg |
| THREONINE | Ȣ===================================== | 77% | 335.0 Mg |
| ISOLEUCINE | Ȣ======================= | 48% | 318.0 Mg |
| LEUCINE | Ȣ============================== | 64% | 566.0 Mg |
| LYSINE | Ȣ==================================== | 77% | 507.0 Mg |
| METHIONINE | Ȣ======================== | 51% | 140.0 Mg |
| CYSTINE | Ȣ===================== | 45% | 124.0 Mg |
| PHENYL-ANINE | Ȣ================================ | 73% | 320.0 Mg |
| TYROSINE | Ȣ============================ | 57% | 248.0 Mg |
| VALINE | Ȣ============================ | 58% | 443.0 Mg |
| HISTIDINE | Ȣ | NO RDA | 325.0 Mg |
| ALCOHOL | Ȣ | NO RDA | 0.000 Gm |
| ASH | Ȣ | NO RDA | 5.990 Gm |
| COPPER | Ȣ=========== | 22% | 0.570 Mg |
| MANGANESE | Ȣ==================================== | 73% | 2.760 Mg |
| IODINE | Ȣ======= | 14% | 22.30 Ug |
| MONO FAT | Ȣ | NO RDA | 0.310 Gm |
| POLY FAT | Ȣ | NO RDA | 3.910 Gm |
| CAFFEINE | Ȣ | NO RDA | 0.000 Mg |
| FLUORIDE | Ȣ== | 5% | 152.0 Ug |
| MOLYBDENUM | Ȣ==================================== | 73% | 240.0 Ug |
| VITAMIN K | Ȣ | 0% | 0.000 Ug |
| SELENIUM | Ȣ==== | 8% | 0.010 Mg |
| BIOTIN | Ȣ===== | 11% | 17.60 Ug |
| CHLORIDE | Ȣ | 0% | 15.50 Mg |
| CHROMIUM | Ȣ============================ | 56% | 0.070 Mg |
| SUGAR | Ȣ | NO RDA | 43.80 Gm |
| FIBER-DIET | Ȣ | NO RDA | 7.890 Gm |
| VIT. E/AT | Ȣ============= | 27% | 2.230 Mg |

```
% RDA:   |0      |20     |40     |60     |80     |100
```

Peach halves used instead of apricot in analysis.

# FRESH FRUIT SLUSH

☆ Make other slush flavors by using other fruit in season and a compatible juice.

---

*2 cups fresh or unsweetened, frozen strawberries*
*2 cups pineapple juice*
*¼ cup orange juice concentrate*
*¼ cup honey*

*Carbonated mineral water*
*(lime flavoring preferable)*

Blend first 4 ingredients in blender till smooth, and pour into ice cube trays. (This mixture can also be poured into popsicle molds and served as a healthy popsicle.) Freeze till solid. Take frozen cubes and blend with enough carbonated mineral water to form a slush consistency.

Even kids' junk food favorites, like slushes and shakes, can be healthfully and satisfactorily duplicated. These drinks are summertime favorites that help everyone to refuel healthfully and beat the heat at the same time.

| SHOPPING LIST | |
|---|---|
| **Regularly Kept in the Kitchen** (Listed in Chapter 14, p. 703) | **Fresh Produce** |
| Honey | Strawberries<br>100% pineapple juice<br>100% orange juice concentrate<br>Sparkling water |

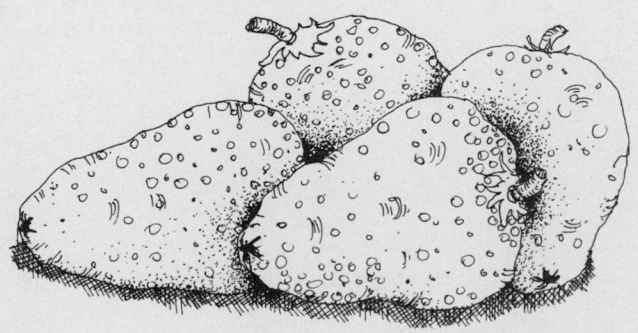

# NUTRITIONAL ANALYSIS FOR ONE SERVING FRESH FRUIT SLUSH

```
NUTRIENT       Type: 14    FEMALE-23 TO 51 YEARS           % RDA    Amount
KCALORIES     A====                                          8%    178.0 Kc
PROTEIN       A=                                             2%    1.160 Gm
CARBOHYDRATE  A                                           NO RDA   45.20 Gm
FAT           A                                           NO RDA   0.140 Gm
FIBER-CRUDE   A                                           NO RDA   0.760 Gm
CHOLESTEROL   A                                           NO RDA   0.000 Mg
SATURATED FA  A                                           NO RDA   0.010 Gm
OLEIC FA      A                                           NO RDA   0.000 Gm
LINOLEIC FA   A                                           NO RDA   0.000 Gm
SODIUM        A                                              0%    9.470 Mg
POTASSIUM     A=====                                        10%    388.0 Mg
MAGNESIUM     A====                                          8%    25.00 Mg
IRON          A===                                           6%    1.080 Mg
ZINC          A                                              1%    0.280 Mg
VITAMIN A     A=                                             2%    85.50 IU
VITAMIN D     A                                              0%    0.000 IU
VIT. E/TOTAL  A                                           NO RDA   0.290 Mg
VITAMIN C     A=================================================  109%  65.50 Mg
THIAMIN       A=======                                      14%    0.140 Mg
RIBOFLAVIN    A==                                            5%    0.070 Mg
NIACIN        A===                                           6%    0.790 Mg
VITAMIN B6    A===                                           7%    0.140 Mg
FOLACIN       A====                                          8%    35.00 Ug
VITAMIN B12   A                                              0%    0.000 Ug
PANTO- ACID   A===                                           6%    0.360 Mg
CALCIUM       A====                                          8%    64.00 Mg
PHOSPHORUS    A=                                             3%    29.20 Mg
TRYPTOPHAN    A=                                             2%    4.500 Mg
THREONINE     A=                                             3%    13.40 Mg
ISOLEUCINE    A                                              1%    11.20 Mg
LEUCINE       A                                              2%    23.10 Mg
LYSINE        A=                                             2%    16.90 Mg
METHIONINE    A                                              0%    2.260 Mg
CYSTINE       A=                                             2%    5.570 Mg
PHENYL-ANINE  A=                                             3%    13.20 Mg
TYROSINE      A=                                             2%    12.40 Mg
VALINE        A                                              1%    14.50 Mg
HISTIDINE     A                                           NO RDA   7.420 Mg
ALCOHOL       A                                           NO RDA   0.000 Gm
ASH           A                                           NO RDA   0.970 Gm
COPPER        A===                                           6%    0.170 Mg
MANGANESE     A====================                         38%    1.460 Mg
IODINE        A                                              0%    0.000 Ug
MONO FAT      A                                           NO RDA   0.020 Gm
POLY FAT      A                                           NO RDA   0.050 Gm
CAFFEINE      A                                           NO RDA   0.000 Mg
FLUORIDE      A                                              0%    21.00 Ug
MOLYBDENUM    A=                                             3%    10.00 Ug
VITAMIN K     A                                              0%    0.000 Ug
SELENIUM      A                                              0%    0.000 Mg
BIOTIN        A                                              0%    0.820 Ug
CHLORIDE      A                                              0%    0.000 Mg
CHROMIUM      A                                              0%    0.000 Mg
SUGAR         A                                           NO RDA   3.870 Gm
FIBER-DIET    A                                           NO RDA   0.000 Gm
VIT. E/AT     A                                              1%    0.150 Mg

   % RDA:  |0      |20     |40     |60     |80    |100
```

Serving amount is for two cups of fruit slush.

# CAROB-BANANA SHAKE

☆ A surprisingly low-calorie, creamy, frosty and rich-tasting shake.

6 *frozen bananas*
1½ *cups nonfat or lowfat milk*
3 *Tbsp. carob powder*
¾ *tsp. vanilla or mint extract*
¾ *tsp. grain coffee*

Place ingredients in blender (cut the frozen bananas into pieces) and blend till smooth. Enjoy a healthy, frosty, nutritious delight.

| SHOPPING LIST | |
|---|---|
| **Regularly Kept in the Kitchen (Listed in Chapter 14, p. 703)** | **Fresh Produce** |
| Lowfat milk<br>Carob powder<br>Vanilla or mint extract<br>Grain coffee | Bananas |

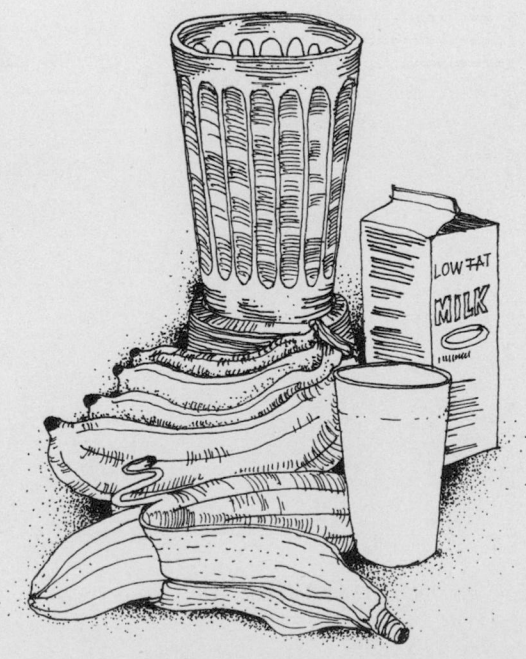

# NUTRITIONAL ANALYSIS FOR ONE
# SERVING CAROB-BANANA SHAKE

| NUTRIENT | Type: 14 FEMALE-23 TO 51 YEARS | % RDA | Amount |
|---|---|---|---|
| KCALORIES | A===== | 10% | 218.0 Kc |
| PROTEIN | A===== | 11% | 5.120 Gm |
| CARBOHYDRATE | A | NO RDA | 50.60 Gm |
| FAT | A | NO RDA | 2.640 Gm |
| FIBER-CRUDE | A | NO RDA | 1.230 Gm |
| CHOLESTEROL | A | NO RDA | 6.750 Mg |
| SATURATED FA | A | NO RDA | 1.420 Gm |
| OLEIC FA | A | NO RDA | 0.460 Gm |
| LINOLEIC FA | A | NO RDA | 0.040 Gm |
| SODIUM | A= | 2% | 49.30 Mg |
| POTASSIUM | A=========== | 23% | 892.0 Mg |
| MAGNESIUM | A=========== | 22% | 66.70 Mg |
| IRON | A== | 4% | 0.740 Mg |
| ZINC | A== | 4% | 0.680 Mg |
| VITAMIN A | A==== | 8% | 332.0 IU |
| VITAMIN D | A========= | 19% | 38.20 IU |
| VIT. E/TOTAL | A | NO RDA | 0.690 Mg |
| VITAMIN C | A============== | 28% | 17.00 Mg |
| THIAMIN | A====== | 12% | 0.120 Mg |
| RIBOFLAVIN | A============== | 29% | 0.350 Mg |
| NIACIN | A==== | 8% | 1.160 Mg |
| VITAMIN B6 | A=========================== | 54% | 1.080 Mg |
| FOLACIN | A==== | 9% | 39.90 Ug |
| VITAMIN B12 | A===== | 11% | 0.330 Ug |
| PANTO- ACID | A====== | 13% | 0.750 Mg |
| CALCIUM | A======== | 17% | 139.0 Mg |
| PHOSPHORUS | A======= | 15% | 127.0 Mg |
| TRYPTOPHAN | A=================== | 39% | 64.60 Mg |
| THREONINE | A======================= | 47% | 206.0 Mg |
| ISOLEUCINE | A=================== | 38% | 254.0 Mg |
| LEUCINE | A========================= | 50% | 439.0 Mg |
| LYSINE | A========================= | 50% | 330.0 Mg |
| METHIONINE | A================== | 36% | 98.40 Mg |
| CYSTINE | A========== | 21% | 59.50 Mg |
| PHENYL-ANINE | A========================= | 51% | 223.0 Mg |
| TYROSINE | A====================== | 44% | 194.0 Mg |
| VALINE | A=================== | 39% | 299.0 Mg |
| HISTIDINE | A | NO RDA | 234.0 Mg |
| ALCOHOL | A | NO RDA | 0.000 Gm |
| ASH | A | NO RDA | 2.110 Gm |
| COPPER | A=== | 7% | 0.180 Mg |
| MANGANESE | A=== | 7% | 0.270 Mg |
| IODINE | A===== | 10% | 15.30 Ug |
| MONO FAT | A | NO RDA | 0.570 Gm |
| POLY FAT | A | NO RDA | 0.220 Gm |
| CAFFEINE | A | NO RDA | 0.000 Mg |
| FLUORIDE | A= | 2% | 68.50 Ug |
| MOLYBDENUM | A===================== | 43% | 140.0 Ug |
| VITAMIN K | A== | 5% | 5.320 Ug |
| SELENIUM | A | 0% | 0.000 Ug |
| BIOTIN | A=== | 6% | 10.30 Ug |
| CHLORIDE | A | 0% | 12.60 Mg |
| CHROMIUM | A==== | 8% | 0.010 Mg |
| SUGAR | A | NO RDA | 25.00 Gm |
| FIBER-DIET | A | NO RDA | 4.200 Gm |
| VIT. E/AT | A=== | 6% | 0.530 Mg |

```
  % RDA:   |0      |20     |40     |60     |80     |100
```

Lowfat milk used instead of nonfat in analysis.

# BUTTERMILK SHAKE

2½ cups cultured buttermilk
3 cups frozen fruit in season (apricots,
    peaches, strawberries, mango and
    pineapple are all excellent)
⅓ to ½ cup honey

Blend all ingredients in blender till smooth and frothy.
Serve immediately. Makes 2 to 3 large servings.

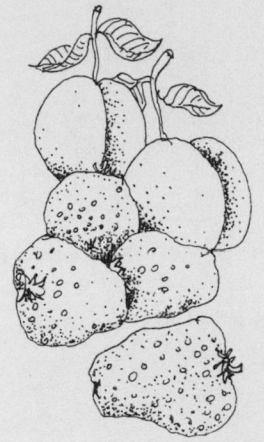

| SHOPPING LIST | |
|---|---|
| **Regularly Kept in the Kitchen**<br>(Listed in Chapter 14, p. 703) | **Fresh Produce** |
| Cultured buttermilk<br>Honey | Frozen fruit of choice |

# INVISIBLE PROTEIN SMOOTHIE

1 cup apple juice or any other fruit juice
2 Tbsp. Bipro powder
Piece of fresh or frozen fruit

Blend all 3 ingredients together in a blender for a smoothie-
type drink. Or, if you prefer to make a juice-type drink with
the protein content of a cup of milk, blend only the first 2
ingredients in a blender (or shake in a tumbler) and omit the
fresh or frozen fruit. Bipro is virtually tasteless and will dissolve in the juice without the strong taste or texture of most
protein powders.

Both of these recipes are good
ways to get some protein in a
snack. The Buttermilk Shake
has a definite cultured milk
taste. Since Bipro is virtually
tasteless (as well as saturated
fat- and cholesterol-free), the
drink will taste like a fruit
drink while providing around 2
to 3 grams more protein than a
cup of milk.

| SHOPPING LIST | |
|---|---|
| **Regularly Kept in the Kitchen**<br>(Listed in Chapter 14, p. 703) | **Fresh Produce** |
| Bipro | 100% fruit juice<br>Fruit of choice |

# PEANUT BUTTER CUPS WITH BRAN

*1 lb. (about 2 cups) peanut butter*
*⅔ cup hard, crystallized honey*
*⅔ cup bran and/or coconut*
*⅓ cup raisins*
*Vanilla (optional)*
*Cinnamon (optional)*

Mix ingredients together thoroughly. Roll into balls or make cups with a 2-tablespoon ice cream scoop. Lay on a tray and allow to sit overnight to harden (bran will absorb moisture). For a special touch, dip in melted carob chips or Carob Fondue sauce (see recipe, p. 235). Makes about 30 candies.

| SHOPPING LIST | |
|---|---|
| Regularly Kept in the Kitchen (Listed in Chapter 14, p. 703) | Fresh Produce |
| Peanut butter<br>Honey<br>Bran<br>Raisins<br>Vanilla extract and cinnamon (optional) | (None) |

This is a good dish for children to make who are too young to be cooking with a flame. Filling cups or covering balls with melted carob chips should be done by an older child or an adult.

# NUTRITIONAL ANALYSIS FOR ONE
# PEANUT BUTTER CUP WITH BRAN

| NUTRIENT | Type: 14 FEMALE-23 TO 51 YEARS | % RDA | Amount |
|---|---|---|---|
| KCALORIES | Ã=== | 6% | 134.0 Kc |
| PROTEIN | Ã===== | 11% | 5.060 Gm |
| CARBOHYDRATE | Ã | NO RDA | 10.60 Gm |
| FAT | Ã | NO RDA | 9.030 Gm |
| FIBER-CRUDE | Ã | NO RDA | 0.700 Gm |
| CHOLESTEROL | Ã | NO RDA | 0.000 Mg |
| SATURATED FA | Ã | NO RDA | 1.710 Gm |
| OLEIC FA | Ã | NO RDA | 3.960 Gm |
| LINOLEIC FA | Ã | NO RDA | 2.480 Gm |
| SODIUM | Ã= | 3% | 80.70 Mg |
| POTASSIUM | Ã= | 3% | 145.0 Mg |
| MAGNESIUM | Ã====== | 12% | 36.40 Mg |
| IRON | Ã= | 2% | 0.520 Mg |
| ZINC | Ã= | 3% | 0.580 Mg |
| VITAMIN A | Ã | 0% | 0.120 IU |
| VITAMIN D | Ã | 0% | 0.000 IU |
| VIT. E/TOTAL | Ã | NO RDA | 3.420 Mg |
| VITAMIN C | Ã | 0% | 0.080 Mg |
| THIAMIN | Ã= | 3% | 0.030 Mg |
| RIBOFLAVIN | Ã | 1% | 0.020 Mg |
| NIACIN | Ã========= | 19% | 2.520 Mg |
| VITAMIN B6 | Ã== | 4% | 0.080 Mg |
| FOLACIN | Ã= | 3% | 14.90 Ug |
| VITAMIN B12 | Ã | 0% | 0.000 Ug |
| PANTO- ACID | Ã= | 3% | 0.180 Mg |
| CALCIUM | Ã | 0% | 7.600 Mg |
| PHOSPHORUS | Ã==== | 9% | 77.60 Mg |
| TRYPTOPHAN | Ã=================== | 37% | 60.50 Mg |
| THREONINE | Ã================ | 33% | 146.0 Mg |
| ISOLEUCINE | Ã============== | 29% | 195.0 Mg |
| LEUCINE | Ã===================== | 43% | 376.0 Mg |
| LYSINE | Ã============== | 29% | 194.0 Mg |
| METHIONINE | Ã========= | 19% | 52.30 Mg |
| CYSTINE | Ã===========  | 23% | 63.70 Mg |
| PHENYL-ANINE | Ã================================= | 65% | 284.0 Mg |
| TYROSINE | Ã============================ | 54% | 237.0 Mg |
| VALINE | Ã============== | 29% | 227.0 Mg |
| HISTIDINE | Ã | NO RDA | 146.0 Mg |
| ALCOHOL | Ã | NO RDA | 0.000 Gm |
| ASH | Ã | NO RDA | 0.630 Gm |
| COPPER | Ã== | 4% | 0.120 Mg |
| MANGANESE | Ã==== | 9% | 0.350 Mg |
| IODINE | Ã | 1% | 1.770 Ug |
| MONO FAT | Ã | NO RDA | 4.210 Gm |
| POLY FAT | Ã | NO RDA | 2.620 Gm |
| CAFFEINE | Ã | NO RDA | 0.000 Mg |
| FLUORIDE | Ã | 0% | 7.430 Ug |
| MOLYBDENUM | Ã==== | 9% | 31.90 Ug |
| VITAMIN K | Ã | 0% | 0.000 Ug |
| SELENIUM | Ã | 0% | 0.000 Mg |
| BIOTIN | Ã== | 4% | 7.100 Ug |
| CHLORIDE | Ã | 0% | 1.590 Mg |
| CHROMIUM | Ã================ | 32% | 0.040 Mg |
| SUGAR | Ã | NO RDA | 0.000 Gm |
| FIBER-DIET | Ã | NO RDA | 0.400 Gm |
| VIT. E/AT | Ã======= | 15% | 1.200 Mg |

% RDA:  |0      |20     |40     |60     |80     |100

Bran used instead of coconut in analysis.

This recipe is appropriately named because this is what Madhava wants to make every time I ask him what he wants to cook. It's good for children to learn to cook as soon as they can do so safely, because in the process of learning how to cook, and with a little practical math, they can also learn about different foods and how foods contribute to, or detract from, health.

# MADHAVA'S FAVORITE CANDY BASE

☆ This makes a taffy-like candy that can be used to make different kinds of chewy candies, caramel or caramel apples.

2 cups honey
¼ cup margarine or butter

Mix both ingredients together over a medium-high heat and cook till it reaches a soft ball stage (when a drop of syrup forms a soft ball after being dropped into a bowl of cold water). At this stage you can make a variety of taffy-like (very chewy) candies by adding different ingredients to it — such as those suggested below — and pouring into an oiled tray to allow to cool.

1) 1¼ cups sesame seeds
   ½ cup unsalted, toasted peanuts

2) ½ tsp. grated orange rind
   ¼ cup chopped, pitted dates
   ½ cup roasted or raw cashew bits
   1 cup sesame seeds

# CARAMEL APPLES

1 recipe Madhava's Favorite Candy Base

2 tsp. vanilla
2 Tbsp. grain coffee
1 cup noninstant, nonfat milk powder

Whole apples

Chopped nuts or seeds (or combination of both)

After heating the honey and butter candy base to soft ball stage, add the next 3 ingredients and mix in thoroughly till smooth. Poke sticks into whole, washed apples which have been wiped dry. Roll apples one at a time in caramel mixture till apple is evenly coated. Immediately roll in chopped nuts or seeds and place stick-side-up on an oiled cookie sheet to cool.

# YUBA CHIPS

☆ Yuba is 53 percent protein, making a more nutritious chip than most sold in supermarkets.

---

*Yuba sheets (cut or broken into bite-sized chips)*

*Oil for deep-frying*

*Nutritional yeast*
*Spike or other vegetable-seasoned salt*

Deep-fry unsoaked yuba pieces in heated oil. Yuba should fry in a matter of seconds and bubble up. Remove from oil and place on paper towels to drain. While chips are still warm, sprinkle with nutritional yeast, Spike or vegetable salt and/or any spicing desired.

# SALAD KABOBS

☆ It may sound like this recipe uses a lot of oil, but bear in mind, a lot of it will be left to use over and over again!

---

½ *cup olive oil*
¼ *cup tarragon vinegar (or any other*
   *herb-seasoned vinegar of your choice)*
2 *Tbsp. lemon juice*
1 *Tbsp. Dijon mustard*
2 *tsp. honey*
1 *tsp. finely minced fresh tarragon*
   *leaves (or fresh herb to match*
   *flavor of seasoned vinegar)*
1 *tsp. Spike or other vegetable-seasoned salt*
¼ *tsp. black pepper*
¼ *tsp. asafetida or ½ clove garlic, crushed*

3 *ears corn-on-the-cob, cut in quarters*
12 *fresh mushrooms*
2 *small zucchini, cut in 1" chunks*
1 *bell pepper, cut in 1" chunks*
2 *tomatoes, sliced in wedges*

Combine first 9 ingredients in a gallon jar and mix till thoroughly blended.

Deep-frying is something I insist on doing rather than the children because a small accident with hot oil will result in a much larger burn than would be gotten by bumping a hand or finger on a hot pot. Although I don't deep-fry often, it's not something I stay away from totally. People in the Far East have deep-fried for thousands of years without problems with cancer or heart disease. I really think that deep-frying once in awhile doesn't hurt when you're not eating meat.

Deep-frying is a quick-cooking method. These yuba chips, or chips made with already-made "poppers" (called "papadams," which can be obtained in East Indian food stores) are a quick, protein-rich snack to make for children or drop-in guests.

Due to old habits and conditioning, we all most likely automatically think of sweets when we think of snacks. Vegetables are ideal snacks because they're high in fiber, vitamins and minerals, and are low in calories.

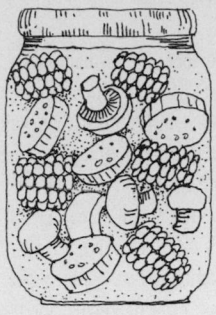

Steam corn-on-the-cob and cut each ear in quarters so each piece is 2" to 3" long. Cut other vegetables and drop into jar with the marinade dressing. Put lid on the jar and gently rotate jar to evenly coat the vegetables. Refrigerate overnight, or at least 4 hours, so vegetables marinate thoroughly. Be sure to rotate and invert jar every now and then. Put vegetables onto kabob sticks, alternating vegetable colors so they're nice and attractive. For a salad, serve on lettuce leaf bed, or store in jar for snacking. Makes about 1 dozen kabobs.

| SHOPPING LIST | |
|---|---|
| **Regularly Kept in the Kitchen** (Listed in Chapter 14, p. 703) | **Fresh Produce** |
| Olive oil | Lemons |
| Tarragon vinegar | Tarragon |
| Dijon mustard | Corn-on-the-cob |
| Honey | Mushrooms |
| Spike | Zucchini |
| Black pepper | Bell pepper |
| Asafetida | Tomatoes |

One overly neglected snack (and essential nutrient) is good, clean water. An ideal way to add a little flavor and beneficial elements is to turn water into Sun Tea (p. 238).

# NUTRITIONAL ANALYSIS FOR ONE SALAD KABOB

```
NUTRIENT        Type: 14    FEMALE-23 TO 51 YEARS          % RDA    Amount
KCALORIES       A===                                         6%     129.0 Kc
PROTEIN         A==                                          4%     2.000 Gm
CARBOHYDRATE    A                                         NO RDA    11.50 Gm
FAT             A                                         NO RDA    9.410 Gm
FIBER-CRUDE     A                                         NO RDA    0.650 Gm
CHOLESTEROL     A                                         NO RDA    0.000 Mg
SATURATED FA    A                                         NO RDA    1.340 Gm
OLEIC FA        A                                         NO RDA    6.410 Gm
LINOLEIC FA     A                                         NO RDA    0.730 Gm
SODIUM          A=                                           3%     86.40 Mg
POTASSIUM       A===                                         7%     279.0 Mg
MAGNESIUM       A===                                         6%     20.50 Mg
IRON            A==                                          4%     0.810 Mg
ZINC            A=                                           2%     0.380 Mg
VITAMIN A       A=====                                      11%     448.0 IU
VITAMIN D       A                                            0%     0.000 IU
VIT. E/TOTAL    A                                         NO RDA    1.710 Mg
VITAMIN C       A===============                            29%     17.50 Mg
THIAMIN         A=====                                      11%     0.110 Mg
RIBOFLAVIN      A=====                                      10%     0.120 Mg
NIACIN          A=====                                      11%     1.500 Mg
VITAMIN B6      A===                                         6%     0.130 Mg
FOLACIN         A==                                          5%     22.80 Ug
VITAMIN B12     A                                            0%     0.000 Ug
PANTO- ACID     A=====                                      10%     0.560 Mg
CALCIUM         A                                            1%     10.70 Mg
PHOSPHORUS      A===                                         7%     60.10 Mg
TRYPTOPHAN      A======                                     12%     20.10 Mg
THREONINE       A========                                   16%     71.00 Mg
ISOLEUCINE      A=====                                      11%     72.40 Mg
LEUCINE         A=========                                  18%     157.0 Mg
LYSINE          A========                                   16%     106.0 Mg
METHIONINE      A======                                     12%     34.70 Mg
CYSTINE         A==                                          5%     16.00 Mg
PHENYL-ANINE    A========                                   17%     77.70 Mg
TYROSINE        A======                                     13%     58.50 Mg
VALINE          A======                                     12%     95.80 Mg
HISTIDINE       A                                         NO RDA    48.20 Mg
ALCOHOL         A                                         NO RDA    0.000 Gm
ASH             A                                         NO RDA    0.680 Gm
COPPER          A=                                           3%     0.080 Mg
MANGANESE       A=                                           2%     0.110 Mg
IODINE          A==                                          5%     8.750 Ug
MONO FAT        A                                         NO RDA    6.700 Gm
POLY FAT        A                                         NO RDA    0.950 Gm
CAFFEINE        A                                         NO RDA    0.000 Mg
FLUORIDE        A                                            1%     28.20 Ug
MOLYBDENUM      A                                            0%     0.000 Ug
VITAMIN K       A                                            0%     1.050 Ug
SELENIUM        A                                            0%     0.000 Mg
BIOTIN          A=                                           2%     4.320 Ug
CHLORIDE        A                                            0%     0.000 Mg
CHROMIUM        A=============                              24%     0.030 Mg
SUGAR           A                                         NO RDA    4.090 Gm
FIBER-DIET      A                                         NO RDA    1.040 Gm
VIT. E/AT       A=======                                    15%     1.270 Mg

    % RDA:   |0      |20     |40     |60     |80    |100
```

It's always interesting how those who take time to use their lives for deep thought almost prophetically make the same observations. Though they live in different parts of the world at different times, their thoughts run parallel. Nearly 3,000 years ago, the sage Lao Tsu wrote —

"For to be over-developed is to hasten decay, and this is against the Tao (the Way), and what is against Tao will soon cease to be."

A few short years ago, the economist E. F. Schumacher voiced the same thought in more contemporary language in his book, Small is Beautiful:

"What is quite clear is that a way of life that bases itself on the materialistic path of permanent, limitless development in a finite environment cannot last long, and that its life expectation is the shorter the more successfully it pursues its expansionist objectives."

# ALL KINDS OF SOUP

Water is the most essential nutrient of all, yet it often goes unconsidered as a snack or in meal-planning. Since our bodies are 45 percent to 65 percent water (infant bodies are about 75 percent), water is an essential nutrient for maintaining human life, secondary only to oxygen. The human body can live only a few minutes without oxygen, up to five days without water (depending on climate and the corresponding rate of dehydration — the loss of 20 percent body fluid is critical), whereas it can survive about five weeks without any other form of nutrients, such as carbohydrates, protein, fats, etc.

Why is water so important? The body gets its oxygen through fluids in the body. All the body's chemical reactions take place within the fluids of the body, and body fluids are the main carrier of nutrients. Water is also needed by the body to keep its air passages, lungs, eyes and other organs moist and cool, and to cushion all the internal organs and joints as well. Water also helps to keep the internal systems cleansed, flushing out body wastes through the kidneys that would otherwise build up as blood poison. In view of all its essential roles, worrying about drinking too much water as a cause of water retention is not only silly, but is a fallacy as well. People with weight problems often blame water retention for unwanted pounds and pudginess. The fact is (for reasons not totally understood by nutrition researchers), drinking good amounts of water helps the body get rid of unwanted water; excessive salt consumption causes water retention.

Although the amount of water needed in a day to maintain optimum health varies according to the amount of water lost (which depends on climate, physical activity and basal metabolic rate of each individual), it's safe to say that adults should consume three-fourths to one gallon. Now that may sound like a lot of water, but it doesn't all have to be gotten by downing a gallon of water a day! There is a lot of water in the foods we eat, from fruits and vegetables, which usually contain over 75 percent water, down to the driest foods we can think of, such as dry cereal and bread, which can contain over one-third water.

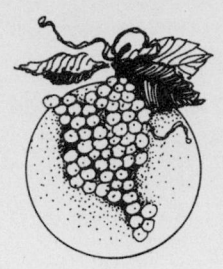

Then, of course, there are other tastier liquids to drink aside from water. As with any other form of nutrient available to us, we are faced again with choices between those which are healthy or unhealthy.

I personally am a fan of the taste of good, clean water (which usually means bottled water in most places in this day and age) to the point that I carry a gallon of water with me wherever I go and keep a gallon in my room as well. But when it comes to other flavored liquids, I choose the healthiest alternative for myself and loved ones. This means alcohol-free "wines" and "beers," caffeine-free herb teas and grain coffees, sodas sweetened with fruit juice instead of white sugar or corn syrup, and a myriad of juices to choose from.

When it comes down to juices, we tend to practice "this-is-better-than-that." Commercial, unsweetened, bottled juices are better than those sweetened with sugar or corn syrup (these we never buy!). There are many excellent juices to choose from on natural food store, and even supermarket, shelves. But even tastier and more nutritious than bottled juices are fresh, unheated fruit and vegetable juices made on the spot at home or at a local juice bar.

Freshly-made fruit and vegetable juices give flavorful, concentrated doses of vitamins and minerals, undamaged by the heating, canning process. Fresh juices are concentrated sources of healthy vitamins and minerals because it takes many pieces of a fruit or vegetable to make only one cup of juice.

While this extra boost of vitamins and minerals has its place as a special rejuvenator on occasion, and is extra helpful when the body is rebuilding and healing, juices are actually a processed food from which essential fiber is removed. While juices are certainly one of the healthier processed foods one can consume (because of the concentrated vitamin and mineral content), there are still some health benefits lost with the fiber.

One healthy way to get a lot of water and fiber in the diet is through soups, which can be served as a side dish, meals in themselves, and even desserts. Participants in a weight-loss study at the Institute of Behavioral Education (King of Prussia, Pennsylvania) found soup to be an efficient weight control. Compared to non-soup eaters, those who made soup a regular part of their meals at least four times a week lost weight more readily and were more likely to have maintained their weight loss a year later. Researchers had logical explanations for this. Soup is (generally) calorically less dense than solid foods, which explains why researchers found that the larger a role soup played in a meal, the fewer calories would be consumed. Another slimming factor about soup is that soup eaters were usually found to take a longer time to eat this less calorically-dense food, which gives the brain a chance to register satiety before too many calories are consumed (see p. 199). Non-soup eaters were found to consume one-third more calories per minute than soup eaters. Applying these findings to everyday life makes the idea of soup as a way to start, or even as the center of, a meal a good one!

# THREE-ONION AND SOME GARDEN COMPANIONS SOUP

☆ A special version of French onion soup.

---

2 Tbsp. safflower oil
2 Tbsp. margarine or butter
4 medium white onions, thinly sliced
4 medium yellow onions, thinly sliced

4 leek bottoms (white part), thinly sliced
2 carrots, cut in matchsticks
1 zuchini, diced in ½" cubes
1 potato, diced in ½" cubes

10 cups water
1 cup dry white wine
5 Morga or other vegetable bouillon cubes
1 bay leaf
2 Tbsp. soy sauce
1 Tbsp. asafetida or 3 cloves garlic, crushed
½ tsp. thyme
¼ tsp. black pepper

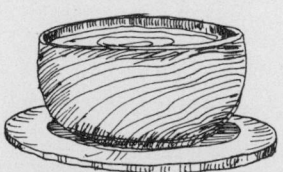

18 1"-thick slices of whole wheat
  French bread, lightly toasted
1 lb. shredded Gruyere or Parmesan cheese,
  or grated mozzarella cheese

Heat a large pot over medium heat and add first 4 ingredients. Saute onions, stirring occasionally (they will have to be stirred more frequently towards the end) till all the onions turn light brown and are completely limp and sticky. This should take ¾ to 1 hour. In the meantime, cut the following vegetables.

Add next 4 vegetables. Saute, stirring frequently to prevent sticking and burning, till onions are a caramel-brown. This should take about a half hour. As the vegetables get closer to being done, you'll find you have to stir them very often.

Add the next 8 ingredients and bring to a boil. Partially cover and turn heat down to simmer for another half hour.

Just before serving, cut French Bread into 1"-thick slices and toast lightly, buttering if desired. Shred or grate cheese.

A few minutes before serving time, preheat oven to 500 degrees and ladle about 2 cups of soup into oven-proof bowls. Drop in 2 to 3 slices of toasted French bread. Liberally sprinkle cheese over the top of toasted bread and soup. Place bowls into the preheated oven and leave there 2 to 3 minutes till cheese melts and browns a bit. Remove from oven onto serving platters and serve immediately.

If you don't have oven-proof dishware, you can get the same effect by making sure that the soup is piping hot. Toast bread, then lay bread on baking tray and sprinkle liberally with cheese. Stick bread and cheese under the broiler till cheese melts and browns a bit. Immediately float 2 to 3 pieces of toast with cheese side up in each bowl. Serve immediately. Makes 6 to 8 servings.

In some countries, onions and garlic are used medicinally. I sometimes make onion soup during the winter to cure or ward off winter colds. If using for this purpose, serve the soup as is and leave out the cheese and bread. For a hot, substantial meal, add the toast and cheese.

| SHOPPING LIST | |
|---|---|
| **Regularly Kept in the Kitchen** (Listed in Chapter 14, p. 703) | **Fresh Produce** |
| Safflower oil | White onions |
| Margarine or butter | Yellow onions |
| Bay leaf | Leeks |
| Soy sauce | Carrots |
| Asafetida | Zucchini |
| Thyme | Potatoes |
| Black pepper | Dry white wine |
| Shredded Gruyere or Parmesan or grated mozzarella cheese | |

| Special Shopping |
|---|
| Vegetable bouillon cubes — found in natural food stores. Whole wheat French bread — found in natural food stores, or make your own (p. 389). |

# NUTRITIONAL ANALYSIS FOR ONE SERVING
## THREE-ONION AND SOME GARDEN COMPANIONS SOUP

| NUTRIENT | Type: 14    FEMALE-23 TO 51 YEARS | % RDA | Amount |
|---|---|---|---|
| KCALORIES | X========================= | 49% | 987.0 Kc |
| PROTEIN | X===================================================== | 112% | 49.30 Gm |
| CARBOHYDRATE | X | NO RDA | 107.0 Gm |
| FAT | X | NO RDA | 42.80 Gm |
| FIBER-CRUDE | X | NO RDA | 4.420 Gm |
| CHOLESTEROL | X | NO RDA | 60.00 Mg |
| SATURATED FA | X | NO RDA | 17.00 Gm |
| OLEIC FA | X | NO RDA | 7.400 Gm |
| LINOLEIC FA | X | NO RDA | 9.280 Gm |
| SODIUM | X===================================================== | 145% | 3198 Mg |
| POTASSIUM | X==================== | 36% | 1365 Mg |
| MAGNESIUM | X============================== | 61% | 183.0 Mg |
| IRON | X===================== | 43% | 7.850 Mg |
| ZINC | X================== | 36% | 5.420 Mg |
| VITAMIN A | X===================================================== | 315% | 12606 IU |
| VITAMIN D | X | 1% | 2.110 IU |
| VIT. E/TOTAL | X | NO RDA | 7.660 Mg |
| VITAMIN C | X====================== | 46% | 28.00 Mg |
| THIAMIN | X=================================== | 72% | 0.720 Mg |
| RIBOFLAVIN | X========================= | 50% | 0.600 Mg |
| NIACIN | X========================== | 51% | 6.690 Mg |
| VITAMIN B6 | X===================== | 42% | 0.840 Mg |
| FOLACIN | X====================== | 45% | 181.0 Ug |
| VITAMIN B12 | X | 0% | 0.020 Ug |
| PANTO- ACID | X================= | 33% | 1.820 Mg |
| CALCIUM | X===================================================== | 149% | 1197 Mg |
| PHOSPHORUS | X===================================================== | 133% | 1067 Mg |
| TRYPTOPHAN | X===================================================== | 361% | 590.0 Mg |
| THREONINE | X===================================================== | 359% | 1563 Mg |
| ISOLEUCINE | X===================================================== | 341% | 2231 Mg |
| LEUCINE | X===================================================== | 446% | 3888 Mg |
| LYSINE | X===================================================== | 517% | 3381 Mg |
| METHIONINE | X===================================================== | 380% | 1036 Mg |
| CYSTINE | X===================================================== | 173% | 472.0 Mg |
| PHENYL-ANINE | X===================================================== | 527% | 2293 Mg |
| TYROSINE | X===================================================== | 511% | 2226 Mg |
| VALINE | X===================================================== | 361% | 2753 Mg |
| HISTIDINE | X | NO RDA | 1484 Mg |
| ALCOHOL | X | NO RDA | 0.000 Gm |
| ASH | X | NO RDA | 9.470 Gm |
| COPPER | X==================== | 41% | 1.030 Mg |
| MANGANESE | X===================================================== | 124% | 4.650 Mg |
| IODINE | X===================================================== | 197% | 296.0 Ug |
| MONO FAT | X | NO RDA | 9.820 Gm |
| POLY FAT | X | NO RDA | 10.40 Gm |
| CAFFEINE | X | NO RDA | 0.000 Mg |
| FLUORIDE | X==== | 9% | 261.0 Ug |
| MOLYBDENUM | X===================================================== | 1292% | 4202 Ug |
| VITAMIN K | X============ | 25% | 27.10 Ug |
| SELENIUM | X======== | 16% | 0.020 Mg |
| BIOTIN | X==== | 9% | 13.70 Ug |
| CHLORIDE | X= | 3% | 133.0 Mg |
| CHROMIUM | X===================================================== | 360% | 0.450 Mg |
| SUGAR | X | NO RDA | 12.10 Gm |
| FIBER-DIET | X | NO RDA | 12.70 Gm |
| VIT. E/AT | X==================================== | 74% | 5.920 Mg |

```
% RDA:   |0      |20     |40     |60     |80     |100
```

Margarine used instead of butter; Parmesan cheese used instead of Gruyere or mozzarella in analysis.

# ELEGANT SOBA SOUP

☆ A whole meal in a bowl!

In Japan, there are literally hundreds of thousands of mom-and-pop run tiny soba shops. Usually all that's sold in these shops is soba soup — hot in the winter and cold in the summer.

12 cups water
1 oz. dry shiitake mushrooms
1 oz. nishime, wakame or kombu seaweed
3 ⅛"-thick slices fresh ginger root

½ cup miso
¼ cup Barbados molasses
2 Tbsp. soy sauce

2 lbs. buckwheat soba noodles
Water for boiling noodles

Simmered shiitake mushrooms, slivered
2 cups deep-fried tofu pouches (aburage)
    or tofu, cut into strips
1 bunch watercress

2 Tbsp. water
2 Tbsp. soy sauce
1 Tbsp. honey
2 cups raw carrot matchsticks
2 cups raw mung bean sprouts
2 cups raw, slivered Chinese snow peas
    or green beans
2 cups raw, slivered scallions

To make soup broth, combine the first 4 ingredients in a large pot and bring to a boil. Turn heat down and simmer 10 minutes. Lift out the seaweed and discard. Lift out mushrooms and keep them for later use. Add the next 3 ingredients to the simmering broth and allow to simmer a few minutes till miso dissolves. Broth is now ready to serve if you want to serve a hot soup.

To serve the soup hot, boil the noodles and prepare vegetable toppings while the broth is cooking. Put cooked noodles into hot broth and top with a little of each vegetable.

If you want to serve a cold soup, allow broth to cool, then refrigerate 6 to 8 hours or overnight. If you are in a hurry to make a cold soup, make a broth concentrate by putting all ingredients into only 4 cups of water and when done cooking, bring the broth level up to 12 cups by adding ice cubes and some cold water.

If you are planning to serve the soup cold, boil noodles about 20 minutes before serving time, pour them into a

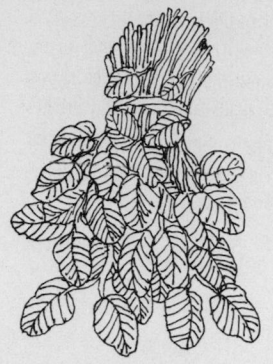

colander and run under cold water till noodles cool all the way through. Place colander inside of a larger bowl that it will fit in, and insert ice cubes throughout the noodles and on the top as well. While noodles are cooking, prepare vegetable toppings. Serve iced noodles into chilled broth (or hot noodles into hot broth), and top with a little of each vegetable topping and the tofu or aburage.

To prepare vegetables, combine water, soy sauce and honey together in a small pot. Simmer slivered shiitake mushrooms (left from soaking) 3 to 5 minutes, then remove from liquid onto large serving platter. Simmer tofu or aburage 3 to 5 minutes, remove from liquid and place onto serving platter with mushrooms. Blanch watercress in remaining liquid till it turns a more brilliant green than when raw. Remove, cut into 2"-long strips and place on same serving platter as mushrooms and tofu or aburage. Prepare raw vegetables by rinsing and draining mung sprouts, cutting carrots into thin matchsticks, and slivering scallions and Chinese snow peas diagonally. Place raw vegetables on serving platter with simmered toppings. A little of each topping should be sprinkled on top of the noodles and broth in each bowl. You can use other vegetables if these aren't available; just bear in mind which are better cooked and which are better raw, and try to get some color variation. Makes 4 to 6 servings.

# STRAWBERRY (OR ANY OTHER TART BERRY) SOUP

Fruit soups make light, refreshing dishes that can be served as meals or desserts. Any fruit or combinations of fruits can be used. These recipes are here just to give an idea of how to make and thicken fruit soups. Fruit soups such as these can be made into a substantial meal by adding chopped pieces of fresh or dried fruit into the soupy liquid.

2 cups fresh or frozen strawberries
1 cup apple juice
2 Tbsp. frozen 100% apple juice concentrate
2 Tbsp. psyllium seed powder

1 cup yogurt

12 fresh or frozen strawberries
Fresh mint leaves (optional)

Blend first 4 ingredients together in blender till smooth. Pour into 2 soup bowls.

Either fold in yogurt with a whisk or simply serve a ½-cup scoop in the middle of the bowl of soup. Drop in 6 whole strawberries in each bowl and garnish with a mint sprig, if desired. Serve immediately. Makes 2 servings.

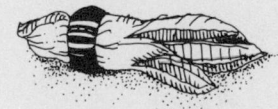

| SHOPPING LIST | |
| --- | --- |
| Regularly Kept in the Kitchen (Listed in Chapter 14, p. 703) | Fresh Produce |
| Yogurt | Strawberries<br>Apple juice<br>Frozen 100% apple juice concentrate<br>Mint leaves (optional) |

| Special Shopping |
| --- |
| Psyllium seed powder — found in most natural food stores. Be sure to get the ground whole seeds and not the whole seeds or ground husks. |

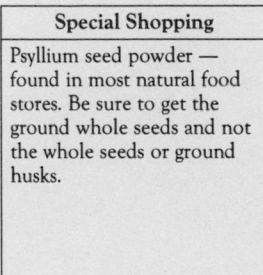

# BLUEBERRY SOUP

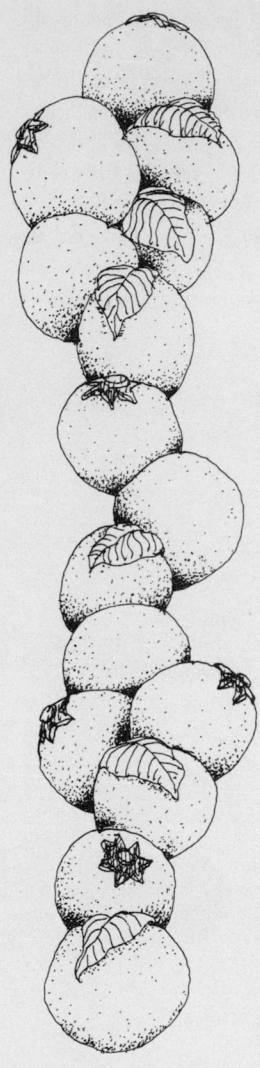

2 cups fresh or frozen blueberries
⅓ cup chilled orange juice
⅛ tsp. nutmeg
⅛ tsp. allspice

1 cup yogurt

1 orange

    Blend first 4 ingredients together till smooth. Pour this into 2 soup bowls.
    Scoop a ½-cup serving of yogurt into the center of each bowl. Peel an orange and divide segments. Arrange half of the orange segments in each bowl in a flower-like pattern on top of the blueberries and yogurt. Serve immediately. Makes 2 servings.

| SHOPPING LIST | |
| --- | --- |
| Regularly Kept in the Kitchen (Listed in Chapter 14, p. 703) | Fresh Produce |
| Nutmeg<br>Allspice<br>Yogurt | Blueberries<br>Orange juice<br>Orange |

# EMERALD FRUIT AMBROSIA

☆ A special, low-calorie, gourmet dessert made with fruit.

1 recipe Mint Sherbeto (see recipe, p. 628)

2⅔ cups Almond Milk or lowfat milk
1 stick agar-agar or ½ cup agar flakes
⅓ cup honey
½ tsp. almond extract

5 ripe peaches, nectarines or mangoes
   (about 4 cups pureed)

*1 cup pitted cherries*
*1 tsp. vanilla extract*

*6 ripe peaches, nectarines or mangoes, sliced thin*
*1 cup orange juice*
*2 Tbsp. honey*

In contrast to the quick, simple fruit soups, here is a fruit soup that takes more preparation. It's perfect for parties and entertaining because it's all prepared ahead of time. All that needs to be done at serving time is assemble the parts.

Make 1 recipe of Mint Sherbeto (see p. 628) a few days ahead of time so cubes get a chance to freeze solid. Within 24 hours before serving time, run mint cubes through a food processor chopper blade or a Champion Juicer so the cubes become aerated and the texture of a sherbet. Immediately place Mint Sherbeto in an airtight container, cover and freeze till time to serve the Ambrosia.

Also, on the day before serving the Ambrosia, combine the next 4 ingredients in a pot and allow to sit 5 to 10 minutes till agar-agar softens. Bring to a boil over medium heat, stirring occasionally. Cook till agar-agar is completely dissolved. Pour into a 9" x 9" cake pan (or similar utensil), allow to cool, then cover with plastic wrap and refrigerate.

A few hours before serving time, blend the next 3 ingredients in a blender to form a smooth puree and refrigerate. Combine next 3 ingredients in a separate container to marinate and refrigerate as well.

At serving time, line up individual bowls (better yet, chill the bowls in the freezer), and get out the 4 different parts of this dish: 1) Mint Sherbeto, 2) Almond Milk gel, 3) fruit puree, and 4) sliced fruit. Cut the Almond Milk gel into very fine ⅛" to ¼" cubes with a knife. In the bottom of each bowl, place a few layers of the sliced fruit, leaving a hole in the center. Place a couple scoops of the Mint Sherbeto in the space provided in the center of the sliced fruit. Ladle a few scoops of the pureed fruit over all of this and top with a generous scoop of the cubed Almond Milk gel. Serve immediately. Makes 6 to 8 larger-sized portions or 12 to 16 dainty dessert-sized portions.

| SHOPPING LIST | |
| --- | --- |
| **Regularly Kept in the Kitchen** (Listed in Chapter 14, p. 703) | **Fresh Produce** |
| Almonds or milk<br>Honey<br>Almond extract<br>Vanilla extract | Mint<br>Lemons<br>Peaches, nectarines or<br>    mangoes<br>Cherries<br>Orange juice |

| Special Shopping |
| --- |
| Agar-agar — found in most natural food stores; also in Japanese and Chinese groceries or Oriental food aisles in supermarkets. |

# NUTRITIONAL ANALYSIS FOR ONE SERVING
# EMERALD FRUIT AMBROSIA

| NUTRIENT | Type: 14  FEMALE-23 TO 51 YEARS | % RDA | Amount |
|---|---|---|---|
| KCALORIES | Å=============== | 29% | 599.0 Kc |
| PROTEIN | Å======== | 16% | 7.260 Gm |
| CARBOHYDRATE | Å | NO RDA | 147.0 Gm |
| FAT | Å | NO RDA | 3.030 Gm |
| FIBER-CRUDE | Å | NO RDA | 3.620 Gm |
| CHOLESTEROL | Å | NO RDA | 7.990 Mg |
| SATURATED FA | Å | NO RDA | 1.490 Gm |
| OLEIC FA | Å | NO RDA | 0.530 Gm |
| LINOLEIC FA | Å | NO RDA | 0.040 Gm |
| SODIUM | Å= | 3% | 66.00 Mg |
| POTASSIUM | Å================ | 32% | 1228 Mg |
| MAGNESIUM | Å=========== | 23% | 70.80 Mg |
| IRON | Å==== | 8% | 1.440 Mg |
| ZINC | Å=== | 6% | 1.010 Mg |
| VITAMIN A | Å================================================= | 249% | 9966 IU |
| VITAMIN D | Å=========== | 22% | 45.30 IU |
| VIT. E/TOTAL | Å | NO RDA | 0.180 Mg |
| VITAMIN C | Å================================================= | 185% | 111.0 Mg |
| THIAMIN | Å============= | 26% | 0.260 Mg |
| RIBOFLAVIN | Å=================== | 38% | 0.460 Mg |
| NIACIN | Å================= | 34% | 4.470 Mg |
| VITAMIN B6 | Å=========== | 22% | 0.440 Mg |
| FOLACIN | Å==== | 9% | 39.00 Ug |
| VITAMIN B12 | Å====== | 13% | 0.390 Ug |
| PANTO- ACID | Å============= | 26% | 1.440 Mg |
| CALCIUM | Å=========== | 23% | 190.0 Mg |
| PHOSPHORUS | Å=========== | 21% | 175.0 Mg |
| TRYPTOPHAN | Å===================== | 45% | 74.40 Mg |
| THREONINE | Å============================== | 63% | 276.0 Mg |
| ISOLEUCINE | Å======================= | 47% | 310.0 Mg |
| LEUCINE | Å============================== | 60% | 529.0 Mg |
| LYSINE | Å================================ | 66% | 435.0 Mg |
| METHIONINE | Å========================== | 54% | 147.0 Mg |
| CYSTINE | Å========= | 18% | 50.70 Mg |
| PHENYL-ANINE | Å============================== | 62% | 270.0 Mg |
| TYROSINE | Å============================ | 56% | 245.0 Mg |
| VALINE | Å========================== | 52% | 401.0 Mg |
| HISTIDINE | Å | NO RDA | 157.0 Mg |
| ALCOHOL | Å | NO RDA | 0.000 Gm |
| ASH | Å | NO RDA | 3.480 Gm |
| COPPER | Å========== | 20% | 0.500 Mg |
| MANGANESE | Å=== | 7% | 0.270 Mg |
| IODINE | Å | 0% | 0.000 Ug |
| MONO FAT | Å | NO RDA | 0.930 Gm |
| POLY FAT | Å | NO RDA | 0.340 Gm |
| CAFFEINE | Å | NO RDA | 0.000 Mg |
| FLUORIDE | Å=== | 6% | 169.0 Ug |
| MOLYBDENUM | Å | 0% | 0.000 Ug |
| VITAMIN K | Å=== | 6% | 6.300 Ug |
| SELENIUM | Å | 0% | 0.000 Mg |
| BIOTIN | Å== | 5% | 7.580 Ug |
| CHLORIDE | Å | 0% | 2.980 Mg |
| CHROMIUM | Å | 0% | 0.000 Mg |
| SUGAR | Å | NO RDA | 18.40 Gm |
| FIBER-DIET | Å | NO RDA | 3.880 Gm |
| VIT. E/AT | Å================ | 33% | 2.660 Mg |

```
% RDA:  |0      |20     |40     |60     |80     |100
```

Fresh mint leaves and mint extract not included in Mint Sherbeto; lowfat milk used instead of Almond Milk recipe. Fruit used in analysis: peaches and mangoes.

# FANTASTIC FIBER

The word is out — dietary fiber is not only essential for good health, but is good news for dieters as well! In a sense, this isn't new news at all. Back in the 1890's, there was a big health and dietary reform movement in America. During that time, a Mr. Kellogg developed a whole grain diet program which was used at Seventh Day Adventist hospital facilities as part of their healing treatment. A little later, Mr. Kellogg and a Mr. Post began producing the first ready-to-eat whole grain breakfast cereals. They would both be completely mortified and scandalized if they could see what the companies they started now sell to Americans to eat for breakfast!

At that time, there were many skeptics who questioned the importance of dietary fiber in the diet. Recent medical and scientific studies have proven dietary fiber to be absolutely essential for good health, and that news has been spread through the mass media so all of us can know about one of the elements we can eat to stay healthy! About 10 years ago, some Western doctors and scientists noted that people in undeveloped countries were virtually free from degenerative diseases like cancer of the colon and other colonic disorders, heart disease and diabetes. They concluded that one factor which helps keep people free from these dietary-related diseases is dietary fiber. When news on their study began appearing in the press, wheat bran became very popular.

Ultimately, how long our bodies last isn't as important as what we do while we are in them. One person who didn't live long, but whose life has had a lasting impact on many is the Buddha. He wrote —
"Better than a hundred years
of ignorance
Is one day spent in reflection.
Better than a hundred years
of idleness
Is one day spent in
determination.
Better to live one day
wondering how all things
arise and pass away.
Better to live one hour seeing
than one whole
life beyond the way.
It is better to conquer
yourself than to win
a thousand battles.
Then the victory is yours.
It cannot be taken from you,
Not by angels or demons,
heaven or hell."

Today our knowledge about dietary fiber is expanding and becoming more complete. Nutrition researchers now know that there are several hundred different kinds of dietary fiber and that each one functions differently in the body.

Nutrition researchers may have yet to identify all the different kinds of dietary fiber and are studying how different ones function in the body, how the way they function is affected by particle size and moisture content, and how pore structure and adhesive properties are affected by cooking. It is known that there are soluble and insoluble dietary fibers. Soluble dietary fiber like pectin, which is found in oats and some fruits, has been shown to lower serum cholesterol levels but seems to slow the progress of food through the digestive tract. On the other hand, insoluble fiber like wheat bran, which doesn't dissolve in hot water, helps speed the movement of food through the digestive tract, thus preventing ailments like constipation, diverticulosis and even colon cancer. Insoluble dietary fiber can aid in slimming by providing bulk, which fills the stomach on few calories and leaves a person feeling full for a long period of time. Because it moves food quickly through the intestinal tract, it keeps the body from absorbing and metabolizing fat.

A word of warning: just as the speedy movement of food through the intestinal tract prevents the absorption of fat from the food, it will also prevent the absorption of other nutrients. For this reason, I don't recommend or personally use bran on a regular basis. If you eat the kind of diet recommended in this book, you'll be getting plenty of dietary fiber. Whole grains, legumes, vegetables and fruit are all high-fiber foods. Heavy consumers of flesh foods get an average of one to two teaspoons of fiber in a day; vegetarians get five to ten times that amount.

However, if you want to do an occasional "housecleaning" or use some bran to speed up the slimming process for a month or so, here are some recipes that will make it easy for you to do so. Eating these bran products is the only "special dieting" practice I recommend. Everything else in this book (changes in diet and a sensible exercise program) are meant to become part of your life for as long as the body lasts!

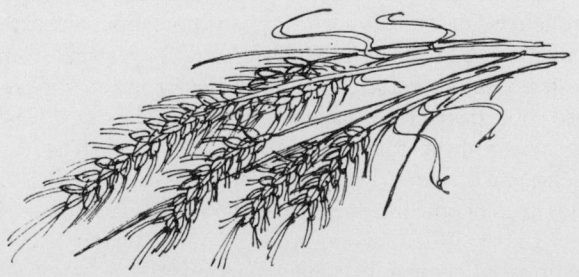

# BRAN "NUTS"

☆ For those who want to supplement their dietary fiber with bran, here is a bran cereal without sugar (most commercial bran cereals contain ⅓ to ½ sugar)!

---

4 cups bran
1 cup honey

¾ cup sliced, raw almonds
½ cup chia or amaranth seeds *(optional)*

Preheat oven to 250 degrees.

Combine first 2 ingredients and mix thoroughly. Using fingertips, sprinkle onto an oiled cookie sheet, breaking into small clumps as you sprinkle (much like making a crumb topping on a cobbler or pie). Just put enough on a cookie sheet to evenly cover with one thin layer. Don't make the layers too thick. This recipe should make enough for 4 cookie sheets.

Sprinkle on the sliced almonds and seeds (if desired). Bake at 250 degrees for 45 minutes. Remove from oven and allow to cool on the cookie sheets, being careful not to pat or touch as it cools. When the bran comes out of the oven it will be soft to the touch, but when cool it will be nice and crunchy. Store in airtight container.

This can be eaten as is, as a cereal, or sprinkled on other foods (certainly more palatable than just plain bran), baked into other dishes, etc. As a breakfast cereal, this recipe makes about twelve ⅓-cup servings.

Bran is a very inexpensive way to supplement dietary fiber. These Bran "Nuts" make it a little easier to get the bran down by making the bran more like nuts instead of sawdust.

Some ways to use Bran "Nuts":
• mixed into cookie batters at the last moment, they cook up just like nuts
• on top of cobblers
• on or in cheesecake crusts
• on puddings or yogurt
• on ice cream
• on fruit salad or slices of fresh fruit
• in peanut butter and jelly sandwiches
• in other breakfast cereals
• in Branola Breakfast Muffins!

| SHOPPING LIST | |
|---|---|
| **Regularly Kept in the Kitchen** (Listed in Chapter 14, p. 703) | **Fresh Produce** |
| Bran Honey Sliced almonds | (None) |

| Special Shopping |
|---|
| Chia or amaranth seeds — found in natural food stores. Date sugar (for Sweeter Bran "Nuts") — found in natural food stores. |

# SWEETER BRAN "NUTS"

*2 cups bran*
*1 cup date sugar*
*¼ cup chia or amaranth seeds*
*¾ cup honey*

Preheat oven to 250 degrees.
Combine ingredients and follow the same directions as in preceding Bran "Nuts" recipe.

For breakfast, slice a banana or other fruit in season and top with ⅓ to ½ cup Branola. Pour a little lowfat, soy or nut milk over all and serve. This may not look like much, but makes for a long-lasting full feeling. The extra chewing the Branola requires allows time for the appestat to register "full."

To use as a dietary aid (only for short periods of time — not as a lifetime habit), ration 1 cup a day. Take the ½ to ⅔ cup not used at breakfast in a little baggie with you and use in another meal and/or snacks during the rest of the day. This will help to keep you feeling full and keep your body from metabolizing a lot of the fat in any of the other food you eat.

# BRANOLA

☆ Tossing in a few additional ingredients turns Bran "Nuts" into a breakfast cereal or dietary aid.

*3¼ cups baked and cooled Bran "Nuts"*
*½ cup diced, dried figs*
*¼ cup diced, dried apricots*

Dice the dried fruit into less than ¼" cubes. Toss into the already baked and cooled Bran "Nuts." This makes twelve ⅓-cup servings.

For a change in taste, a variation on this cereal can be made by adding ¼ teaspoon cinnamon to the Bran "Nuts" before baking them, and replacing the dried figs and apricots with ¾ cup diced, dried apple.

| Special Shopping |
| --- |
| Unsulfured, dried figs and apricots — found in natural food stores. |

| SHOPPING LIST | |
| --- | --- |
| **Regularly Kept in the Kitchen** (Listed in Chapter 14, p. 703) | **Fresh Produce** |
| | |

See shopping list for Bran "Nuts."

# NUTRITIONAL ANALYSIS FOR ONE SERVING BRANOLA

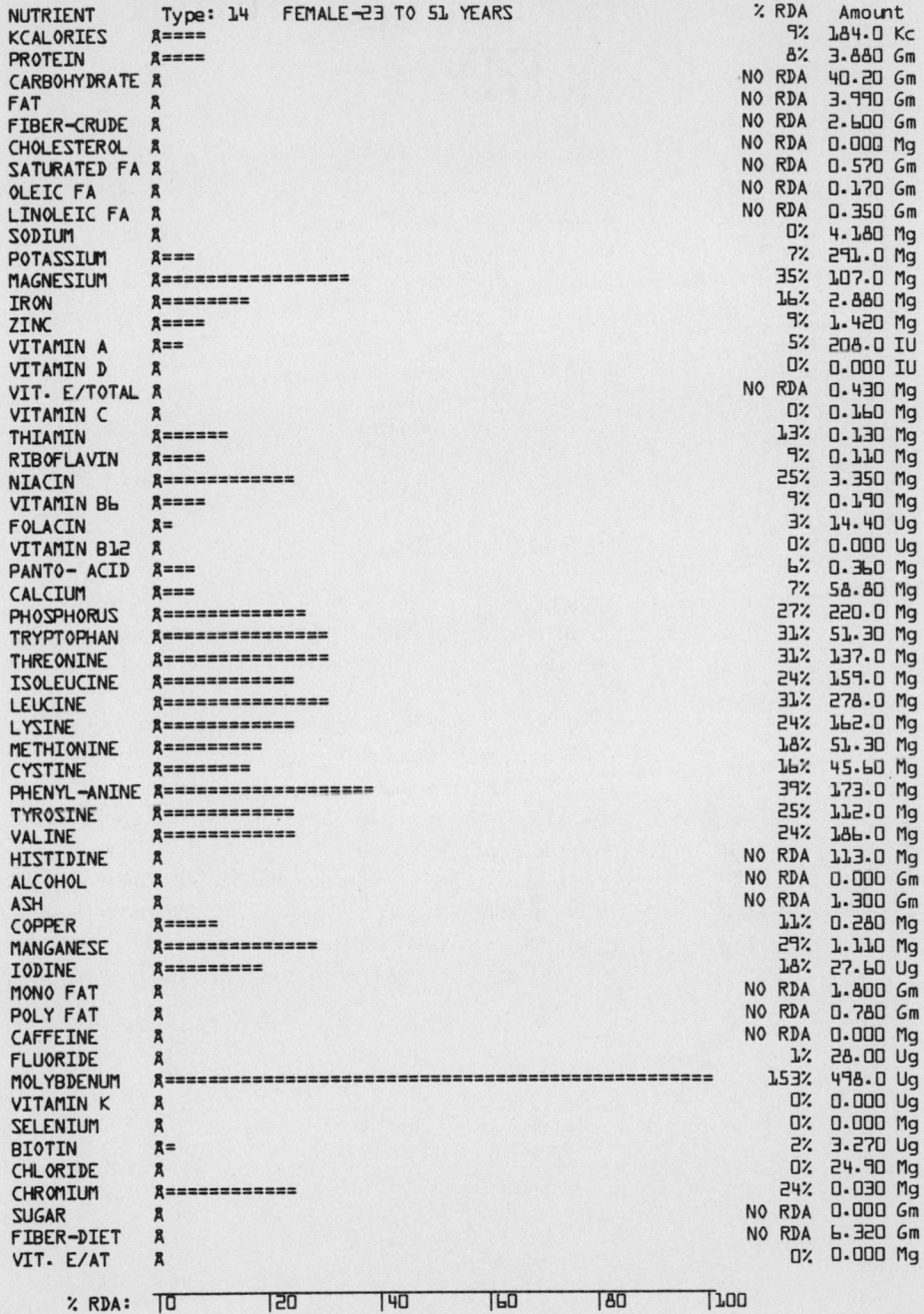

| NUTRIENT | Type: 14   FEMALE-23 TO 51 YEARS | % RDA | Amount |
|---|---|---|---|
| KCALORIES | A==== | 9% | 184.0 Kc |
| PROTEIN | A==== | 8% | 3.880 Gm |
| CARBOHYDRATE | A | NO RDA | 40.20 Gm |
| FAT | A | NO RDA | 3.990 Gm |
| FIBER-CRUDE | A | NO RDA | 2.600 Gm |
| CHOLESTEROL | A | NO RDA | 0.000 Mg |
| SATURATED FA | A | NO RDA | 0.570 Gm |
| OLEIC FA | A | NO RDA | 0.170 Gm |
| LINOLEIC FA | A | NO RDA | 0.350 Gm |
| SODIUM | A | 0% | 4.180 Mg |
| POTASSIUM | A=== | 7% | 291.0 Mg |
| MAGNESIUM | A================== | 35% | 107.0 Mg |
| IRON | A======== | 16% | 2.880 Mg |
| ZINC | A==== | 9% | 1.420 Mg |
| VITAMIN A | A== | 5% | 208.0 IU |
| VITAMIN D | A | 0% | 0.000 IU |
| VIT. E/TOTAL | A | NO RDA | 0.430 Mg |
| VITAMIN C | A | 0% | 0.160 Mg |
| THIAMIN | A====== | 13% | 0.130 Mg |
| RIBOFLAVIN | A==== | 9% | 0.110 Mg |
| NIACIN | A============ | 25% | 3.350 Mg |
| VITAMIN B6 | A==== | 9% | 0.190 Mg |
| FOLACIN | A= | 3% | 14.40 Ug |
| VITAMIN B12 | A | 0% | 0.000 Ug |
| PANTO- ACID | A=== | 6% | 0.360 Mg |
| CALCIUM | A=== | 7% | 58.80 Mg |
| PHOSPHORUS | A============= | 27% | 220.0 Mg |
| TRYPTOPHAN | A=============== | 31% | 51.30 Mg |
| THREONINE | A=============== | 31% | 137.0 Mg |
| ISOLEUCINE | A============ | 24% | 159.0 Mg |
| LEUCINE | A================ | 31% | 278.0 Mg |
| LYSINE | A============ | 24% | 162.0 Mg |
| METHIONINE | A========= | 18% | 51.30 Mg |
| CYSTINE | A======== | 16% | 45.60 Mg |
| PHENYL-ANINE | A================== | 39% | 173.0 Mg |
| TYROSINE | A============ | 25% | 112.0 Mg |
| VALINE | A============ | 24% | 186.0 Mg |
| HISTIDINE | A | NO RDA | 113.0 Mg |
| ALCOHOL | A | NO RDA | 0.000 Gm |
| ASH | A | NO RDA | 1.300 Gm |
| COPPER | A===== | 11% | 0.280 Mg |
| MANGANESE | A============== | 29% | 1.110 Mg |
| IODINE | A========= | 18% | 27.60 Ug |
| MONO FAT | A | NO RDA | 1.800 Gm |
| POLY FAT | A | NO RDA | 0.780 Gm |
| CAFFEINE | A | NO RDA | 0.000 Mg |
| FLUORIDE | A | 1% | 28.00 Ug |
| MOLYBDENUM | A==================================================== | 153% | 498.0 Ug |
| VITAMIN K | A | 0% | 0.000 Ug |
| SELENIUM | A | 0% | 0.000 Mg |
| BIOTIN | A= | 2% | 3.270 Ug |
| CHLORIDE | A | 0% | 24.90 Mg |
| CHROMIUM | A============ | 24% | 0.030 Mg |
| SUGAR | A | NO RDA | 0.000 Gm |
| FIBER-DIET | A | NO RDA | 6.320 Gm |
| VIT. E/AT | A | 0% | 0.000 Mg |

```
    % RDA:  |0      |20      |40      |60      |80      |100
```

Optional chia seeds included in analysis for Bran "Nuts."

# BRANOLA BREAKFAST MUFFINS

☆ A muffin to serve for breakfast or as a dessert.

¾ cup Branola or Bran "Nuts"
1½ cups cultured buttermilk

2 cups whole wheat flour
1½ tsp. baking soda
1½ tsp. baking powder

⅓ cup margarine or butter
⅓ cup yogurt
2 Tbsp. honey

1 cup diced, pitted dates

Preheat oven to 400 degrees.

Mix first 2 ingredients together and allow to sit while assembling the rest of the ingredients (should only take about 5 minutes).

Sift next 3 ingredients together in a separate bowl.

Cream next 3 ingredients together in another bowl. When smooth, add dry ingredients and mix till dry lumps are gone. Fold in the bran (which was left soaking in buttermilk) along with the diced, pitted dates.

Spoon into oiled or paper cup-lined muffin tins, being sure to fill only halfway. Bake at 400 degrees for 20 minutes or till a toothpick inserted in middle comes out clean. Makes 1 dozen standard-sized muffins and about 6 giant-sized ones.

One large-size bran muffin will provide about a tablespoon of bran.

| SHOPPING LIST | |
|---|---|
| **Regularly Kept in the Kitchen** (Listed in Chapter 14, p. 703) | **Fresh Produce** |
| Cultured buttermilk Whole wheat flour Baking soda Baking powder Butter or margarine Honey Yogurt Pitted dates | (None) |
| Also see shopping list for Bran "Nuts" or Branola. | |

# NUTRITIONAL ANALYSIS FOR ONE
# LARGE BRANOLA BREAKFAST MUFFIN

| NUTRIENT | Type: 14   FEMALE-23 TO 51 YEARS | % RDA | Amount |
|----------|----------------------------------|-------|--------|
| KCALORIES | Ã========== | 20% | 413.0 Kc |
| PROTEIN | Ã=========== | 22% | 10.10 Gm |
| CARBOHYDRATE | Ã | NO RDA | 70.10 Gm |
| FAT | Ã | NO RDA | 13.10 Gm |
| FIBER-CRUDE | Ã | NO RDA | 2.460 Gm |
| CHOLESTEROL | Ã | NO RDA | 3.010 Mg |
| SATURATED FA | Ã | NO RDA | 2.430 Gm |
| OLEIC FA | Ã | NO RDA | 0.350 Gm |
| LINOLEIC FA | Ã | NO RDA | 0.540 Gm |
| SODIUM | Ã=========== | 23% | 507.0 Mg |
| POTASSIUM | Ã======= | 15% | 580.0 Mg |
| MAGNESIUM | Ã================= | 34% | 104.0 Mg |
| IRON | Ã======= | 15% | 2.730 Mg |
| ZINC | Ã====== | 12% | 1.930 Mg |
| VITAMIN A | Ã====== | 13% | 537.0 IU |
| VITAMIN D | Ã | 0% | 0.000 IU |
| VIT. E/TOTAL | Ã | NO RDA | 1.980 Mg |
| VITAMIN C | Ã | 1% | 0.770 Mg |
| THIAMIN | Ã================ | 32% | 0.320 Mg |
| RIBOFLAVIN | Ã========= | 19% | 0.230 Mg |
| NIACIN | Ã============== | 28% | 3.650 Mg |
| VITAMIN B6 | Ã======= | 14% | 0.280 Mg |
| FOLACIN | Ã==== | 8% | 32.10 Ug |
| VITAMIN B12 | Ã=== | 7% | 0.210 Ug |
| PANTO- ACID | Ã========== | 20% | 1.150 Mg |
| CALCIUM | Ã============ | 25% | 205.0 Mg |
| PHOSPHORUS | Ã========================= | 50% | 407.0 Mg |
| TRYPTOPHAN | Ã====================================== | 77% | 126.0 Mg |
| THREONINE | Ã======================================== | 80% | 348.0 Mg |
| ISOLEUCINE | Ã==================================== | 72% | 471.0 Mg |
| LEUCINE | Ã============================================ | 87% | 765.0 Mg |
| LYSINE | Ã=================================== | 70% | 461.0 Mg |
| METHIONINE | Ã===============================•==== | 65% | 178.0 Mg |
| CYSTINE | Ã============================== | 61% | 166.0 Mg |
| PHENYL-ANINE | Ã========================================================= | 112% | 491.0 Mg |
| TYROSINE | Ã===========================•================== | 85% | 372.0 Mg |
| VALINE | Ã=================================== | 71% | 546.0 Mg |
| HISTIDINE | Ã | NO RDA | 236.0 Mg |
| ALCOHOL | Ã | NO RDA | 0.000 Gm |
| ASH | Ã | NO RDA | 2.460 Gm |
| COPPER | Ã======= | 15% | 0.390 Mg |
| MANGANESE | Ã================================ | 65% | 2.460 Mg |
| IODINE | Ã================================================= | 138% | 208.0 Ug |
| MONO FAT | Ã | NO RDA | 5.580 Gm |
| POLY FAT | Ã | NO RDA | 3.560 Gm |
| CAFFEINE | Ã | NO RDA | 0.000 Mg |
| FLUORIDE | Ã | 1% | 30.60 Ug |
| MOLYBDENUM | Ã================================================ | 795% | 2586 Ug |
| VITAMIN K | Ã= | 3% | 3.550 Ug |
| SELENIUM | Ã==== | 8% | 0.010 Mg |
| BIOTIN | Ã= | 3% | 4.610 Ug |
| CHLORIDE | Ã= | 2% | 85.10 Mg |
| CHROMIUM | Ã================================================= | 200% | 0.250 Mg |
| SUGAR | Ã | NO RDA | 19.50 Gm |
| FIBER-DIET | Ã | NO RDA | 9.930 Gm |
| VIT. E/AT | Ã== | 4% | 0.320 Mg |

```
% RDA:  |0      |20     |40     |60     |80     |100
```

Branola used instead of Bran "Nuts"; margarine used instead of butter in analysis.

Some people find bran a little rough to digest. Another food you can try that will clean the body out is psyllium seeds. I like to use psyllium seeds ground to a powder because they can easily be made into palatable puddings. The puddings can either be fruit- or fruit juice-based. See the recipes for general ideas, and don't be afraid to make flavor and fruit combinations of your choice!

# BERRY-SILLY PUDDING

*2 cups chopped, pitted cherries (and/or*
*berries in season) and their juice*
*2 Tbsp. psyllium seed powder*
*¼ cup honey*
*1 tsp. almond extract*
*1 tsp. lemon juice*

Mix all ingredients together thoroughly. Let sit in refrigerator 25 to 30 minutes before serving to allow psyllium seed powder to expand and jell. Serve in individual dessert cups as a pudding or use to make parfaits.

To make parfaits, pour a layer of Berry-Silly Pudding into a dessert or parfait cup. Sprinkle with Bran "Nuts" or toasted, sliced almonds to cover the entire surface of this layer. Then top with a layer of vanilla yogurt and another thin layer of Branola. Repeat whole order of layering once more, leaving top layer of yogurt plain. Garnish with mint leaf and one whole cherry. Refrigerate till serving time.

As a pudding, makes four ½-cup servings; as a parfait, makes 8 servings.

| Special Shopping |
|---|
| Psyllium seed powder — found in natural food stores. Be sure to get the ground whole seeds and not the ground husks. |

| SHOPPING LIST | |
|---|---|
| **Regularly Kept in the Kitchen** (Listed in Chapter 14, p. 703) | **Fresh Produce** |
| Honey<br>Almond extract | Cherries<br>Lemon |

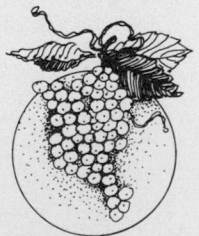

# JUICE-BASED PSYLLIUM SEED PUDDING

*2 cups fresh or bottled, unsweetened fruit juice*
*Few pieces fresh fruit in season*
*3 Tbsp. psyllium seed powder*

Blend ingredients together in blender till psyllium seed powder is thoroughly mixed in. Pour from blender into salad mold or individual bowls and refrigerate a few hours before serving.

# KEIKIS* IN THE KITCHEN

Why does the United Nations exist? Because amidst all the strife and havoc in this world, everyone would really like to establish world peace and brotherhood. Real brotherhood isn't possible unless there is a common father. On the bodily level, each of us has a different father, so real brotherhood is only possible if we are able to look past all our external bodily differences and understand that each and every one of us is a child of the Supreme Father. That's why in the Bible, John states, "If a man says, 'I love God' and hateth his brother, he is a liar."

Allowing your offspring to join you in the kitchen to help cook at your side can make a little more mess than would be made if it was just you in the kitchen, but it's certainly worth the little bit of extra clean-up. Giving a child the opportunity to make, or assist in making, his own snacks and meals from a very early age develops more than just the ability to cook. Cooking can get anyone's creative juices flowing and also reward the child cook (as well as the adult) with the satisfaction of having completed a project. The parent and child cooking together, helping one another, gives both valuable time together to be relating and interacting.

While cooking, there's plenty of time to talk about why people can't live on soda and candy, what foods are healthy or not, where foods come from, etc. Since everyone has to eat, and what is eaten affects each person's health, knowing what foods are healthy and how to prepare them is important for everyone to learn. Hopefully, laying a good foundation like this in early childhood will lead to a lifetime of healthy eating.

*Keikis is Hawaiian for *children*.

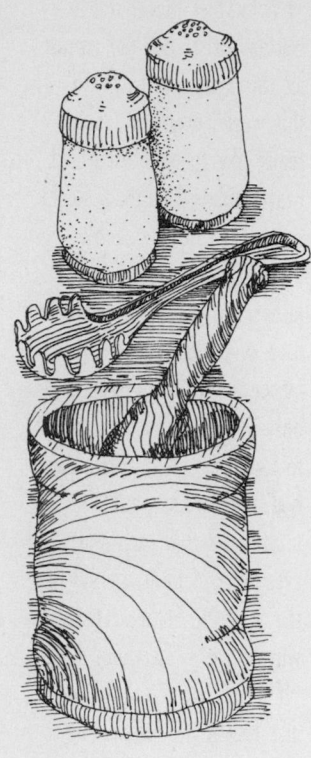

Having children in the kitchen means both the adult and child must learn to think about safety. Safety rules and the amount of supervision a child needs is really a commonsense matter and will vary from child to child according to their ability. Some parents may be shocked to read this, but I don't really think there's any way a child can be in the kitchen regularly and not burn or cut a finger. Maybe it's because as an adult I still do these things. Little hurts like this can help a young child learn what you're talking about when you say, "Don't touch that — it'll burn" or "Don't use this or stick your hand in that because it'll cut your fingers off." One or two small hurts really do teach a child to be careful. I try to supervise in the kitchen to avoid major injuries or disasters and also to avoid disease by teaching cleanliness. For example —

• Teach children not to wear clothes that will catch on fire easily while cooking; for little girls, tie hair back.
• I've never allowed young children to deep-fry or even to pull up a chair to stand by and watch deep-frying.
• Very small children aren't allowed to run electrical appliances by themselves until they're old enough to understand and follow the rules — like not to touch electrical appliances with wet hands, not to stick fingers or utensils in them while motor is running, etc.
• Any knife sharper than a butter knife isn't allowed until the child has the coordination to handle one. To go along with this, only give children using butter knives very soft things to cut.
• For cleanliness, always wash hands before coming into the kitchen, and no eating or licking fingers, hands or stirring utensils.

These few basics and any other rules you feel necessary can help to make your child's time in the kitchen a safe, happy learning experience. Here are some of our children's favorite recipes and some of their thoughts on food.

I'm often asked if our children ever feel tempted to eat meat, etc., or feel deprived because we've never fed them certain foods. As can be seen from their own words, meat has never been a temptation because our reasons for not eating meat go beyond just the well-being of our own bodies. I must admit that from time to time the older three eat something with sugar in it at friends' houses, but they are always sure to read labels to be sure they're not consuming foods that they feel are more important to avoid. Even the babies, who can't read yet, know the importance of reading labels and always ask me to read them labels in stores or if people give them food.

# CANDIED SWEET POTATOES

☆ A good vegetable side dish — but my children love it as a dessert, especially when it's baked in a bun!

---

4 cups (approximately) 1" chunks of sweet potato

2 Tbsp. butter or margarine
¼ cup honey
¼ cup Barbados molasses
1 Tbsp. lemon juice
⅛ tsp. finely grated lemon rind
1 tsp. vanilla

Steam sweet potato chunks till they can be poked with a fork; be careful not to over-cook so they crumble and break apart easily when touched. Turn off heat. In a small pot, combine last 6 ingredients and bring to a gentle boil over medium heat. Cook 2 to 3 minutes till mixture almost reaches the soft-ball stage (when dripped in cold water, drops will form soft balls). Pour steamed sweet potato pieces into sauce and gently mix in, trying to avoid cutting or breaking up the chunks. Cover and simmer over low heat for about 5 minutes. Remove cover and simmer another 5 to 10 minutes, stirring gently every now and then. Makes about 4 servings.

To make stuffed buns that can be served for dessert, mix ½ cup chopped, pitted dates, ¼ cup toasted pecans and ¼ cup macaroon coconut into Candied Sweet Potatoes and form buns as directed in Hot and Sweet Bun Filling.

| SHOPPING LIST | |
|---|---|
| Regularly Kept in the Kitchen (Listed in Chapter 14, p. 703) | Fresh Produce |
| Butter or margarine<br>Honey<br>Barbados molasses<br>Vanilla | Sweet potatoes<br>Lemon |

# BASIC BREAD DOUGH
from Kathy Cooks . . . Naturally (KCN), p. 31

1 Tbsp bulk dry yeast or 1 envelope Fleischmann's, etc.
1¼ cups warm water

1 Tbsp. oil
¼ cup honey
⅓ tsp. salt

3 cups whole wheat flour
½ tsp. baking powder

Put yeast in warm water and let sit a few minutes till it dissolves. Add next 3 ingredients. Sift in dry ingredients and mix well. Turn dough onto floured counter and knead till it forms a soft, firm ball. Shape dough into desired shapes, put on oiled baking sheet or bread pan and set in oven on warm or pilot light for 10 minutes. Leaving bread in oven, turn up to 400 degrees and bake for 20 to 25 minutes. Test to see if it's done by tapping with fingernail, listening for a hollow sound.

As the name of the recipe indicates, this is a good basic bread that can be used in a number of different ways. One thing that can be done with it is to make stuffed buns as directed in the Hot and Sweet Bun Filling recipe. Some other fillings to try —
• Leftover stir-fried tofu and vegetables.
• Leftover steamed vegetables with fresh herbs and Swiss cheese.
• Leftover pizza toppings and sauce.
• Any flavorful wet vegetable dish like Creamy Curry (p. 44), Palak Tofu-Paneer (p. 589) or Eggplant Supreme Curry (p. 586).
• Tofu Cream Cheese (p. 169) spread ½" to ¾" thick, topped with fresh tomato slices and minced, fresh basil.
• For dessert, your favorite pie filling.

Besides making stuffed buns, you might try using the Basic Bread Dough for making —
- Loaves of bread (KCN, p. 31).
- Crescent rolls, like in KCN (p. 311).
- Cinnamon Rolls, (KCN p. 433).
- Pinwheels cooked in different fruit sauces, like Plum Pinwheels (KCN, p. 224).

Hi, I'm Kathy's 10-year-old son. I'm in fairly good shape — my friend and I were the only two kids who were able to complete the Marine Commando Crawl out of a lot of kids from different schools — and I didn't have to chew on an animal's muscle to get in shape. I have never craved to eat meat although my friends try to persuade me to. They say things like, "How can you survive without eating meat?" Some of my friends' parents say that anyone who doesn't eat meat is a fanatic. They are the fanatics because they keep believing when the facts go against eating meat. Most people say you need meat to have muscles. Well, they're wrong. If you could see the body of one of my friends, you'd be able to see the benefit of eating meat on his muscles: there is none. He's all skin and bones. I personally don't think animals were placed on the earth to be slaughtered, sold, cooked and eaten. I think animals were put on earth to be watched over, taken care of and not to be eaten.

— Madhava, age 10 (1986)

# HOT AND SWEET BUN FILLING

2 Tbsp. butter or margarine
1½ cups finely diced onion
1½ cups finely diced bell pepper
1 cup finely diced celery
¼ cup finely diced jalapeno peppers
4 bay leaves
1 Tbsp. oregano
1 tsp. ground cumin
1 tsp. asafetida or garlic powder
1 tsp. thyme
½ tsp. cayenne
½ tsp. black pepper
½ tsp. white pepper

1 lb. tempeh, crumbled
1 cup vegetable broth or 1 vegetable bouillon
   cube dissolved in 1 cup water
1 Tbsp. soy sauce

1 recipe Candied Sweet Potatoes

Combine first 13 ingredients in a small skillet over high heat and cook for 5 minutes, stirring constantly to prevent sticking and burning on bottom of skillet. Mix in next 3 ingredients thoroughly, cover and simmer over low heat for about 10 minutes, stirring occasionally to keep from sticking and burning. Turn off heat and gently fold in Candied Sweet Potatoes.

Use this filling to stuff Basic Bread recipe by breaking bread dough into ½-cup-sized balls. Oil hands and baking tray, flatten dough out in palm of hand so it's ¼" thick. Scoop ½ cup of filling into center of dough and bring edges of dough up and over filling. Pinch dough together so filling is completely encased in dough. Place pinched side down on oiled cookie sheet, or place on a small square of wax paper and then into a steamer. Cook by baking at 350 degrees for 20 to 25 minutes, or steam for 30 to 45 minutes. Makes 6 filled buns. This is delicious served as an entree topped with Hot Cajun Sauce. It also makes a handy dish to pack in a portable lunch. This filling is probably too hot for the tastes of young children, but delicious portable buns can be made for children's school lunches by using more suitable fillings (see note, p. 692).

# HOT CAJUN SAUCE

☆  A sauce for those who like it hot!

2 Tbsp. butter or margarine
¼ cup whole wheat flour

½ tsp. cayenne
½ tsp. white pepper
½ tsp. black pepper
½ tsp. asafetida or garlic powder
¾ cup finely diced celery
½ cup finely diced bell pepper
¼ cup finely diced onion
¼ cup finely chopped jalapeno peppers
3 bay leaves

3 cups water
1 Tbsp. Vegex Bouillon Extract

Toast first 2 ingredients in a small skillet, stirring constantly till flour begins to brown and the aroma of toasted flour can be smelled. Add next 9 ingredients and cook over medium flame for 2 to 3 minutes, stirring constantly. Remove from heat and mix into last 2 ingredients till flour "dissolves." Put over heat and stir constantly till mixture comes to a boil and thickens; lower heat and simmer about 10 minutes.

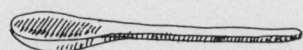

## Special Shopping

Vegex Bouillon Extract — found in natural food stores. I prefer the bouillon extract to the Vegex bouillon cubes, as the cubes have sugar in them! Just goes to show, label-reading is a good habit to get into no matter where you shop!

## SHOPPING LIST

| Regularly Kept in the Kitchen (Listed in Chapter 14, p. 703) | Fresh Produce |
| --- | --- |
| Butter or margarine<br>Whole wheat flour<br>Cayenne<br>White and black pepper<br>Asafetida<br>Bay leaves | Celery<br>Bell pepper<br>Onion<br>Jalapeno peppers |

# NUTRITIONAL ANALYSIS FOR ONE BUN
## (made from Basic Bread Dough)
## WITH HOT AND SWEET BUN FILLING AND HOT CAJUN SAUCE

```
NUTRIENT      Type: 14   FEMALE-23 TO 51 YEARS                    % RDA   Amount
KCALORIES     A===================                                 38%   763.0 Kc
PROTEIN       A===============================                     62%   27.40 Gm
CARBOHYDRATE  A                                                  NO RDA  124.0 Gm
FAT           A                                                  NO RDA  21.20 Gm
FIBER-CRUDE   A                                                  NO RDA  6.120 Gm
CHOLESTEROL   A                                                  NO RDA  0.000 Mg
SATURATED FA  A                                                  NO RDA  3.310 Gm
OLEIC FA      A                                                  NO RDA  1.650 Gm
LINOLEIC FA   A                                                  NO RDA  5.280 Gm
SODIUM        A==================                                  36%   807.0 Mg
POTASSIUM     A=================                                   35%   1339 Mg
MAGNESIUM     A============================                        56%   170.0 Mg
IRON          A=====================                               43%   7.760 Mg
ZINC          A============                                        24%   3.660 Mg
VITAMIN A     A=======================================================  536%  21465 IU
VITAMIN D     A                                                    0%   0.000 IU
VIT. E/TOTAL  A                                                  NO RDA  8.920 Mg
VITAMIN C     A=====================================================  123%  74.10 Mg
THIAMIN       A================================                    64%   0.640 Mg
RIBOFLAVIN    A=================                                   35%   0.420 Mg
NIACIN        A==============================                      62%   8.180 Mg
VITAMIN B6    A=====================                               43%   0.870 Mg
FOLACIN       A====================                                40%   163.0 Ug
VITAMIN B12   A=======                                             15%   0.460 Ug
PANTO- ACID   A===================                                 39%   2.170 Mg
CALCIUM       A==============                                      29%   232.0 Mg
PHOSPHORUS    A==================================                  69%   555.0 Mg
TRYPTOPHAN    A==================================================  220%  359.0 Mg
THREONINE     A==================================================  220%  958.0 Mg
ISOLEUCINE    A==================================================  194%  1268 Mg
LEUCINE       A==================================================  231%  2013 Mg
LYSINE        A==================================================  190%  1241 Mg
METHIONINE    A==================================================  143%  389.0 Mg
CYSTINE       A==================================================  171%  466.0 Mg
PHENYL-ANINE  A==================================================  306%  1333 Mg
TYROSINE      A==================================================  225%  980.0 Mg
VALINE        A==================================================  170%  1302 Mg
HISTIDINE     A                                                  NO RDA  611.0 Mg
ALCOHOL       A                                                  NO RDA  0.000 Gm
ASH           A                                                  NO RDA  5.060 Gm
COPPER        A=========================                           50%   1.270 Mg
MANGANESE     A=================================================   135%  5.070 Mg
IODINE        A=================================================   404%  606.0 Ug
MONO FAT      A                                                  NO RDA  6.940 Gm
POLY FAT      A                                                  NO RDA  8.980 Gm
CAFFEINE      A                                                  NO RDA  0.000 Mg
FLUORIDE      A=                                                   2%   62.60 Ug
MOLYBDENUM    A=================================================  1525%  4958 Ug
VITAMIN K     A                                                    0%   0.000 Ug
SELENIUM      A====================                                40%   0.050 Mg
BIOTIN        A=======                                             15%   23.80 Ug
CHLORIDE      A===                                                 7%   255.0 Mg
CHROMIUM      A=================================================   568%  0.710 Mg
SUGAR         A                                                  NO RDA  8.200 Gm
FIBER-DIET    A                                                  NO RDA  23.70 Gm
VIT. E/AT     A====================================                73%   5.910 Mg

   % RDA:    |0      |20     |40     |60     |80     |100
```

Margarine used instead of butter in analysis.

Many of my friends are "Christians" that go to church on Sunday, but they must not read the Bible a whole lot. Quite often they ask me why I don't eat meat, and once I told them that I didn't eat meat because it hurt the animals. To that they said, "That's what they're here for. God made them for us to eat." According to what they say, the Bible is either misquoting God or has been altered over the years. I think it's really that they don't read the Bible, because if they did they would have seen this quote: "And God said, 'Behold, I have given you every herb-bearing seed which is upon the earth, and every tree in which is the fruit of a tree-yielding seed; to you it shall be for meat.' " How could they miss it — it's only on the first page?!
— Valmiki, age 13 (1986)

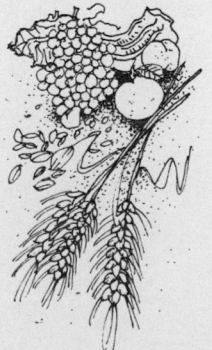

# QUICK VEGIE STEW

☆ A wet stew that Valmiki has made on his own since he was about 8 years old — that's how easy it is to make!

1 qt. sugarless commercial spaghetti sauce
   or tomato sauce

1 lb. tofu, cubed
4 cups ½" -¾" diced zucchini
1 bell pepper, diced
2 cups broken string beans
½ lb. mushrooms, split

½ lb. cheese, grated

Turn medium heat on under large pot with your favorite sugarless spaghetti or tomato sauce in it and leave on as you cut and add next 5 ingredients (should take about 5 minutes). When all vegetables are added, cover and simmer 10 to 15 minutes till sauce begins to boil. Gently stir in grated cheese or sprinkle on surface of vegetables. Cover and cook just till cheese melts.

Delicious served on top of whole grain pastas, brown rice or whole grain toast. Makes 6 to 8 servings.

This can be packed in a thermos to be taken in a lunch bag. Since it's rather soupy, I like to stir a few tablespoons of a raw whole grain into boiling hot stew in the thermos (leave an inch or two from the top for expansion), cover and pack. By the time you're ready for lunch, the grain will be cooked (that is, provided at least an hour will pass between the time you pack the thermos and the time you'll eat its contents)! Any whole grain can be cooked in a thermos in this way, with the addition of any boiling soup, wet stew, or just plain water! Don't forget: thermoses can also be used to keep dishes cold (like smoothies, yogurt, etc.).

| SHOPPING LIST | |
|---|---|
| Regularly Kept in the Kitchen (Listed in Chapter 14, p. 703) | Fresh Produce |
| Sugarless spaghetti sauce<br>Tofu<br>Cheese | Zucchini<br>Bell pepper<br>String beans<br>Mushrooms |

# NUTRITIONAL ANALYSIS FOR ONE SERVING QUICK VEGIE STEW

```
NUTRIENT        Type: 14    FEMALE-23 TO 51 YEARS              % RDA   Amount
KCALORIES       A========                                      15%    303.0 Kc
PROTEIN         A================================             60%    26.40 Gm
CARBOHYDRATE    A                                            NO RDA   23.80 Gm
FAT             A                                            NO RDA   13.00 Gm
FIBER-CRUDE     A                                            NO RDA   1.320 Gm
CHOLESTEROL     A                                            NO RDA   21.60 Mg
SATURATED FA    A                                            NO RDA   4.890 Gm
OLEIC FA        A                                            NO RDA   2.370 Gm
LINOLEIC FA     A                                            NO RDA   1.640 Gm
SODIUM          A=====                                         10%    237.0 Mg
POTASSIUM       A=========                                     17%    666.0 Mg
MAGNESIUM       A===============                               28%    86.90 Mg
IRON            A==========================                    51%    9.360 Mg
ZINC            A==========                                    18%    2.700 Mg
VITAMIN A       A============                                  23%    954.0 IU
VITAMIN D       A                                              0%     0.000 IU
VIT. E/TOTAL    A                                            NO RDA   0.110 Mg
VITAMIN C       A==========================                    51%    31.00 Mg
THIAMIN         A=============                                 26%    0.260 Mg
RIBOFLAVIN      A==================                            35%    0.430 Mg
NIACIN          A==========                                    19%    2.570 Mg
VITAMIN B6      A======                                        12%    0.250 Mg
FOLACIN         A=========                                     16%    67.40 Ug
VITAMIN B12     A=====                                         10%    0.310 Ug
PANTO- ACID     A=========                                     19%    1.070 Mg
CALCIUM         A==================================================   99%    793.0 Mg
PHOSPHORUS      A=========================                     50%    403.0 Mg
TRYPTOPHAN      A================================================   134%    220.0 Mg
THREONINE       A================================================   214%    932.0 Mg
ISOLEUCINE      A================================================   173%   1132 Mg
LEUCINE         A================================================   225%   1965 Mg
LYSINE          A================================================   291%   1901 Mg
METHIONINE      A================================================   165%    451.0 Mg
CYSTINE         A=============================================     88%    241.0 Mg
PHENYL-ANINE    A================================================   266%   1160 Mg
TYROSINE        A================================================   227%    991.0 Mg
VALINE          A================================================   170%   1303 Mg
HISTIDINE       A                                            NO RDA   755.0 Mg
ALCOHOL         A                                            NO RDA   0.000 Gm
ASH             A                                            NO RDA   3.410 Gm
COPPER          A========                                      16%    0.420 Mg
MANGANESE       A===============                               29%    1.100 Mg
IODINE          A==========================================    85%    128.0 Ug
MONO FAT        A                                            NO RDA   3.200 Gm
POLY FAT        A                                            NO RDA   4.060 Gm
CAFFEINE        A                                            NO RDA   0.000 Mg
FLUORIDE        A                                              1%     33.20 Ug
MOLYBDENUM      A================================================   408%   1329 Ug
VITAMIN K       A                                              0%     0.000 Ug
SELENIUM        A====                                          8%     0.010 Mg
BIOTIN          A                                              1%     2.790 Ug
CHLORIDE        A==                                            4%     143.0 Mg
CHROMIUM        A================================================   192%   0.240 Mg
SUGAR           A                                            NO RDA   2.250 Gm
FIBER-DIET      A                                            NO RDA   0.560 Gm
VIT. E/AT       A==                                            5%     0.450 Mg

    % RDA:    |0      |20     |40     |60     |80     |100
```

Tomato sauce used instead of commercial spaghetti sauce in analysis.

Meat is a food for fools. The only people who eat meat are those who have nothing better to do than spend money for the pain and suffering of other living creatures. I've been a vegetarian all my life and have no craving to eat a dead animal — to tear apart somebody's flesh. The popular band "The Smiths" sing a song stressing that killing animals for the pleasure of our palates is just pure murder . . . This expresses very well how I feel about eating meat.

— Chibiabos, age 17 (1986)

MEAT IS MURDER
Heifer whines could be
human cries,
closer comes the screaming knife.
This beautiful creature must die.
This beautiful creature must die.
A death for no reason,
and death for no reason is
MURDER.
And the flesh you so fancifully fry
is not succulent, tasty or kind.
It's death for no reason,
and death for no reason is
MURDER.
And the calf that you carve
with a smile is MURDER,
and the turkey you festively slice
is MURDER.
Do you know how animals die?
Kitchen aromas
aren't very homey.
It's not comforting,
cheery or kind.
It's sizzling blood
and the unholy stench of
MURDER.
It's not "natural," "normal"
or kind.
The flesh you so fancifully fry,
the meat in your mouth as you
savor the flavor of MURDER.
No, no, no, it's MURDER.
No, no, no, it's MURDER.
Who hears when animals cry?

---

### Special Shopping

Bragg's Liquid Aminos — found in natural food stores; resembles soy sauce in flavor but doesn't taste as salty.

# ONE OF CHIBI'S RICE DISHES

☆ My oldest son, 17-year-old Chibiabos, is easy to please (at least when it comes to eating!). He's happy as long as there's a pot of rice. He'll eat it for breakfast, lunch and dinner — a taste he acquired on a visit to the Philippines. He fixes rice in many different ways. This is a favorite which is simple and quick.

---

2 Tbsp. butter, margarine or olive oil
3½ cups cooked, leftover brown rice

¼ cup Bragg's Liquid Aminos or 1 Tbsp. soy sauce
¼ cup nutritional yeast

½ avocado, diced

Saute first 2 ingredients together till rice is warmed, but don't fry so long that the rice begins to crisp. Add next 2 ingredients to rice and mix in thoroughly. Remove from heat and gently toss in avocado. Makes 1 Chibiabos-sized serving or 2 to 3 servings for anyone else.

| SHOPPING LIST | |
|---|---|
| Regularly Kept in the Kitchen (Listed in Chapter 14, p. 703) | Fresh Produce |
| Butter or margarine<br>Brown rice<br>Nutritional yeast | Avocado |

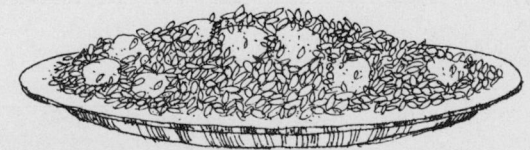

# FRESH JOHN'S FUDGE

☆ We named this light, fresh fudge after two people
named John whom we can thank for knowledge of two
of the ingredients: Johnny Appleseed for the apples
and St. John the Baptist for the carob. The stories of
both of these men's lives are inspirational ones to tell
children too!

---

*1 cup ground or finely chopped, moist dates*
*1 cup coarsely grated sweet apple*
*½ cup carob powder*
*½ cup raw cashew or almond butter*

*¼ cup noninstant, nonfat milk powder (optional)*

*Nut meal*

Combine first 4 ingredients (and noninstant milk powder
if you want to use it — it'll make the candy a little firmer);
mix and knead thoroughly. Oil clean hands and roll into balls
(or other shapes), roll in nut meal and set on platter. Makes
about 2½ cups of batter.

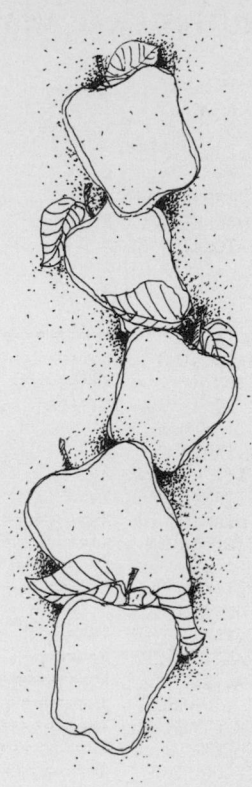

| SHOPPING LIST | |
|---|---|
| **Regularly Kept in the Kitchen** (Listed in Chapter 14, p. 703) | **Fresh Produce** |
| Dates<br>Carob<br>Raw cashew or almond butter<br>Noninstant, nonfat milk powder<br>Nuts | Apple |

Since three-year-old Chintamani
can cut (with a butter knife),
put things in pots, help to stir,
measure, etc., this is a recipe
she can make almost all by herself. She has learned to grate
carefully so she won't nick her
fingers in the process. I usually
help her a bit with measuring
and she makes the little candy
shapes — except when she's
lazy. Then she just scoops it
into a bowl with a spoon.

# NUTRITIONAL ANALYSIS FOR ONE SERVING FRESH JOHN'S FUDGE

```
NUTRIENT        Type: 14    FEMALE-23 TO 51 YEARS              % RDA    Amount
KCALORIES       A=========                                     17%     356.0 Kc
PROTEIN         A===============                               29%     13.10 Gm
CARBOHYDRATE    A                                              NO RDA   52.80 Gm
FAT             A                                              NO RDA   15.40 Gm
FIBER-CRUDE     A                                              NO RDA   2.190 Gm
CHOLESTEROL     A                                              NO RDA   1.200 Mg
SATURATED FA    A                                              NO RDA   2.780 Gm
OLEIC FA        A                                              NO RDA   0.030 Gm
LINOLEIC FA     A                                              NO RDA   0.010 Gm
SODIUM          A                                              1%      41.00 Mg
POTASSIUM       A==========                                    20%     778.0 Mg
MAGNESIUM       A===============                               30%     91.30 Mg
IRON            A=========                                     17%     3.190 Mg
ZINC            A=====                                         11%     1.770 Mg
VITAMIN A       A                                              0%      33.50 IU
VITAMIN D       A                                              0%      0.000 IU
VIT. E/TOTAL    A                                              NO RDA   0.230 Mg
VITAMIN C       A=                                             2%      1.700 Mg
THIAMIN         A=========                                     18%     0.180 Mg
RIBOFLAVIN      A==================                            37%     0.450 Mg
NIACIN          A=========                                     17%     2.300 Mg
VITAMIN B6      A=====                                         10%     0.200 Mg
FOLACIN         A===                                           7%      28.50 Ug
VITAMIN B12     A====                                          8%      0.240 Ug
PANTO- ACID     A=======                                       14%     0.810 Mg
CALCIUM         A============                                  24%     192.0 Mg
PHOSPHORUS      A====================                          40%     321.0 Mg
TRYPTOPHAN      A==================================================    131%    215.0 Mg
THREONINE       A==================================================    116%    508.0 Mg
ISOLEUCINE      A=============================================         94%     619.0 Mg
LEUCINE         A==================================================    122%    1068 Mg
LYSINE          A==================================================    95%     621.0 Mg
METHIONINE      A=====================================                 76%     208.0 Mg
CYSTINE         A=======================================               80%     218.0 Mg
PHENYL-ANINE    A==================================================    154%    673.0 Mg
TYROSINE        A==================================================    104%    455.0 Mg
VALINE          A==================================================    101%    774.0 Mg
HISTIDINE       A                                              NO RDA   352.0 Mg
ALCOHOL         A                                              NO RDA   0.000 Gm
ASH             A                                              NO RDA   2.550 Gm
COPPER          A=============                                 26%     0.670 Mg
MANGANESE       A=                                             2%      0.110 Mg
IODINE          A==========                                    21%     32.80 Ug
MONO FAT        A                                              NO RDA   9.060 Gm
POLY FAT        A                                              NO RDA   2.680 Gm
CAFFEINE        A                                              NO RDA   0.000 Mg
FLUORIDE        A                                              0%      15.20 Ug
MOLYBDENUM      A==============================================        92%     300.0 Ug
VITAMIN K       A                                              0%      0.000 Ug
SELENIUM        A                                              0%      0.000 Mg
BIOTIN          A=                                             2%      3.120 Ug
CHLORIDE        A                                              0%      26.90 Mg
CHROMIUM        A================                              32%     0.040 Mg
SUGAR           A                                              NO RDA   25.60 Gm
FIBER-DIET      A                                              NO RDA   5.900 Gm
VIT. E/AT       A                                              1%      0.130 Mg

% RDA:    |0      |20     |40     |60     |80     |100
```

Cashew butter used instead of almond; optional noninstant nonfat milk powder included in analysis. Type of nut meal used: almond. Recipe makes five ½-cup servings.

Although they don't have any recipes to contribute, two-year-old Guyatri and the brand new baby Sesha do have something to add here.

Two-year-old Guyatri loves to help in the kitchen and sometimes is happy to just observe and make a running commentary. There are many nights that he has single-handedly (enthusiastically and proudly) made the dinner salad all by himself. He tears washed lettuce leaves, then selects other ingredients himself from the refrigerator, rinses and cuts them. His usual selections — sprouts, tomatoes, mushrooms, bell peppers, pitted olives — are all soft enough for him to cut with a butter knife.

Right now Sesha's contribution to mealtime is keeping everyone happy and smiling in the kitchen with her cheerful disposition. She's too young at this point to even eat food, much less prepare it! I've given all of my babies only breast milk for the first six months of their lives. It would take a whole book, like the La Leche League's *The Womanly Art of Breastfeeding*, to give all the reasons why this food provided by nature is the best that exists for babies, but I can't resist listing a few that I hope will convince you to feed your baby in this way as well.

• Colostrum, which is there in the first two to three days after birth before the milk comes in, contains antibodies, proteins and vitamins that are specially "formulated" by nature to give the newborn baby protection against bacteria, germs and other elements of its new environment.

• Statistics show that breastfeeding decreases infant mortality.

• Human mother's milk is easier for an infant to assimilate and digest than any formula, cow's milk or other animal's milk; therefore, breastfed babies have fewer digestive problems.

• Breastfed babies are less susceptible to infections and diseases because mother's milk contains antibodies.

• Breastfeeding encourages the growth of beneficial bacteria in the baby's digestive tract and prevents constipation (many formula-fed babies have problems with constipation).

• Breastfeeding prevents anemia in both mother and child.

• Breastfeeding builds a healthier body for future life. Breastfed babies are less likely to develop allergies in later life, breastfeeding develops good facial and dental structure, and breastfed babies rarely grow up to be obese people.

# CHAPTER 14

# SHOPPING TO STOCK
# KATHY'S KITCHEN
# (AND YOURS TOO, I HOPE)

Throughout the book, the shopping lists at the end of each recipe are divided into three categories. The "Special" list includes foods that I don't keep regularly stocked in my kitchen and generally must be gotten somewhere besides a supermarket. The "Fresh" list contains fresh produce and a few items I don't regularly stock in my kitchen that can easily be found in any supermarket.

The "Regularly" list is comprised of food items that I keep on a regular basis in my kitchen, re-stocking when I begin to run out. Some items are easy to find; others might be new to you and you might have to look for them somewhere beyond your local supermarket. (Some items I've listed as being available in natural food stores might be in your local supermarket's health food aisle.) Here's a list of the items I regularly stock in my kitchen and any information I thought might be useful about them. Outside of these items, you'll find that just about all you'll need to buy is fresh produce and a few "special" items every now and then. You'll find that some of the items are more expensive than something else that could be used but is unhealthy. In the long-run, shopping for healthy foods will cost you less because many of the most often used items (like whole wheat flour, brown rice, tofu, beans, etc.) are extremely inexpensive, and using healthy items that are a little more expensive saves money on doctor bills!

**Arrowroot.** Found in natural food stores; also sold, bottled, in some supermarket spice racks but is very expensive bought in this way. This is what I use part-for-part instead of cornstarch. Besides the fact that many dried corn kernels are soaked in a sulfur dioxide solution which leaves sulfur residues in many corn products, including cornstarch, arrowroot is superior to cornstarch nutritionally. One hundred grams of arrowroot contains about 19 milligrams of calcium (compared to zero in cornstarch), up to 54 milligrams of phosphorus (zero in cornstarch) and three times the amount of protein and iron as cornstarch for about 20 fewer calories.

**Baking powder.** The good habit of label reading comes in handy here. Be sure to get baking powder without any alum or aluminum compound in it (aluminum ammonium sulfate, sodium aluminum sulfate, etc.). This kind of baking powder can sometimes be found in supermarkets, but always in natural food stores.

**Baking soda.** Just good old baking soda that can be found in any supermarket.

**Baking yeast.** The little envelopes found in supermarkets are fine, but if you do or plan to do a lot of baking, it's much more economical to buy the large half- or one-pound-sized bags that are sold in most natural food stores.

**Barbados molasses.** See p. 204; can be found in supermarket and natural food stores.

**Bipro.** This is what I use instead of the egg replacer mentioned in *Kathy Cooks . . . Naturally* because the "Jolly Joan Egg Replacer" is no longer available. Even if it were, I would use Bipro because the old egg replacer made from different starches replaced only the texture of eggs in cooking and not the nutritional value. Bipro replaces the texture of eggs in cooking and is such a pure protein that it can be whipped like egg whites. Made by a special ionization process that extracts only the protein from whey, Bipro is a 97 percent pure protein that's virtually cholesterol-, fat- and lactose-free. Since the amino acid structure of whey most closely resembles human mother's milk, it's an easily assimilated protein for the human body. I was so excited when I found out about the product that I contacted the company which underwrote one of the "Kathy's Kitchen" series. Unfortunately for all concerned, the plant that the company was building took longer to construct than planned, so Bipro isn't out on store shelves — yet! Most likely when it is manufactured, it will appear in natural food stores. You can write me for information.

**Bran.** This inexpensive form of supplementary fiber can always be found in natural food stores.

**Brown rice.** More people eating whole grains have placed brown rice on supermarket shelves where it's always less expensive than in natural food stores. There are many varieties of brown rice; I personally prefer the long grain variety.

**Butter or margarine.** Which one of these is the healthier one to use is debatable. For the sake of avoiding saturated fat, many people are advised (by the likes of the American Heart Association) to use margarine. The problem with most margarines is that most contain a lot of chemical additives and are made from hydrogenated vegetable oils. Anyone with any knowledge of the molecular structure of fats knows that saturated fats are ones in which the carbon atoms are saturated with hydrogen atoms; unsaturated fats have fewer hydrogen molecules. To make unsaturated fats harden when cooled, manufacturers pump hydrogen molecules into them — essentially turning unsaturated fats into saturated fats which are then colored, flavored, preserved, etc., with all sorts of chemical additives. If this is the kind of margarine you're getting, butter is the healthier choice. I've found a margarine in natural food stores that I feel all right about using which is made solid with the use of soy meal and only partially hydrogenated vegetable oil and is free of chemicals and artificial colorings.

**Carob.** It's surprising that this healthier alternative to chocolate (pp. 221 - 222) is still only available in natural food stores.

**Cheese.** I look for uncolored, rennetless cheese in natural food stores, kosher markets and some supermarkets. There is a large enough variety of flavors of these to make just about any dish with cheese in it that you want. Just remember, some cheeses contain more cholesterol and saturated fat than others (p. 308).

**Corn meal.** The corn meal sold in supermarkets is a refined product; get the whole grain corn meal in natural food stores.

**Cottage cheese.** I use a rennetless, lowfat cottage cheese sold in natural food stores. Nutritional graphs for recipes in this book containing cottage cheese are for a two percent lowfat cottage cheese.

**Cultured dairy products (like cultured buttermilk, kefir and yogurt).** All are less expensive when made at home. Cultured buttermilk can be bought in all supermarkets. Buying kefir and yogurt without sugar in them may call for shopping in natural food stores.

**Date sugar.** Although it has its limitations (p. 203), it's one of the healthiest sweeteners, being made from dried fruit. Unfortunately it's not even sold in all natural food stores, but I've found the larger, better stocked stores usually carry it.

**Dried fruit.** With the exception of raisins, I get all my dried fruit at natural food stores to avoid sulfur dioxide

(p. 649). Natural food stores also carry a larger selection of dried fruit: apples, apricots, bananas, cherries, currants, dates, figs, nectarines, papayas, mangoes, peaches, pears, pineapple, prunes, raisins and even star fruit!

**Dry shiitake mushrooms.** Can be found in Chinese or Japanese groceries, Oriental food aisles in supermarkets and natural food stores. This is one of those expensive items that's made affordable by the low cost of everyday items like whole grains, legumes, etc.

**Eggless mayonnaise.** Available in natural food stores; but the Tofu Mayonnaise (p. 332) that can be made at home is more nutritious and less expensive.

**Grain coffee.** This caffeine-free coffee is not a new idea. Postum is the one that has been available in all supermarkets since I was a young girl. Natural food stores usually have a number of different brands to choose from.

**Herb teas.** Caffeine-free herb teas that used to be available only in natural food stores have become such a popular beverage that tea companies like Lipton's even make a line of different flavored herb teas! There's such a large selection of flavors that you should never be able to tire of herb teas.

**Honey.** Available in supermarkets and natural food stores; although I think the honey in natural food stores is, in general, of better quality.

Look for ones that specify no heat was used in extracting the honey from the comb.

**Kelp powder.** Even though I don't use this a lot in recipes, it's a mineral- and flavor-packed condiment (if you like seafood) to keep on the table instead of a salt shaker.

**Lecithin.** This substance is naturally found in some foods (soybeans are a rich source) and is also manufactured in our livers. Lecithin keeps the cholesterol in our bloodstreams in an emulsified state so it flows freely through the veins and prevents deposits from forming on artery walls. It can be healthfully supplemented by using liquid or granular lecithin in food preparation. I use it as an emulsifier to improve the texture of many dishes. It can be found in different forms in natural food stores.

**Legumes.** A short mention of legumes here is a little misleading because they play a major role in many of our meals (see p. 470). There is a great variety available in all supermarkets, although I've found them to be cheaper in bulk bins in natural food stores and co-ops. Oriental and East Indian food stores often have many interesting and different tasting legumes available. Garbanzo beans, lentils, pinto beans, mung and adzuki beans are probably the legumes I use most often, but I do like to get different kinds and experiment with them every now and then.

**Milk.** I get lowfat milk (my children refuse to drink nonfat milk because they say it tastes like water) and try as much as possible to get milk from dairies that have a reputation for taking good care of their cows and don't feed them doses of antibiotics as preventive maintenance.

**Miso.** This fermented soy food adds lots of nutrients as well as flavor to dishes (see p. 366). I usually end up getting mine in natural food stores since I'm there anyway, and that way I'm sure to avoid getting a synthetic imposter. If buying miso in a supermarket or Oriental food store, be on guard for the words "pasteurized" (it kills the beneficial bacteria that grow and make their home in miso in the fermenting process) and "temperature controlled" (this indicates a synthetically made miso). Also look for information on how long the miso has been aged (natural miso will be aged anywhere from 1½ to three years).

**Mustard.** I stock both Dijon-style mustard and American-style mustard because my children don't care much for the hotness of Dijon mustard. Unless Dijon mustard is specified in a recipe, American-style mustard should be used.

**Noninstant, nonfat milk powder.** Found in natural food stores. I prefer to get this kind because it makes thicker homemade yogurts, buttermilk, etc.

**Nuts and seeds.** I am always careful to buy my choice of nuts and seeds (and whole grains) in a natural food store that has a lot of traffic because that ensures a quick turnover of merchandise on the shelves. This is important with nuts, seeds and whole grains because the oils in them get rancid fairly quickly. I always buy my nuts and seeds in their raw, whole, de-shelled form, making nut meals, chopping or roasting as needed. If you don't use nuts, seeds or whole grain flours much, it's a good idea to store them in the refrigerator in an airtight container. The nuts and seeds I buy most often are almonds, cashews, peanuts, walnuts or pecans, and sunflower and sesame seeds.

**Nut butters.** Although there are unhydrogenated peanut butters (ones in which the oil separates and comes to the top) available in supermarkets, you'll find a wealth of different flavored nut butters in natural food stores. I personally prefer raw and roasted almond and cashew butter and raw sesame tahini.

**Nutritional yeast.** The nutritional content and flavor vary a great deal from brand to brand, so it may take some label reading and tasting before you settle on the one you like. At home I use the KAL Brewer's Yeast Flakes most often because it has a nice, cheesy flavor. We used the nutritional information for this KAL yeast in our computer, so the nutritional analyses for recipes with nutritional yeast in them are based on KAL yeast. The nutrients will be different if you use another type of nutritional yeast.

**Olive oil.** Although the olive oil in natural food stores or supermarkets will do, you have to shop in an Italian market at least once to appreciate how many different grades and tastes of olive oil there are!

**Popcorn.** One of those commonly found foods that I feel is healthy enough for my children to make and snack on.

**Refried beans.** Just the fact that I keep these canned beans in my kitchen is evidence of how food industries are becoming more "health conscious" to be able to continue to sell to a public that is trying to eat healthier foods. A few years ago I would have been hard-pressed to name any pre-made food that I bought. Today natural food stores are filling up with more healthy convenience foods than ever before. Even though they're more expensive than refried beans if I make them from scratch, I keep a few cans of Rosarita vegetarian refried beans on hand for quick snacks or days when I'm not together enough to pull a meal together.

**Rolled oats.** This is one healthy whole grain product that has survived all the food fads and trends that sweep through the supermarket. Good old Quaker Oats are just as good as (and usually less expensive than) oats sold in natural food stores.

**Safflower or sunflower oil.** These are the two most unsaturated oils and fortunately the two most neutral tasting as well. I usually get mine in natural food stores, but the "Hollywood" line of oils that can be found in most supermarket cooking oil sections offers a good selection of cold-pressed vegetable oils.

**Salt.** I buy sea salt in natural food stores. We use so little in food that we go through one container every year or two, unless the boys are especially reckless and we have a lot of wounds to soak.

**Seasonings and spices.** These are quite prominent on my shopping list and in my kitchen. If you analyze it, my recipes are made up from a few basic ingredients that are spiced and seasoned in many different ways. Because the spices and herbs in supermarkets are so expensive (you're paying for the packaging), I prefer getting mine in natural food stores or co-ops and some East Indian food stores where they can be bought in bulk. The ones that I use most are —

Allspice
Anise seeds
Basil
Bay leaves
Black pepper
Caraway
Cayenne
Chili powder
Cinnamon (ground and stick)
Coriander (ground and whole)
Cumin (ground and whole)
Curry powder
Dill weed
Fines Herbes

Ginger powder
Ground cloves
Italian Herb Seasoning
Mace
Mustard (powder and seeds)
Nutmeg
Oregano
Paprika
Parsley flakes
Poppy seeds
Poultry seasoning
Red chili seeds
Rosemary
Saffron
Sage
Savory
Tarragon
Thyme
Turmeric
White pepper

Liquid smoke
Almond and vanilla extract

The seasonings worth their own mention are —
• Asafetida — because it's so hard to find. If you can't find it, onions and garlic will give the same flavor (the nice thing about asafetida is it will give the onion or garlic taste without the lingering odor). It can be found in natural food stores with very complete herb sections and in East Indian food stores where it's often called "hing."
• Spike — because I use it so much in my recipes and it

really will make a difference in flavor if any other vegetable-seasoned salt is used. This mixture of herbs, spices, fruits and salt can be found in natural food stores.
• Seaweed — there are different varieties of these vegetables of the sea. The dried, packaged ones are the ones you'll most likely use unless you live close to a clean ocean — and even then all these varieties won't be available to you. Kombu, nishime, wakame and nori (laver) seaweed sheets are available in Japanese food stores where dulse is usually available in addition to all the above.

**Soy sauce (sometimes called "tamari").** Real, naturally brewed soy sauces are available in Oriental food stores and aisles in supermarkets, and in natural food stores. Reading labels is crucial so you can be sure to get soy sauces that are preservative-free and are real soy sauces. "Hydrolyzed soy protein," "caramel coloring" and "corn syrup" are all dead giveaways that what you're looking at is a synthetic, chemically formulated, imitation soy sauce.

**Sugarless, meat-free (that includes lard) spaghetti sauce, tomato puree and tomato sauce.** Available in supermarkets — just read the labels. I usually get mine in supermarkets because they're less expensive there than in natural food stores.

**Tempeh.** This soy food (pp. 140-141) that's new to

the American market is not even available in all natural food stores. I make a point to get a case whenever I go to a store that stocks it and store it in the freezer till I need it.

**Toasted sesame oil.** This rich-flavored oil made from toasted sesame seeds used to be found only in Oriental food stores or supermarket aisles, but I've noticed it more and more in natural food stores lately. There is a great difference in flavor between this and the cold-pressed sesame oil made from raw sesame seeds, so when a recipe calls for toasted sesame oil, be sure to use this — sometimes labeled as "dark sesame oil" or "Oriental sesame oil."

**Tofu.** Since I wrote my first book (*Kathy Cooks . . . Naturally*), tofu has become so popular that it's now found in almost every supermarket and natural food store. All the recipes in this book use "Chinese firm" tofu unless otherwise specified. The nutritional tables in the book make use of the nutritional analysis of tofu curdled with calcium sulfate. If the tofu you use is curdled with something else (it will be indicated on the label), it will be much, much lower in calcium.

**Vinegar.** The basic requirement is that it's naturally brewed and contains no chemical additives. The old stand-by, apple cider vinegar, is a must. There is also a wide spectrum of rice vinegars, wine vinegars, herb- and fruit-flavored vinegars (p. 545)

that are worth trying; you'll find each has its own distinctive flavor.

**Wheat germ.** Natural food stores and consumers who know what they're doing will store this in the refrigerator to prevent the valuable wheat germ oil from turning rancid.

**Whole wheat bread.** I can't bake as much or as quickly as my family can eat bread! I'm grateful that there are now 100 percent whole wheat breads on shelves of natural food stores and most supermarkets! Label reading is important here. "Wheat flour" and "unbleached wheat flour" are other words for refined white flour; watch out for sugar and corn syrup (which is basically wet white sugar) in some apparently wholesome products.

**Whole wheat flour.** This may come as a surprise to many, but for years I've used the Gold Medal whole wheat flour that's sold in supermarkets. It's not even a 100 percent whole wheat flour; a quick look at the label reveals that it is two percent malted barley flour, which is a healthy ingredient, as it is dried and ground, sprouted barley (p. 531). Although organically grown foods are the ideal, in many cases they are often hard to find or beyond my budget. But in the case of whole wheat flour, I choose to use this flour because it's hard to find an organically grown flour that's milled as fine as this is.

**Yuba.** All of us have experienced heating milk and see-

ing the film that forms on the top. "Yuba" is what the Japanese call the film that forms on top of soy milk, which is lifted off and dried to use as a food. As all soy products are, yuba is a cholesterol- and saturated fat-free source of protein that can be prepared in a lot of different ways. Unfortunately, yuba is one of those food items that takes a little extra effort to obtain. I usually get mine at Chinese groceries in Chinatowns where it's called "dried bean curd." Dried bean curd comes in two forms: flat, thin, paper-like sheets and in rope shapes. Because it's a dried food that requires no special storage, whenever I go to get some, I buy a case so it'll be on hand for awhile.

# INFORMATION INDEX

# E

724

# DEAR READERS,

I'm making the following ingredients that are used in this book available through mail-order because of the many letters I've received expressing difficulty at finding these products.

## 1. ASAFETIDA ...

### Exotic Spicing from the East

A unique powdered spice from India that tastes like onion and garlic but doesn't leave an after-taste, odor on the breath, cause belching or upset stomach. Asafetida is an herbal substance derived from the resin of the asafetida tree.

Each canister of asafetida is 1.75 oz. (50 grams) net weight and comes in the compounded powder form containing gum arabic, wheat, rice flour, and asafetida.

*Please allow 4 to 6 weeks for delivery. Canadian orders are welcome at the same prices below. Please remit your payment in International or World Money Order only or Canadian Money Order drawn on a U.S. bank. U.S. currency only.*

## 2. BIPRO ...

### The Rolls Royce of Protein Powders

The purest protein powder in the world today, containing 97% pure protein, Bipro is an odorless, tasteless protein powder extracted from cheese whey through an ionization process that leaves the protein undamaged and in its natural state. Whey protein is very close in amino acid structure to human mother's milk and is assimilated very easily. Though it is a dairy by-product, Bipro contains no cholesterol, saturated fat, or lactose.

Besides being an excellent protein supplement that can be used as most ordinary powders, Bipro has amazing qualities that allow it to be cooked as a food. It can be used as a cholesterol-free replacement for eggs in baking, or to jell or thicken foods, and can even be whipped into meringues. As an egg replacer, Bipro contains six times the amount of protein in one egg, without the cholesterol or saturated fat.

---

*PRICES BELOW INCLUDE SHIPPING & HANDLING*

Please, send your check or money order made payable to...

## KATHY HOSHIJO
P.O. Box 1122 • Glendale, CA 91209

Please send me the following:

| **1. ASAFETIDA** | EACH | TOTAL |
|---|---|---|
| _____ 2-can sample packet (s) .......................................$6.00 | | $_____ |
| _____ 10-can jumbo packet (s).....................................$22.40 | | $_____ |

| **2. BIPRO** | | |
|---|---|---|
| _____ 1-pound packet (s) ............................................$17.98 | | $_____ |
| Enclosed is my total payment of ..............$_____ | | |

NAME_____

STREET ADDRESS_____
(Cannot deliver to P.O. Box)

CITY_____ STATE_____ ZIP_____